THE HEATH INTRODUCTION TO DRAMA

THE HEATH INTRODUCTION TO DRAMA

FIFTH EDITION

Jordan Y. Miller
University of Rhode Island

D. C. HEATH AND COMPANY
Lexington, Massachusetts Toronto

Address editorial correspondence to:

D. C. Heath and Company
125 Spring Street
Lexington, MA 02173

Acquisitions Editor:	Paul A. Smith
Developmental Editor:	Linda M. Bieze
Production Editor:	Bryan Woodhouse
Designer:	Kenneth Hollman
Photo Researcher:	Ann Barnard
Production Coordinator:	Lisa Merrill
Permissions Editor:	Margaret Roll

For permission to use copyrighted materials, grateful acknowledgment is made to the copyright holders listed on pages v–vi, which are hereby considered an extension of this copyright page.

Published simultaneously in Canada.

Printed in the United States of America.

International Standard Book Number: 0-669-35506-2

Library of Congress Catalog Number: 95-68033

56789-DOC-00 99 98

TEXT CREDITS

Oedipus Rex: An English Version by Dudley Fitts and Robert Fitzgerald. Copyright ©1949 by Harcourt Brace & Company and renewed ©1977 by Cornelia Fitts and Robert Fitzgerald. Reprinted by permission of the publisher. *Caution:* All rights, including professional, amateur, motion picture, recitation, lecturing, public reading, radio broadcasting, and television are strictly reserved. Inquiries on all rights should be addressed to Harcourt Brace & Company, Orlando, FL 32887.

Lysistrata: An English Version by Dudley Fitts. Copyright ©1954 by Harcourt Brace & Company and renewed ©1982 by Cornelia Fitts. *Caution:* All rights, including professional, amateur, motion picture, recitation, lecturing, public reading, radio broadcasting, and television are strictly reserved. Inquiries on all rights should be addressed to Harcourt Brace & Company, Orlando, FL 32887.

The Second Shepherds' Play, a modernized version by John Gassner from *A Treasury of the Theatre, Vol. 1,* edited by John Gassner. Copyright ©1935, 1940, 1950, 1951, 1963 by Simon & Schuster, Inc. Reprinted by permission of Simon & Schuster, Inc.

Hamlet by William Shakespeare, edited by Willard Farnham. Copyright ©1957 by Penguin Books Inc. on notes and introduction; renewed copyright ©1985 by Diana Farnham O'Herir, Anthony E. Farnham, and Nicholas H. Farnham. Used by permission of Penguin, a division of Penguin Books USA Inc.

Tartuffe by Molière, translation copyright ©1963, 1962, and 1961 and renewed 1991, 1990, and 1989 by Richard Wilbur, reprinted by permission of Harcourt Brace & Company. CAUTION: Professionals and amateurs are hereby warned that this translation, being fully protected under the copyright laws of the United States of America, the British Empire, including the Dominion of Canada, and all other countries which are signatories to the Universal Copyright Convention and the International Copyright Union, is subject to royalty. All rights, including professional, amateur, motion picture, recitation, lecturing, public reading, radio broadcasting, and television, are strictly reserved. Particular emphasis is laid on the question of readings, permission for which must be secured from the author's agent in writing. Inquiries on professional rights (except for amateur rights) should be addressed to Curtis Brown, Ltd., 10 Astor Place, New York, NY 10003; inquiries on translation rights should be addressed to Harcourt Brace & Company, Permissions Dept., Orlando, FL 32887.

A Doll's House by Henrik Ibsen, translation by Otto Reinert. Copyright ©1977 Otto Reinert. Reprinted by permission.

The Cherry Orchard by Anton Chekhov, translated by Stark Young. Copyright ©1939, 1941, 1947, 1950, 1956. All rights reserved. Used by permission of Flora Roberts, Inc.

Desire Under the Elms by Eugene O'Neill from *The Plays of Eugene O'Neill.* Copyright ©1924 and renewed 1952 by Eugene O'Neill. Reprinted by permission of Random House, Inc.

The Glass Menagerie by Tennessee Williams. Copyright ©1945 by Tennessee Williams and Edwina D. Williams and renewed 1973 by Tennessee Williams.. Reprinted by permission of Random House, Inc.

Death of a Salesman by Arthur Miller. Copyright ©1949, renewed ©1977 by Arthur Miller. Used by permission of Viking Penguin, a division of Penguin Books USA Inc.

The Dumb Waiter by Harold Pinter. Copyright ©1960, 1988 by Harold Pinter. Used by permision of Grove/Atlantic, Inc.

"Dream Deferred" by Langston Hughes, from *The Panther and The Lash.* Copyright 1951 by Langston Hughes. Reprinted by permission of Alfred A. Knopf, Inc.

A Raisin in the Sun by Lorraine Hansburry. Copyright ©1958 by Robert Nemiroff as an unpublished play. Copyright ©1959, 1966, 1984 by Robert Nemiroff. Reprinted by permission of Random House, Inc.

Sticks and Bones by David Rabe. Copyright ©1969, 1972, 1973 by David Rabe.

'Night Mother by Marsha Norman. Copyright ©1983 by Marsha Norman. Reprinted by permission of Hill and Wang, a division of Farrar, Strauss & Giroux, Inc. *Caution*: Professionals and amateurs are hereby warned that *'Night Mother* by Marsha Norman, being fully protected under the Copyright Laws of the United States of America and all other countries of the Berne and Universal Copyright Conventions, is

PREFACE

The eighteen plays in the fifth edition of *The Heath Introduction to Drama* introduce students to an exceptional representation of dramatic works in a manageable, chronological format. Seven new plays in the fifth edition increase the anthology's range, which now spans the play-writing tradition from Sophocles to August Wilson. Its variety makes the volume flexible enough for use in both Introduction to Drama and Introduction to Literature courses. Both the array of plays and their expanded introductions give students a keen sense of the history of the genre and of the historical context of each piece—all in a volume of class-tested plays that costs twenty to forty percent less than comparable anthologies.

Highlights of this edition include:

- multicultural and women's issues strongly represented through the works of playwrights Susan Glaspell, Lorraine Hansberry, Marsha Norman, and August Wilson;
- additional historical eras of drama—medieval, eighteenth-century, and theatre of the absurd—represented, respectively, by *The Second Shepherds' Play,* Richard Brinsley Sheridan's *The School for Scandal,* and Harold Pinter's *The Dumb Waiter;*
- important works by contemporary playwrights, including David Rabe's *Sticks and Bones* and Marsha Norman's *'night Mother.*

The "Introduction: On Drama" imparts a dual perspective on the study of drama—as a literary genre and as a performing art. The Introduction, the introductory notes, and the Selected Bibliography (as in previous editions) and a Selected Filmography (new in this edition) are the work of Jordan Y. Miller.

For their many helpful suggestions we are grateful to the devoted users of *The Heath Introduction to Drama.* We have been aided in developing this anthology by the sensitive and practical suggestions of the following instructors: Bob Alexander, Point Park College; Janice Anderson, Scott Community College; Charles Berst, University of California—Los Angeles; Douglas Cole, Northwestern University; Merle Fifield, Ball State University; Thomas Gay, Youngstown State University; Mary Gibson, Santa Barbara City College; Janet M. Green, Kent State University—Ashtabula; James Hunt, University of Illinois; Maude M. Jennings, Ball State University; Dorothy Kish, Point Park College; Archibald Leyasmeyer, University of Minnesota; William Lindblad, Ball State University;

T. Patrick Lynch, S. J., St. Peter's College; John F. McElroy, St. Peter's College; Kathleen Monahan, St. Peter's College; Erin Mooney, University of New Orleans; Mary T. Roberti, Monroe County Community College; Cathy Stathakos, Chaminade University; and Warren Westcott, Francis Marion University.

We trust that instructors will find this anthology eminently teachable, that students will find the works included here an enlightening introduction to drama, and that all who use this book will find the plays as enjoyable as its editors do.

Paul A. Smith, Senior Editor
D. C. Heath and Company

CONTENTS

THE HEATH INTRODUCTION TO DRAMA

INTRODUCTION: ON DRAMA

Concerning the Drama, the Theatre, and the Play

Ever since some prehistoric hunter returned from the chase to elaborate on the size of the saber-toothed tiger that got away, the human animal has delighted in putting on a show. We know from such surviving evidence as Europe's cave paintings and various artifacts of primitive masks, wigs, and costumes that men and women since prehistory have possessed a keen sense of the beauties and emotional stimulation of human and beast in motion. The essence of theatre has been with us in tribal dance or religious ecstasy from far back in time, whether we have shaken the rattle and sung the songs ourselves, or have witnessed the proceedings in awed fear or happy delight in the give-and-take which is the fundamental nature of the art.

Everything that follows in this book is a direct descendant of that probable first theatrical show. The fact that, in a comparative instant of history, we have developed the ability to put it all down in the scratchings we call written language and have come to possess thereby what we call a "body of dramatic literature" does not alter the basic primitive formula. Every major culture has, at one time or another, possessed a highly developed tradition of theatre. The survival of this tradition in the form of the written word, in considerable quantity in Western culture, less so in others, has provided unique insights into those cultures available in no other form of art.

The reading of "dramatic literature" is a dismally poor alternative to the theatrical experience itself. There is no way to substitute for the interrelationship that exists between those who *do* and those who *watch*. The drama—that is, the story—be it literal truth or fantastic embellishment, simultaneously demands that the interpreter bring it to life as theatre and that the audience react appreciatively. In that manner the full impact of the art has been manifested. But for all practical purposes we have no alternative to reading the written words, strictly second best as that choice may be. Doing so can be made most rewarding by a constant awareness of that interrelationship. Every written piece in this book was designed first and foremost for *performance*.

Furthermore, every work contained here is a great piece of *entertainment*. Whatever sophisticated social or religious theme, whatever erudite subject, propagandistic motive, or moral didacticism that may be apparent in any single play does not alter the fact that to witness a theatrical performance in a Greek amphitheatre holding 15,000 spectators or in a tiny converted nightclub with room for fewer than 200 is to be entertained. This does not imply mere passing amusement, an aspect of theatre valid enough in its own right. It does, however, imply that we who watch expect to experience some form of emotional pleasure. We can be excited, mystified, intrigued, challenged, frightened, or horrified, and we can be driven to tears or laughter, concurrently, consecutively, or entirely independently, but one thing is sure: we will have enjoyed the experience that has been offered to us, for we have, in short, been entertained.

How It Is Said

The drama, the theatre, and the play are so closely related in their broad connotations as to be, on occasion, interchangeable. For our purposes here, however, they will be separately identified in order to establish a sharper distinction among their meanings. Each element demands a different appreciation, and each performs a distinct function. We shall restrict the term *drama* to the written text, created by the *dramatist,*[1] who brings the idea to life on paper. But unlike the artistry of other writers, things do not end there. Once the pages are filled, the work of the novelist, the poet, or the essayist has, to all intents and purposes, been concluded. For the dramatist, on the other hand, the ordeal has just begun. Before it's all over, there looms ahead the intervention of the many elements of *theatre* and the transformation into the production of the *play.* The trip will not be smooth.

Regardless, then, of its eventual metamorphosis in the theatre, what appears in performance is essentially the artistic inspiration of the dramatist, whose source may be religion and its faith and morals, whence all Western drama originated, or it may be a sociological problem, a philosophical question, a political viewpoint, or, indeed, almost anything that strikes the artist's fancy.

Further, the type of drama remains the prerogative of the dramatist, whose choice now begins to place him or her in a somewhat different creative area from other writers. For the novelist there are choices as well: whether to be serious or comic, to create pure fiction or to re-create history, and whether to do so in one hundred or one thousand pages. The poet, too, chooses whether to write a lyric, a sonnet, a narrative epic, or something in between. The dramatist, however, is creating for that special medium, the theatre, and while the work may be developed along any desired lines from the highest tragedy to the lowest farce, there are restraints imposed by certain limitations of the medium. Its long traditions, as we shall see, convey specialized meaning to such terms as *tragedy* and *comedy* and, of course, assume a number of physical restrictions. When the dramatist makes the choice of *style,* the manner in which the creation is to be staged, there will be far more problems than those facing colleagues working in other genres. Although they, of course, may manipulate their language to suggest anything from literal transcription of contemporary speech to the most imaginative

[1]If you prefer the term *playwright*—maker of plays—well and good, although we're going to regard the *play* as the entire finished product put on before an audience.

stream of consciousness, or may choose to describe the most vivid photographic detail or expand into the realms of heightened symbolism or utter fantasy, the dramatist must conceive of style far beyond the printed page and into the life and visible arena of the stage, where not only what is said but how it is delivered to and visualized by the audience in both sight and sound become primary considerations. As in the choice of *type,* so in the choice of *style* the dramatist must face the realities of the medium and be prepared to function within the strict limitations it presents.

What Is to Be Said

As Aristotle pointed out some 2300 years ago in writing that first great piece of dramatic criticism, *The Poetics,* in the fourth century B.C., the most important element of tragedy (to him all serious drama was tragedy) is the *fable,* or more colloquially, the *story.* Some people call it plot, but whatever you want to call it there can be little argument with Aristotle that what goes on, together with the way it happens, is the single most important consideration for the dramatist in putting the idea across. This story, unless conveying the most abstract of messages, must begin at a clearly defined point, proceed to develop in a logical fashion, and arrive at a conclusion that follows equally logically upon what has happened. Herein the dramatist encounters the most serious constraint upon the artistic development of the story, an absolute limit that other literary artists never have to worry about: *time.*

The many convolutions into which a novelist may enter in the course of telling a tale in whatever length desired are not the privilege of the conventional Western dramatist. Following the traditions that have existed since the time of ancient Greece, all must be told within a very few hours of time upon the stage. Further, within that time, everything must be done all at once. Those who watch cannot put the story down, pick it up tomorrow, and go back to Chapter One to remind themselves of what has happened. Moreover, there is a limit in the physical endurance of the audience who must sit or stand, or even crouch, during the entire presentation. The dramatist places heavy demands of concentration upon the audience, but it, in turn, has its own strict demands. If too much must be repeated to make a point, the audience will quickly become bored and lose its attention. If the story leaps too many gaps or the dramatist assumes too much in the ability of the audience to comprehend what is going on, the viewers will become muddled, confused, and disappointed. Within the strict confines of time the dramatist must therefore arrive at what is being said in a linear progression that keeps the audience constantly alert and attentive.

Who Says It

However important the story, it can be conveyed only through the *characters,* those who indicate to the audience what is going on as they speak and move about within the physical restrictions of the stage and within the limits of time. The novelist can use up any number of pages to inform the reader about who is who, or provide a descriptive list for ready reference as, for instance, in some editions of Tolstoy's *War and Peace,* in which a convenient supplement lists all the names and relationships of everyone who appears. The dramatist must do everything quickly and clearly; it's almost impossible to keep checking on everybody in the program's cast of characters, particularly in a darkened auditorium, and there's no way to go back to Chapter One. The audience left at final curtain trying to figure out who all those people were and what they were doing will depart unsatisfied, and the play will fail.

The dramatist must be careful not to clutter the stage with crowds and complicated action, which can become an impossible logistics problem. The alarums and excursions of Shakespeare's battle scenes, properly handled, are far more effective with a handful of participants than any try at verisimilitude could ever be. But probably more important to the dramatist is how many principal characters, the ones on whom the audience's interest centers, can be accommodated within the time allotted for proper identification and establishment of relationships. The dramatist does have one distinct advantage over the novelist, which is the privilege of instant visibility. Once the characters have made their entrances and established who or what they are, they will be recognized promptly the next time around.

Because of the visual element and the fact that a story is being told by live bodies, moving and speaking, the dramatist must maintain a constant awareness of the physical appearance and capabilities of the characters. How will they look together? What variations are desirable and possible? Is there need for some kind of characteristic that costume or makeup can't convey, such as a dwarf or a very young child? Will the character need to fly, like Peter Pan? Will there perhaps be an animal, like Harvey, the giant rabbit, who *never* appears,[2] or like the birds in Aristophanes' ancient Greek comedy of that name, who do? Within the closely limited time will the characters age? or get younger? or become something else, in the frog-into-prince or Beauty-and-the-Beast tradition? Will the audience accept it or be turned off? The novelist can do anything in this regard, but the dramatist must plan with extreme care what every single character, living and breathing on a stage, will be, whether human, divine, supernatural, or four-legged.

The Method of Saying It

The behavior of characters onstage, their movements, facial expressions, reactions to others, and so on, contribute substantially to the development of the

[2]In the very early tryout days of Mary Chase's phenomenally successful farce in 1944 Harvey, who gave the play its title, was fully visible, but an actor in a six-foot rabbit suit could not make the fantasy work and the idea was dropped.

story, but unless it is to be told entirely in pantomime, the vital element that enables us to pursue the study of dramatic literature is the *dialogue.*

Dramatic dialogue is a tightly controlled use of the language that demands a very special writing talent. The total artistic creation relies ultimately on the strength of the dialogue to carry everything along. The dramatist who creates it must have an innate consciousness of what will work onstage, possessing a *sense of theatre* that transcends the mere placing of words on paper. Without this sense, virtually impossible to define, the play will be in trouble. Being a successful writer of fiction is no guarantee of success in the theatre, as Henry James, the great novelist, discovered as he wrote play after play without any success whatever. He possessed no sense of the theatre in relating his story through dialogue alone. Ironically, many of his stories adapted by others became critical successes and popular theatre pieces.

From opening curtain to final exit, everything that goes on must be revealed through what people say to each other. During some periods of theatre history audiences relied on dialogue to convey almost everything, including the locale and the time of day, as when Horatio in the opening of *Hamlet* tells the spectators, standing in broad daylight, that dawn is breaking. But more importantly, dialogue exists as the only means by which characters may develop and establish relationships. In all manner of speeches from long poetic soliloquies to contemporary gutter language, the only way we can learn what characters think of themselves and each other is the way they talk and what they say.

Dialogue presents a paradox in the theatre. Because it keeps up incessantly throughout the drama, it becomes essentially unreal. On the other hand, even in blank verse or heroic couplets, the dialogue must still *appear* real. The fact that nobody actually talks that way is totally irrelevant. It must *seem* that they talk that way, no matter how they say it. The Greeks and the Elizabethans wrote mostly in verse (dramatists then were always regarded as poets), and today we write almost entirely in prose, which at times can be highly poetic, but however it is written, effective dialogue must have a sense of the rhythms and patterns of speech that are appropriate to the speakers and the particular dramatic situation in which they are placed. Characters in the great dramas do not just talk; they speak a highly literate dramatic dialogue. It holds the audience, it tells the story, it reveals the character, and it exposes the theme and idea. The quality of what everybody says to everybody else is what finally comes through as the essence of great *dramatic literature.*

Where It Is Said

Unless, in the manner of Browning or Shelley or one or two others, the dramatist wants to end it all here and publish a "closet" drama, meant only to be read, there is still a long road ahead. The drama, as written, contains within it the dramatic situations conceived by the dramatist, including everything we've talked about so far, but however brilliant the concept it will go nowhere until it is put in motion. What happens from here on out is *theatre,* the visual and the audible within the three-dimensional physical structure that holds the performance. Now the time arrives when the dramatist will witness the awful truth of what takes place when the artistic vision conceived on paper comes to life. Although most of what takes place may please and delight, there is a considerable chance for shock and dismay. Most modern dramatists who have lived to see their works enacted have, at one time or another, suffered the horrifying trauma of one who witnesses the sacrificial slaughter of a loved one. There were, at one time, those who wrote the script, acted in the performance, and even owned the company and the theatre they played in, so they could hold the drama reasonably close to their initial concept. In the contemporary theatre this kind of impresario has disappeared, and a great army of individuals charged with putting on the production subject the dramatist's work to their own wills and skills in order to place it in front of the audience for which it was originally designed.

The prime mover among the many who will eventually place their stamp upon the drama in the playhouse is the *director,* the single individual who has the final say on what appears. Virtually unheard of until the twentieth century, directors have achieved such prominence in the modern theatre that they may receive billing equal to and perhaps even above the dramatist or the star, with commensurate high pay. The final production is the director's ultimate responsibility; it may succeed in driving the audience out of the theatre, the play out the window, and the dramatist off the roof, but what the director says goes.

All others involved in mounting the final production function under the director's guidance. This includes approval of the setting, which provides the appropriate area in which the characters move, conceived by the scene designer, who may well be a highly accomplished and independent-thinking professional artist, and built by the stage technician and construction crew. So that everybody is fully visible (or invisible, if so demanded), the director must approve the lighting, designed and supervised by another professional artist whose conceptions are carried out by the electrician and another crew. Costumes, created by yet another artist (who can be, and frequently is, the scene designer as well), and constructed by still another crew, must also receive the director's approval. And so with sound or any other special effects. Everybody and everything must function flawlessly together, all under the eye and ear of the director, creating the whole stage picture, which we lump together under the term *mise-en-scène,* all meant not to dominate the drama but to serve it.

In addition to these aspects of the stage spectacle, there is a very important element that remains the director's primary responsibility and *raison d'être*—the choice of the actors who must be moved around the stage to project as well as possible everything that the dramatist has to say. The director and the writer, if available, may often work together in mounting a production, but more than one dramatist has been forced to watch the characters, interpreted by the actors chosen by and under the guidance of the director, become something quite apart from original intentions. Lighting, setting, sound, even costumes, are one thing, but the living and thinking actors, under a living and thinking director, observed by the living and thinking dramatist who thought everything up, can be quite another. On rare occasions a writer may dominate a director. George Bernard Shaw and Eugene O'Neill were two twentieth-century dramatists of such strength and fame that their word was law, and they could, and did, frequently overrule directors who dared stray from a play's original concept. Generally, however, the director is the ultimate boss.

Who Hears It Said

Unlike all other art forms, the drama demands a very special participant for its full effect and enjoyment: the *audience.* It is the group of people out front who finally turn everything that has been accomplished up to now into the mutual experience of the *play.* No artist outside the theatre is concerned with pleasing numbers of people simultaneously. Outside of the theatre the admiration of a work of art is a very personal thing, experienced on a one-to-one basis. The painter, the composer, or almost any other artist you can name other than the dramatist, conceives of the audience, broad-based or numerous as it may be, as encountering and reacting to the work as single individuals, unrelated to the surrounding crowd. Enjoying a symphony or admiring the beauties of ballet does not depend upon others being present at the same time. In no other art form is there anything comparable to the instantaneous and continuing action and reaction between the performers and the spectators who form a unit, a living entity, that reacts entirely independently from the separate psyches that make up the individual human components. The sense of mass participation in spectator sports, where the individual identity becomes melded into and altered by the "mob" psychology, is well known, but in art only the theatre expects and receives that same participation.

The psychology of the theatre, functioning on this basis of simultaneous mass experience, does not differentiate among the sizes of the audiences so much as it does the capacity of the areas that hold them. The proper response comes best when the house, however large or small, is full, or at least seems to be. The spark that flies all the way between stage and gallery will ignite effectively only if everyone's there. The play, to work, needs audience response. If there's nobody there, the actors know it; the spark doesn't fly back, and the house turns into an echo chamber. Besides, if you're sitting out front alone, with rows of empty seats between you and the rest of the crowd, it's not easy to catch the spark and throw it back.

The poet Samuel Taylor Coleridge was a drama and theatre critic who explained in very simple terms what actually happens in the theatre. Watching a play, he said, involves a tacit agreement between actors and audience to enter into a *willing suspension of disbelief.* It works in both directions. On the part of the actor it involves a sincere belief in the role, a belief that must be conveyed to the audience. John Smith believes in Hamlet, but he knows, all the same, that he himself is *not* Hamlet. But he does not disbelieve that he is Hamlet, either, knowing that the belief in the role is a vital part of the illusion that he, John Smith, really is Hamlet after all. The audience, while it must believe in what is going on in front of it, knows full well, on the other hand, that Hamlet is, in reality, merely John Smith. Still, it puts that reality aside and *refuses to disbelieve* that it is watching Hamlet and not John Smith. The audience knows that John Smith will get up and walk away after the curtain comes down; it also knows that Hamlet won't. In Coleridge's terms one neither denies what is happening nor truly believes what is happening. One remains suspended, accepting as truth neither illusion nor reality. In the enjoyment of the performance, it's just a matter of agreeing not *not* to believe.

In order for the suspension of disbelief to function properly, a balance must exist between performer and spectator in a kind of two-way stretch. Pulling one way is *empathy;* pulling the other is the maintenance of *aesthetic distance.*

Empathy means emotional identification, a "going out to" the characters by the audience. Although none of us will have met a fraction of the problems of an Oedipus or a Hamlet, we know that each is suffering physical and emotional pain in the same manner as all humankind. Thus we identify as fellow human beings, regardless of the circumstances, so long as our sympathies and understanding, our ultimate belief in the characters and the incidents portrayed, are kept within reasonable bounds. Failure of empathy can be the fault of the dramatist, whose characters appear too gross, too repulsive, extravagant, or ridiculous. It can be the fault of the director, whose control over what is said and done may be so unimaginative, exaggerated, or dull that the audience refuses to accept the theatrical validity of what it sees. Or it can be the fault of the actors who just don't "come across" and who fail to convince. The audience must constantly believe in what it sees. The whole thing must be convincingly plausible, even if it's set on Mars. The audience, in short, must be kept interested and sympathetic.

Against this force is the equal and opposite reaction, *aesthetic distance.* While moving constantly toward the stage in emotional, that is, empathic belief, the audience must simultaneously pull back in the realization that what it witnesses is art, not life. However vivid the stage picture, the audience must never lose that sense of remaining outside, at a distance. Excessive violence, for instance, can alter the balance very quickly. If the audience feels that the actor—not the character, but the actor—is really suffering, so that the difference between illusion and reality is indistinguishable, aesthetic distance can be lost. If the situation onstage is unclear and the audience cannot distinguish between a planned event, something written into the play, or an accidental event, resulting, say, from an actor's lapsed memory, empathy and aesthetic distance both suffer. Children and animals are notorious destroyers of the empathy–aesthetic distance balance. Will they behave? Does the child know his or her lines? Or, on the other side: How well trained they are! How brilliantly they perform! The animal is judged against its human counterpart, and the child against the adult. The illusion, laboriously established, can easily disintegrate.

It's relatively easy to put on a show. It's not all that difficult to mount a good play, but it's very nearly impossible to write, stage, and perform a piece of dramatic and theatrical art that will survive as genuinely great literature. The hurdles are nigh insurmountable, but when they are successfully leaped, there emerges an *Oedipus Rex* or a *Hamlet.* There's an irony behind many of the greatest works of dramatic art. We read them and we go to see them performed, and we praise them for their durability, their insights, their poetry, their stories, their universality. It's hard, sometimes, to remember how many were originally written and performed only for the moment, with survival in an enduring body of dramatic literature very likely never considered. The ancient Greeks staged their plays as part of a religious festival and, once performed, the dramas were normally never revived. Shakespeare was in the business for the money, and he had to keep hopping to help provide his acting company with good playable scripts. If somebody had not safely stored that manuscript of Sophocles in some ancient vault, we might never have known of Oedipus. If Ben Jonson, seeing the First Folio through the press, had not been determined to keep the memory of his friend Shakespeare alive, we would have missed about half of that marvelous collection. Instantaneous, ephemeral, existing only for the time it takes to watch, a hybrid of all the arts, a bastard art claimed as nobody's child but everybody's responsibility, the greatest *drama* survives through its language on a printed page, but it must not be permanently entombed there. Somewhat like the butterfly, encased within its cocoon, the drama is ready for the performer's art, for the *theatre,* emerging from its chrysalis to display its fragile beauty in that single exciting moment of becoming a *play,* before it once more disappears.

Concerning the Form, the Type, and the Style

Literature other than that created for the stage has no particular bounds imposed upon it with regard to the way it is put together or the way it treats its subject matter. The dramatist, however, even beyond the matters of time and space, has further restrictions imposed to a far greater degree than upon other writers, since the drama is constructed and shaped within fairly close limits controlled by factors relating almost wholly to drama and theatre alone.

The Way It's Put Together

If the story is the *soul* of drama, the heart is the *agon,* or *argument,* and it is the *conflict* surrounding the argument that becomes the pulse. The two sides of the conflict, the pros and cons of the agon, center around the *protagonistic* forces and the *antagonistic* forces. The *protagonist* may be one person or many, and the *antagonist* may be a person, a group, a thing, or a force—supernatural, natural, or divine.

The manner by which the argument is developed becomes the structure, or the *form,* of the play. First of all, there has to be a starting point, known as the *point of attack,* at which moment the dramatist leads the audience into the picture. This can start at the beginning of things, in an *accretive plot,* with the essentials cumulatively revealed as they actually occur, thus permitting both the audience and the characters to discover what's going on at the same time. This is the method Shakespeare uses in *Hamlet.* Or it can start at the middle of things, or even very near the end, in a *climactic plot,* with the forward progress of the story gradually revealing the essentials that have already transpired. This is the method Sophocles uses in *Oedipus.*

No matter where the point of attack takes place, the first thing the dramatist has to do is to establish what is going on and who is involved, which is done through the technique of *exposition,* the exposing of the facts. This can involve a variety of approaches, from the maid and visitor routine of characters telling each other, and thus telling the audience, what the basic situation is, much as Chekhov uses in *The Cherry Orchard,* to the direct and immediate involvement in fast-developing action that Shakespeare employs in the opening of *Hamlet.* Exposition must be revealed clearly and slowly enough for the audience to retain the necessary information in order to relate it to subsequent scenes, and dramatic exposition can continue well into the play, through several scenes, as the past is revealed, the present explained, and characters introduced and assimilated. Then, once everything is sufficiently established, the conflict heads toward its climax and eventual resolution, and the dramatist cannot return to any further exposition without confusing the audience and muddying up what has already been said.

Having established where things stand, the dramatist proceeds with the *complications* that provide the depth and breadth of the conflict. These proceed through the *rising action,* a literal building of interest through suspense, emotional reaction, deepening mystery, and so on. It is the time for plottings and counterplottings, intrigues and conspiracies, accumulation of incidents and development of character. Revelations from the past, forebodings and foreshadowings of the future begin carrying the conflict toward the play's high point, its *climax.* Here everything is pulled together. The protagonist and antagonist have established their sides of the agon and have, in one way or another, met head on. This is the point toward which everything has aimed, and the confrontation of protagonist and antagonist results in a climactic showdown, serious or comic, which is termed the *obligatory scene,* the one that everybody knows must happen. It is, in other words, a turning point, after which nothing new can be added. Any high point in the story hereafter becomes *anticlimactic,* and is in serious danger of losing any dramatic effect it may have. There may be a lot of the play left, or it may all terminate very quickly, but once reached, the climax is a point of no return. It can be but a moment, as when Oedipus finally learns the truth of who and what he is, very late in the play, or it can be a series of events, as in *Hamlet,* somewhat past the middle, from the mousetrap play scene to the killing of Polonius.

Following the climax everything heads downward in *falling action,* the period when the action unravels. Now we can see how it all comes out, for there is no more building toward a suspenseful moment in the manner of the rising action. Things fall into place, and the play heads toward the conclusion, or *denouement,* or, as the Greeks put it, particularly as it pertains to tragedy, the *catastrophe.* Then it's all over, the bodies are removed, the lovers embrace, and everybody goes home.

A great number of plays follow the exposition-to-denouement routine in almost perfect balance, capable of being graphically illustrated, scene by scene, act by act, in a uniformly parabolic curve. Such plays have been given the label "well made," and because the structure rather than the theme or idea or character became the most important aspect, emphasizing mass popular entertainment rather than good dramatic literature, the term "well made" has long been one of critical disfavor. But all great plays are essentially "well made," as you will discover in the brilliant structure of plays as diverse as *Oedipus, Hamlet,* or *A Doll's House.* It is what the dramatist does with the story in developing the conflict, how well defined the protagonist and antagonist, that makes the real difference. That parabola may be perfectly formed or completely erratic in its rise and fall. That is not what really matters. Mix everything up, change things around, invent new ways of displaying them, be as "well-made" or experimental as you please, but by the time the last curtain comes down, the dramatist must have established the conflict, developed both sides of the argument, and reached a reasonable conclusion—all involving the elements we have discussed here, for the basic structure, the form of the play, whatever else, remains a whole made out of these very fundamental parts.

What Kind of Play It Is

Polonius gives Hamlet a pretty good catalog of the variety of entertainment provided by the strolling players who happen by Elsinore:

> The best actors in the world, either for tragedy, comedy, history, pastoral, pastoral-comical, historical-pastoral, tragical-historical, tragical-comical-historical-pastoral, scene individable, or poem unlimited. Seneca cannot be too heavy, nor Plautus too light. For the law of writ and the liberty, these are the only men.

Apparently the performers of that day could, upon occasion, do just about everything.

What Polonius was describing, of course, was a variety of dramatic *types,* or individual kinds of plays. Whether or not all the multiple combinations he cites would be recognizable definitions today remains a question, but Polonius touched upon the full spectrum of his own time from the most serious classical to the lightest contemporary approach. He well knew that there could be extensive intermingling of the serious and comic and he recognized the difficulty of pigeonholing any single play, but he was equally aware that what he said conveyed meaning to the Prince in terms of the dramatic types that lay within the players' repertoire.

Tragedy and *comedy* were common terms in fifth-century Greece, as we know from Aristotle. They remain today as the most all-inclusive identifications of type, though there are important variations. The Elizabethans, as Polonius states, were familiar with *historical* plays as in the Richard and Henry sequences of Shakespeare, but the term *tragedy* was used almost universally to mean the serious treatment of a subject. Throughout the Renaissance the *pastoral* was a major form, dealing, as in Shakespeare's *As You Like It,* with shepherds, shepherdesses, and the "pure" country life. But pastorals are essentially comedies and, as a distinct type, have not survived.

On the serious side in today's definitions of type are the three broadly general terms of *tragedy, melodrama,* and *drama,* sometimes called a "*straight play,*" or, in more precise critical terms, the "*middle genre*" or *drame.* On the lighter side are *comedy* and *farce.* Recognizing, like Polonius, that nothing falls easily into one place, we can still fairly easily put the bulk of dramatic art into one of these five broad definitions.[3]

Dramatic tragedy is not what nearly everybody will say it is—a sad play with an unhappy ending. The root of tragedy has nothing at all to do with death or sadness, for it comes down to us from the Greek *tragos,* or goat, plus *aeidein,* to sing, or, simply put, "song of the goat." The goat was sacred to Dionysus, god of wine and fertility in whose name were held the early festivals of song and dance out of which the drama grew. The whole concept of tragedy as we shall now define it is a product of Greek civilization and remains virtually unknown outside the West, for it is founded upon a very special view which the Greeks held concerning humanity and its relationship to the gods. The Greek gods were not animals or freakish creatures. They were human beings in perfect form, immortal to be sure, but subject to every passion of love, hate, jealousy, rage, and sensual delight endured by men and women on earth. The Greeks admired the human body, male and female, and in the great classic age which concerns us here painted and sculpted it undraped, to be revealed, not hidden. Not only did they marvel at its physical beauty, but at the accomplishments it could achieve. There was, in fact, such admiration for the human creature that the Greeks created their gods in an idealized image of themselves—beautiful, handsome, radiant, powerful. Developing naturally from this concept was the realization that Zeus, the king of gods, could be stricken with helpless infatuation for a nubile earthling, and that Hera, his wife, the goddess queen, could be violently jealous. The

[3]The *tragi-comedy,* a serious play approaching tragedy but with a "happy" ending, is sometimes identified as a sixth type.

gods did not necessarily act with common sense and good judgment, any more than their human counterparts, but when they did act, it was along human lines which could be readily understood if not entirely appreciated by ordinary mortals. And the gods were not completely independent, for they were subject to the final act of the Fates, the three sisters who spun out the thread of life, drew it to its full length, and cut it, an event the gods could not alter.

Bearing this in mind, we can fairly easily see how the idea of tragedy developed. It is an assertion of humanity's fundamental greatness. It demonstrates the individual's ability to rise to heights of human dignity in the face of an antagonistic force that he or she knows will finally end in actual or symbolic death. The protagonist of the tragedy may commit the most heinous deeds, knowingly or unknowingly, but because the gods are as they are, capable of carrying grudges and taking offense in the same manner as their mortal counterparts, they may impose outrageous curses upon the perpetrator, including the family unto several generations. The point of tragedy is that the protagonist, male or female, when faced with the inevitability of the fact that the arrayed antagonistic forces are to cause a literal or figurative death, can rise to the occasion and assert magnificence as a human being, defying those forces and, in the end, bringing them to bay or often destroying them. The tragic protagonist is doomed, and there is no possibility of escape. We watch in awe as, finally, in full recognition of the inevitable, he or she proceeds toward that doom. Thereafter comes a balance of forces, a tranquility, a laying to rest, and an absolute finality. Nothing comes afterward. The end is complete. What the protagonist has done in the process of the struggle is what counts. Without hope of rescue or relief, absolutely alone against the forces that will destroy, the tragic protagonist, whatever foul deeds may have been committed or whatever human foolishness may have been displayed, rises to the ultimate in courage and defiance, demonstrating the potential godlike quality that lies within humanity, but which only legendary figures in tragedy can ever approach.

Tragedy is not saddening and depressing in the ordinary sense of a fatal accident or some destructive human or natural catastrophe. Tragedy is positive and optimistic in its view of the heights the human being can reach. There is considerable distinction, as well, between the tragic protagonist and the martyr. The martyr suffers and dies for a particular cause and may consciously seek death. The tragic protagonist, on the contrary, has every reason to live and makes a heroic struggle to survive, but as long as there is survival, there is no tragedy. Only in death does the tragic grandeur emerge. The death of the tragic protagonist is, however, a kind of passion—not necessarily religious, for that would enter into the area of martyrdom—but there is a certain kinship in the great sacrifice involved. In tragedy, humanity has sacrificed something it can ill afford to lose. But the protagonist, displaying greatness, actually approaches the godlike, and the sacrifice is a kind of reverse act, an offering not for the benefit of the gods but for the benefit of humankind—a proof of ultimate human worthiness.

Such tears as may be shed at the final catastrophe are not tears of sadness, but of compassion. There can be profound emotional involvement, but there remains the fundamental optimism that must be present at the end of the best of tragedy. We have witnessed how near the gods a person can be. Aristotle gets involved in this whole matter of emotion when he speaks briefly of tragic *catharsis,* or *purgation* as sometimes translated, and the arousal in the audience of *pity* and *terror,* or *fear.* What he seems to be saying is that in viewing a tragedy one is moved by a compassionate pity toward the protagonist for what is being endured, and it is not a sentimental pity, nor merely a "pitiful" reaction. Similarly, one experiences an emotional reaction akin to terror from a realization of the magnitude of the forces and their power in bringing down the struggling protagonist. By the end, when tranquility has been restored, the audience has gone through a kind of cleansing, a kind of spiritual purgation, in the realization of how great the human creature can be on occasion.

What kind of person is the ideal tragic protagonist? Certainly the protagonist is human and cannot be a god, but must also, at the same time, be of a certain noble stature. Originally this meant royalty or similar high personages, whose deaths could make empires tremble and kingdoms crumble. Today, of course, if we are to assert that tragedy can exist, there must still be contained within the protagonist, however ordinary or lowborn, that element of human greatness involving stature far beyond the ordinary.

The tragic protagonist cannot be evil or villainous by nature, a person whose death the audience welcomes as justified, nor flawlessly good, for then death becomes truly pitiable and shocking, displeasing to those who watch. What makes the difference is that the protagonist is afflicted, as Hamlet says, from "some vicious mole of nature" that can and will destroy. In other words, for all the potential, the protagonist inwardly bears the *tragic flaw* that leads to ultimate destruction. To the Greeks *hubris,* or excessive pride, more often than not could drive a tragic protagonist to his or her fate. But whether you call it pride, arrogance, vanity, or whatever, within the human psyche must rest the seeds of doom. In the end, the protagonist finally recognizes what is happening and neither cringes nor flees, but turns and shouts defiance, much as Macbeth in his final moments, who welcomes his advancing adversary with, "Lay on, Macduff/ And damn'd be him that first cries, 'Hold, enough!'"

Throughout tragedy runs the constant thread of *irony.* The variations are almost endless, but the force of tragic irony contributes substantially to the final impact of the tragic experience. Irony can involve the audience, aware of what is going to happen, or aware of why it is happening from a knowledge of the past, while the protagonist remains in ignorance. It can involve the twists and turns of fate when the harder the protagonist seeks to avoid the catastrophe, as in the case of Oedipus, the faster it arrives. It can involve human procrastination or unthinking impulsiveness, as in Hamlet's refusal to kill the king when he has the chance, or in his killing of Polonius, whom he takes to be the king while knowing full well it cannot *possibly* be the king.

The dramatist who ends up with merely a "sad" play with an "unhappy" ending, is not writing tragedy at all. If the catastrophe brings only sorrow, lacking awe; if it brings pathos instead of majesty, depression instead of elevation; or if the dramatist moralizes upon the fate of the protagonist and speaks of "justice," the play is not entertaining the tragic view.

Melodrama, like tragedy, has come to mean something quite different from its original semantic roots. A combination of *melo,* music, plus *drama,* it means "a play with music." The term originated some time during the eighteenth century when the popular theatre of the day, offering entertainment outside the limited number of duly licensed theatres in London or the aristocratic, more "classical" theatres in Paris, made extensive use of background and incidental music. The subject matter of these theatrical diversions was full of blood and thunder with lots of broad and exciting action. By the end of the eighteenth century, when melodrama as a theatrical type emerged in both England and France, a great many of these characteristics were inherited, together with the most significant tradition of innocent maidens persecuted by villains and saved by handsome heroes.

The difference between a tragedy that, like *Oedipus* or *Hamlet,* may rely upon the sensational events and excitement of what we now call melodrama, and a true melodrama lies in the degree of emphasis. Action in a tragedy is an integral part of the progression toward a final catastrophe, whereas melodrama creates action for its own sake. Characters in tragedy are well developed, more "rounded out"; those in melodrama are flat and instantly recognizable so that the action and the fast-developing plot can move along unencumbered. The end of a tragedy is unrelated to justice and retribution as such; melodrama punishes the bad and rewards the good. Melodrama anticipates that things will all work out in the end, thus creating hope. Tragedy, as we know, provides its central figure with no hope and no way out.

The nontragic, nonmelodramatic, noncomic play known as the *middle genre,* the "*straight*" *drama,* or the *drame,* is a product of literary realism. It achieves its hold on its audience by means of its treatment of men and women who may be king or commoner, rich or poor, in terms of their essential everyday humanity, encountering neither Hamlet's slings and arrows of outrageous fortune nor the arbitrary sensations of a contrived melodrama but facing the challenges of daily existence in the milieu of a familiar and easily recognizable society, reasonably contemporary to that in which the audience itself exists. It avoids the extravagances of tragedy or melodrama at either end, and can present its protagonist as one who may, upon occasion, refuse to shout and who may even run, hide, whimper, or beg. Such characters and the action that they encounter are no less attractive as dramatic figures than their tragic or melodramatic counterparts. In fact, the logic and the rationale of what they are and what they experience may win audiences far more easily and send them home far more satisfied, for they will have seen before them individuals far closer to what they are themselves.

Aristotle's limited observations about comedy still hold true, for he said that tragedy shows people as greater than they are, whereas comedy shows them as less than they are. One thing is certain: Aristotle or not, comedy keeps reminding us how unlike the gods we are, all of our noblest urges notwithstanding.

The popular idea is that comedy is "funny," and that it has a "happy ending." In general, yes. But a comedy can have death and suffering of all kinds. The main thing that distinguishes it from serious drama is the *detached point of view.* Any comic situation carried through to its logical conclusion would probably end in disaster, but comedy forces us to keep our distance, compelling us to recognize that the pain is not damaging nor the disaster permanent. Comedy does not let those who watch become emotionally involved. The moment that we do so, the comedy has ended.

Comedy continually emphasizes the inferior, second-rate nature of most of us, pulling us down from the heights with a reminder of our vulnerability and the foolishness of our posturing. It does this by tripping us up with the sudden reversal, the unexpected twist, the ludicrous juxtaposition and gross exaggeration. Comedy makes us fall flat on our face, and although we who hit the ground with a thud may not like it and may fail to see the joke, those watching see it as ridiculous, and they refuse to feel the pain. It is in this action-reaction combination that comedy treads a very narrow emotional line. Things that have made people laugh may not have changed through history, but artistic taste in dramatic comedy has altered. Physical defects, race, or mental instability no longer work as comic devices among sophisticated audiences in the manner they once did. We do not hire hunchbacks to be our jesters anymore, nor go to the insane asylum of a Sunday afternoon to watch the inmates perform, as the Elizabethans would do at Bethlehem (Bedlam) Hospital. Still with us, however, basically unaltered and effective as ever, is the sex joke in its infinity of variations, along with the pratfall, the pie-in-the-face routine, the wisecrack and the witty epigram.

The extremes of comedy are generally identified as "high" and "low." *High comedy* in its best form, defined from time to time as *social comedy, comedy of manners,* or *drawing-room comedy,* is intellectual in its appeal, relying heavily upon sex, sophistication, and brilliant wit. High comedy is mostly dramatic, rather than theatrical, with very little action. It is static, given to words more than deeds. Most of the characters are fairly well rounded, and they are aware of the fact that they are playing an elaborate game in a comic world. The game, however, is taken very seriously, and the rules by which it operates bring laughter through the reversal of normally expected values. At the other end is *farce,* which includes many of the same qualities as melodrama, but the result is meant for fun and laughter, in toto and without exception. Farce is considered "low" comedy, but that does not mean inferiority. High comedy has a fairly narrow intellectual appeal, while low comedy, in farce, has a broad and anti-intellectual appeal. Incident piles on incident; the jokes, the sight gags and wisecracks come thick and fast. Farce is theatrical, and its premise is that of a wacky world without much sense, inhabited by a lot of zany people, where logic and reason have no known function. The more a sane rationale is sought by characters within a farce, the more it is likely to escape and, hence, the more the laughter. Farce, like melodrama, is visceral. The "belly laugh" means just that.

The large in-between area, neither "high" nor "low," is inhabited by "straight" comedy or, as much of it can also be defined, the *comedy of sensibility.* Those who inhabit this middle genre of comedy are, like their counterparts in the "straight" drama or *drame,* comparatively unsophisticated people who can, in the course of events, experience death and suffering as well as fun and games. Plot development depends mostly on its emphasis on character behavior and attitude, avoiding the vulgarities of farce as well as the intellectual appeal of high comedy. This broad range of the comic shows the fundamental charm of average, plodding, ordinary people, but the characters maintain their comic character, permitting the audience no opportunity for lingering sentimentality, even if the pain and suffering get a little close to home. As Henri Bergson has said in his famous essay on laughter, when we laugh, especially in this type of comedy, we put affection aside and silence our pity. The heart, he said, must undergo "a momentary anesthesia."

The Manner in Which It's Done

Style refers to the *manner* and *method* in which a drama is originally conceived and written and in which it is produced onstage. There are dramatic as well as theatrical styles, each typical of a given period in history, each complementing the other. The drama of one era, such as the Greek, or the Elizabethan, or the Restoration, was designed for production in a specific kind of theatre building, and the building itself was designed to accommodate the drama it received. Until well into the nineteenth century, the style of drama and the style of theatre worked in harmony to present the audience with a style of play relatively unaltered in form for periods of 75 to 100 years or more. Regardless of subject, theme, character, or incident, the general style of what we call Shakespearean (or Elizabethan), for instance, remained consistent in costuming, staging, theatre structure, and dramaturgy from the opening of the first commercial theatre, the open-air structure patterned after Elizabethan innyards, in 1576 until all theatres were closed by the Puritans in 1642. Likewise, from the time of the reopening of the theatres by Charles II in 1660, the style that we have come to call Restoration and Eighteenth Century remained relatively constant in dramatic form and structure, in subject matter and theme, and, in the increasingly large indoor opera-house type of theatre with its horseshoe galleries and sloping stage. In the twentieth century all this changed; today style is no longer so rigidly associated with a particular time and place but involves an almost limitless variety of methods of writing and staging, unrestricted by custom or theatre structure.

Four fairly broad basic styles are now associated with the writing of drama and its production in the theatre. They have significant meanings and connotations in today's theatre, even though variations, combinations, and overlappings are everywhere apparent.

Classic

The *classic style* is carefully structured in its dramaturgy in the manner of Greek tragedy which, like all ancient Greek art, followed clean structural lines conceived, like the Parthenon and other classic temples, primarily for the aesthetic effect. In keeping with the traditions of classic Greek drama, the classic style restricts its subject matter to a single story, avoiding side issues and subplots, devoted mainly to heroic legendary or historical myths and tales. Behavior on stage is decorous and lacks overt physical violence, nearly all of which takes place offstage, though to be sure the physical and mental agonies, such as suffered by an Oedipus, are in full view. Action is held in the main to a single place and a single time. Dialogue is elevated in tone, highly poetic, carefully planned in long set speeches alternating with passages of quick exchange of lines between the major characters. Staging itself is uncluttered, with the whole production, writing included, suggesting the smoothness of polished marble, the grace of fluted columns, the dignity of the Acropolis, the magnificence of a sculptured god or goddess. The dramatist who entertains the *classic* view is interested in the relationship of larger-than-life characters to the gods (or God, or Fate, or Nature, or the Universe) as well as to each other, and also frequently raises profound philosophical questions about human behavior and the forces that control it. Though not necessarily synonymous, the classic and tragic views work very closely together.

Romantic

The *romantic style* chooses its emphasis quite differently. The romanticist sees humankind as essentially good, unaffected by curses from malevolent gods and untainted by original sin, and finds that the rigid uniformity of subject matter, theme, and decor of the classic style is overly restrictive and innovatively stifling. Instead of the artificialities and the stately decorum of the classic view, the romantic outlook calls for originality, freedom to innovate and to move about in time and space, and to entertain high adventure and multiple plotlines. This means, especially in staging, a lot of color, spectacle, exciting adventure, and derring-do. It means the free appeal directly to the emotions, so apparent in melodrama, the dramatic style most obviously an exponent of the romantic.

Central to the philosophy of the romantic is the idea that many human problems are caused by the veneer imposed by "civilization," thus hiding one's true nature. Strip it away and underneath will be revealed not the horrors of a soul doomed by primal curse or original sin to eternal damnation but the source of human kindness and goodness. "Natural man" to the romanticist is pure and uncontaminated. Hence the romanticist looks to nature itself, to the woods, fields, streams, to the winds, rains, storms, and sunshine for the understanding of humanity. In addition—because, in retrospect, the past invariably seems to have been a time of "better days"—the romanticist is historically oriented, recalling the times when men were men and challenges were met with honor and dignity.[4] The romantic attitude involves delight in playing upon the senses, emphasizing sentiment, nostalgia, and the emotionalism of undying love and eternal devotion, and remains basically optimistic.

The romanticist also maintains an equal fascination with the powers of evil and the mysteries of death. The hold upon the mind of evil deeds and Satanic acts is ever gripping; there is far more dramatic appeal in the Hellish than in the Heavenly. What is death? Whence comes it? Can it be overcome? What exists on the other side of the grave? The romantic seeks to know, and revels in the fantastic, the supernatural, the magical, and the exotic, often with settings in secluded vales, on treacherous shores, atop craggy mountains, or in far distant and mysterious lands.

Realistic and Naturalistic

The classicist writes of royalty and nobility, viewing them with awe and a certain fearful respect. The romanticist becomes involved with sentiments and emotions in the treatment of individuals and nature, preferring the ideal, trusting in nature and natural goodness. The literary artist drawn to the realities of life and death, in the ordinary individual man and woman as part and product of their surroundings, their civilization, their society, quite apart from moral aspects of sin and retribution and punishing gods, displays interest in one of the stylistic Siamese twins of *realism* and *naturalism.* The metaphorical joining of these two terms is not without good reason. Trying to separate them reveals so many overlappings and duplications that contemporary critics use them almost interchangeably. They are, however, separate entities in enough ways to make them exist individually, if not entirely independently.

Realism, then, as we apply it to the drama, takes humanity pretty much as it is in the society in which it operates, with that society in turn presented as a product of the men and women in it. The subject matter thus becomes a transcription of reality, placing on stage individuals and their surroundings through language and action as they would be found in real life, performing against the

[4]The romanticist often cannot resist altering history, preferring the ideal of what ought to have been, rather than what actually happened. The German romanticist Friedrich Schiller wrote a version of the Joan of Arc story in 1801 and sent his heroine to her death in battle. His 1800 version of Mary of Scotland brings Mary and Elizabeth together in a key confrontation that never took place. We are still affected in the same manner today. The 1970 movie version of the same story brought the two queens together twice.

background of a fully articulated, illusionistic stage setting. Within the theatre the characters become isolated from the audience behind the proscenium arch where, through the brilliance of electric lighting, the one great invention which forever changed the basic concepts of staging and provided controlled illumination never before available to the theatrical producer, they address each other as if in complete privacy. Asides, soliloquies, and declamatory speeches, the hallmarks of nearly all drama of the past, disappear. The characters become those with whom the audience has a close personal identity. The realist, writing of what transpires in the actual world, presents characters for what they are as the product of their own society, unromanticized and unsentimentalized. The realist strips nothing away, presenting what is seen as in the eye of the camera. The characters are made into rounded, three-dimensional individuals, neither wholly good nor wholly evil but wholly human, appearing strong or fragile, heroic or fearful as the situation demands.

The dialogue of realism is keyed to the idiom of the time. Poetry gives way to the cadences of ordinary speech. Action flows naturally upon previous action, avoiding all arbitrary twists of plot merely for the effect they may create. Realistic drama recognizes that the events portrayed did not begin with the rise, nor do they end with the fall, of the curtain. Of course the realist must be selective about what is placed upon the stage, for this is art, however "real" the illusion. This presents one of the major challenges for the realistic dramatist, who must learn how to balance the illusion of reality with the creativity of art. Recognizing the impossibility of placing reality literally onstage, the dramatist must determine how to convey the sense of reality, through art, while still keeping it "artless." How does one contrive "reality"? The coincidences and accidents that make up reality will appear as contrivances artificially introduced for effect if the dramatist is not careful. Life may lead an individual up one blind alley after another, but too many of them in a "realistic" play will make an audience restless, dissatisfied at having been fooled too many times. The dramatic realist knows that art is art and life is life. Each can only suggest, not become, the other. What the dramatist writes and places on the stage must remain reasonably real, for it is only *realistic;* it cannot be *reality.* It must be, in fact, a highly contrived art that consistently must mask its contrivances. It must eliminate the imaginative play of the mind while compelling the audience to imagine that the illusion is real. It is art that does not appear to be art; it is "reality" that is not reality.

The emphasis of *naturalism* is somewhat different. It makes use of the same subject matter, but regards the characters it treats in a more objective or even scientific sense. To the naturalistic writer characters are subjects for close analysis, a kind of artistic dissection. The naturalist is interested in the fundamental nature of what makes men and women function, not so much as characters in society but as creatures in the natural world. According to the naturalist's perspective, society has imposed upon the individual a certain pattern of behavior made up of the customs and taboos of "civilization." If that veneer is removed, man stands revealed in his animalistic primitiveness, interested primarily in the three urges of natural gratification: eating, evacuation, and sex. The naturalist, dwelling upon these things and, unlike the realist, not particularly selective, preferring to reveal all, has often been accused of being a mere sensationalist, a seeker of horrors. The defense against this charge rests upon the need to remove society's veneer in order to get to the analysis itself and to probe the forces of nature that have made the individuals what they are. As a result, life, as seen by the naturalist, tends to become a jungle. Sex becomes an animal battle, often to the death. The naturalist writer avoids the subjective emotional involvement of the romanticist, sees little to be gained from lessons of the past, and regards the future with pessimism, as opposed to the realist counterpart who is neither a pessimist nor an optimist. The eternal "progress" toward a better world seen by the romanticist is not a part of human nature to the naturalist, who sees very little possibility of people's becoming better.

Recognizing that the forces of nature that make men and women direct products of the natural environment can be devastating, the naturalist can offer no particular solutions, being uncertain even as to whether there *are* any. The realist, in treating the social problems of the day, often takes a stand, advocates a cause, perhaps even offers a solution. Still, much of the difference between the artistic realist and the artistic naturalist comes down to a degree of emphasis. Henrik Ibsen, regarded as the first great dramatic realist, once explained the difference between himself and Émile Zola, widely recognized as one of the greatest naturalists at the end of the nineteenth century. In words to this effect, Ibsen said, "When I go down into the sewer I go to clean it out. When Zola goes down, he takes a bath."

Stylization—Expressionism, Impressionism, Absurdism

Realism (we shall use the single term from now on) has become the commonly accepted definition of the style of "modern" drama, which means from the time of Ibsen in the 1870s and 1880s until the present, and any departure in writing or staging has come to be known as *stylization.* Stylization works in two directions, involving the staging of contemporary plays and revivals of plays from the past. A contemporary subject treated dramatically or theatrically in nonrealistic fashion, as discussed below, is regarded as "stylized." On the other hand, the staging of a Shakespearean play in nineteenth-century Edwardian costume and setting, as has been done with *Much Ado About Nothing,* or the portrayal of a Hamlet or Macbeth in strictly modern costume is also "stylized." Our interest here, however, is in the departures from realism that modern theatre techniques in sound and lighting have made possible, opening up a wide variety of inventive possibilities for the dramatist.

Foremost among the forms of stylization is *expressionism.* First acknowledged in a 1902 drama by the Swedish ultrarealist, August Strindberg, entitled *The Dream Play,* this style placed upon the stage a graphic picture of a nightmare in which time, place, and characters interchanged, blended, and disappeared in the fashion of a long dream. It was the theatrical *expression* of a very subjective viewpoint of life. That is what the expressionist does, taking reality and expressing it not as life *is* but as it *seems.* If the artist finds a man to be a cipher in the monolith of big business he can be called, in the manner of Elmer Rice in his expressionistic play *The Adding Machine* of 1924, Mr. Zero, with equally undistinguished friends Mr. and Mrs. One, Two, and Three. If men or women seem indistinguishable from the machines they operate, make them speak and move as mechanical automatons. If they seem to make no sense in what they say and do in daily living, make their voices monotonous, singsong, metallic, or staccato. Give them gibberish to say. If escape is hopeless, display them in a world that is being closed in by constricting scenery. If you are an expressionist, *express* your views and display them to the fullest extent of dramatic and theatrical distortion, exaggeration, or caricature.

Expressionism is socially oriented in its philosophy, critical in serious as well as comic vein, concerned with the present, and fearful of the future that may or may not arrive. It is a thoroughly pessimistic view in one perspective, but realizing that what occurs is a result of humankind's own actions, expressionism has an air of hope that things might be corrected before it is too late. Like the naturalist, however, the expressionist doesn't have much faith in what the past can teach, and the present bodes ill for the questionable future.

Expressionism as an independent style was popular for only two or three decades at the beginning of the twentieth century, but its effects have remained a permanent legacy in the theatre. Today, the "style" of a play can range from the starkest literal realism in setting, characters, and dialogue to the most highly imaginative expression of the author's innermost thoughts and attitudes. The expressionist opened up the use of the stage, including even the theatre auditorium itself as an acting area, and imposed no limits whatever on dramatic or theatrical technique. The result is that the "offshoots" (or, at least, the parallel developments) of styles like *impressionism* and *absurdism* are equally at home in the modern theatre. The *impressionist* with a view of life from a particular vantage point, through the haze of physical or psychical distance, can make use of sights and sounds, dialogue and actions not wholly real, not wholly unreal, to create not a distorted "*ex*pression" but a highly personal "*im*pression." The *absurdist* can view the world as a ridiculous dark joke, with life as a pointless existentialist exercise, a baffling endurance contest with unknown disinterested forces, an absurdity on the face of it, and can send the characters through a thoroughly stylized world to make this point. And all because the expressionist, making use of the miracle controls of electric lighting and eventually of mobile stages—revolving, elevator, or what not—and electronic sound, proceeded in an independent and imaginative way, whereas the realist sought to present life as it really is. But both were doing the same thing. Each created a style, each based that style on the same premises about humanity and its place in society. The outward, literal, objective presentation is *realism.* The inward, imaginative, subjective presentation is *expressionism.* Independently and collectively they have brought the contemporary drama and the contemporary theatre a lot of excitement and intellectual stimulation.

The prehistoric hunter's retelling of exploits before the cave fire was a type of dramatic experience that had its own form and style, created in the mind, presented with embellishments of sight and sound, ending in a presentation before an audience. There was a *drama,* there was *theatre,* and there was a *play.* Things haven't changed much since. They've just become more complicated.

Everything you will read in this volume has proven its worth, deserving by one means or another to be known as great literature—a special literature for a special kind of experience. Each drama that you read will affect you differently, as it did every man or woman who came to watch or the critic who came to judge since the first one was displayed two and a half thousand years ago. These dramas represent artistic accomplishments that rank among the finest creations of the human mind. But they were meant first and foremost to *entertain.* They must be approached as sources of aesthetic pleasure, for which reason they were created in the first place.

So read.

Enjoy.

Jordan Y. Miller

OEDIPUS REX

(c. 430 B.C.)

SOPHOCLES (496–406 B.C.)

The presentation of tragedies was one of the most important events during the ancient Greek celebration of the Festival of Dionysus. Many poets contributed their works, but only 32 completed plays have survived from the more than 170 known to have been written by the three great tragic poets of the fifth century B.C.: Aeschylus (c. 513–c. 456), Sophocles (496–406), and Euripides (c. 485–c. 407). Everything else, including plays by other writers, except for some titles and assorted fragments, has been lost, but references by Aristotle in particular suggest that the extant plays were among the best. An important aspect is the detailed knowledge they provide about many of the wonderful Greek myths, in addition to some interesting insights into fifth-century Greek society and its attitude toward the gods.

The Dionysiac was a religious festival honoring Dionysus, youngest of the Olympian deities and the god of wine and revelry. Dionysus wore a wreath of vine leaves in his hair and traditionally died and was reborn in the pattern of the seasonal production of the vines themselves. It was a happy occasion, during which the often licentious comedies were performed as well (see the introduction to *Lysistrata*); but even during this carefree wide-open celebration, the appearance of the tragedies was a serious matter indeed. Staged in groups of three, written by the same poet, often (but not always) treating a single subject, these trilogies portrayed the lives and deeds, good and bad, of great legendary and mythical figures, both male and female.

The origin of the magnificent dramas that have come down to us can be traced with reasonable accuracy back to very early celebrations at the tombs or other sacred precincts of these famous individuals, when exalted songs called *dithyrambs* were sung antiphonally by a chorus and a leader. Participants wore goat skins and smeared their faces with the wine lees that settled out at the bottom of the bottles, creating a mask-like effect. Over the years the leader entered into dialogue with the chorus in extolling the particular hero. The poet Thespis (sixth century B.C., exact dates unknown) is traditionally credited with adding a separate performer who could talk with both chorus and leader, immediately opening possibilities for significant dramatic dialogue. Aeschylus added a second and Sophocles a third, so that opportunities were provided for more complex dialogue and heightened drama.

With additional actors, the plays no longer simply sang *about* the heroes and heroines, but brought them directly onto the stage as protagonists. As the three actors assumed increasing importance (all were men and could play multiple roles, male or female) the chorus was pushed into the background. Its singing and dancing served as scene dividers, a kind of act curtain, with the rendition of background information, odes, and lamentations pertinent to the story. Unfortunately, we have no idea what the music was like, what accompaniment, if any, was provided, or how the movement or dances were performed. But we do know the passages were carefully divided into equal parts called *strophe* and *antistrophe,* as you will note in the text of the *Oedipus.* The leader still entered into dialogue with the actors, but his purpose was more reactive than active as he often advised the characters to calm down, take action, or do whatever seemed appropriate at the time. In fact, in some plays the chorus stood around and debated what ought to be done about the apparent murder and mayhem occurring offstage, but which it was unable to stop. *Oedipus Rex* provides one of the best examples of the use of the chorus and leader as they comment about the unfolding events among themselves and with others.

As an outgrowth of the use of wine lees, all performers wore masks completely covering their heads and clearly defining their characters or even their moods. The mask worn by Oedipus in the last scene showed the result of his bloody self-inflicted wounds. High headdresses (*onkos*) and elevated boots (*kothornos*) supplemented the elaborate costumes. In keeping with the Greek sense of decorum and because quick movements and fast action were prevented by the heavy robes of the costumes, the violence often demanded by the story was relegated to offstage action and vivid onstage descriptions of the unseen horrors, generally delivered by a messenger. All of the tragedies, though widely varying in subject and individual style, held to rigid patterns of scenes and choral passages, limited to a single plotline and time sequence, often within a single day. Regardless of the situation or how inappropriate its presence might appear, the chorus was never abandoned, always remaining an integral part of the dramatic pattern.

Because the Dionysiac was a festival of universal importance, unlike the Olympic Games, which women could not attend (many events were held in the nude), women apparently could attend the plays. One account states that the costumes and masks of the Furies in Aeschylus's *The Eumenides* were so horrifying that pregnant women in the audience were reported to have miscarried. Furthermore, the plays were often very costly to mount, so that wealthy citizens considered it an honor to underwrite a play, even to the point of bankruptcy. A highly regarded prize, normally a laurel wreath, was awarded to the poet of the year's best play. As far as we know, plays were given a single performance and never subsequently revived. But for all the fame thus gained, it is interesting to note that other things were often considered more important. Aeschylus, for instance, wanted to be remembered in his epitaph not for his plays but for his participation in the Battle of Marathon, when the Greeks turned back the invading Persians in 490 B.C.

The tale of the House of Thebes is one of the two great Greek myths of families cursed by the gods. The other, the House of Atreus, forms the subject of three plays by Aeschylus. Known collectively as the *Oresteia* (458 B.C.), this only surviving trilogy involves the blood feud within the family of King Agamemnon, hero of the Trojan War, his wife and murderer, Clytemnestra, and their avenging children, Electra and Orestes. The cycle of plays by Sophocles concerning King Oedipus and his family exists in three separate works: the *Oedipus,* first in sequence but second to be written; *Oedipus at Colonus* (c. 406 B.C.), his last play; and *Antigone* (c. 446 B.C.). Together with Aeschylus's *The Seven Against Thebes* (467 B.C.), they provide the full story of this tremendously exciting and powerfully moving legend.

The Greek gods seldom acted without provocation, but when they brought their wrath upon a mortal it could be devastating through several generations. So it is with the House of Thebes. Somewhere in the dim past the founder of the city, King Kadmos, somehow offended the gods; the reason remains obscure. A curse fell upon his seed, bringing its greatest destruction to the family of the fourth generation, King Oedipus. This play is the story of his tragic final hours as king.

Oedipus Rex (also known as *Oedipus Tyrannos* and *Oedipus the King*), favored by critics ever since Aristotle, is probably the greatest tragedy ever written. The central figure of the king—powerful, respected, impetuous, given to emotional extravagances and violent outbursts, subject to the fatal flaw of pride—emerges as the finest example of the classic tragic protagonist. Doomed even before his birth to commit the most heinous and repulsive of crimes, this giant figure still arouses the emotions. His terrifying experiences demand compassionate understanding from the audience as he struggles to make the discoveries that will tell him the truth while rushing him headlong into his frightful destruction. Of exceeding noble stature but fatefully human, he rises in his final symbolic death to the heights that give tragedy its deepest meaning.

As a play the *Oedipus* is brilliantly structured, one of the enduringly great examples of effective dramatic art. From the opening exchange between the king and the suppliants to the terrifying climax, the dramatist has complete control of his action and the development of his characters. Each central figure is fully realized, prompted by recognizable human motives. Each scene rises successfully toward the catastrophe, piling up the evidence, compelling the participants, even the frightened Iokastê, on whom the truth dawns early, to reject its terrible implications, arriving at the almost unbearable but inevitable revelation. In true classic sense, the play proceeds relentlessly in uncluttered fashion, its lines as severe and orderly as a Greek temple. The ironies multiply; the trap around the doomed protagonist steadily closes. Knowing all the while the fate that must come, still we cringe, hold our breath, and find ourselves gripped by the mounting tensions. The effect of the poetic language, even in translation, is powerfully moving as it carries the dialogue along with dignity and steady pace.

The plays of Aeschylus frequently sought out the deeper meanings behind the struggles of men and women against primal forces and the ensuing search for reason and rational behavior. Euripedes often reduced his legendary figures to realistic, almost everyday, proportions. Sophocles survives in but seven plays in which the poet expressed his great concern for men and women struggling to find their individual identities and to establish an understandable relationship with impersonal gods and disinterested fate. His major protagonists are worthy heroic figures, and his tragedy is the best we have.

Oedipus Rex SOPHOCLES

An English version by Dudley Fitts and Robert Fitzgerald

CHARACTERS

OEDIPUS, *King of Thebes, supposed son of Polybos and Meropê, King and Queen of Corinth*
IOKASTÊ, *wife of Oedipus and widow of the late King Laïos*
KREON, *brother of Iokastê, a prince of Thebes*
TEIRESIAS, *a blind seer who serves Apollo*
PRIEST
MESSENGER, *from Corinth*
SHEPHERD, *former servant of Laïos*
SECOND MESSENGER, *from the palace*
CHORUS OF THEBAN ELDERS
CHORAGOS, *leader of the Chorus*
ANTIGONÊ *and* **ISMENÊ**, *young daughters of Oedipus and Iokastê. They appear in the Exodos but do not speak.*
SUPPLIANTS, GUARDS, SERVANTS

THE SCENE. *Before the palace of* OEDIPUS, *King of Thebes. A central door and two lateral doors open onto a platform that runs the length of the façade. On the platform, right and left, are altars; and three steps lead down into the "orchestra" or chorus-ground. At the beginning of the action these steps are crowded by suppliants who have brought branches and chaplets of olive leaves and who sit in various attitudes of despair.* OEDIPUS *enters.*

Prologue

OEDIPUS My children, generations of the living
In the line of Kadmos,[1] nursed at his ancient hearth:
Why have you strewn yourselves before these altars
In supplication, with your boughs and garlands?
The breath of incense rises from the city
With a sound of prayer and lamentation.
Children,
I would not have you speak through messengers,
And therefore I have come myself to hear you—
I, Oedipus, who bear the famous name.
(*to a* PRIEST) You, there, since you are eldest in the company,

[1]founder of Thebes

Speak for them all, tell me what preys upon you,
Whether you come in dread, or crave some blessing:
Tell me, and never doubt that I will help you
In every way I can; I should be heartless
Were I not moved to find you suppliant here.

PRIEST Great Oedipus, O powerful king of Thebes!
You see how all the ages of our people
Cling to your altar steps: here are boys
Who can barely stand alone, and here are priests
By weight of age, as I am a priest of God,
And young men chosen from those yet unmarried;
As for the others, all that multitude,
They wait with olive chaplets in the squares,
At the two shrines of Pallas, and where Apollo
Speaks in the glowing embers.
Your own eyes
Must tell you: Thebes is tossed on a murdering sea
And can not lift her head from the death surge.
A rust consumes the buds and fruits of the earth;
The herds are sick; children die unborn,
And labor is vain. The god of plague and pyre
Raids like detestable lightning through the city,
And all the house of Kadmos is laid waste,
All emptied, and all darkened: Death alone
Battens upon the misery of Thebes.

You are not one of the immortal gods, we know;
Yet we have come to you to make our prayer
As to the man surest in mortal ways
And wisest in the ways of God. You saved us
From the Sphinx, that flinty singer, and the tribute
We paid to her so long; yet you were never
Better informed than we, nor could we teach you:
A god's touch, it seems, enabled you to help us.

Therefore, O mighty power, we turn to you:
Find us our safety, find us a remedy,
Whether by counsel of the gods or of men.
A king of wisdom tested in the past
Can act in a time of troubles, and act well.
Noblest of men, restore
Life to your city! Think how all men call you
Liberator for your boldness long ago;
Ah, when your years of kingship are remembered,

Let them not say *We rose, but later fell—*
Keep the State from going down in the storm!
Once, years ago, with happy augury,
You brought us fortune; be the same again!
No man questions your power to rule the land:
But rule over men, not over a dead city!
Ships are only hulls, high walls are nothing,
When no life moves in the empty passageways.

OEDIPUS Poor children! You may be sure I know
All that you longed for in your coming here.
I know that you are deathly sick; and yet,
Sick as you are, not one is as sick as I.
Each of you suffers in himself alone
His anguish, not another's; but my spirit
Groans for the city, for myself, for you.

I was not sleeping, you are not waking me.
No, I have been in tears for a long while
And in my restless thought walked many ways.
In all my search I found one remedy,
And I have adopted it: I have sent Kreon,
Son of Menoikeus, brother of the queen,
To Delphi, Apollo's place of revelation,
To learn there, if he can,
What act or pledge of mine may save the city.
I have counted the days, and now, this very day,
I am troubled, for he has overstayed his time.
What is he doing? He has been gone too long.
Yet whenever he comes back, I should do ill
Not to take any action the god orders.

PRIEST It is a timely promise. At this instant
They tell me Kreon is here.

OEDIPUS O Lord Apollo!
May his news be fair as his face is radiant!

PRIEST Good news, I gather! he is crowned with bay,
The chaplet is thick with berries.

OEDIPUS We shall soon know;
He is near enough to hear us now.

(*Enter* KREON.)

O prince:
Brother: son of Menoikeus:
What answer do you bring us from the god?

KREON A strong one. I can tell you, great afflictions
Will turn out well, if they are taken well.
OEDIPUS What was the oracle? These vague words
Leave me still hanging between hope and fear.
KREON Is it your pleasure to hear me with all these
Gathered around us? I am prepared to speak,
But should we not go in?
OEDIPUS Speak to them all,
It is for them I suffer, more than for myself.
KREON Then I will tell you what I heard at Delphi.
In plain words
The god commands us to expel from the land of Thebes
An old defilement we are sheltering.
It is a deathly thing, beyond cure;
We must not let it feed upon us longer.
OEDIPUS What defilement? How shall we rid ourselves of it?
KREON By exile or death, blood for blood. It was
Murder that brought the plague-wind on the city.
OEDIPUS Murder of whom? Surely the god has named him?
KREON My lord: Laïos once ruled this land,
Before you came to govern us.
OEDIPUS I know;
I learned of him from others; I never saw him.
KREON He was murdered; and Apollo commands us now
To take revenge upon whoever killed him.
OEDIPUS Upon whom? Where are they? Where shall we find a clue
To solve that crime, after so many years?
KREON Here in this land, he said. Search reveals
Things that escape an inattentive man.
OEDIPUS Tell me: Was Laïos murdered in his house,
Or in the fields, or in some foreign country?
KREON He said he planned to make a pilgrimage.
He did not come home again.
OEDIPUS And was there no one,
No witness, no companion, to tell what happened?
KREON They were all killed but one, and he got away
So frightened that he could remember one thing only.
OEDIPUS What was the one thing? One may be the key
To everything, if we resolve to use it.
KREON He said that a band of highwaymen attacked them,
Outnumbered them, and overwhelmed the king.
OEDIPUS Strange, that a highwayman should be so daring—
Unless some faction here bribed him to do it.

KREON We thought of that. But after Laïos' death
New troubles arose and we had no avenger.
OEDIPUS What troubles could prevent your hunting down
the killers?
KREON The riddling Sphinx's song
Made us deaf to all mysteries but her own.
OEDIPUS Then once more I must bring what is dark to light.
It is most fitting that Apollo shows,
As you do, this compunction for the dead.
You shall see how I stand by you, as I should,
Avenging this country and the god as well,
And not as though it were for some distant friend,
But for my own sake, to be rid of evil.
Whoever killed King Laïos might—who knows?—
Lay violent hands even on me—and soon.
I act for the murdered king in my own interest.

Come, then, my children: leave the altar steps,
Lift up your olive boughs!
One of you go
And summon the people of Kadmos to gather here.
I will do all that I can; you may tell them that.

(*Exit a* PAGE.)

So, with the help of God,
We shall be saved—or else indeed we are lost.
PRIEST Let us rise, children. It was for this we came,
And now the king has promised it.
Phoibos[2] has sent us an oracle; may he descend
Himself to save us and drive out the plague.

(*Exeunt* OEDIPUS *and* KREON *into the palace by the central door. The* PRIEST *and the* SUPPLIANTS *disperse R and L. After a short pause the* CHORUS *enters the* orchestra.)

---

[2]Apollo

Párodos[3]

Strophe 1

CHORUS What is God singing in his profound
Delphi of gold and shadow?
What oracle for Thebes, the sunwhipped city?
Fear unjoints me, the roots of my heart tremble.
Now I remember, O Healer, your power, and wonder:
Will you send doom like a sudden cloud, or weave it
Like nightfall of the past?
Speak to me, tell me, O
Child of golden Hope, immortal Voice.

Antistrophe 1

Let me pray to Athenê, the immortal daughter of Zeus,
And to Artemis her sister
Who keeps her famous throne in the market ring,
And to Apollo, archer from distant heaven—
O gods, descend! Like three streams leap against
The fires of our grief, the fires of darkness;
Be swift to bring us rest!
As in the old time from the brilliant house
Of air you stepped to save us, come again!

Strophe 2

Now our afflictions have no end,
Now all our stricken host lies down
And no man fights off death with his mind;
The noble plowland bears no grain,
And groaning mothers can not bear—
See, how our lives like birds take wing,
Like sparks that fly when a fire soars,
To the shore of the god of evening.

---

[3]The song or ode chanted by the chorus on its entry. It is accompanied by dancing and music played on a flute. The chorus in this play represents elders of the city of Thebes. Chorus members remain onstage (on a level lower than the principal actors) for the remainder of the play. The choral odes and dances serve to separate one scene from another (there was no curtain in Greek theatre) as well as to comment on the action, reinforce the emotion, and interpret the situation. The chorus also performs dance movements during certain portions of the scenes themselves. *Strophe* and *antistrophe* are terms denoting the movement and counter-movement of the chorus from one side of its playing area to the other. When the chorus participates in dialogue with the other characters, its lines are spoken by the Choragos, its leader.

Antistrophe 2

The plague burns on, it is pitiless,
Though pallid children laden with death
Lie unwept in the stony ways,
And old gray women by every path
Flock to the strand about the altars
There to strike their breasts and cry
Worship of Phoibos in wailing prayers:
Be kind, God's golden child!

Strophe 3

There are no swords in this attack by fire,
No shields, but we are ringed with cries.
Send the besieger plunging from our homes
Into the vast sea-room of the Atlantic
Or into the waves that foam eastward of Thrace—
For the day ravages what the night spares—
Destroy our enemy, lord of the thunder!
Let him be riven by lightning from heaven!

Antistrophe 3

Phoibos Apollo, stretch the sun's bowstring,
That golden cord, until it sing for us,
Flashing arrows in heaven!
Artemis, Huntress,
Race with flaring lights upon our mountains!
O scarlet god, O golden-banded brow,
O Theban Bacchos in a storm of Maenads,

(*Enter* OEDIPUS, *C.*)

Whirl upon Death, that all the Undying hate!
Come with blinding torches, come in joy!

Scene I

OEDIPUS Is this your prayer? It may be answered. Come,
Listen to me, act as the crisis demands,
And you shall have relief from all these evils.

Until now I was a stranger to this tale,
As I had been a stranger to the crime.

Could I track down the murderer without a clue?
But now, friends,
As one who became a citizen after the murder,
I make this proclamation to all Thebans:
If any man knows by whose hand Laïos, son of Labdakos,
Met his death, I direct that man to tell me everything,
No matter what he fears for having so long withheld it.
Let it stand as promised that no further trouble
Will come to him, but he may leave the land in safety.

Moreover: If anyone knows the murderer to be foreign,
Let him not keep silent: he shall have his reward from me.
However, if he does conceal it; if any man
Fearing for his friend or for himself disobeys this edict,
Hear what I propose to do:

I solemnly forbid the people of this country,
Where power and throne are mine, ever to receive that man
Or speak to him, no matter who he is, or let him
Join in sacrifice, lustration, or in prayer.
I decree that he be driven from every house,
Being, as he is, corruption itself to us: the Delphic
Voice of Apollo has pronounced this revelation.
Thus I associate myself with the oracle
And take the side of the murdered king.

As for the criminal, I pray to God—
Whether it be a lurking thief, or one of a number—
I pray that that man's life be consumed in evil and wretchedness.
And as for me, this curse applies no less
If it should turn out that the culprit is my guest here,
Sharing my hearth.
                                        You have heard the penalty.
I lay it on you now to attend to this
For my safe, for Apollo's, for the sick
Sterile city that heaven has abandoned.
Suppose the oracle had given you no command:
Should this defilement go uncleansed for ever?
You should have found the murderer: your king,
A noble king, had been destroyed!
                                                            Now I,
Having the power that he held before me,
Having his bed, begetting children there

Upon his wife, as he would have, had he lived—
Their son would have been my children's brother,
If Laïos had had luck in fatherhood!
(And now his bad fortune has struck him down)—
I say I take the son's part, just as though
I were his son, to press the fight for him
And see it won! I'll find the hand that brought
Death to Labdakos' and Polydoros' child,
Heir of Kadmos' and Agenor's line.[4]
And as for those who fail me,
May the gods deny them the fruit of the earth,
Fruit of the womb, and may they rot utterly!
Let them be wretched as we are wretched, and worse!

For you, for loyal Thebans, and for all
Who find my actions right, I pray the favor
Of justice, and of all the immortal gods.

CHORAGOS Since I am under oath, my lord, I swear
I did not do the murder, I can not name
The murderer. Phoibos ordained the search;
Why did he not say who the culprit was?

OEDIPUS An honest question. But no man in the world
Can make the gods do more than the gods will.

CHORAGOS There is an alternative, I think—

OEDIPUS Tell me.
Any or all, you must not fail to tell me.

CHORAGOS A lord clairvoyant to the lord Apollo,
As we all know, is the skilled Teiresias.
One might learn much about this from him, Oedipus.

OEDIPUS I am not wasting time:
Kreon spoke of this, and I have sent for him—
Twice, in fact; it is strange that he is not here.

CHORAGOS The other matter—that old report—seems useless.

OEDIPUS What was that? I am interested in all reports.

CHORAGOS The king was said to have been killed by highwaymen.

OEDIPUS I know. But we have no witnesses to that.

CHORAGOS If the killer can feel a particle of dread,
Your curse will bring him out of hiding!

OEDIPUS No.
The man who dared that act will fear no curse.

---

[4]father, grandfather, great-grandfather, and great-great-grandfather of Laïos

(*Enter the blind seer* TEIRESIAS, *led by a* PAGE.)

CHORAGOS But there is one man who may detect the criminal.
This is Teiresias, this is the holy prophet
In whom, alone of all men, truth was born.
OEDIPUS Teiresias: seer: student of mysteries,
Of all that's taught and all that no man tells,
Secrets of Heaven and secrets of the earth:
Blind though you are, you know the city lies
Sick with plague; and from this plague, my lord,
We find that you alone can guard or save us.

Possibly you did not hear the messengers?
Apollo, when we sent to him,
Sent us back word that this great pestilence
Would lift, but only if we established clearly
The identity of those who murdered Laïos.
They must be killed or exiled.
Can you use
Birdflight[5] or any art of divination
To purify yourself, and Thebes, and me
From this contagion? We are in your hands.
There is no fairer duty
Than that of helping others in distress.
TEIRESIAS How dreadful knowledge of the truth can be
When there's no help in truth! I knew this well,
But did not act on it: else I should not have come.
OEDIPUS What is troubling you? Why are your eyes so cold?
TEIRESIAS Let me go home. Bear your own fate, and I'll
Bear mine. It is better so: trust what I say.
OEDIPUS What you say is ungracious and unhelpful
To your native country. Do not refuse to speak.
TEIRESIAS When it comes to speech, your own is neither temperate
Nor opportune. I wish to be more prudent.
OEDIPUS In God's name, we all beg you—
TEIRESIAS You are all ignorant.
No; I will never tell you what I know.
Now it is my misery; then, it would be yours.
OEDIPUS What! You do know something, and will not tell us?
You would betray us all and wreck the State?
TEIRESIAS I do not intend to torture myself, or you.
Why persist in asking? You will not persuade me.

[5]Prophets predicted the future or divined the unknown by observing the flight of birds.

OEDIPUS What a wicked old man you are! You'd try a stone's
Patience! Out with it! Have you no feeling at all?
TEIRESIAS You call me unfeeling. If you could only see
The nature of your own feelings . . .
OEDIPUS Why,
Who would not feel as I do? Who could endure
Your arrogance toward the city?
TEIRESIAS What does it matter?
Whether I speak or not, it is bound to come.
OEDIPUS Then, if "it" is bound to come, you are bound to tell me.
TEIRESIAS No, I will not go on. Rage as you please.
OEDIPUS Rage? Why not!
And I'll tell you what I think:
You planned it, you had it done, you all but
Killed him with your own hands; if you had eyes,
I'd say the crime was yours, and yours alone.
TEIRESIAS So? I charge you, then,
Abide by the proclamation you have made:
From this day forth
Never speak again to these men or to me;
You yourself are the pollution of this country.
OEDIPUS You dare say that! Can you possibly think you have
Some way of going free, after such insolence?
TEIRESIAS I have gone free. It is the truth that sustains me.
OEDIPUS Who taught you shamelessness? It was not your craft.
TEIRESIAS You did. You made me speak. I did not want to.
OEDIPUS Speak what? Let me hear it again more clearly.
TEIRESIAS Was it not clear before? Are you tempting me?
OEDIPUS I did not understand it. Say it again.
TEIRESIAS I say that you are the murderer whom you seek.
OEDIPUS Now twice you have spat out infamy. You'll pay for it!
TEIRESIAS Would you care for more? Do you wish to be really angry?
OEDIPUS Say what you will. Whatever you say is worthless.
TEIRESIAS I say you live in hideous shame with those
Most dear to you. You can not see the evil.
OEDIPUS Can you go on babbling like this for ever?
TEIRESIAS I can, if there is power in truth.
OEDIPUS There is:
But not for you, not for you,
You sightless, witless, senseless, mad old man!
TEIRESIAS You are the madman. There is no one here
Who will not curse you soon, as you curse me.
OEDIPUS You child of total night! I would not touch you;
Neither would any man who sees the sun.

TEIRESIAS True: it is not from you my fate will come.
That lies within Apollo's competence,
As it is his concern.
OEDIPUS Tell me, who made
These fine discoveries? Kreon? or someone else?
TEIRESIAS Kreon is no threat. You weave your own doom.
OEDIPUS Wealth, power, craft of statesmanship!
Kingly position, everywhere admired!
What savage envy is stored up against these,
If Kreon, whom I trusted, Kreon my friend,
For this great office which the city once
Put in my hands unsought—if for this power
Kreon desires in secret to destroy me!

He has bought this decrepit fortune-teller, this
Collector of dirty pennies, this prophet fraud—
Why, he is no more clairvoyant than I am!
Tell us:
Has your mystic mummery ever approached the truth?
When that hellcat the Sphinx was performing here,
What help were you to these people?
Her magic was not for the first man who came along:
It demanded a real exorcist. Your birds—
What good were they? or the gods, for the matter of that?
But I came by,
Oedipus, the simple man, who knows nothing—
I thought it out for myself, no birds helped me!
And this is the man you think you can destroy,
That you may be close to Kreon when he's king!
Well, you and your friend Kreon, it seems to me,
Will suffer most. If you were not an old man,
You would have paid already for your plot.
CHORAGOS We can not see that his words or yours
Have been spoken except in anger, Oedipus,
And of anger we have no need. How to accomplish
The god's will best: that is what most concerns us.
TEIRESIAS You are a king. But where argument's concerned
I am your man, as much a king as you.
I am not your servant, but Apollo's.
I have no need of Kreon or Kreon's name.

Listen to me. You mock my blindness, do you?
But I say that you, with both your eyes, are blind:
You can not see the wretchedness of your life,

Nor in whose house you live, no, nor with whom.
Who are your father and mother? Can you tell me?
You do not even know the blind wrongs
That you have done them, on earth and in the world below.
But the double lash of your parents' curse will whip you
Out of this land some day, with only night
Upon your precious eyes.
Your cries then—where will they not be heard?
What fastness of Kithairon[6] will not echo them?
And that bridal-descant of yours—you'll know it then,
The song they sang when you came here to Thebes
And found your misguided berthing.
All this, and more, that you can not guess at now,
Will bring you to yourself among your children.

Be angry, then. Curse Kreon. Curse my words.
I tell you, no man that walks upon the earth
Shall be rooted out more horribly than you.

OEDIPUS Am I to bear this from him?—Damnation
Take you! Out of this place! Out of my sight!
TEIRESIAS I would not have come at all if you had not asked me.
OEDIPUS Could I have told that you'd talk nonsense, that
You'd come here to make a fool of yourself, and of me?
TEIRESIAS A fool? Your parents thought me sane enough.
OEDIPUS My parents again!—Wait: who were my parents?
TEIRESIAS This day will give you a father, and break your heart.
OEDIPUS Your infantile riddles! Your damned abracadabra!
TEIRESIAS You were a great man once at solving riddles.
OEDIPUS Mock me with that if you like; you will find it true.
TEIRESIAS It was true enough. It brought about your ruin.
OEDIPUS But if it saved this town?
TEIRESIAS (*to the* PAGE) Boy, give me your hand.
OEDIPUS Yes, boy; lead him away.
—While you are here
We can do nothing. Go; leave us in peace.
TEIRESIAS I will go when I have said what I have to say.
How can you hurt me? And I tell you again:
The man you have been looking for all this time,
The damned man, the murderer of Laïos,
That man is in Thebes. To your mind he is foreign-born,
But it will soon be shown that he is a Theban,
A revelation that will fail to please.

[6] the mountain where Oedipus was taken to be exposed as an infant

A blind man,
Who has his eyes now; a penniless man, who is rich now;
And he will go tapping the strange earth with his staff.
To the children with whom he lives now he will be
Brother and father—the very same; to her
Who bore him, son and husband—the very same
Who came to his father's bed, wet with his father's blood.

Enough. Go think that over.
If later you find error in what I have said,
You may say that I have no skill in prophecy.

(*Exit* TEIRESIAS, *led by his* PAGE. OEDIPUS *goes into the palace.*)

Ode I

Strophe 1

CHORUS The Delphic stone of prophecies
Remembers ancient regicide
And a still bloody hand.
That killer's hour of flight has come.
He must be stronger than riderless
Coursers of untiring wind,
For the son[7] of Zeus armed with his father's thunder
Leaps in lightning after him;
And the Furies hold his track, the sad Furies.

Antistrophe 1

Holy Parnassos'[8] peak of snow
Flashes and blinds that secret man,
That all shall hunt him down:
Though he may roam the forest shade
Like a bull gone wild from pasture
To rage through glooms of stone.
Doom comes down on him; flight will not avail him;
For the world's heart calls him desolate,
And the immortal voices follow, for ever follow.

[7]Apollo [8]mountain sacred to Apollo

Strophe 2

But now a wilder thing is heard
From the old man skilled at hearing Fate in the wing-beat of a bird.
Bewildered as a blown bird, my soul hovers and can not find
Foothold in this debate, or any reason or rest of mind.
But no man ever brought—none can bring
Proof of strife between Thebes' royal house,
Labdakos' line, and the son of Polybos;
And never until now has any man brought word
Of Laïos' dark death staining Oedipus the King.

Antistrophe 2

Divine Zeus and Apollo hold
Perfect intelligence alone of all tales ever told;
And well though this diviner works, he works in his own night;
No man can judge that rough unknown or trust in second sight,
For wisdom changes hands among the wise.
Shall I believe my great lord criminal
At a raging word that a blind old man let fall?
I saw him, when the carrion woman[9] faced him of old,
Prove his heroic mind. These evil words are lies.

Scene II

KREON Men of Thebes:
I am told that heavy accusations
Have been brought against me by King Oedipus.

I am not the kind of man to bear this tamely.

If in these present difficulties
He holds me accountable for any harm to him
Through anything I have said or done—why, then,
I do not value life in this dishonor.
It is not as though this rumor touched upon
Some private indiscretion. The matter is grave.
The fact is that I am being called disloyal
To the State, to my fellow citizens, to my friends.

CHORAGOS He may have spoken in anger, not from his mind.

KREON But did you not hear him say I was the one
Who seduced the old prophet into lying?

---

[9]the Sphinx

CHORAGOS The thing was said; I do not know how seriously.
KREON But you were watching him! Were his eyes steady?
Did he look like a man in his right mind?
CHORAGOS I do not know.
I can not judge the behavior of great men.
But here is the king himself.

(*Enter* OEDIPUS.)

OEDIPUS So you dared come back.
Why? How brazen of you to come to my house,
You murderer!
Do you think I do not know
That you plotted to kill me, plotted to steal my throne?
Tell me, in God's name: am I coward, a fool,
That you should dream you could accomplish this?
A fool who could not see your slippery game?
A coward, not to fight back when I saw it?
You are the fool, Kreon, are you not? hoping
Without support or friends to get a throne?
Thrones may be won or bought: you could do neither.
KREON Now listen to me. You have talked; let me talk, too.
You can not judge unless you know the facts.
OEDIPUS You speak well: there is one fact; but I find it hard
To learn from the deadliest enemy I have.
KREON That above all I must dispute with you.
OEDIPUS That above all I will not hear you deny.
KREON If you think there is anything good in being stubborn
Against all reason, then I say you are wrong.
OEDIPUS If you think a man can sin against his own kind
And not be punished for it, I say you are mad.
KREON I agree. But tell me: What have I done to you?
OEDIPUS You advised me to send for that wizard, did you not?
KREON I did. I should do it again.
OEDIPUS Very well. Now tell me:
How long has it been since Laïos—
KREON What of Laïos?
OEDIPUS Since he vanished in that onset by the road?
KREON It was long ago, a long time.
OEDIPUS And this prophet,
Was he practicing here then?
KREON He was; and with honor, as now.
OEDIPUS Did he speak of me at that time?

KREON He never did,
At least, not when I was present.
OEDIPUS But . . . the enquiry?
I suppose you held one?
KREON We did, but we learned nothing.
OEDIPUS Why did the prophet not speak against me then?
KREON I do not know; and I am the kind of man
Who holds his tongue when he has no facts to go on.
OEDIPUS There's one fact that you know, and you could tell it.
KREON What fact is that? If I know it, you shall have it.
OEDIPUS If he were not involved with you, he could not say
That it was I who murdered Laïos.
KREON If he says that, you are the one that knows it!—
But now it is my turn to question you.
OEDIPUS Put your questions. I am no murderer.
KREON First, then: You married my sister?
OEDIPUS I married your sister.
KREON And you rule the kingdom equally with her?
OEDIPUS Everything that she wants she has from me.
KREON And I am the third, equal to both of you?
OEDIPUS That is why I call you a bad friend.
KREON No. Reason it out, as I have done.
Think of this first: Would any sane man prefer
Power, with all a king's anxieties,
To that same power and the grace of sleep?
Certainly not I.
I have never longed for the king's power—only his rights.
Would any wise man differ from me in this?
As matters stand, I have my way in everything
With your consent, and no responsibilities.
If I were king, I should be a slave to policy.

How could I desire a scepter more
Than what is now mine—untroubled influence?
No, I have not gone mad; I need no honors,
Except those with the perquisites I have now.
I am welcome everywhere; every man salutes me,
And those who want your favor seek my ear,
Since I know how to manage what they ask.
Should I exchange this ease for that anxiety?
Besides, no sober mind is treasonable.
I hate anarchy
And never would deal with any man who likes it.
Test what I have said. Go to the priestess

At Delphi, ask if I quoted her correctly.
And as for this other thing: if I am found
Guilty of treason with Teiresias,
Then sentence me to death. You have my word
It is a sentence I should cast my vote for—
But not without evidence!
You do wrong
When you take good men for bad, bad men for good.
A true friend thrown aside—why, life itself
Is not more precious!
In time you will know this well:
For time, and time alone, will show the just man,
Though scoundrels are discovered in a day.
CHORAGOS This is well said, and a prudent man would ponder it.
Judgments too quickly formed are dangerous.
OEDIPUS But is he not quick in his duplicity?
And shall I not be quick to parry him?
Would you have me stand still, hold my peace, and let
This man win everything, through my inaction?
KREON And you want—what is it, then? To banish me?
OEDIPUS No, not exile. It is your death I want,
So that all the world may see what treason means.
KREON You will persist, then? You will not believe me?
OEDIPUS How can I believe you?
KREON Then you are a fool.
OEDIPUS To save myself?
KREON In justice, think of me.
OEDIPUS You are evil incarnate.
KREON But suppose that you are wrong?
OEDIPUS Still I must rule.
KREON But not if you rule badly.
OEDIPUS O city, city!
KREON It is my city, too!
CHORAGOS Now, my lords, be still. I see the queen,
Iokastê, coming from her palace chambers;
And it is time she came, for the sake of you both.
This dreadful quarrel can be resolved through her.

(*Enter* IOKASTÊ.)

IOKASTÊ Poor foolish men, what wicked din is this?
With Thebes sick to death, is it not shameful
That you should rake some private quarrel up?
(*to* OEDIPUS) Come into the house.

—And you, Kreon, go now:
Let us have no more of this tumult over nothing.
KREON Nothing? No, sister: what your husband plans for me
Is one of two great evils: exile or death.
OEDIPUS He is right.
Why, woman I have caught him squarely
Plotting against my life.
KREON No! Let me die
Accurst if ever I have wished you harm!
IOKASTÊ Ah, believe it, Oedipus!
In the name of the gods, respect this oath of his
For my sake, for the sake of these people here!

Strophe 1

CHORAGOS Open your mind to her, my lord. Be ruled by her, I beg you!
OEDIPUS What would you have me do?
CHORAGOS Respect Kreon's word. He has never spoken like a fool,
And now he has sworn an oath.
OEDIPUS You know what you ask?
CHORAGOS I do.
OEDIPUS Speak on, then.
CHORAGOS A friend so sworn should not be baited so,
In blind malice, and without final proof.
OEDIPUS You are aware, I hope, that what you say
Means death for me, or exile at the least.

Strophe 2

CHORAGOS No, I swear by Helios, first in Heaven!
May I die friendless and accurst,
The worst of deaths, if ever I meant that!
It is the withering fields
That hurt my sick heart:
Must we bear all these ills,
And now your bad blood as well?
OEDIPUS Then let him go. And let me die, if I must,
Or be driven by him in shame from the land of Thebes.
It is your unhappiness, and not his talk,
That touches me.
As for him—
Wherever he goes, hatred will follow him.
KREON Ugly in yielding, as you were ugly in rage!
Natures like yours chiefly torment themselves.

OEDIPUS Can you not go? Can you not leave me?
KREON I can.
You do not know me; but the city knows me,
And in its eyes I am just, if not in yours.

(*Exit* KREON.)

Antistrophe 1

CHORAGOS Lady Iokastê, did you not ask the King to go to his chambers?
IOKASTÊ First tell me what has happened.
CHORAGOS There was suspicion without evidence; yet it rankled
As even false charges will.
IOKASTÊ On both sides?
CHORAGOS On both.
IOKASTÊ But what was said?
CHORAGOS Oh let it rest, let it be done with!
Have we not suffered enough?
OEDIPUS You see to what your decency has brought you:
You have made difficulties where my heart saw none.

Antistrophe 2

CHORAGOS Oedipus, it is not once only I have told you—
You must know I should count myself unwise
To the point of madness, should I now forsake you—
You, under whose hand,
In the storm of another time,
Our dear land sailed out free.
But now stand fast at the helm!
IOKASTÊ In God's name, Oedipus, inform your wife as well:
Why are you so set in this hard anger?
OEDIPUS I will tell you, for none of these men deserves
My confidence as you do. It is Kreon's work,
His treachery, his plotting against me.
IOKASTÊ Go on, if you can make this clear to me.
OEDIPUS He charges me with the murder of Laïos.
IOKASTÊ Has he some knowledge? Or does he speak from hearsay?
OEDIPUS He would not commit himself to such a charge,
But he has brought in that damnable soothsayer
To tell his story.
IOKASTÊ Set your mind at rest.
If it is a question of soothsayers, I tell you

That you will find no man whose craft gives knowledge
Of the unknowable.
Here is my proof:
An oracle was reported to Laïos once
(I will not say from Phoibos himself, but from
His appointed ministers, at any rate)
That his doom would be death at the hands of his own son—
His son, born of his flesh and of mine!

Now, you remember the story: Laïos was killed
By marauding strangers where three highways meet;
But his child had not been three days in this world
Before the king had pierced the baby's ankles
And left him to die on a lonely mountainside.

Thus, Apollo never caused that child
To kill his father, and it was not Laïos' fate
To die at the hands of his son, as he had feared.
This is what prophets and prophecies are worth!
Have no dread of them.
It is God himself
Who can show us what he wills, in his own way.

OEDIPUS How strange a shadowy memory crossed my mind,
Just now while you were speaking; it chilled my heart.

IOKASTÊ What do you mean? What memory do you speak of?

OEDIPUS If I understand you, Laïos was killed
At a place where three roads meet.

IOKASTÊ So it was said;
We have no later story.

OEDIPUS Where did it happen?

IOKASTÊ Phokis, it is called: at a place where the Theban Way
Divides into the roads toward Delphi and Daulia.

OEDIPUS When?

IOKASTÊ We had the news not long before you came
And proved the right to your succession here.

OEDIPUS Ah, what net has God been weaving for me?

IOKASTÊ Oedipus! Why does this trouble you?

OEDIPUS Do not ask me yet.
First, tell me how Laïos looked, and tell me
How old he was.

IOKASTÊ He was tall, his hair just touched
With white; his form was not unlike your own.

OEDIPUS I think that I myself may be accurst
By my own ignorant edict.

IOKASTÊ You speak strangely.
It makes me tremble to look at you, my king.
OEDIPUS I am not sure that the blind man can not see.
But I should know better if you were to tell me—
IOKASTÊ Anything—though I dread to hear you ask it.
OEDIPUS Was the king lightly escorted, or did he ride
With a large company, as a ruler should?
IOKASTÊ There were five men with him in all: one was a herald.
And a single chariot, which he was driving.
OEDIPUS Alas, that makes it plain enough!
But who—
Who told you how it happened?
IOKASTÊ A household servant,
The only one to escape.
OEDIPUS And is he still
A servant of ours?
IOKASTÊ No; for when he came back at last
And found you enthroned in the place of the dead king,
He came to me, touched my hand with his, and begged
That I would send him away to the frontier district
Where only the shepherds go—
As far away from the city as I could send him.
I granted his prayer; for although the man was a slave,
He had earned more than this favor at my hands.
OEDIPUS Can he be called back quickly?
IOKASTÊ Easily.
But why?
OEDIPUS I have taken too much upon myself
Without enquiry; therefore I wish to consult him.
IOKASTÊ Then he shall come.
But am I not one also
To whom you might confide these fears of yours?
OEDIPUS That is your right; it will not be denied you,
Now least of all; for I have reached a pitch
Of wild foreboding. Is there anyone
To whom I should sooner speak?

Polybos of Corinth is my father.
My mother is a Dorian: Meropê.
I grew up chief among the men of Corinth
Until a strange thing happened—
Not worth my passion, it may be, but strange.
At a feast, a drunken man maundering in his cups

Cries out that I am not my father's son![1]
I contained myself that night, though I felt anger
And a sinking heart. The next day I visited
My father and mother, and questioned them. They stormed,
Calling it all the slanderous rant of a fool;
And this relieved me. Yet the suspicion
Remained always aching in my mind;
I knew there was talk; I could not rest;
And finally, saying nothing to my parents,
I went to the shrine at Delphi.

The god dismissed my question without reply;
He spoke of other things.
                                        Some were clear,
Full of wretchedness, dreadful, unbearable:
As, that I should lie with my own mother, breed
Children from whom all men would turn their eyes;
And that I should be my father's murderer.

I heard all this, and fled. And from that day
Corinth to me was only in the stars
Descending in that quarter of the sky,
As I wandered farther and farther on my way
To a land where I should never see the evil
Sung by the oracle. And I came to this country
Where, so you say, King Laïos was killed.

I will tell you all that happened there, my lady.

There were three highways
Coming together at a place I passed;
And there a herald came towards me, and a chariot
Drawn by horses, with a man such as you describe
Seated in it. The groom leading the horses
Forced me off the road at his lord's command;
But as this charioteer lurched over towards me
I struck him in my rage. The old man saw me
And brought his double goad down upon my head
As I came abreast.
                                        He was paid back, and more!
Swinging my club in this right hand I knocked him

[1]Oedipus perhaps interprets this as an allegation that he is a bastard, the son of Meropê but not of Polybos. The implication, at any rate, is that he is not of royal birth, not the legitimate heir to the throne of Corinth.

Out of his car, and he rolled on the ground.
                                                I killed him.
I killed them all.
Now if that stranger and Laïos were—kin,
Where is a man more miserable than I?
More hated by the gods? Citizen and alien alike
Must never shelter me or speak to me—
I must be shunned by all.
                                And I myself
Pronounced this malediction upon myself!

Think of it: I have touched you with these hands,
These hands that killed your husband. What defilement!

Am I all evil, then? It must be so,
Since I must flee from Thebes, yet never again
See my own countrymen, my own country,
For fear of joining my mother in marriage
And killing Polybos, my father.
                                        Ah,
If I was created so, born to this fate,
Who could deny the savagery of God?

O holy majesty of heavenly powers!
May I never see that day! Never!
Rather let me vanish from the race of men
Than know the abomination destined me!

CHORAGOS We too, my lord, have felt dismay at this.
But there is hope: you have yet to hear the shepherd.

OEDIPUS Indeed, I fear no other hope is left me.

IOKASTÊ What do you hope from him when he comes?

OEDIPUS   This much:
If his account of the murder tallies with yours,
Then I am cleared.

IOKASTÊ   What was it that I said
Of such importance?

OEDIPUS   Why, "marauders," you said,
Killed the king, according to this man's story.
If he maintains that still, if there were several,
Clearly the guilt is not mine: I was alone.
But if he says one man, singlehanded, did it,
Then the evidence all points to me.

IOKASTÊ You may be sure that he said there were several;
And can he call back that story now? He can not.
The whole city heard it as plainly as I.
But suppose he alters some detail of it:
He can not ever show that Laïos's death
Fulfilled the oracle: for Apollo said
My child was doomed to kill him; and my child—
Poor baby!—it was my child that died first.
No. From now on, where oracles are concerned,
I would not waste a second thought on any.
OEDIPUS You may be right.
But come: let someone go
For the shepherd at once. This matter must be settled.
IOKASTÊ I will send for him.
I would not wish to cross you in anything,
And surely not in this.—Let us go in.

(Exeunt into the palace.)

Ode II

Strophe I

CHORUS Let me be reverent in the ways of right,
Lowly the paths I journey on;
Let all my words and actions keep
The laws of the pure universe
From highest Heaven handed down.
For Heaven is their bright nurse,
Those generations of the realms of light;
Ah, never of mortal kind were they begot,
Nor are they slaves of memory, lost in sleep:
Their Father is greater than Time, and ages not.

Antistrophe I

The tyrant is a child of Pride
Who drinks from his great sickening cup
Recklessness and vanity,
Until from his high crest headlong
He plummets to the dust of hope.
That strong man is not strong.
But let no fair ambition be denied;
May God protect the wrestler for the State

In government, in comely policy,
Who will fear God, and on His ordinance wait.

Strophe 2

Haughtiness and the high hand of disdain
Tempt and outrage God's holy law;
And any mortal who dares hold
No immortal Power in awe
Will be caught up in a net of pain:
The price for which his levity is sold.
Let each man take due earnings, then,
And keep his hands from holy things,
And from blasphemy stand apart—
Else the crackling blast of heaven
Blows on his head, and on his desperate heart.
Though fools will honor impious men,
In their cities no tragic poet sings.

Antistrophe 2

Shall we lose faith in Delphi's obscurities,
We who have heard the world's core
Discredited, and the sacred wood
Of Zeus at Elis praised no more?
The deeds and the strange prophecies
Must make a pattern yet to be understood.
Zeus, if indeed you are lord of all,
Throned in light over night and day,
Mirror this in your endless mind:
Our masters call the oracle
Words on the wind, and the Delphic vision blind!
Their hearts no longer know Apollo,
And reverence for the gods has died away.

Scene III

(*Enter* IOKASTÊ.)

IOKASTÊ Princes of Thebes, it has occurred to me
To visit the altars of the gods, bearing
These branches as a suppliant, and this incense.
Our king is not himself: his noble soul
Is overwrought with fantasies of dread,
Else he would consider

The new prophecies in the light of the old.
He will listen to any voice that speaks disaster,
And my advice goes for nothing.

(*She approaches the altar, R.*)

To you, then, Apollo,
Lycéan lord, since you are nearest, I turn in prayer.
Receive these offerings, and grant us deliverance
From defilement. Our hearts are heavy with fear
When we see our leader distracted, as helpless sailors
Are terrified by the confusion of their helmsman.

(*Enter* MESSENGER.)

MESSENGER Friends, no doubt you can direct me:
Where shall I find the house of Oedipus,
Or, better still, where is the king himself?
CHORAGOS It is this very place, stranger; he is inside.
This is his wife and mother of his children.
MESSENGER I wish her happiness in a happy house,
Blest in all the fulfillment of her marriage.
IOKASTÊ I wish as much for you: your courtesy
Deserves a like good fortune. But now, tell me:
Why have you come? What have you to say to us?
MESSENGER Good news, my lady, for your house and your husband.
IOKASTÊ What news? Who sent you here?
MESSENGER I am from Corinth.
The news I bring ought to mean joy for you,
Though it may be you will find some grief in it.
IOKASTÊ What is it? How can it touch us in both ways?
MESSENGER The word is that the people of the Isthmus
Intend to call Oedipus to be their king.
IOKASTÊ But old King Polybos—is he not reigning still?
MESSENGER No. Death holds him in his sepulchre.
IOKASTÊ What are you saying? Polybos is dead?
MESSENGER If I am not telling the truth, may I die myself.
IOKASTÊ (*to a* MAIDSERVANT) Go in, go quickly; tell this to your master.

O riddlers of God's will, where are you now!
This was the man whom Oedipus, long ago,
Feared so, fled so, in dread of destroying him—
But it was another fate by which he died.

(*Enter* OEDIPUS, *C.*)

OEDIPUS Dearest Iokastê, why have you sent for me?
IOKASTÊ Listen to what this man says, and then tell me
What has become of the solemn prophecies.
OEDIPUS Who is this man? What is his news for me?
IOKASTÊ He has come from Corinth to announce your father's death!
OEDIPUS Is it true, stranger? Tell me in your own words.
MESSENGER I can not say it more clearly: the king is dead.
OEDIPUS Was it by treason? Or by an attack of illness?
MESSENGER A little thing brings old men to their rest.
OEDIPUS It was sickness, then?
MESSENGER Yes, and his many years.
OEDIPUS Ah!
Why should a man respect the Pythian hearth,[2] or
Give heed to the birds that jangle above his head?
They prophesied that I should kill Polybos,
Kill my own father; but he is dead and buried,
And I am here—I never touched him, never,
Unless he died of grief for my departure,
And thus, in a sense, through me. No. Polybos
Has packed the oracles off with him underground.
They are empty words.
IOKASTÊ Had I not told you so?
OEDIPUS You had; it was my faint heart that betrayed me.
IOKASTÊ From now on never think of those things again.
OEDIPUS And yet—must I not fear my mother's bed?
IOKASTÊ Why should anyone in this world be afraid,
Since Fate rules us and nothing can be foreseen?
A man should live only for the present day.

Have no more fear of sleeping with your mother:
How many men, in dreams, have lain with their mothers!
No reasonable man is troubled by such things.
OEDIPUS That is true; only—
If only my mother were not still alive!
But she is alive. I can not help my dread.
IOKASTÊ Yet this news of your father's death is wonderful.
OEDIPUS Wonderful. But I fear the living woman.
MESSENGER Tell me, who is this woman that you fear?
OEDIPUS It is Meropê, man; the wife of King Polybos.
MESSENGER Meropê? Why should you be afraid of her?
OEDIPUS An oracle of the gods, a dreadful saying.
MESSENGER Can you tell me about it or are you sworn to silence?

[2]Delphi

OEDIPUS I can tell you, and I will.
Apollo said through his prophet that I was the man
Who should marry his own mother, shed his father's blood
With his own hands. And so, for all these years
I have kept clear of Corinth, and no harm has come—
Though it would have been sweet to see my parents again.
MESSENGER And is this the fear that drove you out of Corinth?
OEDIPUS Would you have me kill my father?
MESSENGER As for that
You must be reassured by the news I gave you.
OEDIPUS If you could reassure me, I would reward you.
MESSENGER I had that in mind, I will confess: I thought
I could count on you when you returned to Corinth.
OEDIPUS No: I will never go near my parents again.
MESSENGER Ah, son, you still do not know what you are doing—
OEDIPUS What do you mean? In the name of God tell me!
MESSENGER —if these are your reasons for not going home.
OEDIPUS I tell you, I fear the oracle may come true.
MESSENGER And guilt may come upon you through your parents?
OEDIPUS That is the dread that is always in my heart.
MESSENGER Can you not see that all your fears are groundless?
OEDIPUS Groundless? Am I not my parents' son?
MESSENGER Polybos was not your father.
OEDIPUS Not my father?
MESSENGER No more your father than the man speaking to you.
OEDIPUS But you are nothing to me!
MESSENGER Neither was he.
OEDIPUS Then why did he call me son?
MESSENGER I will tell you:
Long ago he had you from my hands, as a gift.
OEDIPUS Then how could he love me so, if I was not his?
MESSENGER He had no children, and his heart turned to you.
OEDIPUS What of you? Did you buy me? Did you find me by chance?
MESSENGER I came upon you in the woody vales of Kithairon.
OEDIPUS And what were you doing there?
MESSENGER Tending my flocks.
OEDIPUS A wandering shepherd?
MESSENGER But your savior, son, that day.
OEDIPUS From what did you save me?
MESSENGER Your ankles should tell you that.
OEDIPUS Ah, stranger, why do you speak of that childhood pain?
MESSENGER I pulled the skewer that pinned your feet together.
OEDIPUS I have had the mark as long as I can remember.
MESSENGER That was why you were given the name you bear.

OEDIPUS God! Was it my father or my mother who did it?
Tell me!

MESSENGER I do not know. The man who gave you to me
Can tell you better than I.

OEDIPUS It was not you that found me, but another?

MESSENGER It was another shepherd gave you to me.

OEDIPUS Who was he? Can you tell me who he was?

MESSENGER I think he was said to be one of Laïos' people.

OEDIPUS You mean the Laïos who was king here years ago?

MESSENGER Yes; King Laïos; and the man was one of his herdsmen.

OEDIPUS Is he still alive? Can I see him?

MESSENGER These men here
Know best about such things.

OEDIPUS Does anyone here
Know this shepherd that he is talking about?
Have you seen him in the fields, or in the town?
If you have, tell me. It is time things were made plain.

CHORAGOS I think the man he means is that same shepherd
You have already asked to see. Iokastê perhaps
Could tell you something.

OEDIPUS Do you know anything
About him, Lady? Is he the man we have summoned?
Is that the man this shepherd means?

IOKASTÊ Why think of him?
Forget this herdsman. Forget it all.
This talk is a waste of time.

OEDIPUS How can you say that,
When the clues to my true birth are in my hands?

IOKASTÊ For God's love, let us have no more questioning!
Is your life nothing to you?
My own is pain enough for me to bear.

OEDIPUS You need not worry. Suppose my mother a slave,
And born of slaves: no baseness can touch you.

IOKASTÊ Listen to me, I beg you: do not do this thing!

OEDIPUS I will not listen; the truth must be made known.

IOKASTÊ Everything that I say is for your own good!

OEDIPUS My own good
Snaps my patience, then! I want none of it.

IOKASTÊ You are fatally wrong! May you never learn who you are!

OEDIPUS Go, one of you, and bring the shepherd here.
Let us leave this woman to brag of her royal name.

IOKASTÊ Ah, miserable!
That is the only word I have for you now.
That is the only word I can ever have.

(*Exit into the palace.*)

CHORAGOS Why has she left us, Oedipus? Why has she gone
In such a passion of sorrow? I fear this silence:
Something dreadful may come of it.

OEDIPUS Let it come!
However base my birth, I must know about it.
The Queen, like a woman, is perhaps ashamed
To think of my low origin. But I
Am a child of Luck; I can not be dishonored.
Luck is my mother; the passing months, my brothers,
Have seen me rich and poor.
If this is so,
How could I wish that I were someone else?
How could I not be glad to know my birth?

Ode III

Strophe

CHORUS If ever the coming time were known
To my heart's pondering,
Kithairon, now by Heaven I see the torches
At the festival of the next full moon,
And see the dance, and hear the choir sing
A grace to your gentle shade:
Mountain where Oedipus was found,
O mountain guard of a noble race!
May the god[3] who heals us lend his aid,
And let that glory come to pass
For our king's cradling-ground.

Antistrophe

Of the nymphs that flower beyond the years,
Who bore you,[4] royal child,
To Pan of the hills or the timberline Apollo,
Cold in delight where the upland clears,
Or Hermês for whom Kyllenê's heights are piled?
Or flushed as evening cloud,
Great Dionysos, roamer of mountains,

---

[3]Apollo [4]The chorus is suggesting that perhaps Oedipus is the son of one of the immortal nymphs and of a god—Pan, Apollo, Hermes, or Dionysos. The "sweet god-ravisher" (p. 60) is the presumed mother.

He—was it he who found you there,
And caught you up in his own proud
Arms from the sweet god-ravisher
Who laughed by the Muses' fountains?

Scene IV

OEDIPUS Sirs: though I do not know the man,
I think I see him coming, this shepherd we want:
He is old, like our friend here, and the men
Bringing him seem to be servants of my house.
But you can tell, if you have ever seen him.

(*Enter* SHEPHERD *escorted by* SERVANTS.)

CHORAGOS I know him, he was Laïos' man. You can trust him.
OEDIPUS Tell me first, you from Corinth: is this the shepherd
We were discussing?
MESSENGER This is the very man.
OEDIPUS (*to* SHEPHERD) Come here. No, look at me. You must answer
Everything I ask.—You belonged to Laïos?
SHEPHERD Yes: born his slave, brought up in his house.
OEDIPUS Tell me: what kind of work did you do for him?
SHEPHERD I was a shepherd of his, most of my life.
OEDIPUS Where mainly did you go for pasturage?
SHEPHERD Sometimes Kithairon, sometimes the hills near-by.
OEDIPUS Do you remember ever seeing this man out there?
SHEPHERD What would he be doing there? This man?
OEDIPUS This man standing here. Have you ever seen him before?
SHEPHERD No. At least, not to my recollection.
MESSENGER And that is not strange, my lord. But I'll refresh
His memory: he must remember when we two
Spent three whole seasons together, March to September,
On Kithairon or thereabouts. He had two flocks;
I had one. Each autumn I'd drive mine home
And he would go back with his to Laïos' sheepfold.—
Is this not true, just as I have described it?
SHEPHERD True, yes; but it was all so long ago.
MESSENGER Well, then: do you remember, back in those days,
That you gave me a baby boy to bring up as my own?
SHEPHERD What if I did? What are you trying to say?
MESSENGER King Oedipus was once that little child.
SHEPHERD Damn you, hold your tongue!

OEDIPUS No more of that!
It is your tongue needs watching, not this man's.
SHEPHERD My king, my master, what is it I have done wrong?
OEDIPUS You have not answered his question about the boy.
SHEPHERD He does not know . . . He is only making trouble . . .
OEDIPUS Come, speak plainly, or it will go hard with you.
SHEPHERD In God's name, do not torture an old man!
OEDIPUS Come here, one of you; bind his arms behind him.
SHEPHERD Unhappy king! What more do you wish to learn?
OEDIPUS Did you give this man the child he speaks of?
SHEPHERD I did.
And I would to God I had died that very day.
OEDIPUS You will die now unless you speak the truth.
SHEPHERD Yet if I speak the truth, I am worse than dead.
OEDIPUS (*to* ATTENDANT) He intends to draw it out, apparently—
SHEPHERD No! I have told you already that I gave him the boy.
OEDIPUS Where did you get him? From your house? From somewhere else?
SHEPHERD Not from mine, no. A man gave him to me.
OEDIPUS Is that man here? Whose house did he belong to?
SHEPHERD For God's love, my king, do not ask me any more!
OEDIPUS You are a dead man if I have to ask you again.
SHEPHERD Then . . . Then the child was from the palace of Laïos.
OEDIPUS A slave child? or a child of his own line?
SHEPHERD Ah, I am on the brink of dreadful speech!
OEDIPUS And I of dreadful hearing. Yet I must hear.
SHEPHERD If you must be told, then. . .
They said it was Laïos' child;
But it is your wife who can tell you about that.
OEDIPUS My wife!—Did she give it to you?
SHEPHERD My lord, she did.
OEDIPUS Do you know why?
SHEPHERD I was told to get rid of it.
OEDIPUS Oh heartless mother!
SHEPHERD But in dread of prophecies . . .
OEDIPUS Tell me.
SHEPHERD It was said that the boy would kill his own father.
OEDIPUS Then why did you give him over to this old man?
SHEPHERD I pitied the baby, my king,
And I thought that this man would take him far away
To his own country.
He saved him—but for what a fate!
For if you are what this man says you are,
No man living is more wretched than Oedipus.

OEDIPUS Ah God!
It was true!
All the prophecies!
—Now,
O Light, may I look on you for the last time!
I, Oedipus,
Oedipus, damned in his birth, in his marriage damned,
Damned in the blood he shed with his own hand!

(*He rushes into the palace.*)

Ode IV

Strophe 1

CHORUS Alas for the seed of men.
What measure shall I give these generations
That breathe on the void and are void
And exist and do not exist?
Who bears more weight of joy
Than mass of sunlight shifting in images,
Or who shall make his thought stay on
That down time drifts away?
Your splendor is all fallen.
O naked brow of wrath and tears,
O change of Oedipus!
I who saw your days call no man blest—
Your great days like ghosts gone.

Antistrophe 1

That mind was a strong bow.
Deep, how deep you drew it then, hard archer,
At a dim fearful range,
And brought dear glory down!
You overcame the stranger[5]—
The virgin with her hooking lion claws—
And though death sang, stood like a tower
To make pale Thebes take heart.
Fortress against our sorrow!
True king, giver of laws,
Majestic Oedipus!

[5]the Sphinx

No prince in Thebes had ever such renown,
No prince won such grace of power.

Strophe 2

And now of all men ever known
Most pitiful is this man's story:
His fortunes are most changed, his state
Fallen to a low slave's
Ground under bitter fate.
O Oedipus, most royal one!
The great door[6] that expelled you to the light
Gave at night—ah, gave night to your glory:
As to the father, to the fathering son.
All understood too late.
How could that queen whom Laïos won,
The garden that he harrowed at his height,
Be silent when that act was done?

Antistrophe 2

But all eyes fail before time's eye,
All actions come to justice there.
Though never willed, though far down the deep past,
Your bed, your dread sirings,
Are brought to book at last.
Child by Laïos doomed to die,
Then doomed to lose that fortunate little death,
Would God you never took breath in this air
That with my wailing lips I take to cry:
For I weep the world's outcast.
I was blind, and now I can tell why:
Asleep, for you had given ease of breath
To Thebes, while the false years went by.

Exodos[7]

(*Enter, from the palace,* SECOND MESSENGER.)

SECOND MESSENGER Elders of Thebes, most honored in this land,
What horrors are yours to see and hear, what weight
Of sorrow to be endured, if, true to your birth,
You venerate the line of Labdakos!

[6]Iokastê's womb [7]final scene

I think neither Istros nor Phasis, those great rivers,
Could purify this place of all the evil
It shelters now, or soon must bring to light—
Evil not done unconsciously, but willed.

The greatest griefs are those we cause ourselves.

CHORAGOS Surely, friend, we have grief enough already;
What new sorrow do you mean?

SECOND MESSENGER The queen is dead.

CHORAGOS O miserable queen! But at whose hand?

SECOND MESSENGER Her own.
The full horror of what happened you can not know,
For you did not see it; but I, who did, will tell you
As clearly as I can how she met her death.

When she had left us,
In passionate silence, passing through the court,
She ran to her apartment in the house,
Her hair clutched by the fingers of both hands.
She closed the doors behind her; then, by that bed
Where long ago the fatal son was conceived—
That son who should bring about his father's death—
We heard her call upon Laïos, dead so many years,
And heard her wail for the double fruit of her marriage,
A husband by her husband, children by her child.

Exactly how she died I do not know:
For Oedipus burst in moaning and would not let us
Keep vigil to the end: it was by him
As he stormed about the room that our eyes were caught.
From one to another of us he went, begging a sword,
Hunting the wife who was not his wife, the mother
Whose womb had carried his own children and himself.
I do not know: it was none of us aided him,
But surely one of the gods was in control!
For with a dreadful cry
He hurled his weight, as though wrenched out of himself,
At the twin doors: the bolts gave, and he rushed in.
And there we saw her hanging, her body swaying
From the cruel cord she had noosed about her neck.
A great sob broke from him, heartbreaking to hear,
As he loosed the rope and lowered her to the ground.

I would blot out from my mind what happened next!
For the king ripped from her gown the golden brooches

That were her ornament, and raised them, and plunged them down
Straight into his own eyeballs, crying, "No more,
No more shall you look on the misery about me,
The horrors of my own doing! Too long you have known
The faces of those whom I should never have seen,
Too long been blind to those for whom I was searching!
From this hour, go in darkness!" And as he spoke,
He struck at his eyes—not once, but many times;
And the blood spattered his beard,
Bursting from his ruined sockets like red hail.

So from the unhappiness of two this evil has sprung,
A curse on the man and woman alike. The old
Happiness of the house of Labdakos
Was happiness enough: where is it today?
It is all wailing and ruin, disgrace, death—all
The misery of mankind that has a name—
And it is wholly and for ever theirs.

CHORAGOS Is he in agony still? Is there no rest for him?

SECOND MESSENGER He is calling for someone to open the doors wide
So that all the children of Kadmos may look upon
His father's murderer, his mother's—no,
I can not say it!
And then he will leave Thebes,
Self-exiled, in order that the curse
Which he himself pronounced may depart from the house.
He is weak, and there is none to lead him,
So terrible is his suffering.
But you will see:
Look, the doors are opening; in a moment
You will see a thing that would crush a heart of stone.

(*The central door is opened;* OEDIPUS, *blinded, is led in.*)

CHORAGOS Dreadful indeed for men to see.
Never have my own eyes
Looked on a sight so full of fear.

Oedipus!
What madness came upon you, what daemon
Leaped on your life with heavier
Punishment than a mortal man can bear?
No: I can not even
Look at you, poor ruined one.

And I would speak, question, ponder,
If I were able. No.
You make me shudder.
OEDIPUS God. God.
Is there a sorrow greater?
Where shall I find harbor in this world?
My voice is hurled far on a dark wind.
What has God done to me?
CHORAGOS Too terrible to think of, or to see.

Strophe 1

OEDIPUS O cloud of night,
Never to be turned away: night coming on,
I can not tell how: night like a shroud!
My fair winds brought me here.
O God. Again
The pain of the spikes where I had sight,
The flooding pain
Of memory, never to be gouged out.
CHORAGOS This is not strange.
You suffer it all twice over, remorse in pain,
Pain in remorse.

Antistrophe 1

OEDIPUS Ah dear friend
Are you faithful even yet, you alone?
Are you still standing near me, will you stay here,
Patient, to care for the blind?
The blind man!
Yet even blind I know who it is attends me,
By the voice's tone—
Though my new darkness hide the comforter.
CHORAGOS Oh fearful act!
What god was it drove you to rake black
Night across your eyes?

Strophe 2

OEDIPUS Apollo. Apollo. Dear
Children, the god was Apollo.
He brought my sick, sick fate upon me.
But the blinding hand was my own!

How could I bear to see
When all my sight was horror everywhere?
CHORAGOS Everywhere; that is true.
OEDIPUS And now what is left?
Images? Love? A greeting even,
Sweet to the senses? Is there anything?
Ah, no, friends: lead me away.
Lead me away from Thebes.
Lead the great wreck
And hell of Oedipus, whom the gods hate.
CHORAGOS Your misery, you are not blind to that.
Would God you had never found it out!

Antistrophe 2

OEDIPUS Death take the man who unbound
My feet on that hillside
And delivered me from death to life! What life?
If only I had died,
This weight of monstrous doom
Could not have dragged me and my darlings down.
CHORAGOS I would have wished the same.
OEDIPUS Oh never to have come here
With my father's blood upon me! Never
To have been the man they call his mother's husband!
Oh accurst! Oh child of evil,
To have entered that wretched bed—
the selfsame one!
More primal than sin itself, this fell to me.
CHORAGOS I do not know what words to offer you.
You were better dead than alive and blind.

OEDIPUS Do not counsel me any more. This punishment
That I have laid upon myself is just.
If I had eyes,
I do not know how I could bear the sight
Of my father, when I came to the house of Death,
Or my mother: for I have sinned against them both
So vilely that I could not make my peace
By strangling my own life.
Or do you think my children,
Born as they were born, would be sweet to my eyes?
Ah never, never! Nor this town with its high walls,
Nor the holy images of the gods.

For I,
Thrice miserable!—Oedipus, noblest of all the line
Of Kadmos, have condemned myself to enjoy
These things no more, by my own malediction
Expelling that man whom the gods declared
To be a defilement in the house of Laïos.
After exposing the rankness of my own guilt,
How could I look men frankly in the eyes?
No, I swear it,
If I could have stifled my hearing at its source,
I would have done it and made all this body
A tight cell of misery, blank to light and sound:
So I should have been safe in my dark mind
Beyond external evil.
Ah Kithairon!
Why did you shelter me? When I was cast upon you,
Why did I not die? Then I should never
Have shown the world my execrable birth.

Ah Polybos! Corinth, city that I believed
The ancient seat of my ancestors: how fair
I seemed, your child! And all the while this evil
Was cancerous within me!
For I am sick
In my own being, sick in my origin.

O three roads, dark ravine, woodland and way
Where three roads met: you, drinking my father's blood,
My own blood, spilled by my own hand: can you remember
The unspeakable things I did there, and the things
I went on from there to do?
O marriage, marriage!
That act that engendered me, and again the act
Performed by the son in the same bed—
Ah, the net
Of incest, mingling fathers, brothers, sons,
With brides, wives, mothers: the last evil
That can be known by men: no tongue can say
How evil!
No. For the love of God, conceal me
Somewhere far from Thebes; or kill me; or hurl me
Into the sea, away from men's eyes for ever.

Come, lead me. You need not fear to touch me.
Of all men, I alone can bear this guilt.

(*Enter* KREON.)

CHORAGOS Kreon is here now. As to what you ask,
He may decide the course to take. He only
Is left to protect the city in your place.
OEDIPUS Alas, how can I speak to him? What right have I
To beg his courtesy whom I have deeply wronged?
KREON I have not come to mock you, Oedipus,
Or to reproach you, either. (*to* ATTENDANTS)
—You, standing there:
If you have lost all respect for man's dignity,
At least respect the flame of Lord Helios:
Do not allow this pollution to show itself
Openly here, an affront to the earth
And Heaven's rain and the light of day. No, take him
Into the house as quickly as you can.
For it is proper
That only the close kindred see his grief.
OEDIPUS I pray you in God's name, since your courtesy
Ignores my dark expectation, visiting
With mercy this man of all men most execrable:
Give me what I ask—for your good, not for mine.
KREON And what is it that you turn to me begging for?
OEDIPUS Drive me out of this country as quickly as may be
To a place where no human voice can ever greet me.
KREON I should have done that before now—only,
God's will had not been wholly revealed to me.
OEDIPUS But his command is plain: the parricide
Must be destroyed. I am that evil man.
KREON That is the sense of it, yes; but as things are,
We had best discover clearly what is to be done.
OEDIPUS You would learn more about a man like me?
KREON You are ready now to listen to the god.
OEDIPUS I will listen. But it is to you
That I must turn for help. I beg you, hear me.

The woman in there—
Give her whatever funeral you think proper:
She is your sister.
—But let me go, Kreon!
Let me purge my father's Thebes of the pollution
Of my living here, and go out to the wild hills,
To Kithairon, that has won such fame with me,
The tomb my mother and father appointed for me,
And let me die there, as they willed I should.

And yet I know
Death will not ever come to me through sickness
Or in any natural way: I have been preserved
For some unthinkable fate. But let that be.

As for my sons, you need not care for them.
They are men, they will find some way to live.
But my poor daughters, who have shared my table,
Who never before have been parted from their father—
Take care of them, Kreon; do this for me.

And will you let me touch them with my hands
A last time, and let us weep together?
Be kind, my lord,
Great prince, be kind!
Could I but touch them,
They would be mine again, as when I had my eyes.

(*Enter* ANTIGONÊ *and* ISMENÊ, *attended.*)

Ah, God!
Is it my dearest children I hear weeping?
Has Kreon pitied me and sent my daughters?
KREON Yes, Oedipus: I knew that they were dear to you
In the old days, and know you must love them still.
OEDIPUS My God bless you for this—and be a friendlier
Guardian to you than he has been to me!

Children, where are you?
Come quickly to my hands: they are your brother's—
Hands that have brought your father's once clear eyes
To this way of seeing—
Ah dearest ones,
I had neither sight nor knowledge then, your father
By the woman who was the source of his own life!
And I weep for you—having no strength to see you—,
I weep for you when I think of the bitterness
That men will visit upon you all your lives.
What homes, what festivals can you attend
Without being forced to depart again in tears?
And when you come to marriageable age,
Where is the man, my daughters, who would dare
Risk the bane that lies on all my children?
Is there any evil wanting? Your father killed
His father; sowed the womb of her who bore him;
Engendered you at the fount of his own existence!

That is what they will say of you.
Then, whom
Can you ever marry? There are no bridegrooms for you,
And your lives must wither away in sterile dreaming.

O Kreon, son of Menoikeus!
You are the only father my daughters have,
Since we, their parents, are both of us gone for ever.
They are your own blood: you will not let them
Fall into beggary and loneliness;
You will keep them from the miseries that are mine!
Take pity on them; see, they are only children,
Friendless except for you. Promise me this,
Great prince, and give me your hand in token of it.

(KREON *clasps his right hand.*)

Children:
I could say much, if you could understand me,
But as it is, I have only this prayer for you:
Live where you can, be as happy as you can—
Happier, please God, than God has made your father.

KREON Enough. You have wept enough. Now go within.
OEDIPUS I must; but it is hard.
KREON Time eases all things.
OEDIPUS You know my mind, then?
KREON Say what you desire.
OEDIPUS Send me from Thebes!
KREON God grant that I may!
OEDIPUS But since God hates me . . .
KREON No, he will grant your wish.
OEDIPUS You promise?
KREON I can not speak beyond my knowledge.
OEDIPUS Then lead me in.
KREON Come now, and leave your children.
OEDIPUS No! Do not take them from me!
KREON Think no longer
That you are in command here, but rather think
How, when you were, you served your own destruction.

(*Exeunt into the house all but the* CHORUS; *the* CHORAGOS *chants directly to the audience.*)

CHORAGOS Men of Thebes: look upon Oedipus.

This is the king who solved the famous riddle
And towered up, most powerful of men.
No mortal eyes but looked on him with envy,
Yet in the end ruin swept over him.

Let every man in mankind's frailty
Consider his last day; and let none
Presume on his good fortune until he find
Life, at his death, a memory without pain.

LYSISTRATA

(411 B.C.)

ARISTOPHANES (c. 450–387 B.C.)

In its examination of a variety of serious themes, ancient tragedy provides a broad spectrum of views which fifth-century Greek society held regarding humankind's relationship with the gods and with each other from the more mystic explorations of Aeschylus to the more realistic style of Euripides. Though lacking in creed or dogma and subject to certain skepticism as to the literal existence of the gods (one of the most serious charges against Socrates was his alleged denial of the pantheon), the Greek religion did command a certain respect for the gods and what they represented, with prescribed rituals of worship and sacrifice carefully executed.

Ancient comedy, on the other hand, was quite a different matter. In its form, structure, and subject it bore little resemblance to tragedy and revealed a great deal about the relative freedom and openness of the "Golden Age" of Athenian democracy. Although open and direct attack upon important political figures or social patterns could still bring retribution, the ability to criticize through the media of pointed satire, parody, and lampoon was abundantly evident in comedy. Moreover, the society's tolerance for political and sexual license upon the stage was clearly demonstrated. To Aristophanes, in particular, nothing was sacred.

There were three types of nontragic plays in the fifth and fourth centuries, two of them unique to their time and never emulated thereafter. The first of these were the so-called *satyr plays,* not generally regarded as true comedies, presented immediately following the tragic trilogy and written by the same poet. They were gross burlesques, often portraying the hero of the tragedy in a ludicrous situation with a chorus of satyrs, lecherous creatures, half man and half animal, appearing in indecent costumes and speaking and acting equally indecently. Only one such play survives, *The Cyclops* (428 B.C.) by Euripides. The origin of the satyr plays remains obscure, and there is no relationship between them and dramatic satire or any form of Greek comedy.

The second type of nontragic play, known as "New Comedy," survives in the many fragments and one complete play by Menander (c. 342–292 B.C.). With no resemblance whatever to the satyr plays or to the earlier "Old Comedy" of

Aristophanes, these plays are essentially romantic stories of ill-used maidens and slave foundlings who eventually meet true love or achieve long-lost fortunes and discover their noble births. In effect, they represent the first domestic comedies and have been imitated ever since from ancient Roman comedy to today's television "sitcoms."

The third type, or "Old Comedy," which concerns us here, is represented by the eleven surviving plays of Aristophanes. It is a combination of farce, striptease, burlesque, music hall routine, fantasy, and serious literary and political satire. It is, in fact, a unique form that did not extend beyond its brief era in history, but it is one of the most delightfully original and entertaining of all comic dramas. The *Lysistrata* is the most eminently producible and the most easily appreciated today, with a plotline and variety of characters that appeal to contemporary audiences. Furthermore, its satire on the idiocies of war and the incompetent bumblers who conduct it is universal and immediately comprehensible.

Tragedies were presented in the mornings at the Festival of Dionysus, and afternoons were apparently reserved for comedy. They, too, followed a fairly rigid structural form, including set choral passages and dancing, and a unique section known as the *parabasis* during which the author presented directly to the audience his own personal views about a variety of things. As in tragedy, all the characters were played by men, and masks with broadly exaggerated comic faces were essential. But the distinguishing aspect of comic costume was the huge leather sex organ, the *phallus,* worn by male figures just beneath the extremely short tunics and in full view at all times.

We should not associate the phallic aspect of Greek comedy with decadence or debilitating immoral social behavior. The Dionysiac Festival was a time of revelry, and Dionysus, as god of the vine, hence wine, was closely associated with fertility and by extension plain, ordinary sex. Although Priapus, son of Aphrodite the goddess of love, possibly fathered by Dionysus, was the god of fertility in man and nature, Dionysus, also known as Bacchus, lent his name to orgies of drinking and sex—Bacchanals—practiced in his honor. The ancient Greek, who accepted the performance of athletic events by nude participants and admired the beauties of the undraped male and female body, entertained a healthy respect for sex as a perfectly natural function, susceptible, as in all civilizations, to a lot of very funny dirty jokes. Once a year the performance of these comedies at the Dionysiac was regarded as an appropriate outlet for a very natural urge.

Two topics subjected to Aristophanes' often biting pen were the Peloponnesian War (431–404 B.C.) and the position of women. Athens experienced its Vietnam in its ill-planned catastrophic conflict against Sparta. When it ended, the Athens of the Golden Age had been destroyed. Unable to mount a frontal attack, Aristophanes raged against the war in his unsparing, often violent, satiric thrusts against the government that backed the war and the generals who led it. In *Peace* (421 B.C.), his war-weary characters attempt to rescue the goddess of peace from captivity so that she can help bring an end to the conflict. In *The Birds* (414 B.C.), he sends his disillusioned citizens seeking escape from the confused earthly world into Cloud-Cuckoo-Land, a world in the sky, run by a hierarchy of feathered (and fantastically costumed) bureaucrats.

But more to the point of *Lysistrata* is Aristophanes' consideration of the position of women. Held in virtual seclusion by her dominating husband, the Greek wife possessed few civil rights; she could not vote or partake in any political process, and remained only a step above the household slaves. Within these restrictions, however, Greek women exerted considerable influence over their spouses (Socrates was purported to have suffered grievously under a shrewish wife) as they supervised and controlled the many domestic functions.

In two plays besides the *Lysistrata,* Aristophanes has great fun with a look at what might occur in a more liberal society. In *Thesmophoriazousae* (410 B.C.), translated as "Women at the Festival," he concentrates on female goings-on during a public holiday, but he raises some very interesting, albeit comic, problems in *Ecclesiazousae* (392 B.C.), or "Women in Parliament," an outrageous "what if" proposition that speculates on the results of women running the government. Even the husband who kept his wife in her "place" at home was not above thoroughly enjoying in public the rambunctious obscenities of Aristophanes' comedy, particularly the *Lysistrata.* It is Aristophanes' best "feminist" play, and gets right down to the basics in the war between men and women.

The *Lysistrata* is emphatically not in itself a "dirty" play. It is, even more than fairly liberal modern translations indicate, a hilariously obscene play, but it is certainly not pornographic. True, the central theme of the sex strike extends the jokes longer and more fully than in any other of Aristophanes' plays, but the wide-open nature of his exploration of the women's use of their ultimate weapon is tremendous fun and wholly free from any sniggering peep-show quality. The scene between the teasing Myrrhine and the desperate Kinesias when played to its fullest is devastatingly funny. Moreover, in demonstrating the difficulties that Lysistrata herself encounters in organizing her battle plan and holding her troops in line, Aristophanes makes very clear that sex is not just one-sided and male-dominated. His women, every bit as much as men, openly desire and thoroughly enjoy the experience. Although the play does present sex as a source for pointed social and political comment, there is no gainsaying that Aristophanes is also providing, fully intentionally, some of the best comic sex sequences in Western drama.

Lysistrata should be read and experienced in production as it was intended: a brilliant satire on sex itself and on the relative position of supposedly dominating men and submissive women turned topsy-turvy in a society gone mad, and as a superb condemnation of the stupidities of the politicians and bureaucrats who have lived in every historical age and who don't know how to stop the troubles they have let themselves in for. If he couldn't stop the foolishness of these bumbling perpetrators in any other way, Aristophanes must have hoped that through the *Lysistrata* he could at least try to laugh it to death.

Lysistrata ARISTOPHANES

An English version by Dudley Fitts

CHARACTERS

LYSISTRATA
KALONIKE } *Athenian women*
MYRRHINE }
LAMPITO, *a Spartan woman*
CHORUS
MAGISTRATE
KINESIAS, *husband of Myrrhine*
SPARTAN HERALD
SPARTAN AMBASSADOR
A SENTRY
ATHENIAN DRUNKARD

The supernumeraries include the BABY SON *of Kinesias;* STRATYLLIS, *a member of the hemichorus of Old Women; various individual speakers, both Spartan and Athenian.*
Until the exodos, *the* CHORUS *is divided into two hemichori: the first, of Old Men; the second, of Old Women. Each of these has its* CHORAGOS. *In the* exodos, *the hemichori return as Athenians and Spartans.*

Athens. First, a public square; later, beneath the walls of the Acropolis; later, a courtyard within the Acropolis. Time: early in 411 B.C.

Athens; a public square; early morning; LYSISTRATA *sola.*

Prologue

LYSISTRATA If someone had invited them to a festival—
Bacchus's, say, or Pan's, or Aphrodite's, or
that Genetyllis business[1]—, you couldn't get through the streets,
what with the drums and the dancing. But now,
not a woman in sight!
Except—oh, yes!

(*Enter* KALONIKE.)

Here's one, at last. Good
morning, Kalonike.

[1]references to cults of love and wine

KALONIKE Good morning, Lysistrata.
Darling,
don't frown so! You'll ruin your face!

LYSISTRATA Never mind my face.
Kalonike,
the way we women behave! Really, I don't blame the men
for what they say about us.

KALONIKE No; I imagine they're right.

LYSISTRATA For example: I call a meeting
to think out a most important matter—and what happens?
The women all stay in bed!

KALONIKE Oh, they'll be along.
It's hard to get away, you know: a husband, a cook,
a child . . . Home life can be *so* demanding!

LYSISTRATA What I have in mind is even more demanding.

KALONIKE Tell me: what is it?

LYSISTRATA Something big.

KALONIKE Goodness! *How* big?

LYSISTRATA Big enough for all of us.

KALONIKE But we're not all here!

LYSISTRATA We would be, if *that's* what was up!
No, Kalonike,
this is something I've been turning over for nights;
and, I may say, sleepless nights.

KALONIKE Can't be so hard, then,
if you've spent so much time on it.

LYSISTRATA Hard or not,
it comes to this: Only we women can save Greece!

KALONIKE Only we women? Poor Greece!

LYSISTRATA Just the same,
it's up to us. First, we must liquidate
the Peloponnesians—

KALONIKE Fun, fun!

LYSISTRATA —and then the Boeotians.

KALONIKE Oh! But not those heavenly eels![2]

LYSISTRATA You needn't worry.
Athens shall have her sea food.—But here's the point:
If we can get the women from those places—
to join us women here, why, we can save
all Greece!

---

[2]Boeotia was famous for its seafood, especially its eels.

KALONIKE But dearest Lysistrata!
How can women do a thing so austere, so
political? We belong at home. Our only armor's
our transparent saffron dresses and
our pretty little shoes!
LYSISTRATA That's it exactly.
Those transparent saffron dresses, those little shoes—
well, there we are!
KALONIKE Oh?
LYSISTRATA Not a single man would lift
his spear—
KALONIKE I'll get my dress from the dyer's tomorrow!
LYSISTRATA —or need a shield—
KALONIKE The sweetest little negligée—
LYSISTRATA —or bring out his sword.
KALONIKE I know where I can buy
the dreamiest sandals!
LYSISTRATA Well, so you see. Now, shouldn't
the women have come?
KALONIKE Come? they should have *flown!*
LYSISTRATA Athenians are always late.
But imagine!
There's no one here from the South Shore.
KALONIKE They go to work early,
I can swear to that.
LYSISTRATA And nobody from Acharnai.
They should have been here hours ago!
KALONIKE Well, you'll get
that awful Theagenes woman: she's been having
her fortune told at Hecate's shrine.[3]
But look!
Someone at last! Can you see who they are?

(*Enter* MYRRHINE *and other women.*)

LYSISTRATA People from the suburbs.
KALONIKE Yes! The entire
membership of the Suburban League!
MYRRHINE Sorry to be late, Lysistrata.
Oh, come,
don't scowl so! Say something!

---

[3]Theagenes was notoriously superstitious; his practice of never leaving home without consulting Hecate is here transferred to his wife.

LYSISTRATA My dear Myrrhine,
what is there to say? After all,
you've been pretty casual about the whole thing.
MYRRHINE Couldn't find
my girdle in the dark, that's all.
But what *is*
"the whole thing"?
LYSISTRATA Wait for the rest of them.
KALONIKE I suppose so. But, look!
Here's Lampito!

(*Enter* LAMPITO *with women from Sparta.*)

LYSISTRATA Darling Lampito,
how pretty you are today! What a nice color!
Goodness, you look as though you could strangle a bull!
LAMPITO Ah think Ah could! It's the work-out
in the gym every day; and, of co'se that dance of ahs
where y' kick yo' own tail.[4]
LYSISTRATA What lovely breasts!
LAMPITO Lawdy, when y' touch me lahk that,
Ah feel lahk a heifer at the altar!
LYSISTRATA And this young lady?
Where is she from?
LAMPITO Boeotia. Social-Register type.
LYSISTRATA Good morning, Boeotian. You're as pretty as
green grass.
KALONIKE And if you look,
you'll find that the lawn has just been cut.
LYSISTRATA And this lady?
LAMPITO From Corinth. But a good woman.
LYSISTRATA Well, in Corinth
anything's possible.
LAMPITO But let's get to work. Which one of you
called this meeting, and why?
LYSISTRATA *I* did.
LAMPITO Well, then:
what's up?
MYRRHINE Yes, what *is* "the whole thing," after all?
LYSISTRATA I'll tell you.—But first, one question.

---

[4]Among the physical exercises practiced by Greek girls was the strenuous *bibasis,* a dance in which the dancer kicked her buttocks with her heels. (Lampito and other Spartans speak with a distinctly "southern" Greek accent; hence the translator's choice of an American southern drawl for comic effect.)

MYRRHINE Ask away!
LYSISTRATA It's your husbands. Fathers of your children. Doesn't it bother you
that they're always off with the Army? I'll stake my life,
not one of you has a man in the house this minute!
KALONIKE Mine's been in Thrace the last five months, keeping an
eye
on that General.[5]
MYRRHINE Mine's been in Pylos for seven.
LAMPITO And mahn,
whenever he gets a *dis*charge, he goes raht back
with that li'l ole speah of his, and enlists again!
LYSISTRATA And not the ghost of a lover to be found!
From the very day the war began—
those Milesians!
I could skin them alive!
—I've not seen so much, even,
as one of those devices they call Widow's Delight.
But there! What's important is: I've found a way
to end the war, are you with me?
MYRRHINE I should *say* so!
Even if I have to pawn my best dress and
drink up the proceeds.[6]
KALONIKE Me, too! Even if they split me
right up the middle, like a flounder.
LAMPITO Ah'm shorely with you.
Ah'd crawl up Taygetos[7] on mah knees
if that'd bring peace.
LYSISTRATA Then here it is.
Women! Sisters!
If we really want our men to make an armistice,
we must be ready to give up—
MYRRHINE Give up what?
Quick, tell us!
LYSISTRATA But *will* you?
MYRRHINE We will, even if it kills us.
LYSISTRATA Then we must give up sleeping with our men. (*long silence*)
Oh? So now you're sorry? Won't look at me?
Doubtful? Pale? All teary-eyed?
But come: be frank with me,
as I've certainly been with you. Will you do it?
MYRRHINE I couldn't. No.
Let the war go on.

---

[5]a certain Eukrates about whom nothing is known [6]Athenian women were frequently satirized for heavy drinking. [7]a rugged mountain range in the Peloponnesus

KALONIKE Nor I. Let the war go on.
LYSISTRATA You, you little flounder,
ready to be split up the middle?
KALONIKE Lysistrata, no!
I'd walk through fire for you—you *know* I would!—, but don't
ask us to give up *that!* Why, there's nothing like it!
LYSISTRATA And you?
BOEOTIAN No. I must say *I'd* rather walk through fire.
LYSISTRATA You little salamanders!
No wonder poets write tragedies about women.
All we want's a quick tumble!
But you from Sparta:
if you stand by me, we may win yet! Will you?
It means so much!
LAMPITO Ah sweah, it means *too* much!
By the Two Goddesses,[8] it does! Asking a girl
to sleep—Heaven knows how long!—in a great big bed
with nobody there but herself! But Ah'll stay with you!
Peace comes first!
LYSISTRATA Spoken like a true Spartan!
KALONIKE But, if—
oh dear!
—if we give up what you tell us to,
will there *be* any peace?
LYSISTRATA Why, mercy, of course there will!
We'll just sit snug in our very thinnest gowns,
perfumed and powdered from top to bottom, and those men
simply won't stand still! And when we say No,
they'll go out of their minds! And there's your peace.
You can take my word for it.
LAMPITO Ah seem to remember
that Colonel Menelaus threw his sword away
when he saw Helen's breast all bare.
KALONIKE But, goodness me!
What if they just get up and leave us?
LYSISTRATA Well,
we'd have to fall back on ourselves, of course.
But they won't.
KALONIKE What if they drag us into the bedroom?
LYSISTRATA Hang on to the door.
KALONIKE What if they slap us?
LYSISTRATA If they do, you'd better give in.
But be sulky about it. Do I have to teach you how?

[8]Demeter and Persephone; a woman's oath

You know there's no fun for men when they have to force you.
There are millions of ways of getting them to see reason.
Don't you worry: a man
doesn't like it unless the girl co-operates.

KALONIKE I suppose so. Oh, all right! We'll go along!

LAMPITO Ah imagine us Spahtans can arrange a peace. But you
Athenians! Why, you're just war-mongerers!

LYSISTRATA Leave that to me.
I know how to make them listen.

LAMPITO Ah don't see how.
After all, they've got their boats; and there's lots of money
piled up in the Acropolis.

LYSISTRATA The Acropolis? Darling,
we're taking over the Acropolis today!
That's the older women's job. All the rest of us
are going to the Citadel to sacrifice—you understand me?
And once there, we're in for good!

LAMPITO Whee! Up the rebels!
Ah can see you're a good strat*ee*gist.

LYSISTRATA Well, then, Lampito,
let's take the oath.

LAMPITO Say it. We'll sweah.

LYSISTRATA This is it.
—But Lord! Where's our Inner Guard? Never mind.
—You see this
shield? Put it down there. Now bring me the victim's entrails.

KALONIKE But the oath?

LYSISTRATA You remember how in Aeschylus' *Seven*[9]
they killed a sheep and swore on a shield? Well, then?

KALONIKE But I don't see how you can swear for peace on a shield.

LYSISTRATA What else do you suggest?

KALONIKE Why not a white horse?
We could swear by that.

LYSISTRATA And where will you get a white horse?

KALONIKE I never thought of that. *What* can we do?

MYRRHINE I have it!
Let's set this big black wine-bowl on the ground
and pour in a gallon or so of Thasian,[1] and swear
not to add one drop of water.

LAMPITO Ah lahk *that* oath!

LYSISTRATA Bring the bowl and the wine-jug.

[9] *The Seven Against Thebes* [1] a popular wine from Thasos

KALONIKE Oh, what a simply *huge* one!

LYSISTRATA Set it down; and, women, place your hands on the gift-offering.

O Goddess of Persuasion! And thou, O Loving-cup!
Look upon this our sacrifice, and
be gracious!

KALONIKE It spills out like blood. How red and pretty it is!

LAMPITO And Ah must say it smells good.

MYRRHINE Let me swear first!

KALONIKE No, by Aphrodite, let's toss for it!

LYSISTRATA Lampito: all of you women: come, touch the bowl, and repeat after me:
I WILL HAVE NOTHING TO DO WITH MY HUSBAND OR MY LOVER

KALONIKE *I will have nothing to do with my husband or my lover*

LYSISTRATA THOUGH HE COME TO ME IN PITIABLE CONDITION

KALONIKE *Though he come to me in pitiable condition*
(Oh, Lysistrata! This is killing me!)

LYSISTRATA I WILL STAY IN MY HOUSE UNTOUCHABLE

KALONIKE *I will stay in my house untouchable*

LYSISTRATA IN MY THINNEST SAFFRON SILK

KALONIKE *In my thinnest saffron silk*

LYSISTRATA AND MAKE HIM LONG FOR ME.

KALONIKE *And make him long for me.*

LYSISTRATA I WILL NOT GIVE MYSELF

KALONIKE *I will not give myself*

LYSISTRATA AND IF HE CONSTRAINS ME

KALONIKE *And if he constrains me*

LYSISTRATA I WILL BE AS COLD AS ICE AND NEVER MOVE

KALONIKE *I will be as cold as ice and never move*

LYSISTRATA I WILL NOT LIFT MY SLIPPERS TOWARD THE CEILING

KALONIKE *I will not lift my slippers toward the ceiling*

LYSISTRATA OR CROUCH ON ALL FOURS LIKE THE LIONESS IN THE CARVING

KALONIKE *Or crouch on all fours like the lioness in the carving*

LYSISTRATA AND IF I KEEP THIS OATH LET ME DRINK FROM THIS BOWL

KALONIKE *And if I keep this oath let me drink from this bowl*

LYSISTRATA IF NOT, LET MY OWN BOWL BE FILLED WITH WATER.

KALONIKE *If not, let my own bowl be filled with water.*
LYSISTRATA You have all sworn?
MYRRHINE We have.
LYSISTRATA Then thus
I sacrifice the victim. (*drinks largely*)
KALONIKE Save some for us!
Here's to you, darling, and to you, and to you! It's all
for us women. (*loud cries off-stage*)
LAMPITO What's all *that* whoozy-goozy?
LYSISTRATA Just what I told you.
The older women have taken the Acropolis. Now you, Lampito,
rush back to Sparta. We'll take care of things here. And
be sure you get organized!
The rest of you girls,
up to the Citadel: and mind you push in the bolts.
KALONIKE But the men? Won't they be after us?
LYSISTRATA Just you leave
the men to me. There's not fire enough in the world
to make me open *my* door.
KALONIKE I hope so, by Aphrodite!
At any rate,
let's remember the League's reputation for hanging on!

(*Exeunt.*)

Párodos

The hillside just under the Acropolis.

(*Enter* CHORUS OF OLD MEN *with burning torches and braziers; much puffing and coughing.*)

MALE CHORAGOS Easy, Drakes, old friend! Don't skin your shoulders
with those damnable big olive-branches. What a job!

Strophe 1

OLD MEN Forward, forward, comrades! Whew!
The things that old age does to you!
Neighbor Strymodoros, would you have thought it?
We've caught it—
And from women, too!
Women that used to board with us, bed with us—
Now, by the gods, they've got ahead of us,

Taken the Acropolis (Heaven knows why!),
Profaned the sacred statuar-y,
And barred the doors,
The aggravating whores!

MALE CHORAGOS Come, Philourgos, quick, pile your brushwood next to the wall there.
These traitors to Athens and to us,
we'll fry each last one of them! And the very first
will be old Lykon's wife.[2]

Antistrophe 1

OLD MEN By Demeter I swear it—(ouch!),
I'll not perform the Kleomenes-crouch!
How he looked—and a good soldier, too—
When out he flew,
that filthy pouch
Of a body of his all stinking and shaggy,
Bare as an eel, except for the bag he
Covered his rear with. Lord, what a mess!
Never a bath in six years, I'd guess!
Unhappy Sparta,
With such a martyr![3]

MALE CHORAGOS What a siege, friends! Seventeen ranks strong
we stood at the Gate, and never a chance for a nap.
And all because of women, whom the gods hate
(and so does Euripides).
It's enough to make a veteran
turn in his medals from Marathon!

Strophe 2

OLD MEN Forward, men! Just up the hillside,
And we're there!
Keep to the path! A yoke of oxen
Wouldn't care
To haul this lumber. Mind the fire,
Or it'll die before we're higher!
Puff! Puff!
This smoke will strangle me, sure enough!

---

[2]Rhodia, a famous belle of the day [3]Kleomenes, a king of Sparta, had captured the Acropolis but had been forced to give it up.

Antistrophe 2

Holy Heracles, I'm blinded,
Sure as fate!
It's Lemnos-fire[4] we've been toting;
And isn't it great
To be singed by this infernal flame?
(Laches, remember the Goddess: for shame!)
Woof! Woof!
A few steps more, and we're under the roof!

MALE CHORAGOS It catches! It's blazing!
Down with your loads!
We'll sizzle 'em now,
By all the gods!
Vine-branches here, quick!
Light 'em up,
And in through the gate with 'em!
If that doesn't stop
Their nonsense—well,
We'll smoke 'em to Hell.
Ker*shoo!*
(What we really need
Is a grad-u-ate,
Top of his class,
From Samos Military State.[5]
Achoo!)
Come, do
Your duty, you!
Pour out your braziers,
Embers ablaze!
But first, Gentlemen, allow me to raise
The paean:
Lady
Victory, now
Assist thine adherents
Here below!
Down with women!
Up with men!
Io triumphe![6]

OLD MEN Amen!

---

[4]Volcanic; Mount Moschylus on the island of Lemnos was the site of Hephaestus' (Vulcan's) forge.
[5]At this time Samos was the headquarters of Athenian military activities. [6]a ritual cry of triumph

(*Enter* CHORUS OF OLD WOMEN *on the walls of the Acropolis, carrying jars of water to extinguish the fire set by the* CHORUS OF OLD MEN.)

FEMALE CHORAGOS Fire, fire!
Quickly, quickly, women, if we're to save ourselves!

Strophe

OLD WOMEN Nikodike, run!
Or Kalyke's done
To a turn, and poor Kratylla's
Smoked like a ham.
Damn
These men and their wars,
Their hateful ways!
I nearly died before I got to the place
Where we fill our jars:
Slaves pushing and jostling—
Such a hustling
I never saw in all my days!

Antistrophe

But here's water at last.
Sisters, make haste
And slosh it down on them,
The silly old wrecks!
Sex
Almighty! What they want's
A hot bath? Send it down!
And thou, Athena of Athens town,
Assist us in drowning their wheezy taunts!
O Trito-born![7] Helmet of Gold!
Help us to cripple their backs, the old
Fools with their semi-incendiary brawn!

(*The* OLD MEN *capture a woman,* STRATYLLIS.)

STRATYLLIS Let me go! Let me go!

FEMALE CHORAGOS You walking corpses,
have you no shame?

[7]Athena; according to some versions of her story, she was born at Lake Tritonis in Libya.

MALE CHORAGOS I wouldn't have believed it!
An army of women in the Acropolis!
FEMALE CHORAGOS So we scare you, do we? Grandpa, you've seen
only our pickets yet!
MALE CHORAGOS Hey, Phaidrias!
Help me with the necks of these jabbering hens!
FEMALE CHORAGOS Down with your pots, girls! We'll need
both hands
if these antiques attack us.
MALE CHORAGOS Want your face kicked in?
FEMALE CHORAGOS Want to try my teeth?
MALE CHORAGOS Look out! I've got a stick!
FEMALE CHORAGOS You lay a half-inch of your stick on Stratyllis,
and you'll never stick again!
MALE CHORAGOS Fall apart!
FEMALE CHORAGOS I'll chew your guts!
MALE CHORAGOS Euripides! Master!
How well you knew women!
FEMALE CHORAGOS Listen to him! Rhodippe,
up with the pots!
MALE CHORAGOS Demolition of God,
what good are your pots?
FEMALE CHORAGOS You refugee from the tomb,
what good is your fire?
MALE CHORAGOS Good enough to make a pyre
to barbecue you!
FEMALE CHORAGOS We'll squizzle your kindling!
MALE CHORAGOS You think so?
FEMALE CHORAGOS Yah! Just hang around a while!
MALE CHORAGOS Want a touch of my torch?
FEMALE CHORAGOS Your torch needs a bath.
MALE CHORAGOS How about you?
FEMALE CHORAGOS Soap for a senile bridegroom!
MALE CHORAGOS Senile? Hold your trap!
FEMALE CHORAGOS Just *you* try to hold it!
MALE CHORAGOS The yammer of women!
FEMALE CHORAGOS The yatter of men!
But you'll never sit in the jury-box again.
MALE CHORAGOS Gentlemen, I beg you, burn off that woman's hair!
FEMALE CHORAGOS Let it come down! (*They empty their pots on the men.*)
MALE CHORAGOS What a way to drown!
FEMALE CHORAGOS Hot, hey?
MALE CHORAGOS Say,
enough!

FEMALE CHORAGOS Dandruff
needs watering. I'll make you
nice and fresh.
MALE CHORAGOS For God's sake, you
sluts, hold off!

Scene I

(*Enter a* MAGISTRATE *accompanied by four constables.*)

MAGISTRATE These degenerate women! What a racket of little
drums,
what a yapping for Adonis on every house-top!
It's like the time in the Assembly when I was listening
to a speech—out of order, as usual—by that fool
Demostratos,[8] all about troops for Sicily,
that kind of nonsense—
and there was his wife
trotting around in circles howling
Alas for Adonis!—
and Demostratos insisting
we must draft every last Zakynthian that can walk—
and his wife up there on the roof,
drunk as an owl, yowling
Oh weep for Adonis!—
and that damned ox Demostratos
mooing away through the rumpus. That's what we get
for putting up with this wretched woman-business!
MALE CHORAGOS Sir, you haven't heard the half of it. They laughed
at us!
Insulted us! They took pitchers of water
and nearly drowned us! We're still wringing out our clothes,
for all the world like unhousebroken brats.
MAGISTRATE And a good thing, by Poseidon!
Whose fault is it these women-folk of ours
get out of hand? We coddle them,
we teach them to be wasteful and loose. You'll see a husband
go into a jeweler's. "Look," he'll say,
"jeweler," he'll say, "you remember that gold choker
"you made for my wife? Well, she went to a dance last night
"and broke the clasp. Now, I've got to go to Salamis,

[8]A well-known demagogue; the speech alludes to the festival in honor of Adonis which four years earlier had coincided with the decision to undertake the disastrous Sicilian expedition. It was believed that the women's madness in lamenting Adonis had influenced the decision.

"and can't be bothered. Run over to my house tonight,
"will you, and see if you can put it together for her."
Or another one
goes to a cobbler—a good strong workman, too,
with an awl that was never meant for child's play. "Here,"
he'll tell him, "one of my wife's shoes is pinching
"her little toe. Could you come up about noon
"and stretch it out for her?"
Well, what do you expect?
Look at me, for example. I'm a Public Officer,
and it's one of my duties to pay off the sailors.
And where's the money? Up there in the Acropolis!
And those blasted women slam the door in my face!
But what are we waiting for?
—Look here, constable,
stop sniffing around for a tavern, and get us
some crowbars. We'll force their gates! As a matter of fact,
I'll do a little forcing myself.

(*Enter* LYSISTRATA, *above, with* MYRRHINE, KALONIKE, *and the* BOEOTIAN.)

LYSISTRATA No need of forcing.
Here I am, of my own accord. And all this talk
about locked doors—! We don't need locked doors,
but just the least bit of common sense.
MAGISTRATE Is that so, ma'am!
—Where's my constable?
—Constable,
arrest that woman, and tie her hands behind her.
LYSISTRATA If he touches me, I swear by Artemis
there'll be one scamp dropped from the public pay-roll tomorrow!
MAGISTRATE Well, constable? You're not afraid, I suppose? Grab her,
two of you, around the middle!
KALONIKE No, by Pandrosos![9]
Lay a hand on her, and I'll jump on you so hard
your guts will come out the back door!
MAGISTRATE That's what *you* think!
Where's the sergeant?—Here, you: tie up that trollop first,
the one with the pretty talk!
MYRRHINE By the Moon-Goddess![1]
Just you try it, and you'd better call a surgeon!
MAGISTRATE Another one!
Officer, seize that woman!

[9]one of the daughters of the founder of Athens; a woman's oath [1]Artemis

I swear
I'll put an end to this riot!

BOEOTIAN By the Taurian,[2]
one inch closer and you won't have a hair on your head!

MAGISTRATE Lord, what a mess! And my constables seem to have left me.
But—women get the best of us? By God, no!
—Scythians![3]
Close ranks and forward march!

LYSISTRATA "Forward," indeed!
By the Two Goddesses, what's the sense in *that?*
They're up against four companies of women
armed from top to bottom.

MAGISTRATE Forward, my Scythians!

LYSISTRATA Forward, yourselves, dear comrades!
You grainlettucebeanseedmarket girls!
You garlicandonionbreadbakery girls!
Give it to 'em! Knock 'em down! Scratch 'em!
Tell 'em what you think of 'em! (*General mêlée; the Scythians yield.*)
—Ah, that's enough!
Sound a retreat; good soldiers don't rob the dead!

MAGISTRATE A nice day *this* has been for the police!

LYSISTRATA Well, there you are.—Did you really think we women
would be driven like slaves? Maybe now you'll admit
that a woman knows something about glory.

MAGISTRATE Glory enough.
especially glory in bottles! Dear Lord Apollo!

MALE CHORAGOS Your Honor, there's no use talking to them. Words
mean nothing whatever to wild animals like these.
Think of the sousing they gave us! and the water
was not, I believe, of the purest.

FEMALE CHORAGOS You shouldn't have come after us. And if you try it again,
you'll be one eye short!—Although, as a matter of fact,
what I like best is just to stay at home and read,
like a sweet little bride: never hurting a soul, no,
never going out. But if you *must* shake hornets' nests,
look out for the hornets!

Strophe

OLD MEN Good God, what can we do?
What are we coming to?

---

[2]again Artemis, who was worshipped at Taurica Chersonesos [3]Athens' finest archers

These women! Who could bear it? But, for that matter, who
Will find
What they had in mind
When they seized Cranaos' city
And held it (more's the pity!)
Against us men of Athens, and our police force, too?

MALE CHORAGOS We might question them, I suppose. But I warn
you, sir,
don't believe anything you hear! It would be un-Athenian
not to get to the bottom of this plot.

MAGISTRATE Very well.
My first question is this: Why, so help you God,
Did you bar the gates of the Acropolis?

LYSISTRATA Why?
To keep the money, of course. No money, no war.

MAGISTRATE You think that money's the cause of war?

LYSISTRATA I do.
Money brought about the Peisandros[4] business
and all the other attacks on the State. Well and good!
They'll not get another cent here!

MAGISTRATE And what will you do?

LYSISTRATA What a question! From now on, we intend
to control the Treasury.

MAGISTRATE Control the Treasury!

LYSISTRATA Why not? Does that seem strange? After all,
we control our household budgets.

MAGISTRATE But that's different!

LYSISTRATA "Different"? What do you mean?

MAGISTRATE I mean simply this:
it's the Treasury that pays for National Defense.

LYSISTRATA Unnecessary. We propose to abolish war!

MAGISTRATE Good God.—And National Security?

LYSISTRATA Leave that to us.

MAGISTRATE You?

LYSISTRATA Us.

MAGISTRATE We're done for, then!

LYSISTRATA Never mind.
We women will save you in spite of yourselves.

MAGISTRATE What nonsense!

LYSISTRATA If you like. But you must accept it, like it or not.

MAGISTRATE Why, this is downright subversion!

---

[4]a politician who, even as Aristophanes was completing this play, was bringing about the revolution of the Four Hundred, which overthrew Athenian democracy

LYSISTRATA Maybe it is.
But we're going to save you, Judge.
MAGISTRATE I don't *want* to be saved!
LYSISTRATA Tut. The death-wish. All the more reason.
MAGISTRATE But the idea
of women bothering themselves about peace and war!
LYSISTRATA Will you listen to me?
MAGISTRATE Yes. But be brief, or I'll—
LYSISTRATA This is no time for stupid threats.
MAGISTRATE By the gods,
I'm losing my mind!
AN OLD WOMAN That's nice. If you do, remember
you've less to lose than *we* have.
MAGISTRATE Quiet, you old buzzard!
Now, Lysistrata: tell me what you're thinking.
LYSISTRATA Glad to.
Ever since this war began
we women have been watching you men, agreeing with you,
keeping our thoughts to ourselves. That doesn't mean
we were happy: we weren't, for we saw how things were going;
but we'd listen to you at dinner
arguing this way and that.
—Oh you, and your big
Top Secrets!—
And then we'd grin like little patriots
(though goodness knows we didn't feel like grinning) and ask you:
"Dear, did the Armistice come up in Assembly today?"
And you'd say, "None of your business! Pipe down!," you'd say.
And so we would.
AN OLD WOMAN *I* wouldn't have, by God!
MAGISTRATE You'd have taken a beating, then!
—Please go on.
LYSISTRATA Well, we'd be quiet. But then, you know, all at once
you men would think up something worse than ever.
Even *I* could see it was fatal. And, "Darling," I'd say,
"have you gone completely mad?" And my husband would look at
me
and say, "Wife, you've got your weaving to attend to.
Mind your tongue, if you don't want a slap. 'War's
a man's affair!'"[5]
MAGISTRATE Good words, and well pronounced!

[5]quoted from Hector's farewell to Andromache, *Iliad*, VI, 492

LYSISTRATA You're a fool if you think so.
It was hard enough
to put up with all this banquet-hall strategy.
But then we'd hear you out in the public square:
"Nobody left for the draft-quota here in Athens?"
you'd say; and, "No," someone else would say, "not a man!"
And so we women decided to rescue Greece.
You might as well listen to us now: you'll have to, later.
MAGISTRATE *You* rescue Greece? Absurd!
LYSISTRATA You're the absurd one!
MAGISTRATE You expect me to take orders from a woman?
LYSISTRATA Heavens, if that's what's bothering you, take my veil,
here, and my girdle, and my market-basket. Go home
to your weaving and your cooking! I tell you, "War's
a woman's affair!"
FEMALE CHORAGOS Down with your pitchers, comrades,
but keep them close at hand. It's time for a rally!

Antistrophe

OLD WOMEN Dance, girls, dance for peace!
Who cares if our knees
Wobble and creak? Shall we not dance for such allies as these?
Their wit! their grace! their beauty!
It's a municipal duty
To dance them luck and happiness who risk their all for Greece!
FEMALE CHORAGOS Women, remember your grandmothers! Remember, you were born
among brambles and nettles! Dance for victory!
LYSISTRATA O Eros, god of delight! O Aphrodite! Cyprian!
Drench us now with the savor of love!
Let these men, getting wind of us, dream such joy
that they'll tail us through all the provinces of Hellas!
MAGISTRATE And if we do?
LYSISTRATA Well, for one thing, we shan't have to watch you
going to market, a spear in one hand, and heaven knows
what in the other.
FEMALE CHORAGOS Nicely said, by Aphrodite!
LYSISTRATA As things stand now, you're neither men nor women.
Armor clanking with kitchen pans and pots—
you sound like a pack of Corybantes![6]
MAGISTRATE A man must do what a man must do.

---

[6]wild and frenzied dancers; attendants of the goddess Cybele

LYSISTRATA So I'm told.
But to see a General, complete with Gorgon-shield,
jingling along the dock to buy a couple of herrings!

FEMALE CHORAGOS *I* saw a Captain the other day—lovely fellow
he was,
nice curly hair—sitting on his horse; and—can you believe it?—
he'd just bought some soup, and was pouring it into his helmet!
And there was a soldier from Thrace
swishing his lance like something out of Euripides,
and the poor fruit-store woman got so scared
that she ran away and let him have his figs free!

MAGISTRATE All this is beside the point.
Will you be so kind
as to tell me how you mean to save Greece?

LYSISTRATA Of course!
Nothing could be simpler.[7]

MAGISTRATE I assure you, I'm all ears.

LYSISTRATA Do you know anything about weaving?
Say the yarn gets tangled: we thread it
this way and that through the skein, up and down,
until it's free. And it's like that with war.
We'll send our envoys
up and down, this way and that, all over Greece,
until it's finished.

MAGISTRATE Yarn? Thread? Skein?
Are you out of your mind? I tell you,
war is a serious business.

LYSISTRATA So serious
that I'd like to go on talking about weaving.

MAGISTRATE All right. Go ahead.

LYSISTRATA The first thing we have to do
is to wash our yarn, get the dirt out of it.
You see? Isn't there too much dirt here in Athens?
You must wash those men away.
Then our spoiled wool—
that's like your job-hunters, out for a life
of no work and big pay. Back to the basket,
citizens or not, allies or not,
or friendly immigrants!
And your colonies?
Hanks of wool lost in various places. Pull them

[7]This extended *agon* (argument) between Lysistrata and The Magistrate is the closest the play comes to presenting the traditional *parabasis* (see p. 74).

together, weave them into one great whole,
and our voters are clothed for ever.

MAGISTRATE It would take a woman
to reduce state questions to a matter of carding and weaving!

LYSISTRATA You fool! Who were the mothers whose sons sailed off
to fight for Athens in Sicily?

MAGISTRATE Enough!
I beg you, do not call back those memories.

LYSISTRATA And then,
instead of the love that every woman needs,
we have only our single beds, where we can dream
of our husbands off with the Army.
Bad enough for wives!
but what about our girls, getting older every day,
and older, and no kisses?

MAGISTRATE Men get older, too.

LYSISTRATA Not in the same sense.
A soldier's discharged,
and he may be bald and toothless, yet he'll find
a pretty young thing to go to bed with.
But a woman!
Her beauty is gone with the first grey hair.
She can spend her time
consulting the oracles and the fortune-tellers,
but they'll never send her a husband.

MAGISTRATE Still, if a man can rise to the occasion—

LYSISTRATA (*furiously*) Rise? Rise, yourself!
Go invest in a coffin!
You've money enough.
I'll bake you
a cake for the Underworld.[8]
And here's your funeral
wreath! (*She pours water upon him.*)

MYRRHINE And here's another! (*more water*)

KALONIKE And here's
my contribution! (*more water*)

LYSISTRATA What are you waiting for?
All aboard Styx Ferry![9]
Charon's calling for you!
It's sailing-time: don't disrupt the schedule!

---

[8]A honey cake was usually placed in the hand of the dead to be given to Cerberus, the three-headed dog guarding the gates of Hades. [9]The Styx was the river over which Charon ferried the souls of the dead.

MAGISTRATE The insolence of women! And to me!
No, by God, I'll go back to court and show
the rest of the Bench the things that might happen to them!

(*Exit* MAGISTRATE.)

LYSISTRATA Really, I suppose we should have laid out his corpse
on the doorstep, in the usual way.
But never mind!
We'll give him the rites of the dead tomorrow morning!

(*Exit* LYSISTRATA *with* MYRRHINE *and* KALONIKE.)

Choral Episode

Strophe I

OLD MEN Sons of Liberty, strip off your clothes for action! Men arise!
Shall we stand here limp and useless while old Cleisthenes'[1] allies
Prod a herd of furious grandmas to attempt to bring to pass
A female restoration of the Reign of Hippias?[2]
Forbid it, gods misogynist!
Return our Treasury, at least!
We must clothe ourselves and feed ourselves to face these civic rages,
And who can do a single thing if they cut off our wages?

MALE CHORAGOS Gentlemen, we are disgraced forever if we allow
these madwomen to jabber about spears and shields
and make friends with the Spartans. What's a Spartan? a wild
wolf's a safer companion any day! No; their plan's
to bring back Dictatorship; and we won't stand for that!
From now on, let's go armed, each one of us
a new Aristogeiton!
And to begin with,
I propose to poke a number of teeth
down the gullet of that harridan over there.

Antistrophe I

OLD WOMAN Hold your tongues, you senile bravoes, or I swear, when you get home

[1]an Athenian of notorious bisexual tendencies

[2]Last of the Athenian tyrants; he had ruled with his brother Hipparchos until the latter's death at the hands of the patriots Aristogeiton and Harmonius; Hippias was killed later at Marathon.

Your own mothers wouldn't know you! Strip for action, ladies, come!
I bore the holy vessels in my eighth year,[3] and at ten
I was pounding out the barley for Athena Goddess,[4] then
They elected me Little Bear
For Artemis at Brauron Fair,[5]
I'd been made a Basket-Carrier[6] by the time I came of age:
So trust me to advise you in this feminist rampage!

FEMALE CHORAGOS As a woman, I pay my taxes to the State,
though I pay them in baby boys. What do you contribute,
you impotent horrors? Nothing but waste:
our Treasury, the so-called Glory of the Persian Wars,
gone! rifled! parceled out for privilege! And you
have the insolence to control public policy,
leading us all to disaster!
No, don't answer back
unless you want the heel of my slipper
slap against that ugly jaw of yours!

Strophe 2

OLD MEN What impudence!
What malevolence!
Comrades, make haste,
All those of you who still are sensitive below the waist!
Off with your clothes, men!
Nobody knows when
We'll put them back on.
Remember Leipsydrion![7]
We may be old,
But let's be bold!

MALE CHORAGOS Give them an inch, and we're done for! We'll have them
launching boats next and planning naval strategy.
Or perhaps they fancy themselves as cavalry!
That's fair enough: women know how to ride,

[3]Four girls of high birth between the ages of seven and eleven were appointed to service in the Temple of Athena in the Acropolis.

[4]At ten a girl of aristocratic family was eligible to be Millmaid and to grind the sacred grain of Athena.

[5]Brauron was a town on the coast of Attica where a ceremony to Artemis was celebrated in which a little girl impersonated a bear.

[6]Girls carried baskets containing precious objects sacred to Athena.

[7]After the patriots had killed Hipparchos, they fled and fortified themselves in Leipsydrion; after a heroic defense they were forced to surrender.

they're good in the saddle. Just think of Mikon's paintings,[8]
all those Amazons wrestling with men! No, it's time
to bridle these wild mares!

Antistrophe 2

OLD WOMEN Hold on, or
You *are* done for,
By the Two Goddesses above!
Strip, strip, my women: we've got the veterans on the move!
Tangle with me, Gramps,
And you'll have cramps
For the rest of your days!
No more beans! No more cheese!
My two legs
Will scramble your eggs!

FEMALE CHORAGOS If Lampito stands by me, and that elegant
Theban girl, Ismenia—what good are *you?*
Pass your laws!
Laws upon laws, you decrepit legislators!
At the worst you're just a nuisance, rationing Boeotian eels
on the Feast of Hecate, making our girls go without!
That was statesmanship! And we'll have to put up with it
until some patriot slits your silly old gizzards!

(*Exeunt omnes.*)

Scene II

The scene shifts to a court within the Acropolis.

(*Reenter* LYSISTRATA.)

FEMALE CHORAGOS But Lysistrata! Leader! Why such a grim face?

LYSISTRATA Oh the behavior of these idiotic women!
There's something about the female temperament
that I can't bear!

FEMALE CHORAGOS What in the world do you mean?

LYSISTRATA Exactly what I say.

FEMALE CHORAGOS What dreadful thing has happened?
Come, tell us: we're all your friends.

LYSISTRATA It isn't easy
to say it; yet, God knows, we can't hush it up.

[8]Mikon was one of the many painters who dealt with the invasion of Attica by the Amazons, a fabulous race of warrior-women.

FEMALE CHORAGOS Well, then? Out with it!
LYSISTRATA To put it bluntly,
we're desperate for men.
FEMALE CHORAGOS Almighty God!
LYSISTRATA Why bring God into it?—No, it's just as I say.
I can't manage them any longer: they've gone man-crazy,
they're all trying to get out.
Why, look:
one of them was sneaking out the back door
over there by Pan's cave,[9] another
was sliding down the walls with rope and tackle;
another was climbing aboard a sparrow,[1] ready to take off
for the nearest brothel—I dragged *her* back by the hair!
They're all finding some reason to leave.
Look there!
There goes another one.
—Just a minute, you!
Where are you off to so fast?
FIRST WOMAN I've got to get home!
I've a lot of Milesian wool, and the worms are spoiling it.
LYSISTRATA Oh bother you and your worms! Get back inside!
FIRST WOMAN I'll be back right away, I swear I will!
I just want to get it stretched out on my bed.
LYSISTRATA You'll do no such thing. You'll stay right here.
FIRST WOMAN And my wool?
You want it ruined?
LYSISTRATA Yes, for all I care.
SECOND WOMAN Oh dear! My lovely new flax from Amorgos—[2]
I left it at home, all uncarded!
LYSISTRATA Another one!
And all she wants is someone to card her flax.
Get back in there!
SECOND WOMAN But I swear by the Moon-Goddess,
the minute I get it done, I'll be back!
LYSISTRATA I say No!
If you, why not all the other women as well?
THIRD WOMAN O Lady Eileithyia![3] Radiant goddess! Thou
intercessor for women in childbirth! Stay, I pray thee,
oh stay this parturition! Shall I pollute
a sacred spot?

---

[9]a grotto on the north side of the Acropolis
[1]a bird sacred to Aphrodite; it had been harnessed to the chariot of the goddess.
[2]an island in the Aegean famed for its flax
[3]The goddess invoked by women at childbirth; it was unlawful to bear children on the Acropolis because it was holy ground.

LYSISTRATA And what's the matter with *you*?
THIRD WOMAN I'm having a baby—any minute now!
LYSISTRATA But you weren't pregnant yesterday.
THIRD WOMAN Well, I am today!
Let me go home for a midwife, Lysistrata:
there's not much time.
LYSISTRATA I never heard such nonsense.
What's that bulging under your cloak?
THIRD WOMAN A little baby boy.
LYSISTRATA It certainly isn't. But it's something hollow,
like a basin or— Why, it's the helmet of Athena!
And you said you were having a baby!
THIRD WOMAN Well, I am! So there!
LYSISTRATA Then why the helmet?
THIRD WOMAN I was afraid that my pains
might begin here in the Acropolis; and I wanted
to drop my chick into it, just as the dear doves do.
LYSISTRATA Lies! Evasions!—But at least one thing's clear:
you can't leave the place before your purification.
THIRD WOMAN But I can't stay here in the Acropolis! Last night I
dreamed
of a snake.[4]
FIRST WOMAN And those horrible owls,[5] the noise they make!
I can't get a bit of sleep; I'm just about dead.
LYSISTRATA You useless girls, that's enough: Let's have no more
lying.
Of course you want your men. But don't you imagine
that they want you just as much? I'll give you my word,
their nights must be pretty hard.
Just stick it out!
A little patience, that's all, and our battle's won.
I have heard an Oracle. Should you like to hear it?
FIRST WOMAN An Oracle? Yes, tell us!
LYSISTRATA Quiet then.—Here
is what it said:
IF EVER THE SWALLOWS, ESCHEWING HOOPOE-BIRDS,
SHALL CONSPIRE TOGETHER TO DENY THEM ALL
ACCESS,
THEIR GRIEF IS FOREVER OVER.
These are the words
from the Shrine itself.
AYE, AND ZEUS WILL REDRESS

[4]The sacred snake of the Acropolis; it was never seen but was believed to guard the holy ground.
[5]birds sacred to Athena

THEIR WRONGS, AND SET THE LOWER ABOVE THE HIGHER.

FIRST WOMAN Does that mean we'll be on top?

LYSISTRATA BUT IF THEY RETIRE,
EACH SWALLOW HER OWN WAY, FROM THIS HOLY PLACE,
LET THE WORLD PROCLAIM NO BIRD OF SORRIER GRACE
THAN THE SWALLOW.

FIRST WOMAN I swear, *that* Oracle makes sense!

LYSISTRATA Now, then, by all the gods,
let's show that we're bigger than these annoyances.
Back to your places! Let's not disgrace the Oracle.

(*Exeunt* LYSISTRATA *and the dissident women; the* CHORUSES *renew their conflict.*)

Choral Episode

Strophe

OLD MEN I know a little story that I learned way back in school
Goes like this:
Once upon a time there was a young man—and no fool—
Named Melanion;[6] and his
One aversi-on was marriage. He loathed the very thought!
So he ran off to the hills, and in a special grot
Raised a dog, and spent his days
Hunting rabbits. And it says
That he never never never did come home.
It might be called a refuge *from* the womb.
All right,
all right,
all right!
We're as pure as young Melanion, and we hate the very sight
Of you sluts!

A MAN How about a kiss, old woman?

A WOMAN Here's an onion in your eye!

A MAN A kick in the guts, then?

A WOMAN Try, old bristle-tail, just try!

A MAN Yet they say Myronides[7]
On hands and knees
Looked just as shaggy fore and aft as I!

---

[6]The suitor of Atalanta, who hated men. The Chorus of Old Men have made him a hater of women.

[7]a famous Athenian general

Antistrophe

OLD WOMEN Well, *I* know a little story, and it's just as good as yours.
Goes like this:
Once there was a man named Timon[8]—a rough diamond, of course,
And that whiskery face of his
Looked like murder in the shrubbery. By God, he was a son
Of the Furies, let me tell you! And what did he do but run
From the world and all its ways,
Cursing mankind! And it says
That his choicest execrations as of then
Were leveled almost wholly at *old* men.
All right,
all right,
all right!
But there's one thing about Timon: he could always stand the sight
Of us "sluts"!

A WOMAN How about a crack in the jaw, Pop?

A MAN I can take it, Ma—no fear!

A WOMAN How about a kick in the face?

A MAN You'd show your venerable rear.

A WOMAN I may be old;
But I've been told
That I've nothing to worry about down there!

Scene III

(*Reenter* LYSISTRATA.)

LYSISTRATA Oh, quick, girls, quick! Come here!

FEMALE CHORAGOS What is it?

LYSISTRATA A man!
A man simply bulging with love!
O Cyprian Queen,
O Paphian, O Cythereian! Hear us and aid us!

FEMALE CHORAGOS Where is this enemy?

LYSISTRATA Over there, by Demeter's shrine.

FEMALE CHORAGOS Damned if he isn't. But who *is* he?

MYRRHINE My husband.
Kinesias.

LYSISTRATA Oh then, get busy! Tease him! Undermine him!
Wreck him! Give him everything—kissing, tickling, nudging,

[8]a famous Athenian misanthrope

whatever you generally torture him with—: give him everything
except what we swore on the wine we would not give.

MYRRHINE Trust me!

LYSISTRATA I do. But I'll help you get him started.
The rest of you women, stay back.

(*Enter* KINESIAS.)

KINESIAS Oh God! Oh my God!
I'm stiff for lack of exercise. All I can do to stand up!

LYSISTRATA Halt! Who are you, approaching our lines?

KINESIAS Me? I.

LYSISTRATA A man?

KINESIAS You have eyes, haven't you?

LYSISTRATA Go away.

KINESIAS Who says so?

LYSISTRATA Officer of the Day.

KINESIAS Officer, I beg you,
by all the gods at once, bring Myrrhine out!

LYSISTRATA Myrrhine? And who, my good sir, are you?

KINESIAS Kinesias. Last name's Pennison. Her husband.

LYSISTRATA Oh, of course. I beg your pardon. We're glad to see you.
We've heard so much about you. Dearest Myrrhine
is always talking about "Kinesias"—never nibbles an egg
or an apple without saying
"Here's to Kinesias!"

KINESIAS Do you really mean it?

LYSISTRATA I do.
When we're discussing men, she always says,
"Well, after all, there's nobody like Kinesias!"

KINESIAS Good God.—Well, then, please send her down here.

LYSISTRATA And what do *I* get out of it?

KINESIAS A standing promise.

LYSISTRATA I'll take it up with her.

(*Exit* LYSISTRATA.)

KINESIAS But be quick about it!
Lord, what's life without a wife? Can't eat. Can't sleep.
Every time I go home, the place is so empty, so
insufferably sad! Love's killing me! Oh,
hurry!

(*Enter* MANES, *a slave, with Kinesias' baby; the voice of* MYRRHINE *is heard offstage.*)

MYRRHINE But of course I love him! Adore him!—but no,
he hates love. No. I won't go down.

(*Enter* MYRRHINE, *above.*)

KINESIAS Myrrhine!
Darlingest little Myrrhine! Come down quick!
MYRRHINE Certainly not.
KINESIAS Not? But why, Myrrhine?
MYRRHINE Why? You don't need me.
KINESIAS Need you? My God, *look* at me!
MYRRHINE So long! (*turns to go*)
KINESIAS Myrrhine, Myrrhine, Myrrhine!
If not for my sake, for our child! (*pinches* BABY)
—All right, you: pipe up!
BABY Mummie! Mummie! Mummie!
KINESIAS You hear that?
Pitiful, I call it. Six days now
with never a bath; no food; enough to break your heart!
MYRRHINE My darlingest child! What a father *you* acquired!
KINESIAS At least come down for his sake!
MYRRHINE I suppose I must.
Oh, this mother business![9]

(*Exit.*)

KINESIAS How pretty she is! And younger!
She's so much nicer when she's bothered!

(MYRRHINE *enters, below.*)

MYRRHINE Dearest child,
you're as sweet as your father's horrid. Give me a kiss.
KINESIAS Now you see how wrong it was to get involved
in this scheming League of women. All this agony
for nothing!
MYRRHINE Keep your hands to yourself!
KINESIAS But our house
going to rack and ruin?
MYRRHINE *I* don't care.
KINESIAS And your knitting
all torn to pieces by the chickens? Don't you care?
MYRRHINE Not at all.
KINESIAS And our vows to Aphrodite?
Oh, *won't* you come back?

---

[9]a line that parodies Euripides' *Iphigenia at Aulis,* 917

MYRRHINE No.—At least, not until you men make a treaty to end the war.

KINESIAS Why, if that's all you want, by God, we'll make your treaty!

MYRRHINE Oh? Very well. When you've done that, I'll come home. But meanwhile, I've sworn an oath.

KINESIAS Don't worry.—Now, let's have fun.

MYRRHINE No! Stop it! I said no!
—Although, of course, I *do* love you.

KINESIAS I know you do. Darling Myrrhine: come, shall we?

MYRRHINE Are you out of your mind? In front of the child?

KINESIAS Take him home, Manes.

(*Exit* MANES *with baby.*)

There. He's gone.
Come on! There's nothing to stop us now.

MYRRHINE You devil! But where?

KINESIAS In Pan's cave. What could be snugger than that?

MYRRHINE But my purification before I go back to the Citadel?

KINESIAS There's always the Klepsydra.[1]

MYRRHINE And my oath?

KINESIAS Leave the oath to me. After all, I'm the man.

MYRRHINE Well . . . if you say so!
I'll go find a bed.

KINESIAS Oh, bother a bed! The ground's good enough for me!

MYRRHINE No. You're a bad man, but you deserve something better than dirt.

(*Exit* MYRRHINE.)

KINESIAS What a love she is! And how thoughtful!

(*Reenter* MYRRHINE.)

MYRRHINE Here's your bed. Now let me get my clothes off.
But, good horrors! We haven't a mattress!

KINESIAS Oh, forget the mattress!

---

[1]a sacred spring near Pan's cave

MYRRHINE No.
Just lying on blankets? Too sordid!
KINESIAS Give me a kiss.
MYRRHINE Just a second.

(*Exit* MYRRHINE.)

KINESIAS I swear, I'll explode!

(*Reenter* MYRRHINE.)

MYRRHINE Here's your mattress.
Go to bed now. I'll just take my dress off.
But look—
where's our pillow?
KINESIAS I don't need a pillow!
MYRRHINE Well, *I* do.

(*Exit* MYRRHINE.)

KINESIAS I don't suppose even Heracles
would stand for this!

(*Reenter* MYRRHINE.)

MYRRHINE There we are. Ups-a-daisy!
KINESIAS So we are. Well, come to bed.
MYRRHINE But I wonder:
is everything ready now?
KINESIAS I can swear to that. Come, darling!
MYRRHINE Just getting out of my girdle.
But remember, now,
what you promised about the treaty!
KINESIAS I'll remember.
MYRRHINE But no coverlet!
KINESIAS Damn it, I'll be
your coverlet!
MYRRHINE Be right back.

(*Exit* MYRRHINE.)

KINESIAS This girl and her coverlets
will be the death of me.

(*Reenter* MYRRHINE.)

MYRRHINE Here we are. Up you go!
KINESIAS Up? I've been up for ages!
MYRRHINE Some perfume?

KINESIAS No, by Apollo!
MYRRHINE Yes, by Aphrodite!
I don't care whether you want it or not.

(*Exit* MYRRHINE.)

KINESIAS For love's sake, hurry!

(*Reenter* MYRRHINE.)

MYRRHINE Here, in your hand. Rub it right in.
KINESIAS Never cared for perfume.
And this is particularly strong. Still, here goes!
MYRRHINE What a nitwit I am! I brought you the Rhodian bottle![2]
KINESIAS Forget it.
MYRRHINE No trouble at all. You just wait here.

(*Exit* MYRRHINE.)

KINESIAS God damn the man who invented perfume!

(*Reenter* MYRRHINE.)

MYRRHINE At last! The right bottle!
KINESIAS I've got the rightest
bottle of all, and it's right here waiting for you.
Darling, forget everything else. Do come to bed!
MYRRHINE Just let me get my shoes off.
—And, by the way,
you'll vote for the treaty?
KINESIAS I'll think about it.

(MYRRHINE *runs away.*)

There! That's done it! Off she runs,
with never a thought for the way I'm feeling. I must
have *some*one, or I'll go mad! Myrrhine
has just about ruined me.
And you, strutting little soldier:
what about you? There's nothing for it, I guess,
but an expedition to old Dog-fox's[3] bordello.
OLD MEN She's left you in a sorry state:
You have my sympathy.
What upright citizen could bear
Your pain? I swear, not I!

[2]from Rhodes
[3]nickname for a famous procurer

Just the look of you, with never a woman
To come to your aid! It isn't human!

KINESIAS The agony!

MALE CHORAGOS Well, why not?
She has you on the spot!

FEMALE CHORAGOS A lovelier girl never breathed, you old sot!

KINESIAS A lovelier girl? Zeus! Zeus!
Produce a hurricane
To hoist these lovely girls aloft
And drop them down again
Bump on our lances! Then they'd know
What they do that makes men suffer so.

(*Exit* KINESIAS.)

Scene IV

(*Enter a* SPARTAN HERALD.)

HERALD Gentlemen, Ah beg you will be so kind
as to direct me to the Central Committee.
Ah have a communication.

(*Reenter* MAGISTRATE.)

MAGISTRATE Are you a man,
or a fertility symbol?

HERALD Ah refuse to answer that question!
Ah'm a certified herald from Spahta, and Ah've come
to talk about an ahmistice.

MAGISTRATE Then why
that spear under your cloak?

HERALD Ah have no speah!

MAGISTRATE You don't walk naturally, with your tunic
poked out so. You have a tumor, maybe,
or a hernia?

HERALD No, by Castor![4]

MAGISTRATE Well,
something's wrong, I can see that. And I don't like it.

HERALD Colonel, Ah resent this.

MAGISTRATE So I see. But what *is* it?

HERALD A scroll
with a message from Spahta.

---

[4]one of Sparta's protective spirits

MAGISTRATE Oh. I've heard about these scrolls.
Well, then, man, speak out: How are things in Sparta?
HERALD Hard, Colonel, hard! We're at a standstill.
Can't seem to think of anything but women.
MAGISTRATE How curious! Tell me, do you Spartans think
that maybe Pan's to blame?
HERALD Pan? No. Lampito and her little naked friends.
They won't let a man come near them.
MAGISTRATE How are you handling it?
HERALD Losing our minds,
if you want to know, and walking around hunched over
like men carrying candles in a gale.
The women have sworn they'll have nothing to do with us
until we get a treaty.
MAGISTRATE Yes, I know.
It's a general uprising, sir, in all parts of Greece.
But as for the answer—
Sir: go back to Sparta
and have them send us your Armistice Commission.
I'll arrange things in Athens.
And I may say
that my standing is good enough to make them listen.
HERALD A man after mah own heart! Sir, Ah thank you!

(*Exit* HERALD.)

Choral Episode

Strophe

OLD MEN Oh these women! Where will you find
A slavering beast that's more unkind?
Where a hotter fire?
Give me a panther, any day!
He's not so merciless as they,
And panthers don't conspire!

Antistrophe

OLD WOMEN We may be hard, you silly old ass,
But who brought you to this stupid pass?
You're the ones to blame.
Fighting with us, your oldest friends,
Simply to serve your selfish ends—
Really, you have no shame!

MALE CHORAGOS No, I'm through with women for ever![5]
FEMALE CHORAGOS If you say so.
Still, you might put some clothes on. You look too absurd
standing around naked. Come, get into this cloak.
MALE CHORAGOS Thank you; you're right. I merely took it off
because I was in such a temper.
FEMALE CHORAGOS That's much better
Now you resemble a man again.
Why have you been so horrid?
And look: there's some sort of insect in your eye!
Shall I take it out?
MALE CHORAGOS An insect, is it? So that's
what's been bothering me! Lord, yes, take it out!
FEMALE CHORAGOS You might be more polite.
—But, heavens!
What an enormous gnat!
MALE CHORAGOS You've saved my life.
That gnat was drilling an artesian well
in my left eye.
FEMALE CHORAGOS Let me wipe
those tears away!—And now: one little kiss?
MALE CHORAGOS Over my dead body!
FEMALE CHORAGOS You're so difficult!
MALE CHORAGOS These impossible women! How they do get around us!
The poet was right: Can't live with them, or without them!
But let's be friends.
And to celebrate, you might lead off with an Ode.

Strophe

OLD WOMEN Let it never be said
That my tongue is malicious:
Both by word and by deed
I would set an example that's noble and gracious.
We've had sorrow and care
Till we're sick of the tune.
Is there anyone here
Who would like a small loan?
My purse is crammed,
As you'll soon find;
And you needn't pay me back if the Peace gets signed!
I've invited to lunch

[5]parodies lines in Euripides' *Hippolytus*

Some Karystian rips—[6]
An esurient bunch,
But I've ordered a menu to water their lips!
I can still make soup
And slaughter a pig.
You're all coming, I hope?
But a bath first, I beg!
Walk right up
As though you owned the place,
And you'll get the front door slammed to in your face!

Scene V

(*Enter* SPARTAN AMBASSADOR, *with entourage.*)

MALE CHORAGOS The Commission has arrived from Sparta.
How oddly
they're walking!
Gentlemen, welcome to Athens!
How is life in Laconia?

AMBASSADOR Need we discuss that?
Simply use your eyes.

OLD MEN The poor man's right:
What a sight!

AMBASSADOR Words fail me.
But come, gentlemen, call in your Commissioners,
and let's get down to a Peace.

MALE CHORAGOS The state we're in! Can't bear
a stitch below the waist. It's a kind of pelvic
paralysis.

AN ATHENIAN Won't somebody call Lysistrata?
She has the answer.

A SPARTAN Yes, there, look at him.
Same thing.
Seh, do y'all feel a certain strain
early in the morning?

ATHENIAN I do, sir. It's worse than a strain.
A few more days, and there's nothing for us but Cleisthenes,
that broken blossom!

MALE CHORAGOS But you'd better get dressed again.
You know these prudes who go around Athens with chisels,
looking for prominent statues.[7]

---

[6]The Karystians were allies of Athens at this time but were disdained for their primitive manners and loose morals.

[7]statues with prominent male sexual organs, or *phalloi*

ATHENIAN Sir, you are right.
SPARTAN He certainly is! Ah'll put mah own clothes back on.

(*Enter* ATHENIAN COMMISSIONERS.)

AN ATHENIAN They're no better off than we are!
—Greetings, Laconians!
SPARTAN (*to one of his own group*) Colonel, we got dressed just in time.
Ah sweah,
if they'd seen us the way we were, there'd have been a new war between the states.
ATHENIAN Call the meeting to order.
Now, Laconians,
what's your proposal?
AMBASSADOR We'd lahk to consider peace.
ATHENIAN Good. That's on our minds, too.
—Summon Lysistrata.
We'll never get anywhere without her.
AMBASSADOR Lysistrata?
Summon Lysis-*any*body![8] Only, summon!
MALE CHORAGOS No need to summon:
here she is, herself.

(*Enter* LYSISTRATA.)

Lysistrata! Lion of women!
This is your hour to be
hard and yielding, outspoken and sly, austere and gentle. You see here
the best brains of Hellas (confused, I admit,
by your devious charming) met as one man
to turn the future over to you.
LYSISTRATA That's fair enough,
unless you men take it into your heads
to turn to each other instead of to me. But I'd know
soon enough if you did!
—Where is that goddess of Peace?
Go, some of you: bring her here.

(*Exeunt two* SERVANTS.)

And now,
summon the Spartan Commission. Treat them courteously:
our husbands have been lax in that respect.

[8]Lysistrata's name means "dissolver of armies."

Take them by the hand, women,
or by anything else, if they seem unwilling.
—Spartans:
you stand here. Athenians: on this side. Now listen to me.

(*Reenter* SERVANTS, *staggering under the weight of a more-than-life-size statue of a naked woman: this is* PEACE.)

I'm only a woman, I know; but I've a mind,
and I can distinguish between sense and foolishness.
I owe the first to my father; the rest
to the local politicians.[9] So much for that.
Now, then.
What I have to say concerns both sides in this war.
We are all Greeks.
Must I remind you of Thermopylae? of Olympia?
of Delphi? names deep in all our hearts?
And yet you men go raiding through the country,
Greek killing Greek, storming down Greek cities—
and all the time the Barbarian across the sea
is waiting for his chance.—That's my first point.

AN ATHENIAN Lord! I can hardly contain myself!

LYSISTRATA And you Spartans:
Was it so long ago that Pericleides
came here to beg our help?[1] I can see him still,
his white face, his sombre gown. And what did he want?
An army from Athens! Messenia
was at your heels, and the sea-god splitting your shores.
Well, Kimon and his men,
four thousand infantry, marched out of here to save you.
What thanks do we get? You come back to murder us.

ATHENIAN Can't trust a Spartan, Lysistrata!

A SPARTAN Ah admit it.
When Ah look at those legs, Ah sweah Ah can't trust mahself!

LYSISTRATA And you, men of Athens:
you might remember that bad time when we were down,
and an army came from Sparta
and sent Hippias and the Thessalians
whimpering back to the hills. That was Sparta,
and only Sparta; without Sparta, we'd now be
cringing helots, not walking about like free men!

---

[9]The preceding four lines are probably quoted from Euripedes' *Melanippe the Wise.*

[1]in 464 B.C. during a revolt in Sparta, when an earthquake had just severely damaged the city

(*From this point, the male responses are less to* LYSISTRATA *than to the statue of* PEACE.)

A SPARTAN An eloquent speech!

AN ATHENIAN An elegant construction!

LYSISTRATA Why are we fighting each other? Why not make peace?

AMBASSADOR Spahta is ready, ma'am,
so long as we get that place back.

LYSISTRATA Place? What place?

AMBASSADOR Ah refer to Pylos.[2]

MAGISTRATE Not while I'm alive, by God!

LYSISTRATA You'd better give in.

MAGISTRATE But—what were we fighting about?

LYSISTRATA Lots of places left.

MAGISTRATE All right. Well, then:
Hog Island first, and that gulf behind there, and the land between
the Legs of Megara.

AMBASSADOR Mah government objects.

LYSISTRATA Over-ruled. Why fuss about a pair of legs?

(*General assent; the statue of* PEACE *is removed.*)

AN ATHENIAN Let's take off our clothes and plow our fields.

A SPARTAN Ah'll fertilize mahn first, by the Heavenly Twins!

LYSISTRATA And so you shall,
once we have peace. If you are serious,
go, both of you, and talk with your allies.

ATHENIAN Too much talk already. We'll stand together!
We've only one end in view. All that we want
is our women: and I speak for our allies.

AMBASSADOR Mah government concurs.

ATHENIAN So does Karystos.

LYSISTRATA Good.—But before you come inside
to join your wives at supper, you must perform
the usual lustration. Then we'll open
our baskets for you, and all that we have is yours.
But you must promise upright good behavior
from this day on. Then each man home with his woman!

ATHENIAN Let's get it over with!

SPARTAN Lead on: Ah follow!

ATHENIAN Quick as a cat can wink!

(*Exeunt all but the* CHORUSES.)

[2]A lost Spartan possession; for the moment political and sexual desires become confused.

Antistrophe

OLD WOMEN Embroideries and
Twinkling ornaments and
Pretty dresses—I hand
Them all over to you, and with never a qualm.
They'll be nice for your daughters
On festival days
When the girls bring the Goddess
The ritual prize.
Come in, one and all:
Take what you will.
I've nothing here so tightly corked that you can't make it spill!
You may search my house,
But you'll not find
The least thing of use,
Unless your two eyes are keener than mine.
Your numberless brats
Are half starved? and your slaves?
Courage, grandpa! I've lots
Of grain left, and big loaves.
I'll fill your guts,
I'll go the whole hog;
But if you come too close to me, remember: 'ware the dog!

(*Exeunt* CHORUSES.)

Exodos

(*An* ATHENIAN DRUNKARD *approaches the gate and is halted by a* SENTRY.)

DRUNKARD Open. The. Door.
SENTRY Now, friend, just shove along!
So you want to sit down! If it weren't such an old joke,
I'd tickle your tail with this torch. Just the sort of thing
that this kind of audience appreciates.
DRUNKARD I. Stay. Right. Here.
SENTRY Oh, all right. But you'll see some funny sights!
DRUNKARD Bring. Them. On.
SENTRY No, what am I thinking of?
The gentlemen from Sparta are just coming back from supper.
Get out of here, or I'll scalp you!

(*Exit* DRUNKARD.)

(*The general company reenters; the two* CHORUSES *now represent* SPARTANS *and* ATHENIANS.)

MAGISTRATE I must say,
I've never tasted a better meal. And those Laconians!
They're gentlemen, by the Lord! Just goes to show:
a drink to the wise is sufficient. And why not?
A sober man's an ass.
Men of Athens, mark my words: the only efficient
Ambassador's a drunk Ambassador. Is that clear?
Look: we go to Sparta,
and when we get there we're dead sober. The result?
Everyone cackling at everyone else. They make speeches;
and even if we understand, we get it all wrong
when we file our reports in Athens. But today—!
Everybody's happy. Couldn't tell the difference
between *Drink to Me Only* and
the *Star Spangled Athens.*
What's a few lies,
washed down in good strong drink?

(*Reenter* DRUNKARD.)

SENTRY God almighty,
he's back again!

DRUNKARD I. Resume. My. Place.

A SPARTAN (*to an* ATHENIAN) I beg you, seh,
take your instrument in your hand and play for us.
Ah'm told
you understand the in*tri*cacies of the floot?
Ah'd lahk to execute a song and dance
in honor of Athens,
and, of course, of Spahta.

(*The following song is a solo—an aria—accompanied by the flute. The* CHORUS OF SPARTANS *begins a slow dance.*)

DRUNKARD Toot. On. Your. Flute.

SPARTAN CHORAGOS Mnemosyne,[3]
Inspire once more the Grecian Muse
To sing of glory glory glory without end.
Sing Artemesion's shore,[4]

[3]goddess of memory and mother of the Muses

[4]where in 480 B.C. the Athenian fleet successfully engaged the Persians, while Leonidas and his Spartans were making their famous stand at Thermopylae

Where Athens fluttered the Persian fleet—
Alalai,[5] that great
Victory! Sing Leonidas and his men,
Those wild boars, sweat and blood
Down in a red drench. Then, then
The barbarians broke, though they had stood
A myriad strong before!
O Artemis,
Virgin Goddess, whose darts
Flash in our forests: approve
This pact of peace, and join our hearts,
From this day on, in love.
Huntress, descend!

LYSISTRATA All that will come in time.
But now, Laconians,
take home your wives. Athenians, take yours.
Each man be kind to his woman; and you, women,
be equally kind. Never again, pray God,
shall we lose our way in such madness.
—And now
let's dance our joy! (*From this point the dance becomes general.*)

CHORUS OF ATHENIANS Dance!
Dance!
Dance, you Graces!
Artemis, dance!
Dance, Phoebus, Lord of dancing!
Dance, Dionysus, in a scurry of Maenads!
Dance, Zeus Thunderer!
Dance, Lady Hera,
Queen of the sky!
Dance, dance, all you gods!
Dance for the dearest, the bringer of peace,
Deathless Aphrodite!

LYSISTRATA Now let us have another song from Sparta.

CHORUS OF SPARTANS From Taygetos' skyey summit,
Laconian Muse, come down!
Sing the glories of Apollo,
Regent of Amyclae Town.
Sing of Leda's Twins,
Those gallant sons,

[5] a war cry

On the banks of Eurotas—
Alalai Evohe![6]
Here's to our girls
With their tangling curls,
Legs a-wriggle,
Bellies a-jiggle,
A riot of hair,
A fury of feet,
Evohe! Evohai! Evohe!
as they pass
Dancing,
dancing,
dancing,
to greet
Athena of the House of Brass![7]

[6]Now an orgiastic war cry; the play now ends with an erotic dance and the mandatory sexual union, in this case of the warring parties.

[7]a famous temple on the acropolis of Sparta

THE SECOND SHEPHERDS' PLAY

(c. 1420)

THE WAKEFIELD MASTER—MODERNIZED VERSION BY JOHN GASSNER

The retelling of legends and myths of the classic Greek drama portrayed by Aeschylus, Sophocles, and Euripides carried over into the Roman era, surviving in the nine tragedies of Seneca (3 B.C.–A.D. 65). The plays of this philosopher and statesman—for a long time as tutor and adviser he held in check the eccentricities of the young emperor Nero—are considerably inferior to their Greek counterparts, but they exerted a strong impact on the emerging drama of the Renaissance (see the introduction to *Hamlet*). Likewise, the situation comedies of Menander and others, of which we know little, provided the basis for the rambunctious farces of Plautus (254–184 B.C.) and the more polished domestic comedies of Terence (195–159 B.C.). Of all the dramatists who may have practiced over the centuries of Rome's existence, only these three have survived in but a handful of plays.

After the death of Seneca, the drama as it had been known in Greece and Rome and as we think of it today, to all intents and purposes ceased to exist. During the Dark Ages of western Europe, roughly from the fall of Rome in A.D. 410 to the end of the first millennium, the drama had disappeared as a literature as well as a form of public entertainment. There was one notable exception in the person of a tenth-century nun, Hroswitha from Saxony, who wrote a number of farces imitative of Roman comedy, but the history of their staging, if any, remains unknown.

Although the early Christian church was vehement in its opposition to anything smacking of theatrical entertainment, ironically the drama, in the same manner derived by the ancient Greeks, found its new origins in the religion of the time, with Christian myth and legend forming its source material. At some time in the tenth century, particularly at Easter and Christmas, the churches began to attempt to make the stories from the Bible more graphic and hence more comprehensible to their mostly illiterate parishioners. Inserted into the regular liturgy were short exchanges of dialogue called *tropes*, based directly on the biblical text. One of these, the *Quem Quaeritis* trope, survives in its entirety. A figure representing the angel guarding the tomb of Jesus asks the approaching women (all, of course, enacted by clergy or monks, because no women were allowed to function in this capacity), "Quem quaeritis, O Christicolae?" ("Whom do you seek, O Christian women?") and the story of Easter proceeds as the resurrection is revealed.

These few words gradually expanded into more complete enactments of entire scenes which we now call *liturgical drama.* Abandoning the simplicity of the brief tropes, they approached full-fledged drama to the point that their increasingly elaborate nature and their growing emphasis on the secular compelled the churches to remove them from the sanctuary into the squares and streets outside. Here from the thirteenth through the fifteenth centuries they flourished to become the great body of Medieval drama popular both on the continent and in England.

These short plays, called *mysteries* or *miracles,* told stories from Creation to Revelation as well as episodes from the lives of various saints. Presented in sequence and known as *cycles,* they appeared on complex platforms in public squares or were carried from place to place on large scenic wagons, often with elaborate costumes and theatrical effects. Frequently mounted by the various trade guilds—the Water Carriers, for instance, might stage the Flood—and frequently taking days to perform, they were major aspects of public holiday entertainment with their vernacular dialogue and often fast-paced, irreverent scenes reflecting everyday life and interpreted by contemporary characters easily recognized by the audience.

Another type of play that developed about the same time but remained popular longer than the mysteries was the *morality play.* Peopled by a variety of personified abstractions such as Good Deeds, Greed, Lust, or Gluttony, and by assorted tempters, devils, angels, and the like, they offered dramatized moral lectures on the evils of sin and the rewards of heaven. The best-known morality play, the fifteenth century *Everyman,* still playable today, sends its central figure of Everyman in search of someone to accompany him to the grave. Only Good Deeds consents to go with him.

Fortunately, large numbers of mystery-cycle plays have survived. *The Second Shepherds' Play* is part of what is known as the Wakefield Cycle (others are the Chester and Coventry cycles), deriving its title as the second Nativity play within the entire series. The author remains anonymous but is sometimes referred to as "The Wakefield Master," although several writers could easily have been involved. It is widely regarded as a nearly perfect example of the popular humor of its age, with its farce among the best within the scores of existing cycle plays. The characters are well articulated and the fast action conveys an amazing sense of realism. Even today it can command extensive laughter with its earthy fun and slapstick routines.

To appreciate what the play is and to understand the sudden shift from hilarity to solemnity, one must understand the conditions of its presentation. It is not a disrespectful play in any sense. It is devoutly religious. In the same manner that the Greeks regarded sex in Aristophanes' comedy, the Middle Ages treated religion as a very immediate and human part of existence. The Bible stories were not only accepted as literal truths but were regarded with a familiarity that enabled worshippers to visualize the characters in scripture in terms of ordinary individuals like themselves.

Therefore, rather than seeing the shepherds as the stilted unreal figures of the standard Sunday school pageant, the writer of *The Second Shepherds' Play* saw them for what they most likely really were: crude, unlettered, ignorant, perpetually overworked, poverty-stricken peasants, bent on satisfying their bellies and getting a warm night's sleep. The shepherds on this hillside are thoroughly comic, and thoroughly human, characters. Among them arrives a thief and con man as slick as any nineteenth-century riverboat cardsharp. Through the shenanigans of Mak, Gill, and the shepherds we go through a marvelously funny parody of the Nativity, replete with anachronistic oaths "by Our Lady" and "by Christ's cross," none of which worried the audiences a whit.

At the end, however, once the angels have arrived, the play switches to a touchingly human Nativity scene, seriously religious, but still retaining the basic humanity of the rest of the play. It is a brilliant concept. Whatever one's faith, *The Second Shepherds' Play* can be enjoyed as the telling of a very ancient religious story in a thoroughly delightful and naively inoffensive manner.

The Second Shepherds' Play

ANONYMOUS

A modernized version by John Gassner

CHARACTERS

FIRST SHEPHERD, *Coll*
SECOND SHEPHERD, *Gib*
THIRD SHEPHERD, *Daw*
MAK
MAK'S WIFE, *Gill*
AN ANGEL
THE VIRGIN MARY
THE INFANT CHRIST

One unchanged setting, consisting of two huts—one representing MAK'S *cottage and the other the manger or stable of the Nativity. The space between the two huts represents the moors or fields. The action occurs in Palestine, but only in name; actually the local color of the play is drawn from the countryside of Wakefield, England.*
The action is continuous; although scene divisions have been added to the original text, there is no need to drop curtains to indicate a lapse of time.

Scene I

The moors.

1ST SHEPHERD Lord, but these weathers are cold, and I am ill-wrapped!
Nearly numb of hand, so long have I napped;
My legs, they fold; my fingers are chapped.
It is not as I would, for I am all lapped
In sorrow.
In storms and tempest,
Now in the east, now in the west,
Woe is him has never rest,
Mid-day or morrow!

But we poor shepherds that walk on the moor,
In faith, we are near-hands out of the door.
No wonder, as it stands, if we be poor,
For the tilth of our lands lies as fallow as a floor,

As ye ken.[1]
We are so lamed,
Overtaxed and blamed,[2]
We are made hand-tamed
By these gentlery-men.

Thus they rob us of our rest, Our Lady them harry!
These men that are tied fast, their plough must tarry.
What men say is for the best, we find it contrary!
Thus are farming-men oppressed, in point to miscarry
Alive:
Thus the lords hold us under,
Thus they bring us in blunder—
It were great wonder,
If ever we should thrive.

Let man but get a painted sleeve or brooch nowadays,
Woe to one that grieves him or once gainsays;
No man dare reprove him that mastery has,
And yet may no man believe one word that he says—
No letter!
He can make purveyance
With boast and braggance,
And all is through maintenance
By men that are better.

There shall come a swain as proud as a po;[3]
And he must borrow my wain, my plow also
That I am full glad to grant before he go:
Thus live we in pain, anger, and woe,
By night and day.
He must have if he wants it
Though I must do without it;
I were better off hanged
Than once say him Nay!

It does me good as I walk thus by my own
Of this world for to talk in manner of moan.
To my sheep I will stalk and listen anon,
There abide on a ridge or sit on a stone
Full soon.
For I think, pardie!

---

[1] know [2] literally "crushed" [3] peacock

True men if they be,
We shall get more company
Ere it be noon.

(*A* Second Shepherd *appears on the moor, without at first noticing the* First Shepherd, *so absorbed is he in his own thoughts.*)

2ND SHEPHERD *Benedicite*[4] and *Dominus!* what may this mean?
Why fares this world thus? Oft have we not seen:
Lord, these weathers are spiteful, and the winds are keen,
And the frosts so hideous they water my een:[5]
No lie it be!
Now in dry, now in wet,
Now in snow, now in sleet,
When my shoes freeze to my feet,
It is not at all easy.

But as far as I know, or yet as I go,
We poor wed men suffer much, we do;
We have sorrow then and then, it falls often so.
Poor Cappel, our hen, both to and fro
She cackles,
But begin she to rock,
To groan or to cluck,
Woe is to him, our cock,
For he is then in shackles!

These men that are wed have not all their will;
When they are set upon, they sigh full still.
God knows they are led full hard and full ill,
In bower or in bed they have their fill
Beside.
My part have I found,
Know my lesson sound:
Woe is him that is bound,
For he must abide.

But now late in our lives—marvel to me!
That I think my heart breaks such wonder to see:
That, as destiny drives, it should so be
That some men will have two wives, and some have three
In store.
To some is woe that have any,

[4]He pronounces this, by contraction of the Latin for "Bless you," as "Bencité". [5]eyes

But so far as I see, I tell ye,
Woe is him that has many,
For he feels sore.

(*addressing the audience*)

But young men awooing, by God that you bought,
Beware of a wedding and mind in your thought
"Had I known" is a thing that serves you nought.
So much still mourning has wedding home brought
And grief,
With many a sharp shower;
For ye may catch in an hour
What shall savor full sour
As long as you live.

For, as ever read I scripture, I have *her* I keep near:
As sharp as a thistle, as rough as a briar;
She is browed like a bristle with sour-looking cheer.
Had she once wet her whistle, she could sing full clear
Her Pater-Noster.
She is as great as a whale,
She has a gallon of gall;
By Him that died for us all,
I would I had run till I lost her!

(*By now he has been observed by the* FIRST SHEPHERD, *who rouses him from his meditations roughly.*)

1ST SHEPHERD God look over the row, you there, that deafly stand!
2ND SHEPHERD (*startled*) Yea, the devil in thy maw!
—In tarrying, friend,
Saw you Daw about?
1ST SHEPHERD Yes, on fallow land
I heard him blow. He comes here at hand
Not far.
Stand still!
2ND SHEPHERD Why?
1ST SHEPHERD For he comes on, hope I.
1ST SHEPHERD He will din us both a lie
Unless we beware.

(*A* THIRD SHEPHERD, *a boy called* DAW, *employed by the* FIRST SHEPHERD, *appears. The weather has put him out of humor.*)

3RD SHEPHERD Christ's cross me speed, and Saint Nicholas!
Thereof had I need: it is worse than it was!
Whoso could, take heed! and let the world pass;
It is ever in dread and brittle as glass,
And slides.
This world fared never so,
With marvels more and more,
Now in weal, now in woe;
And everything rides!

Was never since Noah's flood such floods seen,
Winds and rains so rude, and storms so keen;
Some stammered, some stood in doubt, as I ween.
Now God turn all to good! I say as I mean
And ponder.
These floods, so they drown
Both fields and town
And bear all down—
That it is a wonder.

We that walk in the nights our cattle to keep,
We see sudden sights when other men sleep—

(*noticing that he is being observed by the other* SHEPHERDS)

But methinks my heart lightens, I see them peep.
Yea, you tall fellows!—I think I'll give my sheep
A turn.

(*He is about to turn away, but changes his mind.*)

But this is ill intent,
For as I walk on this bent
I may lightly repent
And stub my toes.

(*pretending to have just seen them*)

Ah, sir, God you save, and you, master mine!

(*coming up to them*)

A drink fain would I have and somewhat to dine.
1ST SHEPHERD Christ's curse, my knave, thou art a lazy swine!
2ND SHEPHERD What, the boy pleases to rave? You'll wait on line
When we have made it.
I'll drum on thy pate!

Though the knave comes late,
Yet is he in state
To dine, if he had it.

3RD SHEPHERD (*grumbling*) Such servants as I, that sweats and swinks,[6]
Eats our bread dry, and that is ill, I thinks!
We are oft wet and weary when master-men winks,
Yet come full lately the dinners and the drinks.
But neatly,
Both our dame and our sire,
When we have run in the mire,
They can nip us of our hire
And pay us full lately.

But hear my oath: For the food that you serve, I say,
I shall do hereafter—work as you pay:
I shall work a little and a little play,
For yet my supper never on my stomach lay
In the fields.
I won't complain, but a heap
With my staff I shall leap;
For a thing bought too cheap
Nothing yields.

1ST SHEPHERD Yea, thou wert a fool, lad, a-wooing to ride
With one that had but little for spending by his side.
2ND SHEPHERD Peace, boy! And no more jangling I'll bide,
Or I shall make thee full sad, by heaven's King, beside,
For thy gauds.[7]
Where are our sheep? Thy japes we scorn.
3RD SHEPHERD Sir, this same day at morn
I left them in the corn
When the bells rang Lauds.

They have pasture good, they cannot go wrong.
1ST SHEPHERD That is right. By the rood, these nights are long!
Yet I would, ere we went, one gave us a song.
2ND SHEPHERD So *I* thought as I stood—to cheer us along.
3RD SHEPHERD I grant!
1ST SHEPHERD Let me sing the tenory.
2ND SHEPHERD And I the treble so high.
3RD SHEPHERD Then the mean falls to me.
Let's start the chant.

[6]Works; his speech is ungrammatical. [7]tricks or jests

(*At this point,* MAK *appears, his cloak thrown over his tunic.*)

MAK (*to himself*) Lord, for Thy names seven, that made the moon and stars on high
Well more than I reckon: Thy will, Lord, leaves me dry
And lacking, so that of my wits I am shy:
Now would God I were in heaven, for there no children cry
So still.[8]
1ST SHEPHERD (*looking around*) Who is that pipes so poor?
MAK (*still grumbling to himself*) Would God knew how I endure:
A man that walks on the moor
Without his will.

(*The* SHEPHERDS *now recognize him as the thief they know.* MAK *is startled, but pretends he does not know them.*)

2ND SHEPHERD Mak, where have you been? Tell us tidings.
3RD SHEPHERD Is *he* come, then let each one take heed to his things.

(*He takes* MAK's *cloak from him and shakes it, to see whether* MAK *has stolen anything.*)

MAK (*spluttering*) What! I be a yeoman, I tell ye, of the king's.
The self and same, sent from a great lording's
And such.
Fie on you! Go hence
Out of my presence;
I must have reverence—
You grieve me much!

1ST SHEPHERD Why make ye it so quaint, Mak? You do wrong.
2ND SHEPHERD Mak, play ye the saint? For this do ye long?
3RD SHEPHERD I know the knave can deceive, the devil him hang!
MAK I shall make complaint and get ye many a thwang
At a word
When I tell my lord how ye do.
1ST SHEPHERD (*sarcastically*) But, Mak, is that true
Come, that southern tooth[9] unscrew
And set it in a turd.

2ND SHEPHERD Mak, the devil in your eye, a stroke will I lend you.

(*He strikes him.*)

[8]so continuously [9]In pretending to be in the king's service, the actor playing Mak may have affected a Southern—that is, London—accent.

3RD SHEPHERD Mak, know ye not me? By God, I could beat ye too.

(*As he too is about to strike him,* MAK *draws back and pretends to have just recognized the* SHEPHERDS.)

MAK God, look—you all three? Methought—how do you do?
Ye are a fair company.
1ST SHEPHERD May we now recognize you?
2ND SHEPHERD Blast your jest-dealing!
When a man so lately goes
What will good men suppose?
Ye have an ill name one knows
For sheep-stealing.

MAK And true as steel I am, know ye not?
But a sickness I feel that holds me full hot:
My belly fares not well, for it is out of estate.
3RD SHEPHERD (*unsympathetically*) Seldom lies the devil dead by the gate!
MAK (*ignoring the thrust*) Therefore,
Full sore am I and ill;
I stand stone-still,
I ate not a tittle
This month and more.

1ST SHEPHERD How fares thy wife? By my hood, tell us true.
MAK She lies lolling by the road, by the fire too,
And a house full of brew she drinks well too.
Ill speed other things that she will shift
To do.
Eats as fast as she can,
And each year that comes to man
She brings forth a brat—an'
Some years, two.

But were I yet more gracious, and richer at will,
Eaten out of house and home I would be still.
Yet she is a foul dear, if ye come at her close;
None there is looks worse, as none knows
Better than I.
Now will ye see what I proffer:
To give all in my coffer
And tomorrow next, to offer
Mass-pence, should she die.

(*The* SHEPHERDS *have begun to feel drowsy during this recital.*)

2ND SHEPHERD So weary with watching is none in this shire:
I would sleep if it cost me a part of my hire.
3RD SHEPHERD And I am cold and naked, and would have a fire.
1ST SHEPHERD I am weary of walking, and I have run in the mire.

(*to the* SECOND SHEPHERD)

Keep the watch, you!
2ND SHEPHERD Nay, I will lie down by,
For I must sleep or die.
3RD SHEPHERD For sleep as good a man's son am I;
It is my due.

(*They begin to lie down to sleep. But the* THIRD SHEPHERD *eyes* MAK *suspiciously.*)

3RD SHEPHERD But, Mak, come hither; between us you shall lie down.
MAK (*unhappily*) But I may hinder your sleep and make you frown.

(*The* SHEPHERDS *force him down and compel him to stretch out among them, in order to prevent him from robbing them.*)

Ah well, no dread I heed:
From my head to my toe,

(*crossing himself*)

Manus tuas commendo,
Pontio Pilato.[1]
Christ's cross me speed.

(*Before long the* THREE SHEPHERDS *are in a deep sleep, and* MAK *disentangles himself and rises.*)

MAK Now were time for a man that lacks what he would
To stalk privily then into the fold
And nimbly to work, though not to be too bold,
For he might regret the bargain if it were told
At the ending.
Now time for to work in the dell,
For he needs good counsel
That fain would fare well
And has but little spending.

(*He begins to work a spell on the sleepers, drawing a circle around them.*)

[1] "Into your hands I commend myself, Pontius Pilate." The humor lies, of course, in the misquotation.

But about you a circle round as the moon,
Till I have done what I will, till that it be noon—
That ye lie stone-still, until I am done;
And now I shall say thereto of good words a rune
Anon:
Over your heads my hand I light;
Out go your eyes, blind be your sight!
And now that it may come out right
I must shift on.

(*He starts to leave in the direction of the sheep further down the field while the* SHEPHERDS *snore.*)

Lord, but they sleep hard—that may one hear . . .
Was I never shepherd, but now I will shear;
Though the flock be scared, yet shall I nip near;
I must draw hitherward and mend our cheer
From sorrow.

(*He spies a sheep that attracts him.*)

A fat sheep, I daresay,
A good fleece, I dare lay;
Repay when I may—

(*seizing the animal*)

But this will I *borrow.*

Scene II

MAK's *cottage: the exterior and the interior.*
At first MAK *stands outside and knocks at the door. Later he enters and the action transpires inside.*

MAK (*knocking*) How, Gill, art thou in? Get us some light.
WIFE Who makes such din this time of the night?
I am set for to spin: I think not I might
Rise a penny to win—a curse on him alight.
So fares she,
A housewife, I ween,
To be raced thus between.
In house may no work be seen
Because of such small chores that be.

MAK Good wife, open the door. Do ye not see what I bring?
WIFE Then let thou draw the latch.

(*as he enters*)

Ah! come in, my sweeting!
MAK (*grumpily*) Yea, and no thought for my long standing!
WIFE (*observing the sheep*) By the naked neck thou art like to get thy hanging.

MAK Get away!
I am worthy my meat,
For in a pinch can I get
More than they that swink and sweat
All day.

Thus if fell to my lot, Gill, I had such grace.
WIFE It were a foul blot to be hanged for the case.
MAK I have escaped oft from as narrow place.
WIFE But so long goes the pot to the water, one says,
At last
Comes it home broken.
MAK Well I know the token;
But let it never be spoken!—
But come and help fast.

(GILL *helps to take the sheep in.*)

I would it were slain and I sat down to eat:
This twelvemonth was I not so fain for sheep-meat.
WIFE Come they ere it be slain and hear the sheep bleat—
MAK Then might I be taken; cold's the sweat I am in, my sweet—
Go, make fast
The outer door.
WIFE (*going to the door*) Yes, Mak,
If they came at thy back—
MAK Then got I from that pack
The devil's own cast.
WIFE (*coming back*) A good jest I have spied, since thou hast none:

(*pointing to the cradle*)

Here shall we hide it till they be gone;
In the cradle may it abide. Let me alone,
And I shall lie beside in childbed and groan.

MAK Well said!
And I shall say you are light
Of a man-child this night.
WIFE How well it is, day bright,
That ever I bred.

This is a good guise and a far cast:
A woman's advice, it helps at the last.
I shall care never who spies, so go thou fast!

MAK (*outside, walking in the fields toward the sleeping* SHEPHERDS)
If I do not come ere they rise, a cold blast
Will blow; back to sleep
I go. Yet sleeps this company,
And I shall slip in privily
As it had never been me
That carried their sheep.

Scene III

The moors.
MAK *slips in among the sleepers. The* SHEPHERDS *begin to stir.*

1ST SHEPHERD (*rising*) *Resurrex a mortruis:*[2] reach me a hand!
Judas carnas dominus! I may not well stand.
My foot sleeps, by Jesus, and I thirst—and
I thought that we laid us full near England.

2ND SHEPHERD (*rising*)
Ah-ye!
Lord, I have slept well!
I am fresh as an eel,
As light I feel
As leaf on tree.

3RD SHEPHERD (*awaking but dazed*) *Ben'cite* be herein; so my body quakes,
My heart is out of my skin with the noise it makes.
Who makes all this din, so my brow aches?
To the door will I win. Hark, fellows, who wakes?
We were four:
See ye anywhere Mak now?

1ST SHEPHERD We were up ere thou.

2ND SHEPHERD Man, I give God a vow
That he went nowhere.

3RD SHEPHERD (*troubled*) Methought he lay wrapped up in a wolf-skin.

1ST SHEPHERD Many are thus wrapped now—that is, within!

2ND SHEPHERD When we had long napped, methought with a gin[3]
A fat sheep he trapped without making a din.

[2]The unlettered shepherd is babbling Latin words he has picked up imperfectly and makes no particular sense. [3]trick

3RD SHEPHERD (*pointing toward* MAK, *who pretends to be asleep*)
Be still:
This dream makes thee wild,
It is but phantom, by the Holy Child![4]
1ST SHEPHERD Now God turn all things mild,
If it be His will.

(*The* SHEPHERDS *rouse* MAK.)

2ND SHEPHERD Rise, Mak, for shame! Ye lie right long.
MAK (*stirring*) Now Christ's Holy Name, be it among
Us! What's this? By Saint James, I am not strong!
I hope I am the same—my neck has lain wrong
All night!

(*as they help him up*)

Many thanks! Since yester-even,
I swear by Saint Steven,
I was flayed by a dream, so driven
That my heart was not right.

Methought my Gill began to croak, full sad
To labor well nigh at first cock—a lad
To add to our flock; and I never glad
To have more to provide, more than ever I had.
Ah, my head!
A house full of young mouths—banes!
The devil knock out their brains!
Woe him that so many brats gains
And so little bread.

I must go home, by your leave; to Gill, I thought.
But first look in my sleeve that I have stolen naught:
I am loth to grieve you or to take from you aught.
3RD SHEPHERD Go forth, and ill may you thrive!

(MAK *leaves.*)

Still I would we sought
This morn
Whether we have all our store.

[4]An anachronism characteristic of naïve folk literature, since the Holy Child has not yet been born. In the next few lines there are other anachronisms: "Christ's Holy Name," "By Saint James," and "by Saint Steven"—or Stephen.

1ST SHEPHERD Good! I will go before.
Let us meet.
2ND SHEPHERD Where?
3RD SHEPHERD At the crooked thorn.

Scene IV

MAK's *cottage.*

MAK (*at his door*) Undo this door! Who is here? How long shall I stand?
WIFE Who makes such a stir, to walk in the moon-waning?
MAK Ah, Gill, what cheer? It is I, Mak, your husband.
WIFE (*grumpily*) Then see we here the devil himself in a band,
Sir Guile!
Lo, he comes with a noise about
As if he were held by the snout,
I may not do my work for that lout
A hand-long while.

MAK Will ye hear what noise she makes for an excuse
And does nothing but play about and stroke her toes!
WIFE Why, who wanders, who wakes, who comes, who goes?
Who brews, who bakes—now who do you suppose?
And more then
That it is pity to behold—
Now in hot, now in cold.
Full woefull is the household
That lacks women.

But what end have ye made with the shepherds, Mak?
MAK The last word that they said when I turned my back,
They would look that they had of their sheep all the pack;
I fear they will not be well pleased when they their sheep lack,
Pardie!
But howso the sport goes
I'm the thief they'll suppose
And come with a full nose
To cry out on me.

But thou must do as thou planned.
WIFE They'll find me able!
I shall swaddle it right in my cradle.
When I sup with the Devil I use the long ladle!
I will lie down straightway. Come wrap me.
MAK (*doing so*) I will.

WIFE (*sharply*)
Behind!—
If Coll and his mate come, to our sorrow,
They will nip us full narrow.
MAK But I may run and cry "Harrow"
If the sheep they find.

WIFE Listen close when they call—they will come anon.
Come and make ready all, and sing thou alone:
Sing "Lullay" you shall, for I must groan
And cry out by the wall on Mary and John
As if sore.
Sing "Lullay" on fast
When you hear them at last,
And if I play a false cast
Trust me no more!

Scene V

The moors, as the SHEPHERDS *meet.*

3RD SHEPHERD Ah, Coll, good morn: why sleep ye not?
1ST SHEPHERD Alas, that ever was I born! We have a foul blot—
A fat wether have we lost.
3RD SHEPHERD God forbid; say it not!
2ND SHEPHERD Who should have done that harm? That were a foul spot.
1ST SHEPHERD
Some knave—beshrew!
I have sought with my dogs
All Horbury shrogs[5]
And of fifteen hogs[6]
I lack one ewe.

3RD SHEPHERD Now trust me if ye will—by Saint Thomas of Kent!,
Either Mak or Gill a hand to it lent.
1ST SHEPHERD Peace, man, be still: I watched when he went;
You slander him ill, you ought to repent
With speed.
2ND SHEPHERD Yet as ever I thrive or be,
Though the good Lord slay me,
I would say it were he
That did the same deed.

[5]By this is meant the thickets of Horbury, about four miles from Wakefield, where the play was given.
[6]young sheep

3RD SHEPHERD Go we thither then, I say, and let us run fleet;
Till I know the truth, may I never bread eat.
1ST SHEPHERD Nor take drink in my head till with him I meet.
2ND SHEPHERD I will take to no bed until I him greet,
My brother!
One promise I will plight:
Till I get him in sight
I will never sleep one night
Where I sleep another.

Scene VI

MAK's *cottage.*
MAK *is heard singing within, while* GILL *is heard groaning as though she were delivering a child.*

3RD SHEPHERD Will you hear how they hack away; our sir likes to croon.
1ST SHEPHERD Heard I never none crack so clear out of tune.
Call on him!
2ND SHEPHERD Mak, undo your door—soon!
MAK Who is that spoke, as if it were noon
Aloft?
Who is that, I say?

(*He opens the door.*)

3RD SHEPHERD Good fellows you'd see, were it day.
MAK As far as ye may,
Friends, speak soft
Over a sick woman's head that is at malease;
I had sooner be dead than cause her dis-ease.
WIFE Go to another place—I cannot breathe; please!
Each foot ye tread goes through my nose with a squeeze,
Woe is me.
1ST SHEPHERD Tell us, Mak, if ye may:
How fare ye, I say?
MAK But are ye in this town today?—
How fare *ye?*
Ye have run in the mire and are wet a bit;
I shall make you a fire, if ye will sit.

(*pointing at his* WIFE)

A nurse I would hire; think ye on it.
Well paid is my hire—my dream this is it,
In season.

I have brats if ye knew
Many more than will do;

(*with resignation*)

But, then, we must drink as we brew,
And that is but reason!

I would ye dined ere you go; methinks that ye sweat.
2ND SHEPHERD Nay, neither drink nor meat will mend us yet.
MAK (*innocently*) Why, sirs, what ails ye?
3RD SHEPHERD Our sheep we must get
That was stolen. It is great loss that we met.

(MAK *offers a drink.*)

MAK Sirs, drink!
Had I been near,
Someone should have bought it full dear.
1ST SHEPHERD Marry, some men think that ye were.
And that makes us think!

2ND SHEPHERD Mak, some men think that it should be ye.
3RD SHEPHERD Either you or your spouse, so say we.
MAK Now if ye have suspicion against my Gill or me,
Come and search our house, and then may ye see
Who had her,
Or if any sheep I got,
Either cow or stot.[7]
And Gill, my wife, rose not
Here since she laid her.

If I am not true and loyal, to God I pray

(*pointing to the cradle, where the sheep—the alleged child—is hidden*)

That *this* be the first meal I shall eat this day.
1ST SHEPHERD Mak, as I may fare well, take heed, I say!
"He learned early to steal that could not say nay."

(*The* SHEPHERDS *start to search the room, but* GILL *waves them away when they approach the cradle near her.*)

WIFE I faint!
Out, thieves, from my dwelling!
Ye come to rob while I am swelling—

[7]bullock

MAK Your hearts should melt now she's yelling
In plaint.

WIFE Away, thieves from my child; over him don't pore.
MAK Knew ye how much she has borne, your hearts would be sore.
Ye do wrong, I warn you, thus to rummage before
A woman that has suffered—but I say no more!
WIFE (*yelling*)
Ah, my middle!
I pray to God so mild,
If I ever you beguiled,
That I *eat* this child
That lies in this cradle.
MAK (*pretending concern for her*) Peace, woman, for God's pain, and cry not so:
Thou spill'st thy brain and fill'st me with woe.
2ND SHEPHERD (*to the other* Two SHEPHERDS) I think our sheep be slain; what find ye two?
3RD SHEPHERD All this is in vain: we may as well go:

(*finding only rags of clothing as he searches*)

Only tatters!
I can find no flesh,
Hard nor soft,
Salt nor fresh,
But two bare platters.

(*But as he approaches the cradle and sniffs the air, he makes a grimace.*)

Yet live cattle, as I may have bliss, nor tame nor wild,
None has smelled so strong as this—this child!
WIFE (*protesting*) Ah no, so God bless and give me joy, this child smells mild.
1ST SHEPHERD We have aimed amiss: We were elsewhere beguiled.

(*He is about to leave.*)

2ND SHEPHERD (*also giving up the search*)
Sir, we are done!
But sir—Our Lady him save!—
Is your child a lad?
MAK (*proudly*) Any lord might him have
This child to his son.

When he wakens he has a grip that is a joy to see.

3RD SHEPHERD Blessings on his lips, and happiness may he see.
But who were his godparents, will ye tell me?
MAK (*floundering*) Blessed be their lips!—
1ST SHEPHERD (*aside*) Now, what will the lie be?
MAK So God them thank,—
Parkin and Gibbon Waller, be it said,
And gentle John Horne in good stead—
He that made the great riot spread,
He with the big shank.

2ND SHEPHERD (*preparing to leave*) Mak, friends will we be, for we are all one.
MAK (*pretending to have been hurt by their suspicions*) *We?* Now
I must hold back, for amends is there none.
Farewell, all three, and very glad to see you gone!

(*The* SHEPHERDS *leave the house, and we see them outside.*)

3RD SHEPHERD "Fair words may there be, but love is there none
This year."
1ST SHEPHERD (*to the 2nd*) Gave ye the child anything?
2ND SHEPHERD No, not a farthing.
3RD SHEPHERD Fast back will I fling:
Await ye me here.

(*He goes back to* MAK'S *cottage, the others following him.*)

Mak, take it to no grief if I come to thy lad.
MAK Nay, ye have grieved me much and made me sad.
3RD SHEPHERD The child it will not grieve, thy little day-star so glad;
Mak, with your leave, let me give the child you have had
But sixpence.
MAK Nay, go away; he sleeps!
3RD SHEPHERD Methinks, it peeps.[8]
MAK When he wakens, he weeps;
I pray you go hence.

(*The other* SHEPHERDS *enter.*)

3RD SHEPHERD (*coming closer*) Give me leave him to kiss and to lift up the clout.

(*He lifts the cover a little.*)

What the devil is this? He has a long snout!
1ST SHEPHERD He is birth-marked amiss; let us not waste time hereabout.

[8]whimpers

2ND SHEPHERD "From an ill-spun woof ever comes foul out."

(*as he looks closer*)

Ay—so!
He is like our sheep.
3RD SHEPHERD How, Gib? May I peep?
1ST SHEPHERD "Nature will still creep
Where it may not go."
2ND SHEPHERD This was a quaint trick and a far cast;
It was a high fraud!
3RD SHEPHERD Yea, sirs, I am aghast!
Let's burn this bawd and bind her fast;
A false scold hangs at the last—
So shalt thou.

(*He has pulled the covers off.*)

Will ye see how they swaddle
His four feet in the middle?
Saw I never in a cradle
A hornèd lad ere now.

MAK (*who stands behind them and does not see the sheep uncovered; still attempting to brazen it out*)
Peace, bid I! And let be your fare;
I am he that him gat and yon woman him bare.[9]
1ST SHEPHERD (*mocking him*) What devil shall he be called, Mak?
Lo, God! Mak's heir!
2ND SHEPHERD An end to all jesting; now God give thee care I say!

(*As she is lying in bed, the* WIFE *does not see that they have completely uncovered the sheep.*)

WIFE As pretty child is he
As sits on woman's knee;
A dilly-down, perdie,
To make one gay.

3RD SHEPHERD I know my sheep by the ear-mark—this good token.
MAK I tell you, sirs, hear me: his nose was broken,
Since, as the priest told me, he was by witchcraft bespoken.
1ST SHEPHERD This is false work and must be avenged; I have spoken:
Get weapon!

---

[9]bore

WIFE The child was taken by an elf—
I saw it myself.
When the clock struck twelve,
Was he mis-shapen.

2ND SHEPHERD Ye two are right deft, and belong in the same bed.
3RD SHEPHERD Since they maintain their theft, let us do them dead.

(*They seize* MAK.)

MAK (*seeing the game is up*) If I trespass again, strike off my head.
I'll let you be the judge!
3RD SHEPHERD (*to the others*) Sirs, instead:
For this trespass
We need neither curse nor spite,
Nor chide nor fight,
But take him forthright
And toss him in canvas.

(*They drag* MAK *outside and toss him lustily in a sheet while he yells with pain.*)

Scene VII

The fields near Bethlehem in Judea.
We see the three SHEPHERDS *again, weary after their sport with* MAK *and tired with walking.*

1ST SHEPHERD Lord, how I am sore and like to burst in the breast!
In faith, I can stand no more, therefore will I rest.
2ND SHEPHERD As a sheep of seven score Mak weighed in my fist;
To sleep anywhere methink I would list.
3RD SHEPHERD Then I pray you,
Lie down on this green.
1ST SHEPHERD (*hesitating*) On these thefts to think I yet mean.
3RD SHEPHERD Whereto should ye be worried lean?
Do as I tell you.

They lie down to sleep; but they have barely done so when an ANGEL *appears above. He first sings the hymn "Gloria in Excelsis," then addresses the* SHEPHERDS.

ANGEL Rise, herdsmen gentle, for now is He born
That shall take from the Fiend what Adam had lorn;[1]
That fiend to overthrow this night is He born;
God is made your Friend. Now at this morn.
He commands,
To Bedlem[2] you go see:

[1] *lorn* lost or forfeited [2] *Bedlem* Bethlehem

There lies that divine He
In a crib that full poorly
Betwixt two beasts stands.

(*The* ANGEL *disappears.*)

1ST SHEPHERD This was a quaint voice that ever yet I heard.
It is a marvel to relate thus to be stirred.
2ND SHEPHERD Of God's son of heaven, he spoke from above,
All the wood was in lightning as he spoke of love:
I thought it fair.
3RD SHEPHERD Of a child heard I tell
In Bedlem; I heard it well.

(*pointing to a star that has begun to blaze*)

Yonder star, above the dell:
Let us follow him there.
2ND SHEPHERD Say, what was his song? Heard ye how he sang it?
Three breves[3] to a long.
3RD SHEPHERD Yes, marry, he thwacked it;
Was no crotchet wrong, nor nothing lacked it.
1ST SHEPHERD For to sing it again right as he trilled it.
I can, if I may.
2ND SHEPHERD Let me see how ye croon,
Or do ye but bark at the moon?
3RD SHEPHERD Hold your tongues! Have done!
1ST SHEPHERD
Hark after me, I say!

(*They try to sing the hymn as best they can.*)

2ND SHEPHERD To Bedlem he bade that we should go;
I am troubled that we tarry too slow.
3RD SHEPHERD Be merry and not sad: of mirth is our song, lo!
Everlasting glad in the rewards that will flow,
No plaint may we make.
1ST SHEPHERD Hie we thither, cheery,
Though we be wet and weary;
To that Child and that Lady
Let us our way take.

2ND SHEPHERD We find by the prophecy—let be your din!—
Of David and Isaiah, and more therein,
As prophesied by clergy, that on a virgin

[3]A *breve* is equal to two whole notes; a *long* is equal to six whole notes; a *crotchet* is a quarter note.

Should He light and lie, to redeem our sin
And slake it.
Our kind from woe
To save—Isaiah said so.—
"*Ecce virgo*
Concipict a child that is naked."[4]

3RD SHEPHERD Full glad may we be, and await that day
That lovely day that He shall with His might sway.
Lord, well for me for once and for aye!
Might I but kneel on my knee some word for to say
To that child.
But the angel said
In a crib is He laid,
He is poorly arrayed,
So meek and mild.

1ST SHEPHERD Patriarchs that have been, and prophets beforne,
They desired to have seen this Child that is born;
But *they* are gone full clean, from life forlorn—
It is *we* shall see him, ere it be morn
By token.
When I see Him and feel,
Then shall I know full well
It is true as steel
What prophets have spoken:

To so poor as we are that he would appear,
We the first to find and be his messenger!

2ND SHEPHERD Go we now, let us fare: the place must be near.

3RD SHEPHERD I am ready and eager: go we together
To that Light!
Lord! If Thy will it be,
Though we are lowly all three,
Grant us of Thy glee,
To comfort Thy wight.[5]

(*They move on, following the star, to Bethlehem.*)

Scene VIII

The stable or manger in Bethlehem.
The SHEPHERDS *enter and kneel before the* VIRGIN *and* CHILD.

[4]"Behold, a virgin shall conceive." (Isaiah, 7:14) [5]creature

1ST SHEPHERD Hail, comely and clean; hail, young child!
Hail, Maker, as I mean, born of maiden so mild!
Thou hast banned, I deem, the devil so wild;
The evil beguiler now goes beguiled.

(*pointing to the* CHILD)

Lo, merry He is!
Lo, he laughs, my sweeting,
A welcome greeting!
I have had my meeting—

(*offering the* CHILD *some cherries*)

Have a bob of cherries?
2ND SHEPHERD Hail, sovereign Saviour, for Thou hast us sought!
Hail, Nursling, leaf and flower, that all things hath wrought!
Hail, full of favor, that made all of nought!

(*offering a bird*)

Hail, I kneel and I cower.—A bird have I brought
Without mar.
Hail, little, tiny mop,
Of our creed thou art the crop;
I would drink from thy cup,
Little day-star.

3RD SHEPHERD Hail, darling dear, full of godhead!
I pray Thee be near when that I have need.
Hail! Sweet is Thy cheer! And my heart would bleed
To see Thee sit here clothed so poor indeed,
With no pennies.
Hail! Thy hand put forth to us all—
I bring thee but a ball;
Take and play with it withall,
And go to the tennis.
THE VIRGIN MARY The Father of heaven, God omnipotent,
That set all aright, His son has He sent.
My name He chose forth, and on me His light spent;
And I conceived Him forthwith through His might as God meant:
And now is the Child born.
May He keep you from woe!
I shall pray Him so.
Tell the glad news as ye go,
And remember this morn.

1ST SHEPHERD Farewell, Lady, so fair to behold
With thy child on thy knee.
2ND SHEPHERD —But he lies full cold.—
Lord, it is well with me! Now we go, ye may behold.
3RD SHEPHERD In truth, already it seems to be told
Full oft.
1ST SHEPHERD What grace we have found.
2ND SHEPHERD Come forth! Now are we won!
3RD SHEPHERD To sing of it we're bound:
Let us sing aloft!

(*They leave the stable, singing.*)

Explicit Pagina Pastorum.

(*Here ends The Shepherds' Pageant.*)

HAMLET

(1600)

WILLIAM SHAKESPEARE (1564–1616)

English Renaissance tragedy, commonly known as Elizabethan, reached its greatest heights during the long reign of Elizabeth I from 1558 to 1603. The highly popular allegorical morality plays, peopled by personified abstractions such as Greed, Lust, Good Deeds, or Humility, as well as by more realistic human characters, thrived during the first half of the sixteenth century as they presented their serious Christian moral lessons, often interspersed with comic, even farcical, routines. A more "academic" drama influenced by classical literature, mainly the Roman drama of Seneca (c. 4 B.C.–A.D. 65), since the Greek classics were mostly unknown, began to develop about mid-century. Although most of the plays of the early Elizabethan era have disappeared, *Gorboduc,* a not very interesting blank-verse drama written in 1562 by Thomas Norton (1532–1584) and Thomas Sackville (1536–1608) is generally regarded as the first English tragedy.

Not until the construction of the first permanent theatre in 1576, known simply as the Theatre, did acting companies, usually the type of roving players employed so effectively by Hamlet, have any regular performance venue, using innyards and other makeshift locales where an audience could assemble. (*Gorboduc* and similar plays were staged in more private quarters such as the Inns of Court.) But once theatre buildings proliferated—the Theatre was followed by the Curtain (1577), the Rose (1587), the Swan (c. 1596), the Globe (1599), and the Fortune (1600), built in the suburb of Southwark on the south, or "bank" side of the Thames to escape the severe restrictions imposed by the City of London—resident acting companies were organized, often performing under the protective aegis of royalty or nobility such as the queen, the lord chamberlain, and others. Simultaneously, the demand for scripts increased. Among those writing serious plays were George Chapman, John Marston, Philip Massinger, Thomas Middleton, John Webster, Cyril Tourner, Ben Jonson, and, of course, the most famous of them all, William Shakespeare.

We need not enter the fray that has continued for centuries as to who actually wrote the plays attributed to Shakespeare of Stratford. *Somebody* of great genius wrote them, and the strongest evidence still points to Shakespeare, so we will let it go at that. We do know that a frustrated playwright named Robert Greene (c. 1560–1592), who aspired to greatness and resented the successes of his rival, wrote a tract called "A Groatsworth of Wit" shortly before he died in which his ire was directed against the intrusive "Shake-scene." But for all his aspirations, Greene was a lesser dramatist whose early death kept him from achieving major stature.

The two writers whose tragedies are most important in considering the precursors of Shakespeare's greatest works are Thomas Kyd (1558–1594) and Christopher Marlowe (1564–1593). Kyd's *The Spanish Tragedy* (c. 1585), a violent and bloody drama of revenge, survives more as a sensational melodrama, its language and actions a kind of rude progenitor of what Shakespeare at his best would produce. There is fairly good evidence that Kyd also wrote an early version of *Hamlet* that Shakespeare vastly improved. The more important figure is Marlowe, who set the tone in character and incident and especially in language that Shakespeare developed soon afterward. The first of Marlowe's important works is his tale of the fearsome, barbaric conquerer from the east, Tamburlaine the Great. *Tamburlaine Part I* appeared in 1587, followed by *Tamburlaine Part II* the next year (the Elizabethans early on established the tradition of sequels so common four hundred years later). Though it romanticizes the ruthless tyrant who forced prisoners to pull his chariot tied to their eyelashes, and gives him a pure love in "the fair Zenocrate," what emerges with vigor is Marlowe's use of dramatic blank verse, his "mighty line," which raised his plays to new levels of dramatic and theatrical excitement. Later, with his *Tragical History of Dr. Faustus* (c. 1589), full of pyrotechnical magic, *The Jew of Malta* (c. 1590), and *Edward II* (1591–1592), Marlowe gave Shakespeare a firm foundation on which to build. Marlowe's death in a tavern brawl in Holland silenced what might have been a voice equal to his successor.

To be sure, Shakespeare did not offer us the perfected brilliance of *Hamlet*—or *Othello, Macbeth,* or *Lear*—out of a clear blue sky, for his earliest so-called tragedy, the horrendous *Titus Andronicus* (c. 1594) (Shakespeare's total contribution to the play is a matter of debate), with its frightful mutilations of severed hands and an extracted tongue, shows the direct influence of Seneca at his wildest. (The severing of Macbeth's head and the putting out of Gloucester's eyes in *Lear* carry on to a lesser extent, fortunately, the tradition of blood and gore.)

But to compare Shakespeare's more human Shylock of *The Merchant of Venice* to Marlowe's Barabas or the Henrys and Richards to Marlowe's Edward is to see the difference between mere greatness and true genius. Shakespeare, as has often been pointed out, was not always original in his choice of topics, but what he did with them is what really matters.

The Elizabethan playgoing public, both men and women, who filled the London theatres was a fairly representative cross-section of the citizenry. (Royalty, including the queen, attended only the private indoor theatres such as Blackfriars near the Court, which will not concern us here.) Those in the more expensive seats in the tiers of balconies may have presented no particular problem, but the "groundlings," standing throughout the play in the heat of the open-air courtyard, who paid their hard-earned pence to attend and who liked a good show with plenty of action, could be a bothersome lot. The "groundlings," as Hamlet notes in his speech to the players, "for the most part are capable of nothing but inexplicable dumb show and noise." This judgment seems a bit harsh, however, because it is clear that audiences loved to hear the rolling cadences of the dramatic verse and were quite capable of following the story line, which often demanded close attention and relative silence.[1]

Shakespeare may have been contemptuous of some elements of his audience, but he was enough a man of the theatre to provide everybody with what they liked to see. For one thing, the Elizabethans took supernatural spirits very seriously, and the ghost of old Hamlet describing his purgatorial trials was readily acceptable. Instant madness through some trauma was equally received, and Ophelia's sudden loss of mind with her wandering speech and eccentric action was fully believable and theatrically effective. Hamlet's "antic disposition" is feigned successfully enough to convince Polonius that the prince is mad ("for thy love" as he tells Ophelia), accepting the common view that instant mental unbalance was possible. Moreover, the audience demanded authenticity, and in a day when gentlemen carried swords and knew how to use them, the simple stage direction "They fight" meant far more than a few seconds of clashing tin hand props. The climactic duel in *Hamlet* required and very probably received a well-rehearsed and breath-catching display of fencing, especially since the audience knew the fateful dangers involved.

Furthermore, in this age when England, like other nations, was ruled by an absolute monarch, audiences were attracted by the tales of kings and princes with their plottings and intrigues, ambitions and frustrations, as objects of far greater interest than any mundane problems of ordinary citizens. The pomp and circumstance of crowned heads, always portrayed in regal costume, gave the apprentices and shopkeepers who could take the time to attend the theatre considerable opportunity to forget their own too often sordid existence as they watched the giant tragic figures proceed to their inevitable dooms. *Hamlet* projects these aspects in fine fashion.

Of minor importance to the play itself but of considerable historical interest are references to the theatre of Shakespeare's time and the performers who appeared in it. The first occurs when Hamlet and Rosencrantz discuss the arrival of the strolling players in Act II, Scene II. Although such groups were not uncommon in England (and remember that, though set in medieval Denmark, the

[1]The recent discovery of the foundations of the Rose Theatre, so far the only Elizabethan playhouse to be unearthed, revealed some interesting facts about the Shakespearean audience. Its main refreshment seems to have been hazelnuts, shells of which were found in profusion, and their continual cracking must have been an annoying interference. It is very likely that the audience was an unpleasantly aromatic lot as well. However, there is no record of an Elizabethan audience getting out of hand to the detriment of the performance.

play's characters and actions are thoroughly English Renaissance), this particular band of actors has departed its regular venue in "the city" (London) where they have apparently been deposed by, or at least have seen their public dwindle because of, the increased popularity of the indoor houses featuring performances by prepubescent choir boys, the "eyrie of children, little eyases," which Rosencrantz holds in considerable contempt. This is Shakespeare's only reference to the "war of the theatres," which was raging at the time and in which many another playwright became involved as they wrote for and against these private theatres which were causing the professional adult companies such misery. That the conflict was noted by Shakespeare, who was normally above such wrangling, indicates how serious it had become.

Information about players and their playing is shown in two other passages. In the same scene the reaction of Polonius to Hamlet's request that the players be "well bestowed"—that is, given the hospitality of the castle—is that he will use them "according to their desert," a clear indication that, like most people, he regards them as a considerably lower level of being. But Hamlet, showing his respect for them, demands "much better." However, the most interesting passages are those in which Hamlet delivers his "speak the speech" directions to the players at the opening of Act III, Scene II. Here are some of the very few indications available to us as to how actors performed during the great period of Elizabethan drama and theatre. Hamlet is intolerant of actors hamming things up by "tear[ing] a passion to tatters" and "saw[ing] the air too much," or of clowns who ad lib and ignore the script. He is one who prefers a kind of realistic acting which does not "o'erstate the modesty of nature." Not that all performers necessarily behaved in the manner that so offends Hamlet "to the soul," but it is quite possible that there were enough such flawed behaviors in the professional theatre that Shakespeare, through Hamlet, considers it important enough to mention.

To define *Hamlet* as the greatest play ever written may be too-strong hyperbole, but it is a superlative drama and a magnificent piece of theatre. It is virtually impossible to perform a thoroughly bad *Hamlet.* The play has so much to offer, is so "actor proof," that no matter how ineffective a particular interpretation may be or however inept the staging, so much comes through that the magnificence of its artistry transcends even the most botched and bowdlerized version.

There has probably been more serious scholarship and more pompous blather written about who, what, and why Hamlet is than about any other person, living, dead, or imagined. Thousands of words in hundreds of documents have explained, analyzed, and dissected this most fascinating of dramatic characters. That a dramatist like William Shakespeare, who may or may not have been educated beyond the most elementary schooling, who was basically a theatre producer and actor grinding out pieces for his company's repertoire, could have created within the framework of some few hours upon the stage an individual so alive in the consciences and minds of generations ever since is one of the great tributes to human artistic genius.

At the heart of things, *Hamlet* is a rip-roaring Elizabethan revenge melodrama. Dark doings behind dismal castle walls—conspiracies, a ghost crying vengeance, an innocent maiden, a faithless wife, a usurping king, treacherous friends, swordplay and derring-do—are all here in profusion, and the play moves from first to last through a series of events that scarcely allow time to catch one's breath. More than that, the story, Aristotle's soul, is perfectly plotted. The opening sequences on the parapets slam the audience into the thick of things from the first lines. Scenes of fervent activity followed by calm; then quick and exciting action, then sober introspection. Brutality and tenderness, a seamy court intrigue, a deadly cat-and-mouse game, a gentle family caught helplessly in the middle—all this and more combine in a totally absorbing tale of noble acts and infamous skulduggery. The characters are revealed in thoroughly convincing depth and breadth, their actions humanly reasonable and comprehensible. And all told in some of the most magnificent dramatic poetry ever written.

Beyond the exciting action, *Hamlet* is, of course, a superb psychological study. Into the unfathomable and increasingly horrible affairs in Elsinore is thrown the young prince, still at the university, unprepared for the deeds he must do, aware of his unquestioned obligation to do them. The tax upon his strength, his mind, his personal philosophy of life is tremendous and eventually overwhelming. The constant peaks and valleys of the trauma through which he moves are fascinating to observe.

It is difficult to fault Hamlet for what might be regarded as his frequent eccentric behavior. With "wild and whirling words" he baffles Horatio after the encounter with the ghost; he is crude to Ophelia in her closet, and insults her in the nunnery scene and at the play; he is contemptuous of Rosencrantz and Guildenstern, and he ridicules Polonius in the fishmonger scene. His assault upon his mother in her bedroom after the mousetrap scene is particularly vicious, and his slaying of the stupidly intrusive Polonius is an act of totally unreasoning violence. But Hamlet, as a sensitive, thinking individual, is a man struggling to maintain his own mental balance in the face of murder, incest, and faithlessness that would severely tax the self-control of the strongest human will.

Finally, *Hamlet* is a tragedy. The prince is doomed, driven by forces beyond his control into the ultimate catastrophe. He wishes to avoid it, seeks to postpone it, becomes increasingly aware that it must come and that he himself must bring it about. Hamlet is no coward, but he blames himself for being one. He is not a procrastinator by nature, yet he fatally procrastinates. He is a thinker who weighs his thoughts and deeds, yet he acts with foolish impetuosity and unthinking cruelty. He commands our passion and our understanding. He is a potentially great man, capable of being a great king, but he must face the task the fates have ordained for him, ultimately realizing that escape is impossible, disaster inevitable. Who cannot weep, not for sentiment but for the tremendous loss, the sacrifice endured, when, as Horatio tells us, "Now cracks a noble heart." As old Hamlet's perturbed spirit has been laid to rest, so we wish, with Horatio, for young Hamlet, that flights of angels sing him to *his* rest.

Hamlet, Prince of Denmark WILLIAM SHAKESPEARE

CHARACTERS

CLAUDIUS, *King of Denmark*
HAMLET, *son to the late, and nephew to the present, King*
POLONIUS, *Lord Chamberlain*
HORATIO, *friend to Hamlet*
LAERTES, *son to Polonius*
VOLTEMAND
CORNELIUS
ROSENCRANTZ
GUILDENSTERN
OSRIC
A GENTLEMAN } *courtiers*
A PRIEST
MARCELLUS
BERNARDO } *officers*
FRANCISCO, *a soldier*
REYNALDO, *servant to Polonius*
PLAYERS
TWO CLOWNS, *gravediggers*
FORTINBRAS, *Prince of Norway*
A NORWEGIAN CAPTAIN
ENGLISH AMBASSADORS
GERTRUDE, *Queen of Denmark, mother to Hamlet*
OPHELIA, *daughter to Polonius*
GHOST OF HAMLET'S FATHER
LORDS, LADIES, OFFICERS, SOLDIERS, SAILORS, MESSENGERS, ATTENDANTS

Act I

Scene I

Elsinore Castle: a sentry-post.

(*Enter* BERNARDO *and* FRANCISCO, *two sentinels.*)

BERNARDO Who's there?
FRANCISCO Nay, answer me. Stand and unfold yourself.
BERNARDO Long live the king!
FRANCISCO Bernardo?
BERNARDO He.

FRANCISCO You come most carefully upon your hour.
BERNARDO 'Tis now struck twelve. Get thee to bed, Francisco.
FRANCISCO For this relief much thanks. 'Tis bitter cold,
And I am sick at heart.
BERNARDO Have you had quiet guard?
FRANCISCO Not a mouse stirring.
BERNARDO Well, good night.
If you do meet Horatio and Marcellus,
The rivals[2] of my watch, bid them make haste.

(*Enter* HORATIO *and* MARCELLUS.)

FRANCISCO I think I hear them. Stand, ho! Who is there?
HORATIO Friends to this ground.
MARCELLUS And liegemen to the Dane.[3]
FRANCISCO Give you good night.
MARCELLUS O, farewell, honest soldier.
Who hath relieved you?
FRANCISCO Bernardo hath my place.
Give you good night.

(*Exit* FRANCISCO.)

MARCELLUS Holla, Bernardo!
BERNARDO Say—
What, is Horatio there?
HORATIO A piece of him.
BERNARDO Welcome, Horatio. Welcome, good Marcellus.
HORATIO What, has this thing appeared again to-night?
BERNARDO I have seen nothing.
MARCELLUS Horatio says 'tis but our fantasy,
And will not let belief take hold of him
Touching this dreaded sight twice seen of us.
Therefore I have entreated him along
With us to watch the minutes of this night,
That, if again this apparition come,
He may approve[4] our eyes and speak to it.
HORATIO Tush, tush, 'twill not appear.
BERNARDO Sit down awhile,
And let us once again assail your ears,
That are so fortified against our story,
What we two nights have seen.
HORATIO Well, sit we down,
And let us hear Bernardo speak of this.

---

[2]sharers [3]King of Denmark [4]confirm

BERNARDO Last night of all,
When yond same star that's westward from the pole[5]
Had made his course t' illume that part of heaven
Where now it burns, Marcellus and myself,
The bell then beating one—

(*Enter* GHOST.)

MARCELLUS Peace, break thee off. Look where it comes again.
BERNARDO In the same figure like the king that's dead.
MARCELLUS Thou art a scholar; speak to it, Horatio.
BERNARDO Looks 'a not like the king? Mark it, Horatio.
HORATIO Most like. It harrows me with fear and wonder.
BERNARDO It would be spoke to.
MARCELLUS Speak to it, Horatio.
HORATIO What art thou that usurp'st this time of night
Together with that fair and warlike form
In which the majesty of buried Denmark[6]
Did sometimes[7] march? By heaven I charge thee, speak.
MARCELLUS It is offended.
BERNARDO See, it stalks away.
HORATIO Stay. Speak, speak. I charge thee, speak.

(*Exit* GHOST.)

MARCELLUS 'Tis gone and will not answer.
BERNARDO How now, Horatio? You tremble and look pale.
Is not this something more than fantasy?
What think you on't?
HORATIO Before my God, I might not this believe
Without the sensible and true avouch
Of mine own eyes.
MARCELLUS Is it not like the king?
HORATIO As thou art to thyself.
Such was the very armor he had on
When he th' ambitious Norway[8] combated.
So frowned he once when, in an angry parle,[9]
He smote the sledded Polacks on the ice.
'Tis strange.
MARCELLUS Thus twice before, and jump[1] at this dead hour,
With martial stalk hath he gone by our watch.
HORATIO In what particular thought to work I know not;
But in the gross and scope[2] of my opinion,

[5]polestar [6]the buried king of Denmark [7]formerly [8]King of Norway [9]parley [1]just, exactly [2]gross scope, general view

This bodes some strange eruption to our state.
MARCELLUS Good now, sit down, and tell me he that knows,
Why this same strict and most observant watch
So nightly toils the subject[3] of the land,
And why such daily cast of brazen cannon
And foreign mart[4] for implements of war,
Why such impress[5] of shipwrights, whose sore task
Does not divide the Sunday from the week.
What might be toward[6] that this sweaty haste
Doth make the night joint-laborer with the day?
Who is't that can inform me?
HORATIO That can I.
At least the whisper goes so. Our last king,
Whose image even but now appeared to us,
Was as you know by Fortinbras of Norway,
Thereto pricked on by a most emulate[7] pride,
Dared to the combat; in which our valiant Hamlet
(For so this side of our known world esteemed him)
Did slay this Fortinbras; who, by a sealed compact
Well ratified by law and heraldry,[8]
Did forfeit, with his life, all those his lands
Which he stood seized[9] of to the conqueror;
Against the which a moiety competent[1]
Was gaged[2] by our king, which had returned
To the inheritance of Fortinbras
Had he been vanquisher, as, by the same comart[3]
And carriage[4] of the article designed,
His fell to Hamlet. Now, sir, young Fortinbras,
Of unimproved[5] mettle hot and full,
Hath in the skirts of Norway here and there
Sharked[6] up a list of lawless resolutes[7]
For food and diet to some enterprise
That hath a stomach[8] in't; which is no other,
As it doth well appear unto our state,
But to recover of us by strong hand
And terms compulsatory those foresaid lands
So by his father lost; and this, I take it,
Is the main motive of our preparations,
The source of this our watch, and the chief head[9]
Of this posthaste and romage[1] in the land.

---

[3]makes toil; subjects [4]trading [5]conscription [6]in preparation [7]jealously rivalling [8]law of heralds regulating combat [9]possessed [1]sufficient portion [2]engaged, staked [3]joint bargain [4]purport [5]unused [6]snatched indiscriminately as the shark takes prey [7]desperadoes [8]show of venturesomeness [9]fountainhead, source [1]intense activity

BERNARDO I think it be no other but e'en so.
Well may it sort[2] that this portentous figure
Comes armèd through our watch so like the king
That was and is the question of these wars.
HORATIO A mote[3] it is to trouble the mind's eye.
In the most high and palmy state of Rome,
A little ere the mightiest Julius fell,
The graves stood tenantless and the sheeted[4] dead
Did squeak and gibber in the Roman streets;
As stars with trains of fire and dews of blood,
Disasters[5] in the sun; and the moist star[6]
Upon whose influence Neptune's empire stands
Was sick almost to doomsday with eclipse.
And even the like precurse[7] of feared events,
As harbingers[8] preceding still[9] the fates
And prologue to the omen[1] coming on,
Have heaven and earth together demonstrated
Unto our climatures[2] and countrymen.

(*Enter* GHOST.)

But soft, behold, lo where it comes again!
I'll cross it,[3] though it blast me.—Stay, illusion.

(*He spreads his arms.*)

If thou hast any sound or use of voice,
Speak to me.
If there be any good thing to be done
That may to thee do ease and grace to me,
Speak to me.
If thou art privy to thy country's fate,
Which happily[4] foreknowing may avoid,
O, speak!
Or if thou hast uphoarded in thy life
Extorted treasure in the womb of earth,
For which, they say, you spirits oft walk in death,

(*The cock crows.*)

Speak of it. Stay and speak. Stop it, Marcellus.
MARCELLUS Shall I strike at it with my partisan?[5]
HORATIO Do, if it will not stand.

[2]suit [3]speck of dust [4]in shrouds [5]ominous signs [6]moon [7]foreshadowing [8]forerunners [9]constantly [1]calamity [2]regions [3]cross its path [4]haply, perchance [5]pike

BERNARDO 'Tis here.
HORATIO 'Tis here.

(*Exit* GHOST.)

MARCELLUS 'Tis gone.
We do it wrong, being so majestical,
To offer it the show of violence,
For it is as the air invulnerable,
And our vain blows malicious mockery.
BERNARDO It was about to speak when the cock crew.
HORATIO And then it started, like a guilty thing
Upon a fearful summons. I have heard
The cock, that is the trumpet to the morn,
Doth with his lofty and shrill-sounding throat
Awake the god of day, and at his warning,
Whether in sea or fire, in earth or air,
Th' extravagant[6] and erring[7] spirit hies
To his confine; and of the truth herein
This present object made probation.[8]
MARCELLUS It faded on the crowing of the cock.
Some say that ever 'gainst[9] that season comes
Wherein our Saviour's birth is celebrated,
This bird of dawning singeth all night long,
And then, they say, no spirit dare stir abroad,
The nights are wholesome, then no planets strike,[1]
No fairy takes,[2] nor witch hath power to charm.
So hallowed and so gracious is that time.
HORATIO So have I heard and do in part believe it.
But look, the morn in russet mantle clad
Walks o'er the dew of yon high eastward hill.
Break we our watch up, and by my advice
Let us impart what we have seen to-night
Unto young Hamlet, for upon my life
This spirit, dumb to us, will speak to him.
Do you consent we shall acquaint him with it,
As needful in our loves, fitting our duty?
MARCELLUS Let's do't, I pray, and this morning know
Where we shall find him most conveniently.

(*Exeunt.*)

---

[6]wandering beyond bounds [7]wandering [8]proof [9]just before [1]work evil by influence [2]bewitches

Scene II

Elsinore Castle: a room of state.

(*Flourish. Enter* CLAUDIUS, *King of Denmark,* GERTRUDE *the Queen,* COUNCILLORS, POLONIUS *and his son* LAERTES, HAMLET, *cum aliis*[3] [*including* VOLTEMAND *and* CORNELIUS].)

KING Though yet of Hamlet our dear brother's death
The memory be green, and that it us befitted
To bear our hearts in grief, and our whole kingdom
To be contracted in one brow of woe,
Yet so far hath discretion fought with nature
That we with wisest sorrow think on him
Together with remembrance of ourselves.
Therefore our sometime sister, now our queen,
Th' imperial jointress[4] to this warlike state,
Have we, as 'twere with a defeated joy,
With an auspicious and a dropping eye,
With mirth in funeral and with dirge in marriage,
In equal scale weighing delight and dole,
Taken to wife. Nor have we herein barred[5]
Your better wisdoms, which have freely gone
With this affair along. For all, our thanks.
Now follows, that you know, young Fortinbras,
Holding a weak supposal of our worth,
Or thinking by our late dear brother's death
Our state to be disjoint and out of frame,
Colleaguèd[6] with this dream of his advantage,
He hath not failed to pester us with message
Importing the surrender of those lands
Lost by his father, with all bands of law,
To our most valiant brother. So much for him.
Now for ourself and for this time of meeting.
Thus much the business is: we have here writ
To Norway, uncle of young Fortinbras—
Who, impotent and bedrid, scarcely hears
Of this his nephew's purpose—to suppress
His further gait[7] herein, in that the levies,
The lists, and full proportions[8] are all made
Out of his subject; and we here dispatch
You, good Cornelius, and you, Voltemand,

[3]with others [4]a woman who has a jointure, or joint tenancy of an estate [5]excluded [6]united [7]going [8]amounts of forces and supplies

For bearers of this greeting to old Norway,
Giving to you no further personal power
To business with the king, more than the scope
Of these delated[9] articles allow.
Farewell, and let your haste commend your duty.

CORNELIUS, VOLTEMAND In that, and all things, will we show our duty.

KING We doubt it nothing. Heartily farewell.

(*Exeunt* VOLTEMAND *and* CORNELIUS.)

And now, Laertes, what's the news with you?
You told us of some suit. What is't, Laertes?
You cannot speak of reason to the Dane[1]
And lose your voice.[2] What wouldst thou beg, Laertes,
That shall not be my offer, not thy asking?
The head is not more native[3] to the heart,
The hand more instrumental[4] to the mouth,
Than is the throne of Denmark to thy father.
What wouldst thou have, Laertes?

LAERTES My dread lord,
Your leave and favor to return to France,
From whence though willingly I came to Denmark
To show my duty in your coronation,
Yet now I must confess, that duty done,
My thoughts and wishes bend again toward France
And bow them to your gracious leave and pardon.

KING Have you your father's leave? What says Polonius?

POLONIUS He hath, my lord, wrung from me my slow leave
By laborsome petition, and at last
Upon his will I sealed my hard consent.
I do beseech you give him leave to go.

KING Take thy fair hour, Laertes. Time be thine,
And thy best graces spend it at thy will.
But now, my cousin[5] Hamlet, and my son—

HAMLET (*aside*) A little more than kin,[6] and less than kind![7]

KING How is it that the clouds still hang on you?

HAMLET Not so, my lord. I am too much in the sun.[8]

QUEEN Good Hamlet, cast thy nighted color off,
And let thine eye look like a friend on Denmark.
Do not for ever with thy vailèd[9] lids

---

[9]detailed [1]King of Denmark [2]speak in vain [3]joined by nature [4]serviceable [5]kinsman more distant than parent, child, brother, or sister [6]related as nephew [7]kindly in feeling, as by kind, or nature, a son would be to his father [8]sunshine of the king's undesired favor (with the punning additional meaning of "place of a son") [9]downcast

Seek for thy noble father in the dust.
Thou know'st 'tis common. All that lives must die,
Passing through nature to eternity.

HAMLET Ay, madam, it is common.

QUEEN If it be,
Why seems it so particular with thee?

HAMLET Seems, madam? Nay, it is. I know not "seems."
'Tis not alone my inky cloak, good mother,
Nor customary suits of solemn black,
Nor windy suspiration of forced breath,
No, nor the fruitful[1] river in the eye,
Nor the dejected havior of the visage,
Together with all forms, moods, shapes of grief,
That can denote me truly. These indeed seem,
For they are actions that a man might play,
But I have that within which passeth show—
These but the trappings and the suits of woe.

KING 'Tis sweet and commendable in your nature, Hamlet,
To give these mourning duties to your father,
But you must know your father lost a father,
That father lost, lost his, and the survivor bound
In filial obligation for some term
To do obsequious[2] sorrow. But to persever[3]
In obstinate condolement is a course
Of impious stubbornness. 'Tis unmanly grief.
It shows a will most incorrect to heaven,
A heart unfortified, a mind impatient,
An understanding simple and unschooled.
For what we know must be and is as common
As any the most vulgar thing to sense,
Why should we in our peevish opposition
Take it to heart? Fie, 'tis a fault to heaven,
A fault against the dead, a fault to nature,
To reason most absurd, whose common theme
Is death of fathers, and who still hath cried,
From the first corse till he that died to-day,
"This must be so." We pray you throw to earth
This unprevailing woe, and think of us
As a father, for let the world take note
You are the most immediate to our throne,
And with no less nobility of love
Than that which dearest father bears his son

---

[1]copious [2]proper to obsequies or funerals [3]persevere (accented on the second syllable, as always in Shakespeare)

Do I impart toward you. For your intent
In going back to school in Wittenberg,
It is most retrograde[4] to our desire,
And we beseech you, bend you to remain
Here in the cheer and comfort of our eye,
Our chiefest courtier, cousin, and our son.
QUEEN Let not thy mother lose her prayers, Hamlet.
I pray thee stay with us, go not to Wittenberg.
HAMLET I shall in all my best obey you, madam.
KING Why, 'tis a loving and a fair reply.
Be as ourself in Denmark. Madam, come.
This gentle and unforced accord of Hamlet
Sits smiling to my heart, in grace whereof
No jocund health that Denmark drinks to-day
But the great cannon to the clouds shall tell,
And the king's rouse[5] the heaven shall bruit[6] again,
Respeaking earthly thunder. Come away.

(*Flourish. Exeunt all but* HAMLET.)

HAMLET O that this too too sullied flesh would melt,
Thaw, and resolve itself into a dew,
Or that the Everlasting had not fixed
His canon[7] gainst self-slaughter. O God, God,
How weary, stale, flat, and unprofitable
Seem to me all the uses of this world!
Fie on't, ah, fie, 'tis an unweeded garden
That grows to seed. Things rank and gross in nature
Possess it merely.[8] That it should come to this,
But two months dead, nay, not so much, not two,
So excellent a king, that was to this
Hyperion[9] to a satyr, so loving to my mother
That he might not beteem[1] the winds of heaven
Visit her face too roughly. Heaven and earth,
Must I remember? Why, she would hang on him
As if increase of appetite had grown
By what it fed on, and yet within a month—
Let me not think on't; frailty, thy name is woman—
A little month, or ere those shoes were old
With which she followed my poor father's body
Like Niobe,[2] all tears, why she, even she—

[4]contrary [5]toast drunk in wine [6]echo [7]law [8]completely [9]the sun god [1]allow [2]The proud mother who boasted of having more children than Leto and was punished when they were slain by Apollo and Artemis, children of Leto; the grieving Niobe was changed by Zeus into a stone, which continually dropped tears.

O God, a beast that wants discourse[3] of reason
Would have mourned longer—married with my uncle,
My father's brother, but no more like my father
Than I to Hercules. Within a month,
Ere yet the salt of most unrighteous tears
Had left the flushing in her gallèd[4] eyes,
She married. O, most wicked speed, to post
With such dexterity to incestuous sheets!
It is not nor it cannot come to good.
But break my heart, for I must hold my tongue.

(*Enter* HORATIO, MARCELLUS, *and* BERNARDO.)

HORATIO Hail to your lordship!
HAMLET I am glad to see you well.
Horatio—or I do forget myself.
HORATIO The same, my lord, and your poor servant ever.
HAMLET Sir, my good friend, I'll change[5] that name with you.
And what make[6] you from Wittenberg, Horatio?
Marcellus?
MARCELLUS My good lord!
HAMLET I am very glad to see you. (*to* BERNARDO) Good even, sir.
But what, in faith, make you from Wittenberg?
HORATIO A truant disposition, good my lord.
HAMLET I would not hear your enemy say so,
Nor shall you do my ear that violence
To make it truster of your own report
Against yourself. I know you are no truant.
But what is your affair in Elsinore?
We'll teach you to drink deep ere you depart.
HORATIO My lord, I came to see your father's funeral.
HAMLET I prithee do not mock me, fellow student.
I think it was to see my mother's wedding.
HORATIO Indeed, my lord, it followed hard upon.
HAMLET Thrift, thrift, Horatio. The funeral baked meats
Did coldly furnish forth the marriage tables.
Would I had met my dearest[7] foe in heaven
Or ever I had seen that day, Horatio!
My father—methinks I see my father.
HORATIO Where, my lord?
HAMLET In my mind's eye, Horatio.
HORATIO I saw him once. 'A was a goodly king.

[3]logical power or process [4]irritated [5]exchange [6]do [7]direst, bitterest

HAMLET 'A was a man, take him for all in all,
I shall not look upon his like again.
HORATIO My lord, I think I saw him yesternight.
HAMLET Saw? who?
HORATIO My lord, the king, your father.
HAMLET The king my father?
HORATIO Season your admiration[8] for a while
With an attent ear till I may deliver
Upon the witness of these gentlemen
This marvel to you.
HAMLET For God's love let me hear!
HORATIO Two nights together had these gentlemen,
Marcellus and Bernardo, on their watch
In the dead waste and middle of the night
Been thus encountered. A figure like your father,
Armèd at point[9] exactly, cap-a-pe,[1]
Appears before them and with solemn march
Goes slow and stately by them. Thrice he walked
By their oppressed and fear-surprisèd eyes
Within his truncheon's[2] length, whilst they, distilled
Almost to jelly with the act of fear,
Stand dumb and speak not to him. This to me
In dreadful secrecy impart they did,
And I with them the third night kept the watch,
Where, as they had delivered, both in time,
Form of the thing, each word made true and good,
The apparition comes. I knew your father.
These hands are not more like.
HAMLET But where was this?
MARCELLUS My lord, upon the platform where we watched.
HAMLET Did you not speak to it?
HORATIO My lord, I did,
But answer made it none. Yet once methought
It lifted up it[3] head and did address
Itself to motion like as it would speak.
But even then the morning cock crew loud,
And at the sound it shrunk in haste away
And vanished from our sight.
HAMLET 'Tis very strange.
HORATIO As I do live, my honored lord, 'tis true,
And we did think it writ down in our duty
To let you know of it.

[8]control your wonder [9]completely [1]from head to foot [2]military commander's baton [3]its

HAMLET Indeed, indeed, sirs, but this troubles me.
Hold you the watch to-night?
ALL We do, my lord.
HAMLET Armed, say you?
ALL Armed, my lord.
HAMLET From top to toe?
ALL My lord, from head to foot.
HAMLET Then saw you not his face?
HORATIO O, yes, my lord. He wore his beaver[4] up.
HAMLET What, looked he frowningly?
HORATIO A countenance more in sorrow than in anger.
HAMLET Pale or red?
HORATIO Nay, very pale.
HAMLET And fixed his eyes upon you?
HORATIO Most constantly.
HAMLET I would I had been there.
HORATIO It would have much amazed you.
HAMLET Very like, very like. Stayed it long?
HORATIO While one with moderate haste might tell[5] a hundred.
BOTH Longer, longer.
HORATIO Not when I saw't.
HAMLET His beard was grizzled,[6] no?
HORATIO It was as I have seen it in his life,
A sable silvered.[7]
HAMLET I will watch to-night.
Perchance 'twill walk again.
HORATIO I warr'nt it will.
HAMLET If it assume my noble father's person,
I'll speak to it though hell itself should gape
And bid me hold my peace. I pray you all,
If you have hitherto concealed this sight,
Let it be tenable[8] in your silence still,
And whatsomever else shall hap to-night,
Give it an understanding but no tongue.
I will requite your loves. So fare you well.
Upon the platform, 'twixt eleven and twelve
I'll visit you.
ALL Our duty to your honor.
HAMLET Your loves, as mine to you. Farewell.

(*Exeunt all but* HAMLET.)

[4]visor or movable faceguard of the helmet [5]count [6]grey [7]black mixed with white [8]held firmly

My father's spirit—in arms? All is not well.
I doubt[9] some foul play. Would the night were come!
Till then sit still, my soul. Foul deeds will rise,
Though all the earth o'erwhelm them, to men's eyes.

(*Exit.*)

Scene III

Elsinore Castle: the chambers of POLONIUS.

(*Enter* LAERTES *and* OPHELIA, *his sister.*)

LAERTES My necessaries are embarked. Farewell.
And, sister, as the winds give benefit
And convoy[1] is assistant, do not sleep,
But let me hear from you.

OPHELIA Do you doubt that?

LAERTES For Hamlet, and the trifling of his favor,
Hold it a fashion and a toy in blood,
A violet in the youth of primy[2] nature,
Forward, not permanent, sweet, not lasting,
The perfume and suppliance[3] of a minute,
No more.

OPHELIA No more but so?

LAERTES Think it no more.
For nature crescent[4] does not grow alone
In thews and bulk, but as this temple[5] waxes
The inward service of the mind and soul
Grows wide withal. Perhaps he loves you now,
And now no soil nor cautel[6] doth besmirch
The virtue of his will,[7] but you must fear,
His greatness weighed,[8] his will is not his own.
(For he himself is subject to his birth.)
He may not, as unvalued persons do,
Carve for himself, for on his choice depends
The safety and health of this whole state,
And therefore must his choice be circumscribed
Unto the voice and yielding[9] of that body
Whereof he is the head. Then if he says he loves you,
It fits your wisdom so far to believe it
As he in his particular act and place

[9]suspect, fear [1]means of transport [2]of the springtime [3]filling sweetness [4]growing [5]the body [6]deceit [7]desire [8]high position considered [9]assent

May give his saying deed, which is no further
Than the main voice of Denmark goes withal.
Then weigh what loss your honor may sustain
If with too credent[1] ear you list his songs,
Or lose your heart, or your chaste treasure open
To his unmastered importunity.
Fear it, Ophelia, fear it, my dear sister,
And keep you in the rear of your affection,[2]
Out of the shot and danger of desire.
The chariest maid is prodigal enough
If she unmask her beauty to the moon.
Virtue itself scapes not calumnious strokes.
The canker[3] galls[4] the infants of the spring
Too oft before their buttons[5] be disclosed,
And in the morn and liquid dew of youth
Contagious blastments[6] are most imminent.
Be wary then; best safety lies in fear.
Youth to itself rebels, though none else near.

OPHELIA I shall the effect of this good lesson keep
As watchman to my heart, but, good my brother,
Do not as some ungracious pastors do,
Show me the steep and thorny way to heaven,
Whiles like a puffed and reckless libertine
Himself the primrose path of dalliance treads
And recks[7] not his own rede.[8]

(*Enter* POLONIUS.)

LAERTES O, fear me not.
I stay too long. But here my father comes.
A double blessing is a double grace;
Occasion smiles upon a second leave.

POLONIUS Yet here, Laertes? Aboard, aboard, for shame!
The wind sits in the shoulder of your sail,
And you are stayed for. There—my blessing with thee,
And these few precepts in thy memory
Look thou character.[9] Give thy thoughts no tongue,
Nor any unproportioned[1] thought his act.
Be thou familiar, but by no means vulgar.
Those friends thou hast, and their adoption tried,
Grapple them unto thy soul with hoops of steel,
But do not dull thy palm with entertainment

[1]credulous [2]feelings, which rashly lead forward into dangers [3]rose worm [4]injures [5]buds [6]blights [7]regards [8]counsel [9]inscribe [1]unadjusted to what is right

Of each new-hatched, unfledged courage.[2] Beware
Of entrance to a quarrel; but being in,
Bear't that th' opposèd may beware of thee.
Give every man thine ear, but few thy voice;
Take each man's censure,[3] but reserve thy judgment.
Costly thy habit as thy purse can buy,
But not expressed in fancy; rich, not gaudy,
For the apparel oft proclaims the man,
And they in France of the best rank and station
Are of a most select and generous chief[4] in that.
Neither a borrower nor a lender be,
For loan oft loses both itself and friend,
And borrowing dulleth edge of husbandry.[5]
This above all, to thine own self be true,
And it must follow as the night the day
Thou canst not then be false to any man.
Farewell. My blessing season[6] this in thee!

LAERTES Most humbly do I take my leave, my lord.

POLONIUS The time invites you. Go, your servants tend.[7]

LAERTES Farewell, Ophelia, and remember well
What I have said to you.

OPHELIA 'Tis in my memory locked,
And you yourself shall keep the key of it.

LAERTES Farewell.

(*Exit* LAERTES.)

POLONIUS What is't, Ophelia, he hath said to you?

OPHELIA So please you, something touching the Lord Hamlet.

POLONIUS Marry,[8] well bethought.
'Tis told me he hath very oft of late
Given private time to you, and you yourself
Have of your audience been most free and bounteous.
If it be so—as so 'tis put on me,
And that in way of caution—I must tell you
You do not understand yourself so clearly
As it behooves my daughter and your honor.
What is between you? Give me up the truth.

OPHELIA He hath, my lord, of late made many tenders[9]
Of his affection to me.

POLONIUS Affection? Pooh! You speak like a green girl,
Unsifted[1] in such perilous circumstance.
Do you believe his tenders, as you call them?

---

[2]man of spirit, young blood [3]judgment [4]eminence [5]thriftiness [6]ripen and make fruitful [7]wait [8]by Mary [9]offers [1]untested

OPHELIA I do not know, my lord, what I should think.
POLONIUS Marry, I will teach you. Think yourself a baby
That you have ta'en these tenders[2] for true pay
Which are not sterling. Tender yourself more dearly,
Or (not to crack the wind of[3] the poor phrase,
Running it thus) you'll tender me a fool.
OPHELIA My lord, he hath importuned me with love
In honorable fashion.
POLONIUS Ay, fashion you may call it. Go to, go to.[4]
OPHELIA And hath given countenance to his speech, my lord,
With almost all the holy vows of heaven.
POLONIUS Ay, springes[5] to catch woodcocks.[6] I do know,
When the blood burns, how prodigal the soul
Lends the tongue vows. These blazes, daughter,
Giving more light than heat, extinct in both
Even in their promise, as it is a-making,
You must not take for fire. From this time
Be something scanter of your maiden presence.
Set your entreatments[7] at a higher rate
Than a command to parley.[8] For Lord Hamlet,
Believe so much in him that he is young,
And with a larger tether may he walk
Than may be given you. In few, Ophelia,
Do not believe his vows, for they are brokers,[9]
Not of that dye which their investments[1] show,
But mere implorators of unholy suits,
Breathing like sanctified and pious bawds,
The better to beguile. This is for all:
I would not, in plain terms, from this time forth
Have you so slander[2] any moment[3] leisure
As to give words or talk with the Lord Hamlet.
Look to't, I charge you. Come your ways.
OPHELIA I shall obey, my lord.

(*Exeunt.*)

---

[2]tenders . . . Tender . . . tender: offers . . . hold in regard . . . present (a word play going through three meanings, the last use of the word yielding further complexity with its valid implications that she will show herself to him as a fool, will show him to the world as a fool, and may go so far as to present him with a baby, which would be a fool because "fool" was an Elizabethan term of endearment especially applicable to an infant as a "little innocent") [3]make wheeze like a horse driven too hard [4]go away, go on (expressing impatience) [5]snares [6]birds believed foolish [7]military negotiations for surrender [8]confer with a besieger [9]middlemen, panders [1]clothes [2]use disgracefully [3]momentary

Scene IV

The sentry-post.

(*Enter* HAMLET, HORATIO, *and* MARCELLUS.)

HAMLET The air bites shrewdly[4]; it is very cold.
HORATIO It is a nipping and an eager[5] air.
HAMLET What hour now?
HORATIO I think it lacks of twelve.
MARCELLUS No, it is struck.
HORATIO Indeed? I heard it not. It then draws near the season
Wherein the spirit held his wont to walk.

(*A flourish of trumpets, and two pieces go off.*)

What does this mean, my lord?
HAMLET The king doth wake to-night and takes his rouse,[6]
Keeps wassail, and the swaggering upspring[7] reels,
And as he drains his draughts of Rhenish[8] down
The kettledrum and trumpet thus bray out
The triumph[9] of his pledge.
HORATIO Is it a custom?
HAMLET Ay, marry, is't,
But to my mind, though I am native here
And to the manner born, it is a custom
More honored in the breach than the observance.[1]
This heavy-headed revel east and west
Makes us traduced and taxed of[2] other nations.
They clepe[3] us drunkards and with swinish phrase
Soil our addition,[4] and indeed it takes
From our achievements, though performed at height,
The pith and marrow of our attribute.[5]
So oft it chances in particular men
That (for some vicious mole[6] of nature in them,
As in their birth, wherein they are not guilty,
Since nature cannot choose his[7] origin)
By the o'ergrowth of some complexion,[8]
Oft breaking down the pales[9] and forts of reason,
Or by some habit that too much o'erleavens[1]
The form of plausive[2] manners—that (these men

---

[4]wickedly [5]sharp [6]carousel [7]a German dance [8]Rhine wine [9]achievement, feat (in downing a cup of wine at one draught) [1]better broken than observed [2]censured by [3]call [4]reputation, title added as a distinction [5]reputation, what is attributed [6]blemish, flaw [7]its [8]part of the make-up, combination of humors [9]barriers, fences [1]works change throughout, as yeast ferments dough [2]pleasing

Carrying, I say, the stamp of one defect,
Being nature's livery,[3] or fortune's star)[4]
Their virtues else, be they as pure as grace,
As infinite as man may undergo,
Shall in the general censure take corruption
From that particular fault. The dram of evil
Doth all the noble substance of a doubt,
To his own scandal.

(*Enter* GHOST.)

HORATIO Look, my lord, it comes.
HAMLET Angels and ministers of grace defend us!
Be thou a spirit of health[5] or goblin[6] damned,
Bring with thee airs from heaven or blasts from hell,
Be thy intents wicked or charitable,
Thou com'st in such a questionable shape
That I will speak to thee. I'll call thee Hamlet,
King, father, royal Dane. O, answer me!
Let me not burst in ignorance, but tell
Why thy canonized[7] bones, hearsèd in death,
Have burst their cerements,[8] why the sepulchre
Wherein we saw thee quietly interred
Hath oped his ponderous and marble jaws
To cast thee up again. What may this mean
That thou, dead corse, again in complete steel,
Revisits thus the glimpses of the moon,
Making night hideous, and we fools of nature[9]
So horridly to shake our disposition
With thoughts beyond the reaches of our souls?
Say, why is this? wherefore? what should we do?

(GHOST *beckons.*)

HORATIO It beckons you to go away with it,
As if it some impartment did desire
To you alone.
MARCELLUS Look with what courteous action
It waves you to a more removèd ground.
But do not go with it.

---

[3]characteristic equipment or provision [4]make-up as formed by stellar influence [5]sound, good [6]fiend [7]buried with the established rites of the Church [8]waxed gravecloths [9]men made conscious of natural limitations by a supernatural manifestation

HORATIO No, by no means.
HAMLET It will not speak. Then will I follow it.
HORATIO Do not, my lord.
HAMLET Why, what should be the fear?
I do not set my life at a pin's fee,
And for my soul, what can it do to that,
Being a thing immortal as itself?
It waves me forth again. I'll follow it.
HORATIO What if it tempt you toward the flood, my lord,
Or to the dreadful summit of the cliff
That beetles[1] o'er his base into the sea,
And there assume some other horrible form,
Which might deprive[2] your sovereignty of reason[3]
And draw you into madness? Think of it.
The very place puts toys[4] of desperation,
Without more motive, into every brain
That looks so many fathoms to the sea
And hears it roar beneath.
HAMLET It waves me still.
Go on. I'll follow thee.
MARCELLUS You shall not go, my lord.
HAMLET Hold off your hands.
HORATIO Be ruled. You shall not go.
HAMLET My fate cries out
And makes each petty artere[5] in this body
As hardy as the Nemean lion's[6] nerve.[7]
Still am I called. Unhand me, gentlemen.
By heaven, I'll make a ghost of him that lets[8] me!
I say, away! Go on. I'll follow thee.

(*Exit* GHOST, *and* HAMLET.)

HORATIO He waxes desperate with imagination.
MARCELLUS Let's follow. 'Tis not fit thus to obey him.
HORATIO Have after. To what issue will this come?
MARCELLUS Something is rotten in the state of Denmark.
HORATIO Heaven will direct it.
MARCELLUS Nay, let's follow him.

(*Exeunt.*)

---

[1]juts out [2]take away [3]state of being ruled by reason [4]fancies [5]artery [6]a lion slain by Hercules in the performance of one of his twelve labors [7]sinew [8]hinders

Scene V

Another part of the fortifications.

(*Enter* GHOST *and* HAMLET.)

HAMLET Whither wilt thou lead me? Speak. I'll go no further.
GHOST Mark me.
HAMLET I will.
GHOST My hour is almost come,
When I to sulph'rous and tormenting flames[9]
Must render up myself.
HAMLET Alas, poor ghost!
GHOST Pity me not, but lend thy serious hearing
To what I shall unfold.
HAMLET Speak. I am bound to hear.
GHOST So art thou to revenge, when thou shalt hear.
HAMLET What?
GHOST I am thy father's spirit,
Doomed for a certain term to walk the night,
And for the day confined to fast[1] in fires,
Till the foul crimes done in my days of nature
Are burnt and purged away. But that I am forbid
To tell the secrets of my prison house,
I could a tale unfold whose lightest word
Would harrow up thy soul, freeze thy young blood,
Make thy two eyes like stars start from their spheres,[2]
Thy knotted and combinèd locks to part,
And each particular hair to stand an[3] end
Like quills upon the fretful porpentine.[4]
But this eternal blazon[5] must not be
To ears of flesh and blood. List, list, O, list!
If thou didst ever thy dear father love—
HAMLET O God!
GHOST Revenge his foul and most unnatural murder.
HAMLET Murder?
GHOST Murder most foul, as in the best it is,
But this most foul, strange, and unnatural.
HAMLET Haste me to know't, that I, with wings as swift
As meditation[6] or the thoughts of love,
May sweep to my revenge.

[9]sufferings in purgatory (not hell) [1]do penance [2]transparent revolving shells in each of which, according to the Ptolemaic astronomy, a planet or other heavenly body was placed [3]on [4]porcupine [5]revelation of eternity [6]thought

GHOST I find thee apt,
And duller shouldst thou be than the fat weed
That roots itself in ease on Lethe[7] wharf,
Wouldst thou not stir in this. Now, Hamlet, hear.
'Tis given out that, sleeping in my orchard,
A serpent stung me. So the whole ear of Denmark
Is by a forgèd process[8] of my death
Rankly abused. But know, thou noble youth,
The serpent that did sting thy father's life
Now wears his crown.

HAMLET O my prophetic soul!
My uncle?

GHOST Ah, that incestuous, that adulterate[9] beast,
With witchcraft of his wit, with traitorous gifts—
O wicked wit and gifts, that have the power
So to seduce!—won to this shameful lust
The will of my most seeming-virtuous queen.
O Hamlet, what a falling-off was there,
From me, whose love was of that dignity
That it went hand in hand even with the vow
I made to her in marriage, and to decline
Upon a wretch whose natural gifts were poor
To those of mine!
But virtue, as it never will be moved,
Though lewdness court it in a shape of heaven,[1]
So lust, though to a radiant angel linked,
Will sate itself in a celestial bed
And prey on garbage.
But soft, methinks I scent the morning air.
Brief let me be. Sleeping within my orchard,
My custom always of the afternoon,
Upon my secure[2] hour thy uncle stole
With juice of cursed hebona[3] in a vial,
And in the porches of my ears did pour
The leperous distilment, whose effect
Holds such an enmity with blood of man
That swift as quicksilver it courses through
The natural gates and alleys of the body,
And with a sudden vigor it doth posset[4]
And curd, like eager[5] droppings into milk,

---

[7]the river in Hades which brings forgetfulness of past life to a spirit who drinks of it [8]falsified official report [9]adulterous [1]angelic disguise [2]carefree, unsuspecting [3]some poisonous plant [4]curdle [5]sour

The thin and wholesome blood. So did it mine,
And a most instant tetter[6] barked[7] about
Most lazar-like[8] with vile and loathsome crust
All my smooth body.
Thus was I sleeping by a brother's hand
Of life, of crown, of queen at once dispatched,
Cut off even in the blossoms of my sin,
Unhouseled,[9] disappointed,[1] unaneled,[2]
No reck'ning made, but sent to my account
With all my imperfections on my head.
O, horrible! O, horrible! most horrible!
If thou hast nature in thee, bear it not.
Let not the royal bed of Denmark be
A couch for luxury[3] and damnèd incest.
But howsomever thou pursues this act,
Taint not thy mind, nor let thy soul contrive
Against thy mother aught. Leave her to heaven
And to those thorns that in her bosom lodge
To prick and sting her. Fare thee well at once.
The glowworm shows the matin[4] to be near
And gins to pale his uneffectual fire.
Adieu, adieu, adieu. Remember me.

(*Exit.*)

HAMLET O all you host of heaven! O earth! What else?
And shall I couple hell? O fie! Hold, hold, my heart,
And you, my sinews, grow not instant old,
But bear me stiffly up. Remember thee?
Ay, thou poor ghost, while memory holds a seat
In this distracted globe.[5] Remember thee?
Yea, from the table[6] of my memory
I'll wipe away all trivial fond records,
All saws[7] of books, all forms,[8] all pressures[9] past
That youth and observation copied there,
And thy commandment all alone shall live
Within the book and volume of my brain,
Unmixed with baser matter. Yes, by heaven!
O most pernicious woman!
O villain, villain, smiling, damnèd villain!

---

[6]eruption [7]covered as with a bark [8]leper-like [9]without the Sacrament [1]unprepared spiritually [2]without extreme unction [3]lust [4]morning [5]head [6]writing tablet, record book [7]wise sayings [8]mental images, concepts [9]impressions

My tables—meet it is I set it down
That one may smile, and smile, and be a villain.
At least I am sure it may be so in Denmark.

(*writes*)

So, uncle, there you are. Now to my word:
It is "Adieu, adieu, remember me."
I have sworn't.

(*Enter* HORATIO *and* MARCELLUS.)

HORATIO My lord, my lord!
MARCELLUS Lord Hamlet!
HORATIO Heavens secure him!
HAMLET So be it!
MARCELLUS Illo, ho, ho,[1] my lord!
HAMLET Hillo, ho, ho, boy! Come, bird, come.
MARCELLUS How is't, my noble lord?
HORATIO What news, my lord?
HAMLET O, wonderful!
HORATIO Good my lord, tell it.
HAMLET No, you will reveal it.
HORATIO Not I, my lord, by heaven.
MARCELLUS Nor I, my lord.
HAMLET How say you then? Would heart of man once think it?
But you'll be secret?
BOTH Ay, by heaven, my lord.
HAMLET There's never a villain dwelling in all Denmark
But he's an arrant knave.
HORATIO There needs no ghost, my lord, come from the grave
To tell us this.
HAMLET Why, right, you are in the right,
And so, without more circumstance[2] at all,
I hold it fit that we shake hands and part:
You, as your business and desires shall point you,
For every man hath business and desire
Such as it is, and for my own poor part,
Look you, I'll go pray.
HORATIO These are but wild and whirling words, my lord.
HAMLET I am sorry they offend you, heartily;
Yes, faith, heartily.
HORATIO There's no offense, my lord.

[1]cry of the falconer to summon his hawk [2]ceremony

HAMLET Yes, by Saint Patrick, but there is, Horatio,
And much offense too. Touching this vision here,
It is an honest[3] ghost, that let me tell you.
For your desire to know what is between us,
O'ermaster't as you may. And now, good friends,
As you are friends, scholars, and soldiers,
Give me one poor request.
HORATIO What is't, my lord? We will.
HAMLET Never make known what you have seen to-night.
BOTH My lord, we will not.
HAMLET Nay, but swear't.
HORATIO In faith,
My lord, not I.
MARCELLUS Nor I, my lord—in faith.
HAMLET Upon my sword.[4]
MARCELLUS We have sworn, my lord, already.
HAMLET Indeed, upon my sword, indeed.

(GHOST *cries under the stage.*)

GHOST Swear.
HAMLET Ha, ha, boy, say'st thou so? Art thou there, truepenny?[5]
Come on. You hear this fellow in the cellarage.
Consent to swear.
HORATIO Propose the oath, my lord.
HAMLET Never to speak of this that you have seen,
Swear by my sword.
GHOST (*beneath*) Swear.
HAMLET Hic et ubique?[6] Then we'll shift our ground.
Come hither, gentlemen,
And lay your hands again upon my sword.
Swear by my sword
Never to speak of this that you have heard.
GHOST (*beneath*) Swear by his sword.
HAMLET Well said, old mole! Canst work i' th' earth so fast?
A worthy pioner![7] Once more remove, good friends.
HORATIO O day and night, but this is wondrous strange!
HAMLET And therefore as a stranger give it welcome.
There are more things in heaven and earth, Horatio,
Than are dreamt of in your philosophy.[8]
But come:
Here as before, never, so help you mercy,

[3]genuine (not a disguised demon) [4]the cross formed by the sword hilt [5]honest old fellow [6]here and everywhere [7]pioneer, miner [8]this philosophy one hears about

How strange or odd some'er I bear myself
(As I perchance hereafter shall think meet
To put an antic[9] disposition on),
That you, at such times seeing me, never shall,
With arms encumb'red[1] thus, or this head-shake,
Or by pronouncing of some doubtful phrase,
As "Well, well, we know," or "We could, an if[2] we would,"
Or "If we list to speak," or "There be, an if they might,"
Or such ambiguous giving out, to note
That you know aught of me—this do swear,
So grace and mercy at your most need help you.

GHOST (*beneath*) Swear.

(*They swear.*)

HAMLET Rest, rest, perturbèd spirit! So, gentlemen,
With all my love I do commend[3] me to you,
And what so poor a man as Hamlet is
May do t' express his love and friending to you,
God willing, shall not lack. Let us go in together,
And still[4] your fingers on your lips, I pray.
The time is out of joint. O cursèd spite
That ever I was born to set it right!
Nay, come, let's go together.

(*Exeunt.*)

Act II

Scene I

The chambers of POLONIUS.

(*Enter old* POLONIUS, *with his man* [REYNALDO].)

POLONIUS Give him this money and these notes, Reynaldo.

REYNALDO I will, my lord.

POLONIUS You shall do marvellous wisely, good Reynaldo,
Before you visit him, to make inquire
Of his behavior.

REYNALDO My lord, I did intend it.

POLONIUS Marry, well said, very well said. Look you, sir,
Enquire me first what Danskers[5] are in Paris,

---

[9]grotesque, mad [1]folded [2]if [3]entrust [4]always [5]Danes

And how, and who, what means,[6] and where they keep,[7]
What company, at what expense; and finding
By this encompassment[8] and drift of question
That they do know my son, come you more nearer
Than your particular demands[9] will touch it.
Take you as 'twere some distant knowledge of him,
As thus, "I know his father and his friends,
And in part him"—do you mark this, Reynaldo?
REYNALDO Ay, very well, my lord.
POLONIUS "And in part him, but," you may say, "not well,
But if't be he I mean, he's very wild
Addicted so and so." And there put on him
What forgeries[1] you please; marry, none so rank
As may dishonor him—take heed of that—
But, sir, such wanton, wild, and usual slips
As are companions noted and most known
To youth and liberty.
REYNALDO As gaming, my lord.
POLONIUS Ay, or drinking, fencing, swearing, quarrelling,
Drabbing.[2] You may go so far.
REYNALDO My lord, that would dishonor him.
POLONIUS Faith, no, as you may season[3] it in the charge.
You must not put another scandal on him,
That he is open to incontinency.[4]
That's not my meaning. But breathe his faults so quaintly[5]
That they may seem the taints of liberty,
The flash and outbreak of a fiery mind,
A savageness in unreclaimèd[6] blood,
Of general assault.[7]
REYNALDO But, my good lord—
POLONIUS Wherefore should you do this?
REYNALDO Ay, my lord,
I would know that.
POLONIUS Marry, sir, here's my drift,
And I believe it is a fetch of warrant.[8]
You laying these slight sullies on my son
As 'twere a thing a little soiled i' th' working,
Mark you,
Your party in converse, him you would sound,
Having ever[9] seen in the prenominate[1] crimes

[6]what their wealth [7]dwell [8]circling about [9]definite questions [1]invented wrongdoings [2]whoring [3]soften [4]extreme sensuality [5]expertly, gracefully [6]untamed [7]assailing all young men [8]allowable trick [9]if he has ever [1]aforementioned

The youth you breathe of guilty, be assured
He closes with you[2] in this consequence:[3]
"Good sir," or so, or "friend," or "gentleman"—
According to the phrase or the addition[4]
Of man and country—

REYNALDO Very good, my lord.

POLONIUS And then, sir, does 'a this—'a does—
What was I about to say? By the mass, I was about to say something! Where did I leave?

REYNALDO At "closes in the consequence," at "friend or so," and "gentleman."

POLONIUS At "closes in the consequence"—Ay, marry!
He closes thus: "I know the gentleman;
I saw him yesterday, or t' other day,
Or then, or then, with such or such, and, as you say,
There was 'a gaming, there o'ertook[5] in's rouse,[6]
There falling out[7] "at tennis"; or perchance,
"I saw him enter such a house of sale,"
Videlicet,[8] a brothel, or so forth.
See you now—
Your bait of falsehood takes this carp of truth,
And thus do we of wisdom and of reach,[9]
With windlasses[1] and with assays of bias,[2]
By indirections find directions[3] out.
So, by my former lecture and advice,
Shall you my son. You have me, have you not?

REYNALDO My lord, I have.

POLONIUS God bye ye,[4] fare ye well.

REYNALDO Good my lord.

POLONIUS Observe his inclination in yourself.

REYNALDO I shall, my lord.

POLONIUS And let him ply his music.

REYNALDO Well, my lord.

POLONIUS Farewell.

(*Exit* REYNALDO.)

(*Enter* OPHELIA.)

How now, Ophelia, what's the matter?

OPHELIA O my lord, my lord, I have been so affrighted!

POLONIUS With what, i' th' name of God?

---

[2]follows your lead to a conclusion [3]following way [4]title [5]overcome with drunkenness [6]carousal [7]quarreling [8]namely [9]far-reaching comprehension [1]roundabout courses [2]devious attacks [3]ways of procedure [4]God be with you, good-bye

OPHELIA My lord, as I was sewing in my closet,[5]
Lord Hamlet, with his doublet[6] all unbraced,[7]
No hat upon his head, his stockings fouled,
Ungartered, and down-gyvèd[8] to his ankle,
Pale as his shirt, his knees knocking each other,
And with a look so piteous in purport
As if he had been loosèd out of hell
To speak of horrors—he comes before me.
POLONIUS Mad for thy love?
OPHELIA My lord, I do not know,
But truly I do fear it.
POLONIUS What said he?
OPHELIA He took me by the wrist and held me hard.
Then goes he to the length of all his arm,
And with his other hand thus o'er his brow
He falls to such perusal of my face
As 'a would draw it. Long stayed he so.
At last, a little shaking of mine arm
And thrice his head thus waving up and down,
He raised a sigh so piteous and profound
As it did seem to shatter all his bulk
And end his being. That done, he lets me go,
And with his head over his shoulder turned
He seemed to find his way without his eyes,
For out o' doors he went without their helps
And to the last bended their light on me.
POLONIUS Come, go with me. I will go seek the king.
This is the very ecstasy[9] of love,
Whose violent property[1] fordoes[2] itself
And leads the will to desperate undertakings
As oft as any passion under heaven
That does afflict our natures. I am sorry.
What, have you given him any hard words of late?
OPHELIA No, my good lord; but as you did command
I did repel his letters and denied
His access to me.
POLONIUS That hath made him mad.
I am sorry that with better heed and judgment
I had not quoted[3] him. I feared he did but trifle
And meant to wrack thee; but beshrew[4] my jealousy.
By heaven, it is as proper to our age

[5]private living-room [6]jacket [7]unlaced [8]fallen down like gyves or fetters on a prisoner's legs
[9]madness [1]quality [2]destroys [3]observed [4]curse

To cast beyond ourselves[5] in our opinions
As it is common for the younger sort
To lack discretion. Come, go we to the king.
This must be known, which, being kept close,[6] might move[7]
More grief to hide than hate to utter love.[8]
Come.

(*Exeunt.*)

Scene II

A chamber in the castle.

(*Flourish. Enter* KING *and* QUEEN, ROSENCRANTZ, *and* GUILDENSTERN [*with others*].)

KING Welcome, dear Rosencrantz and Guildenstern.
Moreover that[9] we much did long to see you,
The need we have to use you did provoke
Our hasty sending. Something have you heard
Of Hamlet's transformation—so call it,
Sith[1] nor th' exterior nor the inward man
Resembles that it was. What it should be,
More than his father's death, that thus hath put him
So much from th' understanding of himself,
I cannot dream of. I entreat you both
That, being of so young days brought up with him,
And sith so neighbored to his youth and havior,[2]
That you vouchsafe your rest here in our court
Some little time, so by your companies
To draw him on to pleasures, and to gather
So much as from occasion you may glean,
Whether aught to us unknown afflicts him thus,
That opened[3] lies within our remedy.

QUEEN Good gentlemen, he hath much talked of you,
And sure I am two men there are not living
To whom he more adheres.[4] If it will please you
To show us so much gentry[5] and good will
As to expend your time with us awhile
For the supply and profit of our hope,

---

[5]find by calculation more significance in something than we ought to [6]secret [7]cause [8]by such hiding of love than there would be hate moved by a revelation of it (a violently condensed putting of the case which is a triumph of special statement for Polonius) [9]besides the fact that [1]since [2]youthful ways of life [3]revealed [4]is more attached [5]courtesy

Your visitation shall receive such thanks
As fits a king's remembrance.

ROSENCRANTZ Both your majesties
Might, by the sovereign power you have of us,
Put your dread pleasures more into command
Than to entreaty.

GUILDENSTERN But we both obey,
And here give up ourselves in the full bent[6]
To lay our service freely at your feet,
To be commanded.

KING Thanks, Rosencrantz and gentle Guildenstern.

QUEEN Thanks, Guildenstern and gentle Rosencrantz.
And I beseech you instantly to visit
My too much changèd son.—Go, some of you,
And bring these gentlemen where Hamlet is.

GUILDENSTERN Heavens make our presence and our practices
Pleasant and helpful to him!

QUEEN Ay, amen!

(*Exeunt* ROSENCRANTZ *and* GUILDENSTERN [*with some* ATTENDANTS].)

(*Enter* POLONIUS.)

POLONIUS Th' ambassadors from Norway, my good lord,
Are joyfully returned.

KING Thou still[7] hast been the father of good news.

POLONIUS Have I, my lord? Assure you, my good liege,
I hold my duty as I hold my soul,
Both to my God and to my gracious king,
And I do think—or else this brain of mine
Hunts not the trail of policy so sure
As it hath used to do—that I have found
The very cause of Hamlet's lunacy.

KING O, speak of that! That do I long to hear.

POLONIUS Give first admittance to th' ambassadors.
My news shall be the fruit[8] to that great feast.

KING Thyself do grace[9] to them and bring them in.

(*Exit* POLONIUS.)

He tells me, my dear Gertrude, he hath found
The head and source of all your son's distemper.

QUEEN I doubt[1] it is no other but the main,
His father's death and our o'erhasty marriage.

---

[6]at the limit of bending (of a bow), to full capacity [7]always [8]dessert [9]honor [1]suspect

KING Well, we shall sift him.

(*Enter* AMBASSADORS [VOLTEMAND *and* CORNELIUS, *with* POLONIUS].)

Welcome, my good friends.
Say, Voltemand, what from our brother Norway?
VOLTEMAND Most fair return of greetings and desires.
Upon our first,[2] he sent out to suppress
His nephew's levies, which to him appeared
To be a preparation 'gainst the Polack,
But better looked into, he truly found
It was against your highness, whereat grieved,
That so his sickness, age, and impotence
Was falsely borne in hand,[3] sends out arrests
On Fortinbras; which he in brief obeys
Receives rebuke from Norway, and in fine[4]
Makes vow before his uncle never more
To give th' assay[5] of arms against your majesty.
Whereon old Norway, overcome with joy,
Gives him threescore thousand crowns in annual fee
And his commission to employ those soldiers,
So levied as before, against the Polack,
With an entreaty, herein further shown,

(*gives a paper*)

That it might please you to give quiet pass
Through your dominions for this enterprise,
On such regards[6] of safety and allowance
As therein are set down.
KING It likes us well;
And at our more considered time[7] we'll read,
Answer, and think upon this business.
Meantime we thank you for your well-took labor.
Go to your rest; at night we'll feast together.
Most welcome home!

(*Exeunt* AMBASSADORS.)

POLONIUS This business is well ended.
My liege and madam, to expostulate[8]
What majesty should be, what duty is,
Why day is day, night night, and time is time,

---

[2]our first words about the matter [3]deceived [4]in the end [5]trial [6]terms [7]convenient time for consideration [8]discuss

Were nothing but to waste night, day, and time.
Therefore, since brevity is the soul of wit,[9]
And tediousness the limbs and outward flourishes,
I will be brief. Your noble son is mad.
Mad call I it, for, to define true madness,
What is't but to be nothing else but mad?
But let that go.

QUEEN More matter, with less art.

POLONIUS Madam, I swear I use no art at all.
That he is mad, 'tis true: 'tis true 'tis pity,
And pity 'tis 'tis true—a foolish figure.[1]
But farewell it, for I will use no art.
Mad let us grant him then, and now remains
That we find out the cause of this effect—
Or rather say, the cause of this defect,
For this effect defective comes by cause.
Thus it remains, and the remainder thus.
Perpend.[2]
I have a daughter (have while she is mine),
Who in her duty and obedience, mark,
Hath given me this. Now gather, and surmise.

(*reads the letter*)

"To the celestial, and my soul's idol, the most beautified Ophelia,"—
That's an ill phrase, a vile phrase; "beautified" is a vile phrase. But you shall hear. Thus:

(*reads*)

"In her excellent white bosom, these, &c."

QUEEN Came this from Hamlet to her?

POLONIUS Good madam, stay awhile. I will be faithful.

(*reads*)

"Doubt thou the stars are fire;
Doubt that the sun doth move;
Doubt[3] truth to be a liar;
But never doubt I love.

O dear Ophelia, I am ill at these numbers.[4] I have not art to reckon my groans, but that I love thee best, O most best, believe it.

[9]understanding [1]figure in rhetoric [2]ponder [3]suspect [4]verses

Adieu.
Thine evermore, most dear lady,
whilst this machine[5] is to[6] him, Hamlet."

This in obedience hath my daughter shown me,
And more above[7] hath his solicitings,
As they fell out by time, by means, and place,
All given to mine ear.

KING But how hath she
Received his love?

POLONIUS What do you think of me?

KING As of a man faithful and honorable.

POLONIUS I would fain prove so. But what might you think,
When I had seen this hot love on the wing
(As I perceived it, I must tell you that,
Before my daughter told me), what might you,
Or my dear majesty your queen here, think,
If I had played the desk or table book,[8]
Or given my heart a winking,[9] mute and dumb,
Or looked upon this love with idle sight?
What might you think? No, I went round[1] to work
And my young mistress thus I did bespeak:
"Lord Hamlet is a prince, out of thy star.[2]
This must not be." And then I prescripts[3] gave her,
That she should lock herself from his resort,
Admit no messengers, receive no tokens.
Which done, she took the fruits of my advice,
And he, repellèd, a short tale to make,
Fell into a sadness, then into a fast,
Thence to a watch,[4] thence into a weakness,
Thence to a lightness,[5] and, by this declension,
Into the madness wherein now he raves,
And all we mourn for.

KING Do you think 'tis this?

QUEEN It may be, very like.

POLONIUS Hath there been such a time—I would fain know that—
That I have positively said "'Tis so,"
When it proved otherwise?

KING Not that I know.

POLONIUS (*pointing to his head and shoulder*)
Take this from this, if this be otherwise.

---

[5]body [6]attached to [7]besides [8]silent receiver [9]closing of the eyes [1]roundly, plainly [2]condition determined by stellar influence [3]instructions [4]sleepless state [5]lightheadedness

If circumstances lead me, I will find
Where truth is hid, though it were hid indeed
Within the center.[6]

KING How may we try it further?

POLONIUS You know sometimes he walks four hours together
Here in the lobby.

QUEEN So he does indeed.

POLONIUS At such a time I'll loose my daughter to him.
Be you and I behind an arras[7] then.
Mark the encounter. If he love her not,
And be not from his reason fallen thereon,[8]
Let me be no assistant for a state
But keep a farm and carters.

KING We will try it.

(*Enter* HAMLET [*reading on a book*].)

QUEEN But look where sadly the poor wretch comes reading.

POLONIUS Away, I do beseech you both, away.

(*Exit* KING *and* QUEEN [*with* ATTENDANTS].)

I'll board[9] him presently.[1] O, give me leave.
How does my good Lord Hamlet?

HAMLET Well, God-a-mercy.[2]

POLONIUS Do you know me, my lord?

HAMLET Excellent well. You are a fishmonger.[3]

POLONIUS Not I, my lord.

HAMLET Then I would you were so honest a man.

POLONIUS Honest, my lord?

HAMLET Ay, sir. To be honest, as this world goes, is to be one man picked out of ten thousand.

POLONIUS That's very true, my lord.

HAMLET For if the sun breed maggots in a dead dog, being a good kissing carrion[4]—Have you a daughter?

POLONIUS I have, my lord.

HAMLET Let her not walk i' th' sun. Conception is a blessing, but as your daughter may conceive, friend, look to't.

POLONIUS (*aside*) How say you by that? Still harping on my daughter. Yet he knew me not at first. 'A said I was a fishmonger. 'A is far gone, far gone. And truly in my youth I suffered much extremity for love, very near this. I'll speak to him again.—What do you read, my lord?

[6]center of the earth and also of the Ptolemaic universe [7]hanging tapestry [8]on that account [9]accost [1]at once [2]thank you (literally, "God have mercy!") [3]seller of harlots, procurer (a cant term used here with a glance at the fishing Polonius is doing when he offers Ophelia as bait) [4]good bit of flesh for kissing

HAMLET Words, words, words.

POLONIUS What is the matter, my lord?

HAMLET Between who?[5]

POLONIUS I mean the matter that you read, my lord.

HAMLET Slanders, sir, for the satirical rogue says here that old men have grey beards, that their faces are wrinkled, their eyes purging thick amber and plum-tree gum, and that they have a plentiful lack of wit, together with most weak hams. All which, sir, though I most powerfully and potently believe, yet I hold it not honesty to have it thus set down, for you yourself, sir, should be old as I am if, like a crab, you could go backward.

POLONIUS (*aside*) Though this be madness, yet there is method in't.—Will you walk out of the air, my lord?

HAMLET Into my grave?

POLONIUS Indeed, that's out of the air. (*aside*) How pregnant[6] sometimes his replies are! a happiness[7] that often madness hits on, which reason and sanity could not so prosperously be delivered of. I will leave him and suddenly contrive the means of meeting between him and my daughter.—My honorable lord, I will most humbly take my leave of you.

HAMLET You cannot, sir, take from me anything that I will more willingly part withal[8]—except my life, except my life, except my life.

(*Enter* GUILDENSTERN *and* ROSENCRANTZ.)

POLONIUS Fare you well, my lord.

HAMLET These tedious old fools!

POLONIUS You go to seek the Lord Hamlet. There he is.

ROSENCRANTZ (*to* POLONIUS) God save you, sir!

(*Exit* POLONIUS.)

GUILDENSTERN My honored lord!

ROSENCRANTZ My most dear lord!

HAMLET My excellent good friends! How dost thou, Guildenstern?
Ah, Rosencrantz! Good lads, how do ye both?

ROSENCRANTZ As the indifferent[9] children of the earth.

GUILDENSTERN Happy in that we are not over-happy.
On Fortune's cap we are not the very button.

HAMLET Nor the soles of her shoe?

ROSENCRANTZ Neither, my lord.

HAMLET Then you live about her waist, or in the middle of her favors?

GUILDENSTERN Faith, her privates[1] we.

HAMLET In the secret parts of Fortune? O, most true! she is a strumpet. What news?

---

[5]matter for a quarrel between what persons (Hamlet's willful misunderstanding) [6]full of meaning [7]aptness of expression [8]with [9]average [1]ordinary men in private, not public, life (with obvious play upon the sexual term "private parts")

ROSENCRANTZ None, my lord, but that the world's grown honest.

HAMLET Then is doomsday near. But your news is not true. (Let me question more in particular.) What have you, my good friends, deserved at the hands of Fortune that she sends you to prison hither?

GUILDENSTERN Prison, my lord?

HAMLET Denmark's a prison.

ROSENCRANTZ Then is the world one.

HAMLET A goodly one; in which there are many confines,[2] wards,[3] and dungeons, Denmark being one o' th' worst.

ROSENCRANTZ We think not so, my lord.

HAMLET Why, then 'tis none to you, for there is nothing either good or bad but drinking makes it so. To me it is a prison.

ROSENCRANTZ Why, then your ambition makes it one. 'Tis too narrow for your mind.

HAMLET O God, I could be hounded in a nutshell and count myself a king of infinite space, were it not that I have bad dreams.

GUILDENSTERN Which dreams indeed are ambition, for the very substance of the ambitious is merely the shadow of a dream.

HAMLET A dream itself is but a shadow.

ROSENCRANTZ Truly, and I hold ambition of so airy and light a quality that it is but a shadow's shadow.

HAMLET Then are our beggars bodies,[4] and our monarchs and outstretched[5] heroes the beggars' shadows. Shall we to th' court? for, by my fay,[6] I cannot reason.

BOTH We'll wait upon[7] you.

HAMLET No such matter. I will not sort you with the rest of my servants, for, to speak to you like an honest man, I am most dreadfully attended. But in the beaten way of friendship, what make[8] you at Elsinore?

ROSENCRANTZ To visit you, my lord; no other occasion.

HAMLET Beggar that I am, I am even poor in thanks, but I thank you; and sure, dear friends, my thanks are too dear a halfpenny.[9] Were you not sent for? Is it your own inclining? Is it a free visitation? Come, come, deal justly with me. Come, come. Nay, speak.

GUILDENSTERN What should we say, my lord?

HAMLET Why, anything—but to th' purpose. You were sent for, and there is a kind of confession in your looks, which your modesties have not craft enough to color. I know the good king and queen have sent for you.

ROSENCRANTZ To what end, my lord?

HAMLET That you must teach me. But let me conjure you by the rights of our fellowship, by the consonancy[1] of our youth, by the obligation of our ever-

[2]places of imprisonment [3]cells [4]solid substances, not shadows (because beggars lack ambition) [5]elongated as shadows (with a corollary implication of far-reaching with respect to the ambitions that make both heroes and monarchs into shadows) [6]faith [7]attend [8]do [9]at a halfpenny [1]accord (in sameness of age)

preserved love, and by what more dear a better proposer[2] can charge you withal,[3] be even[4] and direct with me whether you were sent for or no.

ROSENCRANTZ (*aside to* GUILDENSTERN) What say you?

HAMLET (*aside*) Nay then, I have an eye of you.—If you love me, hold not off.

GUILDENSTERN My lord, we were sent for.

HAMLET I will tell you why. So shall my anticipation prevent[5] your discovery,[6] and your secrecy to the king and queen moult no feather.[7] I have of late—but wherefore I know not—lost all my mirth, forgone all custom of exercises; and indeed, it goes so heavily with my disposition that this goodly frame the earth seems to me a sterile promontory; this most excellent canopy, the air, look you, this brave o'erhanging firmament,[8] this majestical roof fretted[9] with golden fire—why, it appeareth nothing to me but a foul and pestilent congregation of vapors. What a piece of work is a man, how noble in reason, how infinite in faculties; in form and moving how express[1] and admirable, in action how like an angel, in apprehension how like a god: the beauty of the world, the paragon of animals! And yet to me what is this quintessence[2] of dust? Man delights not me—nor woman neither, though by your smiling you seem to say so.

ROSENCRANTZ My lord, there was no such stuff in my thoughts.

HAMLET Why did ye laugh then, when I said "Man delights not me"?

ROSENCRANTZ To think, my lord, if you delight not in man, what lenten[3] entertainment the players shall receive from you. We coted[4] them on the way, and hither are they coming to offer you service.

HAMLET He that plays the king shall be welcome—his majesty shall have tribute of me—, the adventurous knight shall use his foil and target,[5] the lover shall not sigh gratis, the humorous man[6] shall end his part in peace, the clown shall make those laugh whose lungs are tickle o' th' sere,[7] and the lady shall say her mind freely, or the blank verse shall halt[8] for't. What players are they?

ROSENCRANTZ Even those you were wont to take such delight in, the tragedians of the city.

HAMLET How chances it they travel? Their residence,[9] both in reputation and profit, was better both ways.

ROSENCRANTZ I think their inhibition[1] comes by the means of the late innovation.[2]

HAMLET Do they hold the same estimation they did when I was in the city? Are they so followed?

ROSENCRANTZ No indeed, are they not.

---

[2]propounder [3]with [4]straight [5]forestall [6]disclosure [7]be left whole [8]sky [9]decorated with fretwork [1]well framed [2]fifth or last and finest essence (an alchemical term) [3]scanty [4]overtook [5]sword and shield [6]eccentric character dominated by one of the humours [7]hair-triggered for the discharge of laughter ("sere": part of a gunlock) [8]go lame [9]residing at the capital [1]impediment to acting in residence (formal prohibition?) [2]new fashion of having companies of boy actors play on the "private" stage (?), political upheaval (?)

HAMLET How comes it? Do they grow rusty?

ROSENCRANTZ Nay, their endeavor keeps in the wonted pace, but there is, sir, an eyrie[3] of children, little eyases,[4] that cry out on the top of question[5] and are most tyranically clapped for't. These are now the fashion, and so beratle[6] the common stages[7] (so they call them) that many wearing rapiers are afraid of goose-quills[8] and dare scarce come thither.

HAMLET What, are they children? Who maintains 'em? How are they escoted?[9] Will they pursue the quality[1] no longer than they can sing?[2] Will they not say afterwards, if they should grow themselves to common players (as it is most like, if their means are no better), their writers do them wrong to make them exclaim against their own succession?

ROSENCRANTZ Faith, there has been much to do on both sides, and the nation holds it no sin to tarre[3] them to controversy. There was, for a while, no money bid for argument[4] unless the poet and the player went to cuffs in the question.

HAMLET Is't possible?

GUILDENSTERN O, there has been much throwing about of brains.

HAMLET Do the boys carry it away?

ROSENCRANTZ Ay, that they do, my lord—Hercules and his load[5] too.

HAMLET It is not very strange, for my uncle is King of Denmark, and those that would make mows[6] at him while my father lived give twenty, forty, fifty, a hundred ducats apiece for his picture in little. 'Sblood,[7] there is something in this more than natural, if philosophy could find it out.

(*a flourish*)

GUILDENSTERN There are the players.

HAMLET Gentlemen, you are welcome to Elsinore. Your hands, come then. Th' appurtenance of welcome is fashion and ceremony. Let me comply with you in this garb,[8] lest my extent[9] to the players (which I tell you must show fairly outwards) should more appear like entertainment than yours. You are welcome. But my uncle-father and aunt-mother are deceived.

GUILDENSTERN In what, my dear lord?

HAMLET I am but mad north-north-west. When the wind is southerly I know a hawk from a handsaw.[1]

---

[3]nest [4]nestling hawks [5]above others on matter of dispute [6]berate [7]"public" theatres of the "common" players, who were organized in companies mainly composed of adult actors (allusion being made to the "War of the Theatres" in Shakespeare's London) [8]pens (of satirists who made out that the London public stage showed low taste) [9]supported [1]profession of acting [2]with unchanged voices [3]incite [4]matter of a play [5]the whole world (with a topical reference to the sign of the Globe Theatre, a representation of Hercules bearing the world on his shoulders) [6]grimaces [7]by God's blood [8]fashion [9]showing of welcome [1]*hawk* mattock or pickaxe (also called "hack"; here used apparently with a play on "hawk": a bird); *handsaw* carpenter's tool (apparently with a play on some corrupt form of "hernshaw"; heron, a bird often hunted with the hawk)

(*Enter* POLONIUS.)

POLONIUS Well be with you, gentlemen.

HAMLET Hark you, Guildenstern—and you too—at each ear a hearer. That great baby you see there is not yet out of his swaddling clouts.[2]

ROSENCRANTZ Happily[3] he is the second time come to them, for they say an old man is twice a child.

HAMLET I will prophesy he comes to tell me of the players. Mark it.—You say right, sir; a Monday morning, 'twas then indeed.

POLONIUS My lord, I have news to tell you.

HAMLET My lord, I have news to tell you. When Roscius[4] was an actor in Rome—

POLONIUS The actors are come hither, my lord.

HAMLET Buzz, buzz.

POLONIUS Upon my honor—

HAMLET Then came each actor on his ass—

POLONIUS The best actors in the world, either for tragedy, comedy, history, pastoral, pastoral-comical, historical-pastoral, tragical-historical, tragical-comical-historical-pastoral; scene individable,[5] or poem unlimited.[6] Seneca[7] cannot be too heavy, nor Plautus[8] too light. For the law of writ[9] and the liberty,[1] these are the only men.

HAMLET O Jephthah,[2] judge of Israel, what a treasure hadst thou!

POLONIUS What treasure had he, my lord?

HAMLET Why,

"One fair daughter, and no more,
The which he lovèd passing[3] well."

POLONIUS (*aside*) Still on my daughter.

HAMLET Am I not i' th' right, old Jephthah?

POLONIUS If you call me Jephthah, my lord, I have a daughter that I love passing well.

HAMLET Nay, that follows not.

POLONIUS What follows then, my lord?

HAMLET Why,

"As by lot, God wot,"

and then, you know,

"It came to pass, as most like it was."

The first row[4] of the pious chanson[5] will show you more, for look where my abridgment[6] comes.

(*Enter the* PLAYERS.)

---

[2]clothes [3]haply, perhaps [4]the greatest of Roman comic actors [5]drama observing the unities [6]drama not observing the unities [7]Roman writer of tragedies [8]Roman writer of comedies [9]orthodoxy determined by critical rules of the drama [1]freedom from such orthodoxy [2]the compelled sacrificer of a dearly beloved daughter (Judges xi) [3]surpassingly (verses are from a ballad on Jephthah) [4]stanza [5]song [6]that which shortens my talk

You are welcome, masters, welcome all.—I am glad to see thee well.—Welcome, good friends.—O, old friend, why, thy face is valanced[7] since I saw thee last. Com'st thou to beard me in Denmark?—What, my young lady[8] and mistress? By'r Lady, your ladyship is nearer to heaven than when I saw you last by the altitude of a chopine.[9] Pray God your voice, like a piece of uncurrent[1] gold, be not cracked within the ring.[2]—Masters, you are all welcome. We'll e'en to't like French falconers, fly at anything we see. We'll have a speech straight. Come, give us a taste of your quality. Come, a passionate speech.

PLAYER What speech, my good lord?

HAMLET I heard thee speak me a speech once, but it was never acted, or if it was, not above once, for the play, I remember, pleased not the million; 'twas caviary[3] to the general,[4] but it was (as I received it, and others, whose judgments in such matters cried in the top of[5] mine) an excellent play, well digested in the scenes, set down with as much modesty as cunning. I remember one said there were no sallets[6] in the lines to make the matter savory, nor no matter in the phrase that might indict the author of affectation, but called it an honest method, as wholesome as sweet, and by very much more handsome than fine. One speech in't I chiefly loved. 'Twas Aeneas' tale to Dido, and thereabout of it especially where he speaks of Priam's slaughter.[7] If it live in your memory, begin at this line—let me see, let me see:

"The rugged Pyrrhus, like th' Hyrcanian beast[8]—"

'Tis not so; it begins with Pyrrhus:

"The rugged Pyrrhus, he whose sable[9] arms,
Black as his purpose, did the night resemble
When he lay couchèd in the ominous[1] horse,[2]
Hath now this dread and black complexion smeared
With heraldry more dismal.[3] Head to foot
Now is he total gules,[4] horridly tricked[5]
With blood of fathers, mothers, daughters, sons,
Baked and impasted with the parching[6] streets,
That lend a tyrannous and a damnèd light
To their lord's murder. Roasted in wrath and fire,
And thus o'ersizèd[7] with coagulate[8] gore,
With eyes like carbuncles, the hellish Pyrrhus
Old grandsire Priam seeks."

So, proceed you.

---

[7]fringed (with a beard) [8]boy who plays women's parts [9]women's thick-soled shoe [1]not legal tender [2]from the edge through the line circling the design on the coin (with a play on "ring": a sound) [3]caviare [4]multitude [5]more authoritatively than [6]salads, highly seasoned passages [7]the fall of Troy (Aeneid II, 506 ff.) [8]tiger [9]black [1]fateful [2]the wooden horse by which the Greeks gained entrance to Troy [3]ill-omened [4]red (heraldic term) [5]decorated in color (heraldic term) [6]because Troy was burning [7]covered as with size, a glutinous material used for filling pores of plaster, etc. [8]clotted

POLONIUS Fore God, my lord, well spoken, with good accent and good discretion.

PLAYER "Anon he finds him,
Striking too short at Greeks. His antique sword,
Rebellious to his arms, lies where it falls,
Repugnant to command. Unequal matched,
Pyrrhus at Priam drives, in rage strikes wide,
But with the whiff and wind of his fell[9] sword
Th' unnervèd father falls. Then senseless[1] Ilium,
Seeming to feel this blow, with flaming top
Stoops to his[2] base, and with a hideous crash
Takes prisoner Pyrrhus' ear. For lo! his sword,
Which was declining on the milky head
Of reverend Priam, seemed i' th' air to stick.
So as a painted[3] tyrant Pyrrhus stood,
And like a neutral to his will and matter[4]
Did nothing.
But as we often see, against[5] some storm,
A silence in the heavens, the rack[6] stand still,
The bold winds speechless, and the orb below
As hush as death, anon the dreadful thunder
Doth rend the region,[7] so after Pyrrhus' pause,
Arousèd vengeance sets him new awork,
And never did the Cyclops'[8] hammers fall
On Mars' armor, forged for proof eterne,[9]
With less remorse than Pyrrhus' bleeding sword
Now falls on Priam.
Out, out, thou strumpet Fortune! All you gods,
In general synod take away her power,
Break all the spokes and fellies[1] from her wheel,
And bowl the round nave[2] down the hill of heaven,
As low as to the fiends."

POLONIUS This is too long.

HAMLET It shall to the barber's, with your beard.—Prithee say on. He's for a jig[3] or a tale of bawdry, or he sleeps. Say on; come to Hecuba.

PLAYER "But who (ah woe!) had seen the mobled[4] queen—"

HAMLET "The mobled queen"?

POLONIUS That's good. "Mobled queen" is good.

PLAYER "Run barefoot up and down, threat'ning the flames
With bisson rheum;[5] a clout[6] upon that head

[9]cruel [1]without feeling [2]its [3]pictured [4]purpose and its realization (between which he stands motionless) [5]just before [6]clouds [7]sky [8]giant workmen who made armor in the smithy of Vulcan [9]eternal protection [1]segments of the rim [2]hub [3]short comic piece with singing and dancing often presented after a play [4]muffled [5]blinding tears [6]cloth

Where late the diadem stood, and for a robe,
About her lank and all o'erteemèd[7] loins,
A blanket in the alarm of fear caught up—
Who this had seen, with tongue in venom steeped
'Gainst Fortune's state[8] would treason have pronounced.
But if the gods themselves did see her then,
When she saw Pyrrhus make malicious sport
In mincing with his sword her husband's limbs,
The instant burst of clamor that she made
(Unless things mortal move them not at all)
Would have made milch[9] the burning eyes[1] of heaven
And passion in the gods."

POLONIUS Look, whe'r[2] he has not turned his color, and has tears in's eyes. Prithee no more.

HAMLET 'Tis well. I'll have thee speak out the rest of this soon.—Good my lord, will you see the players well bestowed?[3] Do you hear? Let them be well used, for they are the abstract and brief chronicles of the time. After your death you were better have a bad epitaph than their ill report while you live.

POLONIUS My lord, I will use them according to their desert.

HAMLET God's bodkin,[4] man, much better! Use every man after his desert, and who shall scape whipping? Use them after your own honor and dignity. The less they deserve, the more merit is in your bounty. Take them in.

POLONIUS Come, sirs.

HAMLET Follow him, friends. We'll hear a play tomorrow. (*aside to* PLAYER) Dost thou hear me, old friend? Can you play "The Murder of Gonzago"?

PLAYER Ay, my lord.

HAMLET We'll ha't to-morrow night. You could for a need study a speech of some dozen or sixteen lines which I would set down and insert in't, could you not?

PLAYER Ay, my lord.

HAMLET Very well. Follow that lord, and look you mock him not.—My good friends, I'll leave you till night. You are welcome to Elsinore.

(*Exeunt* POLONIUS *and* PLAYERS.)

ROSENCRANTZ Good my lord.

(*Exeunt* ROSENCRANTZ *and* GUILDENSTERN.)

HAMLET Ay, so, God bye to you.—Now I am alone.
O, what a rogue and peasant slave am I!
Is it not monstrous that this player here,
But in a fiction, in a dream of passion,

---

[7]overproductive of children [8]government of worldly events [9]tearful (milk-giving) [1]stars [2]whether [3]lodged [4]by God's little body

Could force his soul so to his own conceit[5]
That from her working all his visage wanned,
Tears in his eyes, distraction in his aspect.
A broken voice, and his whole function[6] suiting
With forms to his conceit? And all for nothing,
For Hecuba!
What's Hecuba to him, or he to Hecuba,
That he should weep for her? What would he do
Had he the motive and the cue for passion
That I have? He would drown the stage with tears
And cleave the general ear with horrid speech,
Make mad the guilty and appal the free,
Confound the ignorant, and amaze indeed
The very faculties of eyes and ears.
Yet I,
A dull and muddy-mettled[7] rascal, peak[8]
Like John-a-dreams,[9] unpregnant[1] of my cause,
And can say nothing. No, not for a king,
Upon whose property and most dear life
A damned defeat was made. Am I a coward?
Who calls me villain? breaks my pate across?
Plucks off my beard and blows it in my face?
Tweaks me by the nose? gives me the lie i' th' throat
As deep as to the lungs? Who does me this?
Ha, 'swounds,[2] I should take it, for it cannot be
But I am pigeon-livered[3] and lack gall
To make oppression bitter, or ere this
I should ha' fatted all the region kites[4]
With this slave's offal.[5] Bloody, bawdy villain!
Remorseless, treacherous, lecherous, kindless[6] villain!
O, vengeance!
Why, what an ass am I! This is most brave,
That I, the son of a dear father murdered,
Prompted to my revenge by heaven and hell,
Must like a whore unpack my heart with words
And fall a-cursing like a very drab,
A stallion![7] Fie upon't, foh! About, my brains.
Hum—
I have heard that guilty creatures sitting at a play
Have by the very cunning of the scene

---

[5]conception, idea [6]action of bodily powers [7]dull-spirited [8]mope [9]a sleepy dawdler [1]barren of realization [2]by God's wounds [3]of dove-like gentleness [4]kites of the air [5]guts [6]unnatural [7]prostitute (male or female)

Been struck so to the soul that presently[8]
They have proclaimed their malefactions.
For murder, though it have no tongue, will speak
With most miraculous organ. I'll have these players
Play something like the murder of my father
Before mine uncle. I'll observe his looks.
I'll tent[9] him to the quick. If 'a do blench,[1]
I know my course. The spirit that I have seen
May be a devil, and the devil hath power
T' assume a pleasing shape, yea, and perhaps
Out of my weakness and my melancholy,
As he is very potent with such spirits,
Abuses[2] me to damn me. I'll have grounds
More relative[3] than this. The play 's the thing
Wherein I'll catch the conscience of the king.

(*Exit.*)

Act III

Scene I

A chamber in the castle.

(*Enter* King, Queen, Polonius, Ophelia, Rosencrantz, Guildenstern, Lords.)

KING And can you by no drift of conference[4]
Get from him why he puts on this confusion,
Grating so harshly all his days of quiet
With turbulent and dangerous lunacy?
ROSENCRANTZ He does confess he feels himself distracted,
But from what cause 'a will by no means speak.
GUILDENSTERN Nor do we find him forward to be sounded,
But with a crafty madness keeps aloof
When we would bring him on to some confession
Of his true state.
QUEEN Did he receive you well?
ROSENCRANTZ Most like a gentleman.
GUILDENSTERN But with much forcing of his disposition.
ROSENCRANTZ Niggard of question, but of our demands
Most free in his reply.

[8]immediately [9]probe [1]flinch [2]deludes [3]pertinent [4]direction of conversation

QUEEN Did you assay[5] him
To any pastime?
ROSENCRANTZ Madam, it so fell out that certain players
We o'erraught[6] on the way. Of these we told him,
And there did seem in him a kind of joy
To hear of it. They are here about the court,
And, as I think, they have already order
This night to play before him.
POLONIUS 'Tis most true,
And he beseeched me to entreat your majesties
To hear and see the matter.
KING With all my heart, and it doth much content me
To hear him so inclined.
Good gentlemen, give him a further edge[7]
And drive his purpose into these delights.
ROSENCRANTZ We shall, my lord.

(*Exeunt* ROSENCRANTZ *and* GUILDENSTERN.)

KING Sweet Gertrude, leave us too,
For we have closely[8] sent for Hamlet hither,
That he, as 'twere by accident, may here
Affront[9] Ophelia.
Her father and myself (lawful espials[1])
Will so bestow ourselves that, seeing unseen,
We may of their encounter frankly judge
And gather by him, as he is behaved,
If't be th' affliction of his love or no
That thus he suffers for.
QUEEN I shall obey you.—
And for your part, Ophelia, I do wish
That your good beauties be the happy cause
Of Hamlet's wildness. So shall I hope your virtues
Will bring him to his wonted way again,
To both your honors.
OPHELIA Madam, I wish it may.

(*Exit* QUEEN.)

POLONIUS Ophelia, walk you here.—Gracious, so please you,
We will bestow ourselves.—

(*to* OPHELIA)

---

[5]try to win [6]overtook [7]keenness of desire [8]privately [9]come face to face with [1]spies

Read on this book,
That show of such an exercise[2] may color[3]
Your loneliness. We are oft to blame in this,
'Tis too much proved, that with devotion's visage
And pious action we do sugar o'er
The devil himself.

KING (*aside*) O, 'tis too true.
How smart a lash that speech doth give my conscience!
The harlot's cheek, beautied with plast'ring art,
Is not more ugly to[4] the thing that helps it
Than is my deed to my most painted word.
O heavy burthen!

POLONIUS I hear him coming. Let's withdraw, my lord.

(*Exeunt* KING *and* POLONIUS.)

(*Enter* HAMLET.)

HAMLET To be, or not to be—that is the question:
Whether 'tis nobler in the mind to suffer
The slings and arrows of outrageous fortune
Or to take arms against a sea of troubles
And by opposing end them. To die, to sleep—
No more—and by a sleep to say we end
The heartache, and the thousand natural shocks
That flesh is heir to. 'Tis a consummation
Devoutly to be wished. To die, to sleep—
To sleep—perchance to dream: ay, there's the rub,[5]
For in that sleep of death what dreams may come
When we have shuffled off[6] this mortal coil,[7]
Must give us pause. There's the respect[8]
That makes calamity of so long life.[9]
For who would bear the whips and scorns of time,
Th' oppressor's wrong, the proud man's contumely
The pangs of despised love, the law's delay,
The insolence of office, and the spurns
That patient merit of th' unworthy takes,
When he himself might his quietus[1] make
With a bare bodkin?[2] Who would fardels[3] bear,
To grunt and sweat under a weary life,
But that the dread of something after death,

---

[2]religious exercise (the book being obviously one of devotion) [3]give an appearance of naturalness to [4]compared to [5]obstacle (literally, obstruction encountered by a bowler's ball) [6]cast off as an encumbrance [7]to-do, turmoil [8]consideration [9]so long-lived [1]settlement (literally, release from debt) [2]dagger [3]burdens

The undiscovered country, from whose bourn[4]
No traveller returns, puzzles the will,
And makes us rather bear those ills we have
Than fly to others that we know not of?
Thus conscience does make cowards of us all,
And thus the native hue of resolution
Is sicklied o'er with the pale cast of thought,
And enterprises of great pitch[5] and moment
With this regard[6] their currents turn awry
And lose the name of action.—Soft you now,
The fair Ophelia!—Nymph, in thy orisons[7]
Be all my sins remembered.

OPHELIA Good my lord,
How does your honor for this many a day?

HAMLET I humbly thank you, well, well, well.

OPHELIA My lord, I have remembrances of yours
That I have longèd long to re-deliver.
I pray you, now receive them.

HAMLET No, not I,
I never gave you aught.

OPHELIA My honored lord, you know right well you did,
And with them words of so sweet breath composed
As made the things more rich. Their perfume lost,
Take these again, for to the noble mind
Rich gifts wax poor when givers prove unkind.
There, my lord.

HAMLET Ha, ha! Are you honest?[8]

OPHELIA My lord?

HAMLET Are you fair?

OPHELIA What means your lordship?

HAMLET That if you be honest and fair, your honesty should admit no discourse to your beauty.

OPHELIA Could beauty, my lord, have better commerce[9] than with honesty?

HAMLET Ay, truly; for the power of beauty will sooner transform honesty from what it is to a bawd than the force of honesty can translate beauty into his likeness. This was sometime a paradox,[1] but now the time gives it proof. I did love you once.

OPHELIA Indeed, my lord, you made me believe so.

HAMLET You should not have believed me, for virtue cannot so inoculate[2] our old stock but we shall relish[3] of it. I loved you not.

OPHELIA I was the more deceived.

---

[4]confine, region [5]height (of a soaring falcon's flight) [6]consideration [7]prayers (because of the book of devotion she reads) [8]chaste [9]intercourse [1]idea contrary to common opinion [2]graft [3]have a flavor (because of original sin)

HAMLET Get thee to a nunnery. Why wouldst thou be a breeder of sinners? I am myself indifferent honest,[4] but yet I could accuse me of such things that it were better my mother had not borne me: I am very proud, revengeful, ambitious, with more offenses at my beck than I have thoughts to put them in, imagination to give them shape, or time to act them in. What should such fellows as I do crawling between earth and heaven? We are arrant knaves all; believe none of us. Go thy ways to a nunnery. Where's your father?

OPHELIA At home, my lord.

HAMLET Let the doors be shut upon him, that he may play the fool nowhere but in's own house. Farewell.

OPHELIA O, help him, you sweet heavens!

HAMLET If thou dost marry, I'll give thee this plague for thy dowry: be thou as chaste as ice, as pure as snow, thou shalt not escape calumny. Get thee to a nunnery. Go, farewell. Or if thou wilt needs marry, marry a fool, for wise men know well enough what monsters[5] you make of them. To a nunnery, go, and quickly too. Farewell.

OPHELIA O heavenly powers, restore him!

HAMLET I have heard of your paintings too, well enough. God hath given you one face, and you make yourselves another. You jig, you amble, and you lisp; you nickname God's creatures and make your wantonness[6] your ignorance.[7] Go to, I'll no more on't; it hath made me mad. I say we will have no more marriage. Those that are married already—all but one—shall live. The rest shall keep as they are. To a nunnery, go.

(*Exit.*)

OPHELIA O, what a noble mind is here o'erthrown!
The courtier's, soldier's, scholar's, eye, tongue, sword,
Th' expectancy and rose[8] of the fair state,
The glass[9] of fashion and the mould of form,
Th' observed of all observers, quite, quite down!
And I, of ladies most deject and wretched,
That sucked the honey of his music vows,
Now see that noble and most sovereign reason
Like sweet bells jangled, out of time and harsh,
That unmatched form and feature of blown youth
Blasted with ecstasy.[1] O, woe is me
T' have seen what I have seen, see what I see!

(*Enter* KING *and* POLONIUS.)

---

[4]moderately respectable [5]unnatural combinations of wisdom and uxorious folly [6]affectation [7]a matter for which you offer the excuse that you don't know any better [8]fair hope [9]mirror [1]madness

KING Love? his affections[2] do not that way tend,
Nor what he spake, though it lacked form a little,
Was not like madness. There's something in his soul
O'er which his melancholy sits on brood,
And I do doubt[3] the hatch and the disclose
Will be some danger; which for to prevent,
I have in quick determination
Thus set it down: he shall with speed to England
For the demand of our neglected tribute.
Haply the seas, and countries different,
With variable objects, shall expel
This something-settled[4] matter in his heart,
Whereon his brains still beating puts him thus
From fashion of himself. What think you on't?

POLONIUS It shall do well. But yet do I believe
The origin and commencement of his grief
Sprung from neglected love.—How now, Ophelia?
You need not tell us what Lord Hamlet said.
We heard it all.—My lord, do as you please,
But if you hold it fit, after the play
Let his queen mother all alone entreat him
To show his grief. Let her be round[5] with him,
And I'll be placed, so please you, in the ear
Of all their conference. If she find him not,
To England send him, or confine him where
Your wisdom best shall think.

KING It shall be so.
Madness in great ones must not unwatched go.

(*Exeunt.*)

Scene II

The hall of the castle.

(*Enter* HAMLET *and three of the* PLAYERS.)

HAMLET Speak the speech, I pray you, as I pronounced it to you, trippingly[6] on the tongue. But if you mouth it, as many of our players do, I had as lief the town crier spoke my lines. Nor do not saw the air too much with your hand, thus, but use all gently, for in the very torrent, tempest, and (as I may say) whirlwind of your passion, you must acquire and beget a temperance that

[2]emotions [3]fear [4]somewhat settled [5]plain-spoken [6]easily

may give it smoothness. O, it offends me to the soul to hear a robustious[7] periwig-pated[8] fellow tear a passion to tatters, to very rags, to split the ears of the groundlings,[9] who for the most part are capable of nothing but inexplicable dumb shows[1] and noise. I would have such a fellow whipped for o'erdoing Termagant.[2] It out-herods Herod.[3] Pray you avoid it.

PLAYER I warrant your honor.

HAMLET Be not too tame neither, but let your own discretion be your tutor. Suit the action to the word, the word to the action, with this special observance, that you o'erstep not the modesty of nature. For anything so overdone is from[4] the purpose of playing, whose end, both at the first and now, was and is, to hold, as 'twere, the mirror up to nature, to show virtue her own feature, scorn her own image, and the very age and body of the time his form and pressure.[5] Now this overdone, or come tardy off,[6] though it make the unskillful laugh, cannot but make the judicious grieve, the censure of the which one[7] must in your allowance o'erweigh a whole theatre of others. O, there be players that I have seen play, and heard others praise, and that highly (not to speak it profanely), that neither having th' accent of Christians, nor the gait of Christian, pagan, nor man, have so strutted and bellowed that I have thought some of Nature's journeymen[8] had made men, and not made them well, they imitated humanity so abominably.

PLAYER I hope we have reformed that indifferently[9] with us, sir.

HAMLET O, reform it altogether! And let those that play your clowns speak no more than is set down for them, for there be of them[1] that will themselves laugh, to set on some quantity of barren spectators to laugh too, though in the mean time some necessary question of the play be then to be considered. That's villainous and shows a most pitiful ambition in the fool that uses it. Go make you ready.

(*Exeunt* PLAYERS.)

(*Enter* POLONIUS, GUILDENSTERN, *and* ROSENCRANTZ.)

How now, my lord? Will the king hear this piece of work?

POLONIUS And the queen too, and that presently.[2]

HAMLET Bid the players make haste.

(*Exit* POLONIUS.)

Will you two help to hasten them?

ROSENCRANTZ Ay, my lord.

---

[7]boisterous [8]wig-wearing (after the custom of actors) [9]spectators who paid least and stood on the ground in the pit or yard of the theatre [1]brief actions without words, forecasting dramatic matter to follow (the play presented later in this scene giving an old-fashioned example) [2]a Saracen "god" in medieval romance and drama [3]the raging tyrant of old biblical plays [4]apart from [5]impressed or printed character [6]brought off slowly and badly [7]the judgment of even one of whom [8]workmen not yet masters of their trade [9]fairly well [1]some of them [2]at once

(*Exeunt they two.*)

HAMLET What, ho, Horatio!

(*Enter* HORATIO.)

HORATIO Here, sweet lord, at your service.
HAMLET Horatio, thou art e'en as just a man
As e'er my conversation coped withal.[3]
HORATIO O, my dear lord—
HAMLET Nay, do not think I flatter.
For what advancement may I hope from thee,
That no revenue hast but thy good spirits
To feed and clothe thee? Why should the poor be flattered?
No, let the candied tongue lick absurd pomp,
And crook the pregnant[4] hinges of the knee
Where thrift[5] may follow fawning. Dost thou hear?
Since my dear soul was mistress of her choice
And could of men distinguish her election,
S' hath sealed[6] thee for herself, for thou hast been
As one in suff'ring all that suffers nothing,
A man that Fortune's buffets and rewards
Hast ta'en with equal thanks; and blest are those
Whose blood[7] and judgment are so well commeddled[8]
That they are not a pipe for Fortune's finger
To sound what stop she please. Give me that man
That is not passion's slave, and I will wear him
In my heart's core, ay, in my heart of heart,
As I do thee. Something too much of this—
There is a play to-night before the king.
One scene of it comes near the circumstance
Which I have told thee, of my father's death.
I prithee, when thou seest that act afoot,
Even with the very comment of thy soul[9]
Observe my uncle. If his occulted[1] guilt
Do not itself unkennel in one speech,
It is a damnèd ghost[2] that we have seen,
And my imaginations are as foul
As Vulcan's stithy.[3] Give him heedful note,
For I mine eyes will rivet to his face,
And after we will both our judgments join
In censure of[4] his seeming.

---

[3]intercourse with men encountered [4]quick to move [5]profit [6]marked [7]passion [8]mixed together [9]thy deepest sagacity [1]hidden [2]evil spirit, devil [3]smithy [4]sentence upon

HORATIO Well, my lord.
If 'a steal aught the while this play is playing,
And scape detecting, I will pay the theft.

(*Enter* TRUMPETS *and* KETTLEDRUMS, KING, QUEEN, POLONIUS, OPHELIA [ROSENCRANTZ, GUILDENSTERN, *and other* LORDS *attendant*].)

HAMLET They are coming to the play. I must be idle.[5] Get you a place.

KING How fares our cousin[6] Hamlet?

HAMLET Excellent, i' faith, of the chameleon's dish.[7] I eat the air, promise-crammed. You cannot feed capons so.

KING I have nothing with this answer, Hamlet. These words are not mine.[8]

HAMLET No, nor mine now. (*to* POLONIUS) My lord, you played once i' th' university, you say?

POLONIUS That did I, my lord, and was accounted a good actor.

HAMLET What did you enact?

POLONIUS I did enact Julius Caesar. I was killed i' th' Capitol; Brutus killed me.

HAMLET It was a brute part of him to kill so capital a calf there. Be the players ready?

ROSENCRANTZ Ay, my lord. They stay upon your patience.[9]

QUEEN Come hither, my dear Hamlet, sit by me.

HAMLET No, good mother. Here's metal more attractive.

POLONIUS (*to the* KING) O ho! do you mark that?

HAMLET Lady, shall I lie in your lap?

(*He lies at* OPHELIA's *feet.*)

OPHELIA No, my lord.

HAMLET I mean, my head upon your lap?

OPHELIA Ay, my lord.

HAMLET Do you think I meant country matters?[1]

OPHELIA I think nothing, my lord.

HAMLET That's a fair thought to lie between maids' legs.

OPHELIA What is, my lord?

HAMLET Nothing.

OPHELIA You are merry, my lord.

HAMLET Who, I?

OPHELIA Ay, my lord.

HAMLET O God, your only jig-maker![2] What should a man do but be merry? For look you how cheerfully my mother looks, and my father died within's two hours.

---

[5]be foolish, act the madman [6]nephew [7]air (which was believed the chameleon's food; Hamlet willfully takes *fares* in the sense of "feeds") [8]not for me as the asker of my question [9]await your indulgence [1]rustic goings-on, barnyard mating (with a play upon a sexual term) [2]writer of jigs

OPHELIA Nay, 'tis twice two months, my lord.

HAMLET So long? Nay then, let the devil wear black, for I'll have a suit of sables.[3] O heavens! die two months ago, and not forgotten yet? Then there's hope a great man's memory may outlive his life half a year. But, by'r Lady, 'a must build churches then, or else shall 'a suffer not thinking on, with the hobby-horse,[4] whose epitaph is "For O, for O, the hobby-horse is forgot!"

(*The trumpets sound. Dumb show follows:*
Enter a KING *and a* QUEEN [*very lovingly*], *the* QUEEN *embracing him, and he her.* [*She kneels; and makes show of protestation unto him.*] *He takes her up, and declines his head upon her neck. He lies him down upon a bank of flowers. She, seeing him asleep, leaves him. Anon come in another man: takes off his crown, kisses it, pours poison in the sleeper's ears, and leaves him. The* QUEEN *returns, finds the* KING *dead, makes passionate action. The poisoner, with some three or four, come in again, seem to condole with her. The dead body is carried away. The poisoner woos the* QUEEN *with gifts; she seems harsh awhile, but in the end accepts love.*)

(*Exeunt.*)

OPHELIA What means this, my lord?

HAMLET Marry, this is miching mallecho[5], it means mischief.

OPHELIA Belike this show imports the argument of the play.

(*Enter* PROLOGUE.)

HAMLET We shall know by this fellow. The players cannot keep counsel; they'll tell all.

OPHELIA Will 'a tell us what this show meant?

HAMLET Ay, or any show that you'll show him. Be not you ashamed to show, he'll not shame to tell you what it means.

OPHELIA You are naught, you are naught.[6] I'll mark the play.

PROLOGUE For us and for our tragedy,
Here stooping to your clemency,
We beg your hearing patiently.

(*Exit.*)

HAMLET Is this a prologue, or the posy[7] of a ring?[8]

OPHELIA 'Tis brief, my lord.

HAMLET As woman's love.

(*Enter* [*two* PLAYERS *as*] KING *and* QUEEN.)

---

[3]black furs (luxurious garb, not for mourning) [4]traditional figure strapped round the waist of a performer in May games and morris dances [5]sneaking iniquity [6]indecent [7]brief motto in rhyme ("poesy") [8]finger ring

[P.] KING Full thirty times hath Phoebus' cart[9] gone round
Neptune's salt wash and Tellus'[1] orbèd ground,
And thirty dozen moons with borrowed[2] sheen
About the world have times twelve thirties been,
Since love our hearts, and Hymen[3] did our hands,
Unite commutual[4] in most sacred bands.
[P.] QUEEN So many journeys may the sun and moon
Make us again count o'er ere love be done!
But woe is me, you are so sick of late,
So far from cheer and from your former state,
That I distrust you.[5] Yet, though I distrust,
Discomfort you, my lord, it nothing must.
For women fear too much, even as they love,
And women's fear and love hold quantity,[6]
In neither aught, or in extremity.
Now what my love is, proof hath made you know,
And as my love is sized, my fear is so.
Where love is great, the littlest doubts are fear;
Where little fears grow great, great love grows there.
[P.] KING Faith, I must leave thee, love, and shortly too;
My operant powers[7] their functions leave to do.
And thou shalt live in this fair world behind,
Honored, beloved, and haply one as kind
For husband shalt thou—
[P.] QUEEN O, confound the rest!
Such love must needs be treason in my breast.
In second husband let me be accurst!
None wed the second but who killed the first.
HAMLET (*aside*) That's wormwood.[8]
[P.] QUEEN The instances[9] that second marriage move
Are base respects of thrift, but none of love.
A second time I kill my husband dead
When second husband kisses me in bed.
[P.] KING I do believe you think what now you speak,
But what we do determine oft we break.
Purpose is but the slave to[1] memory,
Of violent birth, but poor validity,[2]
Which now like fruit unripe sticks on the tree,
But fall unshaken when they mellow be.
Most necessary 'tis that we forget

---

[9]the sun's chariot [1]Roman goddess of the earth [2]taken from the sun [3]Greek god of marriage [4]mutually [5]fear for you [6]proportion [7]active bodily forces [8]a bitter herb [9]motives [1]dependent upon for life [2]strength

To pay ourselves what to ourselves is debt.
What to ourselves in passion we propose,
The passion ending, doth the purpose lose.
The violence of either grief or joy
Their own enactures[3] with themselves destroy.
Where joy most revels, grief doth most lament;
Grief joys, joy grieves, on slender accident.
This world is not for aye, nor 'tis not strange
That even our loves should with our fortunes change,
For 'tis a question left us yet to prove,
Whether love lead fortune, or else fortune love.
The great man down, you mark his favorite flies,
The poor advanced makes friends of enemies;
And hitherto doth love on fortune tend,
For who not needs shall never lack a friend,
And who in want a hollow friend doth try,
Directly seasons him[4] his enemy.
But, orderly to end where I begun,
Our wills and fates do so contrary run
That our devices still[5] are overthrown;
Our thoughts are ours, their ends none of our own.
So think thou wilt no second husband wed,
But die thy thoughts when thy first lord is dead.

[P.] QUEEN Nor earth to me give food, nor heaven light,
Sport and repose lock from me day and night,
To desperation turn my trust and hope,
An anchor's[6] cheer in prison be my scope,
Each opposite that blanks[7] the face of joy
Meet what I would have well, and it destroy,
Both here and hence[8] pursue me lasting strife,
If, once a widow, ever I be wife!

HAMLET If she should break it now!

[P.] KING 'Tis deeply sworn. Sweet, leave me here awhile.
My spirits grow dull, and fain I would beguile
The tedious day with sleep.

[P.] QUEEN Sleep rock thy brain,

(*He sleeps.*)

And never come mischance between us twain!

(*Exit.*)

---

[3]fulfillments [4]ripens him into [5]always [6]hermit's [7]blanches, makes pale [8]in the next world

HAMLET Madam, how like you this play?

QUEEN The lady doth protest too much, methinks.

HAMLET O, but she'll keep her word.

KING Have you heard the argument?[9] Is there no offense in't?

HAMLET No, no, they do but jest, poison in jest; no offense i' th' world.

KING What do you call the play?

HAMLET "The Mousetrap." Marry, how? Tropically.[1] This play is the image of a murder done in Vienna. Gonzago is the duke's name; his wife, Baptista. You shall see anon. 'Tis a knavish piece of work, but what o' that? Your majesty, and we that have free[2] souls, it touches us not. Let the galled[3] jade[4] winch;[5] our withers[6] are unwrung.

(*Enter* LUCIANUS.)

This is one Lucianus, nephew to the king.

OPHELIA You are as good as a chorus,[7] my lord.

HAMLET I could interpret between you and your love, if I could see the puppets[8] dallying.

OPHELIA You are keen, my lord, you are keen.

HAMLET It would cost you a groaning to take off my edge.

OPHELIA Still better, and worse.

HAMLET So you must take your husbands.—Begin, murderer. Leave thy damnable faces and begin. Come, the croaking raven doth bellow for revenge.

LUCIANUS Thoughts black, hands apt, drugs fit, and time agreeing,
Confederate season,[9] else no creature seeing,
Thou mixture rank, of midnight weeds collected,
With Hecate's[1] ban[2] thrice blasted, thrice infected,
Thy natural magic and dire property
On wholesome life usurps immediately.

(*Pours the poison in his ears.*)

HAMLET 'A poisons him i' th' garden for his estate. His name's Gonzago. The story is extant, and written in very choice Italian. You shall see anon how the murderer gets the love of Gonzago's wife.

OPHELIA The king rises.

HAMLET What, frighted with false fire?[3]

QUEEN How fares my lord?

POLONIUS Give o'er the play.

KING Give me some light. Away!

POLONIUS Lights, lights, lights!

---

[9]plot summary [1]in the way of a trope or figure (with a play on "trapically") [2]guiltless [3]sore-backed [4]horse [5]wince [6]shoulders [7]one in a play who explains the action [8]you and your lover as in a puppet show [9]the occasion being my ally [1]goddess of witchcraft and black magic [2]curse [3]a firing of a gun charged with powder but no shot, a blank discharge

(*Exeunt all but* HAMLET *and* HORATIO.)

HAMLET Why, let the strucken deer go weep,
The hart ungallèd play.
For some must watch, while some must sleep;
Thus runs the world away.

Would not this, sir, and a forest of feathers[4]—if the rest of my fortunes turn Turk[5] with me—with two Provincial roses[6] on my razed[7] shoes, get me a fellowship in a cry[8] of players, sir?

HORATIO Half a share.

HAMLET A whole one, I.
For thou dost know, O Damon dear,
This realm dismantled was
Of Jove himself; and now reigns here
A very, very—peacock.

HORATIO You might have rhymed.

HAMLET O good Horatio, I'll take the ghost's word for a thousand pound. Didst perceive?

HORATIO Very well, my lord.

HAMLET Upon the talk of the poisoning?

HORATIO I did very well note him.

HAMLET Aha! Come, some music! Come, the recorders![9]
For if the king like not the comedy,
Why then, belike he likes it not, perdy.[1]
Come, some music!

(*Enter* ROSENCRANTZ *and* GUILDENSTERN.)

GUILDENSTERN Good my lord, vouchsafe me a word with you.

HAMLET Sir, a whole history.

GUILDENSTERN The king, sir—

HAMLET Ay, sir, what of him?

GUILDENSTERN Is in his retirement marvellous distempered.[2]

HAMLET With drink, sir?

GUILDENSTERN No, my lord, with choler.[3]

HAMLET Your wisdom should show itself more richer to signify this to the doctor, for for me to put him to his purgation would perhaps plunge him into more choler.

GUILDENSTERN Good my lord, put your discourse into some frame,[4] and start not so wildly from my affair.

HAMLET I am tame, sir; pronounce.

---

[4]plumes for actors' costumes [5]turn renegade, like a Christian turning Muslim [6]ribbon rosettes [7]decorated with cut patterns [8]pack [9]musical instruments of the flute class [1]by God ("*par dieu*") [2]out of temper, vexed (twisted by Hamlet into "deranged") [3]anger (twisted by Hamlet into "biliousness") [4]logical order

GUILDENSTERN The queen, your mother, in most great affliction of spirit hath sent me to you.

HAMLET You are welcome.

GUILDENSTERN Nay, good my lord, this courtesy is not of the right breed. If it shall please you to make me a wholesome answer, I will do your mother's commandment. If not, your pardon and my return shall be the end of my business.

HAMLET Sir, I cannot.

ROSENCRANTZ What, my lord?

HAMLET Make you a wholesome answer; my wit's diseased. But, sir, such answer as I can make, you shall command, or rather, as you say, my mother. Therefore no more, but to the matter. My mother, you say—

ROSENCRANTZ Then thus she says: your behavior hath struck her into amazement and admiration.[5]

HAMLET O wonderful son, that can so stonish a mother! But is there no sequel at the heels of this mother's admiration? Impart.

ROSENCRANTZ She desires to speak with you in her closet[6] ere you go to bed.

HAMLET We shall obey, were she ten times our mother. Have you any further trade with us?

ROSENCRANTZ My lord, you once did love me.

HAMLET And so still, by these pickers and stealers.[7]

ROSENCRANTZ Good my lord, what is your cause of distemper? You do surely bar the door upon your own liberty, if you deny your griefs to your friend.

HAMLET Sir, I lack advancement.

ROSENCRANTZ How can that be, when you have the voice of the king himself for your succession in Denmark?

HAMLET Ay, sir, but "while the grass grows"[8] the proverb is something musty.

(*Enter the* PLAYER *with recorders.*)

O, the recorders. Let me see one. To withdraw[9] with you—why do you go about to recover the wind[1] of me, as if you would drive me into a toil?[2]

GUILDENSTERN O my lord, if my duty be too bold, my love is too unmannerly.[3]

HAMLET I do not well understand that. Will you play upon this pipe?

GUILDENSTERN My lord, I cannot.

HAMLET I pray you.

GUILDENSTERN Believe me, I cannot.

HAMLET I do beseech you.

GUILDENSTERN I know no touch of it, my lord.

---

[5]wonder [6]private room [7]hands [8](a proverb, ending: "the horse starves") [9]step aside [1]come up to windward like a hunter [2]snare [3]leads me beyond the restraint of good manners

HAMLET It is as easy as lying. Govern these ventages[4] with your fingers and thumb, give it breath with your mouth, and it will discourse most eloquent music. Look you, these are the stops.

GUILDENSTERN But these cannot I command to any utt'rance of harmony. I have not the skill.

HAMLET Why, look you now, how unworthy a thing you make of me! You would play upon me, you would seem to know my stops, you would pluck out the heart of my mystery, you would sound me from my lowest note to the top of my compass; and there is much music, excellent voice, in this little organ, yet cannot you make it speak. 'Sblood, do you think I am easier to be played on than a pipe? Call me what instrument you will, though you can fret[5] me, you cannot play upon me.

(*Enter* POLONIUS.)

God bless you, sir!

POLONIUS My lord, the queen would speak with you, and presently.[6]

HAMLET Do you see yonder cloud that's almost in shape of a camel?

POLONIUS By th' mass and 'tis, like a camel indeed.

HAMLET Methinks it is like a weasel.

POLONIUS It is backed like a weasel.

HAMLET Or like a whale.

POLONIUS Very like a whale.

HAMLET Then I will come to my mother by and by.[7] (*aside*) They fool me to the top of my bent.—I will come by and by.

POLONIUS I will say so.

(*Exit.*)

HAMLET "By and by" is easily said. Leave me, friends.

(*Exeunt all but* HAMLET.)

'Tis now the very witching time of night,
When churchyards yawn, and hell itself breathes out
Contagion to this world. Now could I drink hot blood
And do such bitter business as the day
Would quake to look on. Soft, now to my mother.
O heart, lose not thy nature; let not ever
The soul of Nero[8] enter this firm bosom.
Let me be cruel, not unnatural;
I will speak daggers to her, but use none.
My tongue and soul in this be hypocrites:

---

[4]holes, vents [5]irritate (with a play on the fret-fingering of certain stringed musical instruments) [6]at once [7]immediately [8]murderer of his mother

How in my words somever she be shent,[9]
To give them seals[1] never, my soul, consent!

(*Exit.*)

Scene III

A chamber in the castle.

(*Enter* KING, ROSENCRANTZ, *and* GUILDENSTERN.)

KING I like him not, nor stands it safe with us
To let his madness range. Therefore prepare you.
I your commission will forthwith dispatch,
And he to England shall along with you.
The terms[2] of our estate[3] may not endure
Hazard so near's as doth hourly grow
Out of his brows.[4]

GUILDENSTERN We will ourselves provide.
Most holy and religious fear it is
To keep those many many bodies safe
That live and feed upon your majesty.

ROSENCRANTZ The single and peculiar[5] life is bound
With all the strength and armor of the mind
To keep itself from noyance,[6] but much more
That spirit upon whose weal depends and rests
The lives of many. The cess[7] of majesty
Dies not alone, but like a gulf[8] doth draw
What's near it with it; or 'tis a massy wheel
Fixed on the summit of the highest mount,
To whose huge spokes ten thousand lesser things
Are mortised and adjoined, which when it falls,
Each small annexment, petty consequence,
Attends[9] the boist'rous ruin. Never alone
Did the king sigh, but with a general groan.

KING Arm[1] you, I pray you, to this speedy voyage,
For we will fetters put upon this fear,
Which now goes too free-footed.

ROSENCRANTZ We will haste us.

(*Exeunt* GENTLEMEN.)

---

[9]reproved [1]authentications in actions [2]circumstances [3]royal position [4]effronteries (apparently with an implication of knitted brows) [5]individual [6]harm [7]cessation, decease [8]whirlpool [9]joins in (like a royal attendant) [1]prepare

(*Enter* POLONIUS.)

POLONIUS My lord, he's going to his mother's closet.
Behind the arras I'll convey myself
To hear the process.[2] I'll warrant she'll tax him home,[3]
And, as you said, and wisely was it said,
'Tis meet that some more audience than a mother,
Since nature makes them partial, should o'erhear
The speech, of vantage.[4] Fare you well, my liege.
I'll call upon you ere you go to bed
And tell you what I know.

KING Thanks, dear my lord.

(*Exit* POLONIUS.)

O, my offense is rank, it smells to heaven;
It hath the primal eldest curse[5] upon't,
A brother's murder. Pray can I not,
Though inclination be as sharp as will.
My stronger guilt defeats my strong intent,
And like a man to double business bound
I stand in pause where I shall first begin,
And both neglect. What if this cursèd hand
Were thicker than itself with brother's blood,
Is there not rain enough in the sweet heavens
To wash it white as snow? Whereto serves mercy
But to confront the visage of offense?[6]
And what's in prayer but this twofold force,
To be forestallèd ere we come to fall,
Or pardoned being down? Then I'll look up.
My fault is past. But, O, what form of prayer
Can serve my turn? "Forgive me my foul murder"?
That cannot be, since I am still possessed
Of those effects[7] for which I did the murder,
My crown, mine own ambition, and my queen.
May one be pardoned and retain th' offense?
In the corrupted currents of this world
Offense's gilded[8] hand may shove by justice,
And oft 'tis seen the wicked prize itself
Buys out the law. But 'tis not so above.
There is no shuffling,[9] there the action[1] lies
In his true nature, and we ourselves compelled,

[2]proceedings [3]thrust home in reprimanding him [4]from an advantageous position [5]that of Cain, who also murdered a brother [6]sin [7]things acquired [8]gold-laden [9]sharp practice, double-dealing [1]legal proceeding (in heaven's court)

Even to the teeth and forehead[2] of our faults,
To give in evidence. What then? What rests?
Try what repentance can. What can it not?
Yet what can it when one cannot repent?
O wretched state! O bosom black as death!
O limèd[3] soul, that struggling to be free
Art more engaged![4] Help, angels! Make assay.[5]
Bow, stubborn knees, and, heart with strings of steel,
Be soft as sinews of the new-born babe.
All may be well.

(*He kneels.*)

(*Enter* HAMLET.)

HAMLET Now might I do it pat,[6] now 'a is a-praying,
And now I'll do't. And so 'a goes to heaven,
And so am I revenged. That would be scanned.
A villain kills my father, and for that
I, his sole son, do this same villain send
To heaven.
Why, this is hire and salary, not revenge.
'A took my father grossly,[7] full of bread,[8]
With all his crimes broad blown,[9] as flush[1] as May;
And how his audit[2] stands, who knows save heaven?
But in our circumstance and course of thought,
'Tis heavy with him; and am I then revenged,
To take him in the purging of his soul,
When he is fit and seasoned for his passage?
No.
Up, sword, and know thou a more horrid hent.[3]
When he is drunk asleep, or in his rage,
Or in th' incestuous pleasure of his bed,
At game a-swearing, or about some act
That has no relish[4] of salvation in't—
Then trip him, that his heels may kick at heaven,
And that his soul may be as damned and black
As hell, whereto it goes. My mother stays.
This physic but prolongs thy sickly days.

(*Exit.*)

---

[2]face-to-face recognition [3]caught in birdlime, a gluey material spread as a bird snare [4]embedded [5]an attempt [6]opportunely [7]in a state of gross unpreparedness [8]worldly sense gratification [9]fully blossomed [1]vigorous [2]account [3]grasping by me on a more horrid occasion [4]flavor

KING (*rises*) My words fly up, my thoughts remain below.
Words without thoughts never to heaven go.

(*Exit.*)

Scene IV

The private chamber of the QUEEN.

(*Enter* [QUEEN] GERTRUDE *and* POLONIUS.)

POLONIUS 'A will come straight. Look you lay[5] home to him.
Tell him his pranks have been too broad[6] to bear with,
And that your grace hath screened and stood between
Much heat and him. I'll silence me even here.
Pray you be round[7] with him.
[HAMLET (*within*) Mother, mother, mother!]
QUEEN I'll warrant you; fear me not. Withdraw; I hear him coming.

(POLONIUS *hides behind the arras.*)

(*Enter* HAMLET.)

HAMLET Now, mother, what's the matter?
QUEEN Hamlet, thou hast thy father much offended.
HAMLET Mother, you have my father much offended.
QUEEN Come, come, you answer with an idle[8] tongue.
HAMLET Go, go, you question with a wicked tongue.
QUEEN Why, how now, Hamlet?
HAMLET What's the matter now?
QUEEN Have you forgot me?
HAMLET No, by the rood,[9] not so!
You are the queen, your husband's brother's wife,
And (would it were not so) you are my mother.
QUEEN Nay, then I'll set those to you that can speak.
HAMLET Come, come, and sit you down. You shall not budge.
You go not till I set you up a glass
Where you may see the inmost part of you.
QUEEN What wilt thou do? Thou wilt not murder me?
Help, ho!
POLONIUS (*behind*) What, ho! help!
HAMLET (*draws*) How now? a rat? Dead for a ducat, dead!

(*makes a pass through the arras and kills* POLONIUS)

[5]thrust [6]unrestrained [7]plain-spoken [8]foolish [9]cross

POLONIUS (*behind*) O, I am slain!
QUEEN O me, what hast thou done?
HAMLET Nay, I know not. Is it the king?
QUEEN O, what a rash and bloody deed is this!
HAMLET A bloody deed—almost as bad, good mother,
As kill a king, and marry with his brother.
QUEEN As kill a king?
HAMLET Ay, lady, it was my word.

(*lifts up the arras and sees* POLONIUS)

Thou wretched, rash, intruding fool, farewell!
I took thee for thy better. Take thy fortune.
Thou find'st to be too busy is some danger.—
Leave wringing of your hands. Peace, sit you down
And let me wring your heart, for so I shall
If it be made of penetrable stuff,
If damnèd custom[1] have not brazed[2] it so
That it is proof[3] and bulwark against sense.[4]
QUEEN What have I done that thou dar'st wag thy tongue
In noise so rude against me?
HAMLET Such an act
That blurs the grace and blush of modesty,
Calls virtue hypocrite, takes off the rose
From the fair forehead of an innocent love,
And sets a blister[5] there, makes marriage vows
As false as dicers' oaths. O, such a deed
As from the body of contraction[6] plucks
The very soul, and sweet religion[7] makes
A rhapsody of words! Heaven's face does glow,
And this solidity and compound mass,[8]
With heated visage, as against[9] the doom,[1]
Is thought-sick at the act.
QUEEN Ay me, what act,
That roars so loud and thunders in the index?[2]
HAMLET Look here upon this picture, and on this,
The counterfeit presentment[3] of two brothers.
See what a grace was seated on this brow:
Hyperion's[4] curls, the front[5] of Jove himself,
An eye like Mars, to threaten and command,
A station[6] like the herald Mercury

[1]habit [2]hardened like brass [3]armor [4]feeling [5]brand (of degradation) [6]the marriage contract [7]sacred marriage vows [8]the earth as compounded of the four elements [9]in expectation of [1]Day of Judgment [2]table of contents preceding the body of a book [3]portrayed representation [4]the sun god [5]forehead [6]attitude in standing

New lighted on a heaven-kissing hill—
A combination and a form indeed
Where every god did seem to set his seal
To give the world assurance of a man.
This was your husband. Look you now what follows.
Here is your husband, like a mildewed ear
Blasting his wholesome brother. Have you eyes?
Could you on this fair mountain leave to feed,
And batten[7] on this moor? Ha! have you eyes?
You cannot call it love, for at your age
The heyday[8] in the blood is tame, it's humble,
And waits upon[9] the judgment, and what judgment
Would step from this to this? Sense[1] sure you have,
Else could you not have motion,[2] but sure that sense
Is apoplexed,[3] for madness would not err,
Nor sense to ecstasy[4] was ne'er so thralled
But it reserved some quantity of choice
To serve in such a difference. What devil was't
That thus hath cozened[5] you at hoodman-blind?[6]
Eyes without feeling, feeling without sight,
Ears without hands or eyes, smelling sans[7] all,
Or but a sickly part of one true sense
Could not so mope.[8]
O shame, where is thy blush? Rebellious hell,
If thou canst mutine[9] in a matron's bones,
To flaming youth let virtue be as wax
And melt in her own fire. Proclaim no shame
When the compulsive[1] ardor gives the charge,[2]
Since frost itself as actively doth burn,
And reason panders will.[3]

QUEEN O Hamlet, speak no more.
Thou turn'st mine eyes into my very soul,
And there I see such black and grainèd[4] spots
As will not leave their tinct.[5]

HAMLET Nay, but to live
In the rank sweat of an enseamèd[6] bed,
Stewed in corruption, honeying and making love
Over the nasty sty—

QUEEN O, speak to me no more.
These words like daggers enter in mine ears.
No more, sweet Hamlet.

---

[7]feed greedily [8]excitement of passion [9]yields to [1]feeling [2]desire, impulse [3]paralyzed [4]madness [5]cheated [6]blindman's buff [7]without [8]be stupid [9]mutiny [1]compelling [2]delivers the attack [3]acts as procurer for desire [4]dyed in grain [5]color [6]grease-laden

HAMLET A murderer and a villain,
A slave that is not twentieth part the tithe[7]
Of your precedent lord, a vice[8] of kings,
A cutpurse[9] of the empire and the rule,
That from a shelf the precious diadem stole
And put it in his pocket—
QUEEN No more.

(*Enter* [*the*] GHOST [*in his nightgown*[1]].)

HAMLET A king of shreds and patches—
Save me and hover o'er me with your wings,
You heavenly guards? What would your gracious figure?
QUEEN Alas, he's mad.
HAMLET Do you not come your tardy son to chide,
That, lapsed in time and passion,[2] lets go by
Th' important acting of your dread command?
O, say!
GHOST Do not forget. This visitation
Is but to whet thy almost blunted purpose.
But look, amazement on thy mother sits.
O, step between her and her fighting soul!
Conceit[3] in weakest bodies strongest works.
Speak to her, Hamlet.
HAMLET How is it with you, lady?
QUEEN Alas, how is't with you,
That you do bend your eye on vacancy,
And with th' incorporal[4] air do hold discourse?
Forth at your eyes your spirits wildly peep,
And as the sleeping soldiers in th' alarm
Your bedded hairs like life in excrements[5]
Start up and stand an[6] end. O gentle son,
Upon the heat and flame of thy distemper[7]
Sprinkle cool patience. Whereon do you look?
HAMLET On him, on him! Look you, how pale he glares!
His form and cause conjoined, preaching to stones,
Would make them capable.[8]—Do not look upon me,
Lest with his piteous action you convert
My stern effects.[9] Then what I have to do
Will want true color—tears perchance for blood.
QUEEN To whom do you speak this?
HAMLET Do you see nothing there?

---

[7]tenth part [8]clownish rogue (like the Vice of the morality plays) [9]skulking thief [1]dressing gown [2]having let the moment slip and passion cool [3]imagination [4]bodiless [5]outgrowths [6]on [7]mental disorder [8]susceptible [9]manifestations of emotion and purpose

QUEEN Nothing at all; yet all that is I see.
HAMLET Nor did you nothing hear?
QUEEN No, nothing but ourselves.
HAMLET Why, look you there! Look how it steals away!
My father, in his habit as he lived!
Look where he goes even now out at the portal!

(*Exit* GHOST.)

QUEEN This is the very coinage of your brain.
This bodiless creation ecstasy[1]
Is very cunning in.
HAMLET Ecstasy?
My pulse as yours doth temperately keep time
And makes as healthful music. It is not madness
That I have uttered. Bring me to the test,
And I the matter will reword, which madness
Would gambol[2] from. Mother, for love of grace,
Lay not that flattering unction[3] to your soul,
That not your trespass but my madness speaks.
It will but skin and film the ulcerous place
Whiles rank corruption, mining[4] all within,
Infects unseen. Confess yourself to heaven,
Repent what's past, avoid what is to come,
And do not spread the compost[5] on the weeds
To make them ranker. Forgive me this my virtue.
For in the fatness[6] of these pursy[7] times
Virtue itself of vice must pardon beg,
Yea, curb[8] and woo for leave to do him good.
QUEEN O Hamlet, thou hast cleft my heart in twain.
HAMLET O, throw away the worser part of it,
And live the purer with the other half.
Good night—but go not to my uncle's bed.
Assume a virtue, if you have it not.
That monster custom, who all sense doth eat,
Of habits devil, is angel yet in this,
That to the use of actions fair and good
He likewise gives a frock or livery[9]
That aptly is put on. Refrain to-night,
And that shall lend a kind of easiness
To the next abstinence; the next more easy;
For use[1] almost can change the stamp[2] of nature,

---

[1]madness [2]shy (like a startled horse) [3]ointment [4]undermining [5]fertilizing mixture [6]gross slackness [7]corpulent [8]bow to [9]characteristic dress (accompanying the suggestion of "garb" in *habits*) [1]habit [2]impression, form

And either [. . .][3] the devil, or throw him out
With wondrous potency. Once more, good night,
And when you are desirous to be blest,
I'll blessing beg of you.—For this same lord,
I do repent; but heaven hath pleased it so,
To punish me with this, and this with me,
That I must be their scourge and minister.
I will bestow[4] him and will answer well
The death I gave him. So again, good night.
I must be cruel only to be kind.
Thus bad begins, and worse remains behind.[5]
One word more, good lady.

QUEEN What shall I do?

HAMLET Not this, by no means, that I bid you do:
Let the bloat[6] king tempt you again to bed,
Pinch wanton on your cheek, call you his mouse,
And let him, for a pair of reechy[7] kisses,
Or paddling in your neck with his damned fingers,
Make you to ravel all this matter out,[8]
That I essentially am not in madness,
But mad in craft. 'Twere good you let him know,
For who that's but a queen, fair, sober, wise,
Would from a paddock,[9] from a bat, a gib,[1]
Such dear concernings[2] hide? Who would do so?
No, in despite of sense and secrecy,
Unpeg the basket on the house's top,
Let the birds fly, and like the famous ape,[3]
To try conclusions,[4] in the basket creep
And break your own neck down.

QUEEN Be thou assured, if words be made of breath,
And breath of life, I have no life to breathe
What thou hast said to me.

HAMLET I must to England; you know that?

QUEEN Alack,
I had forgot. 'Tis so concluded on.

HAMLET There's letters sealed, and my two schoolfellows,
Whom I will trust as I will adders fanged,
They bear the mandate,[5] they must sweep my way
And marshal me to knavery. Let it work.
For 'tis the sport to have the enginer[6]
Hoist[7] with his own petar,[8] and 't shall go hard

[3]A word is apparently omitted here. [4]stow, hide [5]to come [6]bloated with sense gratification [7]filthy [8]ravel . . . out: disentangle [9]toad [1]tomcat [2]matters of great personal significance [3](one in a story now unknown) [4]experiments [5]order [6]engineer, constructor of military engines or works [7]blown up [8]petard, bomb or mine

But I will delve one yard below their mines
And blow them at the moon. O, 'tis most sweet
When in one line two crafts directly meet.
This man shall set me packing.[9]
I'll lug the guts into the neighbor room.
Mother, good night. Indeed, this counsellor
Is now most still, most secret, and most grave,
Who was in life a foolish prating knave.
Come, sir, to draw toward an end with you.
Good night, mother.

(*Exit the* QUEEN. *Then exit* HAMLET, *tugging in* POLONIUS.)

Act IV

Scene I

A chamber in the castle.

(*Enter* KING *and* QUEEN, *with* ROSENCRANTZ *and* GUILDENSTERN.)

KING There's matter in these sighs. These profound heaves
You must translate; 'tis fit we understand them.
Where is your son?

QUEEN Bestow this place on us a little while.

(*Exeunt* ROSENCRANTZ *and* GUILDENSTERN.)

Ah, mine own lord, what have I seen to-night!

KING What, Gertrude? How does Hamlet?

QUEEN Mad as the sea and wind when both contend
Which is the mightier. In his lawless fit,
Behind the arras hearing something stir,
Whips out his rapier, cries, "A rat, a rat!"
And in this brainish apprehension[1] kills
The unseen good old man.

KING O heavy deed!
It had been so with us, had we been there.
His liberty is full of threats to all,
To you yourself, to us, to every one.
Alas, how shall this bloody deed be answered?
It will be laid to us, whose providence[2]
Should have kept short, restrained, and out of haunt[3]

---

[9]traveling in a hurry (with a play upon his "packing" or shouldering of Polonius's body and also upon his "packing" in the sense of "plotting" or "contriving") [1]headstrong conception [2]foresight [3]association with others

This mad young man. But so much was our love
We would not understand what was most fit,
But, like the owner of a foul disease,
To keep it from divulging,[4] let it feed
Even on the pith of life. Where is he gone?

QUEEN To draw apart the body he hath killed;
O'er whom his very madness, like some ore[5]
Among a mineral[6] of metals base,
Shows itself pure. 'A weeps for what is done.

KING O Gertrude, come away!
The sun no sooner shall the mountains touch
But we will ship him hence, and this vile deed
We must with all our majesty and skill
Both countenance and excuse. Ho, Guildenstern!

(*Enter* ROSENCRANTZ *and* GUILDENSTERN.)

Friends both, go join you with some further aid.
Hamlet in madness hath Polonius slain,
And from his mother's closet hath he dragged him.
Go seek him out; speak fair, and bring the body
Into the chapel. I pray you haste in this.

(*Exeunt* ROSENCRANTZ *and* GUILDENSTERN.)

Come, Gertrude, we'll call up our wisest friends
And let them know both what we mean to do
And what's untimely done [. . .][7]
Whose whisper o'er the world's diameter,
As level[8] as the cannon to his blank[9]
Transports his poisoned shot, may miss our name
And hit the woundless air. O, come away!
My soul is full of discord and dismay.

(*Exeunt.*)

Scene II

A passage in the castle.

(*Enter* HAMLET.)

HAMLET Safely stowed.

GENTLEMEN (*within*) Hamlet! Lord Hamlet!

---

[4]becoming known [5]vein of gold [6]mine [7]incomplete line; Capell suggests "So, haply, slander"
[8]with as direct aim [9]mark, central white spot on a target

HAMLET But soft, what noise? Who calls on Hamlet? O, here they come.

(*Enter* ROSENCRANTZ, GUILDENSTERN, *and others.*)

ROSENCRANTZ What have you done, my lord, with the dead body?

HAMLET Compounded it with dust, whereto 'tis kin.

ROSENCRANTZ Tell us where 'tis, that we may take it thence
And bear it to the chapel.

HAMLET Do not believe it.

ROSENCRANTZ Believe what?

HAMLET That I can keep your counsel and not mine own. Besides, to be demanded of a sponge, what replication[1] should be made by the son of a king?

ROSENCRANTZ Take you me for a sponge, my lord?

HAMLET Ay, sir, that soaks up the king's countenance,[2] his rewards, his authorities. But such officers do the king best service in the end. He keeps them, like an ape, in the corner of his jaw, first mouthed, to be last swallowed. When he needs what you have gleaned, it is but squeezing you and, sponge, you shall be dry again.

ROSENCRANTZ I understand you not, my lord.

HAMLET I am glad of it. A knavish speech sleeps in[3] a foolish ear.

ROSENCRANTZ My lord, you must tell us where the body is and go with us to the king.

HAMLET The body is with the king, but the king is not with the body. The king is a thing—

GUILDENSTERN A thing, my lord?

HAMLET Of nothing.[4] Bring me to him. Hide fox, and all after.[5]

(*Exeunt.*)

Scene III

A chamber in the castle.

(*Enter* KING, *and two or three.*)

KING I have sent to seek him and to find the body.
How dangerous is it that this man goes loose!
Yet must not we put the strong law on him;
He's loved of the distracted[6] multitude,
Who like not in their judgment, but their eyes,
And where 'tis so, th' offender's scourge[7] is weighed,
But never the offense. To bear all smooth and even,
This sudden sending him away must seem

---

[1]reply [2]favor [3]means nothing to [4]Cf. Prayer Book, Psalm cxliv, 4, "Man is like a thing of naught: his time passeth away like a shadow." [5]Hide . . . after: (apparently well-known words from some game of hide-and-seek) [6]confused [7]punishment

Deliberate pause.[8] Diseases desperate grown
By desperate appliance are relieved,
Or not at all.

(*Enter* Rosencrantz, Guildenstern, *and all the rest.*)

How now? What hath befallen?

ROSENCRANTZ Where the dead body is bestowed, my lord,
We cannot get from him.

KING But where is he?

ROSENCRANTZ Without, my lord; guarded, to know your pleasure.

KING Bring him before us.

ROSENCRANTZ Ho! Bring in the lord.

(*They enter* [*with* Hamlet].)

KING Now, Hamlet, where's Polonius?

HAMLET At supper.

KING At supper? Where?

HAMLET Not where he eats, but where 'a is eaten. A certain convocation of politic worms[9] are e'en at him. Your worm is your only emperor for diet.[1] We fat all creatures else to fat us, and we fat ourselves for maggots. Your fat king and your lean beggar is but variable service[2]—two dishes, but to one table. That's the end.

KING Alas, alas!

HAMLET A man may fish with the worm that hath eat of a king, and eat of the fish that hath fed of that worm.

KING What dost thou mean by this?

HAMLET Nothing but to show you how a king may go a progress[3] through the guts of a beggar.

KING Where is Polonius?

HAMLET In heaven. Send thither to see. If your messenger find him not there, seek him i' th' other place yourself. But if indeed you find him not within this month, you shall nose him as you go up the stairs into the lobby.

KING (*to* Attendants) Go seek him there.

HAMLET 'A will stay till you come.

(*Exeunt* Attendants.)

[8]something done with much deliberation [9]political and craftily scheming worms (such as Polonius might well attract) [1]food and drink (perhaps with a play upon a famous "convocation," the Diet of Worms opened by the Emperor Charles V on January 28, 1521, before which Luther appeared) [2]different servings of one food [3]royal journey of state

KING Hamlet, this deed, for thine especial safety,
Which we do tender[4] as we dearly[5] grieve
For that which thou hast done, must send thee hence
With fiery quickness. Therefore prepare thyself.
The bark is ready and the wind at help,
Th' associates tend,[6] and everything is bent[7]
For England.

HAMLET For England?

KING Ay, Hamlet.

HAMLET Good.

KING So is it, if thou knew'st our purposes.

HAMLET I see a cherub[8] that sees them. But come, for England! Farewell, dear mother.

KING Thy loving father, Hamlet.

HAMLET My mother—father and mother is man and wife, man and wife is one flesh, and so, my mother. Come, for England!

(*Exit.*)

KING Follow him at foot;[9] tempt him with speed aboard.
Delay it not; I'll have him hence to-night.
Away! for everything is sealed and done
That else leans on[1] th' affair. Pray you make haste.

(*Exeunt all but the* KING.)

And, England,[2] if my love thou hold'st at aught—
As my great power thereof may give thee sense,
Since yet thy cicatrice looks raw and red
After the Danish sword, and thy free awe[3]
Pays homage to us—thou mayst not coldly set[4]
Our sovereign process,[5] which imports at full
By letters congruing[6] to that effect
The present[7] death of Hamlet. Do it, England,
For like the hectic[8] in my blood he rages,
And thou must cure me. Till I know 'tis done,
Howe'er my haps,[9] my joys were ne'er begun.

(*Exit.*)

---

[4]hold dear [5]intensely [6]wait [7]set in readiness (like a bent bow) [8]one of the cherubim (angels with a distinctive quality of knowledge) [9]at heel, close [1]is connected with [2]King of England [3]voluntary show of respect [4]esteem [5]formal command [6]agreeing [7]instant [8]a continuous fever [9]fortunes

Scene IV

A coastal highway.

(*Enter* FORTINBRAS *with his* ARMY *over the stage.*)

FORTINBRAS Go, captain, from me greet the Danish king.
Tell him that by his license Fortinbras
Craves the conveyance[1] of a promised march
Over his kingdom. You know the rendezvous.
If that his majesty would aught with us,
We shall express our duty in his eye,[2]
And let him know so.

CAPTAIN I will do't, my lord.

FORTINBRAS Go softly[3] on.

(*Exeunt all but the* CAPTAIN.)

(*Enter* HAMLET, ROSENCRANTZ, GUILDENSTERN, *and others.*)

HAMLET Good sir, whose powers[4] are these?

CAPTAIN They are of Norway, sir.

HAMLET How purposed, sir, I pray you?

CAPTAIN Against some part of Poland.

HAMLET Who commands them, sir?

CAPTAIN The nephew to old Norway, Fortinbras.

HAMLET Goes it against the main[5] of Poland, sir,
Or for some frontier?

CAPTAIN Truly to speak, and with no addition,[6]
We go to gain a little patch of ground
That hath in it no profit but the name.
To pay[7] five ducats, five, I would not farm it,
Nor will it yield to Norway or the Pole
A ranker[8] rate, should it be sold in fee.[9]

HAMLET Why, then the Polack never will defend it.

CAPTAIN Yes, it is already garrisoned.

HAMLET Two thousand souls and twenty thousand ducats
Will not debate the question of this straw.
This is th' imposthume[1] of much wealth and peace,
That inward breaks, and shows no cause without
Why the man dies. I humbly thank you, sir.

CAPTAIN God bye you, sir.

---

[1]escort [2]presence [3]slowly [4]forces [5]main body [6]exaggeration [7]for a yearly rental of [8]more abundant [9]outright [1]abscess

(*Exit.*)

ROSENCRANTZ Will't please you go, my lord?
HAMLET I'll be with you straight. Go a little before.

(*Exeunt all but* HAMLET.)

How all occasions do inform[2] against me
And spur my dull revenge! What is a man,
If his chief good and market of[3] his time
Be but to sleep and feed? A beast, no more.
Sure he that made us with such large discourse,[4]
Looking before and after, gave us not
That capability and godlike reason
To fust[5] in us unused. Now, whether it be
Bestial oblivion,[6] or some craven scruple
Of thinking too precisely on th' event—[7]
A thought which, quartered, hath but one part wisdom
And ever three parts coward—I do not know
Why yet I live to say, "This thing's to do,"
Sith I have cause, and will, and strength, and means
To do't. Examples gross[8] as earth exhort me.
Witness this army of such mass and charge,[9]
Led by a delicate and tender prince,
Whose spirit, with divine ambition puffed,
Makes mouths[1] at the invisible event,
Exposing what is mortal and unsure
To all that fortune, death, and danger dare,
Even for an eggshell. Rightly to be great
Is not to stir without great argument,
But greatly to find quarrel in a straw[2]
When honor 's at the stake. How stand I then,
That have a father killed, a mother stained,
Excitements of my reason and my blood,
And let all sleep, while to my shame I see
The imminent death of twenty thousand men
That for a fantasy[3] and trick[4] of fame
Go to their graves like beds, fight for a plot
Whereon the numbers cannot try the cause,[5]
Which is not tomb enough and continent[6]

---

[2]take shape [3]compensation for [4]power of thought [5]grow moldy [6]forgetfulness [7]outcome [8]large and evident [9]expense [1]makes faces scornfully [2]greatly . . . straw: to recognize the great argument even in some small matter [3]fanciful image [4]toy [5]find space in which to settle the issue by battle [6]receptacle

To hide the slain? O, from this time forth,
My thoughts be bloody, or be nothing worth!

(*Exit.*)

Scene V

A chamber in the castle.

(*Enter* HORATIO, [QUEEN] GERTRUDE, *and a* GENTLEMAN.)

QUEEN I will not speak with her.
GENTLEMAN She is importunate, indeed distract.[7]
Her mood will needs be pitied.
QUEEN What would she have?
GENTLEMAN She speaks much of her father, says she hears
There's tricks[8] i' th' world, and hems, and beats her heart,
Spurns enviously[9] at straws,[1] speaks things in doubt
That carry but half sense. Her speech is nothing.
Yet the unshapèd use[2] of it doth move
The hearers to collection,[3] they aim[4] at it,
And botch[5] the words up fit to their own thoughts,
Which, as her winks and nods and gestures yield them,
Indeed would make one think there might be thought,
Though nothing sure, yet much unhappily.
HORATIO 'Twere good she were spoken with, for she may strew
Dangerous conjectures in ill-breeding minds.
QUEEN Let her come in.

(*Exit* GENTLEMAN.)

(*aside*)

To my sick soul (as sin's true nature is)
Each toy[6] seems prologue to some great amiss.[7]
So full of artless[8] jealousy[9] is guilt
It spills[1] itself in fearing to be spilt.

(*Enter* OPHELIA [*distracted*].)

OPHELIA Where is the beauteous majesty of Denmark?
QUEEN How now, Ophelia?
OPHELIA (*She sings.*)
How should I your true-love know

---

[7]insane [8]deceits [9]kicks spitefully, takes offense [1]trifles [2]disordered manner [3]attempts at shaping meaning [4]guess [5]patch [6]trifle [7]calamity [8]unskillfully managed [9]suspicion [1]destroys

From another one?
By his cockle hat[2] and staff
And his sandal shoon.[3]

QUEEN Alas, sweet lady, what imports this song?

OPHELIA Say you? Nay, pray you mark.

Song

He is dead and gone, lady,
He is dead and gone;
At his head a grass-green turf,
At his heels a stone.
O, ho!

QUEEN Nay, but Ophelia—

OPHELIA Pray you mark.
(*sings*) White his shroud as the mountain snow—

(*Enter* KING.)

QUEEN Alas, look here, my lord.

OPHELIA

Song

Larded[4] all with sweet flowers;
Which bewept to the grave did not go
With true-love showers.

KING How do you, pretty lady?

OPHELIA Well, God dild[5] you! They say the owl[6] was a baker's daughter. Lord, we know what we are, but know not what we may be. God be at your table!

KING Conceit[7] upon her father.

OPHELIA Pray let's have no words of this, but when they ask you what it means, say you this:

Song

To-morrow is Saint Valentine's day.
All in the morning betime,[8]
And I a maid at your window,
To be your Valentine.

---

[2]hat bearing a cockle shell, worn by a pilgrim who had been to the shrine of St James of Compostela [3]shoes [4]garnished [5]yield, repay [6]an owl into which, according to a folktale, a baker's daughter was transformed because of her failure to show whole-hearted generosity when Christ asked for bread in the baker's shop [7]thought [8]early

Then up he rose and donned his clo'es
And dupped[9] the chamber door,
Let in the maid, that out a maid
Never departed more.

KING Pretty Ophelia!

OPHELIA Indeed, la, without an oath, I'll make an end on't:

(*sings*) By Gis[1] and by Saint Charity,
Alack, and fie for shame!
Young men will do't if they come to't.
By Cock,[2] they are to blame.
Quoth she, "Before you tumbled me,
You promised me to wed."
He answers:
"So would I 'a' done, by yonder sun,
And thou hadst not come to my bed."

KING How long hath she been thus?

OPHELIA I hope all will be well. We must be patient, but I cannot choose but weep to think they would lay him i' th' cold ground. My brother shall know of it; and so I thank you for your good counsel. Come, my coach! Good night, ladies, good night. Sweet ladies, good night, good night.

(*Exit.*)

KING Follow her close; give her good watch, I pray you.

(*Exit* HORATIO.)

O, this is the poison of deep grief; it springs
All from her father's death—and now behold!
O Gertrude, Gertrude,
When sorrows come, they come not single spies,
But in battalions: first, her father slain;
Next, your son gone, and he most violent author
Of his own just remove; the people muddied,[3]
Thick and unwholesome in their thoughts and whispers
For good Polonius' death, and we have done but greenly[4]
In hugger-mugger[5] to inter him; poor Ophelia
Divided from herself and her fair judgment,
Without the which we are pictures or mere beasts;
Last, and as much containing as all these,
Her brother is in secret come from France,
Feeds on his wonder, keeps himself in clouds,[6]

---

[9]opened [1]Jesus [2]God (with a perversion of the name not uncommon in oaths) [3]stirred up and confused [4]foolishly [5]secrecy and disorder [6]obscurity

And wants[7] not buzzers[8] to infect his ear
With pestilent speeches of his father's death,
Wherein necessity, of matter beggared,[9]
Will nothing stick[1] our person to arraign[2]
In ear and ear. O my dear Gertrude, this,
Like to a murd'ring piece,[3] in many places
Gives me superfluous death.

(*a noise within*)

(*Enter a* MESSENGER.)

QUEEN Alack, what noise is this?

KING Attend, where are my Switzers?[4] Let them guard the door. What is the matter?

MESSENGER Save yourself, my lord.
The ocean, overpeering of[5] his list,[6]
Eats not the flats with more impiteous[7] haste
Than young Laertes, in a riotous head,[8]
O'erbears your officers. The rabble call him lord,
And, as the world were now but to begin,
Antiquity forgot, custom not known,
The ratifiers and props of every word,[9]
They cry, "Choose we! Laertes shall be king!"
Caps, hands, and tongues applaud it to the clouds,
"Laertes shall be king! Laertes king!"

(*a noise within*)

QUEEN How cheerfully on the false trail they cry!
O, this is counter,[1] you false Danish dogs!

KING The doors are broke.

(*Enter* LAERTES *with others.*)

LAERTES Where is this king?—Sirs, stand you all without.

ALL No, let's come in.

LAERTES I pray you give me leave.

ALL We will, we will.

LAERTES I thank you. Keep the door.

(*Exeunt his* FOLLOWERS.)

O thou vile king,
Give me my father.

---

[7]lacks [8]whispering talebearers [9]unprovided with facts [1]in no way hesitate [2]accuse [3]cannon loaded with shot meant to scatter [4]hired Swiss guards [5]rising to look over and pass beyond [6]boundary [7]pitiless [8]armed force [9]promise [1]hunting backward on the trail

QUEEN Calmly, good Laertes.
LAERTES That drop of blood that's calm proclaims me bastard,
Cries cuckold to my father, brands the harlot
Even here between the chaste unsmirchèd brows
Of my true mother.
KING What is the cause, Laertes,
That thy rebellion looks so giant-like?
Let him go, Gertrude. Do not fear[2] our person.
There's such divinity doth hedge a king
That treason can but peep to[3] what it would,
Acts little of his will. Tell me, Laertes,
Why thou art thus incensed. Let him go, Gertrude.
Speak, man.
LAERTES Where is my father?
KING Dead.
QUEEN But not by him.
KING Let him demand his fill.
LAERTES How came he dead? I'll not be juggled with.
To hell allegiance, vows to the blackest devil,
Conscience and grace to the profoundest pit!
I dare damnation. To this point I stand,
That both the worlds[4] I give to negligence,[5]
Let come what comes, only I'll be revenged
Most throughly[6] for my father.
KING Who shall stay you?
LAERTES My will, not all the world's.
And for my means, I'll husband them so well
They shall go far with little.
KING Good Laertes,
If you desire to know the certainty
Of your dear father, is't writ in your revenge
That swoopstake[7] you will draw both friend and foe,
Winner and loser?
LAERTES None but his enemies.
KING Will you know them then?
LAERTES To his good friends thus wide I'll ope my arms
And like the kind life-rend'ring[8] pelican
Repast them with my blood.
KING Why, now you speak
Like a good child and a true gentleman.

[2]fear for [3]through the barrier [4]whatever may result in this world or the next [5]disregard [6]thoroughly [7]sweepstake, taking all stakes on the gambling table [8]life-yielding (because the mother pelican supposedly took blood from her breast with her bill to feed her young)

That I am guiltless of your father's death,
And am most sensibly[9] in grief for it,
It shall as level[1] to your judgment 'pear
As day does to your eye.
(*a noise within:*) "Let her come in!"

LAERTES How now? What noise is that?

(*Enter* OPHELIA.)

O heat, dry up my brains; tears seven times salt
Burn out the sense and virtue of mine eye!
By heaven, thy madness shall be paid by weight
Till our scale turn the beam.[2] O rose of May,
Dear maid, kind sister, sweet Ophelia!
O heavens, is't possible a young maid's wits
Should be as mortal as an old man's life?
Nature is fine[3] in love, and where 'tis fine,
It sends some precious instance[4] of itself
After the thing it loves.

OPHELIA

Song

They bore him barefaced on the bier
Hey non nony, nony, hey nony
And in his grave rained many a tear—
Fare you well, my dove!

LAERTES Hadst thou thy wits, and didst persuade revenge,
It could not move thus.

OPHELIA You must sing "A-down a-down, and you call him a-down-a." O, how the wheel[5] becomes it! It is the false steward, that stole his master's daughter.

LAERTES This nothing 's more than matter.[6]

OPHELIA There's rosemary, that's for remembrance. Pray you, love, remember. And there is pansies, that's for thoughts.

LAERTES A document[7] in madness, thoughts and remembrance fitted.

OPHELIA There's fennel[8] for you, and columbines.[9] There's rue[1] for you, and here's some for me. We may call it herb of grace o' Sundays. O, you must wear your rue with a difference. There's a daisy.[2] I would give you some violets,[3] but they withered all when my father died. They say 'a made a good end.
(*sings*) For bonny sweet Robin is all my joy.

[9]feelingly [1]plain [2]bar of a balance [3]refined to purity [4]token [5]burden, refrain [6]more meaningful than sane speech [7]lesson [8]symbol of flattery [9]symbol of thanklessness [1]symbol of repentance [2]symbol of dissembling [3]symbol of faithfulness

LAERTES Thought and affliction, passion, hell itself,
She turns to favor[4] and to prettiness.

OPHELIA

Song

And will 'a not come again?
And will 'a not come again?
No, no, he is dead;
Go to thy deathbed;
He never will come again.
His beard was as white as snow,
All flaxen was his poll.[5]
He is gone, he is gone,
And we cast away moan.
God 'a' mercy on his soul!
And of[6] all Christian souls, I pray God. God bye you.

(*Exit.*)

LAERTES Do you see this, O God?

KING Laertes, I must commune with your grief,
Or you deny me right. Go but apart,
Make choice of whom your wisest friends you will,
And they shall hear and judge 'twixt you and me.
If by direct or by collateral[7] hand
They find us touched,[8] we will our kingdom give,
Our crown, our life, and all that we call ours,
To you in satisfaction; but if not,
Be you content to lend your patience to us,
And we shall jointly labor with your soul
To give it due content.

LAERTES Let this be so.
His means of death, his obscure funeral—
No trophy,[9] sword, nor hatchment[1] o'er his bones,
No noble rite nor formal ostentation[2]—
Cry to be heard, as 'twere from heaven to earth,
That[3] I must call't in question.

KING So you shall;
And where th' offense is, let the great axe fall.
I pray you go with me.

(*Exeunt.*)

[4]charm [5]head [6]on [7]indirect [8]with the crime [9]memorial [1]coat of arms [2]ceremony [3]so that

Scene VI

A chamber in the castle.

(*Enter* HORATIO *and others.*)

HORATIO What are they that would speak with me?

GENTLEMAN Seafaring men, sir. They say they have letters for you.

HORATIO Let them come in.

(*Exit* ATTENDANT.)

I do not know from what part of the world
I should be greeted, if not from Lord Hamlet.

(*Enter* SAILORS.)

SAILOR God bless you, sir.

HORATIO Let him bless thee too.

SAILOR 'A shall, sir, an't please him. There's a letter for you, sir—it came from th' ambassador that was bound for England—if your name be Horatio, as I am let to know it is.

HORATIO (*reads the letter*) "Horatio, when thou shalt have overlooked[4] this, give these fellows some means[5] to the king. They have letters for him. Ere we were two days old at sea, a pirate of very warlike appointment[6] gave us chase. Finding ourselves too slow of sail, we put on a compelled valor, and in the grapple I boarded them. On the instant they got clear of our ship; so I alone became their prisoner. They have dealt with me like thieves of mercy,[7] but they knew what they did: I am to do a good turn for them. Let the king have the letters I have sent, and repair thou to me with as much speed as thou wouldest fly death. I have words to speak in thine ear will make thee dumb; yet are they much too light for the bore[8] of the matter. These good fellows will bring thee where I am. Rosencrantz and Guildenstern hold their course for England. Of them I have much to tell thee.
Farewell.

He that thou knowest thine, Hamlet."

Come, I will give you way for these your letters,
And do't the speedier that you may direct me
To him from whom you brought them.

(*Exeunt.*)

---

[4]surveyed, scanned [5]of access [6]equipment [7]merciful thieves [8]caliber (as of a gun)

Scene VII

A chamber in the castle.

(*Enter* King *and* Laertes.)

KING Now must your conscience my acquittance seal,
And you must put me in your heart for friend,
Sith you have heard, and with a knowing ear,
That he which hath your noble father slain
Pursued my life.
LAERTES It well appears. But tell me
Why you proceeded not against these feats[9]
So crimeful and so capital[1] in nature,
As by your safety, wisdom, all things else,
You mainly[2] were stirred up.
KING O, for two special reasons,
Which may to you perhaps seem much unsinewed,
But yet to me they're strong. The queen his mother
Lives almost by his looks, and for myself—
My virtue or my plague, be it either which—
She is so conjunctive[3] to my life and soul
That, as the star moves not but in his sphere,
I could not but by her. The other motive
Why to a public count[4] I might not go
Is the great love the general gender[5] bear him,
Who, dipping all his faults in their affection,
Would, like the spring that turneth wood to stone,
Convert his gyves[6] to graces; so that my arrows,
Too slightly timbered for so loud a wind,
Would have reverted to my bow again,
And not where I had aimed them.
LAERTES And so have I a noble father lost,
A sister driven into desp'rate terms,[7]
Whose worth, if praises may go back again,[8]
Stood challenger on mount[9] of all the age
For her perfections. But my revenge will come.
KING Break not your sleeps for that. You must not think
That we are made of stuff so flat and dull
That we can let our beard be shook with danger,
And think it pastime. You shortly shall hear more.

---

[9]deeds [1]punishable by death [2]powerfully [3]closely united [4]trial, accounting [5]common people [6]fetters [7]circumstances [8]to her better circumstances [9]on a height

I loved your father, and we love ourself,
And that, I hope, will teach you to imagine—

(*Enter a* MESSENGER *with letters.*)

How now? What news?
MESSENGER Letters, my lord, from Hamlet:
These to your majesty, this to the queen.
KING From Hamlet? Who brought them?
MESSENGER Sailors, my lord, they say; I saw them not.
They were given me by Claudio: he received them
Of him that brought them.
KING Laertes, you shall hear them.—
Leave us.

(*Exit* MESSENGER.)

(*reads*) "High and mighty, you shall know I am set naked[1] on your kingdom. To-morrow shall I beg leave to see your kingly eyes; when I shall (first asking your pardon thereunto) recount the occasion of my sudden and more strange return. Hamlet."
What should this mean? Are all the rest come back?
Or is it some abuse,[2] and no such thing?
LAERTES Know you the hand?
KING 'Tis Hamlet's character.[3] "Naked"!
And in a postscript here, he says "alone."
Can you devise[4] me?
LAERTES I am lost in it, my lord. But let him come.
It warms the very sickness in my heart
That I shall live and tell him to his teeth,
"Thus diddest thou."
KING If it be so, Laertes,
(As how should it be so? how otherwise?)
Will you be ruled by me?
LAERTES Ay, my lord,
So you will not o'errule me to a peace.
KING To thine own peace. If he be now returned,
As checking at[5] his voyage, and that he means
No more to undertake it, I will work him
To an exploit now ripe in my device,
Under the which he shall not choose but fall;
And for his death no wind of blame shall breathe,

---

[1]destitute [2]imposture [3]handwriting [4]explain to [5]turning aside from (like a falcon turning from its quarry for other prey)

But even his mother shall uncharge the practice[6]
And call it accident.

LAERTES My lord, I will be ruled;
The rather if you could devise it so
That I might be the organ.[7]

KING It falls right.
You have been talked of since your travel much,
And that in Hamlet's hearing, for a quality
Wherein they say you shine. Your sum of parts
Did not together pluck such envy from him
As did that one, and that, in my regard,
Of the unworthiest siege.[8]

LAERTES What part is that, my lord?

KING A very riband[9] in the cap of youth,
Yet needful too, for youth no less becomes
The light and careless livery[1] that it wears
Than settled age his sables[2] and his weeds,[3]
Importing health[4] and graveness. Two months since
Here was a gentleman of Normandy.
I have seen myself, and served against, the French,
And they can well[5] on horseback, but this gallant
Had witchcraft in't. He grew unto his seat,
And to such wondrous doing brought his horse
As had he been incorpsed[6] and demi-natured[7]
With the brave beast. So far he topped[8] my thought[9]
That I, in forgery[1] of shapes and tricks,
Come short of what he did.

LAERTES A Norman was't?

KING A Norman.

LAERTES Upon my life, Lamord.

KING The very same.

LAERTES I know him well. He is the brooch[2] indeed
And gem of all the nation.

KING He made confession[3] of you,
And gave you such a masterly report
For art and exercise in your defense,
And for your rapier most especial,
That he cried out 'twould be a sight indeed
If one could match you. The scrimers[4] of their nation

---

[6]acquit the stratagem of being a plot [7]instrument [8]seat, rank [9]decoration [1]distinctive attire [2]dignified robes richly furred with sable [3]distinctive garments [4]welfare, prosperity [5]can perform well [6]made one body [7]made sharer of nature half and half (as man shares with horse in the centaur) [8]excelled [9]imagination of possibilities [1]invention [2]ornament [3]admitted the rival accomplishments [4]fencers

He swore had neither motion, guard, nor eye,
If you opposed them. Sir, this report of his
Did Hamlet so envenom with his envy
That he could nothing do but wish and beg
Your sudden coming o'er to play with you.
Now, out of this—

LAERTES What out of this, my lord?

KING Laertes, was your father dear to you?
Or are you like the painting of a sorrow,
A face without a heart?

LAERTES Why ask you this?

KING Not that I think you did not love your father,
But that I know love is begun by time,
And that I see, in passages of proof,[5]
Time qualifies[6] the spark and fire of it.
There lives within the very flame of love
A kind of wick or snuff[7] that will abate it,
And nothing is at a like goodness still,[8]
For goodness, growing to a plurisy,[9]
Dies in his own too-much. That we would do
We should do when we would, for this "would" changes,
And hath abatements and delays as many
As there are tongues, are hands, are accidents,
And then this "should" is like a spendthrift sigh,
That hurts[1] by easing. But to the quick[2] o' th' ulcer—
Hamlet comes back; what would you undertake
To show yourself your father's son in deed
More than in words?

LAERTES To cut his throat i' th' church!

KING No place indeed should murder sanctuarize,[3]
Revenge should have no bounds. But, good Laertes,
Will you do this? Keep close within your chamber.
Hamlet returned shall know you are come home.
We'll put on[4] those shall praise your excellence
And set a double varnish on the fame
The Frenchman gave you, bring you in fine[5] together
And wager on your heads. He, being remiss,[6]
Most generous, and free from all contriving,
Will not peruse[7] the foils, so that with ease,
Or with a little shuffling, you may choose

---

[5]incidents of experience [6]weakens [7]unconsumed portion of the burned wick [8]always [9]excess [1]shortens life by drawing blood from the heart (as was believed) [2]sensitive flesh [3]protect from punishment, give sanctuary to [4]instigate [5]finally [6]negligent [7]scan

A sword unbated,[8] and, in a pass of practice,[9]
Requite him for your father.

LAERTES I will do't,
And for that purpose I'll anoint my sword.
I bought an unction[1] of a mountebank,[2]
So mortal that, but dip a knife in it,
Where it draws blood no cataplasm[3] so rare,
Collected from all simples[4] that have virtue
Under the moon, can save the thing from death
That is but scratched withal.[5] I'll touch my point
With this contagion, that, if I gall[6] him slightly,
It may be death.

KING Let's further think of this,
Weigh what convenience both of time and means
May fit us to our shape.[7] If this should fail,
And that our drift[8] look[9] through our bad performance,
'Twere better not assayed. Therefore this project
Should have a back or second, that might hold
If this did blast in proof.[1] Soft, let me see.
We'll make a solemn wager on your cunnings—
I ha't!
When in your motion you are hot and dry—
As make your bouts more violent to that end—
And that he calls for drink, I'll have preferred[2] him
A chalice for the nonce,[3] whereon but sipping,
If he by chance escape your venomed stuck,[4]
Our purpose may hold there.—But stay, what noise?

(*Enter* QUEEN.)

QUEEN One woe doth tread upon another's heel,
So fast they follow. Your sister's drowned, Laertes.

LAERTES Drowned! O, where?

QUEEN There is a willow grows askant[5] the brook,
That shows his hoar[6] leaves in the glassy stream.
Therewith fantastic garlands did she make
Of crowflowers, nettles, daisies, and long purples,
That liberal[7] shepherds give a grosser name,
But our cold maids do dead men's fingers call them.
There on the pendent boughs her crownet[8] weeds

---

[8]not blunted [9]thrust made effective by trickery [1]ointment [2]quack-doctor [3]poultice [4]herbs [5]with it [6]scratch [7]plan [8]intention [9]show [1]burst during trial (like a faulty cannon) [2]offered [3]occasion [4]thrust [5]alongside [6]grey [7]free-spoken, licentious [8]coronet

Clamb'ring to hang, an envious sliver broke,
When down her weedy trophies and herself
Fell in the weeping brook. Her clothes spread wide,
And mermaid-like awhile they bore her up,
Which time she chanted snatches of old lauds,[9]
As one incapable of[1] her own distress,
Or like a creature native and indued[2]
Unto that element. But long it could not be
Till that her garments, heavy with their drink,
Pulled the poor wretch from her melodious lay
To muddy death.

LAERTES Alas, then she is drowned?

QUEEN Drowned, drowned.

LAERTES Too much of water hast thou, poor Ophelia,
And therefore I forbid my tears; but yet
It is our trick;[3] nature her custom holds,
Let shame say what it will. When these are gone,
The woman[4] will be out. Adieu, my lord.
I have a speech o' fire, that fain would blaze
But that this folly drowns it.

(*Exit.*)

KING Let's follow, Gertrude.
How much I had to do to calm his rage!
Now fear I this will give it start again;
Therefore let's follow.

(*Exeunt.*)

Act V

Scene I

A churchyard.

(*Enter two* CLOWNS.[5])

CLOWN Is she to be buried in Christian burial[6] when she willfully seeks her own salvation?

OTHER I tell thee she is. Therefore make her grave straight.[7] The crowner[8] hath sate on her, and finds it Christian burial.

---

[9]hymns [1]insensible to [2]endowed [3]way (i.e., to shed tears when sorrowful) [4]unmanly part of nature [5]rustics [6]in consecrated ground with the prescribed service of the Church (a burial denied to suicides) [7]straightway, at once [8]coroner

CLOWN How can that be, unless she drowned herself in her own defense?

OTHER Why, 'tis found so.

CLOWN It must be *se offendendo;*[9] it cannot be else. For here lies the point: if I drown myself wittingly, it argues an act, and an act hath three branches—it is to act, to do, and to perform. Argal,[1] she drowned herself wittingly.

OTHER Nay, but hear you, Goodman Delver.[2]

CLOWN Give me leave. Here lies the water—good. Here stands the man—good. If the man go to this water and drown himself, it is, will he nill he,[3] he goes, mark you that. But if the water come to him and drown him, he drowns not himself. Argal, he that is not guilty of his own death shortens not his own life.

OTHER But is this law?

CLOWN Ay marry, is't—crowner's quest[4] law.

OTHER Will you ha' the truth on't? If this had not been a gentlewoman, she should have been buried out o' Christian burial.

CLOWN Why, there thou say'st.[5] And the more pity that great folk should have count'nance[6] in this world to drown or hang themselves more than their even-Christen.[7] Come, my spade. There is no ancient gentlemen but gard'-ners, ditchers, and grave-makers. They hold up Adam's profession.

OTHER Was he a gentleman?

CLOWN 'A was the first that ever bore arms.

OTHER Why, he had none.[8]

CLOWN What, art a heathen? How dost thou understand the Scripture? The Scripture says Adam digged. Could he dig without arms? I'll put another question to thee. If thou answerest me not to the purpose, confess thyself—

OTHER Go to.

CLOWN What is he that builds stronger than either the mason, the shipwright, or the carpenter?

OTHER The gallows-maker, for that frame outlives a thousand tenants.

CLOWN I like thy wit well, in good faith. The gallows does well. But how does it well? It does well to those that do ill. Now thou dost ill to say the gallows is built stronger than the church. Argal, the gallows may do well to thee. To't again, come.

OTHER Who builds stronger than a mason, a shipwright, or a carpenter?

CLOWN Ay, tell me that, and unyoke.[9]

OTHER Marry, now I can tell.

CLOWN To't.

OTHER Mass,[1] I cannot tell.

CLOWN Cudgel thy brains no more about it, for your dull ass will not mend his pace with beating. And when you are asked this question next, say "a grave-

---

[9]a clownish transformation of "*se defendendo,*" "in self-defense" [1]for "*ergo,*" "therefore" [2]Digger [3]willy-nilly [4]inquest [5]you have it right [6]privilege [7]fellow Christian [8]had no gentleman's coat of arms [9]unharness your powers of thought after a good day's work [1]by the Mass

maker." The houses he makes last till doomsday. Go, get thee in, and fetch me a stoup[2] of liquor.

(*Exit* OTHER CLOWN.)

(*Enter* HAMLET *and* HORATIO [*as* CLOWN *digs and sings*].)

Song

In youth when I did love, did love,
Methought it was very sweet
To contract—O—the time for—a—my behove,[3]
O, methought there—a—was nothing—a—meet.

HAMLET Has this fellow no feeling of his business, that 'a sings at grave-making?

HORATIO Custom hath made it in him a property[4] of easiness.[5]

HAMLET 'Tis e'en so. The hand of little employment hath the daintier sense.[6]

CLOWN

Song

But age with his stealing steps
Hath clawed me in his clutch,
And hath shipped me intil[7] the land,
As if I had never been such.

(*throws up a skull*)

HAMLET That skull had a tongue in it, and could sing once. How the knave jowls[8] it to the ground, as if 'twere Cain's jawbone, that did the first murder! This might be the pate of a politician,[9] which this ass now o'erreaches;[1] one that would circumvent God, might it not?

HORATIO It might, my lord.

HAMLET Or of a courtier, which could say "Good morrow, sweet lord! How dost thou, sweet lord?" This might be my Lord Such-a-one, that praised my Lord Such-a-one's horse when 'a meant to beg it, might it not?

HORATIO Ay, my lord.

HAMLET Why, e'en so, and now my Lady Worm's, chapless,[2] and knocked about the mazzard[3] with a sexton's spade. Here's fine revolution, an we had the trick to see't. Did these bones cost no more the breeding but to play at loggets[4] with 'em? Mine ache to think on't.

---

[2]large mug [3]behoof, benefit [4]peculiarity [5]easy acceptability [6]more delicate feeling (because the hand is less calloused) [7]into [8]hurls [9]crafty schemer [1]gets the better of (with a play upon the literal meaning) [2]lacking the lower chap or jaw [3]head [4]small pieces of wood thrown in a game

CLOWN

Song

A pickaxe and a spade, a spade,
For and[5] a shrouding sheet;
O, a pit of clay for to be made
For such a guest is meet.

(*throws up another skull*)

HAMLET There's another. Why may not that be the skull of a lawyer? Where be his quiddities[6] now, his quillities,[7] his cases, his tenures,[8] and his tricks? Why does he suffer this mad knave now to knock him about the sconce[9] with a dirty shovel, and will not tell him of his action of battery? Hum! This fellow might be in's time a great buyer of land, with his statutes, his recognizances,[1] his fines,[2] his double vouchers,[3] his recoveries. Is this the fine[4] of his fines, and the recovery of his recoveries, to have his fine pate full of fine dirt? Will his vouchers vouch him no more of his purchases, and double ones too, than the length and breadth of a pair of indentures?[5] The very conveyances[6] of his lands will scarcely lie in this box, and must th' inheritor himself have no more, ha?

HORATIO Not a jot more, my lord.

HAMLET Is not parchment made of sheepskins?

HORATIO Ay, my lord, and of calveskins too.

HAMLET They are sheep and calves which seek out assurance in that. I will speak to this fellow. Whose grave 's this, sirrah?

CLOWN Mine, sir.
(*sings*) O, a pit of clay for to be made
For such a guest is meet.

HAMLET I think it be thine indeed, for thou liest in't.

CLOWN You lie out on't, sir, and therefore 'tis not yours. For my part, I do not lie in't, yet it is mine.

HAMLET Thou dost lie in't, to be in't and say it is thine. 'Tis for the dead, not for the quick;[7] therefore thou liest.

CLOWN 'Tis a quick lie, sir; 'twill away again from me to you.

HAMLET What man dost thou dig it for?

CLOWN For no man, sir.

HAMLET What woman then?

CLOWN For none neither.

---

[5]and [6]subtleties (from scholastic *quidditas,* meaning the distinctive nature of anything) [7]nice distinctions [8]holdings of property [9]head [1]legal documents or bonds acknowledging debt [2]modes of converting estate tail into fee simple [3]persons vouched or called on to warrant a title [4]end (introducing a word play involving four meanings of "fine") [5]deed or legal agreement in duplicate [6]deeds [7]living

HAMLET Who is to be buried in't?

CLOWN One that was a woman, sir; but, rest her soul, she's dead.

HAMLET How absolute[8] the knave is! We must speak by the card,[9] or equivocation[1] will undo us. By the Lord, Horatio, this three years I have taken note of it, the age is grown so picked[2] that the toe of the peasant comes so near the heel of the courtier he galls[3] his kibe.[4]—How long hast thou been a grave-maker?

CLOWN Of all the days i' th' year, I came to't that day that our last king Hamlet overcame Fortinbras.

HAMLET How long is that since?

CLOWN Cannot you tell that? Every fool can tell that. It was the very day that young Hamlet was born—he that is mad, and sent into England.

HAMLET Ay, marry, why was he sent into England?

CLOWN Why, because 'a was mad. 'A shall recover his wits there; or, if'a do not, 'tis no great matter there.

HAMLET Why?

CLOWN 'Twill not be seen in him there. There the men are as mad as he.

HAMLET How came he mad?

CLOWN Very strangely, they say.

HAMLET How strangely?

CLOWN Faith, e'en with losing his wits.

HAMLET Upon what ground?

CLOWN Why, here in Denmark. I have been sexton here, man and boy, thirty years.

HAMLET How long will a man lie i' th' earth ere he rot?

CLOWN Faith, if'a be not rotten before 'a die (as we have many pocky[5] corses now-a-days that will scarce hold the laying in), 'a will last you some eight year or nine year. A tanner will last you nine year.

HAMLET Why he more than another?

CLOWN Why, sir, his hide is so tanned with his trade that 'a will keep out water a great while, and your water is a sore decayer of your whoreson dead body. Here's a skull now hath lien you i' th' earth three-and-twenty years.

HAMLET Whose was it?

CLOWN A whoreson mad fellow's it was. Whose do you think it was?

HAMLET Nay, I know not.

CLOWN A pestilence on him for a mad rogue! 'A poured a flagon of Rhenish[6] on my head once. This same skull, sir, was—sir—Yorick's skull, the king's jester.

HAMLET This?

CLOWN E'en that.

---

[8]positive [9]by the card on which the points of the mariner's compass are marked, absolutely to the point [1]ambiguity [2]refined, spruce [3]chafes [4]chilblain [5]rotten (literally, corrupted by pox, or syphilis) [6]Rhine wine

HAMLET Let me see. (*takes the skull*) Alas, poor Yorick! I knew him, Horatio, a fellow of infinite jest, of most excellent fancy. He hath borne me on his back a thousand times. And now how abhorred in my imagination it is! My gorge rises at it. Here hung those lips that I have kissed I know not how oft. Where be your gibes now? Your gambols, your songs, your flashes of merriment that were wont to set the table on a roar? Not one now to mock your own grinning? Quite chapfall'n?[7] Now get you to my lady's chamber, and tell her, let her paint an inch thick, to this favor[8] she must come. Make her laugh at that. Prithee, Horatio, tell me one thing.

HORATIO What's that, my lord?

HAMLET Dost thou think Alexander looked o' this fashion i' th' earth?

HORATIO E'en so.

HAMLET And smelt so? Pah!

(*puts down the skull*)

HORATIO E'en so, my lord.

HAMLET To what base uses we may return, Horatio! Why may not imagination trace the noble dust of Alexander till 'a find it stopping a bunghole?

HORATIO 'Twere to consider too curiously,[9] to consider so.

HAMLET No, faith, not a jot, but to follow him thither with modesty[1] enough, and likelihood to lead it; as thus: Alexander died, Alexander was buried, Alexander returneth to dust; the dust is earth; of earth we make loam; and why of that loam whereto he was converted might they not stop a beer barrel?

Imperious[2] Caesar, dead and turned to clay,
Might stop a hole to keep the wind away.
O, that that earth which kept the world in awe
Should patch a wall t' expel the winter's flaw![3]
But soft, but soft awhile! Here comes the king—

(*Enter* KING, QUEEN, LAERTES, *and the* CORSE [*with* LORDS *attendant and a* DOCTOR OF DIVINITY *as* PRIEST].)

The queen, the courtiers. Who is this they follow?
And with such maimèd rites? This doth betoken
The corse they follow did with desp'rate hand
Fordo[4] it[5] own life. 'Twas of some estate.[6]
Couch[7] we awhile, and mark.

(*retires with* HORATIO)

LAERTES What ceremony else?

---

[7]lacking the lower chap, or jaw (with a play on the sense "down in the mouth," "dejected") [8]countenance, aspect [9]minutely [1]moderation [2]imperial [3]gust of wind [4]destroy [5]its [6]rank [7]hide

HAMLET That is Laertes,
A very noble youth. Mark.
LAERTES What ceremony else?
DOCTOR Her obsequies have been as far enlarged
As we have warranty. Her death was doubtful,
And, but that great command o'ersways the order,
She should in ground unsanctified have lodged
Till the last trumpet. For charitable prayers,
Shards,[8] flints, and pebbles should be thrown on her.
Yet here she is allowed her virgin crants,[9]
Her maiden strewments,[1] and the bringing home[2]
Of bell and burial.
LAERTES Must there no more be done?
DOCTOR No more be done.
We should profane the service of the dead
To sing a requiem and such rest to her
As to peace-parted souls.
LAERTES Lay her i' th' earth,
And from her fair and unpolluted flesh
May violets spring! I tell thee, churlish priest,
A minist'ring angel shall my sister be
When thou liest howling.
HAMLET What, the fair Ophelia?
QUEEN Sweets to the sweet! Farewell.

(*scatters flowers*)

I hoped thou shouldst have been my Hamlet's wife.
I thought thy bride-bed to have decked, sweet maid,
And not have strewed thy grave.
LAERTES O, treble woe
Fall ten times treble on that cursèd head
Whose wicked deed thy most ingenious[3] sense
Deprived thee of! Hold off the earth awhile,
Till I have caught her once more in mine arms.

(*leaps in the grave*)

Now pile your dust upon the quick and dead
Till of this flat a mountain you have made
T' o'ertop old Pelion[4] or the skyish head
Of blue Olympus.

---

[8]broken pieces of pottery [9]garland [1]strewings of the grave with flowers [2]laying to rest [3]of quickest apprehension [4]a mountain in Thessaly, like Olympus and also Ossa (the allusion being to the war in which the Titans fought the gods and attempted to heap Ossa and Olympus on Pelion, or Pelion and Ossa on Olympus, in order to scale heaven)

HAMLET (*coming forward*) What is he whose grief
Bears such an emphasis? whose phrase of sorrow
Conjures[5] the wand'ring stars,[6] and makes them stand
Like wonder-wounded hearers? This is I,
Hamlet the Dane.

(*leaps in after* LAERTES)

LAERTES The devil take thy soul!

(*grapples with him*)

HAMLET Thou pray'st not well.
I prithee take thy fingers from my throat,
For, though I am not splenitive[7] and rash,
Yet have I in me something dangerous,
Which let thy wisdom fear. Hold off thy hand.
KING Pluck them asunder.
QUEEN Hamlet, Hamlet!
ALL Gentlemen!
HORATIO Good my lord, be quiet.

(ATTENDANTS *part them, and they come out of the grave.*)

HAMLET Why, I will fight with him upon this theme
Until my eyelids will no longer wag.
QUEEN O my son, what theme?
HAMLET I loved Ophelia. Forty thousand brothers
Could not with all their quantity of love
Make up my sum. What wilt thou do for her?
KING O, he is mad, Laertes.
QUEEN For love of God, forbear him.
HAMLET 'Swounds, show me what thou't do.
Woo't[8] weep? woo't fight? woo't fast? woo't tear thyself?
Woo't drink up esill?[9] eat a crocodile?
I'll do't. Dost thou come here to whine?
To outface me with leaping in her grave?
Be buried quick[1] with her, and so will I.
And if thou prate of mountains, let them throw
Millions of acres on us, till our ground,
Singeing his pate against the burning zone,
Make Ossa like a wart! Nay, an thou'lt mouth,
I'll rant as well as thou.

---

[5]charms, puts a spell upon [6]planets [7]of fiery temper (the spleen being considered the seat of anger) [8]wilt (thou) [9]vinegar [1]alive

QUEEN This is mere[2] madness;
And thus a while the fit will work on him.
Anon, as patient as the female dove
When that her golden couplets[3] are disclosed,[4]
His silence will sit drooping.

HAMLET Hear you, sir.
What is the reason that you use me thus?
I loved you ever. But it is no matter.
Let Hercules himself do what he may,
The cat will mew, and dog will have his day.

KING I pray thee, good Horatio, wait upon him.

(*Exit* HAMLET *and* HORATIO.)

(*to* LAERTES)

Strengthen your patience in[5] our last night's speech.
We'll put the matter to the present push.[6]
Good Gertrude, set some watch over your son.—
This grave shall have a living monument.
An hour of quiet shortly shall we see;
Till then in patience our proceeding be.

(*Exeunt.*)

Scene II

The hall of the castle.

(*Enter* HAMLET *and* HORATIO.)

HAMLET So much for this, sir; now shall you see the other.
You do remember all the circumstance?

HORATIO Remember it, my lord!

HAMLET Sir, in my heart there was a kind of fighting
That would not let me sleep. Methought I lay
Worse than the mutines[7] in the bilboes.[8] Rashly,
And praised be rashness for it—let us know,
Our indiscretion sometime serves us well
When our deep plots do pall,[9] and that should learn us
There's a divinity that shapes our ends,
Rough-hew[1] them how we will—

HORATIO That is most certain.

[2]absolute [3]pair of fledglings [4]hatched [5]by calling to mind [6]immediate trial [7]mutineers [8]fetters [9]fail [1]shape roughly in trial form

HAMLET Up from my cabin,
My sea-gown scarfed about me, in the dark
Groped I to find out them, had my desire,
Fingered[2] their packet, and in fine[3] withdrew
To mine own room again, making so bold,
My fears forgetting manners, to unseal
Their grand commission; where I found, Horatio—
Ah, royal knavery!—an exact command,
Larded[4] with many several sorts of reasons,
Importing[5] Denmark's health, and England's too,
With, ho! such bugs[6] and goblins in my life,[7]
That on the supervise,[8] no leisure bated,[9]
No, not to stay the grinding of the axe,
My head should be struck off.
HORATIO Is't possible?
HAMLET Here's the commission; read it at more leisure.
But wilt thou hear me how I did proceed?
HORATIO I beseech you.
HAMLET Being thus benetted round with villainies,
Or[1] I could make a prologue to my brains,
They had begun the play. I sat me down,
Devised a new commission, wrote it fair.
I once did hold it, as our statists[2] do,
A baseness to write fair,[3] and labored much
How to forget that learning, but, sir, now
It did me yeoman's service.[4] Wilt thou know
Th' effect[5] of what I wrote?
HORATIO Ay, good my lord.
HAMLET An earnest conjuration from the king,
As England was his faithful tributary,
As love between them like the palm might flourish,
As peace should still her wheaten garland[6] wear
And stand a comma[7] 'tween their amities,
And many such-like as's of great charge,[8]
That on the view and knowing of these contents,
Without debatement further, more or less,
He should the bearers put to sudden death,
Not shriving time[9] allowed.

---

[2]filched [3]finally [4]enriched [5]relating to [6]bugbears [7]to be encountered as dangers if I should be allowed to live [8]perusal [9]deducted, allowed [1]ere [2]statesmen [3]with professional clarity (like a clerk or a scrivener, not like a gentleman) [4]stout service such as yeomen footsoldiers gave as archers [5]purport [6]adornment of fruitful agriculture [7]connective (because it indicates continuity of thought in a sentence) [8]burden (with a double meaning to fit a play that makes *as's* into "asses") [9]time for confession and absolution

HORATIO How was this sealed?
HAMLET Why, even in that was heaven ordinant.[1]
I had my father's signet in my purse,
Which was the model[2] of that Danish seal,
Folded the writ up in the form of th' other,
Subscribed it, gave't th' impression,[3] placed it safely,
The changeling never known. Now, the next day
Was our sea-fight, and what to this was sequent[4]
Thou know'st already.
HORATIO So Guildenstern and Rosencrantz go to't.
HAMLET Why, man, they did make love to this employment.
They are not near my conscience; their defeat
Does by their own insinuation[5] grow.
'Tis dangerous when the baser nature comes
Between the pass[6] and fell[7] incensèd points
Of mighty opposites.
HORATIO Why, what a king is this!
HAMLET Does it not, think thee, stand[8] me now upon—
He that hath killed my king, and whored my mother,
Popped in between th' election[9] and my hopes,
Thrown out his angle[1] for my proper[2] life,
And with such coz'nage[3]—is't not perfect conscience
To quit[4] him with this arm? And is't not to be damned
To let this canker[5] of our nature come
In further evil?
HORATIO It must be shortly known to him from England
What is the issue of the business there.
HAMLET It will be short; the interim is mine,
And a man's life's no more than to say "one."
But I am very sorry, good Horatio,
That to Laertes I forgot myself,
For by the image of my cause I see
The portraiture of his. I'll court his favors.
But sure the bravery[6] of his grief did put me
Into a tow'ring passion.
HORATIO Peace, who comes here?

(*Enter* OSRIC, *a courtier.*)

OSRIC Your lordship is right welcome back to Denmark.
HAMLET I humbly thank you, sir. (*aside to* HORATIO) Dost know this waterfly?

---

[1]controlling [2]counterpart [3]i.e. of the signet [4]subsequent [5]intrusion [6]thrust [7]fierce [8]rest incumbent [9]to the kingship (the Danish kingship being elective) [1]fishing line [2]own [3]cozenage, trickery [4]repay [5]cancer, ulcer [6]ostentatious display

HORATIO (*aside to* HAMLET) No, my good lord.

HAMLET (*aside to* HORATIO) Thy state is the more gracious, for 'tis a vice to know him. He hath much land, and fertile. Let a beast be lord of beasts, and his crib shall stand at the king's mess.[7] 'Tis a chough,[8] but, as I say, spacious in the possession of dirt.

OSRIC Sweet lord, if your lordship were at leisure, I should impart a thing to you from his majesty.

HAMLET I will receive it, sir, with all diligence of spirit. Put your bonnet to his right use. 'Tis for the head.

OSRIC I thank your lordship, it is very hot.

HAMLET No, believe me, 'tis very cold; the wind is northerly.

OSRIC It is indifferent[9] cold, my lord, indeed.

HAMLET But yet methinks it is very sultry and hot for my complexion.[1]

OSRIC Exceedingly, my lord; it is very sultry, as 'twere—I cannot tell how. But, my lord, his majesty bade me signify to you that 'a has laid a great wager on your head. Sir, this is the matter—

HAMLET I beseech you remember.[2]

(HAMLET *moves him to put on his hat.*)

OSRIC Nay, good my lord; for mine ease,[3] in good faith. Sir, here is newly come to court Laertes—believe me, an absolute gentleman, full of most excellent differences,[4] of very soft society[5] and great showing.[6] Indeed, to speak feelingly[7] of him, he is the card[8] or calendar[9] of gentry,[1] for you shall find in him the continent[2] of what part a gentleman would see.

HAMLET Sir, his definement[3] suffers no perdition[4] in you, though, I know, to divide him inventorially would dozy[5] th' arithmetic of memory, and yet but yaw[6] neither[7] in respect of[8] his quick sail. But, in the verity of extolment, I take him to be a soul of great article,[9] and his infusion[1] of such dearth[2] and rareness as, to make true diction of him, his semblable[3] is his mirror, and who else would trace[4] him, his umbrage,[5] nothing more.

OSRIC Your lordship speaks most infallibly of him.

HAMLET The concernancy,[6] sir? Why do we wrap the gentleman in our more rawer[7] breath?

OSRIC Sir?

HORATIO Is't not possible to understand in another tongue? You will to't,[8] sir, really.

---

[7]table [8]jackdaw, chatterer [9]somewhat [1]temperament [2]remember you have done all that courtesy demands [3]I keep my hat off just for comfort (a conventional polite phrase) [4]differentiating characteristics, special qualities [5]gentle manners [6]noble appearance [7]appropriately [8]map [9]guide [1]gentlemanliness [2]all-containing embodiment (with an implication of geographical continent to go with *card*) [3]definition [4]loss [5]dizzy, stagger [6]hold to a course unsteadily like a ship that steers wild [7]for all that [8]in comparison with [9]scope, importance [1]essence [2]scarcity [3]likeness (i.e., only true likeness) [4]follow [5]shadow [6]relevance [7]cruder speech [8]get to an understanding

HAMLET What imports the nomination[9] of this gentleman?

OSRIC Of Laertes?

HORATIO (*aside to* HAMLET) His purse is empty already. All's golden words are spent.

HAMLET Of him, sir.

OSRIC I know you are not ignorant—

HAMLET I would you did, sir; yet, in faith, if you did, it would not much approve me.[1] Well, sir?

OSRIC You are not ignorant of what excellence Laertes is—

HAMLET I dare not confess that, lest I should compare[2] with him in excellence; but to know a man well were to know himself.

OSRIC I mean, sir, for his weapon; but in the imputation laid on him by them, in his meed[3] he's unfellowed.

HAMLET What's his weapon?

OSRIC Rapier and dagger.

HAMLET That's two of his weapons—but well.

OSRIC The king, sir, hath wagered with him six Barbary horses, against the which he has impawned,[4] as I take it, six French rapiers and poniards, with their assigns,[5] as girdle, hangers,[6] and so. Three of the carriages, in faith, are very dear to fancy,[7] very responsive[8] to the hilts, most delicate carriages, and of very liberal conceit.[9]

HAMLET What call you the carriages?

HORATIO (*aside to* HAMLET) I knew you must be edified by the margent[1] ere you had done.

OSRIC The carriages, sir, are the hangers.

HAMLET The phrase would be more germane to the matter if we could carry a cannon by our sides. I would it might be hangers till then. But on! Six Barbary horses against six French swords, their assigns, and three liberal-conceited carriages—that's the French bet against the Danish. Why is this all impawned, as you call it?

OSRIC The king, sir, hath laid, sir, that in a dozen passes between yourself and him he shall not exceed you three hits; he hath laid on twelve for nine, and it would come to immediate trial if your lordship would vouchsafe the answer.

HAMLET How if I answer no?

OSRIC I mean, my lord, the opposition of your person in trial.

HAMLET Sir, I will walk here in the hall. If it please his majesty, it is the breathing time[2] of day with me. Let the foils be brought, the gentleman willing, and the king hold his purpose, I will win for him an[3] I can; if not, I will gain nothing but my shame and the odd hits.

---

[9]mention [1]be to my credit [2]compete [3]worth [4]staked [5]appurtenances [6]straps by which the sword hangs from the belt [7]finely designed [8]corresponding closely [9]tasteful design, refined conception [1]margin (i.e., explanatory notes there printed) [2]exercise hour [3]if

OSRIC Shall I redeliver you e'en so?

HAMLET To this effect, sir, after what flourish your nature will.

OSRIC I commend my duty to your lordship.

HAMLET Your, yours. (*Exit* OSRIC.) He does well to commend it himself; there are no tongues else for's turn.

HORATIO This lapwing[4] runs away with the shell on his head.

HAMLET 'A did comply,[5] sir, with his dug[6] before 'a sucked it. Thus has he, and many more of the same bevy[7] that I know the drossy[8] age dotes on, only got the tune of the time and, out of an habit of encounter, a kind of yeasty collection, which carries them through and through the most fanned and winnowed[9] opinions; and do but blow them to their trial, the bubbles are out.

(*Enter a* LORD.)

LORD My lord, his majesty commended him to you by young Osric, who brings back to him that you attend him in the hall. He sends to know if your pleasure hold to play with Laertes, or that you will take longer time.

HAMLET I am constant to my purposes; they follow the king's pleasure. If his fitness speaks, mine is ready; now or whensoever, provided I be so able as now.

LORD The king and queen and all are coming down.

HAMLET In happy time.[1]

LORD The queen desires you to use some gentle entertainment[2] to Laertes before you fall to play.

HAMLET She well instructs me.

(*Exit* LORD.)

HORATIO You will lose this wager, my lord.

HAMLET I do not think so. Since he went into France I have been in continual practice. I shall win at the odds. But thou wouldst not think how ill all's here about my heart. But it is no matter.

HORATIO Nay, good my lord—

HAMLET It is but foolery, but it is such a kind of gaingiving[3] as would perhaps trouble a woman.

HORATIO If your mind dislike anything, obey it. I will forestall their repair hither and say you are not fit.

HAMLET Not a whit, we defy augury. There is special providence in the fall of a sparrow. If it be now, 'tis not to come; if it be not to come, it will be now; if it be not now, yet it will come. The readiness is all.[4] Since no man of aught he leaves knows, what is't to leave betimes? Let be.

---

[4]a bird reputed to be so precocious as to run as soon as hatched [5]observe formalities of courtesy [6]mother's nipple [7]company [8]frivolous [9]select and refined [1]I am happy (a polite response) [2]words of reception or greeting [3]misgiving [4]all that matters

(*A table prepared. Enter* TRUMPETS, DRUMS, *and* OFFICERS *with cushions;* KING, QUEEN, OSRIC, *and all the* STATE, *with foils, daggers, and stoups of wine borne in; and* LAERTES.)

KING Come, Hamlet, come, and take this hand from me.

(*The* KING *puts* LAERTES' *hand into* HAMLET'S.)

HAMLET Give me your pardon, sir. I have done you wrong,
But pardon't, as you are a gentleman.
This presence[5] knows, and you must needs have heard,
How I am punished with a sore distraction.
What I have done
That might your nature, honor, and exception[6]
Roughly awake, I here proclaim was madness.
Was't Hamlet wronged Laertes? Never Hamlet.
If Hamlet from himself be ta'en away,
And when he's not himself does wrong Laertes,
Then Hamlet does it not, Hamlet denies it.
Who does it then? His madness. If't be so,
Hamlet is of the faction[7] that is wronged;
His madness is poor Hamlet's enemy.
Sir, in this audience,
Let my disclaiming from a purposed evil
Free me so far in your most generous thoughts
That I have shot my arrow o'er the house
And hurt my brother.

LAERTES I am satisfied in nature,[8]
Whose motive in this case should stir me most
To my revenge. But in my terms of honor[9]
I stand aloof, and will no reconcilement
Till by some elder masters of known honor
I have a voice[1] and precedent of peace
To keep my name ungored.[2] But till that time
I do receive your offered love like love,
And will not wrong it.

HAMLET I embrace it freely,
And will this brother's wager frankly play.
Give us the foils. Come on.

LAERTES Come, one for me.

---

[5]assembly [6]disapproval [7]body of persons taking a side in a contention [8]natural feeling as a person [9]position as a man of honor [1]authoritative statement [2]uninjured

HAMLET I'll be your foil,[3] Laertes. In mine ignorance
Your skill shall, like a star i' th' darkest night,
Stick fiery off[4] indeed.
LAERTES You mock me, sir.
HAMLET No, by this hand.
KING Give them the foils, young Osric. Cousin Hamlet,
You know the wager?
HAMLET Very well, my lord.
Your grace has laid the odds o' th' weaker side.
KING I do not fear it, I have seen you both;
But since he is bettered, we have therefore odds.
LAERTES This is too heavy; let me see another.
HAMLET This likes me well. These foils have all a length?

(*prepare to play*)

OSRIC Ay, my good lord.
KING Set me the stoups of wine upon that table.
If Hamlet give the first or second hit,
Or quit[5] in answer of the third exchange,
Let all the battlements their ordnance fire.
The king shall drink to Hamlet's better breath,
And in the cup an union[6] shall he throw
Richer than that which four successive kings
In Denmark's crown have worn. Give me the cups,
And let the kettle[7] to the trumpet speak,
The trumpet to the cannoneer without,
The cannons to the heavens, the heaven to earth,
"Now the king drinks to Hamlet." Come, begin.

(*trumpets the while*)

And you, the judges, bear a wary eye.
HAMLET Come on, sir.
LAERTES Come, my lord.

(*They play.*)

HAMLET One.
LAERTES No.
HAMLET Judgment?
OSRIC A hit, a very palpable hit.

---

[3]setting that displays a jewel advantageously (with a play upon the meaning "weapon") [4]show in brilliant relief [5]repay by a hit [6]pearl [7]kettledrum

(DRUM, TRUMPETS, *and* SHOT. *Flourish; a piece goes off.*)

LAERTES Well, again.
KING Stay, give me drink. Hamlet, this pearl is thine.
Here's to thy health. Give him the cup.
HAMLET I'll play this bout first; set it by awhile.
Come. (*They play.*) Another hit. What say you?
LAERTES A touch, a touch; I do confess't.
KING Our son shall win.
QUEEN He's fat,[8] and scant of breath.
Here, Hamlet, take my napkin,[9] rub thy brows.
The queen carouses[1] to thy fortune, Hamlet.
HAMLET Good madam!
KING Gertrude, do not drink.
QUEEN I will, my lord; I pray you pardon me.

(*drinks*)

KING (*aside*) It is the poisoned cup; it is too late.
HAMLET I dare not drink yet, madam—by and by.
QUEEN Come, let me wipe thy face.
LAERTES My lord, I'll hit him now.
KING I do not think't.
LAERTES (*aside*) And yet it is almost against my conscience.
HAMLET Come for the third, Laertes. You but dally.
I pray you pass with your best violence;
I am afeard you make a wanton[2] of me.
LAERTES Say you so? Come on.

(*They play.*)

OSRIC Nothing neither way.
LAERTES Have at you now!

(*In scuffling they change rapiers, and both are wounded with the poisoned weapon.*)

KING Part them. They are incensed.
HAMLET Nay, come—again!

(*The* QUEEN *falls.*)

OSRIC Look to the queen there, ho!
HORATIO They bleed on both sides. How is it, my lord?
OSRIC How is't, Laertes?

---

[8]not physically fit, out of training [9]handkerchief [1]drinks a toast [2]pampered child

LAERTES Why, as a woodcock[3] to mine own springe,[4] Osric.
I am justly killed with mine own treachery.
HAMLET How does the queen?
KING She sounds[5] to see them bleed.
QUEEN No, no, the drink, the drink! O my dear Hamlet!
The drink, the drink! I am poisoned.

(*dies*)

HAMLET O villainy! Ho! let the door be locked.
Treachery! Seek it out.

(LAERTES *falls.*)

LAERTES It is here, Hamlet. Hamlet, thou art slain;
No med'cine in the world can do thee good.
In thee there is not half an hour's life.
The treacherous instrument is in thy hand,
Unbated[6] and envenomed. The foul practice[7]
Hath turned itself on me. Lo, here I lie,
Never to rise again. Thy mother 's poisoned.
I can no more. The king, the king 's to blame.
HAMLET The point envenomed too?
Then venom, to thy work.

(*hurts the* KING)

ALL Treason! treason!
KING O, yet defend me, friends, I am but hurt.
HAMLET Here, thou incestuous, murd'rous, damnèd Dane,
Drink off this potion. Is thy union here?
Follow my mother.

(KING *dies.*)

LAERTES He is justly served.
It is a poison tempered[8] by himself.
Exchange forgiveness with me, noble Hamlet.
Mine and my father's death come not upon thee,
Nor thine on me!

(*dies*)

HAMLET Heaven make thee free of it! I follow thee.
I am dead, Horatio. Wretched queen, adieu!

[3]a bird reputed to be stupid and easily trapped [4]trap [5]swoons [6]unblunted [7]stratagem [8]mixed

You that look pale and tremble at this chance,
That are but mutes[9] or audience to this act,
Had I but time—as this fell sergeant,[1] Death,
Is strict in his arrest—O, I could tell you—
But let it be. Horatio, I am dead;
Thou livest; report me and my cause aright
To the unsatisfied.

HORATIO Never believe it.
I am more an antique Roman than a Dane.
Here's yet some liquor left.

HAMLET As th' art a man,
Give me the cup. Let go. By heaven, I'll ha't!
O God, Horatio, what a wounded name,
Things standing thus unknown, shall live behind me!
If thou didst ever hold me in thy heart,
Absent thee from felicity awhile,
And in this harsh world draw thy breath in pain,
To tell my story.

(*A march afar off.*)

What warlike noise is this?

OSRIC Young Fortinbras, with conquest come from Poland,
To the ambassadors of England gives
This warlike volley.

HAMLET O, I die, Horatio!
The potent poison quite o'ercrows[2] my spirit.
I cannot live to hear the news from England,
But I do prophesy th' election[3] lights
On Fortinbras. He has my dying voice.[4]
So tell him, with th' occurrents,[5] more and less,
Which have solicited[6]—the rest is silence.

(*dies*)

HORATIO Now cracks a noble heart. Good night, sweet prince,
And flights of angels sing thee to thy rest!

(*march within*)

Why does the drum come hither?

(*Enter* FORTINBRAS, *with the* AMBASSADORS [*and with his train of* DRUM, COLORS, *and* ATTENDANTS].)

[9]actors in a play who speak no lines [1]sheriff's officer [2]triumphs over (like a victor in a cockfight) [3]to the throne [4]vote [5]occurrences [6]incited, provoked

FORTINBRAS Where is this sight?
HORATIO What is it you would see?
If aught of woe or wonder, cease your search.
FORTINBRAS This quarry[7] cries on[8] havoc.[9] O proud Death,
What feast is toward[1] in thine eternal cell
That thou so many princes at a shot
So bloodily hast struck?
AMBASSADOR The sight is dismal;
And our affairs from England come too late.
The ears are senseless that should give us hearing
To tell him his commandment is fulfilled,
That Rosencrantz and Guildenstern are dead.
Where should we have our thanks?
HORATIO Not from his mouth,
Had it th' ability of life to thank you.
He never gave commandment for their death.
But since, so jump[2] upon this bloody question,
You from the Polack wars, and you from England,
Are here arrived, give order that these bodies
High on a stage[3] be placèd to the view,
And let me speak to th' yet unknowing world
How these things came about. So shall you hear
Of carnal, bloody, and unnatural acts,
Of accidental judgments,[4] casual[5] slaughters,
Of deaths put on[6] by cunning and forced cause,
And, in this upshot, purposes mistook
Fall'n on th' inventors' heads. All this can I
Truly deliver.
FORTINBRAS Let us haste to hear it,
And call the noblest to the audience.
For me, with sorrow I embrace my fortune.
I have some rights of memory[7] in this kingdom,
Which now to claim my vantage[8] doth invite me.
HORATIO Of that I shall have also cause to speak,
And from his mouth whose voice will draw on more.[9]
But let this same be presently[1] performed,
Even while men's minds are wild, lest more mischance
On[2] plots and errors happen.

---

[7]pile of dead (literally, of dead deer gathered after the hunt) [8]proclaims loudly [9]indiscriminate killing and destruction such as would follow the order "havoc," or "pillage," given to an army [1]forthcoming [2]precisely [3]platform [4]retributions [5]not humanly planned (reinforcing *accidental*) [6]instigated [7]traditional and kept in mind [8]advantageous opportunity [9]more voices, or votes, for the kingship [1]immediately [2]on the basis of

FORTINBRAS Let four captains
Bear Hamlet like a soldier to the stage,
For he was likely, had he been put on,[3]
To have proved most royal; and for his passage[4]
The soldiers' music and the rites of war
Speak loudly for him.
Take up the bodies. Such a sight as this
Becomes the field, but here shows much amiss.
Go, bid the soldiers shoot.

(*Exeunt* [*marching; after the which a peal of ordinance are shot off*].)

---

[3]set to perform in office [4]death

TARTUFFE

(1669)

MOLIÈRE (JEAN-BAPTISTE POQUELIN) (1622–1673)

Like its counterpart in England, French drama grew out of the mystery and miracle plays of the medieval stage. They, in turn, had developed from drama based on church liturgy and performed inside the church itself, but physical restrictions eventually forced everything into the open air of the public square or marketplace. By the thirteenth century as the liturgical drama faded, dialogue in the mysteries and moralities became more and more vernacular, characters were drawn from contemporary life, and the farcical antics of various fools, imps, and devils hastened the departure from the original religious basis. Most of what was written remains anonymous, and performers were amateurs. We do know that one Adam de la Halle (c. 1240–c. 1280) wrote a play about Robin Hood called *Le Jeu de Robin et Marion,* a wholly secular piece, the earliest known of its kind.

By the early fifteenth century, French drama permanently broke its clerical ties and proceeded to develop on its own. Although mysteries and moralities were still performed, a distinctive French variety of drama was beginning simultaneously, a lasting form of comedy that was to evolve into the hilarities of French farce. In 1470 the anonymous *Maître Pierre Pathelin,* still performable today, wholly unliterate but vastly entertaining, helped set the pattern. By 1548 performances of plays combining religious elements with the profane were banned, and the secular took over completely.

From then on, the development of the French drama, both tragic and comic, followed a somewhat different path from that taken in England. English drama, with many of the same roots, had progressed from troupes of strolling players into the great professional companies of the permanent London theatres of Marlowe, Shakespeare, and Jonson. The finest works of English Renaissance drama came at the end of the sixteenth century and the early part of the seventeenth. Artistically, with nothing similar to offer, the French theatre lagged considerably behind.

Furthermore, unlike the familiar open-air Elizabethan playhouse, the French theatre was always indoors. By the last quarter of the sixteenth century it had settled into the Hôtel de Burgogne in Paris, with its long, narrow, candlelit hall holding seats and boxes as well as standing room in the "pit" (and even, to the constant interference of the action, seats on the stage itself) and the Hôtel d'Argent. Paris thus hosted but two acting companies at the beginning of the seventeenth century, a substantial difference from the half-dozen or so in London. Moreover, their appeal was considerably different: they catered to a higher level of society, which had no place for the petty shopkeepers and apprentices who crowded in to see the works of Shakespeare.

There are few dramatists or plays of importance from this period, another marked contrast to the comparatively large number in England. Not until 1636 when Pierre Corneille (1606–1684) produced *Le Cid,* dramatizing the exploits of the famous Spanish hero, did the "great age" of French drama begin. Jean Racine (1636–1699) with his most famous work, *Phèdre,* a retelling of the classic tragedy of the passion of the wife of Theseus for her stepson Hippolytus, brought the great age to a close. In between stood the third genius, Molière, creator of some of the finest comedy in European stage literature.

How and why Jean-Baptiste Poquelin adopted his stage name of Molière is obscure. Son of a prosperous father who was upholsterer to the king, well-educated and heir apparent to his father's business, he abandoned his middle-class heritage and, hardly out of his teens, ran away to join a company of actors. For the rest of his life he remained in the theatre as the most famous writer, producer, and actor of his time. After roaming the countryside with varied success, in 1658 his troupe became the third acting company in Paris, gaining fame in their presentation of all of Molière's plays between 1659 and 1673.

The modern appeal of the greater portion of the French tragedies of Molière's day has never been strong outside France. A lot has to do with the rigid adherence to the structure, form, and style of the ancient classics, which were regarded as works of perfection. Their imitation was obligatory if one were to create a "proper" tragedy. This meant adherence to the three "unities" of time, place, and action, broadly adapted from Aristotle's *Poetics* as absolutes of dramatic law. Subject matter was restricted to myths and legends, including the Bible. French Renaissance tragedies, except for a few like *Le Cid* and *Phèdre,* which contain some memorable characters, are insufferably boring and now rest in history's musty storerooms. Not so Molière.

There is probably no other writer of comedy in any age who can compare with this giant figure who stands so far above any of his contemporaries. Single-handedly he turned the genre of French farce—artificial, without literary merit, full of stock two-dimensional characters—into a highly literate form, a comedy of permanent worth, often bitingly satiric, with telling thrusts at the idiosyncrasies of the society of his day, or *any* day. They maintain a popularity that goes on and on, as fresh and amusing as when they were written.

The comedies of Molière are as "classic" as the tragedies, written in the best tradition of the new Greek comedies of Menander as seen through the eyes of the Romans Plautus and Terence. The endless struggles of young lovers to overcome the stupidities of aging guardians, particularly fathers or husbands, the farcical intrigues of plots and counterplots, and the impossibly happy endings are "classic" comedy situations.

There was another notable source upon which Molière drew freely, particularly in his earlier plays—the *commedia dell'arte.* Originating in Italy it became popular throughout Europe, including England, from the sixteenth to the early eighteenth century. Its impromptu knockabout slapstick was performed by exaggerated stock figures, their faces often covered by a full or half mask, all aspects which Molière frequently adapted with skill.

The full genius of Molière was, however, entirely his own, even as he borrowed from other sources. His comedies displayed his contempt for and intolerance of society's artificialities, its pretenses, and especially its hypocrisies. He was able to ridicule those in ordinary society and in the higher levels of the court and to make all who were the butt of his thrusts, including the king, laugh as they watched their own ridiculous behavior in the stupid, pompous, single-minded characters he introduced—all, that is, except for one very important segment: the church, which *Tartuffe* mightily offended.

Molière's first successful play, staged in Paris in 1659, was *Les Précieuses ridicules,* a farce including a number of *commedia* routines. The behavior of its two "precious" young ladies, Cathos and Magdalon, remains a fine example of the affectations so consciously followed by those who wished to be regarded as proper practitioners of high society's code of precosity.

L'Ecole des femmes (*The School for Wives*) (1662), Molière's first full-length comedy, a static treatment of the theme of May–December marriages and the wisdom of providing women with a decent education and the right to choose a mate, with Molière and his wife in the leads, proved as successful as *Les Précieuses ridicules.* There is speculation that because Molière had recently married the much younger daughter of his former mistress, he was making a personal moral point, but if so, it does not cause the play to suffer.

Between 1664 and 1673 Molière created his most famous characters in plays that are constantly revived by the Comédie Française and by professionals and amateurs everywhere. *Le Misanthrope* (1667), a brilliant high comic satire of the folly of searching for human perfection, introduces the self-centered purist, Alceste, the personification of misanthropy, and the witty and beautiful Célimène, the best portrait of an independent-minded French Renaissance woman. Infatuated against his better judgment, Alceste does his best to persuade Célimène to change her coquettish ways and leave behind the artificialities of a society thriving on gossip, intrigue, and particularly dishonesty. In the end, he departs alone for his desert isle refuge, but not without a good deal of audience sympathy for the legitimacy of his tenets. But no society can function as purely as Alceste would have it, and Célimène, remaining behind, a willing prisoner of her affectations and a society that supports her, commands equal understanding.

Molière's continual concern about medicine and its quackery (his health was never strong, as his early death attests) was aired in *Le Médicin malgré lui* (*The Doctor in Spite of Himself*) (1666), a throwback to rowdy farce, as Sganarelle, the irresponsible bottle-loving rogue, becomes, against his will and amidst a great deal of bashing around, a famous "doctor," as gag follows upon gag in sheer fun.

L'Avare (*The Miser*) in 1668, deriving its source from Plautus's *Aulularia* (*The Pot of Gold*), presented the quintessence of miserliness in the ridiculous and often repugnant Harpagon, who would deprive himself and all around him of a decent life in his fanatical protection of his riches. *Le Bourgeois gentilhomme* (*The Would-be Gentleman*) (1670) introduced in M. Jourdain one of the theatre's most famous social climbers. In a day when "gentlemen" by definition came from noble or aristocratic stock, the ordinary businessman or entrepreneur had little chance of reaching the distinguished "gentlemanly" level. Now fabulously rich, aspiring to all the best that society can afford, M. Jourdain parades before himself and family all that money can buy in a desperate and, of course, highly comic attempt to reach his goal. Finally, *Le Malade imaginaire* (*The Imaginary Invalid*) in 1673 gives us Argan, the hypochondriac, suffering his primitive treatment by repeated purges administered by his appropriately named doctor, Purgon, who goes through a variety of farcical scenes in the play's exposure of wild and generally useless medical practices.

But it is in the central figure of *Tartuffe* that Molière created probably his best-known character, and the play rivals *Le Misanthrope* as the artist's most famous creation, but it took several years and considerable rewriting before he arrived at the final version of 1669. The cause of all the trouble was Molière's problems with the clergy. Any hint of attacking the sacred precepts of the church was immediately countered by easily offended clerics, especially when it was a satire shown on the sinful stage. Baffled by the narrow tunnel vision of the opposition, Molière did his best to eliminate the most offensive passages but to no avail. Louis XIV had found no problem with the first version, but succumbing to pressure he forbade its continuation. Finally, after three petitions directly to the king, the monarch overruled the opposition and the play proceeded. The attendant notoriety called far more public attention than would otherwise have been the case, and *Tartuffe* became an immediate hit.

The play could not survive today on notoriety alone. It was never conceived as a narrow tract or mere invective against the established church. As a play designed to entertain an audience, its characters and incidents are meant, as Molière explained in his preface to the published version, to expose the behavior of corrupt individuals who screen their offensive vices behind a facade of purity and goodness, and to portray the often inexplicable willingness of those who would be hoodwinked and almost destroyed in their blind admiration of what should be the transparent excesses of con men.

Perhaps both Orgon and Tartuffe are unreal characters whose behavior is extravagantly unbelievable. But through scenes often bordering on low farce—

Tartuffe's pursuit of Elmire while Orgon hides under the table is a good example—Molière sends his leading figures through actions that reveal a lot about them, even as they behave outrageously. Orgon would seem to have been deprived of his senses in his obsession with this villain, but at the same time his behavior can be explained in terms of human willingness to accept a fraud as the real thing.

It is the central figure of Tartuffe who commands our closest attention. He is given one of the longest built-up entrances in all of drama, not entering the stage until the third act. We have learned a lot about him, including his gluttony, for one thing, and his pious entrance as he speaks of hair shirt and scourge quickly reveals his insincerity. As his character unfolds, it is easy to regard him as little more than an out-and-out villain, but the inner nature of his gross sensuality takes over in his action toward Elmire and somewhat subdues the villainous stereotype. Further, in his human greed his craftiness overextends itself in his abortive attempt to secure the family fortune. As Harold Block, an editor and translator of Molière, puts it, it is wrong to see Tartuffe merely as a monster, but he is without doubt a dangerous crook.

A common subtitle for the play is "The Hypocrite." Perhaps the pious people of the church felt that even a suggestion of religious hypocrisy was not a suitable subject for ridicule, somehow fearing that the play cast aspersions on practices of the faith that Tartuffe proclaims but, of course, does not practice. Perhaps the better subtitle is another that is often used, "The Imposter." The wretched man is a fake and a fraud in every element of his outward nature, and he emerges as one of the great dramatic imposters, a very large figure in the gallery of stage scoundrels.

The *deus ex machina* ending can cause a certain amount of eyebrow lifting. It would seem to twist the whole situation around merely to create a happy ending out of an impossibly bad situation. The denouement does not arise from what has already transpired as the gods suddenly intrude without warning to save the worthy unfortunate family. But this is still a comedy, and it has made its point about human failings on both sides; it is time that the villain gets his proper punishment. The best way to bring it all together in a happy ending is to make use of a king who could not possibly permit this kind of evil to endure. The artist's thanks to the sovereign who had finally permitted the play to appear could not have been better conveyed.

We have been fortunate in this country to have had the talents of Richard Wilbur as translator, for his rhymed-couplet versions have retained the lilt of the original poetry and the spontaneous freshness and spirit that Molière injected into his very funny plays.

Tartuffe MOLIÈRE (JEAN-BAPTISTE POQUELIN)

Translated by Richard Wilbur

CHARACTERS

MADAME PERNELLE, *Orgon's mother*
ORGON, *Elmire's husband*
ELMIRE, *Orgon's wife*
DAMIS, *Orgon's son, Elmire's stepson*
MARIANE, *Orgon's daughter, Elmire's stepdaughter, in love with Valère*
VALÈRE, *in love with Mariane*
CLÉANTE, *Orgon's brother-in-law*
TARTUFFE, *a hypocrite*
DORINE, *Mariane's lady's-maid*
MONSIEUR LOYAL, *a bailiff*
A POLICE OFFICER
FLIPOTE, *Madame Pernelle's maid*

The scene throughout: ORGON's *house in Paris.*

Act I

Scene I MADAME PERNELLE *and* FLIPOTE, *her maid,* ELMIRE, MARIANE, DORINE, DAMIS, CLÉANTE.

MADAME PERNELLE Come, come, Flipote; it's time I left this place.
ELMIRE I can't keep up, you walk at such a pace.
MADAME PERNELLE Don't trouble, child; no need to show me out.
It's not your manners I'm concerned about.
ELMIRE We merely pay you the respect we owe.
But Mother, why this hurry? Must you go?
MADAME PERNELLE I must. This house appalls me. No one in it
Will pay attention for a single minute.
Children, I take my leave much vexed in spirit.
I offer good advice, but you won't hear it.
You all break in and chatter on and on.
It's like a madhouse with the keeper gone.
DORINE If . . .
MADAME PERNELLE
Girl, you talk too much, and I'm afraid
You're far too saucy for a lady's-maid.
You push in everywhere and have your say.

DAMIS But . . .

MADAME PERNELLE
You, boy, grow more foolish every day.
To think my grandson should be such a dunce!
I've said a hundred times, if I've said it once,
That if you keep the course on which you've started,
You'll leave your worthy father broken-hearted.

MARIANE I think . . .

MADAME PERNELLE And you, his sister, seem so pure,
So shy, so innocent, and so demure.
But you know what they say about still waters.
I pity parents with secretive daughters.

ELMIRE Now, Mother . . .

MADAME PERNELLE And as for you, child, let me add
That your behavior is extremely bad,
And a poor example for these children, too.
Their dear, dead mother did far better than you.
You're much too free with money, and I'm distressed
To see you so elaborately dressed.
When it's one's husband that one aims to please,
One has no need of costly fripperies.

CLÉANTE Oh, Madam, really . . .

MADAME PERNELLE You are her brother, Sir,
And I respect and love you; yet if I were
My son, this lady's good and pious spouse,
I wouldn't make you welcome in my house.
You're full of worldly counsels which, I fear,
Aren't suitable for decent folk to hear.
I've spoken bluntly, Sir; but it behooves us
Not to mince words when righteous fervor moves us.

DAMIS Your man Tartuffe is full of holy speeches . . .

MADAME PERNELLE And practices precisely what he preaches.
He's a fine man, and should be listened to.
I will not hear him mocked by fools like you.

DAMIS Good God! Do you expect me to submit
To the tyranny of that carping hypocrite?
Must we forgo all joys and satisfactions
Because that bigot censures all our actions?

DORINE To hear him talk—and he talks all the time—
There's nothing one can do that's not a crime.
He rails at everything, your dear Tartuffe.

MADAME PERNELLE Whatever he reproves deserves reproof.
He's out to save souls, and all of you
Must love him, as my son would have you do.

DAMIS Ah no, Grandmother, I could never take
To such a rascal, even for my father's sake.
That's how I feel, and I shall not dissemble.
His every action makes me seethe and tremble
With helpless anger, and I have no doubt
That he and I will shortly have it out.

DORINE Surely it is a shame and a disgrace
To see this man usurp the master's place—
To see this beggar who, when first he came,
Had not a shoe or shoestring to his name
So far forget himself that he behaves
As if the house were his, and we his slaves.

MADAME PERNELLE Well, mark my words, your souls would fare far better
If you obeyed his precepts to the letter.

DORINE You see him as a saint. I'm far less awed;
In fact, I see right through him. He's a fraud.

MADAME PERNELLE Nonsense!

DORINE His man Laurent's the same, or worse;
I'd not trust either with a penny purse.

MADAME PERNELLE I can't say what his servant's morals may be;
His own great goodness I can guarantee.
You all regard him with distaste and fear
Because he tells you what you're loath to hear,
Condemns your sins, points out your moral flaws,
And humbly strives to further Heaven's cause.

DORINE If sin is all that bothers him, why is it
He's so upset when folk drop in to visit?
Is Heaven so outraged by a social call
That he must prophesy against us all?
I'll tell you what I think: if you ask me,
He's jealous of my mistress' company.

MADAME PERNELLE
Rubbish! (*to* ELMIRE) He's not alone, child, in complaining
Of all of your promiscuous entertaining.
Why, the whole neighborhood's upset, I know,
By all these carriages that come and go,
With crowds of guests parading in and out
And noisy servants loitering about.
In all of this, I'm sure there's nothing vicious;
But why give people cause to be suspicious?

CLÉANTE They need no cause; they'll talk in any case.
Madam, this world would be a joyless place
If, fearing what malicious tongues might say,
We locked our doors and turned our friends away.

And even if one did so dreary a thing,
D'you think those tongues would cease their chattering?
One can't fight slander; it's a losing battle;
Let us instead ignore their tittle-tattle.
Let's strive to live by conscience' clear decrees,
And let the gossips gossip as they please.

DORINE If there is talk against us, I know the source:
It's Daphne and her little husband, of course.
Those who have greatest cause for guilt and shame
Are quickest to besmirch a neighbor's name.
When there's a chance for libel, they never miss it;
When something can be made to seem illicit
They're off at once to speak the joyous news,
Adding to fact what fantasies they choose.
By talking up their neighbor's indiscretions
They seek to camouflage their own transgressions,
Hoping that others' innocent affairs
Will lend a hue of innocence to theirs,
Or that their own black guilt will come to seem
Part of a general shady color-scheme.

MADAME PERNELLE All that is quite irrelevant. I doubt
That anyone's more virtuous and devout
Than dear Orante; and I'm informed that she
Condemns your mode of life most vehemently.

DORINE Oh, yes, she's strict, devout, and has no taint
Of worldliness; in short, she seems a saint.
But it was time which taught her that disguise;
She's thus because she can't be otherwise.
So long as her attractions could enthrall,
She flounced and flirted and enjoyed it all,
But now that they're no longer what they were
She quits a world which fast is quitting her,
And wears a veil of virtue to conceal
Her bankrupt beauty and her lost appeal.
That's what becomes of old coquettes today:
Distressed when all their lovers fall away,
They see no recourse but to play the prude,
And so confer a style on solitude.
Thereafter, they're severe with everyone,
Condemning all our actions, pardoning none,
And claiming to be pure, austere, and zealous
When, if the truth were known, they're merely jealous,
And cannot bear to see another know
The pleasures time has forced them to forgo.

MADAME PERNELLE (*initially to* ELMIRE)
That sort of talk is what you like to hear;
Therefore you'd have us all keep still, my dear,
While Madam rattles on the livelong day.
Nevertheless, I mean to have my say.
I tell you that you're blest to have Tartuffe
Dwelling, as my son's guest, beneath this roof;
That Heaven has sent him to forestall its wrath
By leading you, once more, to the true path;
That all he reprehends is reprehensible,
And that you'd better heed him, and be sensible.
These visits, balls, and parties in which you revel
Are nothing but inventions of the Devil.
One never hears a word that's edifying:
Nothing but chaff and foolishness and lying,
As well as vicious gossip in which one's neighbor
Is cut to bits with epee, foil, and saber.
People of sense are driven half-insane
At such affairs, where noise and folly reign
And reputations perish thick and fast.
As a wise preacher said on Sunday last,
Parties are Towers of Babylon, because
The guests all babble on with never a pause;
And then he told a story which, I think . . .

(*to* CLÉANTE:)

I heard that laugh, Sir, and I saw that wink!
Go find your silly friends and laugh some more!
Enough; I'm going; don't show me to the door.
I leave this household much dismayed and vexed;
I cannot say when I shall see you next.

(*slapping* FLIPOTE:)

Wake up, don't stand there gaping into space!
I'll slap some sense into that stupid face.
Move, move, you slut.

Scene II CLÉANTE, DORINE.

CLÉANTE I think I'll stay behind;
I want no further pieces of her mind.
How that old lady . . .

DORINE Oh, what wouldn't she say
If she could hear you speak of her that way!
She'd thank you for the *lady,* but I'm sure
She'd find the *old* a little premature.

CLÉANTE My, what a scene she made, and what a din!
And how this man Tartuffe has taken her in!

DORINE Yes, but her son is even worse deceived;
His folly must be seen to be believed.
In the late troubles, he played an able part
And served his king with wise and loyal heart,
But he's quite lost his senses since he fell
Beneath Tartuffe's infatuating spell.
He calls him brother, and loves him as his life,
Preferring him to mother, child, or wife.
In him and him alone will he confide;
He's made him his confessor and his guide;
He pets and pampers him with love more tender
Than any pretty maiden could engender,
Gives him the place of honor when they dine,
Delights to see him gorging like a swine,
Stuffs him with dainties till his guts distend,
And when he belches, cries "God bless you, friend!"
In short, he's mad; he worships him; he dotes;
His deeds he marvels at, his words he quotes,
Thinking each act a miracle, each word
Oracular as those that Moses heard.
Tartuffe, much pleased to find so easy a victim,
Has in a hundred ways beguiled and tricked him,
Milked him of money, and with his permission
Established here a sort of Inquisition.
Even Laurent, his lackey, dares to give
Us arrogant advice on how to live;
He sermonizes us in thundering tones
And confiscates our ribbons and colognes.
Last week he tore a kerchief into pieces
Because he found it pressed in a *Life of Jesus:*
He said it was a sin to juxtapose
Unholy vanities and holy prose.

Scene III ELMIRE, MARIANE, DAMIS, CLÉANTE, DORINE.

ELMIRE (*to* CLÉANTE) You did well not to follow; she stood in the door
And said *verbatim* all she'd said before.

I saw my husband coming. I think I'd best
Go upstairs now, and take a little rest.
CLÉANTE I'll wait and greet him here; then I must go.
I've really only time to say hello.
DAMIS Sound him about my sister's wedding, please.
I think Tartuffe's against it, and that he's
Been urging Father to withdraw his blessing.
As you well know, I'd find that most distressing.
Unless my sister and Valère can marry,
My hopes to wed *his* sister will miscarry,
And I'm determined . . .
DORINE He's coming.

Scene IV ORGON, CLÉANTE, DORINE.

ORGON Ah, Brother, good-day.
CLÉANTE Well, welcome back. I'm sorry I can't stay.
How was the country? Blooming, I trust, and green?
ORGON Excuse me, Brother; just one moment.

(*to* DORINE:)

Dorine . . .

(*to* CLÉANTE:)

To put my mind at rest, I always learn
The household news the moment I return.

(*to* DORINE:)

Has all been well, these two days I've been gone?
How are the family? What's been going on?
DORINE Your wife, two days ago, had a bad fever,
And a fierce headache which refused to leave her.
ORGON Ah. And Tartuffe?
DORINE Tartuffe? Why, he's round and red,
Bursting with health, and excellently fed.
ORGON Poor fellow!
DORINE That night, the mistress was unable
To take a single bite at the dinner-table.
Her headache-pains, she said, were simply hellish.
ORGON Ah. And Tartuffe?
DORINE He ate his meal with relish,
And zealously devoured in her presence
A leg of mutton and a brace of pheasants.

ORGON Poor fellow!
DORINE Well, the pains continued strong,
And so she tossed and tossed the whole night long,
Now icy-cold, now burning like a flame.
We sat beside her bed till morning came.
ORGON Ah. And Tartuffe?
DORINE Why, having eaten, he rose
And sought his room, already in a doze,
Got into his warm bed, and snored away
In perfect peace until the break of day.
ORGON Poor fellow!
DORINE After much ado, we talked her
Into dispatching someone for the doctor.
He bled her, and the fever quickly fell.
ORGON Ah. And Tartuffe?
DORINE He bore it very well.
To keep his cheerfulness at any cost,
And make up for the blood *Madame* had lost,
He drank, at lunch, four beakers full of port.
ORGON Poor fellow!
DORINE Both are doing well, in short.
I'll go and tell *Madame* that you've expressed
Keen sympathy and anxious interest.

Scene V ORGON, CLÉANTE.

CLÉANTE That girl was laughing in your face, and though
I've no wish to offend you, even so
I'm bound to say that she had some excuse.
How can you possibly be such a goose?
Are you so dazed by this man's hocus-pocus
That all the world, save him, is out of focus?
You've given him clothing, shelter, food, and care;
Why must you also . . .
ORGON Brother, stop right there.
You do not know the man of whom you speak.
CLÉANTE I grant you that. But my judgment's not so weak
That I can't tell, by his effect on others . . .
ORGON Ah, when you meet him, you two will be like brothers!
There's been no loftier soul since time began.
He is a man who . . . a man who . . . an excellent man.
To keep his precepts is to be reborn,
And view this dunghill of a world with scorn.
Yes, thanks to him I'm a changed man indeed.

Under his tutelage my soul's been freed
From earthly loves, and every human tie:
My mother, children, brother, and wife could die,
And I'd not feel a single moment's pain.

CLÉANTE That's a fine sentiment, Brother; most humane.

ORGON Oh, had you seen Tartuffe as I first knew him,
Your heart, like mine, would have surrendered to him.
He used to come into our church each day
And humbly kneel nearby, and start to pray.
He'd draw the eyes of everybody there
By the deep fervor of his heartfelt prayer;
He's sign and weep, and sometimes with a sound
Of rapture he would bend and kiss the ground;
And when I rose to go, he'd run before
To offer me holy-water at the door.
His serving-man, no less devout than he,
Informed me of his master's poverty;
I gave him gifts, but in his humbleness
He'd beg me every time to give him less.
"Oh, that's too much," he'd cry, "too much by twice!
I don't deserve it. The half, Sir, would suffice."
And when I wouldn't take it back, he'd share
Half of it with the poor, right then and there.
At length, Heaven prompted me to take him in
To dwell with us, and free our souls from sin.
He guides our lives, and to protect my honor
Stays by my wife, and keeps an eye upon her;
He tells me whom she sees, and all she does,
And seems more jealous than I ever was!
And how austere he is! Why, he can detect
A mortal sin where you would least suspect;
In smallest trifles, he's extremely strict.
Last week, his conscience was severely pricked
Because, while praying, he had caught a flea
And killed it, so he felt, too wrathfully.

CLÉANTE Good God, man! Have you lost your common sense—
Or is this all some joke at my expense?
How can you stand there and in all sobriety . . .

ORGON Brother, your language savors of impiety.
Too much free-thinking's made your faith unsteady,
And as I've warned you many times already,
'Twill get you into trouble before you're through.

CLÉANTE So I've been told before by dupes like you:
Being blind, you'd have all others blind as well;

The clear-eyed man you call an infidel,
And he who sees through humbug and pretense
Is charged, by you, with want of reverence.
Spare me your warnings, Brother; I have no fear
Of speaking out, for you and Heaven to hear,
Against affected zeal and pious knavery.
There's true and false in piety, as in bravery,
And just as those whose courage shines the most
In battle, are the least inclined to boast,
So those whose hearts are truly pure and lowly
Don't make a flashy show of being holy.
There's a vast difference, so it seems to me,
Between true piety and hypocrisy:
How do you fail to see it, may I ask?
Is not a face quite different from a mask?
Cannot sincerity and cunning art,
Reality and semblance, be told apart?
Are scarecrows just like men, and do you hold
That a false coin is just as good as gold?
Ah, Brother, man's a strangely fashioned creature
Who seldom is content to follow Nature,
But recklessly pursues his inclination
Beyond the narrow bounds of moderation,
And often, by transgressing Reason's laws,
Perverts a lofty aim or noble cause.
A passing observation, but it applies.

ORGON I see, dear Brother, that you're profoundly wise;
You harbor all the insight of the age.
You are our one clear mind, our only sage,
The era's oracle, its Cato too,
And all mankind are fools compared to you.

CLÉANTE Brother, I don't pretend to be a sage,
Nor have I all the wisdom of the age.
There's just one insight I would dare to claim:
I know that true and false are not the same;
And just as there is nothing I more revere
Than a soul whose faith is steadfast and sincere,
Nothing that I more cherish and admire
Than honest zeal and true religious fire,
So there is nothing that I find more base
Than specious piety's dishonest face—
Than these bold mountebanks, these histrios
Whose impious mummeries and hollow shows
Exploit our love of Heaven, and make a jest

Of all that men think holiest and best;
These calculating souls who offer prayers
Not to their Maker, but as public wares,
And seek to buy respect and reputation
With lifted eyes and sighs of exaltation;
These charlatans, I say, whose pilgrim souls
Proceed, by way of Heaven, toward earthly goals,
Who weep and pray and swindle and extort,
Who preach the monkish life, but haunt the court,
Who make their zeal the partner of their vice—
Such men are vengeful, sly, and cold as ice,
And when there is an enemy to defame
They cloak their spite in fair religion's name,
Their private spleen and malice being made
To seem a high and virtuous crusade,
Until, to mankind's reverent applause,
They crucify their foe in Heaven's cause.
Such knaves are all too common; yet, for the wise,
True piety isn't hard to recognize,
And, happily, these present times provide us
With bright examples to instruct and guide us.
Consider Ariston and Périandre;
Look at Oronte, Alcidamas, Clitandre;
Their virtue is acknowledged; who could doubt it?
But you won't hear them beat the drum about it.
They're never ostentatious, never vain,
And their religion's moderate and humane;
It's not their way to criticize and chide:
They think censoriousness a mark of pride,
And therefore, letting others preach and rave,
They show, by deeds, how Christians should behave.
They think no evil of their fellow man,
But judge of him as kindly as they can.
They don't intrigue and wangle and conspire;
To lead a good life is their one desire;
The sinner wakes no rancorous hate in them;
It is the sin alone which they condemn;
Nor do they try to show a fiercer zeal
For Heaven's cause than Heaven itself could feel.
These men I honor, these men I advocate
As models for us all to emulate.
Your man is not their sort at all, I fear:
And, while your praise of him is quite sincere,
I think that you've been dreadfully deluded.

ORGON Now then, dear Brother, is your speech concluded?
CLÉANTE Why, yes.
ORGON Your servant, Sir. (*He turns to go.*)
CLÉANTE No, Brother; wait.
There's one more matter. You agreed of late
That young Valère might have your daughter's hand.
ORGON I did.
CLÉANTE And set the date, I understand.
ORGON Quite so.
CLÉANTE You've now postponed it; is that true?
ORGON No doubt.
CLÉANTE The match no longer pleases you?
ORGON Who knows?
CLÉANTE D'you mean to go back on your word?
ORGON I won't say that.
CLÉANTE Has anything occurred
Which might entitle you to break your pledge?
ORGON Perhaps.
CLÉANTE Why must you hem, and haw, and hedge?
The boy asked me to sound you in this affair . . .
ORGON It's been a pleasure.
CLÉANTE But what shall I tell Valère?
ORGON Whatever you like.
CLÉANTE But what have you decided?
What are your plans?
ORGON I plan, Sir, to be guided
By Heaven's will.
CLÉANTE Come, Brother, don't talk rot.
You've given Valère your word; will you keep it, or not?
ORGON Good day.
CLÉANTE This looks like poor Valère's undoing;
I'll go and warn him that there's trouble brewing.

Act II

Scene I ORGON, MARIANE.

ORGON Mariane.
MARIANE Yes, father?
ORGON A word with you; come here.
MARIANE What are you looking for?
ORGON (*peering into a small closet*) Eavesdroppers, dear.
I'm making sure we shan't be overheard.
Someone in there could catch our every word.

Ah, good, we're safe. Now, Mariane, my child,
You're a sweet girl who's tractable and mild,
Whom I hold dear, and think most highly of.
MARIANE I'm deeply grateful, Father, for your love.
ORGON That's well said, Daughter; and you can repay me
If, in all things, you'll cheerfully obey me.
MARIANE To please you, Sir, is what delights me best.
ORGON Good, good. Now, what d'you think of Tartuffe, our guest?
MARIANE I, Sir?
ORGON Yes. Weigh your answer; think it through.
MARIANE Oh, dear. I'll say whatever you wish me to.
ORGON That's wisely said, my Daughter. Say of him, then,
That he's the very worthiest of men,
And that you're fond of him, and would rejoice
In being his wife, if that should be my choice.
Well?
MARIANE What?
ORGON What's that?
MARIANE I . . .
ORGON Well?
MARIANE Forgive me, pray.
ORGON Did you not hear me?
MARIANE Of *whom,* Sir, must I say
That I am fond of him, and would rejoice
In being his wife, if that should be your choice?
ORGON Why, of Tartuffe.
MARIANE But, Father, that's false, you know.
Why would you have me say what isn't so?
ORGON Because I am resolved it shall be true.
That it's my wish should be enough for you.
MARIANE You can't mean, Father . . .
ORGON Yes, Tartuffe shall be
Allied by marriage to this family,
And he's to be your husband, is that clear?
It's a father's privilege . . .

Scene II DORINE, ORGON, MARIANE.

ORGON (*to* DORINE) What are you doing in here?
Is curiosity so fierce a passion
With you, that you must eavesdrop in this fashion?
DORINE There's lately been a rumor going about—
Based on some hunch or chance remark, no doubt—

That you mean Mariane to wed Tartuffe.
I've laughed it off, of course, as just a spoof.
ORGON You find it so incredible?
DORINE Yes, I do.
I won't accept that story, even from you.
ORGON Well, you'll believe it when the thing is done.
DORINE Yes, yes, of course. Go on and have your fun.
ORGON I've never been more serious in my life.
DORINE Ha!
ORGON Daughter, I mean it; you're to be his wife.
DORINE No, don't believe your father; it's all a hoax.
ORGON See here, young woman . . .
DORINE Come, Sir, no more jokes;
You can't fool us.
ORGON How dare you talk that way?
DORINE All right, then; we believe you, sad to say.
But how a man like you, who looks so wise
And wears a moustache of such splendid size,
Can be so foolish as to . . .
ORGON Silence, please!
My girl, you take too many liberties.
I'm master here, as you must not forget.
DORINE Do let's discuss this calmly; don't be upset.
You can't be serious, Sir, about this plan.
What should that bigot want with Mariane?
Praying and fasting ought to keep him busy.
And then, in terms of wealth and rank, what is he?
Why should a man of property like you
Pick out a beggar son-in-law?
ORGON That will do.
Speak of his poverty with reverence.
His is a pure and saintly indigence
Which far transcends all worldly pride and pelf.
He lost his fortune, as he says himself,
Because he cared for Heaven alone, and so
Was careless of his interests here below.
I mean to get him out of his present straits
And help him to recover his estates—
Which, in his part of the world, have no small fame.
Poor though he is, he's a gentleman just the same.
DORINE Yes, so he tells us; and, Sir, it seems to me
Such pride goes very ill with piety.
A man whose spirit spurns this dungy earth

Ought not to brag of lands and noble birth;
Such worldly arrogance will hardly square
With meek devotion and the life of prayer.
. . . But this approach, I see, has drawn a blank;
Let's speak, then, of his person, not his rank.
Doesn't it seem to you a trifle grim
To give a girl like her to a man like him?
When two are so ill-suited, can't you see
What the sad consequence is bound to be?
A young girl's virtue is imperiled, Sir,
When such a marriage is imposed on her;
For if one's bridegroom isn't to one's taste,
It's hardly an inducement to be chaste,
And many a man with horns upon his brow
Has made his wife the thing that she is now.
It's hard to be a faithful wife, in short,
To certain husbands of a certain sort,
And he who gives his daughter to a man she hates
Must answer for her sins at Heaven's gates.
Think, Sir, before you play so risky a role.

ORGON This servant-girl presumes to save my soul!

DORINE You would do well to ponder what I've said.

ORGON Daughter, we'll disregard this dunderhead.
Just trust your father's judgment. Oh, I'm aware
That I once promised you to young Valère;
But now I hear he gambles, which greatly shocks me;
What's more, I've doubts about his orthodoxy.
His visits to church, I note, are very few.

DORINE Would you have him go at the same hours as you,
And kneel nearby, to be sure of being seen?

ORGON I can dispense with such remarks, Dorine.

(*to* MARIANE:)

Tartuffe, however, is sure of Heaven's blessing,
And that's the only treasure worth possessing.
This match will bring you joys beyond all measure;
Your cup will overflow with every pleasure;
You two will interchange your faithful loves
Like two sweet cherubs, or two turtle-doves.
No harsh word shall be heard, no frown be seen,
And he shall make you happy as a queen.

DORINE And she'll make him a cuckold, just wait and see.

ORGON What language!

DORINE Oh, he's a man of destiny;
He's *made* for horns, and what the stars demand
Your daughter's virtue surely can't withstand.
ORGON Don't interrupt me further. Why can't you learn
That certain things are none of your concern?
DORINE It's for your own sake that I interfere.

(*She repeatedly interrupts* ORGON *just as he is turning to speak to his daughter:*)

ORGON Most kind of you. Now, hold your tongue, d'you hear?
DORINE If I didn't love you . . .
ORGON Spare me your affection.
DORINE I'll love you, Sir, in spite of your objection.
ORGON Blast!
DORINE I can't bear, Sir, for your honor's sake,
To let you make this ludicrous mistake.
ORGON You mean to go on talking?
DORINE If I didn't protest
This sinful marriage, my conscience couldn't rest.
ORGON If you don't hold your tongue, you little shrew . . .
DORINE What, lost your temper? A pious man like you?
ORGON Yes! Yes! You talk and talk. I'm maddened by it.
Once and for all, I tell you to be quiet.
DORINE Well, I'll be quiet. But I'll be thinking hard.
ORGON Think all you like, but you had better guard
That saucy tongue of yours, or I'll . . .

(*turning back to* MARIANE:)

Now, child,
I've weighed this matter fully.
DORINE (*aside*) It drives me wild
That I can't speak.

(ORGON *turns his head, and she is silent.*)

ORGON Tartuffe is no young dandy,
But, still, his person . . .
DORINE (*aside*) Is as sweet as candy.
ORGON Is such that, even if you shouldn't care
For his other merits . . .

(*He turns and stands facing* DORINE, *arms crossed.*)

DORINE (*aside*) They'll make a lovely pair.
If I were she, no man would marry me
Against my inclination, and go scot-free.

He'd learn, before the wedding-day was over,
How readily a wife can find a lover.
ORGON (*to* DORINE) It seems you treat my orders as a joke.
DORINE Why, what's the matter? 'Twas not to you I spoke.
ORGON What *were* you doing?
DORINE Talking to myself, that's all.
ORGON Ah! (*aside*) One more bit of impudence and gall,
And I shall give her a good slap in the face.

(*He puts himself in position to slap her;* DORINE, *whenever he glances at her, stands immobile and silent:*)

Daughter, you shall accept, and with good grace,
The husband I've selected . . . Your wedding day . . .

(*to* DORINE:)

Why don't you talk to yourself?
DORINE I've nothing to say.
ORGON Come, just one word.
DORINE No thank you, Sir. I pass.
ORGON Come, speak; I'm waiting.
DORINE I'd not be such an ass.
ORGON (*turning to* MARIANE) In short, dear Daughter, I mean to be obeyed,
And you must bow to the sound choice I've made.
DORINE (*moving away*) I'd not wed such a monster, even in jest.

(ORGON *attempts to slap her, but misses.*)

ORGON Daughter, that maid of yours is a thorough pest;
She makes me sinfully annoyed and nettled.
I can't speak further; my nerves are too unsettled.
She's so upset me by her insolent talk,
I'll calm myself by going for a walk.

Scene III DORINE, MARIANE.

DORINE (*returning*) Well, have you lost your tongue, girl? Must I play
Your part, and say the lines you ought to say?
Faced with a fate so hideous and absurd,
Can you not utter one dissenting word?
MARIANE What good would it do? A father's power is great.
DORINE Resist him now, or it will be too late.
MARIANE But . . .
DORINE Tell him one cannot love at a father's whim;
That you shall marry for yourself, not him;

That since it's you who are to be the bride,
It's you, not he, who must be satisfied;
And that if his Tartuffe is so sublime,
He's free to marry him at any time.
MARIANE I've bowed so long to Father's strict control,
I couldn't oppose him now, to save my soul.
DORINE Come, come, Mariane. Do listen to reason, won't you?
Valère has asked your hand. Do you love him, or don't you?
MARIANE Oh, how unjust of you! What can you mean
By asking such a question, dear Dorine?
You know the depth of my affection for him;
I've told you a hundred times how I adore him.
DORINE I don't believe in everything I hear;
Who knows if your professions were sincere?
MARIANE They were, Dorine, and you do me wrong to doubt it;
Heaven knows that I've been all too frank about it.
DORINE You love him, then?
MARIANE Oh, more than I can express.
DORINE And he, I take it, cares for you no less?
MARIANE I think so.
DORINE And you both, with equal fire,
Burn to be married?
MARIANE That is our one desire.
DORINE What of Tartuffe, then? What of your father's plan?
MARIANE I'll kill myself, if I'm forced to wed that man.
DORINE I hadn't thought of that recourse. How splendid!
Just die, and all your troubles will be ended!
A fine solution. Oh, it maddens me
To hear you talk in that self-pitying key.
MARIANE Dorine, how harsh you are! It's most unfair.
You have no sympathy for my despair.
DORINE I've none at all for people who talk drivel
And, faced with difficulties, whine and snivel.
MARIANE No doubt I'm timid, but it would be wrong . . .
DORINE True love requires a heart that's firm and strong.
MARIANE I'm strong in my affection for Valère,
But coping with my father is his affair.
DORINE But if your father's brain has grown so cracked
Over his dear Tartuffe that he can retract
His blessing, though your wedding day was named,
It's surely not Valère who's to be blamed.
MARIANE If I defied my father, as you suggest,
Would it not seem unmaidenly, at best?
Shall I defend my love at the expense

Of brazenness and disobedience?
Shall I parade my heart's desires, and flaunt . . .

DORINE No, I ask nothing of you. Clearly you want
To be Madame Tartuffe, and I feel bound
Not to oppose a wish so very sound.
What right have I to criticize the match?
Indeed, my dear, the man's a brilliant catch.
Monsieur Tartuffe! Now, there's a man of weight!
Yes, yes, Monsieur Tartuffe, I'm bound to state,
Is quite a person; that's not to be denied;
'Twill be no little thing to be his bride.
The world already rings with his renown;
He's a great noble—in his native town;
His ears are red, he has a pink complexion,
And all in all, he'll suit you to perfection.

MARIANE Dear God!

DORINE Oh, how triumphant you will feel
At having caught a husband so ideal!

MARIANE Oh, do stop teasing, and use your cleverness
To get me out of this appalling mess.
Advise me, and I'll do whatever you say.

DORINE Ah no, a dutiful daughter must obey
Her father, even if he weds her to an ape.
You've a bright future; why struggle to escape?
Tartuffe will take you back where his family lives,
To a small town aswarm with relatives—
Uncles and cousins whom you'll be charmed to meet.
You'll be received at once by the elite,
Calling upon the bailiff's wife, no less—
Even, perhaps, upon the mayoress,
Who'll sit you down in the *best* kitchen chair.
Then, once a year, you'll dance at the village fair
To the drone of bagpipes—two of them, in fact—
And see a puppet-show, or an animal act.
Your husband . . .

MARIANE Oh, you turn my blood to ice!
Stop torturing me, and give me your advice.

DORINE (*threatening to go*) Your servant, Madam.

MARIANE Dorine, I beg of you . . .

DORINE No, you deserve it; this marriage must go through.

MARIANE Dorine!

DORINE No.

MARIANE Not Tartuffe! You know I think him . . .

DORINE Tartuffe's your cup of tea, and you shall drink him.

MARIANE I've told you everything, and relied . . .
DORINE No. You deserve to be tartuffified.
MARIANE Well, since you mock me and refuse to care,
I'll henceforth seek my solace in despair:
Despair shall be my counsellor and friend,
And help me bring my sorrows to an end.

(*She starts to leave.*)

DORINE There, now, come back; my anger has subsided.
You do deserve some pity, I've decided.
MARIANE Dorine, if Father makes me undergo
This dreadful martyrdom, I'll die, I know.
DORINE Don't fret; it won't be difficult to discover
Some plan of action . . . But here's Valère, your lover.

Scene IV VALÈRE, MARIANE, DORINE.

VALÈRE Madam, I've just received some wondrous news
Regarding which I'd like to hear your views.
MARIANE What news?
VALÈRE You're marrying Tartuffe.
MARIANE I find
That Father does have such a match in mind.
VALÈRE Your father, Madam . . .
MARIANE . . . has just this minute said
That it's Tartuffe he wishes me to wed.
VALÈRE Can he be serious?
MARIANE Oh, indeed he can;
He's clearly set his heart upon the plan.
VALÈRE And what position do you propose to take,
Madam?
MARIANE Why—I don't know.
VALÈRE For heaven's sake—
You don't know?
MARIANE No.
VALÈRE Well, well!
MARIANE Advise me, do.
VALÈRE Marry the man. That's my advice to you.
MARIANE That's your advice?
VALÈRE Yes.
MARIANE Truly?
VALÈRE Oh, absolutely.
You couldn't choose more wisely, more astutely.

MARIANE Thanks for this counsel; I'll follow it, of course.
VALÈRE Do, do; I'm sure 'twill cost you no remorse.
MARIANE To give it didn't cause your heart to break.
VALÈRE I gave it, Madam, only for your sake.
MARIANE And it's for your sake that I take it, Sir.
DORINE (*withdrawing to the rear of the stage*)
Let's see which fool will prove the stubborner.
VALÈRE So! I am nothing to you, and it was flat
Deception when you . . .
MARIANE Please, enough of that.
You've told me plainly that I should agree
To wed the man my father's chosen for me,
And since you've deigned to counsel me so wisely,
I promise, Sir, to do as you advise me.
VALÈRE Ah, no, 'twas not by me that you were swayed.
No, your decision was already made;
Though now, to save appearances, you protest
That you're betraying me at my behest.
MARIANE Just as you say.
VALÈRE Quite so. And I now see
That you were never truly in love with me.
MARIANE Alas, you're free to think so if you choose.
VALÈRE I choose to think so, and here's a bit of news:
You've spurned my hand, but I know where to turn
For kinder treatment, as you shall quickly learn.
MARIANE I'm sure you do. Your noble qualities
Inspire affection . . .
VALÈRE Forget my qualities, please.
They don't inspire you overmuch, I find.
But there's another lady I have in mind
Whose sweet and generous nature will not scorn
To compensate me for the loss I've borne.
MARIANE I'm no great loss, and I'm sure that you'll transfer
Your heart quite painlessly from me to her.
VALÈRE I'll do my best to take it in my stride.
The pain I feel at being cast aside
Time and forgetfulness may put an end to.
Or if I can't forget, I shall pretend to.
No self-respecting person is expected
To go on loving once he's been rejected.
MARIANE Now, that's a fine, high-minded sentiment.
VALÈRE One to which any sane man would assent.
Would you prefer it if I pined away
In hopeless passion till my dying day?

Am I to yield you to a rival's arms
And not console myself with other charms?
MARIANE Go then, console yourself; don't hesitate.
I wish you to; indeed, I cannot wait.
VALÈRE You wish me to?
MARIANE Yes.
VALÈRE That's the final straw.
Madam, farewell. Your wish shall be my law.

(*He starts to leave, and then returns, this repeatedly:*)

MARIANE Splendid.
VALÈRE (*coming back again*)
This breach, remember, is of your making;
It's you who've driven me to the step I'm taking.
MARIANE Of course.
VALÈRE (*coming back again*)
Remember, too, that I am merely
Following your example.
MARIANE I see that clearly.
VALÈRE Enough. I'll go and do your bidding, then.
MARIANE Good.
VALÈRE (*coming back again*)
You shall never see my face again.
MARIANE Excellent.
VALÈRE (*walking to the door, then turning about*)
Yes?
MARIANE What?
VALÈRE What's that? What did you say?
MARIANE Nothing. You're dreaming.
VALÈRE Ah. Well, I'm on my way.
Farewell, Madame.

(*He moves slowly away.*)

MARIANE Farewell.
DORINE (*to* MARIANE) If you ask me,
Both of you are as mad as mad can be.
Do stop this nonsense, now. I've only let you
Squabble so long to see where it would get you.
Whoa there, Monsieur Valère!

(*She goes and seizes* VALÈRE *by the arm; he makes a great show of resistance.*)

VALÈRE What's this, Dorine?
DORINE Come here.

VALÈRE No, no, my heart's too full of spleen.
Don't hold me back; her wish must be obeyed.
DORINE Stop!
VALÈRE It's too late now; my decision's made.
DORINE Oh, pooh!
MARIANE (*aside*) He hates the sight of me, that's plain.
I'll go, and so deliver him from pain.
DORINE (*leaving* VALÈRE, *running after* MARIANE)
And now *you* run away! Come back.
MARIANE No, no.
Nothing you say will keep me here. Let go!
VALÈRE (*aside*) She cannot bear my presence, I perceive.
To spare her further torment, I shall leave.
DORINE (*leaving* MARIANE, *running after* VALÈRE)
Again! You'll not escape, Sir; don't you try it.
Come here, you two. Stop fussing, and be quiet.

(*She takes* VALÈRE *by the hand, then* MARIANE, *and draws them together.*)

VALÈRE (*to* DORINE) What do you want of me?
MARIANE (*to* DORINE) What is the point of this?
DORINE We're going to have a little armistice.

(*to* VALÈRE:)

Now, weren't you silly to get so overheated?
VALÈRE Didn't you see how badly I was treated?
DORINE (*to* MARIANE) Aren't you a simpleton, to have lost your head?
MARIANE Didn't you hear the hateful things he said?
DORINE (*to* VALÈRE) You're both great fools. Her sole desire, Valère,
Is to be yours in marriage. To that I'll swear.

(*to* MARIANE:)

He loves you only, and he wants no wife
But you, Mariane. On that I'll stake my life.
MARIANE (*to* VALÈRE) Then why you advised me so, I cannot see.
VALÈRE (*to* MARIANE) On such a question, why ask advice of *me?*
DORINE Oh, you're impossible. Give me your hands, you two.

(*to* VALÈRE:)

Yours first.
VALÈRE (*giving* DORINE *his hand*)
But why?

DORINE (*to* MARIANE) And now a hand from you.
MARIANE (*also giving* DORINE *her hand*)
What are you doing?
DORINE There: a perfect fit.
You suit each other better than you'll admit.

(VALÈRE *and* MARIANE *hold hands for some time without looking at each other.*)

VALÈRE (*turning toward* MARIANE)
Ah, come, don't be so haughty. Give a man
A look of kindness, won't you, Mariane?

(MARIANE *turns toward* VALÈRE *and smiles.*)

DORINE I tell you, lovers are completely mad!
VALÈRE (*to* MARIANE) Now come, confess that you were very bad
To hurt my feelings as you did just now.
I have a just complaint, you must allow.
MARIANE *You* must allow that you were most unpleasant . . .
DORINE Let's table that discussion for the present;
Your father has a plan which must be stopped.
MARIANE Advise us, then; what means must we adopt?
DORINE We'll use all manner of means, and all at once.

(*to* MARIANE:)

Your father's addled; he's acting like a dunce.
Therefore you'd better humor the old fossil.
Pretend to yield to him, be sweet and docile,
And then postpone, as often as necessary,
The day on which you have agreed to marry.
You'll thus gain time, and time will turn the trick.
Sometimes, for instance, you'll be taken sick,
And that will seem good reason for delay;
Or some bad omen will make you change the day—
You'll dream of muddy water, or you'll pass
A dead man's hearse, or break a looking-glass.
If all else fails, no man can marry you
Unless you take his ring and say "I do."
But now, let's separate. If they should find
Us talking here, our plot might be divined.

(*to* VALÈRE:)

Go to your friends, and tell them what's occurred,
And have them urge her father to keep his word.
Meanwhile, we'll stir her brother into action,

And get Elmire, as well, to join our faction.
Good-bye.
VALÈRE (*to* MARIANE)
Though each of us will do his best,
It's your true heart on which my hopes shall rest.
MARIANE (*to* VALÈRE) Regardless of what Father may decide,
None but Valère shall claim me as his bride.
VALÈRE Oh, how those words content me! Come what will . . .
DORINE Oh, lovers, lovers! Their tongues are never still.
Be off, now.
VALÈRE (*turning to go, then turning back*)
One last word . . .
DORINE No time to chat:
You leave by this door; and *you* leave by that.

(DORINE *pushes them, by the shoulders, toward opposing doors.*)

Act III

Scene I DAMIS, DORINE.

DAMIS May lightning strike me even as I speak,
May all men call me cowardly and weak,
If any fear or scruple holds me back
From settling things, at once, with that great quack!
DORINE Now, don't give way to violent emotion.
You father's merely talked about this notion,
And words and deeds are far from being one.
Much that is talked about is never done.
DAMIS No, I must stop that scoundrel's machinations;
I'll go and tell him off; I'm out of patience.
DORINE Do calm down and be practical. I had rather
My mistress dealt with him—and with your father.
She has some influence with Tartuffe, I've noted.
He hangs upon her words, seems most devoted,
And may, indeed, be smitten by her charm.
Pray Heaven it's true! 'Twould do our cause no harm.
She sent for him, just now, to sound him out
On this affair you're so incensed about;
She'll find out where he stands, and tell him too,
What dreadful strife and trouble will ensue
If he lends countenance to your father's plan.
I couldn't get in to see him, but his man

Says that he's almost finished with his prayers.
Go, now. I'll catch him when he comes downstairs.

DAMIS I want to hear this conference, and I will.

DORINE No, they must be alone.

DAMIS Oh, I'll keep still.

DORINE Not you. I know your temper. You'd start a brawl,
And shout and stamp your foot and spoil it all.
Go on.

DAMIS I won't; I have a perfect right . . .

DORINE Lord, you're a nuisance! He's coming; get out of sight.

(DAMIS *conceals himself in a closet at the rear of the stage.*)

Scene II TARTUFFE, DORINE.

TARTUFFE (*observing* DORINE, *and calling to his manservant offstage*)
Hang up my hair-shirt, put my scourge in place,
And pray, Laurent, for Heaven's perpetual grace.
I'm going to the prison now, to share
My last few coins with the poor wretches there.

DORINE (*aside*) Dear God, what affectation! What a fake!

TARTUFFE You wished to see me?

DORINE Yes . . .

TARTUFFE (*taking a handkerchief from his pocket*) For mercy's sake,
Please take this handkerchief, before you speak.

DORINE What?

TARTUFFE Cover that bosom, girl. The flesh is weak,
And unclean thoughts are difficult to control.
Such sights as that can undermine the soul.

DORINE Your soul, it seems, has very poor defenses,
And flesh makes quite an impact on your senses.
It's strange that you're so easily excited;
My own desires are not so soon ignited,
And if I saw you naked as a beast,
Not all your hide would tempt me in the least.

TARTUFFE Girl, speak more modestly; unless you do,
I shall be forced to take my leave of you.

DORINE Oh, no, it's I who must be on my way;
I've just one little message to convey.
Madame is coming down, and begs you, Sir,
To wait and have a word or two with her.

TARTUFFE Gladly.

DORINE (*aside*) *That* had a softening effect!
I think my guess about him was correct.

TARTUFFE Will she be long?
DORINE No: that's her step I hear.
Ah, here she is, and I shall disappear.

Scene III ELMIRE, TARTUFFE.

TARTUFFE May Heaven, whose infinite goodness we adore,
Preserve your body and soul forevermore,
And bless your days, and answer thus the plea
Of one who is its humblest votary.
ELMIRE I thank you for that pious wish, but please,
Do take a chair and let's be more at ease.

(*They sit down.*)

TARTUFFE I trust that you are once more well and strong?
ELMIRE Oh, yes: the fever didn't last for long.
TARTUFFE My prayers are too unworthy, I am sure,
To have gained from Heaven this most gracious cure;
But lately, Madam, my every supplication
Has had for object your recuperation.
ELMIRE You shouldn't have troubled so. I don't deserve it.
TARTUFFE Your health is priceless, Madam, and to preserve it
I'd gladly give my own, in all sincerity.
ELMIRE Sir, you outdo us all in Christian charity.
You've been most kind. I count myself your debtor.
TARTUFFE 'Twas nothing, Madam. I long to serve you better.
ELMIRE There's a private matter I'm anxious to discuss.
I'm glad there's no one here to hinder us.
TARTUFFE I too am glad; it floods my heart with bliss
To find myself alone with you like this.
For just this chance I've prayed with all my power—
But prayed in vain, until this happy hour.
ELMIRE This won't take long, Sir, and I hope you'll be
Entirely frank and unconstrained with me.
TARTUFFE Indeed, there's nothing I had rather do
Than bare my inmost heart and soul to you.
First, let me say that what remarks I've made
About the constant visits you are paid
Were prompted not by any mean emotion,
But rather by a pure and deep devotion,
A fervent zeal . . .
ELMIRE No need for explanation.
Your sole concern, I'm sure, was my salvation.

TARTUFFE (*taking* ELMIRE's *hand and pressing her fingertips*)
Quite so; and such great fervor do I feel . . .
ELMIRE Ooh! Please! You're pinching!
TARTUFFE 'Twas from excess of zeal.
I never meant to cause you pain, I swear.
I'd rather . . .

(*He places his hand on* ELMIRE's *knee.*)

ELMIRE What can your hand be doing there?
TARTUFFE Feeling your gown; what soft, fine-woven stuff!
ELMIRE Please, I'm extremely ticklish. That's enough.

(*She draws her chair away;* TARTUFFE *pulls his after her.*)

TARTUFFE (*fondling the lace collar of her gown*)
My, my, what lovely lacework on your dress!
The workmanship's miraculous, no less.
I've not seen anything to equal it.
ELMIRE Yes, quite. But let's talk business for a bit.
They say my husband means to break his word
And give his daughter to you, Sir. Had you heard?
TARTUFFE He did once mention it. But I confess
I dream of quite a different happiness.
It's elsewhere, Madam, that my eyes discern
The promise of that bliss for which I yearn.
ELMIRE I see: you care for nothing here below.
TARTUFFE Ah, well—my heart's not made of stone, you know.
ELMIRE All your desires mount heavenward, I'm sure,
In scorn of all that's earthly and impure.
TARTUFFE A love of heavenly beauty does not preclude
A proper love for earthly pulchritude;
Our senses are quite rightly captivated
By perfect works our Maker has created.
Some glory clings to all that Heaven has made;
In you, all Heaven's marvels are displayed.
On that fair face, such beauties have been lavished,
The eyes are dazzled and the heart is ravished;
How could I look on you, O flawless creature,
And not adore the Author of all Nature,
Feeling a love both passionate and pure
For you, his triumph of self-portraiture?
At first, I trembled lest that love should be
A subtle snare that Hell had laid for me;
I vowed to flee the sight of you, eschewing

A rapture that might prove my soul's undoing;
But soon, fair being, I became aware
That my deep passion could be made to square
With rectitude, and with my bounden duty.
I thereupon surrendered to your beauty.
It is, I know, presumptuous on my part
To bring you this poor offering of my heart,
And it is not my merit, Heaven knows,
But your compassion on which my hopes repose.
You are my peace, my solace, my salvation;
On you depends my bliss—or desolation;
I bide your judgment and, as you think best,
I shall be either miserable or blest.

ELMIRE Your declaration is most gallant, Sir,
But don't you think it's out of character?
You'd have done better to restrain your passion
And think before you spoke in such a fashion.
It ill becomes a pious man like you . . .

TARTUFFE I may be pious, but I'm human too:
With your celestial charms before his eyes,
A man has not the power to be wise.
I know such words sound strangely, coming from me,
But I'm no angel, nor was meant to be,
And if you blame my passion, you must needs
Reproach as well the charms on which it feeds.
Your loveliness I had no sooner seen
Than you became my soul's unrivalled queen;
Before your seraph glance, divinely sweet,
My heart's defenses crumbled in defeat,
And nothing fasting, prayer, or tears might do
Could stay my spirit from adoring you.
My eyes, my sighs have told you in the past
What now my lips make bold to say at last,
And if, in your great goodness, you will deign
To look upon your slave, and ease his pain,—
If, in compassion for my soul's distress,
You'll stoop to comfort my unworthiness,
I'll raise to you, in thanks for that sweet manna,
An endless hymn, an infinite hosanna.
With me, of course, there need be no anxiety,
No fear of scandal or of notoriety.
These young court gallants, whom all the ladies fancy,
Are vain in speech, in action rash and chancy;
When they succeed in love, the world soon knows it;

No favor's granted them but they disclose it
And by the looseness of their tongues profane
The very altar where their hearts have lain.
Men of my sort, however, love discreetly,
And one may trust our reticence completely.
My keen concern for my good name insures
The absolute security of yours;
In short, I offer you, my dear Elmire,
Love without scandal, pleasure without fear.

ELMIRE I've heard your well-turned speeches to the end,
And what you urge I clearly apprehend.
Aren't you afraid that I may take a notion
To tell my husband of your warm devotion,
And that, supposing he were duly told,
His feelings toward you might grow rather cold?

TARTUFFE I know, dear lady, that your exceeding charity
Will lead your heart to pardon my temerity;
That you'll excuse my violent affection
As human weakness, human imperfection;
And that—O fairest!—you will bear in mind
That I'm but flesh and blood, and am not blind.

ELMIRE Some women might do otherwise, perhaps,
But I shall be discreet about your lapse;
I'll tell my husband nothing of what's occurred
If, in return, you'll give your solemn word
To advocate as forcefully as you can
The marriage of Valère and Mariane,
Renouncing all desire to dispossess
Another of his rightful happiness,
And . . .

Scene IV Damis, Elmire, Tartuffe.

DAMIS (*emerging from the closet where he has been hiding*)
No! We'll not hush up this vile affair;
I heard it all inside that closet there,
Where Heaven, in order to confound the pride
Of this great rascal, prompted me to hide.
Ah, now I have my long-awaited chance
To punish his deceit and arrogance,
And give my father clear and shocking proof
Of the black character of his dear Tartuffe.

ELMIRE Ah no, Damis! I'll be content if he
Will study to deserve my leniency.

I've promised silence—don't make me break my word;
To make a scandal would be too absurd.
Good wives laugh off such trifles, and forget them;
Why should they tell their husbands, and upset them?
DAMIS You have your reasons for taking such a course,
And I have reasons, too, of equal force.
To spare him now would be insanely wrong.
I've swallowed my just wrath for far too long
And watched this insolent bigot bringing strife
And bitterness into our family life.
Too long he's meddled in my father's affairs,
Thwarting my marriage-hopes, and poor Valère's.
It's high time that my father was undeceived,
And now I've proof that can't be disbelieved—
Proof that was furnished me by Heaven above.
It's too good not to take advantage of.
This is my chance, and I deserve to lose it
If, for one moment, I hesitate to use it.
ELMIRE Damis . . .
DAMIS No, I must do what I think right.
Madam, my heart is bursting with delight.
And, say whatever you will, I'll not consent
To lose the sweet revenge on which I'm bent.
I'll settle matters without more ado;
And here, most opportunely, is my cue.

Scene V ORGON, DAMIS, TARTUFFE, ELMIRE.

DAMIS Father, I'm glad you've joined us. Let us advise you
Of some fresh news which doubtless will surprise you.
You've just now been repaid with interest
For all your loving-kindness to our guest.
He's proved his warm and grateful feelings toward you;
It's with a pair of horns he would reward you.
Yes, I surprised him with your wife, and heard
His whole adulterous offer, every word.
She, with her all too gentle disposition,
Would not have told you of his proposition;
But I shall not make terms with brazen lechery,
And feel that not to tell you would be treachery.
ELMIRE And I hold that one's husband's peace of mind
Should not be spoilt by tattle of this kind.
One's honor doesn't require it: to be proficient
In keeping men at bay is quite sufficient.

These are my sentiments, and I wish, Damis,
That you had heeded me and held your peace.

Scene VI ORGON, DAMIS, TARTUFFE.

ORGON Can it be true, this dreadful thing I hear?
TARTUFFE Yes, Brother, I'm a wicked man, I fear:
A wretched sinner, all depraved and twisted,
The greatest villain that has ever existed.
My life's one heap of crimes, which grows each minute;
There's naught but foulness and corruption in it;
And I perceive that Heaven, outraged by me,
Has chosen this occasion to mortify me.
Charge me with any deed you wish to name;
I'll not defend myself, but take the blame.
Believe what you are told, and drive Tartuffe
Like some base criminal from beneath your roof;
Yes, drive me hence, and with a parting curse;
I shan't protest, for I deserve far worse.
ORGON (*to* DAMIS) Ah, you deceitful boy, how dare you try
To stain his purity with so foul a lie?
DAMIS What! Are you taken in by such a bluff?
Did you not hear . . . ?
ORGON Enough, you rogue, enough!
TARTUFFE Ah, Brother, let him speak: you're being unjust.
Believe his story; the boy deserves your trust.
Why, after all, should you have faith in me?
How can you know what I might do, or be?
Is it on my good actions that you base
Your favor? Do you trust my pious face?
Ah, no, don't be deceived by hollow shows;
I'm far, alas, from being what men suppose;
Though the world takes me for a man of worth,
I'm truly the most worthless man on earth.

(*to* DAMIS:)

Yes, my dear son, speak out now: call me the chief
Of sinners, a wretch, a murderer, a thief;
Load me with all the names men most abhor;
I'll not complain; I've earned them all, and more;
I'll kneel here while you pour them on my head
As a just punishment for the life I've led.
ORGON (*to* TARTUFFE) This is too much, dear Brother.

(*to* DAMIS:)

Have you no heart?
DAMIS Are you so hoodwinked by this rascal's art . . . ?
ORGON Be still, you monster.

(*to* TARTUFFE:)

Brother, I pray you, rise.

(*to* DAMIS:)

Villain!
DAMIS But . . .
ORGON Silence!
DAMIS Can't you realize . . . ?
ORGON Just one word more, and I'll tear you limb from limb.
TARTUFFE In God's name, Brother, don't be harsh with him.
I'd rather far be tortured at the stake
Than see him bear one scratch for my poor sake.
ORGON (*to* DAMIS) Ingrate!
TARTUFFE If I must beg you, on bended knee,
To pardon him . . .
ORGON (*falling to his knees, addressing* TARTUFFE)
Such goodness cannot be!

(*to* DAMIS:)

Now, *there's* true charity!
DAMIS What, you . . . ?
ORGON Villain, be still!
I know your motives; I know you wish him ill:
Yes, all of you—wife, children, servants, all—
Conspire against him and desire his fall,
Employing every shameful trick you can
To alienate me from this saintly man.
Ah, but the more you seek to drive him away,
The more I'll do to keep him. Without delay,
I'll spite this household and confound its pride
By giving him my daughter as his bride.
DAMIS You're going to force her to accept his hand?
ORGON Yes, and this very night, d'you understand?
I shall defy you all, and make it clear
That I'm the one who gives the orders here.
Come, wretch, kneel known and clasp his blessed feet,
And ask his pardon for your black deceit.

DAMIS I ask that swindler's pardon? Why, I'd rather . . .
ORGON So! You insult him, and defy your father!
A stick! A stick! (*to* TARTUFFE:) No, no—release me, do.

(*to* DAMIS:)

Out of my house this minute! Be off with you,
And never dare set foot in it again.
DAMIS Well, I shall go, but . . .
ORGON Well, go quickly, then.
I disinherit you; an empty purse
Is all you'll get from me—except my curse!

Scene VII ORGON, TARTUFFE.

ORGON How he blasphemed your goodness! What a son!
TARTUFFE Forgive him, Lord, as I've already done.

(*to* ORGON:)

You can't know how it hurts when someone tries
To blacken me in my dear Brother's eyes.
ORGON Ahh!
TARTUFFE The mere thought of such ingratitude
Plunges my soul into so dark a mood . . .
Such horror grips my heart . . . I gasp for breath,
And cannot speak, and feel myself near death.
ORGON (*He runs, in tears, to the door through which he has just driven his son.*)
You blackguard! Why did I spare you? Why did I not
Break you in little pieces on the spot?
Compose yourself, and don't be hurt, dear friend.
TARTUFFE These scenes, these dreadful quarrels, have got to end.
I've much upset your household, and I perceive
That the best thing will be for me to leave.
ORGON What are you saying!
TARTUFFE They're all against me here;
They'd have you think me false and insincere.
ORGON Ah, what of that? Have I ceased believing in you?
TARTUFFE Their adverse talk will certainly continue,
And charges which you now repudiate
You may find credible at a later date.
ORGON No, Brother, never.
TARTUFFE Brother, a wife can sway
Her husband's mind in many a subtle way.
ORGON No, no.

TARTUFFE To leave at once is the solution;
Thus only can I end their persecution.
ORGON No, no, I'll not allow it; you shall remain.
TARTUFFE Ah, well; 'twill mean much martyrdom and pain,
but if you wish it . . .
ORGON Ah!
TARTUFFE Enough; so be it.
But one thing must be settled, as I set it.
For your dear honor, and for our friendship's sake,
There's one precaution I feel bound to take.
I shall avoid your wife, and keep away . . .
ORGON No, you shall not, whatever they may say.
It pleases me to vex them, and for spite
I'd have them see you with her day and night.
What's more, I'm going to drive them to despair
By making you my only son and heir;
This very day, I'll give to you alone
Clear deed and title to everything I own.
A dear, good friend and son-in-law-to-be
Is more than wife, or child, or kin to me,
Will you accept my offer, dearest son?
TARTUFFE In all things, let the will of Heaven be done.
ORGON Poor fellow! Come, we'll go draw up the deed.
Then let them burst with disappointed greed!

Act IV

Scene I CLÉANTE, TARTUFFE.

CLÉANTE Yes, all the town's discussing it, and truly,
Their comments do not flatter you unduly.
I'm glad we've met, Sir, and I'll give my view
Of this sad matter in a word or two.
As for who's guilty, that I shan't discuss;
Let's say it was Damis who caused the fuss;
Assuming, then, that you have been ill-used
By young Damis, and groundlessly accused,
Ought not a Christian to forgive, and ought
He not to stifle every vengeful thought?
Should you stand by and watch a father make
His only son an exile for your sake?
Again I tell you frankly, be advised:
The whole town, high and low, is scandalized;
This quarrel must be mended, and my advice is

Not to push matters to a further crisis.
No, sacrifice your wrath to God above,
And help Damis regain his father's love.

TARTUFFE Alas, for my part I should take great joy
In doing so. I've nothing against the boy.
I pardon all, I harbor no resentment;
To serve him would afford me much contentment.
But Heaven's interest will not have it so:
If he comes back, then I shall have to go.
After his conduct—so extreme, so vicious—
Our further intercourse would look suspicious.
God knows what people would think! Why, they'd describe
My goodness to him as a sort of bribe;
They'd say that out of guilt I made pretense
Of loving-kindness and benevolence—
That, fearing my accuser's tongue, I strove
To buy his silence with a show of love.

CLÉANTE Your reasoning is badly warped and stretched,
And these excuses, Sir, are most far-fetched.
Why put yourself in charge of Heaven's cause?
Does Heaven need our help to enforce its laws?
Leave vengeance to the Lord, Sir; while we live,
Our duty's not to punish, but forgive;
And what the Lord commands, we should obey
Without regard to what the world may say.
What! Shall the fear of being misunderstood
Prevent our doing what is right and good?
No, no: let's simply do what Heaven ordains,
And let no other thoughts perplex our brains.

TARTUFFE Again, Sir, let me say that I've forgiven
Damis, and thus obeyed the laws of Heaven;
But I am not commanded by the Bible
To live with one who smears my name with libel.

CLÉANTE Were you commanded, Sir, to indulge the whim
Of poor Orgon, and to encourage him
In suddenly transferring to your name
A large estate to which you have no claim?

TARTUFFE 'Twould never occur to those who know me best
To think I acted from self-interest.
The treasures of this world I quite despise;
Their specious glitter does not charm my eyes;
And if I have resigned myself to taking
The gift which my dear Brother insists on making,
I do so only, as he well understands,

Lest so much wealth fall into wicked hands,
Lest those to whom it might descend in time
Turn it to purposes of sin and crime,
And not, as I shall do, make use of it
For Heaven's glory and mankind's benefit.

CLÉANTE Forget these trumped-up fears. Your argument
Is one the rightful heir might well resent;
It *is* a moral burden to inherit
Such wealth, but give Damis a chance to bear it.
And would it not be worse to be accused
Of swindling, than to see that wealth misused?
I'm shocked that you allowed Orgon to broach
This matter, and that you feel no self-reproach:
Does true religion teach that lawful heirs
May freely be deprived of what is theirs?
And if the Lord has told you in your heart
That you and young Damis must dwell apart,
Would it not be the decent thing to beat
A generous and honorable retreat,
Rather than let the son of the house be sent,
For your convenience, into banishment?
Sir, if you wish to prove the honesty
Of your intentions . . .

TARTUFFE Sir, it is half-past three.
I've certain pious duties to attend to,
And hope my prompt departure won't offend you.

CLÉANTE (*alone*) Damn.

Scene II ELMIRE, MARIANE, CLÉANTE, DORINE.

DORINE Stay, Sir, and help Mariane, for Heaven's sake!
She's suffering so, I fear her heart will break.
Her father's plan to marry her off tonight
Has put the poor child in a desperate plight.
I hear him coming. Let's stand together, now,
And see if we can't change his mind, somehow,
About this match we all deplore and fear.

Scene III ORGON, ELMIRE, MARIANE, CLÉANTE, DORINE.

ORGON Hah! Glad to find you all assembled here.

(*to* MARIANE:)

This contract, child, contains your happiness,
And what it says I think your heart can guess.

MARIANE (*falling to her knees*)
Sir, by that Heaven which sees me here distressed,
And by whatever else can move your breast,
Do not employ a father's power, I pray you,
To crush my heart and force it to obey you,
Nor by your harsh commands oppress me so
That I'll begrudge the duty which I owe—
And do not so embitter and enslave me
That I shall hate the very life you gave me.
If my sweet hopes must perish, if you refuse
To give me to the one I've dared to choose,
Spare me at least—I beg you, I implore—
The pain of wedding one whom I abhor;
And do not, by a heartless use of force,
Drive me to contemplate some desperate course.

ORGON (*feeling himself touched by her*)
Be firm, my soul. No human weakness, now.

MARIANE I don't resent your love for him. Allow
Your heart free rein, Sir; give him your property,
And if that's not enough, take mine from me;
He's welcome to my money; take it, do,
But don't, I pray, include my person too.
Spare me, I beg you; and let me end the tale
Of my sad days behind a convent veil.

ORGON A convent! Hah! When crossed in their amours,
All lovesick girls have the same thought as yours.
Get up! The more you loathe the man, and dread him,
The more ennobling it will be to wed him.
Marry Tartuffe, and mortify your flesh!
Enough; don't start that whimpering afresh.

DORINE But why . . . ?

ORGON Be still, there. Speak when you're spoken to.
Not one more bit of impudence out of you.

CLÉANTE If I may offer a word of counsel here . . .

ORGON Brother, in counseling you have no peer;
All your advice is forceful, sound, and clever;
I don't propose to follow it, however.

ELMIRE (*to* ORGON) I am amazed, and don't know what to say;
Your blindness simply takes my breath away.
You are indeed bewitched, to take no warning
From our account of what occurred this morning.

ORGON Madam, I know a few plain facts, and one
Is that you're partial to my rascal son;
Hence, when he sought to make Tartuffe the victim
Of a base lie, you dared not contradict him.
Ah, but you underplayed your part, my pet;
You should have looked more angry, more upset.
ELMIRE When men make overtures, must we reply
With righteous anger and a battle-cry?
Must we turn back their amorous advances
With sharp reproaches and with fiery glances?
Myself, I find such offers merely amusing,
And make no scenes and fusses in refusing;
My taste is for good-natured rectitude,
And I dislike the savage sort of prude
Who guards her virtue with her teeth and claws,
And tears men's eyes out for the slightest cause:
The Lord preserve me from such honor as that,
Which bites and scratches like an alley-cat!
I've found that a polite and cool rebuff
Discourages a lover quite enough.
ORGON I know the facts, and I shall not be shaken.
ELMIRE I marvel at your power to be mistaken.
Would it, I wonder, carry weight with you
If I could *show* you that our tale was true?
ORGON Show me?
ELMIRE Yes.
ORGON Rot.
ELMIRE Come, what if I found a way
To make you see the facts as plain as day?
ORGON Nonsense.
ELMIRE Do answer me; don't be absurd.
I'm not now asking you to trust our word.
Suppose that from some hiding-place in here
You learned the whole sad truth by eye and ear—
What would you say of your good friend, after that?
ORGON Why, I'd say . . . nothing, by Jehoshaphat!
It can't be true.
ELMIRE You've been too long deceived,
And I'm quite tired of being disbelieved.
Come now: let's put my statements to the test,
And you shall see the truth made manifest.
ORGON I'll take that challenge. Now do your uttermost.
We'll see how you make good your empty boast.
ELMIRE (*to* DORINE) Send him to me.

DORINE He's crafty; it may be hard
To catch the cunning scoundrel off his guard.
ELMIRE No, amorous men are gullible. Their conceit
So blinds them that they're never hard to cheat.
Have him come down

(*to* CLÉANTE *and* MARIANE:)

Please leave us, for a bit.

Scene IV ELMIRE, ORGON.

ELMIRE Pull up this table, and get under it.
ORGON What?
ELMIRE It's essential that you be well-hidden.
ORGON Why there?
ELMIRE Oh, Heavens! Just do as you are bidden.
I have my plans; we'll soon see how they fare.
Under the table, now; and once you're there,
Take care that you are neither seen nor heard.
ORGON Well, I'll indulge you, since I gave my word
To see you through this infantile charade.
ELMIRE Once it is over, you'll be glad we played.

(*to her husband, who is now under the table:*)

I'm going to act quite strangely, now, and you
Must not be shocked at anything I do.
Whatever I may say, you must excuse
As part of that deceit I'm forced to use.
I shall employ sweet speeches in the task
Of making that imposter drop his mask;
I'll give encouragement to his bold desires,
And furnish fuel to his amorous fires.
Since it's for your sake, and for his destruction,
That I shall seem to yield to his seduction,
I'll gladly stop whenever you decide
That all your doubts are fully satisfied.
I'll count on you, as soon as you have seen
What sort of man he is, to intervene,
And not expose me to his odious lust
One moment longer than you feel you must.
Remember: you're to save me from my plight
Whenever . . . He's coming! Hush! Keep out of sight!

Scene V Tartuffe, Elmire, Orgon.

TARTUFFE You wish to have a word with me, I'm told.
ELMIRE Yes. I've a little secret to unfold.
Before I speak, however, it would be wise
To close that door, and look about for spies.

(Tartuffe *goes to the door, closes it, and returns.*)

The very last thing that must happen now
Is a repetition of this morning's row.
I've never been so badly caught off guard.
Oh, how I feared for you! You saw how hard
I tried to make that troublesome Damis
Control his dreadful temper, and hold his peace.
In my confusion, I didn't have the sense
Simply to contradict his evidence;
But as it happened, that was for the best,
And all has worked out in our interest.
This storm has only bettered your position;
My husband doesn't have the least suspicion,
And now, in mockery of those who do,
He bids me be continually with you.
And that is why, quite fearless of reproof,
I now can be alone with my Tartuffe,
And why my heart—perhaps too quick to yield—
Feels free to let its passion be revealed.
TARTUFFE Madam, your words confuse me. Not long ago,
You spoke in quite a different style, you know.
ELMIRE Ah, Sir, if that refusal made you smart,
It's little that you know of woman's heart,
Or what that heart is trying to convey
When it resists in such a feeble way!
Always, at first, our modesty prevents
The frank avowal of tender sentiments;
However high the passion which inflames us,
Still, to confess its power somehow shames us.
Thus we reluct, at first, yet in a tone
Which tells you that our heart is overthrown,
That what our lips deny, our pulse confesses,
And that, in time, all noes will turn to yesses.
I fear my words are all too frank and free,
And a poor proof of woman's modesty;
But since I'm started, tell me, if you will—
Would I have tried to make Damis be still,
Would I have listened, calm and unoffended,

Until your lengthy offer of love was ended,
And been so very mild in my reaction,
Had your sweet words not given me satisfaction?
And when I tried to force you to undo
The marriage-plans my husband has in view,
What did my urgent pleading signify
If not that I admired you, and that I
Deplored the thought that someone else might own
Part of a heart I wished for mine alone?

TARTUFFE Madam, no happiness is so complete
As when, from lips we love, come words so sweet;
Their nectar floods my every sense, and drains
In honeyed rivulets through all my veins.
To please you is my joy, my only goal;
Your love is the restorer of my soul;
And yet I must beg leave, now, to confess
Some lingering doubts as to my happiness.
Might not this be a trick? Might not the catch
Be that you wish me to break off the match
With Mariane, and so have feigned to love me?
I shan't quite trust your fond opinion of me
Until the feelings you've expressed so sweetly
Are demonstrated somewhat more concretely,
And you have shown, by certain kind concessions,
That I may put my faith in your professions.

ELMIRE (*She coughs, to warn her husband.*)
Why be in such a hurry? Must my heart
Exhaust its bounty at the very start?
To make that sweet admission cost me dear,
But you'll not be content, it would appear,
Unless my store of favors is disbursed
To the last farthing, and at the very first.

TARTUFFE The less we merit, the less we dare to hope,
And with our doubts, mere words can never cope.
We trust no promised bliss till we receive it;
Not till a joy is ours can we believe it.
I, who so little merit your esteem,
Can't credit this fulfillment of my dream,
And shan't believe it, Madam, until I savor
Some palpable assurance of your favor.

ELMIRE My, how tyrannical your love can be,
And how it flusters and perplexes me!
How furiously you take one's heart in hand,
And make your every wish a fierce command!
Come, must you hound and harry me to death?

Will you not give me time to catch my breath?
Can it be right to press me with such force,
Give me no quarter, show me no remorse,
And take advantage, by your stern insistence,
Of the fond feelings which weaken my resistance?

TARTUFFE Well, if you look with favor upon my love,
Why, then, begrudge me some clear proof thereof?

ELMIRE But how can I consent without offense
To Heaven, toward which you feel such reverence?

TARTUFFE If Heaven is all that holds you back, don't worry.
I can remove that hindrance in a hurry.
Nothing of that sort need obstruct our path.

ELMIRE Must one not be afraid of Heaven's wrath?

TARTUFFE Madam, forget such fears, and be my pupil,
And I shall teach you how to conquer scruple.
Some joys, it's true, are wrong in Heaven's eyes;
Yet Heaven is not averse to compromise;
There is a science, lately formulated,
Whereby one's conscience may be liberated,
And any wrongful act you care to mention
May be redeemed by purity of intention.
I'll teach you, Madam, the secrets of that science;
Meanwhile, just place on me your full reliance.
Assuage my keen desires, and feel no dread:
The sin, if any, shall be on my head.

(ELMIRE *coughs, this time more loudly.*)

You've a bad cough.

ELMIRE Yes, yes. It's bad indeed.

TARTUFFE (*producing a little paper bag*)
A bit of licorice may be what you need.

ELMIRE No, I've a stubborn cold, it seems. I'm sure it
Will take much more than licorice to cure it.

TARTUFFE How aggravating.

ELMIRE Oh, more than I can say.

TARTUFFE If you're still troubled, think of things this way:
No one shall know our joys, save us alone,
And there's no evil till the act is known;
It's scandal, Madam, which makes it an offense,
And it's no sin to sin in confidence.

ELMIRE (*having coughed once more*) Well, clearly I must do as you require,
And yield to your importunate desire.
It is apparent, now, that nothing less

Will satisfy you, and so I acquiesce.
To go so far is much against my will;
I'm vexed that it should come to this; but still,
Since you are so determined on it, since you
Will not allow mere language to convince you,
And since you ask for concrete evidence, I
See nothing for it, now, but to comply.
If this is sinful, if I'm wrong to do it,
So much the worse for him who drove me to it.
The fault can surely not be charged to me.

TARTUFFE Madam, the fault is mine, if fault there be,
And . . .

ELMIRE Open the door a little, and peek out;
I wouldn't want my husband poking about.

TARTUFFE Why worry about the man? Each day he grows
More gullible; one can lead him by the nose.
To find us here would fill him with delight,
And if he saw the worse, he'd doubt his sight.

ELMIRE Nevertheless, do step out for a minute
Into the hall, and see that no one's in it.

Scene VI ORGON, ELMIRE.

ORGON (*coming out from under the table*)
That man's a perfect monster, I must admit!
I'm simply stunned. I can't get over it.

ELMIRE What, coming out so soon? How premature!
Get back in hiding, and wait until you're sure.
Stay till the end, and be convinced completely;
We mustn't stop till things are proved concretely.

ORGON Hell never harbored anything so vicious!

ELMIRE Tut, don't be hasty. Try to be judicious.
Wait, and be certain that there's no mistake.
No jumping to conclusions, for Heaven's sake!

(*She places* ORGON *behind her, as* TARTUFFE *reenters.*)

Scene VII TARTUFFE, ELMIRE, ORGON.

TARTUFFE (*not seeing* ORGON)
Madam, all things have worked out to perfection;
I've given the neighboring rooms a full inspection;
No one's about; and now I may at last . . .

ORGON (*intercepting him*) Hold on, my passionate fellow, not so fast!

I should advise a little more restraint.
Well, so you thought you'd fool me, my dear saint!
How soon you wearied of the saintly life—
Wedding my daughter, and coveting my wife!
I've long suspected you, and had a feeling
That soon I'd catch you at your double-dealing.
Just now, you've given me the evidence galore;
It's quite enough; I have no wish for more.

ELMIRE (*to* TARTUFFE) I'm sorry to have treated you so slyly,
But circumstances forced me to be wily.

TARTUFFE Brother, you can't think . . .

ORGON No more talk from you:
Just leave this household, without more ado.

TARTUFFE What I intended . . .

ORGON That seems fairly clear.
Spare me your falsehoods and get out of here.

TARTUFFE No, I'm the master, and you're the one to go!
This house belongs to me, I'll have you know,
And I shall show you that you can't hurt *me*
By this contemptible conspiracy,
That those who cross me know not what they do,
And that I've means to expose and punish you,
Avenge offended Heaven, and make you grieve
That ever you dared order me to leave.

Scene VIII ELMIRE, ORGON.

ELMIRE What was the point of all that angry chatter?

ORGON Dear God, I'm worried. This is no laughing matter.

ELMIRE How so?

ORGON I fear I understood his drift.
I'm much disturbed about that deed of gift.

ELMIRE You gave him . . . ?

ORGON Yes, it's all been drawn and signed.
But one thing more is weighing on my mind.

ELMIRE What's that?

ORGON I'll tell you; but first let's see if there's
A certain strong-box in his room upstairs.

Act V

Scene I ORGON, CLÉANTE.

CLÉANTE Where are you going so fast?

ORGON God knows!

CLÉANTE Then wait;
Let's have a conference, and deliberate
On how this situation's to be met.
ORGON That strong-box has me utterly upset;
This is the worst of many, many shocks.
CLÉANTE Is there some fearful mystery in that box?
ORGON My poor friend Argas brought that box to me
With his own hands, in utmost secrecy;
'Twas on the very morning of his flight.
It's full of papers which, if they came to light,
Would ruin him—or such is my impression.
CLÉANTE Then why did you let it out of your possession?
ORGON Those papers vexed my conscience, and it seemed best
To ask the counsel of my pious guest.
The cunning scoundrel got me to agree
To leave the strong-box in his custody,
So that, in case of an investigation,
I could employ a slight equivocation
And swear I didn't have it, and thereby,
At no expense to conscience, tell a lie.
CLÉANTE It looks to me as if you're out on a limb.
Trusting him with that box, and offering him
That deed of gift, were actions of a kind
Which scarcely indicate a prudent mind.
With two such weapons, he has the upper hand,
And since you're vulnerable, as matters stand,
You erred once more in bringing him to bay.
You should have acted in some subtler way.
ORGON Just think of it: behind that fervent face,
A heart so wicked, and a soul so base!
I took him in, a hungry beggar, and then . . .
Enough, by God! I'm through with pious men:
Henceforth I'll hate the whole false brotherhood,
And persecute them worse than Satan could.
CLÉANTE Ah, there you go—extravagant as ever!
Why can you not be rational? You never
Manage to take the middle course, it seems,
But jump, instead, between absurd extremes.
You've recognized your recent grave mistake
In falling victim to a pious fake;
Now, to correct that error, must you embrace
An even greater error in its place,
And judge our worthy neighbors as a whole
By what you've learned of one corrupted soul?
Come, just because one rascal made you swallow

A show of zeal which turned out to be hollow,
Shall you conclude that all men are deceivers,
And that, today, there are no true believers?
Let atheists make that foolish inference;
Learn to distinguish virtue from pretense,
Be cautious in bestowing admiration,
And cultivate a sober moderation.
Don't humor fraud, but also don't asperse
True piety; the latter fault is worse,
And it is best to err, if err one must,
As you have done, upon the side of trust.

Scene II DAMIS, ORGON, CLÉANTE.

DAMIS Father, I hear that scoundrel's uttered threats
Against you; that he pridefully forgets
How, in his need, he was befriended by you,
And means to use your gifts to crucify you.
ORGON It's true, my boy. I'm too distressed for tears.
DAMIS Leave it to me, Sir; let me trim his ears.
Faced with such insolence, we must not waver.
I shall rejoice in doing you the favor
Of cutting short his life, and your distress.
CLÉANTE What a display of young hotheadedness!
Do learn to moderate your fits of rage.
In this just kingdom, this enlightened age,
One does not settle things by violence.

Scene III MADAME PERNELLE, MARIANE, ELMIRE, DORINE, DAMIS, ORGON, CLÉANTE.

MADAME PERNELLE I hear strange tales of very strange events.
ORGON Yes, strange events which these two eyes beheld.
The man's ingratitude is unparalleled.
I save a wretched pauper from starvation,
House him, and treat him like a blood relation,
Shower him every day with my largesse,
Give him my daughter, and all that I possess;
And meanwhile the unconscionable knave
Tries to induce my wife to misbehave;
And not content with such extreme rascality,
Now threatens me with my own liberality,
And aims, by taking base advantage of

The gifts I gave him out of Christian love,
To drive me from my house, a ruined man,
And make me end a pauper, as he began.

DORINE Poor fellow!

MADAME PERNELLE No, my son, I'll never bring
Myself to think him guilty of such a thing.

ORGON How's that?

MADAME PERNELLE The righteous always were maligned.

ORGON Speak clearly, Mother. Say what's on your mind.

MADAME PERNELLE I mean that I can smell a rat, my dear.
You know how everybody hates him, here.

ORGON That has no bearing on the case at all.

MADAME PERNELLE I told you a hundred times, when you were small,
That virtue in this world is hated ever;
Malicious men may die, but malice never.

ORGON No doubt that's true, but how does it apply?

MADAME PERNELLE They've turned you against him by a clever lie.

ORGON I've told you, I was there and saw it done.

MADAME PERNELLE Ah, slanderers will stop at nothing, Son.

ORGON Mother, I'll lose my temper . . . For the last time,
I tell you I was witness to the crime.

MADAME PERNELLE The tongues of spite are busy night and noon,
And to their venom no man is immune.

ORGON You're talking nonsense. Can't you realize
I saw it; saw it; saw it with my eyes?
Saw, do you understand me? Must I shout it
Into your ears before you'll cease to doubt it?

MADAME PERNELLE Appearances can deceive, my son. Dear me,
We cannot always judge by what we see.

ORGON Drat! Drat!

MADAME PERNELLE One often interprets things awry;
Good can seem evil to a suspicious eye.

ORGON Was I to see his pawing at Elmire
As an act of charity?

MADAME PERNELLE Till his guilt is clear,
A man deserves the benefit of the doubt.
You should have waited, to see how things turned out.

ORGON Great God in Heaven, what more proof did I need?
Was I to sit there, watching, until he'd . . .
You drive me to the brink of impropriety.

MADAME PERNELLE No, no, a man of such surpassing piety
Could not do such a thing. You cannot shake me.
I don't believe it, and you shall not make me.

ORGON You vex me so that, if you weren't my mother,
I'd say to you . . . some dreadful thing or other.
DORINE It's your turn now, Sir, not to be listened to;
You'd not trust us, and now she won't trust you.
CLÉANTE My friends, we're wasting time which should be spent
In facing up to our predicament.
I fear that scoundrel's threats weren't made in sport.
DAMIS Do you think he'd have the nerve to go to court?
ELMIRE I'm sure he won't; they'd find it all too crude
A case of swindling and ingratitude.
CLÉANTE Don't be too sure. He won't be at a loss
To give his claims a high and righteous gloss;
And clever rogues with far less valid cause
Have trapped their victims in a web of laws.
I say again that to antagonize
A man so strongly armed was most unwise.
ORGON I know it; but the man's appalling cheek
Outraged me so, I couldn't control my pique.
CLÉANTE I wish to Heaven that we could devise
Some truce between you, or some compromise.
ELMIRE If I had known what cards he held, I'd not
Have roused his anger by my little plot.
ORGON (*to* DORINE, *as* M. LOYAL *enters*)
What is that fellow looking for? Who is he?
Go talk to him—and tell him that I'm busy.

Scene IV MONSIEUR LOYAL, MADAME PERNELLE, ORGON, DAMIS, MARIANE, DORINE, ELMIRE, CLÉANTE.

MONSIEUR LOYAL Good day, dear sister. Kindly let me see
Your master.
DORINE He's involved with company,
And cannot be disturbed just now, I fear.
MONSIEUR LOYAL I hate to intrude; but what has brought me here
Will not disturb your master, in any event.
Indeed, my news will make him most content.
DORINE Your name?
MONSIEUR LOYAL Just say that I bring greetings from
Monsieur Tartuffe, on whose behalf I've come.
DORINE (*to* ORGON) Sir, he's a very gracious man, and bears
A message from Tartuffe, which, he declares,
Will make you most content.
CLÉANTE Upon my word,
I think this man had best be seen, and heard.

ORGON Perhaps he has some settlement to suggest.
How shall I treat him? What manner would be best?
CLÉANTE Control your anger, and if he should mention
Some fair adjustment, give him your full attention.
MONSIEUR LOYAL Good health to you, good Sir. May Heaven confound
Your enemies, and may your joys abound.
ORGON (*aside, to* CLÉANTE) A gentle salutation: it confirms
My guess that he is here to offer terms.
MONSIEUR LOYAL I've always held your family most dear;
I served your father, Sir, for many a year.
ORGON Sir, I must ask your pardon; to my shame,
I cannot now recall your face or name.
MONSIEUR LOYAL Loyal's my name; I come from Normandy,
And I'm a bailiff, in all modesty.
For forty years, praise God, it's been my boast
To serve with honor in that vital post,
And I am here, Sir, if you will permit
The liberty, to serve you with this writ . . .
ORGON To—*what?*
MONSIEUR LOYAL Now, please, Sir, let us have no friction:
It's nothing but an order of eviction.
You are to move your goods and family out
And make way for new occupants, without
Deferment or delay, and give the keys . . .
ORGON I? Leave this house?
MONSIEUR LOYAL Why yes, Sir, if you please.
This house, Sir, from the cellar to the roof,
Belongs now to the good Monsieur Tartuffe,
And he is lord and master of your estate
By virtue of a deed of present date,
Drawn in due form, with clearest legal phrasing . . .
DAMIS Your insolence is utterly amazing!
MONSIEUR LOYAL Young man, my business here is not with you,
But with your wise and temperate father, who,
Like every worthy citizen, stands in awe
Of justice, and would never obstruct the law.
ORGON But . . .
MONSIEUR LOYAL Not for a million, Sir, would you rebel
Against authority; I know that well.
You'll not make trouble, Sir, or interfere
With the execution of my duties here.
DAMIS Someone may execute a smart tattoo
On that black jacket of yours, before you're through.

MONSIEUR LOYAL Sir, bid your son be silent. I'd much regret
Having to mention such a nasty threat
Of violence, in writing my report.
DORINE (*aside*) This man Loyal's a most disloyal sort!
MONSIEUR LOYAL I love all men of upright character,
And when I agreed to serve these papers, Sir,
It was your feelings that I had in mind.
I couldn't bear to see the case assigned
To someone else, who might esteem you less
And so subject you to unpleasantness.
ORGON What's more unpleasant than telling a man to leave
His house and home?
MONSIEUR LOYAL You'd like a short reprieve?
If you desire it, Sir, I shall not press you,
But wait until tomorrow to dispossess you.
Splendid. I'll come and spend the night here, then,
Most quietly, with half a score of men.
For form's sake, you might bring me, just before
You go to bed, the keys to the front door.
My men, I promise, will be on their best
Behavior, and will not disturb your rest.
But bright and early, Sir, you must be quick
And move out all your furniture, every stick:
The men I've chosen are both young and strong,
And with their help it shouldn't take you long.
In short, I'll make things pleasant and convenient,
And since I'm being so extremely lenient,
Please show me, Sir, a like consideration,
And give me your entire cooperation.
ORGON (*aside*) I may be all but bankrupt, but I vow
I'd give a hundred louis, here and now,
Just for the pleasure of landing one good clout
Right on the end of that complacent snout.
CLÉANTE Careful; don't make things worse.
DAMIS My bootsole itches
To give that beggar a good kick in the breeches.
DORINE Monsieur Loyal, I'd love to hear the whack
Of a stout stick across your fine broad back.
MONSIEUR LOYAL Take care: a woman too may go to jail if
She uses threatening language to a bailiff.
CLÉANTE Enough, enough, Sir. This must not go on.
Give me that paper, please, and then begone.
MONSIEUR LOYAL Well, *au revoir*. God give you all good cheer!
ORGON May God confound you, and him who sent you here!

Scene V ORGON, CLÉANTE, MARIANE, ELMIRE, MADAME PERNELLE, DORINE, DAMIS.

ORGON Now, Mother, was I right or not? This writ
Should change your notion of Tartuffe a bit.
Do you perceive his villainy at last?
MADAME PERNELLE I'm thunderstruck. I'm utterly aghast.
DORINE Oh, come, be fair. You mustn't take offense
At this new proof of his benevolence.
He's acting out of selfless love, I know.
Material things enslave the soul, and so
He kindly has arranged your liberation
From all that might endanger your salvation.
ORGON Will you not ever hold your tongue, you dunce?
CLÉANTE Come, you must take some action, and at once.
ELMIRE Go tell the world of the low trick he's tried.
The deed of gift is surely nullified
By such behavior, and public rage will not
Permit the wretch to carry out his plot.

Scene VI VALÈRE, ORGON, CLÉANTE, ELMIRE, MARIANE, MADAME PERNELLE, DAMIS, DORINE.

VALÈRE Sir, though I hate to bring you more bad news,
Such is the danger that I cannot choose.
A friend who is extremely close to me
And knows my interest in your family
Has, for my sake, presumed to violate
The secrecy that's due to things of state,
And sends me word that you are in a plight
From which your one salvation lies in flight,
That scoundrel who's imposed upon you so
Denounced you to the King an hour ago
And, as supporting evidence, displayed
The strong-box of a certain renegade
Whose secret papers, so he testified,
You had disloyally agreed to hide.
I don't know just what charges may be pressed,
But there's a warrant out for your arrest;
Tartuffe has been instructed, furthermore,
To guide the arresting officer to your door.
CLÉANTE He's clearly done this to facilitate
His seizure of your house and your estate.
ORGON That man, I must say, is a vicious beast!

VALÈRE You can't afford to delay, Sir, in the least.
My carriage is outside, to take you hence;
This thousand louis should cover all expense.
Let's lose no time, or you shall be undone;
The sole defense, in this case, is to run.
I shall go with you all the way, and place you
In a safe refuge to which they'll never trace you.
ORGON Alas, dear boy, I wish that I could show you
My gratitude for everything I owe you.
But now is not the time; I pray the Lord
That I may live to give you your reward.
Farewell, my dears; be careful . . .
CLÉANTE Brother, hurry.
We shall take care of things; you needn't worry.

Scene VII THE OFFICER, TARTUFFE, VALÈRE, ORGON, ELMIRE, MARIANE, MADAME PERNELLE, DORINE, CLÉANTE, DAMIS.

TARTUFFE Gently, Sir, gently; stay right where you are.
No need for haste; your lodging isn't far.
You're off to prison, by order of the Prince.
ORGON This is the crowning blow, you wretch; and since
It means my total ruin and defeat,
Your villainy is now at last complete.
TARTUFFE You needn't try to provoke me; it's no use.
Those who serve Heaven must expect abuse.
CLÉANTE You are indeed most patient, sweet, and blameless.
DORINE How he exploits the name of Heaven! It's shameless.
TARTUFFE Your taunts and mockeries are all for naught;
To do my duty is my only thought.
MARIANE Your love of duty is most meritorious,
And what you've done is little short of glorious.
TARTUFFE All deeds are glorious, Madam, which obey
The sovereign prince who sent me here today.
ORGON I rescued you when you were destitute;
Have you forgotten that, you thankless brute?
TARTUFFE No, no, I well remember everything;
But my first duty is to serve my King.
That obligation is so paramount
That other claims, beside it, do not count;
And for it I would sacrifice my wife,
My family, my friend, or my own life.
ELMIRE Hypocrite!

DORINE All that we most revere, he uses
To cloak his plots and camouflage his ruses.

CLÉANTE If it is true that you are animated
By pure and loyal zeal, as you have stated,
Why was this zeal not roused until you'd sought
To make Orgon a cuckold, and been caught?
Why weren't you moved to give your evidence
Until your outraged host had driven you hence?
I shan't say that the gift of all his treasure
Ought to have damped your zeal in any measure;
But if he is a traitor, as you declare,
How could you condescend to be his heir?

TARTUFFE (*to the* OFFICER)
Sir, spare me all this clamor, it's growing shrill.
Please carry out your orders, if you will.

OFFICER Yes, I've delayed too long, Sir. Thank you kindly.
You're just the proper person to remind me.
Come, you are off to join the other boarders
In the King's prison, according to his orders.

TARTUFFE Who? I, Sir?

OFFICER Yes.

TARTUFFE To prison? This can't be true!

OFFICER I owe an explanation, but not to you.

(*to* ORGON:)

Sir, all is well; rest easy, and be grateful.
We serve a Prince to whom all sham is hateful,
A Prince who sees into our inmost hearts,
And can't be fooled by any trickster's arts.
His royal soul, though generous and human,
Views all things with discernment and acumen;
His sovereign reason is not lightly swayed,
And all his judgments are discreetly weighed.
He honors righteous men of every kind,
And yet his zeal for virtue is not blind,
Nor does his love of piety numb his wits
And make him tolerant of hypocrites.
'Twas hardly likely that this man could cozen
A King who's foiled such liars by the dozen.
With one keen glance, the King perceived the whole
Perverseness and corruption of his soul,
And thus high Heaven's justice was displayed:
Betraying you, the rogue stood self-betrayed.

The King soon recognized Tartuffe as one
Notorious by another name, who'd done
So many vicious crimes that one could fill
Ten volumes with them, and be writing still.
But to be brief: our sovereign was appalled
By this man's treachery toward you, which he called
The last, worst villainy of a vile career,
And bade me follow the imposter here
To see how gross his impudence could be,
And force him to restore your property.
Your private papers, by the King's command,
I hereby seize and give into your hand.
The King, by royal order, invalidates
The deed which gave this rascal your estates,
And pardons, furthermore, your grave offense
In harboring an exile's documents.
By these decrees, our Prince rewards you for
Your loyal deeds in the late civil war,
And shows how heartfelt is his satisfaction
In recompensing any worthy action,
How much he prizes merit, and how he makes
More of men's virtues than of their mistakes.

DORINE Heaven be praised!

MADAME PERNELLE I breathe again, at last.

ELMIRE We're safe.

MARIANE I can't believe the danger's past.

ORGON (*to* TARTUFFE)
Well, traitor, now you see . . .

CLÉANTE Ah, Brother, please,
Let's not descend to such indignities.
Leave the poor wretch to his unhappy fate,
And don't say anything to aggravate
His present woes; but rather hope that he
Will soon embrace an honest piety,
And mend his ways, and by a true repentance
Move our just King to moderate his sentence.
Meanwhile, go kneel before your sovereign's throne
And thank him for the mercies he has shown.

ORGON Well said: let's go at once and, gladly kneeling,
Express the gratitude which all are feeling.
Then, when that first great duty has been done,
We'll turn with pleasure to a second one,
And give Valère, whose love has proven so true,
The wedded happiness which is his due.

THE SCHOOL FOR SCANDAL

(1777)

RICHARD BRINSLEY SHERIDAN (1751–1816)

The English theatre that we know as Elizabethan or Shakespearean (actually it outlived both the queen and the dramatist by half a century) experienced a metamorphosis that completely changed the physical structure of the theatre, the drama written for it, and the actors who performed in it. The cause was the revolt of Parliament against King Charles I that began a civil war in 1642 between the Puritan forces of Oliver Cromwell (the Roundheads) and the Royalist forces (the Cavaliers). The defeated king was beheaded in 1649 and his young son was spirited off to France for safety. England was then governed as a commonwealth by the Cromwellian iron fist under strict Puritanical rule bent on eliminating all vestiges of the royal past, particularly as it affected religion. (In its zeal to enforce a rigid austerity of faith and to abandon all forms of frivolity and idolatry, the government, among other measures, forbade the celebration of Christmas as pagan. In addition, a nationwide rampage was conducted that destroyed or seriously defaced many of the great churches and abbeys that had survived the assaults of Henry VIII in his break with Rome in the first half of the sixteenth century.) One of the first royal institutions to be eliminated was the theatre. In 1642 all London theatre buildings were closed. They disappeared so completely that not until the 1980s with the discovery of the foundations for the Rose Theatre was it possible to determine where they had been located.

After Elizabeth's death in 1603, James VI of Scotland became King James I, followed by Charles I in 1625. Theatre and drama continued unabated, but the Marlowe-Shakespeare-Jonson tradition in tragedy began to undergo a notable change, turning to melodramatic sensationalism for its own sake. John Webster (?–1634) with *The Duchess of Malfi* (1614), Thomas Middleton (c. 1570–1627) with *The Changeling* (1622), and John Ford (1586–1639) with *'Tis Pity She's a Whore* (c. 1627) stand out amidst a number of lesser figures. Comedy thrived in the works of Francis Beaumont (c. 1584–1616) and John Fletcher (1579–1625), with their satiric and best-remembered *The Knight of the Burning Pestle* (1607), Philip Massinger (1583–1640) with *A New Way to Pay Old Debts* (c. 1625), and John Shirley (1596–1666), who wrote right up to the closing of the theatres, with *The Gamester* (1633).

All this activity ceased abruptly in 1642, and for the next eighteen years the public theatre vanished. The government tolerated limited private theatricals, often in school productions, and William Davenant's elaborately staged "entertainment with music," *The Siege of Rhodes* in 1656, often regarded as the first English opera, was permitted a public production. To all intents and purposes, however, there was no theatre, the acting companies broke up, and nothing was written as the theatre buildings decayed and collapsed.

True to the policy of any dictator, Oliver Cromwell, who ruled England as its Lord Protector from 1653 to 1658, had made ineffective provision for a transfer of power. His son Richard assumed the mantle upon his father's death, but he totally lacked Cromwell's skills, and after scarcely a year the whole structure was falling apart. Ever since their defeat in the civil war, the nobility and the aristocracy had chafed under Cromwellian tyranny, remaining loyal to the exiled young prince. With Cromwell's death and the ineptness of his son's stumbling rule, conflict was brewing; but when Charles II, now 30 years old and considered capable of assuming the throne, was asked to return in 1660, opposition faded. The monarchy was restored in a bloodless revolt, the English society took up where it had left off before the revolt—almost, but not quite. The struggles of the civil war and the ensuing eighteen years could not erase the hard lines that had been drawn between the greater mass of the populace, who still maintained fairly rigid Puritan principles, and the lesser number of those at the top who functioned in a courtly society wholly alien to the world of the ordinary citizen. Nowhere was this more apparent than in the theatre.

Charles II had spent his youth from age twelve until his return at age thirty amidst a continental society not greatly unlike that which he had fled. This included patronizing the French theatre that welcomed the plays of Corneille and would soon produce Molière and Racine. The king brought back with him a great love for the theatre, and within a few months of his return he had issued patents to Davenant and to Thomas Killigrew for the establishment of two companies of players.

However, the two theatres—the legitimate houses authorized by the crown as the only ones permitted to function in London—were vastly different from what had gone before in almost every way. Seldom in the history of art has such abrupt change been experienced within so short a period. It was not a gradual evolution, but a sudden turnaround that permanently altered the form, the style, and the appeal of the English theatre. From 1660 onward, the London theatre behaved as if the great popular theatre of the previous seventy-five years had never existed. By the time the king had returned there had been a distinct loss of interest in the theatre by those who had previously supported it, and the audience that chose to return became essentially what it has been ever since, privileged and relatively affluent, supporting a theatre whose plays are limited in appeal and relatively expensive to attend. Where five or six theatres flourished before 1642, now only two were permitted to exist, and they experienced recurring problems not only in securing enough plays, but in acquiring audiences to fill them on any regular basis.

Performing at first in makeshift facilities such as indoor tennis courts, the two acting companies moved into newly constructed buildings, first at Lincoln's Inn Fields in 1661 and the Theatre Royal near Covent Garden in 1663. Patterned after the continental style, they were indoors and candlelit, and so could function in all seasons, immune to the vagaries of the English weather. The auditorium held backless benches in the pit, which we now call the orchestra, the tiers of boxes in the familiar opera house horseshoe arrangement. The stage was deep enough to accommodate scenery, unknown to the outdoor Shakespearean theatre, permitting interior and exterior scenes as needed. The front of the stage, the apron, thrust into the auditorium so that the actors delivered their lines directly to the audience, always visible since there was no way of darkening the house. And for the first time in English history, the reigning monarch attended the public theatre, sitting high in the royal box.

The most notable innovation, and for some of the purists of the time the most controversial, was the introduction of women into the acting companies. Gone for good were the young boys who formerly played Juliet or Lady Macbeth. Beautiful actresses in equally beautiful costumes now became as famous as the men. In fact, King Charles became enamored of them and took the glamorous Nell Gwynne as his most famous mistress.

The plays for this new theatre went through a change as complete as the buildings themselves. At first there were revivals of Shakespeare, Jonson, Shirley, and others, there being nothing else available, but their style and their themes did not seem to fit the demands of the new audiences. What developed in the forty-odd years from Charles's return to the end of the century was the body of plays we call Restoration drama. While its tragedies remained unimaginative imitations of the continental neoclassical style, the Restoration provided the English language with some of its finest moments of high comedy.

Released from the iron grip of Puritanism, the comedies of the Restoration broke just about every moral rule in the book. Set within the dilettante society that patronized them, the plays dwelt on sexual intrigue, adultery, deception and deceit (the "dissembling" so often mentioned by the characters), cheating of all kinds, and the acquisition of money and position by whatever means available, fair or foul. Love meant the pursuit of women (and of men by the more licentious ladies) generally in order to bed them in or out of wedlock, but once married, the vows meant little to spouses of either sex, who, tiring of their legal ties to one another, played a dangerous but exciting game of clandestine affairs. The ultra sophistication of these plays set the style of what has ever since been called the *comedy of manners,* because they reflected the more liberated aspects of the society they portrayed and were usually set in salons or the drawing rooms of mansions and country houses.

Two male character types that gave their distinctive mark to Restoration comedy appeared almost at once. John Dryden (1631–1700), poet and critic as well as prolific dramatist, whose best-remembered comedy is probably *Marriage à la Mode* (1672), introduced the male prototype, the "wild gallant," who was to become the central figure in many plays to follow. Generally handsome and witty, often coarse and crude, epitomizing the less savory side of society, the gallant entered into his sexual encounters with vigorous abandon, letting damaged reputations and broken hearts fall where they might.

In 1676 William Wycherley (c. 1640–1716) in *The Country Wife* introduced one of the most famous of the gallants, the somewhat less wild but still exceedingly licentious Horner, whose pursuit of the innocent young wife of a foolish old husband runs through the play in a series of extremely funny sequences. Horner's enticement of his willing victims to view his china collection is a wonderful prototype of the modern inducement to "come up and see my etchings." Also in 1676 *The Man of Mode, or Sir Fopling Flutter* by Sir George Etherege (1635?–1691) created one of the best examples of the heartless "hero" in Dorminant. The play's title, however, emphasizes the second of the two notable Restoration male figures, the fop, or "coxcomb"—the ridiculous overdressed fool who pranced and simpered through the action as the kind of individual whose gross exaggeration in his attempts to behave in the accepted social manner was the object of contemptuous laughter both onstage and off.

To read the whole body of Restoration comedy is to encounter a considerable amount of repetition in characters and action and frequently a lot of inferior writing. By the end of the century the plotlines had worn thin and audiences had begun to demand something less morally repugnant. An offended clergyman, Jeremy Collier, wrote a widely read tract, "On the Profaneness and Immorality of the English Stage" in 1698, which may have had some influence, but the tide had already begun to turn. With the "glorious revolution" of 1688, when Charles's Catholic brother James II was deposed and replaced by the more sedate and proper William of Orange and his queen, Mary, the excesses of the Restoration had pretty well run their course. But not until 1700, with *The Way of the World* by William Congreve (1670–1729), a brilliant portrayal of the folkways and mores of a society that existed mostly in fond memory, did Restoration comedy reach its apogee. The dashingly handsome Mirabell represents the best of the Restoration gallants, more polished and considerably less coarse, but still given to some complex "dissembling" in pursuit of his ladylove, the exquisite Millamant, herself the epitome of the out-and-out flirt dangling her suitors, including the infatuated Mirabell, like puppets on a string.

These glamorous figures of Congreve and all of Restoration comedy live in a world of wealth and idleness, vitally concerned with *having* money but totally averse to *earning* it. They inherit wealth, marry it, if need be steal it, but heaven forbid that they should ever lower themselves to *work* for it! Here is a universe in which the Ten Commandments give way to the 10,000 commandments of social behavior. These people seduce and abandon at will; both male and female are ashamed if caught in the act, not because of their indiscretions, but because they have been found out, which is the real sin. They are neither moral nor immoral; they are *amoral.* They offer lip service to traditional social proprieties but proceed to ignore them without remorse.

The comedies written for the theatre between 1660 and 1700, although bearing notable similarities to the social satires of Molière, were not written by theatre professionals like Molière (except for Dryden, who was much more than just a dramatist) but by dilettantes who dabbled in the theatre by writing a play or two and then quitting. Furthermore, these dramatists were members of the society about which they wrote, and the best of their work remains among the finest examples of high comedy in any language, resting in an exclusive niche of their own. Funny, bitingly satiric at times, often wryly cynical, sometimes scabrous and savagely brutal, their sparkling, if frequently ribald, exposés of the wicked ways of the world still entertain.

As the comedy of the Restoration faded during the last years of the seventeenth century and the first half of the eighteenth, it was replaced by a spate of highly sentimental comedies in which wild gallants were properly reformed into kind and loving husbands and flirtatious women saw the foolishness of their ways. Dubbed "comedies of tears," with their often lacrymous and mostly unconvincing resolutions producing happiness "too great for laughter," they became as monotonous in their goody-goodyness as Restoration comedy had been in its licentiousness. As early as 1704 Colley Cibber (1671–1757), whose *Apology* for his life contains some fine accounts of the drama and theatre of his day, wrote one of the most famous, *The Careless Husband.* Equal to it in lasting fame was *The Conscious Lovers* (1722) by Sir Richard Steele (1672–1729).

With sentimentality dominating the English comic stage for nearly six decades, the quality of the output remained inferior to what had preceded it up to 1700, and most of the plays remain in library archives or specialized anthologies. In 1768, however, a new and bold step was taken to break the stranglehold with the introduction of "laughing comedy" by Oliver Goldsmith (1728–1774). A successful novelist and poet, he had argued strongly against the decline of the true comic spirit, and furthered his point by producing *The Good Natured Man.* This was followed in 1774 by the hilarious *She Stoops to Conquer,* a favorite piece for revival to this day.

The most successful of the writers of laughing comedy was Richard Brinsley Sheridan, remembered mainly for three perennially popular plays. The first, *The Rivals* (1775), pokes great fun at romantic intrigues and sentimentality, with a twisted plot of mistaken identity, which finds the hero challenged to a duel with himself. It also introduced the most famous mangler of the English language, Mrs. Malaprop. *The Critic* (1779) is a fine spoof of pompous actors, producers, and critics, but his most famous remains *The School for Scandal.* Like so many of his predecessors, he wrote very few plays but was directly involved with the stage as the not-very-successful manager of the Drury Lane Theatre. From 1780 to 1812 he was also a member of Parliament and known as one of its finest orators.

The School for Scandal has many of the earmarks of seventeenth-century comedy, but its tone is vastly different. In the first place, though there are intrigues and dissembling, the coarse nature of Restoration comedy is missing. Charles Surface, for instance, never considering working for a living, goes through the actions of a wastrel using up his limited inheritance by indulging in wild living, but he is proven otherwise in his regard for his uncles and his behavior with Maria. She, in turn, eschews the flirtatious ways of her comic forebears and will have nothing to do with Mrs. Candour and her ilk in the infamous scandal school. Joseph Surface, as the dominating elder brother, has the appearance of a scoundrel, but he is far more the clumsy fool than an inveterate seducer. Once exposed in the play's most famous sequence, the "screen scene," he is revealed for what he is and promptly put in his place.

The May-December marriage of Sir Peter and Lady Teazle is a classic of its kind, open to every sort of intrigue and deceit, but Sir Peter, though foolish, is really a lovable if doddering character, and Lady Teazle, not above a little dallying on the side, is basically a good woman who finally wakes up to the good life she has had and will continue to have with her husband. The unsavory characters in the form of Snake, Lady Sneerwell, Mrs. Candour, and others are far more comic than vicious, and their devotion to rumor and innuendo is a wonderful picture of all such gossipy neighbors.

This is a true comedy, a reflection on human foibles and faults with amusing ridicule and gentle satire. It is meant for laughter, and its leading characters are well developed and humane. The happy ending is not superimposed at the last minute as an arbitrary solution but comes naturally out of what has gone before. It is a joyful play, probably the most famous of all English comedies, with relevance in any age, because its action and its characters successfully transcend time.

The School for Scandal

RICHARD BRINSLEY SHERIDAN

CHARACTERS

SIR PETER TEAZLE
SIR OLIVER SURFACE
SIR HARRY BUMPER
SIR BENJAMIN BACKBITE
JOSEPH SURFACE
CHARLES SURFACE
CARELESS
SNAKE
CRABTREE
ROWLEY
MOSES
TRIP
LADY TEAZLE
LADY SNEERWELL
MRS. CANDOUR
MARIA
GENTLEMEN, MAID, AND SERVANTS

SCENE: *London.*

Prologue

Written by Mr. Garrick[1]

A School for Scandal! tell me, I beseech you,
Needs there a school this modish art to teach you?
No need of lessons now, the knowing think;
We might as well be taught to eat and drink.
Caused by a dearth of scandal, should the vapours
Distress our fair ones—let them read the papers;
Their powerful mixtures such disorders hit;
Crave what you will—there's *quantum sufficit.*
"Lord!" cries my Lady Wormwood (who loves tattle,
And puts much salt and pepper in her prattle),

[1]David Garrick (1717–1779) was a prominent English actor who appeared in early productions of the play.

Just risen at noon, all night at cards when threshing
Strong tea and scandal—"Bless me, how refreshing!
Give me the papers, Lisp—how bold and free! (*sips*)
Last night Lord L. (sips) was caught with Lady D.
For aching heads what charming sal volatile! (*sips*)
If Mrs B. will still continue flirting,
We hope she'll DRAW, *or we'll* UNDRAW *the curtain.*
Fine satire, poz—in public all abuse it,
But, by ourselves (*sips*), our praise we can't refuse it.
Now, Lisp, read you—there, at that dash and star:"
"Yes, ma'am—*A certain lord had best beware,*
Who lives not twenty miles from Grosvenor Square;
For, should he Lady W. find willing,
Wormwood is bitter"—"Oh! that's me! the villain!
Throw it behind the fire, and never more
Let that vile paper come within my door."
Thus at our friends we laugh, who feel the dart;
To reach our feelings, we ourselves must smart.
Is our young bard so young, to think that he
Can stop the full spring-tide of calumny?
Knows he the world so little, and its trade?
Alas! the devil's sooner raised than laid.
So strong, so swift, the monster there's no gagging:
Cut Scandal's head off, still the tongue is wagging.
Proud of your smiles once lavishly bestowed,
Again our young Don Quixote takes the road:
To show his gratitude he draws his pen,
And seeks this hydra, Scandal, in his den.
For your applause all perils he would through—
He'll fight—that's write—a cavalliero true,
Till every drop of blood—that's ink—is spilt for you.

Act I

SCENE I LADY SNEERWELL's *Dressing-room.*

LADY SNEERWELL *discovered at her toilet;* SNAKE *drinking chocolate.*

LADY SNEERWELL The paragraphs, you say, Mr Snake, were all inserted?

SNAKE They were, madam; and, as I copied them myself in a feigned hand, there can be no suspicion whence they came.

LADY SNEERWELL Did you circulate the report of Lady Brittle's intrigue with Captain Boastall?

SNAKE That's in as fine a train as your ladyship could wish. In the common course of things, I think it must reach Mrs Clackitt's ears within four-and-twenty hours; and then, you know, the business is as good as done.

LADY SNEERWELL Why, truly, Mrs Clackitt has a very pretty talent, and a great deal of industry.

SNAKE True, madam, and has been tolerably successful in her day. To my knowledge, she has been the cause of six matches being broken off, and three sons being disinherited; of four forced elopements, and as many close confinements; nine separate maintenances, and two divorces. Nay, I have more than once traced her causing a *tête-à-tête* in the "Town and County Magazine," when the parties, perhaps, had never seen each other's face before in the course of their lives.

LADY SNEERWELL She certainly has talents, but her manner is gross.

SNAKE 'Tis very true. She generally designs well, has a free tongue and a bold invention; but her colouring is too dark, and her outlines often extravagant. She wants that delicacy of tint, and mellowness of sneer, which distinguish your ladyship's scandal.

LADY SNEERWELL You are partial, Snake.

SNAKE Not in the least; everybody allows that Lady Sneerwell can do more with a word or look than many can with the most laboured detail, even when they happen to have a little truth on their side to support it.

LADY SNEERWELL Yes, my dear Snake; and I am no hypocrite to deny the satisfaction I reap from the success of my efforts. Wounded myself, in the early part of my life, by the envenomed tongue of slander, I confess I have since known no pleasure equal to the reducing others to the level of my own reputation.

SNAKE Nothing can be more natural. But, Lady Sneerwell, there is one affair in which you have lately employed me, wherein, I confess, I am at a loss to guess your motives.

LADY SNEERWELL I conceive you mean with respect to my neighbour, Sir Peter Teazle, and his family?

SNAKE I do. Here are two young men, to whom Sir Peter has acted as a kind of guardian since their father's death; the eldest possessing the most amiable character, and universally well spoken of—the youngest, the most dissipated and extravagant young fellow in the kingdom, without friends or character; the former an avowed admirer of your ladyship, and apparently your favourite; the latter attached to Maria, Sir Peter's ward, and confessedly beloved by her. Now, on the face of these circumstances, it is utterly unaccountable to me, why you, the widow of a city knight, with a good jointure, should not close with the passion of a man of such character and expectations as Mr Surface; and more so why you should be so uncommonly earnest to destroy the mutual attachment subsisting between his brother Charles and Maria.

LADY SNEERWELL Then, at once to unravel this mystery, I must inform you that love has no share whatever in the intercourse between Mr Surface and me.

SNAKE No!

LADY SNEERWELL His real attachment is to Maria, or her fortune; but, finding in his brother a favoured rival, he has been obliged to mask his pretensions, and profit by my assistance.

SNAKE Yet still I am more puzzled why you should interest yourself in his success.

LADY SNEERWELL Heavens! how dull you are! Cannot you surmise the weakness which I hitherto, through shame, have concealed even from you? Must I confess that Charles—that libertine, that extravagant, that bankrupt in fortune and reputation—that he it is for whom I am thus anxious and malicious, and to gain whom I would sacrifice every thing?

SNAKE Now, indeed, your conduct appears consistent: but how came you and Mr Surface so confidential?

LADY SNEERWELL For our mutual interest. I have found him out a long time since. I know him to be artful, selfish, and malicious—in short, a sentimental knave; while with Sir Peter, and indeed with all his acquaintance, he passes for a youthful miracle of prudence, good sense, and benevolence.

SNAKE Yes; yet Sir Peter vows he has not his equal in England; and, above all, he praises him as a man of sentiment.

LADY SNEERWELL True; and with the assistance of his sentiment and hypocrisy he has brought Sir Peter entirely into his interest with regard to Maria; while poor Charles has no friend in the house—though, I fear, he has a powerful one in Maria's heart, against whom we must direct our schemes.

(*Enter* SERVANT.)

SERVANT Mr Surface.

LADY SNEERWELL Show him up. (*Exit Servant.*) He generally calls about this time. I don't wonder at people giving him to me for a lover.

(*Enter* JOSEPH SURFACE.)

JOSEPH SURFACE My dear Lady Sneerwell, how do you do today? Mr Snake, your most obedient.

LADY SNEERWELL Snake has just been rallying me on our mutual attachment, but I have informed him of our real views. You know how useful he has been to us; and, believe me, the confidence is not ill-placed.

JOSEPH SURFACE Madam, it is impossible for me to suspect a man of Mr Snake's sensibility and discernment.

LADY SNEERWELL Well, well, no compliments now; but tell me when you saw your mistress, Maria—or, what is more material to me, your brother.

JOSEPH SURFACE I have not seen either since I left you; but I can inform you that they never meet. Some of your stories have taken a good effect on Maria.

LADY SNEERWELL Ah, my dear Snake! the merit of this belongs to you. But do your brother's distresses increase?

JOSEPH SURFACE Every hour. I am told he has had another execution in the house yesterday. In short, his dissipation and extravagance exceed any thing I have ever heard of.

LADY SNEERWELL Poor Charles!

JOSEPH SURFACE True, madam; notwithstanding his vices, one can't help feeling for him. Poor Charles! I'm sure I wish it were in my power to be of any essential service to him; for the man who does not share in the distresses of a brother, even though merited by his own misconduct, deserves—

LADY SNEERWELL O Lud! you are going to be moral, and forget that you are among friends.

JOSEPH SURFACE Egad, that's true! I'll keep that sentiment till I see Sir Peter. However, it is certainly a charity to rescue Maria from such a libertine, who if he is to be reclaimed, can be so only by a person of your ladyship's superior accomplishments and understanding.

SNAKE I believe, Lady Sneerwell, here's company coming: I'll go and copy the letter I mentioned to you. Mr Surface, your most obedient.

JOSEPH SURFACE Sir, your very devoted. (*Exit* SNAKE.) Lady Sneerwell, I am very sorry you have put any farther confidence in that fellow.

LADY SNEERWELL Why so?

JOSEPH SURFACE I have lately detected him in frequent conference with old Rowley, who was formerly my father's steward, and has never, you know, been a friend of mine.

LADY SNEERWELL And do you think he would betray us?

JOSEPH SURFACE Nothing more likely; take my word for't, Lady Sneerwell, that fellow hasn't virtue enough to be faithful even to his own villany. Ah, Maria!

(*Enter* MARIA.)

LADY SNEERWELL Maria, my dear, how do you do? What's the matter?

MARIA Oh! there's that disagreeable lover of mine, Sir Benjamin Backbite, has just called at my guardian's, with his odious uncle, Crabtree; so I slipped out, and ran hither to avoid them.

LADY SNEERWELL Is that all?

JOSEPH SURFACE If my brother Charles had been of the party, madam, perhaps you would not have been so much alarmed.

LADY SNEERWELL Nay, now you are severe; for I dare swear the truth of the matter is, Maria heard you were here. But, my dear, what has Sir Benjamin done, that you should avoid him so?

MARIA Oh, he has done nothing—but 'tis for what he has said: his conversation is a perpetual libel on all his acquaintance.

JOSEPH SURFACE Ay, and the worst of it is, there is no advantage in not knowing him; for he'll abuse a stranger just as soon as his best friend: and his uncle's as bad.

LADY SNEERWELL Nay, but we should make allowance; Sir Benjamin is a wit and a poet.

MARIA For my part, I own, madam, wit loses its respect with me, when I see it in company with malice. What do you think, Mr Surface?

JOSEPH SURFACE Certainly, madam; to smile at the jest which plants a thorn in another's breast is to become a principal in the mischief.

LADY SNEERWELL Psha! there's no possibility of being witty without a little ill nature: the malice of a good thing is the barb that makes it stick. What's your opinion, Mr Surface?

JOSEPH SURFACE To be sure, madam; that conversation, where the spirit of raillery is suppressed, will ever appear tedious and insipid.

MARIA Well, I'll not debate how far scandal may be allowable; but in a man, I am sure, it is always contemptible. We have pride, envy, rivalship, and a thousand motives to depreciate each other; but the male slanderer must have the cowardice of a woman before he can traduce one.

(*Reenter* SERVANT.)

SERVANT Mrs Candour is below, and, if your ladyship's at leisure, will leave her carriage.

LADY SNEERWELL Beg her to walk in. (*Exit* SERVANT.) Now, Maria, here is a character to your taste; for, though Mrs Candour is a little talkative, every body allows her to be the best natured and best sort of woman.

MARIA Yes, with a very gross affectation of good nature and benevolence, she does more mischief than the direct malice of old Crabtree.

JOSEPH SURFACE I' faith that's true, Lady Sneerwell: whenever I hear the current running against the characters of my friends, I never think them in such danger as when Candour undertakes their defence.

LADY SNEERWELL Hush!—here she is!

(*Enter* MRS CANDOUR.)

MRS CANDOUR My dear Lady Sneerwell, how have you been this century?—Mr Surface, what news do you hear?—though indeed it is no matter, for I think one hears nothing else but scandal.

JOSEPH SURFACE Just so, indeed, ma'am.

MRS CANDOUR Oh, Maria! child,—what, is the whole affair off between you and Charles? His extravagance, I presume—the town talks of nothing else.

MARIA I am very sorry, ma'am, the town has so little to do.

MRS CANDOUR True, true, child: but there's no stopping people's tongues. I own I was hurt to hear it, as I indeed was to learn, from the same quarter, that your guardian, Sir Peter, and Lady Teazle have not agreed lately as well as could be wished.

MARIA 'Tis strangely impertinent for people to busy themselves so.

MRS CANDOUR Very true, child: but what's to be done? People will talk—there's no preventing it. Why, it was but yesterday I was told that Miss Gadabout had eloped with Sir Filigree Flirt. But, Lord! there's no minding what one hears; though, to be sure, I had this from very good authority.

MARIA Such reports are highly scandalous.

MRS CANDOUR So they are, child—shameful, shameful! But the world is so censorious, no character escapes. Lord, now who would have suspected your friend, Miss Prim, of an indiscretion? Yet such is the ill nature of people, that they say her uncle stopped her last week, just as she was stepping into the York Mail with her dancing-master.

MARIA I'll answer for 't there are no grounds for that report.

MRS CANDOUR Ah, no foundation in the world, I dare swear; no more, probably, than for the story circulated last month, of Mrs Festino's affair with Colonel Cassino—though, to be sure, that matter was never rightly cleared up.

JOSEPH SURFACE The licence of invention some people take is monstrous indeed.

MARIA 'Tis so; but, in my opinion, those who report such things are equally culpable.

MRS CANDOUR To be sure they are; tale-bearers are as bad as the tale-makers—'tis an old observation, and a very true one: but what's to be done, as I said before? how will you prevent people from talking? To-day, Mrs Clackitt assured me, Mr and Mrs Honeymoon were at last become mere man and wife, like the rest of their acquaintance. She likewise hinted that a certain widow, in the next street, had got rid of her dropsy and recovered her shape in a most surprising manner. And at the same time Miss Tattle, who was by, affirmed that Lord Buffalo had discovered his lady at a house of no extraordinary fame; and that Sir Harry Bouquet and Tom Saunter were to measure swords on a similar provocation. But, Lord, do you think I would report these things! No, no! tale-bearers, as I said before, are just as bad as the tale-makers.

JOSEPH SURFACE Ah! Mrs Candour, if every body had your forbearance and good nature!

MRS CANDOUR I confess, Mr Surface, I cannot bear to hear people attacked behind their backs; and when ugly circumstances come out against our acquaintance, I own I always love to think the best. By the by, I hope 'tis not true that your brother is absolutely ruined?

JOSEPH SURFACE I am afraid his circumstances are very bad indeed, ma'am.

MRS CANDOUR Ah! I heard so—but you must tell him to keep up his spirits; every body almost is in the same way: Lord Spindle, Sir Thomas Splint, Captain Quinze, and Mr Nickit—all up, I hear, within this week; so, if Charles is undone, he'll find half his acquaintance ruined too, and that, you know, is a consolation.

JOSEPH SURFACE Doubtless, ma'am—a very great one.

(*Reenter* SERVANT.)

SERVANT Mr Crabtree and Sir Benjamin Backbite. (*Exit.*)

LADY SNEERWELL So, Maria, you see your lover pursues you; positively you sha'nt escape.

(*Enter* CRABTREE *and* SIR BENJAMIN BACKBITE.)

CRABTREE Lady Sneerwell, I kiss your hand. Mrs Candour, I don't believe you are acquainted with my nephew, Sir Benjamin Backbite? Egad, ma'am, he has a pretty wit, and is a pretty poet too. Isn't he, Lady Sneerwell?

SIR BENJAMIN Oh, fie, uncle!

CRABTREE Nay, egad it's true; I back him at a rebus or a charade against the best rhymer in the kingdom. Has your ladyship heard the epigram he wrote last week on Lady Frizzle's feather catching fire?—Do, Benjamin, repeat it, or the charade you made last night extempore at Mrs Drozie's conversazione. Come, now, your first is the name of a fish, your second a great naval commander, and—

SIR BENJAMIN Uncle, now—pr'thee—

CRABTREE I'faith, ma'am, 'twould surprise you to hear how ready he is at all these sorts of things.

LADY SNEERWELL I wonder, Sir Benjamin, you never publish any thing.

SIR BENJAMIN To say truth, ma'am, 'tis very vulgar to print; and as my little productions are mostly satires and lampoons on particular people, I find they circulate more by giving copies in confidence to the friends of the parties. However, I have some love elegies, which, when favoured with this lady's smiles, I mean to give the public. (*pointing to* MARIA)

CRABTREE (*to* MARIA) 'Fore heaven, ma'am, they'll immortalize you!—you will be handed down to posterity, like Petrarch's Laura, or Waller's Sacharissa.

SIR BENJAMIN (*to* MARIA) Yes, madam, I think you will like them, when you shall see them on a beautiful quarto page, where a neat rivulet of text shall meander through a meadow of margin. 'Fore Gad they will be the most elegant things of their kind!

CRABTREE But, ladies, that's true—have you heard the news?

MRS CANDOUR What, sir, do you mean the report of—

CRABTREE No, ma'am, that's not it.—Miss Nicely is going to be married to her own footman.

MRS CANDOUR Impossible!

CRABTREE Ask Sir Benjamin.

SIR BENJAMIN 'Tis very true, ma'am: every thing is fixed, and the wedding liveries bespoke.

CRABTREE Yes—and they do say there were pressing reasons for it.

LADY SNEERWELL Why, I have heard something of this before.

MRS CANDOUR It can't be—and I wonder any one should believe such a story of so prudent a lady as Miss Nicely.

SIR BENJAMIN O Lud! ma'am, that's the very reason 'twas believed at once. She has always been so cautious and so reserved, that every body was sure there was some reason for it at bottom.

MRS CANDOUR Why, to be sure, a tale of scandal is as fatal to the credit of a prudent lady of her stamp as a fever is generally to those of the strongest constitutions. But there is a sort of puny sickly reputation, that is always ailing, yet will outlive the robuster characters of a hundred prudes.

SIR BENJAMIN True, madam, there are valetudinarians in reputation as well as constitution, who, being conscious of their weak part, avoid the least breath of air, and supply their want of stamina by care and circumspection.

MRS CANDOUR Well, but this may be all a mistake. You know, Sir Benjamin, very trifling circumstances often give rise to the most injurious tales.

CRABTREE That they do, I'll be sworn, ma'am. Did you ever hear how Miss Piper came to lose her lover and her character last summer at Tunbridge?—Sir Benjamin, you remember it?

SIR BENJAMIN Oh, to be sure!—the most whimsical circumstance.

LADY SNEERWELL How was it, pray?

CRABTREE Why, one evening, at Mrs Ponto's assembly, the conversation happened to turn on the breeding Nova Scotia sheep in this country. Says a young lady in company, "I have known instances of it; for Miss Letitia Piper, a first cousin of mine, had a Nova Scotia sheep that produced her twins." "What!" cries the Lady Dowager Dundizzy (who you know is as deaf as a post), "has Miss Piper had twins?" This mistake, as you may imagine, threw the whole company into a fit of laughter. However, 'twas the next morning everywhere reported, and in a few days believed by the whole town, that Miss Letitia Piper had actually been brought to bed of a fine boy and a girl: and in less than a week there were some people who could name the father, and the farm-house where the babies were put to nurse.

LADY SNEERWELL Strange, indeed!

CRABTREE Matter of fact, I assure you. O Lud! Mr Surface, pray it is true that your uncle, Sir Oliver, is coming home?

JOSEPH SURFACE Not that I know of, indeed, sir.

CRABTREE He has been in the East Indies a long time. You can scarcely remember him, I believe? Sad comfort, whenever he returns, to hear how your brother has gone on!

JOSEPH SURFACE Charles has been imprudent, sir, to be sure; but I hope no busy people have already prejudiced Sir Oliver against him. He may reform.

SIR BENJAMIN To be sure he may: for my part, I never believed him to be so utterly void of principle as people say; and, though he has lost all his friends, I am told nobody is better spoken of by the Jews.

CRABTREE That's true, egad, nephew. If the Old Jewry was a ward, I believe Charles would be an alderman: no man more popular there, 'fore Gad! I hear he pays as many annuities as the Irish tontine; and that, whenever he is sick, they have prayers for the recovery of his health in all the synagogues.

SIR BENJAMIN Yet no man lives in greater splendour. They tell me, when he entertains his friends he will sit down to dinner with a dozen of his own securities; have a score of tradesmen waiting in the antechamber, and an officer behind every guest's chair.

JOSEPH SURFACE This may be entertainment to you, gentlemen, but you pay very little regard to the feelings of a brother.

MARIA (*aside*) Their malice is intolerable! (*aloud*) Lady Sneerwell, I must wish you a good morning: I'm not very well. (*Exit.*)

MRS CANDOUR O dear! she changes colour very much.

LADY SNEERWELL Do, Mrs Candour, follow her: she may want your assistance.

MRS CANDOUR That I will, with all my soul, ma'am.—Poor dear girl, who knows what her situation may be! (*Exit.*)

LADY SNEERWELL 'Twas nothing but that she could not bear to hear Charles reflected on, notwithstanding their difference.

SIR BENJAMIN The young lady's *penchant* is obvious.

CRABTREE But, Benjamin, you must not give up the pursuit for that: follow her, and put her into good humour. Repeat her some of your own verses. Come, I'll assist you.

SIR BENJAMIN Mr Surface, I did not mean to hurt you; but depend on't your brother is utterly undone.

CRABTREE O Lud, ay! undone as ever man was—can't raise a guinea!

SIR BENJAMIN And everything sold, I'm told, that was movable.

CRABTREE I have seen one that was at his house. Not a thing left but some empty bottles that were overlooked, and the family pictures, which I believe are framed in the wainscots.

SIR BENJAMIN And I'm very sorry also to hear some bad stories against him. (*going*)

CRABTREE Oh, he has done many mean things, that's certain.

SIR BENJAMIN But, however, as he's your brother— (*going*)

CRABTREE We'll tell you all another opportunity.

(*Exeunt* CRABTREE *and* SIR BENJAMIN.)

LADY SNEERWELL Ha! ha! 'tis very hard for them to leave a subject they have not quite run down.

JOSEPH SURFACE And I believe the abuse was no more acceptable to your ladyship than Maria.

LADY SNEERWELL I doubt her affections are farther engaged than we imagine. But the family are to be here this evening, so you may as well dine where you are, and we shall have an opportunity of observing farther; in the meantime, I'll go and plot mischief, and you shall study sentiment.

(*Exeunt.*)

Scene II *A Room in* SIR PETER TEAZLE'S *House.*

(*Enter* SIR PETER TEAZLE.)

SIR PETER When an old bachelor marries a young wife, what is he to expect? 'Tis now six months since Lady Teazle made me the happiest of men—and I have been the most miserable dog ever since! We tiffed a little going to church, and fairly quarrelled before the bell had done ringing. I was more than once nearly choked with gall during the honeymoon, and had lost all comfort in life before my friends had done wishing me joy. Yet I chose with caution—a girl bred wholly in the country, who never knew luxury beyond one silk gown, nor dissipation above the annual gala of a race ball. Yet she now plays her part in all the extravagant fopperies of fashion and the town, with as ready a grace as if she never had seen a bush or a grass-plot out of Grosvenor Square! I am sneered at by all my acquaintance, and paragraphed in the newspapers. She dissipates my fortune, and contradicts all my humours; yet the worst of it is, I doubt I love her, or I should never bear all this. However, I'll never be weak enough to own it.

(*Enter* ROWLEY.)

ROWLEY Oh! Sir Peter, your servant: how is it with you, sir?

SIR PETER Very bad, Master Rowley, very bad. I meet with nothing but crosses and vexations.

ROWLEY What can have happened since yesterday?

SIR PETER A good question to a married man!

ROWLEY Nay, I'm sure, Sir Peter, your lady can't be the cause of your uneasiness.

SIR PETER Why, has any body told you she was dead?

ROWLEY Come, come, Sir Peter, you love her, notwithstanding your tempers don't exactly agree.

SIR PETER But the fault is entirely hers, Master Rowley. I am, myself, the sweetest-tempered man alive, and hate a teasing temper; and so I tell her a hundred times a day.

ROWLEY Indeed!

SIR PETER Ay; and what is very extraordinary, in all our disputes she is always in the wrong! But Lady Sneerwell, and the set she meets at her house, encourage the perverseness of her disposition. Then, to complete my vexation,

Maria, my ward, whom I ought to have the power of a father over, is determined to turn rebel too, and absolutely refuses the man whom I have long resolved on for her husband; meaning, I suppose, to bestow herself on his profligate brother.

ROWLEY You know, Sir Peter, I have always taken the liberty to differ with you on the subject of these two young gentlemen. I only wish you may not be deceived in your opinion of the elder. For Charles, my life on't! he will retrieve his errors yet. Their worthy father, once my honoured master, was, at his years, nearly as wild a spark; yet, when he died, he did not leave a more benevolent heart to lament his loss.

SIR PETER You are wrong, Master Rowley. On their father's death, you know, I acted as a kind of guardian to them both, till their uncle Sir Oliver's liberality gave them an early independence. Of course, no person could have more opportunities of judging of their hearts, and I was never mistaken in my life. Joseph is indeed a model for the young men of the age. He is a man of sentiment, and acts up to the sentiments he professes; but for the other, take my word for't, if he had any grain of virtue by descent, he has dissipated it with the rest of his inheritance. Ah! my old friend, Sir Oliver, will be deeply mortified when he finds how part of his bounty has been misapplied.

ROWLEY I am sorry to find you so violent against the young man, because this may be the most critical period of his fortune. I came hither with news that will surprise you.

SIR PETER What! let me hear.

ROWLEY Sir Oliver is arrived, and at this moment in town.

SIR PETER How! you astonish me! I thought you did not expect him this month.

ROWLEY I did not: but his passage has been remarkably quick.

SIR PETER Egad, I shall rejoice to see my old friend. 'Tis sixteen years since we met. We have had many a day together:—but does he still enjoin us not to inform his nephews of his arrival?

ROWLEY Most strictly. He means, before it is known, to make some trial of their dispositions.

SIR PETER Ah! there needs no art to discover their merits—however, he shall have his way; but, pray, does he know I am married?

ROWLEY Yes, and will soon wish you joy.

SIR PETER What, as we drink health to a friend in a consumption! Ah! Oliver will laugh at me. We used to rail at matrimony together, but he has been steady to his text. Well, he must be soon at my house, though—I'll instantly give orders for his reception. But, Master Rowley, don't drop a word that Lady Teazle and I ever disagree.

ROWLEY By no means.

SIR PETER For I should never be able to stand Noll's jokes; so I'll have him think, Lord forgive me! that we are a very happy couple.

ROWLEY I understand you:—but then you must be very careful not to differ while he is in the house with you.

SIR PETER Egad, and so we must—and that's impossible. Ah! Master Rowley, when an old bachelor marries a young wife, he deserves—no—the crime carries its punishment along with it.

Act II

SCENE I *A Room in* SIR PETER TEAZLE'S *House.*

(*Enter* SIR PETER *and* LADY TEAZLE.)

SIR PETER Lady Teazle, Lady Teazle, I'll not bear it!

LADY TEAZLE Sir Peter, Sir Peter, you may bear it or not, as you please; but I ought to have my own way in every thing, and, what's more, I will too. What! though I was educated in the country, I know very well that women of fashion in London are accountable to nobody after they are married.

SIR PETER Very well, ma'am, very well; so a husband is to have no influence, no authority?

LADY TEAZLE Authority! No, to be sure: if you wanted authority over me, you should have adopted me, and not married me: I'm sure you were old enough.

SIR PETER Old enough!—ay, there it is. Well, well, Lady Teazle, though my life may be made unhappy by your temper, I'll not be ruined by your extravagance!

LADY TEAZLE My extravagance! I'm sure I'm not more extravagant than a woman of fashion ought to be.

SIR PETER No, no, madam, you shall throw away no more sums on such unmeaning luxury. 'Slife! to spend as much to furnish your dressing-room with flowers in winter as would suffice to turn the Pantheon into a greenhouse, and give a *fête champêtre* at Christmas.

LADY TEAZLE And am I to blame, Sir Peter, because flowers are dear in cold weather? You should find fault with the climate, and not with me. For my part, I'm sure I wish it was spring all the year round, and that roses grew under our feet!

SIR PETER Oons! madam—if you had been born to this, I shouldn't wonder at you talking thus; but you forget what your situation was when I married you.

LADY TEAZLE No, no, I don't; 'twas a very disagreeable one, or I should never have married you.

SIR PETER Yes, yes, madam, you were then in somewhat a humbler style—the daughter of a plain country squire. Recollect, Lady Teazle, when I saw you first sitting at your tambour, in a pretty figured linen gown, with a bunch of keys at your side, your hair combed smooth over a roll, and your apartment hung round with fruits in worsted, of your own working.

LADY TEAZLE Oh, yes! I remember it very well, and a curious life I led. My daily occupation to inspect the dairy, superintend the poultry, make extracts from the family receipt-book, and comb my aunt Deborah's lapdog.

SIR PETER Yes, yes, ma'am, 'twas so indeed.

LADY TEAZLE And then you know, my evening amusements! To draw patterns for ruffles, which I had not materials to make up; to play Pope Joan with the curate; to read a sermon to my aunt; or to be stuck down to an old spinet to strum my father to sleep after a fox-chase.

SIR PETER I am glad you have so good a memory. Yes, madam, these were the recreations I took you from! but now you must have your coach—*vis-à-vis*—and three powdered footmen before your chair; and, in the summer, a pair of white cats to draw you to Kensington Gardens. No recollection, I suppose, when you were content to ride double, behind the butler, on a docked coach-horse.

LADY TEAZLE No—I swear I never did that: I deny the butler and the coach-horse.

SIR PETER This, madam, was your situation; and what have I done for you? I have made you a woman of fashion, of fortune, of rank—in short, I have made you my wife.

LADY TEAZLE Well, then, and there is but one thing more you can make me to add to the obligation, this is—

SIR PETER My widow, I suppose?

LADY TEAZLE Hem! hem!

SIR PETER I thank you, madam—but don't flatter yourself, for, though your ill conduct may disturb my peace of mind, it shall never break my heart, I promise you: however, I am equally obliged to you for the hint.

LADY TEAZLE Then why will you endeavour to make yourself so disagreeable to me, and thwart me in every little elegant expense?

SIR PETER 'Slife, madam, I say, had you any of these little elegant expenses when you married me?

LADY TEAZLE Lud, Sir Peter! would you have me be out of the fashion?

SIR PETER The fashion, indeed! what had you to do with the fashion before you married me?

LADY TEAZLE For my part, I should think you would like to have your wife thought a woman of taste.

SIR PETER Ay—there again—taste! Zounds! madam, you had no taste when you married me!

LADY TEAZLE That's very true, indeed, Sir Peter! and, after having married you, I should never pretend to taste again, I allow. But now, Sir Peter, since we have finished our daily jangle, I presume I may go to my engagement at Lady Sneerwell's.

SIR PETER Ay, there's another precious circumstance—a charming set of acquaintance you have made there!

LADY TEAZLE Nay, Sir Peter, they are all people of rank and fortune, and remarkably tenacious of reputation.

SIR PETER Yes, egad, they are tenacious of reputation with a vengeance; for they don't choose anybody should have a character but themselves! Such a crew! Ah! many a wretch has rid on a hurdle who has done less mischief than these utterers of forged tales, coiners of scandal, and clippers of reputation.

LADY TEAZLE What, would you restrain the freedom of speech?

SIR PETER Ah! they have made you just as bad as any one of the society.

LADY TEAZLE Why, I believe I do bear a part with a miserable grace.

SIR PETER Grace indeed!

LADY TEAZLE But I vow I bear no malice against the people I abuse: when I say an ill-natured thing, 'tis out of pure good humour; and I take it for granted they deal exactly in the same manner with me. But, Sir Peter, you know you promised to come to Lady Sneerwell's too.

SIR PETER Well, well, I'll call in, just to look after my own character.

LADY TEAZLE Then, indeed, you must make haste after me, or you'll be too late. So goodbye to ye. (*Exit.*)

SIR PETER So—I have gained much by my intended expostulation! Yet with what a charming air she contradicts every thing I say, and how pleasantly she shows her contempt for my authority! Well, though I can't make her love me, there is great satisfaction in quarrelling with her; and I think she never appears to such advantage as when she is doing every thing in her power to plague me. (*Exit.*)

SCENE II *A Room in* LADY SNEERWELL'S *House.* LADY SNEERWELL, MRS CANDOUR, CRABTREE, SIR BENJAMIN BACKBITE, *and* JOSEPH SURFACE, *discovered.*

LADY SNEERWELL Nay, positively, we will hear it.

JOSEPH SURFACE Yes, yes, the epigram, by all means.

SIR BENJAMIN O plague on't, uncle! 'tis mere nonsense.

CRABTREE No, no; 'fore Gad, very clever for an extempore!

SIR BENJAMIN But, ladies, you should be acquainted with the circumstance. You must know, that one day last week, as Lady Better Curricle was taking the dust in Hyde Park, in a sort of duodecimo phaeton, she desired me to write some verses on her ponies; upon which, I took out my pocket-book, and in a moment produced the following:—

Sure never were seen two such beautiful ponies;
Other horses are clowns, but these macaronies:
To give them this title I'm sure can't be wrong,
Their legs are so slim, and their tails are so long.

CRABTREE There, ladies, done in the smack of a whip, and on horseback too.

JOSEPH SURFACE A very Phoebus, mounted—indeed, Sir Benjamin!

SIR BENJAMIN Oh dear, sir! trifles—trifles.

(*Enter* LADY TEAZLE *and* MARIA.)

MRS CANDOUR I must have a copy.

LADY SNEERWELL Lady Teazle, I hope we shall see Sir Peter?

LADY TEAZLE I believe he'll wait on your ladyship presently.

LADY SNEERWELL Maria, my love, you look grave. Come, you shall sit down to piquet with Mr Surface.

MARIA I take very little pleasure in cards—however, I'll do as your ladyship pleases.

LADY TEAZLE I am surprised Mr Surface should sit down with her; I thought he would have embraced this opportunity of speaking to me before Sir Peter came. (*aside*)

MRS CANDOUR Now, I'll die, but you are so scandalous, I'll forswear your society.

LADY TEAZLE What's the matter, Mrs Candour?

MRS CANDOUR They'll not allow our friend Miss Vermilion to be handsome.

LADY SNEERWELL Oh, surely she is a pretty woman.

CRABTREE I am very glad you think so, ma'am.

MRS CANDOUR She has a charming fresh colour.

LADY TEAZLE Yes, when it is fresh put on.

MRS CANDOUR Oh, fie! I'll swear her colour is natural: I have seen it come and go!

LADY TEAZLE I dare swear you have, ma'am: it goes off at night, and comes again in the morning.

SIR BENJAMIN True, ma'am, it not only comes and goes; but, what's more, egad, her maid can fetch and carry it!

MRS CANDOUR Ha! ha! ha! how I hate to hear you talk so! But surely, now, her sister is, or was, very handsome.

CRABTREE Who? Mrs Evergreen? O Lord! she's six-and-fifty if she's an hour!

MRS CANDOUR Now positively you wrong her; fifty-two or fifty-three is the utmost—and I don't think she looks more.

SIR BENJAMIN Ah! there's no judging by her looks, unless one could see her face.

LADY SNEERWELL Well, well, if Mrs Evergreen does take some pains to repair the ravages of time, you must allow she effects it with great ingenuity; and surely that's better than the careless manner in which the widow Ochre caulks her wrinkles.

SIR BENJAMIN Nay, now, Lady Sneerwell, you are severe upon the widow. Come, come, 'tis not that she paints so ill—but, when she has finished her face, she joins it on so badly to her neck, that she looks like a mended statue, in which the connoisseur may see at once that the head is modern, though the trunk's antique.

CRABTREE Ha! ha! ha! Well said, nephew!

MRS CANDOUR Ha! ha! ha! Well, you make me laugh; but I vow I hate you for it. What do you think of Miss Simper?

SIR BENJAMIN Why, she has very pretty teeth.

LADY TEAZLE Yes; and on that account, when she is neither speaking nor laughing (which very seldom happens), she never absolutely shuts her mouth, but leaves it always a-jar, as it were—thus. (*shows her teeth*)

MRS CANDOUR How can you be so ill-natured?

LADY TEAZLE Nay, I allow even that's better than the pains Mrs Prim takes to conceal her losses in front. She draws her mouth till it positively resembles the aperture of a poor's-box, and all her words appear to slide out edgewise, as it were—thus: *How do you do madam? Yes, madam.* (*mimics*)

LADY SNEERWELL Very well, Lady Teazle; I see you can be a little severe.

LADY TEAZLE In defence of a friend it is but justice. But here comes Sir Peter to spoil our pleasantry.

(*Enter* SIR PETER TEAZLE.)

SIR PETER Ladies, your most obedient. (*aside*) Mercy on me, here is the whole set! a character dead at every word, I suppose.

MRS CANDOUR I am rejoiced you are come, Sir Peter. They have been so censorious—and Lady Teazle as bad as any one.

SIR PETER That must be very distressing to you, indeed, Mrs Candour.

MRS CANDOUR Oh, they will allow good qualities to nobody; not even good nature to our friend Mrs Pursy.

LADY TEAZLE What, the fat dowager who was at Mrs Quadrille's last night?

MRS CANDOUR Nay, her bulk is her misfortune; and, when she takes so much pains to get rid of it, you ought not to reflect on her.

MRS CANDOUR That's very true, indeed.

LADY TEAZLE Yes, I know she almost lives on acids and small whey; laces herself by pulleys; and often, in the hottest noon in summer, you may see her on a little squat pony, with her hair plaited up behind like a drummer's and puffing round the Ring on a full trot.

MRS CANDOUR I thank you, Lady Teazle, for defending her.

SIR PETER Yes, a good defence, truly.

MRS CANDOUR Truly, Lady Teazle is as censorious as Miss Sallow.

CRABTREE Yes, and she is a curious being to pretend to be censorious—an awkward gawky, without any one good point under heaven.

MRS CANDOUR Positively you shall not be so very severe. Miss Sallow is a near relation of mine by marriage, and, as for her person, great allowance is to be made; for, let me tell you, a woman labours under many disadvantages who tries to pass for a girl of six-and-thirty.

LADY SNEERWELL Though, surely, she is handsome still—and for the weakness in her eyes, considering how much she reads by candlelight, it is not to be wondered at.

MRS CANDOUR True, and then as to her manner; upon my word I think it is particularly graceful, considering she never had the least education: for you know her mother was a Welsh milliner, and her father a sugar-baker at Bristol.

SIR BENJAMIN Ah! you are both of you too good-natured!

SIR PETER Yes, damned good-natured! This their own relation! mercy on me! (*aside*)

MRS CANDOUR For my part, I own I cannot bear to hear a friend ill spoken of.

SIR PETER No, to be sure!

SIR BENJAMIN Oh! you are of a moral turn. Mrs Candour and I can sit for an hour and hear Lady Stucco talk sentiment.

LADY TEAZLE Nay, I vow Lady Stucco is very well with the dessert after dinner; for she's just like the French fruit one cracks for mottoes—made up of paint and proverb.

MRS CANDOUR Well, I will never join in ridiculing a friend; and so I constantly tell my cousin Ogle, and you all know what pretensions she has to be critical on beauty.

CRABTREE Oh, to be sure! she has herself the oddest countenance that ever was seen; 'tis a collection of features from all the different countries of the globe.

SIR BENJAMIN So she has, indeed—an Irish front—

CRABTREE Caledonian locks—

SIR BENJAMIN Dutch nose—

CRABTREE Austrian lips—

SIR BENJAMIN Complexion of a Spaniard—

CRABTREE And teeth *à la Chinoise*—

SIR BENJAMIN In short, her face resembles a *table d'hôte* at Spa—where no two guests are of a nation—

CRABTREE Or a congress at the close of a general war—wherein all the members, even to her eyes, appear to have a different interest, and her nose and chin are the only parties likely to join issue.

MRS CANDOUR Ha! ha! ha!

SIR PETER Mercy on my life!—a person they dine with twice a week! (*aside*)

MRS CANDOUR Nay, but I vow you shall not carry the laugh off so—for give me leave to say, that Mrs Ogle—

SIR PETER Madam, madam, I beg your pardon—there's no stopping these good gentlemen's tongues. But when I tell you, Mrs Candour, that the lady they are abusing is a particular friend of mine, I hope you'll not take her part.

LADY SNEERWELL Ha! ha! ha! well said, Sir Peter! but you are a cruel creature—too phlegmatic yourself for a jest, and too peevish to allow wit in others.

SIR PETER Ah, madam, true wit is more nearly allied to good nature than your ladyship is aware of.

LADY TEAZLE True, Sir Peter: I believe they are so near akin that they can never be united.

SIR BENJAMIN Or rather, suppose them man and wife, because one seldom sees them together.

LADY TEAZLE But Sir Peter is such an enemy to scandal, I believe he would have it put down by parliament.

SIR PETER 'Fore heaven, madam, if they were to consider the sporting with reputation of as much importance as poaching on manors, and pass an act for the preservation of fame, as well as game, I believe many would thank them for the bill.

LADY SNEERWELL O Lud! Sir Peter; would you deprive us of our privileges?

SIR PETER Ay, madam; and then no person should be permitted to kill characters and run down reputations, but qualified old maids and disappointed widows.

LADY SNEERWELL Go, you monster!

MRS CANDOUR But surely, you would not be quite so severe on those who only report what they hear?

SIR PETER Yes, madam, I would have law merchant for them too; and in all cases of slander currency, whenever the drawer of the lie was not to be found, the injured parties should have a right to come on any of the indorsers.

CRABTREE Well, for my part, I believe there never was a scandalous tale without some foundation.

LADY SNEERWELL Come, ladies, shall we sit down to cards in the next room?

(*Enter* SERVANT, *who whispers to* SIR PETER.)

SIR PETER I'll be with them directly. (*Exit* SERVANT.) I'll get away unperceived. (*aside*)

LADY SNEERWELL Sir Peter, you are not going to leave us?

SIR PETER Your ladyship must excuse me; I'm called away by particular business. But I leave my character behind me. (*Exit.*)

SIR BENJAMIN Well—certainly, Lady Teazle, that lord of yours is a strange being: I could tell you some stories of him would make you laugh heartily if he were not your husband.

LADY TEAZLE Oh, pray don't mind that; come, do let's hear them. (*Exeunt all but* JOSEPH SURFACE *and* MARIA.)

JOSEPH SURFACE Maria, I see you have no satisfaction in this society.

MARIA How is it possible I should? If to raise malicious smiles at the infirmities or misfortunes of those who have never injured us be the province of wit or humour, Heaven grant me a double portion of dulness!

JOSEPH SURFACE Yet they appear more ill-natured than they are; they have no malice at heart.

MARIA Then is their conduct still more contemptible; for, in my opinion, nothing could excuse the intemperance of their tongues but a natural and uncontrollable bitterness of mind.

JOSEPH SURFACE Undoubtedly, madam; and it has always been a sentiment of mine, that to propagate a malicious truth wantonly is more despicable than to falsify from revenge. But can you, Maria, feel thus for others, and be unkind to me alone? Is hope to be denied the tenderest passion?

MARIA Why will you distress me by renewing this subject?

JOSEPH SURFACE Ah, Maria! you would not treat me thus, and oppose your guardian, Sir Peter's will, but that I see that profligate Charles is still a favoured rival.

MARIA Ungenerously urged! But, whatever my sentiments are for that unfortunate young man, be assured I shall not feel more bound to give him up, because his distresses have lost him the regard even of a brother.

JOSEPH SURFACE Nay, but, Maria, do not leave me with a frown: by all that is honest, I swear— (*kneels*)

(*Reenter* LADY TEAZLE *behind.*)

(*aside*) Gad's life, here's Lady Teazle. (*aloud to* MARIA) You must not—no, you shall not—for, though I have the greatest regard for Lady Teazle—

MARIA Lady Teazle!

JOSEPH SURFACE Yet were Sir Peter to suspect—

LADY TEAZLE (*coming forward*) What is this, pray? Does he take her for me?—Child, you are wanted in the next room. (*Exit* MARIA.) What is all this, pray?

JOSEPH SURFACE Oh, the most unlucky circumstance in nature! Maria has somehow suspected the tender concern I have for your happiness, and threatened to acquaint Sir Peter with her suspicions, and I was just endeavoring to reason with her when you came in.

LADY TEAZLE Indeed! but you seemed to adopt a very tender mode of reasoning—do you usually argue on your knees?

JOSEPH SURFACE Oh, she's a child, and I thought a little bombast—But, Lady Teazle, when are you to give me your judgment on my library, as you promised?

LADY TEAZLE No, no; I begin to think it would be imprudent, and you know I admit you as a lover no farther than fashion requires.

JOSEPH SURFACE True—a mere Platonic cicisbeo, what every wife is entitled to.

LADY TEAZLE Certainly, one must not be out of the fashion. However, I have so many of my country prejudices left, that, though Sir Peter's ill humour may vex me ever so, it never shall provoke me to—

JOSEPH SURFACE The only revenge in your power. Well, I applaud your moderation.

LADY TEAZLE Go—you are an insinuating wretch! But we shall be missed—let us join the company.

JOSEPH SURFACE But we had best not return together.

LADY TEAZLE Well, don't stay; for Maria sha'n't come to hear any more of your reasoning, I promise you. (*Exit.*)

JOSEPH SURFACE A curious dilemma, truly, my politics have run me into! I wanted, at first, only to ingratiate myself with Lady Teazle, that she might not be my enemy with Maria; and I have, I don't know how, become her serious lover. Sincerely I begin to wish I had never made such a point of gaining so very good a character, for it has led me into so many cursed rogueries that I doubt I shall be exposed at last.

(*Exit.*)

SCENE III *A Room in* SIR PETER TEAZLE'S *House.*

(*Enter* SIR OLIVER SURFACE *and* ROWLEY.)

SIR OLIVER Ha! ha! ha! so my old friend is married, hey?—a young wife out of the country. Ha! ha! ha! that he should have stood bluff to old bachelor so long, and sink into a husband at last!

ROWLEY But you must not rally him on the subject, Sir Oliver; 'tis a tender point, I assure you, though he has been married only seven months.

SIR OLIVER Then he has been just half a year on the stool of repentance!—Poor Peter! But you say he has entirely given up Charles—never sees him, hey?

ROWLEY His prejudice against him is astonishing, and I am sure greatly increased by a jealousy of him with Lady Teazle, which he has industriously been led into by a scandalous society in the neighbourhood, who have contributed not a little to Charles's ill name. Whereas the truth is, I believe, if the lady is partial to either of them, his brother is the favourite.

SIR OLIVER Ay, I know there are a set of malicious, prating, prudent gossips, both male and female, who murder characters to kill time, and will rob a young fellow of his good name before he has years to know the value of it. But I am not to be prejudiced against my nephew by such, I promise you! No, no: if Charles has done nothing false or mean, I shall compound for his extravagance.

ROWLEY Then, my life on't, you will reclaim him. Ah, sir, it gives me new life to find that your heart is not turned against him, and that the son of my good old master has one friend, however, left.

SIR OLIVER What! shall I forget, Master Rowley, when I was at his years myself? Egad, my brother and I were neither of us very prudent youths; and yet, I believe, you have not seen many better men than your old master was?

ROWLEY Sir, 'tis this reflection gives me assurance that Charles may yet be a credit to his family. But here comes Sir Peter.

SIR OLIVER Egad, so he does! Mercy on me! he's greatly altered, and seems to have a settled married look! One may read husband in his face at this distance!

(*Enter* SIR PETER TEAZLE.)

SIR PETER Ha! Sir Oliver—my old friend! Welcome to England a thousand times!

SIR OLIVER Thank you, thank you, Sir Peter! and i' faith I am glad to find you well, believe me!

SIR PETER Oh! 'tis a long time since we met—fifteen years, I doubt, Sir Oliver, and many a cross accident in the time.

SIR OLIVER Ay, I have had my share. But what! I find you are married, hey, my old boy? Well, well, it can't be helped; and so—I wish you joy with all my heart!

SIR PETER Thank you, thank you, Sir Oliver.—Yes, I have entered into—the happy state; but we'll not talk of that now.

SIR OLIVER True, true, Sir Peter; old friends should not begin on grievances at first meeting. No, no, no.

ROWLEY (*aside to* SIR OLIVER) Take care, pray, sir.

SIR OLIVER Well, so one of my nephews is a wild rogue, hey?

SIR PETER Wild! Ah! my old friend, I grieve for your disappointment there; he's a lost young man, indeed. However, his brother will make you amends; Joseph is, indeed, what a youth should be—every body in the world speaks well of him.

SIR OLIVER I am sorry to hear it; he has too good a character to be an honest fellow. Every body speaks well of him! Psha! then he has bowed as low to knaves and fools as to the honest dignity of genius and virtue.

SIR PETER What, Sir Oliver! do you blame him for not making enemies?

SIR OLIVER Yes, if he has merit enough to deserve them.

SIR PETER Well, well—you'll be convinced when you know him. 'Tis edification to hear him converse; he professes the noblest sentiments.

SIR OLIVER Oh, plague of his sentiments! If he salutes me with a scrap of morality in his mouth, I shall be sick directly. But, however, don't mistake me, Sir Peter; I don't mean to defend Charles's errors: but, before I form my judgment of either of them, I intend to make a trial of their hearts; and my friend Rowley and I have planned something for the purpose.

ROWLEY And Sir Peter shall own for once he has been mistaken.

SIR PETER Oh, my life on Joseph's honour!

SIR OLIVER Well—come, give us a bottle of good wine, and we'll drink the lads' health, and tell you our scheme.

SIR PETER *Allons*, then!

SIR OLIVER And don't, Sir Peter, be so severe against your old friend's son. Odds my life! I am not sorry that he has run out of the course a little: for my part, I hate to see prudence clinging to the green suckers of youth; 'tis like ivy round a sapling, and spoils the growth of the tree.

(*Exeunt.*)

Act III

SCENE I *A Room in* SIR PETER TEAZLE'S *House.*

(*Enter* SIR PETER TEAZLE, SIR OLIVER SURFACE, *and* ROWLEY.)

SIR PETER Well, then, we will see this fellow first, and have our wine afterwards. But how is this, Master Rowley? I don't see the jest of your scheme.

ROWLEY Why, sir, this Mr Stanley, whom I was speaking of, is nearly related to them by their mother. He was once a merchant in Dublin, but has been ruined by a series of undeserved misfortunes. He has applied, by letter, since his confinement, both to Mr Surface and Charles: from the former he has received nothing but evasive promises of future service, while Charles has done all that his extravagance has left him power to do; and he is, at this time, endeavouring to raise a sum of money, part of which, in the midst of his own distresses, I know he intends for the service of poor Stanley.

SIR OLIVER Ah! he is my brother's son.

SIR PETER Well, but how is Sir Oliver personally to—

ROWLEY Why, sir, I will inform Charles and his brother that Stanley has obtained permission to apply personally to his friends; and, as they have neither of them ever seen him, let Sir Oliver assume his character, and he will have a fair opportunity of judging, at least, of the benevolence of their dispositions: and believe me, sir, you will find in the youngest brother one who, in the midst of folly and dissipation, has still, as our immortal bard expresses it,—

"a heart to pity, and a hand,
Open as day, for melting charity."

SIR PETER Psha! What signifies his having an open hand or purse either, when he has nothing left to give? Well, well, make the trial, if you please. But where is the fellow whom you brought for Sir Oliver to examine, relative to Charles's affairs?

ROWLEY Below, waiting his commands, and no one can give him better intelligence.—This, Sir Oliver is a friendly Jew, who, to do him justice, has done every thing in his power to bring your nephew to a proper sense of his extravagance.

SIR PETER Pray let us have him in.

ROWLEY Desire Mr Moses to walk up stairs.

(*calls to* SERVANT)

SIR PETER But, pray, why should you suppose he will speak the truth?

ROWLEY Oh, I have convinced him that he has no chance of recovering certain sums advanced to Charles but through the bounty of Sir Oliver, who he knows is arrived; so that you may depend on his fidelity to his own interests. I have another evidence in my power, one Snake, whom I have detected in a matter little short of forgery, and shall shortly produce to remove some of your prejudices, Sir Peter, relative to Charles and Lady Teazle.

SIR PETER I have heard too much on that subject.

ROWLEY Here comes the honest Israelite.

(*Enter* MOSES.)

—This is Sir Oliver.

SIR OLIVER I understand you have lately had great dealings with my nephew Charles?

MOSES Yes, Sir Oliver, I have done all I could for him; but he was ruined before he came to me for assistance.

SIR OLIVER That was unlucky, truly; for you have had no opportunity of showing your talents.

MOSES None at all; I hadn't the pleasure of knowing his distresses till he was some thousands worse than nothing.

SIR OLIVER Unfortunate, indeed! But I suppose you have done all in your power for him, honest Moses?

MOSES Yes, he knows that. This very evening I was to have brought him a gentleman from the city, who does not know him, and will, I believe, advance him some money.

SIR PETER What, one Charles has never had money from before?

MOSES Yes, Mr Premium, of Crutched Friars, formerly a broker.

SIR PETER Egad, Sir Oliver, a thought strikes me!—Charles, you say, does not know Mr Premium?

MOSES Not at all.

SIR PETER Now then, Sir Oliver, you may have a better opportunity of satisfying yourself than by an old romancing tale of a poor relation: go with my friend Moses, and represent Premium, and then, I'll answer for it, you'll see your nephew in all his glory.

SIR OLIVER Egad, I like this idea better than the other, and I may visit Joseph afterwards as old Stanley.

SIR PETER True—so you may.

ROWLEY Well, this is taking Charles rather at a disadvantage, to be sure. However, Moses, you understand Sir Peter, and will be faithful?

MOSES You may depend upon me. (*looks at his watch*) This is near the time I was to have gone.

SIR OLIVER I'll accompany you as soon as you please, Moses—But hold! I have forgot one thing—how the plague shall I be able to pass for a Jew?

MOSES There's no need—the principal is Christian.

SIR OLIVER Is he? I'm very sorry to hear it. But, then again, ain't I rather too smartly dressed to look like a money lender?

SIR PETER Not at all; 'twould not be out of character, if you went in your own carriage—would it, Moses?

MOSES Not in the least.

SIR OLIVER Well, but how must I talk; there's certainly some cant of usury and mode of treating that I ought to know?

SIR PETER Oh, there's not much to learn. The great point, as I take it, is to be exorbitant enough in your demands. Hey, Moses?

MOSES Yes, that's a very great point.

SIR OLIVER I'll answer for't I'll not be wanting in that. I'll ask him eight or ten per cent. on the loan, at least.

MOSES If you ask him no more than that, you'll be discovered immediately.

SIR OLIVER Hey! what, the plague! how much then?

MOSES That depends upon the circumstances. If he appears not very anxious for the supply, you should require only forty or fifty per cent.; but if you find him in great distress, and want the moneys very bad, you may ask double.

SIR PETER A good honest trade you're learning, Sir Oliver!

SIR OLIVER Truly, I think so—and not unprofitable.

MOSES Then, you know, you haven't the moneys yourself, but are forced to borrow them for him of a friend.

SIR OLIVER Oh! I borrow it of a friend, do I?

MOSES And your friend is an unconscionable dog: but you can't help that.

SIR OLIVER My friend an unconscionable dog, is he?

MOSES Yes, and he himself has not the moneys by him, but is forced to sell stock at a great loss.

SIR OLIVER He is forced to sell stock at a great loss, is he? Well, that's very kind of him.

SIR PETER I' faith, Sir Oliver—Mr Premium, I mean—you'll soon be master of the trade. But, Moses! would not you have him run out a little against the Annuity Bill? That would be in character, I should think.

MOSES Very much.

ROWLEY And lament that a young man now must be at years of discretion before he is suffered to ruin himself?

MOSES Ay, great pity!

SIR PETER And abuse the public for allowing merit to an act whose only object is to snatch misfortune and imprudence from the rapacious gripe of usury, and give the minor a chance of inheriting his estate without being undone by coming into possession.

SIR OLIVER So, so—Moses shall give me farther instructions as we go together.

SIR PETER You will not have much time, for your nephew lives hard by.

SIR OLIVER Oh, never fear! my tutor appears so able, that though Charles lived in the next street, it must be my own fault if I am not a complete rogue before I turn the corner. (*Exit with* MOSES.)

SIR PETER So, now, I think Sir Oliver will be convinced: you are partial, Rowley, and would have prepared Charles for the other plot.

ROWLEY No, upon my word, Sir Peter.

SIR PETER Well, go bring me this Snake, and I'll hear what he has to say presently. I see Maria, and want to speak with her. (*Exit* ROWLEY.) I should be glad to be convinced my suspicions of Lady Teazle and Charles were unjust. I have never yet opened my mind on this subject to my friend Joseph—I am determined I will do it—he will give me his opinion sincerely.

(*Enter* MARIA.)

So, child, has Mr Surface returned with you?

MARIA No, sir; he was engaged.

SIR PETER Well, Maria, do you not reflect, the more you converse with that amiable young man, what return his partiality for you deserves?

MARIA Indeed, Sir Peter, your frequent importunity on this subject distresses me extremely—you compel me to declare, that I know no man who has ever paid me a particular attention whom I would not prefer to Mr Surface.

SIR PETER So—here's perverseness! No, no, Maria, 'tis Charles only whom you would prefer. 'Tis evident his vices and follies have won your heart.

MARIA This is unkind, sir. You know I have obeyed you in neither seeing nor corresponding with him: I have heard enough to convince me that he is unworthy my regard. Yet I cannot think it culpable, if while my understanding severely condemns his vices, my heart suggests some pity for his distresses.

SIR PETER Well, well, pity him as much as you please; but give your heart and hand to a worthier object.

MARIA Never to his brother!

SIR PETER Go, perverse and obstinate! But take care, madam; you have never yet known what the authority of a guardian is: don't compel me to inform you of it.

MARIA I can only say, you shall not have just reason. 'Tis true, by my father's will, I am for a short period bound to regard you as his substitute; but must cease to think you so, when you would compel me to be miserable.

(*Exit.*)

SIR PETER Was ever man so crossed as I am, every thing conspiring to fret me! I had not been involved in matrimony a fortnight, before her father, a hale and hearty man, died, on purpose, I believe, for the pleasure of plaguing me with the care of his daughter.—(LADY TEAZLE *sings without.*) But here comes my helpmate! She appears in great good humour. How happy I should be if I could tease her into loving me, though but a little!

(*Enter* LADY TEAZLE.)

LADY TEAZLE Lud! Sir Peter, I hope you haven't been quarrelling with Maria? It is not using me well to be ill-humoured when I am not by.

SIR PETER Ah, Lady Teazle, you might have the power to make me good humoured at all times.

LADY TEAZLE I am sure I wish I had; for I want you to be in a charming sweet temper at this moment. Do be good humoured now, and let me have two hundred pounds, will you?

SIR PETER Two hundred pounds; what, ain't I to be in a good humour without paying for it! But speak to me thus, and i' faith there's nothing I could refuse you. You shall have it; but seal me a bond for the repayment.

LADY TEAZLE Oh, no—there—my note of hand will do as well. (*offering her hand*)

SIR PETER And you shall no longer reproach me with not giving you an independent settlement. I mean shortly to surprise you: but shall we always live thus, hey?

LADY TEAZLE If you please. I'm sure I don't care how soon we leave off quarrelling, provided you'll own you were tired first.

SIR PETER Well—then let our future contest be, who shall be most obliging.

LADY TEAZLE I assure you, Sir Peter, good nature becomes you. You look now as you did before we were married, when you used to walk with me under the elms, and tell me stories of what a gallant you were in your youth, and chuck me under the chin, you would; and asked me if I thought I could love an old fellow, who would deny me nothing—didn't you?

SIR PETER Yes, yes, and you were as kind and attentive—

LADY TEAZLE Ay, so I was, and would always take your part, when my acquaintance used to abuse you, and turn you into ridicule.

SIR PETER Indeed!

LADY TEAZLE Ay, and when my cousin Sophy has called you a stiff, peevish old bachelor, and laughed at me for thinking of marrying one who might be my father, I have always defended you, and said, I didn't think you so ugly by any means.

SIR PETER Thank you.

LADY TEAZLE And I dared say you'd make a very good sort of a husband.

SIR PETER And you prophesied right; and we shall now be the happiest couple—

LADY TEAZLE And never differ again?

SIR PETER No, never!—though at the same time, indeed, my dear Lady Teazle, you must watch your temper very seriously; for in all our little quarrels, my dear, if you recollect, my love, you always began first.

LADY TEAZLE I beg your pardon, my dear Sir Peter: indeed, you always gave the provocation.

SIR PETER Now see, my angel! take care—contradicting isn't the way to keep friends.

LADY TEAZLE Then don't you begin it, my love!

SIR PETER There, now! you—you are going on. You don't perceive, my life, that you are just doing the very thing which you know always makes me angry.

LADY TEAZLE Nay, you know, if you will be angry without any reason, my dear—

SIR PETER There! now you want to quarrel again.

LADY TEAZLE No, I'm sure I don't: but, if you will be so peevish—

SIR PETER There now! who begins first?

LADY TEAZLE Why, you, to be sure. I said nothing—but there's no bearing your temper.

SIR PETER No, no, madam: the fault's in your own temper.

LADY TEAZLE Ay, you are just what my cousin Sophy said you would be.

SIR PETER Your cousin Sophy is a forward, impertinent gipsy.

LADY TEAZLE You are a great bear, I'm sure, to abuse my relations.

SIR PETER Now may all the plagues of marriage be doubled on me, if ever I try to be friends with you any more!

LADY TEAZLE So much the better.

SIR PETER No, no, madam: 'tis evident you never cared a pin for me, and I was a madman to marry you—a pert, rural coquette, that had refused half the honest squires in the neighborhood!

LADY TEAZLE And I am sure I was a fool to marry you—an old dangling bachelor, who was single at fifty, only because he never could meet with any one who would have him.

SIR PETER Ay, ay, madam; but you were pleased enough to listen to me: you never had such an offer before.

LADY TEAZLE No! didn't I refuse Sir Tivy Terrier, who every body said would have been a better match? for his estate is just as good as yours, and he has broke his neck since we have been married.

SIR PETER I have done with you, madam! You are an unfeeling, ungrateful—but there's an end of everything. I believe you capable of everything that is bad. Yes, madam, I now believe the reports relative to you and Charles, madam. Yes, madam, you and Charles are, not without grounds—

LADY TEAZLE Take care, Sir Peter! you had better not insinuate any such thing! I'll not be suspected without cause, I promise you.

SIR PETER Very well, madam! very well! A separate maintenance as soon as you please. Yes, madam, or a divorce! I'll make an example of myself for the benefit of all old bachelors. Let us separate, madam.

LADY TEAZLE Agreed! agreed! And now, my dear Sir Peter, we are of a mind once more, we may be the happiest couple, and never differ again, you know: ha! ha! ha! Well, you are going to be in a passion, I see, and I shall only interrupt you—so, bye! bye! (*Exit.*)

SIR PETER Plagues and tortures! can't I make her angry either! Oh, I am the most miserable fellow! But I'll not bear her presuming to keep her temper: no! she may break my heart, but she shan't keep her temper. (*Exit.*)

SCENE II *A Room in* CHARLES SURFACE'S *House.*

(*Enter* TRIP, MOSES, *and* SIR OLIVER SURFACE.)

TRIP Here, Master Moses! if you'll stay a moment I'll try whether—what's the gentleman's name?

SIR OLIVER Mr Moses, what is my name? (*aside to* MOSES)

MOSES Mr Premium.

TRIP Premium—very well. (*Exit taking snuff.*)

SIR OLIVER To judge by the servants, one wouldn't believe the master was ruined. But what!—sure, this was my brother's house?

MOSES Yes, sir; Mr Charles bought it of Mr Joseph, with the furniture, pictures, &c., just as the old gentleman left it. Sir Peter thought it a piece of extravagance in him.

SIR OLIVER In my mind, the other's economy in selling it to him was more reprehensible by half.

(*Reenter* TRIP.)

TRIP My master says you must wait, gentlemen: he has company, and can't speak with you yet.

SIR OLIVER If he knew who it was wanted to see him, perhaps he would not send such a message.

TRIP Yes, yes, sir; he knows you are here—I did not forget little Premium: no, no, no.

SIR OLIVER Very well; and I pray, sir, what may be your name?

TRIP Trip, sir; my name is Trip, at your service.

SIR OLIVER Well, then, Mr Trip, you have a pleasant sort of place here, I guess?

TRIP Why, yes—here are three or four of us pass our time agreeably enough; but then our wages are sometimes a little in arrear—and not very great either—but fifty pounds a year, and find our own bags and bouquets.

SIR OLIVER Bags and bouquets! halters and bastinadoes! (*aside*)

TRIP And *à propos,* Moses, have you been able to get me that little bill discounted?

SIR OLIVER Wants to raise money too!—mercy on me! Has his distresses too, I warrant, like a lord, and affects creditors and duns. (*aside*)

MOSES 'Twas not to be done, indeed, Mr Trip.

TRIP Good lack, you surprise me! My friend Brush has indorsed it, and I thought when he put his name at the back of a bill 'twas the same as cash.

MOSES No, 'twouldn't do.

TRIP A small sum—but twenty pounds. Hark'ee, Moses, do you think you couldn't get it me by way of annuity?

SIR OLIVER An annuity! ha! ha! a footman raise money by way of annuity. Well done, luxury, egad! (*aside*)

MOSES Well, but you must insure your place.

TRIP Oh, with all my heart! I'll insure my place, and my life too, if you please.

SIR OLIVER It's more than I would your neck. (*aside*)

MOSES But is there nothing you could deposit?

TRIP Why, nothing capital of my master's wardrobe has dropped lately; but I could give you a mortgage on some of his winter clothes, with equity of redemption before November—or you shall have the reversion of the French velvet, or a post-obit on the blue and silver;—these, I should think, Moses, with a few pair of point ruffles, as a collateral security—hey, my little fellow?

MOSES Well, well. (*Bell rings.*)

TRIP Egad, I heard the bell. I believe, gentlemen, I can now introduce you. Don't forget the annuity, little Moses! This way, gentlemen, I'll insure my place, you know.

SIR OLIVER (*aside*) If the man be a shadow of the master, this is the temple of dissipation indeed!

(*Exeunt.*)

SCENE III *Another Room in the same.* CHARLES SURFACE, SIR HARRY BUMPER, CARELESS, *and* GENTLEMEN, *discovered drinking.*

CHARLES SURFACE 'Fore heaven, 'tis true!—there's the great degeneracy of the age. Many of our acquaintance have taste, spirit, and politeness; but, plague on 't, they won't drink.

CARELESS It is so, indeed, Charles! they give into all the substantial luxuries of the table, and abstain from nothing but wine and wit. Oh, certainly society suffers by it intolerably! for now, instead of the social spirit of raillery that used to mantle over a glass of bright Burgundy, their conversation is become just like the Spa-water they drink, which has all the pertness and flatulency of champagne, without its spirit or flavour.

1 GENTLEMAN But what are they to do who love play better than wine?

CARELESS True! there's Sir Harry diets himself for gaming, and is now under a hazard regimen.

CHARLES SURFACE Then he'll have the worst of it. What! you wouldn't train a horse for the course by keeping him from corn? For my part, egad, I am never so successful as when I am a little merry: let me throw on a bottle of champagne, and I never lose.

ALL Hey, what?

CARELESS At least I never feel my losses, which is exactly the same thing.

2 GENTLEMAN Ay, that I believe.

CHARLES SURFACE And then, what man can pretend to be a believer in love, who is an abjurer of wine? 'Tis the test by which the lover knows his own heart. Fill a dozen bumpers to a dozen beauties, and she that floats at the top is the maid that has bewitched you.

CARELESS Now then, Charles, be honest, and give us your real favourite.

CHARLES SURFACE Why, I have withheld her only in compassion to you. If I toast her, you must give a round of her peers, which is impossible—on earth.

CARELESS Oh! then we'll find some canonised vestals or heathen goddesses that will do, I warrant.

CHARLES SURFACE Here, then, bumpers, you rogues! bumpers! Maria! Maria!—

SIR HARRY Maria who?

CHARLES SURFACE Oh, damn the surname!—'tis too formal to be registered in Love's calendar—Maria!

ALL Maria!

CHARLES SURFACE But now, Sir Harry, beware, we must have beauty superlative.

CARELESS Nay, never study, Sir Harry: we'll stand to the toast, though your mistress should want an eye, and you know you have a song will excuse you.

SIR HARRY Egad, so I have! and I'll give him the song instead of the lady. (*sings*)

Here's to the maiden of bashful fifteen;
  Here's to the widow of fifty;

Here's to the flaunting extravagant quean,
And here's to the housewife that's thrifty.

Chorus. Let the toast pass—
Drink to the lass,
I'll warrant she'll prove an excuse for the glass.

Here's to the charmer whose dimples we prize;
Now to the maid who has none, sir:
Here's to the girl with a pair of blue eyes,
And here's to the nymph with but one, sir.
Chorus. Let the toast pass, &c.

Here's to the maid with a bosom of snow:
Now to her that's as brown as a berry:
Here's to the wife with a face full of woe,
And now to the damsel that's merry.
Chorus. Let the toast pass, &c.

For let 'em be clumsy, or let 'em be slim,
Young or ancient, I care not a feather;
So fill a pint bumper quite up to the brim,
So fill up your glasses, nay, fill to the brim,
And let us e'en toast them together.
Chorus. Let the toast pass, &c.

ALL Bravo! bravo!

(*Enter* TRIP, *and whispers* CHARLES SURFACE.)

CHARLES SURFACE Gentlemen, you must excuse me a little.—Careless, take the chair, will you?

CARELESS Nay, pr'ythee, Charles, what now? This is one of your peerless beauties, I suppose, has dropped in by chance?

CHARLES SURFACE No, faith! To tell you the truth, 'tis a Jew and a broker, who are come by appointment.

CARELESS Oh, damn it! let's have the Jew in.

1 GENTLEMAN Ay, and the broker too, by all means.

2 GENTLEMAN Yes, yes, the Jew and the broker.

CHARLES SURFACE Egad, with all my heart!—Trip, bid the gentlemen walk in. (*Exit* TRIP.) Though there's one of them a stranger, I can tell you.

CARELESS Charles, let us give them some generous Burgundy, and perhaps they'll grow conscientious.

CHARLES SURFACE Oh, hang 'em, no! wine does but draw forth a man's natural qualities; and to make them drink would only be to whet their knavery.

(*Reenter* TRIP, *with* SIR OLIVER SURFACE *and* MOSES.)

CHARLES SURFACE So, honest Moses; walk in, pray, Mr Premium—that's the gentleman's name, isn't it, Moses?

MOSES Yes, sir.

CHARLES SURFACE Set chairs, Trip.—Sit down, Mr Premium.—Glasses, Trip. (TRIP *gives chairs and glasses, and exit.*) Sit down, Moses.—Come, Mr Premium, I'll give you a sentiment; here's *Success to usury!*—Moses, fill the gentleman a bumper.

MOSES Success to usury! (*drinks*)

CARELESS Right, Moses—usury is prudence and industry, and deserves to succeed.

SIR OLIVER Then here's—All the success it deserves! (*drinks*)

CARELESS No, no, that won't do! Mr Premium, you have demurred at the toast, and must drink it in a pint bumper.

1 GENTLEMAN A pint bumper, at least.

MOSES Oh, pray, sir, consider—Mr Premium's a gentleman.

CARELESS And therefore loves good wine.

2 GENTLEMAN Give Moses a quart glass—this is mutiny, and a high contempt for the chair.

CARELESS Here, now for 't! I'll see justice done to the last drop of my bottle.

SIR OLIVER Nay, pray, gentlemen—I did not expect this usage.

CHARLES SURFACE No, hang it, you shan't; Mr Premium's a stranger.

SIR OLIVER Odd! I wish I was well out of their company. (*aside*)

CARELESS Plague on 'em then! if they won't drink, we'll not sit down with them. Come, Harry, the dice are in the next room.—Charles, you'll join us when you have finished your business with the gentlemen?

CHARLES SURFACE I will! I will! (*Exeunt* SIR HARRY BUMPER *and* GENTLEMEN; CARELESS *following.*) Careless!

CARELESS (*returning*) Well!

CHARLES SURFACE Perhaps I may want you.

CARELESS Oh, you know I am always ready: word, note, or bond, 'tis all the same to me. (*Exit.*)

MOSES Sir, this is Mr Premium, a gentleman of the strictest honour and secrecy; and always performs what he undertakes. Mr Premium, this is—

CHARLES SURFACE Psha! have done. Sir, my friend Moses is a very honest fellow, but a little slow at expression: he'll be an hour giving us our titles. Mr Premium, the plain state of the matter is this: I am an extravagant young fellow who wants to borrow money; you I take to be a prudent old fellow, who have got money to lend. I am blockhead enough to give fifty per cent, sooner than not have it; and you, I presume, are rogue enough to take a hundred if you can get it. Now, sir, you see we are acquainted at once, and may proceed to business without further ceremony.

SIR OLIVER Exceeding frank, upon my word. I see, sir, you are not a man of many compliments.

CHARLES SURFACE Oh, no, sir! plain dealing in business I always think best.

SIR OLIVER Sir, I like you better for it. However, you are mistaken in one thing; I have no money to lend, but I believe I could procure some of a friend; but then he's an unconscionable dog. Isn't he, Moses? And must sell stock to accommodate you. Mustn't he, Moses?

MOSES Yes, indeed! You know I always speak the truth, and scorn to tell a lie!

CHARLES SURFACE Right. People that speak truth generally do. But these are trifles, Mr Premium. What! I know money isn't to be bought without paying for 't!

SIR OLIVER Well, but what security could you give? You have no land, I suppose?

CHARLES SURFACE Not a mole-hill, nor a twig, but what's in the bough-pots out of the window!

SIR OLIVER Nor any stock, I presume?

CHARLES SURFACE Nothing but live stock—and that's only a few pointers and ponies. But pray, Mr Premium, are you acquainted at all with any of my connexions?

SIR OLIVER Why, to say truth, I am.

CHARLES SURFACE Then you must know that I have a devilish rich uncle in the East Indies, Sir Oliver Surface, from whom I have the greatest expectations?

SIR OLIVER That you have a wealthy uncle, I have heard; but how your expectations will turn out is more, I believe, than you can tell.

CHARLES SURFACE Oh, no!—there can be no doubt. They tell me I'm a prodigious favourite, and that he talks of leaving me every thing.

SIR OLIVER Indeed! this is the first I've heard of it.

CHARLES SURFACE Yes, yes, 'tis just so. Moses knows 'tis true; don't you, Moses?

MOSES Oh, yes! I'll swear to't.

SIR OLIVER Egad, they'll persuade me presently I'm at Bengal. (*aside*)

CHARLES SURFACE Now I propose, Mr Premium, if it's agreeable to you, a post-obit on Sir Oliver's life: though at the same time the old fellow has been so liberal to me, that I give you my word, I should be very sorry to hear that any thing had happened to him.

SIR OLIVER Not more than I should, I assure you. But the bond you mention happens to be just the worst security you could offer me—for I might live to a hundred and never see the principal.

CHARLES SURFACE Oh, yes, you would! the moment Sir Oliver dies, you know, you would come on me for the money.

SIR OLIVER Then I believe I should be the most unwelcome dun you ever had in your life.

CHARLES SURFACE What! I suppose you're afraid that Sir Oliver is too good a life?

SIR OLIVER No, indeed I am not; though I have heard he is as hale and healthy as any man of his years in Christendom.

CHARLES SURFACE There again, now, you are misinformed. No, no, the climate has hurt him considerably, poor uncle Oliver. Yes, yes, he breaks apace, I'm told—and is so much altered lately that his nearest relations would not know him.

SIR OLIVER No! Ha! ha! ha! so much altered lately that his nearest relations would not know him! Ha! ha! ha! egad—ha! ha! ha!

CHARLES SURFACE Ha! ha!—you're glad to hear that, little Premium?

SIR OLIVER No, no, I'm not.

CHARLES SURFACE Yes, yes, you are—ha! ha! ha!—you know that mends your chance.

SIR OLIVER But I'm told Sir Oliver is coming over; nay, some say he is actually arrived.

CHARLES SURFACE Psha! sure I must know better than you whether he's come or not. No, no, rely on't he's at this moment at Calcutta. Isn't he, Moses?

MOSES Oh, yes, certainly.

SIR OLIVER Very true, as you say, you must know better than I, though I have it from pretty good authority. Haven't I, Moses?

MOSES Yes, most undoubted!

SIR OLIVER But, sir, as I understand you want a few hundreds immediately, is there nothing you could dispose of?

CHARLES SURFACE How do you mean?

SIR OLIVER For instance, now, I have heard that your father left behind him a great quantity of massy old plate.

CHARLES SURFACE O Lud! that's gone long ago. Moses can tell you how better than I can.

SIR OLIVER (*aside*) Good lack! all the family race-cups and corporation-bowls! (*aloud*) Then it was also supposed that his library was one of the most valuable and compact.

CHARLES SURFACE Yes, yes, so it was—vastly too much so for a private gentleman. For my part, I was always of a communicative disposition, so I thought it a shame to keep so much knowledge to myself.

SIR OLIVER (*aside*) Mercy upon me! learning that had run in the family like an heir-loom! (*aloud*) Pray, what are become of the books?

CHARLES SURFACE You must inquire of the auctioneer, Master Premium, for I don't believe even Moses can direct you.

MOSES I know nothing of books.

SIR OLIVER So, so, nothing of the family property left, I suppose?

CHARLES SURFACE Not much, indeed; unless you have a mind to the family pictures. I have got a room full of ancestors above; and if you have a taste for old paintings, egad, you shall have 'em a bargain!

SIR OLIVER Hey! what the devil! sure, you wouldn't sell your forefathers, would you?

CHARLES SURFACE Every man of them, to the best bidder.

SIR OLIVER What! your great-uncles and aunts?

CHARLES SURFACE Ay, and my great-grandfathers and grandmothers too.

SIR OLIVER (*aside*) Now I give him up! (*aloud*) What the plague, have you no bowels for your own kindred? Odds life! do you take me for Shylock in the play, that you would raise money of me on your own flesh and blood?

CHARLES SURFACE Nay, my little broker, don't be angry: what need you care, if you have your money's worth?

SIR OLIVER Well, I'll be the purchaser: I think I can dispose of the family canvas. (*aside*) Oh, I'll never forgive him this! never!

(*Reenter* CARELESS.)

CARELESS Come, Charles, what keeps you?

CHARLES SURFACE I can't come yet. I'faith, we are going to have a sale above stairs; here's little Premium will buy all my ancestors!

CARELESS Oh, burn your ancestors!

CHARLES SURFACE No, he may do that afterwards, if he pleases. Stay, Careless, we want you: egad, you shall be auctioneer—so come along with us.

CARELESS Oh, have with you, if that's the case. I can handle a hammer as well as a dice-box! Going! going!

SIR OLIVER Oh, the profligates! (*aside*)

CHARLES SURFACE Come, Moses, you shall be appraiser, if we want one. Gad's life, little Premium, you don't seem to like the business?

SIR OLIVER Oh yes, I do, vastly! Ha! ha! ha! yes, yes, I think it a rare joke to sell one's family by auction—ha! ha! (*aside*) Oh, the prodigal!

CHARLES SURFACE To be sure! when a man wants money, where the plague should he get assistance, if he can't make free with his own relations!

SIR OLIVER I'll never forgive him; never! never! (*Exeunt.*)

Act IV

SCENE I *A Picture Room in* CHARLES SURFACE'S *House.*

(*Enter* CHARLES SURFACE, SIR OLIVER SURFACE, MOSES, *and* CARELESS.)

CHARLES SURFACE Walk in, gentlemen, pray walk in;—here they are, the family of the Surfaces, up to the Conquest.

SIR OLIVER And, in my opinion, a goodly collection.

CHARLES SURFACE Ay, ay, these are done in the true spirit of portrait-painting; no *volontière grace* or expression. Not like the works of your modern Raphaels, who give you the strongest resemblance, yet contrive to make your portrait independent of you; so that you may sink the original and not hurt the picture. No, no; the merit of these is the inveterate likeness—all stiff and awkward as the originals, and like nothing in human nature besides.

SIR OLIVER Ah! we shall never see such figures of men again.

CHARLES SURFACE I hope not. Well, you see, Master Premium, what a domestic character I am; here I sit of an evening surrounded by my family. But come, get to your pulpit, Mr Auctioneer; here's an old gouty chair of my grandfather's will answer the purpose.

CARELESS Ay, ay, this will do. But, Charles, I haven't a hammer; and what's an auctioneer without his hammer?

CHARLES SURFACE Egad, that's true. What parchment have we here? Oh, our genealogy in full. (*taking pedigree down*) Here, Careless, you shall have no common bit of mahogany, here's the family tree for you, you rogue! This shall be your hammer, and now you may knock down my ancestors with their own pedigree.

SIR OLIVER What an unnatural rogue!—an *ex post facto* parricide! (*aside*)

CARELESS Yes, yes, here's a list of your generation indeed; faith, Charles, this is the most convenient thing you could have found for the business, for 'twill not only serve as a hammer, but a catalogue into the bargain. Come, begin—A-going, a-going, a-going!

CHARLES SURFACE Bravo, Careless! Well, here's my great-uncle, Sir Richard Raveline, a marvellous good general in his day, I assure you. He served in all the Duke of Marlborough's wars, and got that cut over his eye at the battle of Malplaquet. What say you, Mr Premium? look at him—there's a hero! not cut out of his feathers, as your modern clipped captains are, but enveloped in wig and regimentals, as a general should be. What do you bid?

SIR OLIVER (*aside to* MOSES) Bid him speak.

MOSES Mr Premium would have you speak.

CHARLES SURFACE Why, then, he shall have him for ten pounds, and I'm sure that's not dear for a staff-officer.

SIR OLIVER (*aside*) Heaven deliver me! his famous uncle Richard for ten pounds! (*aloud*) Very well, sir, I take him at that.

CHARLES SURFACE Careless, knock down my uncle Richard.—Here, now, is a maiden sister of his, my great-aunt Deborah, done by Kneller, in his best manner and esteemed a very formidable likeness. There she is, you see, a shepherdess feeding her flock. You shall have her for five pounds ten—the sheep are worth the money.

SIR OLIVER (*aside*) Ah! poor Deborah! a woman who set such a value on herself! (*aloud*) Five pounds ten—she's mine.

CHARLES SURFACE Knock down my aunt Deborah! Here, now, are two that were a sort of cousins of theirs.—You see, Moses, these pictures were done some time ago, when beaux wore wigs, and the ladies their own hair.

SIR OLIVER Yes, truly, head-dresses appear to have been a little lower in those days.

CHARLES SURFACE Well, take that couple for the same.

MOSES 'Tis a good bargain.

CHARLES SURFACE Careless!—This, now, is a grandfather of my mother's, a learned judge, well known on the western circuit.—What do you rate him at, Moses?

MOSES Four guineas.

CHARLES SURFACE Four guineas! Gad's life, you don't bid me the price of his wig.—Mr Premium, you have more respect for the woolsack; do let us knock his lordship down at fifteen.

SIR OLIVER By all means.

CARELESS Gone!

CHARLES SURFACE And there are two brothers of his, William and Walter Blunt, Esquires, both members of parliament, and noted speakers; and, what's very extraordinary, I believe, this is the first time they were ever bought or sold.

SIR OLIVER That is very extraordinary, indeed! I'll take them at your own price, for the honour of parliament.

CARELESS Well said, little Premium! I'll knock them down at forty.

CHARLES SURFACE Here's a jolly fellow—I don't know what relation, but he was mayor of Norwich: take him at eight pounds.

SIR OLIVER No, no; six pounds will do for the mayor.

CHARLES SURFACE Come, make it guineas, and I'll throw you the two aldermen there into the bargain.

SIR OLIVER They're mine.

CHARLES SURFACE Careless, knock down the mayor and aldermen. But, plague on't! we shall be all day retailing in this manner; do let us deal wholesale: what say you, little Premium? Give me three hundred pounds for the rest of the family in the lump.

CARELESS Ay, ay, that will be the best way.

SIR OLIVER Well, well, any thing to accommodate you; they are mine. But there is one portrait which you have always passed over.

CARELESS What, that ill-looking little fellow over the settee.

SIR OLIVER Yes, sir, I mean that; though I don't think him so ill-looking a little fellow, by any means.

CHARLES SURFACE What, that? Oh; that's my uncle Oliver! 'twas done before he went to India.

CARELESS Your uncle Oliver! Gad, then you'll never be friends, Charles. That, now, to me, is as stern a looking rogue as ever I saw; an unforgiving eye, and a damned disinheriting countenance! an inveterate knave, depend on't. Don't you think so, little Premium?

SIR OLIVER Upon my soul, sir, I do not; I think it is as honest a looking face as any in the room, dead or alive. But I suppose uncle Oliver goes with the rest of the lumber?

CHARLES SURFACE No, hang it! I'll not part with poor Noll. The old fellow has been very good to me, and egad, I'll keep his picture while I've a room to put it in.

SIR OLIVER (*aside*) The rogue's my nephew after all! (*aloud*) But, sir, I have somehow taken a fancy to that picture.

CHARLES SURFACE I'm sorry for't, for you certainly will not have it. Oons, haven't you got enough of them?

SIR OLIVER (*aside*) I forgive him every thing! (*aloud*) But, sir, when I take a whim in my head, I don't value money. I'll give you as much for that as for all the rest.

CHARLES SURFACE Don't tease me, master broker; I tell you I'll not part with it, and there's an end of it.

SIR OLIVER (*aside*) How like his father the dog is! (*aloud*) Well, well, I have done. (*aside*) I did not perceive it before, but I think I never saw such a striking resemblance. (*aloud*) Here is a draft for your sum.

CHARLES SURFACE Why, 'tis for eight hundred pounds!

SIR OLIVER You will not let Sir Oliver go?

CHARLES SURFACE Zounds! no! I tell you, once more.

SIR OLIVER Then never mind the difference, we'll balance that another time. But give me your hand on the bargain; you are an honest fellow, Charles—I beg pardon, sir, for being so free.—Come, Moses.

CHARLES SURFACE Egad, this is a whimsical old fellow!—But hark'ee, Premium, you'll prepare lodgings for these gentlemen.

SIR OLIVER Yes, yes, I'll send for them in a day or two.

CHARLES SURFACE But hold; do now send a genteel conveyance for them, for, I assure you, they were most of them used to ride in their own carriages.

SIR OLIVER I will, I will—for all but Oliver.

CHARLES SURFACE Ay, all but the little nabob.

SIR OLIVER You're fixed on that?

CHARLES SURFACE Peremptorily.

SIR OLIVER (*aside*) A dear extravagant rogue! (*aloud*) Good day!—Come, Moses. (*aside*) Let me hear now who dares call him profligate. (*Exit with* MOSES.)

CARELESS Why, this is the oddest genius of the sort I ever met with!

CHARLES SURFACE Egad, he's the prince of brokers, I think. I wonder how the devil Moses got acquainted with so honest a fellow.—Ha! here's Rowley.—Do, Careless, say I'll join the company in a few moments.

CARELESS I will—but don't let that old blockhead persuade you to squander any of that money on old musty debts, or any such nonsense; for tradesmen, Charles, are the most exorbitant fellows.

CHARLES SURFACE Very true, and paying them is only encouraging them.

CARELESS Nothing else.

CHARLES SURFACE Ay, ay, never fear. (*Exit* CARELESS.) So! this was an odd old fellow, indeed. Let me see, two-thirds of these five hundred and thirty odd pounds are mine by right. 'Fore heaven! I find one's ancestors are more valuable relations than I took them for!—Ladies and gentlemen, your most obedient and very grateful servant. (*bows ceremoniously to the pictures*)

(*Enter* ROWLEY.)

Ha! old Rowley! egad, you are just come in time to take leave of your old acquaintance.

ROWLEY Yes, I heard they were a-going. But I wonder you can have such spirits under so many distresses.

CHARLES SURFACE Why, there's the point! my distresses are so many, that I can't afford to part with my spirits; but I shall be rich and splenetic, all in good time. However, I suppose you are surprised that I am not more sorrowful at parting with so many near relations; to be sure, 'tis very affecting, but you see they never move a muscle, so why should I?

ROWLEY There's no making you serious a moment.

CHARLES SURFACE Yes, faith, I am so now. Here, my honest Rowley, here, get me this changed directly, and take a hundred pounds of it immediately to old Stanley.

ROWLEY A hundred pounds! Consider only—

CHARLES SURFACE Gad's life, don't talk about it! poor Stanley's wants are pressing, and, if you don't make haste, we shall have some one call that has a better right to the money.

ROWLEY Ah! there's the point! I never will cease dunning you with the old proverb—

CHARLES SURFACE *Be just before you're generous.*—Why, so I would if I could; but Justice is an old, hobbling beldame, and I can't get her to keep pace with Generosity, for the soul of me.

ROWLEY Yet, Charles, believe me, one hour's reflection—

CHARLES SURFACE Ay, ay, it's very true; but, hark'ee, Rowley, while I have, by Heaven I'll give; so, damn your economy! and now for hazard.

SCENE II *Another Room in the Same.*

(*Enter* SIR OLIVER SURFACE *and* MOSES.)

MOSES Well, sir, I think, as Sir Peter said, you have seen Mr Charles in high glory; 'tis great pity he's so extravagant.

SIR OLIVER True, but he would not sell my picture.

MOSES And loves wine and women so much.

SIR OLIVER But he would not sell my picture.

MOSES And games so deep.

SIR OLIVER But he would not sell my picture. Oh, here's Rowley.

(*Enter* ROWLEY.)

ROWLEY So, Sir Oliver, I find you have made a purchase—

SIR OLIVER Yes, yes, our young rake has parted with his ancestors like old tapestry.

ROWLEY And here has he commissioned me to redeliver you part of the purchase money—I mean, though, in your necessitous character of old Stanley.

MOSES Ah! there is the pity of all; he is so damned charitable.

ROWLEY And I left a hosier and two tailors in the hall, who, I'm sure, won't be paid, and this hundred would satisfy them.

SIR OLIVER Well, well, I'll pay his debts, and his benevolence too. But now I am no more a broker, and you shall introduce me to the elder brother as old Stanley.

ROWLEY Not yet awhile; Sir Peter, I know, means to call there about this time.

(*Enter* TRIP.)

TRIP Oh, gentlemen, I beg pardon for not showing you out; this way—Moses, a word. (*Exit with* MOSES.)

SIR OLIVER There's a fellow for you! Would you believe it, that puppy intercepted the Jew on our coming, and wanted to raise money before he got to his master!

ROWLEY Indeed!

SIR OLIVER Yes, they are now planning an annuity business. Ah, Master Rowley, in my days servants were content with the follies of their masters, when they were worn a little threadbare; but now they have their vices, like their birthday clothes, with the gloss on. (*Exeunt.*)

SCENE III *A Library in* JOSEPH SURFACE'S *House.*

(*Enter* JOSEPH SURFACE *and* SERVANT.)

JOSEPH SURFACE No letter from Lady Teazle?

SERVANT No, sir.

JOSEPH SURFACE (*aside*) I am surprised she has not sent, if she is prevented from coming. Sir Peter certainly does not suspect me. Yet I wish I may not lose the heiress, through the scrape I have drawn myself into with the wife; however, Charles's imprudence and bad character are great points in my favour. (*knocking without*)

SERVANT Sir, I believe that must be Lady Teazle.

JOSEPH SURFACE Hold! See whether it is or not, before you go to the door: I have a particular message for you if it should be my brother.

SERVANT 'Tis her ladyship, sir; she always leaves her chair at the milliner's in the next street.

JOSEPH SURFACE Stay, stay; draw that screen before the window—that will do;—my opposite neighbour is a maiden lady of so curious a temper—(SERVANT *draws the screen, and exit.*) I have a difficult hand to play in this affair. Lady Teazle has lately suspected my views on Maria; but she must by no means be let into that secret,—at least, till I have her more in my power.

(*Enter* LADY TEAZLE.)

LADY TEAZLE What, sentiment in soliloquy now? Have you been very impatient? O Lud! don't pretend to look grave. I vow I couldn't come before.

JOSEPH SURFACE O madam, punctuality is a species of constancy very unfashionable in a lady of quality.

(*places chairs, and sits after* LADY TEAZLE *is seated*)

LADY TEAZLE Upon my word, you ought to pity me. Do you know Sir Peter is grown so ill-natured to me of late, and so jealous of Charles too—that's the best of the story, isn't it?

JOSEPH SURFACE I am glad my scandalous friends keep that up. (*aside*)

LADY TEAZLE I am sure I wish he would let Maria marry him, and then perhaps he would be convinced; don't you, Mr Surface?

JOSEPH SURFACE (*aside*) Indeed I do not. (*aloud*) Oh, certainly I do! for then my dear Lady Teazle would also be convinced how wrong her suspicions were of my having any design on the silly girl.

LADY TEAZLE Well, well, I'm inclined to believe you. But isn't it provoking, to have the most ill-natured things said of one? And there's my friend Lady Sneerwell has circulated I don't know how many scandalous tales of me, and all without any foundation too; that's what vexes me.

JOSEPH SURFACE Ay, madam, to be sure, that is the provoking circumstance—without foundation; yes, yes, there's the mortification, indeed; for when a scandalous story is believed against one, there certainly is no comfort like the consciousness of having deserved it.

LADY TEAZLE No, to be sure, then I'd forgive their malice; but to attack me, who am really so innocent, and who never say an ill-natured thing of any body—that is, of any friend; and then Sir Peter, too, to have him so peevish, and so suspicious, when I know the integrity of my own heart—indeed 'tis monstrous!

JOSEPH SURFACE But, my dear Lady Teazle, 'tis your own fault if you suffer. When a husband entertains a groundless suspicion of his wife, and withdraws his confidence from her, the original compact is broken, and she owes it to the honour of her sex to endeavour to outwit him.

LADY TEAZLE Indeed! So that, if he suspects me without cause, it follows, that the best way of curing his jealousy is to give him reason for't?

JOSEPH SURFACE Undoubtedly—for your husband should never be deceived in you: and in that case it becomes you to be frail in compliment to his discernment.

LADY TEAZLE To be sure, what you say is very reasonable, and when the consciousness of my innocence—

JOSEPH SURFACE Ah, my dear madam, there is the great mistake! 'tis this very conscious innocence that is of the greatest prejudice to you. What is it makes you negligent of forms, and careless of the world's opinion? why, the consciousness of your own innocence. What makes you thoughtless in your conduct, and apt to run into a thousand little imprudences? why, the consciousness of your own innocence. What makes you impatient of Sir Peter's temper, and outrageous at his suspicions? why, the consciousness of your innocence.

LADY TEAZLE 'Tis very true!

JOSEPH SURFACE Now, my dear Lady Teazle, if you would but once make a trifling *faux pas,* you can't conceive how cautious you would grow, and how ready to humour and agree with your husband.

LADY TEAZLE Do you think so?

JOSEPH SURFACE Oh, I am sure on't; and then you would find all scandal would cease at once, for—in short, your character at present is like a person in a plethora, absolutely dying from too much health.

LADY TEAZLE So, so; then I perceive your prescription is, that I must sin in my own defence, and part with my virtue to preserve my reputation?

JOSEPH SURFACE Exactly so, upon my credit, ma'am.

LADY TEAZLE Well, certainly this is the oddest doctrine, and the newest receipt for avoiding calumny!

JOSEPH SURFACE An infallible one, believe me. Prudence, like experience, must be paid for.

LADY TEAZLE Why, if my understanding were once convinced—

JOSEPH SURFACE Oh, certainly, madam, your understanding should be convinced. Yes, yes—Heaven forbid I should persuade you to do any thing you thought wrong. No, no, I have too much honour to desire it.

LADY TEAZLE Don't you think we may as well leave honour out of the argument? (*rises*)

JOSEPH SURFACE Ah, the ill effects of your country education, I see, still remain with you.

LADY TEAZLE I doubt they do indeed; and I will fairly own to you, that if I could be persuaded to do wrong, it would be by Sir Peter's ill usage sooner than your honourable logic, after all.

JOSEPH SURFACE Then, by this hand, which he is unworthy of— (*taking her hand*)

(*Reenter* SERVANT.)

'Sdeath, you blockhead—what do you want?

SERVANT I beg your pardon, sir, but I thought you would not choose Sir Peter to come up without announcing him.

JOSEPH SURFACE Sir Peter!—Oons—the devil!

LADY TEAZLE Sir Peter! O Lud! I'm ruined! I'm ruined!

SERVANT Sir, 'twasn't I let him in.

LADY TEAZLE Oh! I'm quite undone! What will become of me? Now, Mr Logic—Oh! mercy, sir, he's on the stairs—I'll get behind here—and if ever I'm so imprudent again— (*goes behind the screen*)

JOSEPH SURFACE Give me that book.

(*Sits down.* SERVANT *pretends to adjust his chair.*)

(*Enter* SIR PETER TEAZLE.)

SIR PETER Ay, ever improving himself—Mr Surface, Mr Surface— (*pats* JOSEPH *on the shoulder*)

JOSEPH SURFACE Oh, my dear Sir Peter, I beg your pardon. (*gaping, throws away the book*) I have been dozing over a stupid book. Well, I am much obliged to you for this call. You haven't been here, I believe, since I fitted up this room. Books, you know, are the only things I am a coxcomb in.

SIR PETER 'Tis very neat indeed. Well, well, that's proper; and you can make even your screen a source of knowledge—hung, I perceive, with maps.

JOSEPH SURFACE Oh, yes, I find great use in that screen.

SIR PETER I dare say you must, certainly, when you want to find anything in a hurry.

JOSEPH SURFACE Ay, or to hide anything in a hurry either. (*aside*)

SIR PETER Well, I have a little private business—

JOSEPH SURFACE You need not stay. (*to* SERVANT)

SERVANT No, sir. (*Exit.*)

JOSEPH SURFACE Here's a chair, Sir Peter—I beg—

SIR PETER Well, now we are alone, there is a subject, my dear friend, on which I wish to unburden my mind to you—a point of the greatest moment to my peace; in short, my good friend, Lady Teazle's conduct of late has made me very unhappy.

JOSEPH SURFACE Indeed! I am very sorry to hear it.

SIR PETER 'Tis but too plain she has not the least regard for me; but, what's worse, I have pretty good authority to suppose she has formed an attachment to another.

JOSEPH SURFACE Indeed! you astonish me!

SIR PETER Yes! and, between ourselves, I think I've discovered the person.

JOSEPH SURFACE How! you alarm me exceedingly.

SIR PETER Ay, my dear friend, I knew you would sympathise with me!

JOSEPH SURFACE Yes, believe me, Sir Peter, such a discovery would hurt me just as much as it would you.

SIR PETER I am convinced of it. Ah! it is a happiness to have a friend whom we can trust even with one's family secrets. But have you no guess who I mean?

JOSEPH SURFACE I haven't the most distant idea. It can't be Sir Benjamin Backbite!

SIR PETER Oh, no! What say you to Charles?

JOSEPH SURFACE My brother! impossible!

SIR PETER Oh, my dear friend, the goodness of your own heart misleads you. You judge of others by yourself.

JOSEPH SURFACE Certainly, Sir Peter, the heart that is conscious of its own integrity is ever slow to credit another's treachery.

SIR PETER True; but your brother has no sentiment—you never hear him talk so.

JOSEPH SURFACE Yet I can't but think Lady Teazle herself has too much principle.

SIR PETER Ay; but what is principle against the flattery of a handsome, lively young fellow?

JOSEPH SURFACE That's very true.

SIR PETER And then, you know, the difference of our ages makes it very improbable that she should have any great affection for me; and if she were to be frail, and I were to make it public, why the town would only laugh at me, the foolish old bachelor, who had married a girl.

JOSEPH SURFACE That's true, to be sure—they would laugh.

SIR PETER Laugh! ay, and make ballads, and paragraphs, and the devil knows what of me.

JOSEPH SURFACE No, you must never make it public.

SIR PETER But then again—that the nephew of my old friend, Sir Oliver, should be the person to attempt such a wrong, hurts me more nearly.

JOSEPH SURFACE Ay, there's the point. When ingratitude barbs the dart of injury, the wound has double danger in it.

SIR PETER Ay—I, that was, in a manner, left his guardian; in whose house he had been so often entertained; who never in my life denied him—my advice!

JOSEPH SURFACE Oh, 'tis not to be credited! There may be a man capable of such baseness, to be sure; but, for my part, till you can give me positive proofs, I cannot but doubt it. However, if it should be proved on him, he is no longer a brother of mine—I disclaim kindred with him: for the man who can break the laws of hospitality, and tempt the wife of his friend, deserves to be branded as the pest of society.

SIR PETER What a difference there is between you! What noble sentiments!

JOSEPH SURFACE Yet I cannot suspect Lady Teazle's honour.

SIR PETER I am sure I wish to think well of her, and to remove all ground of quarrel between us. She has lately reproached me more than once with having made no settlement on her; and, in our last quarrel, she almost hinted that she should not break her heart if I was dead. Now, as we seem to differ in our ideas of expense, I have resolved she shall have her own way, and be her own mistress in that respect for the future; and, if I were to die, she will find I have not been inattentive to her interest while living. Here, my friend, are the drafts of two deeds, which I wish to have your opinion on. By one, she will enjoy eight hundred a year independent while I live; and, by the other, the bulk of my fortune at my death.

JOSEPH SURFACE This conduct, Sir Peter, is indeed truly generous. (*aside*) I wish it may not corrupt my pupil.

SIR PETER Yes, I am determined she shall have no cause to complain, though I would not have her acquainted with the latter instance of my affection yet awhile.

JOSEPH SURFACE Nor I, if I could help it. (*aside*)

SIR PETER And now, my dear friend, if you please, we will talk over the situation of your hopes with Maria.

JOSEPH SURFACE (*softly*) Oh, no, Sir Peter; another time, if you please.

SIR PETER I am sensibly chagrined at the little progress you seem to make in her affections.

JOSEPH SURFACE (*softly*) I beg you will not mention it. What are my disappointments when your happiness is in debate! (*aside*) 'Sdeath, I shall be ruined every way!

SIR PETER And though you are averse to my acquainting Lady Teazle with your passion, I'm sure she's not your enemy in the affair.

JOSEPH SURFACE Pray, Sir Peter, now oblige me. I am really too much affected by the subject we have been speaking of to bestow a thought on my own concerns. The man who is entrusted with his friend's distresses can never—

(*Reenter* SERVANT.)

Well, sir?

SERVANT Your brother, sir, is speaking to a gentleman in the street, and says he knows you are within.

JOSEPH SURFACE 'Sdeath, blockhead, I'm not within—I'm out for the day.

SIR PETER Stay—hold—a thought has struck me:—you shall be at home.

JOSEPH SURFACE Well, well, let him come up. (*Exit* SERVANT.) He'll interrupt Sir Peter, however. (*aside*)

SIR PETER Now, my good friend, oblige me, I entreat you. Before Charles comes, let me conceal myself somewhere, then do you tax him on the point we have been talking, and his answer may satisfy me at once.

JOSEPH SURFACE Oh, fie, Sir Peter! would you have me join in so mean a trick?—to trepan my brother too?

SIR PETER Nay, you tell me you are sure he is innocent; if so you do him the greatest service by giving him an opportunity to clear himself, and you will set my heart at rest. Come, you shall not refuse me: (*going up*) here, behind the screen will be—Hey! what the devil! there seems to be one listener here already—I'll swear I saw a petticoat!

JOSEPH SURFACE Ha! ha! ha! Well, this is ridiculous enough. I'll tell you, Sir Peter, though I hold a man of intrigue to be a most despicable character, yet, you know, it does not follow that one is to be an absolute Joseph either! Hark'ee, 'tis a little French milliner, a silly rogue that plagues me; and having some character to lose, on your coming, sir, she ran behind the screen.

SIR PETER Ah, Joseph! Joseph! Did I ever think that you—But, egad, she has overheard all I have been saying of my wife.

JOSEPH SURFACE Oh, 'twill never go any farther, you may depend upon it!

SIR PETER No! then, faith, let her hear it out.—Here's a closet will do as well.

JOSEPH SURFACE Well, go in there.

SIR PETER Sly rogue! sly rogue! (*goes into the closet*)

JOSEPH SURFACE A narrow escape, indeed! and a curious situation I'm in, to part man and wife in this manner.

LADY TEAZLE (*peeping*) Couldn't I steal off?

JOSEPH SURFACE Keep close, my angel!

SIR PETER (*peeping*) Joseph, tax him home.

JOSEPH SURFACE Back, my dear friend!

LADY TEAZLE (*peeping*) Couldn't you lock Sir Peter in?

JOSEPH SURFACE Be still, my life!

SIR PETER (*peeping*) You're sure the little milliner won't blab?

JOSEPH SURFACE In, in, my dear Sir Peter!—'Fore Gad, I wish I had a key to the door.

(*Enter* CHARLES SURFACE.)

CHARLES SURFACE Holla! brother, what has been the matter? Your fellow would not let me up at first. What! have you had a Jew or a wench with you?

JOSEPH SURFACE Neither, brother, I assure you.

CHARLES SURFACE But what has made Sir Peter steal off? I thought he had been with you.

JOSEPH SURFACE He was, brother; but, hearing you were coming, he did not choose to stay.

CHARLES SURFACE What! was the old gentleman afraid I wanted to borrow money of him?

JOSEPH SURFACE No, sir; but I am sorry to find, Charles, you have lately given that worthy man grounds for great uneasiness.

CHARLES SURFACE Yes, they tell me I do that to a great many worthy men. But how so, pray?

JOSEPH SURFACE To be plain with you, brother, he thinks you are endeavouring to gain Lady Teazle's affections from him.

CHARLES SURFACE Who, I? O Lud! not I, upon my word.—Ha! ha! ha! so the old fellow has found out that he has got a young wife, has he?—or, what is worse, Lady Teazle has found out she has an old husband?

JOSEPH SURFACE This is no subject to jest on, brother. He who can laugh—

CHARLES SURFACE True, true, as you were going to say—then, seriously, I never had the least idea of what you charge me with, upon my honour.

JOSEPH SURFACE Well, it will give Sir Peter great satisfaction to hear this. (*raising his voice*)

CHARLES SURFACE To be sure, I once thought the lady seemed to have taken a fancy to me; but, upon my soul, I never gave her the least encouragement. Besides, you know my attachment to Maria.

JOSEPH SURFACE But sure, brother, even if Lady Teazle had betrayed the fondest partiality for you—

CHARLES SURFACE Why, look'ee, Joseph, I hope I shall never deliberately do a dishonourable action; but if a pretty woman was purposely to throw herself in my way—and that pretty woman married to a man old enough to be her father—

JOSEPH SURFACE Well!

CHARLES SURFACE Why, I believe I should be obliged to—

JOSEPH SURFACE What?

CHARLES SURFACE To borrow a little of your morality, that's all. But, brother, do you know now that you surprise me exceedingly, by naming me with Lady Teazle; for, i' faith, I always understood you were her favourite.

JOSEPH SURFACE Oh, for shame, Charles! This retort is foolish.

CHARLES SURFACE Nay, I swear I have seen you exchange such significant glances—

JOSEPH SURFACE Nay, nay, sir, this is no jest.

CHARLES SURFACE Egad, I'm serious! Don't you remember one day, when I called here—

JOSEPH SURFACE Nay, pr'ythee, Charles—

CHARLES SURFACE And found you together—

JOSEPH SURFACE Zounds, sir, I insist—

CHARLES SURFACE And another time when your servant—

JOSEPH SURFACE Brother, brother, a word with you! (*aside*) Gad, I must stop him.

CHARLES SURFACE Informed, I say, that—

JOSEPH SURFACE Hush! I beg your pardon, but Sir Peter has overheard all we have been saying. I knew you would clear yourself, or I should not have consented.

CHARLES SURFACE How, Sir Peter! Where is he?

JOSEPH SURFACE Softly, there! (*points to the closet*)

CHARLES SURFACE Oh, 'fore Heaven, I'll have him out. Sir Peter, come forth!

JOSEPH SURFACE No, no—

CHARLES SURFACE I say, Sir Peter, come into court. (*pulls in Sir Peter*) What! my old guardian!—What! turn inquisitor, and take evidence incog.? Oh, fie! Oh, fie!

SIR PETER Give me your hand, Charles—I believe I have suspected you wrongfully; but you mustn't be angry with Joseph—'twas my plan!

CHARLES SURFACE Indeed!

SIR PETER But I acquit you. I promise you I don't think near so ill of you as I did: what I have heard has given me great satisfaction.

CHARLES SURFACE Egad, then, 'twas lucky you didn't hear any more. Wasn't it, Joseph?

SIR PETER Ah! you would have retorted on him.

CHARLES SURFACE Ah, ay, that was a joke.

SIR PETER Yes, yes, I know his honour too well.

CHARLES SURFACE But you might as well have suspected him as me in this matter, for all that. Mightn't he, Joseph?

SIR PETER Well, well, I believe you.

JOSEPH SURFACE Would they were both out of the room. (*aside*)

SIR PETER And in future, perhaps, we may not be such strangers.

(*Reenter* SERVANT, *and whispers to* JOSEPH SURFACE.)

SERVANT Lady Sneerwell is below, and says she will come up.

JOSEPH SURFACE Lady Sneerwell! Gad's life! she must not come here. (*Exit* SERVANT.) Gentlemen, I beg pardon—I must wait on you down stairs: here is a person come on particular business.

CHARLES SURFACE Well, you can see him in another room. Sir Peter and I have not met a long time, and I have something to say to him.

JOSEPH SURFACE (*aside*) They must not be left together. (*aloud*) I'll send Lady Sneerwell away, and return directly. (*aside to* SIR PETER) Sir Peter, not a word of the French milliner.

SIR PETER (*aside to* JOSEPH SURFACE) I! not for the world! (*Exit* JOSEPH SURFACE.) Ah, Charles, if you associated more with your brother, one might indeed hope for your reformation. He is a man of sentiment. Well, there is nothing in the world so noble as a man of sentiment.

CHARLES SURFACE Psha! he is too moral by half; and so apprehensive of his good name, as he calls it, that I suppose he would as soon let a priest into his house as a wench.

SIR PETER No, no,—come, come,—you wrong him. No, no! Joseph is no rake, but he is no such saint either, in that respect. (*aside*) I have a great mind to tell him—we should have such a laugh at Joseph.

CHARLES SURFACE Oh, hang him! he's a very anchorite, a young hermit!

SIR PETER Hark'ee—you must not abuse him: he may chance to hear of it again, I promise you.

CHARLES SURFACE Why, you won't tell him?

SIR PETER No—but—this way. (*aside*) Egad, I'll tell him. (*aloud*) Hark'ee—have you a mind to have a good laugh at Joseph?

CHARLES SURFACE I should like it of all things.

SIR PETER Then, i'faith, we will! I'll be quit with him for discovering me. He had a girl with him when I called. (*whispers*)

CHARLES SURFACE What! Joseph? you jest.

SIR PETER Hush!—a little French milliner—and the best of the jest is—she's in the room now.

CHARLES SURFACE The devil she is!

SIR PETER Hush! I tell you. (*points to the screen*)

CHARLES SURFACE Behind the screen! 'Slife, let's unveil her!

SIR PETER No, no, he's coming:—you sha'n't, indeed!

CHARLES SURFACE Oh, egad, we'll have a peep at the little milliner!

SIR PETER Not for the world!—Joseph will never forgive me.

CHARLES SURFACE I'll stand by you—

SIR PETER Odds, here he is!

(CHARLES SURFACE *throws down the screen.*)

(*Reenter* JOSEPH SURFACE.)

CHARLES SURFACE Lady Teazle, by all that's wonderful.

SIR PETER Lady Teazle, by all that's damnable!

CHARLES SURFACE Sir Peter, this is one of the smartest French milliners I ever saw. Egad, you seem all to have been diverting yourselves here at hide and seek, and I don't see who is out of the secret. Shall I beg your ladyship to inform me? Not a word!—Brother, will you be pleased to explain this matter? What! is Morality dumb too?—Sir Peter, though I found you in the dark, perhaps you are not so now! All mute!—Well—though I can make nothing of the affair, I suppose you perfectly understand one another; so I'll leave you to yourselves. (*going*) Brother, I'm sorry to find you have given that worthy man grounds for so much uneasiness.—Sir Peter! there's nothing in the world so noble as a man of sentiment! (*Exit.*)

JOSEPH SURFACE Sir Peter—notwithstanding—I confess—that appearances are against me—if you will afford me your patience—I make no doubt—but I shall explain every thing to your satisfaction.

SIR PETER If you please, sir.

JOSEPH SURFACE The fact is, sir, that Lady Teazle, knowing my pretensions to your ward Maria—I say, sir, Lady Teazle, being apprehensive of the jealousy of your temper—and knowing my friendship to the family—she, sir, I say—called here—in order that—I might explain these pretensions—but on your coming—being apprehensive—as I said—of your jealousy—she withdrew—and this, you may depend on it, is the whole truth of the matter.

SIR PETER A very clear account, upon my word; and I dare swear the lady will vouch for every article of it.

LADY TEAZLE For not one word of it, Sir Peter!

SIR PETER How! don't you think it worth while to agree in the lie?

LADY TEAZLE There is not one syllable of truth in what that gentleman has told you.

SIR PETER I believe you, upon my soul, ma'am!

JOSEPH SURFACE (*aside to* LADY TEAZLE) 'Sdeath, madam, will you betray me?

LADY TEAZLE Good Mr Hypocrite, by your leave, I'll speak for myself.

SIR PETER Ay, let her alone, sir; you'll find she'll make out a better story than you, without prompting.

LADY TEAZLE Hear me, Sir Peter!—I came here on no matter relating to your ward, and even ignorant of this gentleman's pretensions to her. But I came, seduced by his insidious arguments, at least to listen to his pretended passion, if not to sacrifice your honour to his baseness.

SIR PETER Now, I believe the truth is coming, indeed!

JOSEPH SURFACE The woman's mad!

LADY TEAZLE No, sir; she has recovered her senses and your own arts have furnished her with the means.—Sir Peter, I do not expect you to credit me—

but the tenderness you expressed for me, when I am sure you could not think I was a witness to it, has so penetrated to my heart, that had I left the place without the shame of this discovery, my future life should have spoken the sincerity of my gratitude. As for that smooth-tongued hypocrite, who would have seduced the wife of his too credulous friend, while he affected honourable addresses to his ward—I behold him now in a light so truly despicable, that I shall never again respect myself for having listened to him. (*Exit.*)

JOSEPH SURFACE Notwithstanding all this, Sir Peter, Heaven knows—

SIR PETER That you are a villain! and so I leave you to your conscience.

JOSEPH SURFACE You are too rash, Sir Peter; you shall hear me. The man who shuts out conviction by refusing to—

SIR PETER Oh, damn your sentiments!

(*Exeunt* SIR PETER *and* JOSEPH SURFACE, *talking.*)

Act V

SCENE I *The Library in* JOSEPH SURFACE'S *House.*

(*Enter* JOSEPH SURFACE *and* SERVANT.)

JOSEPH SURFACE Mr Stanley! and why should you think I would see him? you must know he comes to ask something.

SERVANT Sir, I should not have let him in, but that Mr Rowley came to the door with him.

JOSEPH SURFACE Psha! blockhead! to suppose that I should now be in a temper to receive visits from poor relations!—Well, why don't you show the fellow up?

SERVANT I will, sir.—Why, sir, it was not my fault that Sir Peter discovered my lady—

JOSEPH SURFACE Go, fool! (*Exit* SERVANT.) Sure Fortune never played a man of my policy such a trick before! My character with Sir Peter, my hopes with Maria, destroyed in a moment! I'm in a rare humour to listen to other people's distresses! I sha'n't be able to bestow even a benevolent sentiment on Stanley.—So! here he comes, and Rowley with him. I must try to recover myself, and put a little charity into my face, however. (*Exit.*)

(*Enter* SIR OLIVER SURFACE *and* ROWLEY.)

SIR OLIVER What! does he avoid us? That was he, was it not?

ROWLEY It was, sir. But I doubt you are come a little too abruptly. His nerves are so weak, that the sight of a poor relation may be too much for him. I should have gone first to break it to him.

SIR OLIVER Oh, plague of his nerves! Yet this is he whom Sir Peter extols as a man of the most benevolent way of thinking!

ROWLEY As to his way of thinking, I cannot pretend to decide; for, to do him justice, he appears to have as much speculative benevolence as any private gentleman in the kingdom, though he is seldom so sensual as to indulge himself in the exercise of it.

SIR OLIVER Yet he has a string of charitable sentiments at his fingers' ends.

ROWLEY Or, rather, at his tongue's end, Sir Oliver; for I believe there is no sentiment he has such faith in as that *Charity begins at home.*

SIR OLIVER And his, I presume, is of that domestic sort which never stirs abroad at all.

ROWLEY I doubt you'll find it so; but he's coming. I mustn't seem to interrupt you; and you know, immediately as you leave him, I come in to announce your arrival in your real character.

SIR OLIVER True; and afterwards you'll meet me at Sir Peter's.

ROWLEY Without losing a moment. (*Exit.*)

SIR OLIVER I don't like the complaisance of his features.

(*Reenter* JOSEPH SURFACE.)

JOSEPH SURFACE Sir, I beg you ten thousand pardons for keeping you a moment waiting.—Mr Stanley, I presume.

SIR OLIVER At your service.

JOSEPH SURFACE Sir, I beg you will do me the honour to sit down—I entreat you, sir.

SIR OLIVER Dear sir—there's no occasion. (*aside*) Too civil by half!

JOSEPH SURFACE I have not the pleasure of knowing you, Mr Stanley; but I am extremely happy to see you look so well. You were nearly related to my mother, I think, Mr Stanley?

SIR OLIVER I was, sir; so nearly that my present poverty, I fear, may do discredit to her wealthy children, else I should not have presumed to trouble you.

JOSEPH SURFACE Dear sir, there needs no apology;—he that is in distress, though a stranger, has a right to claim kindred with the wealthy. I am sure I wish I was one of that class, and had it in my power to offer you even a small relief.

SIR OLIVER If your uncle, Sir Oliver, were here, I should have a friend.

JOSEPH SURFACE I wish he was, sir, with all my heart; you should not want an advocate with him, believe me, sir.

SIR OLIVER I should not need one—my distresses would recommend me. But I imagined his bounty would enable you to become the agent of his charity.

JOSEPH SURFACE My dear sir, you were strangely misinformed. Sir Oliver is a worthy man, a very worthy man; but avarice, Mr Stanley, is the vice of age. I will tell you, my good sir, in confidence, what he has done for me has been a mere nothing; though people, I know, have thought otherwise, and for my part, I never chose to contradict the report.

SIR OLIVER What! has he never transmitted you bullion—rupees—pagodas?

JOSEPH SURFACE Oh, dear sir, nothing of the kind! No, no; a few presents now and then—china, shawls, congou tea, avadavats and Indian crackers—little more, believe me.

SIR OLIVER Here's gratitude for twelve thousand pounds!—Avadavats and Indian crackers! (*aside*)

JOSEPH SURFACE Then, my dear sir, you have heard, I doubt not, of the extravagance of my brother: there are very few would credit what I have done for that unfortunate young man.

SIR OLIVER Not I, for one! (*aside*)

JOSEPH SURFACE The sums I have lent him! Indeed I have been exceedingly to blame; it was an amiable weakness; however, I don't pretend to defend it—and now I feel it doubly culpable, since it has deprived me of the pleasure of serving you, Mr Stanley, as my heart dictates.

SIR OLIVER (*aside*) Dissembler! (*aloud*) Then, sir, you can't assist me?

JOSEPH SURFACE At present, it grieves me to say, I cannot; but, whenever I have the ability, you may depend upon hearing from me.

SIR OLIVER I am extremely sorry—

JOSEPH SURFACE Not more than I, believe me; to pity, without the power to relieve, is still more painful than to ask and be denied.

SIR OLIVER Kind sir, your most obedient humble servant.

JOSEPH SURFACE You leave me deeply affected, Mr Stanley.—William, be ready to open the door. (*calls to* SERVANT)

SIR OLIVER Oh, dear sir, no ceremony.

JOSEPH SURFACE Your very obedient.

SIR OLIVER Your most obsequious.

JOSEPH SURFACE You may depend upon hearing from me, whenever I can be of service.

SIR OLIVER Sweet sir, you are too good!

JOSEPH SURFACE In the meantime I wish you health and spirits.

SIR OLIVER Your ever grateful and perpetual humble servant.

JOSEPH SURFACE Sir, yours as sincerely.

SIR OLIVER (*aside*) Now I am satisfied. (*Exit.*)

JOSEPH SURFACE This is one bad effect of a good character; it invites application from the unfortunate, and there needs no small degree of address to gain the reputation of benevolence without incurring the expense. The silver ore of pure charity is an expensive article in the catalogue of a man's good qualities; whereas the sentimental French plate I use instead makes just as good a show, and pays no tax.

(*Reenter* ROWLEY.)

ROWLEY Mr Surface, your servant: I was apprehensive of interrupting you, though my business demands immediate attention, as this note will inform you.

JOSEPH SURFACE Always happy to see Mr Rowley,—a rascal. (*aside; reads the letter*) Sir Oliver Surface!—My uncle arrived!

ROWLEY He is, indeed: we have just parted—quite well, after a speedy voyage, and impatient to embrace his worthy nephew.

JOSEPH SURFACE I am astonished!—William! stop Mr Stanley, if he's not gone. (*calls to* SERVANT)

ROWLEY Oh! he's out of reach, I believe.

JOSEPH SURFACE Why did you not let me know this when you came in together?

ROWLEY I thought you had particular business. But I must be gone to inform your brother, and appoint him here to meet your uncle. He will be with you in a quarter of an hour.

JOSEPH SURFACE So he says. Well, I am strangely overjoyed at his coming. (*aside*) Never, to be sure, was anything so damned unlucky!

ROWLEY You will be delighted to see how well he looks.

JOSEPH SURFACE Oh! I'm overjoyed to hear it. (*aside*) Just at this time!

ROWLEY I'll tell him how impatiently you expect him.

JOSEPH SURFACE Do, do; pray give my best duty and affection. Indeed, I cannot express the sensations I feel at the thought of seeing him. (*Exit* ROWLEY.) Certainly his coming just at this time is the cruellest piece of ill fortune. (*Exit.*)

SCENE II *A Room in* SIR PETER TEAZLE'S *House.*

(*Enter* MRS CANDOUR *and* MAID.)

MAID Indeed, ma'am, my lady will see nobody at present.

MRS CANDOUR Did you tell her it was her friend Mrs Candour?

MAID Yes, ma'am; but she begs you will excuse her.

MRS CANDOUR Do go again; I shall be glad to see her, if it be only for a moment, for I am sure she must be in great distress. (*Exit* MAID.) Dear heart, how provoking! I'm not mistress of half the circumstances! We shall have the whole affair in the newspapers, with the names of the parties at length, before I have dropped the story at a dozen houses.

(*Enter* SIR BENJAMIN BACKBITE.)

Oh, dear Sir Benjamin! you have heard, I suppose—

SIR BENJAMIN Of Lady Teazle and Mr Surface—

MRS CANDOUR And Sir Peter's discovery—

SIR BENJAMIN Oh, the strangest piece of business, to be sure!

MRS CANDOUR Well, I never was so surprised in my life. I am so sorry for all parties, indeed.

SIR BENJAMIN Now, I don't pity Sir Peter at all: he was so extravagantly partial to Mr Surface.

MRS CANDOUR Mr Surface! Why, 'twas with Charles Lady Teazle was detected.

SIR BENJAMIN No, no, I tell you: Mr Surface is the gallant.

MRS CANDOUR No such thing! Charles is the man. 'Twas Mr Surface brought Sir Peter on purpose to discover them.

SIR BENJAMIN I tell you I had it from one—

MRS CANDOUR and I have it from one—

SIR BENJAMIN Who had it from one, who had it—

MRS CANDOUR From one immediately. But here comes Lady Sneerwell; perhaps she knows the whole affair.

(*Enter* LADY SNEERWELL.)

LADY SNEERWELL So, my dear Mrs Candour, here's a sad affair of our friend Lady Teazle!

MRS CANDOUR Ay, my dear friend, who would have thought—

LADY SNEERWELL Well, there is no trusting appearances; though, indeed, she was always too lively for me.

MRS CANDOUR To be sure, her manners were a little too free; but then she was so young!

LADY SNEERWELL And had, indeed, some good qualities.

MRS CANDOUR So she had, indeed. But have you heard the particulars?

LADY SNEERWELL No; but every body says that Mr Surface—

SIR BENJAMIN Ay, there; I told you Mr Surface was the man.

MRS CANDOUR No, no: indeed the assignation was with Charles.

LADY SNEERWELL With Charles! You alarm me, Mrs Candour!

MRS CANDOUR Yes, yes; he was the lover. Mr Surface, to do him justice, was only the informer.

SIR BENJAMIN Well, I'll not dispute with you, Mrs Candour; but, be it which it may, I hope that Sir Peter's wound will not—

MRS CANDOUR Sir Peter's wound! Oh, mercy! I didn't hear a word of their fighting.

LADY SNEERWELL Nor I, a syllable.

SIR BENJAMIN No! what, no mention of the duel?

MRS CANDOUR Not a word.

SIR BENJAMIN Oh, yes: they fought before they left the room.

LADY SNEERWELL Pray, let us hear.

MRS CANDOUR Ay, do oblige us with the duel.

SIR BENJAMIN Sir, says Sir Peter, immediately after the discovery, *you are a most ungrateful fellow.*

MRS CANDOUR Ay, to Charles—

SIR BENJAMIN No, no—to Mr Surface—*a most ungrateful fellow; and old as I am, sir,* says he, *I insist on immediate satisfaction.*

MRS CANDOUR Ay, that must have been to Charles; for 'tis very unlikely Mr Surface should fight in his own house.

SIR BENJAMIN Gad's life, ma'am, not at all—*giving me immediate satisfaction.*—On this, ma'am, Lady Teazle, seeing Sir Peter in such danger, ran out of the room in strong hysterics, and Charles after her, calling out for hartshorn and water; then, madam, they began to fight with swords—

(*Enter* CRABTREE.)

CRABTREE With pistols, nephew, pistols! I have it from undoubted authority.

MRS CANDOUR Oh, Mr Crabtree, then it is all true!

CRABTREE Too true, indeed, madam, and Sir Peter is dangerously wounded—

SIR BENJAMIN By a thrust in segoon quite through his left side—

CRABTREE By a bullet lodged in the thorax.

MRS CANDOUR Mercy on me! Poor Sir Peter!

CRABTREE Yes, madam; though Charles would have avoided the matter, if he could.

MRS CANDOUR I told you who it was; I knew Charles was the person.

SIR BENJAMIN My uncle, I see, knows nothing of the matter.

CRABTREE But Sir Peter taxed him with basest ingratitude—

SIR BENJAMIN That I told you, you know—

CRABTREE Do, nephew, let me speak!—and insisted on immediate—

SIR BENJAMIN Just as I said—

CRABTREE Odd's life, nephew, allow others to know something too! A pair of pistols lay on the bureau (for Mr Surface, it seems, had come home the night before late from Salthill, where he had been to see the Montem with a friend, who has a son at Eton), so, unluckily, the pistols were left charged.

SIR BENJAMIN I heard nothing of this.

CRABTREE Sir Peter forced Charles to take one, and they fired, it seems, pretty nearly together. Charles's shot took effect, as I tell you, and Sir Peter's missed; but, what is very extraordinary, the ball struck against a little bronze Shakespeare that stood over the fire place, grazed out of the window at a right angle, and wounded the postman, who was just coming to the door with a double letter from Northamptonshire.

SIR BENJAMIN My uncle's account is more circumstantial, I confess; but I believe mine is the true one, for all that.

LADY SNEERWELL (*aside*) I am more interested in this affair than they imagine, and must have better information. (*Exit.*)

SIR BENJAMIN Ah! Lady Sneerwell's alarm is very easily accounted for.

CRABTREE Yes, yes, they certainly do say—but that's neither here nor there.

MRS CANDOUR But, pray, where is Sir Peter at present?

CRABTREE Oh! they brought him home, and he is now in the house, though the servants are ordered to deny him.

MRS CANDOUR I believe so, and Lady Teazle, I suppose, attending him.

CRABTREE Yes, yes; and I saw one of the faculty enter just before me.

SIR BENJAMIN Hey! who comes here?

CRABTREE Oh, this is he: the physician, depend on't.

MRS CANDOUR Oh, certainly! it must be the physician; and now we shall know.

(*Enter* SIR OLIVER SURFACE.)

CRABTREE Well, doctor, what hopes?

MRS CANDOUR Ay, doctor, how's your patient?

SIR BENJAMIN Now, doctor, isn't it a wound with a small-sword?

CRABTREE A bullet lodged in the thorax, for a hundred!

SIR OLIVER Doctor! a wound with a small-sword! and a bullet in the thorax!—Oons! are you mad, good people?

SIR BENJAMIN Perhaps, sir, you are not a doctor?

SIR OLIVER Truly, I am to thank you for my degree, if I am.

CRABTREE Only a friend of Sir Peter's, then, I presume. But, sir, you must have heard of his accident?

SIR OLIVER Not a word!

CRABTREE Not of his being dangerously wounded?

SIR OLIVER The devil he is!

SIR BENJAMIN Run through the body—

CRABTREE Shot in the breast—

SIR BENJAMIN By one Mr Surface—

CRABTREE Ay, the younger.

SIR OLIVER Hey! what the plague! you seem to differ strangely in your accounts: however, you agree that Sir Peter is dangerously wounded.

SIR BENJAMIN Oh, yes, we agree in that.

CRABTREE Yes, yes, I believe there can be no doubt of that.

SIR OLIVER Then, upon my word, for a person in that situation, he is the most imprudent man alive; for here he comes, walking as if nothing at all was the matter.

(*Enter* SIR PETER TEAZLE.)

Odd's heart, Sir Peter! you are come in good time, I promise you; for we had just given you over!

SIR BENJAMIN (*aside to* CRABTREE) Egad, uncle, this is the most sudden recovery!

SIR OLIVER Why, man! what do you out of bed with a small-sword through your body, and a bullet lodged in your thorax?

SIR PETER A small-sword and a bullet!

SIR OLIVER Ay; these gentlemen would have killed you without law or physic, and wanted to dub me a doctor, to make me an accomplice.

SIR PETER Why, what is all this?

SIR BENJAMIN We rejoice, Sir Peter, that the story of the duel is not true, and are sincerely sorry for your other misfortune.

SIR PETER So, so; all over the town already! (*aside*)

CRABTREE Though, Sir Peter, you were certainly vastly to blame to marry at your years.

SIR PETER Sir, what business is that of yours?

MRS CANDOUR Though, indeed, as Sir Peter made so good a husband, he's very much to be pitied.

SIR PETER Plague on your pity, ma'am! I desire none of it.

SIR BENJAMIN However, Sir Peter, you must not mind the laughing and jests you will meet with on the occasion.

SIR PETER Sir, sir! I desire to be master in my own house.

CRABTREE 'Tis no uncommon case, that's one comfort.

SIR PETER I insist on being left to myself: without ceremony, I insist on your leaving my house directly!

MRS CANDOUR Well, well, we are going; and depend on't, we'll make the best report of it we can. (*Exit.*)

SIR PETER Leave my house!

CRABTREE And tell how hardly you've been treated. (*Exit.*)

SIR PETER Leave my house!

SIR BENJAMIN And how patiently you bear it. (*Exit.*)

SIR PETER Fiends! vipers! furies! Oh! that their own venom would choke them!

SIR OLIVER They are very provoking indeed, Sir Peter.

(*Enter* ROWLEY.)

ROWLEY I heard high words: what has ruffled you, sir?

SIR PETER Psha! what signifies asking? Do I ever pass a day without my vexations?

ROWLEY Well, I'm not inquisitive.

SIR OLIVER Well, Sir Peter, I have seen both my nephews in the manner we proposed.

SIR PETER A precious couple they are!

ROWLEY Yes, and Sir Oliver is convinced that your judgment was right, Sir Peter.

SIR OLIVER Yes, I find Joseph is indeed the man, after all.

ROWLEY Ay, as Sir Peter says, he is a man of sentiment.

SIR OLIVER And acts up to the sentiments he professes.

ROWLEY It certainly is edification to hear him talk.

SIR OLIVER Oh, he's a model for the young men of the age!—but how's this, Sir Peter? you don't join us in your friend Joseph's praise, as I expected?

SIR PETER Sir Oliver, we live in a damned wicked world, and the fewer we praise the better.

ROWLEY What! do you say so, Sir Peter, who were never mistaken in your life?

SIR PETER Psha! plague on you both! I see by your sneering you have heard the whole affair. I shall go mad among you!

ROWLEY Then, to fret you no longer, Sir Peter, we are indeed acquainted with it all. I met Lady Teazle coming from Mr Surface's so humbled, that she deigned to request me to be her advocate with you.

SIR PETER And does Sir Oliver know all this?

SIR OLIVER Every circumstance.

SIR PETER What, of the closet and the screen, hey?

SIR OLIVER Yes, yes, and the little French milliner. Oh, I have been vastly diverted with the story! ha! ha! ha!

SIR PETER 'Twas very pleasant.

SIR OLIVER I never laughed more in my life, I assure you: ah! ah! ah!

SIR PETER Oh, vastly diverting! ha! ha! ha!

ROWLEY To be sure, Joseph with his sentiments! ha! ha! ha!

SIR PETER Yes, yes, his sentiments! ha! ha! ha! Hypocritical villain!

SIR OLIVER Ay, and that rogue Charles to pull Sir Peter out of the closet: ha! ha! ha!

SIR PETER Ha! ha! 'twas devilish entertaining, to be sure!

SIR OLIVER Ha! ha! ha! Egad, Sir Peter, I should like to have seen your face when the screen was thrown down: ha! ha!

SIR PETER Yes, yes, my face when the screen was thrown down: ha! ha! ha! Oh, I must never show my head again!

SIR OLIVER But come, come, it isn't fair to laugh at you neither, my old friend; though, upon my soul, I can't help it.

SIR PETER Oh, pray don't restrain your mirth on my account: it does not hurt me at all! I laugh at the whole affair myself. Yes, yes, I think being a standing jest for all one's acquaintance a very happy situation. Oh, yes, and then of a morning to read the paragraphs about Mr S———, Lady T———, and Sir P———, will be so entertaining!

ROWLEY Without affectation, Sir Peter, you may despise the ridicule of fools. But I see Lady Teazle going towards the next room; I am sure you must desire a reconciliation as earnestly as she does.

SIR OLIVER Perhaps my being here prevents her coming to you. Well, I'll leave honest Rowley to mediate between you; but he must bring you all presently to Mr Surface's, where I am now returning, if not to reclaim a libertine, at least to expose hypocrisy.

SIR PETER I'll be present at your discovering yourself there with all my heart; though 'tis a vile unlucky place for discoveries.

ROWLEY We'll follow. (*Exit* SIR OLIVER SURFACE.)

SIR PETER She is not coming here, you see, Rowley.

ROWLEY No, but she has left the door of that room open, you perceive. See, she is in tears.

SIR PETER Certainly a little mortification appears very becoming in a wife. Don't you think it will do her good to let her pine a little?

ROWLEY Oh, this is ungenerous in you!

SIR PETER Well, I know not what to think. You remember the letter I found of hers evidently intended for Charles?

ROWLEY A mere forgery, Sir Peter! laid in your way on purpose. This is one of the points which I intend Snake shall give you conviction of.

SIR PETER I wish I were once satisfied of that. She looks this way. What a remarkably elegant turn of the head she has! Rowley, I'll go to her.

ROWLEY Certainly.

SIR PETER Though, when it is known that we are reconciled, people will laugh at me ten times more.

ROWLEY Let them laugh, and retort their malice only by showing them you are happy in spite of it.

SIR PETER I' faith, so I will! and, if I'm not mistaken, we may yet be the happiest couple in the country.

ROWLEY Nay, Sir Peter, he who once lays aside suspicion—

SIR PETER Hold, Master Rowley! if you have any regard for me, never let me hear you utter any thing like a sentiment: I have had enough of them to serve me the rest of my life. (*Exeunt.*)

SCENE III *The Library of* JOSEPH SURFACE'S *House.*

(*Enter* JOSEPH SURFACE *and* LADY SNEERWELL.)

LADY SNEERWELL Impossible! Will not Sir Peter immediately be reconciled to Charles, and of course no longer oppose his union with Maria? The thought is distraction to me.

JOSEPH SURFACE Can passion furnish a remedy?

LADY SNEERWELL No, nor cunning either. Oh, I was a fool, an idiot, to league with such a blunderer!

JOSEPH SURFACE Sure, Lady Sneerwell, I am the greatest sufferer; yet you see I bear the accident with calmness.

LADY SNEERWELL Because the disappointment doesn't reach your heart; your interest only attached you to Maria. Had you felt for her what I have for that ungrateful libertine, neither your temper nor hypocrisy could prevent your showing the sharpness of your vexation.

JOSEPH SURFACE But why should your reproaches fall on me for this disappointment?

LADY SNEERWELL Are you not the cause of it? Had you not a sufficient field for your roguery in imposing upon Sir Peter, and supplanting your brother, but you must endeavour to seduce his wife? I hate such an avarice of crimes; 'tis an unfair monopoly, and never prospers.

JOSEPH SURFACE Well, I admit I have been to blame. I confess I deviated from the direct road of wrong, but I don't think we're so totally defeated neither.

LADY SNEERWELL No!

JOSEPH SURFACE You tell me you have made a trial of Snake since we met, and that you still believe him faithful to us?

LADY SNEERWELL I do believe so.

JOSEPH SURFACE And that he has undertaken, should it be necessary, to swear and prove, that Charles is at this time contracted by vows and honour to your ladyship, which some of his former letters to you will serve to support?

LADY SNEERWELL This, indeed, might have assisted.

JOSEPH SURFACE Come, come; it is not too late yet. (*knocking at the door*) But hark! this is probably my uncle, Sir Oliver: retire to that room; we'll consult farther when he is gone.

LADY SNEERWELL Well, but if he should find you out too?

JOSEPH SURFACE Oh, I have no fear of that. Sir Peter will hold his tongue for his own credit's sake—and you may depend on it I shall soon discover Sir Oliver's weak side!

LADY SNEERWELL I have no diffidence of your abilities: only be constant to one roguery at a time.

JOSEPH SURFACE I will, I will! (*Exit* LADY SNEERWELL.) So! 'tis confounded hard, after such bad fortune, to be baited by one's confederate in evil. Well, at all events, my character is so much better than Charles's, that I certainly—hey!—what—this is not Sir Oliver, but old Stanley again. Plague on't that he should return to tease me just now! I shall have Sir Oliver come and find him here—and—

(*Enter* SIR OLIVER SURFACE.)

Gad's life, Mr Stanley, why have you come back to plague me at this time? You must not stay now, upon my word.

SIR OLIVER Sir, I hear your uncle Oliver is expected here, and though he has been so penurious to you, I'll try what he'll do for me.

JOSEPH SURFACE Sir, 'tis impossible for you to stay now, so I must beg—Come any other time, and I promise you, you shall be assisted.

SIR OLIVER No: Sir Oliver and I must be acquainted.

JOSEPH SURFACE Zounds, sir! then I insist on your quitting the room directly.

SIR OLIVER Nay, sir—

JOSEPH SURFACE Sir, I insist on't!—Here, William! show this gentleman out. Since you compel me, sir, not one moment—this is such insolence. (*going to push him out*)

(*Enter* CHARLES SURFACE.)

CHARLES SURFACE Heyday! what's the matter now? What the devil, have you got hold of my little broker here? Zounds, brother, don't hurt little Premium. What's the matter, my little fellow?

JOSEPH SURFACE So! he has been with you too, has he?

CHARLES SURFACE To be sure, he has. Why, he's as honest a little—But sure, Joseph, you have not been borrowing money too, have you?

JOSEPH SURFACE Borrowing! no! But, brother, you know we expect Sir Oliver here every—

CHARLES SURFACE O Gad, that's true! Noll mustn't find the little broker here, to be sure.

JOSEPH SURFACE Yet Mr Stanley insists—

CHARLES SURFACE Stanley! why his name's Premium.

JOSEPH SURFACE No, sir, Stanley.

CHARLES SURFACE No, no, Premium.

JOSEPH SURFACE Well, no matter which—but—

CHARLES SURFACE Ay, ay, Stanley or Premium, 'tis the same thing, as you say; for I suppose he goes by half a hundred names, besides A. B. at the coffee-house. (*knocking*)

JOSEPH SURFACE 'Sdeath! here's Sir Oliver at the door.—Now I beg, Mr Stanley—

CHARLES SURFACE Ay, ay, and I beg, Mr Premium—

SIR OLIVER Gentlemen—

JOSEPH SURFACE Sir, by Heaven you shall go!

CHARLES SURFACE Ay, out with him, certainly!

SIR OLIVER This violence—

JOSEPH SURFACE Sir, 'tis your own fault.

CHARLES SURFACE Out with him, to be sure.

(*both forcing* SIR OLIVER *out*)

(*Enter* SIR PETER *and* LADY TEAZLE, MARIA, *and* ROWLEY.)

SIR PETER My old friend, Sir Oliver—hey! What in the name of wonder—here are dutiful nephews—assault their uncle at a first visit!

LADY TEAZLE Indeed, Sir Oliver, 'twas well we came in to rescue you.

ROWLEY Truly it was; for I perceive, Sir Oliver, the character of old Stanley was no protection to you.

SIR OLIVER Nor of Premium either: the necessities of the former could not extort a shilling from that benevolent gentleman; and with the other I stood a chance of faring worse than my ancestors, and being knocked down without being bid for.

JOSEPH SURFACE Charles!

CHARLES SURFACE Joseph!

JOSEPH SURFACE 'Tis now complete!

CHARLES SURFACE Very.

SIR OLIVER Sir Peter, my friend, and Rowley too—look on that elder nephew of mine. You know what he has already received from my bounty; and you also know how gladly I would have regarded half my fortune as held in trust for him: judge then my disappointment in discovering him to be destitute of truth, charity, and gratitude!

SIR PETER Sir Oliver, I should be more surprised at this declaration, if I had not myself found him to be mean, treacherous, and hypocritical.

LADY TEAZLE And if the gentleman pleads not guilty to these, pray let him call me to his character.

SIR PETER Then, I believe, we need add no more: if he knows himself, he will consider it as the most perfect punishment, that he is known to the world.

CHARLES SURFACE If they talk this way to Honesty, what will they say to me, by and by? (*aside*)

(SIR PETER, LADY TEAZLE, *and* MARIA *retire.*)

SIR OLIVER As for that prodigal, his brother, there—

CHARLES SURFACE Ay, now comes my turn: the damned family pictures will ruin me! (*aside*)

JOSEPH SURFACE Sir Oliver—uncle, will you honour me with a hearing?

CHARLES SURFACE Now, if Joseph would make one of his long speeches, I might recollect myself a little. (*aside*)

SIR OLIVER (*to* JOSEPH SURFACE) I suppose you would undertake to justify yourself?

JOSEPH SURFACE I trust I could.

SIR OLIVER (*to* CHARLES SURFACE) Well, sir!—and you could justify yourself too, I suppose?

CHARLES SURFACE Not that I know of, Sir Oliver.

SIR OLIVER What!—Little Premium has been let too much into the secret, I suppose?

CHARLES SURFACE True, sir; but they were family secrets, and should not be mentioned again, you know.

ROWLEY Come, Sir Oliver, I know you cannot speak of Charles's follies with anger.

SIR OLIVER Odd's heart, no more I can; nor with gravity either. Sir Peter, do you know the rogue bargained with me for all his ancestors; sold me judges and generals by the foot, and maiden aunts as cheap as broken china.

CHARLES SURFACE To be sure, Sir Oliver, I did make a little free with the family canvas, that's the truth on't. My ancestors may rise in judgment against me, there's no denying it; but believe me sincere when I tell you—and upon my soul I would not say so if I was not—that if I do not appear mortified at the exposure of my follies, it is because I feel at this moment the warmest satisfaction in seeing you, my liberal benefactor.

SIR OLIVER Charles, I believe you. Give me your hand again: the ill-looking little fellow over the settee has made your peace.

CHARLES SURFACE Then, sir, my gratitude to the original is still increased.

LADY TEAZLE (*advancing*) Yet, I believe, Sir Oliver, here is one Charles is still more anxious to be reconciled to. (*pointing to* MARIA)

SIR OLIVER Oh, I have heard of his attachment there; and, with the young lady's pardon, if I construe right—that blush—

SIR PETER Well, child, speak your sentiments!

MARIA Sir, I have little to say, but that I shall rejoice to hear that he is happy; for me, whatever claim I had to his attention, I willingly resign to one who has a better title.

CHARLES SURFACE How, Maria!

SIR PETER Heyday! what's the mystery now? While he appeared an incorrigible rake, you would give your hand to no one else; and now that he is likely to reform I'll warrant you won't have him!

MARIA His own heart and Lady Sneerwell know the cause.

CHARLES SURFACE Lady Sneerwell!

JOSEPH SURFACE Brother, it is with great concern I am obliged to speak on this point, but my regard to justice compels me, and Lady Sneerwell's injuries can no longer be concealed. (*opens the door*)

(*Enter* LADY SNEERWELL.)

SIR PETER So! another French milliner! Egad, he has one in every room in the house, I suppose!

LADY SNEERWELL Ungrateful Charles! Well may you be surprised, and feel for the indelicate situation your perfidy has forced me into.

CHARLES SURFACE Pray, uncle, is this another plot of yours? For, as I have life, I don't understand it.

JOSEPH SURFACE I believe, sir, there is but the evidence of one person more necessary to make it extremely clear.

SIR PETER And that person, I imagine, is Mr Snake—Rowley, you were perfectly right to bring him with us, and pray let him appear.

ROWLEY Walk in, Mr Snake.

(*Enter* SNAKE.)

I thought his testimony might be wanted: however, it happens unluckily, that he comes to confront Lady Sneerwell, not to support her.

LADY SNEERWELL A villain! Treacherous to me at last! Speak, fellow, have you too conspired against me?

SNAKE I beg your ladyship ten thousand pardons: you paid me extremely liberally for the lie in question; but I unfortunately have been offered double to speak the truth.

SIR PETER Plot and counter-plot, egad! I wish your ladyship joy of your negociation.

LADY SNEERWELL The torments of shame and disappointment on you all! (*going*)

LADY TEAZLE Hold, Lady Sneerwell—before you go, let me thank you for the trouble you and that gentleman have taken, in writing letters from me to Charles, and answering them yourself; and let me also request you to make my respects to the scandalous college of which you are president, and inform them that Lady Teazle, licentiate, begs leave to return the diploma they granted her, as she leaves off practice, and kills characters no longer.

LADY SNEERWELL You too, madam!—provoking—insolent! May your husband live these fifty years! (*Exit.*)

SIR PETER Oons! what a fury!

LADY TEAZLE A malicious creature, indeed!

SIR PETER What! not for her last wish?

LADY TEAZLE Oh, no!

SIR OLIVER Well, sir, and what have you to say now?

JOSEPH SURFACE Sir, I am so confounded, to find that Lady Sneerwell could be guilty of suborning Mr Snake in this manner, to impose on us all, that I know not what to say: however, lest her revengeful spirit should prompt her to injure my brother, I had certainly better follow her directly. For the man who attempts to— (*Exit.*)

SIR PETER Moral to the last!

SIR OLIVER Ay, and marry her, Joseph, if you can. Oil and vinegar!—egad you'll do very well together.

ROWLEY I believe we have no more occasion for Mr Snake at present?

SNAKE Before I go, I beg pardon once for all, for whatever uneasiness I have been the humble instrument of causing to the parties present.

SIR PETER Well, well, you have made atonement by a good deed at last.

SNAKE But I must request of the company, that it shall never be known.

SIR PETER Hey! what the plague! are you ashamed of having done a right thing once in your life?

SNAKE Ah, sir, consider—I live by the badness of my character; and, if it were once known that I had been betrayed into an honest action, I should lose every friend I have in the world.

SIR OLIVER Well, well—we'll not traduce you by saying any thing in your praise, never fear. (*Exit* SNAKE.)

SIR PETER There's a precious rogue!

LADY TEAZLE See, Sir Oliver, there needs no persuasion now to reconcile your nephew and Maria.

SIR OLIVER Ay, ay, that's as it should be, and, egad, we'll have the wedding tomorrow morning.

CHARLES SURFACE Thank you, dear uncle.

SIR PETER What, you rogue! don't you ask the girl's consent first?

CHARLES SURFACE Oh, I have done that a long time—a minute ago—and she has looked yes.

MARIA For shame, Charles!—I protest, Sir Peter, there has not been a word—

SIR OLIVER Well, then, the fewer the better; may your love for each other never know abatement.

SIR PETER And may you live as happily together as Lady Teazle and I intend to do!

CHARLES SURFACE Rowley, my old friend, I am sure you congratulate me; and I suspect that I owe you much.

SIR OLIVER You do, indeed, Charles.

SIR PETER Ay, honest Rowley always said you would reform.

CHARLES SURFACE Why, as to reforming, Sir Peter, I'll make no promises, and that I take to be a proof that I intend to set about it. But here shall be my monitor—my gentle guide.—

Ah! can I leave the virtuous path those eyes illumine?
Though thou, dear maid, shouldst waive thy beauty's sway,
Thou still must rule, because I will obey:
An humble fugitive from Folly view,
No sanctuary near but Love and you:

(*to the audience*)

You can, indeed, each anxious fear remove,
For even Scandal dies, if you approve.

(*Exeunt omnes.*)

Epilogue

By Mr. Colman

SPOKEN BY LADY TEAZLE

I, who was late so volatile and gay,
Like a trade-wind must now blow all one way,
Bend all my cares, my studies, and my vows,
To one dull rusty weathercock—my spouse!
So wills our virtuous bard—the motley Bayes
Of crying epilogues and laughing plays!
Old bachelors, who marry smart young wives,
Learn from our play to regulate your lives:
Each bring his dear to town, all faults upon her—
London will prove the very source of honour.
Plunged fairly in, like a cold bath it serves,
When principles relax, to brace the nerves:
Such is my case; and yet I must deplore
That the gay dream of dissipation 's o'er.

And say, ye fair! was ever lively wife,
Born with a genius for the highest life,
Like me untimely blasted in her bloom,
Like me condemn'd to such a dismal doom?
Save money—when I just knew how to waste it!
Leave London—just as I began to taste it!
  Must I then watch the early crowing cock,
The melancholy ticking of a clock;
In a lone rustic hall for ever pounded,
With dogs, cats, rats, and squalling brats surrounded.
With humble curate can I now retire,
(While good Sir Peter boozes with the squire)
And at backgammon mortify my soul,
That pants for loo, or flutters at a vole?
Seven's the main! Dear sound that must expire.
Lost at hot cockles round a Christmas fire;
The transient hour of fashion too soon spent,
Farewell the tranquil mind, farewell content!
Farewell the plumèd head, the cushioned tête,
That takes the cushion from its proper seat!
That spirit-stirring drum!—card drums I mean,
Spadille—odd trick—pam—basto—king and queen!
And you, ye knockers, that, with brazen throat,
The welcome visitors' approach denote;
Farewell all quality of high renown,
Pride, pomp, and circumstance of glorious town!
Farewell! your revels I partake no more,
And Lady Teazle's occupation 's o'er!
All this I told our bard; he smiled, and said 'twas clear,
I ought to play deep tragedy next year.
Meanwhile he drew wise morals from his play,
And in these solemn periods stalked away:—
"Blessed were the fair like you; her faults who stopped
And closed her follies when the curtain dropped!
No more in vice or error to engage,
Or play the fool at large on life's great stage."

A DOLL'S HOUSE

(1879)

HENRIK IBSEN (1828–1906)

The Continental theatre of the seventeenth and eighteenth centuries, aside from the "great age" of the French drama of Corneille, Molière, and Racine, has left a limited heritage with nothing to rival what took place during the same period in England. In France comedies were mostly poor imitations of Molière and tragedies were still mired in neoclassicism. The most familiar name is Voltaire (François Marie Arouet) (1694–1778), among whose many plays *Zaire* (1732) is perhaps the best known. The two plays of Pierre-Augustus Beaumarchais (1732–1799), *Le Barbier de Séville* (1775) and *Le Mariage de Figaro* (1781), while deservedly popular in their own right, have achieved their classic proportions in the operas by Rossini and Mozart.

We must leap well into the nineteenth century to find names of lasting significance, and two of them endure more as novelists than as playwrights. Thoroughly tired of the traditional classicism that was suffocating serious French drama, Victor Hugo (1802–1885) fired his first salvo against it in his "Preface to *Cromwell*" in 1827, a proclamation of the tenets of dramatic romanticism. In 1830 he literally blasted the classic concepts to bits in *Hernani.* Its romantic melodramatics, replete with intrigues plotted in dark caves at night, mysterious veiled figures flitting in and out of hidden recesses, a raging storm, heroic deeds accompanied by dialogue of equally heroic proportions, love and honor in the extreme, and the hero's sacrifice of his own life on principle, shattered the tragic unities and all that they implied. The result on opening night was a riot inside the theatre between the die-hard classicists and the upstart romantics, neither giving quarter. Alexandre Dumas, père (1803–1870) with *Antony* (1831) was likewise in the romantic tradition, but Dumas, fils (1824–1895) surpassed his father and most of the romantic dramatists with the story of Marguerite Gautier, the doomed courtesan redeemed by love, in *La Dame aux caméllias* in 1852, now almost universally known in the English theatre as *Camille.* As the basis of Verdi's perennial operatic favorite, *La Traviata,* it has endured, but it has been permanently impressed on public memory by Greta Garbo's unforgettable film version of 1936.

Two names from nineteenth-century French drama stand out, not for the quality of what they created but for how they did it. The first was Eugène Scribe (1791–1861) and the second was Victorien Sardou (1831–1908). Except for Sardou's *La Tosca* (1887), which survives in Puccini's 1900 opera, almost nothing of their output is remembered today. Writing to please the tastes of the growing middle-class audience seeking simple entertainment, concerned with little but popular success, they built their prodigious output (Sardou wrote, singly or in collaboration, over 400 plays) around a predictable pattern that has ever since exerted an influence far out of proportion to its negligible literary merit: the "well-made play." Action rose and fell from exposition through complications and climax to easily anticipated denouement that pulled everything neatly together as uniformly as a bell curve on a graph. Unimaginative characters moved through unsophisticated stories of everyday life, and, with names and places altered, everything was as interchangeable as manufactured precision parts, which, in effect, they were, the successful product of a thoroughly superficial theatrical craftsmanship. The formula for the well-made play has never really disappeared, as the cops and robbers, cowboys (or cavalry) and Indians, boy-meets-loses-gets-girl routines of stock motion picture and television shows will readily attest.

The Italian theatre remained in the doldrums of the classical unities, producing only two dramatists with any recognition today—Vittorio Alfieri (1749–1803) in tragedy und Carlo Goldoni (1707–1793) in comedy. Johann Wolfgang Goethe (1749–1832) brought German drama to prominence, writing in the tradition of *Sturm und Drang*—storm and stress—a movement of eighteenth-century German literature dwelling on the more violent and stressful aspects of romanticism. His *Egmont* of 1789 is recalled mainly by Beethoven's overture, but the two parts of *Faust,* the first appearing in 1801 and the second after the author's death in 1832, have firmly established Goethe as one of the nineteenth century's greatest continental dramatists. The tale of the aging philosopher who sells himself to the Devil for youth, wealth, and sex is a permanent part of the human legend. In one or both parts it can hold an audience in fascinated horror, a truly thrilling dramatic piece. Gounod's lyrical opera of 1859 has remained a favorite in the major houses of the world.

Goethe's contemporary, Friedrich Schiller (1754–1805), is also one of the most well known of the German dramatists. Two of his romantic tragedies play fast and loose with history as *Maria Stuart* (1800) inserts a tensely dramatic face-to-face meeting between Mary of Scotland and Elizabeth of England, an event which, of course, never occurred, and *Die Jungfrau von Orleans* (1801) sends Joan of Arc to her death not as a martyr at the stake but in battle. *Wilhelm Tell* (1804) maintains its fame through Rossini's overture to his 1829 opera.[1]

[1]It is difficult to avoid discussion of the very personification of everything in nineteenth-century German theatre without mention of Richard Wagner (1813–1883), but his importance lies in opera. His librettos, however, which he wrote himself for all of his operas, retain considerable merit.

Beginning in the late eighteenth century, the most notable trend of European drama was toward bourgeois, or middle-class, drama. As theatres rapidly multiplied, the classic repertoire carried limited appeal to the man or woman in the street. The romanticism of Jean-Jacques Rousseau (1712–1778), which held that people are inherently good and devoid of the evils of original sin (an important contribution to the "Enlightenment" or "Age of Reason" rapidly taking hold in the middle of the eighteenth century), was paralleled by the humanism and antimonarchial republicanism of Denis Diderot (1713–1784). The bloody French Revolution of 1789 with its cry of Liberté, Egalité, Fraternité, preceded by the remarkable success of the American Revolution of 1775–1781, ushered in the "era of the common man." Topics of contemporary social concern—business practices, justice, equality (or inequality) of the sexes, exploitation of the poor and of children—so vivid in the popular novels of Charles Dickens in England, provided the subject matter of popular dramatic entertainment. In other words, European drama was encountering the beginnings of an entirely new form: realism.

The turn toward the best of dramatic realism came from a most unlikely and previously unnoted part of Europe—Scandinavia. In the last quarter of the nineteenth century, attention turned north to the theatres of Oslo, Bergen, and Stockholm, to the Norwegian realist Henrik Ibsen and the Swedish naturalist August Strindberg. Their impact was profound and their influence into the twentieth century permanent.

Strindberg, who lived from 1849 to 1912, wrote some of the most powerful naturalistic plays, which centered on the deadly jungle battle of the sexes. The misogynist playwright created a frightening image of emasculating females and their helpless male victims, first in *The Father* (1887), with its coldly-cruel wife who drives her intellectual husband into madness by raising the question of their daughter's paternity. It was followed by *Miss Julie* (1888), a chilling two-scene study of sexual aggression, seduction, and death involving the arrogant aristocratic Julie and her father's subservient but virile valet and *The Dance of Death* (1901), an almost macabre portrayal of the deadly battle that is marriage.

It is Henrik Ibsen, however, who is widely regarded as the "father" of modern drama because of his highly realistic plays devoted to the contemporary political and social problems of the 1870s and 1880s. He did not begin his long career as dramatist and man of the theatre in the realistic tradition. At first he stayed with history, including poetic Norse sagas, while simultaneously working in various theatrical managerial capacities. He was always deeply interested in Norwegian politics and social conditions, although he spent a considerable amount of time abroad, where his first major work, the poetic and mystical *Brand*, was written in 1865. It was a look into the psychology of the questioning minister of the play's title who was driven to seek but was unable to find the answers to questions about the nature of truth. His last poetic play, *Peer Gynt* (1867), which traces the loss of the ne'er-do-well hero's soul through a series of fantastic scenes of witchcraft, trolls, and magic, accompanied by Grieg's famous incidental music, has remained permanently challenging to those who would revive it.

Abandoning these more exotic forms, Ibsen turned to the style and theme with which we now commonly associate him—dramatic realism, beginning with *Pillars of Society* (1877), a close look at the lies upon which public life is often based. But it was *A Doll's House* that fired the dramatic shot heard round the world, in which he sent the young wife, Nora, out into the Norwegian cold, slamming the door on home and children as she broke with the social forces that had kept her a plaything in her husband's house.

Ibsen has frequently been regarded as the first writer to espouse seriously the "liberation" of women. The haughty frigid heroine of *Hedda Gabler* (1890) can be seen as one who, because of her sex, has been denied the ability to become other than a beautiful fixture in the gloomy mansion of her doltish husband. She has thus been driven into channels that divert her considerable energies toward the fatal domination of a particularly weak man and to the taking of her own life when she refuses to surrender to the sexual blackmail of a long-time acquaintance. *Rosmersholm* (1886), with its "liberated" woman whose conscience can permit her to live happily with a man out of wedlock, regardless of social mores, and *The Master Builder* (1892), with the free spirit of a woman who inspires a man literally to climb the heights of his final creation, from which he falls to his death, can be regarded as exposing a narrow-minded society as the perpetrator of major offenses against women, but such interpretations must be held within limits.

Ibsen was not so much an advocate of women's lib in the general sense of the term today as he was a strong advocate of the right of individuals, irrespective of sex, to assert their own human dignity and integrity as persons, regardless of the forces that society brought to bear on them to hold their lives to the established patterns of morality.

Thus it would probably be a misinterpretation of *A Doll's House* to regard it as a polemic that advocates freeing women in general from the bonds of social deprivation and injustice, or of summarily releasing them from the confining restrictions of their domestic and conjugal obligations. It is, however, the first widely recognized and acclaimed "problem play," with which Ibsen was to be firmly identified during the rest of his career. Although a problem, or conflict (Aristotle's *agon*), has been acknowledged as essential to the development of any dramatic work, rather than acting as mere catalyst or motivating factor, the problem now becomes central, and its exploration and analysis within the framework of the existing society, though not necessarily its resolution, become the dramatist's primary consideration.

To be sure, Nora, at first, is unaware of her problem, and she accepts with apparent contentment her identity as "bustling squirrel," surreptitiously eating forbidden macaroons and twittering about, a "little songbird" whom her husband plainly regards as a featherhead. Her role as helpmate, charming little mother, and dainty dancing figure is expected by those around her and practiced to the full by Nora herself. True, she has, in the past, acted with indiscretion to save her husband's life, but then, should not any devoted spouse risk life and limb to preserve the well-being of the man she has sworn to love, honor, and, no doubt, obey?

Nora's ultimate realization of what she represents in an unthinking, male-dominated society brings into sharp focus the problem that she, and many like her, must face: how to establish one's own identity and live with self-respect intact when confronted with sinister threats from the outside and a totally uncomprehending, self-centered husband who cannot see beyond his own narrow personal concerns, blind to the sacrifices offered on his behalf.

Nora's decision to abandon home, husband, and children might be seen as a sudden and irresponsible act, but one cannot condemn her in the face of Helmer's almost incredibly stupid reaction to what she has done and what she now confronts. Although the world, at the time, may have shuddered at the impact of that door slam, Nora's determination to cease playing her doll's role and to assert herself has long since vindicated her. Regardless of what she may have to endure outside the "comfort" of her toy house (Ibsen himself refused to speculate as to Nora's fate), we must admire and praise her for her final awareness of the impossibility of her predicament and to support her in her firm assertion that she has a right to be herself, notwithstanding the consequences that society may wish to force upon her.

A Doll's House — HENRIK IBSEN

A translation by Otto Reinert

CHARACTERS

TORVALD HELMER, *a lawyer*
NORA, *his wife*
DR. RANK
MRS. LINDE
KROGSTAD
THE HELMERS' THREE SMALL CHILDREN
ANNE-MARIE, *the children's nurse*
A HOUSEMAID
A PORTER

SCENE. *The Helmers' living room.*

Act I

A pleasantly, tastefully but not expensively furnished, living room. A door on the rear wall, right, leads to the front hall, another door, left, to HELMER*'s study. Between the two doors a piano. A third door in the middle of the left wall; further front a window. Near the window a round table and a small couch. Towards the rear of the right wall a fourth door; further front a tile stove with a rocking chair and a couple of armchairs in front of it. Between the stove and the door a small table. Copperplate etchings on the walls. A whatnot with porcelain figurines and other small objects. A small bookcase with de luxe editions. A rug on the floor; fire in the stove. Winter day.*

The doorbell rings, then the sound of the front door opening. NORA, *dressed for outdoors, enters, humming cheerfully. She carries several packages, which she puts down on the table, right. She leaves the door to the front hall open; there a* PORTER *is seen holding a Christmas tree and a basket. He gives them to the* MAID *who has let them in.*

NORA Be sure to hide the Christmas tree, Helene. The children mustn't see it before tonight when we've trimmed it. (*opens her purse; to the* PORTER:) How much?

PORTER Fifty ore.

NORA Here's a crown. No, keep the change. (*The* PORTER *thanks her, leaves.* NORA *closes the door. She keeps laughing quietly to herself as she takes off her coat, etc. She takes a bag of macaroons from her pocket and eats a couple. She walks cautiously over to the door to the study and listens.*) Yes, he's home. (*resumes her humming, walks over to the table, right*)

HELMER (*in his study*) Is that my little lark twittering out there?

NORA (*opening some packages*) That's right.

HELMER My squirrel bustling about?

NORA Yes.

HELMER When did squirrel come home?

NORA Just now. (*puts the bag of macaroons back in her pocket, wipes her mouth*) Come out here, Torvald. I want to show you what I've bought.

HELMER I'm busy! (*After a little while he opens the door and looks in, pen in hand.*) Bought, eh? All that? So little wastrel has been throwing money around again?

NORA Oh but Torvald, this Christmas we can be a little extravagant, can't we? It's the first Christmas we don't have to scrimp.

HELMER I don't know about that. We certainly don't have money to waste.

NORA Yes, Torvald, we do. A little, anyway. Just a tiny little bit? Now that you're going to get that big salary and make lots and lots of money.

HELMER Starting at New Year's, yes. But payday isn't till the end of the quarter.

NORA That doesn't matter. We can always borrow.

HELMER Nora! (*goes over to her and playfully pulls her ear*) There you go being irresponsible again. Suppose I borrowed a thousand crowns today and you spent it all for Christmas and on New Year's Eve a tile hit me in the head and laid me out cold.

NORA (*putting her hand over his mouth*) I won't have you say such horrid things.

HELMER But suppose it happened. Then what?

NORA If it did, I wouldn't care whether we owed money or not.

HELMER But what about the people I borrowed from?

NORA Who cares about them! They are strangers.

HELMER Nora, Nora, you *are* a woman! No, really! You know how I feel about that. No debts! A home in debt isn't a free home, and if it isn't free it isn't beautiful. We've managed nicely so far, you and I, and that's the way we'll go on. It won't be for much longer.

NORA (*walks over toward the stove*) All right, Torvald. Whatever you say.

HELMER (*follows her*) Come, come, my little songbird mustn't droop her wings. What's this? Can't have a pouty squirrel in the house, you know. (*takes out his wallet*) Nora, what do you think I have here?

NORA (*turns around quickly*) Money!

HELMER Here. (*gives her some bills*) Don't you think I know Christmas is expensive?

NORA (*counting*) Ten—twenty—thirty—forty. Thank you, thank you, Torvald. This helps a lot.

HELMER I certainly hope so.

NORA It does, it does. But I want to show you what I got. It was cheap, too. Look. New clothes for Ivar. And a sword. And a horse and trumpet for Bob. And a doll and a little bed for Emmy. It isn't any good, but it wouldn't last, anyway. And here's some dress material and scarves for the maids. I feel bad about old Anne-Marie, though. She really should be getting much more.

HELMER And what's in here?

NORA (*cries*) Not till tonight!

HELMER I see. But now what does my little prodigal have in mind for herself?

NORA Oh, nothing. I really don't care.

HELMER Of course you do. Tell me what you'd like. Within reason.

NORA Oh, I don't know. Really, I don't. The only thing—

HELMER Well?

NORA (*fiddling with his buttons, without looking at him*) If you really want to give me something, you might—you could—

HELMER All right, let's have it.

NORA (*quickly*) Some money, Torvald. Just as much as you think you can spare. Then I'll buy myself something one of these days.

HELMER No, really Nora—

NORA Oh yes, please, Torvald. Please? I'll wrap the money in pretty gold paper and hang it on the tree. Won't that be nice?

HELMER What's the name for little birds that are always spending money?

NORA Wastrels, I know. But please let's do it my way, Torvald. Then I'll have time to decide what I need most. Now that's sensible, isn't it?

HELMER (*smiling*) Oh, very sensible. That is, if you really bought yourself something you could use. But it all disappears in the household expenses or you buy things you don't need. And then you come back to me for more.

NORA Oh, but Torvald—

HELMER That's the truth, dear little Nora, and you know it. (*puts his arm around her*) My wastrel is a little sweetheart, but she *does* go through an awful lot of money awfully fast. You've no idea how expensive it is for a man to keep a wastrel.

NORA That's not fair, Torvald. I really save all I can.

HELMER (*laughs*) Oh, I believe that. All you can. Meaning, exactly nothing!

NORA (*hums, smiles mysteriously*) You don't know all the things we songbirds and squirrels need money for, Torvald.

HELMER You know, you're funny. Just like your father. You're always looking for ways to get money, but as soon as you do it runs through your fingers and you can never say what you spent it for. Well, I guess I'll just have to take you the way you are. It's in your blood. Yes, that sort of thing is hereditary, Nora.

NORA In that case, I wish I had inherited many of Daddy's qualities.

HELMER And I don't want you any different from just what you are—my own sweet little songbird. Hey!—I think I just noticed something. Aren't you looking—what's the word?—a little—sly—?

NORA I am?

HELMER You definitely are. Look at me.

NORA (*looks at him*) Well?

HELMER (*wagging a finger*) Little sweet-tooth hasn't by any chance been on a rampage today, has she?

NORA Of course not. Whatever makes you think that?

HELMER A little detour by the pastryshop maybe?

NORA No, I assure you, Torvald—

HELMER Nibbled a little jam?

NORA Certainly not!

HELMER Munched a macaroon or two?

NORA No, really, Torvald, I honestly—

HELMER All right. Of course I was only joking.

NORA (*walks toward the table, right*) You know I wouldn't do anything to displease you.

HELMER I know. And I have your promise. (*over to her*) All right, keep your little Christmas secrets to yourself, Nora darling. They'll all come out tonight, I suppose, when we light the tree.

NORA Did you remember to invite Rank?

HELMER No, but there's no need to. He knows he'll have dinner with us. Anyway, I'll see him later this morning. I'll ask him then. I did order some good wine. Oh Nora, you've no idea how much I'm looking forward to tonight!

NORA Me, too. And the children Torvald! They'll have such a good time!

HELMER You know, it *is* nice to have a good, safe job and a comfortable income. Feels good just thinking about it. Don't you agree?

NORA Oh, it's wonderful!

HELMER Remember last Christmas? For three whole weeks you shut yourself up every evening till long after midnight making ornaments for the Christmas tree and I don't know what else. Some big surprise for all of us, anyway. I'll be damned if I've ever been so bored in my whole life!

NORA I wasn't bored at all!

HELMER (*smiling*) But you've got to admit you didn't have much to show for it in the end.

NORA Oh, don't tease me again about that! Could I help it that the cat got in and tore up everything?

HELMER Of course you couldn't, my poor little Nora. You just wanted to please the rest of us, and that's the important thing. But I *am* glad the hard times are behind us. Aren't you?

NORA Oh yes. I think it's just wonderful.

HELMER This year, I won't be bored and lonely. And you won't have to strain your dear eyes and your delicate little hands—

NORA (*claps her hands*) No I won't, will I Torvald? Oh, how wonderful, how lovely, to hear you say that! (*puts her arm under his*) Let me tell you how I think we should arrange things, Torvald. Soon as Christmas is over—(*The doorbell rings.*) Someone's at the door. (*straightens things up a bit*) A caller, I suppose. Bother!

HELMER Remember, I'm not home for visitors.

THE MAID (*in the door to the front hall*) Ma'am, there's a lady here—

NORA All right. Ask her to come in.

THE MAID (*to* HELMER) And the Doctor just arrived.

HELMER Is he in the study?

THE MAID Yes, sir.

(HELMER *exits into his study.* THE MAID *shows* MRS. LINDE *in and closes the door behind her as she leaves.* MRS. LINDE *is in travel dress.)*

MRS. LINDE (*timid and a little hesitant*) Good morning, Nora.

NORA (*uncertainly*) Good morning.

MRS. LINDE I don't believe you know who I am.

NORA No—I'm not sure—Though I know I should—Of course! Kristine! It's you!

MRS. LINDE Yes, it's me.

NORA And I didn't even recognize you! I had no idea. (*in a lower voice*) You've changed, Kristine.

MRS. LINDE I'm sure I have. It's been nine or ten long years.

NORA Has it really been that long? Yes, you're right. I've been so happy these last eight years. And now you're here. Such a long trip in the middle of winter. How brave!

MRS. LINDE I got in on the steamer this morning.

NORA To have some fun over the holidays, of course. That's lovely. For we are going to have fun. But take off your coat! You aren't cold, are you? (*helps her*) There, now! Let's sit down here by the fire and just relax and talk. No, you sit there. I want the rocking chair. (*takes her hands*) And now you've got your old face back. It was just for a minute, right at first—Though you are a little more pale, Kristine. And maybe a little thinner.

MRS. LINDE And much, much older, Nora.

NORA Maybe a little older. Just a teeny-weeny bit, not much. (*interrupts herself, serious*) Oh, but how thoughtless of me, chatting away like this! Sweet, good Kristine, can you forgive me?

MRS. LINDE Forgive you what, Nora?

NORA (*in a low voice*) You poor dear, you lost your husband, didn't you?

MRS. LINDE Three years ago, yes.

NORA I know. I saw it in the paper. Oh please believe me, Kristine. I really meant to write you, but I never got around to it. Something was always coming up.

MRS. LINDE Of course, Nora. I understand.

NORA No, that wasn't very nice of me. You poor thing, all you must have been through. And he didn't leave you much, either, did he?

MRS. LINDE No.

NORA And no children?

MRS. LINDE No.

NORA Nothing at all, in other words?

MRS. LINDE Not so much as a sense of loss—a grief to live on—

NORA (*incredulous*) But Kristine, how can that *be?*

MRS. LINDE (*with a sad smile, strokes* NORA*'s hair*) That's the way it sometimes is, Nora.

NORA All alone. How awful for you. I have three darling children. You can't see them right now, though; they're out with their nurse. But now you must tell me everything—

MRS. LINDE No, no; I'd rather listen to you.

NORA No, you begin. Today I won't be selfish. Today I'll think only of you. Except there's one thing I've just got to tell you first. Something marvelous that's happened to us just these last few days. You haven't heard, have you?

MRS. LINDE No; tell me.

NORA Just think. My husband's been made manager of the Mutual Bank.

MRS. LINDE Your husband—! Oh, I'm so glad!

NORA Yes, isn't that great? You see, private law practice is so uncertain, especially when you won't have anything to do with cases that aren't—you know—quite nice. And of course Torvald won't do that and I quite agree with him. Oh, you've no idea how delighted we are! He takes over at New Year's, and he'll be getting a big salary and all sorts of extras. From now on we'll be able to live in quite a different way—exactly as we like. Oh, Kristine! I feel so carefree and happy! It's lovely to have lots and lots of money and not have to worry about a thing! Don't you agree?

MRS. LINDE It would be nice to have enough at any rate.

NORA No, I don't mean just enough. I mean lots and lots!

MRS. LINDE (*smiles*) Nora, Nora, when are you going to be sensible? In school you spent a great deal of money.

NORA (*quietly laughing*) Yes, and Torvald says I still do. (*raises her finger at* MRS. LINDE) But "Nora, Nora" isn't so crazy as you all think. Believe me, we've had nothing to be extravagant with. We've both had to work.

MRS. LINDE You too?

NORA Yes. Oh, it's been little things, mostly—sewing, crocheting, embroidery—that sort of thing. (*casually*) And other things too. You know, of course, that Torvald left government service when we got married? There was no chance of promotion in his department, and of course he had to make more money than he had been making. So for the first few years he worked altogether too hard. He had to take jobs on the side and work night and day. It turned out to be too much for him. He became seriously ill. The doctors told him he needed to go south.

MRS. LINDE That's right; you spent a year in Italy, didn't you?

NORA Yes, we did. But you won't believe how hard it was to get away. Ivar had just been born. But of course we had to go. Oh, it was a wonderful trip. And it saved Torvald's life. But it took a lot of money, Kristine.

MRS. LINDE I'm sure it did.

NORA Twelve hundred specie dollars. Four thousand eight hundred crowns. That's a lot of money.

MRS. LINDE Yes. So it's lucky you have it when something like that happens.

NORA Well, actually we got the money from Daddy.

MRS. LINDE I see. That was about the time your father died, I believe.

NORA Yes, just about then. And I couldn't even go and take care of him. I was expecting little Ivar any day. And I had poor Torvald to look after, desperately sick and all. My dear, good Daddy! I never saw him again, Kristine. That's the saddest thing that's happened to me since I got married.

MRS. LINDE I know you were very fond of him. But then you went to Italy?

NORA Yes, for now we had the money, and the doctors urged us to go. So we left about a month later.

MRS. LINDE And when you came back your husband was well again?

NORA Healthy as a horse!

MRS. LINDE But—the doctor?

NORA What do you mean?

MRS. LINDE I thought the maid said it was the doctor, that gentleman who came the same time I did.

NORA Oh, that's Dr. Rank. He doesn't come as a doctor. He's our closest friend. He looks in at least once every day. No, Torvald hasn't been sick once since then. And the children are strong and healthy, too, and so am I. (*jumps up and claps her hands*) Oh God, Kristine! Isn't it wonderful to be alive and happy! Isn't it just lovely!—But now I'm being mean again, talking only about myself and my things. (*sits down on a footstool close to* MRS. LINDE *and puts her arm on her lap*) Please don't be angry with me! Tell me, is it really true that you didn't care for your husband? Then why did you marry him?

MRS. LINDE Mother was still alive then, but she was bedridden and helpless. And I had my two younger brothers to look after. I didn't think I had the right to turn him down.

NORA No, I suppose not. So he had money then?

MRS. LINDE He was quite well off, I think. But it was an uncertain business, Nora. When he died, the whole thing collapsed and there was nothing left.

NORA And then—?

MRS. LINDE Well, I had to manage as best I could. With a little store and a little school and anything else I could think of. The last three years have been one long work day for me, Nora, without any rest. But now it's over. My poor mother doesn't need me any more. She's passed away. And the boys are on their own too. They've both got jobs and support themselves.

NORA What a relief for you—

MRS. LINDE No, not relief. Just a great emptiness. Nobody to live for any more. (*gets up restlessly*) That's why I couldn't stand it any longer in that little hole. Here in town it has to be easier to find something to keep me busy and occupy my thoughts. With a little luck I should be able to find a permanent job, something in an office—

NORA Oh but Kristine, that's exhausting work, and you look worn out already. It would be much better for you to go to a resort.

MRS. LINDE (*walks over to the window*) I don't have a Daddy who can give me the money, Nora.

NORA (*getting up*) Oh, don't be angry with me.

MRS. LINDE (*over to her*) Dear Nora, don't *you* be angry with *me*. That's the worst thing about my kind of situation: you become so bitter. You've nobody to work for, and yet you have to look out for yourself, somehow. You've got to keep on living, and so you become selfish. Do you know—when you told me about your husband's new position I was delighted not so much for your sake as for my own.

NORA Why was that? Oh, I see. You think maybe Torvald can give you a job?

MRS. LINDE That's what I had in mind.

NORA And he will too, Kristine. Just leave it to me. I'll be ever so subtle about it. I'll think of something nice to tell him, something he'll like. Oh I so much want to help you.

MRS. LINDE That's very good of you, Nora—making an effort like that for me. Especially since you've known so little trouble and hardship in your own life.

NORA I—?—have known so little—?

MRS. LINDE (*smiling*) Oh well, a little sewing or whatever it was. You're still a child, Nora.

NORA (*with a toss of her head, walks away*) You shouldn't sound so superior.

MRS. LINDE I shouldn't?

NORA You're just like all the others. None of you think I'm good for anything really serious.

MRS. LINDE Well, now—

NORA That I've never been through anything difficult.

MRS. LINDE But Nora! You just told me all your troubles!

NORA That's nothing! (*lowers her voice*) I haven't told you about *it*.

MRS. LINDE It? What's that? What do you mean?

NORA You patronize me, Kristine, and that's not fair. You're proud that you worked so long and so hard for your mother.

MRS. LINDE I don't think I patronize anyone. But it *is* true that I'm both proud and happy that I could make mother's last years comparatively easy.

NORA And you're proud of all you did for your brothers.

MRS. LINDE I think I have the right to be.

NORA And so do I. But now I want to tell you something, Kristine. I have something to be proud and happy about too.

MRS. LINDE I don't doubt that for a moment. But what exactly do you mean?

NORA Not so loud! Torvald mustn't hear—not for anything in the world. Nobody must know about this, Kristine. Nobody but you.

MRS. LINDE But what is it?

NORA Come here. (*pulls her down on the couch beside her*) You see, I *do* have something to be proud and happy about. I've saved Torvald's life.

MRS. LINDE Saved—? how do you mean—"saved"?

NORA I told you about our trip to Italy. Torvald would have died if he hadn't gone.

MRS. LINDE I understand that. And so your father gave you the money you needed.

NORA (*smiles*) Yes, that's what Torvald and all the others think. But—

MRS. LINDE But what?

NORA Daddy didn't give us a penny. *I* raised that money.

MRS. LINDE *You* did? That whole big amount?

NORA Twelve hundred specie dollars. Four thousand eight hundred crowns. *Now* what do you say?

MRS. LINDE But Nora, how could you? Did you win in the state lottery?

NORA (*contemptuously*) State lottery! (*snorts*) What is so great about that?

MRS. LINDE Where did it come from then?

NORA (*humming and smiling, enjoying her secret*) Hmmm. Tra-la-la-la-la!

MRS. LINDE You certainly couldn't have borrowed it.

NORA Oh? And why not?

MRS. LINDE A wife can't borrow money without her husband's consent.

NORA (*with a toss of her head*) Oh, I don't know—take a wife with a little bit of a head for business—a wife who knows how to manage things—

MRS. LINDE But Nora, I don't understand at all—

NORA You don't have to. I didn't say I borrowed the money, did I? I could have gotten it some other way. (*leans back*) An admirer may have given it to me. When you're as tolerably good-looking as I am—

MRS. LINDE Oh, you're crazy.

NORA I think you're dying from curiosity, Kristine.

MRS. LINDE I'm beginning to think you've done something very foolish, Nora.

NORA (*sits up*) Is it foolish to save your husband's life?

MRS. LINDE I say it's foolish to act behind his back.

NORA But don't you see: he couldn't be told! You're missing the whole point, Kristine. We couldn't even let him know how seriously ill he was. The doctors came to *me* and told me his life was in danger, that nothing could save him but a stay in the south. Don't you think I tried to work on him? I told him how lovely it would be if I could go abroad like other young wives. I cried and begged. I said he'd better remember what condition I was in, that he had to be nice to me and do what I wanted. I even hinted he could borrow the money. But that almost made him angry with me. He told me I was being irresponsible and that it was his duty as my husband not to give in to my moods and whims—I think that's what he called it. All right, I said to myself, you've got to be saved somehow, and so I found a way—

MRS. LINDE And your husband never learned from your father that the money didn't come from him?

NORA Never. Daddy died that same week. I thought of telling him all about it and ask him not to say anything. But since he was so sick—It turned out I didn't have to—

MRS. LINDE And you've never told your husband?

NORA Of course not! Good heavens, how could I? He, with his strict principles! Besides, you know how men are. Torvald would find it embarrassing and humiliating to learn that he owed me anything. It would upset our whole relationship. Our happy, beautiful home would no longer be what it is.

MRS. LINDE Aren't you ever going to tell him?

NORA (*reflectively, half smiling*) Yes—one day, maybe. Many, many years from now, when I'm no longer young and pretty. Don't laugh! I mean when Torvald no longer feels about me the way he does now, when he no longer thinks it's fun when I dance for him and put on costumes and recite for him. Then it will be good to have something in reserve—(*interrupts herself*) Oh, I'm just being silly! That day will never come.—Well, now, Kristine, what do you think of my great secret? Don't you think I'm good for something too?—By the way, you wouldn't believe all the worry I've had because of it. It's been very hard to meet my obligations on schedule. You see, in business there's something called quarterly interest and something called installments on the principal, and those are terribly hard to come up with. I've had to save a little here and a little there, whenever I could. I couldn't use much of the housekeeping money, for Torvald has to eat well. And I couldn't use what I got for clothes for the children. They have to look nice, and I didn't think it would be right to spend less than I got—the sweet little things!

MRS. LINDE Poor Nora! So you had to take it from your own allowance!

NORA Yes, of course. After all, it was my affair. Every time Torvald gave me money for a new dress and things like that, I never used more than half of it. I always bought the cheapest, simplest things for myself. Thank God, everything looks good on me, so Torvald never noticed. But it was hard many times, Kristine, for it's fun to have pretty clothes. Don't you think?

MRS. LINDE Certainly.

NORA Anyway, I had other ways of making money too. Last winter I was lucky enough to get some copying work. So I locked the door and sat up writing every night till quite late. God! I often got so tired—! But it was great fun, too, working and making money. It was almost like being a man.

MRS. LINDE But how much have you been able to pay off this way?

NORA I couldn't tell you exactly. You see, it's very difficult to keep track of business like that. All I know is I have been paying off as much as I've been able to scrape together. Many times I just didn't know what to do. (*smiles*) Then I used to imagine a rich old gentleman had fallen in love with me—

MRS. LINDE What! What old gentleman?

NORA Phooey! And now he was dead and they were reading his will, and there it said in big letters, "All my money is to be paid in cash immediately to the charming Mrs. Nora Helmer."

MRS. LINDE But dearest Nora—who *was* this old gentleman?

NORA For heaven's sake, Kristine, don't you see? There *was* no old gentleman. He was just somebody I made up when I couldn't think of any way to raise the money. But never mind him. The old bore can be anyone he likes to for all I care. I have no use for him or his last will, for now I don't have a single worry in the world. (*jumps up*) Dear God, what a lovely thought this is! To be able to play and have fun with the children, to have everything nice and pretty in the house, just the way Torvald likes it! Not a care! And soon spring will be here, and the air will be blue and high. Maybe we can travel again. Maybe I'll see the ocean again! Oh, yes, yes!—it's wonderful to be alive and happy!

(*The doorbell rings.*)

MRS. LINDE (*getting up*) There's the doorbell. Maybe I better be going.

NORA No, please stay. I'm sure it's just someone for Torvald—

THE MAID (*in the hall door*) Excuse me, ma'am. There's a gentleman here who'd like to see Mr. Helmer.

NORA You mean the bank manager.

THE MAID Sorry, ma'am; the bank manager. But I didn't know—since the Doctor is with him—

NORA Who is the gentleman?

KROGSTAD (*appearing in the door*) It's just me, Mrs. Helmer.

(MRS. LINDE *starts, looks, turns away toward the window.*)

NORA (*takes a step toward him, tense, in a low voice*) You? What do you want? What do you want with my husband?

KROGSTAD Bank business—in a way. I have a small job in the Mutual, and I understand your husband is going to be our new boss—

NORA So, it's just—

KROGSTAD Just routine business, ma'am. Nothing else.

NORA All right. In that case, why don't you go through the door to the office.

(*Dismisses him casually as she closes the door. Walks over to the stove and tends the fire.*)

MRS. LINDE Nora—who was that man?

NORA His name's Krogstad. He's a lawyer.

MRS. LINDE So it *was* him.

NORA Do you know him?

MRS. LINDE I used to—many years ago. For a while he clerked in our part of the country.

NORA Right. He did.

MRS. LINDE He has changed a great deal.

NORA I believe he had a very unhappy marriage.

MRS. LINDE And now he's a widower, isn't he?

NORA With many children. There now; it's burning nicely again. (*closes the stove and moves the rocking chair a little to the side*)

MRS. LINDE They say he's into all sorts of business.

NORA Really? Maybe so. I wouldn't know. But let's not think about business. It's such a bore.

DR. RANK (*appears in the door to* HELMER*'s study*) No. I don't want to be in the way. I'd rather talk to your wife a bit. (*closes the door and notices* MRS. LINDE) Oh, I beg your pardon. I believe I'm in the way here too.

NORA No, not at all. (*introduces them*) Dr. Rank. Mrs. Linde.

RANK Aha. A name often heard in this house. I believe I passed you on the stairs coming up.

MRS. LINDE Yes. I'm afraid I climb stairs very slowly. They aren't good for me.

RANK I see. A slight case of inner decay, perhaps?

MRS. LINDE Overwork, rather.

RANK Oh, is that all? And now you've come to town to relax at all the parties?

MRS. LINDE I have come to look for a job.

RANK A proven cure for overwork, I take it?

MRS. LINDE One has to live, Doctor.

RANK Yes, that seems to be the common opinion.

NORA Come on, Dr. Rank—you want to live just as much as the rest of us.

RANK Of course I do. Miserable as I am, I prefer to go on being tortured as long as possible. All my patients feel the same way. And that's true of the moral invalids too. Helmer is talking with a specimen right this minute.

MRS. LINDE (*in a low voice*) Ah!

NORA What do you mean?

RANK Oh, this lawyer, Krogstad. You don't know him. The roots of his character are decayed. But even he began by saying something about having *to live*—as if it were a matter of the highest importance.

NORA Oh? What did he want with Torvald?

RANK I don't really know. All I heard was something about the bank.

NORA I didn't know that Krog—that this Krogstad had anything to do with the Mutual Bank.

RANK Yes, he seems to have some kind of job there. (*to* MRS. LINDE) I don't know if you are familiar in your part of the country with the kind of person who is always running around trying to sniff out cases of moral decrepitude and as soon as he finds one puts the individual under observation in some excellent position or other. All the healthy ones are left out in the cold.

MRS. LINDE I should think it's the sick who need looking after the most.

RANK (*shrugs his shoulders*) There we are. That's the attitude that turns society into a hospital.

(NORA, *absorbed in her own thoughts, suddenly starts giggling and clapping her hands.*)

RANK What's so funny about that? Do you even know what society is?

NORA What do I care about your stupid society! I laughed at something entirely different—something terribly amusing. Tell me, Dr. Rank—all the employees in the Mutual Bank, from now on they'll all be dependent on Torvald, right?

RANK Is that what you find so enormously amusing?

NORA (*smiles and hums*) That's my business, that's my business! (*walks around*) Yes, I do think it's fun that we—that Torvald is going to have so much influence on so many people's lives. (*brings out the bag of macaroons*) Have a macaroon, Dr. Rank.

RANK Well, well—macaroons. I thought they were banned around here.

NORA Yes, but these were some that Kristine gave me.

MRS. LINDE What! I?

NORA That's all right. Don't look so scared. You couldn't know that Torvald won't let me have them. He's afraid they'll ruin my teeth. But who cares! Just once in a while—! Right, Dr. Rank? Have one! (*puts a macaroon into his mouth*) You too, Kristine. And one for me. A very small one. Or at most two. (*walks around again*) Yes, I really feel very, very happy. Now there's just one thing I'm dying to do.

RANK Oh, and what's that?

NORA Something I'm dying to say so Torvald could hear.

RANK And why can't you?

NORA I don't dare to, for it's not nice.

MRS. LINDE Not nice?

RANK In that case, I guess you'd better not. But surely to the two of us—? What is it you'd like to say for Helmer to hear?

NORA I want to say, "Goddammit!"

RANK Are you out of your mind!

MRS. LINDE For heaven's sake, Nora!

RANK Say it. Here he comes.

NORA (*hiding the macaroons*) Shhh!

(HELMER *enters from his study, carrying his hat and overcoat.*)

NORA (*going to him*) Well, dear, did you get rid of him?

HELMER Yes, he just left.

NORA Torvald, I want you to meet Kristine. She's just come to town.

HELMER Kristine—? I'm sorry; I don't think—

NORA Mrs. Linde, Torvald dear. Mrs. Kristine Linde.

HELMER Ah, yes. A childhood friend of my wife's, I suppose.

MRS. LINDE Yes, we've known each other for a long time.

NORA Just think; she has come all this way just to see you.

HELMER I'm not sure I understand—

MRS. LINDE Well, not really—

NORA You see, Kristine is an absolutely fantastic secretary, and she would so much like to work for a competent executive and learn more than she knows already—

HELMER Very sensible, I'm sure, Mrs. Linde.

NORA So when she heard about your appointment—there was a wire—she came here as fast as she could. How about it, Torvald? Couldn't you do something for Kristine? For my sake. Please?

HELMER Quite possibly. I take it you're a widow, Mrs. Linde?

MRS. LINDE Yes.

HELMER And you've had office experience?

MRS. LINDE Some—yes.

HELMER In that case I think it's quite likely that I'll be able to find you a position.

NORA (*claps her hands*) I knew it! I knew it!

HELMER You've arrived at a most opportune time, Mrs. Linde.

MRS. LINDE Oh, how can I ever thank you—

HELMER Not at all, not at all. (*puts his coat on*) But today you'll have to excuse me—

RANK Wait a minute; I'll come with you. (*gets his fur coat from the front hall, warms it by the stove*)

NORA Don't be long, Torvald.

HELMER An hour or so; no more.

NORA Are you leaving, too, Kristine?

MRS. LINDE (*putting on her things*) Yes, I'd better go and find a place to stay.

HELMER Good. Then we'll be going the same way.

NORA (*helping her*) I'm sorry this place is so small, but I don't think we very well could—

MRS. LINDE Of course! Don't be silly, Nora. Goodbye, and thank you for everything.

NORA Goodbye. We'll see you soon. You'll be back this evening, of course. And you too, Dr. Rank; right? If you feel well enough? Of course you will. Just wrap yourself up.

(*General small talk as all exit into the hall. Children's voices are heard on the stairs.*)

NORA There they are! There they are! (*She runs and opens the door. The nurse* ANNE-MARIE *enters with the children.*)

NORA Come in! Come in! (*bends over and kisses them*) Oh, you sweet, sweet darlings! Look at them, Kristine! Aren't they beautiful?

RANK No standing around in the draft!

HELMER Come along, Mrs. Linde. This place isn't fit for anyone but mothers right now.

(DR. RANK, HELMER, *and* MRS. LINDE *go down the stairs. The* NURSE *enters the living room with the children.* NORA *follows, closing the door behind her.*)

NORA My, how nice you all look! Such red cheeks! Like apples and roses. (*The children all talk at the same time.*) You've had so much fun? I bet you have.

Oh, isn't that nice! You pulled both Emmy and Bob on your sleigh? Both at the same time? That's very good, Ivar. Oh, let me hold her for a minute, Anne-Marie. My sweet little doll baby! (*takes the smallest of the children from the* NURSE *and dances with her*) Yes, yes, of course; Mama'll dance with you too, Bob. What? You threw snowballs? Oh, I wish I'd been there! No, no; *I* want to take their clothes off, Anne-Marie. Please let me; I think it's so much fun. You go on in. You look frozen. There's hot coffee on the stove.

(*The* NURSE *exits into the room to the left.* NORA *takes the children's wraps off and throws them all around. They all keep telling her things at the same time.*)

NORA Oh, really? A big dog ran after you? But it didn't bite you. Of course not. Dogs don't bite sweet little doll babies. Don't peek at the packages, Ivar! What's in them? Wouldn't you like to know! No, no; that's something terrible! Play? You want to play? What do you want to play? Okay, let's play hide-and-seek. Bob hides first. You want *me* to? All right. I'll go first.

(*Laughing and shouting,* NORA *and the children play in the living room and in the adjacent room, right. Finally,* NORA *hides herself under the table; the children rush in, look for her, can't find her. They hear her low giggle, run to the table, lift the rug that covers it, see her. General hilarity. She crawls out, pretends to scare them. New delight. In the meantime there has been a knock on the door between the living room and the front hall, but nobody has noticed. Now the door is opened halfway.* KROGSTAD *appears. He waits a little. The play goes on.*)

KROGSTAD Pardon me, Mrs. Helmer—

NORA (*with a muted cry turns around, jumps up*) Ah! What do you want?

KROGSTAD I'm sorry. The front door was open. Somebody must have forgotten to close it—

NORA (*standing up*) My husband isn't here, Mr. Krogstad.

KROGSTAD I know.

NORA So what do you want?

KROGSTAD I'd like a word with you.

NORA With—? (*to the children*) Go in to Anne-Marie. What? No, the strange man won't do anything bad to Mama. When he's gone we'll play some more.

(*She takes the children into the room to the left and closes the door.*)

NORA (*tense, troubled*) You want to speak with me?

KROGSTAD Yes I do.

NORA Today—? It isn't the first of the month yet.

KROGSTAD No, it's Christmas Eve. It's up to you what kind of holiday you'll have.

NORA What do you want? I can't possibly—

KROGSTAD Let's not talk about that just yet. There's something else. You do have a few minutes, don't you?

NORA Yes. Yes, of course. That is,—

KROGSTAD Good. I was sitting in Olsen's restaurant when I saw your husband go by.

NORA Yes—?

KROGSTAD —with a lady.

NORA What of it?

KROGSTAD May I be so free as to ask: wasn't that lady Mrs. Linde?

NORA Yes.

KROGSTAD Just arrived in town?

NORA Yes, today.

KROGSTAD She's a good friend of yours, I understand?

NORA Yes, she is. But I fail to see—

KROGSTAD I used to know her myself.

NORA I know that.

KROGSTAD So you know about that. I thought as much. In that case, let me ask you a simple question. Is Mrs. Linde going to be employed in the bank?

NORA What makes you think you have the right to cross-examine me like this, Mr. Krogstad—you, one of my husband's employees? But since you ask, I'll tell you. Yes, Mrs. Linde is going to be working in the bank. And it was I who recommended her, Mr. Krogstad. Now you know.

KROGSTAD So I was right.

NORA (*walks up and down*) After all, one does have a little influence, you know. Just because you're a woman, it doesn't mean that—Really, Mr. Krogstad, people in a subordinate position should be careful not to offend someone who—oh well—

KROGSTAD —has influence?

NORA Exactly.

KROGSTAD (*changing his tone*) Mrs. Helmer, I must ask you to be good enough to use your influence on my behalf.

NORA What do you mean?

KROGSTAD I want you to make sure that I am going to keep my subordinate position in the bank.

NORA I don't understand. Who is going to take your position away from you?

KROGSTAD There's no point in playing ignorant with me, Mrs. Helmer. I can very well appreciate that your friend would find it unpleasant to run into me. So now I know who I can thank for my dismissal.

NORA But I assure you—

KROGSTAD Never mind. Just want to say you still have time. I advise you to use your influence to prevent it.

NORA But Mr. Krogstad, I don't have any influence—none at all.

KROGSTAD No? I thought you just said—

NORA Of course I didn't mean it that way. I! Whatever makes you think that I have any influence of that kind on my husband?

KROGSTAD I went to law school with your husband. I have no reason to think that the bank manager is less susceptible than other husbands.

NORA If you're going to insult my husband, I'll ask you to leave.

KROGSTAD You're brave, Mrs. Helmer.

NORA I'm not afraid of you any more. After New Year's I'll be out of this thing with you.

KROGSTAD (*more controlled*) Listen, Mrs. Helmer. If necessary I'll fight as for my life to keep my little job in the bank.

NORA So it seems.

KROGSTAD It isn't just the money; that's really the smallest part of it. There is something else—Well, I guess I might as well tell you. It's like this. I'm sure you know, like everybody else, that some years ago I committed—an impropriety.

NORA I believe I've heard it mentioned.

KROGSTAD The case never came to court, but from that moment all doors were closed to me. So I took up the kind of business you know about. I had to do something, and I think I can say about myself that I have not been among the worst. But now I want to get out of all that. My sons are growing up. For their sake I must get back as much of my good name as I can. This job in the bank was like the first rung on the ladder. And now your husband wants to kick me down and leave me back in the mud again.

NORA But I swear to you, Mr. Krogstad; it's not at all in my power to help you.

KROGSTAD That's because you don't want to. But I have the means to force you.

NORA You don't mean you're going to tell my husband I owe you money?

KROGSTAD And if I did?

NORA That would be a mean thing to do. (*almost crying*) That secret, which is my joy and my pride—for him to learn about it in such a coarse and ugly manner—to learn it from *you*—! It would be terribly unpleasant for me.

KROGSTAD Just unpleasant?

NORA (*heatedly*) But go ahead! Do it! It will be worse for you than for me. When my husband realizes what a bad person you are, you'll be sure to lose your job.

KROGSTAD I asked you if it was just domestic unpleasantness you were afraid of?

NORA When my husband finds out, of course he'll pay off the loan, and then we won't have anything more to do with you.

KROGSTAD (*stepping closer*) Listen, Mrs. Helmer—either you have a very bad memory, or you don't know much about business. I think I had better straighten you out on a few things.

NORA What do you mean?

KROGSTAD When your husband was ill, you came to me to borrow twelve hundred dollars.

NORA I knew nobody else.

KROGSTAD I promised to get you the money—

NORA And you did.

KROGSTAD I promised to get you the money on certain conditions. At the time you were so anxious about your husband's health and so set on getting him away that I doubt very much that you paid much attention to the details of our transaction. That's why I remind you of them now. Anyway, I promised to get you the money if you would sign an I.O.U., which I drafted.

NORA And which I signed.

KROGSTAD Good. But below your signature I added a few lines, making your father security for the loan. Your father was supposed to put his signature to those lines.

NORA Supposed to—? He did.

KROGSTAD I had left the date blank. That is, your father was to date his own signature. You recall that, don't you, Mrs. Helmer?

NORA I guess so—

KROGSTAD I gave the note to you. You were to mail it to your father. Am I correct?

NORA Yes.

KROGSTAD And of course you did so right away, for no more than five or six days later you brought the paper back to me, signed by your father. Then I paid you the money.

NORA Well? And haven't I been keeping up with the payments?

KROGSTAD Fairly well, yes. But to get back to what we were talking about—those were difficult days for you, weren't they, Mrs. Helmer?

NORA Yes, they were.

KROGSTAD Your father was quite ill, I believe.

NORA He was dying.

KROGSTAD And died shortly afterwards?

NORA That's right.

KROGSTAD Tell me, Mrs. Helmer; do you happen to remember the date of your father's death? I mean the exact day of the month?

NORA Daddy died on September 29.

KROGSTAD Quite correct. I have ascertained that fact. That's why there is something peculiar about this (*takes out a piece of paper*), which I can't account for.

NORA Peculiar? How? I don't understand—

KROGSTAD It seems very peculiar, Mrs. Helmer, that your father signed this promissory note three days after his death.

NORA How so? I don't see what—

KROGSTAD Your father died on September 29. Now look. He has dated his signature October 2. Isn't that odd?

(NORA *remains silent.*)

KROGSTAD Can you explain it?

(NORA *is still silent.*)

KROGSTAD I also find it striking that the date and the month and the year are not in your father's handwriting but in a hand I think I recognize. Well, that might be explained. Your father may have forgotten to date his signature and somebody else may have done it here, guessing at the date before he had learned of your father's death. That's all right. It's only the signature itself that matters. And that is genuine, isn't it, Mrs. Helmer? Your father *did* put his name to this note?

NORA (*after a brief silence tosses her head back and looks defiantly at him*) No, he didn't. *I* wrote Daddy's name.

KROGSTAD Mrs. Helmer—do you realize what a dangerous admission you just made?

NORA Why? You'll get your money soon.

KROGSTAD Let me ask you something. Why didn't you mail this note to your father?

NORA Because it was impossible. Daddy was sick—you know that. If I had asked him to sign it, I would have had to tell him what the money was for. But I couldn't tell him, as sick as he was, that my husband's life was in danger. That was impossible. Surely you can see that.

KROGSTAD Then it would have been better for you if you had given up your trip abroad.

NORA No, that was impossible! That trip was to save my husband's life. I couldn't give it up.

KROGSTAD But didn't you realize that what you did amounted to fraud against me?

NORA I couldn't let that make any difference. I didn't care about you at all. I hated the way you made all those difficulties for me, even though you knew the danger my husband was in. I thought you were cold and unfeeling.

KROGSTAD Mrs. Helmer, obviously you have no clear idea of what you have done. Let me tell you that what I did that time was no more and no worse. And it ruined my name and reputation.

NORA You! Are you trying to tell me that you did something brave once in order to save your wife's life?

KROGSTAD The law doesn't ask about motives.

NORA Then it's a bad law.

KROGSTAD Bad or not—if I produce this note in court you'll be judged according to the law.

NORA I refuse to believe you. A daughter shouldn't have the right to spare her dying old father worry and anxiety? A wife shouldn't have the right to save her husband's life? I don't know the laws very well, but I'm sure that somewhere they make allowance for cases like that. And you, a lawyer, don't know that? I think you must be a bad lawyer, Mr. Krogstad.

KROGSTAD That may be. But business—the kind of business you and I have with one another—don't you think I know something about that? Very well. Do what you like. But let me tell you this: if I'm going to be kicked out again, you'll keep me company. (*He bows and exits through the front hall.*)

NORA (*pauses thoughtfully; then, with a defiant toss of her head*) Oh, nonsense! Trying to scare me like that! I'm not all that silly. (*starts picking up the children's clothes; soon stops*) But—? No! That's impossible! I did it for love!

THE CHILDREN (*in the door to the left*) Mama, the strange man just left. We saw him.

NORA Yes, yes; I know. But don't tell anybody about the strange man. Do you hear? Not even Daddy.

THE CHILDREN We won't. But now you'll play with us again, won't you, Mama?

NORA No, not right now.

THE CHILDREN But Mama—you promised.

NORA I know, but I can't just now. Go to your own room. I've so much to do. Be nice now, my little darlings. Do as I say. (*She nudges them gently into the other room and closes the door. She sits down on the couch, picks up a piece of embroidery, makes a few stitches, then stops.*) No! (*throws the embroidery down, goes to the hall door and calls out*) Helene! Bring the Christmas tree in here, please! (*goes to the table, left, opens the drawer, halts*) No—that's impossible!

THE MAID (*with the Christmas tree*) Where do you want it, ma'am?

NORA There. The middle of the floor.

THE MAID You want anything else?

NORA No, thanks. I have everything I need. (THE MAID *goes out.* NORA *starts trimming the tree.*) I want candles—and flowers—That awful man! Oh, nonsense! There's nothing wrong. This will be a lovely tree. I'll do everything you want me to, Torvald. I'll sing for you—dance for you—

(HELMER, *a bundle of papers under his arm, enters from outside.*)

NORA Ah—you're back already?

HELMER Yes. Has anybody been here?

NORA Here? No.

HELMER That's funny. I saw Krogstad leaving just now.

NORA Oh? Oh yes, that's right. Krogstad was here for just a moment.

HELMER I can tell from your face that he came to ask you to put in a word for him.

NORA Yes.

HELMER And it was supposed to be your own idea, wasn't it? You were not to tell me he'd been here. He asked you that too, didn't he?

NORA Yes, Torvald, but—

NORA Nora, Nora, how could you! Talk to a man like that and make him promises! And lying to me about it afterwards—!

NORA Lying—?

HELMER Didn't you say nobody had been here? (*shakes his finger at her*) My little songbird must never do that again. Songbirds are supposed to have clean beaks to chirp with—no false notes. (*puts his arms around her waist*) Isn't that so? Of course it is. (*lets her go*) And that's enough about that. (*sits down in front of the fireplace*) Ah, it's nice and warm in here. (*begins to leaf through his papers*)

NORA (*busy with the tree; after a brief pause*) Torvald.

HELMER Yes.

NORA I'm looking forward so much to the Stenborgs' costume party day after tomorrow.

HELMER And I can't wait to find out what you're going to surprise me with.

NORA Oh, that silly idea!

HELMER Oh?

NORA I can't think of anything. It all seems so foolish and pointless.

HELMER Ah, my little Nora admits that?

NORA (*behind his chair, her arms on the back of the chair*) Are you very busy, Torvald?

HELMER Well—

NORA What are all those papers?

HELMER Bank business.

NORA Already?

HELMER I've asked the board to give me the authority to make certain changes in organization and personnel. That's what I'll be doing over the holidays. I want it all settled before New Year's.

NORA So that's why this poor Krogstad—

HELMER Hm.

NORA (*leisurely playing with the hair on his neck*) If you weren't so busy, Torvald, I'd ask you for a great big favor.

HELMER Let's hear it, anyway.

NORA I don't know anyone with better taste than you, and I want so much to look nice at the party. Couldn't you sort of take charge of me, Torvald, and decide what I'll wear—Help me with my costume?

HELMER Aha! Little Lady Obstinate is looking for someone to rescue her?

NORA Yes, Torvald. I won't get anywhere without your help.

HELMER All right. I'll think about it. We'll come up with something.

NORA Oh, you *are* nice! (*goes back to the Christmas tree; a pause*) Those red flowers look so pretty.—Tell me, was it really all that bad what this Krogstad fellow did?

HELMER He forged signatures. Do you have any idea what that means?

NORA Couldn't it have been because he felt he had to?

HELMER Yes, or like so many others he may simply have been thoughtless. I'm not so heartless as to condemn a man absolutely because of a single imprudent act.

NORA Of course not, Torvald!

HELMER People like him can redeem themselves morally by openly confessing their crime and taking their punishment.

NORA Punishment—?

HELMER But that was not the way Krogstad chose. He got out of it with tricks and evasions. That's what has corrupted him.

NORA So you think that if—?

HELMER Can't you imagine how a guilty person like that has to lie and fake and dissemble wherever he goes—putting on a mask before everybody he's close to, even his own wife and children. It's this thing with the children that's the worst part of it, Nora.

NORA Why is that?

HELMER Because when a man lives inside such a circle of stinking lies he brings infection into his own home and contaminates his whole family. With every breath of air his children inhale the germs of something ugly.

NORA (*moving closer behind him*) Are you so sure of that?

HELMER Of course I am. I have seen enough examples of that in my work. Nearly all young criminals have had mothers who lied.

NORA Why mothers—particularly?

HELMER Most often mothers. But of course fathers tend to have the same influence. Every lawyer knows that. And yet, for years this Krogstad has been poisoning his own children in an atmosphere of lies and deceit. That's why I call him a lost soul morally. (*reaches out for her hands*) And that's why my sweet little Nora must promise me never to take his side again. Let's shake on that.—What? What's this? Give me your hand. There! Now that's settled. I assure you, I would find it impossible to work in the same room with that man. I feel literally sick when I'm around people like that.

NORA (*withdraws her hand and goes to the other side of the Christmas tree*) It's so hot in here. And I have so much to do.

HELMER (*gets up and collects his papers*) Yes, and I really should try to get some of this reading done before dinner. I must think about your costume too. And maybe just possibly I'll have something to wrap in gilt paper and hang on the Christmas tree. (*puts his hand on her head*) Oh my adorable little songbird! (*enters his study and closes the door*)

NORA (*after a pause, in a low voice*) It's all a lot of nonsense. It's not that way at all. It's impossible. It has to be impossible.

THE NURSE (*in the door, left*) The little ones are asking ever so nicely if they can't come in and be with their mama.

NORA No, no no! Don't let them in here! You stay with them, Anne-Marie.

THE NURSE If you say so, ma'am. (*closes the door*)

NORA (*pale with terror*) Corrupt my little children—! Poison my home—? (*Brief pause; she lifts her head.*) That's not true. Never. Never in a million years.

Act II

The same room. The Christmas tree is in the corner by the piano, stripped, shabby-looking, with burnt-down candles. NORA*'s outside clothes are on the couch.* NORA *is alone. She walks around restlessly. She stops by the couch and picks up her coat.*

NORA (*drops the coat again*) There's somebody now! (*goes to the door, listens*) No. Nobody. Of course not—not on Christmas. And not tomorrow either.[2]—But perhaps—(*opens the door and looks*) No, nothing in the mailbox. All empty. (*comes forward*) How silly I am! Of course he isn't serious. Nothing like that could happen. After all, I have three small children.

(*The* NURSE *enters from the room, left, carrying a big carton.*)

THE NURSE Well, at last I found it—the box with your costume.

NORA Thanks. Just put it on the table.

NURSE (*does so*) But it's all a big mess, I'm afraid.

NORA Oh, I wish I could tear the whole thing to little pieces!

NURSE Heavens! It's not as bad as all that. It can be fixed all right. All it takes is a little patience.

NORA I'll go over and get Mrs. Linde to help me.

NURSE Going out again? In this awful weather? You'll catch a cold.

NORA That might not be such a bad thing. How are the children?

NURSE The poor little dears are playing with their presents, but—

NORA Do they keep asking for me?

NURSE Well, you know, they're used to being with their mamma.

NORA I know. But Anne-Marie, from now on I can't be with them as much as before.

NURSE Oh well. Little children get used to everything.

NORA You think so? Do you think they'll forget their mamma if I were gone altogether?

NURSE Goodness me—gone altogether?

NORA Listen, Anne-Marie—something I've wondered about. How could you bring yourself to leave your children with strangers?

NURSE But I had to, if I were to nurse you.

NORA Yes, but how could you *want* to?

NURSE When I could get such a nice place? When something like that happens to a poor young girl, she'd better be grateful for whatever she gets. For *he* didn't do a thing for me—the louse!

NORA But your daughter has forgotten all about you, hasn't she?

NURSE Oh no! Not at all! She wrote to me both when she was confirmed and when she got married.

NORA (*putting her arms around her neck*) You dear old thing—you were a good mother to me when I was little.

---

[2]In Norway both December 25 and 26 are legal holidays.

NURSE Poor little Nora had no one else, you know.

NORA And if my little ones didn't, I know you'd—oh, I'm being silly! (*opens the carton*) Go in to them, please. I really should—. Tomorrow you'll see how pretty I'll be.

NURSE I know. There won't be anybody at that party half as pretty as you, ma'am. (*goes out, left*)

NORA (*begins to take clothes out of the carton; in a moment she throws it all down*) If only I dared to go out. If only I knew nobody would come. That nothing would happen while I was gone.—How silly! Nobody'll come. Just don't think about it. Brush the muff. Beautiful gloves. Beautiful gloves. Forget it. Forget it. One, two, three, four, five, six—(*cries out*) There they are! (*moves toward the door, stops irresolutely*)

(MRS. LINDE *enters from the hall. She has already taken off her coat.*)

NORA Oh, it's you, Kristine. There's no one else out there, is there? I'm so glad you're here.

MRS. LINDE They told me you'd asked for me.

NORA I just happened to walk by. I need your help with something—badly. Let's sit here on the couch. Look. Torvald and I are going to a costume party tomorrow night—at Consul Stenborg's upstairs—and Torvald wants me to go as a Neapolitan fisher girl and dance the tarantella. I learned it when we were on Capri.

MRS. LINDE Well, well! So you'll be putting on a whole show?

NORA Yes, Torvald thinks I should. Look, here's the costume. Torvald had it made for me while we were there. But it's all so torn and everything. I just don't know—

MRS. LINDE Oh, that can be fixed. It's not that much. The trimmings have come loose in a few places. Do you have needle and thread? Ah, here we are. All set.

NORA I really appreciate it, Kristine.

MRS. LINDE (*sewing*) So you'll be in disguise tomorrow night, eh? You know—I may come by for just a moment, just to look at you.—Oh dear. I haven't even thanked you for the nice evening last night.

NORA (*gets up, moves around*) Oh, I don't know. I don't think last night was as nice as it usually is.—You should have come to town a little earlier, Kristine.—Yes, Torvald knows how to make it nice and pretty around here.

MRS. LINDE You too, I should think. After all, you're your father's daughter. By the way, is Dr. Rank always as depressed as he was last night?

NORA No, last night was unusual. He's a very sick man, you know—very sick. Poor Rank, his spine is rotting away. Tuberculosis, I think. You see, his father was a nasty old man with mistresses and all that sort of thing. Rank has been sickly ever since he was a little boy.

MRS. LINDE (*dropping her sewing to her lap*) But dearest, Nora, where have you learned about things like that?

NORA (*still walking about*) Oh, you know—with three children you sometimes get to talk with—other wives. Some of them know quite a bit about medicine. So you pick up a few things.

MRS. LINDE (*resumes her sewing; after a brief pause*) Does Dr. Rank come here every day?

NORA Every single day. He's Torvald's oldest and best friend, after all. And my friend too, for that matter. He's part of the family, almost.

MRS. LINDE But tell me, is he quite sincere? I mean, isn't he the kind of man who likes to say nice things to people?

NORA No, not at all. Rather the opposite, in fact. What makes you say that?

MRS. LINDE When you introduced us yesterday, he told me he'd often heard my name mentioned in this house. But later on it was quite obvious that your husband really had no idea who I was. So how could Dr. Rank—?

NORA You're right, Kristine, but I can explain that. You see, Torvald loves me so very much that he wants me all to himself. That's what he says. When we were first married he got almost jealous when I as much as mentioned anybody from back home that I was fond of. So of course I soon stopped doing that. But with Dr. Rank I often talk about home. You see, he likes to listen to me.

MRS. LINDE Look here, Nora. In many ways you're still a child. After all, I'm quite a bit older than you and have had more experience. I want to give you a piece of advice. I think you should get out of this thing with Dr. Rank.

NORA Get out of what thing?

MRS. LINDE Several things in fact, if you want my opinion. Yesterday you said something about a rich admirer who was going to give you money—

NORA One who doesn't exist, unfortunately. What of it?

MRS. LINDE Does Dr. Rank have money?

NORA Yes, he does.

MRS. LINDE And no dependents?

MRS. LINDE No. But—?

MRS. LINDE And he comes here every day?

NORA Yes, I told you that already.

MRS. LINDE But how can that sensitive man be so tactless?

NORA I haven't the slightest idea what you're talking about.

MRS. LINDE Don't play games with me, Nora. Don't you think I know who you borrowed the twelve hundred dollars from?

NORA Are you out of your mind! The very idea—! A friend of both of us who sees us every day—! What a dreadfully uncomfortable position that would be!

MRS. LINDE So it really isn't Dr. Rank?

NORA Most certainly not! I would never have dreamed of asking him—not for a moment. Anyway, he didn't have any money then. He inherited it afterwards.

MRS. LINDE Well, I still think it may have been lucky for you, Nora dear.

NORA The idea! It would never have occurred to me to ask Dr. Rank—. Though I'm sure that if I *did* ask him—

MRS. LINDE But of course you wouldn't.

NORA Of course not. I can't imagine that that would ever be necessary. But I am quite sure that if I told Dr. Rank—

MRS. LINDE Behind your husband's back?

NORA I must get out of—this other thing. That's also behind his back. I *must* get out of it.

MRS. LINDE That's what I told you yesterday. But—

NORA (*walking up and down*) A man manages these things so much better than a woman—

MRS. LINDE One's husband, yes.

NORA Silly, silly! (*stops*) When you've paid off all you owe, you get your I.O.U. back; right?

MRS. LINDE Yes, of course.

NORA And you can tear it into a hundred thousand little pieces and burn it—that dirty, filthy, paper!

MRS. LINDE (*looks hard at her, puts down her sewing, rises slowly*) Nora—you're hiding something from me.

NORA Can you tell?

MRS. LINDE Something's happened to you, Nora, since yesterday morning. What is it?

NORA (*going to her*) Kristine! (*listens*) Shhh. Torvald just came back. Listen. Why don't you go in to the children for a while. Torvald can't stand having sewing around. Get Anne-Marie to help you.

MRS. LINDE (*gathers some of the sewing things together*) All right, but I'm not leaving here till you and I have talked.

(*She goes out left, as* HELMER *enters from the front hall.*)

NORA (*toward him*) I have been waiting and waiting for you, Torvald.

HELMER Was that the dressmaker?

NORA No, it was Kristine. She's helping me with my costume. Oh Torvald, just wait till you see how nice I'll look!

HELMER I told you. Pretty good idea I had, wasn't it?

NORA Lovely! And wasn't it nice of me to go along with it?

HELMER (*his hands under her chin*) Nice? To do what your husband tells you? All right, you little rascal; I know you didn't mean it that way. But don't let me interrupt you. I suppose you want to try it on.

NORA And you'll be working?

HELMER Yes. (*shows her a pile of papers*) Look. I've been down to the bank. (*is about to enter his study*)

NORA Torvald.

HELMER (*halts*) Yes?

NORA What if your little squirrel asked you ever so nicely—

HELMER For what?

NORA Would you do it?

HELMER Depends on what it is.

NORA Squirrel would run around and do all sorts of fun tricks if you'd be nice and agreeable.

HELMER All right. What is it?

NORA Lark would chirp and twitter in all the rooms, up and down—

HELMER So what? Lark does that anyway.

NORA I'll be your elfmaid and dance for you in the moonlight, Torvald.

HELMER Nora, don't tell me it's the same thing you mentioned this morning?

NORA (*closer to him*) Yes, Torvald. I beg you!

HELMER You really have the nerve to bring that up again?

NORA Yes. You've just got to do as I say. You *must* let Krogstad keep his job.

HELMER My dear Nora. It's his job I intend to give to Mrs. Linde.

NORA I know. And that's ever so nice of you. But can't you just fire somebody else?

HELMER This is incredible! You just don't give up do you? Because you make some foolish promise, *I* am supposed to—!

NORA That's not the reason, Torvald. It's for your own sake. That man writes for the worst newspapers. You've said so yourself. There's no telling what he may do to you. I'm scared to death of him.

HELMER Ah, I understand. You're afraid because of what happened before.

NORA What do you mean?

HELMER You're thinking of your father, of course.

NORA Yes. Yes, you're right. Remember the awful things they wrote about Daddy in the newspapers. I really think they might have forced him to resign if the ministry hadn't sent you to look into the charges and if you hadn't been so helpful and understanding.

HELMER My dear little Nora, there is a world of difference between your father and me. Your father's official conduct was not above reproach. Mine is, and I intend for it to remain that way as long as I hold my position.

NORA Oh, but you don't know what vicious people like that may think of. Oh, Torvald! Now all of us could be so happy together here in our own home, peaceful and carefree. Such a good life, Torvald, for you and me and the children! That's why I implore you—

HELMER And it's exactly because you plead for him that you make it impossible for me to keep him. It's already common knowledge in the bank that I intend to let Krogstad go. If it gets out that the new manager has changed his mind because of his wife—

NORA Yes? What then?

HELMER No, of course, that wouldn't matter at all as long as little Mrs. Pighead here got her way! Do you want me to make myself look ridiculous before my whole staff—make people think I can be swayed by just anybody—by outsiders? Believe me, I would soon enough find out what the consequences would be! Besides, there's another thing that makes it absolutely impossible for Krogstad to stay on in the bank now that I'm in charge.

NORA What's that?

HELMER I suppose in a pinch I could overlook his moral shortcomings—

NORA Yes, you could; couldn't you, Torvald?

HELMER And I understand he's quite a good worker, too. But we've known each other for a long time. It's one of those imprudent relationships you get into when you're young that embarrass you for the rest of your life. I guess I might as well be frank with you: he and I are on a first name basis. And that tactless fellow never hides the fact even when other people are around. Rather, he seems to think it entitles him to be familiar with me. Every chance he gets he comes out with his damn "Torvald, Torvald." I'm telling you, I find it most awkward. He would make my position in the bank intolerable.

NORA You don't really mean any of this, Torvald.

HELMER Oh? I don't? And why not?

NORA No, for it's all so petty.

HELMER What! Petty? You think I'm being petty!

NORA No, I *don't* think you are petty, Torvald dear. That's exactly why I—

HELMER Never mind. You think my reasons are petty, so it follows that I must be petty too. Petty! Indeed! By God, I'll put an end to this right now! (*opens the door to the front hall and calls out*) Helene!

NORA What are you doing?

HELMER (*searching among his papers*) Making a decision. (THE MAID *enters.*) Here. Take this letter. Go out with it right away. Find somebody to deliver it. But quick. The address is on the envelope. Wait. Here's money.

THE MAID Very good sir. (*She takes the letter and goes out.*)

HELMER (*collecting his papers*) There now, little Mrs Obstinate!

NORA (*breathless*) Torvald—what was that letter?

HELMER Krogstad's dismissal.

NORA Call it back, Torvald! There's still time! Oh Torvald, please—call it back! For my sake, for your own sake, for the sake of the children! Listen to me, Torvald! Do it! You don't know what you're doing to all of us!

HELMER Too late.

NORA Yes. Too late.

HELMER Dear Nora, I forgive you this fear you're in, although it really is an insult to me. Yes, it is! It's an insult to think that I am scared of a shabby scrivener's revenge. But I forgive you, for it's such a beautiful proof how much you love me. (*takes her in his arms*) And that's the way it should be, my sweet darling. Whatever happens, you'll see that when things get really rough I have both strength and courage. You'll find out that I am man enough to shoulder the whole burden.

NORA (*terrified*) What do you mean by that?

HELMER All of it, I tell you—

NORA (*composed*) You'll never have to do that.

HELMER Good. Then we'll share the burden, Nora—like husband and wife, the way it ought to be. (*caresses her*) Now are you satisfied? There, there, there. Not that look in your eyes—like a frightened dove. It's all your own foolish imagination.—Why don't you practice the tarantella—and your tambourine, too. I'll be in the inner office and close both doors, so I won't hear you. You can make as much noise as you like. (*turning in the doorway*) And when Rank comes, tell him where to find me. (*He nods to her, enters his study carrying his papers, and closes the door.*)

NORA (*transfixed by terror, whispers*) He would do it. He'll do it. He'll do it in spite of the whole world.—No, this mustn't happen. Anything rather than that! There must be a way!—(*The doorbell rings.*) Dr. Rank! Anything rather than that! Anything—anything at all.

(*She passes her hand over her face, pulls herself together, and opens the door to the hall.* DR. RANK *is out there, hanging up his coat. Darkness begins to fall during the following scene.*)

NORA Hello there, Dr. Rank. I recognized your ringing. Don't go in to Torvald yet. I think he's busy.

RANK And you?

NORA (*as he enters and she closes the door behind him*) You know I always have time for you.

RANK Thanks. I'll make use of that as long as I can.

NORA What do you mean by that—As long as you can?

RANK Does that frighten you?

NORA Well, it's a funny expression. As if something was going to happen.

RANK Something is going to happen that I've long been expecting. But I admit I hadn't thought it would come quite so soon.

NORA (*seizes his arm*) What is it you've found out? Dr. Rank—tell me!

RANK (*sits down by the stove*) I'm going downhill fast. There's nothing to do about that.

NORA (*with audible relief*) So it's *you*—

RANK Who else? No point in lying to myself. I'm in worse shape than any of my other patients, Mrs. Helmer. These last few days I've been making up my inner status. Bankrupt. Chances are that within a month I'll be rotting up in the cemetery.

NORA Shame on you! Talking that horrid way!

RANK The thing itself is horrid—damn horrid. The worst of it, though, is all that other horror that comes first. There is only one more test I need to make. After that I'll have a pretty good idea when I'll start coming apart. There is something I want to say to you. Helmer's refined nature can't stand anything hideous. I don't want him in my sick room.

NORA Oh, but Dr. Rank—

RANK I don't want him there. Under no circumstances. I'll close my door to him. As soon as I have full certainty that the worst is about to begin I'll give you my card with a black cross on it. Then you'll know the last horror of destruction has started.

NORA Today you're really quite impossible. And I had hoped you'd be in a particularly good mood.

RANK With death on my hands? Paying for someone else's sins? Is there justice in that? And yet there isn't a single family that isn't ruled by the same law of ruthless retribution, in one way or another.

NORA (*puts her hands over her ears*) Poppycock! Be fun! Be fun!

RANK Well, yes. You may just as well laugh at the whole thing. My poor, innocent spine is suffering from my father's frolics as a young lieutenant.

NORA (*over by the table, left*) Right. He was addicted to asparagus and good liver paté, wasn't he?

RANK And truffles.

NORA Of course. Truffles. And oysters too, I think.

RANK And oysters. Obviously.

NORA And all the port and champagne that go with it. It's really too bad that goodies like that ruin your backbone.

RANK Particularly an unfortunate backbone that never enjoyed any of it.

NORA Ah yes, that's the saddest part of it all.

RANK (*looks searchingly at her*) Hm—

NORA (*after a brief pause*) Why did you smile just then?

RANK No, it was you that laughed.

NORA No, it was you that smiled, Dr. Rank!

RANK (*gets up*) You're more of a mischief-maker than I thought.

NORA I feel in the mood for mischief today.

RANK So it seems.

NORA (*with both her hands on his shoulders*) Dear, dear Dr. Rank, don't you go and die and leave Torvald and me.

RANK Oh, you won't miss me for very long. Those who go away are soon forgotten.

NORA (*with an anxious look*) Do you believe that?

RANK You'll make new friends, and then—

NORA Who'll make new friends?

RANK Both you and Helmer, once I'm gone. You yourself seem to have made a good start already. What was this Mrs. Linde doing here last night?

NORA Aha—Don't tell me you're jealous of poor Kristine?

RANK Yes, I am. She'll be my successor in this house. As soon as I have made my excuses, that woman is likely to—

NORA Shh—not so loud. She's in there.

RANK Today too? There you are!

NORA She's mending my costume. My God, you really *are* unreasonable. (*sits down on the couch*) Now be nice, Dr. Rank. Tomorrow you'll see how beautifully I'll dance, and then you are to pretend I'm dancing just for you—and for Torvald too, of course. (*takes several items out of the carton*) Sit down, Dr. Rank; I want to show you something.

RANK (*sitting down*) What?

NORA Look.

RANK Silk stockings.

NORA Flesh-colored. Aren't they lovely? Now it's getting dark in here, but tomorrow—No, no. You only get to see the foot. Oh well, you might as well see all of it.

RANK Hmm.

NORA Why do you look so critical? Don't you think they'll fit?

RANK That's something I can't possibly have a reasoned opinion about.

NORA (*looks at him for a moment*) Shame on you. (*slaps his ear lightly with the stocking*) That's what you get. (*puts the things back in the carton*)

RANK And what other treasures are you going to show me?

NORA Nothing at all, because you're naughty. (*She hums a little and rummages in the carton.*)

RANK (*after a brief silence*) When I sit here like this, talking confidently with you, I can't imagine—I can't possibly imagine what would have become of me if I hadn't had you and Helmer.

NORA (*smiles*) Well, yes—I do believe you like being with us.

RANK (*in a lower voice, lost in thought*) And then to have to go away from it all—

NORA Nonsense. You are not going anywhere.

RANK (*as before*) —and not to leave behind as much as a poor little token of gratitude, hardly a brief memory of someone missed, nothing but a vacant place that anyone can fill.

NORA And what if I were to ask you—? No—

RANK Ask me what?

NORA For a great proof of your friendship—

RANK Yes, yes—?

NORA No, I mean—for an enormous favor—

RANK Would you really for once make me as happy as all that?

NORA But you don't even know what it is.

RANK Well, then; tell me.

NORA Oh, but I can't, Dr. Rank. It's altogether too much to ask—It's advice and help and a favor—

RANK So much the better. I can't even begin to guess what it is you have in mind. So for heaven's sake tell me! Don't you trust me?

NORA Yes, I trust you more than anyone else I know. You are my best and most faithful friend. I know that. So I will tell you. All right, Dr. Rank. There is something you can help me prevent. You know how much Torvald loves me—beyond all words. Never for a moment would he hesitate to give his life for me.

RANK (*leaning over to her*) Nora—do you really think he's the only one—?

NORA (*with a slight start*) Who—?

RANK —would gladly give his life for you.

NORA (*heavily*) I see.

RANK I have sworn an oath to myself to tell you before I go. I'll never find a better occasion.—All right, Nora; now you know. And now you also know that you can confide in me more than in anyone else.

NORA (*gets up; in a calm, steady voice*) Let me get by.

RANK (*makes room for her but remains seated*) Nora—

NORA (*in the door to the front hall*) Helene, bring the lamp in here, please. (*walks over to the stove*) Oh, dear Dr. Rank. That really wasn't very nice of you.

RANK (*gets up*) That I have loved you as much as anybody—was that not nice?

NORA No; not that. But that you told me. There was no need for that.

RANK What do you mean? Have you known—?

(*The* MAID *enters with the lamp, puts it on the table, and goes out.*)

RANK Nora—Mrs. Helmer—I'm asking you: did you know?

NORA Oh, how can I tell what I knew and didn't know! I really can't say—But that you could be so awkward, Dr. Rank! Just when everything was so comfortable.

RANK Well, anyway, now you know that I'm at your service with my life and soul. And now you must speak.

NORA (*looks at him*) After what just happened?

RANK I beg of you—let me know what it is.

NORA There is nothing I can tell you now.

RANK Yes, yes. You mustn't punish me this way. Please let me do for you whatever anyone *can* do.

NORA Now there is nothing you can do. Besides, I don't think I really need any help, anyway. It's probably just my imagination. Of course that's all it is. I'm sure of it! (*sits down in the rocking chair, looks at him, smiles*) Well, well, well, Dr. Rank! What a fine gentleman you turned out to be! Aren't you ashamed of yourself, now that we have light?

RANK No, not really. But perhaps I ought to leave—and not come back?

NORA Don't be silly; of course not! You'll come here exactly as you have been doing. You know perfectly well that Torvald can't do without you.

RANK Yes, but what about you?

NORA Oh, I always think it's perfectly delightful when you come.

RANK That's the very thing that misled me. You are a riddle to me. It has often seemed to me that you'd just as soon be with me as with Helmer.

NORA Well, you see, there are people you love, and then there are other people you'd almost rather be with.

RANK Yes, there is something in that.

NORA When I lived at home with Daddy, of course I loved him most. But I always thought it was so much fun to sneak off down to the maids' room, for they never gave me good advice and they always talked about such fun things.

RANK Aha! So it's *their* place I have taken.

NORA (*jumps up and goes over to him*) Oh dear, kind Dr. Rank, you know very well I didn't mean it that way. Can't you see that with Torvald it is the way it used to be with Daddy?

(*The* MAID *enters from the front hall.*)

THE MAID Ma'am! (*whispers to her and gives her a caller's card*)

NORA (*glances at the card*) Ah! (*puts it in her pocket*)

RANK Anything wrong?

NORA No, no; not at all. It's nothing—just my new costume—

RANK But your costume is lying right there!

NORA Oh yes, that one. But this is another one. I ordered it. Torvald mustn't know—

RANK Aha. So that's the great secret.

NORA That's it. Why don't you go in to him, please. He's in the inner office. And keep him there for a while—

RANK Don't worry. He won't get away. (*enters* HELMER'S *study*)

NORA (*to the* MAID) You say he's waiting in the kitchen?

THE MAID Yes. He came up the back stairs.

NORA But didn't you tell him there was somebody with me?

THE MAID Yes, but he wouldn't listen.

NORA He won't leave?

THE MAID No, not till he's had a word with you, ma'am.

NORA All right. But try not to make any noise. And, Helene—don't tell anyone he's here. It's supposed to be a surprise for my husband.

THE MAID I understand, ma'am—(*She leaves.*)

NORA The terrible is happening. It's happening, after all. No, no, no. It can't happen. It won't happen. (*She bolts the study door.*)

(*The* MAID *opens the front hall door for* KROGSTAD *and closes the door behind him. He wears a fur coat for traveling, boots, and a fur hat.*)

NORA (*toward him*) Keep your voice down. My husband's home.

KROGSTAD That's all right.

NORA What do you want?

KROGSTAD To find out something.

NORA Be quick, then. What is it?

KROGSTAD I expect you know I've been fired.

NORA I couldn't prevent it, Mr. Krogstad. I fought for you as long and as hard as I could but it didn't do any good.

KROGSTAD Your husband doesn't love you any more than that? He knows what I can do to you, and yet he runs the risk—

NORA Surely you didn't think I'd tell him?

KROGSTAD No, I really didn't. It wouldn't be like Torvald Helmer to show that kind of guts—

NORA Mr. Krogstad, I insist that you show respect for my husband.

KROGSTAD By all means. All due respect. But since you're so anxious to keep this a secret, may I assume that you are a little better informed than yesterday about exactly what you have done?

NORA Better than *you* could ever teach me.

KROGSTAD Of course. Such a bad lawyer as I am—

NORA What do you want of me?

KROGSTAD I just wanted to find out how you are, Mrs. Helmer. I've been thinking about you all day. You see, even a bill collector, a pen pusher, a—anyway, someone like me—even he has a little of what they call a heart.

NORA Then show it. Think of my little children.

KROGSTAD Have you and your husband thought of mine? Never mind. All I want to tell you is that you don't need to take this business too seriously. I have no intention of bringing charges right away.

NORA Oh no, you wouldn't; would you? I knew you wouldn't.

KROGSTAD The whole thing can be settled quite amiably. Nobody else needs to know anything. It will be between the three of us.

NORA My husband must never find out about this.

KROGSTAD How are you going to prevent that? Maybe you can pay me the balance on the loan?

NORA No, not right now.

KROGSTAD Or do you have a way of raising the money one of these next few days?

NORA None I intend to make use of.

KROGSTAD It wouldn't do you any good, anyway. Even if you had the cash in your hand right this minute, I wouldn't give you your note back. It wouldn't make any difference *how* much money you offered me.

NORA Then you'll have to tell me what you plan to use the note *for.*

KROGSTAD Just keep it; that's all. Have it on hand, so to speak. I won't say a word to anybody else. So if you've been thinking about doing something desperate—

NORA I have.

KROGSTAD —like leaving house and home—

NORA I have!

KROGSTAD —or even something worse—

NORA How did you know?

KROGSTAD —then: don't.

NORA How did you know I was thinking of *that?*

KROGSTAD Most of us do, right at first. I did, too, but when it came down to it I didn't have the courage—

NORA (*tonelessly*) Nor do I.

KROGSTAD (*relieved*) See what I mean? I thought so. You don't either.

NORA I don't. I don't.

KROGSTAD Besides, it would be very silly of you. Once that first domestic blowup is behind you—. Here in my pocket is a letter for your husband.

NORA Telling him everything?

KROGSTAD As delicately as possible.

NORA (*quickly*) He mustn't get that letter. Tear it up. I'll get you the money somehow.

KROGSTAD Excuse me, Mrs. Helmer, I thought I just told you—

NORA I'm not talking about the money I owe you. Just let me know how much money you want from my husband, and I'll get it for you.

KROGSTAD I want no money from your husband.

NORA Then, what *do* you want?

KROGSTAD I'll tell you, Mrs. Helmer. I want to rehabilitate myself; I want to get up in the world; and your husband is going to help me. For a year and a half I haven't done anything disreputable. All that time I have been struggling with the most miserable circumstances. I was content to work my way up step by step. Now I've been kicked out, and I'm no longer satisfied just getting my old job back. I want more than that; I want to get to the top. I'm being quite serious. I want the bank to take me back but in a higher position. I want your husband to create a new job for me—

NORA He'll never do that!

KROGSTAD He will. I know him. He won't dare not to. And once I'm back inside and he and I are working together, you'll see! Within a year I'll be the manager's right hand. It will be Nils Krogstad and not Torvald Helmer who'll be running the Mutual Bank!

NORA You'll never see that happen!

KROGSTAD Are you thinking of—?

NORA Now I *do* have the courage.

KROGSTAD You can't scare me. A fine, spoiled lady like you—

NORA You'll see, you'll see!

KROGSTAD Under the ice, perhaps? Down into that cold, black water? Then spring comes, and you float up again—hideous, can't be identified, hair all gone—

NORA You don't frighten me.

KROGSTAD Nor you me. One doesn't do that sort of thing, Mrs. Helmer. Besides, what good would it do? He'd still be in my power.

NORA Afterwards? When I'm no longer—?

KROGSTAD Aren't you forgetting that your reputation would be in my hands?

(NORA *stares at him, speechless.*)

KROGSTAD All right; now I've told you what to expect. So don't do anything foolish. When Helmer gets my letter I expect to hear from him. And don't you forget that it's your husband himself who forces me to use such means again. That I'll never forgive him. Goodbye, Mrs. Helmer. (*goes out through the hall*)

NORA (*at the door, opens it a little, listens*) He's going. And no letter. Of course not! That would be impossible. (*opens the door more*) What's he doing? He's still there. Doesn't go down. Having second thoughts—? Will he—?

(*The sound of a letter dropping into the mailbox. Then* KROGSTAD*'s steps are heard going down the stairs, gradually dying away.*)

NORA (*with a muted cry runs forward to the table by the couch; brief pause*) In the mailbox. (*tiptoes back to the door to the front hall*) There it is. Torvald, Torvald—now we're lost!

MRS. LINDE (*enters from the left, carrying* NORA*'s Capri costume*) There now. I think it's all fixed. Why don't we try it on you—

NORA (*in a low, hoarse voice*) Kristine, come here.

MRS. LINDE What's wrong with you? You look quite beside yourself.

NORA Come over here. Do you see that letter? There, look—through the glass in the mailbox.

MRS. LINDE Yes, yes; I see it.

NORA That letter is from Krogstad.

MRS. LINDE Nora—it was Krogstad who lent you the money!

NORA Yes, and now Torvald will find out about it.

MRS. LINDE Oh believe me, Nora. That's the best thing for both of you.

NORA There's more to it than you know. I forged a signature—

MRS. LINDE Oh my God—!

NORA I just want to tell you this, Kristine, that you must be my witness.

MRS. LINDE Witness? How? Witness to what?

NORA If I lose my mind—and that could very well happen—

MRS. LINDE Nora!

NORA —or if something were to happen to me—something that made it impossible for me to be here—

MRS. LINDE Nora, Nora! You're not yourself!

NORA —and if someone were to take all the blame, assume the whole responsibility—Do you understand—?

MRS. LINDE Yes, yes; but how can you think—!

NORA Then you are to witness that that's not so, Kristine. I am not beside myself. I am perfectly rational, and what I'm telling you is that nobody else has known about this. I've done it all by myself, the whole thing. Just remember that.

MRS. LINDE I will. But I don't understand any of it.

NORA Oh, how could you! For it's the wonderful that's about to happen.

MRS. LINDE The wonderful?

NORA Yes, the wonderful. But it's so terrible, Kristine. It mustn't happen for anything in the whole world!

MRS. LINDE I'm going over to talk to Krogstad right now.

NORA No, don't. Don't go to him. He'll do something bad to you.

MRS. LINDE There was a time when he would have done anything for me.

NORA He!

MRS. LINDE Where does he live?

NORA Oh, I don't know—Yes, wait a minute—(*reaches into her pocket*)—here's his card.—But the letter, the letter—!

HELMER (*in his study, knocks on the door*) Nora!

NORA (*cries out in fear*) Oh, what is it? What do you want?

HELMER That's all right. Nothing to be scared about. We're not coming in. For one thing, you've bolted the door, you know. Are you modeling your costume?

NORA Yes, yes; I am. I'm going to be so pretty, Torvald.

MRS. LINDE (*having looked at the card*) He lives just around the corner.

NORA Yes, but it's no use. Nothing can save us now. The letter is in the mailbox.

MRS. LINDE And your husband has the key?

NORA Yes. He always keeps it with him.

MRS. LINDE Krogstad must ask for his letter back, unread. He's got to think up some pretext or other—

NORA But this is just the time of day when Torvald—

MRS. LINDE Delay him. Go in to him. I'll be back as soon as I can. (*She hurries out through the hall door.*)

NORA (*walks over to* HELMER*'s door, opens it, and peeks in*) Torvald.

HELMER (*still offstage*) Well, well! So now one's allowed in one's own living room again. Come on, Rank. Now we'll see—(*in the doorway*) But what's this?

NORA What, Torvald dear?

HELMER Rank prepared me for a splendid metamorphosis.

RANK (*in the doorway*) That's how I understood it. Evidently I was mistaken.

NORA Nobody gets to admire me in my costume before tomorrow.

HELMER But, dearest Nora—you look all done in. Have you been practicing too hard?

NORA No, I haven't practiced at all.

HELMER But you'll have to, you know.

NORA I know it, Torvald. I simply must. But I can't do a thing unless you help me. I have forgotten everything.

HELMER Oh it will all come back. We'll work on it.

NORA Oh yes, please, Torvald. You just have to help me. Promise? I am so nervous. That big party—. You mustn't do anything else tonight. Not a bit of business. Don't even touch a pen. Will you promise, Torvald?

HELMER I promise. Tonight I'll be entirely at your service—you helpless little thing.—Just a moment, though. First I want to—(*goes to the door to the front hall*)

NORA What are you doing out there?

HELMER Just looking to see if there's any mail.

NORA No, no! Don't, Torvald!

HELMER Why not?

NORA Torvald, I beg you. There is no mail.

HELMER Let me just look, anyway. (*is about to go out*)

(NORA *by the piano, plays the first bars of the tarantella dance.*)

HELMER (*halts at the door*) Aha!

NORA I won't be able to dance tomorrow if I don't get to practice with you.

HELMER (*goes to her*) Are you really all that scared, Nora dear?

NORA Yes, so terribly scared. Let's try it right now. There's still time before we eat. Oh please, sit down and play for me, Torvald. Teach me, coach me, the way you always do.

HELMER Of course I will, my darling, if that's what you want. (*sits down at the piano*)

(NORA *takes the tambourine out of the carton, as well as a long, many-colored shawl. She quickly drapes the shawl around herself, then leaps into the middle of the floor.*)

NORA Play for me! I want to dance!

(HELMER *plays and* NORA *dances.* DR. RANK *stands by the piano behind* HELMER *and watches.*)

HELMER (*playing*) Slow down, slow down!

NORA Can't!

HELMER Not so violent, Nora!

NORA It has to be this way.

HELMER (*stops playing*) No, no. This won't do at all.

NORA (*laughing, swinging her tambourine*) What did I tell you?

RANK Why don't you let me play?

HELMER (*getting up*) Good idea. Then I can direct her better.

(RANK *sits down at the piano and starts playing.* NORA *dances more and more wildly.* HELMER *stands over by the stove, repeatedly correcting her. She doesn't seem to hear. Her hair comes loose and falls down over her shoulders. She doesn't notice but keeps on dancing.* MRS. LINDE *enters.*)

MRS. LINDE (*stops by the door, dumbfounded*) Ah—!

NORA (*dancing*) We're having such fun, Kristine!

HELMER My dearest Nora, you're dancing as if it were a matter of life and death!

NORA It is! It is!

HELMER Rank, stop. This is sheer madness. Stop, I say!

(RANK *stops playing;* NORA *suddenly stops dancing.*)

HELMER (*goes over to her*) If I hadn't seen it I wouldn't have believed it. You've forgotten every single thing I ever taught you.

NORA (*tosses away the tambourine*) See? I told you.

HELMER Well! You certainly need coaching.

NORA Didn't I tell you I did? Now you've seen for yourself. I'll need your help till the very minute we're leaving for the party. Will you promise, Torvald?

HELMER You can count on it.

NORA You're not to think of anything except me—not tonight and not tomorrow. You're not to read any letters—not to look in the mailbox—

HELMER Ah, I see. You're still afraid of that man.

NORA Yes—yes, that too.

HELMER Nora, I can tell from looking at you. There's a letter from him out there.

NORA I don't know. I think so. But you're not to read it now. I don't want anything ugly to come between us before it's all over.

RANK (*to* HELMER *in a low voice*) Better not argue with her.

HELMER (*throws his arm around her*) The child shall have her way. But tomorrow night, when you've done your dance—

NORA Then you'll be free.

THE MAID (*in the door, right*) Dinner can be served any time, ma'am.

NORA We want champagne, Helene.

THE MAID Very good, ma'am. (*goes out*)

HELMER Aha! Having a party, eh?

NORA Champagne from now till sunrise! (*calls out*) And some macaroons, Helene. Lots!—just this once.

HELMER (*taking her hands*) There, there—I don't like this wild—frenzy—Be my own sweet little lark again, the way you always are.

NORA Oh, I will. But you go on in. You too, Dr. Rank. Kristine, please help me put up my hair.

RANK (*in a low voice to* HELMER *as they go out*) You don't think she is—you know—expecting—?

HELMER Oh no. Nothing like that. It's just this childish fear I was telling you about. (*They go out, right.*)

NORA Well?

MRS. LINDE Left town.

NORA I saw it in your face.

MRS. LINDE He'll be back tomorrow night. I left him a note.

NORA You shouldn't have. I don't want you to try to stop anything. You see, it's a kind of ecstasy, too, this waiting for the wonderful.

MRS. LINDE But what is it you're waiting *for?*

NORA You wouldn't understand. Why don't you go in to the others. I'll be there in a minute.

(MRS. LINDE *enters the dining room, right.*)

NORA (*stands still for a little while, as if collecting herself; she looks at her watch*) Five o'clock. Seven hours till midnight. Twenty-four more hours till next midnight. Then the tarantella is over. Twenty-four plus seven—thirty-one more hours to live.

HELMER (*in the door, right*) What's happening to my little lark?

NORA (*to him, with open arms*) Here's your lark!

Act III

The same room. The table by the couch and the chairs around it have been moved to the middle of the floor. A lighted lamp is on the table. The door to the front hall is open. Dance music is heard from upstairs.

MRS. LINDE *is seated by the table, idly leafing through the pages of a book. She tries to read but seems unable to concentrate. Once or twice she turns her head in the direction of the door, anxiously listening.*

MRS. LINDE (*looks at her watch*) Not yet. It's almost too late. If only he hasn't— (*listens again*) Ah! There he is. (*She goes to the hall and opens the front door carefully. Quiet footsteps on the stairs. She whispers.*) Come in. There's nobody here.

KROGSTAD (*in the door*) I found your note when I got home. What's this all about?

MRS. LINDE I've got to talk to you.

KROGSTAD Oh? And it has to be here?

MRS. LINDE It couldn't be at my place. My room doesn't have a separate entrance. Come in. We're quite alone. The maid is asleep and the Helmers are at a party upstairs.

KROGSTAD (*entering*) Really? The Helmers are dancing tonight, are they?

MRS. LINDE And why not?

KROGSTAD You're right. Why not, indeed.

MRS. LINDE All right, Krogstad. Let's talk, you and I.

KROGSTAD I didn't know we had anything to talk about.

MRS. LINDE We have much to talk about.

KROGSTAD I didn't think so.

MRS. LINDE No, because you've never really understood me.

KROGSTAD What was there to understand? What happened was perfectly commonplace. A heartless woman jilts a man when she gets a more attractive offer.

MRS. LINDE Do you think I'm all that heartless? And do you think it was easy for me to break with you?

KROGSTAD No?

MRS. LINDE You really thought it was?

KROGSTAD If it wasn't, why did you write the way you did that time?

MRS. LINDE What else could I do? If I had to make a break, I also had the duty to destroy whatever feelings you had for me.

KROGSTAD (*clenching his hands*) So that's the way it was. And you did—*that*—just for money!

MRS. LINDE Don't forget I had a helpless mother and two small brothers. We couldn't wait for you, Krogstad. You know yourself how uncertain your prospects were then.

KROGSTAD All right. But you still didn't have the right to throw me over for somebody else.

MRS. LINDE I don't know. I have asked myself that question many times. Did I have that right?

KROGSTAD (*in a lower voice*) When I lost you I lost my footing. Look at me now. A shipwrecked man on a raft.

MRS. LINDE Rescue may be near.

KROGSTAD It *was* near. Then you came between.

MRS. LINDE I didn't know that, Krogstad. Only today did I find out it's your job I'm taking over in the bank.

KROGSTAD I believe you when you say so. But now that you *do* know, aren't you going to step aside?

MRS. LINDE No, for it wouldn't do you any good.

KROGSTAD Whether it would or not—*I* would do it.

MRS. LINDE I have learned common sense. Life and hard necessity have taught me that.

KROGSTAD And life has taught me not to believe in pretty speeches.

MRS. LINDE Then life has taught you a very sensible thing. But you do believe in actions, don't you?

KROGSTAD How do you mean?

MRS. LINDE You referred to yourself just now as a shipwrecked man.

KROGSTAD It seems to me I had every reason to do so.

MRS. LINDE And I am a shipwrecked woman. No one to grieve for, no one to care for.

KROGSTAD You made your choice.

MRS. LINDE I had no other choice that time.

KROGSTAD Let's say you didn't. What then?

MRS. LINDE Krogstad, how would it be if we two shipwrecked people got together?

KROGSTAD What's this!

MRS. LINDE Two on one wreck are better off than each on his own.

KROGSTAD Kristine!

MRS. LINDE Why do you think I came to town?

KROGSTAD Surely not because of me?

MRS. LINDE If I'm going to live at all I must work. All my life, for as long as I can remember, I have worked. That's been my one and only pleasure. But now that I'm all alone in the world I feel nothing but this terrible emptiness and desolation. There is no joy in working just for yourself. Krogstad—give me someone and something to work for.

KROGSTAD I don't believe this. Only hysterical females go in for that kind of high-minded self-sacrifice.

MRS. LINDE Did you ever know me to be hysterical?

KROGSTAD You really could do this? Listen—do you know about my past? All of it?

MRS. LINDE Yes, I do.

KROGSTAD Do you also know what people think of me around here?

MRS. LINDE A little while ago you sounded as if you thought that together with me you might have become a different person.

KROGSTAD I'm sure of it.

MRS. LINDE Couldn't that still be?

KROGSTAD Kristine—do you know what you are doing? Yes, I see you do. And you think you have the courage—?

MRS. LINDE I need someone to be a mother to, and your children need a mother. You and I need one another. Nils, I believe in you—in the real you. Together with you I dare to do anything.

KROGSTAD (*seizes her hands*) Thanks, thanks, Kristine—Now I know I'll raise myself in the eyes of others—Ah, but I forget—!

MRS. LINDE (*listening*) Shh!—there's the tarantella. You must go; hurry!

KROGSTAD Why? What is it?

MRS. LINDE Do you hear what they're playing up there? When that dance is over they'll be down.

KROGSTAD All right. I'm leaving. The whole thing is pointless, anyway. Of course you don't know what I'm doing to the Helmers.

MRS. LINDE Yes, Krogstad; I do know.

KROGSTAD Still, you're brave enough—?

MRS. LINDE I very well understand to what extremes despair can drive a man like you.

KROGSTAD If only it could be undone!

MRS. LINDE It could, for your letter is still out there in the mailbox.

KROGSTAD Are you sure?

MRS. LINDE Quite sure. But—

KROGSTAD (*looks searchingly at her*) Maybe I'm beginning to understand. You want to save your friend at any cost. Be honest with me. That's it, isn't it?

MRS. LINDE Krogstad, you may sell yourself once for somebody else's sake, but you don't do it twice.

KROGSTAD I'll demand my letter back.

MRS. LINDE No, no.

KROGSTAD Yes, of course. I'll wait here till Helmer comes down. Then I'll ask him for my letter. I'll tell him it's just about my dismissal—that he shouldn't read it.

MRS. LINDE No, Krogstad. You are not to ask for that letter back.

KROGSTAD But tell me—wasn't that the real reason you wanted to meet me here?

MRS. LINDE At first it was, because I was so frightened. But that was yesterday. Since then I have seen the most incredible things going on in this house. Helmer must learn the whole truth. This miserable secret must come out in the open; those two must come to a full understanding. They simply can't continue with all this concealment and evasion.

KROGSTAD All right; if you want to take that chance. But there is one thing I *can* do, and I'll do that right now.

MRS. LINDE (*listening*) But hurry! Go! The dance is over. We aren't safe another minute.

KROGSTAD I'll be waiting for you downstairs.

MRS. LINDE Yes, do. You must see me home.

KROGSTAD I've never been so happy in my whole life. (*He leaves through the front door. The door between the living room and the front hall remains open.*)

MRS. LINDE (*straightens up the room a little and gets her things ready*) What a change! Oh yes!—what a change! People to work for—to live for—a home to bring happiness to. I can't wait to get to work—! If only they'd come soon—(*listens*) Ah, there they are. Get my coat on—(*puts on her coat and hat*)

(HELMER*'s and* NORA*'s voices are heard outside. A key is turned in the lock, and* HELMER *almost forces* NORA *into the hall. She is dressed in her Italian costume, with a big black shawl over her shoulders. He is in evening dress under an open black cloak.*)

NORA (*in the door, still resisting*) No, no, no! I don't want to! I want to go back upstairs. I don't want to leave so early.

HELMER But dearest Nora—

NORA Oh please, Torvald—please! I'm asking you as nicely as I can—just another hour!

HELMER Not another minute, sweet. You know we agreed. There now. Get inside. You'll catch a cold out here. (*She still resists, but he guides her gently into the room.*)

MRS. LINDE Good evening.

NORA Kristine!

HELMER Ah, Mrs. Linde. Still here?

MRS. LINDE I know. I really should apologize, but I so much wanted to see Nora in her costume.

NORA You've been waiting up for me?

MRS. LINDE Yes, unfortunately I didn't get here in time. You were already upstairs, but I just didn't feel like leaving till I had seen you.

HELMER (*removing* NORA*'s shawl*) Yes, do take a good look at her, Mrs. Linde. I think I may say she's worth looking at. Isn't she lovely?

MRS. LINDE She certainly is—

HELMER Isn't she a miracle of loveliness, though? That was the general opinion at the party, too. But dreadfully obstinate—that she is, the sweet little thing. What can we do about that? Will you believe it—I practically had to use force to get her away.

NORA Oh Torvald, you're going to be sorry you didn't give me even half an hour more.

HELMER See what I mean, Mrs. Linde? She dances the tarantella—she is a tremendous success—quite deservedly so, though perhaps her performance was a little too natural—I mean, more than could be reconciled with the rules of art. But all right! The point is: she's a success, a tremendous success. So should I let her stay after that? Weaken the effect? Of course not. So I take my lovely little Capri girl—I might say, my capricious little Capri girl—under my arm—a quick turn around the room—a graceful bow in all directions, and—as they say in the novels—the beautiful apparition is gone. A finale should always be done for effect, Mrs. Linde, but there doesn't seem to be any way of getting that into Nora's head. Poooh—! It's hot in here. (*throws his cloak down on a chair and opens the door to his room*) Why, it's dark in here! Of course. Excuse me—(*goes inside and lights a couple of candles*)

NORA (*in a hurried, breathless whisper*) Well?

MRS. LINDE (*in a low voice*) I have talked to him.

NORA And—?

MRS. LINDE Nora—you've got to tell your husband everything.

NORA (*no expression in her voice*) I knew it.

MRS. LINDE You have nothing to fear from Krogstad. But you must speak.

NORA I'll say nothing.

MRS. LINDE Then the letter will.

NORA Thank you, Kristine. Now I know what I have to do. Shh!

HELMER (*returning*) Well, Mrs. Linde, have you looked your fill?

MRS. LINDE Yes. And now I'll say goodnight.

HELMER So soon? Is that your knitting?

MRS. LINDE (*takes it*) Yes, thank you. I almost forgot.

HELMER So you knit, do you?

MRS. LINDE Oh yes.

HELMER You know—you ought to take up embroidery instead.

MRS. LINDE Oh? Why?

HELMER Because it's so much more beautiful. Look. You hold the embroidery so—in your left hand. Than with your right you move the needle—like this—in an easy, elongated arc—you see?

MRS. LINDE Maybe you're right—

HELMER Knitting, on the other hand, can never be anything but ugly. Look here: arms pressed close to the sides—the needles going up and down—there's something Chinese about it somehow—. That really was an excellent champagne they served us tonight.

MRS. LINDE Well, goodnight! Nora. And don't be obstinate any more.

HELMER Well said, Mrs. Linde!

MRS. LINDE Goodnight, sir.

HELMER (*sees her to the front door*) Goodnight, goodnight. I hope you'll get home all right? I'd be very glad to—but of course you don't have far to walk, do you? Goodnight, goodnight. (*She leaves. He closes the door behind her and returns to the living room.*) There! At last we got rid of her. She really is an incredible bore, that woman.

NORA Aren't you very tired, Torvald?

HELMER No, not in the least.

NORA Not sleepy either?

HELMER Not at all. Quite the opposite. I feel enormously—animated. How about you? Yes, you do look tired and sleepy.

NORA Yes, I am very tired. Soon I'll be asleep.

HELMER What did I tell you? I was right, wasn't I? Good thing I didn't let you stay any longer.

NORA Everything you do is right.

HELMER (*kissing her forehead*) Now my little lark is talking like a human being. But did you notice what splendid spirits Rank was in tonight?

NORA Was he? I didn't notice. I didn't get to talk with him.

HELMER Nor did I—hardly. But I haven't seen him in such a good mood for a long time. (*looks at her, comes closer to her*) Ah! It does feel good to be back in our own home again, to be quite alone with you—my young, lovely, ravishing woman!

NORA Don't look at me like that, Torvald!

HELMER Am I not to look at my most precious possession? All that loveliness that is mine, nobody's but mine, all of it mine.

NORA (*walks to the other side of the table*) I won't have you talk to me like that tonight.

HELMER (*follows her*) The Tarantella is still in your blood. I can tell. That only makes you all the more alluring. Listen! The guests are beginning to leave. (*softly*) Nora—soon the whole house will be quiet.

NORA Yes, I hope so.

HELMER Yes, don't you, my darling? Do you know—when I'm at a party with you, like tonight—do you know why I hardly ever talk to you, why I keep away from you, only look at you once in a while—a few stolen glances—do you know why I do that? It's because I pretend that you are my secret love, my young, secret bride-to-be, and nobody has the slightest suspicion that there is anything between us.

NORA Yes, I know. All your thoughts are with me.

HELMER Then when we're leaving and I lay your shawl around your delicate young shoulders—around that wonderful curve of your neck—then I imagine you're my young bride, that we're coming away from the wedding, that I am taking you to my home for the first time—that I am alone with you for the first time—quite alone with you, you young, trembling beauty! I have desired you all evening—there hasn't been a longing in me that hasn't been for you. When you were dancing the tarantella, chasing, inviting—my blood was on fire; I couldn't stand it any longer—that's why I brought you down so early—

NORA Leave me now, Torvald. Please! I don't want all this.

HELMER What do you mean? You're only playing your little teasing bird game with me; aren't you, Nora? Don't want to? I'm your husband, aren't I?

(*There is a knock on the front door.*)

NORA (*with a start*) Did you hear that—?

HELMER (*on his way to the hall*) Who is it?

RANK (*outside*) It's me. May I come in for a moment?

HELMER (*in a low voice, annoyed*) Oh, what does he want now? (*aloud*) Just a minute. (*opens the door*) Well! How good of you not to pass by our door.

RANK I thought I heard your voice, so I felt like saying hello. (*looks around*) Ah yes—this dear, familiar room. What a cozy, comfortable place you have here, you two.

HELMER Looked to me as if you were quite comfortable upstairs too.

RANK I certainly was. Why not? Why not enjoy all you can in this world? As much as you can for as long as you can, anyway. Excellent wine.

HELMER The champagne, particularly.

RANK You noticed that too? Incredible how much I managed to put away.

NORA Torvald drank a lot of champagne tonight, too.

RANK Did he?

NORA Yes, he did, and then he's always so much fun afterwards.

RANK Well, why not have some fun in the evening after a well spent day?

HELMER Well spent? I'm afraid I can't claim that.

RANK (*slapping him lightly on the shoulder*) But you see, I can!

NORA Dr. Rank, I believe you must have been conducting a scientific test today.

RANK Exactly.

HELMER What do you know—little Nora talking about scientific tests!

NORA May I congratulate you on the result?

RANK You may indeed.

NORA It was a good one?

RANK The best possible for both doctor and patient—certainty.

NORA (*a quick query*) Certainty?

RANK Absolute certainty. So why shouldn't I have myself an enjoyable evening afterwards?

NORA I quite agree with you, Dr. Rank. You should.

HELMER And so do I. If only you don't pay for it tomorrow.

RANK Oh well—you get nothing for nothing in this world.

NORA Dr. Rank—you are fond of costume parties, aren't you?

RANK Yes, particularly when there is a reasonable number of amusing disguises.

NORA Listen—what are the two of us going to be the next time?

HELMER You frivolous little thing! Already thinking about the next party!

RANK You and I? That's easy. You'll be Fortune's Child.

HELMER Yes, but what is a fitting costume for that?

RANK Let your wife appear just the way she always is.

HELMER Beautiful. Very good indeed. But how about yourself? Don't you know what you'll go as?

RANK Yes, my friend. I know precisely what I'll be.

HELMER Yes?

RANK At the next masquerade I'll be invisible.

HELMER That's a funny idea.

RANK There's a certain black hat—you've heard about the hat that makes you invisible, haven't you? You put that on, and nobody can see you.

HELMER (*suppressing a smile*) I guess that's right.

RANK But I'm forgetting what I came for. Helmer, give me a cigar—one of your dark Havanas.

HELMER With the greatest pleasure. (*offers him his case*)

RANK (*takes one and cuts off the tip*) Thanks.

NORA (*striking a match*) Let me give you a light.

RANK Thanks. (*She holds the match; he lights his cigar.*) And now goodbye!

HELMER Goodbye, goodbye, my friend.

NORA Sleep well, Dr. Rank.

RANK I thank you.

NORA Wish me the same.

RANK You? Well, if you really want me to—. Sleep well. And thanks for the light. (*He nods to both of them and goes out.*)

HELMER (*in a low voice*) He had had quite a bit to drink.

NORA (*absently*) Maybe so.

(HELMER *takes out his keys and goes out into the hall.*)

NORA Torvald—what are you doing out there?

HELMER Emptying the mailbox. It is quite full. There wouldn't be room for the newspapers in the morning—

NORA Are you going to work tonight?

HELMER You know very well I won't.—Say! What's this? Somebody's been at the lock.

NORA The lock—?

HELMER Yes. Why, I wonder. I hate to think that any of the maids—. Here's a broken hairpin. It's one of yours. Nora.

NORA (*quickly*) Then it must be one of the children.

HELMER You better make damn sure they stop that. Hm, hm.—There! I got it open, finally. (*gathers up the mail, calls out to the kitchen*) Helene?—Oh Helene—turn out the light here in the hall, will you? (*He comes back into the living room and closes the door.*) Look how it's been piling up. (*shows her the bundle of letters, starts leafing through it*) What's this?

NORA (*by the window*) The letter! Oh no, no, Torvald!

HELMER Two calling cards—from Rank.

NORA From Dr. Rank?

HELMER (*looking at them*) "Doctor medicinae Rank." They were on top. He must have put them there when he left just now.

NORA Anything written on them?

HELMER A black cross above the name. What a macabre idea. Like announcing his own death.

NORA That's what it is.

HELMER Hm? You know about this? Has he said anything to you?

NORA That card means he has said goodbye to us. He'll lock himself up to die.

HELMER My poor friend. I knew of course he wouldn't be with me very long. But so soon—. And hiding himself away like a wounded animal—

NORA When it has to be, it's better it happens without words. Don't you think so, Torvald?

HELMER (*walking up and down*) He'd grown so close to us. I find it hard to think of him as gone. With his suffering and loneliness he was like a clouded background for our happy sunshine. Well, it may be better this way. For him, at any rate. (*stops*) And perhaps for us, too, Nora. For now we have nobody but each other. (*embraces her*) Oh you—my beloved wife! I feel I just can't hold you close enough. Do you know, Nora—many times I have wished some great danger threatened you, so I could risk my life and blood and everything—everything, for your sake.

NORA (*frees herself and says in a strong and firm voice*) I think you should go and read your letters now, Torvald.

HELMER No, no—not tonight. I want to be with you, my darling.

NORA With the thought of your dying friend—?

HELMER You are right. This has shaken both of us. Something not beautiful has come between us. Thoughts of death and dissolution. We must try to get over it—out of it. Till then—we'll each go to our own room.

NORA (*her arms around his neck*) Torvald—goodnight! Goodnight!

HELMER (*kisses her forehead*) Goodnight, my little songbird. Sleep well, Nora. Now I'll read my letters. (*He goes into his room, carrying the mail; closes the door.*)

NORA (*her eyes desperate, her hands groping, finds Helmer's black cloak and throws it around her; she whispers, quickly, brokenly, hoarsely*) Never see him again. Never. Never. Never. (*puts her shawl over her head*) And never see the children again, either. Never; never.—The black, icy water—fathomless—this—! If only it was all over.—Now he has it. Now he's reading it. No, no; not yet. Torvald—goodbye—you—the children—

(*She is about to hurry through the hall, when* HELMER *flings open the door to his room and stands there with an open letter in his hand.*)

HELMER Nora!

NORA (*cries out*) Ah—!

HELMER What is it? You know what's in this letter?

NORA Yes, I do! Let me go! Let me out!

HELMER (*holds her back*) Where do you think you're going?

NORA (*trying to tear herself loose from him*) I won't let you save me, Torvald!

HELMER (*tumbles back*) True! Is it true what he writes? Oh my God! No, no—this can't possibly be true.

NORA It is true. I have loved you more than anything else in the whole world.

HELMER Oh, don't give me any silly excuses.

NORA (*taking a step toward him*) Torvald—!

HELMER You wretch! What have you done!

NORA Let me go. You are not to sacrifice yourself for me. You are not to take the blame.

HELMER No more playacting. (*locks the door to the front hall*) You'll stay here and answer me. Do you understand what you have done? Answer me! Do you understand?

NORA (*gazes steadily at him with an increasingly frozen expression*) Yes. Now I'm beginning to understand.

HELMER (*walking up and down*) What a dreadful awakening. All these years—all these eight years—she, my pride and my joy—a hypocrite, a liar—oh worse! worse!—a criminal! Oh, the bottomless ugliness in all this! Damn! Damn! Damn!

(NORA, *silent, keeps gazing at him.*)

HELMER (*stops in front of her*) I ought to have guessed that something like this would happen. I should have expected it. All your father's loose principles—Silence! You have inherited every one of your father's loose principles. No religion, no morals, no sense of duty—. Now I am being punished for my leniency with him. I did it for your sake, and this is how you pay me back.

NORA Yes. This is how.

HELMER You have ruined all my happiness. My whole future—that's what you have destroyed. Oh, it's terrible to think about. I am at the mercy of an unscrupulous man. He can do with me whatever he likes, demand anything of me, command me and dispose of me just as he pleases—I dare not say a word! To go down so miserably, to be destroyed—all because of an irresponsible woman!

NORA When I am gone from the world, you'll be free.

HELMER No noble gestures, please. Your father was always full of such phrases too. What good would it do me if you were gone from the world, as you put it? Not the slightest good at all. He could still make the whole thing public, and if he did, people would be likely to think I had been your accomplice. They might even think it was my idea—that it was I who urged you to do it! And for all this I have you to thank—you, whom I've borne on my hands through all the years of our marriage. *Now* do you understand what you've done to me?

NORA (*with cold calm*) Yes.

HELMER I just can't get it into my head that this is happening; it's all so incredible. But we have to come to terms with it somehow. Take your shawl off. Take it off, I say! I have to satisfy him one way or another. The whole affair must be kept quiet at whatever cost.—And as far as you and I are concerned, nothing must seem to have changed. I'm talking about appearances, of course. You'll go on living here; that goes without saying. But I won't let you bring up the children; I dare not trust you with them.—Oh! Having to say this to one I have loved so much, and whom I still—! But all that is past. It's not a question of happiness any more but of hanging on to what can be salvaged—pieces, appearances—(*The doorbell rings.*)

HELMER (*jumps*) What's that? So late. Is the worst—? Has he—! Hide, Nora! Say you're sick.

(NORA *doesn't move.* HELMER *opens the door to the hall.*)

THE MAID (*half dressed, out in the hall*) A letter for your wife, sir.

HELMER Give it to me. (*takes the letter and closes the door*) Yes, it's from him. But I won't let you have it. I'll read it myself.

NORA Yes—you read it.

HELMER (*by the lamp*) I hardly dare. Perhaps we're lost, both you and I. No; I've got to know. (*tears the letter open, glances through it, looks at an enclosure; a cry of joy*) Nora!

(NORA *looks at him with a question in her eyes.*)

HELMER Nora!—No, I must read it again.—Yes, yes; it is so! I'm saved! Nora, I'm saved!

NORA And I?

HELMER You too, of course; we're both saved, both you and I. Look! He's returning your note. He writes that he's sorry, he regrets, a happy turn in his life—oh, it doesn't matter what he writes. We're saved, Nora! Nobody can do anything to you now. Oh Nora, Nora—. No, I want to get rid of this disgusting thing first. Let me see—(*looks at the signature*) No, I don't want to see it. I don't want it to be more than a bad dream, the whole thing. (*tears up the note and both letters, throws the pieces in the stove, and watches them burn*) There! Now it's gone.—He wrote that ever since Christmas Eve—. Good God, Nora, these must have been three terrible days for you.

NORA I have fought a hard fight these last three days.

HELMER And been in agony and seen no other way out than—. No, we won't think of all that ugliness. We'll just rejoice and tell ourselves it's over, it's all over! Oh, listen to me, Nora. You don't seem to understand. It's over. What *is* it? Why do you look like that—that frozen expression on your face? Oh my poor little Nora, don't you think I know what it is? You can't make yourself believe that I have forgiven you. But I have, Nora; I swear to you, I have forgiven you for everything. Of course I know that what you did was for love of me.

NORA That is true.

HELMER You have loved me the way a wife ought to love her husband. You just didn't have the wisdom to judge the means. But do you think I love you any less because you don't know how to act on your own? Of course not. Just lean on me. I'll advise you; I'll guide you. I wouldn't be a man if I didn't find you twice as attractive because of your womanly helplessness. You mustn't pay any attention to the hard words I said to you right at first. It was just that first shock when I thought everything was collapsing all around me. I have forgiven you, Nora. I swear to you—I really have forgiven you.

NORA I thank you for your forgiveness. (*She goes out through the door, right.*)

HELMER No, stay—(*looks into the room she entered*) What are you doing in there?

NORA (*within*) Getting out of my costume.

HELMER (*by the open door*) Good, good. Try to calm down and compose yourself, my poor little frightened songbird. Rest safely; I have broad wings to cover you with. (*walks around near the door*) What a nice and cozy home we have, Nora. Here's shelter for you. Here I'll keep you safe like a hunted dove I have rescued from the hawk's talons. Believe me: I'll know how to quiet your beating heart. It will happen by and by, Nora; you'll see. Why, tomorrow you'll look at all this in quite a different light. And soon everything will be just the way it was before. I won't need to keep reassuring you that I have forgiven you; you'll feel it yourself. Did you really think I could have abandoned you, or even reproached you? Oh, you don't know a real man's heart, Nora. There is something unspeakably sweet and satisfactory for a man to know deep in himself that he has forgiven his wife—forgiven her in all the fullness of his honest heart. You see, that way she becomes his very own all over again—in a double sense, you might say. He has, so to speak, given her a second birth; it is as if she had become his wife and his child, both. From now on that's what you'll be to me, you lost and helpless creature. Don't worry about a thing, Nora. Only be frank with me, and I'll be your will and your conscience.—What's this? You're not in bed? You've changed your dress—!

NORA (*in an everyday dress*) Yes, Torvald. I have changed my dress.

HELMER But why—now—this late—?

NORA I'm not going to sleep tonight.

HELMER But my dear Nora—

NORA (*looks at her watch*) It isn't all that late. Sit down here with me, Torvald. You and I have much to talk about. (*sits down at the table*)

HELMER Nora—what is this all about? That rigid face—

NORA Sit down. This will take a while. I have much to say to you.

HELMER (*sits down, facing her across the table*) You worry me, Nora. I don't understand you.

NORA No, that's just it. You don't understand me. And I have never understood you—not till tonight. No, don't interrupt me. Just listen to what I have to say.—This is a settling of accounts, Torvald.

HELMER What do you mean by that?

NORA (*after a brief silence*) Doesn't one thing strike you, now that we are sitting together like this?

HELMER What would that be?

NORA We have been married for eight years. Doesn't it occur to you that this is the first time that you and I, husband and wife, are having a serious talk?

HELMER Well—serious—. What do you mean by that?

NORA For eight whole years—longer, in fact—ever since we first met, we have never talked seriously to each other about a single serious thing.

HELMER You mean I should forever have been telling you about worries you couldn't have helped me with anyway?

NORA I am not talking about worries. I'm saying we have never tried seriously to get to the bottom of anything together.

HELMER But dearest Nora, I hardly think that would have been something *you*—

NORA That's the whole point. You have never understood me. Great wrong has been done to me, Torvald. First by Daddy and then by you.

HELMER What! By us two? We who have loved you more deeply than anyone else?

NORA (*shakes her head*) You never loved me—neither Daddy nor you. You only thought it was fun to be in love with me.

HELMER But, Nora—what an expression to use!

NORA That's the way it has been, Torvald. When I was home with Daddy, he told me all his opinions, and so they became my opinions too. If I disagreed with him I kept it to myself, for he wouldn't have liked that. He called me his little doll baby, and he played with me the way I played with my dolls. Then I came to your house—

HELMER What a way to talk about our marriage!

NORA (*imperturbably*) I mean that I passed from Daddy's hands into yours. You arranged everything according to your taste, and so I came to share it—or I pretended to; I'm not sure which. I think it was a little of both, now one and now the other. When I look back on it now, it seems to me I've been living here like a pauper—just a hand-to-mouth kind of existence. I have earned my keep by doing tricks for you, Torvald. But that's the way you wanted it. You have great sins against me to answer for, Daddy and you. It's your fault that nothing has become of me.

HELMER Nora, you're being both unreasonable and ungrateful. Haven't you been happy here?

NORA No, never. I thought I was, but I wasn't.

HELMER Not—not happy!

NORA No; just having fun. And you have always been very good to me. But our home has never been more than a playroom. I have been your doll wife here, just the way I used to be Daddy's doll child. And the children have been my dolls. I thought it was fun when you played with me, just as they thought it was fun when I played with them. That's been our marriage, Torvald.

HELMER There is something in what you are saying—exaggerated and hysterical though it is. But from now on things will be different. Playtime is over; it's time for growing up.

NORA Whose growing up—mine or the children's?

HELMER Both yours and the children's, Nora darling.

NORA Oh Torvald, you're not the man to bring me up to be the right kind of wife for you.

HELMER How can you say that?

NORA And I—? What qualifications do I have for bringing up the children?

HELMER Nora!

NORA You said so yourself a minute ago—that you didn't dare to trust me with them.

HELMER In the first flush of anger, yes. Surely, you're not going to count that.

NORA But you were quite right. I am *not* qualified. Something else has to come first. Somehow I have to grow up myself. And you are not the man to help me do that. That's a job I have to do by myself. And that's why I'm leaving you.

HELMER (*jumps up*) What did you say!

NORA I have to be by myself if I am to find out about myself and about all the other things too. So I can't stay here with you any longer.

HELMER Nora, Nora!

NORA I'm leaving now. I'm sure Kristine will put me up for tonight.

HELMER You're out of your mind! I won't let you! I forbid you!

NORA You can't forbid me anything any more; it won't do any good. I'm taking my own things with me. I won't accept anything from you, either now or later.

HELMER But this is madness!

NORA Tomorrow I'm going home—I mean back to my old home town. It will be easier for me to find some kind of job there.

HELMER Oh, you blind, inexperienced creature—!

NORA I must see to it that I get experience, Torvald.

HELMER Leaving your home, your husband, your children! Not a thought of what people will say!

NORA I can't worry about that. All I know is that I have to leave.

HELMER Oh, this is shocking! Betraying your most sacred duties like this!

NORA And what do you consider my most sacred duties?

HELMER Do I need to tell you that? They are your duties to your husband and your children.

NORA I have other duties equally sacred.

HELMER You do not. What duties would they be?

NORA My duties to myself.

HELMER You are a wife and a mother before you are anything else.

NORA I don't believe that any more. I believe I am first of all a human being, just as much as you—or at any rate that I must try to become one. Oh, I know very well that most people agree with you, Torvald, and that it says something like that in all the books. But what people say and what the books say is no longer enough for me. I have to think about these things myself and see if I can't find the answers.

HELMER You mean to tell me you don't know what your proper place in your own home is? Don't you have a reliable guide in such matters? Don't you have religion?

NORA Oh but Torvald—I don't really know what religion is.

HELMER What are you saying!

NORA All I know is what the Reverend Hansen told me when he prepared me for confirmation. He said that religion was *this* and it was *that.* When I get by myself, away from here, I'll have to look into that, too. I have to decide if what the Reverend Hansen said was right, or anyway if it is right for *me.*

HELMER Oh, this is unheard of in a young woman! If religion can't guide you, let me appeal to your conscience. For surely you have moral feelings? Or—answer me—maybe you don't?

NORA Well, you see, Torvald, I don't really know what to say. I just don't know. I am confused about these things. All I know is that my ideas are quite different from yours. I have just found out that the laws are different from what I thought they were, but in no way can I get it into my head that those laws are right. A woman shouldn't have the right to spare her dying old father or save her husband's life! I just can't believe that.

HELMER You speak like a child. You don't understand the society you live in.

NORA No, I don't. But I want to find out about it. I have to make up my mind who is right, society or I.

HELMER You are sick, Nora; you have a fever. I really don't think you are in your right mind.

NORA I have never felt so clearheaded and sure of myself as I do tonight.

HELMER And clearheaded and sure of yourself you're leaving your husband and children?

NORA Yes.

HELMER Then there is only one possible explanation.

NORA What?

HELMER You don't love me any more.

NORA No, that's just it.

HELMER Nora! Can you say that?

NORA I am sorry, Torvald, for you have always been so good to me. But I can't help it. I don't love you any more.

HELMER (*with forced composure*) And this too is a clear and sure conviction?

NORA Completely clear and sure. That's why I don't want to stay here any more.

HELMER And are you ready to explain to me how I came to forfeit your love?

NORA Certainly I am. It was tonight, when the wonderful didn't happen. That was when I realized you were not the man I thought you were.

HELMER You have to explain. I don't understand.

NORA I have waited patiently for eight years, for I wasn't such a fool that I thought the wonderful is something that happens any old day. Then this—thing—came crashing in on me, and then there wasn't a doubt in my mind that now—now comes the wonderful. When Krogstad's letter was in that mailbox, never for a moment did it even occur to me that you would submit to his conditions. I was so absolutely certain that you would say to him: make the whole thing public—tell everybody. And when that had happened—

HELMER Yes, then what? When I had surrendered my wife to shame and disgrace—!

NORA When that had happened, I was absolutely certain that you would stand up and take the blame and say, "I'm the guilty one."

HELMER Nora!

NORA You mean I never would have accepted such a sacrifice from you? Of course not. But what would my protests have counted against yours. *That* was the wonderful I was hoping for in terror. And to prevent that I was going to kill myself.

HELMER I'd gladly work nights and days for you, Nora—endure sorrow and want for your sake. But nobody sacrifices his *honor* for his love.

NORA A hundred thousand women have done so.

HELMER Oh, you think and talk like a silly child.

NORA All right. But you don't think and talk like the man I can live with. When you had gotten over your fright—not because of what threatened *me* but because of the risk to *you*—and the whole danger was past, then you acted as if nothing at all had happened. Once again I was your little songbird, your doll, just as before, only now you had to handle her even more carefully, because she was so frail and weak. (*rises*) Torvald—that moment I realized that I had been living here for eight years with a stranger and had borne him three children—Oh, I can't stand thinking about it! I feel like tearing myself to pieces!

HELMER (*heavily*) I see it, I see it. An abyss has opened up between us.—Oh but Nora—surely it can be filled?

NORA The way I am now I am no wife for you.

HELMER I have it in me to change.

NORA Perhaps—if your doll is taken from you.

HELMER To part—to part from you! No, no, Nora! I can't grasp that thought!

NORA (*goes out, right*) All the more reason why it has to be. (*She returns with her outdoor clothes and a small bag, which she sets down on the chair by the table.*)

HELMER Nora, Nora! Not now! Wait till tomorrow.

NORA (*putting on her coat*) I can't spend the night in a stranger's rooms.

HELMER But couldn't we live here together like brother and sister—?

NORA (*tying on her hat*) You know very well that wouldn't last long—. (*wraps her shawl around her*) Goodbye, Torvald. I don't want to see the children. I know I leave them in better hands than mine. The way I am now I can't be anything to them.

HELMER But some day, Nora—some day—?

NORA How can I tell? I have no idea what's going to become of me.

HELMER But you're still my wife, both as you are now and as you will be.

NORA Listen, Torvald—when a wife leaves her husband's house, the way I am doing now, I have heard he has no more legal responsibilities for her. At any rate, I now release you from all responsibility. You are not to feel yourself obliged to me for anything, and I have no obligations to you. There has to be full freedom on both sides. Here is your ring back. Now give me mine.

HELMER Even this?

NORA Even this.

HELMER Here it is.

NORA There. So now it's over. I'm putting the keys here. The maids know everything about the house—better than I. Tomorrow, after I'm gone, Kristine will come over and pack my things from home. I want them sent after me.

HELMER Over! It's all over! Nora, will you never think of me?

NORA I'm sure I'll often think of you and the children and this house.

HELMER May I write to you, Nora?

NORA No—never. I won't have that.

HELMER But send you things—? You must let me.

NORA Nothing, nothing.

HELMER —help you, when you need help—?

NORA I told you, no; I won't have it. I'll accept nothing from strangers.

HELMER Nora—can I never again be more to you than a stranger?

NORA (*picks up her bag*) Oh Torvald—then the most wonderful of all would have to happen—

HELMER Tell me what that would be—!

NORA For that to happen, both you and I would have to change so that—Oh Torvald, I no longer believe in the wonderful.

HELMER But I *will* believe. Tell me! Change, so that—?

NORA So that our living together would become a true marriage. Goodbye. (*She goes out through the hall.*)

HELMER (*sinks down on a chair near the door and covers his face with his hands*) Nora! Nora! (*looks around him and gets up*) All empty. She's gone. (*with sudden hope*) The most wonderful—?!

(*From downstairs comes the sound of a heavy door slamming shut.*)

THE CHERRY ORCHARD

(1904)

ANTON CHEKHOV (1860–1904)

There is not much that can be said for Russian drama and theatre before the nineteenth century. The sprawling giant of a country hovering over eastern Europe, its heritage as much Asiatic as European, took a long time to become a part of the Western literary family. Neither the Eastern (Byzantine) rites nor Roman Catholicism, struggling to achieve dominance, approved of sectarian art or anything associated with profane entertainments. Russia was a feudal society, a slave state in its support of serfdom, and only a tiny minority lived at the top and enjoyed any of the privileges of the more sophisticated societies developing in England and on the continent. The great mass of the population remained essentially illiterate.

Within Russia, the Russian language was regarded as barbaric; members of the privileged society and the court preferred the more "civilized" tongues, mainly French, spoken well into the nineteenth century by the educated elite. There was little or no desire to further a native Russian art outside the church. Peter the Great, who ruled from 1682 to 1725, made a few gestures toward establishing a popular theatre, but not much came of his efforts. However, the drama that did eventually emerge was able to survive heavy-handed censorship, inferior scripts, a lack of acting talent, and limited public interest, eventually to gain, in partnership with the great novelists of the nineteenth century such as Dostoyevski, Tolstoi, and Turgenev, a prestige equal in quality if not quantity to the rest of Europe.

The invasion of Russia by Napoleon, finally thwarted by his expulsion in 1812, aroused intense patriotism among the Russian people and a national consciousness hitherto unknown. Suddenly the Russian language, previously held in such contempt, was acceptable for literary expression. The first to use it was Alexander Pushkin (1799–1837), whose *Boris Godunov* (1825), is familiar today in Moussorgski's opera. The play's theme of a tyrant in conflict with his subjects was considered so dangerous that it was not staged until 1870.

Nikolai Gogol (1809–1852), noted for his novel on Russian provincial life, *Dead Souls* (1842), is best remembered for his satire on corruption and incompetence in government bureaucracy, *The Inspector General* of 1836. Its farcical complications surrounding a case of mistaken identity that places a penniless derelict in a high position of authority have never lost their appeal or the aptness of their barbs. Ivan Turgenev (1818–1883) is generally regarded as Chekhov's most important predecessor. His *A Month in the Country* of 1850 (not produced until 1872 because of the usual censorship complications) derived its dramatic conflict from the inner nature of the characters rather than from external factors, a style to be so brilliantly perfected by Chekhov.

Maxim Gorki (1868–1936) was a Soviet hero whose literary output belongs almost entirely in the post-Revolutionary period. He became an early Bolshevik organizer and his works, most of them sufficiently revolutionary to please the Soviet authorities, were controversial enough before the Revolution to keep him in constant trouble with the censors. His *The Lower Depths* (1902) is probably the greatest naturalistic play in modern drama, and it has maintained its reputation everywhere. Gorki was deeply concerned about social injustices and inequalities. His overpowering portrayal of life in the fetid underworld of a Moscow cellar flophouse has never been equaled in its unrelenting naturalistic portrayal, not only in the horrors of this repelling refuge, but in the derelicts, down-and-outs, criminals, and other lost souls who live and die there in the worst of human degradation. It is also a play that ridicules the ludicrous attempts of do-gooders to bring solace and hope to these people through the ministrations of the central character, Luka, whose well-intentioned but ill-conceived plans only backfire and bring peace to no one.

Gorki was closely associated with the Moscow Art Theatre, whose theatre building was dedicated to him, but unlike Chekhov, who was equally important to its establishment and growth, he survived to see the theatre become one of the world's most renowned producing companies. To appreciate its importance some historical background is helpful.

The most direct influence came from a German group that fostered a stage revolution of its own. The Meiningen Players, organized by George, Duke of Saxe-Meiningen, entered the theatrical scene in 1874. Before that time, there had been almost no attempt to coordinate all the aspects of costume, scene, and cast into any kind of unified whole. The idea of a *director,* one individual in charge of the overall production, the person who bore final responsibility for what appeared on opening night, did not exist. Major actors stood apart, poorly integrated into the rest of the cast. Costumes were generally historically inauthentic, and scenery was one of the lesser artistic concerns. Crowd scenes, when needed, were mostly mob scenes. Between 1874 and 1890, Meiningen put an end to all this chaos. He created a stage picture that could convey to an audience the sense that everything occurring on stage had a believable reality. Meiningen's approach was perfectly adapted to the realism and naturalism of Ibsen, Strindberg, and, of course, Chekhov, and his accomplishments have left their permanent mark on Western drama ever since.

The tiny experimental Théâtre Libre of André Antoine founded in Paris in 1887 to give the new realistic plays a proper milieu was directly influenced by

Saxe-Meiningen, followed by The Frei Bühne (free theatre) in Berlin in 1888, but the Moscow Art Theatre was most directly affected. Konstantin Stanislavski (1863–1938), an actor and producer who became as well one of the foremost teachers of acting, found the Meiningen style to be precisely what the professional theatre needed. In 1898, therefore, he helped to found the Moscow Art Theatre; its impact on the theatre, not only of that time, but ever since, has been profound. Stanislavski's acting theories, which he diligently taught to his acting companies, are spelled out in detail in his two famous books, *My Life in Art* (1924) and especially in *An Actor Prepares* (1926), still the "bible" of a very large number of professional actors.

Stanislavsky and the Moscow Art Theatre demanded, as had Saxe-Meiningen, a fully authentic *mise en scène,* historically accurate in costume, setting, props, and all, and precise control of crowd scenes that Meiningen had perfected. Its strongest emphasis was placed on his insistence that the actor convey the immediacy of the character's experience in order to project the sense of absolute reality in the individual's behavior, based as much as possible on the performer's personal awareness of and identification with the character he or she was creating. This theory that the actor in effect *becomes* the character, rather than merely interpreting it, demanded a concentration on the role and a meticulousness in rehearsal that had never before been practiced. Stanislavski's school of acting has always been controversial, but it still exists, particularly in America, as the basis of "method" acting.

Although the fame of many of the playwrights who preceded Chekhov has been limited beyond Russia, Chekhov is the outstanding exception. His short stories, farces, and longer plays are studied and produced everywhere. This good, gentle physician, doomed to die of consumption at a distressingly early age, wrote four plays, *The Seagull* (1896), *Uncle Vanya* (1899), *The Three Sisters* (1901), and *The Cherry Orchard,* uniformly regarded as among our finest pieces of dramatic realism. It is a very special kind of realism, and it makes unusual demands upon the actors who perform and the audience who watches. At first encounter, these dramas strike one as virtually plotless discussions of unrequited love and frustrated careers among a group of self-centered directionless human beings existing in genteel poverty who do nothing but sit around decaying country estates, attempting, mostly without success, to entertain or make love to each other, and drinking endless glasses of tea. Their creator regarded them as comedies.

What Chekhov has written, in fact, *are* some of the best examples of the realistic comedy of sensibility. With great sensitivity and sympathy, he portrays a modestly high level of Russian society whose members are caught amidst rapid social change that will soon see the end of their calm and indolent world. They are pitiful people, distressed in their inability to figure out what is happening while remaining resentfully incapable of adjusting. They are ultimately doomed, but they are charming, refined people whose mundane daily existences the dramatist transforms into effective and highly literate drama. Their encounters may be far removed from our own, but their emotional reactions are not, and Chekhov is able to convey their humdrum, superficial existence through a downbeat but universally appealing portrayal of the human experience.

The underwritten nature of Chekhov's script and the resultant underplaying was at first a complete failure. *The Seagull,* initially produced in the conventional commercial venue of the Imperial Theatre, was utterly incomprehensible to an audience incapable of understanding what Chekhov was trying to do. In fact, the results were so dismal that Chekhov vowed to return to his medical practice and forget the stage altogether. A different interpretation was mandatory, and fortunately for Chekhov and for European drama, it was found in the move to the Moscow Art Theatre. There the play became so successful that a seagull has become the theatre's permanent logo.

It is not difficult to understand the early puzzled reaction to *The Seagull's* approach to comedy. The characters as such are not funny. In fact, their indolence and obvious boredom with themselves and with each other as they wander aimlessly around a decaying country estate create no overt comic action. But in spite of their pitiful struggles and a needless death at the end, the characters are consistently comic because, in best comic fashion, they are strictly second-rate, always hoping for greatness, never remotely able to reach it. Fully realized by the author, created with considerable depth, they live a sadly comic life, with their fates pathetic but not tragic. They speak and act as ordinary creatures who watch their lives slip out from under them, with no way of stopping the erosion. The tone is set in the play's first lines when Masha, asked why she always wears black, replies matter of factly, "I am in mourning for my life."

In *Uncle Vanya* a weary collection of insignificant people—a student, a doctor, a retired professor, all fairly standard Chekhovian figures—come and go inside and outside a dreary country house, getting nowhere in particular, grating on each other's nerves. And in *The Three Sisters* the young ladies do little more than yearn to go to Moscow, prepare to go to Moscow, and never succeed in departing.

Yet all this is, in truth, a gross oversimplification of what Chekhov is doing. Every one of his four important plays creates an impact on an audience at once comic and pitiful, an impact that hits the viewer as the revelation of some very deep and human emotional problems—those experienced by everyone in the comedy of life. The laughs in Chekhov are not loud or prolonged; they are quieter, more inward and introspective as audiences experience a sympathetic identity with the characters as human beings who will never be much better than conventionally mediocre.

Chekhov's plays support no stars. They demand something entirely new to the theatre of their time: carefully controlled *ensemble* acting. There is no leading part, no single major character. The group is the collective protagonist, and the actor who performs Chekhov must surrender any artistic ego to that group. At the same time, he or she must maintain the individual characterization needed to be set apart from all the others. The performer must recognize how

Chekhov loves the people he has created, refusing to criticize but realizing their quiet desperation. He offers them for what they are, ordinary people, unimportant to the world around them, desperately important to themselves, while those among whom they exist continually look the other way.

The Cherry Orchard, arguably Chekhov's best, is the perfect play in which to study the playwright's unique demands on his performers. The actor in Chekhov must portray, for instance, a Madame Ranevskaya who is not actually a simpleton in her wasteful extravagances and her inability to recognize that her fortune is gone, but one who is a thoroughly sympathetic woman whose foolishness we may not condone but we at least comprehend. Gayeff and his incessant billiards must come across as confused, charmingly absent-minded, but certainly not crazy. Lopahin, as confused as all the rest, must evoke sympathy, not antagonism, for he is far from being a villain. He may lack taste and "good breeding," but his search for security and social status as the son of a serf is legitimate. All of the characters are a touching lot, intrinsically comic without being particularly funny. Yet it is impossible not to laugh at them. We are both amused and bemused. Emotionally we identify with them while we seethe in frustration at their disturbing reality. And that's the problem in watching Chekhov. As an audience we yearn for action, for something to happen. If we remain disciplined in our observance, however, we recognize the storm and stress that make for genuinely effective drama.

A Note Concerning Characters' Names

All Russian names have three parts: (1) the given, or as it is often called, the Christian name, (2) the patronymic, taken from the name of the father and indicating the gender, and (3) the family name. Thus Yermolay Alexeevich means Yermolay, son (the *evich* means the person is male) of Alexe, and Lyuboff Andreevna means Lyuboff, daughter (the *evna* means the person is female) of Andre. Characters may address each other by the first name only, often by both the given name and the patronymic, and then, to confuse matters further, by the diminutive, or nickname, as in the case of Pyotr, generally addressed as Petya. Also confusing to the reader is the use of the last name to identify speakers, as in Lopahin, Trofimoff, Gayeff, and others. The reader will need a little perseverance to keep everybody straight.

The Cherry Orchard — ANTON CHEKHOV

Translated by Stark Young

CHARACTERS

YERMOLAY ALEXEEVICH LOPAHIN, *a merchant*
DUNYASHA, *a maid*
SEMYON PANTELEEVICH EPIHODOFF, *a clerk*
FIERS, *a valet, an old man of eighty-seven*
LYUBOFF ANDREEVNA RANEVSKAYA, *a landowner*
ANYA, *her daughter, seventeen years old*
CHARLOTTA IVANOVNA, *a governess*
VARYA, *Madam Ranevskaya's adopted daughter, twenty-four years old*
LEONID ANDREEVICH GAYEFF, *brother of Madam Ranevskaya*
BORIS BORISOVICH SEMYONOFF-PISHTCHIK, *a landowner*
YASHA, *a young valet*
PYOTR SERGEEVICH TROFIMOFF, *a student*
A STRANGER WHO PASSES BY
THE STATION-MASTER
A POST-OFFICE CLERK
VISITORS
SERVANTS

Act I

A room that is still called the nursery. One of the doors leads into ANYA*'s room. Dawn, the sun will soon be rising. It is May, the cherry trees are in blossom but in the orchard it is cold, with a morning frost. The windows in the room are closed.* DUNYASHA *enters with a candle and* LOPAHIN *with a book in his hand.*

LOPAHIN The train got in, thank God! What time is it?

DUNYASHA It's nearly two. (*blows out his candle*) It's already daylight.

LOPAHIN But how late was the train? Two hours at least. (*yawning and stretching*) I'm a fine one, I am, look what a fool thing I did! I drove here on purpose just to meet them at the station, and then all of a sudden I'd overslept myself! Fell asleep in my chair. How provoking!—You could have waked me up.

DUNYASHA I thought you had gone. (*listening*) Listen, I think they are coming now.

LOPAHIN (*listening*) No—No, there's the luggage and one thing and another. (*a pause*) Lyuboff Andreevna has been living abroad five years. I don't know what she is like now—She is a good woman. An easy-going, simple woman. I remember when I was a boy about fifteen, my father, who is at rest—in those days he ran a shop here in the village—hit me in the face with his fist, my nose was bleeding—We'd come to the yard together for something or other, and he was a little drunk. Lyuboff Andreevna, I can see her now, still so young, so slim, led me to the washbasin here in this very room, in the nursery. "Don't cry," she says, "little peasant, it will be well in time for your wedding"—(*a pause*) Yes, little peasant—My father was a peasant truly, and here I am in a white waistcoat and yellow shoes. Like a pig rooting in a pastry shop—I've got this rich, lots of money, but if you really stop and think of it, I'm just a peasant— (*turning the pages of a book*) Here I was reading a book and didn't get a thing out of it. Reading and went to sleep. (*a pause*)

DUNYASHA And all night long the dogs were not asleep, they know their masters are coming.

LOPAHIN What is it, Dunyasha, you're so—

DUNYASHA My hands are shaking. I'm going to faint.

LOPAHIN You're just so delicate, Dunyasha. And all dressed up like a lady, and your hair all done up! Mustn't do that. Must know your place.

(EPIHODOFF *enters, with a bouquet: he wears a jacket and highly polished boots with a loud squeak. As he enters he drops the bouquet.*)

EPIHODOFF (*picking up the bouquet*) Look, the gardener sent these, he says to put them in the dining room.

(*giving the bouquet to* DUNYASHA)

LOPAHIN And bring me some kvass.

DUNYASHA Yes, sir.

(*goes out*)

EPIHODOFF There is a morning frost now, three degrees of frost (*sighing*) and the cherries all in bloom. I cannot approve of our climate—I cannot. Our climate can never quite rise to the occasion. Listen, Yermolay Alexeevich, allow me to subtend, I bought myself, day before yesterday, some boots and they, I venture to assure you, squeak so that it is impossible. What could I grease them with?

LOPAHIN Go on. You annoy me.

EPIHODOFF Every day some misfortune happens to me. But I don't complain, I am used to it and I even smile.

(DUNYASHA *enters, serves* LOPAHIN *the kvass.*)

EPIHODOFF I'm going. (*stumbling over a chair and upsetting it*) There (*as if triumphant*), there, you see, pardon the expression, a circumstance like that, among others—It is simply quite remarkable.

(*goes out*)

DUNYASHA And I must tell you, Yermolay Alexeevich, that Epihodoff has proposed to me.

LOPAHIN Ah!

DUNYASHA I don't know really what to—He is a quiet man but sometimes when he starts talking, you can't understand a thing he means. It's all very nice, and full of feeling, but just doesn't make any sense. I sort of like him. He loves me madly. He's a man that's unfortunate, every day there's something or other. They tease him around here, call him twenty-two misfortunes—

LOPAHIN (*cocking his ear*) Listen, I think they are coming—

DUNYASHA They are coming! But what's the matter with me—I'm cold all over.

LOPAHIN They're really coming. Let's go meet them. Will she recognize me? It's five years we haven't seen each other.

DUNYASHA (*excitedly*) I'm going to faint this very minute. Ah, I'm going to faint!

(*Two carriages can be heard driving up to the house.* LOPAHIN *and* DUNYASHA *hurry out. The stage is empty. In the adjoining rooms a noise begins.* FIERS *hurries across the stage, leaning on a stick; he has been to meet* LYUBOFF ANDREEVNA, *and wears an old-fashioned livery and a high hat; he mutters something to himself, but you cannot understand a word of it. The noise offstage gets louder and louder. A voice: "Look! Let's go through here—"* LYUBOFF ANDREEVNA, ANYA *and* CHARLOTTA IVANOVNA, *with a little dog on a chain, all of them dressed for traveling,* VARYA, *in a coat and kerchief,* GAYEFF, SEMYONOFF-PISHTCHIK, LOPAHIN, DUNYASHA, *with a bundle and an umbrella, servants with pieces of luggage—all pass through the room.*)

ANYA Let's go through here. Mama, do you remember what room this is?

LYUBOFF ANDREEVNA (*happily, through her tears*) The nursery!

VARYA How cold it is, my hands are stiff. (*to* LYUBOFF ANDREEVNA) Your rooms, the white one and the violet, are just the same as ever, Mama.

LYUBOFF ANDREEVNA The nursery, my dear beautiful room—I slept here when I was little— (*crying*) And now I am like a child— (*kisses her brother and* VARYA, *then her brother again*) And Varya is just the same as ever, looks like a nun. And I knew Dunyasha— (*kisses* DUNYASHA)

GAYEFF The train was two hours late. How's that? How's that for good management?

CHARLOTTA (*to* PISHTCHIK) My dog he eats nuts too.

PISHTCHIK (*astonished*) Think of that!

(*Everybody goes out except* ANYA *and* DUNYASHA.)

DUNYASHA We waited so long— (*taking off* ANYA's *coat and hat*)

ANYA I didn't sleep all four nights on the way. And now I feel so chilly.

DUNYASHA It was Lent when you left, there was some snow then, there was frost, and now? My darling (*laughing and kissing her*), I waited so long for you, my joy, my life—I'm telling you now, I can't keep from it another minute.

ANYA (*wearily*) There we go again—

DUNYASHA The clerk Epihodoff, proposed to me after Holy Week.

ANYA You're always talking about the same thing— (*arranging her hair*) I've lost all my hairpins— (*She is tired to the point of staggering.*)

DUNYASHA I just don't know what to think. He loves me, loves me so!

ANYA (*looks in through her door, tenderly*) My room, my windows, it's just as if I had never been away. I'm home! Tomorrow morning I'll get up, I'll run into the orchard—Oh, if I only could go to sleep! I haven't slept all the way, I was tormented by anxiety.

DUNYASHA Day before yesterday, Pyotr Sergeevich arrived.

ANYA (*joyfully*) Petya!

DUNYASHA He's asleep in the bathhouse, he lives there. I am afraid, he says, of being in the way. (*taking her watch from her pocket and looking at it*) Somebody ought to wake him up. It's only that Varvara Mikhailovna told us not to. Don't you wake him up, she said.

(VARYA *enters with a bunch of keys at her belt.*)

VARYA Dunyasha, coffee, quick—Mama is asking for coffee.

DUNYASHA This minute.

(*goes out*)

VARYA Well, thank goodness, you've come back. You are home again. (*caressingly*) My darling is back! My precious is back!

ANYA I've had such a time.

VARYA I can imagine!

ANYA I left during Holy Week, it was cold then. Charlotta talked all the way and did her tricks. Why did you fasten Charlotta on to me—?

VARYA But you couldn't have traveled alone, darling; not at seventeen!

ANYA We arrived in Paris, it was cold there and snowing. I speak terrible French. Mama lived on the fifth floor; I went to see her; there were some French people in her room, ladies, an old priest with his prayer book, and the place was full of tobacco smoke—very dreary. Suddenly I began to feel sorry for Mama, so sorry, I drew her to me, held her close and couldn't let her go. Then Mama kept hugging me, crying—yes—

VARYA (*tearfully*) Don't—oh, don't—

ANYA Her villa near Mentone she had already sold, she had nothing left, nothing. And I didn't have a kopeck left. It was all we could do to get here. And Mama doesn't understand! We sit down to dinner at a station and she orders, insists on the most expensive things and gives the waiters rouble tips. Charlotta does the same. Yasha too demands his share; it's simply dreadful. Mama has her butler, Yasha, we've brought him here—

VARYA I was the wretch.

ANYA Well, how are things? Has the interest on the mortgage been paid?

VARYA How could we?

ANYA Oh, my God, my God—!

VARYA In August the estate is to be sold—

ANYA My God—!

LOPAHIN (*looking in through the door and mooing like a cow*) Moo-o-o— (*goes away*)

VARYA (*tearfully*) I'd land him one like that— (*shaking her fist*)

ANYA (*embracing* VARYA *gently*) Varya, has he proposed? (VARYA *shakes her head.*) But he loves you—Why don't you have it out with him, what are you waiting for?

VARYA I don't think anything will come of it for us. He is very busy, he hasn't any time for me—And doesn't notice me. God knows, it's painful for me to see him—Everybody talks about our marriage, everybody congratulates us, and the truth is, there's nothing to it—it's all like a dream— (*in a different tone*) You have a brooch looks like a bee.

ANYA (*sadly*) Mama bought it. (*going toward her room, speaking gaily, like a child*) And in Paris I went up in a balloon!

VARYA My darling is back! My precious is back! (DUNYASHA *has returned with the coffee pot and is making coffee.* VARYA *is standing by the door.*) Darling, I'm busy all day long with the house and I go around thinking things. If only you could be married to a rich man, I'd be more at peace too, I would go all by myself to a hermitage—then to Kiev—to Moscow, and I'd keep going like that from one holy place to another—I would go on and on. Heavenly!

ANYA The birds are singing in the orchard. What time is it now?

VARYA It must be after two. It's time you were asleep, darling. (*going into* ANYA'S *room*) Heavenly!

(YASHA *enters with a lap robe and a traveling bag.*)

YASHA (*crossing the stage airily*) May I go through here?

DUNYASHA We'd hardly recognize you, Yasha; you've changed so abroad!

YASHA Hm—And who are you?

DUNYASHA When you left here, I was like that— (*her hand so high from the floor*) I'm Dunyasha, Fyodor Kozoyedoff's daughter. You don't remember!

YASHA Hm—You little peach!

(*Looking around before he embraces her, she shrieks and drops a saucer;* YASHA *hurries out.*)

VARYA (*at the door, in a vexed tone*) And what's going on here?

DUNYASHA (*tearfully*) I broke a saucer—

VARYA That's good luck.

ANYA (*emerging from her room*) We ought to tell Mama beforehand: Petya is here—

VARYA I told them not to wake him up.

ANYA (*pensively*) Six years ago our father died, a month later our brother Grisha was drowned in the river, such a pretty little boy, just seven. Mama couldn't bear it, she went away, went away without ever looking back— (*shuddering*) How I understand her, if she only knew I did. (*a pause*) And Petya Trofimoff was Grisha's tutor, he might remind—

(FIERS *enters; he is in a jacket and white waistcoat.*)

FIERS (*going to the coffee urn, busy with it*) The mistress will have her breakfast here— (*putting on white gloves*) Is the coffee ready? (*to* DUNYASHA, *sternly*) You! What about the cream?

DUNYASHA Oh, my God—

(*hurrying out*)

FIERS (*busy at the coffee urn*) Oh, you good-for-nothing—! (*muttering to himself*) Come back from Paris—And the master used to go to Paris by coach— (*laughing*)

VARYA Fiers, what are you—?

FIERS At your service. (*joyfully*) My mistress is back! It's what I've been waiting for! Now I'm ready to die— (*crying for joy*)

(LYUBOFF ANDREEVNA, GAYEFF *and* SEMYONOFF-PISHTCHIK *enter;* SEMYONOFF-PISHTCHIK *is in a podyovka*[1] *of fine cloth and sharovary.*[2] GAYEFF *enters; he makes gestures with his hands and body as if he were playing billiards.*)

LYUBOFF ANDREEVNA How is it? Let me remember—Yellow into the corner! Duplicate in the middle!

GAYEFF I cut into the corner. Sister, you and I slept here in this very room once, and now I am fifty-one years old, strange as that may seem—

LOPAHIN Yes, time passes.

GAYEFF What?

LOPAHIN Time, I say, passes.

GAYEFF And it smells like patchouli here.

ANYA I'm going to bed. Good night, Mama. (*kissing her mother*)

LYUBOFF ANDREEVNA My sweet little child. (*kissing her hands*) You're glad you are home? I still can't get myself together.

ANYA Good-by, Uncle.

GAYEFF (*kissing her face and hands*) God be with you. How like your mother you are! (*to his sister*) Lyuba, at her age you were exactly like her.

(ANYA *shakes hands with* LOPAHIN *and* PISHTCHIK, *goes out and closes the door behind her.*)

---

[1]short tunic worn under a coat or jacket [2]loose, bloused trousers, the legs of which are tied at the ankle or tucked into the boots

LYUBOFF ANDREEVNA She's very tired.

PISHTCHIK It is a long trip, I imagine.

VARYA (*to* LOPAHIN *and* PISHTCHIK) Well, then, sirs? It's going on three o'clock, time for gentlemen to be going.

LYUBOFF ANDREEVNA (*laughing*) The same old Varya. (*drawing her to her and kissing her*) There, I'll drink my coffee, then we'll all go. (FIERS *puts a small cushion under her feet.*) Thank you, my dear. I am used to coffee. Drink it day and night. Thank you, my dear old soul. (*kissing* FIERS)

VARYA I'll go see if all the things have come.

(*goes out*)

LYUBOFF ANDREEVNA Is it really me sitting here? (*laughing*) I'd like to jump around and wave my arms. (*covering her face with her hands*) But I may be dreaming! God knows I love my country, love it deeply, I couldn't look out of the car window, I just kept crying. (*tearfully*) However, I must drink my coffee. Thank you, Fiers, thank you, my dear old friend. I'm so glad you're still alive.

FIERS Day before yesterday.

GAYEFF He doesn't hear well.

LOPAHIN And I must leave right now. It's nearly five o'clock in the morning, for Kharkov. What a nuisance! I wanted to look at you—talk—You are as beautiful as ever.

PISHTCHIK (*breathing heavily*) Even more beautiful—In your Paris clothes—It's a feast for the eyes—

LOPAHIN Your brother, Leonid Andreevich here, says I'm a boor, a peasant money grubber, but that's all the same to me, absolutely. Let him say it. All I wish is you'd trust me as you used to, and your wonderful, touching eyes would look at me as they did. Merciful God! My father was a serf; belonged to your grandfather and your father; but you, your own self, you did so much for me once that I've forgotten all that and love you like my own kin—more than my kin.

LYUBOFF ANDREEVNA I can't sit still—I can't. (*jumping up and walking about in great excitement*) I'll never live through this happiness—Laugh at me, I'm silly—My own little bookcase—! (*kissing the bookcase*) My little table!

GAYEFF And in your absence the nurse here died.

LYUBOFF ANDREEVNA (*sitting down and drinking coffee*) Yes, may she rest in Heaven! They wrote me.

GAYEFF And Anastasy died. Cross-eyed Petrushka left me and lives in town now at the police officer's. (*taking out of his pocket a box of hard candy and sucking a piece*)

PISHTCHIK My daughter, Dashenka—sends you her greetings—

LOPAHIN I want to tell you something very pleasant, cheerful. (*glancing at his watch*) I'm going right away. There's no time for talking. Well, I'll make it two or three words. As you know, your cherry orchard is to be sold for your debts; the auction is set for August 22nd, but don't you worry, my dear, you just sleep in peace, there's a way out of it. Here's my plan. Please listen to me. Your estate is only thirteen miles from town. They've run the railroad by it. Now if the cherry orchard and the land along the river were cut up into building lots and leased for summer cottages, you'd have at the very lowest twenty-five thousand roubles per year income.

GAYEFF Excuse me, what rot!

LYUBOFF ANDREEVNA I don't quite understand you, Yermolay Alexeevich.

LOPAHIN At the very least you will get from the summer residents twenty-five roubles per year for a two-and-a-half acre lot and if you post a notice right off, I'll bet you anything that by autumn you won't have a single patch of land free, everything will be taken. In a word, my congratulations, you are saved. The location is wonderful, the river's so deep. Except, of course, it all needs to be tidied up, cleared—For instance, let's say, tear all the old buildings down and this house, which is no good any more, and cut down the old cherry orchard—

LYUBOFF ANDREEVNA Cut down? My dear, forgive me, you don't understand at all. If there's one thing in the whole province that's interesting—not to say remarkable—it's our cherry orchard.

LOPAHIN The only remarkable thing about this cherry orchard is that it's very big. There's a crop of cherries once every two years and even that's hard to get rid of. Nobody buys them.

GAYEFF This orchard is even mentioned in the encyclopedia.

LOPAHIN (*glancing at his watch*) If we don't cook up something and don't get somewhere, the cherry orchard and the entire estate will be sold at auction on the twenty-second of August. Do get it settled then! I swear there is no other way out. Not a one!

FIERS There was a time, forty-fifty years ago when the cherries were dried, soaked, pickled, cooked into jam and it used to be—

GAYEFF Keep quiet, Fiers.

FIERS And it used to be that the dried cherries were shipped by the wagon-load to Moscow and to Kharkov. And the money there was! And the dried cherries were soft then, juicy, sweet, fragrant—They had a way of treating them then—

LYUBOFF ANDREEVNA And where is that way now?

FIERS They have forgotten it. Nobody remembers it.

PISHTCHIK (*to* LYUBOFF ANDREEVNA) What's happening in Paris? How is everything? Did you eat frogs?

LYUBOFF ANDREEVNA I ate crocodiles.

PISHTCHIK Think of it—!

LOPAHIN Up to now in the country there have been only the gentry and the peasants, but now in summer the villa people too are coming in. All the towns, even the least big ones, are surrounded with cottages. In about twenty years very likely the summer resident will multiply enormously. He merely drinks tea on the porch now, but it might well happen that on this two-and-a-half acre lot of his, he'll go in for farming, and then your cherry orchard would be happy, rich, splendid—

GAYEFF (*getting hot*) What rot!

(VARYA *and* YASHA *enter.*)

VARYA Here, Mama. Two telegrams for you. (*choosing a key and opening the old bookcase noisily*) Here they are.

LYUBOFF ANDREEVNA From Paris. (*tearing up the telegrams without reading them*) Paris, that's all over—

GAYEFF Do you know how old this bookcase is, Lyuba? A week ago I pulled out the bottom drawer and looked, and there the figures were burned on it. The bookcase was made exactly a hundred years ago. How's that? Eh? You might celebrate its jubilee. It's an inanimate object, but all the same, be that as it may, it's a bookcase.

PISHTCHIK (*in astonishment*) A hundred years—! Think of it—!

GAYEFF Yes—quite something— (*shaking the bookcase*) Dear, honored bookcase! I saluted your existence, which for more than a hundred years has been directed toward the clear ideals of goodness and justice; your silent appeal to fruitful endeavor has not flagged in all the course of a hundred years, sustaining (*tearfully*) through the generations of our family, our courage and our faith in a better future and nurturing in us ideals of goodness and of a social consciousness.

(*a pause*)

LOPAHIN Yes.

LYUBOFF ANDREEVNA You're the same as ever, Lenya.

GAYEFF (*slightly embarrassed*) Carom to the right into the corner pocket. I cut into the side pocket!

LOPAHIN (*glancing at his watch*) Well, it's time for me to go.

YASHA (*handing medicine to* LYUBOFF ANDREEVNA) Perhaps you'll take the pills now—

PISHTCHIK You should never take medicaments, dear madam—They do neither harm nor good—Hand them here, dearest lady. (*He takes the pillbox, shakes the pills out into his palm, blows on them, puts them in his mouth and washes them down with kvass.*) There! Now!

LYUBOFF ANDREEVNA (*startled*) Why, you've lost your mind!

PISHTCHIK I took all the pills.

LOPAHIN Such a glutton! (*Everyone laughs.*)

FIERS The gentleman stayed with us during Holy Week, he ate half a bucket of pickles— (*muttering*)

LYUBOFF ANDREEVNA What is he muttering about?

VARYA He's been muttering like that for three years. We're used to it.

YASHA In his dotage.

(CHARLOTTA IVANOVNA *in a white dress—she is very thin, her corset laced very tight—with a lorgnette at her belt, crosses the stage.*)

LOPAHIN Excuse me, Charlotta Ivanovna, I haven't had a chance yet to welcome you. (*trying to kiss her hand*)

CHARLOTTA (*drawing her hand away*) If I let you kiss my hand, 'twould be my elbow next, then my shoulder—

LOPAHIN No luck for me today. (*Everyone laughs.*) Charlotta Ivanovna, show us a trick!

CHARLOTTA No. I want to go to bed.

(*She goes out.*)

LOPAHIN In three weeks we shall see each other. (*kissing* LYUBOFF ANDREEVNA'S *hand*) Till then, good-by. It's time. (*to* GAYEFF) See you soon. (*kissing* PISHTCHIK) See you soon. (*shaking* VARYA'S *hand, then* FIER'S *and* YASHA'S) I don't feel like going. (*to* LYUBOFF ANDREEVNA) If you think it over and make up your mind about the summer cottages, let me know and I'll arrange a loan of something like fifty thousand roubles. Think it over seriously.

VARYA (*angrily*) Do go on, anyhow, will you!

LOPAHIN I'm going, I'm going—

(*He goes out.*)

GAYEFF Boor. However, pardon—Varya is going to marry him, it's Varya's little fiancé.

VARYA Don't talk too much, Uncle.

LYUBOFF ANDREEVNA Well, Varya, I should be very glad. He's a good man.

PISHTCHIK A man, one must say truthfully—A most worthy—And my Dashenka—says also that—she says all sorts of things— (*snoring but immediately waking up*) Nevertheless, dearest lady, oblige me—With a loan of two hundred and forty roubles—Tomorrow the interest on my mortgage has got to be paid—

VARYA (*startled*) There's not any money, none at all.

LYUBOFF ANDREEVNA Really, I haven't got anything.

PISHTCHIK I'll find it, somehow. (*laughing*) I never give up hope. There, I think to myself, all is lost, I am ruined and lo and behold—a railroad is put through my land and—they paid me. And then, just watch, something else will turn up—if not today, then tomorrow—Dashenka will win two hundred thousand—She has a ticket.

LYUBOFF ANDREEVNA We've finished the coffee, now we can go to bed.

FIERS (*brushing* GAYEFF'S *clothes, reprovingly*) You put on the wrong trousers again. What am I going to do with you!

VARYA (*softly*) Anya is asleep. (*opening the window softly*) Already the sun's rising—it's not cold. Look, Mama! What beautiful trees! My Lord, what air! The starlings are singing!

GAYEFF (*opening another window*) The orchard is all white. You haven't forgotten, Lyuba? That long lane there runs straight—as a strap stretched out. It glistens on moonlight nights. Do you remember? You haven't forgotten it?

LYUBOFF ANDREEVNA (*looking out of the window on to the orchard*) Oh, my childhood, my innocence! I slept in this nursery and looked out on the orchard from here, every morning happiness awoke with me, it was just as it is now, then, nothing has changed. (*laughing with joy*) All, all white! Oh, my orchard! After a dark, rainy autumn and cold winter, you are young again and full of happiness. The heavenly angels have not deserted you—If I only could lift the weight from my breast, from my shoulders, if I could only forget my past!

GAYEFF Yes, and the orchard will be sold for debt, strange as that may seem.

LYUBOFF ANDREEVNA Look, our dear mother is walking through the orchard—In a white dress! (*laughing happily*) It's she.

GAYEFF Where?

VARYA God be with you, Mama!

LYUBOFF ANDREEVNA There's not anybody, it only seemed so. To the right, as you turn to the summerhouse, a little white tree is leaning there, looks like a woman— (TROFIMOFF *enters, in a student's uniform, well worn, and glasses.*) What a wonderful orchard! The white masses of blossoms, the sky all blue.

TROFIMOFF Lyuboff Andreevna! (*She looks around at him.*) I will just greet you and go immediately. (*kissing her hand warmly*) I was told to wait until morning, but I hadn't the patience—

(LYUBOFF ANDREEVNA *looks at him puzzled.*)

VARYA (*tearfully*) This is Petya Trofimoff—

TROFIMOFF Petya Trofimoff, the former tutor of your Grisha—Have I really changed so?

(LYUBOFF ANDREEVNA *embraces him, crying quietly.*)

GAYEFF (*embarrassed*) There, there, Lyuba.

VARYA (*crying*) I told you, Petya, to wait till tomorrow.

LYUBOFF ANDREEVNA My Grisha—My boy—Grisha—Son—

VARYA What can we do, Mama? It's God's will.

TROFIMOFF (*in a low voice tearfully*) There, there—

LYUBOFF ANDREEVNA (*weeping softly*) My boy was lost, drowned—Why? Why, my friend? (*more quietly*) Anya is asleep there, and I am talking so loud—Making so much noise—But why, Petya? Why have you lost your looks? Why do you look so much older?

TROFIMOFF A peasant woman on the train called me a mangy-looking gentleman.

LYUBOFF ANDREEVNA You were a mere boy then, a charming young student, and now your hair's not very thick any more and you wear glasses. Are you really a student still? (*going to the door*)

TROFIMOFF Very likely I'll be a perennial student.

LYUBOFF ANDREEVNA (*kissing her brother, then* VARYA) Well, go to bed—You've grown older too, Leonid.

PISHTCHIK (*following her*) So that's it, we are going to bed now. Oh, my gout! I'm staying here—I'd like, Lyuboff Andreevna, my soul, tomorrow morning—Two hundred and forty roubles—

GAYEFF He's still at it.

PISHTCHIK Two hundred and forty roubles—To pay interest on the mortgage.

LYUBOFF ANDREEVNA I haven't any money, my dove.

PISHTCHIK I'll pay it back, my dear—It's a trifling sum—

LYUBOFF ANDREEVNA Oh, very well, Leonid will give—You give it to him, Leonid.

GAYEFF Oh, certainly, I'll give it to him. Hold out your pockets.

LYUBOFF ANDREEVNA What can we do, give it, he needs it—He'll pay it back.

(LYUBOFF ANDREEVNA, TROFIMOFF, PISHTCHIK *and* FIERS *go out.* GAYEFF, VARYA, *and* YASHA *remain.*)

GAYEFF My sister hasn't yet lost her habit of throwing money away. (*to* YASHA) Get away, my good fellow, you smell like hens.

YASHA (*with a grin*) And you are just the same as you used to be, Leonid Andreevich.

GAYEFF What? (*to* VARYA) What did he say?

VARYA (*to* YASHA) Your mother has come from the village, she's been sitting in the servants' hall ever since yesterday, she wants to see you—

YASHA The devil take her!

VARYA Ach, shameless creature!

YASHA A lot I need her! She might have come tomorrow.

(*goes out*)

VARYA Mama is just the same as she was, she hasn't changed at all. If she could, she'd give away everything she has.

GAYEFF Yes—If many remedies are prescribed for an illness, you may know the illness is incurable. I keep thinking, I wrack my brains, I have many remedies, a great many, and that means, really, I haven't any at all. It would be fine to inherit a fortune from somebody, it would be fine to marry off our Anya to a very rich man, it would be fine to go to Yaroslavl and try our luck with our old aunt, the Countess. Auntie is very, very rich.

VARYA (*crying*) If God would only help us!

GAYEFF Don't bawl! Auntie is very rich but she doesn't like us. To begin with, Sister married a lawyer, not a nobleman— (ANYA *appears at the door.*) Married not a nobleman and behaved herself, you could say, not very virtuously. She is good, kind, nice, I love her very much, but no matter how much you allow for the extenuating circumstances, you must admit she's a depraved woman. You feel it in her slightest movement.

VARYA (*whispering*) Anya is standing in the door there.

GAYEFF What? (*a pause*) It's amazing, something got in my right eye. I am beginning to see poorly. And on Thursday, when I was in the District Court—

(ANYA *enters.*)

VARYA But why aren't you asleep, Anya?

ANYA I don't feel like sleeping. I can't.

GAYEFF My little girl— (*kissing* ANYA's *face and hands*) My child— (*tearfully*) You are not my niece, you are my angel, you are everything to me. Believe me, believe—

ANYA I believe you, Uncle. Everybody loves you, respects you—But dear Uncle, you must keep quiet, just keep quiet—What were you saying, just now, about my mother, about your own sister? What did you say that for?

GAYEFF Yes, yes— (*putting her hand up over his face*) Really, it's terrible! My God! Oh, God, save me! And today I made a speech to the bookcase—So silly! And it was only when I finished it that I could see it was silly.

VARYA It's true, Uncle, you ought to keep quiet. Just keep quiet. That's all.

ANYA If you kept quiet, you'd have more peace.

GAYEFF I'll keep quiet. (*kissing* ANYA's *and* VARYA's *hands*) I'll keep quiet. Only this, it's about business. On Thursday I was in the District Court; well, a few of us gathered around and a conversation began about this and that, about lots of things; apparently it will be possible to arrange a loan on a promissory note to pay the bank the interest due.

VARYA If the Lord would only help us!

GAYEFF Tuesday I shall go and talk it over again. (*to* VARYA) Don't bawl! (*to* ANYA) Your mother will talk to Lopahin; of course, he won't refuse her . . . And as soon as you rest up, you will go to Yaroslavl to your great-aunt, the Countess. There, that's how we will move from three directions, and the business is in the bag. We'll pay the interest. I am convinced of that— (*putting a hard candy in his mouth*) On my honor I'll swear, by anything you like, that the estate shall not be sold! (*excitedly*) By my happiness, I swear! Here's my hand, call me a worthless, dishonorable man, if I allow it to come up for auction! With all my soul I swear it!

ANYA (*A quieter mood returns to her; she is happy.*) How good you are, Uncle, how clever! (*embracing her uncle*) I feel easy now! I feel easy! I'm happy!

FIERS (*enters, reproachfully*) Leonid Andreevich, you have no fear of God! When are you going to bed?

GAYEFF Right away, right away. You may go, Fiers. For this once I'll undress myself. Well, children, beddy bye—More details tomorrow, and now, go to bed (*kissing* ANYA *and* VARYA). I am a man of the eighties—It is a period that's not admired, but I can say, nevertheless, that I've suffered no little for my convictions in the course of my life. It is not for nothing that the peasant loves me. One must know the peasant! One must know from what—

ANYA Again, Uncle!

VARYA You, Uncle dear, keep quiet.

FIERS (*angrily*) Leonid Andreevich!

GAYEFF I'm coming, I'm coming—Go to bed. A double bank into the side pocket! A clean shot—

(*goes out,* FIERS *hobbling after him*)

ANYA I feel easy now. I don't feel like going to Yaroslavl; I don't like Great-aunt, but still I feel easy. Thanks to Uncle. (*sits down*)

VARYA I must get to sleep. I'm going. And there was unpleasantness here during your absence. In the old servants' quarters, as you know, live only the old servants: Yephemushka, Polya, Yevstignay, well, and Karp. They began to let every sort of creature spend the night with them—I didn't say anything. But then I hear they've spread the rumor that I'd given orders to feed them nothing but beans. Out of stinginess, you see—And all that from Yevstignay—Very well, I think to myself. If that's the way it is, I think to myself, then you just wait. I call in Yevstignay— (*yawning*) He comes—How is it, I say, that you, Yevstignay—You're such a fool— (*glancing at* ANYA) Anitchka!— (*a pause*) Asleep! (*takes* ANYA *by her arm*) Let's go to bed—Come on!— (*leading her*) My little darling fell asleep! Come on— (*They go. Far away beyond the orchard a shepherd is playing on a pipe.* TROFIMOFF *walks across the stage and, seeing* VARYA *and* ANYA, *stops.*) Shh—She is asleep—asleep—Let's go, dear.

ANYA (*softly, half dreaming*) I'm so tired—All the bells!—Uncle—dear—And Mama and Uncle—Varya.

VARYA Come on, my dear, come on. (*They go into* ANYA's *room.*).

TROFIMOFF (*tenderly*) My little sun! My spring!

Act II

A field. An old chapel, long abandoned, with crooked walls, near it a well, big stones that apparently were once tombstones, and an old bench. A road to the estate of GAYEFF *can be seen. On one side poplars rise, casting their shadows, the cherry orchard begins there. In the distance a row of telegraph poles; and far, far away, faintly traced on the horizon, is a large town, visible only in the clearest weather. The sun will soon be down.* CHARLOTTA, YASHA, *and* DUNYASHA *are sitting on the bench;* EPIHODOFF *is standing near and playing the guitar; everyone sits lost in thought.* CHARLOTTA *wears an old peak cap [fourrage];*[3] *she has taken a rifle from off her shoulders and is adjusting the buckle on the strap.*

CHARLOTTA (*pensively*) I have no proper passport, I don't know how old I am—it always seems to me I'm very young. When I was a little girl, my father and mother traveled from fair to fair and gave performances, very good ones. And I did *salto mortale*[4] and different tricks. And when Papa and Mama died, a German lady took me to live with her and began teaching me. Good. I grew up. And became a governess. But where I came from and who

[3]for hunting [4]leap of death

I am I don't know—Who my parents were, perhaps they weren't even married—I don't know. (*taking a cucumber out of her pocket and beginning to eat it*) I don't know a thing. (*a pause*) I'd like so much to talk but there's not anybody. I haven't anybody.

EPIHODOFF (*playing the guitar and singing*) "What care I for the noisy world, what care I for friends and foes."—How pleasant it is to play the mandolin!

DUNYASHA That's a guitar, not a mandolin. (*looking into a little mirror and powdering her face*)

EPIHODOFF For a madman who is in love this is a mandolin— (*singing*) "If only my heart were warm with the fire of requited love." (*Yasha sings with him.*)

CHARLOTTA How dreadfully these people sing—Phooey! Like jackals.

DUNYASHA (*to* YASHA) All the same what happiness to have been abroad.

YASHA Yes, of course. I cannot disagree with you. (*yawning and then lighting a cigar*)

EPIHODOFF That's easily understood. Abroad everything long since attained its complete development.

YASHA That's obvious.

EPIHODOFF I am a cultured man. I read all kinds of remarkable books, but the trouble is I cannot discover my own inclinations, whether to live or to shoot myself, but nevertheless, I always carry a revolver on me. Here it is— (*showing a revolver*)

CHARLOTTA That's done. Now I am going. (*slinging the rifle over her shoulder*) You are a very clever man, Epihodoff, and a very terrible one; the women must love you madly. Brrrr-r-r-r! (*going*) These clever people are all so silly, I haven't anybody to talk with. I'm always alone, alone, I have nobody and—Who I am, why I am, is unknown—

(*goes out without hurrying*)

EPIHODOFF Strictly speaking, not touching on other subjects, I must state about myself, in passing, that fate treats me mercilessly, as a storm does a small ship. If, let us suppose, I am mistaken, then why, to mention one instance, do I wake up this morning, look and there on my chest is a spider of terrific size—There, like that. (*showing the size with both hands*) And also I take some kvass to drink and in it I find something in the highest degree indecent, such as a cockroach. (*a pause*) Have you read Buckle?[5] (*a pause*) I desire to trouble you, Avdotya Feodorovna, with a couple of words.

DUNYASHA Speak.

EPIHODOFF I have a desire to speak with you alone— (*sighing*)

DUNYASHA (*embarrassed*) Very well—But bring me my cape first—by the cupboard—It's rather damp here—

[5]Henry Thomas Buckle (1821–1862), English historian who proposed a scientific method for writing history

EPIHODOFF Very well—I'll fetch it—Now I know what I should do with my revolver— (*takes the guitar and goes out playing*)

YASHA Twenty-two misfortunes! Between us he's a stupid man, it must be said. (*yawning*)

DUNYASHA God forbid he should shoot himself. (*a pause*) I've grown so uneasy, I'm always fretting. I was only a girl when I was taken into the master's house, and now I've lost the habit of simple living—and here are my hands white, white as a lady's. I've become so delicate, fragile, ladylike, afraid of everything—Frightfully so. And, Yasha, if you deceive me, I don't know what will happen to my nerves.

YASHA (*kissing her*) You little cucumber! Of course every girl must behave properly. What I dislike above everything is for a girl to conduct herself badly.

DUNYASHA I have come to love you passionately, you are educated, you can discuss anything. (*a pause*)

YASHA (*yawning*) Yes, sir—To my mind it is like this: If a girl loves someone, it means she is immoral. (*a pause*) It is pleasant to smoke a cigar in the clear air— (*listening*) They are coming here—It is the ladies and gentlemen— (DUNYASHA *impulsively embraces him.*)

YASHA Go to the house, as though you had been to bathe in the river, go by this path, otherwise, they might meet you and suspect me of making a rendezvous with you. That I cannot tolerate.

DUNYASHA (*with a little cough*) Your cigar has given me the headache.

(*goes out*)

(YASHA *remains, sitting near the chapel.* LYUBOFF ANDREEVNA, GAYEFF *and* LOPAHIN *enter.*)

LOPAHIN We must decide definitely, time doesn't wait. Why, the matter's quite simple. Are you willing to lease your land for summer cottages or are you not? Answer in one word, yes or no? Just one word!

LYUBOFF ANDREEVNA Who is it smokes those disgusting cigars out here—? (*sitting down*)

GAYEFF The railroad running so near is a great convenience. (*sitting down*) We made a trip to town and lunched there—Yellow in the side pocket! Perhaps I should go in the house first and play one game—

LYUBOFF ANDREEVNA You'll have time.

LOPAHIN Just one word! (*imploringly*) Do give me your answer!

GAYEFF (*yawning*) What?

LYUBOFF ANDREEVNA (*looking in her purse*) Yesterday there was lots of money in it. Today there's very little. My poor Varya! For the sake of economy she feeds everybody milk soup, and in the kitchen the old people get nothing but beans, and here I spend money—senselessly— (*dropping her purse and scattering gold coins*) There they go scattering! (*She is vexed.*)

YASHA Allow me, I'll pick them up in a second. (*picking up the coins*)

LYUBOFF ANDREEVNA If you will, Yasha. And why did I go in town for lunch—? Your restaurant with its music is trashy, the tablecloths smell of soap—Why drink so much, Lyonya? Why eat so much? Why talk so much? Today in the restaurant you were talking a lot again, and all of it beside the point. About the seventies, about the decadents. And to whom? Talking to waiters about the decadents!

LOPAHIN Yes.

GAYEFF (*waving his hand*) I am incorrigible, that's evident— (*to* YASHA, *irritably*) What is it?—You are forever swirling around in front of us!

YASHA (*laughing*) I cannot hear your voice without laughing.

GAYEFF (*to his sister*) Either I or he—

LYUBOFF ANDREEVNA Go away, Yasha. Go on—

YASHA (*giving* LYUBOFF ANDREEVNA *her purse*) I am going right away. (*barely suppressing his laughter*) This minute.

(*goes out*)

LOPAHIN The rich Deriganoff intends to buy your estate. They say he is coming personally to the auction.

LYUBOFF ANDREEVNA And where did you hear that?

LOPAHIN In town they are saying it.

GAYEFF Our Yaroslavl aunt promised to send us something, but when and how much she will send, nobody knows—

LOPAHIN How much will she send? A hundred thousand? Two hundred?

LYUBOFF ANDREEVNA Well—maybe ten, fifteen thousand—we'd be thankful for that.

LOPAHIN Excuse me, but such light-minded people as you are, such odd, unbusinesslike people, I never saw. You are told in plain Russian that your estate is being sold up and you just don't seem to take it in.

LYUBOFF ANDREEVNA But what are we to do? Tell us what?

LOPAHIN I tell you every day. Every day I tell you the same thing. Both the cherry orchard and the land have got to be leased for summer cottages, it has to be done right now, quick—The auction is right under your noses. Do understand! Once you finally decide that there are to be summer cottages, you will get all the money you want, and then you'll be saved.

LYUBOFF ANDREEVNA Summer cottages and summer residents—it is so trivial, excuse me.

GAYEFF I absolutely agree with you.

LOPAHIN I'll either burst out crying, or scream, or faint. I can't bear it! You are torturing me! (*to* GAYEFF) You're a perfect old woman!

GAYEFF What?

LOPAHIN A perfect old woman! (*about to go*)

LYUBOFF ANDREEVNA (*alarmed*) No, don't go, stay, my lamb, I beg you. Perhaps we will think of something!

LOPAHIN What is there to think about?

LYUBOFF ANDREEVNA Don't go, I beg you. With you here it is more cheerful anyhow— (*a pause*) I keep waiting for something, as if the house were about to tumble down on our heads.

GAYEFF (*deep in thought*) Double into the corner pocket—Bank into the wide pocket—

LYUBOFF ANDREEVNA We have sinned so much—

LOPAHIN What sins have you—?

GAYEFF (*puts a hard candy into his mouth*) They say I've eaten my fortune up in hard candies— (*laughing*)

LYUBOFF ANDREEVNA Oh, my sins—I've always thrown money around like mad, recklessly, and I married a man who accumulated nothing but debts. My husband died from champagne—he drank fearfully—and to my misfortune I fell in love with another man. I lived with him, and just at that time—it was my first punishment—a blow over the head: right here in the river my boy was drowned and I went abroad—went away for good, never to return, never to see this river again—I shut my eyes, ran away, beside myself, and he after me—mercilessly, brutally. I bought a villa near Mentone, because he fell ill there, and for three years I knew no rest day or night, the sick man exhausted me, my soul dried up. And last year when the villa was sold for debts, I went to Paris and there he robbed me of everything, threw me over, took up with another woman; I tried to poison myself—so stupid, so shameful—And suddenly I was seized with longing for Russia, for my own country, for my little girl— (*wiping away her tears*) Lord, Lord, have mercy, forgive me my sins! Don't punish me any more! (*getting a telegram out of her pocket*) I got this today from Paris, he asks forgiveness, begs me to return— (*tears up the telegram*) That sounds like music somewhere.

(*listening*)

GAYEFF It is our famous Jewish orchestra. You remember, four violins, a flute and double bass.

LYUBOFF ANDREEVNA Does it still exist? We ought to get hold of it sometime and give a party.

LOPAHIN (*listening*) Can't hear it— (*singing softly*) "And for money the Germans will frenchify a Russian." (*laughing*) What a play I saw yesterday at the theatre, very funny!

LYUBOFF ANDREEVNA And most likely there was nothing funny about it. You shouldn't look at plays, but look oftener at yourselves. How gray all your lives are, what a lot of idle things you say!

LOPAHIN That's true. It must be said frankly this life of ours is idiotic— (*a pause*) My father was a peasant, an idiot, he understood nothing, he taught me nothing, he just beat me in his drunken fits and always with a stick. At bottom I am just as big a dolt and idiot as he was. I wasn't taught anything, my handwriting is vile, I write like a pig—I am ashamed for people to see it.

LYUBOFF ANDREEVNA You ought to get married, my friend.

LOPAHIN Yes—That's true.

LYUBOFF ANDREEVNA To our Varya, perhaps. She is a good girl.

LOPAHIN Yes.

LYUBOFF ANDREEVNA She comes from simple people, and she works all day long, but the main thing is she loves you. And you, too, have liked her a long time.

LOPAHIN Why not? I am not against it—She's a good girl. (*a pause*)

GAYEFF They are offering me a position in a bank. Six thousand a year—Have you heard that?

LYUBOFF ANDREEVNA Not you! You stay where you are—

(FIERS *enters, bringing an overcoat.*)

FIERS (*to* GAYEFF) Pray, Sir, put this on, it's damp.

GAYEFF (*putting on the overcoat*) You're a pest, old man.

FIERS That's all right—This morning you went off without letting me know. (*looking him over*)

LYUBOFF ANDREEVNA How old you've grown, Fiers!

FIERS At your service.

LOPAHIN She says you've grown very old!

FIERS I've lived a long time. They were planning to marry me off before your papa was born. (*laughing*) And at the time the serfs were freed I was already the head footman. I didn't want to be freed then, I stayed with the masters—(*a pause*) And I remember, everybody was happy, but what they were happy about they didn't know themselves.

LOPAHIN In the old days it was fine. At least they flogged.

FIERS (*not hearing*) But, of course. The peasants stuck to the masters, the masters stuck to the peasants, and now everything is all smashed up, you can't tell about anything.

GAYEFF Keep still, Fiers. Tomorrow I must go to town. They have promised to introduce me to a certain general who might make us a loan.

LOPAHIN Nothing will come of it. And you can rest assured you won't pay the interest.

LYUBOFF ANDREEVNA He's just raving on. There aren't any such generals.

(TROFIMOFF, ANYA, *and* VARYA *enter.*)

GAYEFF Here they come.

ANYA There is Mama sitting there.

LYUBOFF ANDREEVNA (*tenderly*) Come, come—My darlings— (*embracing* ANYA *and* VARYA) If you only knew how I love you both! Come sit by me—there—like that.

(*Everybody sits down.*)

LOPAHIN Our perennial student is always strolling with the young ladies.

TROFIMOFF It's none of your business.

LOPAHIN He will soon be fifty and he's still a student.

TROFIMOFF Stop your stupid jokes.

LOPAHIN But why are you so peevish, you queer duck?

TROFIMOFF Don't you pester me.

LOPAHIN (*laughing*) Permit me to ask you, what do you make of me?

TROFIMOFF Yermolay Alexeevich, I make this of you: you are a rich man, you'll soon be a millionaire. Just as it is in the metabolism of nature, a wild beast is needed to eat up everything that comes his way; so you, too, are needed.

(*Everyone laughs.*)

VARYA Petya, you'd better tell us about the planets.

LYUBOFF ANDREEVNA No, let's go on with yesterday's conversation.

TROFIMOFF What was it about?

GAYEFF About the proud man.

TROFIMOFF We talked a long time yesterday, but didn't get anywhere. In a proud man, in your sense of the word, there is something mystical. Maybe you are right, from your standpoint, but if we are to discuss it in simple terms, without whimsy, then what pride can there be, is there any sense in it, if man physiologically is poorly constructed, if in the great majority he is crude, unintelligent, profoundly miserable. One must stop admiring oneself. One must only work.

GAYEFF All the same, you will die.

TROFIMOFF Who knows? And what does it mean—you will die? Man may have a hundred senses, and when he dies only the five that are known to us may perish, and the remaining ninety-five go on living.

LYUBOFF ANDREEVNA How clever you are, Petya!

LOPAHIN (*ironically*) Terribly!

TROFIMOFF Humanity goes forward, perfecting its powers. Everything that's unattainable now will some day become familiar, understandable; it is only that one must work and must help with all one's might those who seek the truth. With us in Russia so far only a very few work. The great majority of the intelligentsia that I know are looking for nothing, doing nothing, and as yet have no capacity for work. They call themselves intelligentsia, are free and easy with the servants, treat the peasants like animals, educate themselves poorly, read nothing seriously, do absolutely nothing; about science they just talk and about art they understand very little. Every one of them is serious, all have stern faces; they all talk of nothing but important things, philosophize, and all the time everybody can see that the workmen eat abominably, sleep without any pillows, thirty or forty to a room, and everywhere there are bedbugs, stench, dampness, moral uncleanness—And apparently with us, all the fine talk is only to divert the attention of ourselves and of others. Show me where we have the day nurseries they are always talking so much about, where are the reading rooms? They only write of these in novels, for the truth is there are not any at all. There is only filth, vulgarity, orientalism—I am afraid of very serious faces and dislike them. I'm afraid of serious conversations. Rather than that let's just keep still.

LOPAHIN You know I get up before five o'clock in the morning and work from morning till night. Well, I always have money, my own and other people's, on hand, and I see what the people around me are. One has only to start doing something to find out how few honest and decent people there are. At times when I can't go to sleep, I think: Lord, thou gavest us immense forests, unbounded fields and the widest horizons, and living in the midst of them we should indeed be giants—

LYUBOFF ANDREEVNA You feel the need for giants—They are good only in fairy tales, anywhere else they only frighten us.

(*At the back of the stage* EPIHODOFF *passes by, playing the guitar.*)

LYUBOFF ANDREEVNA (*lost in thought*) Epihodoff is coming—

ANYA (*lost in thought*) Epihodoff is coming.

GAYEFF The sun has set, ladies and gentlemen.

TROFIMOFF Yes.

GAYEFF (*not loud and as if he were declaiming*) Oh, Nature, wonderful, you gleam with eternal radiance, beautiful and indifferent, you, whom we call Mother, combine in yourself both life and death, you give life and you take it away.

VARYA (*beseechingly*) Uncle!

ANYA Uncle, you're doing it again!

TROFIMOFF You'd better bank the yellow into the side pocket.

GAYEFF I'll be quiet, quiet.

(*All sit absorbed in their thoughts. There is only the silence.* FIERS *is heard muttering to himself softly. Suddenly a distant sound is heard, as if from the sky, like the sound of a snapped string, dying away, mournful.*)

LYUBOFF ANDREEVNA What's that?

LOPAHIN I don't know. Somewhere far off in a mine shaft a bucket fell. But somewhere very far off.

GAYEFF And it may be some bird—like a heron.

TROFIMOFF Or an owl—

LYUBOFF ANDREEVNA (*shivering*) It's unpleasant, somehow. (*a pause*)

FIERS Before the disaster it was like that. The owl hooted and the samovar hummed without stopping, both.

GAYEFF Before what disaster?

FIERS Before the emancipation.

(*a pause*)

LYUBOFF ANDREEVNA You know, my friends, let's go. Twilight is falling. (*to* ANYA) You have tears in your eyes—What is it, my dear little girl? (*embracing her*)

ANYA It's just that, Mama. It's nothing.

TROFIMOFF Somebody is coming.

(*A stranger appears in a shabby white cap, and an overcoat; he is a little drunk.*)

THE STRANGER Allow me to ask you, can I go straight through here to the station?

GAYEFF You can. Go by that road.

THE STRANGER I am heartily grateful to you. (*coughing*) The weather is splendid— (*declaiming*) Brother of mine, suffering brother—Go out to the Volga, whose moans— (*to* VARYA) Mademoiselle, grant a hungry Russian man some thirty kopecks— (VARYA *is frightened and gives a shriek.*)

LOPAHIN (*angrily*) There's a limit to everything.

LYUBOFF ANDREEVNA (*flustered*) Take this—Here's this for you— (*searching in her purse*) No silver—It's all the same, here's a gold piece for you—

THE STRANGER I am heartily grateful to you.

(*goes out*)

(*laughter*)

VARYA (*frightened*) I'm going—I'm going—Oh, Mama, you poor little Mama! There's nothing in the house for people to eat, and you gave him a gold piece.

LYUBOFF ANDREEVNA What is to be done with me, so silly? I shall give you all I have in the house. Yermolay Alexeevich, you will lend me some this once more!—

LOPAHIN Agreed.

LYUBOFF ANDREEVNA Let's go, ladies and gentlemen, it's time. And here, Varya, we have definitely made a match for you, I congratulate you.

VARYA (*through her tears*) Mama, that's not something to joke about.

LOPAHIN Achmelia, get thee to a nunnery.[6]

GAYEFF And my hands are trembling; it is a long time since I have played billiards.

LOPAHIN Achmelia, Oh nymph, in thine orisons be all my sins remember'd—[7]

LYUBOFF ANDREEVNA Let's go, my dear friends, it will soon be suppertime.

VARYA He frightened me. My heart is thumping so!

LOPAHIN I remind you, ladies and gentlemen: August 22nd the cherry orchard will be auctioned off. Think about that!—Think!—

---

[6]Shakespeare, *Hamlet,* III.i. [7]*Hamlet,* III.i.

(*All go out except* Trofimoff *and* Anya.)

ANYA (*laughing*) My thanks to the stranger, he frightened Varya, now we are alone.

TROFIMOFF Varya is afraid we might begin to love each other and all day long she won't leave us to ourselves. With her narrow mind she cannot understand that we are above love. To sidestep the petty and illusory, which prevent our being free and happy, that is the aim and meaning of our life. Forward! We march on irresistibly toward the bright star that burns there in the distance. Forward! Do not fall behind, friends!

ANYA (*extending her arms upward*) How well you talk! (*a pause*) It's wonderful here today!

TROFIMOFF Yes, the weather is marvelous.

ANYA What have you done to me, Petya, why don't I love the cherry orchard any longer the way I used to? I loved it so tenderly, it seemed to me there was not a better place on earth than our orchard.

TROFIMOFF All Russia is our orchard. The earth is immense and beautiful, and on it are many wonderful places. (*a pause*) Just think, Anya: your grandfather, great-grandfather and all your ancestors were slave owners, in possession of living souls, and can you doubt that from every cherry in the orchard, from every leaf, from every trunk, human beings are looking at you, can it be that you don't hear their voices? To possess living souls, well, that depraved all of you who lived before and who are living now, so that your mother and you, and your uncle no longer notice that you live by debt, at somebody else's expense, at the expense of those very people whom you wouldn't let past your front door—We are at least two hundred years behind the times, we have as yet absolutely nothing, we have no definite attitude toward the past, we only philosophize, complain of our sadness or drink vodka. Why, it is quite clear that to begin to live in the present we must first atone for our past, must be done with it; and we can atone for it only through suffering, only through uncommon, incessant labor. Understand that, Anya.

ANYA The house we live in ceased to be ours long ago, and I'll go away, I give you my word.

TROFIMOFF If you have the household keys, throw them in the well and go away. Be free as the wind.

ANYA (*transported*) How well you said that!

TROFIMOFF Believe me, Anya, believe me! I am not thirty yet, I am young, I am still a student, but I have already borne so much! Every winter I am hungry, sick, anxious, poor as a beggar, and—where has destiny not chased me, where haven't I been! And yet, my soul has always, every minute, day and night, been full of inexplicable premonitions. I have a premonition of happiness, Anya, I see it already—

ANYA (*pensively*) The moon is rising.

(EPIHODOFF *is heard playing on the guitar, always the same sad song. The moon rises. Somewhere near the poplars* VARYA *is looking for* ANYA *and calling:* "ANYA! *Where are you?*")

TROFIMOFF Yes, the moon is rising. (*a pause*) Here is happiness, here it comes, comes always nearer and nearer, I hear its footsteps now. And if we shall not see it, shall not come to know it, what does that matter? Others will see it!

VARYA (*off*) Anya! Where are you?

TROFIMOFF Again, that Varya! (*angrily*) It's scandalous!

ANYA Well, let's go to the river. It's lovely there.

TROFIMOFF Let's go. (*they go out*)

VARYA (*off*) Anya! Anya!

Act III

The drawing room, separated by an arch from the ballroom. A chandelier is lighted. A Jewish orchestra is playing—the same that was mentioned in Act II. Evening. In the ballroom they are dancing grand rond.[8] *The voice of* SEMYONOFF-PISHTCHIK: *"Promenade à une paire!"*[9] *They enter the drawing room; in the first couple are* PISHTCHIK *and* CHARLOTTA IVANOVNA; *in the second,* TROFIMOFF *and* LYUBOFF ANDREEVNA; *in the third,* ANYA *with the* POST-OFFICE CLERK; *in the fourth,* VARYA *with the* STATION-MASTER, *et cetera—* VARYA *is crying softly and wipes away her tears while she is dancing.* DUNYASHA *is the last couple through the drawing room.* PISHTCHIK *shouts: "Grand rond, balancez!"*[1] *and "Les Cavaliers à genoux et remerciez vos dames!"*[2]

(FIERS *in a frock coat goes by with seltzer water on a tray.* PISHTCHIK *and* TROFIMOFF *come into the drawing room.*)

PISHTCHIK I am full-blooded, I have had two strokes already, and dancing is hard for me, but as they say, if you are in a pack of dogs, you may bark and bark, but you must still wag your tail. At that, I have the health of a horse. My dear father—he was a great joker—may he dwell in Heaven—used to talk as if our ancient line, the Semyonoff-Pishtchiks, were descended from the very horse that Caligula made a Senator— (*sitting down*) But here's my trouble: I haven't any money. A hungry dog believes in nothing but meat— (*snoring but waking at once*) And the same way with me—I can't talk about anything but money.

TROFIMOFF Well, to tell you the truth, there is something of a horse about your figure.

PISHTCHIK Well—a horse is a fine animal—You can sell a horse—

(*The sound of playing billiards comes from the next room.* VARYA *appears under the arch to the ballroom.*)

---

[8]great circle, a dance [9]promenade by single couple [1]a technical dance movement [2]"Gentlemen, kneel and thank your ladies"

TROFIMOFF (*teasing*) Madam Lopahin! Madam Lopahin!

VARYA (*angrily*) A mangy-looking gentleman!

TROFIMOFF Yes, I am a mangy-looking gentleman, and proud of it!

VARYA (*in bitter thought*) Here we have gone and hired musicians and what are we going to pay them with?

(*goes out*)

TROFIMOFF (*to* PISHTCHIK) If the energy you have wasted in the course of your life trying to find money to pay the interest had gone into something else, you could very likely have turned the world upside down before you were done with it.

PISHTCHIK Nietzsche—the philosopher—the greatest—the most celebrated—a man of tremendous mind—says in his works that one may make counterfeit money.

TROFIMOFF And have you read Nietzsche?

PISHTCHIK Well—Dashenka told me. And I'm in such a state now that I could make counterfeit money myself—Day after tomorrow three hundred and ten roubles must be paid—one hundred and thirty I've on hand— (*feeling in his pockets, alarmed*) The money is gone! I have lost the money! (*tearfully*) Where is the money? (*joyfully*) Here it is, inside the lining—I was in quite a sweat—

(LYUBOFF ANDREEVNA *and* CHARLOTTA IVANOVNA *come in.*)

LYUBOFF ANDREEVNA (*humming lazginka, a Georgian dance*) Why does Leonid take so long? What's he doing in town? (*to* DUNYASHA) Dunyasha, offer the musicians some tea—

TROFIMOFF In all probability the auction did not take place.

LYUBOFF ANDREEVNA And the musicians came at an unfortunate moment and we planned the ball at an unfortunate moment—Well, it doesn't matter. (*sitting down and singing softly*)

CHARLOTTA (*gives* PISHTCHIK *a deck of cards*) Here is a deck of cards for you, think of some one card.

PISHTCHIK I have thought of one.

CHARLOTTA Now, shuffle the deck. Very good. Hand it here; oh, my dear Monsieur Pishtchik. *Ein, zwei, drei!* Now look for it, it's in your coat pocket—

PISHTCHIK (*getting a card out of his coat pocket*) The eight of spades, that's absolutely right! (*amazed*) Fancy that!

CHARLOTTA (*holding a deck of cards in her palm; to* TROFIMOFF) Tell me quick now, which card is on top?

TROFIMOFF What is it? Well—the Queen of Spades.

CHARLOTTA Right! (*to* PISHTCHIK) Well? Which card's on top?

PISHTCHIK The Ace of Hearts.

CHARLOTTA Right! (*Strikes the deck against her palm; the deck of cards disappears.*) And what beautiful weather we are having today!

(*A mysterious feminine voice answers her, as if from under the floor: "Oh yes. The weather is splendid, madame." "You are so nice, you're my ideal—" The voice: "Madame, you too please me greatly."*)

THE STATION-MASTER (*applauding*) Madam Ventriloquist, bravo!

PISHTCHIK (*amazed*) Fancy that! Most charming Charlotta Ivanovna—I am simply in love with you.

CHARLOTTA In love? (*shrugging her shoulders*) Is it possible that you can love? *Guter Mensch aber schlechter Musikant.*[3]

TROFIMOFF (*slapping* PISHTCHIK *on the shoulder*) You horse, you—

CHARLOTTA I beg your attention, one more trick. (*taking a lap robe from the chair*) Here is a very fine lap robe—I want to sell it— (*shaking it out*) Wouldn't somebody like to buy it?

PISHTCHIK (*amazed*) Fancy that!

CHARLOTTA *Ein, zwei, drei!*

(*She quickly raises the lowered robe, behind it stands* ANYA, *who curtseys, runs to her mother, embraces her and runs back into the ballroom amid the general delight.*)

LYUBOFF ANDREEVNA (*applauding*) Bravo, bravo—!

CHARLOTTA Now again! *Ein, zwei, drei!*

(*Lifting the robe; behind it stands* VARYA, *she bows.*)

PISHTCHIK (*amazed*) Fancy that!

CHARLOTTA That's all. (*throwing the robe at* PISHTCHIK, *curtseying and running into the ballroom.*)

PISHTCHIK (*hurrying after her*) You little rascal—What a girl! What a girl!

(*goes out*)

LYUBOFF ANDREEVNA And Leonid is not here yet. What he's doing in town so long, I don't understand! Everything is finished there, either the estate is sold by now, or the auction didn't take place. Why keep it from us so long?

VARYA (*trying to comfort her*) Uncle has bought it, I am sure of that.

TROFIMOFF (*mockingly*) Yes.

VARYA Great-aunt sent him power of attorney to buy it in her name and transfer the debt. She did this for Anya. And I feel certain, God willing, that Uncle will buy it.

LYUBOFF ANDREEVNA Our Yaroslavl great-aunt has sent fifteen thousand to buy the estate in her name—She doesn't trust us, but that wouldn't be enough to pay the interest even— (*covering her face with her hands*) Today my fate will be decided, my fate—

TROFIMOFF (*teasing* VARYA) Madam Lopahin!

---

[3]"A good man, but a sloppy musician"

VARYA (*angrily*) Perennial student! You have already been expelled from the University twice.

LYUBOFF ANDREEVNA But why are you angry, Varya? He teases you about Lopahin, what of it? Marry Lopahin if you want to, he is a good man, interesting. If you don't want to, don't marry him; darling, nobody is making you do it.

VARYA I look at this matter seriously, Mama, one must speak straight out. He's a good man, I like him.

LYUBOFF ANDREEVNA Then marry him. What there is to wait for I don't understand!

VARYA But I can't propose to him myself, Mama. It's two years now; everyone has been talking to me about him, everyone talks, and he either remains silent or jokes. I understand. He's getting rich, he's busy with his own affairs, and has no time for me. If there were money, ever so little, even a hundred roubles, I would drop everything, and go far away. I'd go to a nunnery.

TROFIMOFF How saintly!

VARYA (*to* TROFIMOFF) A student should be intelligent! (*in a low voice, tearfully*) How homely you have grown, Petya, how old you've got. (*to* LYUBOFF ANDREEVNA, *no longer crying*) It is just that I can't live without working, Mama. I must be doing something every minute.

YASHA (*enters, barely restraining his laughter*) Epihodoff has broken a billiard cue!—

(*goes out*)

VARYA But why is Epihodoff here? Who allowed him to play billiards? I don't understand these people—

(*goes out*)

LYUBOFF ANDREEVNA Don't tease her, Petya; you can see she has troubles enough without that.

TROFIMOFF She is just too zealous. Sticking her nose into things that are none of her business. All summer she gave us no peace, neither me nor Anya; she was afraid a romance would spring up between us. What business is that of hers? And besides I haven't shown any signs of it. I am so remote from triviality. We are above love!

LYUBOFF ANDREEVNA Well, then, I must be beneath love. (*very anxiously*) Why isn't Leonid here? Just to tell us whether the estate is sold or not? Calamity seems to me so incredible that I don't know what to think, I'm lost—I could scream this minute—I could do something insane. Save me, Petya. Say something, do say. . . .

TROFIMOFF Whether the estate is sold today or is not sold—is it not the same? There is no turning back, the path is all grown over. Calm yourself, my dear, all that was over long ago. One mustn't deceive oneself, one must for once at least in one's life look truth straight in the eye.

LYUBOFF ANDREEVNA What truth? You see where the truth is and where the untruth is, but as for me, it's as if I had lost my sight, I see nothing. You boldly decide all important questions, but tell me, my dear boy, isn't that because you are young and haven't had time yet to suffer through any one of your problems? You look boldly ahead, and isn't that because you don't see and don't expect anything terrible, since life is still hidden from your young eyes? You are braver, more honest, more profound than we are, but stop and think, be magnanimous, have a little mercy on me, just a little. Why, I was born here. My father and mother lived here and my grandfather. I love this house, I can't imagine my life without the cherry orchard and if it is very necessary to sell it, then sell me along with the orchard— (*embracing* TROFIMOFF *and kissing him on the forehead*) Why, my son was drowned here— (*crying*) Have mercy on me, good, kind man.

TROFIMOFF You know I sympathize with you from the bottom of my heart.

LYUBOFF ANDREEVNA But that should be said differently, differently— (*Taking out her handkerchief; a telegram falls on the floor.*) My heart is heavy today, you can't imagine how heavy. It is too noisy for me here, my soul trembles at every sound, I tremble all over and yet I can't go off to myself, when I am alone the silence frightens me. Don't blame me, Petya—I love you as one of my own. I should gladly have given you Anya's hand, I assure you, only, my dear, you must study and finish your course. You do nothing. Fate simply flings you about from place to place, and that's so strange—Isn't that so? Yes? And you must do something about your beard, to make it grow somehow— (*laughing*) You look funny!

TROFIMOFF (*picking up the telegram*) I do not desire to be beautiful.

LYUBOFF ANDREEVNA This telegram is from Paris. I get one every day. Yesterday and today too. That wild man has fallen ill again, something is wrong again with him—He asks forgiveness, begs me to come, and really I ought to make a trip to Paris and stay awhile near him. Your face looks stern, Petya, but what is there to do, my dear, what am I to do, he is ill, he is alone, unhappy, and who will look after him there, who will keep him from doing the wrong thing, who will give him his medicine on time? And what is there to hide or keep still about? I love him, that's plain. I love him, love him—It's a stone about my neck, I'm sinking to the bottom with it, but I love that stone and live without it I cannot. (*pressing* TROFIMOFF's *hand*) Don't think harshly of me, Petya, don't say anything to me, don't—

TROFIMOFF (*tearfully*) Forgive my frankness, for God's sake! Why, he picked your bones.

LYUBOFF ANDREEVNA No, no, no, you must not talk like that. (*stopping her ears*)

TROFIMOFF But he is a scoundrel, only you, you are the only one that doesn't know it. He is a petty scoundrel, a nonentity—

LYUBOFF ANDREEVNA (*angry but controlling herself*) You are twenty-six years old or twenty-seven, but you are still a schoolboy in the second grade!

TROFIMOFF Very well!

LYUBOFF ANDREEVNA You should be a man—at your age you should understand people who love. And you yourself should love someone—you should fall in love! (*angrily*) Yes, yes! And there is no purity in you; you are simply smug, a ridiculous crank, a freak—

TROFIMOFF (*horrified*) What is she saying!

LYUBOFF ANDREEVNA "I am above love!" You are not above love, Petya, you are, as our Fiers would say, just a good-for-nothing. Imagine, at your age, not having a mistress—!

TROFIMOFF (*horrified*) This is terrible! What is she saying! (*goes quickly into the ballroom, clutching his head*) This is horrible—I can't bear it, I am going—(*goes out but immediately returns*) All is over between us. (*goes out into the hall*)

LYUBOFF ANDREEVNA (*shouting after him*) Petya, wait! You funny creature, I was joking! Petya! (*In the hall someone can be heard running up the stairs and suddenly falling back down with a crash.* ANYA *and* VARYA *scream but immediately begin laughing.*) What's that?

ANYA (*runs in, laughing*) Petya fell down the stairs! (*runs out*)

LYUBOFF ANDREEVNA What a funny boy that Petya is—! (*The* STATION-MASTER *stops in the center of the ballroom and begins to recite "The sinner" by A. Tolstoi. They listen to him but he has recited only a few lines when the strains of a waltz are heard from the hall and the recitation is broken off. They all dance.* TROFIMOFF, ANYA, VARYA *and* LYUBOFF ANDREEVNA *come in from the hall.*) But, Petya—but, dear soul—I beg your forgiveness—Let's go dance.

(*She dances with* TROFIMOFF. ANYA *and* VARYA *dance.* FIERS *enters, leaving his stick by the side door.* YASHA *also comes into the drawing room and watches the dancers.*)

YASHA What is it, Grandpa?

FIERS I don't feel very well. In the old days there were generals, barons, admirals dancing at our parties, and now we send for the post-office clerk and the stationmaster, and even they are none too anxious to come. Somehow I've grown feeble. The old master, the grandfather, treated everybody with sealing-wax for all sicknesses. I take sealing-wax every day, have done so for twenty-odd years or more; it may be due to that that I'm alive.

YASHA You are tiresome, Grandpa. (*yawning*) Why don't you go off and die?

FIERS Aw, you—good-for-nothing!— (*muttering*)

(TROFIMOFF *and* LYUBOFF ANDREEVNA *dance in the ballroom and then in the drawing room.*)

LYUBOFF ANDREEVNA *Merci.* I'll sit down awhile— (*sitting down*) I'm tired.

ANYA (*enters, agitated*) And just now in the kitchen some man was saying that the cherry orchard had been sold today.

LYUBOFF ANDREEVNA Sold to whom?

ANYA He didn't say who to. He's gone.

(*Dancing with* TROFIMOFF, *they pass into the ballroom.*)

YASHA It was some old man babbling there. A stranger.

FIERS And Leonid Andreevich is still not here, he has not arrived. The overcoat he has on is light, mid-season—let's hope he won't catch cold. Ach, these young things!

LYUBOFF ANDREEVNA I shall die this minute. Go, Yasha, find out who it was sold to.

YASHA But he's been gone a long time, the old fellow. (*laughing*)

LYUBOFF ANDREEVNA (*with some annoyance*) Well, what are you laughing at? What are you so amused at?

YASHA Epihodoff is just too funny. An empty-headed man. Twenty-two misfortunes!

LYUBOFF ANDREEVNA Fiers, if the estate is sold, where will you go?

FIERS Wherever you say, there I'll go.

LYUBOFF ANDREEVNA Why do you look like that? Aren't you well? You know you ought to go to bed—

FIERS Yes— (*with a sneer*) I go to bed and without me who's going to serve, who'll take care of things? I'm the only one in the whole house.

YASHA (*to* LYUBOFF ANDREEVNA) Lyuboff Andreevna, let me ask a favor of you, do be so kind! If you ever go back to Paris, take me with you, please do! It's impossible for me to stay here. (*looking around him, and speaking in a low voice*) Why talk about it? You can see for yourself it's an uncivilized country, an immoral people and not only that, there's the boredom of it. The food they give us in that kitchen is abominable and there's that Fiers, too, walking about and muttering all kinds of words that are out of place. Take me with you, be so kind!

PISHTCHIK (*enters*) Allow me to ask you—for a little waltz, most beautiful lady— (LYUBOFF ANDREEVNA *goes with him.*) Charming lady, I must borrow a hundred and eighty roubles from you—will borrow— (*dancing*) a hundred and eighty roubles— (*They pass into the ballroom.*)

YASHA (*singing low*) "Wilt thou know the unrest in my soul!"

(*In the ballroom a figure in a gray top hat and checked trousers waves both hands and jumps about; there are shouts of "Bravo,* CHARLOTTA IVANOVNA*!"*)

DUNYASHA (*stopping to powder her face*) The young lady orders me to dance—there are a lot of gentlemen and very few ladies—but dancing makes my head swim and my heart thump. Fiers, Nikolaevich, the post-office clerk said something to me just now that took my breath away.

(*The music plays more softly.*)

FIERS What did he say to you?

DUNYASHA You are like a flower, he says.

YASHA (*yawning*) What ignorance—!

(*goes out*)

DUNYASHA Like a flower—I am such a sensitive girl, I love tender words awfully.

FIERS You'll be getting your head turned.

(EPIHODOFF *enters.*)

EPIHODOFF Avdotya Feodorovna, you don't want to see me—It's as if I were some sort of insect. (*sighing*) Ach, life!

DUNYASHA What do you want?

EPIHODOFF Undoubtedly you may be right. (*sighing*) But of course, if one considers it from a given point of view, then you, I will allow myself so to express it, forgive my frankness, absolutely led me into a state of mind. I know my fate, every day some misfortune happens to me, but I have long since become accustomed to that, and so I look on my misfortunes with a smile. You gave me your word and, although I—

DUNYASHA I beg you, we'll talk later on, but leave me now in peace. I'm in a dream now. (*playing with her fan*)

EPIHODOFF I have something wrong happen every day—I will allow myself so to express it—I just smile, I even laugh.

VARYA (*enters from the ballroom*) You are not gone yet, Semyon? What a really disrespectful man you are! (*to* DUNYASHA) Get out of here, Dunyasha. (*to* EPIHODOFF) You either play billiards and break a cue or you walk about the drawing room like a guest.

EPIHODOFF Allow me to tell you, you cannot make any demands on me.

VARYA I'm not making any demands on you, I'm talking to you. All you know is to walk from place to place but not do any work. We keep a clerk, but what for, nobody knows.

EPIHODOFF (*offended*) Whether I work, whether I walk, whether I eat, or whether I play billiards are matters to be discussed only by people of understanding and my seniors.

VARYA You dare to say that to me! (*flying into a temper*) You dare? So I don't understand anything? Get out of here! This minute!

EPIHODOFF (*alarmed*) I beg you to express yourself in a delicate manner.

VARYA (*beside herself*) This very minute, get out of here! Get out! (*He goes to the door; she follows him.*) Twenty-two misfortunes! Don't you dare breathe in here! Don't let me set eyes on you! (EPIHODOFF *has gone out, but his voice comes from outside the door: "I shall complain about you."*) Ah, you are coming back? (*grabbing the stick that* FIERS *put by the door*) Come on, come—come on, I'll show you—Ah, you are coming? You are coming? Take that then—!

(*She swings the stick, at the very moment when* LOPAHIN *is coming in.*)

LOPAHIN Most humbly, I thank you.

VARYA (*angrily and ironically*) I beg your pardon!

LOPAHIN It's nothing at all. I humbly thank you for the pleasant treat.

VARYA It isn't worth your thanks. (*moving away, then looking back and asking gently*) I haven't hurt you?

LOPAHIN No, it's nothing. There's a great bump coming though.

(*Voices in the ballroom:* "LOPAHIN *has come back.*" "YERMOLAY ALEXEEVICH!")

PISHTCHIK (*enters*) See what we see, hear what we hear—! (*He and* LOPAHIN *kiss one another.*) You smell slightly of cognac, my dear, my good old chap. And we are amusing ourselves here too.

LYUBOFF ANDREEVNA (*enters*) Is that you, Yermolay Alexeevich? Why were you so long? Where is Leonid?

LOPAHIN Leonid Andreevich got back when I did, he's coming.

LYUBOFF ANDREEVNA (*agitated*) Well, what? Was there an auction? Do speak!

LOPAHIN (*embarrassed, afraid of showing the joy he feels*) The auction was over by four o'clock—We were late for the train, had to wait till half-past nine. (*sighing heavily*) Ugh, my head's swimming a bit!

(GAYEFF *enters; with his right hand he carries his purchases; with his left he wipes away his tears.*)

LYUBOFF ANDREEVNA Lyona, what? Lyona, eh? (*impatiently, with tears in her eyes*) Quick, for God's sake—

GAYEFF (*not answering her, merely waving his hand; to* FIERS, *crying*) Here, take it—There are anchovies, some Kertch herrings—I haven't eaten anything all day—What I have suffered! (*The door into the billiard room is open; you hear the balls clicking and* YASHA's *voice: "Seven and eighteen!"* GAYEFF's *expression changes; he is no longer crying.*) I'm terribly tired. You help me change, Fiers.

(*Goes to his room through the ballroom,* FIERS *behind him.*)

PISHTCHIK What happened at the auction? Go on, tell us!

LYUBOFF ANDREEVNA Is the cherry orchard sold?

LOPAHIN It's sold.

LYUBOFF ANDREEVNA Who bought it?

LOPAHIN I bought it. (*A pause.* LYUBOFF ANDREEVNA *is overcome. She would have fallen had she not been standing near the chair and table.* VARYA *takes the keys from her belt, throws them on the floor in the middle of the drawing room and goes out.*) I bought it. Kindly wait a moment, ladies and gentlemen, everything is muddled up in my head, I can't speak— (*laughing*) We arrived at the auction, Deriganoff was already there. Leonid Andreevich had only fifteen thousand and Deriganoff right off bids thirty over and above indebtedness. I see how things are, I match him with forty thousand. He forty-five. I fifty-five. That is to say he raises it by fives, I by tens.—So it ended. Over and above the indebtedness, I bid up to ninety thousand, it was knocked down to me. The cherry orchard is mine now. Mine! (*guffawing*) My God, Lord, the cherry orchard is mine! Tell me I'm drunk, out of my head, that I'm imagining all this— (*stamps his feet*) Don't laugh at me! If only my father and grandfather could rise from their graves and see this whole business, see how their Yermolay, beaten, half-illiterate Yermolay, who used to run around barefoot in winter, how that very Yermolay has bought an estate that nothing in the world can beat. I bought the estate where grandfather and father were slaves, where you wouldn't even let me in the kitchen. I am asleep, it's only some dream of mine, it only seems so to me—That's nothing but the fruit of your imagination, covered with the darkness of the unknown— (*picking up the keys, with a gentle smile*) She threw down the keys, wants to show she is not mistress any more— (*jingling the keys*) Well, it's all the same. (*The orchestra is heard tuning up.*) Hey, musicians, play, I want to hear you! Come on, everybody, and see how Yermolay Lopahin will swing the ax in the cherry orchard, how the trees will fall to the ground! We are going to build villas and our grandsons and great-grandsons will see a new life here—Music, play! (*The music is playing.* LYUBOFF ANDREEVNA *has sunk into a chair, crying bitterly.* LOPAHIN *reproachfully.*) Why, then, didn't you listen to me? My poor dear, it can't be undone now. (*with tears*) Oh, if this could all be over soon, if somehow our awkward, unhappy life would be changed!

PISHTCHIK (*taking him by the arm, in a low voice*) She is crying. Come on in the ballroom, let her be by herself—Come on—

(*taking him by the arm and leading him into the ballroom*)

LOPAHIN What's the matter? Music, there, play up! (*sarcastically*) Everything is to be as I want it! Here comes the new squire, the owner of the cherry orchard. (*Quite accidentally, he bumps into the little table, and very nearly upsets the candelabra.*) I can pay for everything!

(*Goes out with* PISHTCHIK. *There is nobody left either in the ballroom or the drawing room but* LYUBOFF ANDREEVNA, *who sits all huddled up and crying bitterly. The music plays softly.* ANYA *and* TROFIMOFF *enter hurriedly.* ANYA *comes up to her mother and kneels in front of her.* TROFIMOFF *remains at the ballroom door.*)

ANYA Mama—! Mama, you are crying? My dear, kind, good Mama, my beautiful, I love you—I bless you. The cherry orchard is sold, it's not ours any more, that's true; but don't cry, Mama, you've your life still left you, you've your good, pure heart ahead of you—Come with me, come on, darling, away from here, come on—We will plant a new orchard, finer than this one, you'll see it, you'll understand; and joy, quiet, deep joy will sink into your heart, like the sun at evening, and you'll smile, Mama! Come, darling, come on!

Act IV

The same setting as in Act I. There are neither curtains on the windows nor are there any pictures on the walls. Only a little furniture remains piled up in one corner as if for sale. A sense of emptiness is felt. Near the outer door, at the rear of the stage, is a pile of suitcases, traveling bags, and so on. The door on the left is open, and through it VARYA's *and* ANYA's *voices are heard.* LOPAHIN *is standing waiting.* YASHA *is holding a tray with glasses of champagne. In the hall* EPIHODOFF *is tying up a box. Offstage at the rear there is a hum. It is the peasants who have come to say good-by.* GAYEFF's *voice: "Thanks, brothers, thank you."*

YASHA The simple folk have come to say good-by. I am of the opinion, Yermolay Alexeevich, that the people are kind enough but don't understand anything.

(*The hum subsides.* LYUBOFF ANDREEVNA *enters through the hall with* GAYEFF; *she is not crying, but is pale, her face quivers, she is not able to speak.*)

GAYEFF You gave them your purse, Lyuba. Mustn't do that! Mustn't do that!

LYUBOFF ANDREEVNA I couldn't help it! I couldn't help it!

(*Both go out.*)

LOPAHIN (*calling through the door after them*) Please, I humbly beg you! A little glass at parting. I didn't think to bring some from town, and at the station I found just one bottle. Please! (*a pause*) Well, then, ladies and gentlemen! You don't want it? (*moving away from the door*) If I'd known that, I wouldn't have bought it. Well, then I won't drink any either. (YASHA *carefully sets the tray down on a chair.*) At least, you have some, Yasha.

YASHA To those who are departing! Pleasant days to those who stay behind! (*drinking*) This champagne is not the real stuff, I can assure you.

LOPAHIN Eight roubles a bottle. (*a pause*) It's devilish cold in here.

YASHA They didn't heat up today, we are leaving anyway. (*laughing*)

LOPAHIN What are you laughing about?

YASHA For joy.

LOPAHIN Outside it's October, but it's sunny and still, like summer. Good for building. (*looking at his watch, then through the door*) Ladies and gentlemen, bear in mind we have forty-six minutes in all till train time! Which means you have to go to the station in twenty minutes. Hurry up a little.

TROFIMOFF (*in an overcoat, entering from outside*) Seems to me it is time to go. The carriages are ready. The devil knows where my rubbers are. They've disappeared. (*in the door*) Anya, my rubbers are not here! I can't find them.

LOPAHIN And I have to go to Kharkov. I'm going on the same train with you. I'm going to live in Kharkov all winter. I've been dilly-dallying along with you, I'm tired of doing nothing. I can't be without work, look, I don't know what to do with my hands here, see, they are dangling somehow, as if they didn't belong to me.

TROFIMOFF We are leaving right away, and you'll set about your useful labors again.

LOPAHIN Here, drink a glass.

TROFIMOFF I shan't.

LOPAHIN It's to Moscow now?

TROFIMOFF Yes. I'll see them off to town, and tomorrow to Moscow.

LOPAHIN Yes—Maybe the professors are not giving their lectures. I imagine they are waiting till you arrive.

TROFIMOFF That's none of your business.

LOPAHIN How many years is it you've been studying at the University?

TROFIMOFF Think of something newer. This is old and flat. (*looking for his rubbers*) You know, perhaps, we shall not see each other again; therefore, permit me to give you one piece of advice at parting! Don't wave your arms! Cure yourself of that habit—of arm waving. And also of building summer cottages, figuring that the summer residents will in time become individual landowners; figuring like that is arm waving too—Just the same, however, I like you. You have delicate soft features like an artist, you have a delicate soft heart—

LOPAHIN (*embracing him*) Good-by, my dear boy. Thanks for everything. If you need it, take some money from me for the trip.

TROFIMOFF Why should I? There's no need for it.

LOPAHIN But you haven't any!

TROFIMOFF I have. Thank you. I got some for a translation. Here it is in my pocket. (*anxiously*) But my rubbers are gone.

VARYA (*from another room*) Take your nasty things!

(*throws a pair of rubbers on to the stage*)

TROFIMOFF But what are you angry about, Varya? Hm—Why, these are not my rubbers.

LOPAHIN In the spring I planted twenty-seven hundred acres of poppies and now I've made forty thousand clear. And when my poppies were in bloom, what a picture it was! So look, as I say, I've made forty thousand, which means I'm offering you a loan because I can afford to. Why turn up your nose? I'm a peasant—I speak straight out.

TROFIMOFF Your father was a peasant, mine—an apothecary—and from that absolutely nothing follows. (LOPAHIN *takes out his wallet.*) Leave it alone, leave it alone—If you gave me two hundred thousand even, I wouldn't take it. I am a free man. And everything that you all value so highly and dearly, both rich man and beggars, has not the slightest power over me, it's like a mere feather floating in the air. I can get along without you, I can pass you by, I am strong and proud. Humanity is moving toward the loftiest truth, toward the loftiest happiness that is possible on earth and I am in the front ranks.

LOPAHIN Will you get there?

TROFIMOFF I'll get there. (*a pause*) I'll get there, or I'll show the others the way to get there.

(*In the distance is heard the sound of an ax on a tree.*)

LOPAHIN Well, good-by, my dear boy. It's time to go. We turn up our noses at one another, but life keeps on passing. When I work a long time without stopping, my thoughts are clearer, and it seems as if I, too, know what I exist for, and, brother, how many people are there in Russia who exist, nobody knows for what! Well, all the same, it's not that that keeps things circulating. Leonid Andreevich, they say, has accepted a position—he'll be in a bank, six thousand a year—the only thing is he won't stay there, he's very lazy—

ANYA (*in the doorway*) Mama begs of you until she's gone, not to cut down the orchard.

TROFIMOFF Honestly, haven't you enough tact to—

(*goes out through the hall*)

LOPAHIN Right away, right away—What people, really!

(*goes out after him*)

ANYA Has Fiers been sent to the hospital?

YASHA I told them to this morning. They must have sent him.

ANYA (*to* EPIHODOFF, *who is passing through the room*) Semyon Panteleevich, please inquire whether or not they have taken Fiers to the hospital.

YASHA (*huffily*) This morning, I told Igor. Why ask ten times over!

EPIHODOFF The venerable Fiers, according to my conclusive opinion, is not worth mending, he ought to join his forefathers. And I can only envy him. (*putting a suitcase on a hatbox and crushing it*) Well, there you are, of course. I knew it.

(*goes out*)

YASHA (*mockingly*) Twenty-two misfortunes—

VARYA (*on the other side of the door*) Have they taken Fiers to the hospital?

ANYA They have.

VARYA Then why didn't they take the letter to the doctor?

ANYA We must send it on after them—

(*goes out*)

VARYA (*from the next room*) Where is Yasha? Tell him his mother has come, she wants to say good-by to him.

YASHA (*waving his hand*) They merely try my patience.

(DUNYASHA *has been busying herself with the luggage; now when* YASHA *is left alone, she goes up to him.*)

DUNYASHA If you'd only look at me once, Yasha. You are going away—leaving me— (*crying and throwing herself on his neck*)

YASHA Why are you crying? (*drinking champagne*) In six days I'll be in Paris again. Tomorrow we will board the express train and dash off out of sight; somehow, I can't believe it. *Vive la France!* It doesn't suit me here—I can't live here—Can't help that. I've seen enough ignorance—enough for me. (*drinking champagne*) Why do you cry? Behave yourself properly, then you won't be crying.

DUNYASHA (*powdering her face, looking into a small mirror*) Send me a letter from Paris. I loved you, Yasha, you know, loved you so! I am a tender creature, Yasha!

YASHA They are coming here. (*bustling about near the suitcases, humming low*)

(LYUBOFF ANDREEVNA, GAYEFF, ANYA *and* CHARLOTTA IVANOVNA *enter.*)

GAYEFF We should be going. There is very little time left. (*looking at* YASHA) Who is it smells like herring!

LYUBOFF ANDREEVNA In about ten minutes let's be in the carriage— (*glancing around the room*) Good-by, dear house, old Grandfather. Winter will pass; spring will be here, but you won't be here any longer, they'll tear you down. How much these walls have seen! (*kissing her daughter warmly*) My treasure, you are beaming, your eyes are dancing like two diamonds. Are you happy? Very?

ANYA Very! It's the beginning of a new life, Mama!

GAYEFF (*gaily*) Yes, indeed, everything is fine now. Before the sale of the cherry orchard, we all were troubled, distressed, and then when the question was settled definitely, irrevocably, we all calmed down and were even cheerful—I'm a bank official. I am a financier now—Yellow ball into the side pocket, anyway, Lyuba, you look better, no doubt about that.

LYUBOFF ANDREEVNA Yes. My nerves are better, that's true. (*They hand her her hat and coat.*) I sleep well. Carry out my things, Yasha. It's time. (*to* ANYA) My little girl, we shall see each other again soon—I am going to Paris, I shall live there on the money your Yaroslavl great-aunt sent for the purchase of the estate—long live Great-aunt! But that money won't last long.

ANYA Mama, you'll come back soon, soon—Isn't that so? I'll prepare myself, pass the examination at high school, and then I'll work, I will help you. We'll read all sorts of books together. Mama, isn't that so? (*kissing her mother's hands*) We'll read in the autumn evenings, read lots of books, and a new, wonderful world will open up before us— (*daydreaming*) Mama, do come—

LYUBOFF ANDREEVNA I'll come, my precious. (*embracing her daughter*)

(LOPAHIN *enters with* CHARLOTTA *who is softly humming a song.*)

GAYEFF Lucky Charlotta: she's singing!

CHARLOTTA (*taking a bundle that looks like a baby wrapped up*) My baby, bye, bye— (*A baby's cry is heard: Ooah, ooah—!*) Hush, my darling, my dear little boy. (*Ooah, ooah—!*) I am so sorry for you! (*throwing the bundle back*) Will you please find me a position? I cannot go on like this.

LOPAHIN We will find something, Charlotta Ivanovna, don't worry.

GAYEFF Everybody is dropping us, Varya is going away.—All of a sudden we are not needed.

CHARLOTTA I have no place in town to live. I must go away. (*humming*) It's all the same—

(PISHTCHIK *enters.*)

LOPAHIN The freak of nature—!

PISHTCHIK (*out of breath*) Ugh, let me catch my breath—I'm exhausted—My honored friends—Give me some water—

GAYEFF After money, I suppose? This humble servant will flee from sin!

(*goes out*)

PISHTCHIK It's a long time since I was here—Most beautiful lady— (*to* LOPAHIN) You here—? Glad to see you—a man of the greatest intellect—Here—Take it— (*giving* LOPAHIN *some money*) Four hundred roubles—That leaves eight hundred and forty I still owe you—

LOPAHIN (*with astonishment, shrugging his shoulders*) I must be dreaming. But where did you get it?

PISHTCHIK Wait—I'm hot—Most extraordinary event. Some Englishmen came and found on my land some kind of white clay— (*to* LYUBOFF ANDREEVNA) And four hundred for you—Beautiful lady—Wonderful lady—(*handing over the money*) The rest later. (*taking a drink of water*) Just now a young man was saying on the train that some great philosopher recommends jumping off roofs—"Jump!" he says, and "therein lies the whole problem." (*with astonishment*) You don't say! Water!

LOPAHIN And what Englishmen were they?

PISHTCHIK I leased them the parcel of land with the clay for twenty-four years—And now, excuse me, I haven't time—I must run along—I'm going to Znoykoff's—To Kardamonoff's—I owe everybody— (*drinking*) I wish you well—I'll drop in on Thursday—

LYUBOFF ANDREEVNA We are moving to town right away, and tomorrow I'm going abroad—

PISHTCHIK What? (*alarmed*) Why to town? That's why I see furniture—Suitcases—Well, no matter— (*tearfully*) No matter—Men of the greatest minds—those Englishmen—No matter—Good luck! God will help you—No matter—Everything in this world comes to an end— (*kissing* LYUBOFF ANDREEVNA's *hand*) And should the report reach you that my end has come, think of that well-known horse and say: "There was once on earth a so and so—Semyonoff Pishtchik—The kingdom of Heaven be his." Most remarkable weather—yes— (*going out greatly disconcerted, but immediately returning and speaking from the door*) Dashenka sends her greetings!

(*goes out*)

LYUBOFF ANDREEVNA And now we can go. I am leaving with two worries. First, that Fiers is sick (*glancing at her watch*) We still have five minutes—

ANYA Mama, Fiers has already been sent to the hospital. Yasha sent him off this morning.

LYUBOFF ANDREEVNA My second worry—is Varya. She is used to getting up early and working, and now without any work she is like a fish out of water. She has grown thin, pale and cries all the time, poor thing— (*a pause*) You know this, Yermolay Alexeevich: I dreamed—of marrying her to you. And there was every sign of your getting married. (*whispering to* ANYA, *who beckons to* CHARLOTTA; *both go out*) She loves you, you are fond of her, and I don't know, don't know why it is you seem to avoid each other—I don't understand it!

LOPAHIN I don't understand it either, I must confess. It's all strange somehow—If there's still time, I am ready right now even—Let's finish it up—and *basta,*[4] but without you I feel I won't propose.

LYUBOFF ANDREEVNA But that's excellent. Surely it takes only a minute. I'll call her at once.

LOPAHIN And to fit the occasion there's the champagne. (*looking at the glasses*) Empty, somebody has already drunk them. (YASHA *coughs.*) That's what's called lapping it up—

LYUBOFF ANDREEVNA (*vivaciously*) Splendid! We'll go out—Yasha, *allez!*[5] I'll call her— (*through the door*) Varya, drop everything and come here. Come on! (*goes out with* YASHA)

---

[4]be done with it [5]go

LOPAHIN (*looking at his watch*) Yes—

(*A pause. Behind the door you hear smothered laughter, whispering; finally* VARYA *enters.*)

VARYA (*looking at the luggage a long time*) That's strange, I just can't find it—

LOPAHIN What are you looking for?

VARYA I packed it myself and don't remember where.

(*a pause*)

LOPAHIN Where do you expect to go now, Varvara Mikhailovna?

VARYA I? To Regulin's. I agreed to go there to look after the house—As a sort of housekeeper.

LOPAHIN That's in Yashnevo? It's nigh on to seventy miles. (*a pause*) And here ends life in this house—

VARYA (*examining the luggage*) But where is it? Either I put it in the trunk, perhaps—Yes, life in this house is ended—it won't be any more—

LOPAHIN And I am going to Kharkov now—By the next train. I've a lot to do. And I am leaving Epihodoff—on the ground here—I've hired him.

VARYA Well!

LOPAHIN Last year at this time it had already been snowing, if you remember, and now it's quiet, it's sunny. It's only that it's cold, about three degrees of frost.

VARYA I haven't noticed. (*a pause*) And besides our thermometer is broken— (*a pause; a voice from the yard through the door*) Yermolay Alexeevich—

LOPAHIN (*as if he had been expecting this call for a long time*) This minute!

(*goes out quickly*)

(VARYA, *sitting on the floor, putting her head on a bundle of clothes, sobs quietly. The door opens,* LYUBOFF ANDREEVNA *enters cautiously.*)

VARYA (*She is not crying any longer, and has wiped her eyes.*) Yes, it's time, Mama. I can get to Regulin's today, if we are just not too late for the train— (*through the door*) Anya, put your things on! (ANYA, *then* GAYEFF *and* CHARLOTTA IVANOVNA *enter.* GAYEFF *has on a warm overcoat, with a hood. The servants gather, also the drivers.* EPIHODOFF *busies himself with the luggage.*) Now we can be on our way.

ANYA (*joyfully*) On our way!

GAYEFF My friends, my dear, kind friends! Leaving this house forever, can I remain silent, can I restrain myself from expressing, as we say, farewell, those feelings that fill now my whole being—

ANYA (*beseechingly*) Uncle!

VARYA Dear Uncle, don't!

GAYEFF (*dejectedly*) Bank the yellow into the side pocket—I am silent—

(TROFIMOFF *and then* LOPAHIN *enter.*)

TROFIMOFF Well, ladies and gentlemen, it's time to go!

LOPAHIN Epihodoff, my coat!

LYUBOFF ANDREEVNA I'll sit here just a minute more. It's as if I had never seen before what the walls in this house are like, what kind of ceilings, and now I look at them greedily, with such tender love—

GAYEFF I remember when I was six years old, on Trinity Day, I sat in this window and watched my father going to Church—

LYUBOFF ANDREEVNA Are all the things taken out?

LOPAHIN Everything, I think. (*putting on his overcoat; to* EPIHODOFF) Epihodoff, you see that everything is in order.

EPIHODOFF (*talking in a hoarse voice*) Don't worry, Yermolay Alexeevich!

LOPAHIN Why is your voice like that?

EPIHODOFF Just drank some water, swallowed something.

YASHA (*with contempt*) The ignorance—

LYUBOFF ANDREEVNA We are going and there won't be a soul left here—

LOPAHIN Till spring.

VARYA (*Pulls an umbrella out from a bundle, it looks as if she were going to hit someone;* LOPAHIN *pretends to be frightened.*) What do you, what do you—I never thought of it.

TROFIMOFF Ladies and gentlemen, let's get in the carriages—It's time! The train is coming any minute.

VARYA Petya, here they are, your rubbers, by the suitcase. (*tearfully*) And how dirty yours are, how old—!

TROFIMOFF (*putting on the rubbers*) Let's go, ladies and gentlemen!

GAYEFF (*greatly embarrassed, afraid he will cry*) The train—The station—Cross into the side, combination off the white into the corner—

LYUBOFF ANDREEVNA Let's go!

LOPAHIN Everybody here? Nobody there? (*locking the side door on the left*) Things are stored here, it must be locked up, let's go!

ANYA Good-by, house! Good-by, the old life!

TROFIMOFF Long live the new life!

(*Goes out with* ANYA. VARYA *casts a glance around the room and, without hurrying, goes out.* YASHA *and* CHARLOTTA, *with her dog, go out.*)

LOPAHIN And so, till spring. Out, ladies and gentlemen—Till we meet.

(*goes out*)

(LYUBOFF ANDREEVNA *and* GAYEFF *are left alone. As if they had been waiting for this, they throw themselves on one another's necks sobbing, but smothering their sobs as if afraid of being heard.*)

GAYEFF (*in despair*) Oh, Sister, Sister—

LYUBOFF ANDREEVNA Oh, my dear, my lovely, beautiful orchard! My life, my youth, my happiness, good-by!

ANYA (ANYA's *voice, gaily, appealingly*) Mama—!

TROFIMOFF (*gaily, excitedly*) Aaooch!

LYUBOFF ANDREEVNA For the last time, just to look at the walls, at the window—My dear mother used to love to walk around in this room—

GAYEFF Oh, Sister, Sister—!

ANYA (*from outside*) Mama—!

TROFIMOFF (*from outside*) Aaooch—!

LYUBOFF ANDREEVNA We are coming!

(*They go out.*)

(*The stage is empty. One hears the keys locking all the doors, then the carriages driving off. It grows quiet. In the silence the dull thud of an ax on a tree, a lonely, mournful sound. Footsteps are heard. From the door on the right* FIERS *appears. He is dressed as usual, in a jacket and a white waistcoat, slippers on his feet. He is sick.*)

FIERS (*going to the door and trying the knob*) Locked. They've gone. (*sitting down on the sofa*) They forgot about me—No matter—I'll sit here awhile—And Leonid Andreevich, for sure, didn't put on his fur coat, he went off with his topcoat— (*sighing anxiously*) And I didn't see to it—The young saplings! (*He mutters something that cannot be understood.*) Life has gone by, as if I hadn't lived at all— (*lying down*) I'll lie down awhile—You haven't got any strength, nothing is left, nothing—Ach, you—good-for-nothing— (*He lies still.*)

(*There is a far-off sound as if out of the sky, the sound of a snapped string, dying away, sad. A stillness falls, and there is only the thud of an ax on a tree, far away in the orchard.*)

MAJOR BARBARA

(1905)

GEORGE BERNARD SHAW (1856–1950)

George Bernard Shaw expressed his contempt for the Scribe and Sardou tradition (see the introduction to *A Doll's House*) of neatly constructed, well-made plays that sat so heavily upon nineteenth-century drama by dubbing it "sardoodledum." All in all, serious English drama in the first three-quarters of the nineteenth century was not very impressive. A few plays, such as Shelley's *The Cenci* (1819) and Browning's *A Blot on the 'Scutcheon* (1843), both "closet" dramas designed more for reading than production, have never had any life on the stage to speak of.

There were, of course, some popular successes, which can still be read with interest, and, in one or two cases, successfully revived. The Irishman Dion Boucicault (1822–1890), popular both in England and America, wrote 125 pieces, adapted and original, now mostly forgotten except for a couple of interesting melodramas. His adaptation of a French drama, *Les Pauvres de Paris,* became *The Poor of Liverpool* or *The Poor of New York,* depending on the country in which it appeared. A relatively serious attempt at an exposé of unscrupulous financiers, it is mainly remembered for the sensational theatricality of a house on fire. *The Octoroon* (1859) remains a remarkable example, though overly melodramatic, of a play with a social consciousness in its portrayal of the beautiful one-eighth black heroine, Zoe, loved by a white suitor but doomed to the slave auction block. In 1867 Thomas W. Robertson dealt with narrow-minded cultural snobbery in *Caste,* notable for its lack of familiar melodramatics and evil villains plus the innovation of solid stage scenery.

In the century's last quarter two dramatists of importance were Henry Arthur Jones (1851–1929) and Sir Arthur Wing Pinero (1855–1934), both now eclipsed by Shaw. Right in the middle of the well-made tradition, their subject matter and the believability of their characters were able to transcend Shaw's nemisis; together they gave English drama a badly needed shot of vitality and excitement in the midst of the proprieties of Victorian England. Jones's best play, *Michael and His Lost Angel* (1896) was so controversial in its priest-hero's confession of his adulterous past that it was quickly withdrawn. Pinero's best-remembered play, *The Second Mrs. Tanqueray* (1893), engages in a serious discussion of entrenched nineteenth-century prejudices, particularly against women.

Standing above all others in the last decade of the nineteenth century were two unashamedly egocentric geniuses who swiftly brought English drama into the modern age. Their often infuriating, not always sound, but constantly challenging social and political philosophies have become permanent legacies in English dramatic literature. One was George Bernard Shaw, and the other was Oscar Wilde (1854–1900).

The high London society in which Wilde moved was fascinated by his sharp wit and delighted by his extravagances in dress and behavior that parodied and often shocked his social peers. Foremost was his notorious advocacy of the philosophy of decadence, that one should enjoy to the utmost the full sensuousness of the life experience, even though it might in the end destroy. His famous decadent novel, *The Picture of Dorian Gray* (1891), and the sordid fable of the story of John the Baptist and the princess who receives his head on a platter in the short play *Salomé* (1894) fully demonstrated the philosophy that not only destroys the protagonists but eventually destroyed Wilde himself.

Wilde's theatrical fame rests on four plays, all easily performable today, that brilliantly reflect the behavior of a social class he knew so well. *Lady Windermere's Fan* (1892) skillfully handles matters of seduction and adultery; *A Woman of No Importance* (1893) dwells on the heroine's apparently shady past; and *An Ideal Husband* (1895) reveals the wife as the real power behind the husband's "ideal" male achievements. The most outstanding quality of these superb comedies is the elegance of the wit, which sparkles and crackles throughout in a torrent of epigrams, those highly intellectual "wisecracks" for which Wilde remains rightfully famous.

Wilde's ultimate fame must rest with *The Importance of Being Earnest* (1895), a play that is most likely the most brilliant comedy in modern English drama. It is the work of a comic genius whose characters behave and speak in a pattern experienced by no known society, but which is at the same time a devastating parody of every aspect of all who have ever aspired to social heights through birth, wealth, or position. The characters are preposterous, especially the unforgettable Lady Bracknell, the mighty upholder of all that is grand and meaningless, but they exhibit magnificently virtually every known social cliché, making use of long-established comic gags in polished language and sophisticated behavior that is audaciously original and explosively funny.

But nobody—Jones, Pinero, Wilde, or anyone else—brought to the English stage the sheer dramatic vigor and intellectual challenge of George Bernard Shaw. It once seemed, as his work expounded on just about everything decade after decade, that he might possibly live forever. He had begun his career as a music and drama critic and as a sometime writer of fiction. He was 36 before his own first play, *Widower's Houses,* was written in 1892, and his greatest plays were done between his forties and seventies. He was still writing acceptable works into his eighties. Opinionated, garrulous, supremely egotistical, considering himself an expert on any given social or political problem, he was, as well, a true theatrical genius in the creation of some of the most superb comedies in the English language. It is the *nature* of his comedy that matters: his *concerns* were always serious, but his *style* was comic. The notoriety of his social consciousness began in 1893 with *Mrs. Warren's Profession,* an outrage to the purists that called down the wrath of the law. (In America it was closed down by the New York police.) The reason? Shaw espoused the heretical view that young women exploited in factories (in this case, their slow poisoning by the radium they painted on watch dials) would be better off in the far more "healthy" atmosphere of the well-controlled brothels operated on the continent by the socially respectable lady of the title. He ridiculed nineteenth-century militarism in *Arms and the Man* (1894) with the soldier nonhero who carries chocolates instead of ammunition in his cartridge case. Medicine and its attendant leanings toward quackery (Shaw had suffered from smallpox but was still adamantly opposed to vaccination) took some criticism, which was not always fair or rational, in *The Doctor's Dilemma* (1911).

As a public figure on the lecture platform, in his outpouring of critical essays, and in his voluminous correspondence (virtually anyone writing him would get a prompt and often acerbic reply by postcard) Shaw was a born performer. It was next to impossible to determine the "real" Shaw, if, indeed, there ever was one, because he behaved continually as if he were on stage. He could at one moment be the bearded Irish pixie and the next the goading, irascible, devilish socialist. In the production of his plays he could command actors, directors, and audiences to do his bidding even across oceans.

Early in his life Shaw joined the Fabian Society in England and was a longtime advocate of state socialism, even, at times when it was dangerously unpopular to do so, supporting Russian Communism. He strongly espoused Ibsen's abandonment of the conventional attitude toward the "womanly woman"—the traditional female who performed at the command of her husband and male-oriented society, imprisoned by the strictures of an unbending and arbitrary morality. He saw strength in the "life force," including that of natural sexuality, which he discussed at considerable length in *Man and Superman* (1903), as a positive, driving element in the world, while assigning his romantic couples to virtually passionless, albeit wholly charming, affairs. Shaw himself advocated celibacy to the point of having endured, so far as is known, a totally abstinent marriage, while carrying on a kind of public, if platonic, love affair of his own with the beautiful actress Mrs. Patrick Campbell, for whom he created *Pygmalion* in 1913, forever with us in *My Fair Lady.* One of the most "liberated" of women appears in his high comedy masterpiece, *Candida,* in 1895. His most magnificent feminine creation, at once a near-tragic and a delightfully comic figure, is in *Saint Joan* of 1923, Shaw's own personal view of one of history's freest and most captive women.

Above all, Shaw regarded poverty as an out-and-out crime. In *Major Barbara* he has written an effective exposé of human hypocrisy in the way society insists on handling its poor, but in a typical tongue-in-cheek Shavian twist, this ardent socialist has assigned his Utopian state, the perfect benevolent society, to the supercapitalist munitions lord. Against the diabolic reasoning of Undershaft, though it is based on the powderkeg of a cannon foundry, the classical scholarly mind of Adolphus ultimately loses, or at least seems to lose, in order to win the hand of the thoroughly do-good Barbara. She, disillusioned in her faith, surrenders as well to the powers of darkness as she sadly discovers that anyone in the world can be bought if the right amount of hard cash comes along. The fortuitous discovery of Adolphus's illegitimacy as a foundling, eligible for the Undershaft fortune, is not without its ironies.

Shaw is at his best in stringing us along, as he does so well in *Major Barbara,* but what fun there is in following him! Who has really been "had" in all of this? The Army? Bill? Barbara and Dolly? All of us and none of us? Whatever the socialist "thinker" that Shaw makes himself out to be, beneath everything is a dramatist who knows his theatre, for which he creates incident and action at their keenest levels, with charmingly attractive characters and brilliantly sophisticated comedy.

The Preface

Shaw's extensive nondramatic writings range from religion and the arts to politics, economics, and philosophy—all, of course, delivered with a strongly personal Shavian didacticism. His *The Quintessence of Ibsenism,* first published in 1891, is one of the earliest significant endorsements of the Norwegian's dramatic realism, written at a time when Ibsen was being roundly condemned as perverse and obscene. In its subsequent revisions, Shaw's staunch support remains among the best critical studies of the playwright.

But with Shaw's popular reputation resting exclusively on his plays, most of his other works remain unread. The major exception, however, is the dramatic prefaces, considered by many to place Shaw among the masters of English prose. Purporting to introduce the plays, these lengthy and discursive essays, sometimes nearly as long as the plays themselves, while centering on the plays' individual themes, often digress far afield. In the aggregate, they express Shaw's philosophy on just about everything.

The Preface to *Major Barbara* is an excellent example. It is a brilliant argument in its support of the importance of money and its denunciation of the "crime" of poverty, attacking along the way the hypocrisies of religion and the outrages of modern social practices. He is, of course, quite right. His well-established points are based on solid evidence, and they are persuasively argued. His superb rationale for the behavior of his characters removes nearly all objections that they are merely talkative mouthpieces for Shaw's own eccentric ideas. His analysis of the Barbara-Bill relationship is exceptionally lucid and convincing, and his explanation of the seeming paradox of the Army's acceptance of tainted money is difficult to deny. His support of Undershaft's "gospel" is remarkably persuasive.

However, let the reader beware!

Shaw seldom, if ever, entertained the possibility of a viable counterargument. Things were to be seen as he saw them, since his own opinion of himself conceived of no other authority. After all, he does assert that he stands on the shoulders of Euripides, Voltaire, Marx, Molière, Goethe, Tolstoy, and Jesus, among others. The end result can be dangerous. The susceptible reader can easily be led down Shaw's garden path by the sheer verbal power displayed, failing to recognize that despite the seeming rightness of the cause and the mesmerizing persuasive logic, there are opposing and equally valid views. Moreover, because the "real" world refuses to behave in Shavian fashion, as Shaw thinks it should, his solutions to society's ills emerge as oversimplified and impossibly idealistic. Shaw is so good in presenting his side that it becomes disarmingly easy to be wholly convinced. There are, after all, modulations that Shaw refuses to recognize, even though the foundation he builds upon is firmly grounded.

Written in 1906, in the year following the opening of the play, the Preface to *Major Barbara* is as startlingly pertinent at the end of the century as it was at the beginning. Shaw was no fool, and certainly no charlatan. He knew well of what he wrote and spoke, and in the manner of all creative artistic geniuses, his basic ideas transcend time and become universal in their recognition of humankind's often deadly foolishness. The problems raised—senseless buildup of armaments, terrorism on an international scale, the vacuities of established religion, and the inanities of social practices—remain frighteningly with us today. One may scoff at Shaw and ridicule his egocentricities, but one simply cannot ignore him. He may be wildly wrong in his narrow-minded attack on medical practices as expressed in his Preface to *The Doctor's Dilemma;* he may not be able to recognize that his insistence that Eliza and Higgins cannot possibly come together at the end of *Pygmalion* is plainly in error, when all the world knows they will because that's clearly the direction the play is written. (Shaw grudgingly acknowledged the popular will and added the present "happy" ending to the film version of *Pygmalion,* also included in *My Fair Lady,* although all definitive texts of the original play omit it.) But even at his most outrageous, Shaw still commands attention.

And finally, regardless of what he says in his prefaces, regardless of their sometimes overbearing philosophical involvements, which suggest that the plays under discussion can emerge only as deadly bores, what Shaw does is what really matters. His expansive philosophical discourse to the contrary, he has succeeded in creating delightfully entertaining pieces of theatre, thoroughly enjoyable on their own merits, without any necessity at all to know a single word of what has gone before.

PREFACE TO *MAJOR BARBARA*

First Aid to Critics

Before dealing with the deeper aspects of *Major Barbara,* let me, for the credit of English literature, make a protest against an unpatriotic habit into which many of my critics have fallen. Whenever my view strikes them as being at all outside the range of, say, an ordinary suburban churchwarden, they conclude that I am echoing *Schopenhauer, Nietzsche, Ibsen, Strindberg, Tolstoy,* or some other heresiarch in northern or eastern Europe.

I confess there is something flattering in this simple faith in my accomplishment as a linguist and my erudition as a philosopher. But I cannot countenance the assumption that life and literature are so poor in these islands that we must go abroad for all dramatic material that is not common and all ideas that are not superficial. I therefore venture to put my critics in possession of certain facts concerning my contact with modern ideas.

About half a century ago, an Irish novelist, Charles Lever, wrote a story entitled A Day's Ride: A Life's Romance. It was published by Charles Dickens in Household Words, and proved so strange to the public taste that Dickens pressed Lever to make short work of it. I read scraps of this novel when I was a child; and it made an enduring impression on me. The hero was a very romantic hero, trying to live bravely, chivalrously, and powerfully by dint of mere romance-fed imagination, without courage, without means, without knowledge, without skill, without anything real except his bodily appetites. Even in my childhood I found in this poor devil's unsuccessful encounters with the facts of life, a poignant quality that romantic fiction lacked. The book, in spite of its first failure, is not dead: I saw its title the other day in the catalogue of Tauchnitz.

Now why is it that when I also deal in the tragi-comic irony of the conflict between real life and the romantic imagination, critics never affiliate me to my countryman and immediate forerunner, Charles Lever, whilst they confidently derive me from a Norwegian author of whose language I do not know three words, and of whom I knew nothing until years after the Shavian *Anschauung* was already unequivocally declared in books full of what came, ten years later, to be perfunctorily labelled Ibsenism? I was not Ibsenist even at second hand; for Lever, though he may have read Henri Beyle, *alias* Stendhal, certainly never read Ibsen. Of the books that made Lever popular, such as Charles O'Malley and Harry Lorrequer, I know nothing but the names and some of the illustrations. But the story of the day's ride and life's romance of Potts (claiming alliance with Pozzo di Borgo) caught me and fascinated me as something strange and significant, though I already knew all about Alnaschar and Don Quixote and Simon Tappertit and many another romantic hero mocked by reality. From the plays of Aristophanes to the tales of Stevenson that mockery has been made familiar to all who are properly saturated with letters.

Where, then, was the novelty in Lever's tale? Partly, I think, in a new seriousness in dealing with Potts's disease. Formerly, the contrast between madness and sanity was deemed comic: Hogarth shows us how fashionable people went in parties to Bedlam[1] to laugh at the lunatics. I myself have had a village idiot exhibited to me as something irresistibly funny. On the stage the madman was once a regular comic figure: that was how Hamlet got his opportunity before Shakespear touched him. The originality of Shakespear's version lay in his taking the lunatic sympathetically and seriously, and thereby making an advance towards the eastern consciousness of the fact that lunacy may be inspiration in disguise, since a man who has more brains than his fellows necessarily appears as mad to them as one who has less. But Shakespear did not do for Pistol and Parolles what he did for Hamlet. The particular sort of madman they represented, the romantic make-believer, lay outside the pale of sympathy in literature: he was pitilessly despised and ridiculed here as he was in the east under the name of Alnaschar, and was doomed to be, centuries later, under the name of Simon Tappertit. When Cervantes relented over Don Quixote, and Dickens relented over Pickwick, they did not become impartial: they simply changed sides, and became friends and apologists where they had formerly been mockers.

In Lever's story there is a real change of attitude. There is no relenting towards Potts: he never gains our affections like Don Quixote and Pickwick: he has not even the infatuate courage of Tappertit. But we dare not laugh at him, because, somehow, we recognize ourselves in Potts. We may, some of us, have enough nerve, enough muscle, enough luck, enough tact or skill or address or knowledge to carry things off better than he did; to impose on the people who saw through him; to fascinate Katinka (who cut Potts so ruthlessly at the end of the story); but for all that, we know that Potts plays an enormous part in ourselves and in the world, and that the social problem is not a problem of storybook heroes of the older pattern, but a problem of Pottses, and of how to make men of them. To fall back on my old phrase, we have the feeling—one that Alnaschar, Pistol, Parolles, and Tappertit never gave us—that Potts is a piece of really scientific natural history as distinguished from funny story telling. His author is not throwing a stone at a creature of another and inferior order, but making a confession, with the effect that the stone hits each of us full in the conscience and causes our self-esteem to smart very sorely. Hence the failure of Lever's book to please the readers of Household Words. That pain in the self-esteem nowadays causes critics to raise a cry of Ibsenism. I therefore assure them that the sensation first came to me from Lever and may have come to him from Beyle, or at least out of the Stendhalian atmosphere. I exclude the hypothesis of complete originality on Lever's part, because a man can no more be completely original in that sense than a tree can grow out of air.

[1]Bedlam is a corruption of Bethlehem, the name of the London insane asylum. Hogarth was the artist engraver who portrayed many vivid scenes of the age.

Another mistake as to my literary ancestry is made whenever I violate the romantic convention that all women are angels when they are not devils; that they are better looking than men; that their part in courtship is entirely passive; and that the human female form is the most beautiful object in nature. Schopenhauer wrote a splenetic essay which, as it is neither polite nor profound, was probably intended to knock this nonsense violently on the head. A sentence denouncing the idolized form as ugly has been largely quoted. The English critics have read that sentence; and I must here affirm, with as much gentleness as the implication will bear, that it has yet to be proved that they have dipped any deeper. At all events, whenever an English playwright represents a young and marriageable woman as being anything but a romantic heroine, he is disposed of without further thought as an echo of Schopenhauer. My own case is a specially hard one, because, when I implore the critics who are obsessed with the Schopenhauerian formula to remember that playwrights, like sculptors, study their figures from life, and not from philosophic essays, they reply passionately that I am not a playwright and that my stage figures do not live. But even so, I may and do ask them why, if they must give the credit of my plays to a philosopher, they do not give it to an English philosopher? Long before I ever read a word by Schopenhauer, or even knew whether he was a philosopher or a chemist, the Socialist revival of the eighteen-eighties brought me into contact, both literary and personal, with Ernest Belfort Bax, an English Socialist and philosophic essayist, whose handling of modern feminism would provoke romantic protests from Schopenhauer himself, or even Strindberg. As a matter of fact I hardly noticed Schopenhauer's disparagements of women when they came under my notice later on, so thoroughly had Bax familiarized me with the homoist attitude, and forced me to recognize the extent to which public opinion, and consequently legislation and jurisprudence, is corrupted by feminist sentiment.

Belfort Bax's essays were not confined to the feminist question. He was a ruthless critic of current morality. Other writers have gained sympathy for dramatic criminals by eliciting the alleged "soul of goodness in things evil"; but Bax would propound some quite undramatic and apparently shabby violation of our commercial law and morality, and not merely defend it with the most disconcerting ingenuity, but actually prove it to be a positive duty that nothing but the certainty of police persecution should prevent every right-minded man from at once doing on principle. The Socialists were naturally shocked, being for the most part morbidly moral people; but at all events they were saved later on from the delusion that nobody but Nietzsche had ever challenged our mercanto-Christian morality. I first heard the name of Nietzsche from a German mathematician, Miss Borchardt, who had read my Quintessence of Ibsenism, and told me that she saw what I had been reading: namely, Nietzsche's Jenseits von Gut und Böse. Which I protest I had never seen, and could not have read with any comfort, for want of the necessary German, if I had seen it.

Nietzsche, like Schopenhauer, is the victim in England of a single much quoted sentence containing the phrase "big blonde beast." On the strength of this alliteration it is assumed that Nietzsche gained his European reputation by a senseless glorification of selfish bullying as the rule of life, just as it is assumed, on the strength of the single word Superman (Übermensch) borrowed by me from Nietzsche, that I look for the salvation of society to the despotism of a single Napoleonic Superman, in spite of my careful demonstration of the folly of that outworn infatuation. But even the less recklessly superficial critics seem to believe that the modern objection to Christianity as a pernicious slave-morality was first put forward by Nietzsche. It was familiar to me before I ever heard of Nietzsche. The late Captain Wilson, author of several queer pamphlets, propagandist of a metaphysical system called Comprehensionism, and inventor of the term "Crosstianity" to distinguish the retrograde element in Christendom, was wont thirty years ago, in the discussions of the Dialectical Society, to protest earnestly against the beatitudes of the Sermon on the Mount as excuses for cowardice and servility, as destructive of our will, and consequently of our honour and manhood. Now it is true that Captain Wilson's moral criticism of Christianity was not a historical theory of it, like Nietzsche's; but this objection cannot be made to Stuart-Glennie, the successor of Buckle as a philosophic historian, who devoted his life to the elaboration and propagation of his theory that Christianity is part of an epoch (or rather an aberration, since it began as recently as 6000 B.C. and is already collapsing) produced by the necessity in which the numerically inferior white races found themselves to impose their domination on the colored races by priestcraft, making a virtue and a popular religion of drudgery and submissiveness in this world not only as a means of achieving saintliness of character but of securing a reward in heaven. Here was the slave-morality view formulated by a Scotch philosopher of my acquaintance long before we all began chattering about Nietzsche.

As Stuart-Glennie traced the evolution of society to the conflict of races, his theory made some sensation among Socialists—that is, among the only people who were seriously thinking about historical evolution at all—by its collision with the class-conflict theory of Karl Marx. Nietzsche, as I gather, regarded the slave-morality as having been invented and imposed on the world by slaves making a virtue of necessity and a religion of their servitude. Stuart-Glennie regarded the slave-morality as an invention of the superior white race to subjugate the minds of the inferior races whom they wished to exploit, and who would have destroyed them by force of numbers if their minds had not been subjugated. As this process is in operation still, and can be studied at first hand not only in our Church schools and in the struggle between our modern proprietary classes and the proletariat, but in the part played by Christian missionaries in reconciling the black races of Africa to their subjugation by European Capitalism, we can judge for ourselves whether the initiative came from above or below. My object here is not to argue the historical point, but simply to make our theatre critics ashamed of their habit of treating Britain as an intellectual void, and assuming that every philosophical idea, every historic theory, every criticism of our moral, religious and juridical institutions, must necessarily be either a foreign import, or else a fantastic sally (in rather questionable taste) totally unrelated to the existing body of thought. I urge them to remember that this body of thought is the slowest of growths and the rarest of blossomings, and that if there be such a thing on the philosophic plane as a matter of course, it is that no individual can make more than a minute contribution to it. In fact, their conception of clever persons parthenogenetically bringing forth complete original cosmogonies by dint of sheer "brilliancy" is part of that ignorant credulity which is the despair of the honest philosopher, and the opportunity of the religious impostor.

The Gospel of St Andrew Undershaft

It is this credulity that drives me to help my critics out with *Major Barbara* by telling them what to say about it. In the millionaire Undershaft I have represented a man who has become intellectually and spiritually as well as practically conscious of the irresistible natural truth which we all abhor and repudiate: to wit, that the greatest of our evils, and the worst of our crimes is poverty, and that our first duty, to which every other consideration should be sacrificed, is not to be poor. "Poor but honest," "the respectable poor," and such phrases are as intolerable and as immoral as "drunken but amiable," "fraudulent but a good after-dinner speaker," "splendidly criminal," or the like. Security, the chief pretence of civilization, cannot exist where the worst of dangers, the danger of poverty, hangs over everyone's head, and where the alleged protection of our persons from violence is only an accidental result of the existence of a police force whose real business is to force the poor man to see his children starve whilst idle people overfeed pet dogs with money that might feed and clothe them.

It is exceedingly difficult to make people realize that an evil is an evil. For instance, we seize a man and deliberately do him a malicious injury: say, imprison him for years. One would not suppose that it needed any exceptional clearness of wit to recognize in this an act of diabolical cruelty. But in England such a recognition provokes a stare of surprise, followed by an explanation that the outrage is punishment or justice or something else that is all right, or perhaps by a heated attempt to argue that we should all be robbed and murdered in our beds if such stupid villainies as sentences of imprisonment were not committed daily. It is useless to argue that even if this were true, which it is not, the alternative to adding crimes of our own to the crimes from which we suffer is not helpless submission. Chickenpox is an evil; but if I were to declare that we must either submit to it or else repress it sternly by seizing everyone who suffers from it and punishing them by inoculation with smallpox, I should be laughed at; for though nobody could deny that the result would be to prevent chickenpox to some extent by making people avoid it much more carefully, and to effect a further apparent prevention by making them conceal it very anxiously, yet people would have sense enough to see that the deliberate propagation of smallpox was a creation of evil, and must therefore be ruled out in favor of purely humane and hygienic measures. Yet in the precisely parallel case of a man breaking into my house and stealing my wife's diamonds I am expected as a matter of course to steal ten years of his life, torturing him all the time. If he tries to defeat that monstrous retaliation by shooting me, my survivors hang him. The net result suggested by the police statistics is that we inflict atrocious injuries on the burglars we catch in order to make the rest take effectual precautions against detection; so that instead of saving our wives' diamonds from burglary we only greatly decrease our chances of ever getting them back, and increase our chances of being shot by the robber if we are unlucky enough to disturb him at his work.

But the thoughtless wickedness with which we scatter sentences of imprisonment, torture in the solitary cell and on the plank bed, and flogging, on moral invalids and energetic rebels, is as nothing compared to the silly levity with which we tolerate poverty as if it were either a wholesome tonic for lazy people or else a virtue to be embraced as St Francis embraced it. If a man is indolent, let him be poor. If he is drunken, let him be poor. If he is not a gentleman, let him be poor. If he is addicted to the fine arts or to pure science instead of to trade and finance, let him be poor. If he chooses to spend his urban eighteen shillings a week or his agricultural thirteen shillings a week on his beer and his family instead of saving it up for his old age, let him be poor. Let nothing be done for "the undeserving": let him be poor. Serve him right! Also—somewhat inconsistently—blessed are the poor!

Now what does this Let Him Be Poor mean? It means let him be weak. Let him be ignorant. Let him become a nucleus of disease. Let him be a standing exhibition and example of ugliness and dirt. Let him have rickety children. Let him be cheap, and drag his fellows down to his own price by selling himself to do their work. Let his habitations turn our cities into poisonous congeries of slums. Let his daughters infect our young men with the diseases of the streets, and his sons revenge him by turning the nation's manhood into scrofula, cowardice, cruelty, hypocrisy, political imbecility, and all the other fruits of oppression and malnutrition. Let the undeserving become still less deserving; and let the deserving lay up for himself, not treasures in heaven, but horrors in hell upon earth. This being so, is it really wise to let him be poor? Would he not do ten times less harm as a prosperous burglar, incendiary, ravisher or murderer, to the utmost limits of humanity's comparatively negligible impulses in these directions? Suppose we were to abolish all penalties for such activities, and decide that poverty is the one thing we will not tolerate—that every adult with less than, say, £365 a year, shall be painlessly but inexorably killed, and every hungry half naked child forcibly fattened and clothed, would not that be an enormous improvement on our existing system, which has already destroyed so many civilizations, and is visibly destroying ours in the same way?

Is there any radicle of such legislation in our parliamentary system? Well, there are two measures just sprouting in the political soil, which may conceivably grow to something valuable. One is the institution of a Legal Minimum Wage. The other, Old Age Pensions. But there is a better plan than either of these. Some time ago I mentioned the subject of Universal Old Age Pensions to my fellow Socialist Cobden-Sanderson, famous as an artist-craftsman in bookbinding and printing. "Why not Universal Pensions for Life?" said Cobden-Sanderson. In saying this, he solved the industrial problem at a stroke. At present we say callously to each citizen "If you want money, earn it" as if his having or not having it were a matter that concerned himself alone. We do not even secure for him the opportunity of earning it: on the contrary, we allow our industry to be organized in open dependence on the maintenance of "a reserve army of unemployed" for the sake of "elasticity." The sensible course would be Cobden-Sanderson's: that is, to give every man enough to live well on, so as to guarantee the community against the possibility of a case of the malignant disease of poverty, and then (necessarily) to see that he earned it.

Undershaft, the hero of *Major Barbara,* is simply a man who, having grasped the fact that poverty is a crime, knows that when society offered him the alternative of poverty or a lucrative trade in death and destruction, it offered him, not a choice between opulent villainy and humble virtue, but between energetic enterprise and cowardly infamy. His conduct stands the Kantian test, which Peter Shirley's does not. Peter Shirley is what we call the honest poor man. Undershaft is what we call the wicked rich one: Shirley is Lazarus, Undershaft Dives.[2] Well, the misery of the world is due to the fact that the great mass of men act and believe as Peter Shirley acts and believes. If they acted and believed as Undershaft acts and believes, the immediate result would be a revolution of incalculable beneficence. To be wealthy, says Undershaft, is with me a point of honor for which I am prepared to kill at the risk of my own life. This preparedness is, as he says, the final test of sincerity. Like Froissart's medieval hero, who saw that "to rob and pill was a good life" he is not the dupe of that public sentiment against killing which is propagated and endowed by people who would otherwise be killed themselves, or of the mouth-honour paid to poverty and obedience by rich and insubordinate do-nothings who want to rob the poor without courage and command them without superiority. Froissart's knight, in placing the achievement of a good life before all the other duties—which indeed are not duties at all when they conflict with it, but plain wickedness—behaved bravely, admirably, and, in the final analysis, public-spiritedly. Medieval society, on the other hand, behaved very badly indeed in organizing itself so stupidly that a good life could be achieved by robbing and pilling. If the knight's contemporaries had been all as resolute as he, robbing and pilling would have been the shortest way to the gallows, just as, if we were all as resolute and clear-sighted as Undershaft, an attempt to live by means of what is called "an independent in-

[2]*Lazarus* was the diseased beggar in Jesus' parable, and *Dives* was the rich man.

come" would be the shortest way to the lethal chamber. But as, thanks to our political imbecility and personal cowardice (fruits of poverty, both), the best imitation of a good life now procurable is life on an independent income, all sensible people aim at securing such an income, and are, of course, careful to legalize and moralize both it and all the actions and sentiments which lead to it and support it as an institution. What else can they do? They know, of course, that they are rich because others are poor. But they cannot help that: it is for the poor to repudiate poverty when they have had enough of it. The thing can be done easily enough: the demonstration to the contrary made by the economists, jurists, moralists and sentimentalists hired by the rich to defend them, or even doing the work gratuitously out of sheer folly and abjectness, impose only on those who want to be imposed on.

The reason why the independent income-tax payers are not solid in defence of their position is that since we are not medieval rovers through a sparsely populated country, the poverty of those we rob prevents our having the good life for which we sacrifice them. Rich men or aristocrats with a developed sense of life—men like Ruskin and William Morris and Kropotkin—have enormous social appetites and very fastidious personal ones. They are not content with handsome houses: they want handsome cities. They are not content with bediamonded wives and blooming daughters: they complain because the charwoman is badly dressed, because the laundress smells of gin, because the sempstress is anemic, because every man they meet is not a friend and every woman not a romance. They turn up their noses at their neighbor's drains, and are made ill by the architecture of their neighbor's houses. Trade patterns made to suit vulgar people do not please them (and they can get nothing else): they cannot sleep nor sit at ease upon "slaughtered" cabinet makers' furniture. The very air is not good enough for them: there is too much factory smoke in it. They even demand abstract conditions: justice, honor, a noble moral atmosphere, a mystic nexus to replace the cash nexus. Finally they declare that though to rob and pill with your own hand on horseback and in steel coat may have been a good life, to rob and pill by the hands of the policeman, the bailiff, and the soldier, and to underpay them meanly for doing it, is not a good life, but rather fatal to all possibility of even a tolerable one. They call on the poor to revolt, and, finding the poor shocked at their ungentlemanliness, despairingly revile the proletariat for its "damned wantlessness" (*verdammte Bedürfnislosigkeit*).

So far, however, their attack on society has lacked simplicity. The poor do not share their tastes nor understand their art-criticisms. They do not want the simple life, nor the esthetic life; on the contrary, they want very much to wallow in all the costly vulgarities from which the elect souls among the rich turn away with loathing. It is by surfeit and not by abstinence that they will be cured of their hankering after unwholesome sweets. What they do dislike and despise and are ashamed of is poverty. To ask them to fight for the difference between the Christmas number of the Illustrated London News and the Kelmscott Chaucer is silly: they prefer the News. The difference between a stockbroker's cheap and dirty starched white shirt and collar and the comparatively costly and carefully dyed blue shirt of William Morris is a difference so disgraceful to Morris in their eyes that if they fought on the subject at all, they would fight in defence of the starch. "Cease to be slaves, in order that you may become cranks" is not a very inspiring call to arms; nor is it really improved by substituting saints for cranks. Both terms denote men of genius; and the common man does not want to live the life of a man of genius: he would much rather live the life of a pet collie if that were the only alternative. But he does want more money. Whatever else he may be vague about, he is clear about that. He may or may not prefer *Major Barbara* to the Drury Lane pantomime;[3] but he always prefers five hundred pounds to five hundred shillings.

Now to deplore this preference as sordid, and teach children that it is sinful to desire money, is to strain towards the extreme possible limit of impudence in lying and corruption in hypocrisy. The universal regard for money is the one hopeful fact in our civilization, the one sound spot in our social conscience. Money is the most important thing in the world. It represents health, strength, honor, generosity and beauty as conspicuously and undeniably as the want of it represents illness, weakness, disgrace, meanness and ugliness. Not the least of its virtues is that it destroys base people as certainly as it fortifies and dignifies noble people. It is only when it is cheapened to worthlessness for some and made impossibly dear to others, that it becomes a curse. In short, it is a curse only in such foolish social conditions that life itself is a curse. For the two things are inseparable: money is the counter that enables life to be distributed socially: it *is* life as truly as sovereigns and bank notes are money. The first duty of every citizen is to insist on having money on reasonable terms; and this demand is not complied with by giving four men three shillings each for ten or twelve hours' drudgery and one man a thousand pounds for nothing. The crying need of the nation is not for better morals, cheaper bread, temperance, liberty, culture, redemption of fallen sisters and erring brothers, nor the grace, love and fellowship of the Trinity, but simply for enough money. And the evil to be attacked is not sin, suffering, greed, priestcraft, kingcraft, demagogy, monopoly, ignorance, drink, war, pestilence, nor any other of the scapegoats which reformers sacrifice, but simply poverty.

Once take your eyes from the ends of the earth and fix them on this truth just under your nose; and Andrew Undershaft's views will not perplex you in the least. Unless indeed his constant sense that he is only the instrument of a Will or Life Force which uses him for purposes wider than his own, may puzzle you. If so, that is because you are walking either in artificial Darwinian darkness, or in mere stupidity. All genuinely religious people have that consciousness. To them

[3]Drury Lane is a large London theatre. At Christmas time many London theatres present "pantomimes," which are ludicrously, often hilariously, embellished musical versions of well-known fairy tales performed by some of the best English actors. They have always been favorites at holiday time with children and adults alike.

Undershaft the Mystic will be quite intelligible, and his perfect comprehension of his daughter the Salvationist and her lover the Euripidean republican natural and inevitable. That, however, is not new, even on the stage. What is new, as far as I know, is that article in Undershaft's religion which recognizes in Money the first need and in poverty the vilest sin of man and society.

This dramatic conception has not, of course, been attained *per saltum*. Nor has it been borrowed from Nietzsche or from any man born beyond the Channel. The late Samuel Butler, in his own department the greatest English writer of the latter half of the XIX century, steadily inculcated the necessity and morality of a conscientious Laodiceanism in religion and of an earnest and constant sense of the importance of money. It drives one almost to despair of English literature when one sees so extraordinary a study of English life as Butler's posthumous *Way of All Flesh* making so little impression that when, some years later, I produce plays in which Butler's extraordinarily fresh, free and future-piercing suggestions have an obvious share, I am met with nothing but vague cacklings about Ibsen and Nietzsche, and am only too thankful that they are not about Alfred de Musset and Georges Sand. Really, the English do not deserve to have great men. They allowed Butler to die practically unknown, whilst I, a comparatively insignificant Irish journalist, was leading them by the nose into an advertisement of me which has made my own life a burden. In Sicily there is a Via Samuele Butler. When an English tourist sees it, he either asks "Who the devil was Samuele Butler?" or wonders why the Sicilians should perpetuate the memory of the author of *Hudibras*.

Well, it cannot be denied that the English are only too anxious to recognize a man of genius if somebody will kindly point him out to them. Having pointed myself out in this manner with some success, I now point out Samuel Butler, and trust that in consequence I shall hear a little less in future of the novelty and foreign origin of the ideas which are now making their way into the English theatre through plays written by Socialists. There are living men whose originality and power are as obvious as Butler's and when they die that fact will be discovered. Meanwhile I recommend them to insist on their own merits as an important part of their own business.

The Salvation Army

When *Major Barbara* was produced in London, the second act was reported in an important northern newspaper as a withering attack on the Salvation Army, and the despairing ejaculation of Barbara deplored by a London daily as a tasteless blasphemy. And they were set right, not by the professed critics of the theatre, but by religious and philosophical publicists like Sir Oliver Lodge and Dr Stanton Coit, and strenuous Nonconformist journalists like William Stead, who not only understood the act as well as the Salvationists themselves, but also saw it in its relation to the religious life of the nation, a life which seems to lie not only outside the sympathy of many of our theatre critics, but actually outside their knowledge of society. Indeed nothing could be more ironically curious than the confrontation *Major Barbara* effected of the theatre enthusiasts with the religious enthusiasts. On the one hand was the playgoer, always seeking pleasure, paying exorbitantly for it, suffering unbearable discomforts for it, and hardly ever getting it. On the other hand was the Salvationist, repudiating gaiety and courting effort and sacrifice, yet always in the wildest spirits, laughing, joking, singing, rejoicing, drumming, and tambourining: his life flying by in a flash of excitement, and his death arriving as a climax of triumph. And, if you please, the playgoer despising the Salvationist as a joyless person, shut out from the heaven of the theatre, self-condemned to a life of hideous gloom; and the Salvationist mourning over the playgoer as over a prodigal with vine leaves in his hair, careening outrageously to hell amid the popping of champagne corks and the ribald laughter of sirens! Could misunderstanding be more complete, or sympathy worse misplaced?

Fortunately, the Salvationists are more accessible to the religious character of the drama than the playgoers to the gay energy and artistic fertility of religion. They can see, when it is pointed out to them, that a theatre, as a place where two or three are gathered together, takes from that divine presence an inalienable sanctity of which the grossest and profanest farce can no more deprive it than a hypocritical sermon by a snobbish bishop can desecrate Westminster Abbey. But in our professional playgoers this indispensable preliminary conception of sanctity seems wanting. They talk of actors as mimes and mummers, and, I fear, think of dramatic authors as liars and pandars, whose main business is the voluptuous soothing of the tired city speculator when what he calls the serious business of the day is over. Passion, the life of drama, means nothing to them but primitive sexual excitement: such phrases as "impassioned poetry" or "passionate love of truth" have fallen quite out of their vocabulary and been replaced by "passional crime" and the like. They assume, as far as I can gather, that people in whom passion has a larger scope are passionless and therefore uninteresting. Consequently they come to think of religious people as people who are not interesting and not amusing. And so, when Barbara cuts the regular Salvation Army jokes, and snatches a kiss from her lover across his drum, the devotees of the theatre think they ought to appear shocked, and conclude that the whole play is an elaborate mockery of the Army. And then either hypocritically rebuke me for mocking, or foolishly take part in the supposed mockery!

Even the handful of mentally competent critics got into difficulties over my demonstration of the economic deadlock in which the Salvation Army finds itself. Some of them thought that the Army would not have taken money from a distiller and a cannon founder: others thought it should not have taken it: all assumed more or less definitely that it reduced itself to absurdity or hypocrisy by taking it. On the first point the reply of the Army itself was prompt and conclusive. As one of its officers said, they would take money from the devil himself and be only too glad to get it out of his hands and into God's. They gratefully acknowledged that publicans not only give them money but allow them to collect it in the bar—sometimes even when there is a Salvation meeting outside preaching teetotalism. In fact, they questioned the verisimilitude of the play, not because Mrs Baines took the money, but because Barbara refused it.

On the point that the Army ought not to take such money, its justification is obvious. It must take the money because it cannot exist without money, and there is no other money to be had. Practically all the spare money in the country consists of a mass of rent, interest, and profit, every penny of which is bound up with crime, drink, prostitution, disease, and all the evil fruits of poverty, as inextricably as with enterprise, wealth, commercial probity, and national prosperity. The notion that you can earmark certain coins as tainted is an unpractical individualist superstition. Nonetheless the fact that all our money is tainted gives a very severe shock to earnest young souls when some dramatic instance of the taint first makes them conscious of it. When an enthusiastic young clergyman of the Established Church first realizes that the Ecclesiastical Commissioners receive the rents of sporting public houses, brothels, and sweating dens; or that the most generous contributor at his last charity sermon was an employer trading in female labor cheapened by prostitution as unscrupulously as a hotel keeper trades in waiters' labor cheapened by tips, or commissionaires' labor cheapened by pensions; or that the only patron who can afford to rebuild his church or his schools or give his boys' brigade a gymnasium or a library is the son-in-law of a Chicago meat King, that young clergyman has, like Barbara, a very bad quarter hour. But he cannot help himself by refusing to accept money from anybody except sweet old ladies with independent incomes and gentle and lovely ways of life. He has only to follow up the income of the sweet ladies to its industrial source, and there he will find Mrs Warren's profession[4] and the poisonous canned meat and all the rest of it. His own stipend has the same root. He must either share the world's guilt or go to another planet. He must save the world's honour if he is to save his own. This is what all the Churches find just as the Salvation Army and Barbara find it in the play. Her discovery that she is her father's accomplice; that the Salvation Army is the accomplice of the distiller and the dynamite maker; that they can no more escape one another than they can escape the air they breathe; that there is no salvation for them through personal righteousness, but only through the redemption of the whole nation from its vicious, lazy, competitive anarchy: this discovery has been made by everyone except the Pharisees and (apparently) the professional playgoers, who still wear their Tom Hood shirts and underpay their washerwoman without the slightest misgiving as to the elevation of their private characters, the purity of their private atmospheres, and their right to repudiate as foreign to themselves the coarse depravity of the garret and the slum. Not that they mean any harm: they

[4]*Mrs Warren's Profession,* title of Shaw's early play (1893), which shocked audiences in England and America and on at least one occasion prompted the arrest of the performers. Its subject concerned the highly respectable Mrs. Warren who kept a string of brothels on the Continent. Her justification was that it was far better to have young girls employed in this manner rather than to have them die in factories such as the notorious watchmaking establishments, which killed off the workers through radium poisoning in painting fluorescent dials.

only desire to be, in their little private way, what they call gentlemen. They do not understand Barbara's lesson because they have not, like her, learnt it by taking their part in the larger life of the nation.

Barbara's Return to the Colors

Barbara's return to the colors may yet provide a subject for the dramatic historian of the future. To get back to the Salvation Army with the knowledge that even the Salvationists themselves are not saved yet: that poverty is not blessed, but a most damnable sin; and that when General Booth[5] chose Blood and Fire for the emblem of Salvation instead of the Cross, he was perhaps better inspired than he knew: such knowledge, for the daughter of Andrew Undershaft, will clearly lead to something hopefuller than distributing bread and treacle at the expense of Bodger.

It is a very significant thing, this instinctive choice of the military form of organization, this substitution of the drum for the organ, by the Salvation Army. Does it not suggest that the Salvationists divine that they must actually fight the devil instead of merely praying at him? At present, it is true, they have not quite ascertained his correct address. When they do, they may give a very rude shock to that sense of security which he has gained from his experience of the fact that hard words, even when uttered by eloquent essayists and lecturers, or carried unanimously at enthusiastic public meetings on the motion of eminent reformers, break no bones. It has been said that the French Revolution was the work of Voltaire, Rousseau and the Encyclopedists. It seems to me to have been the work of men who had observed that virtuous indignation, caustic criticism, conclusive argument and instructive pamphleteering, even when done by the most earnest and witty literary geniuses, were as useless as praying, things going steadily from bad to worse whilst the Social Contract and the pamphlets of Voltaire were at the height of their vogue. Eventually, as we know, perfectly respectable citizens and earnest philanthropists connived at the September massacres because hard experience had convinced them that if they contented themselves with appeals to humanity and patriotism, the aristocracy, though it would read their appeals with the greatest enjoyment and appreciation, flattering and admiring the writers, would none the less continue to conspire with foreign monarchists to undo the revolution and restore the old system with every circumstance of savage vengeance and ruthless repression of popular liberties.

The nineteenth century saw the same lesson repeated in England. It had its Utilitarians, its Christian Socialists, its Fabians (still extant): it had Bentham, Mill, Dickens, Ruskin, Carlyle, Butler, Henry George, and Morris. And the end of all their efforts is the Chicago described by Mr Upton Sinclair, and the London

[5]William Booth, founder of the Salvation Army, was its first General.

in which the people who pay to be amused by my dramatic representation of Peter Shirley turned out to starve at forty because there are younger slaves to be had for his wages, do not take, and have not the slightest intention of taking, any effective step to organize society in such a way as to make that everyday infamy impossible. I, who have preached and pamphleteered like any Encyclopedist, have to confess that my methods are no use, and would be no use if I were Voltaire, Rousseau, Bentham, Marx, Mill, Dickens, Carlyle, Ruskin, Butler, and Morris all rolled into one, with Euripides, More, Montaigne, Molière, Beaumarchais, Swift, Goethe, Ibsen, Tolstoy, Jesus and the prophets all thrown in (as indeed in some sort I actually am, standing as I do on all their shoulders). The problem being to make heroes out of cowards, we paper apostles and artist-magicians have succeeded only in giving cowards all the sensations of heroes whilst they tolerate every abomination, accept every plunder, and submit to every oppression. Christianity, in making a merit of such submission, has marked only that depth in the abyss at which the very sense of shame is lost. The Christian has been like Dickens' doctor in the debtor's prison, who tells the newcomer of its ineffable peace and security: no duns; no tyrannical collectors of rates, taxes, and rent; no importunate hopes nor exacting duties; nothing but the rest and safety of having no farther to fall.

Yet in the poorest corner of this soul-destroying Christendom vitality suddenly begins to germinate again. Joyousness, a sacred gift long dethroned by the hellish laughter of derision and obscenity, rises like a flood miraculously out of the fetid dust and mud of the slums; rousing marches and impetuous dithyrambs rise to the heavens from people among whom the depressing noise called "sacred music" is a standing joke; a flag with Blood and Fire on it is unfurled, not in murderous rancor, but because fire is beautiful and blood is vital and splendid red; Fear, which we flatter by calling Self, vanishes; and transfigured men and women carry their gospel through a transfigured world, calling their leader General, themselves captains and brigadiers, and their whole body an Army: praying, but praying only for refreshment, for strength to fight, and for needful MONEY (a notable sign, that); preaching, but not preaching submission; daring ill-usage and abuse, but not putting up with more of it than is inevitable; and practising what the world will let them practise, including soap and water, color and music. There is danger in such activity; and where there is danger there is hope. Our present security is nothing, and can be nothing, but evil made irresistible.

Weaknesses of the Salvation Army

For the present, however, it is not my business to flatter the Salvation Army. Rather must I point out to it that it has almost as many weaknesses as the Church of England itself. It is building up a business organization which will compel it eventually to see that its present staff of enthusiast-commanders shall be succeeded by a bureaucracy of men of business who will be no better than bishops, and perhaps a good deal more unscrupulous. That has always happened sooner or later to great orders founded by saints; and the order founded by St William Booth is not exempt from the same danger. It is even more dependent than the Church on rich people who would cut off supplies at once if it began to preach that indispensable revolt against poverty which must also be a revolt against riches. It is hampered by a heavy contingent of pious elders who are not really Salvationists at all, but Evangelicals of the old school. It still, as Commissioner Howard affirms, "sticks to Moses," which is flat nonsense at this time of day if the Commissioner means, as I am afraid he does, that the Book of Genesis contains a trustworthy scientific account of the origin of species, and that the god to whom Jephthah sacrificed his daughter is any less obviously a tribal idol than Dagon or Chemosh.

Further, there is still too much other-worldliness about the Army. Like Frederick's grenadier, the Salvationist wants to live for ever (the most monstrous way of crying for the moon); and though it is evident to anyone who has ever heard General Booth and his best officers that they would work as hard for human salvation as they do at present if they believed that death would be the end of them individually, they and their followers have a bad habit of talking as if the Salvationists were heroically enduring a very bad time on earth as an investment which will bring them in dividends later on in the form, not of a better life to come for the whole world, but of an eternity spent by themselves personally in a sort of bliss which would bore any active person to a second death. Surely the truth is that the Salvationists are unusually happy people. And is it not the very diagnostic of true salvation that it shall overcome the fear of death? Now the man who has come to believe that there is no such thing as death, the change so called being merely the transition to an exquisitely happy and utterly careless life, has not overcome the fear of death at all: on the contrary, it has overcome him so completely that he refuses to die on any terms whatever. I do not call a Salvationist really saved until he is ready to lie down cheerfully on the scrap heap, having paid scot and lot and something over, and let his eternal life pass on to renew its youth in the battalions of the future.

Then there is the nasty lying habit called confession, which the Army encourages because it lends itself to dramatic oratory, with plenty of thrilling incident. For my part, when I hear a convert relating the violences and oaths and blasphemies he was guilty of before he was saved, making out that he was a very terrible fellow then and is the most contrite and chastened of Christians now, I believe him no more than I believe the millionaire who says he came up to London or Chicago as a boy with only three halfpence in his pocket. Salvationists have said to me that Barbara in my play would never have been taken in by so transparent a humbug as Snobby Price; and certainly I do not think Snobby could have taken in any experienced Salvationist on a point on which the Salvationist did not wish to be taken in. But on the point of conversion all Salvationists wish to be taken in; for the more obvious the sinner the more obvious the miracle of his conversion. When you advertise a converted burglar or reclaimed drunkard as one of the attractions at an experience meeting, your burglar can hardly have been too burglarious or your drunkard too drunken. As long as such attractions are relied on, you will have your Snobbies claiming to have beaten their mothers when they were as a matter of prosaic fact habitually beaten by them, and your Rummies of the tamest respectability pretending to a past of reckless and dazzling vice. Even when confessions are sincerely autobiographic we should beware of assuming that the impulse to make them was pious or that the interest of the hearers is wholesome. As well might we assume that the poor people who insist on shewing disgusting ulcers to district visitors are convinced hygienists, or that the curiosity which sometimes welcomes such exhibitions is a pleasant and creditable one. One is often tempted to suggest that those who pester our police superintendents with confessions of murder might very wisely be taken at their word and executed, except in the few cases in which a real murderer is seeking to be relieved of his guilt by confession and expiation. For though I am not, I hope, an unmerciful person, I do not think that the inexorability of the deed once done should be disguised by any ritual, whether in the confessional or on the scaffold.

And here my disagreement with the Salvation Army, and with all propagandists of the Cross (which I loathe as I loathe all gibbets) becomes deep indeed. Forgiveness, absolution, atonement, are figments: punishment is only a pretence of canceling one crime by another; and you can no more have forgiveness without vindictiveness than you can have a cure without a disease. You will never get a high morality from people who conceive that their misdeeds are revocable and pardonable, or in a society where absolution and expiation are officially provided for us all. The demand may be very real; but the supply is spurious. Thus Bill Walker, in my play, having assaulted the Salvation Lass, presently finds himself overwhelmed with an intolerable conviction of sin under the skilled treatment of Barbara. Straightway he begins to try to unassault the lass and deruffianize his deed, first by getting punishment for it in kind, and, when that relief is denied him, by fining himself a pound to compensate the girl. He is foiled both ways. He finds the Salvation Army is inexorable as fact itself. It will not punish him: it will not take his money. It will not tolerate a redeemed ruffian: it leaves him no means of salvation except ceasing to be a ruffian. In doing this, the Salvation Army instinctively grasps the central truth of Christianity and discards its central superstition: that central truth being the vanity of revenge and punishment, and that central superstition the salvation of the world by the gibbet.

For, be it noted, Bill has assaulted an old and starving woman also; and for this worse offence he feels no remorse whatever, because she makes it clear that her malice is as great as his own. "Let her have the law of me, as she said she would," says Bill: "what I done to her is no more on what you might call my conscience than sticking a pig." This shows a perfectly natural and wholesome state of mind on his part. The old woman, like the law she threatens him with, is perfectly ready to play the game of retaliation with him: to rob him if he steals, to flog him if he strikes, to murder him if he kills. By example and precept the law and public opinion teach him to impose his will on others by anger, violence, and cruelty, and to wipe off the moral score by punishment. That is sound Crosstianity. But this Crosstianity has got entangled with something which Barbara calls Christianity, and which unexpectedly causes her to refuse to play the hangman's game of Satan casting out Satan. She refuses to prosecute a drunken ruffian; she converses on equal terms with a blackguard to whom no lady should be seen speaking in the public street: in short, she imitates Christ. Bill's conscience reacts to this just as naturally as it does to the old woman's threats. He is placed in a position of unbearable moral inferiority, and strives by every means in his power to escape from it, whilst he is still quite ready to meet the abuse of the old woman by attempting to smash a mug on her face. And that is the triumphant justification of Barbara's Christianity as against our system of judicial punishment and the vindictive villain-thrashings and "poetic justice" of the romantic stage.

For the credit of literature it must be pointed out that the situation is only partly novel. Victor Hugo long ago gave us the epic of the convict and the bishop's candlesticks, of the Crosstian policeman annihilated by his encounter with the Christian Valjean. But Bill Walker is not, like Valjean, romantically changed from a demon into an angel. There are millions of Bill Walkers in all classes of society today; and the point which I, as a professor of natural psychology, desire to demonstrate, is that Bill, without any change in his character or circumstances whatsoever, will react one way to one sort of treatment and another way to another.

In proof I might point to the sensational object lesson provided by our commercial millionaires today. They begin as brigands: merciless, unscrupulous, dealing out ruin and death and slavery to their competitors and employees, and facing desperately the worst that their competitors can do to them. The history of the English factories, the American Trusts, the exploitation of African gold, diamonds, ivory and rubber, outdoes in villainy the worst that has ever been imagined of the buccaneers of the Spanish Main. Captain Kidd would have marooned a modern Trust magnate for conduct unworthy of a gentleman of fortune. The law every day seizes on unsuccessful scoundrels of this type and punishes them with a cruelty worse than their own, with the result that they come out of the torture house more dangerous than they went in, and renew their evil doing (nobody will employ them at anything else) until they are again seized, again tormented, and again let loose, with the same result.

But the successful scoundrel is dealt with very differently, and very Christianly. He is not only forgiven: he is idolized, respected, made much of, all but worshipped. Society returns him good for evil in the most extravagant overmeasure. And with what result? He begins to idolize himself, to respect himself, to live up to the treatment he receives. He preaches sermons; he writes books of the most edifying advice to young men, and actually persuades himself that he got on by taking his own advice; he endows educational institutions; he supports charities; he dies finally in the odor of sanctity, leaving a will which is a monument of public spirit and bounty. And all this without any change in his character. The spots of the leopard and the stripes of the tiger are as brilliant as ever, but the conduct of the world towards him has changed; and his conduct has changed accordingly. You have only to reverse your attitude towards him—to lay hands on his property, revile him, assault him, and he will be a brigand again in a moment, as ready to crush you as you are to crush him, and quite as full of pretentious moral reasons for doing it.

In short, when Major Barbara says that there are no scoundrels, she is right: there are no absolute scoundrels, though there are impracticable people of whom I shall treat presently. Every reasonable man (and woman) is a potential scoundrel and a potential good citizen. What a man is depends on his character; but what he does and what we think of what he does, depends on his circumstances. The characteristics that ruin a man in one class make him eminent in another. The characters that behave differently in different circumstances behave alike in similar circumstances. Take a common English character like that of Bill Walker. We meet Bill everywhere: on the judicial bench, on the episcopal bench, in the Privy Council, at the War Office and Admiralty, as well as in the Old Bailey dock or in the ranks of casual unskilled labor. And the morality of Bill's characteristics varies with these various circumstances. The faults of the burglar are the qualities of the financier: the manners and habits of a duke would cost a city clerk his situation. In short, though character is independent of circumstances, conduct is not; and our moral judgments of character are not: both are circumstantial. Take any condition of life in which the circumstances are for a mass of men practically alike: felony, the House of Lords, the factory, the stables, the gipsy encampment or where you please! In spite of diversity of character and temperament, the conduct and morals of the individuals in each group are as predictable and as alike in the main as if they were a flock of sheep, morals being mostly only social habits and circumstantial necessities. Strong people know this and count upon it. In nothing have the master-minds of the world been distinguished from the ordinary suburban season-ticket holder more than in their straightforward perception of the fact that mankind is practically a single species, and not a menagerie of gentlemen and bounders, villains and heroes, cowards and daredevils, peers and peasants, grocers and aristocrats, artisans and laborers, washerwomen and duchesses, in which all the grades of income and caste represent distinct animals who must not be introduced to one another or intermarry. Napoleon constructing a galaxy of generals and courtiers, and even of monarchs, out of his collection of social nobodies; Julius Caesar appointing as governor of Egypt the son of a freedman—one who but a short time before would have been legally disqualified for the post even of a private soldier in the Roman army; Louis XI making his barber his privy councillor: all these had in their different ways a firm hold of the scientific fact of human equality, expressed by Barbara in the Christian formula that all men are children of one father. A man who believes that men are naturally divided into upper and lower and middle classes morally is making exactly the same mistake as the man who believes that they are naturally divided in the same way socially. And just as our persistent attempts to found political institutions on a basis of social inequality have always produced long periods of destructive friction relieved from time to time by violent explosions of revolution; so the attempt—will Americans please note—to found moral institutions on a basis of moral inequality can lead to nothing but unnatural Reigns of the Saints relieved by licentious Restorations; to Americans who have made divorce a public institution turning the face of Europe into one huge sardonic smile by refusing to stay in the same hotel with a Russian man of genius who has changed wives without the sanction of South Dakota; to grotesque hypocrisy, cruel persecution, and final utter confusion of conventions and compliances with benevolence and respectability. It is quite useless to declare that all men are born free if you deny that they are born good. Guarantee a man's goodness and his liberty will take care of itself. To guarantee his freedom on condition that you approve of his moral character is formally to abolish all freedom whatsoever, as every man's liberty is at the mercy of a moral indictment which any fool can trump up against everyone who violates custom, whether as a prophet or as a rascal. This is the lesson Democracy has to learn before it can become anything but the most oppressive of all the priesthoods.

Let us now return to Bill Walker and his case of conscience against the Salvation Army. Major Barbara, not being a modern Tetzel, or the treasurer of a hospital, refuses to sell absolution to Bill for a sovereign. Unfortunately, what the Army can afford to refuse in the case of Bill Walker, it cannot refuse in the case of Bodger. Bodger is master of the situation because he holds the purse strings. "Strive as you will," says Bodger, in effect: "me you cannot do without. You cannot save Bill Walker without my money." And the Army answers, quite rightly under the circumstances, "We will take money from the devil himself sooner than abandon the work of Salvation." So Bodger pays his conscience-money and gets the absolution that is refused to Bill. In real life Bill would perhaps never know this. But I, the dramatist whose business it is to show the connexion between things that seem apart and unrelated in the haphazard order of events in real life, have contrived to make it known to Bill, with the result that the Salvation Army loses its hold of him at once.

But Bill may not be lost, for all that. He is still in the grip of the facts and of his own conscience, and may find his taste for blackguardism permanently spoiled. Still, I cannot guarantee that happy ending. Walk through the poorer quarters of our cities on Sunday when the men are not working, but resting and chewing the cud of their reflections. You will find one expression common to every mature face: the expression of cynicism. The discovery made by Bill Walker about the Salvation Army has been made by everyone there. They have found that every man has his price; and they have been foolishly or corruptly taught to mistrust and despise him for that necessary and salutary condition of social existence. When they learn that General Booth, too, has his price, they do not admire him because it is a high one, and admit the need of organizing society so that he shall get it in an honorable way: they conclude that his character is unsound and that all religious men are hypocrites and allies of their sweaters and oppressors. They know that the large subscriptions which help to support the Army are endowments, not of religion, but of the wicked doctrine of docility in poverty and humility under oppression; and they are rent by the most agonizing of all the doubts of the soul, the doubt whether their true salvation must not come from their most abhorrent passions, from murder, envy, greed, stubbornness, rage, and terrorism, rather than from public spirit, reasonableness, humanity, generosity, tenderness, delicacy, pity and kindness. The confirmation of that doubt, at which our newspapers have been working so hard for years past, is the morality of militarism; and the justification of militarism is that circumstances may at any time make it the true morality of the moment. It is by producing such moments that we produce violent and sanguinary revolutions, such as the one now in progress in Russia and the one which Capitalism in England and America is daily and diligently provoking.

At such moments it becomes the duty of the Churches to evoke all the powers of destruction against the existing order. But if they do this, the existing order must forcibly suppress them. Churches are suffered to exist only on condition that they preach submission to the State as at present capitalistically organized. The Church of England itself is compelled to add to the thirty-six articles in which it formulates its religious tenets, three more in which it apologetically protests that the moment any of these articles comes in conflict with the State it is to be entirely renounced, abjured, violated, abrogated and abhorred, the policeman being a much more important person than any of the Persons of the Trinity. And this is why no tolerated Church nor Salvation Army can ever win the entire confidence of the poor. It must be on the side of the police and the military, no matter what it believes or disbelieves; and as the police and the military are the instruments by which the rich rob and oppress the poor (on legal and moral principles made for the purpose), it is not possible to be on the side of the poor and of the police at the same time. Indeed the religious bodies, as the almoners of the rich, become a sort of auxiliary police, taking off the insurrectionary edge of poverty with coals and blankets, bread and treacle, and soothing and cheering the victims with hopes of immense and inexpensive happiness in another world when the process of working them to premature death in the service of the rich is complete in this.

Christianity and Anarchism

Such is the false position from which neither the Salvation Army nor the Church of England nor any other religious organization whatever can escape except through a reconstitution of society. Nor can they merely endure the State passively, washing their hands of its sins. The State is constantly forcing the consciences of men by violence and cruelty. Not content with exacting money from us for the maintenance of its soldiers and policemen, its gaolers and executioners, it forces us to take an active personal part in its proceedings on pain of becoming ourselves the victims of its violence. As I write these lines, a sensational example is given to the world. A royal marriage has been celebrated, first by sacrament in a cathedral, and then by a bullfight having for its main amusement the spectacle of horses gored and disembowelled by the bull, after which, when the bull is so exhausted as to be no longer dangerous, he is killed by a cautious matador. But the ironic contrast between the bullfight and the sacrament of marriage does not move anyone. Another contrast—that between the splendor, the happiness, the atmosphere of kindly admiration surrounding the young couple, and the price paid for it under our abominable social arrangements in the misery, squalor and degradation of millions of other young couples—is drawn at the same moment by a novelist, Mr Upton Sinclair, who chips a corner of the veneering from the huge meat packing industries of Chicago, and shows it to us as a sample of what is going on all over the world underneath the top layer of prosperous plutocracy. One man is sufficiently moved by that contrast to pay his own life as the price of one terrible blow at the responsible parties. His poverty has left him ignorant enough to be duped by the pretence that the innocent young bride and bridegroom, put forth and crowned by plutocracy as the heads of a State in which they have less personal power than any policeman, and less influence than any Chairman of a Trust, are responsible. At them accordingly he launches his sixpennorth of fulminate, missing his mark, but scattering the bowels of as many horses as any bull in the arena, and slaying twenty-three persons, besides wounding ninety-nine. And of all these, the horses alone are innocent of the guilt he is avenging: had he blown all Madrid to atoms with every adult person in it, not one could have escaped the charge of being an accessory, before, at, and after the fact, to poverty and prostitution, to such wholesale massacre of infants as Herod never dreamt of, to plague, pestilence and famine, battle, murder and lingering death—perhaps not one who had not helped, through example, precept, connivance, and even clamor, to teach the dynamiter his well-learnt gospel of hatred and vengeance, by approving every day of sentences of years of imprisonment so infernal in their unnatural stupidity and panic-stricken cruelty, that their advocates can disavow neither the dagger nor the bomb without stripping the mask of justice and humanity from themselves also.

Be it noted that at this very moment there appears the biography of one of our dukes, who, being a Scot, could argue about politics, and therefore stood out as a great brain among our aristocrats. And what, if you please, was his grace's favorite historical episode, which he declared he never read without intense satisfaction? Why, the young General Bonapart's pounding of the Paris mob to pieces in 1795, called in playful approval by our respectable classes "the whiff of grapeshot," though Napoleon, to do him justice, took a deeper view of it, and would fain have had it forgotten. And since the Duke of Argyll was not a demon, but a man of like passions with ourselves, by no means rancorous or cruel as men go, who can doubt that all over the world proletarians of the ducal kidney are now revelling in "the whiff of dynamite" (the flavor of the joke seems to evaporate a little, does it not?) because it was aimed at the class they hate even as our argute duke hated what he called the mob.

In such an atmosphere there can be only one sequel to the Madrid explosion. All Europe burns to emulate it. Vengeance! More blood! Tear "the Anarchist beast" to shreds. Drag him to the scaffold. Imprison him for life. Let all civilized States band together to drive his like off the face of the earth; and if any State refuses to join, make war on it. This time the leading London newspaper, anti-Liberal and therefore anti-Russian in politics, does not say "Serve you right" to the victims, as it did, in effect, when Bobrikoff, and De Plehve, and Grand Duke Sergius, were in the same manner unofficially fulminated into fragments. No: fulminate our rivals in Asia by all means, ye brave Russian revolutionaries; but to aim at an English princess! monstrous! hideous! hound down the wretch to his doom; and observe, please, that we are a civilized and merciful people, and, however much we may regret it, must not treat him as Ravaillac and Damiens were treated. And meanwhile, since we have not yet caught him, let us soothe our quivering nerves with the bullfight, and comment in a courtly way on the unfailing tact and good taste of the ladies of our royal houses, who, though presumably of full normal natural tenderness, have been so effectually broken in to fashionable routine that they can be taken to see the horses slaughtered as helplessly as they could no doubt be taken to a gladiator show, if that happened to be the mode just now.

Strangely enough, in the midst of this raging fire of malice, the one man who still has faith in the kindness and intelligence of human nature is the fulminator, now a hunted wretch, with nothing, apparently, to secure his triumph over all the prisons and scaffolds of infuriate Europe except the revolver in his pocket and his readiness to discharge it at a moment's notice into his own or any other head. Think of him setting out to find a gentleman and a Christian in the multitude of human wolves howling for his blood. Think also of this: that at the very first essay he finds what he seeks, a veritable grandee of Spain, a noble, high-thinking, unterrified, malice-void soul, in the guise—of all masquerades in the world!—of a modern editor. The Anarchist wolf, flying from the wolves of plutocracy, throws himself on the honor of the man. The man, not being a wolf (nor a London editor), and therefore not having enough sympathy with his exploit to be made bloodthirsty by it, does not throw him back to the pursuing wolves—gives him, instead, what help he can to escape, and sends him off acquainted at last with a force that goes deeper than dynamite, though you cannot buy so much of it for sixpence. That righteous and honorable high human deed is not wasted on Europe, let us hope, though it benefits the fugitive wolf only for a moment. The plutocratic wolves presently smell him out. The fugitive shoots the unlucky wolf whose nose is nearest; shoots himself; and then convinces the world, by his photograph, that he was no monstrous freak of reversion to the tiger, but a good looking young man with nothing abnormal about him except his appalling courage and resolution (that is why the terrified shriek Coward at him): one to whom murdering a happy young couple on their wedding morning would have been an unthinkably unnatural abomination under rational and kindly human circumstances.

Then comes the climax of irony and blind stupidity. The wolves, balked of their meal of fellowwolf, turn on the man, and proceed to torture him, after their manner, by imprisonment, for refusing to fasten his teeth in the throat of the dynamiter and hold him down until they came to finish him.

Thus, you see, a man may not be a gentleman nowadays even if he wishes to. As to being a Christian, he is allowed some latitude in that matter, because, I repeat, Christianity has two faces. Popular Christianity has for its emblem a gibbet, for its chief sensation a sanguinary execution after torture, for its central mystery an insane vengeance bought off by a trumpery expiation. But there is a nobler and profounder Christianity which affirms the sacred mystery of Equality, and forbids the glaring futility and folly of vengeance, often politely called punishment or justice. The gibbet part of Christianity is tolerated. The other is criminal felony. Connoisseurs in irony are well aware of the fact that the only editor in England who denounces punishment as radically wrong, also repudiates Christianity; calls his paper The Freethinker; and has been imprisoned for "bad taste" under the law against blasphemy.

Sane Conclusions

And now I must ask the excited reader not to lose his head on one side or the other, but to draw a sane moral from these grim absurdities. It is not good sense to propose that laws against crime should apply to principals only and not to accessories whose consent, counsel, or silence may secure impunity to the principal. If you institute punishment as part of the law, you must punish people for refusing to punish. If you have a police, part of its duty must be to compel everybody to assist the police. No doubt if your laws are unjust, and your policemen agents of oppression, the result will be an unbearable violation of the private consciences of citizens. But that cannot be helped: the remedy is, not to license everybody to thwart the law if they please, but to make laws that will command the public assent, and not to deal cruelly and stupidly with law-breakers. Everybody disapproves of burglars; but the modern burglar, when caught and overpowered by a householder, usually appeals, and often, let us hope, with success, to his captor not to deliver him over to the useless horrors of penal servitude. In other cases the law-breaker escapes because those who could give him up do not consider his breach of the law a guilty action. Sometimes, even, private tribunals are formed in opposition to the official tribunals; and these private tribunals employ assassins as executioners, as was done, for example, by Mahomet before he had established his power officially, and by the Ribbon lodges of Ireland in their long struggle with the landlords. Under such circumstances, the assassin goes free although everybody in the district knows who he is and what he has done. They do not betray him, partly because they justify him exactly as the regular Government justifies its official executioner, and partly because they would themselves be assassinated if they betrayed him: another method learnt from the official government. Given a tribunal, employing a slayer who has no personal quarrel with the slain; and there is clearly no moral difference between official and unofficial killing.

In short, all men are anarchists with regard to laws which are against their consciences, either in the preamble or in the penalty. In London our worst anarchists are the magistrates, because many of them are so old and ignorant that when they are called upon to administer any law that is based on ideas or knowledge less than half a century old, they disagree with it, and being mere ordinary homebred private Englishmen without any respect for law in the abstract, naively set the example of violating it. In this instance the man lags behind the law; but when the law lags behind the man, he becomes equally an anarchist. When some huge change in social conditions, such as the industrial revolution of the eighteenth and nineteenth centuries, throws our legal and industrial institutions out of date, Anarchism becomes almost a religion. The whole force of the most energetic geniuses of the time in philosophy, economics, and art, concentrates itself on demonstrations and reminders that morality and law are only conventions, fallible and continually obsolescing. Tragedies in which the heroes are bandits, and comedies in which law-abiding and conventionally moral folk are compelled to satirize themselves by outraging the conscience of the spectators every time they do their duty, appear simultaneously with economic treatises entitled "What is Property? Theft!" and with histories of "The Conflict between Religion and Science."

Now this is not a healthy state of things. The advantages of living in society are proportionate, not to the freedom of the individual from a code, but to the complexity and subtlety of the code he is prepared not only to accept but to uphold as a matter of such vital importance that a lawbreaker at large is hardly to be tolerated on any plea. Such an attitude becomes impossible when the only men who can make themselves heard and remembered throughout the world spend all their energy in raising our gorge against current law, current morality, current respectability, and legal property. The ordinary man, uneducated in social theory even when he is schooled in Latin verse, cannot be set against all the laws of his country and yet persuaded to regard law in the abstract as vitally necessary to society. Once he is brought to repudiate the laws and institutions he knows, he will repudiate the very conception of law and the very groundwork of institutions, ridiculing human rights, extolling brainless methods as "historical," and tolerating nothing except pure empiricism in conduct, with dynamite as the basis of politics and vivisection as the basis of science. That is hideous; but what is to be done? Here am I, for instance, by class a respectable man, by common sense a hater of waste and disorder, by intellectual constitution legally minded to the verge of pedantry, and by temperament apprehensive and economically disposed to the limit of oldmaidishness; yet I am, and have always been, and shall now always be, a revolutionary writer, because our laws make law impossible;

our liberties destroy all freedom; our property is organized robbery; our morality is an impudent hypocrisy; our wisdom is administered by inexperienced or malexperienced dupes, our power wielded by cowards and weaklings, and our honor false in all its points. I am an enemy of the existing order for good reasons; but that does not make my attacks any less encouraging or helpful to people who are its enemies for bad reasons. The existing order may shriek that if I tell the truth about it, some foolish person may drive it to become still worse by trying to assassinate it. I cannot help that, even if I could see what worse it could do than it is already doing. And the disadvantage of that worst even from its own point of view is that society, with all its prisons and bayonets and whips and ostracisms and starvations, is powerless in the face of the Anarchist who is prepared to sacrifice his own life in the battle with it. Our natural safety from the cheap and devastating explosives which every Russian student can make, and every Russian grenadier has learnt to handle in Manchuria, lies in the fact that brave and resolute men, when they are rascals, will not risk their skins for the good of humanity, and, when they are not, are sympathetic enough to care for humanity, abhorring murder, and never committing it until their consciences are outraged beyond endurance. The remedy is, then, simply not to outrage their consciences.

Do not be afraid that they will not make allowances. All men make very large allowances indeed before they stake their own lives in a war to the death with society. Nobody demands or expects the millennium. But there are two things that must be set right, or we shall perish, like Rome, of soul atrophy disguised as empire.

The first is that the daily ceremony of dividing the wealth of the country among its inhabitants shall be so conducted that no crumb shall, save as a criminal's ration, go to any able-bodied adults who are not producing by their personal exertions not only a full equivalent for what they take, but a surplus sufficient to provide for their superannuation and pay back the debt due for their nurture.

The second is that the deliberate infliction of malicious injuries which now goes on under the name of punishment be abandoned; so that the thief, the ruffian, the gambler, and the beggar, may without inhumanity be handed over to the law, and made to understand that a State which is too humane to punish will also be too thrifty to waste the life of honest men in watching or restraining dishonest ones. That is why we do not imprison dogs. We even take our chance of their first bite. But if a dog delights to bark and bite, it goes to the lethal chamber. That seems to me sensible. To allow the dog to expiate his bite by a period of torment, and then let him loose in a much more savage condition (for the chain makes a dog savage) to bite again and expiate again, having meanwhile spent a great deal of human life and happiness in the task of chaining and feeding and tormenting him, seems to me idiotic and superstitious. Yet that is what we do to men who bark and bite and steal. It would be far more sensible to put up with their vices, as we put up with their illnesses, until they give more trouble than they are worth, at which point we should, with many apologies and expressions of sympathy, and some generosity in complying with their last wishes, place them in the lethal chamber and get rid of them. Under no circumstances should they be allowed to expiate their misdeeds by a manufactured penalty, to subscribe to a charity, or to compensate the victims. If there is to be no punishment there can be no forgiveness. We shall never have real moral responsibility until everyone knows that his deeds are irrevocable, and that his life depends on his usefulness. Hitherto, alas! humanity has never dared face these hard facts. We frantically scatter conscience money and invent systems of conscience banking, with expiatory penalties, atonements, redemptions, salvations, hospital subscription lists and what not, to enable us to contract-out of the moral code. Not content with the old scapegoat and sacrificial lamb, we deify human saviors, and pray to miraculous virgin intercessors. We attribute mercy to the inexorable; soothe our consciences after committing murder by throwing ourselves on the bosom of divine love; and shrink even from our own gallows because we are forced to admit that it, at least, is irrevocable—as if one hour of imprisonment were not as irrevocable as any execution!

If a man cannot look evil in the face without illusion, he will never know what it really is, or combat it effectually. The few men who have been able (relatively) to do this have been called cynics, and have sometimes had an abnormal share of evil in themselves, corresponding to the abnormal strength of their minds; but they have never done mischief unless they intended to do it. That is why great scoundrels have been beneficent rulers whilst amiable and privately harmless monarchs have ruined their countries by trusting to the hocus-pocus of innocence and guilt, reward and punishment, virtuous indignation and pardon, instead of standing up to the facts without either malice or mercy. Major Barbara stands up to Bill Walker in that way, with the result that the ruffian who cannot get hated, has to hate himself. To relieve this agony he tries to get punished; but the Salvationist whom he tries to provoke is as merciless as Barbara, and only prays for him. Then he tries to pay, but can get nobody to take his money. His doom is the doom of Cain, who, failing to find either a savior, a policeman, or an almoner to help him to pretend that his brother's blood no longer cried from the ground, had to live and die a murderer. Cain took care not to commit another murder, unlike our railway shareholders (I am one) who kill and maim shunters by hundreds to save the cost of automatic couplings, and make atonement by annual subscriptions to deserving charities. Had Cain been allowed to pay off his score, he might possibly have killed Adam and Eve for the mere sake of a second luxurious reconciliation with God afterwards. Bodger, you may depend on it, will go on to the end of his life poisoning people with bad whisky, because he can always depend on the Salvation Army or the Church of England to negotiate a redemption for him in consideration of a trifling percentage of his profits.

There is a third condition too, which must be fulfilled before the great teachers of the world will cease to scoff at its religions. Creeds must become intellectually honest. At present there is not a single credible established religion in the world. That is perhaps the most stupendous fact in the whole world-situation. This play of mine, *Major Barbara,* is, I hope, both true and inspired; but whoever says that it all happened, and that faith in it and understanding of it consist in believing that it is a record of an actual occurrence, is, to speak according to Scripture, a fool and a liar, and is hereby solemnly denounced and cursed as such by me, the author, to all posterity.

London, June 1906

Major Barbara GEORGE BERNARD SHAW

Act I

It is after dinner in January 1906, in the library in Lady Britomart Undershaft's *house in Wilton Crescent. A large and comfortable settee is in the middle of the room, upholstered in dark leather. A person sitting on it (it is vacant at present) would have, on his right,* Lady Britomart's *writing table, with the lady herself busy at it; a smaller writing table behind him on his left; the door behind him on* Lady Britomart's *side; and a window with a window seat directly on his left. Near the window is an armchair.*

Lady Britomart *is a woman of fifty or thereabouts, well dressed and yet careless of her dress, well bred and quite reckless of her breeding, well mannered and yet appallingly outspoken and indifferent to the opinion of her interlocutors, amiable and yet peremptory, arbitrary, and high-tempered to the last bearable degree, and withal a very typical managing matron of the upper class, treated as a naughty child until she grew into a scolding mother, and finally settling down with plenty of practical ability and worldly experience, limited in the oddest way with domestic and class limitations, conceiving the universe exactly as if it were a large house in Wilton Crescent, though handling her corner of it very effectively on that assumption, and being quite enlightened and liberal as to the books in the library, the pictures on the walls, the music in the portfolios, and the articles in the papers.*

Her son, Stephen, *comes in. He is a gravely correct young man under 25, taking himself very seriously, but still in some awe of his mother, from childish habit and bachelor shyness rather than from any weakness of character.*

STEPHEN Whats the matter?

LADY BRITOMART Presently, Stephen.

(Stephen *submissively walks to the settee and sits down. He takes up a Liberal weekly called The Speaker.*)

LADY BRITOMART Dont begin to read, Stephen. I shall require all your attention.

STEPHEN It was only while I was waiting—

LADY BRITOMART Dont make excuses, Stephen. (*He puts down The Speaker.*) Now! (*She finishes her writing; rises; and comes to the settee.*) I have not kept you waiting very long, I think.

STEPHEN Not at all, mother.

LADY BRITOMART Bring me my cushion. (*He takes the cushion from the chair at the desk and arranges it for her as she sits down on the settee.*) Sit down. (*He sits down and fingers his tie nervously.*) Dont fiddle with your tie, Stephen: there is nothing the matter with it.

STEPHEN I beg your pardon. (*He fiddles with his watch chain instead.*)

LADY BRITOMART Now are you attending to me, Stephen?

STEPHEN Of course, mother.

LADY BRITOMART No: it's not of course. I want something much more than your everyday matter-of-course attention. I am going to speak to you very seriously, Stephen. I wish you would let that chain alone.

STEPHEN (*hastily relinquishing the chain*) Have I done anything to annoy you, mother? If so, it was quite unintentional.

LADY BRITOMART (*astonished*) Nonsense! (*with some remorse*) My poor boy, did you think I was angry with you?

STEPHEN What is it, then, mother? You are making me very uneasy.

LADY BRITOMART (*squaring herself at him rather aggressively*) Stephen: may I ask how soon you intend to realize that you are a grown-up man, and that I am only a woman?

STEPHEN (*amazed*) Only a—

LADY BRITOMART Dont repeat my words, please: it is a most aggravating habit. You must learn to face life seriously, Stephen. I really cannot bear the whole burden of our family affairs any longer. You must advise me: you must assume the responsibility.

STEPHEN I!

LADY BRITOMART Yes, you, of course. You were 24 last June. Youve been at Harrow and Cambridge. Youve been to India and Japan. You must know a lot of things, now; unless you have wasted your time most scandalously. Well, advise me.

STEPHEN (*much perplexed*) You know I have never interfered in the household—

LADY BRITOMART No: I should think not. I dont want you to order the dinner.

STEPHEN I mean in our family affairs.

LADY BRITOMART Well, you must interfere now for they are getting quite beyond me.

STEPHEN (*troubled*) I have thought sometimes that perhaps I ought; but really, mother, I know so little about them; and what I do know is so painful! it is so impossible to mention some things to you—(*He stops, ashamed.*)

LADY BRITOMART I suppose you mean your father.

STEPHEN (*almost inaudibly*) Yes.

LADY BRITOMART My dear: we cant go on all our lives not mentioning him. Of course you were quite right not to open the subject until I asked you to; but you are old enough now to be taken into my confidence, and to help me to deal with him about the girls.

STEPHEN But the girls are all right. They are engaged.

LADY BRITOMART (*complacently*) Yes: I have made a very good match for Sarah. Charles Lomax will be a millionaire at 35. But that is ten years ahead; and in the meantime his trustees cannot under the terms of his father's will allow him more than £800 a year.

STEPHEN But the will says also that if he increases his income by his own exertions, they may double the increase.

LADY BRITOMART Charles Lomax's exertions are much more likely to decrease his income than to increase it. Sarah will have to find at least another £800 a year for the next ten years; and even then they will be as poor as church mice. And what about Barbara? I thought Barbara was going to make the most brilliant career of all of you. And what does she do? Joins the Salvation Army; discharges her maid; lives on a pound a week and walks in one evening with a professor of Greek whom she has picked up in the street, and who pretends to be a Salvationist, and actually plays the big drum for her in public because he has fallen head over ears in love with her.

STEPHEN I was certainly rather taken aback when I heard they were engaged. Cusins is a very nice fellow, certainly: nobody would ever guess that he was born in Australia; but—

LADY BRITOMART Oh, Adolphus Cusins will make a very good husband. After all, nobody can say a word against Greek: it stamps a man at once as an educated gentleman. And my family, thank Heaven, is not a pig-headed Tory one. We are Whigs, and believe in liberty. Let snobbish people say what they please: Barbara shall marry, not the man they like, but the man *I* like.

STEPHEN Of course I was thinking only of his income. However, he is not likely to be extravagant.

LADY BRITOMART Dont be too sure of that, Stephen. I know your quiet, simple, refined, poetic people like Adolphus: quite content with the best of everything! They cost more than your extravagant people, who are always as mean as they are second rate. No: Barbara will need at least £2000 a year. You see it means two additional households. Besides, my dear, you must marry soon. I dont approve of the present fashion of philandering bachelors and late marriages; and I am trying to arrange something for you.

STEPHEN It's very good of you, mother; but perhaps I had better arrange that for myself.

LADY BRITOMART Nonsense! you are much too young to begin matchmaking: you would be taken in by some pretty little nobody. Of course I dont mean that you are not to be consulted: you know that as well as I do. (STEPHEN *closes his lips and is silent.*) Now dont sulk, Stephen.

STEPHEN I am not sulking, mother. What has all this got to do with—with—with my father?

LADY BRITOMART My dear Stephen: where is the money to come from? It is easy enough for you and the other children to live on my income as long as we are in the same house; but I cant keep four families in four separate houses. You know how poor my father is: he has barely seven thousand a year now; and really, if he were not the Earl of Stevenage, he would have to give up society. He can do nothing for us. He says, naturally enough, that it is absurd that he should be asked to provide for the children of a man who is rolling in money. You see, Stephen, your father must be fabulously wealthy, because there is always a war going on somewhere.

STEPHEN You need not remind me of that, mother. I have hardly ever opened a newspaper in my life without seeing our name in it. The Undershaft torpedo! The Undershaft quick firers! The Undershaft ten inch! the Undershaft disappearing rampart gun! the Undershaft submarine! and now the Undershaft aerial battleship! At Harrow they called me the Woolwich Infant. At Cambridge it was the same. A little brute at King's who was always trying to get up revivals, spoilt my Bible—your first birthday present to me—by writing under my name, "Son and heir to Undershaft and Lazarus, Death and Destruction Dealers: address Christendom and Judea." But that was not so bad as the way I was kowtowed to everywhere because my father was making millions by selling cannons.

LADY BRITOMART It is not only the cannons, but the war loans that Lazarus arranges under cover of giving credit for the cannons. You know, Stephen, it's perfectly scandalous. Those two men, Andrew Undershaft and Lazarus, positively have Europe under their thumbs. That is why your father is able to behave as he does. He is above the law. Do you think Bismarck or Gladstone or Disraeli could have openly defied every social and moral obligation all their lives as your father has? They simply wouldnt have dared. I asked Gladstone to take it up. I asked The Times to take it up. I asked the Lord Chamberlain to take it up. But it was just like asking them to declare war on the Sultan. They wouldnt. They said they couldnt touch him. I believe they were afraid.

STEPHEN What could they do? He does not actually break the law.

LADY BRITOMART Not break the law! He is always breaking the law. He broke the law when he was born: his parents were not married.

STEPHEN Mother! Is that true?

LADY BRITOMART Of course it's true: that was why we separated.

STEPHEN He married without letting you know that!

LADY BRITOMART (*rather taken aback by this inference*) Oh no. To do Andrew justice, that was not the sort of thing he did. Besides, you know the Undershaft motto: Unashamed. Everybody knew.

STEPHEN But you said that was why you separated.

LADY BRITOMART Yes, because he was not content with being a foundling himself: he wanted to disinherit you for another foundling. That was what I couldnt stand.

STEPHEN (*ashamed*) Do you mean for—for—for—

LADY BRITOMART Dont stammer, Stephen. Speak distinctly.

STEPHEN But this is so frightful to me, mother. To have to speak to you about such things!

LADY BRITOMART It's not pleasant for me, either, especially if you are still so childish that you must make it worse by a display of embarrassment. It is only in the middle classes, Stephen, that people get into a state of dumb helpless horror when they find that there are wicked people in the world. In our class, we have to decide what is to be done with wicked people; and nothing should disturb our self-possession. Now ask your question properly.

STEPHEN Mother: have you no consideration for me? For Heaven's sake either treat me as a child, as you always do, and tell me nothing at all or tell me everything and let me take it as best I can.

LADY BRITOMART Treat you as a child! What do you mean? It is most unkind and ungrateful of you to say such a thing. You know I have never treated any of you as children. I have always made you my companions and friends, and allowed you perfect freedom to do and say whatever you like, so long as you liked what I could approve of.

STEPHEN (*desperately*) I daresay we have been the very imperfect children of a very perfect mother; but I do beg you to let me alone for once, and tell me about this horrible business of my father wanting to set me aside for another son.

LADY BRITOMART (*amazed*) Another son! I never said anything of the kind. I never dreamt of such a thing. This is what comes of interrupting me.

STEPHEN But you said—

LADY BRITOMART (*cutting him short*) Now be a good boy, Stephen, and listen to me patiently. The Undershafts are descended from a foundling in the parish of St Andrew Undershaft in the city. That was long ago, in the reign of James the First. Well, this foundling was adopted by an armorer and gunmaker. In the course of time the foundling succeeded to the business; and from some notion of gratitude, or some vow or something, he adopted another foundling, and left the business to him. And that foundling did the same. Ever since that, the cannon business has always been left to an adopted foundling named Andrew Undershaft.

STEPHEN But did they never marry? Were there no legitimate sons?

LADY BRITOMART Oh yes: they married just as your father did; and they were rich enough to buy land for their own children and leave them well provided for. But they always adopted and trained some foundling to succeed them in the business; and of course they always quarrelled with their wives furiously over it. Your father was adopted in that way and he pretends to consider himself bound to keep up the tradition and adopt somebody to leave the business to. Of course I was not going to stand that. There may have been some reason for it when the Undershafts could only marry women in their own class, whose sons were not fit to govern great estates. But there could be no excuse for passing over my son.

STEPHEN (*dubiously*) I am afraid I should make a poor hand of managing a cannon foundry.

LADY BRITOMART Nonsense! you could easily get a manager and pay him a salary.

STEPHEN My father evidently had no great opinion of my capacity.

LADY BRITOMART Stuff, child! you were only a baby: it had nothing to do with your capacity. Andrew did it on principle, just as he did every perverse and wicked thing on principle. When my father remonstrated, Andrew actually told him to his face that history tells us of only two successful institutions: one the Undershaft firm, and the other the Roman Empire under the Antonines. That was because the Antonine emperors all adopted their successors. Such rubbish! The Stevenages are as good as the Antonines, I hope: and you are a Stevenage. But that was Andrew all over. There you have the man! Always clever and unanswerable when he was defending nonsense and wickedness: always awkward and sullen when he had to behave sensibly and decently!

STEPHEN Then it was on my account that your home life was broken up, mother. I am sorry.

LADY BRITOMART Well, dear, there were other differences. I really cannot bear an immoral man. I am not a Pharisee, I hope; and I should not have minded his merely doing wrong things: we are none of us perfect. But your father didnt exactly do wrong things: he said them and thought them: that was what was so dreadful. He really had a sort of religion of wrongness. Just as one doesnt mind men practising immorality so long as they own that they are in the wrong by preaching morality; so I couldnt forgive Andrew for preaching immorality while he practised morality. You would all have grown up without principles, without any knowledge of right and wrong, if he had been in the house. You know, my dear, your father was a very attractive man in some ways. Children did not dislike him; and he took advantage of it to put the wickedest ideas into their heads, and make them quite unmanageable. I did not dislike him myself: very far from it; but nothing can bridge over moral disagreement.

STEPHEN All this simply bewilders me, mother. People may differ about matters of opinion, or even about religion; but how can they differ about right and wrong? Right is right; and wrong is wrong; and if a man cannot distinguish them properly, he is either a fool or a rascal: thats all.

LADY BRITOMART (*touched*) That's my own boy (*She pats his cheek.*)! Your father never could answer that: he used to laugh and get out of it under cover of some affectionate nonsense. And now that you understand the situation, what do you advise me to do?

STEPHEN Well, what can you do?

LADY BRITOMART I must get the money somehow.

STEPHEN We cannot take money from him. I had rather go and live in some cheap place like Bedford Square or even Hampstead than take a farthing of his money.

LADY BRITOMART But after all, Stephen, our present income comes from Andrew.

STEPHEN (*shocked*) I never knew that.

LADY BRITOMART Well, you surely didnt suppose your grandfather had anything to give me. The Stevenages could not do everything for you. We gave you social position. Andrew had to contribute something. He had a very good bargain, I think.

STEPHEN (*bitterly*) We are utterly dependent on him and his cannons, then?

LADY BRITOMART Certainly not: the money is settled. But he provided it. So you see it is not a question of taking money from him or not: it is simply a question of how much. I dont want any more for myself.

STEPHEN Nor do I.

LADY BRITOMART But Sarah does; and Barbara does. That is, Charles Lomax and Adolphus Cusins will cost them more. So I must put my pride in my pocket and ask for it, I suppose. That is your advice, Stephen, is it not?

STEPHEN No.

LADY BRITOMART (*sharply*) Stephen!

STEPHEN Of course if you are determined—

LADY BRITOMART I am not determined: I ask your advice; and I am waiting for it. I will not have all the responsibility thrown on my shoulders.

STEPHEN (*obstinately*) I would die sooner than ask him for another penny.

LADY BRITOMART (*resignedly*) You mean that *I* must ask him. Very well, Stephen: it shall be as you wish. You will be glad to know that your grandfather concurs. But he thinks I ought to ask Andrew to come here and see the girls. After all, he must have some natural affection for them.

STEPHEN Ask him here!!!

LADY BRITOMART Do not repeat my words, Stephen. Where else can I ask him?

STEPHEN I never expected you to ask him at all.

LADY BRITOMART Now dont tease, Stephen. Come! you see that it is necessary that he should pay us a visit, dont you?

STEPHEN (*reluctantly*) I suppose so, if the girls cannot do without his money.

LADY BRITOMART Thank you, Stephen: I knew you would give me the right advice when it was properly explained to you. I have asked your father to come this evening. (STEPHEN *bounds from his seat.*) Dont jump, Stephen: it fidgets me.

STEPHEN (*in utter consternation*) Do you mean to say that my father is coming here tonight—that he may be here at any moment?

LADY BRITOMART (*looking at her watch*) I said nine. (*He gasps. She rises.*) Ring the bell, please. (STEPHEN *goes to the smaller writing table; presses a button on it; and sits at it with his elbows on the table and his head in his hands, outwitted and overwhelmed.*) It is ten minutes to nine yet; and I have to prepare the girls. I asked Charles Lomax and Adolphus to dinner on purpose that they might be here. Andrew had better see them in case he should cherish any delusion as to their being capable of supporting their wives. (*The butler enters:* LADY BRITOMART *goes behind the settee to speak to him.*) Morrison: go up to the drawing room and tell everybody to come down here at once. (MORRISON *withdraws.* LADY BRITOMART *turns to* STEPHEN.) Now remember, Stephen: I shall need all your countenance and authority. (*He rises and tries to recover some vestige of these attributes.*) Give me a chair, dear. (*He pushes a chair forward from the wall to where she stands, near the smaller writing table. She sits down; and he goes to the armchair, into which he throws himself.*) I dont know how Barbara will take it. Ever since they made her a major in the Salvation Army she has developed a propensity to have her own way and order people about which quite cows me sometimes. It's not ladylike: I'm sure I dont know where she picked it up. Anyhow, Barbara shant bully me but still it's just as well that your father should be here before she has time to refuse to meet him or make a fuss. Dont look nervous, Stephen: it will only encourage Barbara to make difficulties. *I* am nervous enough, goodness knows; but I dont shew it.

SARAH *and* **BARBARA** *come in with their respective young men,* **CHARLES LOMAX** *and* **ADOLPHUS CUSINS. SARAH** *is slender, bored, and mundane.* **BARBARA** *is robuster, jollier, much more energetic.* **SARAH** *is fashionably dressed:* **BARBARA** *is in Salvation Army uniform.* **LOMAX,** *a young man about town, is like many other young men about town. He is afflicted with a frivolous sense of humor which plunges him at the most inopportune moments into paroxysms of imperfectly suppressed laughter.* **CUSINS** *is a spectacled student, slight, thin haired, and sweet voiced, with a more complex form of* **LOMAX'S** *complaint. His sense of humor is intellectual and subtle, and is complicated by an appalling temper. The lifelong struggle of a benevolent temperament and a high conscience against impulses of inhuman ridicule and fierce impatience has set up a chronic strain which has visibly wrecked his constitution. He is a most implacable, determined, tenacious, intolerant person who by mere force of character presents himself as—and indeed actually is—considerate, gentle, explanatory, even mild and apologetic, capable possibly of murder, but not of cruelty or coarseness. By the operation of some instinct which is not merciful enough to blind him with the illusions of love, he is obstinately bent on marrying* **BARBARA. LOMAX** *likes* **SARAH** *and thinks it will be rather a lark to marry her. Consequently he has not attempted to resist* **LADY BRITOMART'S** *arrangements to that end.*

All four look as if they had been having a good deal of fun in the drawing room. The girls enter first, leaving the swains outside. **SARAH** *comes to the settee.* **BARBARA** *comes in after her and stops at the door.*

BARBARA Are Cholly and Dolly to come in?

LADY BRITOMART (*forcibly*) Barbara: I will not have Charles called Cholly: the vulgarity of it positively makes me ill.

BARBARA It's all right, mother: Cholly is quite correct nowadays. Are they to come in?

LADY BRITOMART Yes, if they will behave themselves.

BARBARA (*through the door*) Come in, Dolly; and behave yourself.

BARBARA *comes to her mother's writing table.* **CUSINS** *enters smiling, and wanders towards* **LADY BRITOMART.**

SARAH (*calling*) Come in, Cholly. (LOMAX *enters, controlling his features very imperfectly, and places himself vaguely between* SARAH *and* BARBARA.)

LADY BRITOMART (*peremptorily*) Sit down, all of you. (*They sit.* CUSINS *crosses to the window and seats himself there.* LOMAX *takes a chair.* BARBARA *sits at the writing table and* SARAH *on the settee.*) I dont in the least know what you are laughing at, Adolphus. I am surprised at you, though I expected nothing better from Charles Lomax.

CUSINS (*in a remarkably gentle voice*) Barbara has been trying to teach me the West Ham Salvation March.

LADY BRITOMART I see nothing to laugh at in that; nor should you if you are really converted.

CUSINS (*sweetly*) You were not present. It was really funny, I believe.

LOMAX Ripping.

LADY BRITOMART Be quiet, Charles. Now listen to me, children. Your father is coming here this evening.

(*General stupefaction.* LOMAX, SARAH, *and* BARBARA *rise:* SARAH *scared, and* BARBARA *amused and expectant.*)

LOMAX (*remonstrating*) Oh I say!

LADY BRITOMART You are not called on to say anything, Charles.

SARAH Are you serious, mother?

LADY BRITOMART Of course I am serious. It is on your account, Sarah, and also on Charles's. (*Silence,* SARAH *sits, with a shrug.* CHARLES *looks painfully unworthy.*) I hope you are not going to object, Barbara.

BARBARA I! why should I? My father has a soul to be saved like everybody else. He's quite welcome as far as I am concerned. (*She sits on the table, and softly whistles "Onward, Christian Soldiers".*)

LOMAX (*still remonstrant*) But really, dont you know! Oh I say!

LADY BRITOMART (*frigidly*) What do you wish to convey, Charles?

LOMAX Well, you must admit that this is a bit thick.

LADY BRITOMART (*turning with ominous suavity to* CUSINS) Adolphus: you are a professor of Greek. Can you translate Charles Lomax's remarks into reputable English for us?

CUSINS (*cautiously*) If I may say so, Lady Brit, I think Charles has rather happily expressed what we feel. Homer, speaking of Autolycus, uses the same phrase. *πυκινὸν δόμον ελθεει§ ν* means a bit thick.

LOMAX (*handsomely*) Not that I mind, you know, if Sarah dont. (*He sits.*)

LADY BRITOMART (*crushingly*) Thank you. Have I your permission, Adolphus, to invite my own husband to my own house?

CUSINS (*gallantly*) You have my unhesitating support in everything you do.

LADY BRITOMART Tush! Sarah: have you nothing to say?

SARAH Do you mean that he is coming regularly to live here?

LADY BRITOMART Certainly not. The spare room is ready for him if he likes to stay for a day or two and see a little more of you; but there are limits.

SARAH Well, he cant eat us, I suppose. *I* dont mind.

LOMAX (*chuckling*) I wonder how the old man will take it.

LADY BRITOMART Much as the old woman will, no doubt, Charles.

LOMAX (*abashed*) I didnt mean—at least—

LADY BRITOMART You didnt think, Charles. You never do; and the result is, you never mean anything. And now please attend to me, children. Your father will be quite a stranger to us.

LOMAX I suppose he hasnt seen Sarah since she was a little kid.

LADY BRITOMART Not since she was a little kid, Charles, as you express it with that elegance of diction and refinement of thought that seem never to desert you. Accordingly—er—(*impatiently*) Now I have forgotten what I was going to say. That comes of your provoking me to be sarcastic, Charles. Adolphus: will you kindly tell me where I was.

CUSINS (*sweetly*) You were saying that as Mr Undershaft has not seen his children since they were babies, he will form his opinion of the way you have brought them up from their behavior tonight, and that therefore you wish us all to be particularly careful to conduct ourselves well, especially Charles.

LADY BRITOMART (*with emphatic approval*) Precisely.

LOMAX Look here, Dolly: Lady Brit didnt say that.

LADY BRITOMART (*vehemently*) I did, Charles. Adolphus's recollection is perfectly correct. It is most important that you should be good; and I do beg you for once not to pair off into opposite corners and giggle and whisper while I am speaking to your father.

BARBARA All right, mother. We'll do you credit. (*She comes off the table, and sits in her chair with ladylike elegance.*)

LADY BRITOMART Remember, Charles, that Sarah will want to feel proud of you instead of ashamed of you.

LOMAX Oh I say! theres nothing to be exactly proud of, dont you know.

LADY BRITOMART Well, try and look as if there was.

(MORRISON, *pale and dismayed, breaks into the room in unconcealed disorder.*)

MORRISON Might I speak a word to you, my lady?

LADY BRITOMART Nonsense! Shew him up.

MORRISON Yes, my lady. (*He goes.*)

LOMAX Does Morrison know who it is?

LADY BRITOMART Of course. Morrison has always been with us.

LOMAX It must be a regular corker for him, dont you know.

LADY BRITOMART Is this a moment to get on my nerves, Charles, with your outrageous expressions?

LOMAX But this is something out of the ordinary, really—

MORRISON (*at the door*) The—er—Mr Undershaft. (*He retreats in confusion.*)

ANDREW UNDERSHAFT *comes in. All rise.* LADY BRITOMART *meets him in the middle of the room behind the settee.*

ANDREW *is, on the surface, a stoutish, easygoing elderly man, with kindly patient manners, and an engaging simplicity of character. But he has a watchful, deliberate, waiting, listening face, and formidable reserves of power, both bodily and mental, in his capacious chest and long head. His gentleness is partly that of a strong man who has learnt by experience that his natural grip hurts ordinary people unless he handles them very carefully, and partly the mellowness of age and success. He is also a little shy in his present very delicate situation.*

LADY BRITOMART Good evening, Andrew.

UNDERSHAFT How d'ye do, my dear.

LADY BRITOMART You look a good deal older.

UNDERSHAFT (*apologetically*) I am somewhat older. (*taking her hand with a touch of courtship*) Time has stood still with you.

LADY BRITOMART (*throwing away his hand*) Rubbish! This is your family.

UNDERSHAFT (*surprised*) Is it so large? I am sorry to say my memory is failing very badly in some things. (*He offers his hand with paternal kindness to* LOMAX.)

LOMAX (*jerkily shaking his hand*) Ahdedoo.

UNDERSHAFT I can see you are my eldest. I am very glad to meet you again, my boy.

LOMAX (*remonstrating*) No, but look here dont you know—(*overcome*) Oh I say!

LADY BRITOMART (*recovering from momentary speechlessness*) Andrew: do you mean to say that you dont remember how many children you have?

UNDERSHAFT Well, I am afraid I—. They have grown so much—er. Am I making any ridiculous mistake? I may as well confess: I recollect only one son. But so many things have happened since, of course—er—

LADY BRITOMART (*decisively*) Andrew: you are talking nonsense. Of course you have only one son.

UNDERSHAFT Perhaps you will be good enough to introduce me, my dear.

LADY BRITOMART This is Charles Lomax, who is engaged to Sarah.

UNDERSHAFT My dear sir, I beg your pardon.

LOMAX Notatall. Delighted, I assure you.

LADY BRITOMART This is Stephen.

UNDERSHAFT (*bowing*) Happy to make your acquaintance, Mr Stephen. Then (*going to* CUSINS) you must be my son. (*taking* CUSINS' *hands in his*) How are you, my young friend? (*to* LADY BRITOMART) He is very like you, my love.

CUSINS You flatter me, Mr. Undershaft. My name is Cusins: engaged to Barbara. (*very explicitly*) This is Major Barbara Undershaft, of the Salvation Army. This is Sarah, your second daughter. This is Stephen Undershaft, your son.

UNDERSHAFT My dear Stephen, I beg your pardon.

STEPHEN Not at all.

UNDERSHAFT Mr. Cusins: I am much indebted to you for explaining so precisely. (*turning to* SARAH) Barbara, my dear—

SARAH (*prompting him*) Sarah.

UNDERSHAFT Sarah, of course. (*They shake hands. He goes over to* BARBARA.) Barbara—I am right this time, I hope?

BARBARA Quite right. (*They shake hands.*)

LADY BRITOMART (*resuming command*) Sit down, all of you. Sit down, Andrew. (*She comes forward and sits on the settee.* CUSINS *also brings his chair forward on her left.* BARBARA *and* STEPHEN *resume their seats.* LOMAX *gives his chair to* SARAH *and goes for another.)*

UNDERSHAFT Thank you, my love.

LOMAX (*conversationally, as he brings a chair forward between the writing table and the settee, and offers it to* UNDERSHAFT) Takes you some time to find out exactly where you are, dont it?

UNDERSHAFT (*accepting the chair, but remaining standing*) That is not what embarrasses me, Mr Lomax. My difficulty is that if I play the part of a father, I shall produce the effect of an intrusive stranger; and if I play the part of a discreet stranger, I may appear a callous father.

LADY BRITOMART There is no need for you to play any part at all, Andrew. You had much better be sincere and natural.

UNDERSHAFT (*submissively*) Yes, my dear: I daresay that will be best. (*He sits down comfortably.*) Well, here I am. Now what can I do for you all?

LADY BRITOMART You need not do anything, Andrew. You are one of the family. You can sit with us and enjoy yourself.

A painfully conscious pause. BARBARA *makes a face at* LOMAX, *whose too long suppressed mirth immediately explodes in agonized neighings.*

LADY BRITOMART (*outraged*) Charles Lomax: if you can behave yourself, behave yourself. If not, leave the room.

LOMAX I'm awfully sorry, Lady Brit; but really you know, upon my soul! (*He sits on the settee between* LADY BRITOMART *and* UNDERSHAFT, *quite overcome.*)

BARBARA Why dont you laugh if you want to, Cholly? It's good for your inside.

LADY BRITOMART Barbara: you have had the education of a lady. Please let your father see that; and dont talk like a street girl.

UNDERSHAFT Never mind me, my dear. As you know, I am not a gentleman; and I was never educated.

LOMAX (*encouragingly*) Nobody'd know it, I assure you. You look all right, you know.

CUSINS Let me advise you to study Greek, Mr Undershaft. Greek scholars are privileged men. Few of them know Greek; and none of them know anything else; but their position is unchallengeable. Other languages are the qualifications of waiters and commercial travelers: Greek is to a man of position what the hallmark is to silver.

BARBARA Dolly: dont be insincere. Cholly: fetch your concertina and play something for us.

LOMAX (*jumps up eagerly, but checks himself to remark doubtfully to* UNDERSHAFT) Perhaps that sort of thing isnt in your line, eh?

UNDERSHAFT I am particularly fond of music.

LOMAX (*delighted*) Are you? Then I'll get it. (*He goes upstairs for the instrument.*)

UNDERSHAFT Do you play, Barbara?

BARBARA Only the tambourine. But Cholly's teaching me the concertina.

UNDERSHAFT Is Cholly also a member of the Salvation Army?

BARBARA No: he says it's bad form to be a dissenter. But I dont despair of Cholly. I made him come yesterday to a meeting at the dock gates, and take the collection in his hat.

UNDERSHAFT (*looks whimsically at his wife*)!!

LADY BRITOMART It is not my doing, Andrew. Barbara is old enough to take her own way. She has no father to advise her.

BARBARA Oh yes she has. There are no orphans in the Salvation Army.

UNDERSHAFT Your father there has a great many children and plenty of experience, eh?

BARBARA (*looking at him with quick interest and nodding*) Just so. How did you come to understand that? (LOMAX *is heard at the door trying the concertina.*)

LADY BRITOMART Come in, Charles. Play us something at once.

LOMAX Righto! (*He sits down in his former place, and preludes.*)

UNDERSHAFT One moment, Mr Lomax. I am rather interested in the Salvation Army. Its motto might be my own: Blood and Fire.

LOMAX (*shocked*) But not your sort of blood and fire, you know.

UNDERSHAFT My sort of blood cleanses: my sort of fire purifies.

BARBARA So do ours. Come down tomorrow to my shelter—the West Ham shelter—and see what we're doing. We're going to march to a great meeting in the Assembly Hall at Mile End. Come and see the shelter and then march with us: it will do you a lot of good. Can you play anything?

UNDERSHAFT In my youth I earned pennies, and even shillings occasionally, in the streets and in public house parlors by my natural talent for stepdancing. Later on, I became a member of the Undershaft orchestral society, and performed passably on the tenor trombone.

LOMAX (*scandalized—putting down the concertina*) Oh I say!

BARBARA Many a sinner has played himself into heaven on the trombone, thanks to the Army.

LOMAX (*to* BARBARA, *still rather shocked*) Yes, but what about the cannon business, dont you know? (*to* UNDERSHAFT) Getting into heaven is not exactly in your line, is it?

LADY BRITOMART Charles!!!

LOMAX Well; but it stands to reason, dont it? The cannon business may be necessary and all that: we cant get on without cannons; but it isnt right, you know. On the other hand, there may be a certain amount of tosh about the Salvation Army—I belong to the Established Church myself—but still you cant deny that it's religion; and you cant go against religion, can you? At least unless youre downright immoral, dont you know.

UNDERSHAFT You hardly appreciate my position, Mr Lomax—

LOMAX (*hastily*) I'm not saying anything against you personally—

UNDERSHAFT Quite so, quite so. But consider for a moment. Here I am, a profiteer in mutilation and murder. I find myself in a specially amiable humor just now because, this morning, down at the foundry, we blew twenty-seven dummy soldiers into fragments with a gun which formerly destroyed only thirteen.

LOMAX (*leniently*) Well, the more destructive war becomes, the sooner it will be abolished, eh?

UNDERSHAFT Not at all. The more destructive war becomes the more fascinating we find it. No, Mr Lomax: I am obliged to you for making the usual excuse for my trade; but I am not ashamed of it. I am not one of those men who keep their morals and their business in watertight compartments. All the spare money my trade rivals spend on hospitals, cathedrals, and other receptacles for conscience money, I devote to experiments and researches in improved methods of destroying life and property. I have always done so; and I always shall. Therefore your Christmas card moralities of peace on earth and goodwill among men are of no use to me. Your Christianity, which enjoins you to resist not evil, and to turn the other cheek, would make me a bankrupt. My morality—my religion—must have a place for cannons and torpedoes in it.

STEPHEN (*coldly—almost sullenly*) You speak as if there were half a dozen moralities and religions to choose from, instead of one true morality and one true religion.

UNDERSHAFT For me there is only one true morality; but it might not fit you, as you do not manufacture aerial battleships. There is only one true morality for every man; but every man has not the same true morality.

LOMAX (*overtaxed*) Would you mind saying that again? I didnt quite follow it.

CUSINS It's quite simple. As Euripides says, one man's meat is another man's poison morally as well as physically.

UNDERSHAFT Precisely.

LOMAX Oh, that! Yes, yes, yes. True. True.

STEPHEN In other words, some men are honest and some are scoundrels.

BARBARA Bosh! There are no scoundrels.

UNDERSHAFT Indeed? Are there any good men?

BARBARA No. Not one. There are neither good men nor scoundrels: there are just children of one Father; and the sooner they stop calling one another names the better. You neednt talk to me: I know them. Ive had scores of them through my hands: scoundrels, criminals, infidels, philanthropists, missionaries, county councillors, all sorts. Theyre all just the same sort of sinner; and theres the same salvation ready for them all.

UNDERSHAFT May I ask have you ever saved a maker of cannons?

BARBARA No. Will you let me try?

UNDERSHAFT Well, I will make a bargain with you. If I go to see you tomorrow in your Salvation Shelter, will you come the day after to see me in my cannon works?

BARBARA Take care. It may end in your giving up the cannons for the sake of the Salvation Army.

UNDERSHAFT Are you sure it will not end in your giving up the Salvation Army for the sake of the cannons?

BARBARA I will take my chance of that.

UNDERSHAFT And I will take my chance of the other. (*They shake hands on it.*) Where is your shelter?

BARBARA In West Ham. At the sign of the cross. Ask anybody in Canning Town. Where are your works?

UNDERSHAFT In Perivale St Andrews. At the sign of the sword. Ask anybody in Europe.

LOMAX Hadnt I better play something?

BARBARA Yes. Give us Onward, Christian Soldiers.

LOMAX Well, thats rather a strong order to begin with, dont you know. Suppose I sing Thourt passing hence, my brother. It's much the same tune.

BARBARA It's too melancholy. You get saved, Cholly; and youll pass hence, my brother, without making such a fuss about it.

LADY BRITOMART Really, Barbara, you go on as if religion were a pleasant subject. Do have some sense of propriety.

UNDERSHAFT I do not find it an unpleasant subject, my dear. It is the only one that capable people really care for.

LADY BRITOMART (*looking at her watch*) Well, if you are determined to have it, I insist on having it in a proper and respectable way. Charles: ring for prayers.

(*General amazement.* STEPHEN *rises in dismay.*)

LOMAX (*rising*) Oh I say!

UNDERSHAFT (*rising*) I am afraid I must be going.

LADY BRITOMART You cannot go now, Andrew: it would be most improper. Sit down. What will the servants think?

UNDERSHAFT My dear: I have conscientious scruples. May I suggest a compromise? If Barbara will conduct a little service in the drawing room, with Mr Lomax as organist, I will attend it willingly. I will even take part, if a trombone can be procured.

LADY BRITOMART Dont mock, Andrew.

UNDERSHAFT (*shocked—to* BARBARA) You dont think I am mocking, my love, I hope.

BARBARA No, of course not; and it wouldnt matter if you were: half the Army came to their first meeting for a lark. (*rising*) Come along. (*She throws her arm round her father and sweeps him out, calling to the others from the threshold.*) Come, Dolly. Come, Cholly.

LADY BRITOMART I will not be disobeyed by everybody. Adolphus: sit down. (*He does not.*) Charles: you may go. You are not fit for prayers: you cannot keep your countenance.

LOMAX Oh I say! (*He goes out.*)

LADY BRITOMART (*continuing*) But you, Adolphus, can behave yourself if you choose to. I insist on your staying.

CUSINS My dear Lady Brit: there are things in the family prayer book that I couldnt bear to hear you say.

LADY BRITOMART What things, pray?

CUSINS Well, you would have to say before all the servants that we have done things we ought not to have done, and left undone things we ought to have done, and that there is no health in us. I cannot bear to hear you doing yourself such an injustice, and Barbara such an injustice. As for myself, I flatly deny it: I have done my best. I shouldnt dare to marry Barbara—I couldnt look you in the face—if it were true. So I must go to the drawing room.

LADY BRITOMART (*offended*) Well, go. (*He starts for the door.*) And remember this, Adolphus (*He turns to listen.*): I have a very strong suspicion that you went to the Salvation Army to worship Barbara and nothing else. And I quite appreciate the very clever way in which you systematically humbug me. I have found you out. Take care Barbara doesnt. Thats all.

CUSINS (*with unruffled sweetness*) Dont tell on me. (*He steals out.*)

LADY BRITOMART Sarah: if you want to go, go. Anything's better than to sit there as if you wished you were a thousand miles away.

SARAH (*languidly*) Very well, mamma. (*She goes.*)

(LADY BRITOMART, *with a sudden flounce, gives way to a little gust of tears.*)

STEPHEN (*going to her*) Mother: whats the matter?

LADY BRITOMART (*swishing away her tears with her handkerchief*) Nothing. Foolishness. You can go with him, too, if you like, and leave me with the servants.

STEPHEN Oh, you mustnt think that, mother. I—I dont like him.

LADY BRITOMART The others do. That is the injustice of a woman's lot. A woman has to bring up her children; and that means to restrain them, to deny them things they want, to set them tasks, to punish them when they do wrong, to do all the unpleasant things. And then the father, who has nothing to do but pet them and spoil them, comes in when all her work is done and steals their affection from her.

STEPHEN He has not stolen our affection from you. It is only curiosity.

LADY BRITOMART (*violently*) I wont be consoled, Stephen. There is nothing the matter with me. (*She rises and goes towards the door.*)

STEPHEN Where are you going, mother?

LADY BRITOMART To the drawing room, of course. (*She goes out. Onward, Christian Soldiers, on the concertina, with tambourine accompaniment, is heard when the door opens.*) Are you coming, Stephen?

STEPHEN No. Certainly not. (*She goes. He sits down on the settee, with compressed lips and an expression of strong dislike.*)

Act II

The yard of the West Ham shelter of the Salvation Army is a cold place on a January morning. The building itself, an old warehouse, is newly whitewashed. Its gabled end projects into the yard in the middle, with a door on the ground floor, and another in the loft above it without any balcony or ladder, but with a pulley rigged over it for hoisting sacks. Those who come from this central gable end into the yard have the gateway leading to the street on their left, with a stone horse-trough just beyond it, and, on the right, a penthouse shielding a table from the weather. There are forms at the table; and on them are seated a man and a woman, both much down on their luck, finishing a meal of bread (one thick slice each, with margarine and golden syrup) and diluted milk.

The man, a workman out of employment, is young, agile, a talker, a poser, sharp enough to be capable of anything in reason except honesty or altruistic considerations of any kind. The woman is a commonplace old bundle of poverty and hard-worn humanity. She looks sixty and probably is forty-five. If they were rich people, gloved and muffed and well wrapped up in furs and overcoats, they would be numbed and miserable; for it is a grindingly cold raw January day; and a glance at the background of grimy warehouses and leaden sky visible over the whitewashed walls of the yard would drive any idle rich person straight to the Mediterranean. But these two, being no more troubled with visions of the Mediterranean than of the moon, and being compelled to keep more of their clothes in the pawnshop, and less on their persons, in winter than in summer, are not depressed by the cold: rather are they stung into vivacity, to which their meal has just now given an almost jolly turn. The man takes a pull at his mug, and then gets up and moves about the yard with his hands deep in his pockets, occasionally breaking into a stepdance.

THE WOMAN Feel better arter your meal, sir?

THE MAN No. Call that a meal! Good enough for you, praps, but wot is it to me, an intelligent workin man.

THE WOMAN Workin man! Wot are you?

THE MAN Painter.

THE WOMAN (*skeptically*) Yus, I dessay.

THE MAN Yus, you dessay! I know. Every loafer that cant do nothink calls isself a painter. Well, I'm a real painter: grainer, finisher, thirty-eight bob a week when I can get it.

THE WOMAN Then why dont you go and get it?

THE MAN I'll tell you why. Fust: I'm intelligent—fffff! it's rotten cold here (*He dances a step or two.*)—yes: intelligent beyond the station o life into which it has pleased the capitalists to call me; and they dont like a man that sees through em. Second, an intelligent bein needs a doo share of appiness; so I drink somethink cruel when I get the chawnce. Third, I stand by my class and do as little as I can so's to leave arf the job for me fellow workers. Fourth, I'm fly enough to know wots inside the law and wots outside it; and inside it I do as the capitalists do: pinch wot I can lay me ands on. In a proper state of society I am sober, industrious and honest: in Rome, so to speak, I do as the Romans do. Wots the consequence? When trade is bad—and it's rotten bad just now—and the employers az to sack arf their men, they generally start on me.

THE WOMAN Whats your name?

THE MAN Price. Bronterre O'Brien Price. Usually called Snobby Price, for short.

THE WOMAN Snobby's a carpenter, aint it? You said you was a painter.

PRICE Not that kind of snob, but the genteel sort. I'm too uppish, owing to my intelligence, and my father being a Chartist and a reading, thinking man: a stationer, too. I'm none of your common hewers of wood and drawers of water; and dont you forget it. (*He returns to his seat at the table, and takes up his mug.*) Wots your name?

THE WOMAN Rummy Mitchens, sir.

PRICE (*quaffing the remains of his milk to her*) Your elth, Miss Mitchens.

RUMMY (*correcting him*) Missis Mitchens.

PRICE Wot! Oh Rummy, Rummy! Respectable married woman, Rummy, gittin rescued by the Salvation Army by pretendin to be a bad un. Same old game!

RUMMY What am I to do? I cant starve. Them Salvation lasses is dear good girls; but the better you are, the worse they likes to think you were before they rescued you. Why shouldnt they av a bit o credit, poor loves? theyre worn to rags by their work. And where would they get the money to rescue us if we was to let on we're no worse than other people? You know what ladies and gentlemen are.

PRICE Thievin swine! Wish I ad their job, Rummy, all the same. Wot does Rummy stand for? Pet name praps?

RUMMY Short for Romola.

PRICE For wot!?

RUMMY Romola. It was out of a new book. Somebody me mother wanted me to grow up like.

PRICE We're companions in misfortune, Rummy. Both on us got names that nobody cawnt pronounce. Consequently I'm Snobby and youre Rummy because Bill and Sally wasnt good enough for our parents. Such is life!

RUMMY Who saved you, Mr. Price? Was it Major Barbara?

PRICE No: I come here on my own. I'm going to be Bronterre O'Brien Price, the converted painter. I know wot they like. I'll tell em how I blasphemed and gambled and wopped my poor old mother—

RUMMY (*shocked*) Used you to beat your mother?

PRICE Not likely. She used to beat me. No matter: you come and listen to the converted painter, and youll hear how she was a pious woman that taught me me prayers at er knee, an how I used to come home drunk and drag her out o bed be er snow white airs, an lam into er with the poker.

RUMMY Thats whats so unfair to us women. Your confessions is just as big lies as ours: you dont tell what you really done no more than us; but you men can tell your lies right out at the meetins and be made much of for it, while the sort o confessions we az to make az to be whispered to one lady at a time. It aint right, spite of all their piety.

PRICE Right! Do you spose the Army'd be allowed if it went and did right? Not much. It combs our air and makes us good little blokes to be robbed and put upon. But I'll play the game as good as any of em. I'll see somebody struck by lightnin, or hear a voice sayin "Snobby Price: where will you spend eternity?" I'll av a time of it, I tell you.

RUMMY You wont be let drink, though.

PRICE I'll take it out in gorspellin, then. I dont want to drink if I can get fun enough any other way.

(JENNY HILL, *a pale, overwrought, pretty Salvation lass of 18, comes in through the yard gate, leading* PETER SHIRLEY, *a half hardened, half worn-out elderly man, weak with hunger.*)

JENNY (*supporting him*) Come! pluck up. I'll get you something to eat. Youll be all right then.

PRICE (*rising and hurrying officiously to take the old man off* JENNY'*s hands*) Poor old man! Cheer up, brother: youll find rest and peace and appiness ere. Hurry up with the food, miss: e's fair done. (JENNY *hurries into the shelter.*) Ere, buck up, daddy! she's fetchin y'a thick slice of breadn treacle, an a mug o skyblue. (*He seats him at the corner of the table.*)

RUMMY (*gaily*) Keep up your old art! Never say die!

SHIRLEY I'm not an old man. I'm only 46. I'm as good as ever I was. The grey patch come in my hair before I was thirty. All it wants is three pennorth o hair dye: am I to be turned on the streets to starve for it? Holy God! I've worked ten to twelve hours a day since I was thirteen, and paid my way all through; and now am I to be thrown into the gutter and my job given to a young man that can do it no better than me because Ive black hair that goes white at the first change?

PRICE (*cheerfully*) No good jawrin about it. Youre ony a jumped-up, jerked-off, orspittle-turned-out incurable of an ole workin man: who cares about you? Eh? Make the thievin swine give you a meal: theyve stole many a one from you. Get a bit o your own back. (JENNY *returns with the usual meal.*) There you are, brother. Awsk a blessin an tuck that into you.

SHIRLEY (*looking at it ravenously but not touching it, and crying like a child*) I never took anything before.

JENNY (*petting him*) Come, come! the Lord sends it to you: he wasn't above taking bread from his friends; and why should you be? Besides, when we find you a job you can pay us for it if you like.

SHIRLEY (*eagerly*) Yes, yes: thats true. I can pay you back: it's only a loan. (*shivering*) Oh Lord! oh Lord! (*He turns to the table and attacks the meal ravenously.*)

JENNY Well, Rummy, are you more comfortable now?

RUMMY God bless you, lovey! youve fed my body and saved my soul, havent you? (JENNY, *touched, kisses her.*) Sit down and rest a bit: you must be ready to drop.

JENNY Ive been going hard since morning. But theres more work than we can do. I mustnt stop.

RUMMY Try a prayer for just two minutes. Youll work all the better after.

JENNY (*her eyes lighting up*) Oh isnt it wonderful how a few minutes prayer revives you! I was quite lightheaded at twelve o'clock, I was so tired; but Major Barbara just sent me to pray for five minutes; and I was able to go on as if I had only just begun. (*to Price*) Did you have a piece of bread?

PRICE (*with unction*) Yes, miss; but Ive got the piece that I value more; and thats the peace that passeth hall hannerstennin.

RUMMY (*fervently*) Glory Hallelujah!

(BILL WALKER, *a rough customer of about 25, appears at the yard gate and looks malevolently at* JENNY.)

JENNY That makes me so happy. When you say that, I feel wicked for loitering here. I must get to work again.

(*She is hurrying to the shelter, when the new-comer moves quickly up to the door and intercepts her. His manner is so threatening that she retreats as he comes at her truculently, driving her down the yard.*)

BILL Aw knaow you. Youre the one that took awy maw girl. Youre the one that set er agen me. Well, I'm gowin to ev er aht. Not that Aw care a carse for er or you: see? Bat Aw'll let er knaow; and Aw'll let you knaow. Aw'm gowing to give her a doin thatll teach er to cat awy from me. Nah in wiv you and tell er to cam aht afore Aw cam in and kick er aht. Tell er Bill Walker wants er. She'll knaow wot thet means; and if she keeps me witin itll be worse. You stop to jawr beck at me: and Aw'll stawt on you: d'ye eah? Theres your wy. In you gow. (*He takes her by the arm and slings her towards the door of the shelter. She falls on her hand and knee.* RUMMY *helps her up again.*)

PRICE (*rising, and venturing irresolutely towards* BILL) Easy there, mate. She aint doin you no arm.

BILL Oo are you callin mite? (*standing over him threateningly*) Youre gowin to stend ap for er, aw yer? Put ap your ends.

RUMMY (*running indignantly to him to scold him*) Oh, you great brute— (*He instantly swings his left hand back against her face. She screams and reels back to the trough, where she sits down, covering her bruised face with her hands and rocking herself and moaning with pain.*)

JENNY (*going to her*) Oh, God forgive you! How could you strike an old woman like that?

BILL (*seizing her by the hair so violently that she also screams, and tearing her away from the old woman*) You Gawd forgimme again an Aw'll Gawd forgive you one on the jawr thetll stop you pryin for a week. (*holding her and turning fiercely on* PRICE) Ev you ennything to sy agen it?

PRICE (*intimidated*) No, matey: she aint anything to do with me.

BILL Good job for you! Aw'd pat two meals into you and fawt you with one finger arter, you stawved cur. (*to* JENNY) Nah are you gowin to fetch aht Mog Ebbijem; or em Aw to knock your fice off you and fetch her meself?

JENNY (*writhing in his grasp*) Oh please someone go in and tell Major Barbara— (*She screams again as he wrenches her head down; and* PRICE *and* RUMMY *flee into the shelter.*)

BILL You want to gow in and tell your Mijor of me, do you?

JENNY Oh please dont drag my hair. Let me go.

BILL Do you or downt you? (*She stifles a scream.*) Yus or nao?

JENNY God give me strength—

BILL (*striking her with his fist in the face*) Gow an shaow her thet, and tell her if she wants one lawk it to cam and interfere with me. (JENNY, *crying with pain, goes into the shed. He goes to the form and addresses the old man.*) Eah: finish your mess; an git aht o mah wy.

SHIRLEY (*springing up and facing him fiercely, with the mug in his hand*) You take a liberty with me, and I'll smash you over the face with the mug and cut your eye out. Aint you satisfied—young whelps like you—with takin the bread out o the mouths of your elders that have brought you up and slaved for you, but you must come shovin and cheekin and bullyin in here, where the bread o charity is sickenin in our stummicks?

BILL (*contemptuously, but backing a little*) Wot good are you, you aold palsy mag? Wot good are you?

SHIRLEY As good as you and better. I'll do a day's work agen you or any fat young soaker of your age. Go and take my job at Horrockses, where I worked for ten year. They want young men there: they cant afford to keep men over forty-five. They're very sorry—give you a character and happy to help you to get anything suited to your years—sure a steady man wont be long out of a job. Well, let em try you. Theyll find the differ. What do you know? Not as much as how to beeyave yourself—layin your dirty fist across the mouth of a respectable woman!

BILL Downt provowk me to ly it acrost yours: d'ye eah?

SHIRLEY (*with blighting contempt*) Yes: you like an old man to hit, dont you, when youve finished with the women. I ain't seen you hit a young one yet.

BILL (*stung*) You loy, you aold soupkitchener, you. There was a yang menn eah. Did Aw offer to itt him or did Aw not?

SHIRLEY Was he starvin or was he not? Was he a man or only a crossed-eyed thief an a loafer? Would you hit my son-in-law's brother?

BILL Oo's ee?

SHIRLEY Todger Fairmile o Balls Pond. Him that won £20 off the Japanese wrastler at the music hall by standin out 17 minutes 4 seconds agen him.

BILL (*sullenly*) Aw'm nao music awl wrastler. Ken he box?

SHIRLEY Yes: an you cant.

BILL Wot! Aw cawnt, cawnt Aw? Wots thet you sy (*threatening him*)?

SHIRLEY (*not budging an inch*) Will you box Todger Fairmile if I put him on to you? Say the word.

BILL (*subsiding with a slouch*) Aw'll stend ap to enny menn alawv, if he was ten Todger Fairmawls. But Aw dont set ap to be a perfeshnal.

SHIRLEY (*looking down on him with unfathomable disdain*) You box! Slap an old woman with the back o your hand! You hadnt even the sense to hit her where the magistrate couldnt see the mark of it, you silly young lump of conceit and ignorance. Hit a girl in the jaw and ony make her cry! If Todger Fairmile's done it, she wouldnt a got up inside o ten minutes, no more than you would if he got on to you. Yah! I'd set about you myself if I had a week's feedin in me instead o two months' starvation. (*He turns his back on him and sits down moodily at the table.*)

BILL (*following him and stooping over him to drive the taunt in*) You loy! youve the bread and treacle in you that you cam eah to beg.

SHIRLEY (*bursting into tears*) Oh God! it's true: I'm only an old pauper on the scrap heap. (*furiously*) But youll come to it yourself; and then youll know. Youll come to it sooner than a teetotaller like me, fillin yourself with gin at this hour o the mornin!

BILL Aw'm nao gin drinker, you oald lawr; but wen Aw want to give my girl a bloomin good awdin Aw lawk to ev a bit o devil in me: see? An eah Aw emm, talkin to a rotten aold blawter like you sted o givin her wot for. (*working himself into a rage*) Aw'm gowin in there to fetch her aht. (*He makes vengefully for the shelter door.*)

SHIRLEY Youre goin to the station on a stretcher, more likely; and they'll take the gin and the devil out of you there when they get you inside. You mind what youre about: the major here is the Earl o Stevenage's granddaughter.

BILL (*checked*) Garn!

SHIRLEY Youll see.

BILL (*his resolution oozing*) Well, Aw aint dan nathin to er.

SHIRLEY Spose she said you did! who'd believe you?

BILL (*very uneasy, skulking back to the corner of the penthouse*) Gawd! theres no jastice in this cantry. To think wot them people can do! Aw'm as good as er.

SHIRLEY Tell her so. It's just what a fool like you would do.

(BARBARA, *brisk and businesslike, comes from the shelter with a note book, and addresses herself to* SHIRLEY. BILL, *cowed, sits down in the corner on a form, and turns his back on them.*)

BARBARA Good morning.

SHIRLEY (*standing up and taking off his hat*) Good morning, miss.

BARBARA Sit down: make yourself at home. (*He hesitates; but she puts a friendly hand on his shoulder and makes him obey.*) Now then! since youve made friends with us, we want to know all about you. Names and addresses and trades.

SHIRLEY Peter Shirley. Fitter. Chucked out two months ago because I was too old.

BARBARA (*not at all surprised*) Youd pass still. Why didnt you dye your hair?

SHIRLEY I did. Me age come out at a coroner's inquest on me daughter.

BARBARA Steady?

SHIRLEY Teetotaller. Never out of a job before. Good worker. And sent to the knackers like an old horse!

BARBARA No matter: if you did your part God will do his.

SHIRLEY (*suddenly stubborn*) My religion's no concern of anybody but myself.

BARBARA (*guessing*) I know. Secularist?

SHIRLEY (*hotly*) Did I offer to deny it?

BARBARA Why should you? My own father's a Secularist, I think. Our Father—yours and mine—fulfils himself in many ways; and I daresay he knew what he was about when he made a Secularist of you. So buck up, Peter! we can always find a job for a steady man like you. (SHIRLEY, *disarmed and a little bewildered, touches his hat. She turns from him to* BILL.) Whats your name?

BILL (*insolently*) Wots thet to you?

BARBARA (*calmly making a note*) Afraid to give his name. Any trade?

BILL Oo's afride to give is nime? (*Doggedly, with a sense of heroically defying the House of Lords in the person of Lord Stevenage.*) If you want to bring a chawge agen me, bring it. (*She waits, unruffled.*) Moy nime's Bill Walker.

BARBARA (*as if the name were familiar; trying to remember how*) Bill Walker? (*recollecting*) Oh, I know: youre the man that Jenny Hill was praying for inside just now. (*She enters his name in her note book.*)

BILL Oo's Jenny Ill? And wot call as she to pry for me?

BARBARA I dont know. Perhaps it was you that cut her lip.

BILL (*defiantly*) Yus, it was me that cat her lip. Aw aint afride o you.

BARBARA How could you be, since youre not afraid of God? Youre a brave man, Mr Walker. It takes some pluck to do our work here; but none of us dare lift our hand against a girl like that, for fear of her father in heaven.

BILL (*sullenly*) I want nan o your kentin jawr. I spowse you think Aw cam eah to beg from you, like this demmiged lot eah. Not me. Aw downt want your bread and scripe and ketlep. Aw dont belive in your Gawd, no more than you do yourself.

BARBARA (*sunnily apologetic and ladylike, as on a new footing with him*) Oh, I beg your pardon for putting your name down, Mr Walker. I didn't understand. I'll strike it out.

BILL (*taking this as a slight, and deeply wounded by it*) Eah! you let maw nime alown. Aint it good enaff to be in your book?

BARBARA (*considering*) Well, you see, theres no use putting down your name unless I can do something for you, is there? Whats your trade?

BILL (*still smarting*) Thets nao concern o yours.

BARBARA Just so. (*very businesslike*) I'll put you down as (*writing*) the man who—struck—poor little Jenny Hill—in the mouth.

BILL (*rising threateningly*) See eah. Awve ed enaff o this.

BARBARA (*quite sunny and fearless*) What did you come to us for?

BILL Aw cam for maw gel, see? Aw cam to tike her aht o this and to brike er jawr for er.

BARBARA (*complacently*) You see I was right about your trade. (BILL, *on the point of retorting furiously, finds himself, to his great shame and terror, in danger of crying instead. He sits down again suddenly.*) Whats her name?

BILL (*dogged*) Er nime's Mog Ebbijem: thets wot her nime is.

BARBARA Mog Habbijam! Oh, she's gone to Canning Town, to our barracks there.

BILL (*fortified by his resentment of* MOG's *perfidy*) Is she? (*vindictively*) Then Aw'm gowin to Kennintahn arter her. (*He crosses to the gate; hesitates; finally comes back at* BARBARA.) Are you loyin to me to git shat o me?

BARBARA I dont want to get shut of you. I want to keep you here and save your soul. Youd better stay: youre going to have a bad time today, Bill.

BILL Oo's gowin to give it to me? You, preps?

BARBARA Someone you dont believe in. But youll be glad afterwards.

BILL (*slinking off*) Aw'll gow to Kennintahn to be aht o reach o your tangue. (*suddenly turning on her with intense malice*) And if Aw downt fawnd Mog there, Aw'll cam beck and do two years for you, selp me Gawd if Aw downt!

BARBARA (*a shade kindlier, if possible*) It's no use, Bill. She's got another bloke.

BILL Wot!

BARBARA One of her own converts. He fell in love with her when he saw her with her soul saved, and her face clean, and her hair washed.

BILL (*surprised*) Wottud she wash it for, the carroty slat? It's red.

BARBARA It's quite lovely now, because she wears a new look in her eyes with it. It's a pity youre too late. The new bloke has put your nose out of joint, Bill.

BILL Aw'll put his nowse aht o joint for him. Not that Aw care a carse for er, mawned thet. But Aw'll teach her to drop me as if Aw was dirt. And Aw'll teach him to meddle with maw Judy. Wots iz bleedin nime?

BARBARA Sergeant Todger Fairmile.

SHIRLEY (*rising with grim joy*) I'll go with him, miss. I want to see them two meet. I'll take him to the infirmary when it's over.

BILL (*to* SHIRLEY, *with undissembled misgiving*) Is thet im you was speakin on?

SHIRLEY Thats him.

BILL Im that wrastled in the music awl?

SHIRLEY The competitions at the National Sportin Club was worth nigh a hundred a year to him. He's gev em up now for religion; so he's a bit fresh for want of the exercise he was accustomed to. He'll be glad to see you. Come along.

BILL Wots is wight?

SHIRLEY Thirteen four. (BILL*'s last hope expires.*)

BARBARA Go and talk to him, Bill. He'll convert you.

SHIRLEY He'll convert your head into a mashed potato.

BILL (*sullenly*) Aw aint afride of im. Aw aint afride of ennybody. Bat e can lick me. She's dan me. (*He sits down moodily on the edge of the horse trough.*)

SHIRLEY You aint going. I thought not. (*He resumes his seat.*)

BARBARA (*calling*) Jenny!

JENNY (*appearing at the shelter door with a plaster on the corner of her mouth*) Yes, Major.

BARBARA Send Rummy Mitchens out to clear away here.

JENNY I think she's afraid.

BARBARA (*her resemblance to her mother flashing out for a moment*) Nonsense! she must do as she's told.

JENNY (*calling into the shelter*) Rummy: the Major says you must come.

(JENNY *comes to* BARBARA, *purposely keeping on the side next* BILL, *lest he should suppose that she shrank from him or bore malice.*)

BARBARA Poor little Jenny! Are you tired? (*looking at the wounded cheeks*) Does it hurt?

JENNY No: it's all right now. It was nothing.

BARBARA (*critically*) It was as hard as he could hit, I expect. Poor Bill! You dont feel angry with him, do you?

JENNY Oh no, no, no: indeed I dont, Major, bless his poor heart! (BARBARA *kisses her; and she runs away merrily into the shelter.* BILL *writhes with an agonizing return of his new and alarming symptoms, but says nothing.* RUMMY MITCHENS *comes from the shelter.*)

BARBARA (*going to meet* RUMMY) Now Rummy, bustle. Take in those mugs and plates to be washed; and throw the crumbs about for the birds.

(RUMMY *takes the three plates and mugs; but* SHIRLEY *takes back his mug from her, as there is still some milk left in it.*)

RUMMY There aint any crumbs. This aint a time to waste good bread on birds.

PRICE (*appearing at the shelter door*) Gentleman come to see the shelter, Major. Says he's your father.

BARBARA All right. Coming. (SNOBBY *goes back into the shelter, followed by* BARBARA.)

RUMMY (*stealing across to* BILL *and addressing him in a subdued voice, but with intense conviction*) I'd av the lor of you, you flat eared pignosed potwalloper, if she'd let me. Youre no gentleman, to hit a lady in the face. (BILL, *with greater things moving in him, takes no notice.*)

SHIRLEY (*following her*) Here! in with you and dont get yourself into more trouble by talking.

RUMMY (*with hauteur*) I aint ad the pleasure o being hintroduced to you, as I can remember. (*She goes into the shelter with the plates.*)

SHIRLEY Thats the—

BILL (*savagely*) Downt you talk to me, d'ye eah? You lea me alown, or Aw'll do you a mischief. Aw'm not dirt under your feet, ennywy.

SHIRLEY (*calmly*) Dont you be afeerd. You aint such prime company that you need expect to be sought after. (*He is about to go into the shelter when* BARBARA *comes out, with* UNDERSHAFT *on her right.*)

BARBARA Oh, there you are, Mr Shirley! (*Between them.*) This is my father: I told you he was a Secularist, didn't I? Perhaps youll be able to comfort one another.

UNDERSHAFT (*startled*) A Secularist! Not the least in the world: on the contrary, a confirmed mystic.

BARBARA Sorry, I'm sure. By the way, papa, what is your religion? in case I have to introduce you again.

UNDERSHAFT My religion? Well, my dear, I am a Millionaire. That is my religion.

BARBARA Then I'm afraid you and Mr Shirley wont be able to comfort one another after all. Youre not a Millionaire, are you, Peter?

SHIRLEY No; and proud of it.

UNDERSHAFT (*gravely*) Poverty, my friend, is not a thing to be proud of.

SHIRLEY (*angrily*) Who made your millions for you? Me and my like. Whats kep us poor? Keepin you rich. I wouldnt have your conscience, not for all your income.

UNDERSHAFT I wouldnt have your income, not for all your conscience, Mr Shirley. (*He goes to the penthouse and sits down on a form.*)

BARBARA (*stopping* SHIRLEY *adroitly as he is about to retort*) You wouldnt think he was my father, would you, Peter? Will you go into the shelter and lend the lasses a hand for a while: we're worked off our feet.

SHIRLEY (*bitterly*) Yes: I'm in their debt for a meal, aint I?

BARBARA Oh, not because youre in their debt, but for love of them, Peter, for love of them. (*He cannot understand, and is rather scandalized.*) There! dont stare at me. In with you; and give that conscience of yours a holiday (*bustling him into the shelter*).

SHIRLEY (*as he goes in*) Ah! it's a pity you never was trained to use your reason, miss. Youd have been a very taking lecturer on Secularism.

(BARBARA *turns to her father.*)

UNDERSHAFT Never mind me, my dear. Go about your work; and let me watch it for a while.

BARBARA All right.

UNDERSHAFT For instance, whats the matter with that outpatient over there?

BARBARA (*looking at* BILL, *whose attitude has never changed, and whose expression of brooding wrath has deepened*) Oh, we shall cure him in no time. Just watch. (*She goes over to* BILL *and waits. He glances up at her and casts his eyes down again, uneasy, but grimmer than ever.*) It would be nice to just stamp on Mog Habbijam's face, wouldnt it, Bill?

BILL (*starting up from the trough in consternation*) It's a loy: Aw never said so. (*She shakes her head.*) Oo taold you wot was in moy mawnd?

BARBARA Only your new friend.

BILL Wot new friend?

BARBARA The devil, Bill. When he gets round people they get miserable, just like you.

BILL (*with a heartbreaking attempt at devil-may-care cheerfulness*) Aw aint miserable. (*He sits down again, and stretches his legs in an attempt to seem indifferent.*)

BARBARA Well, if youre happy, why dont you look happy, as we do?

BILL (*his legs curling back in spite of him*) Aw'm eppy enaff, Aw tell you. Woy cawnt you lea me alown? Wot ev I dan to you? Aw aint smashed your fice, ev Aw?

BARBARA (*softly: wooing his soul*) It's not me thats getting at you, Bill.

BILL Oo else is it?

BARBARA Somebody that doesnt intend you to smash women's faces, I suppose. Somebody or something that wants to make a man of you.

BILL (*blustering*) Mike a menn o me! Aint Aw a menn? eh? Oo sez Aw'm not a menn?

BARBARA Theres a man in you somewhere, I suppose. But why did he let you hit poor little Jenny Hill? That wasnt very manly of him, was it?

BILL (*tormented*) Ev dan wiv it, Aw tell you. Chack it. Aw'm sick o your Jenny Ill and er silly little fice.

BARBARA Then why do you keep thinking about it? Why does it keep coming up against you in your mind? Youre not getting converted, are you?

BILL (*with conviction*) Not ME. Not lawkly.

BARBARA Thats right, Bill. Hold out against it. Put out your strength. Dont lets get you cheap. Todger Fairmile said he wrestled for three nights against his salvation harder than he ever wrestled with the Jap at the music hall. He gave in to the Jap when his arm was going to break. But he didnt give in to his salvation until his heart was going to break. Perhaps youll escape that. You havnt any heart, have you?

BILL Wot d'ye mean? Woy aint Aw got a awt the sime as ennybody else?

BARBARA A man with a heart wouldnt have bashed poor little Jenny's face, would he?

BILL (*almost crying*) Ow, will you lea me alown? Ev Aw ever offered to meddle with you, that you cam neggin and provowkin me lawk this? (*He writhes convulsively from his eyes to his toes.*)

BARBARA (*with a steady soothing hand on his arm and a gentle voice that never lets him go*) It's your soul thats hurting you, Bill, and not me. Weve been through it all ourselves. Come with us, Bill. (*He looks wildly round.*) To brave manhood on earth and eternal glory in heaven. (*He is on the point of breaking down.*) Come. (*A drum is heard in the shelter; and* BILL, *with a gasp, escapes from the spell as* BARBARA *turns quickly.* ADOLPHUS *enters from the shelter with a big drum.*) Oh! there you are, Dolly. Let me introduce a new friend of mine, Mr Bill Walker. This is my bloke, Bill: Mr Cusins. (CUSINS *salutes with his drumstick.*)

BILL Gowin to merry im?

BARBARA Yes.

BILL (*fervently*) Gawd elp im! Gaw-aw-aw-awd elp im!

BARBARA Why? Do you think he wont be happy with me?

BILL Awve aony ed to stend it for a mawnin: e'll ev to stend it for a lawftawm.

CUSINS That is a frightful reflection, Mr Walker. But I cant tear myself away from her.

BILL Well, Aw ken. (*to* BARBARA) Eah do you knaow where Aw'm gowin to, and wot Aw'm gowin to do?

BARBARA Yes: youre going to heaven; and youre coming back here before the week's out to tell me so.

BILL You loy. Aw'm gowin to Kennintahn, to spit in Todger Fairmawl's eye. Aw beshed Jenny Ill's fice; an nar Aw'll git me aown fice beshed and cam bec and shaow it to er. Ee'll itt me ardern Aw itt her. Thatll mike us square. (*to* ADOLPHUS) Is thet fair or is it not? Youre a genlmn: you oughter knaow.

BARBARA Two black eyes wont make one white one, Bill.

BILL Aw didnt awst you. Cawnt you never keep your mahth shat? Oy awst the genlmn.

CUSINS (*reflectively*) Yes: I think youre right, Mr Walker. Yes: I should do it. Its curious: it's exactly what an ancient Greek would have done.

BARBARA But what good will it do?

CUSINS Well, it will give Mr. Fairmile some exercise; and it will satisfy Mr Walker's soul.

BILL Rot! there aint nao sach a thing as a saoul. Ah kin you tell wevver Awve a saoul or not? You never seen it.

BARBARA Ive seen it hurting you when you went against it.

BILL (*with compressed aggravation*) If you was maw gel and took the word awt o me mahth lawk thet, Aw'd give you sathink youd feel urtin, Aw would. (*to* ADOLPHUS) You tike maw tip, mite. Stop er jawr or youll doy afoah your tawm (*with intense expression*) Wore aht: thets wot youll be: wore aht. (*He goes away through the gate.*)

CUSINS (*looking after him*) I wonder!

BARBARA Dolly! (*indignant, in her mother's manner*)

CUSINS Yes, my dear, it's very wearing to be in love with you. If it lasts, I quite think I shall die young.

BARBARA Should you mind?

CUSINS Not at all. (*He is suddenly softened, and kisses her over the drum, evidently not for the first time, as people cannot kiss over a big drum without practice.* UNDERSHAFT *coughs.*)

BARBARA It's all right, papa, weve not forgotten you. Dolly: explain the place to papa: I havent time. (*She goes busily into the shelter.*)

(UNDERSHAFT *and* ADOLPHUS *now have the yard to themselves.* UNDERSHAFT, *seated on a form, and still keenly attentive, looks hard at* ADOLPHUS. ADOLPHUS *looks hard at him.*)

UNDERSHAFT I fancy you guess something of what is in my mind, Mr Cusins. (CUSINS *flourishes his drumsticks as if in the act of beating a lively rataplan, but makes no sound.*) Exactly so. But suppose Barbara finds you out!

CUSINS You know, I do not admit that I am imposing on Barbara. I am quite genuinely interested in the views of the Salvation Army. The fact is, I am a sort of collector of religions; and the curious thing is that I find I can believe them all. By the way, have you any religion?

UNDERSHAFT Yes.

CUSINS Anything out of the common?

UNDERSHAFT Only that there are two things necessary to Salvation.

CUSINS (*disappointed, but polite*) Ah, the Church Catechism. Charles Lomax also belongs to the Established Church.

UNDERSHAFT The two things are—

CUSINS Baptism and—

UNDERSHAFT No. Money and gunpowder.

CUSINS (*surprised, but interested*) That is the general opinion of our governing classes. The novelty is in hearing any man confess it.

UNDERSHAFT Just so.

CUSINS Excuse me: is there any place in your religion for honor, justice, truth, love, mercy and so forth?

UNDERSHAFT Yes: they are the graces and luxuries of a rich, strong, and safe life.

CUSINS Suppose one is forced to choose between them and money or gunpowder?

UNDERSHAFT Choose money and gunpowder; for without enough of both you cannot afford the others.

CUSINS That is your religion?

UNDERSHAFT Yes.

(*The cadence of this reply makes a full close in the conversation.* CUSINS *twists his face dubiously and contemplates* UNDERSHAFT. UNDERSHAFT *contemplates him.*)

CUSINS Barbara wont stand that. You will have to choose between your religion and Barbara.

UNDERSHAFT So will you, my friend. She will find out that that drum of yours is hollow.

CUSINS Father Undershaft: you are mistaken: I am a sincere Salvationist. You do not understand the Salvation Army. It is the army of joy, of love, of courage: it has banished the fear and remorse and despair of the old hell-ridden evangelical sects: it marches to fight the devil with trumpet and drum, with music and dancing, with banner and palm, as becomes a sally from heaven by its happy garrison. It picks the waster out of the public house and makes a man of him: it finds a worm wriggling in a back kitchen, and lo! a woman! Men and woman of rank too, sons and daughters of the Highest. It takes the poor professor of Greek, the most artificial and self-suppressed of human creatures, from his meal of roots, and lets loose the rhapsodist in him; reveals the true worship of Dionysos to him; sends him down the public street drumming dithyrambs. (*He plays a thundering flourish on the drum.*)

UNDERSHAFT You will alarm the shelter.

CUSINS Oh, they are accustomed to these sudden ecstasies. However, if the drum worries you— (*He pockets the drumsticks; unhooks the drum and stands it on the ground opposite the gateway.*)

UNDERSHAFT Thank you.

CUSINS You remember what Euripides says about your money and gunpowder?

UNDERSHAFT No.

CUSINS (*declaiming*)

One and another
In money and guns may outpass his brother;
And men in their millions float and flow
And seethe with a million hopes as leaven;
And they win their will; or they miss their will;
And their hopes are dead or are pined for still;
But who'er can know
As the long days go
That to live is happy, has found his heaven.

My translation: what do you think of it?

UNDERSHAFT I think, my friend, that if you wish to know, as the long days go, that to live is happy, you must first acquire money enough for a decent life, and power enough to be your own master.

CUSINS You are damnably discouraging. (*He resumes his declamation.*)

Is it so hard a thing to see
That the spirit of God—whate'er it be—
The law that abides and changes not, ages long,
The Eternal and Nature-born: these things be strong?

What else is Wisdom? What of Man's endeavor,
Of God's high grace so lovely and so great?
To stand from fear set free? to breathe and wait?
To hold a hand uplifted over Fate?
And shall not Barbara be loved for ever?

UNDERSHAFT Euripides mentions Barbara, does he?

CUSINS It is a fair translation. The word means Loveliness.

UNDERSHAFT May I ask—as Barbara's father—how much a year she is to be loved for ever on?

CUSINS As for Barbara's father, that is more your affair than mine. I can feed her by teaching Greek: that is about all.

UNDERSHAFT Do you consider it a good match for her?

CUSINS (*with polite obstinacy*) Mr Undershaft: I am in many ways a weak, timid, ineffectual person: and my health is far from satisfactory. But whenever I feel that I must have anything, I get it, sooner or later. I feel that way about Barbara. I dont like marriage: I feel intensely afraid of it; and I dont know what I shall do with Barbara or what she will do with me. But I feel that I and nobody else must marry her. Please regard that as settled.—Not that I wish to be arbitrary; but why should I waste your time in discussing what is inevitable?

UNDERSHAFT You mean that you will stick at nothing: not even the conversion of the Salvation Army to the worship of Dionysos.

CUSINS The business of the Salvation Army is to save, not to wrangle about the name of the pathfinder. Dionysos or another: what does it matter?

UNDERSHAFT (*rising and approaching him*) Professor Cusins: you are a young man after my own heart.

CUSINS Mr Undershaft: you are, as far as I am able to gather, a most infernal old rascal; but you appeal very strongly to my sense of ironic humor.

(UNDERSHAFT *mutely offers his hand. They shake.*)

UNDERSHAFT (*suddenly concentrating himself*) And now to business.

CUSINS Pardon me. We are discussing religion. Why go back to such an uninteresting and unimportant subject as business?

UNDERSHAFT Religion is our business at present, because it is through religion alone that we can win Barbara.

CUSINS Have you, too, fallen in love with Barbara?

UNDERSHAFT Yes, with a father's love.

CUSINS A father's love for a grown-up daughter is the most dangerous of all infatuations. I apologize for mentioning my own pale, coy, mistrustful fancy in the same breath with it.

UNDERSHAFT Keep to the point. We have to win her; and we are neither of us Methodists.

CUSINS That doesnt matter. The power Barbara wields here—the power that wields Barbara herself—is not Calvinism, not Presbyterianism, not Methodism—

UNDERSHAFT Not Greek Paganism either, eh?

CUSINS I admit that. Barbara is quite original in her religion.

UNDERSHAFT (*triumphantly*) Aha! Barbara Undershaft would be. Her inspiration comes from within herself.

CUSINS How do you suppose it got there?

UNDERSHAFT (*in towering excitement*) It is the Undershaft inheritance. I shall hand on my torch to my daughter. She shall make my converts and preach my gospel—

CUSINS What! Money and gunpowder!

UNDERSHAFT Yes, money and gunpowder. Freedom and power. Command of life and command of death.

CUSINS (*urbanely; trying to bring him down to earth*) This is extremely interesting, Mr Undershaft. Of course you know that you are mad.

UNDERSHAFT (*with redoubled force*) And you?

CUSINS Oh, mad as a hatter. You are welcome to my secret since I have discovered yours. But I am astonished. Can a madman make cannons?

UNDERSHAFT Would anyone else than a madman make them? And now (*with surging energy*) question for question. Can a sane man translate Euripides?

CUSINS No.

UNDERSHAFT (*seizing him by the shoulder*) Can a sane woman make a man of a waster or a woman of a worm?

CUSINS (*reeling before the storm*) Father Colossus—Mammoth Millionaire—

UNDERSHAFT (*pressing him*) Are there two mad people or three in this Salvation shelter today?

CUSINS You mean Barbara is as mad as we are?

UNDERSHAFT (*pushing him lightly off and resuming his equanimity suddenly and completely*) Pooh, Professor! let us call things by their proper names. I am a millionaire; you are a poet: Barbara is a savior of souls. What have we three to do with the common mob of slaves and idolators? (*He sits down again with a shrug of contempt for the mob.*)

CUSINS Take care! Barbara is in love with the common people. So am I. Have you never felt the romance of that love?

UNDERSHAFT (*cold and sardonic*) Have you ever been in love with Poverty, like St Francis? Have you ever been in love with Dirt, like St Simeon! Have you ever been in love with disease and suffering, like our nurses and philanthropists? Such passions are not virtues, but the most unnatural of all the vices. This love of the common people may please an earl's granddaughter and a university professor; but I have been a common man and a poor man; and it has no romance for me. Leave it to the poor to pretend that poverty is a blessing: leave it to the coward to make a religion of his cowardice by preaching humility: we know better than that. We three must stand together above the common people: how else can we help their children to climb up beside us? Barbara must belong to us, not to the Salvation Army.

CUSINS Well, I can only say that if you think you will get her away from the Salvation Army by talking to her as you have been talking to me, you dont know Barbara.

UNDERSHAFT My friend: I never ask for what I can buy.

CUSINS (*in a white fury*) Do I understand you to imply that you can buy Barbara?

UNDERSHAFT No; but I can buy the Salvation Army.

CUSINS Quite impossible.

UNDERSHAFT You shall see. All religious organizations exist by selling themselves to the rich.

CUSINS Not the Army. That is the Church of the poor.

UNDERSHAFT All the more reason for buying it.

CUSINS I dont think you quite know what the Army does for the poor.

UNDERSHAFT Oh yes I do. It draws their teeth: that is enough for me as a man of business.

CUSINS Nonsense! It makes them sober—

UNDERSHAFT I prefer sober workmen. The profits are larger.

CUSINS — honest—

UNDERSHAFT Honest workmen are the most economical.

CUSINS — attached to their homes—

UNDERSHAFT So much the better: they will put up with anything sooner than change their shop.

CUSINS — happy—

UNDERSHAFT An invaluable safeguard against revolution.

CUSINS —unselfish—

UNDERSHAFT Indifferent to their own interests, which suits me exactly.

CUSINS — with their thoughts on heavenly things—

UNDERSHAFT (*rising*) And not on Trade Unionism nor Socialism. Excellent.

CUSINS (*revolted*) You really are an infernal old rascal.

UNDERSHAFT (*indicating* PETER SHIRLEY, *who has just come from the shelter and strolled dejectedly down the yard between them*) And this is an honest man!

SHIRLEY Yes; and what av I got by it? (*He passes on bitterly and sits on the form, in the corner of the penthouse.*)

(SNOBBY PRICE, *beaming sanctimoniously, and* JENNY HILL, *with a tambourine full of coppers, come from the shelter and go to the drum, on which* JENNY *begins to count the money.*)

UNDERSHAFT (*replying to* SHIRLEY) Oh, your employers must have got a good deal by it from first to last. (*He sits on the table, with one foot on the side form,* CUSINS, *overwhelmed, sits down on the same form nearer the shelter.*

BARBARA *comes from the shelter to the middle of the yard. She is excited and a little overwrought.*)

BARBARA Weve just had a splendid experience meeting at the other gate in Cripps's lane. Ive hardly ever seen them so much moved as they were by your confession, Mr. Price.

PRICE I could almost be glad of my past wickedness if I could believe that it would elp to keep hathers stright.

BARBARA So it will, Snobby. How much, Jenny?

JENNY Four and tenpence, Major.

BARBARA Oh Snobby, if you had given your poor mother just one more kick, we should have got the whole five shillings!

PRICE If she heard you say that, miss, she'd be sorry I didnt. But I'm glad. Oh what a joy it will be to her when she hears I'm saved!

UNDERSHAFT Shall I contribute the odd twopence, Barbara? The millionaire's mite, eh? (*He takes a couple of pennies from his pocket.*)

BARBARA How did you make that twopence?

UNDERSHAFT As usual. By selling cannons, torpedoes, submarines, and my new patent Grand Duke hand grenade.

BARBARA Put it back in your pocket. You cant buy your salvation here for twopence: you must work it out.

UNDERSHAFT Is twopence not enough? I can afford a little more, if you press me.

BARBARA Two million millions would not be enough. There is bad blood on your hands; and nothing but good blood can cleanse them. Money is no use. Take it away. (*She turns to* CUSINS.) Dolly: you must write another letter for me to the papers. (*He makes a wry face.*) Yes: I know you dont like it; but it must be done. The starvation this winter is beating us: everybody is unemployed. The General says we must close this shelter if we cant get more money. I force the collections at the meetings until I am ashamed: dont I, Snobby?

PRICE It's a fair treat to see you work it, miss. The way you got them up from three-and-six to four-and-ten with that hymn, penny by penny and verse by verse, was a caution. Not a Cheap Jack on Mile End Waste could touch you at it.

BARBARA Yes; but I wish we could do without it. I am getting at last to think more of the collection than of the people's souls. And what are those hatfuls of pence and halfpence? We want thousands! tens of thousands! hundreds of thousands! I want to convert people, not to be always begging for the Army in a way I'd die sooner than beg for myself.

UNDERSHAFT (*in profound irony*) Genuine unselfishness is capable of anything, my dear.

BARBARA (*unsuspectingly, as she turns away to take the money from the drum and put it in a cash bag she carries*) Yes, isn't it? (UNDERSHAFT *looks sardonically at* CUSINS.)

CUSINS (*aside to* UNDERSHAFT) Mephistopheles! Machiavelli!

BARBARA (*tears coming into her eyes as she ties the bag and pockets it*) How are we to feed them? I cant talk religion to a man with bodily hunger in his eyes. (*almost breaking down*) It's frightful.

JENNY (*running to her*) Major, dear—

BARBARA (*rebounding*) No: dont comfort me. It will be all right. We shall get the money.

UNDERSHAFT How?

JENNY By praying for it, of course. Mrs Baines says she prayed for it last night; and she has never prayed for it in vain: never once. (*She goes to the gate and looks out into the street.*)

BARBARA (*who has dried her eyes and regained her composure*) By the way, dad, Mrs Baines has come to march with us to our big meeting this afternoon and she is very anxious to meet you, for some reason or other. Perhaps she'll convert you.

UNDERSHAFT I shall be delighted, my dear.

JENNY (*at the gate: excitedly*) Major! Major! here's that man back again.

BARBARA What man?

JENNY The man that hit me. Oh, I hope he's coming back to join us.

(BILL WALKER, *with frost on his jacket, comes through the gate, his hands deep in his pockets and his chin sunk between his shoulders, like a cleaned-out gambler. He halts between* BARBARA *and the drum.*)

BARBARA Hullo, Bill! Back already!

BILL (*nagging at her*) Bin talkin ever sence, ev you?

BARBARA Pretty nearly. Well, has Todger paid you out for poor Jenny's jaw?

BILL Nao e aint.

BARBARA I thought your jacket looked a bit snowy.

BILL Sao it is snaowy. You want to knaow where the snaow cam from, downt you?

BARBARA Yes.

BILL Well, it cam from orf the grahnd in Pawkinses Corner in Kennintahn. It got rabbed orf be maw shaoulders: see?

BARBARA Pity you didnt rub some off with your knees, Bill! That would have done you a lot of good.

BILL (*with sour mirthless humor*) Aw was sivin anather menn's knees at the tawm. E was kneelin on moy ed, e was.

JENNY Who was kneeling on your head?

BILL Todger was. E was pryin for me: pryin camfortable wiv me as a cawpet. Sow was Mog. Sao was the aol bloomin meeting. Mog she sez "Ow Lawd brike is stabborn sperrit; bat downt urt is dear art." Thet was wot she said. "Downt urt is dear art"! An er blowk—thirteen stun four!—kneelin wiv all is wight on me. Fanny, aint it?

JENNY Oh no. We're so sorry, Mr Walker.

BARBARA (*enjoying it frankly*) Nonsense! of course it's funny. Served you right, Bill! You must have done something to him first.

BILL (*doggedly*) Aw did wot Aw said Aw'd do. Aw spit in is eye. E looks ap at the skoy and sez, "Ow that Aw should be fahnd worthy to be spit upon for the gospel's sike!" e sez; an Mog sez "Glaory Allelloolier!"; and then e called me Braddher, an dahned me as if Aw was a kid and he was me mather worshin me a Setterda nawt. Aw ednt jast nao shaow wiv im at all. Arf the street pryed; an the tather arf larfed fit to split theirselves. (*to* BARBARA) There are you settisfawd nah?

BARBARA (*her eyes dancing*) Wish I'd been there, Bill.

BILL Yus: youd a got in a hextra bit o talk on me, wouldnt you?

JENNY I'm so sorry, Mr Walker.

BILL (*fiercely*) Downt you gow being sorry for me: youve no call. Listen eah. Aw browk your jawr.

JENNY No, it didnt hurt me: indeed it didnt, except for a moment. It was only that I was frightened.

BILL Aw downt want to be forgive be you, or be ennybody. Wot Aw did Aw'll py for. Aw trawd to gat me aown jawr browk to settisfaw you—

JENNY (*distressed*) Oh no—

BILL (*impatiently*) Tell y' Aw did: cawnt you listen to wots being taold you? All Aw got be it was being mide a sawt of in the pablic street for me pines. Well, if Aw cawnt settisfaw you one wy, Aw ken anather. Listen eah! Aw ed two quid sived agen the frost; an Awve a pahnd of it left. A mite o mawn last week ed words with the judy e's gowing to merry. E give er wot-for; an e's bin fawned fifteen bob. E ed a rawt to itt er cause they was gowin to be merrid; but Aw ednt nao rawt to itt you; sao put anather fawv bob on an call it a pahnd's worth. (*He produces a sovereign.*) Eahs the manney. Tike it, and lets ev no more o your forgivin an prying and your Mijor jawrin me. Let wot Aw dan be dan an pide for; and let there be a end of it.

JENNY Oh, I couldn't take it, Mr Walker. But if you would give a shilling or two to poor Rummy Mitchens! you really did hurt her; and she's old.

BILL (*contemptuously*) Not lawkly. Aw'd give her anather as soon as look at er. Let her ev the lawr o me as she threatened! She aint forgiven me: not mach. Wot Aw dan to er is not on me mawned—wot she (*indicating* BARBARA) mawt call on me conscience—no more than stickin a pig. It's this Christian gime o yours that Aw wownt ev plyed agen me: this bloomin forgivin an neggin an jawrin that mikes a menn thet sore that iz lawf's a burdn to im. Aw wownt ev it, Aw tell you; sao tike your manney and stop thraowin your silly beshed fice hap agen me.

JENNY Major: may I take a little of it for the Army?

BARBARA No: the Army is not to be bought. We want your soul, Bill; and we'll take nothing less.

BILL (*bitterly*) Aw knaow. Me an maw few shillins is not good enaff for you. Youre a earl's grendorter, you are. Nathink less than a andered pahnd for you.

UNDERSHAFT Come, Barbara! you could do a great deal of good with a hundred pounds. If you will set this gentleman's mind at ease by taking his pound, I will give the other ninety-nine.

(BILL, *dazed by such opulence, instinctively touches his cap.*)

BARBARA Oh, youre too extravagant, papa. Bill offers twenty pieces of silver. All you need offer is the other ten. That will make the standard price to buy anybody who's for sale. I'm not; and the Army's not. (*to* BILL) Youll never have another quiet moment, Bill, until you come around to us. You cant stand out against your salvation.

BILL (*sullenly*) Aw cawnt stend aht agen music awl wrastlers and awtful tangued women. Awve offered to py. Aw can do no more. Tike it or leave it. There it is. (*He throws the sovereign on the drum, and sits down on the horse trough. The coin fascinates* SNOBBY PRICE, *who takes an early opportunity of dropping his cap on it.*)

(MRS BAINES *comes from the shelter. She is dressed as a Salvation Army Commissioner. She is an earnest looking woman of about 40, with a caressing, urgent voice, and an appealing manner.*)

BARBARA This is my father, Mrs Baines. (UNDERSHAFT *comes from the table, taking his hat off with marked civility.*) Try what you can do with him. He wont listen to me, because he remembers what a fool I was when I was a baby. (*She leaves them together and chats with* JENNY.)

MRS BAINES Have you been shewn over the shelter, Mr Undershaft? You know the work we're doing, of course.

UNDERSHAFT (*very civilly*) The whole nation knows it, Mrs Baines.

MRS BAINES No, sir: the whole nation does not know it, or we should not be crippled as we are for want of money to carry our work through the length and breadth of the land. Let me tell you that there would have been rioting this winter in London but for us.

UNDERSHAFT You really think so?

MRS BAINES I know it. I remember 1886, when you rich gentlemen hardened your hearts against the cry of the poor. They broke the windows of your clubs in Pall Mall.

UNDERSHAFT (*gleaming with approval of their method*) And the Mansion House Fund went up next day from thirty thousand pounds to seventy-nine thousand! I remember quite well.

MRS BAINES Well, wont you help me to get at the people? They wont break windows then. Come here, Price. Let me shew you to this gentleman (PRICE *comes to be inspected*). Do you remember the window breaking?

PRICE My ole father thought it was the revolution, maam.

MRS BAINES Would you break windows now?

PRICE Oh no, maam. The windows of eaven av bin opened to me. I know now that the rich man is a sinner like myself.

RUMMY (*appearing above at the loft door*) Snobby Price!

SNOBBY Wot is it?

RUMMY Your mother's askin for you at the other gate in Cripps's Lane. She's heard about your confession. (PRICE *turns pale.*)

MRS BAINES Go, Mr Price; and pray with her.

JENNY You can go through the shelter, Snobby.

PRICE (*to* MRS BAINES) I couldnt face her now, maam, with all the weight of my sins fresh on me. Tell her she'll find her son at ome, waitin for her in prayer. (*He skulks off through the gate, incidentally stealing the sovereign on his way out by picking up his cap from the drum.*)

MRS BAINES (*with swimming eyes*) You see how we take the anger and the bitterness against you out of their hearts, Mr Undershaft.

UNDERSHAFT It is certainly most convenient and gratifying to all large employers of labor, Mrs Baines.

MRS BAINES Barbara: Jenny: I have good news: most wonderful news. (JENNY *runs to her.*) My prayers have been answered. I told you they would, Jenny, didnt I?

JENNY Yes, yes.

BARBARA (*moving nearer to the drum*) Have we got money enough to keep the shelter open?

MRS BAINES I hope we shall have enough to keep all the shelters open. Lord Saxmundham has promised us five thousand pounds—

BARBARA Hooray!

JENNY Glory!

MRS BAINES —if—

BARBARA "If?" If what?

MRS BAINES —if five other gentlemen will give a thousand each to make it up to ten thousand.

BARBARA Who is Lord Saxmundham? I never heard of him.

UNDERSHAFT (*who has pricked up his ears at the peer's name, and is now watching* BARBARA *curiously*) A new creation, my dear. You have heard of Sir Horace Bodger?

BARBARA Bodger! Do you mean the distiller? Bodger's whisky!

UNDERSHAFT That is the man. He is one of the greatest of our public benefactors. He restored the cathedral at Hakington. They made him a baronet for that. He gave half a million to the funds of his party: they made him a baron for that.

SHIRLEY What will they give him for the five thousand?

UNDERSHAFT There is nothing left to give him. So the five thousand, I should think, is to save his soul.

MRS BAINES Heaven grant it may! Oh Mr Undershaft, you have some very rich friends. Cant you help us towards the other five thousand? We are going to hold a great meeting this afternoon at the Assembly Hall in the Mile End Road. If I could only announce that one gentleman had come forward to support Lord Saxmundham, others would follow. Dont you know somebody? couldnt you? wouldnt you? (*her eyes fill with tears*) oh, think of those poor people, Mr Undershaft: think of how much it means to them, and how little to a great man like you.

UNDERSHAFT (*sardonically gallant*) Mrs Baines: you are irresistible. I cant disappoint you; and I cant deny myself the satisfaction of making Bodger pay up. You shall have your five thousand pounds.

MRS BAINES Thank God!

UNDERSHAFT You dont thank me?

MRS BAINES Oh sir, dont try to be cynical: dont be ashamed of being a good man. The Lord will bless you abundantly; and our prayers will be like a strong fortification round you all the days of your life. (*with a touch of caution*) You will let me have the cheque to shew at the meeting, wont you? Jenny: go in and fetch a pen and ink. (JENNY *runs to the shelter door.*)

UNDERSHAFT Do not disturb Miss Hill: I have a fountain pen. (JENNY *halts. He sits at the table and writes the cheque.* CUSINS *rises to make room for him. They all watch him silently.*)

BILL (*cynically, aside to* BARBARA, *his voice and accent horribly debased*) Wot prawce selvytion nah?

BARBARA Stop. (UNDERSHAFT *stops writing: they all turn to her in surprise.*) Mrs Baines: are you really going to take this money?

MRS BAINES (*astonished*) Why not, dear?

BARBARA Why not! Do you know what my father is? Have you forgotten that Lord Saxmundham is Bodger the whisky man? Do you remember how we implored the County Council to stop him from writing Bodger's Whisky in letters of fire against the sky; so that the poor drink-ruined creatures on the Embankment could not wake up from their snatches of sleep without being reminded of their deadly thirst by that wicked sky sign? Do you know that the worst thing I have had to fight here is not the devil, but Bodger, Bodger, Bodger, with his whisky, his distilleries, and his tied houses? Are you going to make our shelter another tied house for him, and ask me to keep it?

BILL Rotten dranken whisky it is too.

MRS BAINES Dear Barbara: Lord Saxmundham has a soul to be saved like any of us. If heaven had found the way to make a good use of his money, are we to set ourselves up against the answer to our prayers?

BARBARA I know he has a soul to be saved. Let him come down here; and I'll do my best to help him to his salvation. But he wants to send his cheque down to buy us, and go on being as wicked as ever.

UNDERSHAFT (*with a reasonableness which* CUSINS *alone perceives to be ironical*) My dear Barbara: alcohol is a very necessary article. It heals the sick—

BARBARA It does nothing of the sort.

UNDERSHAFT Well, it assists the doctor: that is perhaps a less questionable way of putting it. It makes life bearable to millions of people who could not endure their existence if they were quite sober. It enables Parliament to do things at eleven at night that no sane person would do at eleven in the morning. Is it Bodger's fault that this inestimable gift is deplorably abused by less than one per cent of the poor? (*He turns again to the table; signs the cheque; and crosses it.*)

MRS BAINES Barbara: will there be less drinking or more if all those poor souls we are saving come tomorrow and find the doors of our shelters shut in their faces? Lord Saxmundham gives us the money to stop drinking—to take his own business from him.

CUSINS (*impishly*) Pure self-sacrifice on Bodger's part, clearly! Bless dear Bodger! (BARBARA *almost breaks down as* ADOLPHUS, *too, fails her.*)

UNDERSHAFT (*tearing out the cheque and pocketing the book as he rises and goes past* CUSINS *to* MRS BAINES) I also, Mrs Baines, may claim a little disinterestedness. Think of my business! think of the widows and orphans! the men and lads torn to pieces with shrapnel and poisoned with lyddite! (MRS BAINES *shrinks; but he goes on remorselessly.*) the oceans of blood, not one drop of which is shed in a really just cause! the ravaged crops! the peaceful peasants forced, women and men, to till their fields under the fire of opposing armies on pain of starvation! the bad blood of the fierce little cowards at home who egg on others to fight for the gratification of their national vanity! All this makes money for me: I am never richer, never busier than when the papers are full of it. Well, it is your work to preach peace on earth and good will to men. (MRS BAINES*'s face lights up again.*) Every convert you make is a vote against war. (*Her lips move in prayer.*) Yet I give you this money to help you to hasten my own commercial ruin. (*He gives her the cheque.*)

CUSINS (*mounting the form in an ecstasy of mischief*) The millennium will be inaugurated by the unselfishness of Undershaft and Bodger. Oh be joyful! (*He takes the drumsticks from his pocket and flourishes them.*)

MRS BAINES (*taking the cheque*) The longer I live the more proof I see that there is an Infinite Goodness that turns everything to the work of salvation sooner or later. Who would have thought that any good could have come out of war and drink? And yet their profits are brought today to the feet of salvation to do its blessed work. (*She is affected to tears.*)

JENNY (*running to* MRS BAINES *and throwing her arms round her*) Oh dear! how blessed, how glorious it all is!

CUSINS (*in a convulsion of irony*) Let us seize this unspeakable moment. Let us march to the great meeting at once. Excuse me just an instant. (*He rushes into the shelter.* JENNY *takes her tambourine from the drum head.*)

MRS BAINES Mr Undershaft: have you ever seen a thousand people fall on their knees with one impulse and pray? Come with us to the meeting. Barbara shall tell them that the Army is saved, and saved through you.

CUSINS (*returning impetuously from the shelter with a flag and a trombone, and coming between* MRS BAINES *and* UNDERSHAFT) You shall carry the flag down the first street, Mrs Baines. (*He gives her the flag.*) Mr Undershaft is a gifted trombonist: he shall intone an Olympian diapason to the West Ham Salvation March. (*Aside to* UNDERSHAFT, *as he forces the trombone on him.*) Blow, Machiavelli, blow.

UNDERSHAFT (*aside to him, as he takes the trombone*) The Trumpet in Zion! (CUSINS *rushes to the drum, which he takes up and puts on.* UNDERSHAFT *continues, aloud.*) I will do my best. I could vamp a bass if I knew the tune.

CUSINS It is a wedding chorus from one of Donizetti's operas; but we have converted it. We convert everything to good here, including Bodger. You remember the chorus. 'For thee immense rejoicing—immenso giubilo—immenso giubilo.' (*with drum obbligato*) Rum tum ti tum tum, tum tum ti ta—

BARBARA Dolly: you are breaking my heart.

CUSINS What is a broken heart more or less here? Dionysos Undershaft has descended. I am possessed.

MRS BAINES Come, Barbara: I must have my dear Major to carry the flag with me.

JENNY Yes, yes, Major darling.

CUSINS (*snatches the tambourine out of* JENNY'S *hand and mutely offers it to* BARBARA)

BARBARA (*coming forward a little as she puts the offer behind her with a shudder, whilst* CUSINS *recklessly tosses the tambourine back to* JENNY *and goes to the gate*) I cant come.

JENNY Not come!

MRS BAINES (*with tears in her eyes*) Barbara: do you think I am wrong to take the money?

BARBARA (*impulsively going to her and kissing her*) No, no: God help you, dear, you must: you are saving the Army. Go; and may you have a great meeting!

JENNY But arnt you coming?

BARBARA No. (*She begins taking off the silver S brooch from her collar.*)

MRS BAINES Barbara: what are you doing?

JENNY Why are you taking your badge off? You cant be going to leave us, Major.

BARBARA (*quietly*) Father: come here.

UNDERSHAFT (*coming to her*) My dear! (*Seeing that she is going to pin the badge on his collar, he retreats to the penthouse in some alarm.*)

BARBARA (*following him*) Don't be frightened. (*She pins the badge on and steps back towards the table, shewing him to the others.*) There! It's not much for £5000, is it?

MRS BAINES Barbara: if you wont come and pray with us, promise me you will pray for us.

BARBARA I cant pray now. Perhaps I shall never pray again.

MRS BAINES Barbara!

JENNY Major!

BARBARA (*almost delirious*) I cant bear any more. Quick march!

CUSINS (*calling to the procession in the street outside*) Off we go. Play up, there! Immenso giubilo. (*He gives the time with his drum; and the band strikes up the march, which rapidly becomes more distant as the procession moves briskly away.*)

MRS BAINES I must go, dear. Youre overworked: you will be all right tomorrow. We'll never lose you. Now Jenny: step out with the old flag. Blood and Fire! (*She marches out through the gate with her flag.*)

JENNY Glory Hallelujah! (*flourishing her tambourine and marching*)

UNDERSHAFT (*to* CUSINS, *as he marches out past him easing the slide of his trombone*) "My ducats and my daughter"!

CUSINS (*following him out*) Money and gunpowder!

BARBARA Drunkenness and Murder! My God: why has thou forsaken me?

(*She sinks on the form with her face buried in her hands. The march passes away into silence.* BILL WALKER *steals across to her.*)

BILL (*taunting*) Wot prawce selvytion nah?

SHIRLEY Don't you hit her when she's down.

BILL She it me wen aw wiz dahn. Waw shouldnt Aw git a bit o me aown beck?

BARBARA (*raising her head*) I didnt take your money, Bill. (*She crosses the yard to the gate and turns her back on the two men to hide her face from them.*)

BILL (*sneering after her*) Naow, it warnt enaff for you. (*Turning to the drum, he misses the money.*) Ellow! If you aint took it sammun else ez. Weres it gorn? Bly me if Jenny Ill didnt tike it arter all!

RUMMY (*screaming at him from the loft*) You lie, you dirty blackguard! Snobby Price pinched it off the drum when he took up his cap. I was up here all the time an see im do it.

BILL Wot! Stowl may manney! Waw didnt you call thief on him, you silly aold macker you?

RUMMY To serve you aht for ittin me acrost the fice. It's cost y'pahnd, that az. (*raising a pœn of squalid triumph*) I done you. I'm even with you. Uve ad it aht o y— (BILL *snatches up* SHIRLEY's *mug and hurls it at her. She slams the loft door and vanishes. The mug smashes against the door and falls in fragments.*)

BILL (*beginning to chuckle*) Tell us, aol menn, wot o'clock this mawnin was it wen im as they call Snobby Prawce was sived?

BARBARA (*turning to him more composedly, and with unspoiled sweetness*) About half past twelve, Bill. And he pinched your pound at a quarter to two. *I* know. Well, you cant afford to lose it. I'll send it to you.

BILL (*his voice and accent suddenly improving*) Not if Aw wiz to stawve for it. Aw aint to be bought.

SHIRLEY Aint you? Youd sell yourself to the devil for a pint o beer; only there aint no devil to make the offer.

BILL (*unashamed*) Sao Aw would, mite, and often ev, cheerful. But she cawnt baw me. (*approaching* BARBARA) You wanted maw soul, did you? Well, you aint got it.

BARBARA I nearly got it, Bill. But weve sold it back to you for ten thousand pounds.

SHIRLEY And dear at the money!

BARBARA No, Peter: it was worth more than money.

BILL (*salvationproof*) It's nao good: you cawnt get rahnd me nah. Aw downt blieve in it; and Awve seen tody that Aw was rawt. (*going*) Sao long, aol soupkitchener! Ta, ta, Mijor Earl's Grendorter! (*turning at the gate*) Wot prawce selvytion nah? Snobby Prawce! Ha! ha!

BARBARA (*offering her hand*) Goodbye, Bill.

BILL (*taken aback, half plucks his cap off; then shoves it on again defiantly*) Get aht. (BARBARA *drops her hand, discouraged. He has a twinge of remorse.*) But thets aw rawt, you knaow. Nathink pasnl. Naow mellice. Sao long, Judy. (*He goes.*)

BARBARA No malice. So long, Bill.

SHIRLEY (*shaking his head*) You make too much of him, miss, in your innocence.

BARBARA (*going to him*) Peter: I'm like you now. Cleaned out, and lost my job.

SHIRLEY Youve youth an hope. Thats two better than me.

BARBARA I'll get you a job, Peter. Thats hope for you: the youth will have to be enough for me. (*She counts her money.*) I have just enough left for two teas at Lockharts, a Rowton doss for you, and my tram and bus home. (*He frowns and rises with offended pride. She takes his arm.*) Dont be proud, Peter: it's sharing between friends. And promise me youll talk to me and not let me cry. (*She draws him toward the gate.*)

SHIRLEY Well, I'm not accustomed to talk to the like of you—

BARBARA (*urgently*) Yes, yes: you must talk to me. Tell me about Tom Paine's books and Bradlaugh's lectures. Come along.

SHIRLEY Ah, if you would only read Tom Paine in the proper spirit, miss! (*They go out through the gate together.*)

Act III

Next day after lunch **LADY BRITOMART** *is writing in the library in Wilton Crescent.* **SARAH** *is reading in the armchair near the window.* **BARBARA**, *in ordinary fashionable dress, pale and brooding, is on the settee.* **CHARLES LOMAX** *enters. He starts on seeing* **BARBARA** *fashionably attired and in low spirits.*

LOMAX Youve left off your uniform!

(BARBARA *says nothing; but an expression of pain passes over her face.*)

LADY BRITOMART (*warning him in low tones to be careful*) Charles!

LOMAX (*much concerned, coming behind the settee and bending sympathetically over* BARBARA) I'm awfully sorry, Barbara. You know I helped you all I could with the concertina and so forth. (*momentously*) Still, I have never shut my eyes to the fact that there is a certain amount of tosh about the Salvation Army. Now the claims of the Church of England—

LADY BRITOMART Thats enough, Charles. Speak of something suited to your mental capacity.

LOMAX But surely the Church of England is suited to all our capacities.

BARBARA (*pressing his hand*) Thank you for your sympathy, Cholly. Now go and spoon with Sarah.

LOMAX (*dragging a chair from the writing table and seating himself affectionately by* SARAH*'s side*) How is my ownest today?

SARAH I wish you wouldnt tell Cholly to do things, Barbara. He always comes straight and does them. Cholly: we're going to the works this afternoon.

LOMAX What works?

SARAH The cannon works.

LOMAX What? your governor's shop!

SARAH Yes.

LOMAX Oh I say!

(CUSINS *enters in poor condition. He also starts visibly when he sees* BARBARA *without her uniform.*)

BARBARA I expected you this morning, Dolly. Didnt you guess that?

CUSINS (*sitting down beside her*) I'm sorry. I have only just breakfasted.

SARAH But weve just finished lunch.

BARBARA Have you had one of your bad nights?

CUSINS No: I had rather a good night: in fact, one of the most remarkable nights I have ever passed.

BARBARA The meeting?

CUSINS No: after the meeting.

LADY BRITOMART You should have gone to bed after the meeting. What were you doing?

CUSINS Drinking.

LADY BRITOMART Adolphus!
SARAH Dolly!
BARBARA Dolly!
LOMAX Oh I say!

LADY BRITOMART What were you drinking, may I ask?

CUSINS A most devilish kind of Spanish burgundy, warranted free from added alcohol: a Temperance burgundy in fact. Its richness in natural alcohol made any addition superfluous.

BARBARA Are you joking, Dolly?

CUSINS (*patiently*) No. I have been making a night of it with the nominal head of this household: that is all.

LADY BRITOMART Andrew made you drunk!

CUSINS No: he only provided the wine. I think it was Dionysos who made me drunk. (*to* BARBARA) I told you I was possessed.

LADY BRITOMART Youre not sober yet. Go home to bed at once.

CUSINS I have never before ventured to reproach you, Lady Brit; but how could you marry the Prince of Darkness?

LADY BRITOMART It was much more excusable to marry him than to get drunk with him. That is a new accomplishment of Andrew's, by the way. He usent to drink.

CUSINS He doesnt now. He only sat there and completed the wreck of my moral basis, the rout of my convictions, the purchase of my soul. He cares for you, Barbara. That is what makes him so dangerous to me.

BARBARA That has nothing to do with it, Dolly. There are larger loves and diviner dreams than the fireside ones. You know that, dont you?

CUSINS Yes: that is our understanding. I know it. I hold to it. Unless he can win me on that holier ground he may amuse me for a while; but he can get no deeper hold, strong as he is.

BARBARA Keep to that; and the end will be right. Now tell me what happened at the meeting?

CUSINS It was an amazing meeting. Mrs Baines almost died of emotion. Jenny Hill simply gibbered with hysteria. The Prince of Darkness played his trombone like a madman: its brazen roarings were like the laughter of the damned. 117 conversions took place then and there. They prayed with the most touching sincerity and gratitude for Bodger, and for the anonymous donor of the £5000. Your father would not let his name be given.

LOMAX That was rather fine of the old man, you know. Most chaps would have wanted the advertisement.

CUSINS He said all the charitable institutions would be down on him like kites on a battle-field if he gave his name.

LADY BRITOMART Thats Andrew all over. He never does a proper thing without giving an improper reason for it.

CUSINS He convinced me that I have all my life been doing improper things for proper reasons.

LADY BRITOMART Adolphus: now that Barbara has left the Salvation Army, you had better leave it too. I will not have you playing that drum in the streets.

CUSINS Your orders are already obeyed, Lady Brit.

BARBARA Dolly: were you ever really in earnest about it? Would you have joined if you had never seen me?

CUSINS (*disingenuously*) Well—er—well, possibly, as a collector of religions—

LOMAX (*cunningly*) Not as a drummer, though, you know. You are a very clear-headed brainy chap, Dolly; and it must have been apparent to you that there is a certain amount of tosh about—

LADY BRITOMART Charles: if you must drivel, drivel like a grown-up man and not like a schoolboy.

LOMAX (*out of countenance*) Well, drivel is drivel, dont you know, whatever a man's age.

LADY BRITOMART In good society in England, Charles, men drivel at all ages by repeating silly formulas with an air of wisdom. Schoolboys make their own formulas out of slang, like you. When they reach your age, and get political private secretaryships and things of that sort, they drop slang and get their formulas out of the Spectator or The Times. You had better confine yourself to The Times. You will find that there is a certain amount of tosh about The Times; but at least its language is reputable.

LOMAX (*overwhelmed*) You are so awfully strong-minded, Lady Brit—

LADY BRITOMART Rubbish! (MORRISON *comes in.*) What is it?

MORRISON If you please, my lady, Mr Undershaft has just drove up to the door.

LADY BRITOMART Well, let him in. (MORRISON *hesitates.*) Whats the matter with you?

MORRISON Shall I announce him, my lady; or is he at home here, so to speak, my lady?

LADY BRITOMART Announce him.

MORRISON Thank you, my lady. You wont mind my asking, I hope. The occasion is in a manner of speaking new to me.

LADY BRITOMART Quite right. Go and let him in.

MORRISON Thank you, my lady. (*He withdraws.*)

LADY BRITOMART Children: go and get ready. (SARAH *and* BARBARA *go upstairs for their out-of-door wraps.*) Charles: go and tell Stephen to come down here in five minutes: you will find him in the drawing room. (CHARLES *goes.*) Adolphus: tell them to send round the carriage in about fifteen minutes. (ADOLPHUS *goes.*)

MORRISON (*at the door*) Mr Undershaft.

(UNDERSHAFT *comes in.* MORRISON *goes out.*)

UNDERSHAFT Alone! How fortunate!

LADY BRITOMART (*rising*) Dont be sentimental, Andrew. Sit down. (*She sits on the settee: he sits beside her, on her left. She comes to the point before he has time to breathe.*) Sarah must have £800 a year until Charles Lomax comes into his property. Barbara will need more, and need it permanently, because Adolphus hasnt any property.

UNDERSHAFT (*resignedly*) Yes, my dear: I will see to it. Anything else? for yourself, for instance?

LADY BRITOMART I want to talk to you about Stephen.

UNDERSHAFT (*rather wearily*) Dont, my dear. Stephen doesnt interest me.

LADY BRITOMART He does interest me. He is our son.

UNDERSHAFT Do you really think so? He has induced us to bring him into the world; but he chose his parents very incongruously, I think. I see nothing of myself in him, and less of you.

LADY BRITOMART Andrew: Stephen is an excellent son, and a most steady, capable, highminded young man. You are simply trying to find an excuse for disinheriting him.

UNDERSHAFT My dear Biddy: the Undershaft tradition disinherits him. It would be dishonest of me to leave the cannon foundry to my son.

LADY BRITOMART It would be most unnatural and improper of you to leave it to anyone else, Andrew. Do you suppose this wicked and immoral tradition can be kept up for ever? Do you pretend that Stephen could not carry on the foundry just as well as all the other sons of the big business houses?

UNDERSHAFT Yes: he could learn the office routine without understanding the business, like all the other sons; and the firm would go by its own momentum until the real Undershaft—probably an Italian or a German—would invent a new method and cut him out.

LADY BRITOMART There is nothing that any Italian or German could do that Stephen could not do. And Stephen at least has breeding.

UNDERSHAFT The son of a foundling! Nonsense!

LADY BRITOMART My son, Andrew! And even you may have good blood in your veins for all you know.

UNDERSHAFT True. Probably I have. That is another argument in favour of a foundling.

LADY BRITOMART Andrew: dont be aggravating. And dont be wicked. At present you are both.

UNDERSHAFT This conversation is part of the Undershaft tradition, Biddy. Every Undershaft's wife has treated him to it ever since the house was founded. It is mere waste of breath. If the tradition be ever broken it will be for an abler man than Stephen.

LADY BRITOMART (*pouting*) Then go away.

UNDERSHAFT (*deprecatory*) Go away!

LADY BRITOMART Yes: go away. If you will do nothing for Stephen, you are not wanted here. Go to your foundling, whoever he is; and look after him.

UNDERSHAFT The fact is, Biddy—

LADY BRITOMART Dont call me Biddy. I dont call you Andy.

UNDERSHAFT I will not call my wife Britomart: it is not good sense. Seriously, my love, the Undershaft tradition has landed me in a difficulty. I am getting on in years; and my partner Lazarus has at last made a stand and insisted that the succession must be settled one way or the other; and of course he is quite right. You see, I havent found a fit successor yet.

LADY BRITOMART (*obstinately*) There is Stephen.

UNDERSHAFT Thats just it: all the foundlings I can find are exactly like Stephen.

LADY BRITOMART Andrew!!

UNDERSHAFT I want a man with no relations and no schooling: that is, a man who would be out of the running altogether if he were not a strong man. And I cant find him. Every blessed foundling nowadays is snapped up in his infancy by Barnardo homes, or School Board officers, or Boards of Guardians; and if he shews the least ability he is fastened on by schoolmasters; trained to win scholarships like a racehorse; crammed with second-hand ideas; drilled and disciplined in docility and what they call good taste; and lamed for life so that he is fit for nothing but teaching. If you want to keep the foundry in the family, you had better find an eligible foundling and marry him to Barbara.

LADY BRITOMART Ah! Barbara! Your Pet! You would sacrifice Stephen to Barbara.

UNDERSHAFT Cheerfully. And you, my dear, would boil Barbara to make soup for Stephen.

LADY BRITOMART Andrew: this is not a question of our likings and dislikings: it is a question of duty. It is your duty to make Stephen your successor.

UNDERSHAFT Just as much as it is your duty to submit to your husband. Come, Biddy! these tricks of the governing class are of no use with me. I am one of the governing class myself; and it is waste of time giving tracts to a missionary. I have the power in this matter; and I am not to be hum-bugged into using it for your purposes.

LADY BRITOMART Andrew: you can talk my head off; but you cant change wrong into right. And your tie is all on one side. Put it straight.

UNDERSHAFT (*disconcerted*) It won't stay unless it's pinned (*he fumbles at it with childish grimaces*)—

(STEPHEN *comes in.*)

STEPHEN (*at the door*) I beg your pardon (*about to retire*).

LADY BRITOMART No: come in, Stephen. (STEPHEN *comes forward to his mother's writing table.*)

UNDERSHAFT (*not very cordially*) Good afternoon.

STEPHEN (*coldly*) Good afternoon.

UNDERSHAFT (*to* LADY BRITOMART) He knows all about the tradition, I suppose?

LADY BRITOMART Yes. (*to* STEPHEN) It is what I told you last night, Stephen.

UNDERSHAFT (*sulkily*) I understand you want to come into the cannon business.

STEPHEN *I* go into trade! Certainly not.

UNDERSHAFT (*opening his eyes, greatly eased in mind and manner*) Oh! in that case—

LADY BRITOMART Cannons are not trade, Stephen. They are enterprise.

STEPHEN I have no intention of becoming a man of business in any sense. I have no capacity for business and no taste for it. I intend to devote myself to politics.

UNDERSHAFT (*rising*) My dear boy: this is an immense relief to me. And I trust it may prove an equally good thing for the country. I was afraid you would consider yourself disparaged and slighted. (*He moves towards* STEPHEN *as if to shake hands with him.*)

LADY BRITOMART (*rising and interposing*) Stephen: I cannot allow you to throw away an enormous property like this.

STEPHEN (*stiffly*) Mother: there must be an end of treating me as a child, if you please. (LADY BRITOMART *recoils, deeply wounded by his tone.*) Until last night I did not take your attitude seriously, because I did not think you meant it seriously. But I find now that you left me in the dark as to matters which you should have explained to me years ago. I am extremely hurt and offended. Any further discussion of my intentions had better take place with my father, as between one man and another.

LADY BRITOMART Stephen! (*She sits down again, her eyes filling with tears.*)

UNDERSHAFT (*with grave compassion*) You see, my dear, it is only the big men who can be treated as children.

STEPHEN I am sorry, mother, that you have forced me—

UNDERSHAFT (*stopping him*) Yes, yes, yes, yes: thats all right, Stephen. She wont interfere with you any more: your independence is achieved: you have won your latchkey. Dont rub it in; and above all, dont apologize. (*He resumes his seat.*) Now what about your future, as between one man and another—I beg your pardon, Biddy: as between two men and a woman.

LADY BRITOMART (*who has pulled herself together strongly*) I quite understand, Stephen. By all means go your own way if you feel strong enough. (STEPHEN *sits down magisterially in the chair at the writing table with an air of affirming his majority.*)

UNDERSHAFT It is settled that you do not ask for the succession to the cannon business.

STEPHEN I hope it is settled that I repudiate the cannon business.

UNDERSHAFT Come, come! dont be so devilishly sulky: it's boyish. Freedom should be generous. Besides, I owe you a fair start in life in exchange for disinheriting you. You cant become prime minister all at once. Havent you a turn for something? What about literature, art, and so forth?

STEPHEN I have nothing of the artist about me, either in faculty or character, thank Heaven!

UNDERSHAFT A philosopher, perhaps? Eh?

STEPHEN I make no such ridiculous pretension.

UNDERSHAFT Just so. Well, there is the army, the navy, the Church, the Bar. The Bar requires some ability. What about the Bar?

STEPHEN I have not studied law. And I am afraid I have not the necessary push—I believe that is the name barristers give to their vulgarity—for success in pleading.

UNDERSHAFT Rather a difficult case, Stephen. Hardly anything left but the stage, is there? (STEPHEN *makes an impatient movement.*) Well, come! is there anything you know or care for?

STEPHEN (*rising and looking at him steadily*) I know the difference between right and wrong.

UNDERSHAFT (*hugely tickled*) You dont say so! What! no capacity for business, no knowledge of law, no sympathy with art, no pretension to philosophy; only a simple knowledge of the secret that has puzzled all the philosophers, baffled all the lawyers, muddled all the men of business, and ruined most of the artists: the secret of right and wrong. Why, man, youre a genius, a master of masters, a god! At twenty-four, too!

STEPHEN (*keeping his temper with difficulty*) You are pleased to be facetious. I pretend to nothing more than any honorable English gentleman claims as his birthright (*he sits down angrily*).

UNDERSHAFT Oh, thats everybody's birthright. Look at poor little Jenny Hill, the Salvation lassie! she would think you were laughing at her if you asked her to stand up in the street and teach grammar or geography or mathematics or even drawing room dancing; but it never occurs to her to doubt that she can teach morals and religion. You are all alike, you respectable people. You cant tell me the bursting strain of a ten-inch gun, which is a very simple matter; but you all think you can tell me the bursting strain of a man under temptation. You darent handle high explosives; but youre all ready to handle honesty and truth and justice and the whole duty of man, and kill one another at that game. What a country! What a world!

LADY BRITOMART (*uneasily*) What do you think he had better do, Andrew?

UNDERSHAFT Oh, just what he wants to do. He knows nothing and he thinks he knows everything. That points clearly to a political career. Get him a private secretaryship to someone who can get him an Under Secretaryship; and then leave him alone. He will find his natural and proper place in the end on the Treasury Bench.

STEPHEN (*springing up again*) I am sorry, sir, that you force me to forget the respect due to you as my father. I am an Englishman and I will not hear the Government of my country insulted. (*He thrusts his hands in his pockets, and walks angrily across to the window.*)

UNDERSHAFT (*with a touch of brutality*) The government of your country! *I* am the government of your country: I, and Lazarus. Do you suppose that you and half a dozen amateurs like you, sitting in a row in that foolish gabble shop, can govern Undershaft and Lazarus? No, my friend: you will do what pays us. You will make war when it suits us, and keep peace when it doesnt. You will find out that trade requires certain measures when we have decided on those measures. When I want anything to keep my dividends up, you will discover that my want is a national need. When other people want something to keep my dividends down, you will call out the police and military. And in return you shall have the support and applause of my newspapers, and the delight of imagining that you are a great statesman. Government of your country! Be off with you, my boy, and play with your caucuses and leading articles and historic parties and great leaders and burning questions and the rest of your toys. *I* am going back to my counting-house to pay the piper and call the tune.

STEPHEN (*actually smiling, and putting his hand on his father's shoulder with indulgent patronage*) Really, my dear father, it is impossible to be angry with you. You dont know how absurd all this sounds to me. You are very properly proud of having been industrious enough to make money; and it is greatly to your credit that you have made so much of it. But it has kept you in circles where you are valued for your money and deferred to for it, instead of in the doubtless very old-fashioned and behind-the-times public school and university where I formed my habits of mind. It is natural for you to think that money governs England; but you must allow me to think I know better.

UNDERSHAFT And what does govern England, pray?

STEPHEN Character, father, character.

UNDERSHAFT Whose character? Yours or mine?

STEPHEN Neither yours nor mine, father, but the best elements in the English national character.

UNDERSHAFT Stephen: Ive found your profession for you. Youre a born journalist. I'll start you with a high-toned weekly review. There!

(*Before* STEPHEN *can reply* SARAH, BARBARA, LOMAX, *and* CUSINS *come in ready for walking.* BARBARA *crosses the room to the window and looks out.* CUSINS *drifts amiably to the armchair.* LOMAX *remains near the door, whilst* SARAH *comes to her mother.*

STEPHEN *goes to the smaller writing table and busies himself with his letters.*)

SARAH Go and get ready, mamma: the carriage is waiting. (LADY BRITOMART *leaves the room.*)

UNDERSHAFT (*to* SARAH) Good day, my dear. Good afternoon, Mr Lomax.

LOMAX (*vaguely*) Ahdedoo.

UNDERSHAFT (*to* CUSINS) Quite well after last night, Euripides, eh?

CUSINS As well as can be expected.

UNDERSHAFT Thats right. (*to* BARBARA) So you are coming to see my death and devastation factory, Barbara?

BARBARA (*at the window*) You came yesterday to see my salvation factory. I promised you a return visit.

LOMAX (*coming forward between* SARAH *and* UNDERSHAFT) You'll find it awfully interesting. Ive been through the Woolwich Arsenal and it gives you a ripping feeling of security, you know, to think of the lot of beggars we could kill if it came to fighting. (*to* UNDERSHAFT, *with sudden solemnity*) Still, it must be rather an awful reflection for you, from the religious point of view as it were. Youre getting on, you know, and all that.

SARAH You dont mind Cholly's imbecility, papa, do you?

LOMAX (*much taken aback*) Oh I say!

UNDERSHAFT Mr Lomax looks at the matter in a very proper spirit, my dear.

LOMAX Just so. Thats all I meant, I assure you.

SARAH Are you coming, Stephen?

STEPHEN Well, I am rather busy—er— (*magnanimously*) Oh well, yes: I'll come. That is, if there is room for me.

UNDERSHAFT I can take two with me in a little motor I am experimenting with for field use. You wont mind its being rather unfashionable. It's not painted yet; but it's bullet proof.

LOMAX (*appalled at the prospect of confronting Wilton Crescent in an unpainted motor*) Oh I say!

SARAH The carriage for me, thank you. Barbara doesnt mind what she's seen in.

LOMAX I say, Dolly, old chap: do you really mind the car being a guy? Because of course if you do I'll go in it. Still—

CUSINS I prefer it.

LOMAX Thanks awfully, old man. Come, my ownest. (*He hurries out to secure his seat in the carriage.* SARAH *follows him.*)

CUSINS (*moodily walking across to* LADY BRITOMART'S *writing table*) Why are we two coming to this Works Department of Hell? that is what I ask myself.

BARBARA I have always thought of it as a sort of pit where lost creatures with blackened faces stirred up smoky fires and were driven and tormented by my father. Is it like that, dad?

UNDERSHAFT (*scandalized*) My dear! It is a spotlessly clean and beautiful hillside town.

CUSINS With a Methodist chapel? Oh do say theres a Methodist chapel.

UNDERSHAFT There are two: a Primitive one and a sophisticated one. There is even an Ethical Society; but it is not much patronized, as my men are all strongly religious. In the High Explosives Sheds they object to the presence of Agnostics as unsafe.

CUSINS And yet they dont object to you!

BARBARA Do they obey all your orders?

UNDERSHAFT I never give them any orders. When I speak to one of them it is "Well, Jones, is the baby doing well? and has Mrs Jones made a good recovery?" "Nicely, thank you, sir." And thats all.

CUSINS But Jones has to be kept in order. How do you maintain discipline among your men?

UNDERSHAFT I dont. They do. You see, the one thing Jones wont stand is any rebellion from the man under him, or any assertion of social equality between the wife of the man with 4 shillings a week less than himself, and Mrs Jones! Of course they all rebel against me, theoretically. Practically, every man of them keeps the man just below him in his place. I never meddle with them. I never bully them. I dont even bully Lazarus. I say that certain things are to be done; but I dont order anybody to do them. I dont say, mind you, that there is no ordering about and snubbing and even bullying. The men snub the boys and order them about; the carmen snub the sweepers; the artisans snub the unskilled laborers; the foremen drive and bully both the laborers and artisans; the assistant engineers find fault with the foremen; the chief engineers drop on the assistants; the departmental managers worry the chiefs; and the clerks have tall hats and hymnbooks and keep up the social tone by refusing to associate on equal terms with anybody. The result is a colossal profit, which comes to me.

CUSINS (*revolted*) You really are a—well, what I was saying yesterday.

BARBARA What was he saying yesterday?

UNDERSHAFT Never mind, my dear. He thinks I have made you unhappy. Have I?

BARBARA Do you think I can be happy in this vulgar silly dress? I! who have worn the uniform. Do you understand what you have done to me? Yesterday I had a man's soul in my hand. I set him in the way of life with his face to salvation. But when we took your money he turned back to drunkenness and derision. (*with intense conviction*) I will never forgive you that. If I had a child, and you destroyed its body with your explosives—if you murdered Dolly with your horrible guns—I could forgive you if my forgiveness would open the gates of heaven to you. But to take a human soul from me, and turn it into the soul of a wolf! that is worse than any murder.

UNDERSHAFT Does my daughter despair so easily? Can you strike a man to the heart and leave no mark on him?

BARBARA (*her face lighting up*) Oh, you are right: he can never be lost now: where was my faith?

CUSINS Oh, clever clever devil!

BARBARA You may be a devil; but God speaks through you sometimes. (*She takes her father's hands and kisses them.*) You have given me back my happiness: I feel it deep down now, though my spirit is troubled.

UNDERSHAFT You have learnt something. That always feels at first as if you had lost something.

BARBARA Well, take me to the factory of death; and let me learn something more. There must be some truth or other behind all this frightful irony. Come, Dolly. (*She goes out.*)

CUSINS My guardian angel! (*to* UNDERSHAFT) Avaunt! (*He follows* BARBARA.)

STEPHEN (*quietly, at the writing table*) You must not mind Cusins, father. He is a very amiable good fellow; but he is a Greek scholar and naturally a little eccentric.

UNDERSHAFT Ah, quite so. Thank you, Stephen. Thank you. (*He goes out.*)

(STEPHEN *smiles patronizingly; buttons his coat responsibly; and crosses the room to the door.* LADY BRITOMART, *dressed for out-of-doors, opens it before he reaches it. She looks round for the others; looks at* STEPHEN *and turns to go without a word.*)

STEPHEN (*embarrassed*) Mother—

LADY BRITOMART Dont be apologetic, Stephen. And dont forget that you have outgrown your mother. (*She goes out.*)

Perivale St Andrews lies between two Middlesex hills, half climbing the northern one. It is an almost smokeless town of white walls, roofs of narrow green slates or red tiles, tall trees, domes, campaniles, and slender chimney shafts, beautifully situated and beautiful in itself. The best view of it is obtained from the crest of a slope about half a mile to the east, where the high explosives are dealt with. The foundry lies hidden in the depths between, the tops of its chimneys sprouting like huge skittles into the middle distance. Across the crest runs an emplacement of concrete, with a firestep, and a parapet which suggests a fortification, because there is a huge cannon of the obsolete Woolwich Infant pattern peering across it at the town. The cannon is mounted on an experimental gun carriage: possibly the original model of the UNDERSHAFT *disappearing rampart gun alluded to by* STEPHEN. *The firestep, being a convenient place to sit, is furnished here and there with straw disc cushions; and at one place there is the additional luxury of a fur rug.*

BARBARA *is standing on the firestep, looking over the parapet towards the town. On her right is the cannon; on her left the end of a shed raised on piles, with a ladder of three or four steps up to the door, which opens outwards and has a little wooden landing at the threshold, with a fire bucket in the corner of the landing. Several dummy soldiers more or less mutilated, with straw protruding from their gashes, have been shoved out of the way under the landing. A few others are nearly upright against the shed; and one has fallen forward and lies, like a grotesque corpse, on the emplacement. The parapet stops short of the shed, leaving a gap which is the beginning of the path down the hill through the foundry to the town. The rug is on the firestep near this gap. Down on the emplacement behind the cannon is a trolley carrying a huge conical bombshell with a red band painted on it. Further to the right is the door of an office, which, like the sheds, is of the lightest possible construction.*

CUSINS *arrives by the path from the town.*

BARBARA Well?

CUSINS Not a ray of hope. Everything perfect! wonderful! real! It only needs a cathedral to be a heavenly city instead of a hellish one.

BARBARA Have you found out whether they have done anything for old Peter Shirley?

CUSINS They have found him a job as gatekeeper and timekeeper. He's frightfully miserable. He calls the time-keeping brainwork, and says he isnt used to it; and his gate lodge is so splendid that he's ashamed to use the rooms, and skulks in the scullery.

BARBARA Poor Peter!

(STEPHEN *arrives from the town. He carries a fieldglass.*)

STEPHEN (*enthusiastically*) Have you two seen the place? Why did you leave us?

CUSINS I wanted to see everything I was not intended to see; and Barbara wanted to make the men talk.

STEPHEN Have you found anything discreditable?

CUSINS No. They call him Dandy Andy and are proud of his being a cunning old rascal; but it's all horribly, frightfully, immorally, unanswerably perfect.

(SARAH *arrives.*)

SARAH Heavens! what a place! (*She crosses to the trolley.*) Did you see the nursing home? (*She sits down on the shell.*)

STEPHEN Did you see the libraries and schools?

SARAH Did you see the ball room and the banqueting chamber in the Town Hall!?

STEPHEN Have you gone into the insurance fund, the pension fund, the building society, the various applications of cooperation!?

(UNDERSHAFT *comes from the office, with a sheaf of telegrams in his hand.*)

UNDERSHAFT Well, have you seen everything? I'm sorry I was called away. (*indicating the telegrams*) Good news from Manchuria.

STEPHEN Another Japanese victory?

UNDERSHAFT Oh, I dont know. Which side wins does not concern us here. No: the good news is that the aerial battleship is a tremendous success. At the first trial it has wiped out a fort with three hundred soldiers in it.

CUSINS (*from the platform*) Dummy soldiers?

UNDERSHAFT (*striding across to* STEPHEN *and kicking the prostrate dummy brutally out of his way*) No: the real thing.

(CUSINS *and* BARBARA *exchange glances. Then* CUSINS *sits on the step and buries his face in his hands.* BARBARA *gravely lays her hand on his shoulder. He looks up at her in whimsical desperation.*)

UNDERSHAFT Well, Stephen, what do you think of the place?

STEPHEN Oh, magnificent. A perfect triumph of modern industry. Frankly, my dear father, I have been a fool: I had no idea of what it all meant: of the wonderful forethought, the power of organization, the administrative capacity, the financial genius, the colossal capital it represents. I have been repeating to myself as I came through your streets "Peace hath her victories no less renowned than War." I have only one misgiving about it all.

UNDERSHAFT Out with it.

STEPHEN Well, I cannot help thinking that all this provision for every want of your workmen may sap their independence and weaken their sense of responsibility. And greatly as we enjoyed our tea at that splendid restaurant—how they gave us all that luxury and cake and jam and cream for threepence I really cannot imagine!—still you must remember that restaurants break up home life. Look at the continent, for instance! Are you sure so much pampering is really good for the men's characters?

UNDERSHAFT Well you see, my dear boy, when you are organizing civilization you have to make up your mind whether trouble and anxiety are good things or not. If you decide that they are, then, I take it, you simply dont organize civilization; and there you are, with trouble and anxiety enough to make us all angels! But if you decide the other way, you may as well go through with it. However, Stephen, our characters are safe here. A sufficient dose of anxiety is always provided by the fact that we may be blown to smithereens at any moment.

SARAH By the way, papa, where do you make the explosives?

UNDERSHAFT In separate little sheds like that one. When one of them blows up, it costs very little, and only the people quite close to it are killed.

(STEPHEN, *who is quite close to it, looks at it rather scaredly, and moves away quickly to the cannon. At the same moment the door of the shed is thrown abruptly open; and a foreman in overalls and list slippers comes out on the little landing and holds the door for* LOMAX, *who appears in the doorway.*)

LOMAX (*with studied coolness*) My good fellow: you neednt get into a state of nerves. Nothing's going to happen to you; and I suppose it wouldnt be the end of the world if anything did. A little bit of British pluck is what you want, old chap. (*He descends and strolls across to* SARAH.)

UNDERSHAFT (*to the foreman*) Anything wrong, Bilton?

BILTON (*with ironic calm*) Gentleman walked into the high explosives shed and lit a cigaret, sir: thats all.

UNDERSHAFT Ah, quite so. (*going over to* LOMAX) Do you happen to remember what you did with the match?

LOMAX Oh come! I'm not a fool. I took jolly good care to blow it out before I chucked it away.

BILTON The top of it was red hot inside, sir.

LOMAX Well, suppose it was! I didnt chuck it into any of your messes.

UNDERSHAFT Think no more of it, Mr Lomax. By the way, would you mind lending me your matches.

LOMAX (*offering his box*) Certainly.

UNDERSHAFT Thanks. (*He pockets the matches.*)

LOMAX (*lecturing to the company generally*) You know, these high explosives dont go off like gunpowder, except when theyre in a gun. When theyre spread loose, you can put a match to them without the least risk: they just burn quietly like a bit of paper. (*warming to the scientific interest of the subject*) Did you know that, Undershaft? Have you ever tried?

UNDERSHAFT Not on a large scale, Mr Lomax. Bilton will give you a sample of guncotton when you are leaving if you ask him. You can experiment with it at home. (BILTON *looks puzzled.*)

SARAH Bilton will do nothing of the sort, papa. I suppose it's your business to blow up the Russians and Japs; but you might really stop short of blowing up poor Cholly. (BILTON *gives it up and retires into the shed.*)

LOMAX My ownest, there is no danger. (*He sits beside her on the shell.*)

(LADY BRITOMART *arrives from the town with a bouquet.*)

LADY BRITOMART (*impetuously*) Andrew: you shouldnt have let me see this place.

UNDERSHAFT Why, my dear?

LADY BRITOMART Never mind why: you shouldnt have: thats all. To think of all that (*indicating the town*) being yours! and that you have kept it to yourself all these years!

UNDERSHAFT It does not belong to me. I belong to it. It is the Undershaft inheritance.

LADY BRITOMART It is not. Your ridiculous cannons and that noisy banking foundry may be the Undershaft inheritance; but all that plate and linen, all that furniture and those houses and orchards and gardens belong to us. They belong to me: they are not a man's business. I wont give them up. You must be out of your senses to throw them all away; and if you persist in such folly, I will call in a doctor.

UNDERSHAFT (*stooping to smell the bouquet*) Where did you get the flowers, my dear?

LADY BRITOMART Your men presented them to me in your William Morris Labor Church.

CUSINS Oh! It needed only that. A Labor Church! (*He mounts the firestep distractedly, and leans with his elbows on the parapet, turning his back to them.*)

LADY BRITOMART Yes, with Morris's words in mosaic letters ten feet high around the dome. NO MAN IS GOOD ENOUGH TO BE ANOTHER MAN'S MASTER. The cynicism of it!

UNDERSHAFT It shocked the men at first, I am afraid. But now they take no more notice of it than of the ten commandments in church.

LADY BRITOMART Andrew: you are trying to put me off the subject of the inheritance by profane jokes. Well, you shant. I dont ask it any longer for Stephen: he has inherited far too much of your perversity to be fit for it. But Barbara has rights as well as Stephen. Why should not Adolphus succeed to the inheritance? I could manage the town for him and he can look after the cannons, if they are really necessary.

UNDERSHAFT I should ask nothing better if Adolphus were a foundling. He is exactly the sort of new blood that is wanted in English business. But he's not a foundling; and theres an end of it. (*He makes for the office door.*)

CUSINS (*turning to them*) Not quite. (*They all turn and stare at him.*) I think—Mind! I am not committing myself in any way as to my future course—but I think the foundling difficulty can be got over. (*He jumps down to the emplacement.*)

UNDERSHAFT (*coming back to him*) What do you mean?

CUSINS Well, I have something to say which is in the nature of a confession.

SARAH
LADY BRITOMART
BARBARA
STEPHEN } Confession!

LOMAX Oh I say!

CUSINS Yes, a confession. Listen, all. Until I met Barbara I thought myself in the main an honorable, truthful man, because I wanted the approval of my conscience more than I wanted anything else. But the moment I saw Barbara, I wanted her far more than the approval of my conscience.

LADY BRITOMART Adolphus!

CUSINS It is true. You accused me yourself, Lady Brit, of joining the Army to worship Barbara; and so I did. She bought my soul like a flower at a street corner; but she bought it for herself.

UNDERSHAFT What! Not for Dionysos or another?

CUSINS Dionysos and all the others are in herself. I adored what was divine in her, and was therefore a true worshipper. But I was romantic about her too. I thought she was a woman of the people, and that a marriage with a professor of Greek would be far beyond the wildest social ambitions of her rank.

LADY BRITOMART Adolphus!!

LOMAX Oh I say!!!

CUSINS When I learnt the horrible truth—

LADY BRITOMART What do you mean by the horrible truth, pray?

CUSINS That she was enormously rich; that her grandfather was an earl; that her father was the Prince of Darkness—

UNDERSHAFT Chut!

CUSINS —and that I was only an adventurer trying to catch a rich wife, then I stooped to deceive her about my birth.

BARBARA (*rising*) Dolly!

LADY BRITOMART Your birth! Now Adolphus, dont dare to make up a wicked story for the sake of these wretched cannons. Remember: I have seen photographs of your parents; and the Agent General for South Western Australia knows them personally and has assured me that they are most respectable married people.

CUSINS So they are in Australia; but here they are outcasts. Their marriage is legal in Australia, but not in England. My mother is my father's deceased wife's sister; and in this island I am consequently a foundling. (*sensation*)

BARBARA Silly! (*She climbs to the cannon, and leans, listening, in the angle it makes with the parapet.*)

CUSINS Is the subterfuge good enough, Machiavelli?

UNDERSHAFT (*thoughtfully*) Biddy: this may be a way out of the difficulty.

LADY BRITOMART Stuff! A man cant make cannons any the better for being his own cousin instead of his proper self. (*She sits down on the rug with a bounce that expresses her downright contempt for their casuistry.*)

UNDERSHAFT (*to* CUSINS) You are an educated man. That is against the tradition.

CUSINS Once in ten thousand times it happens that the schoolboy is a born master of what they try to teach him. Greek has not destroyed my mind: it has nourished it. Besides, I did not learn it at an English public school.

UNDERSHAFT Hm! Well, I cannot afford to be too particular: you have cornered the foundling market. Let it pass. You are eligible, Euripides: you are eligible.

BARBARA Dolly: yesterday morning, when Stephen told us all about the tradition, you became very silent, and you have been strange and excited ever since. Were you thinking of your birth then?

CUSINS When the finger of Destiny suddenly points at a man in the middle of his breakfast, it makes him thoughtful.

UNDERSHAFT Aha! You have had your eye on the business, my young friend, have you?

CUSINS Take care! There is an abyss of moral horror between me and your accursed aerial battleships.

UNDERSHAFT Never mind the abyss for the present. Let us settle the practical details and leave your final decision open. You know that you will have to change your name. Do you object to that?

CUSINS Would any man named Adolphus—any man called Dolly!—object to be called something else?

UNDERSHAFT Good. Now, as to money! I propose to treat you handsomely from the beginning. You shall start at a thousand a year.

CUSINS (*with sudden heat, his spectacles twinkling with mischief*) A thousand! You dare offer a miserable thousand to the son-in-law of a millionaire! No, by Heavens, Machiavelli! you shall not cheat me. You cannot do without me; and I can do without you. I must have two thousand five hundred a year for two years. At the end of that time, if I am a failure, I go. But if I am a success, and stay on, you must give me the other five thousand.

UNDERSHAFT What other five thousand?

CUSINS To make the two years up to five thousand a year. The two thousand five hundred is only half pay in case I should turn out a failure. The third year I must have ten per cent on the profits.

UNDERSHAFT (*taken aback*) Ten per cent! Why, man, do you know what my profits are?

CUSINS Enormous, I hope: otherwise I shall require twenty-five per cent.

UNDERSHAFT But, Mr Cusins, this is a serious matter of business. You are not bringing any capital into the concern.

CUSINS What! no capital! Is my mastery of Greek no capital? Is my access to the subtlest thought, the loftiest poetry yet attained by humanity, no capital? My character! my intellect! my life! my career! what Barbara calls my soul! are these no capital? Say another word; and I double my salary.

UNDERSHAFT Be reasonable—

CUSINS (*peremptorily*) Mr Undershaft: you have my terms. Take them or leave them.

UNDERSHAFT (*recovering himself*) Very well, I note your terms; and I offer you half.

CUSINS (*disgusted*) Half!

UNDERSHAFT (*firmly*) Half.

CUSINS You call yourself a gentleman; and you offer me half!

UNDERSHAFT I do not call myself a gentleman; but I offer you half.

CUSINS This to your future partner! your successor! your son-in-law!

BARBARA You are selling your own soul, Dolly, not mine. Leave me out of the bargain, please.

UNDERSHAFT Come! I will go a step further for Barbara's sake. I will give you three fifths; but that is my last word.

CUSINS Done!

LOMAX Done in the eye! Why, *I* get only eight hundred, you know.

CUSINS By the way, Mac, I am a classical scholar not an arithmetical one. Is three fifths more than half or less?

UNDERSHAFT More, of course.

CUSINS I would have taken two hundred and fifty. How you can succeed in business when you are willing to pay all that money to a University don who is obviously not worth a junior clerk's wages!—well! What will Lazarus say?

UNDERSHAFT Lazarus is a gentle romantic Jew who cares for nothing but string quartets and stalls at fashionable theatres. He will be blamed for your rapacity in money matters, poor fellow! as he has hitherto been blamed for mine. You are a shark of the first order, Euripides. So much the better for the firm!

BARBARA Is the bargain closed, Dolly? Does your soul belong to him now?

CUSINS No: the price is settled: that is all. The real tug of war is still to come. What about the moral question?

LADY BRITOMART There is no moral question in the matter at all, Adolphus. You must simply sell cannons and weapons to people whose cause is right and just, and refuse them to foreigners and criminals.

UNDERSHAFT (*determinedly*) No: none of that. You must keep the true faith of an Armorer, or you dont come in here.

CUSINS What on earth is the true faith of an Armorer?

UNDERSHAFT To give arms to all men who offer an honest price for them, without respect of persons or principles: to aristocrat and republican, to Nihilist and Tsar, to Capitalist and Socialist, to Protestant and Catholic, to burglar and policeman, to black man, white man and yellow man, to all sorts and conditions, all nationalities, all faiths, all follies, all causes and all crimes. The first Undershaft wrote up in his shop IF GOD GAVE THE HAND, LET NOT MAN WITHHOLD THE SWORD. The second wrote up ALL HAVE THE RIGHT TO FIGHT: NONE HAVE THE RIGHT TO JUDGE. The third wrote up TO MAN THE WEAPON: TO HEAVEN THE VICTORY. The fourth had no literary turn; so he did not write up anything; but he sold cannons to Napoleon under the nose of George the Third. The fifth wrote up PEACE SHALL NOT PREVAIL SAVE WITH A SWORD IN HER HAND. The sixth, my master, was the best of all. He wrote up NOTHING IS EVER DONE IN THIS WORLD UNTIL MEN ARE PREPARED TO KILL ONE ANOTHER IF IT IS NOT DONE. After that, there was nothing left for the seventh to say. So he wrote up, simply, UNASHAMED.

CUSINS My good Machiavelli. I shall certainly write something up on the wall; only, as I shall write it in Greek, you wont be able to read it. But as to your Armorer's faith, if I take my neck out of the noose of my own morality I am not going to put it into the noose of yours. I shall sell cannons to whom I please and refuse them to whom I please. So there!

UNDERSHAFT From the moment when you become Andrew Undershaft, you will never do as you please again. Dont come here lusting for power, young man.

CUSINS If power were my aim I should not come here for it. You have no power.

UNDERSHAFT None of my own, certainly.

CUSINS I have more power than you, more will. You do not drive this place: it drives you. And what drives the place?

UNDERSHAFT (*enigmatically*) A will of which I am a part.

BARBARA (*startled*) Father! Do you know what you are saying; or are you laying a snare for my soul?

CUSINS Dont listen to his metaphysics, Barbara. The place is driven by the most rascally part of society, the money hunters, the pleasure hunters, the military promotion hunters; and he is their slave.

UNDERSHAFT Not necessarily. Remember the Armorer's Faith. I will take an order from a good man as cheerfully as from a bad one. If you good people prefer preaching and shirking to buying my weapons and fighting the rascals, dont blame me. I can make cannons: I cannot make courage and conviction. Bah! you tire me, Euripides, with your morality mongering. Ask Barbara: she understands. (*He suddenly reaches up and takes* BARBARA'S *hands, looking powerfully into her eyes.*) Tell him, my love, what power really means.

BARBARA (*hypnotized*) Before I joined the Salvation Army, I was in my own power and the consequence was that I never knew what to do with myself. When I joined it, I had not time enough for all the things I had to do.

UNDERSHAFT (*approvingly*) Just so. And why was that, do you suppose?

BARBARA Yesterday I should have said, because I was in the power of God. (*She resumes her self-possession, withdrawing her hands from his with a power equal to his own.*) But you came and shewed me that I was in the power of Bodger and Undershaft. Today I feel—oh! how can I put it into words? Sarah: do you remember the earthquake at Cannes, when we were little children?—how little the surprise of the first shock mattered compared to the dread and horror of waiting for the second? That is how I feel in this place today. I stood on the rock I thought eternal; and without a word of warning it reeled and crumbled under me. I was safe with an infinite wisdom watching me, an army marching to Salvation with me; and in a moment, at a stroke of your pen in a cheque book, I stood alone; and the heavens were empty. That was the first shock of the earthquake: I am waiting for the second.

UNDERSHAFT Come, come, my daughter! dont make too much of your little tinpot tragedy. What do we do here when we spend years of work and thought and thousands of pounds of solid cash on a new gun or an aerial battleship that turns out just a hairsbreadth wrong after all? Scrap it. Scrap it without wasting another hour or another pound on it. Well, you have made for yourself something that you call a morality or a religion or what not. It doesnt fit the facts. Well, scrap it. Scrap it and get one that does fit. That is what is wrong with the world at present. It scraps its obsolete steam engines and dynamos; but it wont scrap its old prejudices and its old moralities and its old religions and its old political constitutions. Whats the result? In machinery it does very well; but in morals and religion and politics it is working at a loss that brings it nearer bankruptcy every year. Dont persist in that folly. If your old religion broke down yesterday, get a newer and a better one for tomorrow.

BARBARA Oh how gladly I would take a better one to my soul! But you offer me a worse one. (*turning on him with sudden vehemence*) Justify yourself: shew me some light through the darkness of this dreadful place, with its beautifully clean workshops, and respectable workmen, and model homes.

UNDERSHAFT Cleanliness and respectability do not need justification, Barbara: they justify themselves. I see no darkness here, no dreadfulness. In your Salvation shelter I saw poverty, misery, cold and hunger. You gave them bread and treacle and dreams of heaven. I give from thirty shillings a week to twelve thousand a year. They find their own dreams but I look after the drainage.

BARBARA And their souls?

UNDERSHAFT I save their souls just as I saved yours.

BARBARA (*revolted*) You saved my soul! What do you mean?

UNDERSHAFT I fed you and clothed you and housed you. I took care that you should have money enough to live handsomely—more than enough; so that you could be wasteful, careless, generous. That saved your soul from the seven deadly sins.

BARBARA (*bewildered*) The seven deadly sins!

UNDERSHAFT Yes, the deadly seven. (*counting on his fingers*) Food, clothing, firing, rent, taxes, respectability and children. Nothing can lift those seven millstones from Man's neck but money and the spirit cannot soar until the millstones are lifted. I lifted them from your spirit. I enabled Barbara to become Major Barbara; and I saved her from the crime of poverty.

CUSINS Do you call poverty a crime?

UNDERSHAFT The worst of crimes. All the other crimes are virtues beside it: all the other dishonors are chivalry itself by comparison. Poverty blights whole cities; spreads horrible pestilences; strikes dead the very souls of all who come within sight, sound, or smell of it. What you call crime is nothing: a murder here and a theft there, a blow now and a curse then: what do they matter? they are only the accidents and illnesses of life: there are not fifty genuine professional criminals in London. But there are millions of poor people, abject people, dirty people, ill fed, ill clothed people. They poison us morally and physically: they kill the happiness of society: they force us to do away with our own liberties and to organize unnatural cruelties for fear they should rise against us and drag us down into their abyss. Only fools fear crime: we all fear poverty. Pah! (*turning on* BARBARA) you talk of your half-saved ruffian in West Ham: you accuse me of dragging his soul back to perdition. Well, bring him to me here; and I will drag his soul back again to salvation for you. Not by words and dreams; but by thirty-eight shillings a week, a sound house in a handsome street and a permanent job. In three weeks he will have a fancy waistcoat; in three months a tall hat and a chapel sitting; before the end of the year he will shake hands with a duchess at a Primrose League meeting, and join the Conservative Party.

BARBARA And will he be the better for that?

UNDERSHAFT You know he will. Dont be a hypocrite, Barbara. He will be better fed, better housed, better clothed, better behaved; and his children will be pounds heavier and bigger. That will be better than an American cloth mattress in a shelter, chopping firewood, eating bread and treacle, and being forced to kneel down from time to time to thank heaven for it: knee drill, I think you call it. It is cheap work converting starving men with a Bible in one hand and a slice of bread in the other. I will undertake to convert West Ham to Mahometanism on the same terms. Try your hand on my men: their souls are hungry because their bodies are full.

BARBARA And leave the east end to starve?

UNDERSHAFT (*his energetic tone dropping into one of bitter and brooding remembrance*) *I* was an east ender. I moralized and starved until one day I swore that I would be a full-fed free man at all costs; that nothing should stop me except a bullet, neither reason nor morals nor the lives of other men. I said "Thou shalt starve ere I starve"; and with that word I became free and great. I was a dangerous man until I had my will: now I am a useful, beneficent, kindly person. That is the history of most self-made millionaires, I fancy. When it is the history of every Englishman we shall have an England worth living in.

LADY BRITOMART Stop making speeches, Andrew. This is not the place for them.

UNDERSHAFT (*punctured*) My dear: I have no other means of conveying my ideas.

LADY BRITOMART Your ideas are nonsense. You got on because you were selfish and unscrupulous.

UNDERSHAFT Not at all. I had the strongest scruples about poverty and starvation. Your moralists are quite unscrupulous about both: they make virtues of them. I had rather be a thief than a pauper. I had rather be a murderer than a slave. I dont want to be either; but if you force the alternative on me, then, by Heaven, I'll choose the braver and more moral one. I hate poverty and slavery worse than any other crimes whatsoever. And let me tell you this. Poverty and slavery have stood up for centuries to your sermons and leading articles: they will not stand up to my machine guns. Dont preach at them: dont reason with them. Kill them.

BARBARA Killing. Is that your remedy for everything?

UNDERSHAFT It is the final test of conviction, the only lever strong enough to overturn a social system, the only way of saying Must. Let six hundred and seventy fools loose in the streets; and three policemen can scatter them. But huddle them together in a certain house in Westminster; and let them go through certain ceremonies and call themselves certain names until at last they get the courage to kill; and your six hundred and seventy fools become a government. Your pious mob fills up ballot papers and imagines it is governing its masters; but the ballot paper that really governs is the paper that has a bullet wrapped up in it.

CUSINS That is perhaps why, like most intelligent people, I never vote.

UNDERSHAFT Vote! Bah! When you vote, you only change the names of the cabinet. When you shoot, you pull down governments, inaugurate new epochs, abolish old orders and set up new. Is that historically true, Mr Learned Man, or is it not?

CUSINS It is historically true. I loathe having to admit it. I repudiate your sentiments. I abhor your nature. I defy you in every possible way. Still, it is true. But it ought not to be true.

UNDERSHAFT Ought! ought! ought! ought! ought! Are you going to spend your life saying ought, like the rest of our moralists? Turn your oughts into shalls, man. Come and make explosives with me. Whatever can blow men up can blow society up. The history of the world is the history of those who had courage enough to embrace this truth. Have you the courage to embrace it, Barbara?

LADY BRITOMART Barbara: I positively forbid you to listen to your father's abominable wickedness. And you, Adolphus, ought to know better than to go about saying that wrong things are true. What does it matter whether they are true if they are wrong?

UNDERSHAFT What does it matter whether they are wrong if they are true?

LADY BRITOMART (*rising*) Children: come home instantly. Andrew: I am exceedingly sorry I allowed you to call on us. You are wickeder than ever. Come at once.

BARBARA (*shaking her head*) It's no use running away from wicked people, mamma.

LADY BRITOMART It is every use. It shews your disapprobation of them.

BARBARA It does not save them.

LADY BRITOMART I can see that you are going to disobey me. Sarah: are you coming home or are you not?

SARAH I daresay it's very wicked of papa to make cannons; but I dont think I shall cut him on that account.

LOMAX (*pouring oil on the troubled waters*) The fact is, you know, there is a certain amount of tosh about this notion of wickedness. It doesnt work. You must look at facts. Not that I would say a word in favor of anything wrong; but then, you see, all sorts of chaps are always doing all sorts of things; and we have to fit them in somehow, dont you know. What I mean is that you cant go cutting everybody; and thats about what it comes to. (*Their rapt attention to his eloquence makes him nervous.*) Perhaps I dont make myself clear.

LADY BRITOMART You are lucidity itself, Charles. Because Andrew is successful and has plenty of money to give to Sarah, you will flatter him and encourage him in his wickedness.

LOMAX (*unruffled*) Well, where the carcase is, there will the eagles be gathered, don't you know. (*to* UNDERSHAFT) Eh? What?

UNDERSHAFT Precisely. By the way, may I call you Charles?

LOMAX Delighted. Cholly is the usual ticket.

UNDERSHAFT (*to* LADY BRITOMART) Biddy—

LADY BRITOMART (*violently*) Dont dare call me Biddy. Charles Lomax: you are a fool. Adolphus Cusins: you are a Jesuit. Stephen: you are a prig. Barbara: you are a lunatic. Andrew: you are a vulgar tradesman. Now you all know my opinion; and my conscience is clear, at all events. (*She sits down with a vehemence that the rug fortunately softens.*)

UNDERSHAFT My dear: you are the incarnation of morality. (*She snorts.*) Your conscience is clear and your duty done when you have called everybody names. Come, Euripides! it is getting late; and we all want to go home. Make up your mind.

CUSINS Understand this, you old demon—

LADY BRITOMART Adolphus!

UNDERSHAFT Let him alone, Biddy. Proceed, Euripides.

CUSINS You have me in a horrible dilemma. I want Barbara.

UNDERSHAFT Like all young men, you greatly exaggerate the difference between one young woman and another.

BARBARA Quite true, Dolly.

CUSINS I also want to avoid being a rascal.

UNDERSHAFT (*with biting contempt*) You lust for personal righteousness, for self-approval, for what you call a good conscience, for what Barbara calls salvation, for what I call patronizing people who are not so lucky as yourself.

CUSINS I do not: all the poet in me recoils from being a good man. But there are things in me that I must reckon with. Pity—

UNDERSHAFT Pity! The scavenger of misery.

CUSINS Well, love.

UNDERSHAFT I know. You love the needy and the outcast: you love the oppressed races, the negro, the Indian ryot, the underdog everywhere. Do you love the Japanese? Do you love the French? Do you love the English?

CUSINS No. Every true Englishman detests the English. We are the wickedest nation on earth; and our success is a moral horror.

UNDERSHAFT That is what comes of your gospel of love, is it?

CUSINS May I not love even my father-in-law?

UNDERSHAFT Who wants your love, man? By what right do you take the liberty of offering it to me? I will have your due heed and respect, or I will kill you. But your love! Damn your impertinence!

CUSINS (*grinning*) I may not be able to control my affections, Mac.

UNDERSHAFT You are fencing, Euripides. You are weakening: your grip is slipping. Come! try your last weapon. Pity and love have broken in your hand: forgiveness is still left.

CUSINS No: forgiveness is a beggar's refuge. I am with you there: we must pay our debts.

UNDERSHAFT Well said. Come! you will suit me. Remember the words of Plato.

CUSINS (*starting*) Plato! You dare quote Plato to me!

UNDERSHAFT Plato says, my friend, that society cannot be saved until either the Professors of Greek take to making gunpowder, or else the makers of gunpowder become Professors of Greek.

CUSINS Oh, tempter, cunning tempter!

UNDERSHAFT Come! choose, man, choose.

CUSINS But perhaps Barbara will not marry me if I make the wrong choice.

BARBARA Perhaps not.

CUSINS (*desperately perplexed*) You hear!

BARBARA Father: do you love nobody?

UNDERSHAFT I love my best friend.

LADY BRITOMART And who is that, pray?

UNDERSHAFT My bravest enemy. That is the man who keeps me up to the mark.

CUSINS You know, the creature is really a sort of poet in his way. Suppose he is a great man, after all!

UNDERSHAFT Suppose you stop talking and make up your mind, my young friend.

CUSINS But you are driving me against my nature. I hate war.

UNDERSHAFT Hatred is the coward's revenge for being intimidated. Dare you make war on war? Here are the means: my friend Mr Lomax is sitting on them.

LOMAX (*springing up*) Oh I say! You dont mean that this thing is loaded, do you? My ownest: come off it.

SARAH (*sitting placidly on the shell*) If I am to be blown up, the more thoroughly it is done the better. Dont fuss, Cholly.

LOMAX (*to* UNDERSHAFT, *strongly remonstrant*) Your own daughter, you know!

UNDERSHAFT So I see. (*to* CUSINS) Well, my friend, may we expect you here at six tomorrow morning?

CUSINS (*firmly*) Not on any account. I will see the whole establishment blown up with its own dynamite before I will get up at five. My hours are healthy, rational hours: eleven to five.

UNDERSHAFT Come when you please: before a week you will come at six and stay until I turn you out for the sake of your health. (*calling*) Bilton! (*He turns to* LADY BRITOMART, *who rises.*) My dear: let us leave these two young people to themselves for a moment. (BILTON *comes from the shed.*) I am going to take you through the guncotton shed.

BILTON (*barring the way*) You cant take anything explosive in here, sir.

LADY BRITOMART What do you mean? Are you alluding to me?

BILTON (*unmoved*) No, maam. Mr Undershaft has the other gentleman's matches in his pocket.

LADY BRITOMART (*abruptly*) Oh! I beg your pardon! (*She goes into the shed.*)

UNDERSHAFT Quite right, Bilton, quite right: here you are. (*He gives* BILTON *the box of matches.*) Come, Stephen. Come, Charles. Bring Sarah. (*He passes into the shed.*)

(BILTON *opens the box and deliberately drops the matches into the firebucket.*)

LOMAX Oh! I say. (BILTON *stolidly hands him the empty box.*) Infernal nonsense! Pure scientific ignorance! (*He goes in.*)

SARAH Am I all right, Bilton?

BILTON Youll have to put on list slippers, miss: thats all. Weve got em inside. (*She goes in.*)

STEPHEN (*very seriously to* CUSINS) Dolly, old fellow, think. Think before you decide. Do you feel that you are a sufficiently practical man? It is a huge undertaking, an enormous responsibility. All this mass of business will be Greek to you.

CUSINS Oh, I think it will be much less difficult than Greek.

STEPHEN Well, I just want to say this before I leave you to yourselves. Dont let anything I have said about right and wrong prejudice you against this great chance in life. I have satisfied myself that the business is one of the highest character and a credit to our country. (*emotionally*) I am very proud of my father. I— (*Unable to proceed, he presses* CUSINS' *hand and goes hastily into the shed, followed by* BILTON.)

(BARBARA *and* CUSINS, *left alone together, look at one another silently.*)

CUSINS Barbara: I am going to accept this offer.

BARBARA I thought you would.

CUSINS You understand, dont you, that I had to decide without consulting you. If I had thrown the burden of the choice on you, you would sooner or later have despised me for it.

BARBARA Yes: I did not want you to sell your soul for me any more than for this inheritance.

CUSINS It is not the sale of my soul that troubles me: I have sold it too often to care about that. I have sold it for a professorship. I have sold it for an income. I have sold it to escape being imprisoned for refusing to pay taxes for hangmen's ropes and unjust wars and things that I abhor. What is all human conduct but the daily and hourly sale of our souls for trifles? What I am now selling it for is neither money nor position nor comfort, but for reality and for power.

BARBARA You know that you will have no power, and that he has none.

CUSINS I know. It is not for myself alone. I want to make power for the world.

BARBARA I want to make power for the world too; but it must be spiritual power.

CUSINS I think all power is spiritual: these cannons will not go off by themselves. I have tried to make spiritual power by teaching Greek. But the world can never be really touched by a dead language and a dead civilization. The people must have power; and the people cannot have Greek. Now the power that is made here can be wielded by all men.

BARBARA Power to burn women's houses down and kill their sons and tear their husbands to pieces.

CUSINS You cannot have power for good without having power for evil too. Even mother's milk nourishes murderers as well as heroes. This power which only tears men's bodies to pieces has never been so horribly abused as the intellectual power, the imaginative power, the poetic, religious power that can enslave men's souls. As a teacher of Greek I gave the intellectual man weapons against the common man. I now want to give the common man weapons against the intellectual man. I love the common people. I want to arm them against the lawyers, the doctors, the priests, the literary men, the professors, the artists, and the politicians, who, once in authority, are more disastrous and tyrannical than all the fools, rascals, and impostors. I want a power simple enough for common men to use, yet strong enough to force the intellectual oligarchy to use its genius for the general good.

BARBARA Is there no higher power than that (*pointing to the shell*)?

CUSINS Yes; but that power can destroy the higher powers just as a tiger can destroy a man: therefore Man must master that power first. I admitted this when the Turks and Greeks were last at war. My best pupil went out to fight for Hellas. My parting gift to him was not a copy of Plato's Republic, but a revolver and a hundred Undershaft cartridges. The blood of every Turk he shot—if he shot any—is on my head as well as on Undershaft's. That act committed me to this place for ever. Your father's challenge has beaten me. Dare I make war on war? I must. I will. And now, is it all over between us?

BARBARA (*touched by his evident dread of her answer*) Silly baby Dolly! How could it be!

CUSINS (*overjoyed*) Then you—you—you—Oh for my drum! (*He flourishes imaginary drumsticks.*)

BARBARA (*angered by his levity*) Take care, Dolly, take care. Oh, if only I could get away from you and from father and from it all! if I could have the wings of a dove and fly away to heaven!

CUSINS And leave me!

BARBARA Yes, you, and all the other naughty mischievous children of men. But I cant. I was happy in the Salvation Army for a moment. I escaped from the world into a paradise of enthusiasm and prayer and soul saving; but the moment our money ran short, it all came back to Bodger: it was he who saved our people; he, and the Prince of Darkness, my papa. Undershaft and Bodger: their hands stretch everywhere: when we feed a starving fellow creature, it is with their bread, because there is no other bread; when we tend the sick, it is in the hospitals they endow; if we turn from the churches they build, we must kneel on the stones of the streets they pave. As long as that lasts, there is no getting away from them. Turning our backs on Bodger and Undershaft is turning our backs on life.

CUSINS I thought you were determined to turn your back on the wicked side of life.

BARBARA There is no wicked side: life is all one. And I never wanted to shirk my share in whatever evil must be endured, whether it be sin or suffering. I wish I could cure you of middle-class ideas, Dolly.

CUSINS (*gasping*) Middle cl—! A snub! A social snub to me from the daughter of a foundling!

BARBARA That is why I have no class, Dolly: I come straight out of the heart of the whole people. If I were middle-class I should turn my back on my father's business; and we should both live in an artistic drawing room, with you reading the reviews in one corner, and I in the other at the piano, playing Schumann: both very superior persons, and neither of us a bit of use. Sooner than that, I would sweep out the guncotton shed, or be one of Bodger's barmaids. Do you know what would have happened if you had refused papa's offer?

CUSINS I wonder!

BARBARA I should have given you up and married the man who accepted it. After all, my dear old mother has more sense than any of you. I felt like her when I saw this place—felt that I must have it—that never, never, never could I let it go; only she thought it was the houses and the kitchen ranges and the linen and china, when it was really all the human souls to be saved: not weak souls in starved bodies, sobbing with gratitude for a scrap of bread and treacle, but fullfed, quarrelsome, snobbish, uppish creatures, all standing on their little rights and dignities, and thinking that my father ought to be greatly obliged to them for making so many money for him—and so he ought. That is where salvation is really wanted. My father shall never throw it in my teeth again that my converts were bribed with bread. (*She is transfigured.*) I have got rid of the bribe of bread. I have got rid of the bribe of heaven. Let God's work be done for its own sake: the work he had to create us to do because it cannot be done except by living men and women. When I die, let him be in my debt, not I in his; and let me forgive him as becomes a woman of my rank.

CUSINS Then the way of life lies through the factory of death?

BARBARA Yes, through the raising of hell to heaven and of man to God, through the unveiling of an eternal light in the Valley of The Shadow. (*seizing him with both hands*) Oh, did you think my courage would never come back? did you believe that I was a deserter? that I, who have stood in the streets, and taken my people to my heart, and talked of the holiest and greatest things with them, could ever turn back and chatter foolishly to fashionable people about nothing in a drawing room? Never, never, never, never: Major Barbara will die with the colors. Oh! and I have my dear little Dolly boy still; and he has found me my place and my work. Glory Hallelujah! (*She kisses him.*)

CUSINS My dearest: consider my delicate health. I cannot stand as much happiness as you can.

BARBARA Yes: it is not easy work being in love with me, is it? But it's good for you. (*She runs to the shed, and calls, childlike.*) Mamma! Mamma! (BILTON *comes out of the shed, followed by* UNDERSHAFT.) I want Mamma.

UNDERSHAFT She is taking off her list slippers, dear. (*He passes on to* CUSINS.) Well? What does she say?

CUSINS She has gone right up into the skies.

LADY BRITOMART (*coming from the shed and stopping on the steps, obstructing* SARAH, *who follows with* LOMAX. BARBARA *clutches like a baby at her mother's skirt*) Barbara: when will you learn to be independent and to act and think for yourself? I know, as well as possible what that cry of "Mamma, Mamma," means. Always running to me!

SARAH (*touching* LADY BRITOMART'S *ribs with her finger tips and imitating a bicycle horn*) Pip! pip!

LADY BRITOMART (*highly indignant*) How dare you say Pip! pip! to me, Sarah? You are both very naughty children. What do you want, Barbara?

BARBARA I want a house in the village to live in with Dolly. (*dragging at the skirt*) Come and tell me which one to take.

UNDERSHAFT (*to* CUSINS) Six o'clock tomorrow morning, Euripides.

TRIFLES

(1917)

SUSAN GLASPELL (1882–1948)

From the founding of Jamestown in 1607 and Plymouth in 1620, introducing theatrical entertainment into the American colonies was not an easy proposition. Puritan sensibilities in New England long remained a formidable opponent to the "ungodly and profane" behavior of theatrical personnel, and even Virginia, presumably more liberal than stiff-necked New England, "resolved to suffer no idle persons" (such as actors) in its midst.

In 1750 Boston saw a production of Otway's *The Orphan,* but the good fathers of Massachusetts reacted predictably by immediately banning such means of "disseminating licentious maxims" tending to "immorality of conduct." In the same year, however, New York did support a 300-seat house, but Philadelphia, then the major colonial city, successfully resisted any theatrical incursions.

With the coming of the revolution there was a flurry of quasitheatrical activity, none of it very good, but all intensely patriotic. The best-remembered today are the dramatic satires by Mercy Otis Warren (1728–1814) attacking the Tories and others in opposition to the revolt, but there is no record of their performance. In 1778 the Continental Congress legislated against "plays and other expensive diversions and entertainments" to effectively stifle any native writing or acting talent, although it is known that American soldiers put on theatricals in camp, and even George Washington was known to enjoy a play.

After hostilities ended, New York audiences witnessed the beginning of real American stage writing on April 16, 1787, with the first professional production of an American-written play on an American subject, *The Contrast,* by Royall Tyler (1757–1826). This mild satire, which was greatly influenced by Sheridan, contrasts the artificial English manners of the day with the more liberal and democratic manners of the new America. It introduced the first significant American character, the bumpkin Jonathan, an ignorant rustic who happens into a performance of *The School for Scandal* and thinks he is seeing the house next door through a hole in the wall. Philadelphia finally succumbed to theatrical entertainment in February 1794 when America's first truly elegant playhouse opened, the 2000-seat Chestnut Street Theatre.

America's first theatrical impresario was the actor, producer, and playwright William Dunlap (1766–1839). His sincere integrity as a serious artist helped to carry the nascent American theatre forward. His sixty-some plays have little to offer to posterity, but his *History of the American Theatre* (1832), though fairly personal and often inaccurate, was the first attempt to bring the American stage some recognition and respectability.

Themes treating the Native American were popular fare in plays of the early nineteenth century, but most of the "noble savages" were impossibly romantic. John Smith and Pocahontas turned up frequently. Stage Yankees, patterned after Jonathan of *The Contrast,* proliferated. Social affectations, this time French rather than English, continued in *Fashion* (1845) by Anna Cora Mowatt (1819–1870), a comedy of manners that can be revived with remarkable ease. And during most of the nineteenth century the American stage portrayed African-American stereotypes as part vaudeville minstrel and part noble savage. Harriet Beecher Stowe's antislavery novel of 1852, *Uncle Tom's Cabin,* adapted to the stage against the author's will, significantly contributed to the distorted picture of the enslaved black.

One who dominated the American stage just before the Civil War was not a native but the Irish-born Dion Boucicault, also famous in England, who wrote nearly 125 foreign adaptations and original plays. His best remains the still-playable *The Octoroon* (1859), a daring treatment of a young white Southern plantation owner's love for the beautiful one-eighth-Negro-blood Zoe. His *The Colleen Bawn* (1860) was the first play to present a sympathetic picture of an Irish character, hitherto, like the Native American, mostly burlesqued and ridiculed. Boucicault, an accomplished actor, made a substantial contribution beyond his writing in his long and successful campaign for enforceable copyright laws to provide dramatists with control over publication and production of their plays as well as a regular income.

After the Civil War, American drama and theatre took remarkable strides forward. Augustin Daly (1838–1899) became the first American to give the director a leading role in the production of plays, and his careful control over all aspects of performance introduced some well-disciplined and refined productions. Bronson Howard (1842–1908) was the first American playwright who made his living solely by writing plays, thanks mainly to the enforcement of copyright laws. Howard's adherence to certain "laws" of dramatic construction shows how difficult it was to overcome long-held traditions. He insisted that these laws were as immutable as those in mathematics; one of his dramatic laws maintained that retribution was inevitable and generally fatal for any woman who erred in leaving the path of sexual purity. The double standard of the inability to forgive the adulterous wife under any circumstances while faithless husbands never suffered remained, unhappily, a "law" too often obeyed.

While Ibsenesque realism was establishing its roots in Europe, American drama, always in arrears, received its most important early proponent of the realistic "problem play" in James A. Herne (1839–1901). He remained close to the common life and the simple fundamentals of everyday existence, although his best play, *Margaret Fleming* (1890), was never very successful because its subject of the "fallen" man, rather than woman, was not quite what the public wanted. William Gillette (1855–1937) wrote *Secret Service* (1895), the best of the Civil War plays. It was his portrayal of Conan Doyle's master detective in *Sherlock Holmes* that began the tradition of the deerstalker cap, the cape, and the meerschaum pipe.

David Belasco (1859–1931) was one of the most well-known and influential theatrical personalities from the end of the nineteenth century through the 1920s. He became famous for his attempts to reproduce the absolute sense of scenic reality by settings in the utmost naturalistic detail. On one occasion he removed an entire room from a New York tenement and placed it on the stage. His only plays still remembered today are *Madame Butterfly* (1900) and *The Girl of the Golden West* (1905), both of them inspirations for the more famous Puccini operas.

William Vaughn Moody (1869–1910), more poet than dramatist, wrote *The Great Divide* in 1906, a play timely in its contrast of the mores of staid and Puritan New England with the freer and less rigid code of the West. Moody's play, in which the heroine chooses a life on the frontier against her family's wishes, is one of the earlier American plays following Ibsen's insistence that one has the right to establish and maintain one's own individual character in the face of strongly entrenched social opposition. Edward Sheldon (1886–1946) ventured into dramatic naturalism with such plays as *Salvation Nell* (1908) and *The Boss* (1911), with characters who often remained as unsavory and unrepentant as when they first entered. *The Nigger* (1909) was a daring discussion of race prejudice in its story of a Southern governor revealed to be a mulatto.

Clyde Fitch (1865–1909) was the first American dramatist to achieve substantial foreign recognition, but he was never able to raise his form of realism above dramatic mediocrity. He was aware of the sounds and patterns of actual speech, and he comprehended the personalities within the American society he knew, placing them in the midst of a recognizable American scene, though often succumbing to a "well-made" tradition that much too conveniently tied everything together at the end. *The City*, produced posthumously in 1909, full of melodramatic and unmotivated incident, remains his best. It introduced incest, drug abuse, and civic corruption into the plot, and the shock of its violent profanity, as the maddened villain uttered "You're a God-damn liar!" to the hero, stunned the audience.

The prewar American theatre began to pay close attention to the new "free" theatres of Europe such as Antoine's Théâtre Libre of Paris and the Frei Bühne of Berlin, and of course the Moscow Art Theatre. From Ireland, where William Butler Yeats and Lady Isabella Gregory had organized in 1899 what was soon to develop into the internationally famous Abbey Theatre of Dublin in 1904, came some powerful impulses. When the group toured America before the war, it mightily impressed an aspiring young dramatist named Eugene O'Neill. Two "art," or "little," theatres in New York can be credited with bringing American drama into the twentieth century by their boldness in producing not only some of the newest and most controversial English and European plays, but in encouraging American playwrights. One was The Washington Square Players organized in 1914 and eventually to become America's foremost producing company, The Theatre Guild. The other was the Provincetown Players.

Washington Square was more professional than the Provincetown Players and included a wide variety of foreign plays in its repertoire. The Provincetown preferred to remain relatively amateur and stayed with American writers. The major impetus came from the husband-and-wife team of George Cram Cook and Susan Glaspell, whose summer home in Provincetown at the tip of Cape Cod was part of a lively colony of poets, novelists, and other artists who held radical points of view concerning art, politics, and personal behavior quite removed from the mainstream.

The first play given by the Provincetown was also the first to be associated with Susan Glaspell. But she and her husband (always known as "Jig") were writers and competent actors, and they collaborated on a two-scene satire on Freudian psychoanalysis called *Suppressed Desires,* which they produced in 1915 in the home of one of their friends. The play has never lost its popularity as a comic exposure of fads and faddists as its heroine gets way over her head in something she knows absolutely nothing about.

In working with the Provincetown, Glaspell became one of the most successful American woman playwrights. In 1919, *Bernice,* a serious psychodrama about the mystery surrounding the apparent suicide of the heroine, established her as a playwright of considerable importance. The symbolic treatment of some serious contemporary problems in *The Verge* (1921) made use of stylized staging and pseudoexpressionistic dialogue to underline the psychological problems of Claire Archer, the central figure, on her way to mental disintegration and final collapse. Glaspell's last play established her permanent reputation—*Alison's House* in 1930 was derived loosely from the life of Emily Dickinson, a sensitive story of a withdrawn spinster's unhappy love affair, which impressively explored a number of psychological truths. It was not well supported by the public but won the Pulitzer Prize for 1930–1931.

Susan Glaspell's best short play and one that carries a very strong impact even today is *Trifles.* Within the brief scope of its one act, Glaspell has created an intensely gripping piece of stage realism. By its very nature, the one-act play sharply limits what the author can do with character and action, demanding that everything be accomplished in a very brief time without much opportunity for development. But Glaspell was able to transcend these restrictions through her careful plotting and her ability to portray ordinary but sympathetic characters in such a brief span of time. Most remarkable, the characters of greatest importance, those involved in the play's hopeless central situation, never appear on stage. The almost photographic detail of the setting combines with action and dialogue to create a dark, forbidding mood that quickly grips the audience.

The whole sordid affair of the deadening life experienced by Mrs. Wright at the hands of her callous, unthinking husband is revealed in excellent theatrical fashion. The women learn a lot from their observations and their instincts, which rise to protect one of their own, while the supposedly clever men seeking clues for the crime's motive deride the "inferior" nature of their womenfolk, whose observation of petty trifles cannot possibly have any importance.

Not limited by any set theatrical form, Susan Glaspell was at home with conventional realism and unconventional stylization. Her name survives as a major figure in the beginnings of modern American drama, and a number of her short plays are still popular with high school, college, and amateur groups. Along with O'Neill, she stands as an important transition figure between the old, more conventional plays that typified American prewar drama and the new and exciting American theatre that was to follow.

Trifles SUSAN GLASPELL

SCENE: *The kitchen in the now abandoned farmhouse of* JOHN WRIGHT, *a gloomy kitchen, and left without having been put in order—the walls covered with a faded wallpaper. Down right is a door leading to the parlor. On the right wall above this door is a built-in kitchen cupboard with shelves in the upper portion and drawers below. In the rear wall at right, up two steps is a door opening onto stairs leading to the second floor. In the rear wall at left is a door to the shed and from there to the outside. Between these two doors is an old-fashioned black iron stove. Running along the left wall from the shed door is an old iron sink and sink shelf, in which is set a hand pump. Downstage of the sink is an uncurtained window. Near the window is an old wooden rocker. Center stage is an unpainted wooden kitchen table with straight chairs on either side. There is a small chair down right. Unwashed pans under the sink, a loaf of bread outside the breadbox, a dish towel on the table—other signs of incompleted work. At the rear the shed door opens and the* SHERIFF *comes in followed by the* COUNTY ATTORNEY *and* HALE. *The* SHERIFF *and* HALE *are men in middle life, the* COUNTY ATTORNEY *is a young man; all are much bundled up and go at once to the stove. They are followed by the two women—the* SHERIFF'S *wife,* MRS. PETERS, *first; she is a slight wiry woman, a thin nervous face.* MRS. HALE *is larger and would ordinarily be called more comfortable looking, but she is disturbed now and looks fearfully about as she enters. The women have come in slowly, and stand close together near the door.*

COUNTY ATTORNEY (*at stove rubbing his hands*) This feels good. Come up to the fire, ladies.

MRS. PETERS (*after taking a step forward*) I'm not—cold.

SHERIFF (*unbuttoning his overcoat and stepping away from the stove to right of table as if to mark the beginning of official business*) Now, Mr. Hale, before we move things about, you explain to Mr. Henderson just what you saw when you came here yesterday morning.

COUNTY ATTORNEY (*crossing down to left of the table*) By the way, has anything been moved? Are things just as you left them yesterday?

SHERIFF (*looking about*) It's just the same. When it dropped below zero last night I thought I'd better send Frank out this morning to make a fire for us—(*sits right of center table*) no use getting pneumonia with a big case on, but I told him not to touch anything except the stove—and you know Frank.

COUNTY ATTORNEY Somebody should have been left here yesterday.

SHERIFF Oh—yesterday. When I had to send Frank to Morris Center for that man who went crazy—I want you to know I had my hands full yesterday. I knew you could get back from Omaha by today and as long as I went over everything here myself —

COUNTY ATTORNEY Well, Mr. Hale, tell just what happened when you came here yesterday morning.

HALE (*crossing down to above table*) Harry and I had started to town with a load of potatoes. We came along the road from my place and as I got here I said, "I'm going to see if I can't get John Wright to go in with me on a party telephone." I spoke to Wright about it once before and he put me off, saying folks talked too much anyway, and all he asked was peace and quiet—I guess you know about how much he talked himself; but I thought maybe if I went to the house and talked about it before his wife, though I said to Harry that I didn't know as what his wife wanted made much difference to John —

COUNTY ATTORNEY Let's talk about that later, Mr. Hale. I do want to talk about that, but tell now just what happened when you got to the house.

HALE I didn't hear or see anything; I knocked at the door, and still it was all quiet inside. I knew they must be up, it was past eight o'clock. So I knocked again, and I thought I heard somebody say, "Come in." I wasn't sure, I'm not sure yet, but I opened the door—this door (*indicating the door by which the two women are still standing*) and there in that rocker— (*pointing to it*) sat Mrs. Wright. (*They all look at the rocker down left.*)

COUNTY ATTORNEY What—what was she doing?

HALE She was rockin' back and forth. She had her apron in her hand and was kind of—pleating it.

COUNTY ATTORNEY And how did she—look?

HALE Well, she looked queer.

COUNTY ATTORNEY How do you mean—queer?

HALE Well, as if she didn't know what she was going to do next. And kind of done up.

COUNTY ATTORNEY (*takes out notebook and pencil and sits left of center table*) How did she seem to feel about your coming?

HALE Why, I don't think she minded—one way or other. She didn't pay much attention. I said, "How do, Mrs. Wright, it's cold, ain't it?" And she said, "Is it?"—and went on kind of pleating at her apron. Well, I was surprised; she didn't ask me to come up to the stove, or to set down, but just sat there, not even looking at me, so I said, "I want to see John." And then she—laughed. I guess you would call it a laugh. I thought of Harry and the team outside, so I said a little sharp: "Can't I see John?" "No," she says, kind o' dull like. "Ain't he home?" says I. "Yes," says she, "he's home." "Then why can't I see him?" I asked her, out of patience. "'Cause he's dead," says she. "*Dead?*" says I. She just nodded her head, not getting a bit excited, but rockin' back and forth. "Why—where is he?" says I, not knowing what to say. She just pointed upstairs—like that. (*himself pointing to the room above*) I started for the stairs, with the idea of going up there. I walked from there to here—then I says, "Why, what did he die of?" "He died of a rope round his neck," says she, and just went on pleatin' at her apron. Well, I went out and called Harry, I thought I might—need help. We went upstairs and there he was lyin'—

COUNTY ATTORNEY I think I'd rather have you go into that upstairs, where you can point it all out. Just go on now with the rest of the story.

HALE Well, my first thought was to get that rope off. It looked . . . (*stops, his face twitches*) . . . but Harry, he went up to him and he said, "No, he's dead all right, and we'd better not touch anything." So we went back downstairs. She was still sitting that same way. "Has anybody been notified?" I asked. "No," says she, unconcerned. "Who did this, Mrs. Wright?" said Harry. He said it business-like—and she stopped pleatin' of her apron. "I don't know," she says. "You don't *know?*" says Harry. "No," says she. "Weren't you sleepin' in the bed with him?" says Harry. "Yes," says she, "but I was on the inside." "Somebody slipped a rope round his neck and strangled him and you didn't wake up?" says Harry. "I didn't wake up," she said after him. We musta looked as if we didn't see how that could be, for after a minute she said, "I sleep sound." Harry was going to ask her more questions but I said maybe we ought to let her tell her story first to the coroner, or the sheriff, so Harry went fast as he could to Rivers' place, where there's a telephone.

COUNTY ATTORNEY And what did Mrs. Wright do when she knew that you had gone for the coroner?

HALE She moved from the rocker to that chair over there (*pointing to a small chair in the down right corner*) and just sat there with her hands held together and looking down. I got a feeling that I ought to make some conversation, so I said I had come in to see if John wanted to put in a telephone, and at that she started to laugh, and then she stopped and looked at me—scared. (*The* COUNTY ATTORNEY, *who has had his notebook out, makes a note.*) I dunno, maybe it wasn't scared. I wouldn't like to say it was. Soon Harry got back, and then Dr. Lloyd came, and you, Mr. Peters, and so I guess that's all I know that you don't.

COUNTY ATTORNEY (*rising and looking around*) I guess we'll go upstairs first—and then out to the barn and around there. (*to the* SHERIFF) You're convinced that there was nothing important here—nothing that would point to any motive?

SHERIFF Nothing here but kitchen things. (*The* COUNTY ATTORNEY, *after again looking around the kitchen, opens the door of a cupboard closet in right wall. He brings a small chair from right; gets up on it and looks on a shelf; pulls his hand away, sticky.*)

COUNTY ATTORNEY Here's a nice mess. (*The women draw nearer up center.*)

MRS. PETERS (*to the other woman*) Oh, her fruit; it did freeze. (*to the* LAWYER) She worried about that when it turned so cold. She said the fire'd go out and her jars would break.

SHERIFF (*rises*) Well, can you beat the women! Held for murder and worryin' about her preserves.

COUNTY ATTORNEY (*getting down from chair*) I guess before we're through she may have something more serious than preserves to worry about. (*crosses down right center*)

HALE Well, women are used to worrying over trifles. (*The two women move a little closer together.*)

COUNTY ATTORNEY (*with the gallantry of a young politician*) And yet, for all their worries, what would we do without the ladies? (*The women do not unbend. He goes below the center table to the sink, takes a dipperful of water from the pail and pouring it into a basin, washes his hands. While he is doing this the* SHERIFF *and* HALE *cross to cupboard, which they inspect. The* COUNTY ATTORNEY *starts to wipe his hands on the roller towel, turns it for a cleaner place.*) Dirty towels! (*kicks his foot against the pans under the sink*) Not much of a housekeeper, would you say, ladies?

MRS. HALE (*stiffly*) There's a great deal of work to be done on a farm.

COUNTY ATTORNEY To be sure. And yet (*with a little bow to her*) I know there are some Dickson County farmhouses which do not have such roller towels. (*He gives it a pull to expose its full length again.*)

MRS. HALE Those towels get dirty awful quick. Men's hands aren't always as clean as they might be.

COUNTY ATTORNEY Ah, loyal to your sex, I see. But you and Mrs. Wright were neighbors. I suppose you were friends, too.

MRS. HALE (*shaking her head*) I've not seen much of her of late years. I've not been in this house—it's more than a year.

COUNTY ATTORNEY (*crossing to women up center*) And why was that? You didn't like her?

MRS. HALE I liked her all well enough. Farmers' wives have their hands full, Mr. Henderson. And then—

COUNTY ATTORNEY Yes—?

MRS. HALE (*looking about*) It never seemed a very cheerful place.

COUNTY ATTORNEY No—it's not cheerful. I shouldn't say she had the home-making instinct.

MRS. HALE Well I don't know as Wright had, either.

COUNTY ATTORNEY You mean that they didn't get on very well?

MRS. HALE No, I don't mean anything. But I don't think a place'd be any cheerfuller for John Wright's being in it.

COUNTY ATTORNEY I'd like to talk more of that a little later. I want to get the lay of things upstairs now. (*He goes past the women to up right where steps lead to a stair door.*)

SHERIFF I suppose anything Mrs. Peters does'll be all right. She was to take in some clothes for her, you know, and a few little things. We left in such a hurry yesterday.

COUNTY ATTORNEY Yes, but I would like to see what you take, Mrs. Peters, and keep an eye out for anything that might be of use to us.

MRS. PETERS Yes, Mr. Henderson. (*The men leave by up right door to stairs. The women listen to the men's steps on the stairs, then look about the kitchen.*)

MRS. HALE (*crossing left to sink*) I'd hate to have men coming into my kitchen, snooping around and criticizing. (*She arranges the pans under sink which the* LAWYER *had shoved out of place.*)

MRS. PETERS Of course it's no more than their duty. (*crosses to cupboard up right*)

MRS. HALE Duty's all right, but I guess that deputy sheriff that came out to make the fire might have got a little of this on. (*gives the roller towel a pull*) Wish I'd thought of that sooner. Seems mean to talk about her for not having things slicked up when she had to come away in such a hurry. (*crosses right to* MRS. PETERS *at cupboard*)

MRS. PETERS (*who has been looking through cupboard, lifts one end of a towel that covers a pan*) She had bread set. (*stands still*)

MRS. HALE (*eyes fixed on a loaf of bread beside the breadbox, which is on a low shelf of the cupboard*) She was going to put this in there. (*picks up loaf, then abruptly drops it, in a manner of returning to familiar things*) It's a shame about her fruit. I wonder if it's all gone. (*gets up on the chair and looks*) I think there's some here that's all right, Mrs. Peters. Yes—here; (*holding it toward the window*) this is cherries, too. (*looking again*) I declare I believe that's the only one. (*gets down, jar in her hand, goes to the sink, and wipes it off on the outside*) She'll feel awful bad after all her hard work in the hot weather. I remember the afternoon I put up my cherries last summer. (*She puts the jar on the big kitchen table, center of the room. With a sigh, is about to sit down in the rocking chair. Before she is seated realizes what chair it is; with a slow look at it, steps back. The chair which she has touched rocks back and forth.* MRS. PETERS *moves to center table and they both watch the chair rock for a moment or two.*)

MRS. PETERS (*shaking off the mood which the empty rocking chair has evoked. Now in a businesslike manner she speaks*) Well, I must get those things from the front room closet. (*She goes to the door at the right, but, after looking into the other room, steps back.*) You coming with me, Mrs. Hale? You could help me carry them. (*They go in the other room, then reappear,* MRS. PETERS *carrying a dress, petticoat, and skirt,* MRS. HALE *following with a pair of shoes.*) My, it's cold in there. (*She puts the clothes on the big table, and hurries to the stove.*)

MRS. HALE (*right of center table examining the skirt*) Wright was close. I think maybe that's why she kept so much to herself. She didn't even belong to the Ladies' Aid. I suppose she felt she couldn't do her part, and then you don't enjoy things when you feel shabby. I heard she used to wear pretty clothes and be lively, when she was Minnie Foster, one of the town girls singing in the choir. But that—oh, that was thirty years ago. This all you was to take in?

MRS. PETERS She said she wanted an apron. Funny thing to want, for there isn't much to get you dirty in jail, goodness knows. But I suppose just to make her feel more natural. (*crosses to cupboard*) She said they was in the top drawer in this cupboard. Yes, here. And then her little shawl that was always hung behind the door. (*opens stair door and looks*) Yes, here it is. (*quickly shuts door leading upstairs*)

MRS. HALE (*abruptly moving toward her*) Mrs. Peters?

MRS. PETERS Yes, Mrs. Hale? (*at up right door*)

MRS. HALE Do you think she did it?

MRS. PETERS (*in a frightened voice*) Oh, I don't know.

MRS. HALE Well, I don't think she did. Asking for an apron and her little shawl. Worrying about her fruit.

MRS. PETERS (*starts to speak, glances up, where footsteps are heard in the room above; in a low voice*) Mr. Peters says it looks bad for her. Mr. Henderson is awful sarcastic in a speech and he'll make fun of her sayin' she didn't wake up.

MRS. HALE Well, I guess John Wright didn't wake when they was slipping that rope under his neck.

MRS. PETERS (*crossing slowly to table and placing shawl and apron on table with other clothing*) No, it's strange. It must have been done awful crafty and still. They say it was such a—funny way to kill a man, rigging it all up like that.

MRS. HALE (*crossing to left of* MRS. PETERS *at table*) That's just what Mr. Hale said. There was a gun in the house. He says that's what he can't understand.

MRS. PETERS Mr. Henderson said coming out that what was needed for the case was a motive, something to show anger, or—sudden feeling.

MRS. HALE (*who is standing by the table*) Well, I don't see any signs of anger around here. (*She put her hand on the dish towel which lies on the table, stands looking down at table, one-half of which is clean, the other half messy.*) It's wiped to here. (*makes a move as if to finish work, then turns and looks at loaf of bread outside of breadbox, drops towel; in that voice of coming back to familiar things*) Wonder how they are finding things upstairs. (*crossing below table to down right*) I hope she had it a little more red-up up there. You know, it seems kind of *sneaking*. Locking her up in town and then coming out here and trying to get her own house to turn against her!

MRS. PETERS But, Mrs. Hale, the law is the law.

MRS. HALE I s'pose 'tis. (*unbuttoning her coat*) Better loosen up your things, Mrs. Peters. You won't feel them when you go out. (MRS. PETERS *takes off her fur tippet, goes to hang it on chair back left of table, stands looking at the work basket on floor near down left window.*)

MRS. PETERS She was piecing a quilt. (*She brings the large sewing basket to the center table and they look at the bright pieces.* MRS. HALE *above the table and* MRS. PETERS *left of it.*)

MRS. HALE It's a log cabin pattern. Pretty, isn't it? I wonder if she was goin' to quilt it or just knot it? (*Footsteps have been heard coming down the stairs. The* SHERIFF *enters followed by* HALE *and the* COUNTY ATTORNEY.)

SHERIFF They wonder if she was going to quilt it or just knot it! (*The men laugh, the women look abashed.*)

COUNTY ATTORNEY (*rubbing his hands over the stove*) Frank's fire didn't do much up there, did it? Well, let's go out to the barn and get that cleared up. (*The men go outside by up left door.*)

MRS. HALE (*resentfully*) I don't know as there's anything so strange, our takin' up our time with little things while we're waiting for them to get the evidence. (*She sits in chair right of table smoothing out a block with decision.*) I don't see as it's anything to laugh about.

MRS. PETERS (*apologetically*) Of course they've got awful important things on their minds. (*pulls up a chair and joins* MRS. HALE *at the left of the table*)

MRS. HALE (*examining another block*) Mrs. Peters, look at this one. Here, this is the one she was working on, and look at the sewing! All the rest of it has been so nice and even. And look at this! It's all over the place! Why, it looks as if she didn't know what she was about! (*After she has said this they look at each other, then start to glance back at the door. After an instant* MRS. HALE *has pulled at a knot and ripped the sewing.*)

MRS. PETERS Oh, what are you doing, Mrs. Hale?

MRS. HALE (*mildly*) Just pulling out a stitch or two that's not sewed very good. (*threading a needle*) Bad sewing always made me fidgety.

MRS. PETERS (*with a glance at door, nervously*) I don't think we ought to touch things.

MRS. HALE I'll just finish up this end. (*suddenly stopping and leaning forward*) Mrs. Peters?

MRS. PETERS Yes, Mrs. Hale?

MRS. HALE What do you suppose she was so nervous about?

MRS. PETERS Oh—I don't know. I don't know as she was nervous. I sometimes sew awful queer when I'm just tired. (MRS. HALE *starts to say something, looks at* MRS. PETERS, *then goes on sewing.*) Well, I must get these things wrapped up. They may be through sooner than we think. (*putting apron and other things together*) I wonder where I can find a piece of paper, and string. (*rises*)

MRS. HALE In that cupboard, maybe.

MRS. PETERS (*crosses right looking in cupboard*) Why, here's a bird-cage. (*holds it up*) Did she have a bird, Miss Hale?

MRS. HALE Why, I don't know whether she did or not—I've not been here for so long. There was a man around last year selling canaries cheap, but I don't know as she took one; maybe she did. She used to sing real pretty herself.

MRS. PETERS (*glancing around*) Seems funny to think of a bird here. But she must have had one, or why would she have a cage? I wonder what happened to it?

MRS. HALE I s'pose maybe the cat got it.

MRS. PETERS No, she didn't have a cat. She's got that feeling some people have about cats—being afraid of them. My cat got in her room and she was real upset and asked me to take it out.

MRS. HALE My sister Bessie was like that. Queer, ain't it?

MRS. PETERS (*examining the cage*) Why, look at this door. It's broke. One hinge is pulled apart. (*takes a step down to* MRS. HALE*'s right*)

MRS. HALE (*looking too*) Looks as if someone must have been rough with it.

MRS. PETERS Why, yes. (*She brings the cage forward and puts it on the table.*)

MRS. HALE (*glancing toward up left door*) I wish if they're going to find any evidence they'd be about it. I don't like this place.

MRS. PETERS But I'm awful glad you came with me, Mrs. Hale. It would be lonesome for me setting here alone.

MRS. HALE It would, wouldn't it? (*dropping her sewing*) But I tell you what I do wish, Mrs. Peters. I wish I had come over sometimes when *she* was here. I—(*looking around the room*)—wish I had.

MRS. PETERS But of course you were awful busy, Mrs. Hale—your house and your children.

MRS. HALE (*rises and crosses left*) I could've come. I stayed away because it weren't cheerful—and that's why I ought to have come. I—(*looking out left window*)—I've never liked this place. Maybe because it's down in a hollow and you don't see the road. I dunno what it is, but it's a lonesome place and always was. I wish I had come over to see Minnie Foster sometimes. I can see now—(*shakes her head*)

MRS. PETERS (*left of table and above it*) Well, you mustn't reproach yourself, Mrs. Hale. Somehow we just don't see how it is with other folks until—something turns up.

MRS. HALE Not having children makes less work—but it makes a quiet house, and Wright out to work all day, and no company when he did come in. (*turning from window*) Did you know John Wright, Mrs. Peters?

MRS. PETERS Not to know him; I've seen him in town. They say he was a good man.

MRS. HALE Yes—good; he didn't drink, and kept his word as well as most, I guess, and paid his debts. But he was a hard man, Mrs. Peters. Just to pass the time of day with him—(*shivers*) Like a raw wind that gets to the bone. (*pauses, her eye falling on the cage*) I should think she woulda wanted a bird. But what do you suppose went with it?

MRS. PETERS I don't know, unless it got sick and died. (*She reaches over and swings the broken door, swings it again; both women watch it.*)

MRS. HALE You weren't raised round here, were you? (MRS. PETERS *shakes her head.*) You didn't know—her?

MRS. PETERS Not till they brought her yesterday.

MRS. HALE She—come to think of it, she was kind of like a bird herself—real sweet and pretty, but kind of timid and—fluttery. How—she—did—change. (*silence; then, as if struck by a happy thought and relieved to get back to everyday things, crosses right above* MRS. PETERS *to cupboard, replaces small chair used to stand on to its original place down right*) Tell you what, Mrs. Peters, why don't you take the quilt in with you? It might take up her mind.

MRS. PETERS Why, I think that's a real nice idea, Mrs. Hale. There couldn't possibly be any objection to it, could there? Now, just what would I take? I wonder if her patches are in here—and her things. (*They look in the sewing basket.*)

MRS. HALE (*crosses to right of table*) Here's some red. I expect this has got sewing things in it. (*brings out a fancy box*) What a pretty box. Looks like something somebody would give you. Maybe her scissors are in here. (*opens box, suddenly puts her hand to her nose*) Why—(MRS. PETERS *bends nearer, then turns her face away.*) There's something wrapped up in this piece of silk.

MRS. PETERS Why, this isn't her scissors.

MRS. HALE (*lifting the silk*) Oh, Mrs. Peters—it's—(MRS. PETERS *bends closer.*)

MRS. PETERS It's the bird.

MRS. HALE But, Mrs. Peters—look at it! Its neck! Look at its neck! It's all—other side *to.*

MRS. PETERS Somebody—wrung—its—neck. (*Their eyes meet. A look of growing comprehension, of horror. Steps are heard outside.* MRS. HALE *slips box under quilt pieces, and sinks into her chair. Enter* SHERIFF *and* COUNTY ATTORNEY. MRS. PETERS *steps down left and stands looking out of window.*)

COUNTY ATTORNEY (*as one turning from serious things to little pleasantries*) Well, ladies, have you decided whether she was going to quilt it or knot it? (*crosses to center above table*)

MRS. PETERS We think she was going to—knot it. (SHERIFF *crosses to right of stove, lifts stove lid and glances at fire, then stands warming hands at stove.*)

COUNTY ATTORNEY Well, that's interesting, I'm sure. (*seeing the bird cage*) Has the bird flown?

MRS. HALE (*putting more quilt pieces over the box*) We think the—cat got it.

COUNTY ATTORNEY (*preoccupied*) Is there a cat? (MRS. HALE *glances in a quick covert way at* MRS. PETERS.)

MRS. PETERS (*turning from window takes a step in*) Well, not *now.* They're superstitious, you know. They leave.

COUNTY ATTORNEY (*to* SHERIFF PETERS, *continuing an interrupted conversation*) No sign at all of anyone having come from the outside. Their own rope. Now let's go up again and go over it piece by piece. (*They start upstairs.*) It would have to have been someone who knew just the—(MRS. PETERS *sits down left of table. The two women sit there not looking at one another, but as if peering into something and at the same time holding back. When they talk now it is in the manner of feeling their way over strange ground, as if afraid of what they are saying, but as if they cannot help saying it.*)

MRS. HALE (*hesitatively and in hushed voice*) She liked the bird. She was going to bury it in that pretty box.

MRS. PETERS (*in a whisper*) When I was a girl—my kitten—there was a boy took a hatchet, and before my eyes—and before I could get there—(*covers her face an instant*) If they hadn't held me back I would have—(*catches herself, looks upstairs where steps are heard, falters weakly*)—hurt him.

MRS. HALE (*with a slow look around her*) I wonder how it would seem never to have had any children around. (*pause*) No, Wright wouldn't like the bird—a thing that sang. She used to sing. He killed that, too.

MRS. PETERS (*moving uneasily*) We don't know who killed the bird.

MRS. HALE I knew John Wright.

MRS. PETERS It was an awful thing done in this house that night, Mrs. Hale. Killing a man while he slept, slipping a rope around his neck that choked the life out of him.

MRS. HALE His neck. Choked the life out of him. (*Her hand goes out and rests on the bird-cage.*)

MRS. PETERS (*with rising voice*) We don't know who killed him. We don't *know.*

MRS. HALE (*her own feeling not interrupted*) If there'd been years and years of nothing, then a bird to sing to you, it would be awful—still, after the bird was still.

MRS. PETERS (*something within her speaking*) I know what stillness is. When we homesteaded in Dakota, and my first baby died—after he was two years old, and me with no other then—

MRS. HALE (*moving*) How soon do you suppose they'll be through looking for the evidence?

MRS. PETERS I know what stillness is. (*pulling herself back*) The law has got to punish crime, Mrs. Hale.

MRS. HALE (*not as if answering that*) I wish you'd seen Minnie Foster when she wore a white dress with blue ribbons and stood up there in the choir and sang. (*a look around the room*) Oh, I *wish* I'd come over here once in a while! That was a crime! That was a crime! Who's going to punish that?

MRS. PETERS (*looking upstairs*) We mustn't—take on.

MRS. HALE I might have known she needed help! I know how things can be—for women. I tell you, it's queer, Mrs. Peters. We live close together and we live far apart. We all go through the same things—it's all just a different kind of the same thing. (*brushes her eyes, noticing the jar of fruit, reaches out for it*) If I was you I wouldn't tell her her fruit was gone. Tell her it *ain't.* Tell her it's all right. Take this in to prove it to her. She—she may never know whether it was broke or not.

MRS. PETERS (*takes the jar, looks about for something to wrap it in; takes petticoat from the clothes brought from the other room, very nervously begins winding this around the jar; in a false voice:*) My, it's a good thing the men couldn't hear us. Wouldn't they just laugh! Getting all stirred up over a little thing like a—dead canary. As if that could have anything to do with—with—wouldn't they *laugh!* (*The men are heard coming downstairs.*)

MRS. HALE (*under her breath*) Maybe they would—maybe they wouldn't.

COUNTY ATTORNEY No, Peters, it's all perfectly clear except a reason for doing it. But you know juries when it comes to women. If there was some definite thing. (*Crosses slowly to above table.* SHERIFF *crosses down right.* MRS. HALE *and* MRS. PETERS *remain seated at either side of table.*) Something to show—something to make a story about—a thing that would connect up with this strange way of doing it—(*The women's eyes meet for an instant. Enter* HALE *from outer door.*)

HALE (*remaining up left by door*) Well, I've got the team around. Pretty cold out there.

COUNTY ATTORNEY I'm going to stay awhile by myself. (*to the* SHERIFF) You can send Frank out for me, can't you? I want to go over everything. I'm not satisfied that we can't do better.

SHERIFF Do you want to see what Mrs. Peters is going to take in? (*The* LAWYER *picks up the apron, laughs.*)

COUNTY ATTORNEY Oh, I guess they're not very dangerous things the ladies have picked out. (*moves a few things about, disturbing the quilt pieces which cover the box, steps back*) No, Mrs. Peters doesn't need supervising. For that matter a sheriff's wife is married to the law. Ever think of it that way, Mrs. Peters?

MRS. PETERS Not—just that way.

SHERIFF (*chuckling*) Married to the law. (*moves to down right door to the other room*) I just want you to come in here a minute, George. We ought to take a look at these windows.

COUNTY ATTORNEY (*scoffingly*) Oh, windows!

SHERIFF We'll be right out, Mr. Hale. (HALE *goes outside. The* SHERIFF *follows the* COUNTY ATTORNEY *into the other room. Then* MRS. HALE *rises, hands tight together, looking intensely at* MRS. PETERS, *whose eyes make a slow turn, finally meeting* MRS. HALE*'s. A moment* MRS. HALE *holds her, then her own eyes point the way to where the box is concealed. Suddenly* MRS. PETERS *throws back quilt pieces and tries to put the box in the bag she is carrying. It is too big. She opens box, starts to take bird out, cannot touch it, goes to pieces, stands there helpless. Sound of a knob turning in the other room.* MRS. HALE *snatches the box and puts it in the pocket of her big coat. Enter* COUNTY ATTORNEY *and* SHERIFF, *who remains down right.*)

COUNTY ATTORNEY (*crosses to up left door facetiously*) Well, Henry, at least we found out that she was not going to quilt it. She was going to—what is it you call it, ladies?

MRS. HALE (*standing center below table facing front, her hand against her pocket*) We call it—knot it, Mr. Henderson.

Curtain

DESIRE UNDER THE ELMS

(1924)

EUGENE O'NEILL (1888–1953)

Eugene O'Neill has survived as America's greatest dramatist, but it was not always certain he would do so. Hailed in the 1920s and 1930s as the hewer of new ways, he produced a body of astonishingly good and frightfully bad plays between the two great wars, demonstrating a theatrical talent of unequaled skill and intensity while also displaying some incredibly inept artistic talent. Both in the quality of what he did and in his thematic and stylistic approach, O'Neill baffled, confused, and infuriated his public, but he always attracted them. Like Shaw, who called him a "banshee Shakespeare," O'Neill eventually attained the ability to make audiences and actors do his bidding in stupendous feats of endurance in the presentation of the multiact five-hour and longer marathons that capped the first half of his career prior to his long "retirement" before and during World War II.

Welcomed as America's first great realist, O'Neill became almost at once our first great expressionist. Seen as the improvisor who would alter the basic concepts of contemporary theatre, he endures as probably the greatest writer of modern naturalistic tragedy. While he lived, his plays were front-page news. Those who liked him would often turn ecstatic; those who did not were known to try to close down his plays as dangerous and immoral obscenities. When he died he had so completely disappeared from public awareness that his funeral passed all but unnoticed, his plays seldom staged. The posthumous production of his later works, now accepted as his best, have returned O'Neill as a dramatic artist of world importance and of permanently high artistic stature.

O'Neill was not only a product of the movement that fostered the development of little theatres in the period before and during World War I, but he, like Glaspell, was a prime mover within it. In fact, it was Jig Cook and Susan Glaspell who recognized the unique talent of this young, shy, and brooding Irishman and welcomed him into the fledgling Provincetown Players. He became almost at once and for several years thereafter the group's most important writer and public drawing card.

The background of Eugene O'Neill would not suggest that he would evolve into America's greatest dramatist, honored the world over, winner of three

Pulitzer Prizes during his lifetime, another posthumously, and the Nobel Prize for literature. He was almost literally born and bred backstage. He was the son of James O'Neill, one of the great matinee idols at the end of the nineteenth century, whose endless playing of the lead role in *The Count of Monte Cristo* earned him a fortune but stifled a career as a classical actor equaling Edwin Booth, with whom he had at one time played. Farmed out to a variety of private secondary schools; surviving less than a year at Princeton; a newspaper stringer in New London, Connecticut; a prospector for gold in Honduras; a sailor on sailing and steam vessels to Europe and South America; married and divorced with a child he never knew until many years later; a derelict in New York waterfront bars and flophouses; associate of whores, pimps, and petty gangsters; heavy drinker and near-alcoholic; victim of incipient tuberculosis—by the time he was twenty-six years old, Eugene O'Neill seemed to have absolutely no future whatever.

But the young O'Neill had always been an avid reader and aspiring poet, as shown in some unimpressive verses written for his New London paper. Although he was turned off by the melodramatic pyrotechnics and sentimentalities of the theatre that welcomed his father, during his 1912–1913 convalescence in a Connecticut sanatorium he became fascinated by the brooding naturalistic plays of Strindberg. He soon began writing on his own, and with his father's help, he published a slim volume in 1914 called *Thirst, and Other One-Act Plays,* which nobody bought then but now is a valuable collector's item. That same year, again backed by his father, he entered George Pierce Baker's English 47 at Harvard, supposedly a composition course but actually a course in playwriting that became famous as the 47 Workshop, which produced many an important American playwright.

O'Neill was not attracted to the conventional dramaturgy taught by Baker. Instead, he shocked his classmates with short plays about adultery, sordid murder, and abortion. He had informed Baker in his application that "I want to be an artist or nothing," and after leaving the class, he stuck to his vow the rest of his life, writing with minor exception only plays, all of them created in his own way, regardless of how they might be viewed by his colleagues or his public.

In 1916 he was introduced to the Provincetown Players as a young man "with a trunkful of plays," one of which, *Bound East for Cardiff,* was read to the group. Upon hearing it, Susan Glaspell wrote, "we knew what we were for." Here was a voice of serious intensity, writing plotless one-act plays with a realistic atmosphere created by language and character in a manner that most members of the Provincetown had never before encountered. The play is set in the cramped quarters of a tramp steamer's forecastle among sailors of a variety of nationalities, speaking in dialects and behaving in manners with which O'Neill as a former seaman was very familiar. On one of the bunks lies a sailor dying of injuries suffered in a fall as the ship slowly plows through a rainy, foggy sea. As his fellow seamen come and go in their duties on deck, his agony and the agony of those who cannot help him are played out until, hallucinating and recalling his rough past, he is finally removed from his misery by death. Action has been minimal, but atmosphere and emotion have been everything. The Provincetown immediately chose the play to open their second season in 1916. From its first production in the group's tiny Wharf Theatre, which held scarcely 60 spectators in an abandoned fish shack on a pier jutting over the water and enveloped with fog as the waves lapped underneath, through many seasons in New York's Greenwich Village, a play by Eugene O'Neill was always a major event.

In February 1920, O'Neill's Pulitzer Prize–winning domestic tragedy of life and death on a New England farm, *Beyond the Horizon,* appeared on Broadway. On November 1 of the same year the highly stylized, expressionistic portrayal of the former Pullman porter turned despot in *The Emperor Jones,* performed by the Provincetown Players, became the year's theatrical sensation. Sophisticated New York playgoers, who normally attended the major Broadway theatres with little interest in what went on in the narrow confines of Greenwich Village, stampeded to see it.

European expressionism had never gained much of a foothold in American drama. Its emphasis on contemporary social and political concerns often appeared too radical and controversial. O'Neill's fascination with Strindberg, whose *The Dream Play* in 1902 has generally been considered the first significant expressionistic play, had led him to his stylized experimentation in *Jones.* Theatrical devices in both sight and sound heightened the mental deterioration of the once proud "emperor" who had suppressed and exploited the black natives whom he held in utter contempt. The constant beating of native drums in the background, first at the rate of a normal heartbeat, then rising in tempo as Jones became more and more panicked in his flight through the jungle, kept the audience continually on edge. Scenery projected against the plaster dome of the theatre, lit to suggest the infinity of the sky, emphasized the forbidding nature of the forest that entrapped the fugitive. Jones's whole life and the life of the race itself were projected onto the stage as Jones shed his imperial trappings and was reduced to a helpless, whimpering creature in a loin cloth. Most important of all, O'Neill had insisted that a black actor, not a white man in blackface, should play the part of Jones—the first time a major role had been assigned to a black actor in American theatre history.

A year after *Jones,* the realistic comedy-drama *Anna Christie,* with a reformed prostitute as the heroine who finds hope and true love in defiance of all of Bronson Howard's "laws," won a second Pulitzer. Then, after stumbling with a couple of critical and popular failures, O'Neill sent out an even more shocking wave with his second expressionistic creation, *The Hairy Ape* (1922), the story of a burly, bullying steamship stoker, Yank. Because of its underlying violent nature and particularly the earthy profanity of its language and despite much critical praise, the mayor of New York City attempted to close it down; and, as is always the case when offended guardians of morality move to deny access to the public, that same public clamored to see it. Because it was known that O'Neill had worked on both sailing and steam vessels, the play seemed to be a naturalistic picture of this grimy life below decks. But *The Hairy Ape* is considerably more than that, with its obvious distortions of reality and its vivid interpretation of what things *seemed* like, a consciously stylized artistic *expression* of reality.

Very early in his career, O'Neill affirmed that he was not interested in the relationship of man to man but of man to God. This did not assume any particular religion or creed, but it was truly a classic tragic concept. *Desire Under the Elms* is O'Neill's first tragedy in the classic sense. It is not Greek in the literal sense of neoclassical imitation, even though it follows the outline of the classic myth of Queen Phaedra and her incestuous passion for her stepson, Hippolytus. The closer imitation of the Greek was to come later in O'Neill's adaptation of *The Oresteia* in *Mourning Becomes Electra* in 1931, transferring the legend to Civil War New England. *Desire Under the Elms* makes use not of the fates but of the natural environment, and instead of gods imposing curses it uses elemental passions beyond the control of the protagonists. There is a primitive force in evidence, seen in the rock-hard unyielding land under the control of an equally hard, unyielding god. The characters are at the mercy of what they are—ignorant, earthy, unlettered, performing with animal lust in the satisfaction of natural urges. They are trapped by what they are as much as is Oedipus, and their escape is equally impossible.

There is great size and stature here. Old Cabot is a huge man, able to challenge his demanding god, yet remaining an absolute child of nature who can find solace among the dumb beasts in the barn. The attraction between Eben and Abbie, first calculated for personal gain, then out of control as a natural force, passes through the walls of the house to create a sinister atmosphere that even old Cabot senses but cannot understand. In the end, the realization of what they have done and the recognition of their fate, which must be shared, compel Eben and Abbie to face the inevitable catastrophe. Ephraim can return to his cows, but destruction is total for the adulterous semi-incestuous lovers who have succumbed to, but at the same time conquered, the elemental forces of their downfall.

Desire Under the Elms EUGENE O'NEILL

CHARACTERS

EPHRAIM CABOT
SIMEON }
PETER } *his sons*
EBEN }
ABBIE PUTNAM
YOUNG GIRL, TWO FARMERS, THE FIDDLER, THE SHERIFF, OTHER FOLK *from the neighboring farms*

The action of the entire play takes place in, and immediately outside of, the CABOT *farmhouse in New England, in the year 1850. The south end of the house faces front to a stone wall with a wooden gate at center opening on a country road. The house is in good condition but in need of paint. Its walls are a sickly grayish, the green of the shutters faded. Two enormous elms are on each side of the house. They bend their trailing branches down over the roof. They appear to protect and at the same time subdue. There is a sinister maternity in their aspect, a crushing, jealous absorption. They have developed from their intimate contact with the life of man in the house an appalling humaneness. They brood oppressively over the house. They are like exhausted women resting their sagging breasts and hands and hair on its roof, and when it rains their tears trickle down monotonously and rot on the shingles.*

There is a path running from the gate around the right corner of the house to the front door. A narrow porch is on this side. The end wall facing us has two windows in its upper story, two larger ones on the floor below. The two upper are those of the father's bedroom and that of the brothers. On the left, ground floor, is the kitchen—on the right, the parlor, the shades of which are always drawn down.

Part I

Scene I

Exterior of the farmhouse. It is sunset of a day at the beginning of summer in the year 1850. There is no wind and everything is still. The sky above the roof is suffused with deep colors, the green of the elms glows, but the house is in shadow, seeming pale and washed out by contrast.

A door opens and EBEN CABOT *comes to the end of the porch and stands looking down the road to the right. He has a large bell in his hand and this he swings mechanically, awakening a deafening clangor. Then he puts his hands on his hips and stares up at the sky. He sighs with a puzzled awe and blurts out with halting appreciation.*

EBEN God! Purty! (*His eyes fall and he stares about him frowningly. He is twenty-five, tall and sinewy. His face is well-formed, good-looking, but its expression is resentful and defensive. His defiant, dark eyes remind one of a wild animal's in captivity. Each day is a cage in which he finds himself trapped but inwardly unsubdued. There is a fierce repressed vitality about him. He has black hair, mustache, a thin curly trace of beard. He is dressed in rough farm clothes.*

He spits on the ground with intense disgust, turns and goes back into the house.

SIMEON *and* PETER *come in from their work in the fields. They are tall men, much older than their half-brother* [SIMEON *is thirty-nine and* PETER *thirty-seven*], *built on a squarer, simpler model, fleshier in body, more bovine and homelier in face, shrewder and more practical. Their shoulders stoop a bit from years of farm work. They clump heavily along in their clumsy thick-soled boots caked with earth. Their clothes, their faces, hands, bare arms and throats are earth-stained. They smell of earth. They stand together for a moment in front of the house and, as if with the one impulse, stare dumbly up at the sky, leaning on their hoes. Their faces have a compressed, unresigned expression. As they look upward, this softens.*)

SIMEON (*grudgingly*) Purty.

PETER Ay-eh.

SIMEON (*suddenly*) Eighteen year ago.

PETER What?

SIMEON Jenn. My woman. She died.

PETER I'd fergot.

SIMEON I rec'lect—now an' agin. Makes it lonesome. She'd hair long's a hoss' tail—an' yaller like gold!

PETER Waal—she's gone. (*this with indifferent finality—then after a pause*) They's gold in the West, Sim.

SIMEON (*still under the influence of sunset—vaguely*) In the sky?

PETER Waal—in a manner o' speakin'—thar's the promise. (*growing excited*) Gold in the sky—in the West—Golden Gate—Californi-a!—Goldest West!—fields o' gold!

SIMEON (*excited in his turn*) Fortunes layin' just atop o' the ground waitin' t' be picked! Solomon's mines, they says! (*For a moment they continue looking up at the sky—then their eyes drop.*)

PETER (*with sardonic bitterness*) Here—it's stones atop o' the ground—stones atop o' stones—makin' stone walls—year atop o' year—him 'n' yew 'n' me 'n' then Eben—makin' stone walls fur him to fence us in!

SIMEON We've wuked. Give our strength. Give our years. Plowed 'em under in the ground—(*He stamps rebelliously.*)—rottin'—makin' soil for his crops! (*a pause*) Waal—the farm pays good for hereabouts.

PETER If we plowed in Californi-a, they'd be lumps o' gold in the furrow!

SIMEON Californi-a's t'other side o' earth, a'most. We got t' calc'late —

PETER (*after a pause*) 'Twould be hard fur me, too, to give up what we've 'arned here by our sweat. (*A pause;* EBEN *sticks his head out of the dining-room window, listening.*)

SIMEON Ay-eh. (*a pause*) Mebbe—he'll die soon.

PETER (*doubtfully*) Mebbe.

SIMEON Mebbe—fur all we knows—he's dead now.

PETER Ye'd need proof.

SIMEON He's been gone two months—with no word.

PETER Left us in the fields an evenin' like this. Hitched up an' druv off into the West. That's plum onnateral. He hain't never been off this farm 'ceptin' t' the village in thirty year or more, not since he married Eben's maw. (*a pause; shrewdly*) I calc'late we might git him declared crazy by the court.

SIMEON He skinned 'em too slick. He got the best o' all on 'em. They'd never b'lieve him crazy. (*a pause*) We got t' wait—till he's under ground.

EBEN (*with a sardonic chuckle*) Honor thy father! (*They turn, startled, and stare at him. He grins, then scowls.*) I pray he's died. (*They stare at him. He continues matter-of-factly.*) Supper's ready.

SIMEON *and* PETER (*together*) Ay-eh.

EBEN (*gazing up at the sky*) Sun's downin' purty.

SIMEON *and* PETER (*together*) Ay-eh. They's gold in the West.

EBEN Ay-eh. (*pointing*) Yonder atop o' the hill pasture, ye mean?

SIMEON *and* PETER (*together*) In Californi-a!

EBEN Hunh? (*stares at them indifferently for a second, then drawls*) Waal—supper's gittin' cold. (*He turns back into kitchen.*)

SIMEON (*startled—smacks his lips*) I air hungry!

PETER (*sniffing*) I smells bacon!

SIMEON (*with hungry appreciation*) Bacon's good!

PETER (*in same tone*) Bacon's bacon! (*They turn, shouldering each other, their bodies bumping and rubbing together as they hurry clumsily to their food, like two friendly oxen toward their evening meal. They disappear around the right corner of house and can be heard entering the door.*)

Scene 2

The color fades from the sky. Twilight begins. The interior of the kitchen is now visible. A pine table is at center, a cookstove in the right rear corner, four rough wooden chairs, a tallow candle on the table. In the middle of the rear wall is fastened a big advertising poster with a ship in full sail and the word "California" in big letters. Kitchen utensils hang from nails. Everything is neat and in order but the atmosphere is of a men's camp kitchen rather than that of a home.

Places for three are laid. EBEN *takes boiled potatoes and bacon from the stove and puts them on the table, also a loaf of bread and a crock of water.* SIMEON *and* PETER *shoulder in, slump down in their chairs without a word.* EBEN *joins them. The three eat in silence for a moment, the two elder as naturally unrestrained as beasts of the field,* EBEN *picking at his food without appetite, glancing at them with a tolerant dislike.*

SIMEON (*suddenly turns to* EBEN) Looky here! Ye'd oughtn't t' said that, Eben.

PETER 'Twa'n't righteous.

EBEN What?

SIMEON Ye prayed he'd died.

EBEN Waal—don't yew pray it? (*a pause*)

PETER He's our Paw.

EBEN (*violently*) Not mine!

SIMEON (*dryly*) Ye'd not let no one else say that about yer Maw! Ha! (*He gives one abrupt sardonic guffaw.* PETER *grins.*)

EBEN (*very pale*) I meant—I hain't his'n—I hain't like him—he hain't me!

PETER (*dryly*) Wait till ye've growed his age!

EBEN (*intensely*) I'm Maw—every drop o' blood! (*A pause. They stare at him with indifferent curiosity.*)

PETER (*reminiscently*) She was good t' Sim 'n' me. A good stepmaw's scurse.

SIMEON She was good t' everyone.

EBEN (*greatly moved, gets to his feet and makes an awkward bow to each of them—stammering*) I be thankful t' ye. I'm her—her heir. (*He sits down in confusion.*)

PETER (*after a pause—judicially*) She was good even t' him.

EBEN (*fiercely*) An' fur thanks he killed her!

SIMEON (*after a pause*) No one never kills nobody. It's allus somethin'. That's the murderer.

EBEN Didn't he slave Maw t' death?

PETER He's slaved himself t' death. He's slaved Sim 'n' me 'n' yew t' death—on'y none o' us hain't died—yit.

SIMEON It's somethin'—drivin' him—t' drive us!

EBEN (*vengefully*) Waal—I hold him t' jedgment! (*then scornfully*) Somethin'! What's somethin'?

SIMEON Dunno.

EBEN (*sardonically*) What's drivin' yew to Californi-a, mebbe? (*They look at him in surprise.*) Oh, I've heerd ye! (*then, after a pause*) But ye'll never go t' the gold fields!

PETER (*assertively*) Mebbe!

EBEN Whar'll ye git the money?

PETER We kin walk. It's an a'mighty ways—Californi-a—but if yew was t' put all the steps we've walked on this farm end t' end we'd be in the moon!

EBEN The Injuns'll skulp ye on the plains.

SIMEON (*with grim humor*) We'll mebbe make 'em pay a hair fur a hair!

EBEN (*decisively*) But t'ain't that. Ye won't never go because ye'll wait here fur yer share o' the farm, thinkin' allus he'll die soon.

SIMEON (*after a pause*) We've a right.

PETER Two-thirds belongs t'us.

EBEN (*jumping to his feet*) Ye've no right! She wa'n't yewr Maw! It was her farm! Didn't he steal it from her? She's dead. It's my farm.

SIMEON (*sardonically*) Tell that t' Paw—when he comes! I'll bet ye a dollar he'll laugh—fur once in his life. Ha! (*He laughs himself in one single mirthless bark.*)

PETER (*amused in turn, echoes his brother*) Ha!

SIMEON (*after a pause*) What've ye got held agin us, Eben? Year arter year it's skulked in yer eye—somethin'.

PETER Ay-eh.

EBEN Ay-eh. They's somethin'. (*suddenly exploding*) Why didn't ye never stand between him 'n' my Maw when he was slavin' her to her grave—t' pay her back fur the kindness she done t' yew? (*There is a long pause. They stare at him in surprise.*)

SIMEON Waal—the stock'd got t' be watered.

PETER 'R they was woodin' t' do.

SIMEON 'R plowin'.

PETER 'R hayin'.

SIMEON 'R spreadin' manure.

PETER 'R weedin'.

SIMEON 'R prunin'.

PETER 'R milkin'.

EBEN (*breaking in harshly*) An' makin' walls—stone atop o' stone—makin' walls till yer heart's a stone ye heft up out o' the way o' growth onto a stone wall t' wall in yer heart!

SIMEON (*matter-of-factly*) We never had no time t' meddle.

PETER (*to* EBEN) Yew was fifteen afore yer Maw died—an' big fur yer age. Why didn't ye never do nothin'?

EBEN (*harshly*) They was chores t' do, wa'n't they? (*a pause—then slowly*) It was on'y arter she died I come to think o' it. Me cookin'—doin' her work—that made me know her, suffer her sufferin'—she'd come back t' help—come back t' bile potatoes—come back t' fry bacon—come back t' bake biscuits—come back all cramped up t' shake the fire, an' carry ashes, her eyes weepin' an' bloody with smoke an' cinders same's they used t' be. She still comes back—stands by the stove thar in the evenin'—she can't find it nateral sleepin' an' restin' in peace. She can't git used t' bein' free—even in her grave.

SIMEON She never complained none.

EBEN She'd got too tired. She'd got too used t' being' too tired. That was what he done. (*with vengeful passion*) An' sooner'r later, I'll meddle. I'll say the thin's I didn't say then t' him! I'll yell 'em at the top o' my lungs. I'll see t' it my Maw gits some rest an' sleep in her grave! (*He sits down again, relapsing into a brooding silence. They look at him with a queer indifferent curiosity.*)

PETER (*after a pause*) Whar in tarnation d'ye s'pose he went, Sim?

SIMEON Dunno. He druv off in the buggy, all spick an' span, with the mare all breshed an' shiny, druv off clackin' his tongue an' wavin' his whip. I remember it right well. I was finishin' plowin', it was spring an' May an' sunset, an' gold in the West, an' he druv off into it. I yells "Whar ye goin', Paw?" an' he hauls up by the stone wall a jiffy. His old snake's eyes was glitterin' in the sun like he'd been drinkin' a jugful an' he says with a mule's grin: "Don't ye run away till I come back!"

PETER Wonder if he knowed we was wantin' fur Californi-a?

SIMEON Mebbe. I didn't say nothin' and he says, lookin' kinder queer an' sick: "I been hearin' the hens cluckin' an' the roosters crowin' all the durn day. I been listenin' t' the cows lowin' an' everythin' else kickin' up till I can't stand it no more. It's spring an' I'm feelin' damned," he says. "Damned like an old bare hickory tree fit on'y fur burnin'," he says. An' then I calc'late I must've looked a mite hopeful, fur he adds real spry and vicious: "But don't git no fool idee I'm dead. I've sworn t' live a hundred an' I'll do it, if on'y t' spite yer sinful greed! An' now I'm ridin' out t' learn God's message t' me in the spring, like the prophets done. An' yew git back t' yer plowin'," he says. An' he druv off singin' a hymn. I thought he was drunk—'r I'd stopped him goin'.

EBEN (*scornfully*) No, ye wouldn't! Ye're scared o' him. He's stronger—inside—than both o' ye put together!

PETER (*sardonically*) An' yew—be yew Samson?

EBEN I'm gittin' stronger. I kin feel it growin' in me—growin' an' growin'—till it'll bust out—! (*He gets up and puts on his coat and a hat. They watch him, gradually breaking into grins.* EBEN *avoids their eyes sheepishly.*) I'm goin' out fur a spell—up the road.

PETER T' the village?

SIMEON T' see Minnie?

EBEN (*defiantly*) Ay-eh!

PETER (*jeeringly*) The Scarlet Woman!

SIMEON Lust—that's what's growin' in ye!

EBEN Waal—she's purty!

PETER She's been purty fur twenty year!

SIMEON A new coat o' paint'll make a heifer out of forty.

EBEN She hain't forty!

PETER If she hain't, she's teeterin' on the edge.

EBEN (*desperately*) What d'yew know —

PETER All they is . . . Sim knew her—an' then me arter —

SIMEON An' Paw kin tell yew somethin' too! He was fust!

EBEN D'ye mean t' say he . . . ?

SIMEON (*with a grin*) Ay-eh! We air his heirs in everythin'!

EBEN (*intensely*) That's more to it! That grows on it! It'll bust soon! (*then violently*) I'll go smash my fist in her face! (*He pulls open the door in rear violently.*)

SIMEON (*with a wink at* PETER—*drawlingly*) Mebbe—but the night's wa'm—purty—by the time ye git thar mebbe ye'll kiss her instead!

PETER Sart'n he will! (*They both roar with coarse laughter.* EBEN *rushes out and slams the door—then the outside front door—comes around the corner of the house and stands still by the gate, staring up at the sky.*)

SIMEON (*looking after him*) Like his Paw.

PETER Dead spit an' image!

SIMEON Dog'll eat dog!

PETER Ay-eh. (*pause; with yearning*) Mebbe a year from now we'll be in Californi-a.

SIMEON Ay-eh. (*A pause. Both yawn.*) Let's git t'bed. (*He blows out the candle. They go out door in rear.* EBEN *stretches his arms up to the sky—rebelliously.*)

EBEN Waal—thar's a star, an' somewhar's they's him, an' here's me, an' thar's Min up the road—in the same night. What if I does kiss her? She's like t'night, she's soft 'n' wa'm, her eyes kin wink like a star, her mouth's wa'm, her arms're wa'm, she smells like a wa'm plowed field, she's purty . . . Ay-eh! By God A'mighty she's purty, an' I don't give a damn how many sins she's sinned afore mine or who she's sinned 'em with, my sin's as purty as any one on 'em! (*He strides off down the road to the left.*)

Scene 3

It is the pitch darkness just before dawn. EBEN *comes in from the left and goes around to the porch, feeling his way, chuckling bitterly and cursing half-aloud to himself.*

EBEN The cussed old miser! (*He can be heard going in the front door. There is a pause as he goes upstairs, then a loud knock on the bedroom door of the brothers.*) Wake up!

SIMEON (*startedly*) Who's thar?

EBEN (*pushing open the door and coming in, a lighted candle in his hand. The bedroom of the brothers is revealed. Its ceiling is the sloping roof. They can stand upright only close to the center dividing wall of the upstairs.* SIMEON *and* PETER *are in a double bed, front.* EBEN'S *cot is to the rear.* EBEN *has a mixture of silly grin and vicious scowl on his face*) I be!

PETER (*angrily*) What in hell's-fire . . . ?

EBEN I got news fur ye! Ha! (*He gives one abrupt sardonic guffaw.*)

SIMEON (*angrily*) Couldn't ye hold it 'til we'd got our sleep?

EBEN It's nigh sunup. (*then explosively*) He's gone an' married agen!

SIMEON *and* PETER (*explosively*) Paw?

EBEN Got himself hitched to a female 'bout thirty-five—an' purty, they says . . .

SIMEON (*aghast*) It's a durn lie!

PETER Who says?

SIMEON They been stringin' ye!

EBEN Think I'm a dunce, do ye? The hull village says. The preacher from New Dover, he brung the news—told it t'our preacher—New Dover, that's whar the old loon got himself hitched—that's whar the woman lived—

PETER (*no longer doubting—stunned*) Waal . . . !

SIMEON (*the same*) Waal . . . !

EBEN (*sitting down on a bed—with vicious hatred*) Ain't he a devil out o' hell? It's jest t' spite us—the damned old mule!

PETER (*after a pause*) Everythin'll go t' her now.

SIMEON Ay-eh. (*a pause—dully*) Waal—if it's done—

PETER It's done us. (*pause—then persuasively*) They's gold in the fields o' Californi-a, Sim. No good a-stayin' here now.

SIMEON Jest what I was a-thinkin'. (*then with decision*) S'well fust's last! Let's light out and git this mornin'.

PETER Suits me.

EBEN Ye must like walkin'.

SIMEON (*sardonically*) If ye'd grow wings on us we'd fly thar!

EBEN Ye'd like ridin' better—on a boat, wouldn't ye? (*fumbles in his pocket and takes out a crumpled sheet of foolscap*) Waal, if ye sign this ye kin ride on a boat. I've had it writ out an' ready in case ye'd ever go. It says fur three hundred dollars t' each ye agree yewr shares o' the farm is sold t' me. (*They look suspiciously at the paper. A pause.*)

SIMEON (*wonderingly*) But if he's hitched agen—

PETER An' whar'd yew git that sum o' money, anyways?

EBEN (*cunningly*) I know whar it's hid. I been waitin'—Maw told me. She knew whar it lay fur years, but she was waitin' . . . It's her'n—the money he hoarded from her farm an' hid from Maw. It's my money by rights now.

PETER Whar's it hid?

EBEN (*cunningly*) Whar yew won't never find it without me. Maw spied on him—'r she'd never knowed. (*A pause. They look at him suspiciously, and he at them.*) Waal, is it fa'r trade?

SIMEON Dunno.

PETER Dunno.

SIMEON (*looking at window*) Sky's grayin'.

PETER Ye better start the fire, Eben.

SIMEON An' fix some vittles.

EBEN Ay-eh. (*then with a forced jocular heartiness*) I'll git ye a good one. If ye're startin' t' hoof it t' Californi-a ye'll need somethin' that'll stick t' yer ribs. (*He turns to the door, adding meaningly:*) But ye kin ride on a boat if ye'll swap. (*He stops at the door and pauses. They stare at him.*)

SIMEON (*suspiciously*) Whar was ye all night?

EBEN (*defiantly*) Up t' Min's. (*then slowly*) Walkin' thar, fust I felt 's if I'd kiss her; then I got a-thinkin' on' what ye'd said o' him an' her an' I says, I'll bust her nose fur that! Then I got t' the village an' heerd the news an' I got madder'n hell an' run all the way t' Min's not knowin' what I'd do—(*He pauses—then sheepishly but more defiantly:*) Waal—when I seen her, I didn't hit her—nor I didn't kiss her nuther—I begun t' beller like a calf an' cuss at the same time, I was so durn mad—an' she got scared—an' I jest grabbed holt an' tuk her! (*proudly*) Yes, sirree! I tuk her. She may've been his'n—an' your'n, too—but she's mine now!

SIMEON (*dryly*) In love, air yew?

EBEN (*with lofty scorn*) Love! I don't take no stock in sech slop!

PETER (*winking at* SIMEON) Mebbe Eben's aimin' t' marry, too.

SIMEON Min'd make a true faithful he'pmeet! (*They snicker.*)

EBEN What do I care fur her—'ceptin' she's round an' wa'm? The p'int is she was his'n—an' now she belongs t' me! (*He goes to the door—then turns—rebelliously.*) An' Min hain't sech a bad un. They's worse'n Min in the world, I'll bet ye! Wait'll we see this cow the Old Man's hitched t'! She'll beat Min, I got a notion! (*He starts to go out.*)

SIMEON (*suddenly*) Mebbe ye'll try t' make her your'n, too?

PETER Ha! (*He gives a sardonic laugh of relish at this idea.*)

EBEN (*spitting with disgust*) Her—here—sleepin' with him—stealin' my Maw's farm! I'd as soon pet a skunk 'r kiss a snake! (*He goes out. The two stare after him suspiciously. A pause. They listen to his steps receding.*)

PETER He's startin' the fire.

SIMEON I'd like t' ride t' Californi-a—but —

PETER Min might o' put some scheme in his head.

SIMEON Mebbe it's all a lie 'bout Paw marryin'. We'd best wait an' see the bride.

PETER An' don't sign nothin' till we does!

SIMEON Nor till we've tested it's good money! (*then with a grin*) But if Paw's hitched we'd be sellin' Eben somethin' we'd never git nohow!

PETER We'll wait an' see. (*then with sudden vindictive anger*) An' till he comes, let's yew 'n' me not wuk a lick, let Eben tend to thin's if he's a mind t', let's us jest sleep an' eat an' drink likker, an' let the hull damned farm go t' blazes!

SIMEON (*excitedly*) By God, we've 'arned a rest! We'll play rich fur a change. I hain't a-going to stir outa bed till breakfast's ready.

PETER An' on the table!

SIMEON (*after a pause—thoughtfully*) What d'ye calc'late she'll be like—our new Maw? Like Eben thinks?

PETER More'n likely.

SIMEON (*vindictively*) Waal—I hope she's a she-devil that'll make him wish he was dead an' livin' in the pit o' hell fur comfort!

PETER (*fervently*) Amen!

SIMEON (*imitating his father's voice*) "I'm ridin' out t' learn God's message t' me in the spring like the prophets done," he says. I'll bet right then an' thar he knew plumb well he was goin' whorin', the stinkin' old hypocrite!

Scene 4

Same as SCENE 2*—shows the interior of the kitchen with a lighted candle on table. It is gray dawn outside.* **SIMEON** *and* **PETER** *are just finishing their breakfast.* **EBEN** *sits before his plate of untouched food, brooding frowningly.*

PETER (*glancing at him rather irritably*) Lookin' glum don't help none.

SIMEON (*sarcastically*) Sorrowin' over his lust o' the flesh!

PETER (*with a grin*) Was she yer fust?

EBEN (*angrily*) None o' yer business. (*a pause*) I was thinkin' o' him. I got a notion he's gittin' near—I kin feel him comin' on like yew kin feel malaria chill afore it takes ye.

PETER It's too early yet.

SIMEON Dunno. He'd like t' catch us nappin'—jest t' have somethin' t' hoss us 'round over.

PETER (*mechanically gets to his feet.* SIMEON *does the same.*) Waal—let's git t' wuk. (*They both plod mechanically toward the door before they realize. Then they stop short.*)

SIMEON (*grinning*) Ye're a cussed fool, Pete—and I be wuss! Let him see we hain't wukin'! We don't give a durn!

PETER (*as they go back to the table*) Not a damned durn! It'll serve t' show him we're done with him. (*They sit down again.* EBEN *stares from one to the other with surprise.*)

SIMEON (*grins at him*) We're aimin' t' start bein' lilies o' the field.

PETER Nary a toil 'r spin 'r lick o' wuk do we put in!

SIMEON Ye're sole owner—till he comes—that's what ye wanted. Waal, ye got t' be sole hand, too.

PETER The cows air bellerin'. Ye better hustle at the milkin'.

EBEN (*with excited joy*) Ye mean ye'll sign the paper?

SIMEON (*dryly*) Mebbe.

PETER Mebbe.

SIMEON We're considerin'. (*peremptorily*) Ye better git t' wuk.

EBEN (*with queer excitement*) It's Maw's farm agen! It's my farm! Them's my cows! I'll milk my durn fingers off fur cows o' mine! (*He goes out door in rear, they stare after him indifferently.*)

SIMEON Like his Paw.

PETER Dead spit 'n' image!

SIMEON Waal—let dog eat dog! (EBEN *comes out of front door and around the corner of the house. The sky is beginning to grow flushed with sunrise.* EBEN *stops by the gate and stares around him with glowing, possessive eyes. He takes in the whole farm with his embracing glance of desire.*)

EBEN It's purty! It's damned purty! It's mine! (*He suddenly throws his head back boldly and glares with hard, defiant eyes at the sky.*) Mine, d'ye hear? Mine! (*He turns and walks quickly off left, rear, toward the barn. The two brothers light their pipes.*)

SIMEON (*putting his muddy boots up on the table, tilting back his chair, and puffing defiantly*) Waal—this air solid comfort—fur once.

PETER Ay-eh. (*He follows suit. A pause. Unconsciously they both sigh.*)

SIMEON (*suddenly*) He never was much o' a hand at milkin', Eben wa'n't.

PETER (*with a snort*) His hands air like hoofs! (*a pause*)

SIMEON Reach down the jug thar! Let's take a swaller. I'm feelin' kind o' low.

PETER Good idee! (*He does so—gets two glasses—they pour out drinks of whisky.*) Here's t' the gold in Californi-a!

SIMEON An' luck t' find it! (*They drink—puff resolutely—sigh—take their feet down from the table.*)

PETER Likker don't pear t' sot right.

SIMEON We hain't used t' it this early. (*A pause. They become very restless.*)

PETER Gittin' close in this kitchen.

SIMEON (*with immense relief*) Let's git a breath o' air. (*They arise briskly and go out rear—appear around house and stop by the gate. They stare up at the sky with a numbed appreciation.*)

PETER Purty!

SIMEON Ay-eh. Gold's t' the East now.

PETER Sun's startin' with us fur the Golden West.

SIMEON (*staring around the farm, his compressed face tightened, unable to conceal his emotion*) Waal—it's our last mornin'—mebbe.

PETER (*the same*) Ay-eh.

SIMEON (*stamps his foot on the earth and addresses it desperately*) Waal—ye've thirty year o' me buried in ye—spread out over ye—blood an' bone an' sweat—rotted away—fertilizin' ye—richin' yer soul—prime manure, by God, that's what I been t' ye!

PETER Ay-eh! An' me!

SIMEON An' yew, Peter. (*He sighs—then spits.*) Waal—no use'n cryin' over spilt milk.

PETER They's gold in the West—an' freedom, mebbe. We been slaves t' stone walls here.

SIMEON (*defiantly*) We hain't nobody's slaves from this out—nor nothin's slaves nuther. (*a pause—restlessly*) Speakin' o' milk, wonder how Eben's managin'?

PETER I s'pose he's managin'.

SIMEON Mebbe we'd ought t' help—this once.

PETER Mebbe. The cows knows us.

SIMEON An' likes us. They don't know him much.

PETER An' the hosses, an' pigs, an' chickens. They don't know him much.

SIMEON They knows us like brothers—an' likes us! (*proudly*) Hain't we raised 'em t' be fust-rate, number one prize stock?

PETER We hain't—not no more.

SIMEON (*dully*) I was fergittin'. (*then resignedly*) Waal, let's go help Eben a spell an' git waked up.

PETER Suits me. (*They are starting off down left, rear, for the barn when* EBEN *appears from there hurrying toward them, his face excited.*)

EBEN (*breathlessly*) Waal—har they be! The old mule an' the bride! I seen 'em from the barn down below at the turnin'.

PETER How could ye tell that far?

EBEN Hain't I as far-sight as he's near-sight? Don't I know the mare 'n' buggy, an' two people settin' in it? Who else . . . ? An' I tell ye I kin feel 'em a-comin', too! (*He squirms as if he had the itch.*)

PETER (*beginning to be angry*) Waal—let him do his own unhitchin'!

SIMEON (*angry in his turn*) Let's hustle in an' git our bundles an' be a-goin' as he's a-comin'. I don't want never t' step inside the door agen arter he's back. (*They both start back around the corner of the house.* EBEN *follows them.*)

EBEN (*anxiously*) Will ye sign it afore ye go?

PETER Let's see the color o' the old skinflint's money an' we'll sign. (*They disappear left. The two brothers clump upstairs to get their bundles.* EBEN *appears in the kitchen, runs to the window, peers out, comes back and pulls up a strip of flooring in under stove, takes out a canvas bag and puts it on table, then sets the floorboard back in place. The two brothers appear a moment after. They carry old carpetbags.*)

EBEN (*puts his hand on bag guardingly*) Have ye signed?

SIMEON (*shows paper in his hand*) Ay-eh. (*greedily*) Be that the money?

EBEN (*opens bag and pours out pile of twenty-dollar gold pieces*) Twenty-dollar pieces—thirty on 'em. Count 'em. (PETER *does so, arranging them in stacks of five, biting one or two to test them.*)

PETER Six hundred. (*He puts them in bag and puts it inside his shirt carefully.*)

SIMEON (*handing paper to* EBEN) Har ye be.

EBEN (*after a glance, folds it carefully and hides it under his shirt—gratefully*) Thank yew.

PETER Thank yew fur the ride.

SIMEON We'll send ye a lump o' gold fur Christmas. (*A pause.* EBEN *stares at them and they at him.*)

PETER (*awkwardly*) Waal—we're a-goin'.

SIMEON Comin' out t' the yard?

EBEN No. I'm waitin' in here a spell. (*Another silence. The brothers edge awkwardly to door in rear—then turn and stand.*)

SIMEON Waal—good-by.

PETER Good-by.

EBEN Good-by. (*They go out. He sits down at the table, faces the stove and pulls out the paper. He looks from it to the stove. His face, lighted up by the shaft of sunlight from the window, has an expression of trance. His lips move. The two brothers come out to the gate.*)

PETER (*looking off toward barn*) Thar he be—unhitchin'.

SIMEON (*with a chuckle*) I'll bet ye he's riled!

PETER An' thar she be.

SIMEON Let's wait 'n' see what our new Maw looks like.

PETER (*with a grin*) An' give him our partin' cuss!

SIMEON (*grinning*) I feel like raisin' fun. I feel light in my head an' feet.

PETER Me, too. I feel like laffin' till I'd split up the middle.

SIMEON Reckon it's the likker?

PETER No. My feet feel itchin' t' walk an' walk—an' jump high over thin's—an'. . . .

SIMEON Dance? (*a pause*)

PETER (*puzzled*) It's plumb onnateral.

SIMEON (*a light coming over his face*) I calc'late it's 'cause school's out. It's holiday. Fur once we're free!

PETER (*dazedly*) Free?

SIMEON The halter's broke—the harness is busted—the fence bars is down—the stone walls air crumblin' an' tumblin'! We'll be kickin' up an' tearin' away down the road!

PETER (*drawing a deep breath—oratorically*) Anybody that wants this stinkin' old rock-pile of a farm kin hev it. 'Tain't our'n, no sirree!

SIMEON (*takes the gate off its hinges and puts it under his arm*) We harby 'bolishes shet gates an' open gates, an' all gates, by thunder!

PETER We'll take it with us fur luck an' let 'er sail free down some river.

SIMEON (*as a sound of voices comes from left, rear*) Har they comes! (*The two brothers congeal into two stiff, grim-visaged statues.* EPHRAIM CABOT *and* ABBIE PUTNAM *come in.* CABOT *is seventy-five, tall and gaunt, with great, wiry, concentrated power, but stoop-shouldered from toil. His face is as hard as if it were hewn out of a boulder, yet there is a weakness in it, a pretty pride in its own narrow strength. His eyes are small, close together, and extremely near-sighted, blinking continually in the effort to focus on objects, their stare having a straining, ingrowing quality. He is dressed in his dismal black Sunday suit.* ABBIE *is thirty-five, buxom, full of vitality. Her round face is pretty but marred by its rather gross sensuality. There is strength and obstinacy in her jaw, a hard determination in her eyes, and about her whole personality the same unsettled, untamed, desperate quality which is so apparent in* EBEN.)

CABOT (*as they enter—a queer strangled emotion in his dry cracking voice*) Har we be t' hum, Abbie.

ABBIE (*with lust for the word*) Hum! (*Her eyes gloating on the house without seeming to see the two stiff figures at the gate.*) It's purty—purty! I can't b'lieve it's r'ally mine.

CABOT (*sharply*) Yewr'n? Mine! (*He stares at her penetratingly. She stares back. He adds relentingly.*) Our'n—mebbe! It was lonesome too long. I was growin' old in the spring. A hum's got t' hev a woman.

ABBIE (*her voice taking possession*) A woman's got t' hev a hum!

CABOT (*nodding uncertainly*) Ay-eh. (*then irritably*) Whar be they? Ain't thar nobody about—'r wukin'—'r nothin'?

ABBIE (*sees the brothers. She returns their stare of cold appraising contempt with interest—slowly.*) Thar's two men loafin' at the gate an' starin' at me like a couple o' strayed hogs.

CABOT (*straining his eyes*) I kin see 'em—but I can't make out. . . .

SIMEON It's Simeon.

PETER It's Peter.

CABOT (*exploding*) Why hain't ye wukin'?

SIMEON (*dryly*) We're waitin' t' welcome ye hum—yew an' the bride!

CABOT (*confusedly*) Huh? Waal—this be yer new Maw, boys. (*She stares at them and they at her.*)

SIMEON (*turns away and spits contemptuously*) I see her!

PETER (*spits also*) An' I see her!

ABBIE (*with the conqueror's conscious superiority*) I'll go in an' look at *my* house. (*She goes slowly around to porch.*)

SIMEON (*with a snort*) *Her* house!

PETER (*calls after her*) Ye'll find Eben inside. Ye better not tell him it's *yewr* house.

ABBIE (*mouthing the name*) Eben. (*then quietly*) I'll tell Eben.

CABOT (*with a contemptuous sneer*) Ye needn't heed Eben. Eben's a dumb fool—like his Maw—soft an' simple!

SIMEON (*with his sardonic burst of laughter*) Ha! Eben's a chip o' yew—spit 'n' image—hard 'n' bitter's a hickory tree! Dog'll eat dog. He'll eat ye yet, old man!

CABOT (*commandingly*) Ye git t' wuk!

SIMEON (*as* ABBIE *disappears in house—winks at* PETER *and says tauntingly*) So that thar's our new Maw, be it? Whar in hell did ye dig her up? (*He and* PETER *laugh.*)

PETER Ha! Ye'd better turn her in the pen with the other sows. (*They laugh uproariously, slapping their thighs.*)

CABOT (*so amazed at their effrontery that he stutters in confusion*) Simeon! Peter! What's come over ye? Air ye drunk?

SIMEON We're free, old man—free o' yew an' the hull damned farm! (*They grow more and more hilarious and excited.*)

PETER An' we're startin' out fur the gold fields o' Californi-a!

SIMEON Ye kin take this place an' burn it!

PETER An' bury it—fur all we cares!

SIMEON We're free, old man! (*He cuts a caper.*)

PETER Free! (*He gives a kick in the air.*)

SIMEON (*in a frenzy*) Whoop!

PETER Whoop! (*They do an absurd Indian war dance about the old man who is petrified between rage and the fear that they are insane.*)

SIMEON We're free as Injuns! Lucky we don't sculp ye!

PETER An' burn yer barn an' kill the stock!

SIMEON An' rape yer new woman! Whoop! (*He and* PETER *stop their dance, holding their sides, rocking with wild laughter.*)

CABOT (*edging away*) Lust fur gold—fur the sinful, easy gold o' Californi-a! It's made ye mad!

SIMEON (*tauntingly*) Wouldn't ye like us to send ye back some sinful gold, ye old sinner?

PETER They's gold besides what's in Californi-a! (*He retreats back beyond the vision of the old man and takes the bag of money and flaunts it in the air above his head, laughing.*)

SIMEON And sinfuller, too!

PETER We'll be voyagin' on the sea! Whoop! (*He leaps up and down.*)

SIMEON Livin' free! Whoop! (*He leaps in turn.*)

CABOT (*suddenly roaring with rage*) My cuss on ye!

SIMEON Take our'n in trade fur it! Whoop!

CABOT I'll hev ye both chained up in the asylum!

PETER Ye old skinflint! Good-by!

SIMEON Ye old blood sucker! Good-by!

CABOT Go afore I . . . !

PETER Whoop! (*He picks a stone from the road.* SIMEON *does the same.*)

SIMEON Maw'll be in the parlor.

PETER Ay-eh! One! Two!

CABOT (*frightened*) What air ye . . . ?

PETER Three! (*They both throw, the stones hitting the parlor window with a crash of glass, tearing the shade.*)

SIMEON Whoop!

PETER Whoop!

CABOT (*in a fury now, rushing toward them*) If I kin lay hands on ye—I'll break yer bones fur ye! (*But they beat a capering retreat before him,* SIMEON *with the gate still under his arm.* CABOT *comes back, panting with impotent rage. Their voices as they go off take up the song of the gold-seekers to the old tune of "Oh, Susannah!"*)

"I jumped aboard the Liza ship,
And traveled on the sea,
And every time I thought of home
I wished it wasn't me!
Oh! Californi-a,
That's the land fur me!
I'm off to Californi-a!
With my wash bowl on my knee."

(*In the meantime, the window of the upper bedroom on right is raised and* ABBIE *sticks her head out. She looks down at* CABOT *with a sigh of relief.*)

ABBIE Waal—that's the last o' them two, hain't it? (*He doesn't answer; then in possessive tones:*) This here's a nice bedroom, Ephraim. It's a r'al nice bed. Is it my room, Ephraim?

CABOT (*grimly—without looking up*) Our'n! (*She cannot control a grimace of aversion and pulls back her head slowly and shuts the window. A sudden horrible thought seems to enter* CABOT'S *head.*) They been up to somethin'! Mebbe—mebbe they've pizened the stock—'r somethin'! (*He almost runs off down toward the barn. A moment later the kitchen door is slowly pushed open and* ABBIE *enters. For a moment she stands looking at* EBEN. *He does not notice her at first. Her eyes take him in penetratingly with a calculating appraisal of his strength as against hers. But under this her desire is dimly awakened by his youth and good looks. Suddenly he becomes conscious of her presence and looks up. Their eyes meet. He leaps to his feet, glowering at her speechlessly.*)

ABBIE (*in her most seductive tones which she uses all through this scene*) Be you—Eben? I'm Abbie—(*She laughs.*) I mean, I'm yer new Maw.

EBEN (*viciously*) No, damn ye!

ABBIE (*as if she hadn't heard—with a queer smile*) Yer Paw's spoke a lot o' yew. . . .

EBEN Ha!

ABBIE Ye mustn't mind him. He's an old man. (*A long pause. They stare at each other.*) I don't want t' pretend playin' Maw t' ye, Eben. (*admiringly*) Ye're too big an' too strong fur that. I want t' be frens with ye. Mebbe with me fur a fren ye'd find ye'd like livin' here better. I kin make it easy fur ye with him, mebbe. (*with a scornful sense of power*) I calc'late I kin git him t' do most anythin' fur me.

EBEN (*with bitter scorn*) Ha! (*They stare again,* EBEN *obscurely moved, physically attracted to her—in forced stilted tones*) Yew kin go t' the devil!

ABBIE (*calmly*) If cussin' me does ye good, cuss all ye've a mind t'. I'm all prepared t' have ye agin me—at fust. I don't blame ye nuther. I'd feel the same at any stranger comin' t' take my Maw's place. (*He shudders. She is watching him carefully.*) Yew must've cared a lot fur yewr Maw, didn't ye? My Maw died afore I'd growed. I don't remember her none. (*a pause*) But yew won't hate me long, Eben. I'm not the wust in the world—an' yew an' me've got a lot in common. I kin tell that by lookin' at ye. Waal—I've had a hard life, too—oceans o' trouble an' nuthin' but wuk fur reward. I was a orphan early an' had t' wuk fur others in other folks' hums. Then I married an' he turned out a drunken spreer an' so he had to wuk fur others an' me too agen in other folks' hums, an' the baby died, an' my husband got sick an' died too, an' I was glad sayin' now I'm free fur once, on'y I diskivered right away all I was free fur was t' wuk agen in other folks' hums, doin' other folks' wuk till I'd most give up hope o' ever doin' my own wuk in my own hum, an' then your Paw come. . . . (CABOT *appears returning from the barn. He comes to the gate and looks down the road the brothers have gone. A faint strain of their retreating voices is heard: "Oh, Californi-a! That's the place for me." He stands glowering, his fist clenched, his face grim with rage.*)

EBEN (*fighting against his growing attraction and sympathy—harshly*) An' bought yew—like a harlot! (*She is stung and flushes angrily. She has been sincerely moved by the recital of her troubles. He adds furiously:*) An' the price he's payin' ye—this farm—was my Maw's, damn ye!—an' mine now!

ABBIE (*with a cool laugh of confidence*) Yewr'n? We'll see 'bout that! (*then strongly*) Waal—what if I did need a hum? What else'd I marry an old man like him fur?

EBEN (*maliciously*) I'll tell him ye said that!

ABBIE (*smiling*) I'll say ye're lyin' a-purpose—an' he'll drive ye off the place!

EBEN Ye devil!

ABBIE (*defying him*) This be my farm—this be my hum—this be my kitchen—!

EBEN (*furiously, as if he were going to attack her*) Shut up, damn ye!

ABBIE (*walks up to him—a queer coarse expression of desire in her face and body—slowly*) An' upstairs—that be my bedroom—an' my bed! (*He stares into her eyes, terribly confused and torn. She adds softly*) I hain't bad nor mean—'ceptin' fur an enemy—but I got t' fight fur what's due me out o' life, if I ever 'spect t' git it. (*then putting her hand on his arm—seductively*) Let's yew 'n' me be frens, Eben.

EBEN (*stupidly—as if hypnotized*) Ay-ey. (*then furiously flinging off her arm*) No, ye durned old witch! I hate ye! (*He rushes out the door.*)

ABBIE (*looks after him smiling satisfiedly—then half to herself, mouthing the word*) Eben's nice. (*She looks at the table, proudly.*) I'll wash up *my* dishes now. (EBEN *appears outside, slamming the door behind him. He comes around corner, stops on seeing his father, and stands staring at him with hate.*)

CABOT (*raising his arms to heaven in the fury he can no longer control*) Lord God o' Hosts, smite the undutiful sons with Thy wust cuss!

EBEN (*breaking in violently*) Yew 'n' yewr God! Allus cussin' folks—allus naggin' 'em!

CABOT (*oblivious to him—summoningly*) God o' the old! God o' the lonesome!

EBEN (*mockingly*) Naggin' His sheep t' sin! T' hell with yewr God! (CABOT *turns. He and* EBEN *glower at each other.*)

CABOT (*harshly*) So it's yew. I might've knowed it. (*shaking his finger threateningly at him*) Blasphemin' fool! (*then quickly*) Why hain't ye t' wuk?

EBEN Why hain't yew? They've went. I can't wuk it all alone.

CABOT (*contemptuously*) Nor noways! I'm wuth ten o' ye yit, old's I be! Ye'll never be more'n half a man! (*then, matter-of-factly*) Waal—let's git t' the barn. (*They go. A last faint note of the "Californi-a" song is heard from the distance.* ABBIE *is washing her dishes.*)

Part II

Scene I

The exterior of the farmhouse, as in PART I*—a hot Sunday afternoon two months later.* **ABBIE**, *dressed in her best, is discovered sitting in a rocker at the end of the porch. She rocks listlessly, enervated by the heat, staring in front of her with bored, half-closed eyes.*

EBEN *sticks his head out of his bedroom window. He looks around furtively and tries to see—or hear—if anyone is on the porch, but although he has been careful to make no noise,* **ABBIE** *has sensed his movement. She stops rocking, her face grows animated and eager, she waits attentively.* **EBEN** *seems to feel her presence, he scowls back his thoughts of her and spits with exaggerated disdain—then withdraws back into the room.* **ABBIE** *waits, holding her breath as she listens with passionate eagerness for every sound within the house.*

EBEN *comes out. Their eyes meet. He falters, he is confused, he turns away and slams the door resentfully. At this gesture,* **ABBIE** *laughs tantalizingly, amused but at the same time piqued and irritated. He scowls, strides off the porch to the path and starts to walk past her to the road with a grand swagger of ignoring her existence. He is dressed in his store suit, spruced up, his face shines from soap and water.* **ABBIE** *leans forward on her chair, her eyes hard and angry now, and, as he passes her, gives a sneering, taunting chuckle.*

EBEN (*stung—turns on her furiously*) What air yew cacklin' 'bout?

ABBIE (*triumphant*) Yew!

EBEN What about me?

ABBIE Ye look all slicked up like a prize bull.

EBEN (*with a sneer*) Waal—ye hain't so durned purty yerself, be ye? (*They stare into each other's eyes, his held by hers in spite of himself, hers glowingly possessive. Their physical attraction becomes a palpable force quivering in the hot air.*)

ABBIE (*softly*) Ye don't mean that, Eben. Ye may think ye mean it, mebbe, but ye don't. Ye can't. It's agin nature, Eben. Ye been fightin' yer nature ever since the day I come—tryin' t' tell yerself I hain't purty t'ye. (*She laughs a low humid laugh without taking her eyes from his. A pause—her body squirms desirously—she murmurs languorously.*) Hain't the sun strong an' hot? Ye kin feel it burnin' into the earth—Nature—makin' thin's grow—bigger 'n' bigger—burnin' inside ye—makin' ye want t' grow—into somethin' else—till ye're jined with it—an' it's your'n—but it owns ye, too—an' makes ye grow bigger—like a tree—like them elums—(*She laughs again softly, holding his eyes. He takes a step toward her, compelled against his will.*) Nature'll beat ye, Eben. Ye might's well own up t' it fust 's last.

EBEN (*trying to break from her spell—confusedly*) If Paw'd hear ye goin' on. . . . (*resentfully*) But ye've made such a damned idjit out o' the old devil . . . ! (ABBIE *laughs.*)

ABBIE Waal—hain't it easier fur yew with him changed softer?

EBEN (*defiantly*) No. I'm fightin' him—fightin' yew—fightin' fur Maw's right t' her hum! (*This breaks her spell for him. He glowers at her.*) An' I'm onto ye. Ye hain't foolin' me a mite. Ye're aimin' t' swaller up everythin' an' make it your'n. Waal, you'll find I'm a heap sight bigger hunk nor yew kin chew! (*He turns from her with a sneer.*)

ABBIE (*trying to regain her ascendancy—seductively*) Eben!

EBEN Leave me be! (*He starts to walk away.*)

ABBIE (*more commandingly*) Eben!

EBEN (*stops—resentfully*) What d'ye want?

ABBIE (*trying to conceal a growing excitement*) Whar air ye goin'?

EBEN (*with malicious nonchalance*) Oh—up the road a spell.

ABBIE T' the village?

EBEN Mebbe.

ABBIE (*excitedly*) T' see that Min, I s'pose?

EBEN Mebbe.

ABBIE (*weakly*) What d'ye want t' waste time on her fur?

EBEN (*revenging himself now—grinning at her*) Ye can't beat Nature, didn't ye say? (*He laughs and again starts to walk away.*)

ABBIE (*bursting out*) An ugly old hake!

EBEN (*with a tantalizing sneer*) She's purtier'n yew be!

ABBIE That every wuthless drunk in the country has. . . .

EBEN (*tauntingly*) Mebbe—but she's better'n yew. She owns up fa'r 'n' squar' t' her doin's.

ABBIE (*furiously*) Don't ye dare compare. . . .

EBEN She don't go sneakin' an' stealin'—what's mine.

ABBIE (*savagely seizing on his weak point*) You'rn? Yew mean—my farm?

EBEN I mean the farm yew sold yerself fur like any other old whore—my farm!

ABBIE (*stung—fiercely*) Ye'll never live t' see the day when even a stinkin' weed on it'll belong t' ye! (*then in a scream*) Git out o' my sight! Go on t' yer slut—disgracin' yer Paw 'n' me! I'll git yer Paw t' horsewhip ye off the place if I want t'! Ye're only livin' here 'cause I tolerate ye! Git along! I hate the sight o' ye! (*She stops, panting and glaring at him.*)

EBEN (*returning her glance in kind*) An' I hate the sight o' yew! (*He turns and strides off up the road. She follows his retreating figure with concentrated hate. Old* CABOT *appears coming up from the barn. The hard, grim expression of his face has changed. He seems in some queer way softened, mellowed. His eyes have taken on a strange, incongruous dreamy quality. Yet there is no hint of physical weakness about him—rather he looks more robust and younger.* ABBIE *sees him and turns away quickly with unconcealed aversion. He comes slowly up to her.*)

CABOT (*mildly*) War yew an' Eben quarrelin' agen?

ABBIE (*shortly*) No.

CABOT Ye was talkin' a'mighty loud. (*He sits down on the edge of porch.*)

ABBIE (*snappishly*) If ye heerd us they hain't no need askin' questions.

CABOT I didn't hear what ye said.

ABBIE (*relieved*) Waal—it wa'n't nothin' t' speak on.

CABOT (*after a pause*) Eben's queer.

ABBIE (*bitterly*) He's the dead spit 'n' image o' yew!

CABOT (*queerly interested*) D'ye think so, Abbie? (*after a pause, ruminatingly*) Me 'n' Eben's allus fit 'n' fit. I never could b'ar him noways. He's so thunderin' soft—like his Maw.

ABBIE (*scornfully*) Ay-eh! 'Bout as soft as yew be!

CABOT (*as if he hadn't heard*) Mebbe I been too hard on him.

ABBIE (*jeeringly*) Waal—ye're gittin' soft now—soft as slop! That's what Eben was sayin'.

CABOT (*his face instantly grim and ominous*) Eben was sayin'? Waal, he'd best not do nothin' t' try me 'r he'll soon diskiver. . . . (*A pause. She keeps her face turned away. His gradually softens. He stares up at the sky.*) Purty, hain't it?

ABBIE (*crossly*) I don't see nothin' purty.

CABOT The sky. Feels like a wa'm field up thar.

ABBIE (*sarcastically*) Air yew aimin' t' buy up over the farm too? (*She snickers contemptuously.*)

CABOT (*strangely*) I'd like t' own my place up thar. (*a pause*) I'm gittin' old, Abbie. I'm gittin' ripe on the bough. (*A pause. She stares at him mystified. He goes on.*) It's allus lonesome cold in the house—even when it's bilin' hot outside. Hain't yew noticed?

ABBIE No.

CABOT It's wa'm down t' the barn—nice smellin' an' warm—with the cows. (*a pause*) Cows is queer.

ABBIE Like yew?

CABOT Like Eben. (*a pause*) I'm gittin' t' feel resigned t' Eben—jest as I got t' feel 'bout his Maw. I'm gittin' t' learn to b'ar his softness—jest like her'n. I calc'late I c'd a'most take t' him—if he wa'n't sech a dumb fool! (*a pause*) I s'pose it's old age a-creepin' in my bones.

ABBIE (*indifferently*) Waal—ye hain't dead yet.

CABOT (*roused*) No, I hain't, yew bet—not by a hell of a sight—I'm sound 'n' tough as hickory! (*then moodily*) But arter three score and ten the Lord warns ye t' prepare. (*a pause*) That's why Eben's come in my head. Now that his cussed sinful brothers is gone their path t' hell, they's no one left but Eben.

ABBIE (*resentfully*) They's me, hain't they? (*agitatedly*) What's all this sudden likin' ye tuk to Eben? Why don't ye say nothin' 'bout me? Hain't I yer lawful wife?

CABOT (*simply*) Ay-eh. Ye be. (*A pause—he stares at her desirously—his eyes grow avid—then with a sudden movement he seizes her hands and squeezes them, declaiming in a queer camp meeting preacher's tempo.*) Yew air my Rose o' Sharon! Behold, yew air fair; yer eyes air doves; yer lips air like scarlet; yer two breasts air like two fawns; yer navel be like a round goblet; yer belly be like a heap o' wheat. . . . (*He covers her hand with kisses. She does not seem to notice. She stares before her with hard angry eyes.*)

ABBIE (*jerking her hands away—harshly*) So ye're plannin' t' leave the farm t' Eben, air ye?

CABOT (*dazedly*) Leave . . . ? (*then with resentful obstinancy*) I hain't a-givin' it t' no one!

ABBIE (*remorselessly*) Ye can't take it with ye.

CABOT (*thinks a moment—then reluctantly*) No, I calc'late not. (*after a pause—with a strange passion*) But if I could, I would, by the Etarnal! 'R if I could, in my dyin' hour, I'd set it afire an' watch it burn—this house an' every ear o' corn an' every tree down t' the last blade o' hay! I'd sit an' know it was all a-dying with me an' no one else'd ever own what was mine, what I'd made out o' nothin' with my own sweat 'n' blood! (*a pause—then he adds with a queer affection*) 'Ceptin' the cows. Them I'd turn free.

ABBIE (*harshly*) An' me?

CABOT (*with a queer smile*) Ye'd be turned free, too.

ABBIE (*furiously*) So that's the thanks I git fur marryin' ye—t' have ye change kind to Eben who hates ye, an' talk o' turnin' me out in the road.

CABOT (*hastily*) Abbie! Ye know I wa'n't. . . .

ABBIE (*vengefully*) Just let me tell ye a thing or two 'bout Eben! Whar's he gone? T' see that harlot, Min! I tried fur t' stop him. Disgracin' yew an' me—on the Sabbath, too!

CABOT (*rather guiltily*) He's a sinner—nateral-born. It's lust eatin' his heart.

ABBIE (*enraged beyond endurance—wildly vindictive*) An' his lust fur me! Kin ye find excuses fur that?

CABOT (*stares at her—after a dead pause*) Lust—fur yew?

ABBIE (*defiantly*) He was tryin' t' make love t' me—when ye heerd us quarrelin'.

CABOT (*stares at her—then a terrible expression of rage comes over his face—he springs to his feet shaking all over*) By the A'mighty God—I'll end him!

ABBIE (*frightened now for* EBEN) No! Don't ye!

CABOT (*violently*) I'll git the shotgun an' blow his soft brains t' the top o' them elums!

ABBIE (*throwing her arms around him*) No, Ephraim!

CABOT (*pushing her away violently*) I will, by God!

ABBIE (*in a quieting tone*) Listen, Ephraim. 'Twa'n't nothin' bad—on'y a boy's foolin'—'twa'n't meant serious—jest jokin' an teasin'. . . .

CABOT Then why did ye say—lust?

ABBIE It must hev sounded wusser'n I meant. An' I was mad at thinkin'—ye'd leave him the farm.

CABOT (*quieter but still grim and cruel*) Waal then, I'll horsewhip him off the place if that much'll content ye.

ABBIE (*reaching out and taking his hand*) No. Don't think o' me! Ye mustn't drive him off. 'Tain't sensible. Who'll ye get to help ye on the farm? They's no one hereabouts.

CABOT (*considers this—then nodding his appreciation*) Ye got a head on ye. (*then irritably*) Waal, let them stay. (*He sits down on the edge of the porch. She sits beside him. He murmurs contemptuously:*) I oughtn't t' git riled so—at that 'ere fool calf. (*a pause*) But har's the p'int. What son o' mine'll keep on here t' the farm—when the Lord does call me? Simeon an' Peter air gone t' hell—an' Eben's follerin' 'em.

ABBIE They's me.

CABOT Ye're on'y a woman.

ABBIE I'm yewr wife.

CABOT That hain't me. A son is me—my blood—mine. Mine ought t' git mine. An' then it's still mine—even though I be six foot under. D'ye see?

ABBIE (*giving him a look of hatred*) Ay-eh. I see. (*She becomes very thoughtful, her face growing shrewd, her eyes studying* CABOT *craftily.*)

CABOT I'm gittin' old—ripe on the bough. (*then with a sudden forced reassurance*) Not but what I hain't a hard nut t' crack even yet—an' fur many a year t' come! By the Etarnal, I kin break most o' the young fellers' backs at any kind o' work any day o' the year!

ABBIE (*suddenly*) Mebbe the Lord'll give *us* a son.

CABOT (*turns and stares at her eagerly*) Ye mean—a son—t' me 'n' yew?

ABBIE (*with a cajoling smile*) Ye're a strong man yet, hain't ye? 'Tain't noways impossible, be it? We know that. Why d'ye stare so? Hain't ye never thought o' that afore? I been thinkin' o' it all along. Ay-ey—an' I been prayin' it'd happen, too.

CABOT (*his face growing full of joyous pride and a sort of religious ecstasy*) Ye been prayin', Abbie?—fur a son?—t' us?

ABBIE Ay-eh. (*with a grim resolution*) I want a son now.

CABOT (*excitedly clutching both of her hands in his*) It'd be the blessin' o' God, Abbie—the blessin' o' God A'mighty on me—in my old age—in my lonesomeness! They hain't nothin' I wouldn't do fur ye then, Abbie. Ye'd hev on'y ask it—anythin' ye'd a mind t'!

ABBIE (*interrupting*) Would ye will the farm t' me then—t' me an' it . . . ?

CABOT (*vehemently*) I'd do anythin' ye axed, I tell ye! I swar it! May I be everlastin' damned t' hell if I wouldn't! (*He sinks to his knees pulling her down with him. He trembles all over with the fervor of his hopes.*) Pray t' the Lord agen, Abbie. It's the Sabbath! I'll jine ye! Two prayers air better nor one. "An' God hearkened unto Rachel"! An' God hearkened unto Abbie! Pray, Abbie! Pray fur him to hearken! (*He bows his head, mumbling. She pretends to do likewise but gives him a side glance of scorn and triumph.*)

Scene 2

About eight in the evening. The interior of the two bedrooms on the top floor is shown— EBEN *is sitting on the side of his bed in the room on the left. On account of the heat he has taken off everything but his undershirt and pants. His feet are bare. He faces front, brooding moodily, his chin propped on his hands, a desperate expression on his face.*

In the other room CABOT *and* ABBIE *are sitting side by side on the edge of their bed, an old four-poster with feather mattress. He is in his night shirt, she in her nightdress. He is still in the queer, excited mood into which the notion of a son has thrown him. Both rooms are lighted dimly and flickeringly by tallow candles.*

CABOT The farm needs a son.

ABBIE I need a son.

CABOT Ay-eh. Sometimes ye air the farm an' sometimes the farm be yew. That's why I clove t' ye in my lonesomeness. (*A pause. He pounds his knee with his fist.*) Me an' the farm has got t' beget a son!

ABBIE Ye'd best go t' sleep. Ye're gittin' thin's all mixed.

CABOT (*with an impatient gesture*) No, I hain't. My mind's clear's a bell. Ye don't know me, that's it. (*He stares hopelessly at the floor.*)

ABBIE (*indifferently*) Mebbe. (*In the next room* EBEN *gets up and paces up and down distractedly.* ABBIE *hears him. Her eyes fasten on the intervening wall with concentrated attention.* EBEN *stops and stares. Their hot glances seem to meet through the wall. Unconsciously he stretches out his arms for her and she half rises. Then aware, he mutters a curse at himself and flings himself face downward on the bed, his clenched fists above his head, his face buried in the pillow.* ABBIE *relaxes with a faint sigh but her eyes remain fixed on the wall; she listens with all her attention for some movement from* EBEN.)

CABOT (*suddenly raises his head and looks at her—scornfully*) Will ye ever know me—'r will any man 'r woman? (*shaking his head*) No. I calc'late 't wa'n't t' be. (*He turns away.* ABBIE *looks at the wall. Then, evidently unable to keep silent about his thoughts, without looking at his wife, he puts out his hand and clutches her knee. She starts violently, looks at him, sees he is not watching her, concentrates again on the wall and pays no attention to what he says.*) Listen, Abbie. When I come here fifty odd year ago—I was jest twenty an' the strongest an' hardest ye ever seen—ten times as strong an' fifty times as hard as Eben. Waal—this place was nothin' but fields o' stones. Folks laughed when I tuk it. They couldn't know what I knowed. When he kin make corn sprout out o' stones, God's livin' in yew! They wa'n't strong enuf fur that! They reckoned God was easy. They laughed. They don't laugh no more. Some died hereabouts. Some went West an' died. They're all under ground—fur follerin' arter an easy God. God hain't easy. (*He shakes his head slowly.*) An' I growed hard. Folks kept allus sayin' he's a hard man like 'twas sinful t' be hard, so's at last I said back at 'em: Waal then, by thunder, ye'll git me hard an' see how ye like it! (*then suddenly*) But I give in t' weakness once. 'Twas arter I'd been here two year. I got weak—despairful—they was so many stones. They was a party leavin', givin' up, goin' West. I jined 'em. We tracked on 'n' on. We come t' broad medders, plains, whar the soil was black an' rich as gold. Nary a stone. Easy. Ye'd on'y to plow an' sow an' then set an' smoke yer pipe an' watch thin's grow. I could o' been a rich man—but somethin' in me fit me an' fit me—the voice o' God sayin': "This hain't wuth nothin' t' Me. Get ye back t' hum!" I got afeerd o' that voice an' I lit out back t' hum here, leavin' my claim an' crops t' whoever'd a mind t' take 'em. Ay-eh. I actoolly give up what was rightful mine! God's hard, not easy! God's in the stones! Build my church on a rock—out o' stones an' I'll be in them! That's what He meant t' Peter! (*He sighs heavily—a pause.*) Stones. I picked 'em up an' piled 'em into walls. Ye kin read the years o' my life in them walls, every day a hefted stone, climbin' over the hills up and down, fencin' in the fields that was mine, whar I'd made thin's grow out o' nothin'—like the will o' God, like the servant o' His hand. It wa'n't easy. It was hard an' He made me hard fur it. (*He pauses.*) All the time I kept gittin' lonesomer. I tuk a wife. She bore Simeon an' Peter. She was a good woman. She wuked hard. We was married twenty year. She never knowed me. She helped but she never knowed what she was helpin'. I was allus lonesome. She died. After that it wa'n't so lonesome fur a spell. (*a pause*) I lost count o' the years. I had no time t' fool away countin' 'em. Sim an' Peter helped. The farm growed. It was all mine! When I thought o' that I didn't feel lonesome. (*a pause*) But ye can't hitch yer mind t' one thin' day an' night. I tuk another wife—Eben's Maw. Her folks was contestin' me at law over my deeds t' the farm—my farm! That's why Eben keeps a'talkin' his fool talk o' this bein' his Maw's farm. She bore Eben. She was purty—but soft. She tried t' be hard. She couldn't. She never knowed me nor nothin'. It was lonesomer 'n hell with her. After a matter o' sixteen odd years, she died. (*a pause*) I lived with the boys. They hated me 'cause I was hard. I hated them 'cause they was soft. They coveted the farm without knowin' what it meant. It made me bitter 'n wormwood. It aged me—them coveting what I'd made fur mine. Then this spring the call come—the voice o' God cryin' in my wilderness, in my lonesomeness—t' go out an' seek an' find! (*turning to her with strange passion*) I sought ye an' I found ye! Yew air my Rose o' Sharon! Yer eyes air like. . . . (*She has turned a blank face, resentful eyes to his. He stares at her for a moment—then harshly:*) Air ye any the wiser fur all I've told ye?

ABBIE (*confusedly*) Mebbe.

CABOT (*pushing her away from him—angrily*) Ye don't know nothin'—nor never will. If ye don't hev a son t' redeem ye . . . (*this in a tone of cold threat*)

ABBIE (*resentfully*) I've prayed, hain't I?

CABOT (*bitterly*) Pray agen—fur understandin'!

ABBIE (*a veiled threat in her tone*) Ye'll have a son out o' me, I promise ye.

CABOT How kin ye promise?

ABBIE I got second-sight mebbe. I kin foretell. (*She gives a queer smile.*)

CABOT I believe ye have. Ye give me the chills sometimes. (*He shivers.*) It's cold in this house. It's oneasy. They's thin's pokin' about in the dark—in the corners. (*He pulls on his trousers, tucking in his night shirt, and pulls on his boots.*)

ABBIE (*surprised*) Whar air ye goin'?

CABOT (*queerly*) Down whar it's restful—whar it's warm—down t' the barn. (*bitterly*) I kin talk t' the cows. They know. They know the farm an' me. They'll give me peace. (*He turns to go out the door.*)

ABBIE (*a bit frightenedly*) Air ye ailin' tonight, Ephraim?

CABOT Growin'. Growin' ripe on the bough. (*He turns and goes, his boots clumping down the stairs.* EBEN *sits up with a start, listening.* ABBIE *is conscious of his movement and stares at the wall.* CABOT *comes out of the house around the corner and stands by the gate, blinking at the sky. He stretches up his hands in a tortured gesture.*) God A'mighty, call from the dark! (*He listens as if expecting an answer. Then his arms drop, he shakes his head and plods off toward the barn.* EBEN *and* ABBIE *stare at each other through the wall.* EBEN *sighs heavily and* ABBIE *echoes it. Both become terribly nervous, uneasy. Finally* ABBIE *gets up and listens, her ear to the wall. He acts as if he saw every move she was making, he becomes resolutely still. She seems driven into a decision—goes out the door in rear determinedly. His eyes follow her. Then as the door of his room is opened softly, he turns away, waits in an attitude of strained fixity.* ABBIE *stands for a second staring at him, her eyes burning with desire. Then with a little cry she runs over and throws her arms about his neck, she pulls his head back and covers his mouth with kisses. At first, he submits dumbly; then he puts his arms about her neck and returns her kisses, but finally, suddenly aware of his hatred, he hurls her away from him, springing to his feet. They stand speechless and breathless, panting like two animals.*)

ABBIE (*at last—painfully*) Ye shouldn't, Eben—ye shouldn't—I'd make ye happy!

EBEN (*harshly*) I don't want t' be happy—from yew!

ABBIE (*helplessly*) Ye do, Eben! Ye do! Why d'ye lie?

EBEN (*viciously*) I don't take t'ye, I tell ye! I hate the sight o' ye!

ABBIE (*with an uncertain troubled laugh*) Waal, I kissed ye anyways—an' ye kissed back—yer lips was burnin'—ye can't lie 'bout that! (*intensely*) If ye don't care, why did ye kiss me back—why was yer lips burnin'?

EBEN (*wiping his mouth*) It was like pizen on 'em (*then tauntingly*) When I kissed ye back, mebbe I thought 'twas someone else.

ABBIE (*wildly*) Min?

EBEN Mebbe.

ABBIE (*torturedly*) Did ye go t' see her? Did ye r'ally go? I thought ye mightn't. Is that why ye throwed me off jest now?

EBEN (*sneeringly*) What if it be?

ABBIE (*raging*) Then ye're a dog, Eben Cabot!

EBEN (*threateningly*) Ye can't talk that way t' me!

ABBIE (*with a shrill laugh*) Can't I? Did ye think I was in love with ye—a weak thin' like yew? Not much! I on'y wanted ye fur a purpose o' my own—an' I'll hev ye fur it yet 'cause I'm stronger'n yew be!

EBEN (*resentfully*) I knowed well it was on'y part o' yer plan t' swaller everythin'!

ABBIE (*tauntingly*) Mebbe!

EBEN (*furious*) Git out o' my room!

ABBIE This air my room an' ye're on'y hired help!

EBEN (*threateningly*) Git out afore I murder ye!

ABBIE (*quite confident now*) I hain't a mite afeerd. Ye want me, don't ye? Yes, ye do! An' yer Paw's son'll never kill what he wants! Look at yer eyes! They's lust fur me in 'em, burnin' 'em up! Look at yer lips now! They're tremblin' an' longin' t' kiss me, an' yer teeth t'bite! (*He is watching her now with a horrible fascination. She laughs a crazy triumphant laugh.*) I'm a-goin' t' make all o' this hum my hum! They's one room hain't mine yet, but it's a-goin' t' be tonight. I'm a-goin' down now an' light up! (*She makes him a mocking bow.*) Won't ye come courtin' me in the best parlor, Mister Cabot?

EBEN (*staring at her—horribly confused—dully*) Don't ye dare! It hain't been opened since Maw died an' was laid out thar! Don't ye . . . ! (*But her eyes are fixed on his so burningly that his will seems to wither before hers. He stands swaying toward her helplessly.*)

ABBIE (*holding his eyes and putting all her will into her words as she backs out the door*) I'll expect ye afore long, Eben.

EBEN (*stares after her for a while, walking toward the door. A light appears in the parlor window. He murmurs:*) In the parlor? (*This seems to arouse connotations for he comes back and puts on his white shirt, collar, half ties the tie mechanically, puts on coat, takes his hat, stands barefooted looking about him in bewilderment, mutters wonderingly.*) Maw! Whar air yew? (*Then he goes slowly toward the door in rear.*)

Scene 3

A few minutes later. The interior of the parlor is shown. A grim, repressed room like a tomb in which the family has been interred alive. ABBIE *sits on the edge of the horsehair sofa. She has lighted all the candles and the room is revealed in all its preserved ugliness. A change has come over the woman. She looks awed and frightened now, ready to run away.*

The door is opened and EBEN *appears. His face wears an expression of obsessed confusion. He stands staring at her, his arms hanging disjointedly from his shoulders, his feet bare, his hat in his hand.*

ABBIE (*after a pause—with a nervous, formal politeness*) Won't ye set?

EBEN (*dully*) Ay-eh. (*Mechanically he places his hat carefully on the floor near the door and sits stiffly beside her on the edge of the sofa. A pause. They both remain rigid, looking straight ahead with eyes full of fear.*)

ABBIE When I fust came in—in the dark—they seemed somethin' here.

EBEN (*simply*) Maw.

ABBIE I kin still feel—somethin'. . . .

EBEN It's Maw.

ABBIE At fust I was feered o' it. I wanted t' yell an' run. Now—since yew come—seems like it's growin' soft an' kind t' me. (*addressing the air—queerly*) Thank yew.

EBEN Maw allus loved me.

ABBIE Mebbe it knows I love yew too. Mebbe that makes it kind t' me.

EBEN (*dully*) I dunno. I should think she'd hate ye.

ABBIE (*with certainty*) No. I kin feel it don't—not no more.

EBEN Hate yer fur stealin' her place—here in her hum—settin' in her parlor whar she was laid— (*He suddenly stops, staring stupidly before him.*)

ABBIE What is it, Eben?

EBEN (*in a whisper*) Seems like Maw didn't want me t' remind ye.

ABBIE (*excitedly*) I knowed, Eben! It's kind t' me! It don't b'ar me no grudges fur what I never knowed an' couldn't help!

EBEN Maw b'ars him a grudge.

ABBIE Waal, so does all o' us.

EBEN Ay-eh. (*with passion*) I does, by God!

ABBIE (*taking one of his hands in hers and patting it*) Thar! Don't git riled thinkin' o' him. Think o' yer Maw who's kind t' us. Tell me about yer Maw, Eben.

EBEN They hain't nothin' much. She was kind. She was good.

ABBIE (*putting one arm over his shoulder. He does not seem to notice—passionately:*) I'll be kind an' good t' ye!

EBEN Sometimes she used t' sing fur me.

ABBIE I'll sing fur ye!

EBEN This was her hum. This was her farm.

ABBIE This is my hum! This is my farm!

EBEN He married her t' steal 'em. She was soft an' easy. He couldn't 'preciate her.

ABBIE He can't 'preciate me!

EBEN He murdered her with his hardness.

ABBIE He's murderin' me!

EBEN She died. (*a pause*) Sometimes she used to sing fur me. (*He bursts into a fit of sobbing.*)

ABBIE (*both arms around him—with wild passion*) I'll sing fur ye! I'll die fur ye! (*In spite of her overwhelming desire for him, there is a sincere maternal love in her manner and voice—a horribly frank mixture of lust and mother love.*) Don't cry, Eben! I'll take yer Maw's place! I'll be everythin' she was t' ye! Let me kiss ye, Eben! (*She pulls his head around. He makes a bewildered pretense of resistance. She is tender.*) Don't be afeered! I'll kiss ye pure, Eben—same's if I was a Maw t' ye—an' ye kin kiss me back 's if yew was my son—my boy—sayin' goodnight t' me! Kiss me, Eben. (*They kiss in restrained fashion. Then suddenly wild passion overcomes her. She kisses him lustfully again and again and he flings his arms about her and returns her kisses. Suddenly, as in the bedroom, he frees himself from her violently and springs to his feet. He is trembling all over, in a strange state of terror.* ABBIE *strains her arms toward him with fierce pleading.*) Don't ye leave me, Eben! Can't ye see it hain't enuf—lovin' ye like a Maw—can't ye see it's got t' be that an' more—much more—a hundred times more—fur me t' be happy—for yew t' be happy?

EBEN (*to the presence he feels in the room*) Maw! Maw! What d'ye want? What air ye tellin' me?

ABBIE She's tellin' ye t' love me. She knows I love ye an' I'll be good t' ye. Can't ye feel it? Don't ye know? She's tellin' ye t' love me, Eben!

EBEN Ah-eh. I feel—mebbe she—but—I can't figger out—why—when ye've stole her place—here in her hum—in the parlor whar she was—

ABBIE (*fiercely*) She knows I love ye!

EBEN (*his face suddenly lighting up with a fierce triumphant grin*) I see it! I sees why. It's her vengeance on him—so's she kin rest quiet in her grave!

ABBIE (*wildly*) Vengeance o' God on the hull o' us! What d'we give a durn? I love ye, Eben! God knows I love ye! (*She stretches out her arms for him.*)

EBEN (*throws himself on his knees beside the sofa and grabs her in his arms—releasing all his pent-up passion*) An' I love yew, Abbie!—now I kin say it! I been dyin' fur want o' ye—every hour since ye come! I love ye! (*Their lips meet in a fierce, bruising kiss.*)

Scene 4

Exterior of the farmhouse. It is just dawn. The front door at right is opened.

EBEN *comes out and walks around to the gate. He is dressed in his working clothes. He seems changed. His face wears a bold and confident expression, he is grinning to himself with evident satisfaction. As he gets near the gate, the window of the parlor is heard opening and the shutters are flung back and* ABBIE *sticks her head out. Her hair tumbles over her shoulders in disarray, her face is flushed, she looks at* EBEN *with tender, languorous eyes and calls softly.*

ABBIE Eben. (*As he turns—playfully*) Jest one more kiss afore ye go. I'm goin' to miss ye fearful all day.

EBEN An' me yew, ye kin bet! (*He goes to her. They kiss several times. He draws away, laughingly.*) Thar. That's enuf, hain't it? Ye won't hev none left fur next time.

ABBIE I got a million o' 'em left fur yew! (*then a bit anxiously*) D'ye r'ally love me Eben?

EBEN (*emphatically*) I like ye better'n any gal I ever knowed! That's gospel!

ABBIE Likin' hain't lovin'.

EBEN Waal then—I love ye. Now air yew satisfied?

ABBIE Ay-eh, I be. (*She smiles at him adoringly.*)

EBEN I better git t' the barn. The old critter's liable t' suspicion an' come sneakin' up.

ABBIE (*with a confident laugh*) Let him! I kin allus pull the wool over his eyes. I'm goin' t' leave the shutters open and let in the sun 'n' air. This room's been dead long enuf. Now it's goin' t' be my room!

EBEN (*frowning*) Ay-eh.

ABBIE We made it our'n last night, didn't we? We give it life—our lovin' did. (*a pause*)

EBEN (*with a strange look*) Maw's gone back t' her grave. She kin sleep now.

ABBIE May she rest in peace! (*then tenderly rebuking*) Ye oughtn't t' talk o' sad thin's—this mornin'.

EBEN It jest come up in my mind o' itself.

ABBIE Don't let it. (*He doesn't answer. She yawns.*) Waal, I'm a-goin' t' steal a wink o' sleep. I'll tell the Old Man I hain't feelin' pert. Let him git his own vittles.

EBEN I see him comin' from the barn. Ye better look smart an' git upstairs.

ABBIE Ay-eh. Good-by. Don't fergit me. (*She throws him a kiss. He grins—then squares his shoulders and awaits his father confidently.* CABOT *walks slowly up from the left, staring up at the sky with a vague face.*)

EBEN (*jovially*) Mornin', Paw. Star-gazin' in daylight?

CABOT Purty, hain't it?

EBEN (*looking around him possessively*) It's a durned purty farm.

CABOT I mean the sky.

EBEN (*grinning*) How d'ye know? Them eyes o' your'n can't see that fur. (*This tickles his humor and he slaps his thigh and laughs.*) Ho-ho! That's a good un!

CABOT (*grimly sarcastic*) Ye're feelin' right chipper, hain't ye? Whar'd ye steal the likker?

EBEN (*good-naturedly*) 'Taint likker. Jest life. (*suddenly holding out his hand—soberly*) Yew 'n' me is quits. Let's shake hands.

CABOT (*suspiciously*) What's come over ye?

EBEN Then don't. Mebbe it's jest as well. (*a moment's pause*) What's come over me? (*queerly*) Didn't ye feel her passin'—goin' back t' her grave?

CABOT (*dully*) Who?

EBEN Maw. She kin rest now an' sleep content. She's quit with ye.

CABOT (*confusedly*) I rested. I slept good—down with the cows. They know how t' sleep. They're teachin' me.

EBEN (*suddenly jovial again*) Good fur the cows! Waal—ye better git t' work.

CABOT (*grimly amused*) Air yew bossin' me, ye calf?

EBEN (*beginning to laugh*) Ah-eh! I'm bossin' yew! Ha-ha-ha! see how ye like it! Ha-ha-ha! I'm the prize rooster o' this roost. Ha-ha-ha! (*He goes off toward the barn laughing.*)

CABOT (*looks after him with scornful pity*) Soft-headed. Like his Maw. Dead spit 'n' image. No hope in him! (*He spits with contemptuous disgust.*) A born fool! (*then matter-of-factly*) Waal—I'm gittin' peckish. (*He goes toward door.*)

Part III

Scene I

A night in late spring the following year. The kitchen and the two bedrooms upstairs are shown. The two bedrooms are dimly lighted by a tallow candle in each. **Eben** *is sitting on the side of the bed in his room, his chin propped on his fists, his face a study of the struggle he is making to understand his conflicting emotions. The noisy laughter and music from below where a kitchen dance is in progress annoy and distract him. He scowls at the floor. In the next room a cradle stands beside the double bed.*

In the kitchen all is festivity. The stove has been taken down to give more room to the dancers. The chairs, with wooden benches added, have been pushed back against the walls. On these are seated, squeezed in tight against one another, farmers and their wives and their young folks of both sexes from the neighboring farms. They are all chattering and laughing loudly. They evidently have some secret joke in common. There is no end of winking, of nudging, of meaning nods of the head toward **Cabot** *who, in a state of extreme hilarious excitement increased by the amount he has drunk, is standing near the rear door where there is a small keg of whisky and serving drinks to all the men. In the left corner, front, dividing the attention with her husband,* **Abbie** *is sitting in a rocking chair, a shawl wrapped about her shoulders. She is very pale, her face is thin and drawn, her eyes are fixed anxiously on the open door in rear as if waiting for someone.*

The **Musician** *is tuning up his fiddle, seated in the far right corner. He is a lanky young fellow with a long, weak face. His pale eyes blink incessantly and he grins about him slyly with a greedy malice.*

ABBIE (*suddenly turning to a young girl on her right*) Whar's Eben?

YOUNG GIRL (*eying her scornfully*) I dunno, Mrs. Cabot. I hain't seen Eben in ages. (*meaningly*) Seems like he's spent most o' his time t' hum since yew come.

ABBIE (*vaguely*) I tuk his Maw's place.

YOUNG GIRL Ay-eh. So I've heerd. (*She turns away to retail this bit of gossip to her mother sitting next to her.* **Abbie** *turns to her left to a big stoutish middle-aged man whose flushed face and staring eyes show the amount of "likker" he has consumed.*)

ABBIE Ye hain't seen Eben, hev ye?

MAN No, I hain't. (*then he adds with a wink*) If yew hain't, who would?

ABBIE He's the best dancer in the county. He'd ought t' come an' dance.

MAN (*with a wink*) Mebbe he's doin' the dutiful an' walkin' the kid t' sleep. It's a boy, hain't it?

ABBIE (*nodding vaguely*) Ay-eh—born two weeks back—purty's a picter.

MAN They all is—t' their Maws. (*then in a whisper, with a nudge and a leer*) Listen, Abbie—if ye ever git tired o' Eben, remember me! Don't fergit now! (*He looks at her uncomprehending face for a second—then grunts disgustedly.*) Waal—guess I'll likker agin. (*He goes over and joins* **Cabot** *who is arguing noisily with an old farmer over cows. They all drink.*)

ABBIE (*this time appealing to nobody in particular*) Wonder what Eben's a-doin'? (*Her remark is repeated down the line with many a guffaw and titter until it reaches the fiddler. He fastens his blinking eyes on* ABBIE.)

FIDDLER (*raising his voice*) Bet I kin tell ye, Abbie, what Eben's doin'! He's down t' the church offerin' up prayers o' thanksgivin'. (*They all titter expectantly.*)

MAN What fur? (*Another titter.*)

FIDDLER 'Cause unto him a—(*He hesitates just long enough.*)—brother is born! (*A roar of laughter. They all look from* ABBIE *to* CABOT. *She is oblivious, staring at the door.* CABOT, *although he hasn't heard the words, is irritated by the laughter and steps forward, glaring about him. There is an immediate silence.*)

CABOT What're ye all bleatin' about—like a flock o' goats? Why don't ye dance, damn ye? I axed ye here t' dance—t' eat, drink an' be merry—an' thar ye set cacklin' like a lot o' wet hens with the pip! Ye've swilled my likker an' guzzled my vittles like hogs, hain't ye? Then dance fur me, can't ye? That's fa'r an' squar', hain't it? (*A grumble of resentment goes around but they are all evidently in too much awe of him to express it openly.*)

FIDDLER (*slyly*) We're waitin' fur Eben. (*a suppressed laugh*)

CABOT (*with a fierce exultation*) T'hell with Eben! Eben's done fur now! I got a new son! (*his mood switching with drunken suddenness*) But ye needn't t' laugh at Eben, none o' ye! He's my blood, if he be a dumb fool. He's better nor any o' yew! He kin do a day's work a'most up t' what I kin—an' that'd put any o' yew pore critters t' shame!

FIDDLER An' he kin do a good night's work, too! (*a roar of laughter*)

CABOT Laugh, ye damn fools! Ye're right jist the same, Fiddler. He kin work day an' night too, like I kin, if need be!

OLD FARMER (*from behind the keg where he is weaving drunkenly back and forth—with great simplicity*) They hain't many t' touch ye, Ephraim—a son at seventy-six. That's a hard man fur ye! I be on'y sixty-eight an' I couldn't do it. (*a roar of laughter in which* CABOT *joins uproariously*)

CABOT (*slapping him on the back*) I'm sorry fur ye, Hi. I'd never suspicion sech weakness from a boy like yew!

OLD FARMER An' I never reckoned yew had it in ye nuther, Ephraim. (*There is another laugh.*)

CABOT (*suddenly grim*) I got a lot in me—a hell of a lot—folks don't know on. (*turning to the* FIDDLER) Fiddle 'er up, durn ye! Give 'em somethin' t' dance t'! What air ye, an ornament? Hain't this a celebration? Then grease yer elbow an' go it!

FIDDLER (*seizes a drink which the* OLD FARMER *holds out to him and downs it*) Here goes! (*He starts to fiddle "Lady of the Lake." Four young fellows and four girls form in two lines and dance a square dance. The* FIDDLER *shouts directions for the different movements, keeping his words in the rhythm of the music and interspersing them with jocular personal remarks to the dancers themselves. The people seated along the walls stamp their feet and clap their hands in unison.* CABOT *is especially active in this respect. Only* ABBIE *remains apathetic, staring at the door as if she were alone in a silent room.*)

FIDDLER Swing your partner t' the right! That's it, Jim! Give her a b'ar hug! Her Maw hain't lookin'. (*laughter*) Change partners! That suits ye, don't it, Essie, now ye got Reub afore ye? Look at her redden up, will ye! Waal, life is short an' so's love, as the feller says. (*laughter*)

CABOT (*excitedly, stamping his foot*) Go it, boys! Go it, gals!

FIDDLER (*with a wink at the others*) Ye're the spryest seventy-six ever I sees, Ephraim! Now if ye'd on'y good eye-sight . . . ! (*Suppressed laughter. He gives* CABOT *no chance to retort but roars.*) Promenade! Ye're walkin' like a bride down the aisle, Sarah! Waal, while they's life they's allus hope, I've heerd tell. Swing your partner to the left! Gosh A'mighty, look at Johnny Cook high-steppin'! They hain't goin' t'be much strength left fur howin' in the corn lot t'morrow. (*laughter*)

CABOT Go it! Go it! (*Then suddenly, unable to restrain himself any longer, he prances into the midst of the dancers, scattering them, waving his arms about wildly.*) Ye're all hoofs! Git out o' my road! Give me room! I'll show ye dancin'. Ye're all too soft! (*He pushes them roughly away. They crowd back toward the walls, muttering, looking at him resentfully.*)

FIDDLER (*jeeringly*) Go it, Ephraim! Go it! (*He starts "Pop Goes the Weasel," increasing the tempo with every verse until at the end he is fiddling crazily as fast as he can go.*)

CABOT (*starts to dance, which he does very well and with tremendous vigor. Then he begins to improvise, cuts incredibly grotesque capers, leaping up and cracking his heels together, prancing around in a circle with body bent in an Indian war dance, then suddenly straightening up and kicking as high as he can with both legs. He is like a monkey on a string. And all the while he intersperses his antics with shouts and derisive comments.*) Whoop! Here's dancin' fur ye! Whoop! See that! Seventy-six, if I'm a day! Hard as iron yet! Beatin' the young 'uns like I allus done! Look at me! I'd invite ye t' dance on my hundredth birthday on'y ye'll all be dead by then. Ye're a sickly generation! Yer hearts air pink, not red! Yer veins is full o' mud an' water! I be the on'y man in the county! Whoop! See that! I'm a Injun! I've killed Injuns in the West afore ye was born—an' skulped 'em too! They's a arrer wound on my backside I c'd show ye! The hull tribe chased me. I outrun 'em all—with the arrer stuck in me! An' I tuk venegeance on 'em. Ten eyes fur an eye, that was my motter! Whoop! Look at me! I kin kick the ceilin' off the room! Whoop!

FIDDLER (*stops playing—exhaustedly*) God A'mighty, I got enuf. Ye got the devil's strength in ye.

CABOT (*delightedly*) Did I beat yew, too? Wa'al, ye played smart. Hev a swig. (*He pours whisky for himself and* FIDDLER. *They drink. The others watch*

CABOT *silently with cold, hostile eyes. There is a dead pause. The* FIDDLER *rests.* CABOT *leans against the keg, panting, glaring around him confusedly. In the room above,* EBEN *gets to his feet and tiptoes out the door in rear, appearing a moment later in the other bedroom. He moves silently, even frightenedly, toward the cradle and stands there looking down at the baby. His face is as vague as his reactions are confused, but there is a trace of tenderness, of interested discovery. At the same moment that he reaches the cradle,* ABBIE *seems to sense something. She gets up weakly and goes to* CABOT.)

ABBIE I'm goin' up t' the baby.

CABOT (*with real solicitude*) Air ye able fur the stairs? D'ye want me t' help ye, Abbie?

ABBIE No. I'm able. I'll be down agen soon.

CABOT Don't ye git wore out! He needs ye, remember—our son does! (*He grins affectionately, patting her on the back. She shrinks from his touch.*)

ABBIE (*dully*) Don't—tech me. I'm goin'—up. (*She goes.* CABOT *looks after her. A whisper goes around the room.* CABOT *turns. It ceases. He wipes his forehead streaming with sweat. He is breathing pantingly.*)

CABOT I'm a-goin' out t' git fresh air. I'm feelin' a mite dizzy. Fiddle up thar! Dance, all o' ye! Here's likker fur them as wants it. Enjoy yerselves. I'll be back. (*He goes, closing the door behind him.*)

FIDDLER (*sarcastically*) Don't hurry none on our account! (*A suppressed laugh. He imitates* ABBIE.) Whar's Eben? (*more laughter*)

A WOMAN (*loudly*) What's happened in this house is plain as the nose on yer face! (ABBIE *appears in the doorway upstairs and stands looking in surprise and adoration at* EBEN *who does not see her.*)

A MAN Ssshh! He's li'ble t' be listenin' at the door. That'd be like him. (*Their voices die to an intensive whispering. Their faces are concentrated on this gossip. A noise as of dead leaves in the wind comes from the room.* CABOT *has come out from the porch and stands by the gate, leaning on it, staring at the sky blinkingly.* ABBIE *comes across the room silently.* EBEN *does not notice her until quite near.*)

EBEN (*starting*) Abbie!

ABBIE Ssshh! (*She throws her arms around him. They kiss—then bend over the cradle together.*) Ain't he purty?—dead spit 'n' image o' yew!

EBEN (*pleased*) Air he? I can't tell none.

ABBIE E-zactly like!

EBEN (*frowningly*) I don't like this. I don't like lettin' on what's mine's his'n. I been doin' that all my life. I'm gittin' t' the end o' b'arin' it!

ABBIE (*putting her finger on his lips*) We're doin' the best we kin. We got t' wait. Somethin's bound t' happen. (*She puts her arms around him.*) I got t' go back.

EBEN I'm goin' out. I can't b'ar it with the fiddle playin' an' the laughin'.

ABBIE Don't git feelin' low. I love ye, Eben. Kiss me. (*He kisses her. They remain in each other's arms.*)

CABOT (*at the gate, confusedly*) Even the music can't drive it out—somethin'. Ye kin feel it droppin' off the elums, climbin' up the roof, sneakin' down the chimney, pokin' in the corners! They's no peace in houses, they's no rest livin' with folks. Somethin's always livin' with ye. (*with a deep sign*) I'll go t' the barn an' rest a spell. (*He goes wearily toward the barn.*)

FIDDLER (*tuning up*) Let's celebrate the old skunk gittin' fooled! We kin have some fun now he's went. (*He starts to fiddle "Turkey in the Straw." There is real merriment now. The young folks get up to dance.*)

Scene 2

A half hour later—exterior.

EBEN *is standing by the gate looking up at the sky, an expression of dumb pain bewildered by itself on his face.* CABOT *appears, returning from the barn, walking wearily, his eyes on the ground. He sees* EBEN *and his whole mood immediately changes. He becomes excited, a cruel, triumphant grin comes to his lips, he strides up and slaps* EBEN *on the back. From within comes the whining of the fiddle and the noise of stamping feet and laughing voices.*

CABOT So har ye be!

EBEN (*startled, stares at him with hatred for a moment—then dully*) Ay-eh.

CABOT (*surveying him jeeringly*) Why hain't ye been in t' dance? They was all axin' fur ye.

EBEN Let 'em ax!

CABOT They's a hull pasel o' purty gals.

EBEN T' hell with 'em!

CABOT Ye'd ought t' be marryin' one o' 'em soon.

EBEN I hain't marryin' no one.

CABOT Ye might 'arn a share o' a farm that way.

EBEN (*with a sneer*) Like yew did, ye mean? I hain't that kind.

CABOT (*stung*) Ye lie! 'Twas yer Maw's folks aimed t' steal my farm from me.

EBEN Other folks don't say so. (*after a pause—defiantly*) An' I got a farm, anyways!

CABOT (*derisively*) Whar?

EBEN (*stamps a foot on the ground*) Har!

CABOT (*throws his head back and laughs coarsely*) Ho-ho! Ye hev, hev ye? Waal, that's a good un!

EBEN (*controlling himself—grimly*) Ye'll see!

CABOT (*stares at him suspiciously, trying to make him out—a pause—then with scornful confidence*) Ay-eh. I'll see. So'll ye. It's ye that's blind—blind as a mole underground. (EBEN *suddenly laughs, one short sardonic bark: "Ha." A pause.* CABOT *peers at him with renewed suspicion.*) Whar air ye hawin' 'bout? (EBEN *turns away without answering.* CABOT *grows angry.*) God A'mighty, yew air a dumb dunce! They's nothin' in that thick skull o' your'n but noise—like a empty keg it be! (EBEN *doesn't seem to hear—*CABOT'*s rage* *grows.*) Yewr farm! God A'mighty! If ye wa'n't a born donkey ye'd know ye'll never own stick nor stone on it, specially now arter him bein' born. It's his'n, I tell ye—his'n arter I die—but I'll live a hundred jest t' fool ye all—an' he'll be growed then—yewr age a'most! (EBEN *laughs again his sardonic "Ha." This drives* CABOT *into a fury.*) Ha? Ye think ye kin git 'round that someways, do ye? Waal, it'll be her'n, too—Abbie's—ye won't git 'round her—she knows yer tricks—she'll be too much fur ye—she wants the farm her'n—she was afeerd o' ye—she told me ye was sneakin' 'round tryin' t' make love t' her t' git her on yer side . . . ye . . . ye mad fool, ye! (*He raises his clenched fists threateningly.*)

EBEN (*is confronting him choking with rage*) Ye lie, ye old skunk! Abbie never said no sech thing!

CABOT (*suddenly triumphant when he sees how shaken* EBEN *is*) She did. An' I says, I'll blow his brains t' the top o' them elums—an' she says no, that hain't sense, who'll ye git t'help ye on the farm in his place—an' then she says yew'n me ought t' have a son—I know we kin, she says—an' I says, if we do, ye kin have anythin' I've got ye've a mind t'. An' she says, I wants Eben cut off so's this farm'll be mine when ye die! (*with terrible gloating*) An' that's what's happened, hain't it? An' the farm's her'n! An' the dust o' the road—that's your'n! Ha! Now who's hawin'?

EBEN (*has been listening, petrified with grief and rage—suddenly laughs wildly and brokenly*) Ha-ha-ha! So that's her sneakin' game—all along!—like I suspicioned at fust—t' swaller it all—an' me, too . . . ! (*madly*) I'll murder her! (*He springs toward the porch but* CABOT *is quicker and gets in between.*)

CABOT No, ye don't!

EBEN Git out o' my road! (*He tries to throw* CABOT *aside. They grapple in what becomes immediately a murderous struggle. The old man's concentrated strength is too much for* EBEN. CABOT *gets one hand on his throat and presses him back across the stone wall. At the same moment,* ABBIE *comes out on the porch. With a stifled cry she runs toward them.*)

ABBIE Eben! Ephraim! (*She tugs at the hand on* EBEN'S *throat.*) Let go, Ephraim! Ye're chokin' him!

CABOT (*removes his hand and flings* EBEN *sideways full length on the grass, gasping and choking. With a cry,* ABBIE *kneels beside him, trying to take his head on her lap, but he pushes her away.* CABOT *stands looking down with fierce triumph*) Ye needn't t've fret, Abbie, I wa'n't aimin' t' kill him. He hain't wuth hangin' fur—not by a hell of a sight! (*more and more triumphantly*) Seventy-six an' him not thirty yit—an' look whar he be fur thinkin' his Paw was easy! No, by God, I hain't easy! An' him upstairs, I'll raise him t' be like me! (*He turns to leave them.*) I'm goin' in an' dance!—sing an' celebrate! (*He walks to the porch—then turns with a great grin.*) I don't calc'late it's left ir him, but if he gits pesky, Abbie, ye jest sing out. I'll come a-runnin' ar' the Etarnal, I'll put him across my knee an' birch him! Ha-ha-ha! (*F into the house laughing. A moment later his loud "whoop" is heard.*)

ABBIE (*tenderly*) Eben. Air ye hurt? (*She tries to kiss him but he pushes her violently away and struggles to a sitting position.*)

EBEN (*gaspingly*) T'hell—with ye!

ABBIE (*not believing her ears*) It's me, Eben—Abbie—don't ye know me?

EBEN (*glowering at her with hatred*) Ay-eh—I know ye—now! (*He suddenly breaks down, sobbing weakly.*)

ABBIE (*fearfully*) Eben—what's happened t' ye—why did ye look at me 's if ye hated me?

EBEN (*violently, between sobs and gasps*) I do hate ye! Ye're a whore—a damn trickin' whore!

ABBIE (*shrinking back horrified*) Eben! Ye don't know what ye're sayin'!

EBEN (*scrambling to his feet and following her—accusingly*) Ye're nothin' but a stinkin' passel o' lies! Ye've been lyin' t' me every word ye spoke, day an' night, since we fust—done it. Ye've kept sayin' ye loved me. . . .

ABBIE (*frantically*) I do love ye! (*She takes his hand but he flings hers away.*)

EBEN (*unheeding*) Ye've made a fool o' me—a sick, dumb fool—a-purpose! Ye've been on'y playin' yer sneakin', stealin' game all along—gittin' me t' lie with ye so's ye'd hev a son he'd think was his'n, an' makin' him promise he'd give ye the farm and let me eat dust, if ye did git him a son! (*staring at her with anguished, bewildered eyes*) They must be a devil livin' in ye! 'Tain't human t' be as bad as that be!

ABBIE (*stunned—dully*) He told yew . . . ?

EBEN Hain't it true? It hain't no good in yew lyin'.

ABBIE (*pleadingly*) Eben, listen—ye must listen—it was long ago—afore we done nothin'—yew was scornin' me—goin' t' see Min—when I was lovin' ye—an' I said it t' him t' git vengeance on ye!

EBEN (*unheedingly. With tortured passion:*) I wish ye was dead! I wish I was dead along with ye afore this come! (*ragingly*) But I'll git my vengeance too! I'll pray Maw t' come back t' help me—t' put her cuss on yew an' him!

ABBIE (*brokenly*) Don't ye, Eben! Don't ye! (*She throws herself on her knees before him, weeping.*) I didn't mean t' do bad t'ye! Fergive me, won't ye?

EBEN (*not seeming to hear her—fiercely*) I'll git squar' with the old skunk—an' yew! I'll tell him the truth 'bout the son he's so proud o'! Then I'll leave ye here t' pizen each other—with Maw comin' out o' her grave at nights—an' I'll go t' the gold fields o' Californi-a whar Sim an' Peter be!

ABBIE (*terrified*) Ye won't—leave me? Ye can't!

EBEN (*with fierce determination*) I'm a-goin', I tell ye! I'll git rich thar an' come back an' fight him fur the farm he stole—an' I'll kick ye both out in the road—t' beg an' sleep in the woods—an' yer son along with ye—t' starve an' die! (*He is hysterical at the end.*)

ABBIE (*with a shudder—humbly*) He's yewr son, too, Eben.

EBEN (*torturedly*) I wish he never was born! I wish he'd die this minit! I wish I'd never sot eyes on him! It's him—yew havin' him—a-purpose t' steal—that's changed everythin'!

ABBIE (*gently*) Did ye believe I loved ye—afore he come?

EBEN Ay-eh—like a dumb ox!

ABBIE An' ye don't believe no more?

EBEN B'lieve a lyin' thief! Ha!

ABBIE (*shudders—then humbly*) An did ye r'ally love me afore?

EBEN (*brokenly*) Ay-eh—an' ye was trickin' me!

ABBIE An' ye don't love me now!

EBEN (*violently*) I hate ye, I tell ye!

ABBIE An' ye're truly goin' West—goin' t' leave me—all account o' him being born?

EBEN I'm a-goin' in the mornin'—or may God strike me t' hell!

ABBIE (*after a pause—with a dreadful cold intensity—slowly*) If that's what his comin's done t' me—killin' yewr love—takin' yew away—my on'y joy—the on'y joy I've ever knowed—like heaven t' me—purtier'n heaven—then I hate him, too, even if I be his Maw!

EBEN (*bitterly*) Lies! Ye love him! He'll steal the farm fur ye! (*brokenly*) But 'tain't the farm so much—not no more—it's yew foolin' me—gittin' me t' love ye—lyin' yew loved me—jest t' git a son t' steal!

ABBIE (*distractedly*) He won't steal! I'd kill him fust! I do love ye! I'll prove t' ye . . . !

EBEN (*harshly*) 'Tain't no use lyin' no more. I'm deaf t' ye! (*He turns away.*) I hain't seein' ye agen. Good-by!

ABBIE (*pale with anguish*) Hain't ye even goin' t' kiss me—not once—arter all we loved?

EBEN (*in a hard voice*) I hain't wantin' t' kiss ye never agen! I'm wantin' t' forgit I ever sot eyes on ye!

ABBIE Eben!—ye mustn't—wait a spell—I want t' tell ye. . . .

EBEN I'm a-goin' in t' git drunk. I'm a-goin' t' dance.

ABBIE (*clinging to his arm—with passionate earnestness*) If I could make it—'s if he'd never come up between us—if I could prove t' ye I wa'n't schemin' t' steal from ye—so's everythin' could be jest the same with us, lovin' each other jest the same, kissin' an' happy the same's we've been happy afore he come—if I could do it—ye'd love me agen, wouldn't ye? Ye'd kiss me agen? Ye wouldn't never leave me, would ye?

EBEN (*moved*) I calc'late not. (*then shaking her hand off his arm—with a bitter smile*) But ye hain't God, be ye?

ABBIE (*exultantly*) Remember ye've promised! (*then with strange intensity*) Mebbe I kin take back one thin' God does!

EBEN (*peering at her*) Ye're gittin' cracked, hain't ye? (*then going towards door*) I'm a-goin' t' dance.

ABBIE (*calls after him intensely*) I'll prove t' ye! I'll prove I love ye better'n. . . . (*He goes in the door, not seeming to hear. She remains standing where she i looking after him—then she finishes desperately:*) Better'n everythin' el the world!

Scene 3

Just before dawn in the morning—shows the kitchen and CABOT'S *bedroom.*

In the kitchen, by the light of a tallow candle on the table, EBEN *is sitting, his chin propped on his hands, his drawn face blank and expressionless. His carpetbag is on the floor beside him. In the bedroom, dimly lighted by a small whale-oil lamp,* CABOT *lies asleep.* ABBIE *is bending over the cradle, listening, her face full of terror yet with an undercurrent of desperate triumph. Suddenly, she breaks down and sobs, appears about to throw herself on her knees beside the cradle; but the old man turns restlessly, groaning in his sleep, and she controls herself, and shrinking away from the cradle with a gesture of horror, backs swiftly toward the door in rear and goes out. A moment later she comes into the kitchen and, running to* EBEN, *flings her arms about his neck and kisses him wildly. He hardens himself, he remains unmoved and cold, he keeps his eyes straight ahead.*

ABBIE (*hysterically*) I done it, Eben! I told ye I'd do it! I've proved I love ye—better'n everythin'—so's ye can't never doubt me no more!

EBEN (*dully*) Whatever ye done, it hain't no good now.

ABBIE (*wildly*) Don't ye say that! Kiss me, Eben, won't ye? I need ye t' kiss me arter what I done! I need ye t' say ye love me!

EBEN (*kisses her without emotion—dully*) That's fur good-by. I'm a-goin' soon.

ABBIE No! No! Ye won't go—not now!

EBEN (*going on with his own thoughts*) I been a-thinkin'—an' I hain't goin' t' tell Paw nothin'. I'll leave Maw t' take vengeance on ye. If I told him, the old skunk'd jest be stinkin' mean enuf to take it out on that baby. (*his voice showing emotion in spite of him*) An' I don't want nothin' bad t' happen t' him. He hain't t' blame fur yew. (*he adds with a certain queer pride*) An' he looks like me! An' by God, he's mine! An' some day I'll be a-comin' back an' . . . !

ABBIE (*too absorbed in her own thoughts to listen to him—pleadingly*) They's no cause fur ye t' go now—they's no sense—it's all the same's it was—they's nothin' come b'tween us now—arter what I done!

EBEN (*something in her voice arouses him. He stares at her a bit frightenedly:*) Ye look mad, Abbie. What did ye do?

ABBIE I—I killed him, Eben.

EBEN (*amazed*) Ye killed him?

ABBIE (*dully*) Ay-eh.

EBEN (*recovering from his astonishment—savagely*) An' serves him right! But we got t' do somethin' quick t' make it look s'if the old skunk'd killed himself when he was drunk. We kin prove by 'em all how drunk he got.

ABBIE (*wildly*) No! No! Not him! (*laughing distractedly*) But that's what I ought t' done, hain't it? I oughter killed him instead! Why didn't ye tell me?

EBEN (*appalled*) Instead? What d'ye mean?

ABBIE Not him.

EBEN (*his face grown ghastly*) Not—not that baby!

ABBIE (*dully*) Ay-eh!

EBEN (*falls to his knees as if he'd been struck—his voice trembling with horror*) Oh, God A'mighty! A'mighty God! Maw, whar was ye, why didn't ye stop her?

ABBIE (*simply*) She went back t' her grave that night we fust done it, remember? I hain't felt her about since. (*A pause.* EBEN *hides his head in his hands, trembling all over as if he had the ague. She goes on dully.*) I left the piller over his little face. Then he killed himself. He stopped breathin'. (*She begins to weep softly.*)

EBEN (*rage beginning to mingle with grief*) He looked like me. He was mine, damn ye!

ABBIE (*slowly and brokenly*) I didn't want t' do it. I hated myself fur doin' it. I loved him. He was so purty—dead spit 'n' image o' yew. But I loved yew more—an' yew was goin' away—far off whar I'd never see ye agen, never kiss ye, never feel ye pressed agin me agen—an' ye said ye hated me fur havin' him—ye said ye hated him an' wished he was dead—ye said if it hadn't been fur him comin' it'd be the same's afore between us.

EBEN (*unable to endure this, springs to his feet in a fury, threatening her, his twitching fingers seeming to reach out for her throat*) Ye lie! I never said—I never dreamed ye'd—I'd cut off my head afore I'd hurt his finger!

ABBIE (*piteously, sinking on her knees*) Eben, don't ye look at me like that—hatin' me—not after what I done fur ye—fur us—so's we could be happy agen —

EBEN (*furiously now*) Shut up, or I'll kill ye! I see yer game now—the same old sneakin' trick—ye're aimin' t' blame me fur the murder ye done!

ABBIE (*moaning—putting her hands over her ears*) Don't ye, Eben! Don't ye! (*She grasps his legs.*)

EBEN (*his mood suddenly changing to horror, shrinks away from her*) Don't ye tech me! Ye're pizen! How could ye—t' murder a pore little critter—Ye must've swapped yer soul t' hell! (*suddenly raging*) Ha! I kin see why ye done it! Not the lies ye jest told—but 'cause ye wanted t' steal agen—steal the last thin' ye'd left me—my part o' him—no, the hull o' him—ye saw he looked like me—ye knowed he was all mine—an' ye couldn't b'ar it—I know ye! Ye killed him fur bein' mine! (*All this has driven him almost insane. He makes a rush past her for the door—then turns—shaking both fists at her, violently.*) But I'll take vengeance now! I'll git the Sheriff! I'll tell him everythin'! Then I'll sing "I'm off to Californi-a!" an' go—gold—Golden Gate—gold sun—fields o' gold in the West! (*This last he half shouts, half croons incoherently, suddenly breaking off passionately.*) I'm a-goin' fur the Sheriff t' come an' git ye! I want ye tuk away, locked up from me! I can't stand t'luk at ye! Murderer an' thief 'r not, ye still tempt me! I'll give ye up t' the Sheriff! (*He turns and runs out, around the corner of house, panting and sobbing, and breaks into a swerving sprint down the road.*)

ABBIE (*struggling to her feet, runs to the door, calling after him*) I love ye, Eben! I love ye! (*She stops at the door weakly, swaying, about to fall.*) I don't care what ye do—if ye'll on'y love me agen— (*She falls limply to the floor in a faint.*)

Scene 4

About an hour later. Same as SCENE 3. *Shows the kitchen and* **CABOT'S** *bedroom. It is after dawn. The sky is brilliant with the sunrise.*

In the kitchen, **ABBIE** *sits at the table, her body limp and exhausted, her head bowed down over her arms, her face hidden. Upstairs,* **CABOT** *is still asleep but awakens with a start. He looks toward the window and gives a snort of surprise and irritation—throws back the covers and begins hurriedly pulling on his clothes. Without looking behind him, he begins talking to* **ABBIE** *whom he supposes beside him.*

CABOT Thunder 'n' lightnin', Abbie! I hain't slept this late in fifty year! Looks 's if the sun was full riz a'most. Must've been the dancin' 'an' likker. Must be gittin' old. I hope Eben's t' wuk. Ye might've tuk the trouble t' rouse me, Abbie. (*He turns—sees no one there—surprised.*) Waal—whar air she? Gittin' vittles, I calc'late. (*He tiptoes to the cradle and peers down—proudly*) Mornin', sonny. Purty's a picter! Sleepin' sound. He don't beller all night like most o' 'em. (*He goes quietly out the door in rear—a few moments later enters kitchen—sees* ABBIE*—with satisfaction.*) So thar ye be. Ye got any vittles cooked?

ABBIE (*without moving*) No.

CABOT (*coming to her, almost sympathetically*) Ye feelin' sick?

ABBIE No.

CABOT (*pats her on shoulder. She shudders.*) Ye'd best lie down a spell. (*half jocularly*) Yer son'll be needin' ye soon. He'd ought t' wake up with a gnashin' appetite, the sound way he's sleepin'.

ABBIE (*shudders—then in a dead voice*) He ain't never goin' to wake up.

CABOT (*jokingly*) Takes after me this mornin'. I ain't slept so late in . . .

ABBIE He's dead.

CABOT (*stares at her—bewilderedly*) What . . .

ABBIE I killed him.

CABOT (*stepping back from her—aghast*) Air ye drunk—'r crazy—'r . . . !

ABBIE (*suddenly lifts her head and turns on him—wildly*) I killed him, I tell ye! I smothered him. Go up an' see if ye don't b'lieve me! (CABOT *stares at her a second, then bolts out the rear door, can be heard bounding up the stairs, and rushes into the bedroom and over to the cradle.* ABBIE *has sunk back lifelessly into her former position.* CABOT *puts his hand down on the body in the crib. An expression of fear and horror comes over his face.*)

CABOT (*shrinking away—tremblingly*) God A'mighty! God A'mighty. (*He stumbles out the door—in a short while returns to the kitchen—comes to* ABBIE*, the stunned expression still on his face—hoarsely.*) Why did ye do it? Why? (*As she doesn't answer, he grabs her violently by the shoulder and shakes her.*) I ax ye why ye done it! Ye'd better tell me 'r . . . !

ABBIE (*gives him a furious push which sends him staggering back and springs to her feet—with wild rage and hatred*) Don't ye dare tech me! What right hev ye t' question me 'bout him? He wa'n't yewr son! Think I'd have a son by yew? I'd die fust! I hate the sight o' ye an' allus did! It's yew I should've murdered, if I'd had good sense! I hate ye! I love Eben. I did from the fust. An' he was Eben's son—mine an' Eben's—not your'n!

CABOT (*stands looking at her dazedly—a pause—finding his words with an effort—dully*) That was it—what I felt—pokin' round the corners—while ye lied—holdin' herself from me—sayin' ye'd a'ready conceived—(*He lapses into crushed silence—then with a strange emotion.*) He's dead, sart'n. I felt his heart. Pore little critter! (*He blinks back one tear, wiping his sleeve across his nose.*)

ABBIE (*hysterically*) Don't ye! Don't ye! (*She sobs unrestrainedly.*)

CABOT (*with a concentrated effort that stiffens his body into a rigid line and hardens his face into a stony mask—through his teeth to himself*) I got t' be—like a stone—a rock o' jedgment! (*A pause. He gets complete control over himself—harshly.*) If he was Eben's, I be glad he air gone! An' mebbe I suspicioned it all along. I felt they was somethin' onnateral—somewhars—the house got so lonesome—an' cold—drivin' me down t' the barn—t' the beasts o' the field. . . . Ay-eh. I must've suspicioned—somethin'. Ye didn't fool me—not altogether, leastways—I'm too old a bird—growin' ripe on the bough. . . . (*He becomes aware he is wandering, straightens again, looks at* ABBIE *with a cruel grin.*) So ye'd liked t' hev murdered me 'stead o' him, would ye? Waal, I'll live to a hundred! I'll live t' see ye hung! I'll deliver ye up t' the jedgment o' God an' the law! I'll git the Sheriff now. (*Starts for the door.*)

ABBIE (*dully*) Ye needn't. Eben's gone fur him.

CABOT (*amazed*) Eben—gone fur the Sheriff?

ABBIE Ay-eh.

CABOT T' inform agen ye?

ABBIE Ah-eh.

CABOT (*considers this—a pause—then in a hard voice*) Waal, I'm thankful fur him savin' me the trouble. I'll git t' wuk. (*He goes to the door—then turns—in a voice full of strange emotion.*) He'd ought t' been my son, Abbie. Ye'd ought t' loved me. I'm a man. If ye'd loved me, I'd never told no Sheriff on ye no matter what ye did, if they was t' brile me alive!

ABBIE (*defensively*) They's more to it nor yew know, makes him tell.

CABOT (*dryly*) Fur yewr sake, I hope they be. (*He goes out—comes around to the gate—stares up at the sky. His control relaxes. For a moment he is old and weary. He murmurs despairingly*) God A'mighty, I be lonesomer'n ever! (*He hears running footsteps from the left, immediately is himself again.* EBEN *runs in, panting exhaustedly, wild-eyed and mad looking. He lurches through the gate.* CABOT *grabs him by the shoulder.* EBEN *stares at him dumbly.*) Did ye tell the Sheriff?

EBEN (*nodding stupidly*) Ay-eh.

CABOT (*gives him a push away that sends him sprawling—laughing with withering contempt*) Good fur ye! A prime chip o' yer Maw ye be! (*He goes toward the barn, laughing harshly.* EBEN *scrambles to his feet. Suddenly* CABOT *turns—grimly threatening.*) Git off this farm when the Sheriff takes her—or, by God, he'll have t' come back an' git me fur murder, too! (*He stalks off.* EBEN *does not appear to have heard him. He runs to the door and comes into the kitchen.* ABBIE *looks up with a cry of anguished joy.* EBEN *stumbles over and throws himself on his knees beside her—sobbing brokenly.*)

EBEN Fergive me!

ABBIE (*happily*) Eben! (*She kisses him and pulls his head over against her breast.*)

EBEN I love ye! Fergive me!

ABBIE (*ecstatically*) I'd fergive ye all the sins in hell fur sayin' that! (*She kisses his head, pressing it to her with a fierce passion of possession.*)

EBEN (*brokenly*) But I told the Sheriff. He's comin' fur ye!

ABBIE I kin b'ar what happens t' me—now!

EBEN I woke him up. I told him. He says, wait 'til I git dressed. I was waiting. I got to thinkin' o' yew. I got to thinkin' how I'd loved ye. It hurt like somethin' was bustin' in my chest an' head. I got t' cryin'. I knowed sudden I loved ye yet, an' allus would love ye!

ABBIE (*caressing his hair—tenderly*) My boy, hain't ye?

EBEN I begun t' run back. I cut across the fields an' through the woods. I thought ye might have time t' run away—with me—an' . . .

ABBIE (*shaking her head*) I got t' take my punishment—t' pay fur my sin.

EBEN Then I want t' share it with ye.

ABBIE Ye didn't do nothin'.

EBEN I put it in yer head. I wisht he was dead! I as much as urged ye t' do it!

ABBIE No. It was me alone!

EBEN I'm as guilty as yew be! He was the child o' our sin.

ABBIE (*lifting her head as if defying God*) I don't repent that sin! I hain't askin' God t' fergive that!

EBEN Nor me—but it led up t' the other—an' the murder ye did, ye did 'count o' me—an' it's my murder, too, I'll tell the Sheriff—an' if ye deny it, I'll say we planned it t'gether—an' they'll all b'lieve me, fur they suspicion everythin' we've done, an' it'll seem likely an' true to 'em. An' it is true—way down. I did help ye—somehow.

ABBIE (*laying her head on his—sobbing*) No! I don't want ye t' suffer!

EBEN I got t' pay fur my part o' the sin! An' I'd suffer wuss leavin' ye, goin' West, thinkin' o' ye day an' night, bein' out when yew was in—(*lowering his voice*)—'r bein' alive when yew was dead. (*a pause*) I want t' share with ye, Abbie—prison 'r death 'r hell 'r anythin'! (*He looks into her eyes and forces a trembling smile.*) If I'm sharin' with ye, I won't feel lonesome, leastways.

ABBIE (*weakly*) Eben! I won't let ye! I can't let ye!

EBEN (*kissing her—tenderly*) Ye can't he'p yerself. I got ye beat fur once!

ABBIE (*forcing a smile—adoringly*) I hain't beat—s'long's I got ye!

EBEN (*hears the sound of feet outside*) Ssshh! Listen! They've come t' take us!

ABBIE No, it's him. Don't give him no chance to fight ye, Eben. Don't say nothin'—no matter what he says. An' I won't neither. (*It is* CABOT. *He comes up from the barn in a great state of excitement and strides into the house and then into the kitchen.* EBEN *is kneeling beside* ABBIE, *his arm around her, hers around him. They stare straight ahead.*)

CABOT (*stares at them, his face hard. A long pause—vindictively*) Ye make a slick pair o' murderin' turtle doves! Ye'd ought t' be both hung on the same limb an' left thar t' swing in the breeze an' rot—a warnin' t' old fools like me t' b'ar their lonesomeness alone—an' fur young fools like ye t' hobble their lust. (*A pause. The excitement returns to his face, his eyes snap, he looks a bit crazy.*) I couldn't work today. I couldn't take no interest. T' hell with the farm! I'm leavin' it! I've turned the cows an' other stock loose! I've druv 'em into the woods whar they kin be free! By freein' 'em, I'm freein' myself! I'm quittin' here today! I'll set fire t' house an' barn an' watch 'em burn, an' I'll leave yer Maw t' haunt the ashes, an' I'll will the fields back t' God, so that nothin' human kin never touch 'em! I'll be a-goin' to Californi-a—t' jine Simeon an' Peter—true sons o' mine if they be dumb fools—an' the Cabots'll find Solomon's Mines t'gether! (*He suddenly cuts a mad caper.*) Whoop! What was the song they sung? "Oh, Californi-a! That's the land fur me." (*He sings this—then gets on his knees by the floorboard under which the money was hid.*) An I'll sail thar on one o' the finest clippers I kin find! I've got the money! Pity ye didn't know whar this was hidden so's ye could steal . . . (*He has pulled up the board. He stares—feels—stares again. A pause of dead silence. He slowly turns, slumping into a sitting position on the floor, his eyes like those of a dead fish, his face the sickly green of an attack of nausea. He swallows painfully several times—forces a weak smile at last.*) So—ye did steal it!

EBEN (*emotionlessly*) I swapped it t' Sim an' Peter fur their share o' the farm—t' pay their passage t' Californi-a.

CABOT (*with one sardonic*) Ha! (*He begins to recover, gets slowly to his feet—strangely.*) I calc'late God give it to 'em—not yew! God's hard, not easy! Mebbe they's easy gold in the West but it hain't God's gold. It hain't fur me. I kin hear His voice warnin' me agen t' be hard an' stay on my farm. I kin see his hand usin' Eben t' steal t' keep me from weakness. I kin feel I be in the palm o' His hand, His fingers guidin' me. (*a pause—then he mutters sadly*) It's a-goin' t' be lonesomer now than ever it war afore—an' I'm gittin' old, Lord—ripe on the bough. . . . (*then stiffening*) Waal—what d'ye want? God's lonesome, hain't He? God's hard an' lonesome! (*A pause. The* SHERIFF *with two men comes up the road from the left. They move cautiously to the door. The* SHERIFF *knocks on it with the butt of his pistol.*)

SHERIFF Open in the name o' the law! (*They start.*)

CABOT They've come fur ye. (*He goes to the rear door.*) Come in, Jim! (*The three men enter.* CABOT *meets them in doorway.*) Jest a minit, Jim. I got 'em safe here. (*The* SHERIFF *nods. He and his companions remain in the doorway.*)

EBEN (*suddenly calls*) I lied this mornin', Jim. I helped her to do it. Ye kin take me, too.

ABBIE (*brokenly*) No!

CABOT Take 'em both. (*He comes forward—stares at* EBEN *with a trace of grudging admiration.*) Purty good—fur yew! Waal, I got t' round up the stock. Good-by.

EBEN Good-by.

ABBIE Good-by. (CABOT *turns and strides past the men—comes out and around the corner of the house, his shoulders squared, his face stony, and stalks grimly toward the barn. In the meantime the* SHERIFF *and men have come into the room.*)

SHERIFF (*embarrassedly*) Waal—we'd best start.

ABBIE Wait. (*turns to* EBEN) I love ye, Eben.

EBEN I love ye, Abbie. (*They kiss. The three men grin and shuffle embarrassedly.* EBEN *takes* ABBIE'S *hand. They go out the door in rear, the men following, and come from the house, walking hand in hand to the gate.* EBEN *stops there and points to the sunrise sky.*) Sun's a-rizin'. Purty, hain't it?

ABBIE Ay-eh. (*They both stand for a moment looking up raptly in attitudes strangely aloof and devout.*)

SHERIFF (*looking around at the farm enviously—to his companion*) It's a jim-dandy farm, no denyin'. Wished I owned it!

THE GLASS MENAGERIE

(1944)

TENNESSEE WILLIAMS (1911–1983)

Before and after World War I and throughout the two decades of peace before the outbreak of World War II in 1939, the drama in England maintained a steady pace of producing respectable, if not great, plays. Until the conflict ended in 1945, drama on the continent all too often reflected the heavy hand of dictatorship, which stifled any artistic expression that conflicted with the official party line. In the United States, however, the story was quite different. During the twenty years between wars, American drama, with O'Neill at the forefront, achieved respect and recognition as the leading force in Western dramatic art. In the following twenty years, both during and following World War II, American dramatists maintained the dominant position while Europe recovered from the effects of the destruction and disruption it had suffered during the nearly six years that modern all-out warfare had imposed upon it.

In England, George Bernard Shaw continued his irascible and unpredictable ways. He produced what is probably his masterwork, *Saint Joan,* in 1924. The serious socially conscious plays of John Galsworthy (1867–1933) treated the struggle of working people on strike in *Strife* (1909), the inequalities of the legal system in *Justice* (1910), and Jew-Gentile prejudices in *Loyalties* (1922). The Abbey Theatre of Dublin excited the world and frequently enraged the Irish, who resented what they considered a degrading picture of themselves in *The Playboy of the Western World* (1907) by John Millington Synge (1871–1909) and in the plays of Sean O'Casey (1880–1964), *Juno and the Paycock* (1924) and *The Plough and the Stars* (1926).

Somerset Maugham (1874–1965) continued the British high comic tradition in *The Circle* (1921) and *The Constant Wife* (1927). *Private Lives* and *Design for Living* (1923) by Noel Coward (1899–1973) were the ultimate in sophistication in their brittle, witty language and the unconventional behavior of their rich and spoiled characters. Sir James M. Barrie (1860–1937), always associated with the boy who never grew up, *Peter Pan* (1904), wrote a series of sometimes mystical, sometimes whimsical comedy-dramas often full of cloying sentiment but frequently with pertinent social commentary. Others, such as Emlyn Williams (1906–1987), J. B. Priestley (1894–1989), and Terence Rattigan

(1911–1977), contributed a variety of melodrama, serious drama, and comedy, becoming familiar names on both sides of the Atlantic as they wrote and produced during and after the war.

On the continent the political uncertainties and the rumblings that presaged the coming second conflict began to take their artistic toll. In Russia the growing despotism and emphasis on "proletarian" art had pretty well ended dramatic progress and only Maxim Gorki's work carries any significance today. Germany, devastated by defeat and the punishing Versailles Treaty, with the impotent Weimar republic gradually falling apart and heading toward the horrors of Hitler and Nazism, had little to offer, although Georg Kaiser (1878–1945) and Ernst Toller (1893–1939) had written some of the most impressive expressionistic plays. Kaiser's *Gas* trilogy (1918–1920) was a terrifyingly accurate prediction of things to come as the Gas that Kills annihilates the world; and Toller's *Man and the Masses* (1920) was a devastating expressionistic picture of mass hysteria. Bertolt Brecht (1898–1956) became famous for his *Threepenny Opera* (1928) with Kurt Weill's music. After he fled Nazi Germany, he remained a staunch Communist, settling for some time in America. His *Mother Courage* (1939) was an outstanding example of the nonrealistic theatre he called "epic." Nobody to speak of stood out in Fascist Italy under the boot of Benito Mussolini except for the Nobel Prize–winning Luigi Pirandello (1867–1936), whose baffling treatment of the unreality of reality and the total illusion of existence still entrances audiences in *Right You Are If You Think You Are* (1918) and *Six Characters in Search of an Author* (1921).

France fared somewhat better. At the end of the nineteenth century Edmond Rostand (1868–1918) composed the forever-popular romantic favorite *Cyrano de Bergerac* (1897). Maurice Maeterlinck (1862–1949) wrote impressionistic poetic dramas full of symbolism in *Pélléas et Mélisande* (1892) and *The Blue Bird* (1909). Jean Giraudoux (1882–1944) retold the Greek myth of Zeus and Alcmene in *Amphitryon 38* (1937). Jean Cocteau (1892–1963) gained fame with his contemporary look at the Oedipus legend in *The Infernal Machine* (1934). The existential poet-philosopher Jean Paul Sartre (1905–1980) let us know that hell is other people in *No Exit* (1944), and Jean Anouilh (1910–1987) took the myth of Oedipus's daughter's defiance of the law in *Antigone* (1944), a modern-dress version drawing obvious parallels to France's defiance of the German occupation.

Between 1920 and 1960 the United States achieved its international fame with a concentration of dramatic artists never seen before and never experienced since. Until the mid-1930s, the figure standing above all others was, of course, Eugene O'Neill. Until 1934, with his rather sad exit from the scene with the total failure of his modern "miracle" play *Days Without End*, his eighteen major plays, both resounding failures and resounding successes, brought him worldwide recognition culminating in the Nobel Prize for Literature in 1936. The two plays most remembered from this period are the nine-act *Strange Interlude* (1928), with its long soliloquy asides and its demand that audiences spend hours in the theatre both before and after dinner, and the equally lengthy trilogy *Mourning Becomes Electra* (1932), with its parallels of Greek tragic curses imposed upon a New England family after the Civil War. *Ah, Wilderness!* (1933), O'Neill's only out-and-out comedy, showed a might-have-been Connecticut Fourth of July and succeeded in convincing the public that O'Neill was, after all, human.

During the 1930s, in the era of the Great Depression, there were loud voices from the Left, most of them expressed in single-minded Communist-slanted pieces of agitation and propaganda, known as *agitprop*, meant to sway the masses but preaching mostly to the converted, almost never appearing in an established Broadway house. The most famous voice was Clifford Odets (1906–1963), once a Communist party member, whose plays, though slanted by his social and political philosophies, were major Broadway productions. *Waiting for Lefty* in 1935 dwelled on the oppression of New York cab drivers voting to strike. Two other plays in the same year, *Awake and Sing* and *Paradise Lost*, established him as the outstanding advocate of the ordinary, hardworking decent citizen caught in and trying to cope with the Depression's suffocating economic catastrophe. From 1935 to 1937 the Federal Theatre Project, born of the Depression-inspired Works Project Administration, originated a unique form of theatre called The Living Newspaper, a newsreellike production based on social and political events of immediate concern, all with a decidedly liberal point of view. Although it was tremendously successful across the nation and never censored by any government bureau, the Federal Theatre was abruptly ended by a nervous, conservative Congress.

The recently ended war prompted Maxwell Anderson (1888–1959) and Laurence Stallings (1894–1965) to write the rousing *What Price Glory?* in 1924, permanently ending the long tradition of romanticizing the soldier's life as a kind of glorified heroism. Although they were only moderately successful, Anderson created a series of pseudo-Elizabethan tragedies in verse, *Elizabeth the Queen* (1930), *Mary of Scotland* (1933), and *Anne of the Thousand Days* (1948). His poetic modern tragedy *Winterset* (1935), concerning doomed young lovers in a New York slum, remains his best play.

Sidney Howard (1891–1939), in *They Knew What They Wanted* (1924), drew an exceptionally sympathetic yet realistic picture of individuals in California's Napa Valley wine-producing district. His portrait of the near-incestuous possessiveness of a mother toward her sons in *The Silver Cord* (1926) was a horrifying portrayal of the parental affliction called "momism." *The Petrified Forest* (1938) by Robert E. Sherwood (1896–1955) created a memorable picture of the deadening effects of the Depression in the symbolism of life on the edge of the Arizona stone forest. *Idiot's Delight* (1936) all too accurately forecast the conflagration to begin in three years. *Abe Lincoln in Illinois* (1938), a believable portrait of Lincoln up to his election, avoided idolizing sanctification. S. N. Behrman (1893–1973) wrote successful high comedies in *The Second Man* (1927) and *Biography* (1932). Elmer Rice (1892–1967) wrote one of the best

American expressionistic plays in *The Adding Machine* (1923), a grim picture of a hopeless nonentity called Mr. Zero mired in a dead-end job. *Street Scene* (1929) was a remarkable picture of life and violence in a lower middle-class New York apartment house on a steaming summer day.

Sidney Kingsley (1906–) wrote two of the best American naturalistic dramas: *Men in White* (1933) depicted life in a large hospital; *Dead End* (1935) placed onstage one of the most striking naturalistic stage settings ever seen in New York, with its luxury apartment house abutting a filthy tenement district. Lillian Hellman (1905–1984) raised questions of pathological lying by a malicious child and suggestions of possible lesbianism in *The Children's Hour* (1934). *The Little Foxes* (1939), also by Hellman, was the well-made play at its best in its introduction of the Hubbard clan of human predators. The sensation of 1937 was John Steinbeck's dramatization of his novel *Of Mice and Men,* a sympathetic treatment of migrant farm workers in California in the midst of the Depression.

The period between the wars was the great age of American comedy, dominated by one man, the author, collaborator, "play doctor," director, and actor George S. Kaufman (1889–1961). With a host of collaborators he rolled out hit after hit: *Beggar on Horseback* (1924), an expressionistic satire on big business; *You Can't Take It with You* (1936), with the unforgettably madcap Vanderhof family; and *The Man Who Came to Dinner* (1939), introducing the eccentric, insufferable Sheridan Whiteside, an outstanding satire aimed at columnist and radio personality Alexander Woollcott.

Philip Barry (1896–1949) wrote the very successful high comedy *The Philadelphia Story* (1939). Clare Booth (1903–1987) savaged her own sex in *The Women* (1936). Howard Lindsay (1889–1968) and Russell Crouse (1893–1966) introduced the red-headed family of Clarence Day in *Life With Father* (1939), the longest-running legitimate play in American history, with 3,224 performances. James Thurber (1894–1965) and Elliott Nugent (1900–1965) dissected the sacred rite of a university homecoming weekend in *The Male Animal* (1940). The most widely loved and best-known American play of all time, *Our Town,* the portrait of life and death in a small New Hampshire town by Thornton Wilder (1897–1975), appeared in 1938. *Harvey* (1944), the comedy fantasy by Mary Chase about a six-foot, one-and-one-half-inch white rabbit that may or may not exist, took America's mind off the global war in its 1,775 performances.

The folk drama of the American South gained prominence in *Porgy* (1927) by DuBose Heyward (1885–1940) and his wife Dorothy (1890–1961), which became the great American opera, *Porgy and Bess* (1935), with music by George Gershwin. *The Green Pastures* (1929) by Marc Connelly (1890–1980) dramatized stories from the Old Testament as they might be told in a Southern black Sunday school. *Tobacco Road* (1933), adapted by Jack Kirkland (1904–1969) from the novel of Georgia sharecroppers by Erskine Caldwell (1903–1987), shocked and mesmerized American audiences as the longest-running American play until it was deposed by *Life With Father.*

Immediately after the war, the American drama carried on its tradition of excellent plays. In 1946 Eugene O'Neill returned with his first play in twelve years, the long-awaited *The Iceman Cometh.* Its initial appearance was not a success, but in 1956 its revival in The Circle-in-the-Square turned it into the longest-running O'Neill play in history, made a star of Jason Robards, established José Quintero as a major director, and helped to reestablish O'Neill as our greatest playwright. His masterpiece, *Long Day's Journey Into Night* (1956), telling for the first time the secrets of his tragic family, permanently established O'Neill as a playwright of truly international importance.

Two new playwrights, rivals of the returned O'Neill, helped prolong American theatrical dominance with their serious near-tragic dramas—Tennessee Williams and Arthur Miller.

Thomas Lanier Williams, nicknamed "Tennessee" for reasons not altogether clear—drifter in and out of jobs, in and out of colleges, abysmally unsuccessful writer of an abysmally unsuccessful play called *Battle of Angels,* almost literally driven out of Boston in 1940, shy, introverted, but determined to become a writer—broke sharply upon the scene in 1944 when the successful Chicago premiere of *The Glass Menagerie* was followed quickly by equal success and critical acclaim in New York. Four years later, one of the great modern American dramatic masterpieces, *A Streetcar Named Desire,* made Marlon Brando an instant star and virtual household name and raised Tennessee Williams to membership in an elite group of postwar American dramatic artists of international reputation. O'Neill, Arthur Miller, and Tennessee Williams still remain the best America has produced.

Williams's dramatic technique relies all too often on overworked themes of decadence in the South, particularly women, strutting young studs, horribly violent deaths and mutilations, and a look at the world and its inhabitants as in one way or another depraved. An effective picture of this world is summarized in the almost purely expressionistic *Camino Real,* an artistic failure in 1953, now regarded as one of Williams's major works. Even at that, Williams was able to compose a substantial body of superior dramatic literature that rightfully earned him his far-reaching artistic reputation. His first commercial success, the charmingly appealing *The Glass Menagerie,* remains among his best efforts.

The Glass Menagerie has the surface qualities of realistic drama with its petty little people and their struggle for meaning and dignity in a shoddy world, but Williams has actually written one of the few truly *impressionistic* plays. The style suggests the quality of a painting by Pissarro, or Monet, or, in music, of Debussy. There is a tremendous amount of mood, a sense of viewing through a glass, perhaps darkly, certainly hazily, and hearing from afar a life experience from a single vantage point. The actions are meant to be seen in the memory of the storyteller who colors it as he sees fit, reveals it as he wishes, creating for us his deeply personal impression of the way it was. We watch the play in certain sequences through a theatrical gauze, and the filminess is thus further heightened. We listen to the chorus figure, Tom, as he steps in and out of his reminiscences at will. It is a prolonged impression, a lengthy look, full of nostalgia, resentment, some hate, certainly regrets, and a lot of love.

Is *The Glass Menagerie* a tragedy? Probably not. It is a drama of compassion, and tragic only in the most pathetic sense, often much too fragile—like Laura's tiny animals—to achieve the necessary strength. There is, of course, an inevitability and sense of unavoidable catastrophe, and there is no way out. These people possess their individual flaws, but we see them with too much conscious emotion for tragedy. The tears raised on Laura's behalf become too sentimental. Amanda may be understandable as the frantic mother seeking a modicum of gentility among the ruins, but she is too much the smothering, monster stage mother. Tom is certainly no tragic protagonist in his detachment.

Still, *The Glass Menagerie* is a forceful play. Williams wants us to understand and to pity these three lost creatures, driven into themselves, each by the others, to a final disintegration of the spirit. In *The Glass Menagerie* all survive, yet all die, making the play, perhaps, simply a tragedy of life itself.

The Glass Menagerie TENNESSEE WILLIAMS

CHARACTERS

AMANDA WINGFIELD, *the mother.*

A little woman of great but confused vitality clinging frantically to another time and place. Her characterization must be carefully created, not copied from type. She is not paranoiac, but her life is paranoia. There is much to admire in AMANDA, *and as much to love and pity as there is to laugh at. Certainly she has endurance and a kind of heroism, and though her foolishness makes her unwittingly cruel at times, there is tenderness in her slight person.*

LAURA WINGFIELD, *her daughter.*

AMANDA, *having failed to establish contact with reality, continues to live vitally in her illusions, but* LAURA'S *situation is even graver. A childhood illness has left her crippled, one leg slightly shorter than the other, and held in a brace. This defect need not be more than suggested on the stage. Stemming from this,* LAURA'S *separation increases till she is like a piece of her own glass collection, too exquisitely fragile to move from the shelf.*

TOM WINGFIELD, *her son, and the narrator of the play.*

A poet with a job in a warehouse. His nature is not remorseless, but to escape from a trap he has to act without pity.

JIM O'CONNOR, *the gentleman caller.*

A nice, ordinary, young man.

SCENE: *An alley in St. Louis.*
PART I: *Preparation for a Gentleman Caller.*
PART II: *The Gentleman Calls.*
TIME: *Now and the Past.*

Scene I

The Wingfield apartment is in the rear of the building, one of those vast hive-like conglomerations of cellular living-units that flower as warty growths in overcrowded urban centers of lower middle-class population and are symptomatic of the impulse of this largest and fundamentally enslaved section of American society to avoid fluidity and differentiation and to exist and function as one interfused mass of automatism.

The apartment faces an alley and is entered by a fire-escape, a structure whose name is a touch of accidental poetic truth, for all of these huge buildings are always burning with the slow and implacable fires of human desperation. The fire-escape is included in the set—that is, the landing of it and steps descending from it.

The scene is memory and is therefore nonrealistic. Memory takes a lot of poetic license. It omits some details; others are exaggerated, according to the emotional value of the articles it touches, for memory is seated predominantly in the heart. The interior is therefore rather dim and poetic.

At the rise of the curtain, the audience is faced with the dark, grim rear wall of the Wingfield tenement. This building, which runs parallel to the footlights, is flanked on both sides by dark, narrow alleys which run into murky canyons of tangled clotheslines, garbage cans and the sinister latticework of neighboring fire-escapes. It is up and down these side alleys that exterior entrances and exits are made, during the play. At the end of TOM*'s opening commentary, the dark tenement wall slowly reveals (by means of a transparency) the interior of the ground floor Wingfield apartment.*

Downstage is the living room, which also serves as a sleeping room for LAURA, *the sofa unfolding to make her bed. Upstage, center, and divided by a wide arch or second proscenium with transparent faded portieres (or second curtain), is the dining room. In an old-fashioned what-not in the living room are seen scores of transparent glass animals. A blown-up photograph of the father hangs on the wall of the living room, facing the audience, to the left of the archway. It is the face of a very handsome young man in a doughboy's First World War cap. He is gallantly smiling, ineluctably smiling, as if to say, "I will be smiling forever."*

The audience hears and sees the opening scene in the dining room through both the transparent fourth wall of the building and the transparent gauze portieres of the dining-room arch. It is during this revealing scene that the fourth wall slowly ascends, out of sight. This transparent exterior wall is not brought down again until the very end of the play, during TOM*'s final speech.*

The narrator is an undisguised convention of the play. He takes whatever license with dramatic convention as is convenient to his purposes.

TOM *enters dressed as a merchant sailor from alley, stage left, and strolls across the front of the stage to the fire-escape. There he stops and lights a cigarette. He addresses the audience.*

TOM Yes, I have tricks in my pocket, I have things up my sleeve. But I am the opposite of a stage magician. He gives you illusion that has the appearance of truth. I give you truth in the pleasant disguise of illusion. To begin with, I turn back time. I reverse it to that quaint period, the thirties, when the huge middle class of America was matriculating in a school for the blind. Their eyes had failed them, or they had failed their eyes, and so they were having their fingers pressed forcibly down by the fiery Braille alphabet of a dissolving economy. In Spain there was revolution. Here there was only shouting and confusion. In Spain there was Guernica. Here there were disturbances of labor, sometimes pretty violent, in otherwise peaceful cities such as Chicago, Cleveland, Saint Louis. . . . This is the social background of the play.

(Music.)

The play is memory. Being a memory play, it is dimly lighted, it is sentimental, it is not realistic. In memory everything seems to happen to music. That explains the fiddle in the wings. I am the narrator of the play, and also a character in it. The other characters are my mother, Amanda, my sister, Laura, and a gentleman caller who appears in the final scenes. He is the most realistic character in the play, being an emissary from a world of reality that we were somehow set apart from. But since I have a poet's weakness for symbols, I am using this character also as a symbol; he is the long delayed but always expected something that we live for. There is a fifth character in the play who doesn't appear except in this larger-than-life photograph over the mantel. This is our father who left us a long time ago. He was a telephone man who fell in love with long distances; he gave up his job with the telephone company and skipped the light fantastic out of town . . . The last we heard of him was a picture post-card from Mazatlan, on the Pacific coast of Mexico, containing a message of two words—"Hello—Goodbye!" and an address. I think the rest of the play will explain itself. . . .

(*Amanda's voice becomes audible through the portieres.*)

(*Legend on screen: "Où sont les neiges."*)

(*He divides the portieres and enters the upstage area.*

AMANDA *and* LAURA *are seated at a drop-leaf table. Eating is indicated by gestures without food or utensils.* AMANDA *faces the audience.* TOM *and* LAURA *are seated in profile.*

The interior has lit up softly and through the scrim we see AMANDA *and* LAURA *seated at the table in the upstage area.*)

AMANDA (*calling*) Tom?

TOM Yes, Mother.

AMANDA We can't say grace until you come to the table!

TOM Coming, Mother. (*He bows slightly and withdraws, reappearing a few moments later in his place at the table.*)

AMANDA (*to her son*) Honey, don't *push* with your *fingers*. If you have to push with something, the thing to push with is a crust of bread. And chew—chew! Animals have sections in their stomachs which enable them to digest food without mastication, but human beings are supposed to chew their food before they swallow it down. Eat food leisurely, son, and really enjoy it. A well-cooked meal has lots of delicate flavors that have to be held in the mouth for appreciation. So chew your food and give your salivary glands a chance to function!

(TOM *deliberately lays his imaginary fork down and pushes his chair back from the table.*)

TOM I haven't enjoyed one bite of this dinner because of your constant directions on how to eat it. It's you that makes me rush through meals with your hawk-like attention to every bite I take. Sickening—spoils my appetite—all this discussion of animals' secretion—salivary glands—mastication!

AMANDA (*lightly*) Temperament like a Metropolitan star! (*He rises and crosses downstage.*) You're not excused from the table.

TOM I am getting a cigarette.

AMANDA You smoke too much.

(LAURA *rises.*)

LAURA I'll bring in the blanc mange.

(*He remains standing with his cigarette by the portieres during the following.*)

AMANDA (*rising*) No, sister, no, sister—you be the lady this time and I'll be the darky.

LAURA I'm already up.

AMANDA Resume your seat, little sister—I want you to stay fresh and pretty—for gentlemen callers!

LAURA I'm not expecting any gentlemen callers.

AMANDA (*crossing out to kitchenette; airily*) Sometimes they come when they are least expected! Why, I remember one Sunday afternoon in Blue Mountain—(*enters kitchenette*)

TOM I know what's coming!

LAURA Yes. But let her tell it.

TOM Again?

LAURA She loves to tell it.

(AMANDA *returns with bowl of dessert.*)

AMANDA One Sunday afternoon in Blue Mountain—your mother received—*seventeen!*—gentlemen callers! Why, sometimes there weren't chairs enough to accommodate them all. We had to send the nigger over to bring in folding chairs from the parish house.

TOM (*remaining at portieres*) How did you entertain those gentlemen callers?

AMANDA I understood the art of conversation!

TOM I bet you could talk.

AMANDA Girls in those days *knew* how to talk, I can tell you.

TOM Yes?

(*Image: Amanda as a girl on a porch greeting callers.*)

AMANDA They knew how to entertain their gentlemen callers. It wasn't enough for a girl to be possessed of a pretty face and a graceful figure—although I wasn't slighted in either respect. She also needed to have a nimble wit and a tongue to meet all occasions.

TOM What did you talk about?

AMANDA Things of importance going on in the world! Never anything coarse or common or vulgar. (*She addresses* TOM *as though he were seated in the vacant chair at the table though he remains by portieres. He plays this scene as though he held the book.*) My callers were gentlemen—all! Among my callers were some of the most prominent young planters of the Mississippi Delta—planters and sons of planters!

(TOM *motions for music and a spot of light on* AMANDA. *Her eyes lift, her face glows, her voice becomes rich and elegiac.*)

(Screen legend: "Où sont les neiges.")

There was young Champ Laughlin who later became vice-president of the Delta Planters Bank. Hadley Stevenson who was drowned in Moon Lake and left his widow one hundred and fifty thousand in Government bonds. There were the Cutrere brothers, Wesley and Bates. Bates was one of my bright particular beaux! He got in a quarrel with that wild Wainright boy. They shot it out on the floor of Moon Lake Casino. Bates was shot through the stomach. Died in the ambulance on his way to Memphis. His widow was also well-provided for, came into eight or ten thousand acres, that's all. She married him on the rebound—never loved her—carried my picture on him the night he died! And there was that boy that every girl in the Delta had set her cap for! That beautiful, brilliant young Fitzhugh boy from Green County!

TOM What did he leave his widow?

AMANDA He never married! Gracious, you talk as though all of my old admirers had turned up their toes to the daisies!

TOM Isn't this the first you mentioned that still survives?

AMANDA That Fitzhugh boy went North and made a fortune—came to be known as the Wolf of Wall Street! He had the Midas touch, whatever he touched turned to gold! And I could have been Mrs. Duncan J. Fitzhugh, mind you! But—I picked your *father!*

LAURA (*rising*) Mother, let me clear the table.

AMANDA No, dear, you go in front and study your typewriter chart. Or practice your shorthand a little. Stay fresh and pretty—It's almost time for our gentlemen callers to start arriving. (*She flounces girlishly toward the kitchenette.*) How many do you suppose we're going to entertain this afternoon?

(TOM *throws down the paper and jumps up with a groan.*)

LAURA (*alone in the dining room*) I don't believe we're going to receive any, Mother.

AMANDA (*reappearing, airily*) What? No one—not one? You must be joking! (LAURA *nervously echoes her laugh. She slips in a fugitive manner through the half-open portieres and draws them gently behind her. A shaft of very clear light is thrown on her face against the faded tapestry of the curtains. Music: "The Glass Menagerie" under faintly; lightly.*) Not one gentleman caller? It can't be true! There must be a flood, there must have been a tornado!

LAURA It isn't a flood, it's not a tornado, Mother. I'm just not popular like you were in Blue Mountain. . . . (TOM *utters another groan.* LAURA *glances at him with a faint, apologetic smile; her voice catching a little.*) Mother's afraid I'm going to be an old maid.

(The scene dims out with "Glass Menagerie" music.)

Scene II

("Laura, Haven't You Ever Liked Some Boy?")

On the dark stage the screen is lighted with the image of blue roses.

Gradually LAURA*'s figure becomes apparent and the screen goes out.*

The music subsides.

LAURA *is seated in the delicate ivory chair at the small clawfoot table.*

She wears a dress of soft violet material for a kimono—her hair tied back from her forehead with a ribbon.

She is washing and polishing her collection of glass.

AMANDA *appears on the fire-escape steps. At the sound of her ascent,* LAURA *catches her breath, thrusts the bowl of ornaments away and seats herself stiffly before the diagram of the typewriter keyboard as though it held her spellbound. Something has happened to* AMANDA*. It is written in her face as she climbs to the landing: a look that is grim and hopeless and a little absurd.*

She has on one of those cheap or imitation velvety-looking cloth coats with imitation fur collar. Her hat is five or six years old, one of those dreadful cloche hats that were worn in the late twenties and she is clasping an enormous black patent-leather pocket-book with nickel clasp and initials. This is her full-dress outfit, the one she usually wears to the D.A.R.

Before entering she looks through the door.

She purses her lips, opens her eyes wide, rolls them upward, and shakes her head.

Then she slowly lets herself in the door. Seeing her mother's expression LAURA *touches her lips with a nervous gesture.*

LAURA Hello, Mother, I was—(*She makes a nervous gesture toward the chart on the wall.* AMANDA *leans against the shut door and stares at* LAURA *with a martyred look.*)

AMANDA Deception? Deception? (*She slowly removes her hat and gloves, continuing the swift suffering stare. She lets the hat and gloves fall on the floor—a bit of acting.*)

LAURA (*shakily*) How was the D.A.R. meeting? (AMANDA *slowly opens her purse and removes a dainty white handkerchief which she shakes out delicately and delicately touches to her lips and nostrils.*) Didn't you go to the D.A.R. meeting, Mother?

AMANDA (*faintly, almost inaudibly*) —No.—No. (*then more forcibly*) I did not have the strength—to go to the D.A.R. In fact, I did not have the courage! I wanted to find a hole in the ground and hide myself in it forever! (*She crosses slowly to the wall and removes the diagram of the typewriter keyboard. She holds it in front of her for a second, staring at it sweetly and sorrowfully—then bites her lips and tears it in two pieces.*)

LAURA (*faintly*) Why did you do that, Mother? (AMANDA *repeats the same procedure with the chart of the Gregg Alphabet.*) Why are you—

AMANDA Why? Why? How old are you, Laura?

LAURA Mother, you know my age.

AMANDA I thought that you were an adult; it seems that I was mistaken. (*She crosses slowly to the sofa and sinks down and stares at* LAURA.)

LAURA Please don't stare at me, Mother.

(AMANDA *closes her eyes and lowers her head. Count ten.*)

AMANDA What are we going to do, what is going to become of us, what is the future?

(*Count ten.*)

LAURA Has something happened, Mother? (AMANDA *draws a long breath and takes out the handkerchief again; dabbing process.*) Mother, has—something happened?

AMANDA I'll be all right in a minute. I'm just bewildered—(*Count five.*)—by life. . . .

LAURA Mother, I wish that you would tell me what's happened.

AMANDA As you know, I was supposed to be inducted into my office at the D.A.R. this afternoon. (IMAGE: A SWARM OF TYPEWRITERS.) But I stopped off at Rubicam's Business College to speak to your teachers about your having a cold and ask them what progress they thought you were making down there.

LAURA Oh. . . .

AMANDA I went to the typing instructor and introduced myself as your mother. She didn't know who you were. Wingfield, she said. We don't have any such student enrolled at the school! I assured her she did, that you had been going to classes since early in January. "I wonder," she said, "if you could be talking about that terribly shy little girl who dropped out of school after only a few days' attendance?" "No," I said, "Laura, my daughter, has been going to school every day for the past six weeks!" "Excuse me," she said. She took the attendance book out and there was your name, unmistakably printed, and all the dates you were absent until they decided that you had dropped out of school. I still said, "No, there must have been some mistake! There must have been some mix-up in the records!" And she said, "No—I remember her perfectly now. Her hand shook so that she couldn't hit the right keys! The first time we gave a speed-test, she broke down completely—was sick at the stomach and almost had to be carried into the wash-room! After that morning she never showed up any more. We phoned the house but never got any answer—while I was working at Famous and Barr, I suppose, demonstrating those—Oh!" I felt so weak I could barely keep on my feet! I had to sit down while they got me a glass of water! Fifty dollars' tuition, all of our plans—my hopes and ambitions for you—just gone up the spout, just gone up the spout like that. (LAURA *draws a long breath and gets awkwardly to her feet. She crosses to the victrola and winds it up.*) What are you doing?

LAURA Oh! (*She releases the handle and returns to her seat.*)

AMANDA Laura, where have you been going when you've gone out pretending that you were going to business college?

LAURA I've just been going out walking.

AMANDA That's not true.

LAURA It is. I just went walking.

AMANDA Walking? Walking? In winter? Deliberately courting pneumonia in that light coat? Where did you walk to, Laura?

LAURA All sorts of places—mostly in the park.

AMANDA Even after you'd started catching that cold?

LAURA It was the lesser of two evils, Mother. (IMAGE: WINTER SCENE IN PARK.) I couldn't go back up. I—threw up—on the floor!

AMANDA From half past seven till after five every day you mean to tell me you walked around in the park, because you wanted to make me think that you were still going to Rubicam's Business College?

LAURA It wasn't as bad as it sounds. I went inside places to get warmed up.

AMANDA Inside where?

LAURA I went in the art museum and the bird-houses at the Zoo. I visited the penguins every day! Sometimes I did without lunch and went to the movies. Lately I've been spending most of my afternoons in the Jewel-box, that big glass house where they raise the tropical flowers.

AMANDA You did all this to deceive me, just for the deception? (LAURA *looks down.*) Why?

LAURA Mother, when you're disappointed, you get that awful suffering look on your face, like the picture of Jesus' mother in the museum!

AMANDA Hush!

LAURA I couldn't face it.

(*Pause. A whisper of strings.*)

(Legend: "The crust of humility.")

AMANDA (*hopelessly fingering the huge pocketbook*) So what are we going to do the rest of our lives? Stay home and watch the parades go by? Amuse ourselves with the glass menagerie, darling? Eternally play those worn-out phonograph records your father left as a painful reminder of him? We won't have a business career—we've given that up because it gave us nervous indigestion! (*laughs wearily*) What is there left but dependency all our lives? I know so well what becomes of unmarried women who aren't prepared to occupy a position. I've seen such pitiful cases in the South—barely tolerated spinsters living upon the grudging patronage of sister's husband or brother's wife!—stuck away in some little mouse-trap of a room—encouraged by one in-law to visit another—little birdlike women without any nest—eating the crust of humility all their life! Is that the future that we've mapped out for ourselves? I swear it's the only alternative I can think of! It isn't a very pleasant alternative, is it? Of course—some girls *do marry.* (LAURA *twists her hands nervously.*) Haven't you ever liked some boy?

LAURA Yes. I liked one once. (*rises*) I came across his picture a while ago.

AMANDA (*with some interest*) He gave you his picture?

LAURA No, it's in the year-book.

AMANDA (*disappointed*) Oh—a high-school boy.

(Screen image: Jim as a high-school hero bearing a silver cup.)

LAURA Yes. His name was Jim. (LAURA *lifts the heavy annual from the claw-foot table.*) Here he is in *The Pirates of Penzance.*

AMANDA (*absently*) The what?

LAURA The operetta the senior class put on. He had a wonderful voice and we sat across the aisle from each other Mondays, Wednesdays and Fridays in the Aud. Here he is with the silver cup for debating! See his grin?

AMANDA (*absently*) He must have had a jolly disposition.

LAURA He used to call me—Blue Roses.

(Image: Blue roses.)

AMANDA Why did he call you such a name as that?

AMANDA When I had that attack of pleurosis—he asked me what was the matter when I came back. I said pleurosis—he thought that I said Blue Roses! So that's what he always called me after that. Whenever he saw me, he'd holler, "Hello, Blue Roses!" I didn't care for the girl that he went out with. Emily Meisenbach. Emily was the best-dressed girl at Soldan. She never struck me, though, as being sincere . . . It says in the Personal Section—they're engaged. That's—six years ago! They must be married by now.

AMANDA Girls that aren't cut out for business careers usually wind up married to some nice man. (*gets up with a spark of revival*) Sister, that's what you'll do!

(LAURA *utters a startled, doubtful laugh. She reaches quickly for a piece of glass.*)

LAURA But, Mother—

AMANDA Yes? (*crossing to photograph*)

LAURA (*in a tone of frightened apology*) I'm—crippled!

(Image: Screen.)

AMANDA Nonsense! Laura, I've told you never, never to use that word. Why, you're not crippled, you just have a little defect—hardly noticeable, even! When people have some slight disadvantage like that, they cultivate other things to make up for it—develop charm—and vivacity—and—*charm!*

That's all you have to do! (*She turns again to the photograph.*) One thing your father had *plenty of*—was *charm!*

(TOM *motions to the fiddle in the wings.*)

(The scene fades out with music.)

Scene III

(Legend on screen: "After the fiasco—")

TOM *speaks from the fire-escape landing.*

TOM After the fiasco at Rubicam's Business College, the idea of getting a gentleman caller for Laura began to play a more important part in Mother's calculations. It became an obsession. Like some archetype of the universal unconscious, the image of the gentleman caller haunted our small apartment. . . . (IMAGE: YOUNG MAN AT DOOR WITH FLOWERS.) An evening at home rarely passed without some allusion to this image, this spectre, this hope. . . . Even when he wasn't mentioned, his presence hung in Mother's preoccupied look and in my sister's frightened, apologetic manner—hung like a sentence passed upon the Wingfields! Mother was a woman of action as well as words. She began to take logical steps in the planned direction. Late that winter and in the early spring—realizing that extra money would be needed to properly feather the nest and plume the bird—she conducted a vigorous campaign on the telephone, roping in subscribers to one of those magazines for matrons called *The Home-maker's Companion,* the type of journal that features the serialized sublimations of ladies of letters who think in terms of delicate cup-like breasts, slim, tapering waists, rich, creamy thighs, eyes like wood-smoke in autumn, fingers that soothe and caress like strains of music, bodies as powerful as Etruscan sculpture.

(Screen image: Glamor magazine cover.)

(AMANDA *enters with phone on long extension cord. She is spotted in the dim stage.*)

AMANDA Ida Scott? This is Amanda Wingfield! We *missed* you at the D.A.R. last Monday! I said to myself: She's probably suffering with that sinus condition! How is that sinus condition? Horrors! Heaven have mercy!—You're a Christian martyr, yes, that's what you are, a Christian martyr! Well, I just now happened to notice that your subscription to the *Companion*'s about to expire! Yes, it expires with the next issue, honey!—just when that wonderful new serial by Bessie Mae Hopper is getting off to such an exciting start. Oh, honey, it's something that you can't miss! You remember how *Gone With the Wind* took everybody by storm? You simply couldn't go out if you hadn't read it. All everybody *talked* was Scarlett O'Hara. Well, this is a book that critics already compare to *Gone With the Wind*. It's the *Gone With the Wind* of the post-World War generation!—What?—Burning?—Oh, honey, don't let them burn, go take a look in the oven and I'll hold the wire! Heavens—I think she's hung up!

(Dim out.)

(Legend on screen: "You think I'm in love with Continental Shoemakers?")

(*Before the stage is lighted, the violent voices of* TOM *and* AMANDA *are heard.*

They are quarreling behind the portieres. In front of them stands LAURA *with clenched hands and panicky expression.*

A clear pool of light on her figure throughout this scene.)

TOM What in Christ's name am I—

AMANDA (*shrilly*) Don't you use that—

TOM Supposed to do!

AMANDA Expression! Not in my—

TOM Ohhh!

AMANDA Presence! Have you gone out of your senses?

TOM I have, that's true, *driven* out!

AMANDA What is the matter with you, you—big—big—IDIOT!

TOM Look—I've got *no thing*, no single thing—

AMANDA Lower your voice!

TOM In my life here that I can call my OWN! Everything is—

AMANDA Stop that shouting!

TOM Yesterday you confiscated my books! You had the nerve to—

AMANDA I took that horrible novel back to the library—yes! That hideous book by that insane Mr. Lawrence. (TOM *laughs wildly.*) I cannot control the output of diseased minds or people who cater to them—(TOM *laughs still more wildly.*) BUT I WON'T ALLOW SUCH FILTH BROUGHT INTO MY HOUSE! No, no, no, no, no!

TOM House, house! Who pays rent on it, who makes a slave of himself to—

AMANDA (*fairly screeching*) Don't you DARE to—

TOM No, no, *I* mustn't say things! *I've* got to just—

AMANDA Let me tell you—

TOM I don't want to hear any more! (*He tears the portieres open. The upstage area is lit with a turgid smoky red glow.*)

(AMANDA*'s hair is in metal curlers and she wears a very old bathrobe, much too large for her slight figure, a relic of the faithless Mr. Wingfield.*

An upright typewriter and a wild disarray of manuscripts is on the dropleaf table. The quarrel was probably precipitated by AMANDA*'s interruption of his creative labor. A chair lying overthrown on the floor.*

Their gesticulating shadows are cast on the ceiling by the fiery glow.)

AMANDA You *will* hear more, you—

TOM No, I won't hear more, I'm going out!

AMANDA You come right back in—

TOM Out, out out! Because I'm—

AMANDA Come back here, Tom Wingfield! I'm not through talking to you!

TOM Oh, go—

LAURA (*desperately*) —Tom!

AMANDA You're going to listen, and no more insolence from you! I'm at the end of my patience! (*He comes back toward her.*)

TOM What do you think I'm at? Aren't I supposed to have any patience to reach the end of, Mother? I know, I know. It seems unimportant to you, what I'm *doing*—what I *want* to do—having a little *difference* between them! You don't think that—

AMANDA I think you've been doing things that you're ashamed of. That's why you act like this. I don't believe that you go every night to the movies. Nobody goes to the movies night after night. Nobody in their right minds goes to the movies as often as you pretend to. People don't go to the movies at nearly midnight, and movies don't let out at two A.M. Come in stumbling. Muttering to yourself like a maniac! You get three hours sleep and then go to work. Oh, I can picture the way you're doing down there. Moping, doping, because you're in no condition.

TOM (*wildly*) No, I'm in no condition!

AMANDA What right have you got to jeopardize your job? Jeopardize the security of us all? How do you think we'd manage if you were—

TOM Listen! You think I'm crazy *about* the *warehouse?* (*He bends fiercely toward her slight figure.*) You think I'm in love with the Continental Shoemakers? You think I want to spend fifty-five *years* down there in that—*celotex interior!* with—*fluorescent—tubes!* Look! I'd rather somebody picked up a crowbar and battered out my brains—than go back mornings! I *go!* Every time you come in yelling that God damn "*Rise and Shine!*" "*Rise and Shine!*" I say to myself "How *lucky dead* people are!" But I get up. I *go!* For sixty-five dollars a month I give up all that I dream of doing and being *ever!* And you say self—*self's* all I ever think of. Why, listen, if self is what I thought of, Mother, I'd be where he is—GONE! (*pointing to father's picture*) As far as the system of transportation reaches! (*He starts past her. She grabs his arm.*) Don't grab me, Mother!

AMANDA Where are you going?

TOM I'm going to the *movies!*

AMANDA I don't believe that lie!

TOM (*crouching toward her, overtowering her tiny figure. She backs away, gasping.*) I'm going to opium dens! Yes, opium dens, dens of vice and criminals' hangouts, Mother. I've joined the Hogan gang, I'm a hired assassin, I carry a tommy-gun in a violin case! I run a string of cat-houses in the Valley! They call me Killer, Killer Wingfield, I'm leading a double-life, a simple, honest warehouse worker by day, by night, a dynamic *czar* of the *underworld,*

Mother. I go to gambling casinos, I spin away fortunes on the roulette table! I wear a patch over one eye and a false mustache, sometimes I put on green whiskers. On those occasions they call me—*El Diablo!* Oh, I could tell you things to make you sleepless! My enemies plan to dynamite this place. They're going to blow us all sky-high some night! I'll be glad, very happy, and so will you! You'll go up, up on a broomstick, over Blue Mountain with seventeen gentlemen callers! You ugly—babbling old—*witch. . . .* (*He goes through a series of violent, clumsy movements, seizing his overcoat, lunging to the door, pulling it fiercely open. The women watch him, aghast. His arm catches in the sleeve of the coat as he struggles to pull it on. For a moment he is pinioned by the bulky garment. With an outraged groan he tears the coat off again, splitting the shoulders of it, and hurls it across the room. It strikes against the shelf of* LAURA*'s glass collection, there is a tinkle of shattering glass.* LAURA *cries out as if wounded.*)

(Music legend: "The Glass Menagerie.")

LAURA (*shrilly*) *My glass!*—menagerie. . . . (*She covers her face and turns away.*)

(*But* AMANDA *is still stunned and stupefied by the "ugly witch" so that she barely notices this occurrence. Now she recovers her speech.*)

AMANDA (*in an awful voice*) I won't speak to you—until you apologize! (*She crosses through portieres and draws them together behind her.* TOM *is left with* LAURA. LAURA *clings weakly to the mantel with her face averted.* TOM *stares at her stupidly for a moment. Then he crosses to shelf. Drops awkwardly to his knees to collect the fallen glass, glancing at* LAURA *as if he would speak but couldn't.*)

"The Glass Menagerie" steals in as

(The scene dims out.)

Scene IV

The interior is dark. Faint light in the alley.

A deep-voiced bell in a church is tolling the hour of five as the scene commences.

TOM *appears at the top of the alley. After each solemn boom of the bell in the tower, he shakes a little noise-maker or rattle as if to express the tiny spasm of man in contrast to the sustained power and dignity of the Almighty. This and the unsteadiness of his advance make it evident that he has been drinking.*

As he climbs the few steps to the fire-escape landing light steals up inside. LAURA *appears in night-dress, observing* TOM*'s empty bed in the front room.*

TOM *fishes in his pockets for the door-key, removing a motley assortment of articles in the search, including a perfect shower of movie-ticket stubs and an empty bottle. At last he finds the key, but just as he is about to insert it, it slips from his fingers. He strikes a match and crouches below the door.*

TOM (*bitterly*) One crack—and it falls through!

(LAURA *opens the door.*)

LAURA Tom! Tom, what are you doing?

TOM Looking for a door-key.

LAURA Where have you been all this time?

TOM I have been to the movies.

LAURA All this time at the movies?

TOM There was a very long program. There was a Garbo picture and a Mickey Mouse and a travelogue and a newsreel and a preview of coming attractions. And there was an organ solo and a collection for the milk-fund—simultaneously—which ended up in a terrible fight between a fat lady and an usher!

LAURA (*innocently*) Did you have to stay through everything?

TOM Of course! And, oh, I forgot! There was a big stage show! The headliner on this stage show was Malvolio the Magician. He performed wonderful tricks, many of them, such as pouring water back and forth between pitchers. First it turned to wine and then it turned to beer and then it turned to whiskey. I know it was whiskey it finally turned into because he needed somebody to come up out of the audience to help him, and I came up—both shows! It was Kentucky Straight Bourbon. A very generous fellow, he gave souvenirs. (*He pulls from his back pocket a shimmering rainbow-colored scarf.*) He gave me this. This is his magic scarf. You can have it, Laura. You wave it over a canary cage and you get a bowl of gold-fish. You wave it over the gold-fish bowl and they fly away canaries. . . . But the wonderfullest trick of all was the coffin trick. We nailed him into a coffin and he got out of the coffin without removing one nail. (*He has come inside.*) There is a trick that would come in handy for me—get me out of this 2 by 4 situation! (*flops onto bed and starts removing shoes*)

LAURA Tom—Shhh!

TOM What you shushing me for?

LAURA You'll wake up Mother.

TOM Goody, goody! Pay 'er back for all those "Rise an' Shines." (*lies down, groaning*) You know it don't take much intelligence to get yourself into a nailed-up coffin, Laura. But who in hell ever got himself out of one without removing one nail?

(*As if in answer, the father's grinning photograph lights up.*)

(*Scene dims out.*)

(*Immediately following: The church bell is heard striking six. At the sixth stroke the alarm clock goes off in* AMANDA*'s room, and after a few moments we hear her calling: "Rise and Shine! Rise and Shine! Laura, go tell your brother to rise and shine!"*)

TOM (*sitting up slowly*) I'll rise—but I won't shine.

(*The light increases.*)

AMANDA Laura, tell your brother his coffee is ready.

(LAURA *slips into front room.*)

LAURA Tom! it's nearly seven. Don't make Mother nervous. (*He stares at her stupidly, beseechingly.*) Tom, speak to Mother this morning. Make up with her, apologize, speak to her!

TOM She won't to me. It's her that started not speaking.

LAURA If you just say you're sorry she'll start speaking.

TOM Her not speaking—is that such a tragedy?

LAURA Please—please!

AMANDA (*calling from kitchenette*) Laura, are you going to do what I asked you to do, or do I have to get dressed and go out myself?

LAURA Going, going—soon as I get on my coat! (*She pulls on a shapeless felt hat with nervous, jerky movement, pleadingly glancing at* TOM. *Rushes awkwardly for coat. The coat is one of* AMANDA'S, *inaccurately made-over, the sleeves too short for* LAURA.) Butter and what else?

AMANDA (*entering upstage*) Just butter. Tell them to charge it.

LAURA Mother, they make such faces when I do that.

AMANDA Sticks and stones may break my bones, but the expression on Mr. Garfinkel's face won't harm us! Tell your brother his coffee is getting cold.

LAURA (*at door*) Do what I asked you, will you, will you, Tom?

(*He looks sullenly away.*)

AMANDA Laura, go now or just don't go at all!

LAURA (*rushing out*) Going—going! (*A second later she cries out.* TOMS *springs up and crosses to the door.* AMANDA *rushes anxiously in.* TOM *opens the door.*)

TOM Laura?

LAURA I'm all right. I slipped, but I'm all right.

AMANDA (*peering anxiously after her*) If anyone breaks a leg on those fire-escape steps, the landlord ought to be sued for every cent he possesses! (*She shuts door, remembers she isn't speaking, and returns to other room.*)

(*As* TOM *enters listlessly for his coffee, she turns her back to him and stands rigidly facing the window on the gloomy gray vault of the areaway. Its light on her face with its aged but childish features is cruelly sharp, satirical as a Daumier print.*)

(*Music under: "Ave Maria."*)

(TOM *glances sheepishly but sullenly at her averted figure and slumps at the table. The coffee is scalding hot; he sips it and gasps and spits it back in the cup. At his gasp,* AMANDA *catches her breath and half turns. Then catches herself and turns back to window.*

TOM *blows on his coffee, glancing sidewise at his mother. She clears her throat.* TOM *clears his. He starts to rise. Sinks back down again, scratches his head, clears his throat again.* Amanda *coughs.* Tom *raises his cup in both hands to blow on it, his eyes staring over the rim of it at his mother for several moments. Then he slowly sets the cup down and awkwardly and hesitantly rises from the chair.*)

TOM (*hoarsely*) Mother. I—I apologize. Mother. (Amanda *draws a quick, shuddering breath. Her face works grotesquely. She breaks into childlike tears.*) I'm sorry for what I said, for everything that I said, I didn't mean it.

AMANDA (*sobbingly*) My devotion has made me a witch and so I make myself hateful to my children!

TOM No, you *don't.*

AMANDA I worry so much, don't sleep, it makes me nervous!

TOM (*gently*) I understand that.

AMANDA I've had to put up a solitary battle all these years. But you're my right-hand bower! Don't fall down, don't fail!

TOM (*gently*) I try, Mother.

AMANDA (*with great enthusiasm*) Try and you will SUCCEED! (*The notion makes her breathless.*) Why, you—you're just *full* of natural endowments! Both of my children—they're *unusual* children! Don't you think I know it? I'm so—*proud!* Happy and—feel I've—so much to be thankful for but—Promise me one thing, son!

TOM What, Mother?

AMANDA Promise, son, you'll—never be a drunkard!

TOM (*turns to her grinning*) I will never be a drunkard, Mother.

AMANDA That's what frightened me so, that you'd be drinking! Eat a bowl of Purina!

TOM Just coffee, Mother.

AMANDA Shredded wheat biscuit?

TOM No. No, Mother, just coffee.

AMANDA You can't put in a day's work on an empty stomach. You've got ten minutes—don't gulp! Drinking too-hot liquids makes cancer of the stomach. . . . Put cream in.

TOM No, thank you.

AMANDA To cool it.

TOM No! No, thank you, I want it black.

AMANDA I know, but it's not good for you. We have to do all that we can to build ourselves up. In these trying times we live in, all that we have to cling to is—each other. . . . That's why it's so important to—Tom, I—I sent out your sister so I could discuss something with you. If you hadn't spoken I would have spoken to you. (*sits down*)

TOM (*gently*) What is it, Mother, that you want to discuss?

AMANDA Laura!

(Tom *puts his cup down slowly.*)

(Legend on screen: "Laura.")

(Music: "The Glass Menagerie.")

TOM —Oh.—Laura . . .

AMANDA (*touching his sleeve*) You know how Laura is. So quiet but—still water runs deep! She notices things and I think she—broods about them. (TOM *looks up.*) A few days ago I came in and she was crying.

TOM What about?

AMANDA You.

TOM Me?

AMANDA She has an idea that you're not happy here.

TOM What gave her that idea?

AMANDA What gives her any idea? However, you do act strangely. I—I'm not criticizing, understand *that!* I know your ambitions do not lie in the warehouse, that like everybody in the whole wide world—you've had to—make sacrifices, but—Tom—Tom—life's not easy, it calls for—Spartan endurance! There's so many things in my heart that I cannot describe to you! I've never told you but I—*loved* your father. . . .

TOM (*gently*) I know that, Mother.

AMANDA And you—when I see you taking after his ways! Staying out late—and—well, you *had* been drinking the night you were in that—terrifying condition! Laura says that you hate the apartment and that you go out nights to get away from it! Is that true, Tom?

TOM No. You say there's so much in your heart that you can't describe to me. That's true of me, too. There's so much in my heart that I can't describe to *you!* So let's respect each other's—

AMANDA But, why—*why*, Tom—are you always so *restless?* Where do you go to, nights?

TOM I—go to the movies.

AMANDA Why do you go to the movies so much, Tom?

TOM I go to the movies because—I like adventure. Adventure is something I don't have much of at work, so I go to the movies.

AMANDA But, Tom, you go to the movies *entirely* too *much!*

TOM I like a lot of adventure.

(AMANDA *looks baffled, then hurt. As the familiar inquisition resumes he becomes hard and impatient again.* AMANDA *slips back into her querulous attitude toward him.*)

(Image on screen: Sailing vessel with Jolly Roger.)

AMANDA Most young men find adventure in their careers.

TOM Then most young men are not employed in a warehouse.

AMANDA The world is full of young men employed in warehouses and offices and factories.

TOM Do all of them find adventure in their careers?

AMANDA They do or they do without it! Not everybody has a craze for adventure.

TOM Man is by instinct a lover, a hunter, a fighter, and none of those instincts are given much play at the warehouse!

AMANDA Man is by instinct! Don't quote instinct to me! Instinct is something that people have got away from! It belongs to animals! Christian adults don't want it!

TOM What do Christian adults want, then, Mother?

AMANDA Superior things! Things of the mind and the spirit! Only animals have to satisfy instincts! Surely your aims are somewhat higher than theirs! Than monkeys—pigs—

TOM I reckon they're not.

AMANDA You're joking. However, that isn't what I wanted to discuss.

TOM (*rising*) I haven't much time.

AMANDA (*pushing his shoulders*) Sit down.

TOM You want me to punch in red at the warehouse, Mother?

AMANDA You have five minutes. I want to talk about Laura.

(Legend: "Plans and provisions.")

TOM All right! What about Laura?

AMANDA We have to be making plans and provisions for her. She's older than you, two years, and nothing has happened. She just drifts along doing nothing. It frightens me terribly how she just drifts along.

TOM I guess she's the type that people call home girls.

AMANDA There's no such type, and if there is, it's a pity! That is unless the home is hers, with a husband!

TOM What?

AMANDA Oh, I can see the handwriting on the wall as plain as I see the nose in front of my face! It's terrifying! More and more you remind me of your father! He was out all hours without explanation—Then *left! Goodbye!* And me with a bag to hold. I saw that letter you got from the Merchant Marine. I know what you're dreaming of. I'm not standing here blindfolded. Very well, then. Then *do* it! But not till there's somebody to take your place.

TOM What do you mean?

AMANDA I mean that as soon as Laura has got somebody to take care of her, married, a home of her own, independent—why, then you'll be free to go wherever you please, on land, on sea, whichever way the wind blows! But until that time you've got to look out for your sister. I don't say me because I'm old and don't matter! I say for your sister because she's young and dependent. I put her in business college—a dismal failure! Frightened her so it made her sick to her stomach. I took her over to the Young People's League at the church. Another fiasco. She spoke to nobody, nobody spoke to her.

Now all she does is fool with those pieces of glass and play those worn-out records. What kind of life is that for a girl to lead?

TOM What can I do about it?

AMANDA Overcome selfishness! Self, self, self is all that you ever think of! (TOM *springs up and crosses to get his coat. It is ugly and bulky. He pulls on a cap with earmuffs.*) Where is your muffler? Put your wool muffler on! (*He snatches it angrily from the closet and tosses it around his neck and pulls both ends tight.*) Tom! I haven't said what I had in mind to ask you.

TOM I'm too late to—

AMANDA (*catching his arm—very importunately; then shyly:*) Down at the warehouse, aren't there some—nice young men?

TOM No!

AMANDA There *must* be—*some* . . .

TOM Mother—

(*Gesture.*)

AMANDA Find out one that's clean-living—doesn't drink and—ask him out for sister!

TOM What?

AMANDA For *sister!* To *meet!* Get *acquainted!*

TOM (*stamping to door*) Oh, my *go-osh!*

AMANDA Will you? (*He opens door; imploringly:*) Will you? (*He starts down.*) Will you? *Will* you, dear?

TOM (*calling back*) YES!

(AMANDA *closes the door hesitantly and with a troubled but faintly hopeful expression.*)

(Screen image: Glamor magazine cover.)

(*Spot* AMANDA *at phone.*)

AMANDA Ella Cartwright? This is Amanda Wingfield! How are you, honey? How is that kidney condition? (*Count five.*) *Horrors!* (*Count five.*) You're a Christian martyr, yes, honey, that's what you are, a Christian martyr! Well, I just happened to notice in my little red book that your subscription to the *Companion* has just run out! I knew that you wouldn't want to miss out on the wonderful serial starting in this new issue. It's by Bessie Mae Hopper, the first thing she's written since *Honeymoon for Three.* Wasn't that a strange and interesting story? Well, this one is even lovelier, I believe. It has a sophisticated society background. It's all about the horsey set on Long Island!

(Fade out.)

Scene V

(Legend on screen: "Annunciation.")

Fade with music.

It is early dusk of a spring evening. Supper has just been finished in the Wingfield apartment. AMANDA *and* LAURA *in light colored dresses are removing dishes from the table, in the upstage area, which is shadowy, their movements formalized almost as a dance or ritual, their moving forms as pale and silent as moths.*

Tom, in white shirt and trousers, rises from the table and crosses toward the fire escape.

AMANDA (*as he passes her*) Son, will you do me a favor?

TOM What?

AMANDA Comb your hair! You look so pretty when your hair is combed! (TOM *slouches on sofa with evening paper; enormous caption "Franco Triumphs."*) There is only one respect in which I would like you to emulate your father.

TOM What respect is that?

AMANDA The care he always took of his appearance. He never allowed himself to look untidy. (*He throws down the paper and crosses to fire escape.*) Where are you going?

TOM I'm going out to smoke.

AMANDA You smoke too much. A pack a day at fifteen cents a pack. How much would that amount to in a month? Thirty times fifteen is how much, Tom? Figure it out and you will be astounded at what you could save. Enough to give you a night-school course in accounting at Washington U! Just think what a wonderful thing that would be for you, son!

(TOM *is unmoved by the thought.*)

TOM I'd rather smoke. (*He steps out on landing, letting the screen door slam.*)

AMANDA (*sharply*) I know! That's the tragedy of it. . . . (*Alone, she turns to look at her husband's picture.*)

(Dance music: "All the world is waiting for the sunrise!")

TOM (*to the audience*) Across the alley from us was the Paradise Dance Hall. On evenings in spring the windows and doors were open and the music came outdoors. Sometimes the lights were turned out except for a large glass sphere that hung from the ceiling. It would turn slowly about and filter the dusk with delicate rainbow colors. Then the orchestra played a waltz or a tango, something that had a slow and sensuous rhythm. Couples would come outside, to the relative privacy of the alley. You could see them kissing behind ash-pits and telephone poles. This was the compensation for lives that passed like mine, without any change or adventure. Adventure and change were imminent in this year. They were waiting around the corner for all these kids. Suspended in the mist over Berchtesgaden, caught in the folds of Chamberlain's umbrella—In Spain there was Guernica! But here there was only hot swing music and liquor, dance halls, bars, and movies, and sex that hung in the gloom like a chandelier and flooded the world with brief, deceptive rainbows. . . . All the world was waiting for bombardments!

(AMANDA *turns from the picture and comes outside.*)

AMANDA (*sighing*) A fire-escape landing's a poor excuse for a porch. (*She spreads a newspaper on a step and sits down, gracefully and demurely as if she were settling into a swing on a Mississippi veranda.*) What are you looking at?

TOM The moon.

AMANDA Is there a moon this evening?

TOM It's rising over Garfinkel's Delicatessen.

AMANDA So it is! A little silver slipper of a moon. Have you made a wish on it yet?

TOM Um-hum.

AMANDA What did you wish for?

TOM That's a secret.

AMANDA A secret, huh? Well, I won't tell mine either. I will be just as mysterious as you.

TOM I bet I can guess what yours is.

AMANDA Is my head so transparent?

TOM You're not a sphinx.

AMANDA No, I don't have secrets. I'll tell you what I wished for on the moon. Success and happiness for my precious children! I wish for that whenever there's a moon, and when there isn't a moon, I wish for it, too.

TOM I thought perhaps you wished for a gentleman caller.

AMANDA Why do you say that?

TOM Don't you remember asking me to fetch one?

AMANDA I remember suggesting that it would be nice for your sister if you brought home some nice young man from the warehouse. I think I've made that suggestion more than once.

TOM Yes, you have made it repeatedly.

AMANDA Well?

TOM We are going to have one.

AMANDA *What?*

TOM A gentleman caller!

(The annunciation is celebrated with music.)

(AMANDA *rises.*)

(Image on screen: Caller with bouquet.)

AMANDA You mean you have asked some nice young man to come over?

TOM Yep. I've asked him to dinner.

AMANDA You really did?

TOM I did!

AMANDA You did, and did he—*accept?*

TOM He did!

AMANDA Well, well—well, well! That's—lovely!

TOM I thought that you would be pleased.

AMANDA It's definite, then?

TOM Very definite.

AMANDA Soon?

TOM Very soon.

AMANDA For heaven's sake, stop putting on and tell me some things, will you?

TOM What things do you want me to tell you?

AMANDA *Naturally* I would like to know when he's *coming!*

TOM He's coming tomorrow.

AMANDA *Tomorrow?*

TOM Yep. Tomorrow.

AMANDA But, Tom!

TOM Yes, Mother?

AMANDA Tomorrow gives me no time!

TOM Time for what?

AMANDA Preparations! Why didn't you phone me at once, as soon as you asked him, the minute that he accepted? Then, don't you see, I could have been getting ready!

TOM You don't have to make any fuss.

AMANDA Oh, Tom, Tom, Tom, of course I have to make a fuss! I want things nice, not sloppy! Not thrown together. I'll certainly have to do some fast thinking, won't I?

TOM I don't see why you have to think at all.

AMANDA You just don't know. We can't have a gentleman caller in a pig-sty! All my wedding silver has to be polished, the monogrammed table linen ought to be laundered! The windows have to be washed and fresh curtains put up. And how about clothes? We have to *wear* something, don't we?

TOM Mother, this boy is no one to make a fuss over!

AMANDA Do you realize he's the first young man we've introduced to your sister? It's terrible, dreadful, disgraceful that poor little sister has never received a single gentleman caller! Tom, come inside! (*She opens the screen door.*)

TOM What for?

AMANDA I want to ask you some things.

TOM If you're going to make such a fuss, I'll call it off, I'll tell him not to come.

AMANDA You certainly won't do anything of the kind. Nothing offends people worse than broken engagements. It simply means I'll have to work like a Turk! We won't be brilliant, but we'll pass inspection. Come on inside. (TOM *follows, groaning.*) Sit down.

TOM Any particular place you would like me to sit?

AMANDA Thank heavens I've got that new sofa! I'm also making payments on a floor lamp I'll have sent out! And put the chintz covers on, they'll brighten things up! Of course I'd hoped to have these walls re-papered. . . . What is the young man's name?

TOM His name is O'Connor.

AMANDA That, of course, means fish—tomorrow is Friday! I'll have that salmon loaf—with Durkee's dressing! What does he do? He works at the warehouse?

TOM Of course! How else would I—

AMANDA Tom, he—doesn't drink?

TOM Why do you ask me that?

AMANDA Your father *did!*

TOM Don't get started on that!

AMANDA He *does* drink, then?

TOM Not that I know of!

AMANDA Make sure, be certain! The last thing I want for my daughter's a boy who drinks!

TOM Aren't you being a little premature? Mr. O'Connor has not yet appeared on the scene!

AMANDA But will tomorrow. To meet your sister, and what do I know about this character? Nothing! Old maids are better off than wives of drunkards!

TOM Oh, my God!

AMANDA Be still!

TOM (*leaning forward to whisper*) Lots of fellows meet girls whom they don't marry!

AMANDA Oh, talk sensibly, Tom—and don't be sarcastic! (*She has gotten a hair-brush.*)

TOM What are you doing?

AMANDA I'm brushing that cow-lick down! What is this young man's position at the warehouse?

TOM (*submitting grimly to the brush and the interrogation*) This young man's position is that of a shipping clerk, Mother.

AMANDA Sounds to me like a fairly responsible job, the sort of a job *you* would be in if you just had more *get-up*. What is his salary? Have you got any idea?

TOM I would judge it to be approximately eighty-five dollars a month.

AMANDA Well—not princely, but—

TOM Twenty more than I make.

AMANDA Yes, how well I know! But for a family man, eighty-five dollars a month is not much more than you can just get by on. . . .

TOM Yes, but Mr. O'Connor is not a family man.

AMANDA He might be, mightn't he? Some time in the future?

TOM I see. Plans and provisions.

AMANDA You are the only young man that I know of who ignores the fact that the future becomes the present, the present the past, and the past turns into everlasting regret if you don't plan for it!

TOM I will think that over and see what I can make of it.

AMANDA Don't be supercilious with your mother! Tell me some more about this—what do you call him?

TOM James D. O'Connor. The D. is for Delaney.

AMANDA Irish on *both* sides! *Gracious!* And doesn't drink?

TOM Shall I call him up and ask him right this minute?

AMANDA The only way to find out about those things is to make discreet inquiries at the proper moment. When I was a girl in Blue Mountain and it was suspected that a young man drank, the girl whose attentions he had been receiving, if any girl *was,* would sometimes speak to the minister of his church, or rather her father would if her father was living, and sort of feel him out on the young man's character. That is the way such things are discreetly handled to keep a young woman from making a tragic mistake!

TOM Then how did you happen to make a tragic mistake?

AMANDA That innocent look of your father's had everyone fooled! He *smiled*—the world was *enchanted!* No girl can do worse than put herself at the mercy of a handsome appearance! I hope that Mr. O'Connor is not too good-looking.

TOM No, he's not too good-looking. He's covered with freckles and hasn't too much of a nose.

AMANDA He's not right-down homely, though?

TOM Not right-down homely. Just medium homely. I'd say.

AMANDA Character's what to look for in a man.

TOM That's what I've always said, Mother.

AMANDA You've never said anything of the kind and I suspect you would never give it a thought.

TOM Don't be suspicious of me.

AMANDA At least I hope he's the type that's up and coming.

TOM I think he really goes in for self-improvement.

AMANDA What reason have you to think so?

TOM He goes to night school.

AMANDA (*beaming*) Splendid! What does he do, I mean study?

TOM Radio engineering and public speaking!

AMANDA Then he has visions of being advanced in the world! Any young man who studies public speaking is aiming to have an executive job some day! And radio engineering? A thing for the future! Both of these facts are very illuminating. Those are the sort of things that a mother should know concerning any young man who comes to call on her daughter. Seriously or—not.

TOM One little warning. He doesn't know about Laura. I didn't let on that we had dark ulterior motives. I just said, why don't you come have dinner with us? He said okay and that was the whole conversation.

AMANDA I bet it was! You're eloquent as an oyster. However, he'll know about Laura when he gets here. When he sees how lovely and sweet and pretty she is, he'll thank his lucky stars he was asked to dinner.

TOM Mother, you mustn't expect too much of Laura.

AMANDA What do you mean?

TOM Laura seems all those things to you and me because she's ours and we love her. We don't even notice she's crippled any more.

AMANDA Don't say crippled! You know that I never allow that word to be used!

TOM But face facts, Mother. She is and—that's not all—

AMANDA What do you mean "not all"?

TOM Laura is very different from other girls.

AMANDA I think the difference is all to her advantage.

TOM Not quite all—in the eyes of others—strangers—she's terribly shy and lives in a world of her own and those things make her seem a little peculiar to people outside the house.

AMANDA Don't say peculiar.

TOM Face the facts. She is.

(The dance-hall music changes to a tango that has a minor and somewhat ominous tone.)

AMANDA In what was is she peculiar—may I ask?

TOM (*gently*) She lives in a world of her own—a world of—little glass ornaments, Mother. . . . (*Gets up.* AMANDA *remains holding brush, looking at him, troubled.*) She plays old phonograph records and—that's about all—(*He glances at himself in the mirror and crosses to door.*)

AMANDA (*sharply*) Where are you going?

TOM I'm going to the movies. (*out screen door*)

AMANDA Not to the movies, every night to the movies! (*follows quickly to screen door*) I don't believe you always go to the movies! (*He is gone.* AMANDA *looks worriedly after him for a moment. Then vitality and optimism return and she turns from the door, crossing to portieres.*) Laura! Laura! (LAURA *answers from kitchenette.*)

LAURA Yes, Mother.

AMANDA Let those dishes go and come in front! (LAURA *appears with dish towel; gaily:*) Laura, come here and make a wish on the moon!

LAURA (*entering*) Moon—moon?

AMANDA A little silver slipper of a moon. Look over your left shoulder, Laura, and make a wish! (LAURA *looks faintly puzzled as if called out of sleep.* AMANDA *seizes her shoulders and turns her at an angle by the door.*) No! Now, darling, *wish!*

LAURA What shall I wish for, Mother?

AMANDA (*her voice trembling and her eyes suddenly filling with tears*) Happiness! Good Fortune!

(The violin rises and the stage dims out.)

Scene VI

(Image: High school hero.)

TOM And so the following evening I brought Jim home to dinner. I had known Jim slightly in high school. In high school Jim was a hero. He had tremendous Irish good nature and vitality with the scrubbed and polished look of white chinaware. He seemed to move in a continual spotlight. He was a star in basketball, captain of the debating club, president of the senior class and the glee club and he sang the male lead in the annual light operas. He was always running or bounding, never just walking. He seemed always at the point of defeating the law of gravity. He was shooting with such velocity through his adolescence that you would logically expect him to arrive at nothing short of the White House by the time he was thirty. But Jim apparently ran into more interference after his graduation from Soldan. His speed had definitely slowed. Six years after he left high school he was holding a job that wasn't much better than mine.

(Image: Clerk.)

He was the only one at the warehouse with whom I was on friendly terms. I was valuable to him as someone who could remember his former glory, who had seen him win basketball games and the silver cup in debating. He knew of my secret practice of retiring to a cabinet of the washroom to work on poems when business was slack in the warehouse. He called me Shakespeare. And while the other boys in the warehouse regarded me with suspicious hostility, Jim took a humorous attitude toward me. Gradually his attitude affected the others, their hostility wore off and they also began to smile at me as people smile at an oddly fashioned dog who trots across their path at some distance.

I knew that Jim and Laura had known each other at Soldan, and I had heard Laura speak admiringly of his voice. I didn't know if Jim remembered her or not. In high school Laura had been as unobtrusive as Jim had been astonishing. If he did remember Laura, it was not as my sister, for when I asked him to dinner, he grinned and said, "You know, Shakespeare, I never thought of you as having folks!"

He was about to discover that I did. . . .

(Light up stage.)

(Legend on screen: "The accent of a coming foot.")

Friday evening. It is about five o'clock of a late spring evening which comes "scattering poems in the sky."

A delicate lemony light is in the Wingfield apartment.

AMANDA *has worked like a Turk in preparation for the gentleman caller. The results are astonishing. The new floor lamp with its rose-silk shade is in place, a colored paper lantern conceals the broken light fixture in the ceiling, new billowing white curtains are at the windows, chintz covers are on chairs and sofa, a pair of new sofa pillows make their initial appearance.*

Open boxes and tissue paper are scattered on the floor.

LAURA *stands in the middle with lifted arms while* AMANDA *crouches before her, adjusting the hem of the new dress, devout and ritualistic. The dress is colored and designed by memory. The arrangement of* LAURA*'s hair is changed; it is softer and more becoming. A fragile, unearthly prettiness has come out in* LAURA: *she is like a piece of translucent glass touched by light, given a momentary radiance, not actual, not lasting.*

AMANDA (*impatiently*) Why are you trembling?

LAURA Mother, you've made me so nervous!

AMANDA How have I made you nervous?

LAURA By all this fuss! You make it seem so important!

AMANDA I don't understand you, Laura. You couldn't be satisfied with just sitting home, and yet whenever I try to arrange something for you, you seem to resist it. (*She gets up.*) Now take a look at yourself. No, wait! Wait just a moment—I have an idea!

LAURA What is it now?

(AMANDA *produces two powder puffs which she wraps in handkerchiefs and stuffs in* LAURA*'s bosom.*)

LAURA Mother, what are you doing?

AMANDA They call them "Gay Deceivers"!

LAURA I won't wear them!

AMANDA You will!

LAURA Why should I?

AMANDA Because, to be painfully honest, your chest is flat.

LAURA You make it seem like we were setting a trap.

AMANDA All pretty girls are a trap, a pretty trap, and men expect them to be. (*Legend: "A pretty trap."*) Now look at yourself, young lady. This is the prettiest you will ever be! I've got to fix myself now! You're going to be surprised by your mother's appearance! (*She crosses through portieres, humming gaily.*)

(LAURA *moves slowly to the long mirror and stares solemnly at herself.*

A wind blows the white curtains inward in a slow, graceful motion and with a faint, sorrowful sighing.)

AMANDA (*off stage*) It isn't dark enough yet. (*She turns slowly before the mirror with a troubled look.*)

(Legend on screen: "This is my sister: celebrate her with strings!" Music.)

AMANDA (*laughing, off*) I'm going to show you something. I'm going to make a spectacular appearance!

LAURA What is it, mother?

AMANDA Possess your soul in patience—you will see! Something I've resurrected from that old trunk! Styles haven't changed so terribly much after all. . . . (*She parts the portieres.*) Now just look at your mother! (*She wears a girlish frock of yellowed voile with a blue silk sash. She carries a bunch of jonquils—the legend of her youth is nearly revived; feverishly:*) This is the dress in which I led the cotillion. Won the cakewalk twice at Sunset Hill, wore one spring to the Governor's ball in Jackson! See how I sashayed around the ballroom, Laura? (*She raises her skirt and does a mincing step around the room.*) I wore it on Sundays for my gentlemen callers! I had it on the day I met your father—I had malaria fever all that spring. The change of climate from East Tennessee to the Delta—weakened resistance—I had a little temperature all the time—not enough to be serious—just enough to make me restless and giddy! Invitations poured in—parties all over the Delta!—"Stay in bed," said Mother, "you have fever!"—but I just wouldn't.—I took quinine but kept on going, going!—Evenings, dances!—Afternoons, long, long, rides! Picnics—lovely!—So lovely, that country in May.—All lacy with dogwood, literally flooded with jonquils!—That was the spring I had the craze for jonquils. Jonquils became an absolute obsession. Mother said, "Honey, there's no more room for jonquils." And still I kept bringing in more jonquils. Whenever, wherever I saw them, I'd say, "Stop! Stop! I see jonquils!" I made the young men help me gather the jonquils! It was a joke, Amanda and her jonquils! Finally there were no more vases to hold them, every available space was filled with jonquils. No vases to hold them? All right, I'll hold them myself! And then I—(*She stops in front of the picture. Music.*) met your father! Malaria fever and jonquils and then—this—boy. . . . (*She switches on the rose-colored lamp.*) I hope they get here before it starts to rain. (*She crosses upstage and places the jonquils in bowl on table.*) I gave your brother a little extra change so he and Mr. O'Connor could take the service car home.

LAURA (*with altered look*) What did you say his name was?

AMANDA O'Connor.

LAURA What is his first name?

AMANDA I don't remember. Oh, yes, I do. It was—Jim!

(LAURA *sways slightly and catches hold of a chair.*)

(Legend on screen: "Not Jim!")

LAURA (*faintly*) Not—Jim!

AMANDA Yes, that was it, it was Jim! I've never known a Jim that wasn't nice!

(Music: Ominous.)

LAURA Are you sure his name is Jim O'Connor?

AMANDA Yes. Why?

LAURA Is he the one that Tom used to know in high school?

AMANDA He didn't say so. I think he just got to know him at the warehouse.

LAURA There was a Jim O'Connor we both knew in high school—(*then, with effort:*) If that is the one that Tom is bringing to dinner—you'll have to excuse me, I won't come to the table.

AMANDA What sort of nonsense is this?

LAURA You asked me once if I'd ever liked a boy. Don't you remember I showed you this boy's picture?

AMANDA You mean the boy you showed me in the year book?

LAURA Yes, that boy.

AMANDA Laura, Laura, were you in love with that boy?

LAURA I don't know, Mother. All I know is I couldn't sit at the table if it was him!

AMANDA It won't be him! It isn't the least bit likely. But whether it is or not, you will come to the table. You will not be excused.

LAURA I'll have to be, Mother.

AMANDA I don't intend to humor your silliness, Laura. I've had too much from you and your brother, both! So just sit down and compose yourself till they come. Tom has forgotten his key so you'll have to let them in, when they arrive.

LAURA (*panicky*) Oh, Mother—*you* answer the door!

AMANDA (*lightly*) I'll be in the kitchen—busy!

LAURA Oh, Mother, please answer the door, don't make me do it!

AMANDA (*crossing into kitchenette*) I've got to fix the dressing for the salmon. Fuss, fuss—silliness!—over a gentleman caller!

(*Door swings shut.* LAURA *is left alone.*)

(Legend: "Terror!")

(*She utters a low moan and turns off the lamp—sits stiffly on the edge of the sofa, knotting her fingers together.*)

(Legend on screen: "The opening of a door!")

(TOM *and* JIM *appear on the fire-escape steps and climb to landing. Hearing their approach,* LAURA *rises with a panicky gesture. She retreats to the portieres.*

The doorbell. LAURA *catches her breath and touches her throat. Low drums.*)

AMANDA (*calling*) Laura, sweetheart! The door!

(LAURA *stares at it without moving.*)

JIM I think we just beat the rain.

TOM Uh-huh. (*He rings again, nervously.* JIM *whistles and fishes for a cigarette.*)

AMANDA (*very, very gaily*) Laura, that is your brother and Mr. O'Connor! Will you let them in, darling?

(LAURA *crosses toward kitchenette door.*)

LAURA (*breathlessly*) Mother—you go to the door!

(AMANDA *steps out of kitchenette and stares furiously at* LAURA. *She points imperiously at the door.*)

LAURA Please, please!

AMANDA (*in a fierce whisper*) What is the matter with you, you silly thing?

LAURA (*desperately*) Please, you answer it, *please!*

AMANDA I told you I wasn't going to humor you, Laura. Why have you chosen this moment to lose your mind?

LAURA Please, please, please, you go!

AMANDA You'll have to go to the door because I can't!

LAURA (*despairingly*) I can't either!

AMANDA Why?

LAURA I'm *sick!*

AMANDA I'm sick, too—of your nonsense! Why can't you and your brother be normal people? Fantastic whims and behavior! (TOM *gives a long ring.*) Preposterous goings on! Can you give me one reason—(*calls out lyrically*) COMING! JUST ONE SECOND!—why should you be afraid to open a door? Now you answer it, Laura!

LAURA Oh, oh, oh . . . (*She returns through the portieres. Darts to the victrola and winds it frantically and turns it on.*)

AMANDA Laura Wingfield, you march right to that door!

LAURA Yes—yes, Mother!

(*A faraway, scratchy rendition of "Dardanella" softens the air and gives her strength to move through it. She slips to the door and draws it cautiously open.*

TOM *enters with the caller,* JIM O'CONNOR.)

TOM Laura, this is Jim. Jim, this is my sister, Laura.

JIM (*stepping inside*) I didn't know that Shakespeare had a sister!

LAURA (*retreating stiff and trembling from the door*) How—how do you do?

JIM (*heartily extending his hand*) Okay!

(LAURA *touches it hesitantly with hers.*)

JIM Your hand's *cold,* Laura!

LAURA Yes, well—I've been playing the victrola. . . .

JIM Must have been playing classical music on it! You ought to play a little hot swing music to warm you up!

LAURA Excuse me—I haven't finished playing the victrola. . . .

(*She turns awkwardly and hurries into the front room. She pauses a second by the victrola. Then catches her breath and darts through the portieres like a frightened deer.*)

JIM (*grinning*) What was the matter?

TOM Oh—with Laura? Laura is—terribly shy.

JIM Shy, huh? It's unusual to meet a shy girl nowadays. I don't believe you ever mentioned you had a sister.

TOM Well, now you know. I have one. Here is the *Post Dispatch.* You want a piece of it?

JIM Uh-huh.

TOM What piece? The comics?

JIM Sports! (*glances at it*) Ole Dizzy Dean is on his bad behavior.

TOM (*disinterest*) Yeah? (*lights cigarette and crosses back to fire-escape door*)

JIM Where are *you* going?

TOM I'm going out on the terrace.

JIM (*goes after him*) You know, Shakespeare—I'm going to sell you a bill of goods!

TOM What goods?

JIM A course I'm taking.

TOM Huh?

JIM In public speaking! You and me, we're not the warehouse type.

TOM Thanks—that's good news. But what has public speaking got to do with it?

JIM It fits you for—executive positions!

TOM Awww.

JIM I tell you it's done a helluva lot for me.

(Image: Executive at desk.)

TOM In what respect?

JIM In every! Ask yourself what is the difference between you an' me and men in the office down front? Brains?—No!—Ability?—No! Then what? Just one little thing—

TOM What is that one little thing?

JIM Primarily it amounts to—social poise! Being able to square up to people and hold your own on any social level!

AMANDA (*off stage*) Tom?

TOM Yes, Mother?

AMANDA Is that you and Mr. O'Connor?

TOM Yes, Mother.

AMANDA Well, you just make yourselves comfortable in there.

TOM Yes, Mother.

AMANDA Ask Mr. O'Connor if he would like to wash his hands.

JIM Aw—no—no—thank you—I took care of that at the warehouse. Tom—

TOM Yes?

JIM Mr. Mendoza was speaking to me about you.

TOM Favorably?

JIM What do you think?

TOM Well—

JIM You're going to be out of a job if you don't wake up.

TOM I am waking up—

JIM You show no signs.

TOM The signs are interior.

(Image on screen: The sailing vessel with Jolly Roger again.)

TOM I'm planning to change. (*He leans over the rail speaking with quiet exhilaration. The incandescent marquees and signs of the first-run movie houses light his face from across the alley. He looks like a voyager.*) I'm right at the point of committing myself to a future that doesn't include the warehouse and Mr. Mendoza or even a night-school course in public speaking.

JIM What are you gassing about?

TOM I'm tired of the movies.

JIM Movies!

TOM Yes, movies! Look at them—(*a wave toward the marvels of Grand Avenue*) All of those glamorous people—having adventures—hogging it all, gobbling the whole thing up! You know what happens? People go to the *movies* instead of *moving!* Hollywood characters are supposed to have all the adventures for everybody in America, while everybody in America sits in a dark room and watches them have them! Yes, until there's a war. That's when adventure becomes available to the masses! *Everyone's* dish, not only Gable's! Then the people in the dark room come out of the dark room to have some adventures themselves—Goody, goody!—It's our turn now, to go to the South Sea Island—to make a safari—to be exotic, far-off!—But I'm not patient. I don't want to wait till then. I'm tired of the *movies* and I am *about* to *move!*

JIM (*incredulously*) Move?

TOM Yes.

JIM When?

TOM Soon!

JIM Where? Where?

(Theme three music seems to answer the question, while Tom thinks it over. He searches among his pockets.)

TOM I'm starting to boil inside. I know I seem dreamy, but inside—well, I'm boiling! Whenever I pick up a shoe, I shudder a little thinking how short life is and what I am doing!—Whatever that means. I know it doesn't mean shoes—except as something to wear on a traveler's feet! (*finds paper*) Look—

JIM What?

TOM I'm a member.

JIM (*reading*) The Union of Merchant Seamen.

TOM I paid my dues this month, instead of the light bill.

JIM You will regret it when they turn the lights off.

TOM I won't be here.

JIM How about your mother?

TOM I'm like my father. The bastard son of a bastard! See how he grins? And he's been absent going on sixteen years!

JIM You're just talking, you drip. How does your mother feel about it?

TOM Shhh!—Here comes Mother! Mother is not acquainted with my plans!

AMANDA (*enters portieres*) Where are you all?

TOM On the terrace, Mother.

(*They start inside. She advances to them.* TOM *is distinctly shocked at her appearance. Even* JIM *blinks a little. He is making his first contact with girlish Southern vivacity and in spite of the night-school course in public speaking is somewhat thrown off the beam by the unexpected outlay of social charm.*

Certain responses are attempted by JIM *but are swept aside by* AMANDA*'s gay laughter and chatter.* TOM *is embarrassed but after the first shock* JIM *reacts very warmly. Grins and chuckles, is altogether won over.*)

(*Image: Amanda as a girl.*)

AMANDA (*coyly smiling, shaking her girlish ringlets*) Well, well, well, so this is Mr. O'Connor. Introductions entirely unnecessary. I've heard so much about you from my boy. I finally said to him, Tom—good gracious!—why don't you bring this paragon to supper? I'd like to meet this nice young man at the warehouse!—Instead of just hearing him sing your praises so much! I don't know why my son is so stand-offish—that's not Southern behavior! Let's sit down and—I think we could stand a little more air in here! Tom, leave the door open. I felt a nice fresh breeze a moment ago. Where has it gone? Mmm, so warm already! And not quite summer, even. We're going to burn up when summer really gets started. However, we're having—we're having a very light supper. I think light things are better fo' this time of year. The same as light clothes are. Light clothes an' light food are what warm weather calls fo'. You know our blood gets so thick during th' winter—it takes a while fo' us to *adjust* ou'selves!—when the season changes . . . It's come so quick this year. I wasn't prepared. All of a sudden—heavens! Already summer!—I ran to the trunk an' pulled out this light dress—Terribly old! Historical almost! But feels so good—so good an' co-ol, y'know. . . .

TOM Mother—

AMANDA Yes, honey?

TOM How about—supper?

AMANDA Honey, you go ask Sister if supper is ready! You know that Sister is in full charge of supper! Tell her you hungry boys are waiting for it. (*to* JIM) Have you met Laura?

JIM She—

AMANDA Let you in? Oh, good, you've met already! It's rare for a girl as sweet an' pretty as Laura to be domestic! But Laura is, thank heavens, not only pretty but also very domestic. I'm not at all. I never was a bit. I never could make a thing but angel-food cake. Well, in the South we had so many servants. Gone, gone, gone. All vestige of gracious living! Gone completely! I wasn't prepared for what the future brought me. All of my gentlemen callers were sons of planters and so of course I assumed that I would be married to one and raise my family on a large piece of land with plenty of servants. But man proposes—and woman accepts the proposal!—To vary that old, old saying a little bit—I married no planter! I married a man who worked for the telephone company!—That gallantly smiling gentleman over there! (*points to the picture*) A telephone man who—fell in love with long-distance!—Now he travels and I don't even know where!—But what am I going on for about my—tribulations? Tell me yours—I hope you don't have any! Tom?

TOM (*returning*) Yes, Mother?

AMANDA Is supper nearly ready?

TOM It looks to me like supper is on the table.

AMANDA Let me look—(*She rises prettily and looks through portieres.*) Oh, lovely!—But where is Sister?

TOM Laura is not feeling well and she says that she thinks she'd better not come to the table.

AMANDA What?—Nonsense!—Laura? Oh, Laura!

LAURA (*off stage, faintly*) Yes, Mother.

AMANDA You really must come to the table. We won't be seated until you come to the table! Come in, Mr. O'Connor. You sit over there and I'll—Laura? Laura Wingfield! You're keeping us waiting, honey! We can't say grace until you come to the table!

(*The back door is pushed weakly open and* LAURA *comes in. She is obviously quite faint, her lips trembling, her eyes wide and staring. She moves unsteadily toward the table.*)

(Legend: "Terror!")

(*Outside a summer storm is coming abruptly. The white curtains billow inward at the windows and there is a sorrowful murmur and deep blue dusk.*

LAURA *suddenly stumbles; she catches at a chair with a faint moan.*)

TOM Laura!

AMANDA Laura! (*There is a clap of thunder.*) *(Legend: "Ah!")* (*despairingly:*) Why, Laura, you *are* sick, darling! Tom, help your sister into the living room, dear! Sit in the living room, Laura—rest on the sofa. Well! (*to the gentleman caller:*) Standing over the hot stove made her ill!—I told her that it was just too warm this evening, but—(TOM *comes back in.* LAURA *is on the sofa.*) Is Laura all right now?

TOM Yes.

AMANDA What *is* that? Rain? A nice cool rain has come up! (*She gives the gentleman caller a frightened look.*) I think we may—have grace—now . . . (TOM *looks at her stupidly.*) Tom, honey—you say grace!

TOM Oh . . . "For these and all thy mercies—" (*They bow their heads,* AMANDA *stealing a nervous glance at* JIM. *In the living room* LAURA, *stretched on the sofa, clenches her hand to her lips, to hold back a shuddering sob.*) God's Holy Name be praised—

(*The scene dims out.*)

Scene VII

(*Legend: "A souvenir."*)

Half an hour later. Dinner is just being finished in the upstage area which is concealed by the drawn portieres.

As the curtain rises LAURA *is still huddled upon the sofa, her feet drawn under her, her head resting on a pale blue pillow, her eyes wide and mysteriously watchful. The new floor lamp with its shade of rose-colored silk gives a soft, becoming light to her face, bringing out the fragile, unearthly prettiness which usually escapes attention. There is a steady murmur of rain, but it is slackening and stops soon after the scene begins; the air outside becomes pale and luminous as the moon breaks out.*

A moment after the curtain rises, the lights in both rooms flicker and go out.

JIM Hey, there, Mr. Light Bulb!

(AMANDA *laughs nervously.*)

(*Legend: "Suspension of a public service."*)

AMANDA Where was Moses when the lights went out? Ha-ha. Do you know the answer to that one, Mr. O'Connor?

JIM No, Ma'am, what's the answer?

AMANDA In the dark! (JIM *laughs appreciably.*) Everybody sit still. I'll light the candles. Isn't it lucky we have them on the table? Where's a match? Which of you gentlemen can provide a match?

JIM Here.

AMANDA Thank you, sir.

JIM Not at all, Ma'am!

AMANDA I guess the fuse has burnt out. Mr. O'Connor, can you tell a burnt-out fuse? I know I can't and Tom is a total loss when it comes to mechanics. (*Sound: Getting up: voices recede a little to kitchenette.*) Oh, be careful you don't bump into something. We don't want our gentleman caller to break his neck. Now wouldn't that be a fine howdy-do?

JIM Ha-ha! Where is the fuse-box?

AMANDA Right here next to the stove. Can you see anything?

JIM Just a minute.

AMANDA Isn't electricity a mysterious thing? Wasn't it Benjamin Franklin who tied a key to a kite? We live in such a mysterious universe, don't we? Some people say that science clears up all mysteries for us. In my opinion it only creates more! Have you found it yet?

JIM No, Ma'am. All these fuses look okay to me.

AMANDA Tom!

TOM Yes, Mother?

AMANDA That light bill I gave you several days ago. The one I told you we got the notices about?

TOM Oh.—Yeah.

(Legend: "Ha!")

AMANDA You didn't neglect to pay it by any chance?

TOM Why, I—

AMANDA Didn't! I might have known it!

JIM Shakespeare probably wrote a poem on that light bill, Mrs. Wingfield.

AMANDA I might have known better than to trust him with it! There's such a high price for negligence in this world!

JIM Maybe the poem will win a ten-dollar prize.

AMANDA We'll just have to spend the remainder of the evening in the nineteenth century, before Mr. Edison made the Mazda lamp!

JIM Candlelight is my favorite kind of light.

AMANDA That shows you're romantic! But that's no excuse for Tom. Well, we got through dinner. Very considerate of them to let us get through dinner before they plunged us into everlasting darkness, wasn't it, Mr. O'Connor?

JIM Ha-ha!

AMANDA Tom, as a penalty for your carelessness you can help me with the dishes.

JIM Let me give you a hand.

AMANDA Indeed you will not!

JIM I ought to be good for something.

AMANDA Good for something? (*Her tone is rhapsodic.*) *You?* Why, Mr. O'Connor, nobody, *nobody's* given me this much entertainment in years—as you have!

JIM Aw, now, Mrs. Wingfield!

AMANDA I'm not exaggerating, not one bit! But Sister is all by her lonesome. You go keep her company in the parlor! I'll give you this lovely old candelabrum that used to be on the altar at the church of the Heavenly Rest. It was melted a little out of shape when the church burnt down. Lightning struck it one spring. Gypsy Jones was holding a revival at the time and he intimated that the church was destroyed because the Episcopalians gave card parties.

JIM Ha-ha.

AMANDA And how about coaxing Sister to drink a little wine? I think it would be good for her! Can you carry both at once?

JIM Sure. I'm Superman!

AMANDA Now, Thomas, get into this apron!

(*The door of kitchenette swings closed on* AMANDA*'s gay laughter; the flickering light approaches the portieres.*

LAURA *sits up nervously as he enters. Her speech at first is low and breathless from the almost intolerable strain of being alone with a stranger.*)

(*The legend: "I don't suppose you remember me at all!"*)

(*In her first speeches in his scene, before* JIM*'s warmth overcomes her paralyzing shyness,* LAURA*'s voice is thin and breathless as though she has just run up a steep flight of stairs.*

JIM*'s attitude is gently humorous. In playing this scene it should be stressed that while the incident is apparently unimportant, it is to* LAURA *the climax of her secret life.*)

JIM Hello, there, Laura.

LAURA (*faintly*) Hello. (*She clears her throat.*)

JIM How are you feeling now? Better?

LAURA Yes. Yes, thank you.

JIM This is for you. A little dandelion wine. (*He extends it toward her with extravagant gallantry.*)

LAURA Thank you.

JIM Drink it—but don't get drunk! (*He laughs heartily.* LAURA *takes the glass uncertainly, laughs shyly.*) Where shall I set the candles?

LAURA Oh—oh, anywhere . . .

JIM How about here on the floor? Any objections?

LAURA No.

JIM I'll spread a newspaper under to catch the drippings. I like to sit on the floor. Mind if I do?

LAURA Oh, no.

JIM Give me a pillow?

LAURA What?

JIM A pillow!

LAURA Oh . . . (*hands him one quickly*)

JIM How about you? Don't you like to sit on the floor?

LAURA Oh—yes.

JIM Why don't you, then?

LAURA I—will.

JIM Take a pillow! (LAURA *does. Sits on the other side of the candelabrum.* JIM *crosses his legs and smiles engagingly at her.*) I can't hardly see you sitting way over there.

LAURA I can—see you.

JIM I know, but that's not fair, I'm in the limelight. (LAURA *moves her pillow closer.*) Good! Now I can see you! Comfortable?

LAURA Yes.

JIM So am I. Comfortable as a cow. Will you have some gum?

LAURA No, thank you.

JIM I think that I will indulge, with your permission. (*musingly unwraps it and holds it up*) Think of the fortune made by the guy that invented the first piece of chewing gum. Amazing, huh? The Wrigley Building is one of the sights of Chicago.—I saw it summer before last when I went up to the Century of Progress. Did you take in the Century of Progress?

LAURA No, I didn't.

JIM Well, it was quite a wonderful exposition. What impressed me most was the Hall of Science. Gives you an idea of what the future will be in America, even more wonderful than the present time is! (*pause; smiling at her:*) Your brother tells me you're shy. Is that right, Laura?

LAURA I—don't know.

JIM I judge you to be an old-fashioned type of girl. Well, I think that's a pretty good type to be. Hope you don't think I'm being too personal—do you?

LAURA (*hastily, out of embarrassment*) I believe I *will* take a piece of gum, if you—don't mind. (*clearing her throat*) Mr. O'Connor, have you—kept up with your singing?

JIM Singing? Me?

LAURA Yes, I remember what a beautiful voice you had.

JIM When did you hear me sing?

(*Voice off stage in the pause.*)

VOICE (*off stage*)

O blow, ye winds, heigh-ho,
A-roving I will go!
I'm off to my love
With a boxing glove—
Ten thousand miles away!

JIM You say you've heard me sing?

LAURA Oh, yes! Yes, very often . . . I—don't suppose you remember me—at all?

JIM (*smiling doubtfully*) You know I have an idea I've seen you before. I had that idea soon as you opened the door. It seemed almost like I was about to remember your name. But the name that I started to call you—wasn't a name! And so I stopped myself before I said it.

LAURA Wasn't it—Blue Roses?

JIM (*springs up, grinning*) Blue Roses! My gosh, yes—Blue Roses! That's what I had on my tongue when you opened the door! Isn't it funny what tricks your memory plays? I didn't connect you with the high school somehow or other. But that's where it was; it was high school. I didn't even know you were Shakespeare's sister! Gosh, I'm sorry.

LAURA I didn't expect you to. You—barely knew me!

JIM But we did have a speaking acquaintance, huh?

LAURA Yes, we—spoke to each other.

JIM When did you recognize me?

LAURA Oh, right away!

JIM Soon as I came in the door?

LAURA When I heard your name I thought it was probably you. I knew that Tom used to know you a little in high school. So when you came in the door—Well, then I was—sure.

JIM Why didn't you *say* something, then?

LAURA (*breathlessly*) I didn't know what to say, I was—too surprised!

JIM For goodness' sakes! You know, this sure is funny!

LAURA Yes! Yes, isn't it, though . . .

JIM Didn't we have a class in something together?

LAURA Yes, we did.

JIM What class was that?

LAURA It was—singing—Chorus!

JIM Aw!

LAURA I saw across the aisle from you in the Aud.

JIM Aw.

LAURA Mondays, Wednesdays and Fridays.

JIM Now I remember—you always came in late.

LAURA Yes, it was so hard for me, getting upstairs. I had that brace on my leg—it clumped so loud!

JIM I never heard any clumping.

LAURA (*wincing at the recollection*) To me it sounded like—thunder!

JIM Well, well, well. I never even noticed.

LAURA And everybody was seated before I came in. I had to walk in front of all those people. My seat was in the back row. I had to go clumping all the way up the aisle with everyone watching!

JIM You shouldn't have been self-conscious.

LAURA I know, but I was. It was always such a relief when the singing started.

JIM Aw, yes. I've placed you now! I used to call you Blue Roses. How was it that I got started calling you that?

LAURA I was out of school a little while with pleurosis. When I came back you asked me what was the matter. I said I had pleurosis—you thought I said Blue Roses. That's what you always called me after that!

JIM I hope you didn't mind.

LAURA Oh, no—I liked it. You see, I wasn't acquainted with many—people. . . .

JIM As I remember you sort of stuck by yourself.

LAURA I—I—never had much luck at—making friends.

JIM I don't see why you wouldn't.

LAURA Well, I—started out badly.

JIM You mean being—

LAURA Yes, it sort of—stood between me—

JIM You shouldn't have let it!

LAURA I know, but it did, and—

JIM You were shy with people!

LAURA I tried not to be but never could—

JIM Overcome it?

LAURA No, I—I never could!

JIM I guess being shy is something you have to work out of kind of gradually.

LAURA (*sorrowfully*) Yes—I guess it—

JIM Takes time!

LAURA Yes—

JIM People are not so dreadful when you know them. That's what you have to remember! And everybody has problems, not just you, but practically everybody has got some problems. You think of yourself as having the only problems, as being the only one who is disappointed. But just look around you and you will see lots of people as disappointed as you are. For instance, I hoped when I was going to high school that I would be further along at this time, six years later, than I am now—You remember that wonderful write-up I had in *The Torch?*

LAURA Yes! (*She rises and crosses to table.*)

JIM It said I was bound to succeed in anything I went into! (LAURA *returns with the annual.*) Holy Jeez! *The Torch!* (*He accepts it reverently. They smile across it with mutual wonder.* LAURA *crouches beside him and they begin to turn through it.* LAURA'S *shyness is dissolving in his warmth.*)

LAURA Here you are in *Pirates of Penzance!*

JIM (*wistfully*) I sang the baritone lead in that operetta.

LAURA (*rapidly*) So—*beautifully!*

JIM (*protesting*) Aw—

LAURA Yes, yes—beautifully—beautifully!

JIM You heard me?

LAURA All three times!

JIM No!

LAURA Yes!

JIM All three performances?

LAURA (*looking down*) Yes.

JIM Why?

LAURA I—wanted to ask you to—autograph my program.

JIM Why didn't you ask me to?

LAURA You were always surrounded by your own friends so much that I never had a chance to.

JIM You should have just—

LAURA Well, I—thought you might think I was—

JIM Thought I might think you was—what?

LAURA Oh—

JIM (*with reflective relish*) I was beleaguered by females in those days.

LAURA You were terribly popular!

JIM Yeah—

LAURA You had such a—friendly way—

JIM I was spoiled in high school.

LAURA Everybody—liked you!

JIM Including you?

LAURA I—yes, I—I did, too—(*She gently closes the book in her lap.*)

JIM Well, well, well!—Give me that program, Laura. (*She hands it to him. He signs it with a flourish.*) There you are—better late than never!

LAURA Oh, I—what a—surprise!

JIM My signature isn't worth very much right now. But some day—maybe—it will increase in value! Being disappointed is one thing and being discouraged is something else. I am disappointed but I am not discouraged. I'm twenty-three years old. How old are you?

LAURA I'll be twenty-four in June.

JIM That's not old age!

LAURA No, but—

JIM You finished high school?

LAURA (*with difficulty*) I didn't go back.

JIM You mean you dropped out?

LAURA I made bad grades in my final examinations. (*She rises and replaces the book and the program; her voice strained:*) How is—Emily Meisenbach getting along?

JIM Oh, that kraut-head!

LAURA Why do you call her that?

JIM That's what she was.

LAURA You're not still—going with her?

JIM I never see her.

LAURA It said in the Personal Section that you were—engaged!

JIM I know, but I wasn't impressed by that—propaganda!

LAURA It wasn't—the truth?

JIM Only in Emily's optimistic opinion!

LAURA Oh—

(Legend: "What have you done since high school?")

(JIM *lights a cigarette and leans indolently back on his elbows smiling at* LAURA *with a warmth and charm which lights her inwardly with altar candles. She remains by the table and turns in her hands a piece of glass to cover her tumult.*)

JIM (*after several reflective puffs on a cigarette*) What have you done since high school? (*She seems not to hear him.*) Huh? (LAURA *looks up.*) I said what have you done since high school, Laura?

LAURA Nothing much.

JIM You must have been doing something these six long years.

LAURA Yes.

JIM Well, then, such as what?

LAURA I took a business course at business college—

JIM How did that work out?

LAURA Well, not very—well—I had to drop out, it gave me—indigestion—

(JIM *laughs gently.*)

JIM What are you doing now?

LAURA I don't do anything—much. Oh, please don't think I sit around doing nothing! My glass collection takes up a good deal of my time. Glass is something you have to take good care of.

JIM What did you say—about glass?

LAURA Collection I said—I have one—(*She clears her throat and turns away again, acutely shy.*)

JIM (*abruptly*) You know what I judge to be the trouble with you? Inferiority complex! Know what that is? That's what they call it when someone low-rates himself! I understand it because I had it, too. Although my case was not so aggravated as yours seems to be. I had it until I took up public speaking, developed my voice, and learned that I had an aptitude for science. Before that time I never thought of myself as being outstanding in any way whatsoever! Now I've never made a regular study of it, but I have a friend who says I can analyze people better than doctors that make a profession of it. I don't claim that to be necessarily true, but I can sure guess a person's psychology, Laura! (*takes out his gum*) Excuse me, Laura. I always take it out when the flavor is gone. I'll use this scrap of paper to wrap it in. I know how it is to get it stuck on a shoe. Yep—that's what I judge to be your principal trouble. A lack of confidence in yourself as a person. You don't have the proper amount of faith in yourself. I'm basing that fact on a number of your remarks and also on certain observations I've made. For instance that clumping you thought was so awful in high school. You say that you even dreaded to walk into class. You see what you did? You dropped out of school, you gave up an education because of a clump, which as far as I know was practically non-existent! A little physical defect is what you have. Hardly noticeable even! Magnified thousands of times by imagination! You know what my strong advice to you is? Think of yourself as *superior* in some way!

LAURA In what way would I think?

JIM Why, man alive, Laura! Just look about you a little. What do you see? A world full of common people! All of 'em born and all of 'em going to die!

Which of them has one-tenth of your good points! Or mine! Or anyone else's, as far as that goes—Gosh! Everybody excels in some one thing. Some in many! (*unconsciously glances at himself in the mirror*) All you've got to do is discover in *what!* Take me, for instance. (*He adjusts his tie at the mirror.*) My interest happens to lie in electro-dynamics. I'm taking a course in radio engineering at night school, Laura, on top of a fairly responsible job at the warehouse. I'm taking that course and studying public speaking.

LAURA Ohhhh.

JIM Because I believe in the future of television! (*turning back to her*) I wish to be ready to go up right along with it. Therefore I'm planning to get in on the ground floor. In fact, I've already made the right connections and all that remains is for the industry itself to get under way! Full steam—(*His eyes are starry.*) *Knowledge*—Zzzzzp! *Money*—Zzzzzzp!—*Power!* That's the cycle democracy is built on! (*His attitude is convincingly dynamic.* LAURA *stares at him, even her shyness eclipsed in her absolute wonder. He suddenly grins.*) I guess you think I think a lot of myself!

LAURA No—o-o-o, I—

JIM Now how about you? Isn't there something you take more interest in than anything else?

LAURA Well, I do—as I said—have my—glass collection—

(*A peal of girlish laughter from the kitchen.*)

JIM I'm not right sure I know what you're talking about. What kind of glass is it?

LAURA Little articles of it, they're ornaments mostly! Most of them are little animals made out of glass, the tiniest little animals in the world. Mother calls them a glass menagerie! Here's an example of one, if you'd like to see it! This one is one of the oldest. It's nearly thirteen. (*He stretches out his hand.*) (*Music: "The Glass Menagerie."*) Oh, be careful—if you breathe, it breaks!

JIM I'd better not take it. I'm pretty clumsy with things.

LAURA Go on, I trust you with him! (*places it in his palm*) There now—you're holding him gently! Hold him over the light, he loves the light! You see how the light shines through him?

JIM It sure does shine!

LAURA I shouldn't be partial, but he is my favorite one.

JIM What kind of thing is this one supposed to be?

LAURA Haven't you noticed the single horn on his forehead?

JIM A unicorn, huh?

LAURA Mmm-hmmm!

JIM Unicorns, aren't they extinct in the modern world?

LAURA I know!

JIM Poor little fellow, he must feel sort of lonesome.

LAURA (*smiling*) Well, if he does he doesn't complain about it. He stays on a shelf with some horses that don't have horns and all of them seem to get along nicely together.

JIM How do you know?

LAURA (*lightly*) I haven't heard any arguments among them!

JIM (*grinning*) No arguments, huh? Well, that's a pretty good sign! Where shall I set him?

LAURA Put him on the table. They all like a change of scenery once in a while!

JIM (*stretching*) Well, well, well, well—Look how big my shadow is when I stretch!

LAURA Oh, oh, yes—it stretches across the ceiling!

JIM (*crossing to the door*) I think it's stopped raining. (*opens fire-escape door*) Where does the music come from?

LAURA From the Paradise Dance Hall across the alley.

JIM How about cutting the rug a little, Miss Wingfield?

AMANDA Oh, I—

JIM Or is your program filled up? Let me have a look at it. (*grasps imaginary card*) Why, every dance is taken! I'll just have to scratch some out. (*Waltz music: "La Golondrina."*) Ahhh, a waltz! (*He executes some sweeping turns by himself, then holds his arms toward* LAURA.)

LAURA (*breathlessly*) I—can't dance!

JIM There you go, that inferiority stuff.

LAURA I've never danced in my life!

JIM Come on, try!

LAURA Oh, but I'd step on you!

JIM I'm not made out of glass.

LAURA How—how—how do we start?

JIM Just leave it to me. You hold your arms out a little.

LAURA Like this?

JIM A little big higher. Right. Now don't tighten up, that's the main thing about it—relax.

LAURA (*laughing breathlessly*) It's hard not to.

JIM Okay.

LAURA I'm afraid you can't budge me.

JIM What do you bet I can't? (*He swings her into motion.*)

LAURA Goodness, yes, you can!

JIM Let yourself go, now, Laura, just let yourself go.

LAURA I'm—

JIM Come on!

LAURA Trying!

JIM Not so stiff—Easy does it!

LAURA I know but I'm—

JIM Loosen th' backbone! There now, that's a lot better.

LAURA Am I?

JIM Lots, lots better! (*He moves her about the room in a clumsy waltz.*)

LAURA Oh, my!

JIM Ha-ha!

LAURA Goodness, yes you can!

JIM Ha-ha-ha! (*They suddenly bump into the table.* JIM *stops.*) What did we hit on?

LAURA Table.

JIM Did something fall off it? I think—

LAURA Yes.

JIM I hope that it wasn't the little glass horse with the horn!

LAURA Yes.

JIM Aw, aw, aw. Is it broken?

LAURA Now it is just like all the other horses.

JIM It's lost its—

LAURA Horn! It doesn't matter. Maybe it's a blessing in disguise.

JIM You'll never forgive me. I bet that that was your favorite piece of glass.

LAURA I don't have favorites much. It's no tragedy, Freckles. Glass breaks so easily. No matter how careful you are. The traffic jars the shelves and things fall off them.

JIM Still I'm awfully sorry that I was the cause.

LAURA (*smiling*) I'll just imagine he had an operation. The horn was removed to make him feel less—freakish! (*They both laugh.*) Now he will feel more at home with the other horses, the ones that don't have horns . . .

JIM Ha-ha, that's very funny! (*suddenly serious:*) I'm glad to see that you have a sense of humor. You know—you're—well—very different! Surprisingly different from anyone else I know! (*His voice becomes soft and hesitant with a genuine feeling.*) Do you mind me telling you that? (LAURA *is abashed beyond speech.*) You make me feel sort of—I don't know how to put it! I'm usually pretty good at expressing things, but—This is something that I don't know how to say! (LAURA *touches her throat and clears it—turns the broken unicorn in her hands.*) (*even softer:*) Has anyone ever told you that you were pretty? *(Pause: Music)* (LAURA *looks up slowly, with wonder, and shakes her head.*) Well, you are! In a very different way from anyone else. And all the nicer because of the difference, too. (*His voice becomes low and husky.* LAURA *turns away, nearly faint with the novelty of her emotions.*) I wish that you were my sister. I'd teach you to have some confidence in yourself. The different people are not like other people, but being different is nothing to be ashamed of. Because other people are not such wonderful people. They're one hundred times one thousand. You're one times one! They walk all over the earth. You just stay here. They're common as—weeds, but—you—well, you're—*Blue Roses!*

(Image on screen: Blue roses.)

(Music changes.)

LAURA But blue is wrong for—roses . . .

JIM It's right for you—You're—pretty!

LAURA In what respect am I pretty?

JIM In all respects—believe me! Your eyes—your hair—are pretty! Your hands are pretty! (*He catches hold of her hand.*) You think I'm making this up because I'm invited to dinner and have to be nice. Oh, I could do that! I could put on an act for you, Laura, and say lots of things without being very sincere. But this time I am. I'm talking to you sincerely. I happened to notice you had this inferiority complex that keeps you from feeling comfortable with people. Somebody needs to build your confidence up and make you proud instead of shy and turning away and—blushing—Somebody ought to—Ought to—*kiss* you, Laura! (*His hand slips slowly up her arm to her shoulder.*) (*Music swells tumultuously.*) (*He suddenly turns her about and kisses her on the lips. When he releases her* LAURA *sinks on the sofa with a bright, dazed look.* JIM *backs away and fishes in his pocket for a cigarette.*) (*Legend on screen: "Souvenir."*) Stumble-john! (*He lights the cigarette, avoiding her look. There is a peal of girlish laughter from* AMANDA *in the kitchen.* LAURA *slowly raises and opens her hand. It still contains the little broken glass animal. She looks at it with a tender, bewildered expression.*) Stumble-john! I shouldn't have done that—That was way off the beam. You don't smoke, do you? (*She looks up, smiling, not hearing the question. He sits beside her a little gingerly. She looks at him speechlessly—waiting. He coughs decorously and moves a little farther aside as he considers the situation and senses her feelings, dimly, with perturbation; gently:*) Would you—care for a—mint? (*She doesn't seem to hear him but her look grows brighter even.*) Peppermint—Life Saver? My pocket's a regular drug store—wherever I go . . . (*He pops a mint in his mouth. Then gulps and decides to make a clean breast of it. He speaks slowly and gingerly.*) Laura, you know, if I had a sister like you, I'd do the same thing as Tom. I'd bring out fellows—introduce her to them. The right type of boys of a type to—appreciate her. Only—well—he made a mistake about me. Maybe I've got no call to be saying this. That may not have been the idea in having me over. But what if it was? There's nothing wrong about that. The only trouble is that in my case—I'm not in a situation to—do the right thing. I can't take down your number and say I'll phone. I can't call up next week and—ask for a date. I thought I had better explain the situation in case you misunderstood it and—hurt your feelings. . . . (*Pause. Slowly, very slowly,* LAURA'S *look changes, her eyes returning slowly from his to the ornament in her palm.*)

(AMANDA *utters another gay laugh in the kitchen.*)

LAURA (*faintly*) You—won't—call again?

JIM No, Laura, I can't. (*He rises from the sofa.*) As I was just explaining, I've—got strings on me, Laura, I've—been going steady! I go out all the time with a girl named Betty. She's a home-girl like you, and Catholic, and Irish, and in a great many ways we—get along fine. I met her last summer on a moonlight boat trip up the river to Alton, on the *Majestic.* Well—right away from the start it was—love! (*Legend: Love!*) (LAURA *sways slightly forward and grips the arm of the sofa. He fails to notice, now enrapt in his own comfortable being.*) Being in love has made a new man of me! (*Leaning stiffly forward, clutching the arm of the sofa,* LAURA *struggles visibly with her storm. But* JIM *is oblivious; she is a long way off.*) The power of love is really pretty tremendous! Love is something that—changes the whole world, Laura! (*The storm abates a little and* LAURA *leans back. He notices her again.*) It happened that Betty's aunt took sick, she got a wire and had to go to Centralia. So Tom—when he asked me to dinner—I naturally just accepted the invitation, not knowing that you—that he—that I—(*He stops awkwardly.*) Huh—I'm a stumble-john! (*He flops back on the sofa. The holy candles in the altar of* LAURA'*s face have been snuffed out! There is a look of almost infinite desolation.* JIM *glances at her uneasily.*) I wish that you would—say something. (*She bites her lip which was trembling and then bravely smiles. She opens her hand again on the broken glass ornament. Then she gently takes his hand and raises it level with her own. She carefully places the unicorn in the palm of his hand, then pushes his fingers closed upon it.*) What are you—doing that for? You want me to have him?—Laura? (*She nods.*) What for?

LAURA A—souvenir . . .

(*She rises unsteadily and crouches beside the victrola to wind it up.*)

(*Legend on screen: "Things have a way of turning out so badly."*)

(*Or image: "Gentleman caller waving goodbye!—gaily."*)

(*At this moment* AMANDA *rushes brightly back in the front room. She bears a pitcher of fruit punch in an old-fashioned cut-glass pitcher and a plate of macaroons. The plate has a gold border and poppies painted on it.*)

AMANDA Well, well, well! Isn't the air delightful after the shower? I've made you children a little liquid refreshment. (*turns gaily to the gentleman caller*) Jim, do you know that song about lemonade?

"Lemonade, lemonade
Made in the shade and stirred with a spade—
Good enough for any old maid!"

JIM (*uneasily*) Ha-ha! No—I never heard it.

AMANDA Why, Laura! You look so serious!

JIM We were having a serious conversation.

AMANDA Good! Now you're better acquainted!

JIM (*uncertainly*) Ha-ha! Yes.

AMANDA You modern young people are much more serious-minded than my generation. I was so gay as a girl!

JIM You haven't changed, Mrs. Wingfield.

AMANDA Tonight I'm rejuvenated! The gaiety of the occasion, Mr. O'Connor! (*She tosses her head with a peal of laughter, spills lemonade.*) Oooo! I'm baptizing myself!

JIM Here—let me—

AMANDA (*setting the pitcher down*) There now. I discovered we had some maraschino cherries. I dumped them in, juice and all!

JIM You shouldn't have gone to that trouble, Mrs. Wingfield.

AMANDA Trouble, trouble? Why it was loads of fun! Didn't you hear me cutting up in the kitchen? I bet your ears were burning! I told Tom how outdone with him I was for keeping you to himself so long a time! He should have brought you over much, much sooner! Well, now that you've found your way, I want you to be a very frequent caller! Not just occasional but all the time. Oh, we're going to have a lot of gay times together! I see them coming! Mmm, just breathe that air! So fresh, and the moon's so pretty! I'll skip back out—I know where my place is when young folks are having a—serious conversation!

JIM Oh, don't go out, Mrs. Wingfield. The fact of the matter is I've got to be going.

AMANDA Going, now? You're joking! Why, it's only the shank of the evening, Mr. O'Connor!

JIM Well, you know how it is.

AMANDA You mean you're a young workingman and have to keep workingmen's hours. We'll let you off early tonight. But only on the condition that next time you stay later. What's the best night for you? Isn't Saturday night the best night for you workingmen?

JIM I have a couple of time-clocks to punch, Mrs. Wingfield. One at morning, another one at night!

AMANDA My, but you *are* ambitious! You work at night, too?

JIM No, Ma'am, not work but—Betty! (*He crosses deliberately to pick up his hat. The band at the Paradise Dance Hall goes into a tender waltz.*)

AMANDA Betty? Betty? Who's—Betty! (*There is an ominous cracking sound in the sky.*)

JIM Oh, just a girl. The girl I go steady with! (*He smiles charmingly. The sky falls.*)

(Legend: "The sky falls.")

AMANDA (*a long-drawn exhalation*) Ohhhh . . . Is it a serious romance, Mr. O'Connor?

JIM We're going to be married the second Sunday in June.

AMANDA Ohhhh—how nice! Tom didn't mention that you were engaged to be married.

JIM The cat's not out of the bag at the warehouse yet. You know how they are. They call you Romeo and stuff like that. (*He stops at the oval mirror to put on his hat. He carefully shapes the brim and the crown to give a discreetly dashing effect.*) It's been a wonderful evening, Mrs. Wingfield. I guess this is what they mean by Southern hospitality.

AMANDA It really wasn't anything at all.

JIM I hope it don't seem like I'm rushing off. But I promised Betty I'd pick her up at the Wabash depot, an' by the time I get my jalopy down there her train'll be in. Some women are pretty upset if you keep 'em waiting.

AMANDA Yes, I know—The tyranny of women! (*extends her hand*) Goodbye, Mr. O'Connor. I wish you luck—and happiness—and success! All three of them, and so does Laura!—Don't you, Laura?

LAURA Yes!

JIM (*taking her hand*) Good-bye, Laura. I'm certainly going to treasure that souvenir. And don't you forget the good advice I gave you. (*raises his voice to a cheery shout*) So long, Shakespeare! Thanks again, ladies—Good night!

(*He grins and ducks jauntily out.*

Still bravely grimacing, AMANDA *closes the door on the gentleman caller. Then she turns back to the room with a puzzled expression. She and* LAURA *don't dare to face each other.* LAURA *crouches beside the victrola to wind it.*)

AMANDA (*faintly*) Things have a way of turning out so badly. I don't believe that I would play the victrola. Well, well—well—Our gentleman caller was engaged to be married! Tom!

TOM (*from back*) Yes, Mother?

AMANDA Come in here a minute. I want to tell you something awfully funny.

TOM (*enters with a macaroon and a glass of the lemonade*) Has the gentleman caller gotten away already?

AMANDA The gentleman caller has made an early departure. What a wonderful joke you played on us!

TOM How do you mean?

AMANDA You didn't mention that he was engaged to be married.

TOM Jim? Engaged?

AMANDA That's what he just informed us.

TOM I'll be jiggered! I didn't know about that.

AMANDA That seems very peculiar.

TOM What's peculiar about it?

AMANDA Didn't you call him your best friend down at the warehouse?

TOM He is, but how did I know?

AMANDA It seems extremely peculiar that you wouldn't know your best friend was going to be married!

TOM The warehouse is where I work, not where I know things about people!

AMANDA You don't know things anywhere! You live in a dream; you manufacture illusions! (*He crosses to door.*) Where are you going?

TOM I'm going to the movies.

AMANDA That's right, now that you've had us make such fools of ourselves. The effort, the preparations, all the expense! The new floor lamp, the rug, the clothes for Laura! All for what? To entertain some other girl's fiancé! Go to the movies, go! Don't think about us, a mother deserted, an unmarried sister who's crippled and has no job! Don't let anything interfere with your selfish pleasure! Just go, go, go—to the movies!

TOM All right, I will! The more you shout about my selfishness to me the quicker I'll go, and I won't go to the movies!

AMANDA Go, then! Then go to the moon—you selfish dreamer!

(TOM *smashes his glass on the floor. He plunges out on the fire-escape, slamming the door,* LAURA *screams—cut off by the door.*

Dance-hall music up. TOM *goes to the rail and grips it desperately, lifting his face in the chill white moonlight penetrating the narrow abyss of the alley.*)

(*Legend on screen: "And so good-bye . . ."*)

(TOM*'s closing speech is timed with the interior pantomime. The interior scene is played as though viewed through soundproof glass.* AMANDA *appears to be making a comforting speech to* LAURA *who is huddled upon the sofa. Now that we cannot hear the mother's speech, her silliness is gone and she has dignity and tragic beauty.* LAURA*'s dark hair hides her face until at the end of the speech she lifts it to smile at her mother.* AMANDA*'s gestures are slow and graceful, almost dancelike, as she comforts the daughter. At the end of her speech she glances a moment at the father's picture—then withdraws through the portieres. At close of* TOM*'s speech,* LAURA *blows out the candles, ending the play.*)

TOM I didn't go to the moon, I went much further—for time is the longest distance between two places—Not long after that I was fired for writing a poem on the lid of a shoe-box. I left Saint Louis. I descended the steps of this fire-escape for a last time and followed, from then on, in my father's footsteps, attempting to find in motion what was lost in space—I traveled around a great deal. The cities swept about me like dead leaves, leaves that were brightly colored but torn away from the branches. I would have stopped, but I was pursued by something. It always came upon me unawares, taking me altogether by surprise. Perhaps it was a familiar bit of music. Perhaps it was only a piece of transparent glass—Perhaps I am walking along a street at night, in some strange city, before I have found companions. I pass the lighted window of a shop where perfume is sold. The window is filled with pieces of colored glass, tiny transparent bottles in delicate colors, like bits of a shattered rainbow. Then all at once my sister touches my shoulder. I turn around and look into her eyes . . . Oh, Laura, Laura, I tried to leave you behind me, but I am more faithful than I intended to be! I reach for a cigarette, I cross the street, I run into the movies or a bar, I buy a drink, I speak to the nearest stranger—anything that can blow your candles out! (LAURA *bends over the candles.*)—for nowadays the world is lit by lightning! Blow out your candles, Laura—and so good-bye. . . .

(*She blows the candles out.*)

(*The scene dissolves.*)

DEATH OF A SALESMAN

(1949)

ARTHUR MILLER (1915–   )

If, among the three great modern American dramatists, the final reputation of Eugene O'Neill rests upon *Long Day's Journey Into Night,* produced posthumously in 1956, and of Tennessee Williams upon *A Streetcar Named Desire,* so will the ultimate judgment of Arthur Miller probably rest upon *Death of a Salesman.*

Death of a Salesman was the theatre sensation of the immediate post–World War II years. *All My Sons* (1947) and *The Crucible* (1953) could well have earned Arthur Miller a distinguished place in American drama, but *Salesman* clearly surpasses them in its portrait of the broken drummer, Willy Loman. If O'Neill was the dramatic artist pursuing the relationship of man to God, Miller is certainly the one who devotes his full energies to exploring the relationship of man to man, particularly father to son, most explicitly and devastatingly in Willy and his family. The father-son love-hate combat predominates in *All My Sons, A View from the Bridge* (1955), and *The Price* (1968), but *Salesman* gives it its most powerful thrust.

Because Willy has quite rightfully been viewed as a kind of universal figure from American business folklore, his play has too often been regarded as the great *American* tragedy, a brutal indictment of "the system," which makes and breaks the best it has, chews it up, spits it out, and leaves it helpless without a sign of appreciation. It builds giant cities that suffocate and drown the little folk in their cottages in shadows that prevent the flowering of the fruits of the earth. It turns good people into burned-out shells. There, but for the Grace of God, go all of us, and God Help Willy Loman.

Death of a Salesman is not, however, a modern tragedy. Society has not destroyed Willy Loman. Willy Loman has destroyed himself. More precisely, he has destroyed an image of himself in his own imagination of what society is and what the business world expects of him. Nowhere are we permitted to see Willy Loman except through his own eyes. He says he was a great salesman. There is not a shred of evidence. Why has the old refrigerator had to last so many years, the old car so many miles? Willy insists that there are great rewards for what he does and he seems at one time to have reaped them. But we see nothing of substance to support his claims. Willy is a sham, through and through, living on what he thinks he is and what he thinks is right, while all along the young Bernard next door gives the lie to Willy's theories of how to raise a family and how to perform in society. The fact that Bernard can argue before the Supreme Court is incomprehensible to the Willy who could see no purpose in the scholarly bookishness of his next-door neighbor's son. And Willy never really sees that Charley is the one who has succeeded, and who has the money to keep Willy alive. How come Willy doesn't have it?

Brother Ben is shown only as Willy sees him. Was he the whiz-kid that Willy makes him out? Or was he as false as Willy? To the very end Willy never realizes what he has done. All that he has discovered is that, despite his shabby sleaziness and the ruin he has brought, Biff loves him. Indeed!

Willy's suicide is not the positive act of tragedy. It is the act of one who still thinks in terms of self-redemption, of being able to "make it up" to those he has done wrong. True, Willy is a man, and maybe he should have some attention paid. But Willy is a very little man in all ways, and while we weep for him and may be deeply moved, he remains with feet of very sticky clay, firmly fastened to the ground, far from the heights demanded of tragedy.

Death of a Salesman ARTHUR MILLER

Certain Private Conversations in Two Acts and a Requiem

CHARACTERS

WILLY LOMAN
LINDA
BIFF
HAPPY
BERNARD
THE WOMAN
CHARLEY
UNCLE BEN
HOWARD WAGNER
JENNY
STANLEY
MISS FORSYTHE
LETTA

The action takes place in WILLY LOMAN*'s house and yard and in various places he visits in the New York and Boston of today.*

Throughout the play, in the stage directions, left and right mean stage left and stage right.

Act I

An Overture

A melody is heard, played upon a flute. It is small and fine, telling of grass and trees and the horizon. The curtain rises.

Before us is the Salesman's house. We are aware of towering, angular shapes behind it, surrounding it on all sides. Only the blue light of the sky falls upon the house and forestage; the surrounding area shows an angry glow of orange. As more light appears, we see a solid vault of apartment houses around the small, fragile-seeming home. An air of the dream clings to the place, a dream rising out of reality. The kitchen at center seems actual enough, for there is a kitchen table with three chairs, and a refrigerator. But no other fixtures are seen. At the back of the kitchen there is a draped entrance, which leads to the living room. To the right of the kitchen, on a level raised two feet, is a bedroom furnished only with a brass bedstead and a straight chair. On a shelf over the bed a silver athletic trophy stands. A window opens onto the apartment house at the side.

Behind the kitchen, on a level raised six and a half feet, is the boys' bedroom, at present barely visible. Two beds are dimly seen, and at the back of the room a dormer window. (This bedroom is above the unseen living room.) At the left a stairway curves up to it from the kitchen.

The entire setting is wholly or, in some places, partially transparent. The roof-line of the house is one-dimensional; under and over it we see the apartment buildings. Before the house lies an apron, curving beyond the forestage into the orchestra. This forward area serves as the back yard as well as the locale of all WILLY'S *imaginings and of his city scenes. Whenever the action is in the present the actors observe the imaginary wall-lines, entering the house only through its door at the left. But in the scenes of the past these boundaries are broken, and characters enter or leave a room by stepping "through" a wall onto the forestage.*

From the right, WILLY LOMAN, *the Salesman, enters, carrying two large sample cases. The flute plays on. He hears but is not aware of it. He is past sixty years of age, dressed quietly. Even as he crosses the stage to the doorway of the house, his exhaustion is apparent. He unlocks the door, comes into the kitchen, and thankfully lets his burden down, feeling the soreness of his palms. A word-sigh escapes his lips—it might be "Oh, boy, oh, boy." He closes the door, then carries his cases out into the living room, through the draped kitchen doorway.*

LINDA, *his wife, has stirred in her bed at the right. She gets out and puts on a robe, listening. Most often jovial, she has developed an iron repression of her exceptions to* WILLY'S *behavior—she more than loves him, she admires him, as though his mercurial nature, his temper, his massive dreams and little cruelties, served her only as sharp reminders of the turbulent longings within him, longings which she shares but lacks the temperament to utter and follow to their end.*

LINDA (*hearing* WILLY *outside the bedroom, calls with some trepidation*) Willy!

WILLY It's all right. I came back.

LINDA Why? What happened? (*slight pause*) Did something happen, Willy?

WILLY No, nothing happened.

LINDA You didn't smash the car, did you?

WILLY (*with casual irritation*) I said nothing happened. Didn't you hear me?

LINDA Don't you feel well?

WILLY I'm tired to the death. (*The flute has faded away. He sits on the bed beside her, a little numb.*) I couldn't make it. I just couldn't make it, Linda.

LINDA (*very carefully, delicately*) Where were you all day? You look terrible.

WILLY I got as far as a little above Yonkers. I stopped for a cup of coffee. Maybe it was the coffee.

LINDA What?

WILLY (*after a pause*) I suddenly couldn't drive any more. The car kept going off the shoulder, y'know?

LINDA (*helpfully*) Oh. Maybe it was the steering again. I don't think Angelo knows the Studebaker.

WILLY No, it's me, it's me. Suddenly I realize I'm goin' sixty miles an hour and I don't remember the last five minutes. I'm—I can't seem to—keep my mind to it.

LINDA Maybe it's your glasses. You never went for your new glasses.

WILLY No, I see everything. I came back ten miles an hour. It took me nearly four hours from Yonkers.

LINDA (*resigned*) Well, you'll just have to take a rest, Willy, you can't continue this way.

WILLY I just got back from Florida.

LINDA But you didn't rest your mind. Your mind is overactive, and the mind is what counts, dear.

WILLY I'll start out in the morning. Maybe I'll feel better in the morning. (*She is taking off his shoes.*) These goddam arch supports are killing me.

LINDA Take an aspirin. Should I get you an aspirin? It'll soothe you.

WILLY (*with wonder*) I was driving along, you understand? And I was fine. I was even observing the scenery. You can imagine, me looking at scenery, on the road every week of my life. But it's so beautiful up there, Linda, the trees are so thick, and the sun is warm. I opened the windshield and just let the warm air bathe over me. And then all of a sudden I'm goin' off the road! I'm tellin' ya, I absolutely forgot I was driving. If I'd've gone the other way over the white line I might've killed somebody. So I went on again—and five minutes later I'm dreamin' again, and I nearly— (*He presses two fingers against his eyes.*) I have such thoughts, I have such strange thoughts.

LINDA Willy, dear. Talk to them again. There's no reason why you can't work in New York.

WILLY They don't need me in New York. I'm the New England man. I'm vital in New England.

LINDA But you're sixty years old. They can't expect you to keep traveling every week.

WILLY I'll have to send a wire to Portland. I'm supposed to see Brown and Morrison tomorrow morning at ten o'clock to show the line. Goddammit, I could sell them! (*He starts putting on his jacket.*)

LINDA (*taking the jacket from him*) Why don't you go down to the place tomorrow and tell Howard you've simply got to work in New York? You're too accommodating, dear.

WILLY If old man Wagner was alive I'd a been in charge of New York now! That man was a prince, he was a masterful man. But that boy of his, that Howard, he don't appreciate. When I went north the first time, the Wagner Company didn't know where New England was!

LINDA Why don't you tell those things to Howard, dear?

WILLY (*encouraged*) I will, I definitely will. Is there any cheese?

LINDA I'll make you a sandwich.

WILLY No, go to sleep. I'll take some milk. I'll be up right away. The boys in?

LINDA They're sleeping. Happy took Biff on a date tonight.

WILLY (*interested*) That so?

LINDA It was so nice to see them shaving together, one behind the other, in the bathroom. And going out together. You notice? The whole house smells of shaving lotion.

WILLY Figure it out. Work a lifetime to pay off a house. You finally own it, and there's nobody to live in it.

LINDA Well, dear, life is a casting off. It's always that way.

WILLY No, no, some people—some people accomplish something. Did Biff say anything after I went this morning?

LINDA You shouldn't have criticized him, Willy, especially after he just got off the train. You mustn't lose your temper with him.

WILLY When the hell did I lose my temper? I simply asked him if he was making any money. Is that a criticism?

LINDA But, dear, how could he make any money?

WILLY (*worried and angered*) There's such an undercurrent in him. He became a moody man. Did he apologize when I left this morning?

LINDA He was crestfallen, Willy. You know how he admires you. I think if he finds himself, then you'll both be happier and not fight any more.

WILLY How can he find himself on a farm? Is that a life? A farmhand? In the beginning, when he was young, I thought, well, a young man, it's good for him to tramp around, take a lot of different jobs. But it's more than ten years now and he has yet to make thirty-five dollars a week!

LINDA He's finding himself, Willy.

WILLY Not finding yourself at the age of thirty-four is a disgrace!

LINDA Shh!

WILLY The trouble is he's lazy, goddammit!

LINDA Willy, please!

WILLY Biff is a lazy bum!

LINDA They're sleeping. Get something to eat. Go on down.

WILLY Why did he come home? I would like to know what brought him home.

LINDA I don't know. I think he's still lost, Willy. I think he's very lost.

WILLY Biff Loman is lost. In the greatest country in the world a young man with such—personal attractiveness, gets lost. And such a hard worker. There's one thing about Biff—he's not lazy.

LINDA Never.

WILLY (*with pity and resolve*) I'll see him in the morning; I'll have a nice talk with him. I'll get him a job selling. He could be big in no time. My God! Remember how they used to follow him around in high school? When he smiled at one of them their faces lit up. When he walked down the street . . . (*He loses himself in reminiscences.*)

LINDA (*trying to bring him out of it*) Willy, dear, I got a new kind of American-type cheese today. It's whipped.

WILLY Why do you get American when I like Swiss?

LINDA I just thought you'd like a change—

WILLY I don't want a change! I want Swiss cheese. Why am I always being contradicted?

LINDA (*with a covering laugh*) I thought it would be a surprise.

WILLY Why don't you open a window in here, for God's sake?

LINDA (*with infinite patience*) They're all open, dear.

WILLY The way they boxed us in here. Bricks and windows, windows and bricks.

LINDA We should've bought the land next door.

WILLY The street is lined with cars. There's not a breath of fresh air in the neighborhood. The grass don't grow any more, you can't raise a carrot in the back yard. They should've had a law against apartment houses. Remember those two beautiful elm trees out there? When I and Biff hung the swing between them?

LINDA Yeah, like being a million miles from the city.

WILLY They should've arrested the builder for cutting those down. They massacred the neighborhood. (*lost*) More and more I think of those days, Linda. This time of year it was lilac and wisteria. And then the peonies would come out, and the daffodils. What fragrance in this room!

LINDA Well, after all, people had to move somewhere.

WILLY No, there's more people now.

LINDA I don't think there's more people. I think—

WILLY There's more people! That's what's ruining this country! Population is getting out of control. The competition is maddening! Smell the stink from that apartment house! And another one on the other side . . . How can they whip cheese?

(*On* WILLY's *last line,* BIFF *and* HAPPY *raise themselves up in their beds, listening.*)

LINDA Go down, try it. And be quiet.

WILLY (*turning to* LINDA, *guiltily*) You're not worried about me, are you, sweetheart?

BIFF What's the matter?

HAPPY Listen!

LINDA You've got too much on the ball to worry about.

WILLY You're my foundation and my support, Linda.

LINDA Just try to relax, dear. You make mountains out of molehills.

WILLY I won't fight with him any more. If he wants to go back to Texas, let him go.

LINDA He'll find his way.

WILLY Sure. Certain men just don't get started till later in life. Like Thomas Edison, I think. Or B. F. Goodrich. One of them was deaf. (*He starts for the bedroom doorway.*) I'll put my money on Biff.

LINDA And Willy—if it's warm Sunday we'll drive in the country. And we'll open the windshield, and take lunch.

WILLY No, the windshields don't open on the new cars.

LINDA But you opened it today.

WILLY Me? I didn't. (*He stops.*) Now isn't that peculiar! Isn't that a remarkable— (*He breaks off in amazement and fright as the flute is heard distantly.*)

LINDA What, darling?

WILLY That is the most remarkable thing.

LINDA What, dear?

WILLY I was thinking of the Chevvy. (*slight pause*) Nineteen twenty-eight . . . when I had that red Chevvy— (*breaks off*) That funny? I coulda sworn I was driving that Chevvy today.

LINDA Well, that's nothing. Something must've reminded you.

WILLY Remarkable. Ts. Remember those days? The way Biff used to simonize that car? The dealer refused to believe there was eighty thousand miles on it. (*He shakes his head.*) Heh! (*to* LINDA) Close your eyes, I'll be right up. (*He walks out of the bedroom.*)

HAPPY (*to* BIFF) Jesus, maybe he smashed up the car again!

LINDA (*calling after* WILLY) Be careful on the stairs, dear! The cheese is on the middle shelf! (*She turns, goes over to the bed, takes his jacket, and goes out of the bedroom.*)

(*Light has risen on the boys' room. Unseen,* WILLY *is heard talking to himself, "Eighty thousand miles," and a little laugh.* BIFF *gets out of bed, comes downstage a bit, and stands attentively.* BIFF *is two years older than his brother* HAPPY, *well built, but in these days bears a worn air and seems less self-assured. He has succeeded less, and his dreams are stronger and less acceptable than* HAPPY's. HAPPY *is tall, powerfully made. Sexuality is like a visible color on him, or a scent that many women have discovered. He, like his brother, is lost, but in a different way, for he has never allowed himself to turn his face toward defeat and is thus more confused and hard-skinned, although seemingly more content.*)

HAPPY (*getting out of bed*) He's going to get his license taken away if he keeps that up. I'm getting nervous about him, y'know, Biff?

BIFF His eyes are going.

HAPPY No, I've driven with him. He sees all right. He just doesn't keep his mind on it. I drove into the city with him last week. He stops at a green light and then it turns red and he goes. (*He laughs.*)

BIFF Maybe he's color-blind.

HAPPY Pop? Why he's got the finest eye for color in the business. You know that.

BIFF (*sitting down on his bed*) I'm going to sleep.

HAPPY You're not still sour on Dad, are you, Biff?

BIFF He's all right, I guess.

WILLY (*underneath them, in the living room*) Yes, sir, eighty thousand miles—eighty-two thousand!

BIFF You smoking?

HAPPY (*holding out a pack of cigarettes*) Want one?

BIFF (*taking a cigarette*) I can never sleep when I smell it.

WILLY What a simonizing job, heh!

HAPPY (*with deep sentiment*) Funny, Biff, y'now? Us sleeping in here again? The old beds. (*He pats his bed affectionately.*) All the talk that went across those two beds, huh? Our whole lives.

BIFF Yeah. Lotta dreams and plans.

HAPPY (*with a deep and masculine laugh*) About five hundred women would like to know what was said in this room.

(*They share a soft laugh.*)

BIFF Remember that big Betsy something—what the hell was her name—over on Bushwick Avenue?

HAPPY (*combing his hair*) With the collie dog!

BIFF That's the one. I got you in there, remember?

HAPPY Yeah, that was my first time—I think. Boy, there was a pig! (*They laugh, almost crudely.*) You taught me everything I know about women. Don't forget that.

BIFF I bet you forgot how bashful you used to be. Especially with girls.

HAPPY Oh, I still am, Biff.

BIFF Oh, go on.

HAPPY I just control it, that's all. I think I got less bashful and you got more so. What happened, Biff? Where's the old humor, the old confidence? (*He shakes* BIFF's *knee.* BIFF *gets up and moves restlessly about the room.*) What's the matter?

BIFF Why does Dad mock me all the time?

HAPPY He's not mocking you, he—

BIFF Everything I say there's a twist of mockery on his face. I can't get near him.

HAPPY He just wants you to make good, that's all. I wanted to talk to you about Dad for a long time, Biff. Something's—happening to him. He—talks to himself.

BIFF I noticed that this morning. But he always mumbled.

HAPPY But not so noticeable. It got so embarrassing I sent him to Florida. And you know something? Most of the time he's talking to you.

BIFF What's he say about me?

HAPPY I can't make it out.

BIFF What's he say about me?

HAPPY I think the fact that you're not settled, that you're still kind of up in the air . . .

BIFF There's one or two other things depressing him, Happy.

HAPPY What do you mean?

BIFF Never mind. Just don't lay it all on me.

HAPPY But I think if you just got started—I mean—is there any future for you out there?

BIFF I tell ya, Hap, I don't know what the future is. I don't know—what I'm supposed to want.

HAPPY What do you mean?

BIFF Well, I spent six or seven years after high school trying to work myself up. Shipping clerk, salesman, business of one kind or another. And it's a measly manner of existence. To get on that subway on the hot mornings in summer. To devote your whole life to keeping stock, or making phone calls, or selling or buying. To suffer fifty weeks of the year for the sake of a two-week vacation, when all you really desire is to be outdoors, with your shirt off. And always to have to get ahead of the next fella. And still—that's how you build a future.

HAPPY Well, you really enjoy it on a farm? Are you content out there?

BIFF (*with rising agitation*) Hap, I've had twenty or thirty different kinds of jobs since I left home before the war, and it always turns out the same. I just realized it lately. In Nebraska when I herded cattle, and the Dakotas, and Arizona, and now in Texas. It's why I came home now, I guess, because I realized it. This farm I work on, it's spring there now, see? And they've got about fifteen new colts. There's nothing more inspiring or—beautiful than the sight of a mare and a new colt. And it's cool there now, see? Texas is cool now, and it's spring. And whenever spring comes to where I am, I suddenly get the feeling, my God, I'm not gettin' anywhere! What the hell am I doing, playing around with horses, twenty-eight dollars a week! I'm thirty-four years old, I oughta be makin' my future. That's when I come running home. And now, I get here, and I don't know what to do with myself. (*after a pause*) I've always made a point of not wasting my life, and everytime I come back here I know that all I've done is to waste my life.

HAPPY You're a poet, you know that, Biff? You're a—you're an idealist!

BIFF No, I'm mixed up very bad. Maybe I oughta get married. Maybe I oughta get stuck into something. Maybe that's my trouble. I'm like a boy. I'm not married, I'm not in business, I just—I'm like a boy. Are you content, Hap? You're a success, aren't you? Are you content?

HAPPY Hell, no!

BIFF Why? You're making money, aren't you?

HAPPY (*moving about with energy, expressiveness*) All I can do now is wait for the merchandise manager to die. And suppose I get to be merchandise manager? He's a good friend of mine, and he just built a terrific estate on Long Island. And he lived there about two months and sold it, and now he's building another one. He can't enjoy it once it's finished. And I know that's just what I would do. I don't know what the hell I'm workin' for. Sometimes I sit in my apartment—all alone. And I think of the rent I'm paying. And it's crazy. But then, it's what I always wanted. My own apartment, a car, and plenty of women. And still, goddammit, I'm lonely.

BIFF (*with enthusiasm*) Listen, why don't you come out West with me?

HAPPY You and I, heh?

BIFF Sure, maybe we could buy a ranch. Raise cattle, use our muscles. Men built like we are should be working out in the open.

HAPPY (*avidly*) The Loman Brothers, heh?

BIFF (*with vast affection*) Sure, we'd be known all over the counties!

HAPPY (*enthralled*) That's what I dream about, Biff. Sometimes I want to just rip my clothes off in the middle of the store and outbox that goddam merchandise manager. I mean I can outbox, outrun, and outlift anybody in that store, and I have to take orders from those common, petty sons-of-bitches till I can't stand it any more.

BIFF I'm tellin' you, kid, if you were with me I'd be happy out there.

HAPPY (*enthused*) See, Biff, everybody around me is so false that I'm constantly lowering my ideals . . .

BIFF Baby, together we'd stand up for one another, we'd have someone to trust.

HAPPY If I were around you—

BIFF Hap, the trouble is we weren't brought up to grub for money. I don't know how to do it.

HAPPY Neither can I!

BIFF Then let's go!

HAPPY The only thing is—what can you make out there?

BIFF But look at your friend. Builds an estate and then hasn't the peace of mind to live in it.

HAPPY Yeah, but when he walks into the store the waves part in front of him. That's fifty-two thousand dollars a year coming through the revolving door, and I got more in my pinky finger than he's got in his head.

BIFF Yeah, but you just said—

HAPPY I gotta show some of those pompous, self-important executives over there that Hap Loman can make the grade. I want to walk into the store the way he walks in. Then I'll go with you, Biff. We'll be together yet, I swear. But take those two we had tonight. Now weren't they gorgeous creatures?

BIFF Yeah, yeah, most gorgeous I've had in years.

HAPPY I get that any time I want, Biff. Whenever I feel disgusted. The only trouble is, it gets like bowling or something. I just keep knockin' them over and it doesn't mean anything. You still run around a lot?

BIFF Naa. I'd like to find a girl—steady, somebody with substance.

HAPPY That's what I long for.

BIFF Go on! You'd never come home.

HAPPY I would! Somebody with character, with resistance! Like Mom, y'know? You're gonna call me a bastard when I tell you this. That girl Charlotte I was with tonight is engaged to be married in five weeks. (*He tries on his new hat.*)

BIFF No kiddin'!

HAPPY Sure, the guy's in line for the vice-presidency of the store. I don't know what gets into me, maybe I just have an overdeveloped sense of competition or something, but I went and ruined her, and furthermore I can't get rid of her. And he's the third executive I've done that to. Isn't that a crummy characteristic? And to top it all, I go to their weddings! (*indignantly, but laughing*) Like I'm not supposed to take bribes. Manufacturers offer me a hundred-dollar bill now and then to throw an order their way. You know how honest I am, but it's like this girl, see. I hate myself for it. Because I don't want the girl, and, still, I take it and—I love it!

BIFF Let's go to sleep.

HAPPY I guess we didn't settle anything, heh?

BIFF I just got one idea that I think I'm going to try.

HAPPY What's that?

BIFF Remember Bill Oliver?

HAPPY Sure, Oliver is very big now. You want to work for him again?

BIFF No, but when I quit he said something to me. He put his arm on my shoulder, and he said, "Biff, if you ever need anything, come to me."

HAPPY I remember that. That sounds good.

BIFF I think I'll go to see him. If I could get ten thousand or even seven or eight thousand dollars I could buy a beautiful ranch.

HAPPY I bet he'd back you. 'Cause he thought highly of you, Biff. I mean, they all do. You're well liked, Biff. That's why I say to come back here, and we both have the apartment. And I'm tellin' you, Biff, any babe you want . . .

BIFF No, with a ranch I could do the work I like and still be something. I just wonder though. I wonder if Oliver still thinks I stole that carton of basketballs.

HAPPY Oh, he probably forgot that long ago. It's almost ten years. You're too sensitive. Anyway, he didn't really fire you.

BIFF Well, I think he was going to. I think that's why I quit. I was never sure whether he knew or not. I know he thought the world of me, though. I was the only one he'd let lock up the place.

WILLY (*below*) You gonna wash the engine, Biff?

HAPPY Shh!

(BIFF *looks at* HAPPY, *who is gazing down, listening.* WILLY *is mumbling in the parlor.*)

HAPPY You hear that?

(*They listen.* WILLY *laughs warmly.*)

BIFF (*growing angry*) Doesn't he know Mom can hear that?

WILLY Don't get your sweater dirty, Biff!

(*A look of pain crosses* BIFF*'s face.*)

HAPPY Isn't that terrible? Don't leave again, will you? You'll find a job here. You gotta stick around. I don't know what to do about him, it's getting embarrassing.

WILLY What a simonizing job!

BIFF Mom's hearing that!

WILLY No kiddin', Biff, you got a date? Wonderful!

HAPPY Go on to sleep. But talk to him in the morning, will you?

BIFF (*reluctantly getting into bed*) With her in the house. Brother!

HAPPY (*getting into bed*) I wish you'd have a good talk with him.

(*The light on their room begins to fade.*)

BIFF (*to himself in bed*) That selfish, stupid . . .

HAPPY Sh . . . Sleep, Biff.

(*Their light is out. Well before they have finished speaking,* WILLY'S *form is dimly seen below in the darkened kitchen. He opens the refrigerator, searches in there, and takes out a bottle of milk. The apartment houses are fading out, and the entire house and surroundings become covered with leaves. Music insinuates itself as the leaves appear.*)

WILLY Just wanna be careful with those girls, Biff, that's all. Don't make any promises. No promises of any kind. Because a girl, y'know, they always believe what you tell 'em, and you're very young, Biff, you're too young to be talking seriously to girls.

(*Light rises on the kitchen.* WILLY, *talking, shuts the refrigerator door and comes downstage to the kitchen table. He pours milk into a glass. He is totally immersed in himself, smiling faintly.*)

WILLY Too young entirely, Biff. You want to watch your schooling first. Then when you're all set, there'll be plenty of girls for a boy like you. (*He smiles broadly at a kitchen chair.*) That so? The girls pay for you? (*He laughs.*) Boy, you must really be makin' a hit.

(WILLY *is gradually addressing—physically—a point offstage, speaking through the wall of the kitchen, and his voice has been rising in volume to that of a normal conversation.*)

WILLY I been wondering why you polish the car so careful. Ha! Don't leave the hubcaps, boys. Get the chamois to the hubcaps. Happy, use newspaper on the windows, it's the easiest thing. Show him how to do it, Biff! You see, Happy? Pad it up, use it like a pad. That's it, that's it, good work. You're doin' all right, Hap. (*He pauses, then nods in approbation for a few seconds, then looks upward.*) Biff, first thing we gotta do when we get time is clip that big branch over the house. Afraid it's gonna fall in a storm and hit the roof. Tell you what. We get a rope and sling her around, and then we climb up there with a couple of saws and take her down. Soon as you finish the car, boys, I wanna see ya. I got a surprise for you, boys.

BIFF (*offstage*) Whatta ya got, Dad?

WILLY No, you finish first. Never leave a job till you're finished—remember that. (*looking toward the "big trees"*) Biff, up in Albany I saw a beautiful hammock. I think I'll buy it next trip, and we'll hang it right between those two elms. Wouldn't that be something? Just swingin' there under those branches. Boy, that would be . . .

(*Young* Biff *and Young* Happy *appear from the direction* Willy *was addressing.* Happy *carries rags and a pail of water.* Biff, *wearing a sweater with a block "S," carries a football.*)

BIFF (*pointing in the direction of the car offstage*) How's that, Pop, professional?

WILLY Terrific. Terrific job, boys. Good work, Biff.

HAPPY Where's the surprise, Pop?

WILLY In the back seat of the car.

HAPPY Boy! (*He runs off.*)

BIFF What is it, Dad? Tell me, what'd you buy?

WILLY (*laughing, cuffs him*) Never mind, something I want you to have.

BIFF (*turns and starts off*) What is it, Hap?

HAPPY (*offstage*) It's a punching bag!

BIFF Oh, Pop!

WILLY It's got Gene Tunney's signature on it!

(Happy *runs onstage with a punching bag.*)

BIFF Gee, how'd you know we wanted a punching bag?

WILLY Well, it's the finest thing for the timing.

HAPPY (*lies down on his back and pedals with his feet*) I'm losing weight, you notice, Pop?

WILLY (*to* Happy) Jumping rope is good too.

BIFF Did you see the new football I got?

WILLY (*examining the ball*) Where'd you get a new ball?

BIFF The coach told me to practice my passing.

WILLY That so? And he gave you the ball, heh?

BIFF Well, I borrowed it from the locker room. (*He laughs confidentially.*)

WILLY (*laughing with him at the theft*) I want you to return that.

HAPPY I told you he wouldn't like it!

BIFF (*angrily*) Well, I'm bringing it back!

WILLY (*stopping the incipient argument, to* Happy) Sure, he's gotta practice with a regulation ball, doesn't he? (*to* Biff) Coach'll probably congratulate you on your initiative!

BIFF Oh, he keeps congratulating my initiative all the time, Pop.

WILLY That's because he likes you. If somebody else took that ball there'd be an uproar. So what's the report, boys, what's the report?

BIFF Where'd you go this time, Dad? Gee we were lonesome for you.

WILLY (*pleased, puts an arm around each boy and they come down to the apron*) Lonesome, heh?

BIFF Missed you every minute.

WILLY Don't say? Tell you a secret, boys. Don't breathe it to a soul. Someday I'll have my own business, and I'll never have to leave home any more.

HAPPY Like Uncle Charley, heh?

WILLY Bigger than Uncle Charley! Because Charley is not—liked. He's liked, but he's not—well liked.

BIFF Where'd you go this time, Dad?

WILLY Well, I got on the road, and I went north to Providence. Met the Mayor.

BIFF The Mayor of Providence!

WILLY He was sitting in the hotel lobby.

BIFF What'd he say?

WILLY He said, "Morning!" And I said, "You got a fine city here, Mayor." And then he had coffee with me. And then I went to Waterbury. Waterbury is a fine city. Big clock city, the famous Waterbury clock. Sold a nice bill there. And then Boston—Boston is the cradle of the Revolution. A fine city. And a couple of other towns in Mass., and on to Portland and Bangor and straight home!

BIFF Gee, I'd love to go with you sometime, Dad.

WILLY Soon as summer comes.

HAPPY Promise?

WILLY You and Hap and I, and I'll show you all the towns. America is full of beautiful towns and fine, upstanding people. And they know me, boys, they know me up and down New England. The finest people. And when I bring you fellas up, there'll be open sesame for all of us, 'cause one thing, boys: I have friends. I can park my car in any street in New England, and the cops protect it like their own. This summer, heh?

BIFF and HAPPY (*together*) Yeah! You bet!

WILLY We'll take our bathing suits.

HAPPY We'll carry your bags, Pop!

WILLY Oh, won't that be something! Me comin' into the Boston stores with you boys carryin' my bags. What a sensation!

(BIFF *is prancing around, practicing passing the ball.*)

WILLY You nervous, Biff, about the game?

BIFF Not if you're gonna be there.

WILLY What do they say about you in school, now that they made you captain?

HAPPY There's a crowd of girls behind him everytime the classes change.

BIFF (*taking* WILLY's *hand*) This Saturday, Pop, this Saturday—just for you, I'm going to break through for a touchdown.

HAPPY You're supposed to pass.

BIFF I'm takin' one play for Pop. You watch me, Pop, and when I take off my helmet, that means I'm breakin' out. Then you watch me crash through that line!

WILLY (*kisses* BIFF) Oh, wait'll I tell this in Boston!

(BERNARD *enters in knickers. He is younger than* BIFF, *earnest and loyal, a worried boy.*)

BERNARD Biff, where are you? You're supposed to study with me today.

WILLY Hey, looka Bernard. What're you lookin' so anemic about, Bernard?

BERNARD He's gotta study, Uncle Willy. He's got Regents next week.

HAPPY (*tauntingly, spinning* BERNARD *around*) Let's box, Bernard!

BERNARD Biff! (*He gets away from* HAPPY.) Listen, Biff, I heard Mr. Birnbaum say that if you don't start studyin' math he's gonna flunk you, and you won't graduate. I heard him!

WILLY You better study with him, Biff. Go ahead now.

BERNARD I heard him!

BIFF Oh, Pop, you didn't see my sneakers! (*He holds up a foot for* WILLY *to look at.*)

WILLY Hey, that's a beautiful job of printing!

BERNARD (*wiping his glasses*) Just because he printed University of Virginia on his sneakers doesn't mean they've got to graduate him, Uncle Willy!

WILLY (*angrily*) What're you talking about? With scholarships to three universities they're gonna flunk him?

BERNARD But I heard Mr. Birnbaum say—

WILLY Don't be a pest, Bernard! (*to his boys*) What an anemic!

BERNARD Okay, I'm waiting for you in my house, Biff.

(BERNARD *goes off. The* LOMANS *laugh.*)

WILLY Bernard is not well liked, is he?

BIFF He's liked, but he's not well liked.

HAPPY That's right, Pop.

WILLY That's just what I mean. Bernard can get the best marks in school, y'understand, but when he gets out in the business world, y'understand, you are going to be five times ahead of him. That's why I thank Almighty God you're both built like Adonises. Because the man who makes an appearance in the business world, the man who creates personal interest, is the man who gets ahead. Be liked and you will never want. You take me, for instance, I never have to wait in line to see a buyer. "Willy Loman is here!" That's all they have to know, and I go right through.

BIFF Did you knock them dead, Pop?

WILLY Knocked 'em cold in Providence, slaughtered 'em in Boston.

HAPPY (*on his back, pedaling again*) I'm losing weight, you notice, Pop?

(LINDA *enters, as of old, a ribbon in her hair, carrying a basket of washing.*)

LINDA (*with youthful energy*) Hello, dear!

WILLY Sweetheart!

LINDA How'd the Chevvy run?

WILLY Chevrolet, Linda, is the greatest car ever built. (*to the boys*) Since when do you let your mother carry wash up the stairs?

BIFF Grab hold there, boy!

HAPPY Where to, Mom?

LINDA Hang them up on the line. And you better go down to your friends, Biff. The cellar is full of boys. They don't know what to do with themselves.

BIFF Ah, when Pop comes home they can wait!

WILLY (*laughs appreciatively*) You better go down and tell them what to do, Biff.

BIFF I think I'll have them sweep out the furnace room.

WILLY Good work, Biff.

BIFF (*goes through wall-line of kitchen to doorway at back and calls down*) Fellas! Everybody sweep out the furnace room! I'll be right down!

VOICES All right! Okay, Biff.

BIFF George and Sam and Frank, come out back! We're hangin' up the wash! Come on, Hap, on the double! (*He and* HAPPY *carry out the basket.*)

LINDA The way they obey him!

WILLY Well, that's training, the training. I'm tellin' you, I was sellin' thousands and thousands, but I had to come home.

LINDA Oh, the whole block'll be at that game. Did you sell anything?

WILLY I did five hundred gross in Providence and seven hundred gross in Boston.

LINDA No! Wait a minute, I've got a pencil. (*She pulls pencil and paper out of her apron pocket.*) That makes your commission . . . Two hundred—my God! Two hundred and twelve dollars!

WILLY Well, I didn't figure it yet, but . . .

LINDA How much did you do?

WILLY Well, I—I did—about a hundred and eighty gross in Providence. Well, no—it came to—roughly two hundred gross on the whole trip.

LINDA (*without hesitation*) Two hundred gross. That's . . . (*She figures.*)

WILLY The trouble was that three of the stores were half closed for inventory in Boston. Otherwise I woulda broke records.

LINDA Well, it makes seventy dollars and some pennies. That's very good.

WILLY What do we owe?

LINDA Well, on the first there's sixteen dollars on the refrigerator—

WILLY Why sixteen?

LINDA Well, the fan belt broke, so it was a dollar eighty.

WILLY But it's brand new.

LINDA Well, the man said that's the way it is. Till they work themselves in, y'know.

(*They move through the wall-line into the kitchen.*)

WILLY I hope we didn't get stuck on that machine.

LINDA They got the biggest ads of any of them!

WILLY I know, it's a fine machine. What else?

LINDA Well, there's nine-sixty for the washing machine. And for the vacuum cleaner there's three and a half due on the fifteenth. Then the roof, you got twenty-one dollars remaining.

WILLY It don't leak, does it?

LINDA No, they did a wonderful job. Then you owe Frank for the carburetor.

WILLY I'm not going to pay that man! That goddam Chevrolet, they ought to prohibit the manufacture of that car!

LINDA Well, you owe him three and a half. And odds and ends, comes to around a hundred and twenty dollars by the fifteenth.

WILLY A hundred and twenty dollars! My God, if business don't pick up I don't know what I'm gonna do!

LINDA Well, next week you'll do better.

WILLY Oh, I'll knock 'em dead next week. I'll go to Hartford. I'm very well liked in Hartford. You know, the trouble is, Linda, people don't seem to take to me.

(*They move onto the forestage.*)

LINDA Oh, don't be foolish.

WILLY I know it when I walk in. They seem to laugh at me.

LINDA Why? Why would they laugh at you? Don't talk that way, Willy.

(WILLY *moves to the edge of the stage.* LINDA *goes into the kitchen and starts to darn stockings.*)

WILLY I don't know the reason for it, but they just pass me by. I'm not noticed.

LINDA But you're doing wonderful, dear. You're making seventy to a hundred dollars a week.

WILLY But I gotta be at it ten, twelve hours a day. Other men—I don't know—they do it easier. I don't know why—I can't stop myself—I talk too much. A man oughta come in with a few words. One thing about Charley. He's a man of few words, and they respect him.

LINDA You don't talk too much, you're just lively.

WILLY (*smiling*) Well, I figure, what the hell, life is short, a couple of jokes. (*to himself*) I joke too much! (*The smile goes.*)

LINDA Why? You're—

WILLY I'm fat. I'm very—foolish to look at, Linda. I didn't tell you, but Christmas time I happened to be calling on F. H. Stewarts, and a salesman I know, as I was going in to see the buyer I heard him say something about—walrus. And I—I cracked him right across the face. I won't take that. I simply will not take that. But they do laugh at me. I know that.

LINDA Darling . . .

WILLY I gotta overcome it. I know I gotta overcome it. I'm not dressing to advantage, maybe.

LINDA Willy, darling, you're the handsomest man in the world—

WILLY Oh, no, Linda.

LINDA To me you are. (*slight pause*) The handsomest.

(*From the darkness is heard the laughter of a woman.* WILLY *doesn't turn to it, but it continues through* LINDA'*s lines.*)

LINDA And the boys, Willy. Few men are idolized by their children the way you are.

(*Music is heard as behind a scrim, to the left of the house.* THE WOMAN, *dimly seen, is dressing.*)

WILLY (*with great feeling*) You're the best there is, Linda, you're a pal, you know that? On the road—on the road I want to grab you sometimes and just kiss the life outa you.

(*The laughter is loud now, and he moves into a brightening area at the left, where* THE WOMAN *has come from behind the scrim and is standing, putting on her hat, looking into a "mirror" and laughing.*)

WILLY 'Cause I get so lonely—especially when business is bad and there's nobody to talk to. I get the feeling that I'll never sell anything again, that I won't make a living for you, or a business, a business for the boys. (*He talks through* THE WOMAN'S *subsiding laughter;* THE WOMAN *primps at the "mirror."*) There's so much I want to make for—

THE WOMAN Me? You didn't make me, Willy. I picked you.

WILLY (*pleased*) You picked me?

THE WOMAN (*who is quite proper-looking,* WILLY'S *age*) I did. I've been sitting at that desk watching all the salesmen go by, day in, day out. But you've got such a sense of humor, and we do have such a good time together, don't we?

WILLY Sure, sure. (*He takes her in his arms.*) Why do you have to go now?

THE WOMAN It's two o'clock . . .

WILLY No, come on in! (*He pulls her.*)

THE WOMAN . . . my sisters'll be scandalized. When'll you be back?

WILLY Oh, two weeks about. Will you come up again?

THE WOMAN Sure thing. You do make me laugh. It's good for me. (*She squeezes his arm, kisses him.*) And I think you're a wonderful man.

WILLY You picked me, heh?

THE WOMAN Sure. Because you're so sweet. And such a kidder.

WILLY Well, I'll see you next time I'm in Boston.

THE WOMAN I'll put you right through to the buyers.

WILLY (*slapping her bottom*) Right. Well, bottoms up!

THE WOMAN (*slaps him gently and laughs*) You just kill me, Willy. (*He suddenly grabs her and kisses her roughly.*) You kill me. And thanks for the stockings. I love a lot of stockings. Well, good night.

WILLY Good night. And keep your pores open!

THE WOMAN Oh, Willy!

(THE WOMAN *bursts out laughing, and* LINDA'S *laughter blends in.* THE WOMAN *disappears into the dark. Now the area at the kitchen table brightens.* LINDA *is sitting where she was at the kitchen table, but now is mending a pair of her silk stockings.*)

LINDA You are, Willy. The handsomest man. You've got no reason to feel that—

WILLY (*coming out of* THE WOMAN's *dimming area and going over to* LINDA) I'll make it all up to you, Linda. I'll—

LINDA There's nothing to make up, dear. You're doing fine, better than—

WILLY (*noticing her mending*) What's that?

LINDA Just mending my stockings. They're so expensive—

WILLY (*angrily, taking them from her*) I won't have you mending stockings in this house! Now throw them out!

(LINDA *puts the stockings in her pocket.*)

BERNARD (*entering on the run*) Where is he? If he doesn't study!

WILLY (*moving to the forestage, with great agitation*) You'll give him the answers!

BERNARD I do, but I can't on a Regents! That's a state exam! They're liable to arrest me!

WILLY Where is he? I'll whip him, I'll whip him!

LINDA And he'd better give back that football, Willy, it's not nice.

WILLY Biff! Where is he? Why is he taking everything?

LINDA He's too rough with the girls, Willy. All the mothers are afraid of him!

WILLY I'll whip him!

BERNARD He's driving the car without a license!

(THE WOMAN's *laugh is heard.*)

WILLY Shut up!

LINDA All the mothers—

WILLY Shut up!

BERNARD (*backing quietly away and out*) Mr. Birnbaum says he's stuck up.

WILLY Get outa here!

BERNARD If he doesn't buckle down he'll flunk math! (*He goes off.*)

LINDA He's right, Willy, you've gotta—

WILLY (*exploding at her*) There's nothing the matter with him! You want him to be a worm like Bernard? He's got spirit, personality . . .

(*As he speaks,* LINDA, *almost in tears, exits into the living room.* WILLY *is alone in the kitchen, wilting and staring. The leaves are gone. It is night again, and the apartment houses look down from behind.*)

WILLY Loaded with it. Loaded! What is he stealing? He's giving it back, isn't he? Why is he stealing? What did I tell him? I never in my life told him anything but decent things.

(HAPPY *in pajamas has come down the stairs;* WILLY *suddenly becomes aware of* HAPPY's *presence.*)

HAPPY Let's go now, come on.

WILLY (*sitting down at the kitchen table*) Huh! Why did she have to wax the floors herself? Everytime she waxes the floors she keels over. She knows that!

HAPPY Shh! Take it easy. What brought you back tonight?

WILLY I got an awful scare. Nearly hit a kid in Yonkers. God! Why didn't I go to Alaska with my brother Ben that time! Ben! That man was a genius, that man was success incarnate! What a mistake! He begged me to go.

HAPPY Well, there's no use in—

WILLY You guys! There was a man started with the clothes on his back and ended up with diamond mines!

HAPPY Boy, someday I'd like to know how he did it.

WILLY What's the mystery? The man knew what he wanted and went out and got it! Walked into a jungle, and comes out, the age of twenty-one, and he's rich! The world is an oyster, but you don't crack it open on a mattress!

HAPPY Pop, I told you I'm gonna retire you for life.

WILLY You'll retire me for life on seventy goddam dollars a week? And your women and your car and your apartment, and you'll retire me for life! Christ's sake, I couldn't get past Yonkers today! Where are you guys, where are you? The woods are burning! I can't drive a car!

(CHARLEY *has appeared in the doorway. He is a large man, slow of speech, laconic, immovable. In all he says, despite what he says, there is pity, and, now, trepidation. He has a robe over pajamas, slippers on his feet. He enters the kitchen.*)

CHARLEY Everything all right?

HAPPY Yeah, Charley, everything's . . .

WILLY What's the matter?

CHARLEY I heard some noise. I thought something happened. Can't we do something about the walls? You sneeze in here, and in my house hats blow off.

HAPPY Let's go to bed, Dad. Come on.

(CHARLEY *signals to* HAPPY *to go.*)

WILLY You go ahead, I'm not tired at the moment.

HAPPY (*to* WILLY) Take it easy, huh? (*He exits.*)

WILLY What're you doin' up?

CHARLEY (*sitting down at the kitchen table opposite* WILLY) Couldn't sleep good. I had a heartburn.

WILLY Well, you don't know how to eat.

CHARLEY I eat with my mouth.

WILLY No, you're ignorant. You gotta know about vitamins and things like that.

CHARLEY Come on, let's shoot. Tire you out a little.

WILLY (*hesitantly*) All right. You got cards?

CHARLEY (*taking a deck from his pocket*) Yeah, I got them. Someplace. What is it with those vitamins?

WILLY (*dealing*) They build up your bones. Chemistry.

CHARLEY Yeah, but there's no bones in a heartburn.

WILLY What are you talkin' about? Do you know the first thing about it?

CHARLEY Don't get insulted.

WILLY Don't talk about something you don't know anything about.

(*They are playing. Pause.*)

CHARLEY What're you doin' home?

WILLY A little trouble with the car.

CHARLEY Oh. (*pause*) I'd like to take a trip to California.

WILLY Don't say.

CHARLEY You want a job?

WILLY I got a job. I told you that. (*after a slight pause*) What the hell are you offering me a job for?

CHARLEY Don't get insulted.

WILLY Don't insult me.

CHARLEY I don't see no sense in it. You don't have to go on this way.

WILLY I got a good job. (*slight pause*) What do you keep comin' in here for?

CHARLEY You want me to go?

WILLY (*after a pause, withering*) I can't understand it. He's going back to Texas again. What the hell is that?

CHARLEY Let him go.

WILLY I got nothin' to give him, Charley. I'm clean, I'm clean.

CHARLEY He won't starve. None a them starve. Forget about him.

WILLY Then what have I got to remember?

CHARLEY You take it too hard. To hell with it. When a deposit bottle is broken you don't get your nickel back.

WILLY That's easy enough for you to say.

CHARLEY That ain't easy for me to say.

WILLY Did you see the ceiling I put up in the living room?

CHARLEY Yeah, that's a piece of work. To put up a ceiling is a mystery to me. How do you do it?

WILLY What's the difference?

CHARLEY Well, talk about it.

WILLY You gonna put up a ceiling?

CHARLEY How could I put up a ceiling?

WILLY Then what the hell are you bothering me for?

CHARLEY You're insulted again.

WILLY A man who can't handle tools is not a man. You're disgusting.

CHARLEY Don't call me disgusting, Willy.

(UNCLE BEN, *carrying a valise and an umbrella, enters the forestage from around the right corner of the house. He is a stolid man, in his sixties, with a mustache and an authoritative air. He is utterly certain of his destiny, and there is an aura of far places about him. He enters exactly as* WILLY *speaks.*)

WILLY I'm getting awfully tired, Ben.

(BEN's *music is heard.* BEN *looks around at everything.*)

CHARLEY Good, keep playing; you'll sleep better. Did you call me Ben?

(BEN *looks at his watch.*)

WILLY That's funny. For a second there you reminded me of my brother Ben.

BEN I only have a few minutes. (*He strolls, inspecting the place.* WILLY *and* CHARLEY *continue playing.*)

CHARLEY You never heard from him again, heh? Since that time?

WILLY Didn't Linda tell you? Couple of weeks ago we got a letter from his wife in Africa. He died.

CHARLEY That so.

BEN (*chuckling*) So this is Brooklyn, eh?

CHARLEY Maybe you're in for some of his money.

WILLY Naa, he had seven sons. There's just one opportunity I had with that man . . .

BEN I must make a train, William. There are several properties I'm looking at in Alaska.

WILLY Sure, sure! If I'd gone with him to Alaska that time, everything would've been totally different.

CHARLEY Go on, you'd froze to death up there.

WILLY What're you talking about?

BEN Opportunity is tremendous in Alaska, William. Surprised you're not up there.

WILLY Sure, tremendous.

CHARLEY Heh?

WILLY There was the only man I ever met who knew the answers.

CHARLEY Who?

BEN How are you all?

WILLY (*taking a pot, smiling*) Fine, fine.

CHARLEY Pretty sharp tonight.

BEN Is Mother living with you?

WILLY No, she died a long time ago.

CHARLEY Who?

BEN That's too bad. Fine specimen of a lady, Mother.

WILLY (*to* CHARLEY) Heh?

BEN I'd hoped to see the old girl.

CHARLEY Who died?

BEN Heard anything from Father, have you?

WILLY (*unnerved*) What do you mean, who died?

CHARLEY (*taking a pot*) What're you talkin' about?

BEN (*looking at his watch*) William, it's half-past eight!

WILLY (*as though to dispel his confusion he angrily stops* CHARLEY'S *hand*) That's my build!

CHARLEY I put the ace—

WILLY If you don't know how to play the game I'm not gonna throw my money away on you!

CHARLEY (*rising*) It was my ace, for God's sake!

WILLY I'm through, I'm through!

BEN When did Mother die?

WILLY Long ago. Since the beginning you never knew how to play cards.

CHARLEY (*picks up the cards and goes to the door*) All right! Next time I'll bring a deck with five aces.

WILLY I don't play that kind of game!

CHARLEY (*turning to him*) You ought to be ashamed of yourself!

WILLY Yeah?

CHARLEY Yeah! (*He goes out.*)

WILLY (*slamming the door after him*) Ignoramus!

BEN (*as* WILLY *comes toward him through the wall-line of the kitchen*) So you're William.

WILLY (*shaking* BEN'S *hand*) Ben! I've been waiting for you so long! What's the answer? How did you do it?

BEN Oh, there's a story in that.

(LINDA *enters the forestage, as of old, carrying the wash basket.*)

LINDA Is this Ben?

BEN (*gallantly*) How do you do, my dear.

LINDA Where've you been all these years? Willy's always wondered why you—

WILLY (*pulling* BEN *away from her impatiently*) Where is Dad? Didn't you follow him? How did you get started?

BEN Well, I don't know how much you remember.

WILLY Well, I was just a baby, of course, only three or four years old—

BEN Three years and eleven months.

WILLY What a memory, Ben!

BEN I have many enterprises, William, and I have never kept books.

WILLY I remember I was sitting under the wagon in—was it Nebraska?

BEN It was South Dakota, and I gave you a bunch of wild flowers.

WILLY I remember you walking away down some open road.

BEN (*laughing*) I was going to find Father in Alaska.

WILLY Where is he?

BEN At that age I had a very faulty view of geography, William. I discovered after a few days that I was heading due south, so instead of Alaska, I ended up in Africa.

LINDA Africa!

WILLY The Gold Coast!

BEN Principally diamond mines.

LINDA Diamond mines!

BEN Yes, my dear. But I've only a few minutes—

WILLY No! Boys! Boys! (*Young* BIFF *and* HAPPY *appear.*) Listen to this. This is your Uncle Ben, a great man! Tell my boys, Ben!

BEN Why, boys, when I was seventeen I walked into the jungle, and when I was twenty-one I walked out. (*He laughs.*) And by God I was rich.

WILLY (*to the boys*) You see what I been talking about? The greatest things can happen!

BEN (*glancing at his watch*) I have an appointment in Ketchikan Tuesday week.

WILLY No, Ben! Please tell about Dad. I want my boys to hear. I want them to know the kind of stock they spring from. All I remember is a man with a big beard, and I was in Mamma's lap, sitting around a fire, and some kind of high music.

BEN His flute. He played the flute.

WILLY Sure, the flute, that's right!

(*New music is heard, a high, rollicking tune.*)

BEN Father was a very great and a very wild-hearted man. We would start in Boston, and he'd toss the whole family into the wagon, and then he'd drive the team right across the country; through Ohio, and Indiana, Michigan, Illinois, and all the Western states. And we'd stop in the towns and sell the flutes that he'd made on the way. Great inventor, Father. With one gadget he made more in a week than a man like you could make in a lifetime.

WILLY That's just the way I'm bringing them up, Ben—rugged, well liked, all-around.

BEN Yeah? (*to* BIFF) Hit that, boy—hard as you can. (*He pounds his stomach.*)

BIFF Oh, no, sir!

BEN (*taking boxing stance*) Come on, get to me! (*He laughs.*)

WILLY Go to it, Biff! Go ahead, show him!

BIFF Okay! (*He cocks his fists and starts in.*)

LINDA (*to* WILLY) Why must he fight, dear?

BEN (*sparring with* BIFF) Good boy! Good boy!

WILLY How's that, Ben, heh?

HAPPY Give him the left, Biff!

LINDA Why are you fighting?

BEN Good boy! (*suddenly comes in, trips* BIFF, *and stands over him, the point of his umbrella poised over* BIFF*'s eye*)

LINDA Look out, Biff!

BIFF Gee!

BEN (*patting* BIFF's *knee*) Never fight fair with a stranger, boy. You'll never get out of the jungle that way. (*taking* LINDA's *hand and bowing*) It was an honor and a pleasure to meet you, Linda.

LINDA (*withdrawing her hand coldly, frightened*) Have a nice—trip.

BEN (*to* WILLY) And good luck with your—what do you do?

WILLY Selling.

BEN Yes. Well . . . (*He raises his hand in farewell to all.*)

WILLY No, Ben, I don't want you to think . . . (*He takes* BEN's *arm to show him.*) It's Brooklyn, I know, but we hunt too.

BEN Really, now.

WILLY Oh, sure, there's snakes and rabbits and—that's why I moved out here. Why, Biff can fell any one of these trees in no time! Boys! Go right over to where they're building the apartment house and get some sand. We're gonna rebuild the entire front stoop right now! Watch this, Ben!

BIFF Yes, sir! On the double, Hap!

HAPPY (*as he and* BIFF *run off*) I lost weight, Pop, you notice?

(CHARLEY *enters in knickers, even before the boys are gone.*)

CHARLEY Listen, if they steal any more from that building the watchman'll put the cops on them!

LINDA (*to* WILLY) Don't let Biff . . .

(BEN *laughs lustily.*)

WILLY You shoulda seen the lumber they brought home last week. At least a dozen six-by-tens worth all kinds a money.

CHARLEY Listen, if that watchman—

WILLY I gave them hell, understand. But I got a couple of fearless characters there.

CHARLEY Willy, the jails are full of fearless characters.

BEN (*clapping* WILLY *on the back, with a laugh at* CHARLEY) And the stock exchange, friend!

WILLY (*joining in* BEN's *laughter*) Where are the rest of your pants?

CHARLEY My wife bought them.

WILLY Now all you need is a golf club and you can go upstairs and go to sleep. (*to* BEN) Great athlete! Between him and his son Bernard they can't hammer a nail!

BERNARD (*rushing in*) The watchman's chasing Biff!

WILLY (*angrily*) Shut up! He's not stealing anything!

LINDA (*alarmed, hurrying off left*) Where is he? Biff, dear! (*She exits.*)

WILLY (*moving toward the left, away from* BEN) There's nothing wrong. What's the matter with you?

BEN Nervy boy. Good!

WILLY (*laughing*) Oh, nerves of iron, that Biff!

CHARLEY Don't know what it is. My New England man comes back and he's bleedin', they murdered him up there.

WILLY It's contacts, Charley, I got important contacts!

CHARLEY (*sarcastically*) Glad to hear it, Willy. Come in later, we'll shoot a little casino. I'll take some of your Portland money. (*He laughs at* WILLY *and exits.*)

WILLY (*turning to* BEN) Business is bad, it's murderous. But not for me, of course.

BEN I'll stop by on my way back to Africa.

WILLY (*longingly*) Can't you stay a few days? You're just what I need, Ben, because I—I have a fine position here, but I—well, Dad left when I was such a baby and I never had a chance to talk to him and I still feel—kind of temporary about myself.

BEN I'll be late for my train.

(*They are at opposite ends of the stage.*)

WILLY Ben, my boys—can't we talk? They'd go into the jaws of hell for me, see, but I—

BEN William, you're being first-rate with your boys. Outstanding, manly chaps!

WILLY (*hanging on to his words*) Oh, Ben, that's good to hear! Because sometimes I'm afraid that I'm not teaching them the right kind of—Ben, how should I teach them?

BEN (*giving great weight to each word, and with a certain vicious audacity*) William, when I walked into the jungle, I was seventeen. When I walked out I was twenty-one. And, by God, I was rich! (*He goes off into darkness around the right corner of the house.*)

WILLY . . .was rich! That's just the spirit I want to imbue them with! To walk into a jungle! I was right! I was right! I was right!

(BEN *is gone, but* WILLY *is still speaking to him as* LINDA, *in nightgown and robe, enters the kitchen, glances around for* WILLY, *then goes to the door of the house, looks out and sees him. Comes down to his left. He looks at her.*)

LINDA Willy, dear? Willy?

WILLY I was right!

LINDA Did you have some cheese? (*He can't answer.*) It's very late, darling. Come to bed, heh?

WILLY (*looking straight up*) Gotta break your neck to see a star in this yard.

LINDA You coming in?

WILLY Whatever happened to that diamond watch fob? Remember? When Ben came from Africa that time? Didn't he give me a watch fob with a diamond in it?

LINDA You pawned it, dear. Twelve, thirteen years ago. For Biff's radio correspondence course.

WILLY Gee, that was a beautiful thing. I'll take a walk.

LINDA But you're in your slippers.

WILLY (*starting to go around the house at the left*) I was right! I was! (*half to* LINDA, *as he goes, shaking his head*) What a man! There was a man worth talking to! I was right!

LINDA (*calling after* WILLY) But in your slippers, Willy!

(WILLY *is almost gone when* BIFF, *in his pajamas, comes down the stairs and enters the kitchen.*)

BIFF What is he doing out there?

LINDA Sh!

BIFF God Almighty, Mom, how long has he been doing this?

LINDA Don't, he'll hear you.

BIFF What the hell is the matter with him?

LINDA It'll pass by morning.

BIFF Shouldn't we do anything?

LINDA Oh, my dear, you should do a lot of things, but there's nothing to do, so go to sleep.

(HAPPY *comes down the stairs and sits on the steps.*)

HAPPY I never heard him so loud, Mom.

LINDA Well, come around more often; you'll hear him. (*She sits down at the table and mends the lining of* WILLY'S *jacket.*)

BIFF Why didn't you ever write me about this, Mom?

LINDA How would I write to you? For over three months you had no address.

BIFF I was on the move. But you know I thought of you all the time. You know that, don't you, pal?

LINDA I know, dear, I know. But he likes to have a letter. Just to know that there's still a possibility for better things.

BIFF He's not like this all the time, is he?

LINDA It's when you come home he's always the worst.

BIFF When I come home?

LINDA When you write you're coming, he's all smiles, and talks about the future, and—he's just wonderful. And then the closer you seem to come, the more shaky he gets, and then, by the time you get here, he's arguing, and he seems angry at you. I think it's just that maybe he can't bring himself to—to open up to you. Why are you so hateful to each other? Why is that?

BIFF (*evasively*) I'm not hateful, Mom.

LINDA But you no sooner come in the door than you're fighting!

BIFF I don't know why. I mean to change. I'm tryin', Mom, you understand?

LINDA Are you home to stay now?

BIFF I don't know. I want to look around, see what's doin'.

LINDA Biff, you can't look around all your life, can you?

BIFF I just can't take hold, Mom. I can't take hold of some kind of a life.

LINDA Biff, a man is not a bird, to come and go with the springtime.

BIFF Your hair . . . (*He touches her hair.*) Your hair got so gray.

LINDA Oh, it's been gray since you were in high school. I just stopped dyeing it, that's all.

BIFF Dye it again, will ya? I don't want my pal looking old. (*He smiles.*)

LINDA You're such a boy! You think you can go away for a year and . . . You've got to get it into your head now that one day you'll knock on this door and there'll be strange people here—

BIFF What are you talking about? You're not even sixty, Mom.

LINDA But what about your father?

BIFF (*lamely*) Well, I meant him too.

HAPPY He admires Pop.

LINDA Biff, dear, if you don't have any feeling for him, then you can't have any feeling for me.

BIFF Sure I can, Mom.

LINDA No. You can't just come to see me, because I love him. (*with a threat, but only a threat, of tears*) He's the dearest man in the world to me, and I won't have anyone making him feel unwanted and low and blue. You've got to make up your mind now, darling, there's no leeway any more. Either he's your father and you pay him that respect, or else you're not to come here. I know he's not easy to get along with—nobody knows that better than me—but . . .

WILLY (*from the left, with a laugh*) Hey, hey, Biffo!

BIFF (*starting to go out after* WILLY) What the hell is the matter with him? (HAPPY *stops him.*)

LINDA Don't—don't go near him!

BIFF Stop making excuses for him! He always, always wiped the floor with you. Never had an ounce of respect for you.

HAPPY He's always had respect for—

BIFF What the hell do you know about it?

HAPPY (*surlily*) Just don't call him crazy!

BIFF He's got no character—Charley wouldn't do this. Not in his own house—spewing out that vomit from his mind.

HAPPY Charley never had to cope with what he's got to.

BIFF People are worse off than Willy Loman. Believe me, I've seen them!

LINDA Then make Charley your father, Biff. You can't do that, can you? I don't say he's a great man. Willy Loman never made a lot of money. His name was never in the paper. He's not the finest character that ever lived. But he's a human being, and a terrible thing is happening to him. So attention must be paid. He's not to be allowed to fall into his grave like an old dog. Attention, attention must be finally paid to such a person. You called him crazy—

BIFF I didn't mean—

LINDA No, a lot of people think he's lost his—balance. But you don't have to be very smart to know what his trouble is. The man is exhausted.

HAPPY Sure!

LINDA A small man can be just as exhausted as a great man. He works for a company thirty-six years this March, opens up unheard-of territories to their trademark, and now in his old age they take his salary away.

HAPPY (*indignantly*) I didn't know that, Mom.

LINDA You never asked, my dear! Now that you get your spending money someplace else you don't trouble your mind with him.

HAPPY But I gave you money last—

LINDA Christmas time, fifty dollars! To fix the hot water it cost ninety-seven fifty! For five weeks he's been on straight commission, like a beginner, an unknown!

BIFF Those ungrateful bastards!

LINDA Are they any worse than his sons? When he brought them business, when he was young, they were glad to see him. But now his old friends, the old buyers that loved him so and always found some order to hand him in a pinch—they're all dead, retired. He used to be able to make six, seven calls a day in Boston. Now he takes his valises out of the car and puts them back and takes them out again and he's exhausted. Instead of walking he talks now. He drives seven hundred miles, and when he gets there no one knows him any more, no one welcomes him. And what goes through a man's mind, driving seven hundred miles home without having earned a cent? Why shouldn't he talk to himself? Why? When he has to go to Charley and borrow fifty dollars a week and pretend to me that it's his pay? How long can that go on? How long? You see what I'm sitting here and waiting for? And you tell me he has no character? The man who never worked a day but for your benefit? When does he get the medal for that? Is this his reward—to turn around at the age of sixty-three and find his sons, who he loved better than his life, one a philandering bum—

HAPPY Mom!

LINDA That's all you are, my baby! (*to* BIFF) And you! What happened to the love you had for him? You were such pals! How you used to talk to him on the phone every night! How lonely he was till he could come home to you!

BIFF All right, Mom. I'll live here in my room, and I'll get a job. I'll keep away from him, that's all.

LINDA No, Biff. You can't stay here and fight all the time.

BIFF He threw me out of this house, remember that.

LINDA Why did he do that? I never knew why.

BIFF Because I know he's a fake and he doesn't like anybody around who knows!

LINDA Why a fake? In what way? What do you mean?

BIFF Just don't lay it all at my feet. It's between me and him—that's all I have to say. I'll chip in from now on. He'll settle for half my pay check. He'll be all right. I'm going to bed. (*He starts for the stairs.*)

LINDA He won't be all right.

BIFF (*turning on the stairs, furiously*) I hate this city and I'll stay here. Now what do you want?

LINDA He's dying, Biff.

(HAPPY *turns quickly to her, shocked.*)

BIFF (*after a pause*) Why is he dying?

LINDA He's been trying to kill himself.

BIFF (*with great horror*) How?

LINDA I live from day to day.

BIFF What're you talking about?

LINDA Remember I wrote you that he smashed up the car again? In February?

BIFF Well?

LINDA The insurance inspector came. He said that they have evidence. That all these accidents in the last year—weren't—weren't—accidents.

HAPPY How can they tell that? That's a lie.

LINDA It seems there's a woman . . . (*She takes a breath as* . . .)

BIFF (*sharply but contained*) What woman?
LINDA (*simultaneously*) . . . and this woman . . .

LINDA What?

BIFF Nothing. Go ahead.

LINDA What did you say?

BIFF Nothing. I just said what woman?

HAPPY What about her?

LINDA Well, it seems she was walking down the road and saw his car. She says that he wasn't driving fast at all, and that he didn't skid. She says he came to that little bridge, and then deliberately smashed into the railing, and it was only the shallowness of the water that saved him.

BIFF Oh, no, he probably just fell asleep again.

LINDA I don't think he fell asleep.

BIFF Why not?

LINDA Last month . . . (*with great difficulty*) Oh, boys, it's so hard to say a thing like this! He's just a big stupid man to you, but I tell you there's more good in him than in many other people. (*She chokes, wipes her eyes.*) I was looking for a fuse. The lights blew out, and I went down the cellar. And behind the fuse box—it happened to fall out—was length of rubber pipe—just short.

HAPPY No kidding?

LINDA There's a little attachment on the end of it. I knew right away. And sure enough, on the bottom of the water heater there's a new little nipple on the gas pipe.

HAPPY (*angrily*) That—jerk.

BIFF Did you have it taken off?

LINDA I'm—I'm ashamed to. How can I mention it to him? Every day I go down and take away that little rubber pipe. But, when he comes home, I put it back where it was. How can I insult him that way? I don't know what to do. I live from day to day, boys. I tell you, I know every thought in his mind. It sounds so old-fashioned and silly, but I tell you he put his whole life into you and you've turned your backs on him. (*She is bent over in the chair, weeping, her face in her hands.*) Biff, I swear to God! Biff, his life is in your hands!

HAPPY (*to* BIFF) How do you like that damned fool!

BIFF (*kissing her*) All right, pal, all right. It's all settled now. I've been remiss. I know that, Mom. But now I'll stay, and I swear to you, I'll apply myself. (*kneeling in front of her, in a fever of self-reproach*) It's just—you see, Mom, I don't fit in business. Not that I won't try. I'll try, and I'll make good.

HAPPY Sure you will. The trouble with you in business was you never tried to please people.

BIFF I know, I—

HAPPY Like when you worked for Harrison's. Bob Harrison said you were tops, and then you go and do some damn fool thing like whistling whole songs in the elevator like a comedian.

BIFF (*against* HAPPY) So what? I like to whistle sometimes.

HAPPY You don't raise a guy to a responsible job who whistles in the elevator!

LINDA Well, don't argue about it now.

HAPPY Like when you'd go off and swim in the middle of the day instead of taking the line around.

BIFF (*his resentment rising*) Well, don't you run off? You take off sometimes, don't you? On a nice summer day?

HAPPY Yeah, but I cover myself!

LINDA Boys!

HAPPY If I'm going to take a fade the boss can call any number where I'm supposed to be and they'll swear to him that I just left. I'll tell you something that I hate to say, Biff, but in the business world some of them think you're crazy.

BIFF (*angered*) Screw the business world!

HAPPY All right, screw it! Great, but cover yourself!

LINDA Hap, Hap!

BIFF I don't care what they think! They've laughed at Dad for years, and you know why? Because we don't belong in this nuthouse of a city! We should be mixing cement on some open plain, or—or carpenters. A carpenter is allowed to whistle!

(WILLY *walks in from the entrance of the house, at left.*)

WILLY Even your grandfather was better than a carpenter. (*Pause. They watch him.*) You never grew up. Bernard does not whistle in the elevator, I assure you.

BIFF (*as though to laugh* WILLY *out of it*) Yeah, but you do, Pop.

WILLY I never in my life whistled in an elevator! And who in the business world thinks I'm crazy?

BIFF I didn't mean it like that, Pop. Now don't make a whole thing out of it, will ya?

WILLY Go back to the West! Be a carpenter, a cowboy, enjoy yourself!

LINDA Willy, he was just saying—

WILLY I heard what he said!

HAPPY (*trying to quiet* WILLY) Hey, Pop, come on now . . .

WILLY (*continuing over* HAPPY'S *line*) They laugh at me, heh? Go to Filene's, go to the Hub, go to Slattery's, Boston. Call out the name Willy Loman and see what happens! Big shot!

BIFF All right, Pop.

WILLY Big!

BIFF All right!

WILLY Why do you always insult me?

BIFF I didn't say a word. (*to* LINDA) Did I say a word?

LINDA He didn't say anything, Willy.

WILLY (*going to the doorway of the living room*) All right, good night, good night.

LINDA Willy, dear, he just decided . . .

WILLY (*to* BIFF) If you get tired hanging around tomorrow, paint the ceiling I put up in the living room.

BIFF I'm leaving early tomorrow.

HAPPY He's going to see Bill Oliver, Pop.

WILLY (*interestedly*) Oliver? For what?

BIFF (*with reserve, but trying, trying*) He always said he'd stake me. I'd like to go into business, so maybe I can take him up on it.

LINDA Isn't that wonderful?

WILLY Don't interrupt. What's wonderful about it? There's fifty men in the City of New York who'd stake him. (*to* BIFF) Sporting goods?

BIFF I guess so. I know something about it and—

WILLY He knows something about it! You know sporting goods better than Spalding, for God's sake! How much is he giving you?

BIFF I don't know, I didn't even see him yet, but—

WILLY Then what're you talkin' about?

BIFF (*getting angry*) Well, all I said was I'm gonna see him, that's all!

WILLY (*turning away*) Ah, you're counting your chickens again.

BIFF (*starting left for the stairs*) Oh, Jesus, I'm going to sleep!

WILLY (*calling after him*) Don't curse in this house!

BIFF (*turning*) Since when did you get so clean?

HAPPY (*trying to stop them*) Wait a . . .

WILLY Don't use that language to me! I won't have it!

HAPPY (*grabbing* BIFF, *shouts*) Wait a minute! I got an idea. I got a feasible idea. Come here, Biff, let's talk this over now, let's talk some sense here. When I was down in Florida last time, I thought of a great idea to sell sporting goods. It just came back to me. You and I, Biff—we have a line, the Loman Line. We train a couple of weeks, and put on a couple of exhibitions, see?

WILLY That's an idea!

HAPPY Wait! We form two basketball teams, see? Two waterpolo teams. We play each other. It's a million dollars' worth of publicity. Two brothers, see? The Loman Brothers. Displays in the Royal Palms—all the hotels. And banners over the ring and the basketball court: "Loman Brothers." Baby, we could sell sporting goods!

WILLY That is a one-million-dollar idea!

LINDA Marvelous!

BIFF I'm in great shape as far as that's concerned.

HAPPY And the beauty of it is, Biff, it wouldn't be like a business. We'd be out playin' ball again . . .

BIFF (*enthused*) Yeah, that's . . .

WILLY Million-dollar . . .

HAPPY And you wouldn't get fed up with it, Biff. It'd be the family again. There'd be the old honor, and comradeship, and if you wanted to go off for a swim or somethin'—well, you'd do it! Without some smart cooky gettin' up ahead of you!

WILLY Lick the world! You guys together could absolutely lick the civilized world.

BIFF I'll see Oliver tomorrow. Hap, if we could work that out . . .

LINDA Maybe things are beginning to—

WILLY (*wildly enthused, to* LINDA) Stop interrupting! (*to* BIFF) But don't wear sport jacket and slacks when you see Oliver.

BIFF No, I'll—

WILLY A business suit, and talk as little as possible, and don't crack any jokes.

BIFF He did like me. Always liked me.

LINDA He loved you!

WILLY (*to* LINDA) Will you stop! (*to* BIFF) Walk in very serious. You are not applying for a boy's job. Money is to pass. Be quiet, fine, and serious. Everybody likes a kidder, but nobody lends him money.

HAPPY I'll try to get some myself, Biff. I'm sure I can.

WILLY I see great things for you kids, I think your troubles are over. But remember, start big and you'll end big. Ask for fifteen. How much you gonna ask for?

BIFF Gee, I don't know—

WILLY And don't say "Gee." "Gee" is a boy's word. A man walking in for fifteen thousand dollars does not say "Gee!"

BIFF Ten, I think, would be top though.

WILLY Don't be so modest. You always started too low. Walk in with a big laugh. Don't look worried. Start off with a couple of your good stories to lighten things up. It's not what you say, it's how you say it—because personality always wins the day.

LINDA Oliver always thought the highest of him—

WILLY Will you let me talk?

BIFF Don't yell at her, Pop, will ya?

WILLY (*angrily*) I was talking, wasn't I?

BIFF I don't like you yelling at her all the time, and I'm tellin' you, that's all.

WILLY What're you, takin' over this house?

LINDA Willy—

WILLY (*turning on her*) Don't take his side all the time, goddammit!

BIFF (*furiously*) Stop yelling at her!

WILLY (*suddenly pulling on his cheek, beaten down, guilt ridden*) Give my best to Bill Oliver—he may remember me. (*He exits through the living-room doorway.*)

LINDA (*her voice subdued*) What'd you have to start that for? (BIFF *turns away.*) You see how sweet he was as soon as you talked hopefully? (*She goes over to* BIFF.) Come up and say good night to him. Don't let him go to bed that way.

HAPPY Come on, Biff, let's buck him up.

LINDA Please, dear. Just say good night. It takes so little to make him happy. Come. (*She goes through the living-room doorway, calling upstairs from within the living room.*) Your pajamas are hanging in the bathroom, Willy!

HAPPY (*looking toward where* LINDA *went out*) What a woman! They broke the mold when they made her. You know that, Biff?

BIFF He's off salary. My God, working on commission!

HAPPY Well, let's face it: he's no hot-shot selling man. Except that sometimes, you have to admit, he's a sweet personality.

BIFF (*deciding*) Lend me ten bucks, will ya? I want to buy some new ties.

HAPPY I'll take you to a place I know. Beautiful stuff. Wear one of my striped shirts tomorrow.

BIFF She got gray. Mom got awful old. Gee, I'm gonna go in to Oliver tomorrow and knock him for a—

HAPPY Come on up. Tell that to Dad. Let's give him a whirl. Come on.

BIFF (*steamed up*) You know, with ten thousand bucks, boy!

HAPPY (*as they go into the living room*) That's the talk, Biff, that's the first time I've heard the old confidence out of you! (*from within the living room, fading off*) You're gonna live with me, kid, and any babe you want just say the word . . .

(*The last lines are hardly heard. They are mounting the stairs to their parents' bedroom.*)

LINDA (*entering her bedroom and addressing* WILLY, *who is in the bathroom. She is straightening the bed for him.*) Can you do anything about the shower? It drips.

WILLY (*from the bathroom*) All of a sudden everything falls to pieces! Goddam plumbing, oughta be sued, those people. I hardly finished putting it in and the thing . . . (*His words rumble off.*)

LINDA I'm just wondering if Oliver will remember him. You think he might?

WILLY (*coming out of the bathroom in his pajamas*) Remember him? What's the matter with you, you crazy? If he'd've stayed with Oliver he'd be on top by now! Wait'll Oliver gets a look at him. You don't know the average caliber any more. The average young man today—(*he is getting into bed*)—is got a caliber of zero. Greatest thing in the world for him was to bum around.

(BIFF *and* HAPPY *enter the bedroom. Slight pause.*)

WILLY (*stops short, looking at* BIFF) Glad to hear it, boy.

HAPPY He wanted to say good night to you, sport.

WILLY (*to* BIFF) Yeah. Knock him dead, boy. What'd you want to tell me?

BIFF Just take it easy, Pop. Good night. (*He turns to go.*)

WILLY (*unable to rest*) And if anything falls off the desk while you're talking to him—like a package or something—don't you pick it up. They have office boys for that.

LINDA I'll make a big breakfast—

WILLY Will you let me finish? (*to* BIFF) Tell him you were in the business in the West. Not farm work.

BIFF All right, Dad.

LINDA I think everything—

WILLY (*going right through her speech*) And don't undersell yourself. No less than fifteen thousand dollars.

BIFF (*unable to bear him*) Okay. Good night, Mom. (*He starts moving.*)

WILLY Because you got a greatness in you, Biff, remember that. You got all kinds a greatness . . . (*He lies back, exhausted.* BIFF *walks out.*)

LINDA (*calling after* BIFF) Sleep well, darling!

HAPPY I'm gonna get married, Mom. I wanted to tell you.

LINDA Go to sleep, dear.

HAPPY (*going*) I just wanted to tell you.

WILLY Keep up the good work. (HAPPY *exits.*) God . . . remember that Ebbets Field game? The championship of the city?

LINDA Just rest. Should I sing to you?

WILLY Yeah. Sing to me. (LINDA *hums a soft lullaby.*) When that team came out—he was the tallest, remember?

LINDA Oh, yes. And in gold.

(BIFF *enters the darkened kitchen, takes a cigarette, and leaves the house. He comes downstage into a golden pool of light. He smokes, staring at the night.*)

WILLY Like a young god. Hercules—something like that. And the sun, the sun all around him. Remember how he waved to me? Right up from the field, with the representatives of three colleges standing by? And the buyers I brought, and the cheers when he came out—Loman, Loman, Loman! God almighty, he'll be great yet. A star like that, magnificent, can never really fade away!

(*The light on* WILLY *is fading. The gas heater begins to glow through the kitchen wall, near the stairs, a blue flame beneath red coils.*)

LINDA (*timidly*) Willy dear, what has he got against you?

WILLY I'm so tired. Don't talk any more.

(BIFF *slowly returns to the kitchen. He stops, stares toward the heater.*)

LINDA Will you ask Howard to let you work in New York?

WILLY First thing in the morning. Everything'll be all right.

(BIFF *reaches behind the heater and draws out a length of rubber tubing. He is horrified and turns his head toward* WILLY*'s room, still dimly lit, from which the strains of* LINDA*'s desperate but monotonous humming rise.*)

WILLY (*staring through the window into the moonlight*) Gee, look at the moon moving between the buildings!

(BIFF *wraps the tubing around his hand and quickly goes up the stairs.*)

Curtain

Act II

Music is heard, gay and bright. The curtain rises as the music fades away. **WILLY,** *in shirt sleeves, is sitting at the kitchen table, sipping coffee, his hat in his lap.* **LINDA** *is filling his cup when she can.*

WILLY Wonderful coffee. Meal in itself.

LINDA Can I make you some eggs?

WILLY No. Take a breath.

LINDA You look so rested, dear.

WILLY I slept like a dead one. First time in months. Imagine, sleeping till ten on a Tuesday morning. Boys left nice and early, heh?

LINDA They were out of here by eight o'clock.

WILLY Good work!

LINDA It was so thrilling to see them leaving together. I can't get over the shaving lotion in this house!

WILLY (*smiling*) Mmm—

LINDA Biff was very changed this morning. His whole attitude seemed to be hopeful. He couldn't wait to get downtown to see Oliver.

WILLY He's heading for a change. There's no question, there simply are certain men that take longer to get—solidified. How did he dress?

LINDA His blue suit. He's so handsome in that suit. He could be a—anything in that suit!

(WILLY *gets up from the table.* LINDA *holds his jacket for him.*)

WILLY There's no question, no question at all. Gee, on the way home tonight I'd like to buy some seeds.

LINDA (*laughing*) That'd be wonderful. But not enough sun gets back there. Nothing'll grow any more.

WILLY You wait, kid, before it's all over we're gonna get a little place out in the country, and I'll raise some vegetables, a couple of chickens . . .

LINDA You'll do it yet, dear.

(WILLY *walks out of his jacket.* LINDA *follows him.*)

WILLY And they'll get married, and come for a weekend. I'd build a little guest house. 'Cause I got so many fine tools, all I'd need would be a little lumber and some peace of mind.

LINDA (*joyfully*) I sewed the lining . . .

WILLY I could build two guest houses, so they'd both come. Did he decide how much he's going to ask Oliver for?

LINDA (*getting him into the jacket*) He didn't mention it, but I imagine ten or fifteen thousand. You going to talk to Howard today?

WILLY Yeah. I'll put it to him straight and simple. He'll just have to take me off the road.

LINDA And Willy, don't forget to ask for a little advance, because we've got the insurance premium. It's the grace period now.

WILLY That's a hundred . . . ?

LINDA A hundred and eight, sixty-eight. Because we're a little short again.

WILLY Why are we short?

LINDA Well, you had the motor job on the car . . .

WILLY That goddam Studebaker!

LINDA And you got one more payment on the refrigerator . . .

WILLY But it just broke again!

LINDA Well, it's old, dear.

WILLY I told you we should've bought a well-advertised machine. Charley bought a General Electric and it's twenty years old and it's still good, that son-of-a-bitch.

LINDA But, Willy—

WILLY Whoever heard of a Hastings refrigerator? Once in my life I would like to own something outright before it's broken! I'm always in a race with the junkyard! I just finished paying for the car and it's on its last legs. The refrigerator consumes belts like a goddam maniac. They time those things. They time them so when you finally paid for them, they're used up.

LINDA (*buttoning up his jacket as he unbuttons it*) All told, about two hundred dollars would carry us, dear. But that includes the last payment on the mortgage. After this payment, Willy, the house belongs to us.

WILLY It's twenty-five years!

LINDA Biff was nine years old when we bought it.

WILLY Well, that's a great thing. To weather a twenty-five year mortgage is—

LINDA It's an accomplishment.

WILLY All the cement, the lumber, the reconstruction I put in this house! There ain't a crack to be found in it any more.

LINDA Well, it served its purpose.

WILLY What purpose? Some stranger'll come along, move in, and that's that. If only Biff would take this house, and raise a family . . . (*He starts to go.*) Good-by, I'm late.

LINDA (*suddenly remembering*) Oh, I forgot! You're supposed to meet them for dinner.

WILLY Me?

LINDA At Frank's Chop House on Forty-eighth near Sixth Avenue.

WILLY Is that so? How about you?

LINDA No, just the three of you. They're gonna blow you to a big meal!

WILLY Don't say! Who thought of that?

LINDA Biff came to me this morning, Willy, and he said, "Tell Dad, we want to blow him to a big meal." Be there six o'clock. You and your two boys are going to have dinner.

WILLY Gee whiz! That's really somethin'. I'm gonna knock Howard for a loop, kid. I'll get an advance, and I'll come home with a New York job. Goddammit, now I'm gonna do it!

LINDA Oh, that's the spirit, Willy!

WILLY I will never get behind a wheel the rest of my life!

LINDA It's changing, Willy, I can feel it changing!

WILLY Beyond a question. G'by, I'm late. (*He starts to go again.*)

LINDA (*calling after him as she runs to the kitchen table for a handkerchief*) You got your glasses?

WILLY (*feels for them, then comes back in*) Yeah, yeah, got my glasses.

LINDA (*giving him the handkerchief*) And a handkerchief.

WILLY Yeah, handkerchief.

LINDA And your saccharine?

WILLY Yeah, my saccharine.

LINDA Be careful on the subway stairs.

(*She kisses him, and a silk stocking is seen hanging from her hand.* WILLY *notices it.*)

WILLY Will you stop mending stockings? At least while I'm in the house. It gets me nervous. I can't tell you. Please.

(LINDA *hides the stocking in her hand as she follows* WILLY *across the forestage in front of the house.*)

LINDA Remember, Frank's Chop House.

WILLY (*passing the apron*) Maybe beets would grow out there.

LINDA (*laughing*) But you tried so many times.

WILLY Yeah. Well, don't work hard today. (*He disappears around the right corner of the house.*)

LINDA Be careful!

(*As* WILLY *vanishes,* LINDA *waves to him. Suddenly the phone rings. She runs across the stage and into the kitchen and lifts it.*)

LINDA Hello? Oh, Biff! I'm so glad you called, I just . . . Yes, sure, I just told him. Yes, he'll be there for dinner at six o'clock, I didn't forget. Listen, I was just dying to tell you. You know that little rubber pipe I told you about? That he connected to the gas heater? I finally decided to go down the cellar this morning and take it away and destroy it. But it's gone! Imagine? He took it away himself, it isn't there! (*She listens.*) When? Oh, then you took it. Oh—nothing, it's just that I'd hoped he'd taken it away himself. Oh, I'm not worried, darling, because this morning he left in such high spirits, it was like the old days! I'm not afraid any more. Did Mr. Oliver see you? . . . Well, you wait there then. And make a nice impression on him, darling. Just don't perspire too much before you see him. And have a nice time with Dad. He may have big news too! . . . That's right, a New York job. And be sweet to him tonight, dear. Be loving to him. Because he's only a little boat looking for a harbor. (*She is trembling with sorrow and joy.*) Oh, that's wonderful, Biff, you'll save his life. Thanks, darling. Just put your arm around him when he comes into the restaurant. Give him a smile. That's the boy . . . Good-by, dear. . . . You got your comb? . . . That's fine. Good-by, Biff dear.

(*In the middle of her speech,* HOWARD WAGNER, *thirty-six, wheels on a small typewriter table on which is a wire-recording machine and proceeds to plug it in. This is on the left forestage. Light slowly fades on* LINDA *as it rises on* HOWARD. HOWARD *is intent on threading the machine and only glances over his shoulder as* WILLY *appears.*)

WILLY Pst! Pst!

HOWARD Hello, Willy, come in.

WILLY Like to have a little talk with you, Howard.

HOWARD Sorry to keep you waiting. I'll be with you in a minute.

WILLY What's that, Howard?

HOWARD Didn't you ever see one of these? Wire recorder.

WILLY Oh. Can we talk a minute?

HOWARD Records things. Just got delivery yesterday. Been driving me crazy, the most terrific machine I ever saw in my life. I was up all night with it.

WILLY What do you do with it?

HOWARD I bought it for dictation, but you can do anything with it. Listen to this. I had it home last night. Listen to what I picked up. The first one is my daughter. Get this. (*He flicks the switch and "Roll out the Barrel" is heard being whistled.*) Listen to that kid whistle.

WILLY That is lifelike, isn't it?

HOWARD Seven years old. Get that tone.

WILLY Ts, ts. Like to ask a little favor if you . . .

(*The whistling breaks off, and the voice of* HOWARD's *daughter is heard.*)

HIS DAUGHTER "Now you, Daddy."

HOWARD She's crazy for me! (*Again the same song is whistled.*) That's me! Ha! (*He winks.*)

WILLY You're very good.

(*The whistling breaks off again. The machine runs silent for a moment.*)

HOWARD Sh! Get this now, this is my son.

HIS SON "The capital of Alabama is Montgomery; the capital of Arizona is Phoenix; the capital of Arkansas is Little Rock; the capital of California is Sacramento . . ." (*and on, and on*)

HOWARD (*holding up five fingers*) Five years old, Willy!

WILLY He'll make an announcer some day!

HIS SON (*continuing*) "The capital . . ."

HOWARD Get that—alphabetical order! (*The machine breaks off suddenly.*) Wait a minute. The maid kicked the plug out.

WILLY It certainly is a—

HOWARD Sh, for God's sake!

HIS SON "It's nine o'clock, Bulova watch time. So I have to go to sleep."

WILLY That really is—

HOWARD Wait a minute! The next is my wife.

(*They wait.*)

HOWARD'S VOICE "Go on, say something." (*pause*) "Well, you gonna talk?"

HIS WIFE "I can't think of anything."

HOWARD'S VOICE "Well, talk—it's turning."

HIS WIFE (*shyly, beaten*) "Hello." (*silence*) "Oh, Howard, I can't talk into this . . ."

HOWARD (*snapping the machine off*) That was my wife.

WILLY That is a wonderful machine. Can we—

HOWARD I tell you, Willy, I'm gonna take my camera, and my bandsaw, and all my hobbies, and out they go. This is the most fascinating relaxation I ever found.

WILLY I think I'll get one myself.

HOWARD Sure, they're only a hundred and a half. You can't do without it. Supposing you wanna hear Jack Benny, see? But you can't be at home at that hour. So you tell the maid to turn the radio on when Jack Benny comes on, and this automatically goes on with the radio . . .

WILLY And when you come home you . . .

HOWARD You can come home twelve o'clock, one o'clock, any time you like, and you get yourself a Coke and sit yourself down, throw the switch, and there's Jack Benny's program in the middle of the night!

WILLY I'm definitely going to get one. Because lots of time I'm on the road, and I think to myself, what I must be missing on the radio!

HOWARD Don't you have a radio in the car?

WILLY Well, yeah, but who ever thinks of turning it on?

HOWARD Say, aren't you supposed to be in Boston?

WILLY That's what I want to talk to you about, Howard. You got a minute? (*He draws a chair in from the wing.*)

HOWARD What happened? What're you doing here?

WILLY Well . . .

HOWARD You didn't crack up again, did you?

WILLY Oh, no. No . . .

HOWARD Geez, you had me worried there for a minute. What's the trouble?

WILLY Well, tell you the truth, Howard. I've come to the decision that I'd rather not travel any more.

HOWARD Not travel! Well, what'll you do?

WILLY Remember, Christmas time, when you had the party here? You said you'd try to think of some spot for me here in town.

HOWARD With us?

WILLY Well, sure.

HOWARD Oh, yeah, yeah. I remember. Well, I couldn't think of anything for you, Willy.

WILLY I tell ya, Howard. The kids are all grown up, y'know. I don't need much any more. If I could take home—well, sixty-five dollars a week, I could swing it.

HOWARD Yeah, but Willy, see I—

WILLY I tell ya why, Howard. Speaking frankly and between the two of us, y'know—I'm just a little tired.

HOWARD Oh, I could understand that, Willy. But you're a road man, Willy, and we do a road business. We've only got a half-dozen salesmen on the floor here.

WILLY God knows, Howard, I never asked a favor of any man. But I was with the firm when your father used to carry you in here in his arms.

HOWARD I know that, Willy, but—

WILLY Your father came to me the day you were born and asked me what I thought of the name of Howard, may he rest in peace.

HOWARD I appreciate that, Willy, but there just is no spot here for you. If I had a spot I'd slam you right in, but I just don't have a single solitary spot.

(*He looks for his lighter.* WILLY *has picked it up and gives it to him. Pause.*)

WILLY (*with increasing anger*) Howard, all I need to set my table is fifty dollars a week.

HOWARD But where am I going to put you, kid?

WILLY Look, it isn't a question of whether I can sell merchandise, is it?

HOWARD No, but it's a business, kid, and everybody's gotta pull his own weight.

WILLY (*desperately*) Just let me tell you a story, Howard—

HOWARD 'Cause you gotta admit, business is business.

WILLY (*angrily*) Business is definitely business, but just listen for a minute. You don't understand this. When I was a boy—eighteen, nineteen—I was already on the road. And there was a question in my mind as to whether selling had a future for me. Because in those days I had a yearning to go to Alaska. See, there were three gold strikes in one month in Alaska, and I felt like going out. Just for the ride, you might say.

HOWARD (*barely interested*) Don't say.

WILLY Oh, yeah, my father lived many years in Alaska. He was an adventurous man. We've got quite a little streak of self-reliance in our family. I thought I'd go out with my older brother and try to locate him, and maybe settle in the North with the old man. And I was almost decided to go, when I met a salesman in the Parker House. His name was Dave Singleman. And he was eighty-four years old, and he'd drummed merchandise in thirty-one states. And old Dave, he'd go up to his room, y'understand, put on his green velvet slippers—I'll never forget—and pick up his phone and call the buyers, and without ever leaving his room, at the age of eighty-four, he made his living. And when I saw that, I realized that selling was the greatest career a man could want. 'Cause what could be more satisfying than to be able to go, at the age of eighty-four, into twenty or thirty different cities, and pick up a phone, and be remembered and loved and helped by so many different people? Do you know? when he died—and by the way he died the death of a salesman, in his green velvet slippers in the smoker of the New York, New Haven and Hartford, going into Boston—when he died, hundreds of salesmen and buyers were at his funeral. Things were sad on a lotta trains for months after that. (*He stands up.* HOWARD *has not looked at him.*) In those days there was personality in it, Howard. There was respect, and comradeship, and gratitude in it. Today, it's all cut and dried, and there's no chance for bringing friendship to bear—or personality. You see what I mean? They don't know me any more.

HOWARD (*moving away, to the right*) That's just the thing, Willy.

WILLY If I had forty dollars a week—that's all I'd need. Forty dollars, Howard.

HOWARD Kid, I can't take blood from a stone, I—

WILLY (*desperation is on him now*) Howard, the year Al Smith was nominated, your father came to me and—

HOWARD (*starting to go off*) I've got to see some people, kid.

WILLY (*stopping him*) I'm talking about your father! There were promises made across this desk! You mustn't tell me you've got people to see—I put thirty-four years into this firm, Howard, and now I can't pay my insurance! You can't eat the orange and throw the peel away—a man is not a piece of fruit! (*after a pause*) Now pay attention. Your father—in 1928 I had a big year. I averaged a hundred and seventy dollars a week in commissions.

HOWARD (*impatiently*) Now, Willy, you never averaged—

WILLY (*banging his hand on the desk*) I averaged a hundred and seventy dollars a week in the year of 1928! And your father came to me—or rather, I was in the office here—it was right over this desk—and he put his hand on my shoulder—

HOWARD (*getting up*) You'll have to excuse me, Willy, I gotta see some people. Pull yourself together. (*going out*) I'll be back in a little while.

(*On* HOWARD's *exit, the light on his chair grows very bright and strange.*)

WILLY Pull myself together! What the hell did I say to him? My God, I was yelling at him! How could I! (WILLY *breaks off, staring at the light, which occupies the chair, animating it. He approaches this chair, standing across the desk from it.*) Frank, Frank, don't you remember what you told me that time? How you put your hand on my shoulder, and Frank . . .

(*He leans on the desk and as he speaks the dead man's name he accidentally switches on the recorder, and instantly:*)

HOWARD'S SON ". . . of New York is Albany. The capital of Ohio is Cincinnati, the capital of Rhode Island is . . ." (*The recitation continues.*)

WILLY (*leaping away with fright, shouting*) Ha! Howard! Howard! Howard!

HOWARD (*rushing in*) What happened?

WILLY (*pointing at the machine, which continues nasally, childishly, with the capital cities*) Shut it off! Shut it off!

HOWARD (*pulling the plug out*) Look, Willy . . .

WILLY (*pressing his hands to his eyes*) I gotta get myself some coffee. I'll get some coffee . . .

(WILLY *starts to walk out.* HOWARD *stops him.*)

HOWARD (*rolling up the cord*) Willy, look . . .

WILLY I'll go to Boston.

HOWARD Willy, you can't go to Boston for us.

WILLY Why can't I go?

HOWARD I don't want you to represent us. I've been meaning to tell you for a long time now.

WILLY Howard, are you firing me?

HOWARD I think you need a good long rest, Willy.

WILLY Howard—

HOWARD And when you feel better, come back, and we'll see if we can work something out.

WILLY But I gotta earn money, Howard. I'm in no position to—

HOWARD Where are your sons? Why don't your sons give you a hand?

WILLY They're working on a very big deal.

HOWARD This is no time for false pride, Willy. You go to your sons and you tell them that you're tired. You've got two great boys, haven't you?

WILLY Oh, no question, no question, but in the meantime . . .

HOWARD Then that's that, heh?

WILLY All right, I'll go to Boston tomorrow.

HOWARD No, no.

WILLY I can't throw myself on my sons. I'm not a cripple!

HOWARD Look, kid, I'm busy this morning.

WILLY (*grasping* HOWARD's *arm*) Howard, you've got to let me go to Boston!

HOWARD (*hard, keeping himself under control*) I've got a line of people to see this morning. Sit down, take five minutes, and pull yourself together, and then go home, will ya? I need the office, Willy. (*He starts to go, turns, remembering the recorder, starts to push off the table holding the recorder.*) Oh, yeah. Whenever you can this week, stop by and drop off the samples. You'll feel better, Willy, and then come back and we'll talk. Pull yourself together, kid, there's people outside.

(HOWARD *exits, pushing the table off left.* WILLY *stares into space, exhausted. Now the music is heard—*BEN's *music—first distantly, then closer, closer. As* WILLY *speaks,* BEN *enters from the right. He carries valise and umbrella.*)

WILLY Oh, Ben, how did you do it? What is the answer? Did you wind up the Alaska deal already?

BEN Doesn't take much time if you know what you're doing. Just a short business trip. Boarding ship in an hour. Wanted to say good-by.

WILLY Ben, I've got to talk to you.

BEN (*glancing at his watch*) Haven't the time, William.

WILLY (*crossing the apron to* BEN) Ben, nothing's working out. I don't know what to do.

BEN Now, look here, William. I've bought timberland in Alaska and I need a man to look after things for me.

WILLY God, timberland! Me and my boys in those grand outdoors!

BEN You've a new continent at your doorstep, William. Get out of these cities, they're full of talk and time payments and courts of law. Screw on your fists and you can fight for a fortune up there.

WILLY Yes, yes! Linda! Linda!

(LINDA *enters as of old, with the wash.*)

LINDA Oh, you're back?

BEN I haven't much time.

WILLY No, wait! Linda, he's got a proposition for me in Alaska.

LINDA But you've got— (*to* BEN) He's got a beautiful job here.

WILLY But in Alaska, kid, I could—

LINDA You're doing well enough, Willy!

BEN (*to* LINDA) Enough for what, my dear?

LINDA (*frightened of* BEN *and angry at him*) Don't say those things to him! Enough to be happy right here, right now. (*to* WILLY, *while* BEN *laughs*) Why must everybody conquer the world? You're well liked, and the boys love you, and someday—(*to* BEN)—why, old man Wagner told him just the other day that if he keeps it up he'll be a member of the firm, didn't he, Willy?

WILLY Sure, sure. I am building something with this firm, Ben, and if a man is building something he must be on the right track, mustn't he?

BEN What are you building? Lay your hand on it. Where is it?

WILLY (*hesitantly*) That's true, Linda, there's nothing.

LINDA Why? (*to* BEN) There's a man eighty-four years old—

WILLY That's right, Ben, that's right. When I look at that man I say, what is there to worry about?

BEN Bah!

WILLY It's true, Ben. All he has to do is go into any city, pick up the phone, and he's making his living and you know why?

BEN (*picking up his valise*) I've got to go.

WILLY (*holding* BEN *back*) Look at this boy!

(BIFF, *in his high school sweater, enters carrying suitcase.* HAPPY *carries* BIFF'S *shoulder guards, gold helmet, and football pants.*)

WILLY Without a penny to his name, three great universities are begging for him, and from there the sky's the limit, because it's not what you do, Ben. It's who you know and the smile on your face! It's contacts, Ben, contacts! The whole wealth of Alaska passes over the lunch table at the Commodore Hotel, and that's the wonder, the wonder of this country, that a man can end with diamonds here on the basis of being liked! (*He turns to* BIFF.) And that's why when you get out on that field today it's important. Because thousands of people will be rooting for you and loving you. (*to* BEN, *who has again begun to leave*) And Ben! when he walks into a business office his name will sound out like a bell and all the doors will open to him! I've seen it, Ben, I've seen it a thousand times! You can't feel it with your hand like timber, but it's there!

BEN Good-by, William.

WILLY Ben, am I right? Don't you think I'm right? I value your advice.

BEN There's a new continent at your doorstep, William. You could walk out rich. Rich! (*He is gone.*)

WILLY We'll do it here, Ben! You hear me? We're gonna do it here!

(*Young* BERNARD *rushes in. The gay music of the Boys is heard.*)

BERNARD Oh, gee, I was afraid you left already!

WILLY Why? What time is it?

BERNARD It's half-past one!

WILLY Well, come on, everybody! Ebbets Field next stop! Where's the pennants? (*He rushes through the wall-line of the kitchen and out into the living-room.*)

LINDA (*to* BIFF) Did you pack fresh underwear?

BIFF (*who has been limbering up*) I want to go!

BERNARD Biff, I'm carrying your helmet, ain't I?

HAPPY No, I'm carrying the helmet.

BERNARD Oh, Biff, you promised me.

HAPPY I'm carrying the helmet.

BERNARD How am I going to get in the locker room?

LINDA Let him carry the shoulder guards. (*She puts her coat and hat on in the kitchen.*)

BERNARD Can I, Biff? 'Cause I told everybody I'm going to be in the locker room.

HAPPY In Ebbets Field it's the clubhouse.

BERNARD I meant the clubhouse. Biff!

HAPPY Biff!

BIFF (*grandly, after a slight pause*) Let him carry the shoulder guards.

HAPPY (*as he gives* BERNARD *the shoulder guards*) Stay close to us now.

(WILLY *rushes in with the pennants.*)

WILLY (*handing them out*) Everybody wave when Biff comes out on the field. (HAPPY *and* BERNARD *run off.*) You set now, boy?

(*The music has died away.*)

BIFF Ready to go, Pop. Every muscle is ready.

WILLY (*at the edge of the apron*) You realize what this means?

BIFF That's right, Pop.

WILLY (*feeling* BIFF'S *muscles*) You're comin' home this afternoon captain of the All-Scholastic Championship Team of the City of New York.

BIFF I got it, Pop. And remember, pal, when I take off my helmet, that touchdown is for you.

WILLY Let's go! (*He is starting out, with his arm around* BIFF, *when* CHARLEY *enters, as of old, in knickers.*) I got no room for you, Charley.

CHARLEY Room? For what?

WILLY In the car.

CHARLEY You goin' for a ride? I wanted to shoot some casino.

WILLY (*furiously*) Casino! (*incredulously*) Don't you realize what today is?

LINDA Oh, he knows, Willy. He's just kidding you.

WILLY That's nothing to kid about!

CHARLEY No, Linda, what's goin' on?

LINDA He's playing in Ebbets Field.

CHARLEY Baseball in this weather?

WILLY Don't talk to him. Come on, come on! (*He is pushing them out.*)

CHARLEY Wait a minute, didn't you hear the news?

WILLY What?

CHARLEY Don't you listen to the radio? Ebbets Field just blew up.

WILLY You go to hell! (CHARLEY *laughs.*) (*pushing them out*) Come on, come on! We're late.

CHARLEY (*as they go*) Knock a homer, Biff, knock a homer!

WILLY (*the last to leave, turning to* CHARLEY) I don't think that was funny, Charley. This is the greatest day of his life.

CHARLEY Willy, when are you going to grow up?

WILLY Yeah, heh? When this game is over, Charley, you'll be laughing out of the other side of your face. They'll be calling him another Red Grange. Twenty-five thousand a year.

CHARLEY (*kidding*) Is that so?

WILLY Yeah, that's so.

CHARLEY Well, then, I'm sorry, Willy. But tell me something.

WILLY What?

CHARLEY Who is Red Grange?

WILLY Put up your hands. Goddam you, put up your hands!

(CHARLEY, *chuckling, shakes his head and walks away, around the left corner of the stage.* WILLY *follows him. The music rises to a mocking frenzy.*)

WILLY Who the hell do you think you are, better than everybody else? You don't know everything, you big, ignorant, stupid . . . Put up your hands!

(*Light rises, on the right side of the forestage, on a small table in the reception room of* CHARLEY'S *office. Traffic sounds are heard.* BERNARD, *now mature, sits whistling to himself. A pair of tennis rackets and an overnight bag are on the floor beside him.*)

WILLY (*offstage*) What are you walking away for? Don't walk away! If you're going to say something say it to my face! I know you laugh at me behind my back. You'll laugh out of the other side of your goddam face after this game. Touchdown! Touchdown! Eighty thousand people! Touchdown! Right between the goal posts.

(BERNARD *is a quiet, earnest, but self-assured young man.* WILLY'S *voice is coming from right upstage now.* BERNARD *lowers his feet off the table and listens.* JENNY, *his father's secretary, enters.*)

JENNY (*distressed*) Say, Bernard, will you go out in the hall?

BERNARD What is that noise? Who is it?

JENNY Mr. Loman. He just got off the elevator.

BERNARD (*getting up*) Who's he arguing with?

JENNY Nobody. There's nobody with him. I can't deal with him any more, and your father gets all upset everytime he comes. I've got a lot of typing to do, and your father's waiting to sign it. Will you see him?

WILLY (*entering*) Touchdown! Touch— (*He sees* JENNY.) Jenny, Jenny, good to see you. How're ya? Workin'? Or still honest?

JENNY Fine. How've you been feeling?

WILLY Not much any more, Jenny. Ha, ha! (*He is surprised to see the rackets.*)

BERNARD Hello, Uncle Willy.

WILLY (*almost shocked*) Bernard! Well, look who's here! (*He comes quickly, guiltily, to* BERNARD *and warmly shakes his hand.*)

BERNARD How are you? Good to see you.

WILLY What are you doing here?

BERNARD Oh, just stopped by to see Pop. Get off my feet till my train leaves. I'm going to Washington in a few minutes.

WILLY Is he in?

BERNARD Yes, he's in his office with the accountant. Sit down.

WILLY (*sitting down*) What're you going to do in Washington?

BERNARD Oh, just a case I've got there, Willy.

WILLY That so? (*indicating the rackets*) You going to play tennis there?

BERNARD I'm staying with a friend who's got a court.

WILLY Don't say. His own tennis court. Must be fine people, I bet.

BERNARD They are, very nice. Dad tells me Biff's in town.

WILLY (*with a big smile*) Yeah, Biff's in. Working on a very big deal, Bernard.

BERNARD What's Biff doing?

WILLY Well, he's been doing very big things in the West. But he decided to establish himself here. Very big. We're having dinner. Did I hear your wife had a boy?

BERNARD That's right. Our second.

WILLY Two boys! What do you know!

BERNARD What kind of a deal has Biff got?

WILLY Well, Bill Oliver—very big sporting-goods man—he wants Biff very badly. Called him in from the West. Long distance, carte blanche, special deliveries. Your friends have their own private tennis court?

BERNARD You still with the old firm, Willy?

WILLY (*after a pause*) I'm—I'm overjoyed to see how you made the grade, Bernard, overjoyed. It's an encouraging thing to see a young man really—really—Looks very good for Biff—very— (*He breaks off, then.*) Bernard— (*He is so full of emotion, he breaks off again.*)

BERNARD What is it, Willy?

WILLY (*small and alone*) What—what's the secret?

BERNARD What secret?

WILLY How—how did you? Why didn't he ever catch on?

BERNARD I wouldn't know that, Willy.

WILLY (*confidentially, desperately*) You were his friend, his boyhood friend. There's something I don't understand about it. His life ended after that Ebbets Field game. From the age of seventeen nothing good ever happened to him.

BERNARD He never trained himself for anything.

WILLY But he did, he did. After high school he took so many correspondence courses. Radio mechanics; television; God knows what, and never made the slightest mark.

BERNARD (*taking off his glasses*) Willy, do you want to talk candidly?

WILLY (*rising, faces* BERNARD) I regard you as a very brilliant man, Bernard. I value your advice.

BERNARD Oh, the hell with the advice, Willy. I couldn't advise you. There's just one thing I've always wanted to ask you. When he was supposed to graduate, and the math teacher flunked him—

WILLY Oh, that son-of-a-bitch ruined his life.

BERNARD Yeah, but, Willy, all he had to do was go to summer school and make up that subject.

WILLY That's right, that's right.

BERNARD Did you tell him not to go to summer school?

WILLY Me? I begged him to go. I ordered him to go!

BERNARD Then why wouldn't he go?

WILLY Why? Why! Bernard, that question has been trailing me like a ghost for the last fifteen years. He flunked the subject, and laid down and died like a hammer hit him!

BERNARD Take it easy, kid.

WILLY Let me talk to you—I got nobody to talk to. Bernard, Bernard, was it my fault? Y'see? It keeps going around in my mind, maybe I did something to him. I got nothing to give him.

BERNARD Don't take it so hard.

WILLY Why did he lay down? What is the story there? You were his friend!

BERNARD Willy, I remember, it was June, and our grades came out. And he'd flunked math.

WILLY That son-of-a-bitch!

BERNARD No, it wasn't right then. Biff just got very angry, I remember, and he was ready to enroll in summer school.

WILLY (*surprised*) He was?

BERNARD He wasn't beaten by it at all. But then, Willy, he disappeared from the block for almost a month. And I got the idea that he'd gone up to New England to see you. Did he have a talk with you then?

(WILLY *stares in silence.*)

BERNARD Willy?

WILLY (*with a strong edge of resentment in his voice*) Yeah, he came to Boston. What about it?

BERNARD Well, just that when he came back—I'll never forget this, it always mystifies me. Because I'd thought so well of Biff, even though he'd always taken advantage of me. I loved him, Willy, y'know? And he came back after that month and took his sneakers—remember those sneakers with "University of Virginia" printed on them? He was so proud of those, wore them every day. And he took them down in the cellar, and burned them up in the furnace. We had a fist fight. It lasted at least half an hour. Just the two of us, punching each other down the cellar, and crying right through it. I've often thought of how strange it was that I knew he'd given up his life. What happened in Boston, Willy?

(WILLY *looks at him as at an intruder.*)

BERNARD I just bring it up because you asked me.

WILLY (*angrily*) Nothing. What do you mean, "What happened?" What's that got to do with anything?

BERNARD Well, don't get sore.

WILLY What are you trying to do, blame it on me? If a boy lays down is that my fault?

BERNARD Now, Willy, don't get—

WILLY Well, don't—don't talk to me that way! What does that mean, "What happened?"

(CHARLEY *enters. He is in his vest, and he carries a bottle of bourbon.*)

CHARLEY Hey, you're going to miss that train. (*He waves the bottle.*)

BERNARD Yeah, I'm going. (*He takes the bottle.*) Thanks, Pop. (*He picks up his rackets and bag.*) Good-by, Willy, and don't worry about it. You know, "If at first you don't succeed . . ."

WILLY Yes, I believe in that.

BERNARD But sometimes, Willy, it's better for a man just to walk away.

WILLY Walk away?

BERNARD That's right.

WILLY But if you can't walk away?

BERNARD (*after a slight pause*) I guess that's when it's tough. (*extending his hand*) Good-by, Willy.

WILLY (*shaking* BERNARD's *hand*) Good-by, boy.

CHARLEY (*an arm on* BERNARD's *shoulder*) How do you like this kid? Gonna argue a case in front of the Supreme Court.

BERNARD (*protesting*) Pop!

WILLY (*genuinely shocked, pained, and happy*) No! The Supreme Court!

BERNARD I gotta run. 'By, Dad!

CHARLEY Knock 'em dead, Bernard!

(BERNARD *goes off.*)

WILLY (*as* CHARLEY *takes out his wallet*) The Supreme Court! And he didn't even mention it!

CHARLEY (*counting out money on the desk*) He don't have to—he's gonna do it.

WILLY And you never told him what to do, did you? You never took any interest in him.

CHARLEY My salvation is that I never took any interest in anything. There's some money—fifty dollars. I got an accountant inside.

WILLY Charley, look . . . (*with difficulty*) I got my insurance to pay. If you can manage it—I need a hundred and ten dollars.

(CHARLEY *doesn't reply for a moment; merely stops moving.*)

WILLY I'd draw it from my bank but Linda would know, and I . . .

CHARLEY Sit down, Willy.

WILLY (*moving toward the chair*) I'm keeping an account of everything, remember. I'll pay every penny back. (*He sits.*)

CHARLEY Now listen to me, Willy.

WILLY I want you to know I appreciate . . .

CHARLEY (*sitting down on the table*) Willy, what're you doin'? What the hell is goin' on in your head?

WILLY Why? I'm simply . . .

CHARLEY I offered you a job. You can make fifty dollars a week. And I won't send you on the road.

WILLY I've got a job.

CHARLEY Without pay? What kind of a job is a job without pay? (*He rises.*) Now, look, kid, enough is enough. I'm no genius but I know when I'm being insulted.

WILLY Insulted!

CHARLEY Why don't you want to work for me?

WILLY What's the matter with you? I've got a job.

CHARLEY Then what're you walkin' in here every week for?

WILLY (*getting up*) Well, if you don't want me to walk in here—

CHARLEY I am offering you a job.

WILLY I don't want your goddam job!

CHARLEY When the hell are you going to grow up?

WILLY (*furiously*) You big ignoramus, if you say that to me again I'll rap you one! I don't care how big you are! (*He's ready to fight.*)

(*pause*)

CHARLEY (*kindly, going to him*) How much do you need, Willy?

WILLY Charley, I'm strapped. I'm strapped. I don't know what to do. I was just fired.

CHARLEY Howard fired you?

WILLY That snotnose. Imagine that? I named him. I named him Howard.

CHARLEY Willy, when're you gonna realize that them things don't mean anything? You named him Howard, but you can't sell that. The only thing you got in this world is what you can sell. And the funny thing is that you're a salesman, and you don't know that.

WILLY I've always tried to think otherwise, I guess. I always felt that if a man was impressive, and well liked, that nothing—

CHARLEY Why must everybody like you? Who liked J. P. Morgan? Was he impressive? In a Turkish bath he'd look like a butcher. But with his pockets on he was very well liked. Now listen, Willy, I know you don't like me, and nobody can say I'm in love with you, but I'll give you a job because—just for the hell of it, put it that way. Now what do you say?

WILLY I—I just can't work for you, Charley.

CHARLEY What're you, jealous of me?

WILLY I can't work for you, that's all, don't ask me why.

CHARLEY (*angered, takes out more bills*) You been jealous of me all your life, you damned fool! Here, pay your insurance. (*He puts the money in* WILLY's *hand.*)

WILLY I'm keeping strict accounts.

CHARLEY I've got some work to do. Take care of yourself. And pay your insurance.

WILLY (*moving to the right*) Funny, y'know? After all the highways, and the trains, and the appointments, and the years, you end up worth more dead than alive.

CHARLEY Willy, nobody's worth nothin' dead. (*after a slight pause*) Did you hear what I said?

(WILLY *stands still, dreaming.*)

CHARLEY Willy!

WILLY Apologize to Bernard for me when you see him. I didn't mean to argue with him. He's a fine boy. They're all fine boys, and they'll end up big—all of them. Someday they'll all play tennis together. Wish me luck, Charley. He saw Bill Oliver today.

CHARLEY Good luck.

WILLY (*on the verge of tears*) Charley, you're the only friend I got. Isn't that a remarkable thing? (*He goes out*)

CHARLEY Jesus!

(CHARLEY *stares after him a moment and follows. All light blacks out. Suddenly raucous music is heard, and a red glow rises behind the screen at right.* STANLEY, *a young waiter, appears, carrying a table, followed by* HAPPY, *who is carrying two chairs.*)

STANLEY (*putting the table down*) That's all right, Mr. Loman, I can handle it myself. (*He turns and takes the chairs from* HAPPY *and places them at the table.*)

HAPPY (*glancing around*) Oh, this is better.

STANLEY Sure, in the front there you're in the middle of all kinds a noise. Whenever you got a party, Mr. Loman, you just tell me and I'll put you back here. Y'know, there's a lotta people they don't like it private, because when they go out they like to see a lotta action around them because they're sick and tired to stay in the house by theirself. But I know you, you ain't from Hackensack. You know what I mean?

HAPPY (*sitting down*) So how's it coming, Stanley?

STANLEY Ah, it's a dog's life. I only wish during the war they'd a took me in the Army. I coulda been dead by now.

HAPPY My brother's back, Stanley.

STANLEY Oh, he come back, heh? From the Far West.

HAPPY Yeah, big cattle man, my brother, so treat him right. And my father's coming too.

STANLEY Oh, your father too!

HAPPY You got a couple of nice lobsters?

STANLEY Hundred per cent, big.

HAPPY I want them with the claws.

STANLEY Don't worry, I don't give you no mice. (HAPPY *laughs.*) How about some wine? It'll put a head on the meal.

HAPPY No. You remember, Stanley, that recipe I brought you from overseas? With the champagne in it?

STANLEY Oh, yeah, sure. I still got it tacked up yet in the kitchen. But that'll have to cost a buck apiece anyways.

HAPPY That's all right.

STANLEY What'd you, hit a number or somethin'?

HAPPY No, it's a little celebration. My brother is—I think he pulled off a big deal today. I think we're going into business together.

STANLEY Great! That's the best for you. Because a family business, you know what I mean?—that's the best.

HAPPY That's what I think.

STANLEY 'Cause what's the difference? Somebody steals? It's in the family. Know what I mean? (*sotto voce*) Like this bartender here. The boss is goin' crazy what kinda leak he's got in the cash register. You put it in but it don't come out.

HAPPY (*raising his head*) Sh!

STANLEY What?

HAPPY You notice I wasn't lookin' right or left, was I?

STANLEY No.

HAPPY And my eyes are closed.

STANLEY So what's the—?

HAPPY Strudel's comin'.

STANLEY (*catching on, looks around*) Ah, no, there's no—

(*He breaks off as a furred, lavishly dressed girl enters and sits at the next table. Both follow her with their eyes.*)

STANLEY Geez, how'd ya know?

HAPPY I got radar or something. (*staring directly at her profile*) Oooooooo . . . Stanley.

STANLEY I think that's for you, Mr. Loman.

HAPPY Look at that mouth. Oh, God. And the binoculars.

STANLEY Geez, you got a life, Mr. Loman.

HAPPY Wait on her.

STANLEY (*going to the* GIRL's *table*) Would you like a menu, ma'am?

GIRL I'm expecting someone, but I'd like a—

HAPPY Why don't you bring her—excuse me, miss, do you mind? I sell champagne, and I'd like you to try my brand. Bring her a champagne, Stanley.

GIRL That's awfully nice of you.

HAPPY Don't mention it. It's all company money. (*He laughs.*)

GIRL That's a charming product to be selling, isn't it?

HAPPY Oh, gets to be like everything else. Selling is selling, y'know.

GIRL I suppose.

HAPPY You don't happen to sell, do you?

GIRL No, I don't sell.

HAPPY Would you object to a compliment from a stranger? You ought to be on a magazine cover.

GIRL (*looking at him a little archly*) I have been.

(STANLEY *comes in with a glass of champagne.*)

HAPPY What'd I say before, Stanley? You see? She's a cover girl.

STANLEY Oh, I could see, I could see.

HAPPY (*to the* GIRL) What magazine?

GIRL Oh, a lot of them. (*She takes the drink.*) Thank you.

HAPPY You know what they say in France, don't you? "Champagne is the drink of the complexion"—Hya, Biff!

(BIFF *has entered and sits with* HAPPY.)

BIFF Hello, kid. Sorry I'm late.

HAPPY I just got here. Uh, Miss—?

GIRL Forsythe.

HAPPY Miss Forsythe, this is my brother.

BIFF Is Dad here?

HAPPY His name is Biff. You might've heard of him. Great football player.

GIRL Really? What team?

HAPPY Are you familiar with football?

GIRL No, I'm afraid I'm not.

HAPPY Biff is quarterback with the New York Giants.

GIRL Well, that is nice, isn't it? (*She drinks.*)

HAPPY Good health.

GIRL I'm happy to meet you.

HAPPY That's my name. Hap. It's really Harold, but at West Point they called me Happy.

GIRL (*now really impressed*) Oh, I see. How do you do? (*She turns her profile.*)

BIFF Isn't Dad coming?

HAPPY You want her?

BIFF Oh, I could never make that.

HAPPY I remember the time that idea would never come into your head. Where's the old confidence, Biff?

BIFF I just saw Oliver—

HAPPY Wait a minute. I've got to see that old confidence again. Do you want her? She's on call.

BIFF Oh, no. (*He turns to look at the* GIRL.)

HAPPY I'm telling you. Watch this. (*turning to the* GIRL) Honey? (*She turns to him.*) Are you busy?

GIRL Well, I am . . . but I could make a phone call.

HAPPY Do that, will you, honey? And see if you can get a friend. We'll be here for a while. Biff is one of the greatest football players in the country.

GIRL (*standing up*) Well, I'm certainly happy to meet you.

HAPPY Come back soon.

GIRL I'll try.

HAPPY Don't try, honey, try hard.

(*The* GIRL *exits.* STANLEY *follows, shaking his head in bewildered admiration.*)

HAPPY Isn't that a shame now? A beautiful girl like that? That's why I can't get married. There's not a good woman in a thousand. New York is loaded with them, kid!

BIFF Hap, look—

HAPPY I told you she was on call!

BIFF (*strangely unnerved*) Cut it out, will ya? I want to say something to you.

HAPPY Did you see Oliver?

BIFF I saw him all right. Now look, I want to tell Dad a couple of things and I want you to help me.

HAPPY What? Is he going to back you?

BIFF Are you crazy? You're out of your goddam head, you know that?

HAPPY Why? What happened?

BIFF (*breathlessly*) I did a terrible thing today, Hap. It's been the strangest day I ever went through. I'm all numb, I swear.

HAPPY You mean he wouldn't see you?

BIFF Well, I waited six hours for him, see? All day. Kept sending my name in. Even tried to date his secretary so she'd get me to him, but no soap.

HAPPY Because you're not showin' the old confidence, Biff. He remembered you, didn't he?

BIFF (*stopping* HAPPY *with a gesture*) Finally, about five o'clock, he comes out. Didn't remember who I was or anything. I felt like such an idiot, Hap.

HAPPY Did you tell him my Florida idea?

BIFF He walked away. I saw him for one minute. I got so mad I could've torn the walls down! How the hell did I ever get the idea I was a salesman there? I even believed myself that I'd been a salesman for him! And then he gave me one look and—I realized what a ridiculous lie my whole life has been! We've been talking in a dream of fifteen years. I was a shipping clerk.

HAPPY What'd you do?

BIFF (*with great tension and wonder*) Well, he left, see. And the secretary went out. I was all alone in the waiting-room. I don't know what came over me, Hap. The next thing I know I'm in his office—paneled walls, everything. I can't explain it. I—Hap, I took his fountain pen.

HAPPY Geez, did he catch you?

BIFF I ran out. I ran down all eleven flights. I ran and ran and ran.

HAPPY That was an awful dumb—what'd you do that for?

BIFF (*agonized*) I don't know, I just—wanted to take something, I don't know. You gotta help me, Hap. I'm gonna tell Pop.

HAPPY You crazy? What for?

BIFF Hap, he's got to understand that I'm not the man somebody lends that kind of money to. He thinks I've been spiting him all these years and it's eating him up.

HAPPY That's just it. You tell him something nice.

BIFF I can't.

HAPPY Say you got a lunch date with Oliver tomorrow.

BIFF So what do I do tomorrow?

HAPPY You leave the house tomorrow and come back at night and say Oliver is thinking it over. And he thinks it over for a couple of weeks, and gradually it fades away and nobody's the worse.

BIFF But it'll go on forever!

HAPPY Dad is never so happy as when he's looking forward to something!

(WILLY *enters.*)

HAPPY Hello, scout!

WILLY Gee, I haven't been here in years!

(STANLEY *has followed* WILLY *in and sets a chair for him.* STANLEY *starts off but* HAPPY *stops him.*)

HAPPY Stanley!

(STANLEY *stands by, waiting for an order.*)

BIFF (*going to* WILLY *with guilt, as to an invalid*) Sit down, Pop. You want a drink?

WILLY Sure, I don't mind.

BIFF Let's get a load on.

WILLY You look worried.

BIFF N-no. (*to* STANLEY) Scotch all around. Make it doubles.

STANLEY Doubles, right. (*He goes.*)

WILLY You had a couple already, didn't you?

BIFF Just a couple, yeah.

WILLY Well, what happened, boy? (*nodding affirmatively, with a smile*) Everything go all right?

BIFF (*takes a breath, then reaches out and grasps* WILLY's *hand*) Pal . . . (*He is smiling bravely, and* WILLY *is smiling, too.*) I had an experience today.

HAPPY Terrific, Pop.

WILLY That so? What happened?

BIFF (*high, slightly alcoholic, above the earth*) I'm going to tell you everything from first to last. It's been a strange day. (*Silence. He looks around, composes himself as best he can, but his breath keeps breaking the rhythm of his voice.*) I had to wait quite a while for him, and—

WILLY Oliver?

BIFF Yeah, Oliver. All day, as a matter of cold fact. And a lot of—instances—facts, Pop, facts about my life came back to me. Who was it, Pop? Who ever said I was a salesman with Oliver?

WILLY Well, you were.

BIFF No, Dad, I was a shipping clerk.

WILLY But you were practically—

BIFF (*with determination*) Dad, I don't know who said it first, but I was never a salesman for Bill Oliver.

WILLY What're you talking about?

BIFF Let's hold on to the facts tonight, Pop. We're not going to get anywhere bullin' around. I was a shipping clerk.

WILLY (*angrily*) All right, now listen to me—

BIFF Why don't you let me finish?

WILLY I'm not interested in stories about the past or any crap of that kind because the woods are burning, boys, you understand? There's a big blaze going on all around. I was fired today.

BIFF (*shocked*) How could you be?

WILLY I was fired, and I'm looking for a little good news to tell your mother, because the woman has waited and the woman has suffered. The gift of it is that I haven't got a story left in my head, Biff. So don't give me a lecture about facts and aspects. I am not interested. Now what've you got to say to me?

(STANLEY *enters with three drinks. They wait until he leaves.*)

WILLY Did you see Oliver?

BIFF Jesus, Dad!

WILLY You mean you didn't go up there?

HAPPY Sure he went up there.

BIFF I did. I—saw him. How could they fire you?

WILLY (*on the edge of his chair*) What kind of a welcome did he give you?

BIFF He won't even let you work on commission?

WILLY I'm out! (*driving*) So tell me, he gave you a warm welcome?

HAPPY Sure, Pop, sure!

BIFF (*driven*) Well, it was kind of—

WILLY I was wondering if he'd remember you. (*to* HAPPY) Imagine, man doesn't see him for ten, twelve years and gives him that kind of a welcome!

HAPPY Damn right!

BIFF (*trying to return to the offensive*) Pop, look—

WILLY You know why he remembered you, don't you? Because you impressed him in those days.

BIFF Let's talk quietly and get this down to the facts, huh?

WILLY (*as though* BIFF *had been interrupting*) Well, what happened? It's great news, Biff. Did he take you into his office or'd you talk in the waiting-room?

BIFF Well, he came in, see, and—

WILLY (*with a big smile*) What'd he say? Betcha he threw his arm around you.

BIFF Well, he kinda—

WILLY He's a fine man. (*to* HAPPY) Very hard man to see, y'know.

HAPPY (*agreeing*) Oh, I know.

WILLY (*to* BIFF) Is that where you had the drinks?

BIFF Yeah, he gave me a couple of—no, no!

HAPPY (*cutting in*) He told him my Florida idea.

WILLY Don't interrupt. (*to* BIFF) How'd he react to the Florida idea?

BIFF Dad, will you give me a minute to explain?

WILLY I've been waiting for you to explain since I sat down here! What happened? He took you into his office and what?

BIFF Well—I talked. And—and he listened, see.

WILLY Famous for the way he listens, y'know. What was his answer?

BIFF His answer was— (*He breaks off, suddenly angry.*) Dad, you're not letting me tell you what I want to tell you!

WILLY (*accusing, angered*) You didn't see him, did you?

BIFF I did see him!

WILLY What'd you insult him or something? You insulted him, didn't you?

BIFF Listen, will you let me out of it, will you just let me out of it!

HAPPY What the hell!

WILLY Tell me what happened!

BIFF (*to* HAPPY) I can't talk to him!

(*A single trumpet note jars the ear. The light of green leaves stains the house, which holds the air of night and a dream. Young* BERNARD *enters and knocks on the door of the house.*)

YOUNG BERNARD (*frantically*) Mrs. Loman, Mrs. Loman!

HAPPY Tell him what happened!

BIFF (*to* HAPPY) Shut up and leave me alone!

WILLY No, no! You had to go and flunk math!

BIFF What math? What're you talking about?

YOUNG BERNARD Mrs. Loman, Mrs. Loman!

(LINDA *appears in the house, as of old.*)

WILLY (*wildly*) Math, math, math!

BIFF Take it easy, Pop!

YOUNG BERNARD Mrs. Loman!

WILLY (*furiously*) If you hadn't flunked you'd've been set by now!

BIFF Now, look, I'm gonna tell you what happened, and you're going to listen to me.

YOUNG BERNARD Mrs. Loman!

BIFF I waited six hours—

HAPPY What the hell are you saying?

BIFF I kept sending in my name but he wouldn't see me. So finally he . . . (*He continues unheard as light fades low on the restaurant.*)

YOUNG BERNARD Biff flunked math!

LINDA No!

YOUNG BERNARD Birnbaum flunked him! They won't graduate him!

LINDA But they have to. He's gotta go to the university. Where is he? Biff! Biff!

YOUNG BERNARD No, he left. He went to Grand Central.

LINDA Grand—You mean he went to Boston!

YOUNG BERNARD Is Uncle Willy in Boston?

LINDA Oh, maybe Willy can talk to the teacher. Oh, the poor, poor boy!

(*Light on house area snaps out.*)

BIFF (*at the table, now audible, holding up a gold fountain pen*) . . . so I'm washed up with Oliver, you understand? Are you listening to me?

WILLY (*at a loss*) Yeah, sure. If you hadn't flunked—

BIFF Flunked what? What're you talking about?

WILLY Don't blame everything on me! I didn't flunk math—you did! What pen?

HAPPY That was awful dumb, Biff, a pen like that is worth—

WILLY (*seeing the pen for the first time*) You took Oliver's pen?

BIFF (*weakening*) Dad, I just explained it to you.

WILLY You stole Bill Oliver's fountain pen!

BIFF I didn't exactly steal it! That's just what I've been explaining to you!

HAPPY He had it in his hand and just then Oliver walked in, so he got nervous and stuck it in his pocket!

WILLY My God, Biff!

BIFF I never intended to do it, Dad!

OPERATOR'S VOICE Standish Arms, good evening!

WILLY (*shouting*) I'm not in my room!

BIFF (*frightened*) Dad, what's the matter? (*He and* HAPPY *stand up.*)

OPERATOR Ringing Mr. Loman for you!

WILLY I'm not there, stop it!

BIFF (*horrified, gets down on one knee before* WILLY) Dad, I'll make good, I'll make good. (WILLY *tries to get to his feet.* BIFF *holds him down.*) Sit down now.

WILLY No, you're no good, you're no good for anything.

BIFF I am, Dad, I'll find something else, you understand? Now don't worry about anything. (*He holds up* WILLY'S *face.*) Talk to me, Dad.

OPERATOR Mr. Loman does not answer. Shall I page him?

WILLY (*attempting to stand, as though to rush and silence the* OPERATOR) No, no, no!

HAPPY He'll strike something, Pop.

WILLY No, no . . .

BIFF (*desperately, standing over* WILLY) Pop, listen! Listen to me! I'm telling you something good. Oliver talked to his partner about the Florida idea. You listening? He—he talked to his partner, and he came to me . . . I'm going to be all right, you hear? Dad, listen to me, he said it was just a question of the amount!

WILLY Then you . . . got it?

HAPPY He's gonna be terrific, Pop!

WILLY (*trying to stand*) Then you got it, haven't you? You got it! You got it!

BIFF (*agonized, holds* WILLY *down*) No, no. Look, Pop. I'm supposed to have lunch with them tomorrow. I'm just telling you this so you'll know that I can still make an impression, Pop. And I'll make good somewhere, but I can't go tomorrow, see?

WILLY Why not? You simply—

BIFF But the pen, Pop!

WILLY You give it to him and tell him it was an oversight!

HAPPY Sure, have lunch tomorrow!

BIFF I can't say that—

WILLY You were doing a crossword puzzle and accidentally used his pen!

BIFF Listen, kid, I took those balls years ago, now I walk in with his fountain pen? That clinches it, don't you see? I can't face him like that! I'll try elsewhere.

PAGE'S VOICE Paging Mr. Loman!

WILLY Don't you want to be anything?

BIFF Pop, how can I go back?

WILLY You don't want to be anything, is that what's behind it?

BIFF (*now angry at* WILLY *for not crediting his sympathy*) Don't take it that way! You think it was easy walking into that office after what I'd done to him? A team of horses couldn't have dragged me back to Bill Oliver!

WILLY Then why'd you go?

BIFF Why did I go? Why did I go! Look at you! Look at what's become of you!

(*Off left,* THE WOMAN *laughs.*)

WILLY Biff, you're going to go to that lunch tomorrow, or—

BIFF I can't go. I've got no appointment!

HAPPY Biff, for . . . !

WILLY Are you spiting me?

BIFF Don't take it that way! Goddammit!

WILLY (*strikes* BIFF *and falters away from the table*) You rotten little louse! Are you spiting me?

THE WOMAN Someone's at the door, Willy!

BIFF I'm no good, can't you see what I am?

HAPPY (*separating them*) Hey, you're in a restaurant! Now cut it out, both of you! (*The girls enter.*) Hello, girls, sit down.

(THE WOMAN *laughs, off left.*)

MISS FORSYTHE I guess we might as well. This is Letta.

THE WOMAN Willy, are you going to wake up?

BIFF (*ignoring* WILLY) How're ya, miss, sit down. What do you drink?

MISS FORSYTHE Letta might not be able to stay long.

LETTA I gotta get up very early tomorrow. I got jury duty. I'm so excited! Were you fellows ever on a jury?

BIFF No, but I been in front of them! (*The girls laugh.*) This is my father.

LETTA Isn't he cute? Sit down with us, Pop.

HAPPY Sit him down, Biff!

BIFF (*going to him*) Come on, slugger, drink us under the table. To hell with it! Come on, sit down, pal.

(*On* BIFF*'s last insistence,* WILLY *is about to sit.*)

THE WOMAN (*now urgently*) Willy, are you going to answer the door!

(THE WOMAN's *call pulls* WILLY *back. He starts right, befuddled.*)

BIFF Hey, where are you going?

WILLY Open the door.

BIFF The door?

WILLY The washroom . . . the door . . . where's the door?

BIFF (*leading* WILLY *to the left*) Just go straight down.

(WILLY *moves left.*)

THE WOMAN Willy, Willy, are you going to get up, get up, get up, get up?

(WILLY *exits left.*)

LETTA I think it's sweet you bring your daddy along.

MISS FORSYTHE Oh, he isn't really your father!

BIFF (*at left, turning to her resentfully*) Miss Forsythe, you've just seen a prince walk by. A fine, troubled prince. A hard-working, unappreciated prince. A pal, you understand? A good companion. Always for his boys.

LETTA That's so sweet.

HAPPY Well, girls, what's the program? We're wasting time. Come on, Biff. Gather round. Where would you like to go?

BIFF Why don't you do something for him?

HAPPY Me!

BIFF Don't you give a damn for him, Hap?

HAPPY What're you talking about? I'm the one who—

BIFF I sense it, you don't give a good goddam about him. (*He takes the rolled-up hose from his pocket and puts it on the table in front of* HAPPY.) Look what I found in the cellar, for Christ's sake. How can you bear to let it go on?

HAPPY Me? Who goes away? Who runs off and—

BIFF Yeah, but he doesn't mean anything to you. You could help him—I can't! Don't you understand what I'm talking about? He's going to kill himself, don't you know that?

HAPPY Don't I know it! Me!

BIFF Hap, help him! Jesus . . . help him . . . Help me, help me, I can't bear to look at his face! (*ready to weep, he hurries out, up right*)

HAPPY (*starting after him*) Where are you going?

MISS FORSYTHE What's he so mad about?

HAPPY Come on, girls, we'll catch up with him.

MISS FORSYTHE (*as* HAPPY *pushes her out*) Say, I don't like that temper of his!

HAPPY He's just a little overstrung, he'll be all right!

WILLY (*off left, as* THE WOMAN *laughs*) Don't answer! Don't answer!

LETTA Don't you want to tell your father—

HAPPY No, that's not my father. He's just a guy. Come on, we'll catch Biff, and, honey, we're going to paint this town! Stanley, where's the check! Hey, Stanley!

(*They exit.* STANLEY *looks toward left.*)

STANLEY (*calling to* HAPPY *indignantly*) Mr. Loman! Mr. Loman!

(STANLEY *picks up a chair and follows them off. Knocking is heard off left.*)

(THE WOMAN *enters, laughing.* WILLY *follows her. She is in a black slip; he is buttoning his shirt. Raw, sensuous music accompanies their speech.*)

WILLY Will you stop laughing? Will you stop?

THE WOMAN Aren't you going to answer the door? He'll wake the whole hotel.

WILLY I'm not expecting anybody.

THE WOMAN Whyn't you have another drink, honey, and stop being so damn self-centered?

WILLY I'm so lonely.

THE WOMAN You know you ruined me, Willy? From now on, whenever you come to the office, I'll see that you go right through to the buyers. No waiting at my desk any more, Willy. You ruined me.

WILLY That's nice of you to say that.

THE WOMAN Gee, you are self-centered! Why so sad? You are the saddest, self-centeredest soul I ever did see-saw. (*She laughs. He kisses her.*) Come on inside, drummer boy. It's silly to be dressing in the middle of the night. (*as knocking is heard*) Aren't you going to answer the door?

WILLY They're knocking on the wrong door.

THE WOMAN But I felt the knocking. And he heard us talking in here. Maybe the hotel's on fire!

WILLY (*his terror rising*) It's a mistake.

THE WOMAN Then tell him to go away!

WILLY There's nobody there.

THE WOMAN It's getting on my nerves, Willy. There's somebody standing out there and it's getting on my nerves!

WILLY (*pushing her away from him*) All right, stay in the bathroom here, and don't come out. I think there's a law in Massachusetts about it, so don't come out. It may be that new room clerk. He looked very mean. So don't come out. It's a mistake, there's no fire.

(*The knocking is heard again. He takes a few steps away from her, and she vanishes into the wing. The light follows him, and now he is facing* YOUNG BIFF, *who carries a suitcase.* BIFF *steps toward him. The music is gone.*)

BIFF Why didn't you answer?

WILLY Biff! What are you doing in Boston?

BIFF Why didn't you answer? I've been knocking for five minutes, I called you on the phone—

WILLY I just heard you. I was in the bathroom and had the door shut. Did anything happen home?

BIFF Dad—I let you down.

WILLY What do you mean?

BIFF Dad . . .

WILLY Biffo, what's this about? (*putting his arm around* BIFF) Come on, let's go downstairs and get you a malted.

BIFF Dad, I flunked math.

WILLY Not for the term?

BIFF The term. I haven't got enough credits to graduate.

WILLY You mean to say Bernard wouldn't give you the answers?

BIFF He did, he tried, but I only got a sixty-one.

WILLY And they wouldn't give you four points?

BIFF Birnbaum refused absolutely. I begged him, Pop, but he won't give me those points. You gotta talk to him before they close the school. Because if he saw the kind of man you are, and you just talked to him in your way, I'm sure he'd come through for me. The class came right before practice, see, and I didn't go enough. Would you talk to him? He'd like you, Pop. You know the way you could talk.

WILLY You're on. We'll drive right back.

BIFF Oh, Dad, good work! I'm sure he'll change it for you!

WILLY Go downstairs and tell the clerk I'm checkin' out. Go right down.

BIFF Yes, sir! See, the reason he hates me, Pop—one day he was late for class so I got up at the blackboard and imitated him. I crossed my eyes and talked with a lithp.

WILLY (*laughing*) You did? The kids like it?

BIFF They nearly died laughing!

WILLY Yeah? What'd you do?

BIFF The thquare root of thixthy twee is . . . (WILLY *bursts out laughing;* BIFF *joins him.*) And in the middle of it he walked in!

(WILLY *laughs and* THE WOMAN *joins in offstage.*)

WILLY (*without hesitation*) Hurry downstairs and—

BIFF Somebody in there?

WILLY No, that was next door.

(THE WOMAN *laughs offstage.*)

BIFF Somebody got in your bathroom!

WILLY No, it's the next room, there's a party—

THE WOMAN (*enters, laughing. She lisps this.*) Can I come in? There's something in the bathtub, Willy, and it's moving!

(WILLY *looks at* BIFF, *who is staring open-mouthed and horrified at* THE WOMAN.)

WILLY Ah—you better go back to your room. They must be finished painting by now. They're painting her room so I let her take a shower here. Go back, go back . . . (*He pushes her.*)

THE WOMAN (*resisting*) But I've got to get dressed, Willy, I can't—

WILLY Get out of here! Go back, go back . . . (*suddenly striving for the ordinary*) This is Miss Francis, Biff, she's a buyer. They're painting her room. Go back, Miss Francis, go back . . .

THE WOMAN But my clothes, I can't go out naked in the hall!

WILLY (*pushing her offstage*) Get outa here! Go back, go back!

(BIFF *slowly sits down on his suitcase as the argument continues offstage.*)

THE WOMAN Where's my stockings? You promised me stockings, Willy!

WILLY I have no stockings here!

THE WOMAN You had two boxes of size nine sheers for me, and I want them!

WILLY Here, for God's sake, will you get outa here!

THE WOMAN (*enters holding a box of stockings*) I just hope there's nobody in the hall. That's all I hope. (*to* BIFF) Are you football or baseball?

BIFF Football.

THE WOMAN (*angry, humiliated*) That's me too. G'night. (*She snatches her clothes from* WILLY, *and walks out.*)

WILLY (*after a pause*) Well, better get going. I want to get to the school first thing in the morning. Get my suits out of the closet, I'll get my valise. (BIFF *doesn't move.*) What's the matter? (BIFF *remains motionless, tears falling.*) She's a buyer. Buys for J. H. Simmons. She lives down the hall—they're painting. You don't imagine— (*He breaks off; after a pause:*) Now listen, pal, she's just a buyer. She sees merchandise in her room and they have to keep it looking just so . . . (*pause; assuming command:*) All right, get my suits. (BIFF *doesn't move.*) Now stop crying and do as I say. I gave you an order. Biff, I gave you an order! Is that what you do when I give you an order? How dare you cry! (*putting his arm around* BIFF) Now look, Biff, when you grow up you'll understand about these things. You mustn't—you mustn't overemphasize a thing like this. I'll see Birnbaum first thing in the morning.

BIFF Never mind.

WILLY (*getting down beside* BIFF) Never mind! He's going to give you those points. I'll see to it.

BIFF He wouldn't listen to you.

WILLY He certainly will listen to me. You need those points for the U. of Virginia.

BIFF I'm not going there.

WILLY Heh? If I can't get him to change that mark you'll make it up in summer school. You've got all summer to—

BIFF (*his weeping breaking from him*) Dad . . .

WILLY (*infected by it*) Oh, my boy . . .

BIFF Dad . . .

WILLY She's nothing to me, Biff. I was lonely, I was terribly lonely.

BIFF You—you gave her Mama's stockings! (*His tears break through and he rises to go.*)

WILLY (*grabbing for* BIFF) I gave you an order!

BIFF Don't touch me, you—liar!

WILLY Apologize for that!

BIFF You fake! You phony little fake! You fake! (*Overcome, he turns quickly and weeping fully goes out with his suitcase.* WILLY *is left on the floor on his knees.*)

WILLY I gave you an order! Biff, come back here or I'll beat you! Come back here! I'll whip you!

(STANLEY *comes quickly in from the right and stands in front of* WILLY.)

WILLY (*shouts at* STANLEY) I gave you an order . . .

STANLEY Hey, let's pick it up, pick it up, Mr. Loman. (*He helps* WILLY *to his feet.*) Your boys left with the chippies. They said they'll see you home.

(*A second* WAITER *watches some distance away.*)

WILLY But we were supposed to have dinner together.

(*Music is heard,* WILLY's *theme.*)

STANLEY Can you make it?

WILLY I'll—sure, I can make it. (*suddenly concerned about his clothes*) Do I—I look all right?

STANLEY Sure, you look all right. (*He flicks a speck off* WILLY's *lapel.*)

WILLY Here—here's a dollar.

STANLEY Oh, your son paid me. It's all right.

WILLY (*putting it in* STANLEY's *hand*) No, take it. You're a good boy.

STANLEY Oh, no, you don't have to . . .

WILLY Here—here's some more, I don't need it any more. (*after a slight pause*) Tell me—is there a seed store in the neighborhood?

STANLEY Seeds? You mean like to plant?

(*As* WILLY *turns,* STANLEY *slips the money back into his jacket pocket.*)

WILLY Yes. Carrots, peas . . .

STANLEY Well, there's hardware stores on Sixth Avenue, but it may be too late now.

WILLY (*anxiously*) Oh, I'd better hurry. I've got to get some seeds. (*He starts off to the right.*) I've got to get some seeds, right away. Nothing's planted. I don't have a thing in the ground.

(WILLY *hurries out as the light goes down.* STANLEY *moves over to the right after him, watches him off. The other* WAITER *has been staring at* WILLY.)

STANLEY (*to the* WAITER) Well, whatta you looking at?

(*The* WAITER *picks up the chairs and moves off right.* STANLEY *takes the table and follows him. The light fades on this area. There is a long pause, the sound of the flute coming over. The light gradually rises on the kitchen, which is empty.* HAPPY *appears at the door of the house, followed by* BIFF. HAPPY *is carrying a large bunch of long-stemmed roses. He enters the kitchen, looks around for* LINDA. *Not seeing her, he turns to* BIFF, *who is just outside the house door, and makes a gesture with his hands, indicating "Not here, I guess." He looks into the living room and freezes. Inside,* LINDA, *unseen, is seated,* WILLY'S *coat on her lap. She rises ominously and quietly and moves toward* HAPPY, *who backs up into the kitchen, afraid.*)

HAPPY Hey, what're you doing up? (LINDA *says nothing but moves toward him implacably.*) Where's Pop? (*He keeps backing to the right, and now* LINDA *is in full view in the doorway to the living room.*) Is he sleeping?

LINDA Where were you?

HAPPY (*trying to laugh it off*) We met two girls, Mom, very fine types. Here, we brought you some flowers. (*offering them to her*) Put them in your room, Ma.

(*She knocks them to the floor at* BIFF'S *feet. He has now come inside and closed the door behind him. She stares at* BIFF, *silent.*)

HAPPY Now what'd you do that for? Mom, I want you to have some flowers—

LINDA (*cutting* HAPPY *off, violently to* BIFF) Don't you care whether he lives or dies?

HAPPY (*going to the stairs*) Come upstairs, Biff.

BIFF (*with a flare of disgust, to* HAPPY) Go away from me! (*to* LINDA) What do you mean, lives or dies? Nobody's dying around here, pal.

LINDA Get out of my sight! Get out of here!

BIFF I wanna see the boss.

LINDA You're not going near him!

BIFF Where is he? (*He moves into the living room and* LINDA *follows.*)

LINDA (*shouting after* BIFF) You invite him for dinner. He looks forward to it all day— (BIFF *appears in his parents' bedroom, looks around, and exits.*) — and then you desert him there. There's no stranger you'd do that to!

HAPPY Why? He had a swell time with us. Listen, when I— (LINDA *comes back into the kitchen.*) —desert him I hope I don't outlive the day!

LINDA Get out of here!

HAPPY Now look, Mom . . .

LINDA Did you have to go to women tonight? You and your lousy rotten whores!

(BIFF *reenters the kitchen.*)

HAPPY Mom, all we did was follow Biff around trying to cheer him up! (*to* BIFF) Boy, what a night you gave me!

LINDA Get out of here, both of you, and don't come back! I don't want you tormenting him any more. Go on now, get your things together! (*to* BIFF) You can sleep in his apartment. (*She starts to pick up the flowers and stops herself.*) Pick up this stuff, I'm not your maid any more. Pick it up, you bum, you!

(HAPPY *turns his back to her in refusal.* BIFF *slowly moves over and gets down on his knees, picking up the flowers.*)

LINDA You're a pair of animals! Not one, not another living soul would have had the cruelty to walk out on that man in a restaurant!

BIFF (*not looking at her*) Is that what he said?

LINDA He didn't have to say anything. He was so humiliated he nearly limped when he came in.

HAPPY But, Mom, he had a great time with us—

BIFF (*cutting him off violently*) Shut up!

(*Without another word,* HAPPY *goes upstairs.*)

LINDA You! You didn't even go in to see if he was all right!

BIFF (*still on the floor in front of* LINDA, *the flowers in his hand; with self-loathing*) No. Didn't. Didn't do a damned thing. How do you like that, heh? Left him babbling in a toilet.

LINDA You louse. You . . .

BIFF Now you hit it on the nose! (*He gets up, throws the flowers in the wastebasket.*) The scum of the earth, and you're looking at him!

LINDA Get out of here!

BIFF I gotta talk to the boss, Mom. Where is he?

LINDA You're not going near him. Get out of this house!

BIFF (*with absolute assurance, determination*) No. We're gonna have an abrupt conversation, him and me.

LINDA You're not talking to him!

(*Hammering is heard from outside the house, off right.* BIFF *turns toward the noise.*)

LINDA (*suddenly pleading*) Will you please leave him alone?

BIFF What's he doing out there?

LINDA He's planting the garden!

BIFF (*quietly*) Now? Oh, my God!

(BIFF *moves outside,* LINDA *following. The light dies down on them and comes up on the center of the apron as* WILLY *walks into it. He is carrying a flashlight, a hoe, and a handful of seed packets. He raps the top of the hoe sharply to fix it firmly, and then moves to the left, measuring off the distance with his foot. He holds the flashlight to look at the seed packets, reading off the instructions. He is in the blue of night.*)

WILLY Carrots . . . quarter-inch apart. Rows . . . one-foot rows. (*He measures it off.*) One foot. (*He puts down a package and measures off.*) Beets. (*He puts down another package and measures again.*) Lettuce. (*He reads the package, puts it down.*) One foot— (*He breaks off as* BEN *appears at the right and moves slowly down to him.*) What a proposition, ts, ts. Terrific, terrific.

'Cause she's suffered, Ben, the woman has suffered. You understand me? A man can't go out the way he came in, Ben, a man has got to add up to something. You can't, you can't— (BEN *moves toward him as though to interrupt.*) You gotta consider, now. Don't answer so quick. Remember, it's a guaranteed twenty-thousand-dollar proposition. Now look, Ben, I want you to go through the ins and outs of this thing with me. I've got nobody to talk to, Ben, and the woman has suffered, you hear me?

BEN (*standing still, considering*) What's the proposition?

WILLY It's twenty thousand dollars on the barrelhead. Guaranteed, gilt-edged, you understand?

BEN You don't want to make a fool of yourself. They might not honor the policy.

WILLY How can they dare refuse? Didn't I work like a coolie to meet every premium on the nose? And now they don't pay off? Impossible!

BEN It's called a cowardly thing, William.

WILLY Why? Does it take more guts to stand here the rest of my life ringing up a zero?

BEN (*yielding*) That's a point, William. (*He moves, thinking, turns.*) And twenty thousand—that *is* something one can feel with the hand, it is there.

WILLY (*now assured, with rising power*) Oh, Ben, that's the whole beauty of it! I see it like a diamond, shining in the dark, hard and rough, that I can pick up and touch in my hand. Not like—like an appointment! This would not be another damned-fool appointment, Ben, and it changes all the aspects. Because he thinks I'm nothing, see, and so he spites me. But the funeral—(*straightening up*) Ben, that funeral will be massive! They'll come from Maine, Massachusetts, Vermont, New Hampshire! All the old-timers with the strange license plates—that boy will be thunderstruck, Ben, because he never realized—I am known! Rhode Island, New York, New Jersey—I am known, Ben, and he'll see it with his eyes once and for all. He'll see what I am, Ben! He's in for a shock, that boy!

BEN (*coming down to the edge of the garden*) He'll call you a coward.

WILLY (*suddenly fearful*) No, that would be terrible.

BEN Yes. And a damned fool.

WILLY No, no, he mustn't, I won't have that! (*He is broken and desperate.*)

BEN He'll hate you, William.

(*The gay music of the Boys is heard.*)

WILLY Oh, Ben, how do we get back to all the great times? Used to be so full of light, and comradeship, the sleigh-riding in winter, and the ruddiness on his cheeks. And always some kind of good news coming up, always something nice coming up ahead. And never even let me carry the valises in the house, and simonizing, simonizing that little red car! Why, why can't I give him something and not have him hate me?

BEN Let me think about it. (*He glances at his watch.*) I still have a little time. Remarkable proposition, but you've got to be sure you're not making a fool of yourself.

(BEN *drifts off upstage and goes out of sight.* BIFF *comes down from the left.*)

WILLY (*suddenly conscious of* BIFF, *turns and looks up at him, then begins picking up the packages of seeds in confusion*) Where the hell is that seed? (*indignantly*) You can't see nothing out here! They boxed in the whole goddam neighborhood!

BIFF There are people all around here. Don't you realize that?

WILLY I'm busy. Don't bother me.

BIFF (*taking the hoe from* WILLY) I'm saying good-by to you, Pop. (WILLY *looks at him, silent, unable to move.*) I'm not coming back any more.

WILLY You're not going to see Oliver tomorrow?

BIFF I've got no appointment, Dad.

WILLY He put his arm around you, and you've got no appointment?

BIFF Pop, get this now, will you? Everytime I've left it's been a fight that sent me out of here. Today I realized something about myself and I tried to explain it to you and I—I think I'm just not smart enough to make any sense out of it for you. To hell with whose fault it is or anything like that. (*He takes* WILLY's *arm.*) Let's just wrap it up, heh? Come on in, we'll tell Mom. (*He gently tries to pull* WILLY *to left.*)

WILLY (*frozen, immobile, with guilt in his voice*) No, I don't want to see her.

BIFF Come on! (*He pulls again, and* WILLY *tries to pull away.*)

WILLY (*highly nervous*) No, no, I don't want to see her.

BIFF (*tries to look into* WILLY's *face, as if to find the answer there*) Why don't you want to see her?

WILLY (*more harshly now*) Don't bother me, will you?

BIFF What do you mean, you don't want to see her? You don't want them calling you yellow, do you? This isn't your fault; it's me, I'm a bum. Now come inside! (WILLY *strains to get away.*) Did you hear what I said to you?

(WILLY *pulls away and quickly goes by himself into the house.* BIFF *follows.*)

LINDA (*to* WILLY) Did you plant, dear?

BIFF (*at the door, to* LINDA) All right, we had it out. I'm going and I'm not writing any more.

LINDA (*going to* WILLY *in the kitchen*) I think that's the best way, dear. 'Cause there's no use drawing it out, you'll just never get along.

(WILLY *doesn't respond.*)

BIFF People ask where I am and what I'm doing, you don't know, and you don't care. That way it'll be off your mind and you can start brightening up again. All right? That clears it, doesn't it? (WILLY *is silent, and* BIFF *goes to him.*) You gonna wish me luck, scout? (*He extends his hand.*) What do you say?

LINDA Shake his hand, Willy.

WILLY (*turning to her, seething with hurt*) There's no necessity to mention the pen at all, y'know.

BIFF (*gently*) I've got no appointment, Dad.

WILLY (*erupting fiercely*) He put his arm around . . . ?

BIFF Dad, you're never going to see what I am, so what's the use of arguing? If I strike oil I'll send you a check. Meantime forget I'm alive.

WILLY (*to* LINDA) Spite, see?

BIFF Shake hands, Dad.

WILLY Not my hand.

BIFF I was hoping not to go this way.

WILLY Well, this is the way you're going. Good-by.

(BIFF *looks at him a moment, then turns sharply and goes to the stairs.*)

WILLY (*stops him with*) May you rot in hell if you leave this house!

BIFF (*turning*) Exactly what is it that you want from me?

WILLY I want you to know, on the train, in the mountains, in the valleys, wherever you go, that you cut down your life for spite!

BIFF No, no.

WILLY Spite, spite, is the word of your undoing! And when you're down and out, remember what did it. When you're rotting somewhere beside the railroad tracks, remember, and don't you dare blame it on me!

BIFF I'm not blaming it on you!

WILLY I won't take the rap for this, you hear?

(HAPPY *comes down the stairs and stands on the bottom step, watching.*)

BIFF That's just what I'm telling you!

WILLY (*sinking into a chair at the table, with full accusation*) You're trying to put a knife in me—don't think I don't know what you're doing!

BIFF All right, phony! Then let's lay it on the line. (*He whips the rubber tube out of his pocket and puts it on the table.*)

HAPPY You crazy—

LINDA Biff! (*She moves to grab the hose, but* BIFF *holds it down with his hand.*)

BIFF Leave it there! Don't move it!

WILLY (*not looking at it*) What is that?

BIFF You know goddam well what that is.

WILLY (*caged, wanting to escape*) I never saw that.

BIFF You saw it. The mice didn't bring it into the cellar! What is this supposed to do, make a hero out of you? This supposed to make me sorry for you?

WILLY Never heard of it.

BIFF There'll be no pity for you, you hear it? No pity!

WILLY (*to* LINDA) You hear the spite!

BIFF No, you're going to hear the truth—what you are and what I am!

LINDA Stop it!

WILLY Spite!

HAPPY (*coming down toward* BIFF) You cut it now!

BIFF (*to* HAPPY) The man don't know who we are! The man is gonna know! (*to* WILLY) We never told the truth for ten minutes in this house!

HAPPY We always told the truth!

BIFF (*turning on him*) You big blow, are you the assistant buyer? You're one of the two assistants to the assistant, aren't you?

HAPPY Well, I'm practically—

BIFF You're practically full of it! We all are! And I'm through with it. (*to* WILLY) Now hear this, Willy, this is me.

WILLY I know you!

BIFF You know why I had no address for three months? I stole a suit in Kansas City and I was in jail. (*to* LINDA, *who is sobbing*) Stop crying. I'm through with it.

(LINDA *turns away from them, her hands covering her face.*)

WILLY I suppose that's my fault!

BIFF I stole myself out of every good job since high school!

WILLY And whose fault is that?

BIFF And I never got anywhere because you blew me so full of hot air I could never stand taking orders from anybody! That's whose fault it is!

WILLY I hear that!

LINDA Don't, Biff!

BIFF It's goddam time you heard that! I had to be boss big shot in two weeks, and I'm through with it!

WILLY Then hang yourself! For spite, hang yourself!

BIFF No! Nobody's hanging himself, Willy! I ran down eleven flights with a pen in my hand today. And suddenly I stopped, you hear me? And in the middle of that office building, do you hear this? I stopped in the middle of that building and I saw—the sky. I saw the things that I love in this world. The work and the food and time to sit and smoke. And I looked at the pen and said to myself, what the hell am I grabbing this for? Why am I trying to become what I don't want to be? What am I doing in an office, making a contemptuous, begging fool of myself, when all I want is out there, waiting for me the minute I say I know who I am! Why can't I say that, Willy? (*He tries to make* WILLY *face him, but* WILLY *pulls away and moves to the left.*)

WILLY (*with hatred, threateningly*) The door of your life is wide open!

BIFF Pop! I'm a dime a dozen, and so are you!

WILLY (*turning on him now in an uncontrolled outburst*) I am not a dime a dozen! I am Willy Loman, and you are Biff Loman!

(BIFF *starts for* WILLY, *but is blocked by* HAPPY. *In his fury,* BIFF *seems on the verge of attacking his father.)*

BIFF I am not a leader of men, Willy, and neither are you. You were never anything but a hard-working drummer who landed in the ash can like all the rest of them! I'm one dollar an hour, Willy! I tried seven states and couldn't raise it. A buck an hour! Do you gather my meaning? I'm not bringing home any prizes any more, and you're going to stop waiting for me to bring them home!

WILLY (*directly to* BIFF) You vengeful, spiteful mut!

(BIFF *breaks from* HAPPY. WILLY, *in fright, starts up the stairs.* BIFF *grabs him.)*

BIFF (*at the peak of his fury*) Pop, I'm nothing! I'm nothing, Pop. Can't you understand that? There's no spite in it any more. I'm just what I am, that's all.

(BIFF'S *fury has spent itself, and he breaks down, sobbing, holding on to* WILLY, *who dumbly fumbles for* BIFF'S *face.)*

WILLY (*astonished*) What're you doing? What're you doing? (*to* LINDA) Why is he crying?

BIFF (*crying, broken*) Will you let me go, for Christ's sake? Will you take that phony dream and burn it before something happens? (*Struggling to contain himself, he pulls away and moves to the stairs.*) I'll go in the morning. Put him—put him to bed. (*Exhausted,* BIFF *moves up the stairs to his room.*)

WILLY (*after a long pause, astonished, elevated*) Isn't that—isn't that remarkable? Biff—he likes me!

LINDA He loves you, Willy!

HAPPY (*deeply moved*) Always did, Pop.

WILLY Oh, Biff! (*staring wildly*) He cried! Cried to me. (*He is choking with his love, and now cries out his promise.*) That boy—that boy is going to be magnificent!

(BEN *appears in the light just outside the kitchen.)*

BEN Yes, outstanding, with twenty thousand behind him.

LINDA (*sensing the racing of his mind, fearfully, carefully*) Now come to bed, Willy. It's all settled now.

WILLY (*finding it difficult not to rush out of the house*) Yes, we'll sleep. Come on. Go to sleep, Hap.

BEN And it does take a great kind of a man to crack the jungle.

(*In accents of dread,* BEN'S *idyllic music starts up.)*

HAPPY (*his arm around* LINDA) I'm getting married, Pop, don't forget it. I'm changing everything. I'm gonna run that department before the year is up. You'll see, Mom. (*He kisses her.*)

BEN The jungle is dark but full of diamonds, Willy.

(WILLY *turns, moves, listening to* BEN.)

LINDA Be good. You're both good boys, just act that way, that's all.

HAPPY 'Night, Pop. (*He goes upstairs.*)

LINDA (*to* WILLY) Come, dear.

BEN (*with greater force*) One must go in to fetch a diamond out.

WILLY (*to* LINDA, *as he moves slowly along the edge of the kitchen, toward the door*) I just want to get settled down, Linda. Let me sit alone for a little.

LINDA (*almost uttering her fear*) I want you upstairs.

WILLY (*taking her in his arms*) In a few minutes, Linda. I couldn't sleep right now. Go on, you look awful tired. (*He kisses her.*)

BEN Not like an appointment at all. A diamond is rough and hard to the touch.

WILLY Go on now. I'll be right up.

LINDA I think this is the only way, Willy.

WILLY Sure, it's the best thing.

BEN Best thing!

WILLY The only way. Everything is gonna be—go on, kid, get to bed. You look so tired.

LINDA Come right up.

WILLY Two minutes.

(LINDA *goes into the living room, then reappears in her bedroom.* WILLY *moves just outside the kitchen door.*)

WILLY Loves me. (*wonderingly*) Always loved me. Isn't that a remarkable thing? Ben, he'll worship me for it!

BEN (*with promise*) It's dark there, but full of diamonds.

WILLY Can you imagine that magnificence with twenty thousand dollars in his pocket?

LINDA (*calling from her room*) Willy! Come up!

WILLY (*calling into the kitchen*) Yes! Yes. Coming! It's very smart, you realize that, don't you, sweetheart? Even Ben sees it. I gotta go, baby. 'By! 'By! (*Going over to* BEN, *almost dancing.*) Imagine? When the mail comes he'll be ahead of Bernard again!

BEN A perfect proposition all around.

WILLY Did you see how he cried to me? Oh, if I could kiss him, Ben!

BEN Time, William, time!

WILLY Oh, Ben, I always knew one way or another we were gonna make it, Biff and I!

BEN (*looking at his watch*) The boat. We'll be late. (*He moves slowly off into the darkness.*)

WILLY (*elegiacally, turning to the house*) Now when you kick off, boy, I want a seventy-yard boot, and get right down the field under the ball, and when you hit, hit low and hit hard, because it's important, boy. (*He swings around and faces the audience.*) There's all kinds of important people in the stands, and the first thing you know . . . (*suddenly realizing he is alone*) Ben! Ben, where do I . . . ? (*He makes a sudden movement of search.*) Ben, how do I . . . ?

LINDA (*calling*) Willy, you coming up?

WILLY (*uttering a gasp of fear, whirling about as if to quiet her*) Sh! (*He turns around as if to find his way; sounds, faces, voices, seem to be swarming in upon him and he flicks at them, crying.*) Sh! Sh! (*Suddenly music, faint and high, stops him. It rises in intensity, almost to an unbearable scream. He goes up and down on his toes, and rushes off around the house.*) Shhh!

LINDA Willy?

(*There is no answer.* LINDA *waits.* BIFF *gets up off his bed. He is still in his clothes.* HAPPY *sits up.* BIFF *stands listening.*)

LINDA (*with real fear*) Willy, answer me! Willy!

(*There is the sound of a car starting and moving away at full speed.*)

LINDA No!

BIFF (*rushing down the stairs*) Pop!

(*As the car speeds off, the music crashes down in a frenzy of sound, which becomes the soft pulsation of a single cello string.* BIFF *slowly returns to his bedroom. He and* HAPPY *gravely don their jackets.* LINDA *slowly walks out of her room. The music has developed into a dead march. The leaves of day are appearing over everything.* CHARLEY *and* BERNARD, *somberly dressed, appear and knock on the kitchen door.* BIFF *and* HAPPY *slowly descend the stairs to the kitchen as* CHARLEY *and* BERNARD *enter. All stop a moment when* LINDA, *in clothes of mourning, bearing a little bunch of roses, comes through the draped doorway into the kitchen. She goes to* CHARLEY *and takes his arm. Now all move toward the audience, through the wall-line of the kitchen. At the limit of the apron,* LINDA *lays down the flowers, kneels, and sits back on her heels. All stare down at the grave.*)

Requiem

CHARLEY It's getting dark, Linda.

(LINDA *doesn't react. She stares at the grave.*)

BIFF How about it, Mom? Better get some rest, heh? They'll be closing the gate soon.

(LINDA *makes no move. Pause.*)

HAPPY (*deeply angered*) He had no right to do that. There was no necessity for it. We would've helped him.

CHARLEY (*grunting*) Hmmm.

BIFF Come along, Mom.

LINDA Why didn't anybody come?

CHARLEY It was a very nice funeral.

LINDA But where are all the people he knew? Maybe they blame him.

CHARLEY Naa. It's a rough world, Linda. They wouldn't blame him.

LINDA I can't understand it. At this time especially. First time in thirty-five years we were just about free and clear. He only needed a little salary. He was even finished with the dentist.

CHARLEY No man only needs a little salary.

LINDA I can't understand it.

BIFF There were a lot of nice days. When he'd come home from a trip; or on Sundays, making the stoop; finishing the cellar; putting on the new porch; when he built the extra bathroom; and put up the garage. You know something, Charley, there's more of him in that front stoop than in all the sales he ever made.

CHARLEY Yeah. He was a happy man with a batch of cement.

LINDA He was so wonderful with his hands.

BIFF He had the wrong dreams. All, all, wrong.

HAPPY (*almost ready to fight* BIFF) Don't say that!

BIFF He never knew who he was.

CHARLEY (*stopping* HAPPY's *movement and reply; to* BIFF) Nobody dast blame this man. You don't understand: Willy was a salesman. And for a salesman, there is no rock bottom to the life. He don't put a bolt to a nut, he don't tell you the law or give you medicine. He's a man way out there in the blue, riding on a smile and a shoeshine. And when they start not smiling back—that's an earthquake. And then you get yourself a couple of spots on your hat, and you're finished. Nobody dast blame this man. A salesman is got to dream, boy. It comes with the territory.

BIFF Charley, the man didn't know who he was.

HAPPY (*infuriated*) Don't say that!

BIFF Why don't you come with me, Happy?

HAPPY I'm not licked that easily. I'm staying right in this city, and I'm gonna beat this racket! (*He looks at* BIFF, *his chin set.*) The Loman Brothers!

BIFF I know who I am, kid.

HAPPY All right, boy. I'm gonna show you and everybody else that Willy Loman did not die in vain. He had a good dream. It's the only dream you can have—to come out number-one man. He fought it out here, and this is where I'm gonna win it for him.

BIFF (*with a hopeless glance at* HAPPY, *bends toward his mother*) Let's go, Mom.

LINDA I'll be with you in a minute. Go on, Charley. (*He hesitates.*) I want to, just for a minute. I never had a chance to say good-by.

(CHARLEY *moves away, followed by* HAPPY. BIFF *remains a slight distance up and left of* LINDA. *She sits there, summoning herself. The flute begins, not far away, playing behind her speech.*)

LINDA Forgive me, dear. I can't cry. I don't know what it is, but I can't cry. I don't understand it. Why did you ever do that? Help me, Willy, I can't cry. It seems to me that you're just on another trip. I keep expecting you. Willy, dear, I can't cry. Why did you do it? I search and search and I search, and I can't understand it, Willy. I made the last payment on the house today. Today, dear. And there'll be nobody home. (*A sob rises in her throat.*) We're free and clear. (*sobbing more fully, released*) We're free. (BIFF *comes slowly toward her.*) We're free . . . We're free . . .

(BIFF *lifts her to her feet and moves out up right with her in his arms.* LINDA *sobs quietly.* BERNARD *and* CHARLEY *come together and follow them, followed by* HAPPY. *Only the music of the flute is left on the darkening stage as over the house the hard towers of the apartment buildings rise into sharp focus, and*)

The Curtain Falls

THE DUMB WAITER

(1957)

HAROLD PINTER (1930–)

In 1961 Martin Esslin, a well-established British theatrical critic and producer, published a study of contemporary drama called *The Theatre of the Absurd,* and thus introduced a new phrase into dramatic criticism that, for better or worse, has stuck as a definition of a particular dramatic style. Esslin included a substantial body of major and minor plays under the "absurd" rubric, and ever since there has been debate as to precisely what the absurd is, whether or not all of the important and lesser works assigned by Esslin to the genre really belong there, and whether or not it is a legitimate dramatic and theatrical category in the first place. As is the case in all such critical debates, no firm conclusions have been reached, nor absolutes determined. The fact remains that the term *absurd* has established itself, however limited the scope may be in the world of literary criticism, and no amount of attempting to discredit it has dislodged it from the theatrical vocabulary.

Generally speaking the absurd assumes a fundamental ridiculousness in the fact of being alive. We know, above all other creatures, that we will eventually die and that whatever we accomplish for ourselves in our instant in eternity is an exercise in futility. We wait endlessly for we know not what; we hope endlessly for something significant to happen, and though constantly deprived of that hope, we never abandon it. There are unseen and uncomprehended forces at work somewhere in the dim background, but nobody knows quite what they are or where they come from. It is a dark and dismal view, but it is often riotously funny. It looks at the maddening quirks of "nature" or whatever it is that rules humankind, and it shows the often idiotic bumblings of human creatures desperately trying to find out what is happening but unable to do so. The world won't stand still, leaving us behind in our ridiculous—our absurd—attempt to make sense of it all. And a string of sounds we call language—meant, we assume, for communication—all too often entirely prevents any meaningful communication whatever.

The absurd is not limited by natural boundaries and can be applied equally in Esslin's terms to English, European, and American drama. Among the best examples are the plays of the Romanian Eugene Ionesco (1912–1994). Among his most familiar plays are his first, *The Bald Soprano* (1950) in one act, and the full-length *Rhinoceros* (1960), both of which had successful runs in America and Europe. In *The Bald Soprano,* Ionesco creates a hilariously insane world in which husbands and wives have difficulty recognizing each other, everybody in one family, male and female, has the same name, clocks tell whatever time pleases them, firemen knock at the door in search of fires to put out, and language is finally reduced to absolute gibberish, with characters at the end of the play exchanging places and beginning the whole routine all over again. In *Rhinoceros,* while rampaging and rapidly multiplying horned beasts ravage a town, the inhabitants calmly debate their origin and numbers of horns, while, in the end, literally becoming rhinoceroses themselves, so that even the single survivor who refuses to succumb stands isolated and alone, ashamed of his soft skin and human features. The world of Ionesco is one in which reason and rational behavior, both human and otherwise, do not exist. Yet under all lies a frighteningly sane view of the world's inanities.

Equally famous is Samuel Beckett (1906–1989), an Irishman who wrote in French and then translated his own work back into English. His *Waiting for Godot* (1954) has become a classic of sorts in its treatment of the seemingly utter futility of life as two tramps wait patiently in an apparent wasteland roadside for the constantly promised arrival of Godot, a mysterious and never seen character who, presumably, will be able to take them out of their totally meaningless, idle lives. A variety of things are tried to while away the time and to combat the unending boredom, including a vaudeville routine with hats, and a serious consideration of committing suicide. Continually deciding to leave and wait no longer, they never move; Godot, of course, never arrives; and the two tramps remain as at the beginning, unable to do anything but wait.

The American Edward Albee (1928–) has written a variety of plays that have variously fitted into the absurd genre, with *The American Dream* a fairly good example. In this one-act piece Mommy, Daddy, and Grandma live in a house whose rooms tend to change places or disappear at random, and all await the arrival of the van that will cart Grandma away to some distant limbo, a move eagerly anticipated by all. Dialogue is frequently non sequitur, and Mommy and Daddy, whose innards are now made up mostly of tubes and such, rendering him impotent, have little to give each other. The play concludes as The American Dream—a muscular, handsome young man whose mind is clearly a vacuum—is introduced to the family as a replacement for the "bumble" (baby) that, years before, Mommy and Daddy had taken apart limb by limb merely because it wasn't what they really wanted. Very funny on the surface, this play is a truly devastating comment on the deterioration of traditional, if unreal, American "family values."

The plays of Briton Harold Pinter fit comfortably within Esslin's tradition of the absurd, but they also have about them an individuality of their own. Their specialty is an air of sinister suspense and undefined lurking horrors in a world almost entirely out of rational control. Tenements, suburban homes, shabby seaside hostelries are invaded by mysterious characters, mostly human but with an air of something unnatural, arriving out of nowhere, sometimes remaining unseen, who force themselves upon their hosts, control their lives, kill and kidnap on occasion, and remain forever unidentified.

In *The Dumb Waiter* Ben and Gus feel most of these Pinteresque effects. They are hoods of some kind, hit men in the hire of some Mr. Big, amusing characters in themselves, but nothing to admire. They are obviously extremely efficient at what they do. They have now been called upon to do it again. They have made their rendezvous, but with whom? The cellar kitchen and lavatory are the depths of something. Hell? Purgatory? Or just an old basement kitchen? Who is upstairs? What prompts the senseless maddening instructions that come clattering down the dumb waiter? These men are conditioned to obey orders. Their frantic attempt to meet the idiotic requests is excruciatingly funny. It is also terribly frightening. Who is pulling the ropes, literally and figuratively? Do they know who's down below? Do they care?

The sinister forces, be they god, devil, society, or nothingness, send down the final directive. Specifics for the hit have arrived. Now the captive servers of the dumb waiter suddenly see their own horrifying involvement. What happened in the hallway? Why did it happen? In Pinter, nobody knows the facts. Not even the audience. And most certainly, not even Pinter.

The Dumb Waiter HAROLD PINTER

SCENE: *A basement room. Two beds, flat against the back wall. A serving hatch, closed, between the beds. A door to the kitchen and lavatory, left. A door to a passage, right.*

(BEN *is lying on a bed, left, reading a paper.* GUS *is sitting on a bed, right, tying his shoelaces, with difficulty. Both are dressed in shirts, trousers and braces.*

Silence.

GUS *ties his laces, rises, yawns and begins to walk slowly to the door, left. He stops, looks down, and shakes his foot.*

BEN *lowers his paper and watches him.* GUS *kneels and unties his shoelace and slowly takes off the shoe. He looks inside it and brings out a flattened matchbox. He shakes it and examines it. Their eyes meet.* BEN *rattles his paper and reads.* GUS *puts the matchbox in his pocket and bends down to put on his shoe. He ties his lace, with difficulty.* BEN *lowers his paper and watches him.* GUS *walks to the door, left, stops, and shakes the other foot. He kneels, unties his shoelace, and slowly takes off the shoe. He looks inside it and brings out a flattened cigarette packet. He shakes it and examines it. Their eyes meet.* BEN *rattles his paper and reads.* GUS *puts the packet in his pocket, bends down, puts on his shoe and ties the lace.*

He wanders off, left.

BEN *slams the paper down on the bed and glares after him. He picks up the paper and lies on his back, reading.*

Silence.

A lavatory chain is pulled twice off, left, but the lavatory does not flush.

Silence.

GUS *reenters, left, and halts at the door, scratching his head.*

BEN *slams down the paper.*)

BEN Kaw!

(*He picks up the paper.*)

What about this? Listen to this!

(*He refers to the paper.*)

A man of eighty-seven wanted to cross the road. But there was a lot of traffic, see? He couldn't see how he was going to squeeze through. So he crawled under a lorry.

GUS He what?

BEN He crawled under a lorry. A stationary lorry.

GUS No?

BEN The lorry started and ran over him.

GUS Go on!

BEN That's what it says here.
GUS Get away.
BEN It's enough to make you want to puke, isn't it?
GUS Who advised him to do a thing like that?
BEN A man of eighty-seven crawling under a lorry!
GUS It's unbelievable.
BEN It's down here in black and white.
GUS Incredible.

(*Silence.*
GUS *shakes his head and exits.* BEN *lies back and reads.*
The lavatory chain is pulled once off left, but the lavatory does not flush.
BEN *whistles at an item in the paper.*
GUS *reenters.*)

I want to ask you something.
BEN What are you doing out there?
GUS Well, I was just—
BEN What about the tea?
GUS I'm just going to make it.
BEN Yes, I will. (*He sits in a chair, ruminatively.*) He's laid on some very nice crockery this time, I'll say that. It's sort of striped. There's a white stripe.

(BEN *reads.*)

It's very nice. I'll say that.

(BEN *turns the page.*)

You know, sort of round the cup. Round the rim. All the rest of it's black, you see. Then the saucer's black, except for right in the middle, where the cup goes, where it's white.

(BEN *reads.*)

Then the plates are the same, you see. Only they've got a black stripe—the plates—right across the middle. Yes, I'm quite taken with the crockery.
BEN (*still reading*) What do you want plates for? You're not going to eat.
GUS I've brought a few biscuits.
BEN Well, you'd better eat them quick.
GUS I always bring a few biscuits. Or a pie. You know I can't drink tea without anything to eat.
BEN Well, make the tea then, will you? Time's getting on.

(GUS *brings out the flattened cigarette packet and examines it.*)

GUS You got any cigarettes? I think I've run out.

(*He throws the packet high up and leans forward to catch it.*)

I hope it won't be a long job, this one.

(*Aiming carefully, he flips the packet under his bed.*)

Oh, I wanted to ask you something.

BEN (*slamming his paper down*) Kaw!

GUS What's that?

BEN A child of eight killed a cat!

GUS Get away.

BEN It's a fact. What about that, eh? A child of eight killing a cat!

GUS How did he do it?

BEN It was a girl.

GUS How did she do it?

BEN She—

(*He picks up the paper and studies it.*)

It doesn't say.

GUS Why not?

BEN Wait a minute. It just says—Her brother, aged eleven, viewed the incident from the toolshed.

GUS Go on!

BEN That's bloody ridiculous.

(*Pause.*)

GUS I bet he did it.

BEN Who?

GUS The brother.

BEN I think you're right.

(*Pause.*)

(*slamming down the paper*) What about that, eh? A kid of eleven killing a cat and blaming it on his little sister of eight! It's enough to—

(*He breaks off in disgust and seizes the paper.* GUS *rises.*)

GUS What time is he getting in touch?

(BEN *reads.*)

What time is he getting in touch?

BEN What's the matter with you? It could be any time. Any time.

GUS (*moves to the foot of* BEN's *bed*) Well, I was going to ask you something.

BEN What?

GUS Have you noticed the time that tank takes to fill?

BEN What tank?
GUS In the lavatory.
BEN No. Does it?
GUS Terrible.
BEN Well, what about it?
GUS What do you think's the matter with it?
BEN Nothing.
GUS Nothing?
BEN It's got a deficient ballcock, that's all.
GUS A deficient what?
BEN Ballcock.
GUS No? Really?
BEN That's what I should say.
GUS Go on! That didn't occur to me.

(GUS *wanders to his bed and presses the mattress.*)

I didn't have a very restful sleep today, did you? It's not much of a bed. I could have done with another blanket too. (*He catches sight of a picture on the wall.*) Hello, what's this? (*peering at it*) "The First Eleven." Cricketers. You seen this, Ben?

BEN (*reading*) What?
GUS The first eleven.
BEN What?
GUS There's a photo here of the first eleven.
BEN What first eleven?
GUS (*studying the photo*) It doesn't say.
BEN What about that tea?
GUS They all look a bit old to me.

(GUS *wanders downstage, looks out front, then all about the room.*)

I wouldn't like to live in this dump. I wouldn't mind if you had a window, you could see what it looked like outside.

BEN What do you want a window for?
GUS Well, I like to have a bit of a view, Ben. It whiles away the time.

(*He walks about the room.*)

I mean, you come into a place when it's still dark, you come into a room you've never seen before, you sleep all day, you do your job, and then you go away in the night again.

(*Pause.*)

I like to get a look at the scenery. You never get the chance in this job.

BEN You get your holidays, don't you?

GUS Only a fortnight.

BEN (*lowering the paper*) You kill me. Anyone would think you're working every day. How often do we do a job? Once a week? What are you complaining about?

GUS Yes, but we've got to be on tap though, haven't we? You can't move out of the house in case a call comes.

BEN You know what your trouble is?

GUS What?

BEN You haven't got any interests.

GUS I've got interests.

BEN What? Tell me one of your interests.

(*Pause.*)

GUS I've got interests.

BEN Look at me. What have I got?

GUS I don't know. What?

BEN I've got my woodwork. I've got my model boats. Have you ever seen me idle? I'm never idle. I know how to occupy my time, to its best advantage. Then when a call comes, I'm ready.

GUS Don't you ever get a bit fed up?

BEN Fed up? What with?

(*Silence.*)

(BEN *reads.* GUS *feels in the pocket of his jacket, which hangs on the bed.*)

GUS You got any cigarettes? I've run out.

(*The lavatory flushes off left.*)

There she goes.

(GUS *sits on his bed.*)

No, I mean, I say the crockery's good. It is. It's very nice. But that's about all I can say for this place. It's worse than the last one. Remember that last place we were in? Last time, where was it? At least there was a wireless there. No, honest. He doesn't seem to bother much about our comfort these days.

BEN When are you going to stop jabbering?

GUS You'd get rheumatism in a place like this, if you stay long.

BEN We're not staying long. Make the tea, will you? We'll be on the job in a minute.

(GUS *picks up a small bag by his bed and brings out a packet of tea. He examines it and looks up.*)

GUS Eh, I've been meaning to ask you.

BEN What the hell is it now?

GUS Why did you stop the car this morning, in the middle of that road?

BEN (*lowering the paper*) I thought you were asleep.

GUS I was, but I woke up when you stopped. You did stop, didn't you?

(*Pause.*)

In the middle of that road. It was still dark, don't you remember? I looked out. It was all misty. I thought perhaps you wanted to kip, but you were sitting up dead straight, like you were waiting for something.

BEN I wasn't waiting for anything.

GUS I must have fallen asleep again. What was all that about then? Why did you stop?

BEN (*picking up the paper*) We were too early.

GUS Early? (*He rises.*) What do you mean? We got the call, didn't we, saying we were to start right away. We did. We shoved out on the dot. So how could we be too early?

BEN (*quietly*) Who took the call, me or you?

GUS You.

BEN We were too early.

GUS Too early for what?

(*Pause.*)

You mean someone had to get out before we got in?

(*He examines the bedclothes.*)

I thought these sheets didn't look too bright. I thought they ponged a bit. I was too tired to notice when I got in this morning. Eh, that's taking a bit of a liberty, isn't it? I don't want to share my bed-sheets. I told you things were going down the drain. I mean, we've always had clean sheets laid on up till now. I've noticed it.

BEN How do you know those sheets weren't clean?

GUS What do you mean?

BEN How do you know they weren't clean? You've spent the whole day in them, haven't you?

GUS What, you mean it might be my pong? (*He sniffs sheets.*) Yes. (*He sits slowly on bed.*) It could be my pong, I suppose. It's difficult to tell. I don't really know what I pong like, that's the trouble.

BEN (*referring to the paper*) Kaw!

GUS Eh, Ben.

BEN Kaw!
GUS Ben.
BEN What?
GUS What town are we in? I've forgotten.
BEN I've told you. Birmingham.
GUS Go on!

(*He looks with interest about the room.*)

That's in the Midlands. The second biggest city in Great Britain. I'd never have guessed.

(*He snaps his fingers.*)

Eh, it's Friday today, isn't it? It'll be Saturday tomorrow.
BEN What about it?
GUS (*excited*) We could go and watch the Villa.
BEN They're playing away.
GUS No, are they? Caarr! What a pity.
BEN Anyway, there's no time. We've got to get straight back.
GUS Well, we have done in the past, haven't we? Stayed over and watched a game, haven't we? For a bit of relaxation.
BEN Things have tightened up, mate. They've tightened up.

(GUS *chuckles to himself.*)

GUS I saw the Villa get beat in a cup tie once. Who was it against now? White shirts. It was one-all at half-time. I'll never forget it. Their opponents won by a penalty. Talk about drama. Yes, it was a disputed penalty. Disputed. They got beat two-one, anyway, because of it. You were there yourself.
BEN Not me.
GUS Yes, you were there. Don't you remember that disputed penalty?
BEN No.
GUS He went down just inside the area. Then they said he was just acting. I didn't think the other bloke touched him myself. But the referee had the ball on the spot.
BEN Didn't touch him! What are you talking about? He laid him out flat!
GUS Not the Villa. The Villa don't play that sort of game.
BEN Get out of it.

(*Pause.*)

GUS Eh, that must have been here, in Birmingham.
BEN What must?
GUS The Villa. That must have been here.
BEN They were playing away.

GUS Because you know who the other team was? It was the Spurs. It was Tottenham Hotspur.
BEN Well, what about it?
GUS We've never done a job in Tottenham.
BEN How do you know?
GUS I'd remember Tottenham.

(BEN *turns on his bed to look at him.*)

BEN Don't make me laugh, will you?

(BEN *turns back and reads.* GUS *yawns and speaks through his yawn.*)

GUS When's he going to get in touch?

(*Pause.*)

Yes, I'd like to see another football match. I've always been an ardent football fan. Here, what about coming to see the Spurs tomorrow?
BEN (*tonelessly*) They're playing away.
GUS Who are?
BEN The Spurs.
GUS Then they might be playing here.
BEN Don't be silly.
GUS If they're playing away they might be playing here. They might be playing the Villa.
BEN (*tonelessly*) But the Villa are playing away.

(*Pause. An envelope slides under the door, right.* GUS *sees it. He stands, looking at it.*)

GUS Ben.
BEN Away. They're all playing away.
GUS Ben, look here.
BEN What?
GUS Look.

(BEN *turns his head and sees the envelope. He stands.*)

BEN What's that?
GUS I don't know.
BEN Where did it come from?
GUS Under the door.
BEN Well, what is it?
GUS I don't know.

(*They stare at it.*)

BEN Pick it up.
GUS What do you mean?
BEN Pick it up!

(GUS *slowly moves towards it, bends, and picks it up.*)

What is it?
GUS An envelope.
BEN Is there anything on it?
GUS No.
BEN Is it sealed?
GUS Yes.
BEN Open it.
GUS What?
BEN Open it!

(GUS *opens it and looks inside.*)

What's in it?

(GUS *empties twelve matches into his hand.*)

GUS Matches.
BEN Matches?
GUS Yes.
BEN Show it to me.

(GUS *passes the envelope.* BEN *examines it.*)

Nothing on it. Not a word.
GUS That's funny, isn't it?
BEN It came under the door?
GUS Must have done.
BEN Well, go on.
GUS Go on where?
BEN Open the door and see if you can catch anyone outside.
GUS Who, me?
BEN Go on!

(GUS *stares at him, puts the matches in his pocket, goes to his bed and brings a revolver from under the pillow. He goes to the door, opens it, looks out and shuts it.*)

GUS No one.

(*He replaces the revolver.*)

BEN What did you see?
GUS Nothing.

BEN They must have been pretty quick.

(GUS *takes the matches from pocket and looks at them.*)

GUS Well, they'll come in handy.
BEN Yes.
GUS Won't they?
BEN Yes, you're always running out, aren't you?
GUS All the time.
BEN Well, they'll come in handy then.
GUS Yes.
BEN Won't they?
GUS Yes, I could do with them. I could do with them too.
BEN You could, eh?
GUS Yes.
BEN Why?
GUS We haven't got any.
BEN Well, you've got some now, haven't you?
GUS I can light the kettle now.
BEN Yes, you're always cadging matches. How many have you got there?
GUS About a dozen.
BEN Well, don't lose them. Red too. You don't even need a box.

(GUS *probes his ear with a match.*)

(*slapping his hand*) Don't waste them! Go on, go and light it.

GUS Eh?
BEN Go and light it.
GUS Light what?
BEN The kettle.
GUS You mean the gas.
BEN Who does?
GUS You do.
BEN (*his eyes narrowing*) What do you mean, I mean the gas?
GUS Well, that's what you mean, don't you? The gas.
BEN (*powerfully*) If I say go and light the kettle I mean go and light the kettle.
GUS How can you light a kettle?
BEN It's a figure of speech! Light the kettle. It's a figure of speech!
GUS I've never heard it.
BEN Light the kettle! It's common usage!
GUS I think you've got it wrong.
BEN (*menacing*) What do you mean?
GUS They say put on the kettle.
BEN (*taut*) Who says?

(*They stare at each other, breathing hard.*)

(*deliberately*) I have never in all my life heard anyone say put on the kettle.

GUS I bet my mother used to say it.

BEN Your mother? When did you last see your mother?

GUS I don't know, about—

BEN Well, what are you talking about your mother for?

(*They stare.*)

Gus, I'm not trying to be unreasonable. I'm just trying to point out something to you.

GUS Yes, but—

BEN Who's the senior partner here, me or you?

GUS You.

BEN I'm only looking after your interests, Gus. You've got to learn, mate.

GUS Yes, but I've never heard—

BEN (*vehemently*) Nobody says light the gas! What does the gas light?

GUS What does the gas—?

BEN (*grabbing him with two hands by the throat, at arm's length*) THE KETTLE, YOU FOOL!

(GUS *takes the hands from his throat.*)

GUS All right, all right.

(*Pause.*)

BEN Well, what are you waiting for?

GUS I want to see if they light.

BEN What?

GUS The matches.

(*He takes out the flattened box and tries to strike.*)

No.

(*He throws the box under the bed.*
BEN *stares at him.*
GUS *raises his foot.*)

Shall I try it on here?

(BEN *stares.* GUS *strikes a match on his shoe. It lights.*)

Here we are.

BEN (*wearily*) Put on the bloody kettle, for Christ's sake.

(BEN *goes to his bed, but, realizing what he has said, stops and half turns. They look at each other.* GUS *slowly exits, left,* BEN *slams his paper down on the bed and sits on it, head in hands.*)

GUS (*entering*) It's going.

BEN What?

GUS The stove.

(GUS *goes to his bed and sits.*)

I wonder who it'll be tonight.

(*Silence.*)

Eh, I've been wanting to ask you something.

BEN (*putting his legs on the bed*) Oh, for Christ's sake.

GUS No. I was going to ask you something.

(*He rises and sits on* BEN*'s bed.*)

BEN What are you sitting on my bed for?

(GUS *sits.*)

What's the matter with you? You're always asking me questions. What's the matter with you?

GUS Nothing.

BEN You never used to ask me so many damn questions. What's come over you?

GUS No, I was just wondering.

BEN Stop wondering. You've got a job to do. Why don't you just do it and shut up?

GUS That's what I was wondering about.

BEN What?

GUS The job.

BEN What job?

GUS (*tentatively*) I thought perhaps you might know something.

(BEN *looks at him.*)

I thought perhaps you—I mean—have you got any idea—who it's going to be tonight?

BEN Who what's going to be?

(*They look at each other.*)

GUS (*at length*) Who it's going to be.

(*Silence.*)

BEN Are you feeling all right?
GUS Sure.
BEN Go and make the tea.
GUS Yes, sure.

(GUS *exits, left,* BEN *looks after him. He then takes his revolver from under the pillow and checks it for ammunition.* GUS *reenters.*)

The gas has gone out.
BEN Well, what about it?
GUS There's a meter.
BEN I haven't got any money.
GUS Nor have I.
BEN You'll have to wait.
GUS What for?
BEN For Wilson.
GUS He might not come. He might just send a message. He doesn't always come.
BEN Well, you'll have to do without it, won't you?
GUS Blimey.
BEN You'll have a cup of tea afterwards. What's the matter with you?
GUS I like to have one before.

(BEN *holds the revolver up to the light and polishes it.*)

BEN You'd better get ready anyway.
GUS Well, I don't know, that's a bit much, you know, for my money.

(*He picks up a packet of tea from the bed and throws it into the bag.*)

I hope he's got a shilling, anyway, if he comes. He's entitled to have. After all, it's his place, he could have seen there was enough gas for a cup of tea.
BEN What do you mean, it's his place?
GUS Well, isn't it?
BEN He's probably only rented it. It doesn't have to be his place.
GUS I know it's his place. I bet the whole house is. He's not even laying on any gas now either.

(GUS *sits on his bed.*)

It's his place all right. Look at all the other places. You go to this address, there's a key there, there's a teapot, there's never a soul in sight—(*He pauses.*) Eh, nobody ever hears a thing, have you ever thought of that? We never get any complaints, do we, too much noise or anything like that? You never see a soul, do you?—except the bloke who comes. You ever noticed that? I wonder if the walls are sound-proof. (*He touches the wall above his *bed.*) Can't tell. All you do is wait, eh? Half the time he doesn't even bother to put in an appearance, Wilson.

BEN Why should he? He's a busy man.

GUS (*thoughtfully*) I find him hard to talk to, Wilson. Do you know that, Ben?

BEN Scrub round it, will you?

(*Pause.*)

GUS There are a number of things I want to ask him. But I can never get round to it, when I see him.

(*Pause.*)

I've been thinking about the last one.

BEN What last one?

GUS That girl.

(BEN *grabs the paper, which he reads.*)

(*rising, looking down at* BEN) How many times have you read that paper?

(BEN *slams the paper down and rises.*)

BEN (*angrily*) What do you mean?

GUS I was just wondering how many times you'd—

BEN What are you doing, criticizing me?

GUS No, I was just—

BEN You'll get a swipe round your earhole if you don't watch your step.

GUS Now look here, Ben—

BEN I'm not looking anywhere! (*He addresses the room.*) How many times have I—! A bloody liberty!

GUS I didn't mean that.

BEN You just get on with it, mate. Get on with it, that's all.

(BEN *gets back on the bed.*)

GUS I was just thinking about that girl, that's all.

(GUS *sits on his bed.*)

She wasn't much to look at, I know, but still. It was a mess though, wasn't it? What a mess. Honest, I can't remember a mess like that one. They don't seem to hold together like men, women. A looser texture, like. Didn't she spread, eh? She didn't half spread. Kaw! But I've been meaning to ask you.

(BEN *sits up and clenches his eyes.*)

Who clears up after we've gone? I'm curious about that. Who does the clearing up? Maybe they don't clear up. Maybe they just leave them there, eh?

What do you think? How many jobs have we done? Blimey, I can't count them. What if they never clear anything up after we've gone.

BEN (*pityingly*) You mutt. Do you think we're the only branch of this organization? Have a bit of common. They got departments for everything.

GUS What cleaners and all?

BEN You birk!

GUS No, it was that girl made me start to think—

(*There is a loud clatter and racket in the bulge of wall between the beds, of something descending. They grab their revolvers, jump up and face the wall. The noise comes to a stop. Silence. They look at each other.* BEN *gestures sharply towards the wall.* GUS *approaches the wall slowly. He bangs it with his revolver. It is hollow.* BEN *moves to the head of his bed, his revolver cocked.* GUS *puts his revolver on his bed and pats along the bottom of the centre panel. He finds a rim. He lifts the panel. Disclosed is a serving-hatch, a "dumb waiter." A wide box is held by pulleys.* GUS *peers into the box. He brings out a piece of paper.*)

BEN What is it?

GUS You have a look at it.

BEN Read it.

GUS (*reading*) Two braised steak and chips. Two sago puddings. Two teas without sugar.

BEN Let me see that. (*He takes the paper.*)

GUS (*to himself*) Two teas without sugar.

BEN Mmnn.

GUS What do you think of that?

BEN Well—

(*The box goes up.* BEN *levels his revolver.*)

GUS Give us a chance! They're in a hurry, aren't they?

(BEN *rereads the note.* GUS *looks over his shoulder.*)

That's a bit—that's a bit funny, isn't it?

BEN (*quickly*) No. It's not funny. It probably used to be a café here, that's all. Upstairs. These places change hands very quickly.

GUS A café?

BEN Yes.

GUS What, you mean this was the kitchen, down here?

BEN Yes, they change hands overnight, these places. Go into liquidation. The people who run it, you know, they don't find it a going concern, they move out.

GUS You mean the people who ran this place didn't find it a going concern and moved out?

BEN Sure.

GUS WELL, WHO'S GOT IT NOW?

(*Silence.*)

BEN What do you mean, who's got it now?
GUS Who's got it now? If they moved out, who moved in?
BEN Well, that all depends—

(*The box descends with a clatter and bang.* BEN *levels his revolver.* GUS *goes to the box and brings out a piece of paper.*)

GUS (*reading*) Soup of the day. Liver and onions. Jam tart.

(*A pause.* GUS *looks at* BEN. BEN *takes the note and reads it. He walks slowly to the hatch.* GUS *follows.* BEN *looks into the hatch but not up it.* GUS *puts his hand on* BEN*'s shoulder.* BEN *throws it off.* GUS *puts his finger to his mouth. He leans on the hatch and swiftly looks up it.* BEN *flings him away in alarm.* BEN *looks at the note. He throws his revolver on the bed and speaks with decision.*)

BEN We'd better send something up.
GUS Eh?
BEN We'd better send something up.
GUS Oh! Yes. Yes. Maybe you're right.

(*They are both relieved at the decision.*)

BEN (*purposefully*) Quick! What have you got in that bag?
GUS Not much.

(GUS *goes to the hatch and shouts up it.*)

Wait a minute!
BEN Don't do that!

(GUS *examines the contents of the bag and brings them out, one by one.*)

GUS Biscuits. A bar of chocolate. Half a pint of milk.
BEN That all?
GUS Packet of tea.
BEN Good.
GUS We can't send the tea. That's all the tea we've got.
BEN Well, there's no gas. You can't do anything with it, can you?
GUS Maybe they can send us down a bob.
BEN What else is there?
GUS (*reaching into bag*) One Eccles cake.
BEN One Eccles cake?
GUS Yes.
BEN You never told me you had an Eccles cake.

GUS Didn't I?
BEN Why only one? Didn't you bring one for me?
GUS I didn't think you'd be keen.
BEN Well, you can't send up one Eccles cake, anyway.
GUS Why not?
BEN Fetch one of those plates.
GUS All right.

(GUS *goes towards the door, left, and stops.*)

Do you mean I can keep the Eccles cake then?
BEN Keep it?
GUS Well, they don't know we've got it, do they?
BEN That's not the point.
GUS Can't I keep it?
BEN No, you can't. Get the plate.

(GUS *exits, left.* BEN *looks in the bag. He brings out a packet of crisps. Enter* GUS *with a plate.*)

(*accusingly, holding up the crisps*) Where did these come from?
GUS What?
BEN Where did these crisps come from?
GUS Where did you find them?
BEN (*hitting him on the shoulder*) You're playing a dirty game, my lad!
GUS I only eat those with beer!
BEN Well, where were you going to get the beer?
GUS I was saving them till I did.
BEN I'll remember this. Put everything on the plate.

(*They pile everything on to the plate. The box goes up without the plate.*)

Wait a minute!

(*They stand.*)

GUS It's gone up.
BEN It's all your stupid fault, playing about!
GUS What do we do now?
BEN We'll have to wait till it comes down.

(BEN *puts the plate on the bed, puts on his shoulder holster, and starts to put on his tie.*)

You'd better get ready.

(GUS *goes to his bed, puts on his tie, and starts to fix his holster.*)

GUS Hey, Ben.
BEN What?
GUS What's going on here?

(*Pause.*)

BEN What do you mean?
GUS How can this be a café?
BEN It used to be a café.
GUS Have you seen the gas stove?
BEN What about it?
GUS It's only got three rings.
BEN So what?
GUS Well, you couldn't cook much on three rings, not for a busy place like this.
BEN (*irritably*) That's why the service is slow!

(BEN *puts on his waistcoat.*)

GUS Yes, but what happens when we're not here? What do they do then? All these menus coming down and nothing going up. It might have been going on like this for years.

(BEN *brushes his jacket.*)

What happens when we go?

(BEN *puts on his jacket.*)

They can't do much business.

(*The box descends. They turn about.* GUS *goes to the hatch and brings out a note.*)

GUS (*reading*) Macaroni Pastitsio. Ormitha Macarounada.
BEN What was that?
GUS Macaroni Pastitsio. Ormitha Macarounada.
BEN Greek dishes.
GUS No.
BEN That's right.
GUS That's pretty high class.
BEN Quick before it goes up.

(GUS *puts the plate in the box.*)

GUS (*calling up the hatch*) Three McVitie and Price! One Lyons Red Label! One Smith's Crisps! One Eccles cake! One Fruit and Nut!
BEN Cadbury's.
GUS (*up the hatch*) Cadbury's!
BEN (*handing the milk*) One bottle of milk.

GUS (*up the hatch*) One bottle of milk! Half a pint! (*He looks at the label.*) Express Dairy! (*He puts the bottle in the box.*)

(*The box goes up.*)

Just did it.

BEN You shouldn't shout like that.

GUS Why not?

BEN It isn't done.

(BEN *goes to his bed.*)

Well, that should be all right, anyway, for the time being.

GUS You think so, eh?

BEN Get dressed, will you? It'll be any minute now.

(GUS *puts on his waistcoat.* BEN *lies down and looks up at the ceiling.*)

GUS This is some place. No tea and no biscuits.

BEN Eating makes you lazy, mate. You're getting lazy, you know that? You don't want to get slack on your job.

GUS Who me?

BEN Slack, mate, slack.

GUS Who me? Slack?

BEN Have you checked your gun? You haven't even checked your gun. It looks disgraceful, anyway. Why don't you ever polish it?

(GUS *rubs his revolver on the sheet.* BEN *takes out a pocket mirror and straightens his tie.*)

GUS I wonder where the cook is. They must have had a few, to cope with that. Maybe they had a few more gas stoves. Eh! Maybe there's another kitchen along the passage.

BEN Of course there is! Do you know what it takes to make an Ormitha Macarounada?

GUS No, what?

BEN An Ormitha—! Buck your ideas up, will you?

GUS Takes a few cooks, eh?

(GUS *puts his revolver in its holster.*)

The sooner we're out of this place the better.

(*He puts on his jacket.*)

Why doesn't he get in touch? I feel like I've been here years. (*He takes his revolver out of its holster to check the ammunition.*) We've never let him down though, have we? We've never let him down. I was thinking only the other day, Ben. We're reliable, aren't we?

(*He puts his revolver back in its holster.*)

Still, I'll be glad when it's over tonight.

(*He brushes his jacket.*)

I hope the bloke's not going to get excited tonight, or anything. I'm feeling a bit off. I've got a splitting headache.

(*Silence.*
The box descends. BEN *jumps up.*
GUS *collects the note.*)

(*reading*) One Bamboo Shoots, Water Chestnuts and Chicken. One Char Siu and Beansprouts.

BEN Beansprouts?

GUS Yes.

BEN Blimey.

GUS I wouldn't know where to begin.

(*He looks back at the box. The packet of tea is inside it. He picks it up.*)

They've sent back the tea.

BEN (*anxious*) What'd they do that for?

GUS Maybe it isn't tea-time.

(*The box goes up. Silence.*)

BEN (*throwing the tea on the bed, and speaking urgently*) Look here. We'd better tell them.

GUS Tell them what?

BEN That we can't do it, we haven't got it.

GUS All right then.

BEN Lend us your pencil. We'll write a note.

(GUS, *turning for a pencil, suddenly discovers the speaking-tube, which hangs on the right wall of the hatch facing his bed.*)

GUS What's this?

BEN What?

GUS This.

BEN (*examining it*) This? It's a speaking-tube.

GUS How long has that been there?

BEN Just the job. We should have used it before, instead of shouting up there.

GUS Funny I never noticed it before.

BEN Well, come on.
GUS What do you do?
BEN See that? That's a whistle.
GUS What, this?
BEN Yes, take it out. Pull it out.

(GUS *does so.*)

That's it.
GUS What do we do now?
BEN Blow into it.
GUS Blow?
BEN It whistles up there if you blow. Then they know you want to speak. Blow.

(GUS *blows. Silence.*)

GUS (*tube at mouth*) I can't hear a thing.
BEN Now you speak! Speak into it!

(GUS *looks at* BEN, *then speaks into the tube.*)

GUS The larder's bare!
BEN Give me that!

(*He grabs the tube and puts it to his mouth.*)

(*speaking with great deference*) Good evening. I'm sorry to—bother you, but we just thought we'd better let you know that we haven't got anything left. We sent up all we had. There's no more food down here.

(*He brings the tube slowly to his ear.*)

What?

(*to mouth*)

What?

(*to ear. He listens. to mouth*)

No, all we had we sent up.

(*to ear. He listens. to mouth*)

Oh, I'm very sorry to hear that.

(*to ear. He listens. to* GUS:)

The Eccles cake was stale.

(*He listens. to* GUS:)

The chocolate was melted.

(*He listens. to* GUS:)

The milk was sour.

GUS What about the crisps?

BEN (*listening*) The biscuits were mouldy.

(*He glares at* GUS. *tube to mouth*)

Well, we're very sorry about that.

(*tube to ear*)

What?

(*to mouth*)

What?

(*to ear*)

Yes. Yes.

(*to mouth*)

Yes certainly. Certainly. Right away.

(*to ear. The voice has ceased. He hangs up the tube.*)

(*excitedly*) Did you hear that?

GUS What?

BEN You know what he said? Light the kettle! Not put on the kettle! Not light the gas! But light the kettle!

GUS How can we light the kettle?

BEN What do you mean?

GUS There's no gas.

BEN (*clapping hand to head*) Now what do we do?

GUS What did he want us to light the kettle for?

BEN For tea. He wanted a cup of tea.

GUS *He* wanted a cup of tea! What about me? I've been wanting a cup of tea all night!

BEN (*despairingly*) What do we do now?

GUS What are we supposed to drink?

(BEN *sits on his bed, staring.*)

What about us?

(BEN *sits.*)

I'm thirsty too. I'm starving. And he wants a cup of tea. That beats the band, that does.

(BEN *lets his head sink on to his chest.*)

I could do with a bit of sustenance myself. What about you? You look as if you could do with something too.

(GUS *sits on his bed.*)

We send him up all we've got and he's not satisfied. No, honest, it's enough to make the cat laugh. Why did you send him up all that stuff? (*thoughtfully*) Why did I send it up?

(*Pause.*)

Who knows what he's got upstairs? He's probably got a salad bowl. They must have something up there. They won't get much from down here. You notice they didn't ask for any salads? They've probably got a salad bowl up there. Cold meat, radishes, cucumbers. Watercress. Roll mops.

(*Pause.*)

Hardboiled eggs.

(*Pause.*)

The lot. They've probably got a crate of beer too. Probably eating my crisps with a pint of beer now. Didn't have anything to say about those crisps, did he? They do all right, don't worry about that. You don't think they're just going to sit there and wait for stuff to come up from down here, do you? That'll get them nowhere.

(*Pause.*)

They do all right.

(*Pause.*)

And he wants a cup of tea.

(*Pause.*)

That's past a joke, in my opinion.

(*He looks over at* BEN, *rises, and goes to him.*)

What's the matter with you? You don't look too bright. I feel like an Alka-Seltzer myself.

(BEN *sits up.*)

BEN (*in a low voice*) Time's getting on.
GUS I know. I don't like doing a job on an empty stomach.
BEN (*wearily*) Be quiet a minute. Let me give you your instructions.
GUS What for? We always do it the same way, don't we?
BEN Let me give you your instructions.

(GUS *sighs and sits next to* BEN *on the bed. The instructions are stated and repeated automatically.*)

When we get the call, you go over and stand behind the door.
GUS Stand behind the door.
BEN If there's a knock on the door you don't answer it.
GUS If there's a knock on the door I don't answer it.
BEN But there won't be a knock on the door.
GUS So I won't answer it.
BEN When the bloke comes in—
GUS When the bloke comes in—
BEN Shut the door behind him.
GUS Shut the door behind him.
BEN Without divulging your presence.
GUS Without divulging my presence.
BEN He'll see me and come towards me.
GUS He'll see you and come towards you.
BEN He won't see you.
GUS (*absently*) Eh?
BEN He won't see you.
GUS He won't see me.
BEN But he'll see me.
GUS He'll see you.
BEN He won't know you're there.
GUS He won't know you're there.
BEN He won't know *you're* there.
GUS He won't know I'm there.
BEN I take out my gun.
GUS You take out your gun.
BEN He stops in his tracks.
GUS He stops in his tracks.
BEN If he turns round—
GUS If he turns round—
BEN You're there.
GUS I'm here.

(BEN *frowns and presses his forehead.*)

You've missed something out.

BEN I know. What?

GUS I haven't taken my gun out, according to you.

BEN You take your gun out—

GUS After I've closed the door.

BEN After you've closed the door.

GUS You've never missed that out before, you know that?

BEN When he sees you behind him—

GUS Me behind him—

BEN And me in front of him—

GUS And you in front of him—

BEN He'll feel uncertain—

GUS Uneasy.

BEN He won't know what to do.

GUS So what will he do?

BEN He'll look at me and he'll look at you.

GUS We won't say a word.

BEN We'll look at him.

GUS He won't say a word.

BEN He'll look at us.

GUS And we'll look at him.

BEN Nobody says a word.

(*Pause.*)

GUS What do we do if it's a girl?

BEN We do the same.

GUS Exactly the same?

BEN Exactly.

(*Pause.*)

GUS We don't do anything different?

BEN We do exactly the same.

GUS Oh.

(GUS *rises, and shivers.*)

Excuse me.

(*He exits through the door on the left.* BEN *remains sitting on the bed, still. The lavatory chain is pulled once off left, but the lavatory does not flush.*

Silence.

GUS *reenters and stops inside the door, deep in thought. He looks at* BEN, *then walks slowly across to his own bed. He is troubled. He stands, thinking. He turns and looks at* BEN. *He moves a few paces towards him.*)

(*slowly in a low, tense voice*) Why did he send us matches if he knew there was no gas?

(*Silence.*

BEN *stares in front of him.* GUS *crosses to the left side of* BEN, *to the foot of his bed, to get to his other ear.*)

Ben. Why did he send us matches if he knew there was no gas?

(BEN *looks up.*)

Why did he do that?

BEN Who?

GUS Who sent us those matches?

BEN What are you talking about?

(GUS *stares down at him.*)

GUS (*thickly*) Who is it upstairs?

BEN (*nervously*) What's one thing to do with another?

GUS Who is it, though?

BEN What's one thing to do with another?

(BEN *fumbles for his paper on the bed.*)

GUS I asked you a question.

BEN Enough!

GUS (*with growing agitation*) I asked you before. Who moved in? I asked you. You said the people who had it before moved out. Well, who moved in?

BEN (*hunched*) Shut up.

GUS I told you, didn't I?

BEN (*standing*) Shut up!

GUS (*feverishly*) I told you before who owned this place, didn't I? I told you.

(BEN *hits him viciously on the shoulder.*)

I told you who ran this place, didn't I?

(BEN *hits him viciously on the shoulder.*)

(*violently*) Well, what's he playing all these games for? That's what I want to know. What's he doing it for?

BEN What games?

GUS (*passionately, advancing*) What's he doing it for? We've been through our tests, haven't we? We got right through our tests, years ago, didn't we? We took them together, don't you remember, didn't we? We've proved ourselves before now, haven't we? We've always done our job. What's he doing all this for? What's the idea? What's he playing these games for?

(*The box in the shaft comes down behind them. The noise is this time accompanied by a shrill whistle, as it falls.* GUS *rushes to the hatch and seizes the note.*)

(*reading*) Scampi!

(*He crumples the note, picks up the tube, takes out the whistle, blows and speaks.*)

WE'VE GOT NOTHING LEFT! NOTHING! DO YOU UNDERSTAND?

(BEN *seizes the tube and flings* GUS *away. He follows* GUS *and slaps him hard, back-handed, across the chest.*)

BEN Stop it! You maniac!
GUS But you heard!
BEN (*savagely*) That's enough! I'm warning you!

(*Silence.*
BEN *hangs the tube. He goes to his bed and lies down. He picks up his paper and reads.*
Silence.
The box goes up.
They turn quickly, their eyes meet. BEN *turns to his paper.*
Slowly GUS *goes back to his bed, and sits.*
Silence.
The hatch falls back into place.
They turn quickly, their eyes meet. BEN *turns back to his paper.*
Silence.
BEN *throws his paper down.*)

BEN Kaw!

(*He picks up the paper and looks at it.*)

Listen to this!

(*Pause.*)

What about that, eh?

(*Pause.*)

Kaw!

(*Pause.*)

Have you ever heard such a thing?
GUS (*dully*) Go on!
BEN It's true.
GUS Get away.

BEN It's down here in black and white.
GUS (*very low*) Is that a fact?
BEN Can you imagine it.
GUS It's unbelievable.
BEN It's enough to make you want to puke, isn't it?
GUS (*almost inaudible*) Incredible.

(BEN *shakes his head. He puts the paper down and rises. He fixes the revolver in his holster.*
GUS *stands up. He goes towards the door on the left.*)

BEN Where are you going?
GUS I'm going to have a glass of water.

(*He exits.* BEN *brushes dust off his clothes and shoes. The whistle in the speaking-tube blows. He goes to it, takes the whistle out and puts the tube to his ear. He listens. He puts it to his mouth.*)

BEN Yes.

(*to ear. He listens. to mouth*)

Straight away. Right.

(*to ear. He listens. to mouth*)

Sure we're ready.

(*to ear. He listens. to mouth*)

Understood. Repeat. He has arrived and will be coming in straight away. The normal method to be employed. Understood.

(*to ear. He listens. to mouth*)

Sure we're ready.

(*to ear. He listens. to mouth*)

Right.

(*He hangs the tube up.*)

Gus!

(*He takes out a comb and combs his hair, adjusts his jacket to diminish the bulge of the revolver. The lavatory flushes off left.* BEN *goes quickly to the door, left.*)

Gus!

(*The door right opens sharply.* BEN *turns, his revolver levelled at the door.*
GUS *stumbles in.*
He is stripped of his jacket, waistcoat, tie, holster and revolver.
He stops, body stooping, his arms at his sides.
He raises his head and looks at BEN.
A long silence.
They stare at each other.)

Curtain

A RAISIN IN THE SUN

(1959)

LORRAINE HANSBERRY (1930–1965)

How to define "black drama" in the United States presents a number of problems. The simplest and most unsatisfactory definition is to describe as a black drama any play in which African Americans appear as major characters involved significantly in the plot. This would encompass the first play to embrace the situation of the black in American society, *The Octoroon* (1859) by Dion Boucicault (1822–1900). Melodramatic in its contrived action and in its predominance of stereotyped characters, good and bad, the play does succeed in dramatizing the helpless and essentially hopeless situation of an individual in white society who is considered to be black, no matter how remotely so. This definition would certainly include the most famous of all black-white melodramas, *Uncle Tom's Cabin* (1852), originally a novel by Harriet Beecher Stowe but known around the world in its unauthorized dramatic form, complete with the docile, ever-forgiving Uncle Tom, the "good" slave owner St. Clare, the impish Topsy, the angelic Little Eva, and the villain of all villains, Simon Legree. But the failure of this oversimplified definition is clear. These are not really "black" dramas. They were written by an Irishman and a white New Englander; their production was in the white commercial theatre, and they totally lacked any pretense at serious insight into the psyche of the captive black or analysis of the social curse of slavery itself. And these plays involved as many white as black characters, and, as originally produced, also involved the portrayal of most blacks by white performers in blackface.

A second definition, more appropriate, but still questionable, would be a play devoted entirely to African Americans within the white society, with black protagonists portrayed by blacks themselves. This definition would include *The Emperor Jones* (1921) and *All God's Chillun Got Wings* (1924) by Eugene O'Neill, the first major American plays to use professional African-American actors not as menials or buffoons but as serious, even tragic, characters. Also included would be *In Abraham's Bosom* (1927) by Paul Green (1894–1981), the drama of a

---

The factual material in this introduction was obtained from a variety of essays in *The Black American Writer*, Vol. II, ed. C. W. E. Bigsby, DeLand, FL, Everett/Edwards, 1969. Copyright by C. W. E. Bigsby.

sensitive, educated black man's struggle to provide proper schooling for the children of his race against the bigoted opposition of Southern whites. Not to be ignored in this definition would be *The Green Pastures* (1930) by Marc Connelly (1890–1980), with its all-black cast interpreting Old Testament stories as seen from a deep-South black Sunday school perspective. Perhaps this definition would also include *They Shall Not Die* (1934) by John Wexley (1902–1985), a dramatization of the infamous Scottsboro case in which young black boys were railroaded through court and convicted of raping a white prostitute. The problem here is that all these plays were written by white dramatists, designed for the commercial theatre attended almost exclusively by affluent white audiences.

It could be assumed, then, that "black drama" as a form of American theatre would be better served if defined strictly as a body of plays written by and about African Americans to be performed by blacks, thus offering the points of view, the insights, of blacks themselves, unconcerned with any distortion or social prejudices associated with white perspectives. Well and good, but this raises the question of audience: for whom, exactly, is such black drama created? Is it meant to be for consumption exclusively by blacks? Is it meant to be designed, staged, and acted solely by blacks who can project the subtleties of racial concerns more effectively than whites? These limitations, it hardly need be said, would severely restrict the potential of black artistry and would deprive the great majority of the public from a distinctive theatre experience. After all, if any permanent national recognition is to be gained by a play it must be achieved in a commercial theatre, centering almost entirely in New York and the Broadway stage, and dominated almost exclusively by whites. It is still mostly whites who operate the mechanics of the theatre building, who cast and direct the plays, and who support them with their audience. It is also primarily the white world that offers the criticism, writes the columns and the articles, and awards the prizes. So perhaps it is best not to attempt to define black drama with any precision but to consider it on the basis of each individual work written by an African-American dramatist.

Dramatic enactments of black social, political, or economic problems at the end of the nineteenth and beginning of the twentieth century held little appeal for a public that preferred to ignore the concerns of such a small percentage of the population. Those that were successful gained their audiences because of the exotic nature of the subject, as in *The Emperor Jones* or *All God's Chillun.* Any attempt at serious examination or analysis of black status in society had nowhere to go on stage, although the appearance of novels or poetry by African-American writers was not uncommon. Frederick Douglass, W. E. B. Du Bois, Langston Hughes, Richard Wright, and Ralph Ellison were familiar names. But publishing novels or poetry is far removed from staging plays. The public nature of the drama and the complications of bringing it before the public created substantial barriers, many of them racially motivated.

There was a play by an African-American written as early as 1858, called *The Escape, or a Leap for Freedom,* composed by a fugitive slave named William Wells

Brown (1814–1884), but no record of its production has been found. It would be a full century before anything approaching a serious legitimate black drama could hold the stage in a prolonged New York run, as did Lorraine Hansberry's *A Raisin in the Sun.*

This does not mean that there was no activity at all within that hundred-year interim. Black theatre groups were established in New York during the first decades of the twentieth century with the hope of providing an outlet for black writers and performers and attracting black audiences. Best known were the Harlem Showcase, the Lafayette Theatre (probably the most successful), the American Negro Theatre, and the Rose McClendon Players. During the brief life of the Federal Theatre Project in the 1930s Depression era, a very active Negro unit presented a wide variety of works, including Shakespeare. Their most sensational production was the "voodoo" *Macbeth,* set in Haiti, with genuine witch doctors in the cast.

Very popular were minstrel shows with their lively song-and-dance numbers and low comedy routines, generally performed by whites in burnt-cork blackface. A kind of parallel to them was the so-called "coon" show, with African-American actors putting on similar performances involving gross stereotypes of blacks as viewed by whites. An interesting aspect of these shows, as historians have pointed out, was the total lack of any love songs between on-stage blacks because of the widely held white view that romance was alien to blacks, given their assumed lack of sexual morals. Two musicals of the first decades of the twentieth century that supposedly brought to white audiences a glimpse into the *real* black culture were *Shuffle Along* (1921), an all-black production, written, staged, and performed entirely by blacks, and the adaptation of the Heywards' play *Porgy* (1927) in *Porgy and Bess* in 1935. But here again, it was created by whites, and Gershwin's score was thoroughly Broadway.

An important production was *Mulatto* in 1935, by the poet Langston Hughes (1902–1967). Its father-son conflict was, of course, nothing particularly new, but the subject of the white parent and black child was enough to generate popular support. African-American drama off Broadway did not succeed much better than that produced uptown. Again, Hughes tried his skills in a musical history of blacks in America in *Don't You Want to be Free* in 1937, with the more successful run of about two months of *Big White Fog* in 1938, by Theodore Ward (1902–1983), a portrayal of African-American frustrations in the late twenties and early thirties.

The 1940s brought renewed hope for the social integration of blacks and whites after both races had fought to eliminate the likes of Hitler and his racist world, but, of course, African Americans remained in segregated military units, receiving very little credit for combat valor and led by a single black general officer. (The ultimate irony of this twisted situation was demonstrated in the South where black soldiers transporting German war prisoners ate in the kitchens of restaurants along the way, while the prisoners were served in the dining rooms.) Frustration, of course, was still the reward, although more attention was being paid to black-white problems in a number of major New York productions. *Our Lan'* (1946) by Theodore Ward drew obvious parallels between freed slaves and their denied promises after the Civil War and returning World War II veterans. The most important production in the early forties was *Native Son* (1941), the novel by Richard Wright (1908–1960) adapted by Paul Green, a powerful presentation of the tremendous inner conflict of Bigger Thomas, living in a Chicago slum, who hates both blacks and whites, both of whom seem bent on maintaining the intolerable status quo.

Anna Lucasta (1944) by Philip Yordan (b. 1914) was a moderately successful sympathetic portrayal of an African-American prostitute, but, ironically, it was originally a Polish story, adapted to the needs of the American Negro Theatre. It featured some of the biggest names in black theatre: Ossie Davis, Ruby Dee, Canada Lee, and Sidney Poitier, all of whom became famous on stage and screen beyond the narrow confines of exclusively black theatre.

In 1956 Loften Mitchell (b. 1919) produced *A Land Beyond the River* in a Greenwich Village theatre. It told the real story of a southern black educator, DeLaine, who attempted to get black children into white schools, an action that had helped persuade the Supreme Court in *Brown v. Board of Education* in 1954 that "separate but equal" was an unconstitutional denial of rights. In 1953 *Take a Giant Step* by Louis Peterson (b. 1922) ran for 76 performances. It concerns an educated northern African American in Philadelphia who loses his childhood white friends as they reach maturity and is unable to adjust to being forced to seek his companions in an all-black environment. The popular African-American singer Eartha Kitt appeared in *Mrs. Patterson* (1957) by Charles Sebree (b. 1914) about the daydreams of a girl who longs for the wealth and excitement she sees in her mother's white employer.

The appearance of Lorraine Hansberry's play in 1959 was an entirely new phenomenon, placing the black playwright and black drama itself in a new perspective. During her short lifetime of 34 years, Lorraine Hansberry contributed only two plays to the American theatre: the first, *A Raisin in the Sun,* won the New York Drama Critics' Circle Award and became an outstanding success both in the theatre and on the screen; the second, *The Sign in Sidney Brustein's Window* (1964), was a commercial failure. (Two other pieces, *Les Blancs,* patched together from an incomplete manuscript, and *To Be Young, Gifted and Black,* a collection of excerpts from other writings, were both posthumous.) Her reputation as a major American dramatist rests solely on these two plays, and almost exclusively on *Raisin.*

Hansberry's position in American drama is unique, for she was representative of two neglected minorities in American dramatic art: she was African-American, and she was a woman. Yet without drawing attention to herself because of either of these situations, she wrote, in *A Raisin in the Sun,* one of the major plays of the 1950s and, indeed, of the modern American drama. It is a play about blacks without being a "black" play; it is a well-made problem play centering on one of the most volatile problems of modern American society—social integration of blacks and whites—without making the problem overbearingly central; and it constantly borders on presenting stereotypical characters in a predictably melodramatic situation without actually descending either into stereotype or into overt melodrama.

There is certainly no question that the basic social problem of the 1950s, that of the driving desire of African Americans to pull themselves out of the stifling debilitation of second-class citizenry living in degrading slums, is the basic motivating factor of the play. Close behind are other problems: the suppressed human dignity of people working in menial positions as servants to The Man, with little or no opportunity for advancement; their frustration at being unable to acquire a good education, and so on, down the familiar line. And, of course, climaxing all of this is the crude attempt by the self-righteous residents of Clybourne Park to buy off these intruders into their lily-white WASP paradise.

Nevertheless, Hansberry has devised a very human and humane play based upon the universal problems of human aspirations and striving toward individual and collective dignity, which are exacerbated by the racial situation but which in no way are related *only* to that situation. One can, in fact, be almost colorblind in looking at *A Raisin in the Sun,* because many of the problems—personal, financial, or otherwise—are those faced by any close-knit family attempting to better themselves when the opportunity, in this case in the form of the $10,000 insurance check, presents itself.

It is clear that this family, despite its being led by the dominating matriarch Lena, was once headed by the absent Big Walter, whose hard work and devotion enabled him to provide a relatively decent home and to purchase a substantial and costly life-insurance policy. It is not a gratuitous gift from the gods, but well earned, well deserved. It can serve this family very well materially.

The use and misuse of the money, through Lena's determination to have a better home with sun, air, and flowers, and through Walter Lee's determination to become the man of the house, provide impetus for the development of the characters, but none of the action of the limited plotline centers primarily around blackness and social prejudice as such. It introduces Lindner's misguided efforts to thwart the move, but any violent or traumatic encounter resulting from the move is relegated to the future, offstage, of no immediate concern.

A Raisin in the Sun is a touching, appealing drama about human beings who happen to be black, written by a dramatist who also happened to be black. But there is no cry to arms, no appeal to resist the white world's sinister prejudices. The Youngers choose to function, if permitted, within the world as it exists, making this move toward the comforts and conveniences that should be the privilege of all. Walter Lee has demonstrated that he *can* be a man, liquor store or not, and Lena has seen that her trust in her son, momentarily set back, is justified. The dream is no longer deferred, and we, admiring their determination, cheer the Youngers on, as we would *any* such family, regardless of their race, creed, or color.

A Raisin in the Sun LORRAINE HANSBERRY

To Mama: in gratitude for the dream

CHARACTERS

RUTH YOUNGER
TRAVIS YOUNGER
WALTER LEE YOUNGER (*Brother*)
BENEATHA YOUNGER
LENA YOUNGER (*Mama*)
JOSEPH ASAGAI
GEORGE MURCHISON
KARL LINDNER
BOBO
MOVING MEN

The action of the play is set in Chicago's Southside, sometime between World War II and the present.

ACT I

SCENE I
Friday morning.

SCENE II
The following morning.

ACT II

SCENE I
Later the same day.

SCENE II
Friday night, a few weeks later.

SCENE III
Saturday, moving day, one week later.

ACT III
An hour later.

What happens to a dream deferred?
Does it dry up
Like a raisin in the sun?
Or fester like a sore—

And then run?
Does it stink like rotten meat?
Or crust and sugar over—
Like a syrupy sweet?

Maybe it just sags
Like a heavy load.

Or does it explode?

Langston Hughes[1]

Act I

Scene I

The **Younger** *living room would be a comfortable and well-ordered room if it were not for a number of indestructible contradictions to this state of being. Its furnishings are typical and undistinguished and their primary feature now is that they have clearly had to accommodate the living of too many people for too many years—and they are tired. Still, we can see that at some time, a time probably no longer remembered by the family (except perhaps for* **Mama***), the furnishings of this room were actually selected with care and love and even hope—and brought to this apartment and arranged with taste and pride.*

That was a long time ago. Now the once loved pattern of the couch upholstery has to fight to show itself from under acres of crocheted doilies and couch covers which have themselves finally come to be more important than the upholstery. And here a table or a chair has been moved to disguise the worn places in the carpet; but the carpet has fought back by showing its weariness, with depressing uniformity, elsewhere on its surface.

Weariness has, in fact, won in this room. Everything has been polished, washed, sat on, used, scrubbed too often. All pretenses but living itself have long since vanished from the very atmosphere of this room.

Moreover, a section of this room, for it is not really a room unto itself, though the landlord's lease would make it seem so, slopes backward to provide a small kitchen area, where the family prepares the meals that are eaten in the living room proper, which must also serve as dining room. The single window that has been provided for these "two" rooms is located in this kitchen area. The sole natural light the family may enjoy in the course of a day is only that which fights its way through this little window.

At left, a door leads to a bedroom which is shared by **Mama** *and her daughter,* **Beneatha***. At right, opposite, is a second room (which in the beginning of the life of this apartment was probably a breakfast room), which serves as a bedroom for* **Walter** *and his wife,* **Ruth**.

Time: Sometime between World War II and the present.

Place: Chicago's Southside.

At rise: It is morning dark in the living room. **Travis** *is asleep on the make-down bed at center. An alarm clock sounds from within the bedroom at right, and presently* **Ruth** *enters*

---

[1]From "Dream Deferred." Copyright 1951 by Langston Hughes. Reprinted from *The Panther and the Lash* by Langston Hughes, by permission of Alfred A. Knopf, Inc.

from that room and closes the door behind her. She crosses sleepily toward the window. As she passes her sleeping son she reaches down and shakes him a little. At the window she raises the shade and a dusky Southside morning light comes in feebly. She fills a pot with water and puts it on to boil. She calls to the boy, between yawns, in a slightly muffled voice.

RUTH *is about thirty. We can see that she was a pretty girl, even exceptionally so, but now it is apparent that life has been little that she expected, and disappointment has already begun to hang in her face. In a few years, before thirty-five even, she will be known among her people as a "settled woman."*

She crosses to her son and gives him a good, final, rousing shake.

RUTH Come on now, boy, it's seven thirty! (*Her son sits up at last, in a stupor of sleepiness.*) I say hurry up, Travis! You ain't the only person in the world got to use a bathroom! (*The child, a sturdy, handsome little boy of ten or eleven, drags himself out of the bed and almost blindly takes his towels and "today's clothes" from drawers and a closet and goes out to the bathroom, which is in an outside hall and which is shared by another family or families on the same floor.* RUTH *crosses to the bedroom door at right and opens it and calls in to her husband.*) Walter Lee! . . . It's after seven thirty! Lemme see you do some waking up in there now! (*She waits.*) You better get up from there, man! It's after seven thirty I tell you. (*She waits again.*) All right, you just go ahead and lay there and next thing you know Travis be finished and Mr. Johnson'll be in there and you'll be fussing and cussing round here like a mad man! And be late too! (*She waits, at the end of patience.*) Walter Lee—it's time for you to get up!

(*She waits another second and then starts to go into the bedroom, but is apparently satisfied that her husband has begun to get up. She stops, pulls the door to, and returns to the kitchen area. She wipes her face with a moist cloth and runs her fingers through her sleep-disheveled hair in a vain effort and ties an apron around her housecoat. The bedroom door at right opens and her husband stands in the doorway in his pajamas, which are rumpled and mismated. He is a lean, intense young man in his middle thirties, inclined to quick nervous movements and erratic speech habits—and always in his voice there is a quality of indictment.*)

WALTER Is he out yet?

RUTH What you mean *out?* He ain't hardly got in there good yet.

WALTER (*wandering in, still more oriented to sleep than to a new day*) Well, what was you doing all that yelling for if I can't even get in there yet? (*stopping and thinking*) Check coming today?

RUTH They *said* Saturday and this is just Friday and I hopes to God you ain't going to get up here first thing this morning and start talking to me 'bout no money—'cause I 'bout don't want to hear it.

WALTER Something the matter with you this morning?

RUTH No—I'm just sleepy as the devil. What kind of eggs you want?

WALTER Not scrambled. (RUTH *starts to scramble eggs.*) Paper come? (RUTH *points impatiently to the rolled up* Tribune *on the table, and he gets it and spreads it out and vaguely reads the front page.*) Set off another bomb yesterday.

RUTH (*maximum indifference*) Did they?

WALTER (*looking up*) What's the matter with you?

RUTH Ain't nothing the matter with me. And don't keep asking me that this morning.

WALTER Ain't nobody bothering you. (*reading the news of the day absently again*) Say Colonel McCormick is sick.

RUTH (*affecting tea-party interest*) Is he now? Poor thing.

WALTER (*sighing and looking at his watch*) Oh, me. (*He waits.*) Now what is that boy doing in that bathroom all this time? He just going to have to start getting up earlier. I can't be being late to work on account of him fooling around in there.

RUTH (*turning on him*) Oh, no he ain't going to be getting up no earlier no such thing! It ain't his fault that he can't get to bed no earlier nights 'cause he got a bunch of crazy good-for-nothing clowns sitting up running their mouths in what is supposed to be his bedroom after ten o'clock at night. . . .

WALTER That's what you mad about, ain't it? The things I want to talk about with my friends just couldn't be important in your mind, could they?

(*He rises and finds a cigarette in her handbag on the table and crosses to the little window and looks out, smoking and deeply enjoying this first one.*)

RUTH (*almost matter of factly, a complaint too automatic to deserve emphasis*) Why you always got to smoke before you eat in the morning?

WALTER (*at the window*) Just look at 'em down there. . . . Running and racing to work . . . (*he turns and faces his wife and watches her a moment at the stove, and then, suddenly*) You look young this morning, baby.

RUTH (*indifferently*) Yeah?

WALTER Just for a second—stirring them eggs. It's gone now—just for a second it was—you looked real young again. (*then, drily*) It's gone now—you look like yourself again.

RUTH Man, if you don't shut up and leave me alone.

WALTER (*looking out to the street again*) First thing a man ought to learn in life is not to make love to no colored woman first thing in the morning. You all some evil people at eight o'clock in the morning.

(TRAVIS *appears in the hall doorway, almost fully dressed and quite wide awake now, his towels and pajamas across his shoulders. He opens the door and signals for his father to make the bathroom in a hurry.*)

TRAVIS (*watching the bathroom*) Daddy, come on!

(WALTER *gets his bathroom utensils and flies out to the bathroom.*)

RUTH Sit down and have your breakfast, Travis.

TRAVIS Mama, this is Friday. (*gleefully*) Check coming tomorrow, huh?

RUTH You get your mind off money and eat your breakfast.

TRAVIS (*eating*) This is the morning we supposed to bring the fifty cents to school.

RUTH Well, I ain't got no fifty cents this morning.

TRAVIS Teacher say we have to.

RUTH I don't care what teacher say. I ain't got it. Eat your breakfast, Travis.

TRAVIS I *am* eating.

RUTH Hush up now and just eat!

(*The boy gives her an exasperated look for her lack of understanding, and eats grudgingly.*)

TRAVIS You think Grandmama would have it?

RUTH No! And I want you to stop asking your grandmother for money, you hear me?

TRAVIS (*outraged*) Gaaaleee! I don't ask her, she just gimme it sometimes!

RUTH Travis Willard Younger—I got too much on me this morning to be—

TRAVIS Maybe Daddy—

RUTH *Travis!*

(*The boy hushes abruptly. They are both quiet and tense for several seconds.*)

TRAVIS (*presently*) Could I maybe go carry some groceries in front of the supermarket for a little while after school then?

RUTH Just hush, I said. (TRAVIS *jabs his spoon into his cereal bowl viciously, and rests his head in anger upon his fists.*) If you through eating, you can get over there and make up your bed.

(*The boy obeys stiffly and crosses the room, almost mechanically, to the bed and more or less carefully folds the covering. He carries the bedding into his mother's room and returns with his books and cap.*)

TRAVIS (*sulking and standing apart from her unnaturally*) I'm gone.

RUTH (*looking up from the stove to inspect him automatically*) Come *here.* (*He crosses to her and she studies his head.*) If you don't take this comb and fix this here head, you better! (TRAVIS *puts down his books with a great sigh of oppression, and crosses to the mirror. His mother mutters under her breath about his "slubbornness."*) 'Bout to march out of here with that head looking just like chickens slept in it! I just don't know where you get your slubborn ways. . . . And get your jacket, too. Looks chilly out this morning.

TRAVIS (*with conspicuously brushed hair and jacket*) I'm gone.

RUTH Get carfare and milk money—(*waving one finger*)—and not a single penny for no caps, you hear me?

TRAVIS (*with sullen politeness*) Yes'm.

(*He turns in outrage to leave. His mother watches after him as in his frustration he approaches the door almost comically. When she speaks to him her voice has become a very gentle tease.*)

RUTH (*mocking; as she thinks he would say it*) Oh, Mama makes me so mad sometimes, I don't know what to do! (*She waits and continues to his back as he stands stock-still in front of the door.*) I wouldn't kiss that woman good-bye for nothing in this world this morning! (*The boy finally turns around and rolls his eyes at her, knowing the mood has changed and he is vindicated; he does not, however, move toward her yet.*) Not for nothing in this world! (*She finally laughs aloud at him and holds out her arms to him and we see that it is a way between them, very old and practiced. He crosses to her and allows her to embrace him warmly but keeps his face fixed with masculine rigidity. She holds him back from her presently and looks at him and runs her fingers over the features of his face. With utter gentleness—*) Now—whose little old angry man are you?

TRAVIS (*the masculinity and gruffness start to fade at last*) Aw gaalee—Mama . . .

RUTH (*mimicking*) Aw—gaaaaalleeeee, Mama! (*She pushes him, with rough playfulness and finality, toward the door.*) Get on out of here or you going to be late.

TRAVIS (*in the face of love, new aggressiveness*) Mama, could I *please* go carry groceries?

RUTH Honey, it's starting to get so cold evenings.

WALTER (*coming in from the bathroom and drawing a make-believe gun from a make-believe holster and shooting at his son*) What is it he wants to do?

RUTH Go carry groceries after school at the supermarket.

WALTER Well, let him go . . .

TRAVIS (*quickly, to the ally*) I *have* to—she won't gimme the fifty cents. . . .

WALTER (*to his wife only*) Why not?

RUTH (*simply, and with flavor*) 'Cause we don't have it.

WALTER (*to* RUTH *only*) What you tell the boys things like that for? (*reaching down into his pants with a rather important gesture*) Here, son—

(*He hands the boy the coin, but his eyes are directed to his wife's.* TRAVIS *takes the money happily.*)

TRAVIS Thanks, Daddy.

(*He starts out.* RUTH *watches both of them with murder in her eyes.* WALTER *stands and stares back at her with defiance, and suddenly reaches into his pocket again on an afterthought.*)

WALTER (*without even looking at his son, still staring hard at his wife*) In fact, here's another fifty cents. . . . Buy yourself some fruit today—or take a taxi-cab to school or something!

TRAVIS Whoopee—

(*He leaps up and clasps his father around the middle with his legs, and they face each other in mutual appreciation; slowly* WALTER LEE *peeks around the boy to catch the violent rays from his wife's eyes and draws his head back as if shot.*)

WALTER You better get down now—and get to school, man.

TRAVIS (*at the door*) O.K. Good-bye. (*He exits.*)

WALTER (*after him, pointing with pride*) That's *my* boy. (*She looks at him with disgust and turns back to her work.*) You know what I was thinking 'bout in the bathroom this morning?

RUTH No.

WALTER How come you always try to be so pleasant!

RUTH What is there to be pleasant 'bout!

WALTER You want to know what I was thinking 'bout in the bathroom or not!

RUTH I know what you thinking 'bout.

WALTER (*ignoring her*) 'Bout what me and Willy Harris was talking about last night.

RUTH (*immediately—a refrain*) Willy Harris is a good-for-nothing loud mouth.

WALTER Anybody who talks to me has got to be a good-for-nothing loud mouth, ain't he? And what you know about who is just a good-for-nothing loud mouth? Charlie Atkins was just a "good-for-nothing loud mouth" too, wasn't he! When he wanted me to go in the dry-cleaning business with him. And now—he's grossing a hundred thousand a year. A hundred thousand dollars a year! You still call *him* a loud mouth!

RUTH (*bitterly*) Oh, Walter Lee. . . . (*She folds her head on her arms over the table.*)

WALTER (*rising and coming to her and standing over her*) You tired, ain't you? Tired of everything. Me, the boy, the way we live—this beat-up hole—everything. Ain't you? (*She doesn't look up, doesn't answer.*) So tired—moaning and groaning all the time, but you wouldn't do nothing to help, would you? You couldn't be on my side that long for nothing, could you?

RUTH Walter, please leave me alone.

WALTER A man needs for a woman to back him up. . . .

RUTH Walter—

WALTER Mama would listen to you. You know she listen to you more than she do me and Bennie. She think more of you. All you have to do is just sit down with her when you drinking your coffee one morning and talking 'bout things like you do and—(*He sits down beside her and demonstrates graphically what he thinks her methods and tone should be.*)—you just sip your coffee, see, and say easy like that you been thinking 'bout that deal Walter Lee is so interested in, 'bout the store and all, and sip some more coffee, like what you saying ain't really that important to you—And the next thing you know, she be listening good and asking you questions and when I come home—I can tell her the details. This ain't no fly-by-night proposition, baby. I mean we figured it out, me and Willy and Bobo.

RUTH (*with a frown*) Bobo?

WALTER Yeah. You see, this little liquor store we got in mind cost seventy-five thousand and we figured the initial investment on the place be 'bout thirty thousand, see. That be ten thousand each. Course, there's a couple of hundred you got to pay so's you don't spend your life just waiting for them clowns to let your license get approved—

RUTH You mean graft?

WALTER (*frowning impatiently*) Don't call it that. See there, that just goes to show you what women understand about the world. Baby, don't *nothing* happen for you in this world 'less you pay *somebody* off!

RUTH Walter, leave me alone! (*She raises her head and stares at him vigorously—then says, more quietly*) *Eat* your eggs, they gonna be cold.

WALTER (*straightening up from her and looking off*) That's it. There you are. Man say to his woman: I got me a dream. His woman say: Eat your eggs. (*sadly, but gaining in power*) Man say: I got to take hold of this here world, baby! And a woman will say: Eat your eggs and go to work. (*passionately now*) Man say: I got to change my life, I'm choking to death, baby! And his woman say— (*in utter anguish as he brings his fists down on his thighs*)—Your eggs is getting cold!

RUTH (*softly*) Walter, that ain't none of our money.

WALTER (*not listening at all or even looking at her*) This morning, I was lookin' in the mirror and thinking about it. . . . I'm thirty-five years old; I been married eleven years and I got a boy who sleeps in the living room—(*very, very quietly*)—and all I got to give him is stories about how rich white people live. . . .

RUTH Eat your eggs, Walter.

WALTER *Damn my eggs . . . damn all the eggs that ever was!*

RUTH Then go to work.

WALTER (*looking up at her*) See—I'm trying to talk to you 'bout myself—(*shaking his head with the repetition*)—and all you can say is eat them eggs and go to work.

RUTH (*wearily*) Honey, you never say nothing new. I listen to you every day, every night and every morning, and you never say nothing new. (*shrugging*) So you would rather *be* Mr. Arnold than be his chauffeur. So—I would *rather* be living in Buckingham Palace.

WALTER That is just what is wrong with the colored woman in this world. . . . Don't understand about building their men up and making 'em feel like they somebody. Like they can do something.

RUTH (*drily, but to hurt*) There *are* colored men who do things.

WALTER No thanks to the colored woman.

RUTH Well, being a colored woman, I guess I can't help myself none.

(*She rises and gets the ironing board and sets it up and attacks a huge pile of rough-dried clothes, sprinkling them in preparation for the ironing and then rolling them into tight fat balls.*)

WALTER (*mumbling*) We one group of men tied to a race of women with small minds.

(*His sister* BENEATHA *enters. She is about twenty, as slim and intense as her brother. She is not as pretty as her sister-in-law, but her lean, almost intellectual face has a handsomeness of its own. She wears a bright-red flannel nightie, and her thick hair stands wildly about her head. Her speech is a mixture of many things; it is different from the rest of the family's insofar as education has permeated her sense of English—and perhaps the Midwest rather than the South has finally—at last—won out in her inflection; but not altogether, because over all of it is a soft slurring and transformed use of vowels which is the decided influence of the Southside. She passes through the room without looking at either* RUTH *or* WALTER *and goes to the outside door and looks, a little blindly, out to the bathroom. She sees that it has been lost to the Johnsons. She closes the door with a sleepy vengeance and crosses to the table and sits down a little defeated.*)

BENEATHA I am going to start timing those people.

WALTER You should get up earlier.

BENEATHA (*her face in her hands; she is still fighting the urge to go back to bed*) Really—would you suggest dawn? Where's the paper?

WALTER (*pushing the paper across the table to her as he studies her almost clinically, as though he has never seen her before*) You a horrible-looking chick at this hour.

BENEATHA (*drily*) Good morning, everybody.

WALTER (*senselessly*) How is school coming?

BENEATHA (*in the same spirit*) Lovely. Lovely. And you know, biology is the greatest. (*looking up at him*) I dissected something that looked just like you yesterday.

WALTER I just wondered if you've made up your mind and everything.

BENEATHA (*gaining in sharpness and impatience*) And what did I answer yesterday morning—and the day before that?

RUTH (*from the ironing board, like someone disinterested and old*) Don't be so nasty, Bennie.

BENEATHA (*still to her brother*) And the day before that and the day before that!

WALTER (*defensively*) I'm interested in you. Something wrong with that? Ain't many girls who decide—

WALTER *and* BENEATHA (*in unison*) —"to be a doctor."

(*Silence.*)

WALTER Have we figured out yet just exactly how much medical school is going to cost?

RUTH Walter Lee, why don't you leave that girl alone and get out of here to work?

BENEATHA (*exits to the bathroom and bangs on the door*) Come on out of there, please! (*She comes back into the room.*)

WALTER (*looking at his sister intently*) You know the check is coming tomorrow.

BENEATHA (*turning on him with a sharpness all her own*) That money belongs to Mama, Walter, and it's for her to decide how she wants to use it. I don't care if she wants to buy a house or a rocket ship or just nail it up somewhere and look at it. It's hers. Not ours—*hers.*

WALTER (*bitterly*) Now ain't that fine! You just got your mother's interest at heart, ain't you, girl? You such a nice girl—but if Mama got that money she can always take a few thousand and help you through school too—can't she?

BENEATHA I have never asked anyone around here to do anything for me!

WALTER No! And the line between asking and just accepting when the time comes is big and wide—ain't it!

BENEATHA (*with fury*) What do you want from me, Brother—that I quit school or just drop dead, which!

WALTER I don't want nothing but for you to stop acting holy 'round here. Me and Ruth done made some sacrifices for you—why can't you do something for the family?

RUTH Walter, don't be dragging me in it.

WALTER You are in it—Don't you get up and go work in somebody's kitchen for the last three years to help put clothes on her back?

RUTH Oh, Walter—that's not fair. . . .

WALTER It ain't that nobody expects you to get on your knees and say thank you, Brother; thank you, Ruth; thank you, Mama—and thank you, Travis, for wearing the same pair of shoes for two semesters—

BENEATHA (*dropping to her knees*) Well—I *do*—all right?—thank everybody . . . and forgive me for ever wanting to be anything at all . . . forgive me, forgive me!

RUTH Please stop it! Your mama'll hear you.

WALTER Who the hell told you you had to be a doctor? If you so crazy 'bout messing 'round with sick people—then go be a nurse like other women—or just get married and be quiet. . . .

BENEATHA Well—you finally got it said. . . . It took you three years but you finally got it said. Walter, give up; leave me alone—it's Mama's money.

WALTER *He was my father, too!*

BENEATHA So what? He was mine, too—and Travis' grandfather—but the insurance money belongs to Mama. Picking on me is not going to make her give it to you to invest in any liquor stores—(*underbreath, dropping into a chair*)—and I for one say, God bless Mama for that!

WALTER (*to* RUTH) See—did you hear? Did you hear!

RUTH Honey, please go to work.

WALTER Nobody in this house is ever going to understand me.

BENEATHA Because you're a nut.

WALTER Who's a nut?

BENEATHA You—you are a nut. Thee is mad, boy.

WALTER (*looking at his wife and his sister from the door, very sadly*) The world's most backward race of people, and that's a fact.

BENEATHA (*turning slowly in her chair*) And then there are all those prophets who would lead us out of the wilderness—(WALTER *slams out of the house.*)—into the swamps!

RUTH Bennie, why you always gotta be pickin' on your brother? Can't you be a little sweeter sometimes?

(*Door opens.* WALTER *walks in.*)

WALTER (*to* RUTH) I need some money for carfare.

RUTH (*looks at him, then warms; teasing, but tenderly*) Fifty cents? (*She goes to her bag and gets money.*) Here, take a taxi!

(WALTER *exits.* MAMA *enters. She is a woman in her early sixties, full-bodied and strong. She is one of those women of a certain grace and beauty who wear it so unobtrusively that it takes a while to notice. Her dark-brown face is surrounded by the total whiteness of her hair, and, being a woman who has adjusted to many things in life and overcome many more, her face is full of strength. She has, we can see, wit and faith of a kind that keep her eyes lit and full of interest and expectancy. She is, in a word, a beautiful woman. Her bearing is perhaps most like the noble bearing of the women of the Hereros of Southwest Africa—rather as if she imagines that as she walks she still bears a basket or a vessel upon her head. Her speech, on the other hand, is as careless as her carriage is precise—she is inclined to slur everything—but her voice is perhaps not so much quiet as simply soft.*)

MAMA Who that 'round here slamming doors at this hour?

(*She crosses through the room, goes to the window, opens it, and brings in a feeble little plant growing doggedly in a small pot on the window sill. She feels the dirt and puts it back out.*)

RUTH That was Walter Lee. He and Bennie was at it again.

MAMA My children and they tempers. Lord, if this little old plant don't get more sun than it's been getting it ain't never going to see spring again. (*She turns from the window.*) What's the matter with you this morning, Ruth? You looks right peaked. You aiming to iron all them things? Leave some for me. I'll get to 'em this afternoon. Bennie honey, it's too drafty for you to be sitting 'round half dressed. Where's your robe?

BENEATHA In the cleaners.

MAMA Well, go get mine and put it on.

BENEATHA I'm not cold, Mama, honest.

MAMA I know—but you so thin. . . .

BENEATHA (*irritably*) Mama, I'm not cold.

MAMA (*seeing the make-down bed as* TRAVIS *has left it*) Lord have mercy, look at that poor bed. Bless his heart—he tries, don't he? (*She moves to the bed* TRAVIS *has sloppily made up.*)

RUTH No—he don't half try at all 'cause he knows you going to come along behind him and fix everything. That's just how come he don't know how to do nothing right now—you done spoiled that boy so.

MAMA Well—he's a little boy. Ain't supposed to know 'bout housekeeping. My baby, that's what he is. What you fix for his breakfast this morning?

RUTH (*angrily*) I feed my son, Lena!

MAMA I ain't meddling—(*underbreath; busy bodyish*)—I just noticed all last week he had cold cereal, and when it starts getting this chilly in the fall a child ought to have some hot grits or something when he goes out in the cold—

RUTH (*furious*) I gave him hot oats—is that all right!

MAMA I ain't meddling. (*pause*) Put a lot of nice butter on it? (RUTH *shoots her an angry look and does not reply.*) He likes lots of butter.

RUTH (*exasperated*) Lena—

MAMA (*to* BENEATHA; MAMA *is inclined to wander conversationally sometimes*) What was you and your brother fussing 'bout this morning?

BENEATHA It's not important, Mama.

(*She gets up and goes to look out at the bathroom, which is apparently free, and she picks up her towels and rushes out.*)

MAMA What was they fighting about?

RUTH Now you know as well as I do.

MAMA (*shaking her head*) Brother still worrying his self sick about that money?

RUTH You know he is.

MAMA You had breakfast?

RUTH Some coffee.

MAMA Girl, you better start eating and looking after yourself better. You almost thin as Travis.

RUTH Lena—

MAMA Un-hunh?

RUTH What are you going to do with it?

MAMA Now don't you start, child. It's too early in the morning to be talking about money. It ain't Christian.

RUTH It's just that he got his heart set on that store—

MAMA You mean that liquor store that Willy Harris want him to invest in?

RUTH Yes—

MAMA We ain't no business people, Ruth. We just plain working folks.

RUTH Ain't nobody business people till they go into business. Walter Lee say colored people ain't never going to start getting ahead till they start gambling on some different kinds of things in the world—investments and things.

MAMA What done got into you, girl? Walter Lee done finally sold you on investing.

RUTH No. Mama, something is happening between Walter and me. I don't know what it is—but he needs something—something I can't give him any more. He needs this chance, Lena.

MAMA (*frowning deeply*) But liquor, honey—

RUTH Well—like Walter say—I spec people going to always be drinking themselves some liquor.

MAMA Well—whether they drinks it or not ain't none of my business. But whether I go into business selling it to 'em *is,* and I don't want that on my ledger this late in life. (*stopping suddenly and studying her daughter-in-law*) Ruth Younger, what's the matter with you today? You look like you could fall over right there.

RUTH I'm tired.

MAMA Then you better stay home from work today.

RUTH I can't stay home. She'd be calling up the agency and screaming at them, "My girl didn't come in today—send me somebody! My girl didn't come in!" Oh, she just have a fit. . . .

MAMA Well, let her have it. I'll just call her up and say you got the flu—

RUTH (*laughing*) Why the flu?

MAMA 'Cause it sounds respectable to 'em. Something white people get, too. They know 'bout the flu. Otherwise they think you been cut up or something when you tell 'em you sick.

RUTH I got to go in. We need the money.

MAMA Somebody would of thought my children done all but starved to death the way they talk about money here late. Child, we got a great big old check coming tomorrow.

RUTH (*sincerely, but also self-righteously*) Now that's your money. It ain't got nothing to do with me. We all feel like that—Walter and Bennie and me—even Travis.

MAMA (*thoughtfully, and suddenly very far away*) Ten thousand dollars—

RUTH Sure is wonderful.

MAMA Ten thousand dollars.

RUTH You know what you should do, Miss Lena? You should take yourself a trip somewhere. To Europe or South America or someplace—

MAMA (*throwing up her hands at the thought*) Oh, child!

RUTH I'm serious. Just pack up and leave! Go on away and enjoy yourself some. Forget about the family and have yourself a ball for once in your life—

MAMA (*drily*) You sound like I'm just about ready to die. Who'd go with me? What I look like wandering 'round Europe by myself?

RUTH Shoot—these here rich white women do it all the time. They don't think nothing of packing up they suitcases and piling on one of them big steamships and—swoosh!—they gone, child.

MAMA Something always told me I wasn't no rich white woman.

RUTH Well—what are you going to do with it then?

MAMA I ain't rightly decided. (*thinking. She speaks now with emphasis.*) Some of it got to be put away for Beneatha and her schoolin'—and ain't nothing going to touch that part of it. Nothing. (*She waits several seconds, trying to make up her mind about something, and looks at* RUTH *a little tentatively before going on.*) Been thinking that we maybe could meet the notes on a little old two-story somewhere, with a yard where Travis could play in the summertime, if we use part of the insurance for a down payment and everybody kind of pitch in. I could maybe take on a little day work again, few days a week—

RUTH (*studying her mother-in-law furtively and concentrating on her ironing, anxious to encourage without seeming to*) Well, Lord knows, we've put enough rent into this here rat trap to pay for four houses by now. . . .

MAMA (*looking up at the words "rat trap" and then looking around and leaning back and sighing—in a suddenly reflective mood—*) "Rat trap"—yes, that's all it is. (*smiling*) I remember just as well the day me and Big Walter moved in here. Hadn't been married but two weeks and wasn't planning on living here no more than a year. (*She shakes her head at the dissolved dream.*) We was going to set away, little by little, don't you know, and buy a little place out in Morgan Park. We had even picked out the house. (*chuckling a little*) Looks right dumpy today. But Lord, child, you should know all the dreams I had 'bout buying that house and fixing it up and making me a little garden in the back—(*She waits and stops smiling.*) And didn't none of it happen. (*dropping her hands in a futile gesture*)

RUTH (*keeps her head down, ironing*) Yes, life can be a barrel of disappointments, sometimes.

MAMA Honey, Big Walter would come in here some nights back then and slump down on that couch there and just look at the rug, and look at me and look at the rug and then back at me—and I'd know he was down then . . . really down. (*After a second very long and thoughtful pause; she is seeing back to times that only she can see.*) And then, Lord, when I lost that baby—little Claude—I almost thought I was going to lose Big Walter too. Oh, that man grieved hisself! He was one man to love his children.

RUTH Ain't nothin' can tear at you like losin' your baby.

MAMA I guess that's how come that man finally worked hisself to death like he done. Like he was fighting his own war with this here world that took his baby from him.

RUTH He sure was a fine man, all right. I always liked Mr. Younger.

MAMA Crazy 'bout his children! God knows there was plenty wrong with Walter Younger—hard-headed, mean, kind of wild with women—plenty wrong with him. But he sure loved his children. Always wanted them to have something—be something. That's where Brother gets all these notions, I reckon. Big Walter used to say, he'd get right wet in the eyes sometimes, lean his head back with the water standing in his eyes and say, "Seem like God didn't see fit to give the black man nothing but dreams—but He did give us children to make them dreams seem worth while." (*She smiles.*) He could talk like that, don't you know.

RUTH Yes, he sure could. He was a good man, Mr. Younger.

MAMA Yes, a fine man—just couldn't never catch up with his dreams, that's all.

(BENEATHA *comes in, brushing her hair and looking up to the ceiling, where the sound of a vacuum cleaner has started up.*)

BENEATHA What could be so dirty on that woman's rugs that she has to vacuum them every single day?

RUTH I wish certain young women 'round here who I could name would take inspiration about certain rugs in a certain apartment I could also mention.

BENEATHA (*shrugging*) How much cleaning can a house need, for Christ's sakes.

MAMA (*not liking the Lord's name used thus*) Bennie!

RUTH Just listen to her—just listen!

BENEATHA Oh, God!

MAMA If you use the Lord's name just one more time—

BENEATHA (*a bit of a whine*) Oh, Mama—

RUTH Fresh—just fresh as salt, this girl!

BENEATHA (*drily*) Well—if the salt loses its savor—

MAMA Now that will do. I just ain't going to have you 'round here reciting the scriptures in vain—you hear me?

BENEATHA How did I manage to get on everybody's wrong side by just walking into a room?

RUTH If you weren't so fresh—

BENEATHA Ruth, I'm twenty years old.

MAMA What time you be home from school today?

BENEATHA Kind of late. (*with enthusiasm*) Madeline is going to start my guitar lessons today.

(MAMA *and* RUTH *look up with the same expression.*)

MAMA Your *what* kind of lessons?

BENEATHA Guitar.

RUTH Oh, Father!

MAMA How come you done taken it in your mind to learn to play the guitar?

BENEATHA I just want to, that's all.

MAMA (*smiling*) Lord, child, don't you know what to do with yourself? How long it going to be before you get tired of this now—like you got tired of that little play-acting group you joined last year? (*looking at* RUTH) And what was it the year before that?

RUTH The horseback-riding club for which she bought that fifty-five-dollar riding habit that's been hanging in the closet ever since!

MAMA (*to* BENEATHA) Why you got to flit so from one thing to another, baby?

BENEATHA (*sharply*) I just want to learn to play the guitar. Is there anything wrong with that?

MAMA Ain't nobody trying to stop you. I just wonders sometimes why you has to flit so from one thing to another all the time. You ain't never done nothing with all that camera equipment you brought home—

BENEATHA I don't flit! I—I experiment with different forms of expression—

RUTH Like riding a horse?

BENEATHA —People have to express themselves one way or another.

MAMA What is it you want to express?

BENEATHA (*angrily*) Me! (MAMA *and* RUTH *look at each other and burst into raucous laughter.*) Don't worry—I don't expect you to understand.

MAMA (*to change the subject*) Who you going out with tomorrow night?

BENEATHA (*with displeasure*) George Murchison again.

MAMA (*pleased*) Oh—you getting a little sweet on him?

RUTH You ask me, this child ain't sweet on nobody but herself—(*underbreath*) Express herself!

(*They laugh.*)

BENEATHA Oh—I like George all right, Mama. I mean I like him enough to go out with him and stuff, but—

RUTH (*for devilment*) What does *and stuff* mean?

BENEATHA Mind your own business.

MAMA Stop picking at her now, Ruth. (*a thoughtful pause, and then a suspicious sudden look at her daughter as she turns in her chair for emphasis*) What *does* it mean?

BENEATHA (*wearily*) Oh, I just mean I couldn't ever really be serious about George. He's—he's so shallow.

RUTH Shallow—what do you mean he's shallow? He's *rich!*

MAMA Hush, Ruth.

BENEATHA I know he's rich. He knows he's rich, too.

RUTH Well—what other qualities a man got to have to satisfy you, little girl?

BENEATHA You wouldn't even begin to understand. Anybody who married Walter could not possibly understand.

MAMA (*outraged*) What kind of way is that to talk about your brother?

BENEATHA Brother is a flip—let's face it.

MAMA (*to* RUTH, *helplessly*) What's a flip?

RUTH (*glad to add kindling*) She's saying he's crazy.

BENEATHA Not crazy. Brother isn't really crazy yet—he—he's an elaborate neurotic.

MAMA Hush your mouth!

BENEATHA As for George. Well. George looks good—he's got a beautiful car and he takes me to nice places and, as my sister-in-law says, he is probably the richest boy I will ever get to know and I even like him sometimes—but if the Youngers are sitting around waiting to see if their little Bennie is going to tie up the family with the Murchisons, they are wasting their time.

RUTH You mean you wouldn't marry George Murchison if he asked you someday? That pretty, rich thing? Honey, I knew you was odd—

BENEATHA No I would not marry him if all I felt for him was what I feel now. Besides, George's family wouldn't really like it.

MAMA Why not?

BENEATHA Oh, Mama—The Murchisons are honest-to-God-real-*live*-rich colored people, and the only people in the world who are more snobbish than rich white people are rich colored people. I thought everybody knew that. I've met Mrs. Murchison. She's a scene!

MAMA You must not dislike people 'cause they well off, honey.

BENEATHA Why not? It makes just as much sense as disliking people 'cause they are poor, and lots of people do that.

RUTH (*a wisdom-of-the-ages manner; to* MAMA) Well, she'll get over some of this—

BENEATHA Get over it? What are you talking about, Ruth? Listen, I'm going to be a doctor. I'm not worried about who I'm going to marry yet—if I ever get married.

MAMA *and* RUTH *If!*

MAMA Now, Bennie—

BENEATHA Oh, I probably will . . . but first I'm going to be a doctor, and George, for one, still think's that's pretty funny. I couldn't be bothered with that, I am going to be a doctor and everybody around here better understand that!

MAMA (*kindly*) 'Course you going to be a doctor, honey, God willing.

BENEATHA (*drily*) God hasn't got a thing to do with it.

MAMA Beneatha—that just wasn't necessary.

BENEATHA Well—neither is God. I get sick of hearing about God.

MAMA Beneatha!

BENEATHA I mean it! I'm just tired of hearing about God all the time. What has He got to do with anything? Does He pay tuition?

MAMA You 'bout to get your fresh little jaw slapped!

RUTH That's just what she needs, all right!

BENEATHA Why? Why can't I say what I want to around here, like everybody else?

MAMA It don't sound nice for a young girl to say things like that—you wasn't brought up that way. Me and your father went to trouble to get you and Brother to church every Sunday.

BENEATHA Mama, you don't understand. It's all a matter of ideas, and God is just one idea I don't accept. It's not important, I am not going out and be immoral or commit crimes because I don't believe in God. I don't even think about it. It's just that I get tired of Him getting credit for all the things the human race achieves through its own stubborn effort. There simply is no blasted God—there is only man and it is he who makes miracles!

(MAMA *absorbs this speech, studies her daughter and rises slowly and crosses to* BENEATHA *and slaps her powerfully across the face. After, there is only silence and the daughter drops her eyes from her mother's face, and* MAMA *is very tall before her.*)

MAMA Now—you say after me, in my mother's house there is still God. (*There is a long pause and* BENEATHA *stares at the floor wordlessly.* MAMA *repeats the phrase with precision and cool emotion.*) In my mother's house there is still God.

BENEATHA In my mother's house there is still God.

(*A long pause.*)

MAMA (*walking away from* BENEATHA, *too disturbed for triumphant posture; stopping and turning back to her daughter*) There are some ideas we ain't going to have in this house. Not long as I am at the head of this family.

BENEATHA Yes, ma'am.

(MAMA *walks out of the room.*)

RUTH (*almost gently, with profound understanding*) You think you a woman, Bennie—but you still a little girl. What you did was childish—so you got treated like a child.

BENEATHA I see. (*quietly*) I also see that everybody thinks it's all right for Mama to be a tyrant. But all the tyranny in the world will never put a God in the heavens! (*She picks up her books and goes out.*)

RUTH (*goes to* MAMA'*s door*) She said she was sorry.

MAMA (*coming out, going to her plant*) They frightens me, Ruth. My children.

RUTH You got good children, Lena. They just a little off sometimes—but they're good.

MAMA No—there's something come down between me and them that don't let us understand each other and I don't know what it is. One done almost lost his mind thinking 'bout money all the time and the other done commence to talk about things I can't seem to understand in no form or fashion. What is it that's changing, Ruth?

RUTH (*soothingly, older than her years*) Now . . . you taking it all too seriously. You just got strong-willed children and it takes a strong woman like you to keep 'em in hand.

MAMA (*looking at her plant and sprinkling a little water on it*) They spirited all right, my children. Got to admit they got spirit—Bennie and Walter. Like this old plant that ain't never had enough sunshine or nothing—and look at it. . . .

(*She has her back to* RUTH, *who has had to stop ironing and lean against something and put the back of her hand to her forehead.*)

RUTH (*trying to keep* MAMA *from noticing*) You . . . sure . . . loves that little old thing, don't you? . . .

MAMA Well, I always wanted me a garden like I used to see sometimes at the back of the houses down home. This plant is close as I ever got to having one. (*She looks out of the window as she replaces the plant.*) Lord, ain't nothing as dreary as the view from this window on a dreary day, is there? Why ain't you singing this morning, Ruth? Sing that "No Ways Tired." That song always lifts me up so—(*She turns at last to see that* RUTH *has slipped quietly into a chair, in a state of semiconsciousness.*) Ruth! Ruth honey—what's the matter with you . . . Ruth!

Curtain

Scene II

It is the following morning; a Saturday morning, and house cleaning is in progress at the **YOUNGERS.** *Furniture has been shoved hither and yon and* **MAMA** *is giving the kitchen-area walls a washing down.* **BENEATHA,** *in dungarees, with a handkerchief tied around her face, is spraying insecticide into the cracks in the walls. As they work, the radio is on and a Southside disc-jockey program is inappropriately filling the house with a rather exotic saxophone blues.* **TRAVIS,** *the sole idle one, is leaning on his arms, looking out of the window.*

TRAVIS Grandmama, that stuff Bennie is using smells awful. Can I go downstairs, please?

MAMA Did you get all them chores done already? I ain't see you doing much.

TRAVIS Yes'm—finished early. Where did Mama go this morning?

MAMA (*looking at* BENEATHA) She had to go on a little errand.

TRAVIS Where?

MAMA To tend to her business.

TRAVIS Can I go outside then?

MAMA Oh, I guess so. You better stay right in front of the house, though . . . and keep a good lookout for the postman.

TRAVIS Yes'm. (*He starts out and decides to give his* AUNT BENEATHA *a good swat on the legs as he passes her.*) Leave them poor little old cockroaches alone, they ain't bothering you none.

(*He runs as she swings the spray gun at him both viciously and playfully.* WALTER *enters from the bedroom and goes to the phone.*)

MAMA Look out there, girl, before you be spilling some of that stuff on that child!

TRAVIS (*teasing*) That's right—look out now! (*He exits.*)

BENEATHA (*drily*) I can't imagine that it would hurt him—it has never hurt the roaches.

MAMA Well, little boys' hides ain't as tough as Southside roaches.

WALTER (*into phone*) Hello—Let me talk to Willy Harris.

MAMA You better get over there behind the bureau. I seen one marching out of there like Napoleon yesterday.

WALTER Hello. Willy? It ain't come yet. It'll be here in a few minutes. Did the lawyer give you the papers?

BENEATHA There's really only one way to get rid of them, Mama—

MAMA How?

BENEATHA Set fire to this building.

WALTER Good. Good. I'll be right over.

BENEATHA Where did Ruth go, Walter?

WALTER I don't know. (*He exits abruptly.*)

BENEATHA Mama, where did Ruth go?

MAMA (*looking at her with meaning*) To the doctor, I think.

BENEATHA The doctor? What's the matter? (*They exchange glances.*) You don't think—

MAMA (*with her sense of drama*) Now I ain't saying what I think. But I ain't never been wrong 'bout a woman neither.

(*The phone rings.*)

BENEATHA (*at the phone*) Hay-lo . . . (*pause, and a moment of recognition*) Well—when did you get back! . . . And how was it? . . . Of course I've missed you—in my way. . . . This morning? No . . . house cleaning and all that and Mama hates it if I let people come over when the house is like this. . . . You *have?* Well, that's different. . . . What is it—Oh, what the hell, come on over. . . . Right, see you then. (*She hangs up.*)

MAMA (*who has listened vigorously, as is her habit*) Who is that you inviting over here with this house looking like this? You ain't got the pride you was born with!

BENEATHA Asagai doesn't care how houses look, Mama—he's an intellectual.

MAMA *Who?*

BENEATHA Asagai—Joseph Asagai. He's an African boy I met on campus. He's been studying in Canada all summer.

MAMA What's his name?

BENEATHA Asagai, Joseph. Ah-sah-guy . . . He's from Nigeria.

MAMA Oh, that's the little country that was founded by slaves way back. . . .

BENEATHA No, Mama—that's Liberia.

MAMA I don't think I never met no African before.

BENEATHA Well, do me a favor and don't ask him a whole lot of ignorant questions about Africans. I mean, do they wear clothes and all that—

MAMA Well, now, I guess if you think we so ignorant 'round here maybe you shouldn't bring your friends here—

BENEATHA It's just that people ask such crazy things. All anyone seems to know about when it comes to Africa is Tarzan—

MAMA (*indignantly*) Why should I know anything about Africa?

BENEATHA Why do you give money at church for the missionary work?

MAMA Well, that's to help save people.

BENEATHA You mean to save them from *heathenism*—

MAMA (*innocently*) Yes.

BENEATHA I'm afraid they need more salvation from the British and the French.

(RUTH *comes in forlornly and pulls off her coat with dejection. They both turn to look at her.*)

RUTH (*dispiritedly*) Well, I guess from all the happy faces—everybody knows.

BENEATHA You pregnant?

MAMA Lord have mercy, I sure hope it's a little old girl. Travis ought to have a sister.

(BENEATHA *and* RUTH *give her a hopeless look for this grandmotherly enthusiasm.*)

BENEATHA How far along are you?

RUTH Two months.

BENEATHA Did you mean to? I mean did you plan it or was it an accident?

MAMA What do you know about planning or not planning?

BENEATHA Oh, Mama.

RUTH (*wearily*) She's twenty years old, Lena.

BENEATHA Did you plan it, Ruth?

RUTH Mind your own business.

BENEATHA It is my business—where is he going to live, on the *roof*? (*There is silence following the remark as the three women react to the sense of it.*) Gee—I didn't mean that, Ruth, honest. Gee, I don't feel like that at all. I—I think it is wonderful.

RUTH (*dully*) Wonderful.

BENEATHA Yes—really.

MAMA (*looking at* RUTH, *worried*) Doctor say everything going to be all right?
RUTH (*far away*) Yes—she says everything is going to be fine. . . .
MAMA (*immediately suspicious*) "She"—What doctor you went to?

(RUTH *folds over, near hysteria.*)

MAMA (*worriedly hovering over* RUTH) Ruth honey—what's the matter with you—you sick?

(RUTH *has her fists clenched on her thighs and is fighting hard to suppress a scream that seems to be rising in her.*)

BENEATHA What's the matter with her, Mama?
MAMA (*working her fingers in* RUTH'S *shoulder to relax her*) She be all right. Women gets right depressed sometimes when they get her way. (*speaking softly, expertly, rapidly*) Now you just relax. That's right . . . just lean back, don't think 'bout nothing at all . . . nothing at all—
RUTH I'm all right. . . .

(*The glassy-eyed look melts and then she collapses into a fit of heavy sobbing. The bell rings.*)

BENEATHA Oh, my God—that must be Asagai.
MAMA (*to* RUTH) Come on now, honey. You need to lie down and rest awhile . . . then have some nice hot food.

(*They exit,* RUTH'S *weight on her mother-in-law.* BENEATHA, *herself profoundly disturbed, opens the door to admit a rather dramatic-looking young man with a large package.*)

ASAGAI Hello, Alaiyo—
BENEATHA (*holding the door open and regarding him with pleasure*) Hello . . . (*long pause*) Well—come in. And please excuse everything. My mother was very upset about my letting anyone come here with the place like this.
ASAGAI (*coming into the room*) You look disturbed too. . . . Is something wrong?
BENEATHA (*still at the door, absently*) Yes . . . we've all got acute ghetto-itus. (*She smiles and comes toward him, finding a cigarette and sitting.*) So—sit down! How was Canada?
ASAGAI (*a sophisticate*) Canadian.
BENEATHA (*looking at him*) I'm very glad you are back.
ASAGAI (*looking back at her in turn*) Are you really?
BENEATHA Yes—very.
ASAGAI Why—you were quite glad when I went away. What happened?
BENEATHA You went away.
ASAGAI Ahhhhhhhh.

BENEATHA Before—you wanted to be so serious before there was time.

ASAGAI How much time must there be before one knows what one feels?

BENEATHA (*stalling this particular conversation, her hands pressed together in a deliberately childish gesture*) What did you bring me?

ASAGAI (*handing her the package*) Open it and see.

BENEATHA (*eagerly opening the package and drawing out some records and the colorful robes of a Nigerian woman*) Oh, Asagai! . . . You got them for me! . . . How beautiful . . . and the records too! (*She lifts out the robes and runs to the mirror with them and holds the drapery up in front of herself.*)

ASAGAI (*coming to her at the mirror*) I shall have to teach you how to drape it properly. (*He flings the material about her for the moment and stands back to look at her.*) Ah—*Oh-pay-gay-day, oh-gbah-mu-shay.* (*a Yoruba exclamation for admiration*) You wear it well . . . very well . . . mutilated hair and all.

BENEATHA (*turning suddenly*) My hair—what's wrong with my hair?

ASAGAI (*shrugging*) Were you born with it like that?

BENEATHA (*reaching up to touch it*) No . . . of course not. (*She looks back to the mirror, disturbed.*)

ASAGAI (*smiling*) How then?

BENEATHA You know perfectly well how . . . as crinkly as yours . . . that's how.

ASAGAI And it is ugly to you that way?

BENEATHA (*quickly*) Oh, no—not ugly . . . (*more slowly, apologetically*) But it's so hard to manage when it's well—raw.

ASAGAI And so to accommodate that—you mutilate it every week?

BENEATHA It's not mutilation!

ASAGAI (*laughing aloud at her seriousness*) Oh . . . please! I am only teasing you because you are so very serious about these things. (*He stands back from her and folds his arms across his chest as he watches her pulling at her hair and frowning in the mirror.*) Do you remember the first time you met me at school? . . . (*He laughs.*) You came up to me and said—and I thought you were the most serious little thing I had ever seen—you said: (*He imitates her.*) "Mr. Asagai—I want very much to talk with you. About Africa. You see, Mr. Asagai, I am looking for my *identity!*" (*He laughs.*)

BENEATHA (*turning to him, not laughing*) Yes—(*Her face is quizzical, profoundly disturbed.*)

ASAGAI (*still teasing and reaching out and taking her face in his hands and turning her profile to him*) Well . . . it is true that this is not so much a profile of a Hollywood queen as perhaps a queen of the Nile—(*a mock dismissal of the importance of the question*) But what does it matter? Assimilationism is so popular in your country.

BENEATHA (*wheeling, passionately, sharply*) I am not an assimilationist!

ASAGAI (*the protest hangs in the room for a moment and* ASAGAI *studies her, his laughter fading*) Such a serious one. (*There is a pause.*) So—you like the robes? You must take excellent care of them—they are from my sister's personal wardrobe.

BENEATHA (*with incredulity*) You—you sent all the way home—for me?

ASAGAI (*with charm*) For you—I would do much more. . . . Well, that is what I came for. I must go.

BENEATHA Will you call me Monday?

ASAGAI Yes . . . We have a great deal to talk about. I mean about identity and time and all that.

BENEATHA Time?

ASAGAI Yes. About how much time one needs to know what one feels.

BENEATHA You never understood that there is more than one kind of feeling which can exist between a man and a woman—or, at least, there should be.

ASAGAI (*shaking his head negatively but gently*) No. Between a man and a woman there need be only one kind of feeling. I have that for you. . . . Now even . . . right this moment. . . .

BENEATHA I know—and by itself—it won't do. I can find that anywhere.

ASAGAI For a woman it should be enough.

BENEATHA I know—because that's what it says in all the novels that men write. But it isn't. Go ahead and laugh—but I'm not interested in being someone's little episode in America or—(*with feminine vengeance*)—one of them! (ASAGAI *has burst into laughter again.*) That's funny as hell, huh!

ASAGAI It's just that every American girl I have known has said that to me. White—black—in this you are all the same. And the same speech, too!

BENEATHA (*angrily*) Yuk, yuk, yuk!

ASAGAI It's how you can be sure that the world's most liberated women are not liberated at all. You all talk about it too much!

(MAMA *enters and is immediately all social charm because of the presence of a guest.*)

BENEATHA Oh—Mama—this is Mr. Asagai.

MAMA How do you do?

ASAGAI (*total politeness to an elder*) How do you do, Mrs. Younger. Please forgive me for coming at such an outrageous hour on a Saturday.

MAMA Well, you are quite welcome. I just hope you understand that our house don't always look like this. (*chatterish*) You must come again. I would love to hear all about—(*not sure of the name*)—your country. I think it's so sad the way our American Negroes don't know nothing about Africa 'cept Tarzan and all that. And all that money they pour into these churches when they ought to be helping you people over there drive out them French and Englishmen done taken away your land.

(*The mother flashes a slightly superior look at her daughter upon completion of the recitation.*)

ASAGAI (*taken aback by this sudden and acutely unrelated expression of sympathy*) Yes . . . yes. . . .

MAMA (*smiling at him suddenly and relaxing and looking him over*) How many miles is it from here to where you come from?

ASAGAI Many thousands.

MAMA (*looking at him as she would* WALTER) I bet you don't half look after yourself, being away from your mama either. I spec you better come 'round here from time to time and get yourself some decent home-cooked meals. . . .

ASAGAI (*moved*) Thank you. Thank you very much. (*They are all quiet, then—*) Well . . . I must go. I will call you Monday, Alaiyo.

MAMA What's that he call you?

ASAGAI Oh—"Alaiyo." I hope you don't mind. It is what you would call a nickname, I think. It is a Yoruba word. I am a Yoruba.

MAMA (*looking at* BENEATHA) I—I thought he was from—

ASAGAI (*understanding*) Nigeria is my country. Yoruba is my tribal origin—

BENEATHA You didn't tell us what Alaiyo means . . . for all I know, you might be calling me Little Idiot or something. . . .

ASAGAI Well . . . let me see . . . I do not know how just to explain it. . . . The sense of a thing can be so different when it changes languages.

BENEATHA You're evading.

ASAGAI No—really it is difficult. . . . (*thinking*) It means . . . it means One for Whom Bread—Food—Is Not Enough. (*He looks at her.*) Is that all right?

BENEATHA (*understanding, softly*) Thank you.

MAMA (*looking from one to the other and not understanding any of it*) Well . . . that's nice. . . . You must come see us again—Mr.—

ASAGAI Ah-sah-guy . . .

MAMA Yes . . . Do come again.

ASAGAI Good-bye. (*He exits.*)

MAMA (*after him*) Lord, that's a pretty thing just went out here! (*insinuatingly, to her daughter*) Yes, I guess I see why we done commence to get so interested in Africa 'round here. Missionaries my aunt Jenny! (*She exits.*)

BENEATHA Oh, Mama! . . .

(*She picks up the Nigerian dress and holds it up to her in front of the mirror again. She sets the headdress on haphazardly and then notices her hair again and clutches at it and then replaces the headdress and frowns at herself. Then she starts to wriggle in front of the mirror as she thinks a Nigerian woman might.* TRAVIS *enters and regards her.*)

TRAVIS You cracking up?

BENEATHA Shut up.

(*She pulls the headdress off and looks at herself in the mirror and clutches at her hair again and squinches her eyes as if trying to imagine something. Then, suddenly, she gets her raincoat and kerchief and hurriedly prepares for going out.*)

MAMA (*coming back into the room*) She's resting now. Travis, baby, run next door and ask Miss Johnson to please let me have a little kitchen cleanser. This here can is empty as Jacob's kettle.

TRAVIS I just come in.

MAMA Do as you told. (*He exits and she looks at her daughter.*) Where you going?

BENEATHA (*halting at the door*) To become a queen of the Nile!

(*She exits in a breathless blaze of glory.* RUTH *appears in the bedroom doorway.*)

MAMA Who told you to get up?

RUTH Ain't nothing wrong with me to be lying in no bed for. Where did Bennie go?

MAMA (*drumming her fingers*) Far as I could make out—to Egypt. (RUTH *just looks at her.*) What time is it getting to?

RUTH Ten twenty. And the mailman going to ring that bell this morning just like he done every morning for the last umpteen years.

(TRAVIS *comes in with the cleanser can.*)

TRAVIS She say to tell you that she don't have much.

MAMA (*angrily*) Lord, some people I could name sure is tight-fisted! (*directing her grandson*) Mark two cans of cleanser down on the list there. If she that hard up for kitchen cleanser, I sure don't want to forget to get her none!

RUTH Lena—maybe the woman is just short on cleanser—

MAMA (*not listening*) —Much baking powder as she done borrowed from me all these years, she could of done gone into the baking business!

(*The bell sounds suddenly and sharply and all three are stunned—serious and silent—mid-speech. In spite of all the other conversations and distractions of the morning, this is what they have been waiting for, even* TRAVIS, *who looks helplessly from his mother to his grandmother.* RUTH *is the first to come to life again.*)

RUTH (*to* TRAVIS) *Get down them steps, boy!*

(TRAVIS *snaps to life and flies out to get the mail.*)

MAMA (*her eyes wide, her hand to her breast*) You mean it done really come?

RUTH (*excitedly*) Oh, Miss Lena!

MAMA (*collecting herself*) Well . . . I don't know what we all so excited about 'round here for. We known it was coming for months.

RUTH That's a whole lot different from having it come and being able to hold it in your hands . . . a piece of paper worth ten thousand dollars. . . . (TRAVIS *bursts back into the room. He holds the envelope high above his head, like a little dancer, his face is radiant and he is breathless. He moves to his grandmother with sudden slow ceremony and puts the envelope into her hands. She accepts it, and then merely holds it and looks at it.*) Come on! Open it . . . Lord have mercy, I wish Walter Lee was here!

TRAVIS Open it, Grandmama!

MAMA (*staring at it*) Now you all be quiet. It's just a check.

RUTH *Open it. . . .*

MAMA (*still staring at it*) Now don't act silly. . . . We ain't never been no people to act silly 'bout no money—

RUTH (*swiftly*) We ain't never had none before—*open it!*

(MAMA *finally makes a good strong tear and pulls out the thin blue slice of paper and inspects it closely. The boy and his mother study it raptly over* MAMA's *shoulders.*)

MAMA *Travis!* (*She is counting off with doubt.*) Is that the right number of zeros?

TRAVIS Yes'm . . . ten thousand dollars. Gaalee, Grandmama, you rich.

MAMA (*She holds the check away from her, still looking at it. Slowly her face sobers into a mask of unhappiness*) Ten thousand dollars. (*She hands it to* RUTH.) Put it away somewhere, Ruth. (*She does not look at* RUTH; *her eyes seem to be seeing something somewhere very far off.*) Ten thousand dollars they give you. Ten thousand dollars.

TRAVIS (*to his mother, sincerely*) What's the matter with Grandmama—don't she want to be rich?

RUTH (*distractedly*) You go out and play now, baby. (TRAVIS *exits.* MAMA *starts wiping dishes absently, humming intently to herself.* RUTH *turns to her, with kind exasperation.*) You're gone and got yourself upset.

MAMA (*not looking at her*) I spec if it wasn't for all you . . . I would just put that money away or give it to the church or something.

RUTH Now what kind of talk is that. Mr. Younger would just be plain mad if he could hear you talking foolish like that.

MAMA (*stopping and staring off*) Yes . . . he sure would. (*sighing*) We got enough to do with that money, all right. (*She halts then, and turns and looks at her daughter-in-law hard;* RUTH *avoids her eyes and* MAMA *wipes her hands with finality and starts to speak firmly to* RUTH.) Where did you go today, girl?

RUTH To the doctor.

MAMA (*impatiently*) Now, Ruth . . . you know better than that. Old Doctor Jones is strange enough in his way but there ain't nothing 'bout him make somebody slip and call him "she"—like you done this morning.

RUTH Well, that's what happened—my tongue slipped.

MAMA You went to see that woman, didn't you?

RUTH (*defensively, giving herself away*) What woman you talking about?

MAMA (*angrily*) That woman who—

(WALTER *enters in great excitement.*)

WALTER Did it come?

MAMA (*quietly*) Can't you give people a Christian greeting before you start asking about money?

WALTER (*to* RUTH) Did it come? (RUTH *unfolds the check and lays it quietly before him, watching him intently with thoughts of her own.* WALTER *sits down and grasps it close and counts off the zeros.*) Ten thousand dollars—(*He turns suddenly, frantically to his mother and draws some papers out of his breast pocket.*) Mama—look. Old Willy Harris put everything on paper—

MAMA Son—I think you ought to talk to your wife. . . . I'll go on out and leave you alone if you want—

WALTER I can talk to her later—Mama, look—

MAMA Son—

WALTER WILL SOMEBODY PLEASE LISTEN TO ME TODAY!

MAMA (*quietly*) I don't 'low no yellin' in this house, Walter Lee, and you know it—(WALTER *stares at them in frustration and starts to speak several times.*) And there ain't going to be no investing in no liquor stores. I don't aim to have to speak on that again.

(*A long pause.*)

WALTER Oh—so you don't aim to have to speak on that again? So *you* have decided. . . . (*crumpling his papers*) Well, *you* tell that to my boy tonight when you put him to sleep on the living-room couch. . . . (*turning to* MAMA *and speaking directly to her*) Yeah—and tell it to my wife, Mama, tomorrow when she has to go out of here to look after somebody else's kids. And tell it to *me,* Mama, every time we need a new pair of curtains and I have to watch *you* go out and work in somebody's kitchen. Yeah, you tell me then!

(WALTER *starts out.*)

RUTH Where you going?

WALTER I'm going out!

RUTH Where?

WALTER Just out of this house somewhere—

RUTH (*getting her coat*) I'll come too.

WALTER I don't want you to come!

RUTH I got something to talk to you about, Walter.

WALTER That's too bad.

MAMA (*still quietly*) Walter Lee—(*She waits and he finally turns and looks at her.*) Sit down.

WALTER I'm a grown man, Mama.

MAMA Ain't nobody said you wasn't grown. But you still in my house and my presence. And as long as you are—you'll talk to your wife civil. Now sit down.

RUTH (*suddenly*) Oh, let him go on out and drink himself to death! He makes me sick to my stomach! (*She flings her coat against him.*)

WALTER (*violently*) And you turn mine too, baby! (RUTH *goes into their bedroom and slams the door behind her.*) That was my greatest mistake—

MAMA (*still quietly*) Walter, what is the matter with you?

WALTER Matter with me? Ain't nothing the matter with *me!*

MAMA Yes there is. Something eating you up like a crazy man. Something more than me not giving you this money. The past few years I been watching it happen to you. You get all nervous acting and kind of wild in the eyes—(WALTER *jumps up impatiently at her words.*) I said sit there now, I'm talking to you!

WALTER Mama—I don't need no nagging at me today.

MAMA Seem like you getting to a place where you always tied up in some kind of knot about something. But if anybody ask you 'bout it you just yell at 'em and bust out the house and go out and drink somewheres. Walter Lee, people can't live with that. Ruth's a good, patient girl in her way—but you getting to be too much. Boy, don't make the mistake of driving that girl away from you.

WALTER Why—what she do for me?

MAMA She loves you.

WALTER Mama—I'm going out. I want to go off somewhere and be by myself for a while.

MAMA I'm sorry 'bout your liquor store, son. It just wasn't the thing for us to do. That's what I want to tell you about—

WALTER I got to go out, Mama—(*He rises.*)

MAMA It's dangerous, son.

WALTER What's dangerous?

MAMA When a man goes outside his home to look for peace.

WALTER (*beseechingly*) Then why can't there never be no peace in this house then?

MAMA You done found it in some other house?

WALTER No—there ain't no woman! Why do women always think there's a woman somewhere when a man gets restless. (*coming to her*) Mama—Mama—I want so many things. . . .

MAMA Yes, son—

WALTER I want so many things that they are driving me kind of crazy. . . . Mama—look at me.

MAMA I'm looking at you. You a good-looking boy. You got a job, a nice wife, a fine boy and—

WALTER A job. (*looks at her*) Mama, a job? I open and close car doors all day long. I drive a man around in his limousine and I say, "Yes, sir; no, sir; very good, sir; shall I take the Drive, sir?" Mama, that ain't no kind of job . . . that ain't nothing at all. (*very quietly*) Mama, I don't know if I can make you understand.

MAMA Understand what, baby?

WALTER (*quietly*) Sometimes it's like I can see the future stretched out in front of me—just plain as day. The future, Mama. Hanging over there at the edge of my days. Just waiting for me—a big, looming blank space—full of *nothing*. Just waiting for *me*. (*pause*) Mama—sometimes when I'm downtown and I pass them cool, quiet-looking restaurants where them white boys are sitting back and talking 'bout things . . . sitting there turning deals worth millions of dollars . . . sometimes I see guys don't look much older than me—

MAMA Son—how come you talk so much 'bout money?

WALTER (*with immense passion*) Because it is life, Mama!

MAMA (*quietly*) Oh—(*very quietly*) So now it's life. Money is life. Once upon a time freedom used to be life—now it's money. I guess the world really do change. . . .

WALTER No—it was always money, Mama. We just didn't know about it.

MAMA No . . . something has changed. (*She looks at him.*) You something new, boy. In my time we was worried about not being lynched and getting to the North if we could and how to stay alive and still have a pinch of dignity too. . . . Now here come you and Beneatha—talking 'bout things we ain't never even thought about hardly, me and your daddy. You ain't satisfied or proud of nothing we done. I mean that you had a home; that we kept you out of trouble till you was grown; that you don't have to ride to work on the back of nobody's streetcar—You my children—but how different we done become.

WALTER You just don't understand, Mama, you just don't understand.

MAMA Son—do you know your wife is expecting another baby? (WALTER *stands, stunned, and absorbs what his mother has said.*) That's what she wanted to talk to you about. (WALTER *sinks down into a chair.*) This ain't for me to be telling—but you ought to know. (*She waits.*) I think Ruth is thinking 'bout getting rid of that child.

WALTER (*slowly understanding*) No—no—Ruth wouldn't do that.

MAMA When the world gets ugly enough—a woman will do anything for her family. *The part that's already living.*

WALTER You don't know Ruth, Mama, if you think she would do that.

(RUTH *opens the bedroom door and stands there a little limp.*)

RUTH (*beaten*) Yes I would too, Walter. (*pause*) I gave her a five-dollar down payment.

(*There is total silence as the man stares at his wife and the mother stares at her son.*)

MAMA (*presently*) Well—(*tightly*) Well—son, I'm waiting to hear you say something. . . . I'm waiting to hear how you be your father's son. Be the man he was. . . . (*pause*) Your wife say she going to destroy your child. And I'm waiting to hear you talk like him and say we a people who give children life, not who destroys them—(*She rises.*) I'm waiting to see you stand up and look like your daddy and say we done give up one baby to poverty and that we ain't going to give up nary another one. . . . I'm waiting.

WALTER Ruth—

MAMA If you a son of mine, tell her! (WALTER *turns, looks at her and can say nothing. She continues, bitterly.*) You . . . you are a disgrace to your father's memory. Somebody get me my hat.

Curtain

Act II

Scene I

Time: Later the same day.

At rise: RUTH *is ironing again. She has the radio going. Presently* BENEATHA'S *bedroom door opens and* RUTH'S *mouth falls and she puts down the iron in fascination.*

RUTH What have we got on tonight!

BENEATHA (*emerging grandly from the doorway so that we can see her thoroughly robed in the costume* ASAGAI *brought*) You are looking at what a well-dressed Nigerian woman wears—(*She parades for* RUTH, *her hair completely hidden by the headdress; she is coquettishly fanning herself with an ornate oriental fan, mistakenly more like Butterfly than any Nigerian that ever was.*) Isn't it beautiful? (*She promenades to the radio and, with an arrogant flourish, turns off the good loud blues that is playing.*) Enough of this assimilationist junk! (RUTH *follows her with her eyes as she goes to the phonograph and puts on a record and turns and waits ceremoniously for the music to come up. Then, with a shout—*) OCOMOGOSIAY!

(RUTH *jumps. The music comes up, a lovely Nigerian melody.* BENEATHA *listens, enraptured, her eyes far away—"back to the past." She begins to dance.* RUTH *is dumfounded.*)

RUTH What kind of dance is that?

BENEATHA A folk dance.

RUTH (*Pearl Bailey*) What kind of folks do that, honey?

BENEATHA It's from Nigeria. It's a dance of welcome.

RUTH Who you welcoming?

BENEATHA The men back to the village.

RUTH Where they been?

BENEATHA How should I know—out hunting or something. Anyway, they are coming back now. . . .

RUTH Well, that's good.

BENEATHA (*with the record*)

Alundi, alundi
Alundi alunya
Jop pu a jeepua
Ang gu soooooooooo

Ai yai yae . . .
Ayehaye—alundi . . .

(WALTER *comes in during this performance; he has obviously been drinking. He leans against the door heavily and watches his sister, at first with distaste. Then his eyes look off—"back to the past"—as he lifts both his fists to the roof, screaming.)*

WALTER YEAH . . . AND ETHIOPIA STRETCH FORTH HER HANDS AGAIN! . . .

RUTH (*drily, looking at him*) Yes—and Africa sure is claiming her own tonight. (*She gives them both up and starts ironing again.*)

WALTER (*all in a drunken, dramatic shout*) Shut up! . . . I'm digging them drums . . . them drums move me! . . . (*He makes his weaving way to his wife's face and leans in close to her.*) In my *heart of hearts*—(*he thumps his chest*)—I am much warrior!

RUTH (*without even looking up*) In your heart of hearts you are much drunkard.

WALTER (*coming away from her and starting to wander around the room, shouting.*) Me and Jomo . . . (*intently, in his sister's face. She has stopped dancing to watch him in this unknown mood.*) That's my man, Kenyatta. (*shouting and thumping his chest*) FLAMING SPEAR! HOT DAMN! (*He is suddenly in possession of an imaginary spear and actively spearing enemies all over the room.*) OCOMOGOSIAY . . . THE LION IS WAKING . . . OWIMOWEH! (*He pulls his shirt open and leaps up on a table and gestures with his spear. The bell rings.* RUTH *goes to answer.*)

BENEATHA (*to encourage* WALTER, *thoroughly caught up with this side of him*) OCOMOGOSIAY, FLAMING SPEAR!

WALTER (*on the table, very far gone, his eyes pure glass sheets; he sees what we cannot, that he is a leader of his people, a great chief, a descendant of Chaka, and that the hour to march has come*) Listen, my black broth—ers—

BENEATHA OCOMOGOSIAY!

WALTER —Do you hear the waters rushing against the shores of the coastlands—

BENEATHA OCOMOGOSIAY!

WALTER —Do you hear the screeching of the cocks in yonder hills beyond where the chiefs meet in council for the coming of the mighty war—

BENEATHA OCOMOGOSIAY!

WALTER —Do you hear the beating of the wings of the birds flying low over the mountains and the low places of our land—

(RUTH *opens the door.* GEORGE MURCHISON *enters.*)

BENEATHA OCOMOGOSIAY!

WALTER —Do you hear the singing of the women, singing the war songs of our fathers to the babies in the great houses . . . singing the sweet war songs? OH, DO YOU HEAR, MY BLACK BROTHERS!

BENEATHA (*completely gone*) We hear you, Flaming Spear—

WALTER Telling us to prepare for the greatness of the time—(*to* GEORGE) Black Brother! (*He extends his hand for the fraternal clasp.*)

GEORGE Black Brother, hell!

RUTH (*having had enough, and embarrassed for the family*) Beneatha, you got company—what's the matter with you? Walter Lee Younger, get down off that table and stop acting like a fool. . . .

(WALTER *comes down off the table suddenly and makes a quick exit to the bathroom.*)

RUTH He's had a little to drink. . . . I don't know what her excuse is.

GEORGE (*to* BENEATHA) Look honey, we're going *to* the theater—we're not going to be *in* it . . . so go change, huh?

RUTH You expect this boy to go out with you looking like that?

BENEATHA (*looking at* GEORGE) That's up to George. If he's ashamed of his heritage—

GEORGE Oh, don't be so proud of yourself, Bennie—just because you look eccentric.

BENEATHA How can something that's natural be eccentric?

GEORGE That's what being eccentric means—being natural. Get dressed.

BENEATHA I don't like that, George.

RUTH Why must you and your brother make an argument out of everything people say?

BENEATHA Because I hate assimilationist Negroes!

RUTH Will somebody please tell me what assimila-whoever means!

GEORGE Oh, it's just a college girl's way of calling people Uncle Toms—but that isn't what it means at all.

BENEATHA (*cutting* GEORGE *off and staring at him as she replies to* RUTH) It means someone who is willing to give up his own culture and submerge himself completely in the dominant, and in this case, *oppressive* culture!

GEORGE Oh, dear, dear, dear! Here we go! A lecture on the African past! On our Great West African Heritage! In one second we will hear all about the great Ashanti empires; the great Songhay civilizations; and the great sculpture of Bénin—and then some poetry in the Bantu—and the whole monologue will end with the word *heritage!* (*nastily*) Let's face it, baby, your heritage is nothing but a bunch of raggedy-assed spirituals and some grass huts!

BENEATHA *Grass huts!* (RUTH *crosses to her and forcibly pushes her toward the bedroom.*) See there . . . you are standing there in your splendid ignorance talking about people who were the first to smelt iron on the face of the earth! (RUTH *is pushing her through the door.*) The Ashanti were performing surgical operations when the English—(RUTH *pulls the door to, with* BENEATHA *on the other side, and smiles graciously at* GEORGE. BENEATHA *opens the door and shouts the end of the sentence defiantly at* GEORGE.)—were still tattooing themselves with blue dragons. . . . (*She goes back inside.*)

RUTH Have a seat, George. (*They both sit.* RUTH *folds her hands rather primly on her lap, determined to demonstrate the civilization of the family.*) Warm, ain't it? I mean for September. (*pause*) Just like they always say about Chicago weather: If it's too hot or cold for you, just wait a minute and it'll change. (*She smiles happily at this cliché of clichés.*) Everybody say it's got to do with them bombs and things they keep setting off. (*pause*) Would you like a nice cold beer?

GEORGE No, thank you. I don't care for beer. (*He looks at his watch.*) I hope she hurries up.

RUTH What time is the show?

GEORGE It's an eight-thirty curtain. That's just Chicago, though. In New York standard curtain time is eight forty. (*He is rather proud of this knowledge.*)

RUTH (*properly appreciating it*) You get to New York a lot?

GEORGE (*offhand*) Few times a year.

RUTH Oh—that's nice. I've never been to New York.

(WALTER *enters. We feel he has relieved himself, but the edge of unreality is still with him.*)

WALTER New York ain't got nothing Chicago ain't. Just a bunch of hustling people all squeezed up together—being "Eastern." (*He turns his face into a screw of displeasure.*)

GEORGE Oh—you've been?

WALTER *Plenty* of times.

RUTH (*shocked at the lie*) Walter Lee Younger!

WALTER (*staring her down*) Plenty! (*pause*) What we got to drink in this house? Why don't you offer this man some refreshment? (*to* GEORGE) They don't know how to entertain people in this house, man.

GEORGE Thank you—I don't really care for anything.

WALTER (*feeling his head; sobriety coming*) Where's Mama?

RUTH She ain't come back yet.

WALTER (*looking* MURCHISON *over from head to toe, scrutinizing his carefully casual tweed sports jacket over cashmere V-neck sweater over soft eyelet shirt and tie, and soft slacks, finished off with white buckskin shoes*) Why all you college boys wear them fairyish-looking white shoes?

RUTH Walter Lee!

(GEORGE MURCHISON *ignores the remark.*)

WALTER (*to* RUTH) Well, they look crazy as hell—white shoes, cold as it is.

RUTH (*crushed*) You have to excuse him—

WALTER No he don't! Excuse me for what? What you always excusing me for! I'll excuse myself when I needs to be excused! (*a pause*) They look as funny as them black knee socks Beneatha wears out of here all the time.

RUTH It's the college *style,* Walter.

WALTER Style, hell. She looks like she got burnt legs or something!

RUTH Oh, Walter—

WALTER (*an irritable mimic*) Oh, Walter! Oh, Walter! (*to* MURCHISON) How's your old man making out? I understand you all going to buy that big hotel on the Drive? (*He finds a beer in the refrigerator, wanders over to* MURCHISON, *sipping and wiping his lips with the back of his hand, and straddling a chair backwards to talk to the other man.*) Shrewd move. Your old man is all right, man. (*tapping his head and half winking for emphasis*) I mean he knows how to operate. I mean he thinks *big,* you know what I mean, I mean for a *home,* you know? But I think he's kind of running out of ideas now. I'd like to talk to him. Listen, man, I got some plans that could turn this city upside down. I mean I think like he does. *Big.* Invest big, gamble big, hell, lose *big* if you have to, you know what I mean. It's hard to find a man on this whole Southside who understands my kind of thinking—you dig? (*He scrutinizes* MURCHISON *again, drinks his beer, squints his eyes and leans in close, confidential, man to man.*) Me and you ought to sit down and talk sometimes, man. Man, I got me some ideas. . . .

MURCHISON (*with boredom*) Yeah—sometimes we'll have to do that, Walter.

WALTER (*understanding the indifference, and offended*) Yeah—well, when you get the time, man. I know you a busy little boy.

RUTH Walter, please—

WALTER (*bitterly, hurt*) I know ain't nothing in this world as busy as you colored college boys with your fraternity pins and white shoes. . . .

RUTH (*covering her face with humiliation*) Oh, Walter Lee—

WALTER I see you all all the time—with the books tucked under your arms—going to your (*British A—a mimic*) "clahsses." And for what! What the hell you learning over there? Filling up your heads—(*counting off on his fingers*)—with the sociology and the psychology—but they teaching you how to be a man? How to take over and run the world? They teaching you how to run a rubber plantation or a steel mill? Naw—just to talk proper and read books and wear white shoes. . . .

GEORGE (*looking at him with distaste, a little above it all*) You're all wacked up with bitterness, man.

WALTER (*intently, almost quietly, between the teeth, glaring at the boy*) And you—ain't you bitter, man? Ain't you just about had it yet? Don't you see no stars gleaming that you can't reach out and grab? You happy?—You contented son-of-a-bitch—you happy? You got it made? Bitter? Man, I'm a volcano. Bitter? Here I am a giant—surrounded by ants! Ants who can't even understand what it is the giant is talking about.

RUTH (*passionately and suddenly*) Oh, Walter—ain't you with nobody!

WALTER (*violently*) No! 'Cause ain't nobody with me! Not even my own mother!

RUTH Walter, that's a terrible thing to say!

(BENEATHA *enters, dressed for the evening in a cocktail dress and earrings.*)

GEORGE Well—hey, you look great.

BENEATHA Let's go, George. See you all later.

RUTH Have a nice time.

GEORGE Thanks. Good night. (*to* WALTER, *sarcastically*) Good night, *Prometheus.* (BENEATHA *and* GEORGE *exit.*)

WALTER (*to* RUTH) Who is Prometheus?

RUTH I don't know. Don't worry about it.

WALTER (*in a fury, pointing after* GEORGE) See there—they get to a point where they can't insult you man to man—they got to talk about something ain't nobody never heard of!

RUTH How do you know it was an insult? (*to humor him*) Maybe Prometheus is a nice fellow.

WALTER Prometheus! I bet there ain't even no such thing! I bet that simple-minded clown—

RUTH Walter—(*She stops what she is doing and looks at him.*)

WALTER (*yelling*) Don't start!

RUTH Start what?

WALTER Your nagging! Where was I? Who was I with? How much money did I spend?

RUTH (*plaintively*) Walter Lee—why don't we just try to talk about it. . . .

WALTER (*not listening*) I been out talking with people who understand me. People who care about the things I got on my mind.

RUTH (*wearily*) I guess that means people like Willy Harris.

WALTER Yes, people like Willy Harris.

RUTH (*with a sudden flash of impatience*) Why don't you all just hurry up and go into the banking business and stop talking about it!

WALTER Why? You want to know why? 'Cause we all tied up in a race of people that don't know how to do nothing but moan, pray and have babies!

(*The line is too bitter even for him and he looks at her and sits down.*)

RUTH Oh, Walter . . . (*softly*) Honey, why can't you stop fighting me?

WALTER (*without thinking*) Who's fighting you? Who even cares about you?

(*This line begins the retardation of his mood.*)

RUTH Well—(*She waits a long time, and then with resignation starts to put away her things.*) I guess I might as well go on to bed. . . . (*more or less to herself*) I don't know where we lost it . . . but we have. . . . (*then, to him*) I—I'm sorry about this new baby, Walter. I guess maybe I better go on and do what I started . . . I guess I just didn't realize how bad things was with us . . . I guess I just didn't really realize—(*She starts out to the bedroom and stops.*) You want some hot milk?

WALTER Hot milk?

RUTH Yes—hot milk.

WALTER Why hot milk?

RUTH 'Cause after all that liquor you come home with you ought to have something hot in your stomach.

WALTER I don't want no milk.

RUTH You want some coffee then?

WALTER No, I don't want no coffee. I don't want nothing hot to drink. (*almost plaintively*) Why you always trying to give me something to eat?

RUTH (*standing and looking at him helplessly*) What else can I give you, Walter Lee Younger?

(*She stands and looks at him and presently turns to go out again. He lifts his head and watches her going away from him in a new mood which began to emerge when he asked her "Who cares about you?"*)

WALTER It's been rough, ain't it, baby? (*She hears and stops but does not turn around and he continues to her back.*) I guess between two people there ain't never as much understood as folks generally thinks there is. I mean like between me and you—(*She turns to face him.*) How we gets to the place where we scared to talk softness to each other. (*He waits, thinking hard himself.*) Why you think it got to be like that? (*He is thoughtful, almost as a child would be.*) Ruth, what is it gets into people ought to be close?

RUTH I don't know, honey. I think about it a lot.

WALTER On account of you and me, you mean? The way things are with us. The way something done come down between us.

RUTH There ain't so much between us, Walter. . . . Not when you come to me and try to talk to me. Try to be with me . . . a little even.

WALTER (*total honesty*) Sometimes . . . sometimes . . . I don't even know how to try.

RUTH Walter—

WALTER Yes?

RUTH (*coming to him, gently and with misgiving, but coming to him*) Honey . . . life don't have to be like this. I mean sometimes people can do things so that things are better. . . . You remember how we used to talk when Travis was born . . . about the way we were going to live . . . the kind of house . . . (*She is stroking his head.*) Well, it's all starting to slip away from us. . . .

(MAMA *enters, and* WALTER *jumps up and shouts at her.*)

WALTER Mama, where have you been?

MAMA My—them steps is longer than they used to be. Whew! (*She sits down and ignores him.*) How you feeling this evening, Ruth?

(RUTH *shrugs, disturbed some at having been prematurely interrupted and watching her husband knowingly.*)

WALTER Mama, where have you been all day?

MAMA (*still ignoring him and leaning on the table and changing to more comfortable shoes*) Where's Travis?

RUTH I let him go out earlier and he ain't come back yet. Boy, is he going to get it!

WALTER Mama!

MAMA (*as if she has heard him for the first time*) Yes, son?

WALTER Where did you go this afternoon?

MAMA I went downtown to tend to some business that I had to tend to.

WALTER What kind of business?

MAMA You know better than to question me like a child, Brother.

WALTER (*rising and bending over the table*) Where were you, Mama? (*bringing his fists down and shouting*) Mama, you didn't go do something with that insurance money, something crazy?

(*The front door opens slowly, interrupting him, and* TRAVIS *peeks his head in, less than hopefully.*)

TRAVIS (*to his mother*) Mama, I—

RUTH "Mama I" nothing! You're going to get it, boy! Get on in that bedroom and get yourself ready!

TRAVIS But I—

MAMA Why don't you all never let the child explain hisself.

RUTH Keep out of it now, Lena.

(MAMA *clamps her lips together, and* RUTH *advances toward her son menacingly.*)

RUTH A thousand times I have told you not to go off like that—

MAMA (*holding out her arms to her grandson*) Well—at least let me tell him something. I want him to be the first one to hear. . . . Come here, Travis. (*The boy obeys, gladly.*) Travis—(*She takes him by the shoulder and looks into his face.*)—you know that money we got in the mail this morning?

TRAVIS Yes'm—

MAMA Well—what do you think your grandmama gone and done with that money?

TRAVIS I don't know, Grandmama.

MAMA (*putting her finger on his nose for emphasis*) She went out and she bought you a house! (*The explosion comes from* WALTER *at the end of the revelation and he jumps up and turns away from all of them in a fury.* MAMA *continues, to* TRAVIS:) You glad about the house? It's going to be yours when you get to be a man.

TRAVIS Yeah—I always wanted to live in a house.

MAMA All right, gimme some sugar then—(TRAVIS *puts his arms around her neck as she watches her son over the boy's shoulder. Then, to* TRAVIS, *after the embrace:*) Now when you say your prayers tonight, you thank God and your grandfather—'cause it was him who give you the house—in his way.

RUTH (*taking the boy from* MAMA *and pushing him toward the bedroom*) Now you get out of here and get ready for your beating.

TRAVIS Aw, Mama—

RUTH Get on in there—(*closing the door behind him and turning radiantly to her mother-in-law*) So you went and did it!

MAMA (*quietly, looking at her son with pain*) Yes, I did.

RUTH (*raising both arms classically*) Praise God! (*Looks at* WALTER *a moment, who says nothing. She crosses rapidly to her husband.*) Please, honey—let me be glad . . . you be glad too. (*She has laid her hands on his shoulders, but he shakes himself free of her roughly, without turning to face her.*) Oh, Walter . . . a home . . . a home . . . a home. (*She comes back to* MAMA.) Well—where is it? How big is it? How much it going to cost?

MAMA Well—

RUTH When we moving?

MAMA (*smiling at her*) First of the month.

RUTH (*throwing back her head with jubilance*) *Praise God!*

MAMA (*tentatively, still looking at her son's back turned against her and* RUTH) It's—it's a nice house too. . . . (*She cannot help speaking directly to him. An imploring quality in her voice, her manner, makes her almost like a girl now.*) Three bedrooms—nice big one for you and Ruth. . . . Me and Beneatha still have to share our room, but Travis have one of his own—and (*with difficulty*) I figure if the—new baby—is a boy, we could get one of them double-decker outfits. . . . And there's a yard with a little patch of dirt where I could maybe get to grow me a few flowers. . . . And a nice big basement. . . .

RUTH Walter honey, be glad—

MAMA (*still to his back, fingering things on the table*) 'Course I don't want to make it sound fancier than it is. . . . It's just a plain little old house—but it's made good and solid—and it will be *ours.* Walter Lee—it makes a difference in a man when he can walk on floors that belong to *him.* . . .

RUTH Where is it?

MAMA (*frightened at this telling*) Well—well—it's out there in Clybourne Park—

(RUTH'S *radiance fades abruptly, and* WALTER *finally turns slowly to face his mother with incredulity and hostility.*)

RUTH Where?

MAMA (*matter-of-factly*) Four o six Clybourne Street, Clybourne Park.

RUTH Clybourne Park? Mama, there ain't no colored people living in Clybourne Park.

MAMA (*almost idiotically*) Well, I guess there's going to be some now.

WALTER (*bitterly*) So that's the peace and comfort you went out and bought for us today!

MAMA (*raising her eyes to meet his finally*) Son—I just tried to find the nicest place for the least amount of money for my family.

RUTH (*trying to recover from the shock*) Well—well—'course I ain't one never been 'fraid of no crackers, mind you—but—well, wasn't there no other houses nowhere?

MAMA Them houses they put up for colored in them areas way out all seem to cost twice as much as other houses. I did the best I could.

RUTH (*Struck senseless with the news, in its various degrees of goodness and trouble, she sits a moment, her fists propping her chin in thought, and then she starts to rise, bringing her fists down with vigor, the radiance spreading from cheek to cheek again.*) Well—well!—All I can say is—if this is my time in life—*my time*—to say goodbye— (*And she builds with momentum as she starts to circle the room with an exuberant, almost tearfully happy release.*)—to these Goddamned cracking walls!— (*She pounds the walls.*) —and these marching *roaches!*— (*She wipes at an imaginary army of marching roaches.*)—and this cramped little closet which ain't now or never was no kitchen! . . . then I say it loud and good, *Hallelujah! and good-bye misery. . . . I don't never want to see your ugly face again! (She laughs joyously, having practically destroyed the apartment, and flings her arms up and lets them come down happily, slowly, reflectively, over her abdomen, aware for the first time perhaps that the life therein pulses with happiness and not despair.*) Lena?

MAMA (*moved, watching with happiness*) Yes, honey?

RUTH (*looking off*) Is there—is there a whole lot of sunlight?

MAMA (*understanding*) Yes, child, there's a whole lot of sunlight.

(*Long pause.*)

RUTH (*collecting herself and going to the door of the room* TRAVIS *is in*) Well—I guess I better see 'bout Travis. (*to* MAMA) Lord, I sure don't feel like whipping nobody today! (*She exits.*)

MAMA (*the mother and son are left alone now and the mother waits a long time, considering deeply, before she speaks*) Son—you—you understand what I done, don't you? (WALTER *is silent and sullen.*) I—I just seen my family falling apart today . . . just falling to pieces in front of my eyes. . . . We couldn't of gone on like we was today. We was going backwards 'stead of forwards—talking 'bout killing babies and wishing each other was dead. . . . When it gets like that in life—you just got to do something different, push on out and do something bigger. . . . (*She waits.*) I wish you say something, son . . . I wish you'd say how deep inside you you think I done the right thing—

WALTER (*crossing slowly to his bedroom door and finally turning there and speaking measuredly*) What you need me to say you done right for? *You* the head of this family. You run our lives like you want to. It was your money and you did what you wanted with it. So what you need for me to say it was all right for? (*bitterly, to hurt her as deeply as he knows is possible*) So you butchered up a dream of mine—you—who always talking 'bout your children's dreams. . . .

MAMA Walter Lee—

(*He just closes the door behind him.* MAMA *sits alone, thinking heavily.*)

Curtain

Scene II

Time: Friday night, a few weeks later.

At rise: Packing crates mark the intention of the family to move. BENEATHA *and* GEORGE *come in, presumably from an evening out again.*

GEORGE O.K. . . . O.K., whatever you say. . . . (*They both sit on the couch. He tries to kiss her. She moves away.*) Look, we've had a nice evening; let's not spoil it, huh? . . .

(*He again turns her head and tries to nuzzle in and she turns away from him, not with distaste but with momentary lack of interest; in a mood to pursue what they were talking about.*)

BENEATHA I'm *trying* to talk to you.

GEORGE We always talk.

BENEATHA Yes—and I love to talk.

GEORGE (*exasperated; rising*) I know it and I don't mind it sometimes . . . I want you to cut it out, see—The moody stuff. I mean. I don't like it. You're a nice-looking girl . . . all over. That's all you need, honey, forget the atmosphere. Guys aren't going to go for the atmosphere—they're going to go for what they see. Be glad for that. Drop the Garbo routine. It doesn't go with you. As for myself, I want a nice—(*groping*)—simple (*thoughtfully*)—sophisticated girl . . . not a poet—O.K.?

(*She rebuffs him again and he starts to leave.*)

BENEATHA Why are you angry?

GEORGE Because this is stupid! I don't go out with you to discuss the nature of "quiet desperation" or to hear all about your thoughts—because the world will go on thinking what it thinks regardless—

BENEATHA Then why read books? Why go to school?

GEORGE (*with artificial patience, counting on his fingers*) It's simple. You read books—to learn facts—to get grades—to pass the course—to get a degree. That's all—it has nothing to do with thoughts.

(*A long pause.*)

BENEATHA I see. (*a longer pause as she looks at him*) Good night, George.

(GEORGE *looks at her a little oddly, and starts to exit. He meets* MAMA *coming in.*)

GEORGE Oh—hello, Mrs. Younger.

MAMA Hello, George, how you feeling?

GEORGE Fine—fine, how are you?

MAMA Oh, a little tired. You know them steps can get you after a day's work. You all have a nice time tonight?

GEORGE Yes—a fine time. Well, good night.

MAMA Good night. (*He exits.* MAMA *closes the door behind her.*) Hello, honey. What you sitting like that for?

BENEATHA I'm just sitting.

MAMA Didn't you have a nice time?

BENEATHA No.

MAMA No? What's the matter?

BENEATHA Mama, George is a fool—honest. (*She rises.*)

MAMA (*hustling around unloading the packages she has entered with; she stops*) Is he, baby?

BENEATHA Yes.

(BENEATHA *makes up* TRAVIS' *bed as she talks.*)

MAMA You sure?

BENEATHA Yes.

MAMA Well—I guess you better not waste your time with no fools.

(BENEATHA *looks up at her mother, watching her put groceries in the refrigerator. Finally she gathers up her things and starts into the bedroom. At the door she stops and looks back at her mother.*)

BENEATHA Mama—

MAMA Yes, baby—

BENEATHA Thank you.

MAMA For what?

BENEATHA For understanding me this time.

(*She exits quickly and the mother stands, smiling a little, looking at the place where* BENEATHA *just stood.* RUTH *enters.*)

RUTH Now don't you fool with any of this stuff, Lena—
MAMA Oh, I just thought I'd sort a few things out.

(*The phone rings.* RUTH *answers.*)

RUTH (*at the phone*) Hello—Just a minute. (*goes to the door*) Walter, it's Mrs. Arnold. (*waits; goes back to the phone; tense*) Hello. Yes, this is his wife speaking . . . He's lying down now. Yes . . . well, he'll be in tomorrow. He's been very sick. Yes—I know we should have called, but we were so sure he'd be able to come in today. Yes—yes, I'm very sorry. Yes . . . Thank you very much. (*She hangs up.* WALTER *is standing in the doorway of the bedroom behind her.*) That was Mrs. Arnold.
WALTER (*indifferently*) Was it?
RUTH She said if you don't come in tomorrow that they are getting a new man. . . .
WALTER Ain't that sad—ain't that crying sad.
RUTH She said Mr. Arnold has had to take a cab for three days. . . . Walter, you ain't been to work for three days! (*This is a revelation to her.*) Where you been, Walter Lee Younger? (WALTER *looks at her and starts to laugh.*) You're going to lose your job.
WALTER That's right . . .
RUTH Oh, Walter, and with your mother working like a dog every day—
WALTER That's sad too—Everything is sad.
MAMA What you been doing for these three days, son?
WALTER Mama—you don't know all the things a man what got leisure can find to do in this city. . . . What's this—Friday night? Well—Wednesday I borrowed Willy Harris' car and I went for a drive . . . just me and myself and I drove and drove . . . Way out . . . way past South Chicago, and I parked the car and I sat and looked at the steel mills all day long. I just sat in the car and looked at them big black chimneys for hours. Then I drove back and I went to the Green Hat. (*pause*) And Thursday—Thursday I borrowed the car again and I got in it and I pointed it the other way and I drove the other way—for hours—way, way up to Wisconsin, and I looked at the farms. I just drove and looked at the farms. Then I drove back and I went to the Green Hat. (*pause*) And today—today I didn't get the car. Today I just walked. All over the South side. And I looked at the Negroes and they looked at me and finally I just sat down on the curb at Thirty-ninth and South Parkway and I just sat there and watched the Negroes go by. And then I went to the Green Hat. You all sad? You all depressed? And you know where I am going right now—

(RUTH *goes out quietly.*)

MAMA Oh, Big Walter, is this the harvest of our days?

WALTER You know what I like about the Green Hat? (*He turns the radio on and a steamy, deep blues pours into the room.*) I like this little cat they got there who blows a sax. . . . He blows. He talks to me. He ain't but 'bout five feet tall and he's got a conked head and his eyes is always closed and he's all music—

MAMA (*rising and getting some papers out of her handbag*) Walter—

WALTER And there's this other guy who plays the piano . . . and they got a sound. I mean they can work on some music. . . . They got the best little combo in the world in the Green Hat. . . . You can just sit there and drink and listen to them three men play and you realize that don't nothing matter worth a damn, but just being there—

MAMA I've helped do it to you, haven't I, son? Walter, I been wrong.

WALTER Naw—you ain't never been wrong about nothing, Mama.

MAMA Listen to me, now. I say I been wrong, son. That I been doing to you what the rest of the world been doing to you. (*She stops and he looks up slowly at her and she meets his eyes pleadingly.*) Walter—what you ain't never understood is that I ain't got nothing, don't own nothing, ain't never really wanted nothing that wasn't for you. There ain't nothing as precious to me. . . . There ain't nothing worth holding on to, money, dreams, nothing else—if it means—if it means it's going to destroy my boy. (*She puts her papers in front of him and he watches her without speaking or moving.*) I paid the man thirty-five hundred dollars down on the house. That leaves sixty-five hundred dollars. Monday morning I want you to take this money and take three thousand dollars and put it in a savings account for Beneatha's medical schooling. The rest you put in a checking account—with your name on it. And from now on any penny that come out of it or that go in it is for you to look after. For you to decide. (*She drops her hands a little helplessly.*) It ain't much, but it's all I got in the world and I'm putting it in your hands. I'm telling you to be the head of this family from now on like you supposed to be.

WALTER (*stares at the money*) You trust me like that, Mama?

MAMA I ain't never stop trusting you. Like I ain't never stop loving you.

(*She goes out, and* WALTER *sits looking at the money on the table as the music continues in its idiom, pulsing in the room. Finally, in a decisive gesture, he gets up, and, in mingled joy and desperation, picks up the money. At the same moment,* TRAVIS *enters for bed.*)

TRAVIS What's the matter, Daddy? You drunk?

WALTER (*sweetly, more sweetly than we have ever known him*) No, Daddy ain't drunk. Daddy ain't going to never be drunk again. . . .

TRAVIS Well, good night, Daddy.

(*The Father has come from behind the couch and leans over, embracing his son.*)

WALTER Son, I feel like talking to you tonight.

TRAVIS About what?

WALTER Oh, about a lot of things. About you and what kind of man you going to be when you grow up. . . . Son—son, what do you want to be when you grow up?

TRAVIS A bus driver.

WALTER (*laughing a little*) A what? Man, that ain't nothing to want to be!

TRAVIS Why not?

WALTER 'Cause, man—it ain't big enough—you know what I mean.

TRAVIS I don't know then. I can't make up my mind. Sometimes Mama asks me that too. And sometimes when I tell her I just want to be like you—she says she don't want me to be like that and sometimes she says she does. . . .

WALTER (*gathering him up in his arms*) You know what, Travis? In seven years you going to be seventeen years old. And things is going to be very different with us in seven years, Travis. . . . One day when you are seventeen I'll come home—home from my office downtown somewhere—

TRAVIS You don't work in no office, Daddy.

WALTER No—but after tonight. After what your daddy gonna do tonight, there's going to be offices—a whole lot of offices. . . .

TRAVIS What you gonna do tonight, Daddy?

WALTER You wouldn't understand yet, son, but your daddy's gonna make a transaction . . . a business transaction that's going to change our lives. . . . That's how come one day when you 'bout seventeen years old I'll come home and I'll be pretty tired, you know what I mean, after a day of conferences and secretaries getting things wrong the way they do . . . 'cause an executive's life is hell, man—(*The more he talks, the farther away he gets.*) And I'll pull the car up on the driveway . . . just a plain black Chrysler, I think, with white walls—no—black tires. More elegant. Rich people don't have to be flashy . . . though I'll have to get something a little sportier for Ruth—maybe a Cadillac convertible to do her shopping in. . . . And I'll come up the steps to the house and the gardener will be clipping away at the hedges and he'll say, "Good evening, Mr. Younger." And I'll say, "Hello, Jefferson, how are you this evening?" And I'll go inside and Ruth will come downstairs and meet me at the door and we'll kiss each other and she'll take my arm and we'll go up to your room to see you sitting on the floor with the catalogues of all the great schools in America around you. . . . All the great schools in the world! And—and I'll say, all right son—it's your seventeenth birthday, what is it you've decided? . . . Just tell me, where you want to go to school and you'll *go.* Just tell me, what it is you want to be—and you'll *be* it . . . . Whatever you want to be—Yessir! (*He holds his arms open for* TRAVIS.) You just name it, son . . . (TRAVIS *leaps into them.*) and I hand you the world!

(WALTER'S *voice has risen in pitch and hysterical promise and on the last line he lifts* TRAVIS *high.*)

Blackout

Scene III

Time: Saturday, moving day, one week later.

Before the curtain rises, **RUTH**'s *voice, a strident, dramatic church alto cuts through the silence.*

It is, in the darkness a triumphant surge, a penetrating statement of expectation: "Oh, Lord, I don't feel no ways tired! Children, oh, glory hallelujah!"

As the curtain rises we see that **RUTH** *is alone in the living room, finishing up the family's packing. It is moving day. She is nailing crates and tying cartons.* **BENEATHA** *enters, carrying a guitar case, and watches her exuberant sister-in-law.*

RUTH Hey!

BENEATHA (*putting away the case*) Hi.

RUTH (*pointing at a package*) Honey—look in that package there and see what I found on sale this morning at the South Center. (RUTH *gets up and moves to the package and draws out some curtains.*) Lookahere—hand-turned hems!

BENEATHA How do you know the window size out there?

RUTH (*who hadn't thought of that*) Oh—Well, they bound to fit something in the whole house. Anyhow, they was too good a bargain to pass up. (RUTH *slaps her head, suddenly remembering something.*) Oh, Bennie—I meant to put a special note on that carton over there. That's your mamma's good china and she wants 'em to be very careful with it.

BENEATHA I'll do it.

(BENEATHA *finds a piece of paper and starts to draw large letters on it.*)

RUTH You know what I'm going to do soon as I get in that new house?

BENEATHA What?

RUTH Honey—I'm going to run me a tub of water up to here. . . . (*with her fingers practically up to her nostrils*) And I'm going to get in it—and I am going to sit . . . and sit . . . and sit in that hot water and the first person who knocks to tell *me* to hurry up and come out—

BENEATHA Gets shot at sunrise.

RUTH (*laughing happily*) You said it, sister! (*noticing how large* BENEATHA *is absent-mindedly making the note*) Honey, they ain't going to read that from no airplane.

BENEATHA (*laughing herself*) I guess I always think things have more emphasis if they are big, somehow.

RUTH (*looking up at her and smiling*) You and your brother seem to have that as a philosophy of life. Lord, that man—done changed so 'round here. You know—you know what we did last night? Me and Walter Lee?

BENEATHA What?

RUTH (*smiling to herself*) We went to the movies. (*looking at* BENEATHA *to see if she understands*) We went to the movies. You know the last time me and Walter went to the movies together?

BENEATHA No.

RUTH Me neither. That's how long it been. (*smiling again*) But we went last night. The picture wasn't much good, but that didn't seem to matter. We went—and we held hands.

BENEATHA Oh, Lord!

RUTH We held hands—and you know what?

BENEATHA What?

RUTH When we come out of the show it was late and dark and all the stores and things was closed up . . . and it was kind of chilly and there wasn't many people on the streets . . . and we was still holding hands, me and Walter.

BENEATHA You're killing me.

(WALTER *enters with a large package. His happiness is deep in him; he cannot keep still with his new-found exuberance. He is singing and wiggling and snapping his fingers. He puts his package in a corner and puts a phonograph record, which he has brought in with him, on the record player. As the music comes up he dances over to* RUTH *and tries to get her to dance with him. She gives in at last to his raunchiness and in a fit of giggling allows herself to be drawn into his mood and together they deliberately burlesque an old social dance of their youth.*)

BENEATHA (*regarding them a long time as they dance, then drawing in her breath for a deeply exaggerated comment which she does not particularly mean*) Talk about—oldddddddddd-fashionedddddd—Negroes!

WALTER (*stopping momentarily*) What kind of Negroes?

(*He says this in fun. He is not angry with her today, nor with anyone. He starts to dance with his wife again.*)

BENEATHA Old-fashioned.

WALTER (*as he dances with* RUTH) You know, when these *New Negroes* have their convention—(*pointing at his sister*)—that is going to be the chairman of the Committee on Unending Agitation. (*He goes on dancing, then stops.*) Race, race, race! . . . Girl, I do believe you are the first person in the history of the entire human race to successfully brainwash yourself. (BENEATHA *breaks up and he goes on dancing. He stops again, enjoying his tease.*) Damn, even the N double A C P takes a holiday sometimes! (BENEATHA *and* RUTH *laugh. He dances with* RUTH *some more and starts to laugh and stops and pantomimes someone over an operating table.*) I can just see that chick someday looking down at some poor cat on an operating table before she starts to slice him, saying . . . (*pulling his sleeves back maliciously*) "By the way, what are your views on civil rights down there? . . ."

(*He laughs at her again and starts to dance happily. The bell sounds.*)

BENEATHA Sticks and stones may break my bones but . . . words will never hurt me!

(BENEATHA *goes to the door and opens it as* WALTER *and* RUTH *go on with the clowning.* BENEATHA *is somewhat surprised to see a quiet-looking middle-aged white man in a business suit holding his hat and a briefcase in his hand and consulting a small piece of paper.*)

MAN Uh—how do you do, miss. I am looking for a Mrs.—(*he looks at the slip of paper*) Mrs. Lena Younger?

BENEATHA (*smoothing her hair with slight embarrassment*) Oh—yes, that's my mother. Excuse me. (*She closes the door and turns to quiet the other two.*) Ruth! Brother! Somebody's here. (*Then she opens the door. The man casts a curious quick glance at all of them.*) Uh—come in please.

MAN (*coming in*) Thank you.

BENEATHA My mother isn't here just now. Is it business?

MAN Yes . . . well, of a sort.

WALTER (*freely, the Man of the House*) Have a seat. I'm Mrs. Younger's son. I look after most of her business matters.

(RUTH *and* BENEATHA *exchange amused glances.*)

MAN (*regarding* WALTER, *and sitting*) Well—my name is Karl Lindner . . .

WALTER (*stretching out his hand*) Walter Younger. This is my wife—(RUTH *nods politely.*)—and my sister.

LINDNER How do you do.

WALTER (*amiably, as he sits himself easily on a chair, leaning with interest forward on his knees and looking expectantly into the newcomer's face*) What can we do for you, Mr. Lindner!

LINDNER (*some minor shuffling of the hat and briefcase on his knees*) Well—I am a representative of the Clybourne Park Improvement Association—

WALTER (*pointing*) Why don't you sit your things on the floor?

LINDNER Oh—yes. Thank you. (*He slides the briefcase and hat under the chair.*) And as I was saying—I am from the Clybourne Park Improvement Association and we have had it brought to our attention at the last meeting that you people—or at least your mother—has bought a piece of residential property at—(*he digs for the slip of paper again*)—four o six Clybourne Street. . . .

WALTER That's right. Care for something to drink? Ruth, get Mr. Lindner a beer.

LINDNER (*upset for some reason*) Oh—no, really. I mean thank you very much, but no thank you.

RUTH (*innocently*) Some coffee?

LINDNER Thank you, nothing at all.

(BENEATHA *is watching the man carefully.*)

LINDNER Well, I don't know how much you folks know about our organization. (*He is a gentle man; thoughtful and somewhat labored in his manner.*) It is one of those community organizations set up to look after—oh, you know, things like block upkeep and special projects and we also have what we call our New Neighbors Orientation Committee. . . .

BENEATHA (*drily*) Yes—and what do they do?

LINDNER (*turning a little to her and then returning the main force to* WALTER) Well—it's what you might call a sort of welcoming committee, I guess. I mean they, we, I'm the chairman of the committee—go around and see the new people who move into the neighborhood and sort of give them the lowdown on the way we do things out in Clybourne Park.

BENEATHA (*with appreciation of the two meanings, which escape* RUTH *and* WALTER) Uh-huh.

LINDNER And we also have the category of what the association calls—(*He looks elsewhere.*)—uh—special community problems. . . .

BENEATHA Yes—and what are some of those?

WALTER Girl, let the man talk.

LINDNER (*with understated relief*) Thank you. I would sort of like to explain this thing in my own way. I mean I want to explain to you in a certain way.

WALTER Go ahead.

LINDNER Yes. Well. I'm going to try to get right to the point. I'm sure we'll all appreciate that in the long run.

BENEATHA Yes.

LINDNER Well—

WALTER Be still now!

LINDNER Well—

RUTH (*still innocently*) Would you like another chair—you don't look comfortable.

LINDNER (*more frustrated than annoyed*) No, thank you very much. Please. Well—to get right to the point I—(*a great breath, and he is off at last*) I am sure you people must be aware of some of the incidents which have happened in various parts of the city when colored people have moved into certain areas—(BENEATHA *exhales heavily and starts tossing a piece of fruit up and down in the air.*) Well—because we have what I think is going to be a unique type of organization in American community life—not only do we deplore that kind of thing—but we are trying to do something about it. (BENEATHA *stops tossing and turns with a new and quizzical interest to the man.*) We feel—(*gaining confidence in his mission because of the interest in the faces of the people he is talking to*)—we feel that most of the trouble in this world, when you come right down to it—(*He hits his knee for emphasis.*)—most of the trouble exists because people just don't sit down and talk to each other.

RUTH (*nodding as she might in church, pleased with the remark*) You can say that again, mister.

LINDNER (*more encouraged by such affirmation*) That we don't try hard enough in this world to understand the other fellow's problem. The other guy's point of view.

RUTH Now that's right.

(BENEATHA *and* WALTER *merely watch and listen with genuine interest.*)

LINDNER Yes—that's the way we feel out in Clybourne Park. And that's why I was elected to come here this afternoon and talk to you people. Friendly like, you know, the way people should talk to each other and see if we couldn't find some way to work this thing out. As I say, the whole business is a matter of *caring* about the other fellow. Anybody can see that you are a nice family of folks, hard-working and honest I'm sure. (BENEATHA *frowns slightly, quizzically, her head tilted regarding him.*) Today everybody knows what it means to be on the outside of *something.* And of course, there is always somebody who is out to take the advantage of people who don't always understand.

WALTER What do you mean?

LINDNER Well—you see our community is made up of people who've worked hard as the dickens for years to build up that little community. They're not rich and fancy people; just hard-working, honest people who don't really have much but those little homes and a dream of the kind of community they want to raise their children in. Now, I don't say we are perfect and there is a lot wrong in some of the things they want. But you've got to admit that a man, right or wrong, has the right to want to have the neighborhood he lives in a certain kind of way. And at the moment the overwhelming majority of our people out there feel that people get along better, take more of a common interest in the life of the community, when they share a common background. I want you to believe me when I tell you that race prejudice simply doesn't enter into it. It is a matter of the people of Clybourne Park believing, rightly or wrongly, as I say, that for the happiness of all concerned that our Negro families are happier when they live in their *own* communities.

BENEATHA (*with a grand and bitter gesture*) This, friends, is the Welcoming Committee!

WALTER (*dumbfounded, looking at* LINDNER) Is this what you came marching all the way over here to tell us?

LINDNER Well, now we've been having a fine conversation. I hope you'll hear me all the way through.

WALTER (*tightly*) Go ahead, man.

LINDNER You see—in the face of all things I have said, we are prepared to make your family a very generous offer. . . .

BENEATHA Thirty pieces and not a coin less!

WALTER Yeah?

LINDNER (*putting on his glasses and drawing a form out of the briefcase*) Our association is prepared, through the collective effort of our people, to buy the house from you at a financial gain to your family.

RUTH Lord have mercy, ain't this the living gall!

WALTER All right, you through?

LINDNER Well, I want to give you the exact terms of the financial arrangement—

WALTER We don't want to hear no exact terms of no arrangements. I want to know if you got any more to tell us 'bout getting together?

LINDNER (*taking off his glasses*) Well—I don't suppose that you feel. . . .

WALTER Never mind how I feel—you got any more to say 'bout how people ought to sit down and talk to each other? . . . Get out of my house, man. (*He turns his back and walks to the door.*)

LINDNER (*looking around at the hostile faces and reaching and assembling his hat and briefcase*) Well—I don't understand why you people are reacting this way. What do you think you are going to gain by moving into a neighborhood where you just aren't wanted and where some elements—well—people can get awful worked up when they feel that their whole way of life and everything they've ever worked for is threatened.

WALTER Get out.

LINDNER (*at the door, holding a small card*) Well—I'm sorry it went like this.

WALTER Get out.

LINDNER (*almost sadly, regarding* WALTER) You just can't force people to change their hearts, son.

(*He turns and puts his card on a table and exits.* WALTER *pushes the door to with stinging hatred, and stands looking at it.* RUTH *just sits and* BENEATHA *just stands. They say nothing.* MAMA *and* TRAVIS *enter.*)

MAMA Well—this all the packing got done since I left out of here this morning. I testify before God that my children got all the energy of the dead. What time the moving men due?

BENEATHA Four o'clock. You had a caller, Mama. (*She is smiling, teasingly.*)

MAMA Sure enough—who?

BENEATHA (*her arms folded saucily*) The Welcoming Committee.

(WALTER *and* RUTH *giggle.*)

MAMA (*innocently*) Who?

BENEATHA The Welcoming Committee. They said they're sure going to be glad to see you when you get there.

WALTER (*devilishly*) Yeah, they said they can't hardly wait to see your face.

(*Laughter.*)

MAMA (*sensing their facetiousness*) What's the matter with you all?

WALTER Ain't nothing the matter with us. We just telling you 'bout the gentleman who came to see you this afternoon. From the Clybourne Park Improvement Association.

MAMA What he want?

RUTH (*in the same mood as* BENEATHA *and* WALTER) To welcome you, honey.

WALTER He said they can't hardly wait. He said the one thing they don't have, that they just *dying* to have out there is a fine family of colored people! (*to* RUTH *and* BENEATHA) Ain't that right!

RUTH *and* BENEATHA (*mockingly*) Yeah! He left his card in case—

(*They indicate the card, and* MAMA *picks it up and throws it on the floor—understanding and looking off as she draws her chair up to the table on which she has put her plant and some sticks and some cord.*)

MAMA Father, give us strength. (*knowingly—and without fun*) Did he threaten us?

BENEATHA Oh—Mama—they don't do it like that any more. He talked Brotherhood. He said everybody ought to learn how to sit down and hate each other with good Christian fellowship.

(*She and* WALTER *shake hands to ridicule the remark.*)

MAMA (*sadly*) Lord, protect us. . . .

RUTH You should hear the money those folks raised to buy the house from us. All we paid and then some.

BENEATHA What they think we going to do—eat 'em?

RUTH No, honey, marry 'em.

MAMA (*shaking her head*) Lord, Lord, Lord. . . .

RUTH Well—that's the way the crackers crumble. Joke.

BENEATHA (*laughingly noticing what her mother is doing*) Mama, what are you doing?

MAMA Fixing my plant so it won't get hurt none on the way. . . .

BENEATHA Mama, you going to take *that* to the new house?

MAMA Uh-huh—

BENEATHA That raggedy-looking old thing?

MAMA (*stopping and looking at her*) It expresses *me*.

RUTH (*with delight, to* BENEATHA) So there, Miss Thing!

(WALTER *comes to* MAMA *suddenly and bends down behind her and squeezes her in his arms with all his strength. She is overwhelmed by the suddenness of it and, though delighted, her manner is like that of* RUTH *with* TRAVIS.)

MAMA Look out now, boy! You make me mess up my thing here!

WALTER (*his face lit, he slips down on his knees beside her, his arms still around her*) Mama . . . you know what it means to climb up in the chariot?

MAMA (*gruffly, very happy*) Get on away from me now. . . .

RUTH (*near the gift-wrapped package, trying to catch* WALTER'S *eye*) Psst—

WALTER What the old song say, Mama. . . .

RUTH Walter—Now? (*She is pointing at the package.*)

WALTER (*speaking the lines, sweetly, playfully, in his mother's face*)

I got wings . . . you got wings . . .
All God's children got wings . . .

MAMA Boy—get out of my face and do some work. . . .

WALTER

When I get to heaven gonna put on my wings.
Gonna fly all over God's heaven . . .

BENEATHA (*teasingly, from across the room*) Everybody talking 'bout heaven ain't going there!

WALTER (*to* RUTH, *who is carrying the box across to them*) I don't know, you think we ought to give her that. . . . Seems to me she ain't been very appreciative around here.

MAMA (*eyeing the box, which is obviously a gift*) What is that?

WALTER (*taking it from* RUTH *and putting it on the table in front of* MAMA) Well—what you all think? Should we give it to her?

RUTH Oh—she was pretty good today.

MAMA I'll good you—(*She turns her eyes to the box again.*)

BENEATHA Open it, Mama.

(*She stands up, looks at it, turns and looks at all of them, and then presses her hands together and does not open the package.*)

WALTER (*sweetly*) Open it, Mama. It's for you. (MAMA *looks in his eyes. It is the first present in her life without its being Christmas. Slowly she opens her package and lifts out, one by one, a brand-new sparkling set of gardening tools.* WALTER *continues, prodding:*) Ruth made up the note—read it . . .

MAMA (*picking up the card and adjusting her glasses*) "To our own Mrs. Miniver—Love from Brother, Ruth and Beneatha." Ain't that lovely. . . .

TRAVIS (*tugging at his father's sleeve*) Daddy, can I give her mine now?

WALTER All right, son. (TRAVIS *flies to get his gift.*) Travis didn't want to go in with the rest of us, Mama. He got his own. (*somewhat amused*) We don't know what it is. . . .

TRAVIS (*racing back in the room with a large hatbox and putting it in front of his grandmother*) Here!

MAMA Lord have mercy, baby. You done gone and bought your grandmother a hat?

TRAVIS (*very proud*) Open it!

(*She does and lifts out an elaborate, but very elaborate, wide gardening hat, and all the adults break up at the sight of it.*)

RUTH Travis, honey, what is that?

TRAVIS (*who thinks it is beautiful and appropriate*) It's a gardening hat! Like the ladies always have on in the magazines when they work in their gardens.

BENEATHA (*giggling fiercely*) Travis—we were trying to make Mama Mrs. Miniver—not Scarlett O'Hara!

MAMA (*indignantly*) What's the matter with you all! This here is a beautiful hat! (*absurdly*) I always wanted me one just like it!

(*She pops it on her head to prove it to her grandson, and the hat is ludicrous and considerably oversized.*)

RUTH Hot dog! Go, Mama!

WALTER (*doubled over with laughter*) I'm sorry, Mama—but you look like you ready to go out and chop you some cotton sure enough!

(*They all laugh except* MAMA, *out of deference to* TRAVIS' *feelings.*)

MAMA (*gathering the boy up to her*) Bless your heart—this is the prettiest hat I ever owned—(WALTER, RUTH, *and* BENEATHA *chime in noisily, festively and insincerely congratulating* TRAVIS *on his gift.*) What are we all standing around here for? We ain't finished packin' yet. Bennie, you ain't packed one book.

(*The bell rings.*)

BENEATHA That couldn't be the movers . . . it's not hardly two good yet—

(BENEATHA *goes into her room.* MAMA *starts for door.*)

WALTER (*turning, stiffening*) Wait—wait—I'll get it. (*He stands and looks at the door.*)

MAMA You expecting company, son?

WALTER (*just looking at the door*) Yeah—yeah. . . .

(MAMA *looks at* RUTH, *and they exchange innocent and unfrightened glances.*)

MAMA (*not understanding*) Well, let them in, son.

BENEATHA (*from her room*) We need some more string.

MAMA Travis—you run to the hardware and get me some string cord.

(MAMA *goes out and* WALTER *turns and looks at* RUTH. TRAVIS *goes to a dish for money.*)

RUTH Why don't you answer the door, man?

WALTER (*suddenly bounding across the floor to her*) 'Cause sometimes it hard to let the future begin! (*stooping down in her face*)

I got wings! You got wings!
All God's children got wings!

(*He crosses to the door and throws it open. Standing there is a very slight little man in a not too prosperous business suit and with haunted frightened eyes and a hat pulled down tightly, brim up, around his forehead.* TRAVIS *passes between the men and exits.* WALTER *leans deep in the man's face, still in his jubilance.*)

When I get to heaven gonna put on my wings.
Gonna fly all over God's heaven . . .

(*The little man just stares at him.*)

Heaven—

(*Suddenly he stops and looks past the little man into the empty hallway.*) Where's Willy, man?

BOBO He ain't with me.

WALTER (*not disturbed*) Oh—come on in. You know my wife.

BOBO (*dumbly, taking off his hat*) Yes—h'you, Miss Ruth.

RUTH (*quietly, a mood apart from her husband already, seeing* BOBO) Hello, Bobo.

WALTER You right on time today. . . . Right on time. That's the way! (*He slaps* BOBO *on his back.*) Sit down . . . lemme hear.

(RUTH *stands stiffly and quietly in back of them, as though somehow she senses death, her eyes fixed on her husband.*)

BOBO (*his frightened eyes on the floor, his hat in his hands*) Could I please get a drink of water, before I tell you about it, Walter Lee?

(WALTER *does not take his eyes off the man.* RUTH *goes blindly to the tap and gets a glass of water and brings it to* BOBO.)

WALTER There ain't nothing wrong, is there?

BOBO Lemme tell you—

WALTER Man—didn't nothing go wrong?

BOBO Lemme tell you—Walter Lee. (*looking at* RUTH *and talking to her more than to* WALTER) You know how it was. I got to tell you how it was. I mean first I got tell you how it was all the way . . . I mean about the money I put in, Walter Lee. . . .

WALTER (*with taut agitation*) What about the money you put in?

BOBO Well—it wasn't much as we told you—me and Willy—(*He stops.*) I'm sorry, Walter. I got a bad feeling about it. I got a real bad feeling about it. . . .

WALTER Man, what you telling me about all this for? . . . Tell me what happened in Springfield. . . .

BOBO Springfield.

RUTH (*like a dead woman*) What was supposed to happen in Springfield?

BOBO (*to her*) This deal that me and Walter went into with Willy—Me and Willy was going to go down to Springfield and spread some money 'round so's we wouldn't have to wait so long for the liquor license. . . . That's what we were going to do. Everybody said that was the way you had to do, you understand, Miss Ruth?

WALTER Man—what happened down there?

BOBO (*a pitiful man, near tears*) I'm trying to tell you, Walter.

WALTER (*screaming at him suddenly*) THEN TELL ME, GOD-DAMMIT . . . WHAT'S THE MATTER WITH YOU?

BOBO Man . . . I didn't go to no Springfield, yesterday.

WALTER (*halted, life hanging in the moment*) Why not?

BOBO (*the long way, the hard way to tell*) 'Cause I didn't have no reasons to. . . .

WALTER Man, what are you talking about!

BOBO I'm talking about the fact that when I got to the train station yesterday morning—eight o'clock like we planned . . . Man—*Willy didn't never show up.*

WALTER Why . . . where was he . . . where is he?

BOBO That's what I'm trying to tell you . . . I don't know . . . I waited six hours . . . I called his house . . . and I waited . . . six hours . . . I waited in that train station six hours . . . (*breaking into tears*) That was all the extra money I had in the world. . . . (*looking up at* WALTER *with tears running down his face*) Man, *Willy is gone.*

WALTER Gone, what you mean Willy is gone? Gone where? You mean he went by himself. You mean he went off to Springfield by himself—to take care of getting the license—(*turns and looks anxiously at* RUTH) You mean maybe he didn't want too many people in on the business down there? (*looks to* RUTH *again, as before*) You know Willy got his own ways. (*looks back to* BOBO) Maybe you was late yesterday and he just went on down there without you. Maybe—maybe—he's been callin' you at home tryin' to tell you what happened or something. Maybe—maybe—he just got sick. He's somewhere—he's got to be somewhere. We just got to find him—me and you got to find him. (*grabs* BOBO *senselessly by the collar and starts to shake him*) We got to!

BOBO (*in sudden angry, frightened agony*) What's the matter with you, Walter! *When a cat take off with your money he don't leave you no maps!*

WALTER (*turning madly, as though he is looking for* WILLY *in the very room*) Willy! . . .Willy . . . don't do it. . . . Please don't do it . . . Man, not with that money . . . Man, please not with that money . . . Oh, God . . . Don't let it be true. . . . (*He is wandering around, crying out for* WILLY *and looking for him or perhaps for help from God.*) Man . . . I trusted you . . . Man, I put my life in your hands. . . . (*He starts to crumple down on the floor as* RUTH *just covers her face in horror.* MAMA *opens the door and comes into the room, with* BENEATHA *behind her.*) Man . . . (*He starts to pound the floor with his fists, sobbing wildly.*) *That money is made out of my father's flesh. . . .*

BOBO (*standing over him helplessly*) I'm sorry, Walter. . . . (*Only* WALTER'S *sobs reply.* BOBO *puts on his hat.*) I had my life staked on this deal, too. . . . (*He exits.*)

MAMA (*to* WALTER) Son— (*She goes to him, bends down to him, talks to his bent head.*) Son . . . Is it gone? Son, I gave you sixty-five hundred dollars. Is it gone? All of it? Beneatha's money too?

WALTER (*lifting his head slowly*) Mama . . . I never . . . went to the bank at all. . . .

MAMA (*not wanting to believe him*) You mean . . . your sister's school money . . . you used that too . . . Walter? . . .

WALTER Yessss! . . . All of it. . . . It's all gone. . . .

(*There is total silence.* RUTH *stands with her face covered with her hands;* BENEATHA *leans forlornly against a wall, fingering a piece of red ribbon from the mother's gift.* MAMA *stops and looks at her son without recognition and then, quite without thinking about it, starts to beat him senselessly in the face.* BENEATHA *goes to them and stops it.*)

BENEATHA Mama!

(MAMA *stops and looks at both of her children and rises slowly and wanders vaguely, aimlessly away from them.*)

MAMA I seen . . . him . . . night after night . . . come in . . . and look at that rug . . . and then look at me . . . the red showing in his eyes . . . the veins moving in his head. . . . I seen him grow thin and old before he was forty . . . working and working and working like somebody's old horse . . . killing himself . . . and you—you give it all away in a day. . . .

BENEATHA Mama—

MAMA Oh, God. . . . (*She looks up to Him.*) Look down here—and show me the strength.

BENEATHA Mama—

MAMA (*plaintively*) Strength. . . .

BENEATHA (*plaintively*) Mama. . . .

MAMA Strength!

Curtain

Act III

An hour later.

At curtain, there is a sullen light of gloom in the living room, gray light not unlike that which began the first scene of Act I. At left we can see WALTER *within his room, alone with himself. He is stretched out on the bed, his shirt out and open, his arms under his head. He does not smoke, he does not cry out, he merely lies there, looking up at the ceiling, much as if he were alone in the world.*

In the living room BENEATHA *sits at the table, still surrounded by the now almost ominous packing crates. She sits looking off. We feel that this is a mood struck perhaps an hour before, and it lingers now, full of the empty sound of profound disappointment. We see on a line from her brother's bedroom the sameness of their attitudes. Presently the bell rings and* BENEATHA *rises without ambition or interest in answering. It is* ASAGAI, *smiling broadly, striding into the room with energy and happy expectation and conversation.*

ASAGAI I came over . . . I had some free time. I thought I might help with the packing. Ah, I like the look of packing crates! A household in preparation for a journey! It depresses some people . . . but for me . . . it is another feeling. Something full of the flow of life, do you understand? Movement, progress . . . It makes me think of Africa.

BENEATHA Africa!

ASAGAI What kind of a mood is this? Have I told you how deeply you move me?

BENEATHA He gave away the money, Asagai. . . .

ASAGAI Who gave away what money?

BENEATHA The insurance money. My brother gave it away.

ASAGAI Gave it away?

BENEATHA He made an investment! With a man even Travis wouldn't have trusted.

ASAGAI And it's gone?

BENEATHA Gone!

ASAGAI I'm very sorry. . . . And you, now?

BENEATHA Me? . . . Me? . . . Me I'm nothing. . . . Me. When I was very small . . . we used to take our sleds out in the wintertime and the only hills we had were the ice-covered stone steps of some houses down the street. And we used to fill them in with snow and make them smooth and slide down them all day . . . and it was very dangerous you know . . . far too steep . . . and sure enough one day a kid named Rufus came down too fast and hit the sidewalk . . . and we saw his face just split open right there in front of us. . . . And I remember standing there looking at his bloody open face thinking that was the end of Rufus. But the ambulance came and they took him to the hospital and they fixed the broken bones and they sewed it all up . . . and the next time I saw Rufus he just had a little line down the middle of his face. . . . I never got over that. . . .

(WALTER *sits up, listening on the bed. Throughout this scene it is important that we feel his reaction at all times, that he visibly respond to the words of his sister and* ASAGAI.)

ASAGAI What?

BENEATHA That was what one person could do for another, fix him up—sew up the problem, make him all right again. That was the most marvelous thing in the world. . . . I wanted to do that. I always thought it was the one concrete thing in the world that a human being could do. Fix up the sick, you know—and make them whole again. This was truly being God. . . .

ASAGAI You wanted to be God?

BENEATHA No—I wanted to cure. It used to be so important to me. I wanted to cure. It used to matter. I used to care. I mean about people and how their bodies hurt. . . .

ASAGAI And you've stopped caring?

BENEATHA Yes—I think so.

ASAGAI Why?

(WALTER *rises, goes to the door of his room and is about to open it, then stops and stands listening, leaning on the door jamb.*)

BENEATHA Because it doesn't seem deep enough, close enough to what ails mankind—I mean this thing of sewing up bodies or administering drugs. Don't you understand? It was a child's reaction to the world. I thought that doctors had the secret to all the hurts. . . . That's the way a child sees things—or an idealist.

ASAGAI Children see things very well sometimes—and idealists even better.

BENEATHA I know that's what you think. Because you are still where I left off—you still care. This is what you see for the world, for Africa. You with the dreams of the future will patch up all Africa—you are going to cure the Great Sore of colonialism with Independence—

ASAGAI Yes!

BENEATHA Yes—and you think that one word is the penicillin of the human spirit: "Independence!" But then what?

ASAGAI That will be the problem for another time. First we must get there.

BENEATHA And where does it end?

ASAGAI End? Who even spoke of an end? To life? To living?

BENEATHA An end to misery!

ASAGAI (*smiling*) You sound like a French intellectual.

BENEATHA No! I sound like a human being who just had her future taken right out of her hands! While I was sleeping in my bed in there, things were happening in this world that directly concerned me—and nobody asked me, consulted me—they just went out and did things—and changed my life. Don't you see there isn't any real progress, Asagai, there is only one large circle that we march in, around and around, each of us with our own little picture—in front of us—our own little mirage that we think is the future.

ASAGAI That is the mistake.

BENEATHA What?

ASAGAI What you just said—about the circle. It isn't a circle—it is simply a long line—as in geometry, you know, one that reaches into infinity. And because we cannot see the end—we also cannot see how it changes. And it is very odd but those who see the changes are called "idealists"—and those who cannot, or refuse to think, they are the "realists." It is very strange, and amusing too, I think.

BENEATHA You—you are almost religious.

ASAGAI Yes . . . I think I have the religion of doing what is necessary in the world—and of worshipping man—because he is so marvelous, you see.

BENEATHA Man is foul! And the human race deserves its misery!

ASAGAI You see: *you* have become the religious one in the old sense. Already, and after such a small defeat, you are worshipping despair.

BENEATHA From now on, I worship the truth—and the truth is that people are puny, small and selfish. . . .

ASAGAI Truth? Why is it that you despairing ones always think that only you have the truth? I never thought to see *you* like that. You! Your brother made a stupid, childish mistake—and you are grateful to him. So that now you can give up the ailing human race on account of it. You talk about what good is struggle; what good is anything? Where are we all going? And why are we bothering?

BENEATHA *And you cannot answer it!* All your talk and dreams about Africa and Independence. Independence and then what? What about all the crooks and petty thieves and just plain idiots who will come into power to steal and plunder the same as before—only now they will be black and do it in the name of the new Independence—You cannot answer that.

ASAGAI (*shouting over her*) *I live the answer!* (*pause*) In my village at home it is the exceptional man who can even read a newspaper . . . or who ever *sees* a book at all. I will go home and much of what I will have to say will seem strange to the people of my village. . . . But I will teach and work and things will happen, slowly and swiftly. At times it will seem that nothing changes at all . . . and then again . . . the sudden dramatic events which make history leap into the future. And then quiet again. Retrogression even. Guns, murder, revolution. And I even will have moments when I wonder if the quiet was not better than all that death and hatred. But I will look about my village at the illiteracy and disease and ignorance and I will not wonder long.

And perhaps . . . perhaps I will be a great man. . . . I mean perhaps I will hold on to the substance of truth and find my way always with the right course . . . and perhaps for it I will be butchered in my bed some night by the servants of the empire. . . .

BENEATHA *The martyr!*

ASAGAI . . . or perhaps I shall live to be a very old man, respected and esteemed in my new nation. . . . And perhaps I shall hold office and this is what I'm trying to tell you, Alaiyo; perhaps the things I believe now for my country will be wrong and outmoded, and I will not understand and do terrible things to have things my way or merely to keep my power. Don't you see that there will be young men and women, not British soldiers then, but my own black countrymen . . . to step out of the shadows some evening and slit my then useless throat? Don't you see they have always been there . . . that they always will be. And that such a thing as my own death will be an advance? They who might kill me even . . . actually replenish me!

BENEATHA Oh, Asagai, I know all that.

ASAGAI Good! Then stop moaning and groaning and tell me what you plan to do.

BENEATHA Do?

ASAGAI I have a bit of a suggestion.

BENEATHA What?

ASAGAI (*rather quietly for him*) That when it is all over—that you come home with me—

BENEATHA (*slapping herself on the forehead with exasperation born of misunderstanding*) Oh—Asagai—at this moment you decide to be romantic!

ASAGAI (*quickly understanding and misunderstanding*) My dear, young creature of the New World—I do not mean across the city—I mean across the ocean; home—to Africa.

BENEATHA (*slowly understanding and turning to him with murmured amazement*) To—to Nigeria?

ASAGAI Yes! . . . (*smiling and lifting his arms playfully*) Three hundred years later the African Prince rose up out of the seas and swept the maiden back across the middle passage over which her ancestors had come—

BENEATHA (*unable to play*) Nigeria?

ASAGAI Nigeria. Home. (*coming to her with genuine romantic flippancy*) I will show you our mountains and our stars; and give you cool drinks from gourds and teach you the old songs and the ways of our people—and, in time, we will pretend that—(*very softly*)—you have only been away for a day—

(*She turns her back to him, thinking. He swings her around and takes her full in his arms in a long embrace which proceeds to passion.*)

BENEATHA (*pulling away*) You're getting me all mixed up—

ASAGAI Why?

BENEATHA Too many things—too many things have happened today. I must sit down and think. I don't know what I feel about anything right this minute. (*She promptly sits down and props her chin on her fist.*)

ASAGAI (*charmed*) All right, I shall leave you. No—don't get up. (*touching her, gently, sweetly*) Just sit awhile and think. . . . Never be afraid to sit awhile and think. (*He goes to door and looks at her.*) How often I have looked at you and said, "Ah—so this is what the New World hath finally wrought. . . ."

(*He exits.* BENEATHA *sits on alone. Presently* WALTER *enters from his room and starts to rummage through things, feverishly looking for something. She looks up and turns in her seat.*)

BENEATHA (*hissingly*) Yes—just look at what the New World hath wrought! . . . Just look! (*She gestures with bitter disgust.*) There he is! *Monsieur le petit bourgeois noir*—himself! There he is—Symbol of a Rising Class! Entrepreneur! Titan of the system! (WALTER *ignores her completely and continues frantically and destructively looking for something and hurling things to floor and tearing things out of their place in his search.* BENEATHA *ignores the eccentricity of his actions and goes on with the monologue of insult.*) Did you dream of yachts on Lake Michigan, Brother? Did you see yourself on that Great Day sitting down at the Conference Table, surrounded by all the mighty bald-headed men in America? All halted, waiting, breathless, waiting for your pronouncements on industry? Waiting for you—Chairman of the Board? (WALTER *finds what he is looking for—a small piece of white paper—and pushes it in his pocket and puts on his coat and rushes out without even having looked at her. She shouts after him.*) I look at you and I see the final triumph of stupidity in the world!

(*The door slams and she returns to just sitting again.* RUTH *comes quickly out of* MAMA's *room.*)

RUTH Who was that?

BENEATHA Your husband.

RUTH Where did he go?

BENEATHA Who knows—maybe he has an appointment at U.S. Steel.

RUTH (*anxiously, with frightened eyes*) You didn't say nothing bad to him, did you?

BENEATHA Bad? Say anything bad to him? No—I told him he was a sweet boy and full of dreams and everything is strictly peachy keen, as the ofay kids say!

(MAMA *enters from her bedroom. She is lost, vague, trying to catch hold, to make some sense of her former command of the world, but it still eludes her. A sense of waste overwhelms her gait; a measure of apology rides on her shoulders. She goes to her plant, which has remained on the table, looks at it, picks it up and takes it to the window sill and sits it outside, and she stands and looks at it a long moment. Then she closes the window, straightens her body with effort and turns around to her children.*)

MAMA Well—ain't it a mess in here, though? (*a false cheerfulness, a beginning of something*) I guess we all better stop moping around and get some work done. All this unpacking and everything we got to do. (RUTH *raises her head slowly in response to the sense of the line; and* BENEATHA *in similar manner turns very slowly to look at her mother.*) One of you all better call the moving people and tell 'em not to come.

RUTH Tell 'em not to come?

MAMA Of course, baby. Ain't no need in 'em coming all the way here and having to go back. They charges for that too. (*She sits down, fingers to her brow, thinking.*) Lord, ever since I was a little girl, I always remembers people saying, "Lena—Lena Eggleston, you aims too high all the time. You needs to slow down and see life a little more like it is. Just slow down some." That's what they always used to say down home—"Lord, that Lena Eggleston is a high-minded thing. She'll get her due one day!"

RUTH No, Lena. . . .

MAMA Me and Big Walter just didn't never learn right.

RUTH Lena, no! We gotta go. Bennie—tell her. . . . (*She rises and crosses to* BENEATHA *with her arms outstretched.* BENEATHA *doesn't respond.*) Tell her we can still move . . . the notes ain't but a hundred and twenty-five a month. We got four grown people in this house—we can work. . . .

MAMA (*to herself*) Just aimed too high all the time—

RUTH (*turning and going to* MAMA *fast—the words pouring out with urgency and desperation*) Lena—I'll work. . . . I'll work twenty hours a day in all the kitchens in Chicago. . . . I'll strap my baby on my back if I have to and scrub all the floors in America and wash all the sheets in America if I have to—but we got to move. . . . We got to get out of here. . . .

(MAMA *reaches out absently and pats* RUTH's *hand.*)

MAMA No—I see things differently now. Been thinking 'bout some of the things we could do to fix this place up some. I seen a second-hand bureau over on Maxwell Street just the other day that could fit right there. (*She points to where the new furniture might go.* RUTH *wanders away from her.*) Would need some new handles on it and then a little varnish and then it look like something brand-new. And—we can put up them new curtains in the kitchen. . . . Why this place be looking fine. Cheer us all up so that we forget trouble ever came. . . . (*to* RUTH) And you could get some nice screens to put up in your room round the baby's bassinet. . . . (*She looks at both of them, pleadingly.*) Sometimes you just got to know when to give up some things . . . and hold on to what you got.

(WALTER *enters from the outside, looking spent and leaning against the door, his coat hanging from him.*)

MAMA Where you been, son?

WALTER (*breathing hard*) Made a call.

MAMA To who, son?

WALTER To The Man.

MAMA What man, baby?

WALTER The Man, Mama. Don't you know who The Man is?

RUTH Walter Lee?

WALTER *The Man.* Like the guys in the streets say—The Man. Captain Boss—Mistuh Charley . . . Old Captain Please Mr. Bossman . . .

BENEATHA (*suddenly*) Lindner!

WALTER That's right! That's good. I told him to come right over.

BENEATHA (*fiercely, understanding*) For what? What do you want to see him for!

WALTER (*looking at his sister*) We going to do business with him.

MAMA What you talking 'bout, son?

WALTER Talking 'bout life, Mama. You all always telling me to see life like it is. Well—I laid in there on my back today . . . and I figured it out. Life just like it is. Who gets and who don't get. (*He sits down with his coat on and laughs.*) Mama, you know it's all divided up. Life is. Sure enough. Between the takers and the "tooken." (*He laughs.*) I've figured it out finally. (*He looks around at them.*) Yeah. Some of us always getting "tooken." (*He laughs.*) People like Willy Harris, they don't never get "tooken." And you know why the rest of us do? 'Cause we all mixed up. Mixed up bad. We get to looking 'round for the right and the wrong; and we worry about it and cry about it and stay up nights trying to figure out 'bout the wrong and the right of things all the time. . . . And all the time, man, them takers is out there operating, just taking and taking. Willy Harris? Shoot—Willy Harris don't even count. He don't even count in the big scheme of things. But I'll say one thing for old Willy Harris . . . he's taught me something. He's taught me to keep my eye on what counts in this world. Yeah—(*shouting out a little*) Thanks, Willy!

RUTH What did you call that man for, Walter Lee?

WALTER Called him to tell him to come on over to the show. Gonna put on a show for the man. Just what he wants to see. You see, Mama, the man came here today and he told us that them people out there where you want us to move—well they so upset they willing to pay us not to move out there. (*He laughs again.*) And—and oh, Mama—you would of been proud of the way me and Ruth and Bennie acted. We told him to get out . . . Lord have mercy! We told the man to get out. Oh, we was some proud folks this afternoon, yeah. (*He lights a cigarette.*) We were still full of that old-time stuff. . . .

RUTH (*coming toward him slowly*) You talking 'bout taking them people's money to keep us from moving in that house?

WALTER I ain't just talking 'bout it, baby—I'm telling you that's what's going to happen.

BENEATHA Oh, God! Where is the bottom! Where is the real honest-to-God bottom so he can't go any farther!

WALTER See—that's old stuff. You and that boy that was here today. You all want everybody to carry a flag and a spear and sing some marching songs, huh? You wanna spend your life looking into things and trying to find the right and the wrong part, huh? Yeah. You know what's going to happen to that boy someday—he'll find himself sitting in a dungeon, locked in forever—and the takers will have the key! Forget it, baby! There ain't no causes—there ain't nothing but taking in this world, and he who takes most is smartest—and it don't make a damn bit of difference *how.*

MAMA You making something inside me cry, son. Some awful pain inside me.

WALTER Don't cry, Mama. Understand. That white man is going to walk in that door able to write checks for more money than we ever had. It's important to him and I'm going to help him . . . I'm going to put on the show, Mama.

MAMA Son—I come from five generations of people who was slaves and sharecroppers—but ain't nobody in my family never let nobody pay 'em no money that was a way of telling us we wasn't fit to walk the earth. We ain't never been that poor. (*raising her eyes and looking at him*) We ain't never been that dead inside.

BENEATHA Well—we are dead now. All the talk about dreams and sunlight that goes on in this house. All dead.

WALTER What's the matter with you all! I didn't make this world! It was give to me this way! Hell, yes, I want me some yachts someday! Yes, I want to hang some real pearls 'round my wife's neck. Ain't she supposed to wear no pearls? Somebody tell me—tell me, who decides which women is suppose to wear pearls in this world. I tell you I am a *man*—and I think my wife should wear pearls in this world!

(*This last line hangs a good while and* WALTER *begins to move about the room. The word "Man" has penetrated his consciousness; he mumbles it to himself repeatedly between strange agitated pauses as he moves about.*)

MAMA Baby, how you going to feel on the inside?

WALTER Fine! . . . Going to feel fine . . . a man. . . .

MAMA You won't have nothing left then, Walter Lee.

WALTER (*coming to her*) I'm going to feel fine, Mama. I'm going to look that son-of-a-bitch in the eyes and say—(*He falters.*)—and say, "All right, Mr. Lindner—(*He falters even more.*)—that's your neighborhood out there. You got the right to keep it like you want. You got the right to have it like you want. Just write the check and—the house is yours." And, and I am going to say—(*His voice almost breaks.*) And you—you people just put the money in my hand and you won't have to live next to this bunch of stinking niggers! . . . (*He straightens up and moves away from his mother, walking around the room.*) Maybe—maybe I'll just get down on my black knees. . . . (*He does so;* RUTH *and* BENNIE *and* MAMA *watch him in frozen horror.*) Captain, Mistuh, Bossman. (*He starts crying.*) A-hee-hee-hee! (*wringing his hands in profoundly anguished imitation*) Yasssssuh! Great White Father, just gi' ussen de money, fo' God's sake, and we's ain't gwine come out deh and dirty up yo' white folks neighborhood. . . .

(*He breaks down completely, then gets up and goes into the bedroom.*)

BENEATHA That is not a man. That is nothing but a toothless rat.

MAMA Yes—death done come in this here house. (*She is nodding, slowly, reflectively.*) Done come walking in my house. On the lips of my children. You what supposed to be my beginning again. You—what supposed to be my harvest. (*to* BENEATHA) You—you mourning your brother?

BENEATHA He's no brother of mine.

MAMA What you say?

BENEATHA I said that that individual in that room is no brother of mine.

MAMA That's what I thought you said. You feeling like you better than he is today? (BENEATHA *does not answer.*) Yes? What you tell him a minute ago? That he wasn't a man? Yes? You give him up for me? You done wrote his epitaph too—like the rest of the world? Well, who give you the privilege?

BENEATHA Be on my side for once! You saw what he just did, Mama! You saw him—down on his knees. Wasn't it you who taught me—to despise any man who would do that. Do what he's going to do.

MAMA Yes—I taught you that. Me and your daddy. But I thought I taught you something else too . . . I thought I taught you to love him.

BENEATHA Love him? There is nothing left to love.

MAMA There is always something left to love. And if you ain't learned that, you ain't learned nothing. (*looking at her*) Have you cried for that boy today? I don't mean for yourself and for the family 'cause we lost the money. I mean for him; what he been through and what it done to him. Child, when do you think is the time to love somebody the most; when they done good and made things easy for everybody? Well, then, you ain't through learning—because that ain't the time at all. It's when he's at his lowest and can't believe in hisself 'cause the world done whipped him so. When you starts measuring somebody, measure him right, child, measure him right. Make sure you done taken into account what hills and valleys he come through before he got to wherever he is.

(TRAVIS *bursts into the room at the end of the speech, leaving the door open.*)

TRAVIS Grandmama—the moving men are downstairs! The truck just pulled up.

MAMA (*turning and looking at him*) Are they, baby? They downstairs?

(*She sighs and sits.* LINDNER *appears in the doorway. He peers in and knocks lightly, to gain attention, and comes in. All turn to look at him.*)

LINDNER (*hat and briefcase in hand*) Uh—hello . . .

(RUTH *crosses mechanically to the bedroom door and opens it and lets it swing open freely and slowly as the lights come up on* WALTER *within, still in his coat, sitting at the far corner of the room. He looks up and out through the room to* LINDNER.)

RUTH He's here.

(*A long minute passes and* WALTER *slowly gets up.*)

LINDNER (*coming to the table with efficiency, putting his briefcase on the table and starting to unfold papers and unscrew fountain pens*) Well, I certainly was glad to hear from you people. (WALTER *has begun the trek out of the room, slowly and awkwardly, rather like a small boy, passing the back of his sleeve across his mouth from time to time.*) Life can really be so much simpler than people let it be most of the time. Well—with whom do I negotiate? You, Mrs. Younger, or your son here? (MAMA *sits with her hands folded on her lap and her eyes closed as* WALTER *advances.* TRAVIS *goes close to* LINDNER *and looks at the papers curiously.*) Just some official papers, sonny.

RUTH Travis, you go downstairs.

MAMA (*opening her eyes and looking into* WALTER's) No. Travis, you stay right here. And you make him understand what you doing, Walter Lee. You teach him good. Like Willy Harris taught you. You show where our five generations done come to. Go ahead, son—

WALTER (*looks down into his boy's eyes;* TRAVIS *grins up at him merrily and* WALTER *draws him beside him with his arm lightly around his shoulders*) Well, Mr. Lindner. (BENEATHA *turns away.*) We called you—(*There is a profound, simple groping quality in his speech.*)—because, well, me and my family—(*He looks around and shifts from one foot to the other.*) Well—we are very plain people. . . .

LINDNER Yes—

WALTER I mean—I have worked as a chauffeur most of my life—and my wife here, she does domestic work in people's kitchens. So does my mother. I mean—we are plain people. . . .

LINDNER Yes, Mr. Younger—

WALTER (*really like a small boy, looking down at his shoes and then up at the man*) And—uh—well, my father, well, he was a laborer most of his life.

LINDNER (*absolutely confused*) Uh, yes—

WALTER (*looking down at his toes once again*) My father almost beat a man to death once because this man called him a bad name or something, you know what I mean?

LINDNER No, I'm afraid I don't.

WALTER (*finally straightening up*) Well, what I mean is that we come from people who had a lot of pride. I mean—we are very proud people. And that's my sister over there and she's going to be a doctor—and we are very proud—

LINDNER Well—I am sure that is very nice, but—

WALTER (*starting to cry and facing the man eye to eye*) What I am telling you is that we called you over here to tell you that we are very proud and that this is—this is my son, who makes the sixth generation of our family in this country, and that we have all thought about your offer and we have decided to move into our house because my father—my father—he earned it. (MAMA *has her eyes closed and is rocking back and forth as though she were in church, with her head nodding the amen yes.*) We don't want to make no trouble for nobody or fight no causes—but we will try to be good neighbors. That's all we got to say. (*He looks the man absolutely in the eyes.*) We don't want your money. (*He turns and walks away from the man.*)

LINDNER (*looking around at all of them*) I take it then that you have decided to occupy.

BENEATHA That's what the man said.

LINDNER (*to* MAMA *in her reverie*) Then I would like to appeal to you, Mrs. Younger. You are older and wiser and understand things better I am sure . . .

MAMA (*rising*) I am afraid you don't understand. My son said we was going to move and there ain't nothing left for me to say. (*shaking her head with double meaning*) You know how these young folks is nowadays, mister. Can't do a thing with 'em. Good-bye.

LINDNER (*folding up his materials*) Well—if you are that final about it. . . . There is nothing left for me to say. (*He finishes. He is almost ignored by the family, who are concentrating on* WALTER LEE. *At the door* LINDNER *halts and looks around.*) I sure hope you people know what you're doing. (*He shakes his head and exits.*)

RUTH (*looking around and coming to life*) Well, for God's sake—if the moving men are here—LET'S GET THE HELL OUT OF HERE!

MAMA (*into action*) Ain't it the truth! Look at all this here mess. Ruth, put Travis' good jacket on him. . . . Walter Lee, fix your tie and tuck your shirt in, you look just like somebody's hoodlum. Lord have mercy, where is my plant? (*She flies to get it amid the general bustling of the family, who are deliberately trying to ignore the nobility of the past moment.*) You all start on down. . . . Travis child, don't go empty-handed. . . . Ruth, where did I put that box with my skillets in it? I want to be in charge of it myself. . . . I'm going to make us the biggest dinner we ever ate tonight. . . . Beneatha, what's the matter with them stockings? Pull them things up, girl. . . .

(The family starts to file out as two moving men appear and begin to carry out the heavier pieces of furniture, bumping into the family as they move about.)

BENEATHA Mama, Asagai—asked me to marry him today and go to Africa—

MAMA (*in the middle of her getting-ready activity*) He did? You ain't old enough to marry nobody—(*seeing the moving men lifting one of her chairs precariously*) Darling, that ain't no bale of cotton, please handle it so we can sit in it again. I had that chair twenty-five years. . . .

(*The movers sigh with exasperation and go on with their work.*)

BENEATHA (*girlishly and unreasonably trying to pursue the conversation*) To go to Africa, Mama—be a doctor in Africa. . . .

MAMA (*distracted*) Yes, baby—

WALTER Africa! What he want you to go to Africa for?

BENEATHA To practice there. . . .

WALTER Girl, if you don't get all them silly ideas out of your head! You better marry yourself a man with some loot. . . .

BENEATHA (*angrily, precisely as in the first scene of the play*) What have you got to do with who I marry!

WALTER Plenty. Now I think George Murchison—

(*He and* BENEATHA *go out yelling at each other vigorously;* BENEATHA *is heard saying that she would not marry* GEORGE MURCHISON *if he were Adam and she were Eve, etc. The anger is loud and real till their voices diminish.* RUTH *stands at the door and turns to* MAMA *and smiles knowingly.*)

MAMA (*fixing her hat at last*) Yeah—they something all right, my children. . . .

RUTH Yeah—they're something. Let's go, Lena.

MAMA (*stalling, starting to look around at the house*) Yes—I'm coming. Ruth—

RUTH Yes?

MAMA (*quietly, woman to woman*) He finally come into his manhood today, didn't he? Kind of like a rainbow after the rain. . . .

RUTH (*biting her lip lest her own pride explode in front of* MAMA) Yes, Lena.

(WALTER'S *voice calls for them raucously.*)

MAMA (*waving* RUTH *out vaguely*) All right, honey—go on down. I be down directly.

(RUTH *hesitates, then exits.* MAMA *stands, at last alone in the living room, her plant on the table before her as the lights start to come down. She looks around at all the walls and ceilings and suddenly, despite herself, while the children call below, a great heaving thing rises in her and she puts her fist to her mouth, takes a final desperate look, pulls her coat about her, pats her hat and goes out. The lights dim down. The door opens and she comes back in, grabs her plant, and goes out for the last time.*)

Curtain

STICKS AND BONES

(1971)

DAVID RABE (1940–)

Plays concerning warfare and its effects on both combatants and noncombatants alike have existed in all of Western dramatic history. The Trojan War was the subject of several ancient Greek plays; *The Trojan Women* by Euripides remains the most notable in its powerful indictment of war and its brutal aftermath. And we have already seen how Aristophanes handled the subject in *Lysistrata.*

The physical aspects of war are impossible to portray with any fidelity because of the obvious limitations of the stage. The mayhem and destruction of battle are best left to the film maker. The dramatist, then, must relegate the conflict itself to the background and thus restrict treatment of the struggle to the actions and reactions of the characters. Renaissance dramatists might call for a brief encounter involving considerable swordplay with a certain amount of running back and forth over the stage (Shakespeare's "alarums and excursions"), but the fighting was unimportant. The fate of the nobles and aristocrats involved became the main problem of dramatized warfare.

In more modern times, the privileged ranks of the commissioned officers replaced the crowned heads, as armies were organized along distinct class lines—that is, officers (gentlemen) and soldiers (rabble). Thus, because officers were by definition "gentlemen," at least on stage they conducted war along traditional rules of gallantry. Surrenders were formal affairs, including the knee-bending delivery of the sword to the conqueror. Women, of course, except for the lowly camp followers, were inviolate and were to be defended and respected by both sides.

The American Revolution provided material for a limited number of dramas. Most of them, whether before or after the conflict, were "dramatic dialogues" rather than legitimate stage pieces. The satires of Mrs. Mercy Otis Warren, including *The Group* (1775), remain the most famous, but whether or not they were ever produced remains a question. The fighting inspired a few efforts, such as the rather undramatic *The Battle of Bunker's Hill* (1776) by Hugh Henry Brackenridge (1748–1816). The only play worth reading today is *André* (1798) by William Dunlap, based on the Benedict Arnold treason. True to form, it is peopled by a noble collection of unbelievably honorable officers whose main concern is not the pursuit of the war but whether or not Major André, Arnold's British counterpart in the conspiracy, should die a soldier's death by being shot or be hanged like the lowly spy he really is. Hanging eventually wins out.

The American Civil War was once called the "noblest war" and the "last war between gentlemen." The "nobility" may be questioned, but its leaders, especially from the South, were the social elite, and Grant's generosity toward the defeated Lee was in the finest gentlemanly tradition. But it was a vicious war, the first truly modern conflict fought over vast territories by huge citizen armies, with widespread destruction of cities and towns and considerable suffering by noncombatant bystanders. Its tremendous slaughter produced the highest ratio of battlefield casualties to the number of combatants and the total population that has ever been known. Its hostilities of brother against brother provided tremendous opportunity for highly charged dramatic themes and theatrical effects.

The two best Civil War plays brought the fighting much closer to the civilians behind the lines, but they still centered around the comings and goings of the officers. *Shenandoah* (1888) by Bronson Howard tells of close friends and lovers torn apart by divided loyalties but all drawn together in the end for a happy and forgiving conclusion.

Secret Service (1895) by William Gillette is set in besieged Richmond and features a secret agent, Capt. Dumont, USA, performing his dark duties as Capt. Thorne, CSA, and falling in love with a Confederate general's daughter. The war comes closer with the steady bombardment in the background, but most of the action involves the ultimate refusal of Dumont, as Thorne, to telegraph counterfeit orders that could destroy the city's defenders—all as a matter of honor toward his Southern lady-love. When captured and unmasked, he stands ready to die but is spared at the last moment by the compassionate general who chooses to imprison rather than shoot him. After all, everybody is a gentleman and due respect must be paid.

The view of warfare as some kind of ennobling and romantic venture was abruptly and permanently ended with Stephen Crane's short novel *The Red Badge of Courage* in 1896. Here for the first time was a literary treatment of the realities of war and the effects upon those engaged in it. The central figure, Henry Fleming, who joins the Union Army with dreams of glory riding a white horse, soon learns that a soldier's life is one of boredom, horror, death, stench, starvation, and excruciating pain. Further, he does what every soldier at one time or another wants to do: turn tail and run to get as far from the carnage as possible. No longer could the brutality of war be disguised as the romantic chivalry that writers knew did not exist, a fact that they had up until then refused to admit on paper.

If there was any "romance" left, it was quickly shattered in the disaster of World War I. The disillusionment of what went on in the infested filth of front-line trenches or in the appalling slaughter of useless frontal attacks made a mockery of the high aims of saving democracy. The price of all this was questioned in the best of the World War I plays, *What Price Glory?* by Laurence Stallings (1894–1968) and Maxwell Anderson (1888–1959), which stunned audiences in 1924 with its revelation that the whole thing is an obscene nightmare in which officers and men share a hideously grim existence, fight over the same sluttish women, and roundly and explicitly curse each other and the top brass, who, they are sure, wouldn't know a war if they saw one. In this play men are hit and scream and blaspheme and die, and they receive orders from above to go right back and do it all over again.

The all-encompassing global struggle of World War II held the threat of direct involvement on the home front as well as the battlefield. Moreover, the jungles and beachheads made the trenches of *What Price Glory?* seem comparatively safe and comfortable, and the frightfulness of Hiroshima's mushroom cloud obliterated any possibility of attempting to re-create the war's violence. The important plays turned from bellowing obscenities or piously sermonizing about war's hideous nature to an examination of the physical and mental agonies encountered by everybody from stripeless private to multistarred general under these wildly unnatural conditions that can be more terrifying than enemy shrapnel or bullets.

In *The Eve of St. Mark* (1942) Maxwell Anderson turned from raucous bawdiness and front-line frightfulness to the portrayal of the underlying emotions of a group of young men uprooted from their comfortable society and suddenly placed in a violent world trained for war. Trapped on a remote Pacific island, facing certain death or capture, without venting their rage or uttering platitudinous nonsense, they do their best to survive and in the end emerge more "heroic" and more human. Arthur Laurents (1918–) in *Home of the Brave* (1846) explores the very strong sense of guilt that often overcomes the individual soldier who survives while watching his buddy die. *Command Decision* (1947) by William Wister Haines (1908–1989) goes no further than a Heavy Bombardment Command Post in England, well to the rear of the fighting. Its high-ranking officers are decent, respectable, thoroughly competent human beings for whom the strain of sending young men and their fabulously costly equipment into the teeth of enemy resistance that inflicts murderous casualties can stretch mental and physical endurance literally to the breaking point. *The Caine Mutiny Court Martial* (1954) by Hermon Wouk (1915–) deals with bravery and cowardice under conditions of utmost violence, yet does it all within the single setting of a stateside military court.

The "police action" of the undeclared war in Korea from 1950 to 1953 saw no significant drama, aside from the phenomenally successful film and television series *M*A*S*H.* Ending in a no-win stalemate and precarious truce, the Korean War became a "forgotten" war despite its bloody nature and nearly 140,000 casualties. On the other hand, the national agony of the Vietnam War spawned plays, motion pictures, and television series defending and attacking the rationale behind a conflict that all the might of a global power could not win and from which it eventually withdrew. Resistance and support at home, in their way, were as violent as anything in the rice paddies or jungles of the Indo-China peninsula.

Standing out among the best drama of the Vietnam era are three plays by David Rabe, each one distinctly different from the others, but each effectively treating the war's effects on the ordinary fighting men both in the barracks and at home. *Streamers* (1976) concerns the behind-the-lines experiences of paratroopers (a "streamer" is a parachute that fails to open properly). *The Basic Training of Pavlo Hummel* (1971) depicts the army life of a young and not particularly bright enlisted man whose lack of purpose and muddled behavior in the midst of a mad world demonstrates his inability to comprehend what's going on around him either in stateside barracks or on the battlefield. A single act, falling on a grenade to protect others, turns him into an instant but unacknowledged hero who, like thousands of others, demands but seldom gets our ultimate respect.

Sticks and Bones brings the national crisis of the Vietnam War directly into the American domestic scene. Those who did not live through the late 1940s and into the 1950s will miss much of the power of Rabe's satire in presenting the cozy domesticity of Ozzie, Harriet, David, and Rick. These were actual people—Ozzie Nelson, successful bandleader, and his vocalist wife, Harriet Hiliard—who struck immediate popularity and ensuing commercial success with their long-running radio and television "adventures." Here was the family that the postwar audience wanted to hear, see, and believe in. Handsome, youthful bread-winning father, confident and understanding, always welcomed home by lovely, perfectly coiffed, unflappable mother. The "adventures" with their two real-life sons were touchingly funny and sweetly sentimental, untarnished by what went on in the "real" world outside, representing the very best of what many Americans felt the country ought to be.

Rabe's use of the Nelson family is a brilliant stroke. True, the play can be successful without the Nelson connection, and some productions have used other names, but Rabe's point is all the more stinging when the origins are known. All the amenities of a good American life are present and the family is close and loving, *except* that one all-American son has experienced and now returns, blinded, from the horrors of the Vietnam debacle, and he shatters the sacred peace, tranquility, and complacency of his home. He is deeply resented for this intrusion as he brings out the strong underlying ugliness of racism and bigotry. It is not a pretty sight.

As Rabe moves into the realm of stylized unreality and nightmare, the audience must make some rather abrupt adjustments, but once the symbolic meanings are recognized, the dramatist's points become clear. But still we must ask: Does Zung really exist? Is she or is she not visible to others? How literally should we take the final ritual sacrifice of David's life? However one looks at it, *Sticks and Bones* is a devastating comment on a variety of levels involving the war, its refugees and survivors, the American family, and a number of social values so long taken for granted.

Author's Note

In any society there is an image of how the perfectly happy family should appear. It is this image that the people in this play wish to preserve above all else. Mom and Dad are not concerned that terrible events have occurred in the world, but rather that David has come home to behave in a manner that makes him no longer lovable. Thus he is keeping them from being the happy family they know they must be. He attacks those aspects of their self-image in which reside all their sense of value and sanity. But, curiously, one of the requisites of their self-image is that everything is fine, and, consequently, for a long time they must not even admit that David is attacking.

Yet everything is being communicated. Often a full, long speech is used in this play where in another, more "realistic" play there would be only a silence during which something was communicated between two people. Here the communication is obvious, because it is directly spoken. Consequently the ignoring of that which is communicated must be equally obvious. David throws a yelling, screaming tantrum over his feelings of isolation and Harriet confidently, cheerfully offers Ezy Sleep sleeping pills in full faith that they will solve his problem. The actors must try to look at what they are ignoring. They must not physically ignore things—turn their backs, avert their eyes, be busy with something else. The point is not that they do not physically see or hear, but that they psychologically ignore. Though they look right at things, though they listen closely, they do not see or hear. The harder they physically focus and concentrate on an event, the clearer their psychological state and the point and nature of the play will be, when in their next moments and speeches they verbally and emotionally ignore or miss what they have clearly looked at. In addition, the actors should try not to take the play overly seriously. The characters (except for David) do not take things seriously until they are forced to, and then they do it for as short a time as they can manage. Let the audience take seriously the jolly way the people go about the curious business of their lives.

Stylization, then, is the main production problem. The forms referred to during the time of writing *Sticks and Bones* were farce, horror movie, TV situation comedy. These should have their effect, though it must be remembered that they are where form was sought, not content. What is poetic in the writing must not be reinforced by deep feeling on the part of the actors, or the writing will hollow into pretension. In a more "realistic" play, where language is thinner, subtext must be supplied or there is no weight. Such deep support of *Sticks and Bones* will make the play ponderous. As a general rule, I think it is true that when an actor's first impulse (the impulse of all his training) is to make a heavy or serious adjustment in a scene, he should reverse himself and head for a lighthearted adjustment. If his first impulse is toward lightheartedness, perhaps he should turn toward a serious tack. A major premise of the play is that stubbing your own big toe is a more disturbing event than hearing of a stranger's suicide.

At the start, the family is happy and orderly, and then David comes home and he is unhappy. As the play progresses, he become happier and they become unhappier. Then, at the end, they are happy.

D.R.

Sticks and Bones DAVID RABE

For Tâm

CHARACTERS

OZZIE
HARRIET
DAVID
RICK
ZUNG (*the Girl*)
FATHER DONALD
SERGEANT MAJOR

Time: Autumn
Place: The family home

Act I

Place: the family home.

Darkness; silence. Slides appear on both sides of the stage: the first is a black-and-white medium close-up of a young man, mood and clothing of the early 1900s; he is lean, reasonably handsome, black hair parted in the center. Voices speak. They are slow and relaxed, with an improvisational quality.

1ST CHILD'S VOICE Who zat?
MAN'S VOICE Grandpa Jacob's father.

New slide: group photo, same era, eight or ten people, all ages.

2ND CHILD'S VOICE Look at 'em all!
1ST CHILD'S VOICE How come they're all so serious?

New slide: small boy, black hair, black knickers.

WOMAN'S VOICE There's Grandpa Oswald as a little boy.
1ST CHILD'S VOICE Grandpa?

New slide: different boy, same pose.

WOMAN'S VOICE And that's his brother Thomas. He died real young.
MAN'S VOICE Scarlet fever.

New slide: young girl, seventeen or eighteen.

And that's his sister Christina.

WOMAN'S VOICE No, that's Grandma.

MAN'S VOICE No.

WOMAN'S VOICE Sure.

New slide: OZZIE *and* HARRIET, *young, 1940s era.*

There's the two of them.

MAN'S VOICE Mmmmm, you're right, because that's Grandpa.

New slide: two boys, five and nine years old.

WOMAN'S VOICE The taller one's David, right?

New slide: color close-up of DAVID *from the last moment of the play, a stricken look.*

1ST CHILD'S VOICE What's that one?

MAN'S VOICE Somebody sick.

1ST CHILD'S VOICE Boy . . . !

New slide: color photo of OZZIE, HARRIET, *and* FATHER DONALD. FATHER DONALD, *wearing a gym suit, his back to the camera, stands holding a basketball in one hand.* OZZIE *and* HARRIET *face him, one on either side.*

2ND CHILD'S VOICE Oh, look at that one!

MAN'S VOICE That's a funny one, isn't it.

WOMAN'S VOICE That's one—I bet somebody took it—they didn't know it was going to be taken.

There is a bright flash and the stage is immediately illuminated. The set is an American home, very modern, with a quality of brightness, green walls, green rug. Stairs lead up to a bedroom—not lighted now—with a hallway leading off to the rest of the upstairs beyond. There is naturalness, yet a sense of space and, oddly, a sense also that this room, these stairs belong in the gloss of an advertisement.

Downstage, a TV on wheels faces upstage, glowing, murmuring. OZZIE, HARRIET, *and* FATHER DONALD*—a slightly rotund, serious man—are standing as they were in the slide last seen.*

FATHER DONALD A feel for it is the big thing. A feel for the ball. You know, I mean, bouncing it, dribbling it. You don't even look at it.

(*Phone rings.*)

OZZIE I'll get it.

FATHER DONALD You can do it, Harriet. Give it a try. (*He bounces the ball to* HARRIET.)

OZZIE Hello? . . .

FATHER DONALD (*as* HARRIET *catches the ball*) That a girl.

HARRIET Oh, Father . . .

OZZIE (*hanging up*) Nobody there.

FATHER DONALD That's what I'm telling you. You gotta help kids. Keeps 'em outa trouble. We help. Organized sports activities; it does 'em a world a good. You know that. And they need you.

OZZIE I was a track and field man. Miler. Dash man—I told you.

(*Phone rings.*)

FATHER DONALD But this is basketball season. (*He moves toward* HARRIET *and then the door, as* OZZIE *goes to the phone, says "Hello," then listens intently.*) You listen to me, you get that husband of yours out there to help us. It'll do him good. Tell him he'd be a good little guard. A play maker.

HARRIET Oh, Father Donald, bless me.

FATHER DONALD Of course. (*He blesses her, holding the ball under his left arm.*) Bye-bye.

HARRIET (*as* FATHER DONALD *goes*) Good-bye, Father.
(*And she turns to look for a moment at* OZZIE *on the phone.*)
Why aren't you talking?
(*Silence: she is looking at him.*)
Ozzie, why aren't you talking?

OZZIE (*slowly lowering the phone*) They're gone. They hung up.

HARRIET You didn't say a word. You said nothing.

OZZIE I said my name.

HARRIET What did they want?

OZZIE I said hello.

HARRIET Were they selling something—is that what they wanted?

OZZIE No, no.

HARRIET Well . . . who was it?

OZZIE What?

HARRIET What are we talking about?

OZZIE The Government. It was . . . you know. . . .

HARRIET Ozzie! (*in fear*) No!

OZZIE (*some weariness in him*) No, he's all right, he's coming home!

HARRIET Why didn't you let me speak? Who was it?

OZZIE No, no.

HARRIET It was David.

OZZIE No, somebody else. Some clerk. I don't know who.

HARRIET You're lying.

OZZIE No. There was just all this static—it was hard to hear. But he was coming home was part of it, and they had his records and papers but I couldn't talk to him directly even though he was right there, standing right there.

HARRIET I don't understand.

OZZIE That's what they said. . . . And he was fine and everything. And he wanted them to say hello for him. He'd lost some weight. He would be sent by truck. I could hear truck engines in the background—revving. They wanted to know my name. I told them.

HARRIET No more?

OZZIE They were very professional. Very brusque . . .

HARRIET No more . . . at all? . . .

(*The front door opens and* RICK *comes in. And the door slams. He is young, seventeen. His hair is long and neat, with sideburns. His clothing is elaborate—very, very up to date. He carries a guitar on his shoulder.*)

RICK Hi, Mom. Hi, Dad.

HARRIET Hi, Rick.

OZZIE Hi, Rick.

HARRIET Ohhh, Ricky, Ricky, your brother's on his way home. David's coming home!

OZZIE We just got a call.

RICK Ohhh, boy!

HARRIET Isn't that wonderful? Isn't it? Your father talked to him. Oh, I bet you're starving. Sit, sit.

OZZIE I talked to *somebody*, Rick.

HARRIET There's fudge and ice cream in the fridge; would you like that?

RICK Oh, yeah, and could I have some soda?

(*She is on her way to the kitchen, nodding.*)

Wow, some news. I'm awful hungry.

OZZIE Never had a doubt. A boy like that—if he leaves, he comes back.

RICK (*as he picks up a comic book*) How about me? What if I left?

OZZIE Absolutely. Absolutely.

(*Silence. Rick reads the comic.*)

I built jeeps . . . tanks, trucks.

RICK What?

OZZIE In the other war, I mean. Number Two. I worked on vehicles. Vehicles were needed and I worked to build them. Sometimes I put on wheels, tightened 'em up. I never . . . served . . . is what I mean. (*Slight pause.*) They got all those people—soldiers, Rick—you see what I mean? They get 'em across the ocean, they don't have any jeeps or tanks or trucks, what are they gonna do, stand around? Wait for a bus on the beachhead? Call a cab?

RICK No public transportation in a war.

OZZIE That's right, that's right.

(HARRIET *enters, carrying fudge and ice cream.*)

HARRIET Oh, Ozzie, Ozzie, do you remember—I just remembered that time David locked himself in that old icebox. We didn't know where he was. We looked all over. We couldn't find him. And then there was this icebox in this clearing . . . out in the middle. I'll bet you don't even remember.

OZZIE Of course I remember.

HARRIET And he leaped to us. So frightened.

OZZIE He couldn't even speak—he couldn't even speak—just these noises.

HARRIET Or that time he fell from that tree.

OZZIE My God, he was somethin'! If he wasn't fallin', he was gettin' hit.

HARRIET And then there was that day we went out into the woods. It was just all wind and clouds. We sailed a kite!

OZZIE I'd nearly forgotten! . . .

RICK Where was I?

HARRIET You were just a baby, Rick. We had a picnic.

RICK I'm gonna get some more soda, okay?

(HARRIET *touches him as he passes.*)

OZZIE What a day that was. I felt great that day.

HARRIET And then Hank came along. Hank Grenweller. He came from out of the woods calling that—

OZZIE That's right.

HARRIET He was happy.

OZZIE We were all happy. Except he'd come to tell us he was going away, leaving. And then we had that race. Wasn't that the day?

HARRIET I don't remember.

OZZIE Hank and me! Hank Grenweller. A foot race. And I beat him. I did it; got him.

HARRIET Noooo.

OZZIE It was only inches, but—

HARRIET Ozzie, he took it easy. He wasn't trying.

OZZIE He had to do his very best. Always. Never less. That was one thing you knew—no matter what he did or said, it was meant and true. All those long talks. Do you ever miss him?

HARRIET He was a fine strong man.

OZZIE I don't know why he left.

HARRIET Do you remember when he showed us this house?

OZZIE I remember when he showed me you.

HARRIET You know that's not true. If it was close—and it was—that race you ran—(*This is not loud: there is intimacy; they are near one another.*) I remember now—it was because he let it be—no other reason. We were all having fun. He didn't want to make you feel badly. He didn't want to ruin all the fun. You know that. You know you do.

RICK (*calling from the kitchen*) You people want some fudge?

HARRIET No, Rick.

OZZIE I don't know he didn't try. I don't know that. (*He stares at* HARRIET.)

HARRIET I think I'll be going up to bed; take a little nap.

RICK Sleepy, Mom?
HARRIET A little. (*She is crossing toward* OZZIE.)
RICK That's a good idea then.
HARRIET Call me.
RICK Okay.
HARRIET Do you know, the day he left? It was a winter day. November, Ozzie. (*She moves toward the stairs.*)
OZZIE I know.
HARRIET I prayed; did you know that? Now he's home.
OZZIE It was a winter day.
HARRIET (*at the top of the stairs*) I know.
RICK (*toying with his guitar*) Night, Mom.

(*She doesn't answer but disappears down the hall. He looks up and yells after her.*)

Night, Mom!
HARRIET (*from off*) Turn off the TV, somebody.

(RICK *crosses to the TV. He turns it off and wheels it back under the stairs.* OZZIE *watches. Silence.*)

OZZIE I knew she was praying. She moves her lips.

(RICK *does not look up. He begins, softly, to strum and tune the guitar.*)

And something else—yes, sir, boy, oh, boy, I tell you, huh? What a day, huh? (*Slight pause.*) They got seventeen hundred million men they gotta deal with, how they gonna do that without any trucks and tanks and jeeps? But I'm some kinda jerk because I wasn't out there blastin' away, huh? I was useful. I put my time to use. I been in fights. Fat Kramer. . . . How we used to fight!

(RICK *strums some notes on the guitar.* OZZIE *stares at him.*)

How come I'm restless? I . . . seen him do some awful, awful things, ole Dave. He was a mean . . . foul-tempered little baby. I'm only glad I was *here* when they sent him off to do his killing. That's right. (*Silence.*) I feel like I swallowed ants, that's how restless I am. Outran a bowlin' ball one time. These guys bet me I couldn't do it and I did, beat it to the pins. Got a runnin' start, then the—

(*A faint, strange rapping sound has stopped him, spun him around.*)

Did you do that?
RICK Somebody knockin'.
OZZIE Knockin'?
RICK The door, Dad.
OZZIE Oh.

RICK You want me to get it?

OZZIE No, no. It's just so late. (*He moves for the door.*)

RICK That's all right.

OZZIE Sure.

(*He opens the door just a crack, as if to stick his head around. But the door is thrust open and a man enters abruptly. He is black or of Spanish descent, and is dressed in the uniform of a sergeant major and wearing many campaign ribbons.*)

SGT. MAJOR Excuse me. Listen to me. I'd like to speak to the father here. I'd like to know who . . . is the father? Could . . . you tell me the address?

OZZIE May I ask who it is who's asking?

SGT. MAJOR I am. I'm asking. What's the address of this house?

OZZIE But I mean, who is it that wants to know?

SGT. MAJOR We called; we spoke. Is this seven-seventeen Dunbar?

OZZIE Yes.

SGT. MAJOR What's wrong with you?

OZZIE Don't you worry about me.

SGT. MAJOR I have your son.

OZZIE What?

SGT. MAJOR Your son.

OZZIE No.

SGT. MAJOR But he is. I have papers, pictures, prints. I know your blood and his. This is the right address. Please. Excuse me. (*He pivots, reaches out into the dark.*) I am very busy. I have your father, David.

(*He draws* DAVID *in—a tall, thin boy, blond and, in the shadows, wearing sunglasses and a uniform of dress greens. In his right hand is a long, white, red-tipped cane. He moves, probing the air, as the sergeant major moves him past Ozzie toward the couch, where he will sit the boy down like a parcel.*)

OZZIE David? . . .

SGT. MAJOR He's blind.

OZZIE What?

SGT. MAJOR Blind.

OZZIE I don't . . . understand.

SGT. MAJOR We're very sorry.

OZZIE (*realizing*) Ohhhhh. Yes. Ohhhh. I see . . . sure. I mean, we didn't know. Nobody said it. I mean, sure, Dave, sure; it's all right—don't you worry. Rick's here, too, Dave—Rick, your brother, tell him hello.

RICK Hi, Dave.

DAVID (*worried*) You said . . . "father."

OZZIE Well . . . there's two of us, Dave; two.

DAVID Sergeant, you said "home." I don't think so.

OZZIE Dave, sure.

DAVID It doesn't feel right.

OZZIE But it is, Dave—me and Rick—Dad and Rick. Harriet! (*Calling up the stairs*) Harriet!

DAVID Let me touch their faces. . . . I can't see. (*rising, his fear increasing*) Let me put my fingers on their faces.

OZZIE (*hurt, startled*) What? Do what?

SGT. MAJOR Will that be all right if he does that?

OZZIE Sure. . . . Sure. . . . Fine.

SGT. MAJOR (*helping* DAVID *to* OZZIE) It will take him time.

OZZIE That's normal and to be expected. I'm not surprised. Not at all. We figured on this. Sure, we did. Didn't we, Rick?

RICK (*occupied with his camera, an Instamatic*) I wanna take some pictures, okay? How are you, Dave?

DAVID What room is this?

OZZIE Middle room, Dave. TV room. TV's in—

HARRIET (*on the stairs*) David! . . . Oh, David! . . . David . . .

(*And* OZZIE, *leaving* DAVID, *hurries toward the stairs and looks up at her as she falters, stops, stares. Rick, moving near, snaps a picture of her.*)

OZZIE Harriet . . . don't be upset. . . . They say . . . Harriet, Harriet . . . he can't see! . . . Harriet . . . they say—he—can't . . . see. That man.

HARRIET (*standing very still*) Can't see? What do you mean?

SGT. MAJOR He's blind.

HARRIET No. Who says? No, no.

OZZIE Look at him. He looks so old. But it's nothing, Harriet, I'm sure.

SGT. MAJOR I hope you people understand.

OZZIE It's probably just how he's tired from his long trip.

HARRIET (*moving toward him*) Oh, you're home now, David.

SGT. MAJOR (*with a large sheet of paper waving in his hands.*) Who's gonna sign this for me, Mister? It's a shipping receipt. I got to have somebody's signature to show you got him. I got to have somebody's name on the paper.

OZZIE Let me. All right?

SGT. MAJOR Just here and here, you see? Your name or mark three times.

(*as they move toward a table and away from* HARRIET, *who is near* DAVID)

OZZIE Fine, listen, would you like some refreshments?

SGT. MAJOR No.

OZZIE I mean while I do this. Cake and coffee. Of course, you do.

SGT. MAJOR No.

OZZIE Sure.

SGT. MAJOR No. I haven't time. I've got to get going. I've got trucks out there backed up for blocks. Other boys. I got to get on to Chicago, and some of them to Denver and Cleveland, Reno, New Orleans, Boston, Trenton, Watts,

Atlanta. And when I get back they'll be layin' all over the grass; layin' there in pieces all over the grass, their backs been broken, their brains jellied, their insides turned into garbage. One-legged boys and no-legged boys. I'm due in Harlem; I got to get to the Bronx and Queens, Cincinnati, Saint Louis, Reading. I don't have time for coffee. I got deliveries to make all across this country.

DAVID (*with* HARRIET, *his hands on her face, a kind of realization*) Nooooooo. . . . Sergeant . . . nooo; there's something wrong; it all feels wrong. Where are you? Are you here? I don't know these people!

SGT. MAJOR That's natural, Soldier; it's natural you feel that way.

DAVID Nooooo.

HARRIET (*attempting to guide him back to a chair*) David, just sit, be still.

DAVID Don't you hear me?

OZZIE Harriet, calm him.

DAVID The air is wrong; the smells and sounds, the wind.

HARRIET David, please, please. What is it? Be still. Please . . .

DAVID GODDAMN YOU, SERGEANT, I AM LONELY HERE! I AM LONELY!

SGT. MAJOR I got to go. (*And he pivots to leave.*)

DAVID (*following the sound of the sergeant major's voice*) Sergeant!

SGT. MAJOR (*whirling, bellowing*) You shut up. You piss-ass soldier, you shut the fuck up!

OZZIE (*walking to the sergeant major, putting his hand on the man's shoulder*) Listen, let me walk you to the door. All right? I'd like to take a look at that truck of yours. All right?

SGT. MAJOR There's more than one.

OZZIE Fine.

SGT. MAJOR It's a convoy.

OZZIE Good.

(*They exit, slamming the door, and Rick, running close behind them, pops it open, leaps out. He calls from off.*)

RICK Sure are lots a trucks, Mom!

HARRIET (*as he reenters*) Are there?

RICK Oh, yeah. Gonna rain some more too. (*And turning, he runs up the stairs.*) See you in the morning. Night, Dave.

HARRIET It's so good to have you here again; so good to see you. You look . . . just . . .

(OZZIE *has slipped back into the room behind her, he stands, looking.*)

fine. You look—

(*She senses* OZZIE'S *presence, turns, immediately, speaking.*)

He bewilders you, doesn't he?

(*And* OZZIE, *jauntily, heads for the stairs.*)

Where are you going?

(*He stops; he doesn't know. And she is happily sad now as she speaks—sad for poor* OZZIE *and* DAVID, *they are so whimsical, so childlike.*)

You thought you knew what was right, all those years, teaching him sports and fighting. Do you understand what I'm trying to say? A mother knows *things* . . . a father cannot ever know them. The measles, smallpox, cuts and bruises. Never have you come upon him in the night as he lay awake and staring . . . praying.

OZZIE I saw him put a knife through the skin of a cat. I saw him cut the belly open.

DAVID Noooo. . . .

HARRIET (*moving toward him in response*) David, David. . . .

DAVID Ricky!

(*There is a kind of accusation in this as if he were saying* RICKY *did the killing of the cat. He says it loudly and directly into her face.*)

HARRIET He's gone to bed.

DAVID I want to leave.

(*There is furniture around him; he is caged. He pokes with his cane.*)

HARRIET What is it?

DAVID Help me. (*He crashes.*)

OZZIE Settle down! Relax.

DAVID I want to leave! I want to leave! I want to leave. I . . .

(*And he smashes into the stairs, goes down, flails, pounding his cane.*)

want to leave.

OZZIE *and* HARRIET Dave! David! Davey!

DAVID . . . . to leave! Please.

(*He is on the floor, breathing. Long, long silence in which they look at him sadly, until* HARRIET *announces the problem's solution.*)

HARRIET Ozzie, get him some medicine. Get him some Ezy Sleep.

OZZIE Good idea.

HARRIET It's in the medicine cabinet; a little blue bottle, little pink pills.

(*And when* OZZIE *is gone up the stairs, there is quiet. She stands over* DAVID.)

It'll give you the sleep you need. Dave—the sleep you remember. You're our child and you're home. Our good . . . beautiful boy.

(*And front door bursts open. There is a small girl in the doorway, an Asian girl. She wears the Vietnamese* ao dai, *black slacks and white tunic slit up the sides. Slowly, she enters, carrying before her a small straw hat.* HARRIET *is looking at the open door.*)

HARRIET What an awful . . . wind. (*She shuts the door.*)

(*Blackout. Guitar music.*)

(*A match flickers as* HARRIET *lights a candle in the night. And the girl silently moves from before the door across the floor to the stairs, where she sits, as* HARRIET *moves toward the stairs and* OZZIE, *asleep sitting up in a chair, stirs.*)

HARRIET Oh! I didn't mean to wake you. I lit a candle so I wouldn't wake you.

(*He stares at her.*)

I'm sorry.

OZZIE I wasn't sleeping.

HARRIET I thought you were.

OZZIE Couldn't. Tried. Couldn't. Thinking. Thoughts running very fast. Trying to remember the night David . . . was made. Do you understand me? I don't know why. But the feeling in me that I had to figure something out and if only I could remember that night . . . the mood . . . I would be able. You're . . . shaking your head.

HARRIET I don't understand.

OZZIE No.

HARRIET Good night.

(*She turns and leaves* OZZIE *sitting there, gazing at the dark. Arriving at* DAVID's *door, she raps softly and then opens the door.* DAVID *is lying unmoving on the bed. She speaks to him.*)

I heard you call.

DAVID What?

HARRIET I heard you call.

DAVID I didn't.

HARRIET Would you like a glass of warm milk?

DAVID I was sleeping.

HARRIET (*after a slight pause*) How about that milk? Would you like some milk?

DAVID I didn't call. I was sleeping.

HARRIET I'll bet you're glad you didn't bring her back. Their skins are yellow, aren't they?

DAVID What?

HARRIET You're troubled, warm milk would help. Do you pray at all any more? If I were to pray now, would you pray with me?

DAVID What . . . do you want?
HARRIET They eat the flesh of dogs.
DAVID I know. I've seen them.
HARRIET Pray with me; pray.
DAVID What . . . do . . . you want?
HARRIET Just to talk, that's all. Just to know that you're home and safe again. Nothing else; only that we're all together, a family. You must be exhausted. Don't worry; sleep. (*She is backing into the hallway. In a whisper:*) Good night.

(*She blows out the candle and is gone, moving down the hall. Meanwhile the girl is stirring, rising, climbing from the living room up toward* DAVID*'s room, which she enters, moving through a wall, and* DAVID *sits up.*)

DAVID Who's there?

(*As she drifts by, he waves the cane at the air.*)

Zung? (*He stands.*) Chào, Cô Zung.

(*He moves for the door, which he opens, and steps into the hall, leaving her behind him in the room.*)

Zung. Chào, Cô Zung.

(*And he moves off up the hallway. She follows*)

Zung! . . .

(*Blackout. Music.*)

(*Lights up. It is a bright afternoon, and* OZZIE *is under the stairs with a screwdriver in his hand, poking about at the TV set.*)

OZZIE C'mon, c'mon. Ohhhh, c'mon, this one more game and ole State's Bowl-bound. C'mon, what is it? Ohhh, hey . . . ohhhhh. . . .
HARRIET (*entering the kitchen carrying a tray with a bowl of soup and a glass of juice.*) Ozzie, take this up to David; make him eat it.
OZZIE Harriet, the TV is broke.
HARRIET What?
OZZIE There's a picture but no sound. I don't—

(*Grabbing her by the arm, he pulls her toward a place before the set.*)

HARRIET Stoppit, you're spilling the soup. (*She pulls free.*)
OZZIE It's Sunday. I want to watch it. I turned it on, picture came on just like normal. I got the volume up full blast.

(*Having set the tray down,* HARRIET *now shoves the TV set deeper under the stairs, deeper into the place where it is kept when not in use.*)

Hey! I want to watch it!

HARRIET I want to talk about David.

OZZIE David's all right.

(*He turns, crosses toward the phone, picks up the phone book.*)

I'm gonna call the repairman.

HARRIET (*following him*) Ozzie, he won't eat. He just lays there. I offer him food, he won't eat it. No, no. The TV repairman won't help, you silly. (*She takes the phone book from him.*) He doesn't matter. There's something wrong with David. He's been home days and days and still he speaks only when spoken to; there's no light in his eye, no smile; he's not happy to be here and not once has he touched me or held me, nor has he even shaken your hand.

(OZZIE *flops down in a chair.*)

OZZIE Oh, I don't mind that. Why should I mind—

HARRIET And now he's talking to himself! What about that? Do you mind that? He mutters in his sleep.

OZZIE (*exasperated*) Ohhhhhh.

HARRIET Yes. And it's not a regular kind of talking at all. It's very strange—very spooky.

OZZIE Spooky?

HARRIET That's right.

OZZIE I never heard him.

HARRIET You sleep too deeply. I took a candle and followed. I was in his room. He lay there, speaking.

OZZIE Speaking what?

HARRIET I don't know. I couldn't understand.

OZZIE Was it words?

HARRIET All kind of funny and fast.

OZZIE Maybe prayer; praying.

HARRIET No. No, it was secret. Oh, Ozzie, I know praying when I hear it and it wasn't praying he was doing. We meant our son to be so different—I don't understand—good and strong. And yet . . . perhaps he is. But there are moments when I see him . . . hiding . . . in that bed behind those awful glasses, and I see the chalkiness that's come into—

OZZIE (*headed for the kitchen, looking for juice to drink.*) Those glasses are simply to ease his discomfort.

HARRIET I hate them.

OZZIE They're tinted glass and plastic. Don't be so damn suspicious.

HARRIET I'm not, I'm not. It's seeing I'm doing, not suspicion. Suspicion fe9hasn't any reasons. It's you—now accusing me for no reason when I'm only worried.

OZZIE (*returning from the kitchen, angered.*) Where's my juice?

HARRIET I want to talk.

OZZIE The hell with David for a minute—I want some juice.

HARRIET Shut up. You're selfish. You're so selfish.

OZZIE (*walking to the tray and juice, attempting to threaten her*) I'll pour it on the floor. I'll break the glass.

(*She turns to move to get the juice.*)

HARRIET A few years ago you might have done that kind of thing.

OZZIE I woke up this morning, I could see so clearly the lovely way you looked when you were young. Beside me this morning, you were having trouble breathing. You kept . . . trying . . . to breathe.

(*She approaches him to hand him the juice.*)

What do you give me when you give me this?

HARRIET I always looked pretty much as I do now. I never looked so different at all.

(DAVID *appears from off upstairs, dressed in a red robe, and descends toward them.*)

DAVID (*sounding happy, yet moving with urgency*) Good morning.

OZZIE Oh, David! Ohhh, good morning. Hello. How do you feel this fine bright morning; how do you feel?

DAVID He was a big man, wasn't he?

OZZIE What?

DAVID Hank. You were talking about Hank Grenweller. I thought you were.

OZZIE Oh, yes. Hank. Very big. Big. A good fine friend, ole Hank.

DAVID You felt when he was with you he filled the room.

OZZIE It was the way he talked that did that. He boomed. His voice just boomed.

DAVID He was here once and you wanted me to sit on his lap, isn't that right? It was after dinner. He was in a chair in the corner.

HARRIET That's right.

DAVID His hand was gone—the bone showed in the skin.

OZZIE My God, what a memory—did you hear that, Harriet? You were only four or five. He'd just had this terrible, awful auto accident. His hand was hurt, not gone.

DAVID No. It was congenital and none of us knew.

OZZIE What?

DAVID That hand. The sickness in it.

OZZIE Congenital?

DAVID Yes.

OZZIE What do you mean? What do you think you mean?

DAVID I'd like some coffee.

(*He is seated now, but not without tension.*)

OZZIE Hank's parents were good fine people, David.

DAVID I know.

OZZIE Well, what are you saying then?

DAVID I'd like that coffee.

HARRIET Of course. And what else with it?

DAVID Nothing.

HARRIET Oh, no, no, you've got to eat. To get back your strength. You must. Pancakes? How do pancakes sound? Or wheat cakes? Or there's eggs? And juice? Orange or prune: or waffles. I bet it's eggs you want. Over, David? Over easy? Scrambled?

DAVID I'm only thirsty.

HARRIET Well, all right then, coffee is what you'll have and I'll just put some eggs on the side; you used to love them so; remember?

(*And picking up the tray, she is off toward the kitchen. There is a pause.*)

OZZIE I mean, I hate to harp on a thing, but I just think you're way off base on Hank, Dave. I just think you're dead wrong.

DAVID He told me.

OZZIE Who?

DAVID Hank.

OZZIE You . . . talked to Hank?

DAVID In California. The day before they shipped me overseas.

OZZIE No, no. He went to Georgia when he left here. We have all his letters postmarked Georgia.

DAVID (*with great urgency*) It was California, I'm telling you. I was in the barracks. The C.Q. came to tell me there was someone to see me. It was Hank asking did I remember him? He'd seen my name on a list and wondered if I was Ozzie's boy. He was dying, he said. The sickness was congenital. We had a long, long talk.

OZZIE But his parents were good fine people, David.

DAVID Don't you understand? We spoke. Why did you make me think him perfect? It was starting in his face the way it started in his hand.

OZZIE Oh! I didn't realize—I didn't know. You weren't blind. You could see. I didn't realize, Dave.

DAVID What?

OZZIE Did he wanna know about me? Did he mention me?

DAVID (*after thinking a moment*) He asked . . . how you were.

OZZIE Well, I'm fine. Sure. You told him.

HARRIET (*entering with a cup of coffee*) It must be so wonderful for you to be home. It must just be so wonderful. A little strange, maybe . . . just a little, but time will take care of all that. It always does. You get sick and you don't know how you're going to get better and then you do. You just do. You must have terrible, awful, ugly dreams, though.

(*Slight pause.*)

OZZIE She said you probably have terrible, awful, ugly dreams . . . though.

DAVID What?

HARRIET Don't you remember when we spoke last night?

DAVID Who?

HARRIET You called to me and then you claimed you hadn't.

DAVID I didn't.

HARRIET Ohhh, we had a lovely conversation, David. Of course you called. You called; we talked. We talked and laughed and it was very pleasant. Could I see behind your glasses?

DAVID What? (*moving away, crossing in flight from them*) Do . . . what?

HARRIET See behind your glasses; see your eyes.

OZZIE Me too, Dave; could we?

DAVID My eyes . . . are ugly.

OZZIE We don't mind.

HARRIET We're your parents, David.

DAVID I think it better if you don't.

OZZIE And something else I've been meaning to ask you—why did you cry out against us that first night—to that stranger, I mean, that sergeant?

HARRIET And you do dream. You do.

OZZIE Sure. You needn't be ashamed.

HARRIET We all do it. All of us.

OZZIE We have things that haunt us.

HARRIET And it would mean nothing at all—it would be of no consequence at all—if only you didn't speak.

DAVID I don't understand.

OZZIE She says she heard you, Dave.

HARRIET I stood outside your door.

DAVID No.

OZZIE A terrible experience for her, Dave; you can see that.

HARRIET Whatever it is, David, tell us.

OZZIE What's wrong?

DAVID No.

HARRIET We'll work it out.

OZZIE You can't know how you hurt us.

DAVID I wasn't asleep.

OZZIE Not until you have children of your own.

HARRIET What?

(*Silence.*)

Not . . . asleep? . . .

DAVID I was awake; lying awake and speaking.

OZZIE Now wait a minute.

DAVID Someone was with me—there in the dark—I don't know what's wrong with me.

HARRIET It was me. I was with you. There's nothing wrong with you.

DAVID No. In my room. I could feel it.

HARRIET I was there.

(*And they have him cornered in another chair.*)

DAVID No.

OZZIE Harriet, wait!

HARRIET What are you saying, "Wait"? I was there.

OZZIE Oh, my God. Oh, Christ, of course. Oh, Dave, forgive us.

HARRIET What?

OZZIE Dave, I understand. It's buddies left behind.

DAVID No.

OZZIE But I do. Maybe your mother can't but I can. Men serving together in war, it's a powerful thing—and I don't mean to sound like I think I know it—all of it, I mean—I don't, I couldn't—but I respect you having had it—I almost envy you having had it, Dave. I mean . . . true comradeship.

DAVID Dad . . .

OZZIE I had just a taste—not that those trucks and factory were any battlefield, but there was a taste of it there—in the jokes we told and the way we saw each other first in the morning. We told dirty, filthy jokes, Dave. We shot pool, played cards, drank beer late every night, singing all these crazy songs.

DAVID That's not right, Dad.

OZZIE But all that's nothing, I'm sure, to what it must be in war. The things you must touch and see. Honor. You must touch honor. And then one of you is hurt, wounded . . . made blind . . .

DAVID No. I had fear of all the kinds of dying that there are when I went from here. And then there was this girl with hands and hair like wings. (*The poetry is like a thing possessing him, a frenzy in which he does not know where he is.*) There were candles above the net of gauze under which we lay. Lizards. Cannon could be heard. A girl to weigh no more than dust.

HARRIET A nurse, right . . . David?

OZZIE No, no, one of them foreign correspondents, English maybe or French.

(*Silence.*)

HARRIET Oh, how lovely! A Wac or Red Cross girl? . . .

DAVID No.

OZZIE Redhead or blonde, Dave?

DAVID No.

(HARRIET *is shaken.*)

OZZIE I mean, what you mean is you whored around a lot. Sure. You whored around. That's what you're saying. You banged some whores . . . had some intercourse. Sure, I mean, that's my point.

(DAVID, *turning away, seems about to rise.*)

Now Dave, take it easy. What I mean is, okay, sure, you shacked up with. I mean, hit on. Hit on, Dave. Dicked. Look at me. I mean, you pronged it, right? Right? Sure, attaboy. (*Patting* DAVID *on the shoulder*) I mean, it's like going to the bathroom. All glands and secretions. Look, Dave, what are you doing?

(*A rage is building in* DAVID, *tension forcing him to stand, his cane pressing the floor.*)

We can talk this over. We can talk this over.

(DAVID, *heading for the stairs, crashes into* OZZIE.)

Don't—goddamnit, don't walk away from me. (*He pushes* DAVID *backward.*) What the hell do you think you're doing? It's what you did. Who the hell you think you are? You screwed it. A yellow whore. Some yellow ass. You put in your prick and humped your ass. You screwed some yellow fucking whore!

(*He has chased* DAVID *backward,* HARRIET *joining in with him.*)

HARRIET That's right, that's right. You were lonely and young and away from home for the very first time in your life, no white girls around—

DAVID They are the color of the earth, and what is white but winter and the earth under it like a suicide?

(HARRIET'S *voice is a high humming in her throat.*)

Why didn't you tell me what I was?

(*And* HARRIET *vomits, her hands at her mouth, her back turning. There is a silence. They stand.* OZZIE *starts toward her, falters, starts, reaches, stops.*)

OZZIE Why . . . don't . . . you ask her to cook something for you, David, will you? Make her feel better . . . okay.

DAVID I think . . . some eggs might be good, Mom.

OZZIE (*wanting to help her*). Hear that, Harriet? David wants some eggs.

HARRIET I'm *all right.*

OZZIE Of course you are. (*Patting her tenderly, he offers his clean white handkerchief.*) Here, here: wipe your mouth; you've got a little something—on the corner, left side. That's it. Whattayou say, David?

HARRIET What's your pleasure, David?

DAVID Scrambled.

OZZIE There you go. Your specialty, his pleasure.

(OZZIE, *between them, claps his hands; off she goes for the kitchen.* OZZIE, *looking about the room like a man in deep water looking for something to keep him afloat, sees a pack of cigarettes.*)

How about a cigarette? (*running to grab them, show them*) Filter, see, I switched. Just a little after you left, and I just find them a lot smoother, actually. I wondered if you'd notice. (*And speaking now, his voice and manner take on a confidence; he demonstrates; he is self-assured.*) The filter's granulated. It's an off-product of corn husks. I light up—I feel like I'm on a ship at sea. Isn't that one hell of a good tasting cigarette? Isn't that one beautiful goddamn cigarette?

(HARRIET *enters with two bowls. One has a grapefruit cut in half; the second has eggs and a spoon sticking out.*)

HARRIET Here's a little grapefruit to tide you over till I get the eggs.

(*And now she stirs the eggs in preparation for scrambling them.*)

Won't be long, I promise—but I was just wondering, wouldn't it be nice if we could all go to church tonight. All together and we could make a little visit in thanksgiving of your coming home.

(DAVID *is putting his cigarette out in his grapefruit. They see.*)

I wouldn't ask that it be long—just—

(*He is rising now, dropping the grapefruit on the chair.*)

I mean, we could go to whatever saint you wanted, it wouldn't . . . matter . . .

(*He has turned his back, is walking toward the stairs.*)

Just in . . . just out . . .

(*He is climbing the stairs.*)

David.

OZZIE Tired . . . Dave?

(*They watch him plodding unfalteringly toward his room.*)

Where you going . . . bathroom?

DAVID No.

OZZIE Oh.

(DAVID *disappears into his room and* HARRIET *whirls and heads for the telephone.* OZZIE, *startled, turns to look at her.*)

Harriet, what's up?

HARRIET I'm calling Father Donald.

OZZIE Father Donald?

HARRIET (*dialing*) We need help, I'm calling for help.

OZZIE Now wait a minute. No; oh, no, we—

HARRIET Do you still refuse to see it? He was involved with one of them. You know what the Bible says about those people. You heard him.

OZZIE Just not Father Donald; please, please. That's all I ask—just—

(*She is obstinate, he sees. She turns her back waiting for someone to answer.*)

Why must everything be personal vengeance?

(*The front door pops open and in comes bounding* RICK, *guitar upon his back.*)

RICK (*happy*) Hi, Mom. Hi, Dad.

HARRIET (*waiting, telephone in hand—overjoyed*) Hi, Rick!

RICK (*happy*) Hi, Mom.

OZZIE (*feeling fine*) Hi, Rick.

RICK Hi, Dad.

OZZIE How you doin', Rick? (*He is happy to see good ole regular Rick.*)

RICK Fine, Dad. You?

OZZIE Fine.

RICK Good.

HARRIET I'll get you some fudge in just a minute, Rick!

RICK Okay. How's Dave doin', Dad?

(*He is fiddling with his camera.*)

OZZIE Dave's doin' fine, Rick.

RICK Boy, I'm glad to hear that. I'm really glad to hear that, because, boy, I'll sure be glad when everything's back to the regular way. Dave's too serious, Dad; don't you think so? That's what I think. Whattayou think, Dad?

(*He snaps a picture of* OZZIE, *who is posing, smiling, while* HARRIET *waves angrily at them.*)

HARRIET SHHHHHHH! *Everybody!* (*And then, more pleasantly she returns to the phone.*) Yes, yes. Oh, Father. I didn't recognize your voice. No, I don't know who. Well, yes, it's about my son, Father, David. Yes. Well, I don't know if you know it or not, but he just got back from the war and he's troubled. Deeply. Yes.

(*As she listens silently for a moment,* RICK, *crouching, snaps a picture of her. She tries to wave him away.*)

Deeply.

(*He moves to another position, another angle, and snaps another picture.*)

Deeply, yes. Oh. So do you think you might be able to stop over some time soon to talk to him or not? Father, any time that would be convenient for you. Yes. Oh, that would be wonderful. Yes. Oh, thank you. And may God reward *you,* Father.

(*Hanging up the phone, she stands a moment, dreaming.*)

OZZIE I say to myself, what does it mean that he is my son? How the hell is it that . . . he . . . is my son? I mean, they say something of you joined to something of me and became . . . him . . . but what kinda goddamn thing is that? One mystery replacing another? Mystery doesn't explain mystery!

RICK (*scarcely looking up from his comic*) Mom, hey, c'mon, how about that fudge, will ya?

HARRIET Ricky, oh, I'm sorry. I forgot.

OZZIE They've got . . . diseases! . . .

HARRIET (*having been stopped by his voice*) What? . . .

OZZIE Dirty, filthy diseases. They got 'em. Those girls. Infections. From the blood of their parents into the very fluids of their bodies. Malaria, TB. An actual rot alive in them . . . gonorrhea, syphilis. There are some who have the plague. He touched them. It's disgusting. It's—

RICK Mom, I'm starving, honest to God; and I'm thirsty too.

HARRIET (*as she scurries off, clapping, for the kitchen*) Yes, of course. Oh, oh.

RICK And bring a piece for Dad, too; Dad looks hungry.

OZZIE No.

RICK Sure, a big sweet chocolate piece of fudge.

OZZIE No. Please. I don't feel well.

RICK It'll do you good.

HARRIET (*entering with fudge and milk in each hand*) Ricky, here, come here.

RICK (*hurrying toward her*) What?

HARRIET (*hands him fudge and milk*) Look good? (*And she moves toward* OZZIE.)

OZZIE And something else—maybe it could just be that he's growing away from us, like we did ourselves, only we thought it would happen in some other way, some lesser way.

HARRIET (*putting the fudge and milk into* OZZIE*'s hands*) What are you talking about, "going away"? He's right upstairs.

OZZIE I don't want that.

HARRIET You said you did.

OZZIE He said I did.

RICK (*having gobbled the fudge and milk*) You want me to drive you, Mom?

HARRIET Would you, Ricky, please?

RICK (*running*) I'll go around and get the car.

HARRIET (*scolding, as* OZZIE *has put the fudge and milk down on a coffee table*) It's all cut and poured, Ozzie; it'll just be a waste.

OZZIE I don't care.

HARRIET You're so childish.

(*She marches off toward the front door, where she takes a light jacket from a hook, starts to slip it on.*)

OZZIE Don't you know I could throw you down onto this floor and make another child live inside you . . . now! . . .

HARRIET I . . . doubt that . . . Ozzie.

OZZIE You want me to do it?

HARRIET (*going out the door*) Ohhh, Ozzie, Ozzie.

OZZIE Sure. Bye-bye. Bye-bye. (*after a pause*) They think they know me and they know nothing. They don't know how I feel. . . . How I'd like to beat Ricky with my fists till his face is ugly! How I'd like to banish David to the streets. . . . How I'd like to cut her tongue from her mouth.

(DAVID *moves around upstairs.*)

I was myself.

(*And now he is clearly speaking to the audience, making them see his value. They are his friends and buddies, and he talks directly to them.*)

I lived in a time beyond anything they can ever know—a time beyond and separate, and I was nobody's goddamn father and nobody's goddamn husband! I was myself! And I could run. I got a scrapbook of victories, a bag of medals and ribbons. In the town in which I lived my name was spoken in the factories and in the fields all around because I was the best there was. I'd beaten the finest anybody had to offer. Summer . . . I would sit out on this old wood porch on the front of our house and my strength was in me, quiet and mine. Round the corner would come some old Model T Ford and scampering up the walk this ancient, bone-stiff, buck-toothed farmer, raw as winter and cawing at me like a crow: they had one for me. Out at the edge of town. A runner from another county. My shoes are in a brown-paper bag at my feet. I snatch 'em up. I set out into the dusk, easy as breathing. There's an old white fence and we run for the sun. . . . For a hundred yards or a thousand yards or a thousand thousand. It doesn't matter. Whatever they want. We run the race they think their speciality and I beat them. They sweat and struggle; I simply glide on, one step beyond, no matter what their effort, and the sun bleeds before me. . . . We cross rivers and deserts; we clamber over mountains. I run the races the farmers arrange and win the bets they make. And then a few days after the race, money comes to me anonymously in the mail; but it's not for the money that I run. In the fields and factories they speak my name when they sit down to their lunches. If there's a prize to be run for, it's me they send for. It's to be the-one-sent-for that I run.

(DAVID *entering from his room, has listened to the latter part of this.*)

DAVID And . . . then . . . you left.

OZZIE (*whirling to look at him*) What?

DAVID I said . . . "And . . . then you left." That town.

OZZIE Left?

DAVID Yes. Went away; traveled.

OZZIE No. What do you mean?

DAVID I mean, you're no longer there; you're here . . . now.

OZZIE But I didn't really *leave* it. I mean, not *leave.* Not really.

DAVID Of course you did. Where are you?

OZZIE That's not the point, Dave. Where I am isn't the point at all.

DAVID But it is. It's everything; all that other is gone. Where are you going?

OZZIE Groceries. Gotta go get groceries. You want anything at the grocery store? (*He looks at his watch.*) It's late. I gotta get busy.

DAVID (*as* OZZIE *exits*) That's all right, Dad. That's fine.

Blackout.

(*The lights rise to brightness, and* RICK *enters from the kitchen, carrying his guitar, plinking a note or two as* HARRIET *emerges also from the kitchen, carrying a bowl of chips and a tray of drinks, and* OZZIE *appears upstairs, coming down the hall carrying an 8-mm movie projector already loaded with film.*)

HARRIET Tune her up now, Rick.

OZZIE What's the movie about anyway?

HARRIET It's probably scenery, don't you think?—trees and fields and those little ponds. Everything over there's so green and lovely. Enough chips, Ricky?

(*All during this, they scurry about with their many preparations.*)

RICK We gonna have pretzels too? 'Cause if there's both pretzels and chips then there's enough chips.

OZZIE (*at the projector*) David shoot it or somebody else? . . . Anybody know? I tried to peek—put a couple of feet up to the light . . .

HARRIET What did you see?

OZZIE Nothing. Couldn't.

HARRIET Well, I'll just bet there's one of those lovely little ponds in it somewhere.

OZZIE Harriet . . . you know when David was talking about that trouble in Hank's hand being congenital, what did you think? You think it's possible? I don't myself. I mean, we knew Hank well. I think it's just something David got mixed up about and nobody corrected him. What do you think? Is that what you think? Whatsamatter? Oh.

(*He stops, startled, as he sees she is waving at him. Looking up the stairs, which are behind him, he sees* DAVID *is there, preparing to descend.* DAVID *wears his robe and a bright-colored tie.*)

HARRIET Hello!

OZZIE Oh. Hey, oh, let me give you a hand. Yes. Yes. You look good. Good to see you.

(*And he is on the move to* DAVID *to help him down the stairs.*)

Yes, sir. I think, all things considered, I think we can figure we're over the hump now and it's all downhill and good from here on in. I mean, we've talked things over, Dave, what do you say? The air's been cleared, that's what I mean—the wounds acknowledged, the healing begun. It's the ones that aren't acknowledged—the ones that aren't talked over—they're the ones that do the deep damage. That's always what happens.

HARRIET (*moving to* DAVID) I've baked a cake, David. Happy, happy being home.

(DAVID, *on his own, finds his way to a chair and sits.*)

OZZIE And we've got pop and ice and chips, and Rick is going to sing some songs.

HARRIET Maybe we can all sing along if we want.

RICK Anything special you'd like to hear, Dave?

OZZIE You just sing what you know, Rick; sing what you care for and you'll do it best.

(*And he and* HARRIET *settle down upon the couch to listen, all smiles.*)

RICK How about "Baby, When I Find You"?

HARRIET Ohhh, that's such a good one.

RICK Dave, you just listen to me go! I'm gonna build! (*He plays an excited lead into the song.*) I'm gonna build, build, build.

(*And he sings.*)

Baby, when I find you,
never gonna stand behind you,

gonna, gonna lead
softly at the start,
gently by the heart,
Sweet . . . Love! . . .

Slipping softly to the sea
you and me both mine
wondrous as a green
growing forest vine. . . .

Baby, when I find you,
never gonna stand behind you,
gonna, gonna lead you
softly at the start,
gently by the heart,
Sweet . . . Love! . . .
Baby, when I find you.

OZZIE (*as both he and* HARRIET *clap and laugh*) Ohhh, great, Rick, great. You burn me up with envy, honest to God.

HARRIET It was just so wonderful. Oh, thank you so much.

RICK I just love to do it so much, you know?

OZZIE Has he got something goin' for him, Dave? Huh? Hey! You don't even have a drink. Take this one; take mine!

(*Now they hurry back and forth from* DAVID *to the table.*)

HARRIET And here's some cake.

OZZIE How 'bout some pretzels, Dave?

RICK Tell me what you'd like to hear.

DAVID I'd like to sing.

(*This stops them. They stare at* DAVID *for a beat of silence.*)

RICK What?

OZZIE What's that?

DAVID I have something I'd like to sing.

RICK Dave, you don't sing.

DAVID (*reaching at the air*) I'd like to use the guitar, if I could.

HARRIET What are you saying?

OZZIE C'mon, you couldn't carry a tune in a bucket and you know it. Rick's the singer, Rick and your mom.

(*Not really listening, thinking that his father has gotten everything back to normal,* RICK *strums and strums the guitar, drifting nearer to* DAVID.)

C'mon, let's go, that all we're gonna hear?

DAVID You're so selfish, Rick. Your hair is black; it glistens. You smile. You sing. People think you are the songs you sing. They never see you. Give me the guitar.

(*And he clamps his hand closed on the guitar, stopping the music.*)

RICK Mom, what's wrong with Dave?

DAVID Give me.

RICK Listen, you eat your cake and drink your drink, and if you still wanna, I'll let you.

(DAVID *stands, straining to take the guitar.*)

DAVID Now!

HARRIET Ozzie, make David behave.

OZZIE Don't you play too roughly. . . .

DAVID Ricky! . . .

RICK I don't think he's playing, Dad.

OZZIE (*as* DAVID, *following* RICK, *bumps into a chair*) You watch out what you're doing . . .

(DAVID *drops his glass on the floor, grabs the guitar.*)

You got cake all over your fingers, you'll get it all sticky, the strings all sticky—(*Struggling desperately to keep his guitar*) Just tell me what you want to hear, I'll do it for you!

HARRIET What is it? What's wrong?

DAVID GIVE ME! (*With great anger*) GIVE ME!

OZZIE David! . . .

(*And* DAVID *wrenches the guitar from* RICK'S *hands, sends* RICK *sprawling, and loops the strap of the guitar over his shoulder, smiling, smiling.*)

HARRIET Ohhhh, no, no, you're ruining everything. What's wrong with you?

OZZIE I thought we were gonna have a nice party—

DAVID I'm singing! We are!

OZZIE No, no, I mean a *nice* party—one where everybody's happy!

DAVID I'm happy. I'm singing. Don't you see them? Don't you see them?

OZZIE Pardon, Dave?

HARRIET What . . . are you saying?

DAVID (*changing, turning*) I have some movies. I thought you . . . knew.

HARRIET Well . . . we . . . do.

OZZIE Movies?

DAVID Yes, I took them.

RICK I thought you wanted to sing.

OZZIE I mean, they're what's planned, Dave. That's what's up. The projector's all wound and ready. I don't know what you had to get so angry for.

HARRIET Let's get everything ready.

OZZIE Sure, sure. No need for all that yelling.

(*He moves to set up the projector.*)

DAVID I'll narrate.

OZZIE Fine, sure. What's it about anyway?

HARRIET Are you in it?

OZZIE Ricky, plug it in. C'mon, c'mon.

DAVID It's a kind of story.

RICK What about my guitar?

DAVID No.

OZZIE We oughta have some popcorn, though.

HARRIET Oh, yes, what a dumb movie house, no popcorn, huh, Rick!

(RICK *switches off the lights.*)

OZZIE Let her rip, Dave.

(DAVE *turns on the projector;* OZZIE *is hurrying to a seat.*)

Ready when you are, C.B.

HARRIET Shhhhhhh!

OZZIE (*a little child playing*) Let her rip, C.B. I want a new contract, C.B.

(*The projector runs for a moment. Note: In proscenium, a screen should be used if possible, or the film may be allowed to seem projected on the fourth wall; in three-quarter or round the screen may be necessary. If the screen is used, nothing must show upon it but a flickering of green.*)

HARRIET Ohhh, what's the matter? It didn't come out, there's nothing there.

DAVID Of course there is.

HARRIET Noooo. . . . It's all funny.

DAVID Look.

OZZIE It's underexposed, Dave.

DAVID (*moving nearer*) No. Look.

HARRIET What?

DAVID They hang in the trees. They hang by their wrists half-severed by the wire.

OZZIE Pardon me, Dave?

HARRIET I'm going to put on the lights.

DAVID NOOOOOO! LOOK! They hang in the greenish haze afflicted by insects; a woman and a man, middle aged. They do not shout or cry. He is too small. Look—he seems all bone, shame in his eyes; his wife even here come with him, skinny also as a broom and her hair is straight and black, hanging to mask her eyes.

(*The girl,* Zung, *drifts into the room.*)

OZZIE I don't know what you're doing, David; there's nothing there.

DAVID LOOK! (*and he points*) They are all bone and pain, uncontoured and ugly but for the peculiar melon-swelling in her middle which is her pregnancy, which they do not see—look! these soldiers who have found her—as they do not see that she is not dead but only dying until saliva and blood bubble at her lips. Look. . . . Yet . . . she dies. Though a doctor is called in to remove the bullet-shot baby she would have preferred . . . to keep since she was dying and it was dead.

(*And* Zung *silently, drifting, departs*)

In fact, as it turned out they would have all been better off left to hang as they had been strung on the wire—he with the back of his head blown off and she, the rifle jammed exactly and deeply up into her, with a bullet fired directly into the child living there. For they ended each buried in a separate place; the husband by chance alone was returned to their village, while the wife was dumped into an alien nearby plot of dirt, while the child, too small a piece of meat, was burned. Put into fire, as the shattered legs and arms cut off of men are burned. There's an oven. It is no ceremony. It is the disposal of garbage! . . .

(Harriet *gets to her feet, marches to the projector, pulls the plug, begins a little lecture.*)

HARRIET It's so awful the things those yellow people do to one another. Yellow people hanging yellow people. Isn't that right? Ozzie, I told you—animals—Christ, burn them. David, don't let it hurt you. All the things you saw. People aren't themselves in war. I mean like that sticking that gun into that poor woman and then shooting that poor little baby, that's not human. That's inhuman. It's inhuman, barbaric and uncivilized and inhuman.

DAVID I'm thirsty.

HARRIET For what? Tell me? Water? Or would you like some milk? How about some milk?

DAVID (*shaking his head*) No.

HARRIET Or would you like some orange juice? All golden and little bits of ice.

OZZIE Just all those words and that film with no picture and these poor people hanging somewhere—so you can bring them home like this house is a meat house—

HARRIET Oh, Ozzie, no, it's not that—no—he's just young, a young boy . . . and he's been through terrible, terrible things and now he's home, with his family he loves, just trying to speak to those he loves—just—

DAVID Yes! That's right. Yes. What I mean is, yes, of course, that's what I am—a young . . . blind man in a room . . . in a house in the dark, raising nothing in a gesture of no meaning toward two voices who are not speaking . . . of a certain . . . incredible . . . *connection!*

(*All stare.* RICK *leaps up, running for the stairs.*)

RICK Listen, everybody. I hate to rush off like this, but I gotta. Night.
HARRIET Good night, Rick.
OZZIE (*simultaneously*) Good night.

(DAVID *moves toward the stairs, looking upward.*)

DAVID Because I talk of certain things . . . don't think I did them. Murderers don't even know that murder happens.
HARRIET What are you saying? No, no. We're a family, that's all—we've had a little trouble—David, you've got to stop—please—no more yelling. Just be happy and home like all the others—why can't you?
DAVID You mean take some old man to a ditch of water, shove his head under, talk of cars and money till his feeble pawing stops, and then head on home to go in and out of doors and drive cars and sing sometimes. I left her like you wanted . . . where people are thin and small all their lives. (*The beginning of realization*) Or did . . . you . . . think it was a . . . place . . . like this? Sinks and kitchens all the world over? Is that what you believe? Water from faucets, light from wires? Trucks, telephones, TV. Ricky sings and sings, but if I were to cut his throat, he would no longer and you would miss him—you would miss his singing. We are hoboes! (*And it is the first time in his life he has ever thought these things.*) We make signs in the dark. You know yours. I understand my own. We share . . . coffee!

(*There is nearly joy in this discovery: a hint of new freedom that might be liberation. And somewhere in the thrill of it he has whirled, his cane has come near to* OZZIE, *frightening him, though* HARRIET *does not notice. Now* DAVID *turns, moving for the stairs, thinking.*)

I'm going up to bed . . . now . . . I'm very . . . tired.
OZZIE Well . . . you have a good sleep, Son. . . .
DAVID Yes, I think I'll sleep in.
OZZIE You do as you please. . . .
DAVID Good night.
HARRIET Good night.
OZZIE Good night.
HARRIET Good night. (*slight pause*) You get a good rest. (*Silence.*) Try . . .

(*Silence.* DAVID *has gone into his room.* OZZIE *and* HARRIET *stand.*)

I'm . . . hungry . . . Ozzie. . . . Are you hungry?

OZZIE Hungry? . . .

HARRIET Yes.

OZZIE No. Oh, no.

HARRIET How do you feel? You look a little peaked. Do you feel all right?

OZZIE I'm fine; I'm fine.

HARRIET You look funny.

OZZIE Really. No. How about yourself?

HARRIET I'm never sick; you know that. Just a little sleepy.

OZZIE Well . . . that's no wonder. It's been a long day.

HARRIET Yes, it has.

OZZIE No wonder.

HARRIET Good night.

(*She is climbing the stairs toward bed.*)

OZZIE Good night.

HARRIET Don't stay up too late now.

OZZIE Do you know when he pointed that cane at me, I couldn't breathe. I felt . . . for an instant I . . . might never breathe. . . .

HARRIET Ohhh . . . I'm so sleepy. So . . . sooooo sleepy. Aren't you sleepy?

OZZIE (*to make her answer*) Harriet! I couldn't breathe.

HARRIET WHAT DO YOU WANT? TEACHING HIM SPORTS AND FIGHTING.

(*This moment—one of almost a primal rage—should be the very first shattering of her motherly self-sacrificing image.*)

WHAT . . . OZZIE . . . DO YOU WANT?

OZZIE Well . . . I was . . . wondering, do we have any aspirin down here . . . or are they all upstairs?

HARRIET I thought you said you felt well.

OZZIE Well, I do, I do. It's just a tiny headache. Hardly worth mentioning.

HARRIET There's aspirin in the desk.

OZZIE (*crossing*) Fine. Big drawer?

HARRIET Second drawer, right-hand side.

OZZIE Get me a glass of water, would you, please?

HARRIET Of course.

(*She gets a glass from a nearby table, a drink left over from the party, and hands it to him.*)

OZZIE Thank you. It's not much of a headache, actually. Actually it's just a tiny headache.

(*He pops the tablets into his mouth and drinks to wash them down.*)

HARRIET Aspirin makes your stomach bleed.

(*He tries to keep from swallowing the aspirin, but it is too late.*)

Did you know that? Nobody knows why. It's part of how it works. It just does it, makes you bleed. This extremely tiny series of hemorrhages in those delicate inner tissues.

(*He is staring at her: there is vengeance in what she is doing.*)

It's like those thin membranes begin, in a very minor way, to sweat blood and you bleed; inside yourself you bleed.

(*She crosses away.*)

OZZIE That's not true. None of that. You made all that up. . . . Where are you going?

(*With a raincoat on, she is moving out the front door.*)

I mean . . . are you going out? Where . . . are you off to?

(*She is gone.*)

Goddamnit, there's something going on around here, don't you want to know what it is? (*yelling at the shut door*) I want to know what it is. (*turning, marching to the phone, dialing*) I want to know what's going on around here. I want to; I do. Want to—got to. Police. That's right, goddamnit—I want one of you people to get on out to seven-seventeen Dunbar and do some checking, some checking at seven-seventeen—What? Ohhh—(*hissing*) Christ! . . . (*and he is pulling a handkerchief from his pocket, and covering the mouthpiece*) I mean, they got a kid living there who just got back from the war and something's going on and I want to know what it. . . . No, I don't wanna give my name—it's them, not me—Hey! Hey!

RICK (*popping in at the hallway at the top of the stairs*) Hey, Dad! How you doin'?

(*Ozzie slams down the phone.*)

OZZIE Oh, Rick! Hi!

RICK Hi! How you doin'?

(*Guitar over his shoulder, he is heading down the stairs and toward the front door.*)

OZZIE Fine. Just fine.

RICK Good.

OZZIE How you doin', Rick?

RICK Well, I'll see you later.

OZZIE (*running*) I WANT YOU TO TEACH ME GUITAR!

RICK (*faltering*) What?

OZZIE I want you to teach me . . . guitar! . . . To play it.

RICK (*as* OZZIE *pulls the guitar from his hands*). Sure. Okay.

OZZIE I want to learn to play it. They've always been a kind of mystery to me, pianos, guitars.

RICK Mystery?

(*And* OZZIE *is trying, awkwardly, desperately, to play.*)

OZZIE I mean, what do you think? Do you ever have to think what your fingers should be doing? What I mean is do you ever have to say—I don't know what—"This finger goes there and this other one does—" I mean, "It's on *this* ridge; now I chord all the strings and then switch it all." See? And do you have to tell yourself, "Now switch it all—first finger this ridge—second finger, down—third—somewhere." I mean, does that kind of thing ever happen? I mean, *How do you play it?* I keep having this notion of wanting some . . . thing . . . some material thing, and I've built it. And then there's this feeling I'm of value, that I'm on my way—I mean, moving—and I'm going to come to something eventually, some kind of achievement. All these feelings of a child . . . in me. . . . They shoot through me and then they're gone and they're not anything . . . anymore. But it's . . . a . . . wall . . . that I want . . . I think. I see myself doing it sometimes . . . all brick and stone . . . coils of steel. And then I finish . . . and the success of it is monumental and people come from far . . . to see . . . to look. They applaud. Ricky . . . teach me . . .

RICK Ahhh . . . what, Dad?

HARRIET Guitar, guitar.

RICK Oh, sure. First you start with the basic C chord. You put the first finger on the second string—

OZZIE But that's what I'm talking about. You don't do that. I know you don't.

RICK (*not understanding*) Oh.

OZZIE You just pick it up and play it. I don't have time for all that you're saying. That's what I've been telling you.

RICK (*on his way for the door*) Well, maybe some other day then. Maybe Mom'll wanna learn, too.

(*All this dialogue is rapid, overlapping.*)

OZZIE No, no.

RICK Just me and you then.

OZZIE Right. Me and you.

RICK I'll see you later.

OZZIE What?

RICK Maybe tomorrow.

OZZIE No.

RICK Well, maybe the next day then.

(*And he is gone out the door.*)

OZZIE NOW! Now!

(*And the door slams shut.*)

I grew too old too quick. I had no choice. It was just a town, I thought, and no one remained to test me. I didn't even know it was leaving I was doing. I thought I'd go away and come back. Not leave. (*And he looks up at* DAVID's *room.*) YOU SONOFABITCH (*running up to* DAVID's *room*), NOT LEAVE! (*He bursts into the room. silence*) Restless, Dave; restless. Got a lot on my mind. Some of us can't just lay around, you know. You said I left that town like I was wrong, but I was right. A man proved himself out there, tested himself. So I went and then I ended up in the goddamn Depression, what about that? I stood in goddamn lines of people begging bread and soup. You're not the only one who's had troubles. All of us, by God, David; think about that a little. (*stepping out the door, slamming it*) Just give somebody besides yourself some goddamn thought for a change.

(*Pause. He talks to the audience again; they are his friends.*)

Lived in goddamn dirty fields, made tents of our coats. The whole length of this country again and again, soot in our fingers, riding the rails, a bum, a hobo, but young. I remember. And then one day . . . on one of those trains, Hank was there, the first time I ever saw him. Hank, the brakeman, and he sees me hunched down in that car and he orders me off. He stands distant, ordering that I jump! . . . I don't understand and then he stops speaking . . . and . . . when he speaks again, pain is in his eyes and voice—"You're a runner," he says. "Christ, I didn't know you were a runner." And he moves to embrace me and with both hands lifts me high above his head—holds me there trembling, then flings me far out and I fall, I roll. All in the air, then slam down breathless, raw from the cinders . . . bruised and dizzy at the outskirts of this town, and I'm here, gone from that other town. I'm here. We become friends, Hank and me, have good times even though things are rough. He likes to point young girls out on the street and tell me how good it feels to touch them. I start thinking of their bodies, having dreams of horses, breasts and crotches. I remember. And then one day the feeling is in me that I must see a train go by and I'll get on it or I won't, something will happen, but halfway down to where I was thrown off, I see how the grass in among the ties is tall, the rails rusted. . . . Grass grows in abundance. No trains any longer come that way; they all go some other way . . . and far behind me Hank is calling, and I turn to see him coming, Harriet young and lovely in his hand, weaving among the weeds. I feel the wonder of her body moving toward me. She's the thing I think I'll enter to find my future. "Hank," I yell, "you sonofabitch! Bring her here. C'mon. Bring her on." Swollen with pride, screaming and yelling, I stand there, I stand: "I'm ready. I'm ready . . . I'm ready."

(*He has come down the stairs. He stands, arms spread, yelling. Blackout. Music.*)

(*Lights slowly up.* Ozzie *sleeps on the couch.* Rick *sits in a chair, looking at his guitar.* Zung *is in* David's *room, sitting on the bed behind* David, *who is slouched in a chair.* Harriet, *dressed in a blue robe, enters from the upstairs hallway and comes down the stairs.*)

HARRIET Have you seen my crossword-puzzle book?

RICK In the bathroom, Mom.

HARRIET Bathroom? . . . Did I leave it there?

(*Turning, she heads back up the stairs.*)

RICK Guess so, Mom.

DAVID (*sitting abruptly up in his chair as if at a sudden, frightening sound*) Who's there? There's someone there?

(Rick *looks up;* David *is standing, poking the air with his cane.*)

Who's there?

(*He opens the door to his room and steps into the hallway.*)

RICK Whatsamatter? It's just me and Dad, and Dad's sleeping.

DAVID Sleeping? Is he?

RICK On the davenport. . . . You want me to wake him?

DAVID Nooo . . . nooo.

(*He moves swiftly to descend to the living room.*)

RICK Hey . . . could I get some pictures, Dave? Would you mind?

DAVID Of course not. No.

RICK (*dashing off up the stairs, while* David *gropes to find the couch*) Let me just go get some film and some flashes, okay.

DAVID (*standing behind the couch on which* Ozzie *sleeps and looking after* Rick) Sure . . .

OZZIE Pardon? Par . . . don?

DAVID (*whispering into his father's ear*) I think you should know I've begun to hate you. I feel the wound of you, yet I don't think you can tell me any more, I . . . must tell you. If I had been an orphan with no one to count on me, I would have stayed there. Now . . . she is everywhere I look. I can see nothing to distract me.

(Ozzie *stirs.*)

You think us good, we steal all you have.

OZZIE Good . . . ole Hank. . . .

DAVID No, no, he has hated us always—always sick with rot.

OZZIE Noooo . . . nooooooo. . . .

DAVID She would tell me you would not like her. She would touch her fingers to her eyes, and she knew how I must feel sometimes as you do.

OZZIE Ohhh, noooo . . . sleeping. . . .

DAVID You must hear me. It is only fraud that keeps us sane, I swear it.

OZZIE David, sleeping! . . . Oh, oh . . .

DAVID It is not innocence I have lost. What is it I have lost?

OZZIE Oh . . . oh . . .

(RICK *has appeared high in the hallway and hesitates there.*)

DAVID Don't you know? Do you see her in your sleep?

RICK (*hurrying down*) I meant to get some good shots at the party, but I never got a chance the way things turned out. You can stay right there.

DAVID (*moving toward the chair on which* RICK's *guitar rests*) I'll sit, all right?

RICK *rushes to save the guitar.*

RICK Sure. How you feelin' anyway, Dave? I mean, honest ta God, I'm hopin' you get better. Everybody is. I mean . . . (*He takes a picture.*) . . . you're not gonna go talkin' anymore crazy like about that guitar and all that, are you? You know what I mean. Not to Mom and Dad anyway. It scares 'em and then I get scared and I don't like it, okay?

(*He moves on, taking more pictures.*)

DAVID Sure. That guitar business wasn't serious anyway, Rick. None of that. It was all just a little joke I felt like playing, a kind of little game. I was only trying to show you how I hate you.

RICK Huh? (*Stunned, he stares.*)

DAVID To see you die is why I live, Rick.

RICK Oh.

HARRIET (*appearing from off upstairs, the crossword-puzzle book in her hands*) Goodness gracious, Ricky, it was just where you said it would be, though I'm sure I don't know how it got there because I didn't put it there. Hello, David.

DAVID Hello.

OZZIE OHHHHHHHHHHHHHHHH! (*Screaming, he comes awake, falling off the couch.*) Oh, boy, what a dream! Oh. . . . (*trying to get to his feet, but collapsing*) Ohhhhhhh! God, leg's asleep. Jesus! (*and he flops about, sits there rubbing his leg*) Ohhhh, everybody. Scared hell out of me, that dream. I hollered. Did you hear me? And my leg's asleep, too.

(*He hits the leg, stomps the floor.* HARRIET *sits on the couch, working her crossword-puzzle book.* RICK, *slumped in a chair, reads a comic.* DAVID, *though, leans forward in his chair. He wants to know the effect of his whispering on his father.*)

Did anybody hear me holler?

HARRIET Not me.

RICK What did you dream about, Dad?

OZZIE I don't remember, but it was awful. (*stomping the foot*) Ohhhh, wake up, wake up. Hank was in it, though. And Dave. They stood over me, whispering—I could feel how they hated me.

RICK That really happened; he really did that, Dad.

OZZIE Who did?

RICK What you said.

OZZIE No. No, I was sleeping. It scared me awful in my sleep. I'm still scared, honest ta God, it was so awful.

DAVID It's that sleeping in funny positions, Dad. It's that sleeping in some place that's not a bed.

OZZIE Pardon?

DAVID Makes you dream funny. What did Hank look like?

HARRIET Ozzie, how do you spell "Apollo"?

OZZIE What?

RICK Jesus, Dad, Schroeder got three home runs, you hear about that? Two in the second of the first and one in the third of the second. Goddamn, if he don't make MVP in the National, I'll eat my socks. You hear about that, Dad?

OZZIE Yes, I did. Yes.

RICK He's somethin'.

OZZIE A pro.

HARRIET Ozzie, can you think of a four letter word that starts with G and ends with B?

RICK Glub.

HARRIET Glub?

OZZIE (*almost simultaneously*) Glub?

RICK It's a cartoon word. Cartoon people say it when they're drowning. G-L-U-B.

OZZIE (*on his feet now*) Ricky. Ricky, I was wondering . . . when I was sleeping, were my eyes open? Was I seeing?

RICK I didn't notice, Dad.

HARRIET *Glub* doesn't work, Rick.

RICK Try *grub.* That's what sourdoughs call their food. It's G-R—

OZZIE WAIT A MINUTE!

RICK G-R—

OZZIE ALL OF YOU WAIT A MINUTE! LISTEN! Listen. I mean, I look for explanations. I look inside myself. For an explanation. I mean, I look inside *my* self. As I would look into water . . . or the sky . . . the ocean. They're silver. Answers . . . silver and elusive . . . like fish. But if you can catch them in the sea . . . hook them as they flash by, snatch them . . . drag them down like birds from the sky . . . against all their struggle . . . when you're adrift . . . and starving . . . they . . . can help you live.

(*He falters; he stands among them, straining to go further, searching for some sign of comprehension in their faces.*)

RICK Mom . . . Dad's hungry . . . I think. He wants some fish, I—

OZZIE SHUT UP!

RICK (*hurt deeply*) Dad?

OZZIE PIECE OF SHIT! SHUT UP! SHUT UP!

HARRIET Ozzie! . . .

OZZIE (*roaring down at* DAVID) I don't want to hear about her. I'm not interested in her. You did what you did and I was no part of it. You understand me? I don't want to hear any more about her! Look at him. Sitting there. Listening. I'm tired of hearing you, Dave. You understand that? I'm tired of hearing you and your crybaby voice and your crybaby stories. And your crybaby slobbering and your . . . (*and his voice is possessed with astonished loathing*) LOOK . . . AT . . . HIM! YOU MAKE ME WANT TO VOMIT! HARRIET! YOU—(*He whirls on* HARRIET.) YOU! Your internal organs—your internal female organs—they've got some kind of poison in them. They're backing up some kind of rot into the world. I think you ought to have them cut out of you. I MEAN, I JUST CAN'T STOP THINKING ABOUT IT. I JUST CAN'T STOP THINKING ABOUT IT. LITTLE BITTY CHINKY KIDS HE WANTED TO HAVE! LITTLE BITTY CHINKY YELLOW KIDS! DIDN'T YOU! FOR OUR GRANDCHILDREN! (*and he slaps* DAVID *with one hand.*) LITTLE BITTY YELLOW PUFFY—(*He breaks, groping for the word.*) . . . creatures! . . . FOR OUR GRANDCHILDREN! (*He slaps* DAVID *again, again.*) THAT'S ALL YOU CARED!

(DAVID *a howl in his throat, has stood up.*)

HARRIET Ohhh, Ozzie, God forgive you the cruelty of your words. All children are God's children.

(DAVID *is standing rigid. The front door blows open, and in a fierce and sudden light* ZUNG *steps forward to the edge of* DAVID's *room, as he looks up at her.*)

DAVID I didn't know you were here. I didn't know. I will buy you clothing. I have lived with them all my life. I will make them not hate you. I will buy you boots.

(*And he is moving toward her, climbing the stairs.*)

They will see you. The seasons will amaze you. Texas is enormous. Ohio is sometimes green. There will be time. We will learn to speak. And it will be as it was in that moment when we looked in the dark and our eyes were tongues that could speak and the hurting . . . all of it . . . stopped, and there was total understanding in you of me and in me of you . . . and . . .

(*Near her now, stepping into his room through the wall, he reaches in a tentative way toward her.*)

such delight in your eyes that I felt it;

(*And she has begun to move away from him.*)

yet . . . I

(*She is moving away and down the stairs.*)

discarded you. I discarded you. Forgive me. You moved to leave as if you were struggling not to move, not to leave. "She's the thing most possibly of value in my life," I said. "She is garbage and filth and I must get her back if I wish to live. Sickness. I must cherish her." Zung, there were old voices inside me I had trusted all my life as if they were my own. I didn't know I shouldn't hear them. So reasonable and calm they seemed a source of wisdom. "She's all of everything impossible made possible, cast her down," they said. "Go home." And I did as they told; and now I know that I am not awake but asleep, and in my sleep . . . there is nothing. . . .

(ZUNG *is now standing before the open door, facing it, about to leave.*)

Nothing! . . . What do you want from me to make you stay? I'll do it. I'll do what you want!

RICK (*in the dark before his father, camera in hand*) Lookee here, Dad. Cheer up! Cheer up!

DAVID (*as* ZUNG *turns to look up at him*) Noooooooo. . . .

(*And there is a flash as* RICK *takes the picture.*)

NOOOOOOOOOOOOOO! STAAAAAAAY!

(*and the door slams shut, leaving* ZUNG *still inside. A slide of* OZZIE *appears on the screen, a close-up of his pained and puzzled face. Music, a falling of notes. The lights are going to black. Perhaps "Intermission" is on the bottom of the slide. The slide blinks out.*)

Act II

Blackness. Slide: color close-up of a man's ruddy, smiling, round face.

1ST CHILD'S VOICE Who zat?
WOMAN'S VOICE I don't know.
MAN'S VOICE Looks like a neighbor.
WOMAN'S VOICE How can you say it's a neighbor? You don't know.

New slide appears: scenery, in color.

2ND CHILD'S VOICE Oh, that's a pretty one.

New slide: Father Donald in a boxing pose, color.

1ST CHILD'S VOICE Oh, lookee that.

MAN'S VOICE Father What's-his-name. You know.

Another slide: Father Donald, slightly different boxing pose.

WOMAN'S VOICE There he is again.
2ND CHILD'S VOICE Wow.

Lights up on the downstairs. **David** *is up in his room on his bed. Downstairs,* **Harriet** *sits on the couch,* **Father Donald** *is on a chair;* **Ozzie** *is in the chair beside him. We have the feeling they have been there a long, long time.*

FATHER DONALD I deal with people and their uneasiness on a regular basis all the time, you see. Everybody I talk to is nervous . . . one way or another . . . so . . . I anticipate no real trouble in dealing with Dave. You have no idea the things people do and then tell me once that confessional door is shut. I'm looking forward actually, to speaking with him. Religion has been sloughed off a lot lately, but I think there's a relevancy much larger than the credit most give. We're growing—and our insights, when we have them, are twofold. I for one have come recently to understand how very often what seems a spiritual problem is in fact a problem of the mind rather than the spirit—not that the two can in fact be separated, though, in theory, they very often are. So what we must do is apply these theories to fact. At which point we would find that mind and spirit are one and I, a priest, am a psychiatrist, and psychiatrists are priests. I mean—I feel like I'm rambling. Am I rambling?

HARRIET Oh, no, Father.

OZZIE Nooo . . . noo.

HARRIET Father, this is hard for me to say, but I . . . feel . . . his problem is he sinned against the sixth commandment with whores.

FATHER DONALD That's very likely over there.

HARRIET And then the threat of death each day made it so much worse.

FATHER DONALD I got the impression from our earlier talk that he'd had a relationship of some duration.

HARRIET A day or two, wouldn't you say, Ozzie?

OZZIE (*distracted, oddly preoccupied with his chair*) A three-day pass I'd say . . . though I don't know, of course.

FATHER DONALD They're doing a lot of psychiatric studies on that phenomenon right now, did you know that?

(*The front door pops open, and in bounds* Rick.)

HARRIET Oh, Rick! . . .

RICK Hi, Mom. Hi, Dad.

OZZIE Hi, Rick.

FATHER DONALD (*rising*) Rick, hello!

RICK Oh, Father Donald . . . hi.

(*No time for* Father Donald, Rick *is speeding for the kitchen.*)

OZZIE Look at him heading for the fudge.

FATHER DONALD Well, he's a good big strong sturdy boy.

RICK (*as he goes out*) Hungry and thirsty.

FATHER DONALD And don't you ever feel bad about it, either!

(*He stands for an instant, a little uncertain what to do.*)

Dave's up in his room, I imagine, so maybe I'll just head on up and have my little chat. He is why I'm here, after all.

HARRIET Fine.

OZZIE (*standing, still distracted, he stares at the chair in which* Father Donald *was sitting*) First door top of the stairs.

FATHER DONALD And could I use the bathroom, please, before I see ole Dave? Got to see a man about a horse.

HARRIET Oh, Father, certainly: it's just down the hall. Fifth door.

OZZIE (*stepping nearer to the chair*) What's wrong with that chair? . . .

HARRIET It's the blue door, Father! . . .

OZZIE I . . . don't like that chair. I think it's stupid . . . looking. . . .

(*as* Rick *enters from the kitchen, eating fudge*)

Ricky, sit. Sit in that chair.

RICK What? . . .

OZZIE Go on, sit, sit.

(Rick *hurries to the chair, sits, eats.* Ozzie *is fixated on the chair.*)

HARRIET Oh, Ricky, take your father's picture, he looks so silly.

OZZIE I just don't think that chair is any good. I just don't think it's comfortable. Father Donald looked ill at east all the while he was sitting there.

HARRIET Well, he had to go to the bathroom, Ozzie, what do you expect?

OZZIE (*to* Ricky) Get up. It's just not right.

(Rick *gets up and* Ozzie *flops into the chair, sits, fidgets.* Rick *goes back out to the kitchen.*)

Noooooo. It's just not a comfortable chair at all, I don't know why.

(*He rises and moves toward the couch.*)

I don't like it. How much did we pay?

HARRIET What do you think you're doing?

OZZIE And this couch isn't comfortable either.

HARRIET It's a lovely couch.

OZZIE (*tests it*) But it isn't comfortable. Noooo. And I'm not really sure it's lovely, either. Did we pay two hundred dollars?

HARRIET What? Oh, more.
OZZIE How much?
HARRIET I don't know, I told you.
OZZIE You don't. I don't. It's gone anyway, isn't it?
HARRIET Ozzie, what does it matter?
OZZIE (*already on the move for the stairs*) I'm going upstairs. I'll be upstairs.
HARRIET Wait a minute.

(*As he keeps moving, up the stairs*)

I want to talk to you. *I think we ought to talk!*

(*Emotion well beneath her voice stops him, turns him.*)

I mean, it's nothing to worry about or anything, but you don't know about it and it's your house, you're involved—so it's just something I mention. You're the man of the house, you ought to know. The police were here . . . earlier today.
OZZIE What? Oh, my God.
HARRIET The police. Two of them. Two. A big and a small . . . they—

(*He is dazed; he doesn't know whether to go up or down, listen or leave. He nods.*)

It was just a little bit ago; not long at all.
OZZIE Jesus Christ. (*He descends.*)
HARRIET Oh, I know, I know. Just out of the blue like that—it's how I felt too. I did, I did.
OZZIE *What—police?*
HARRIET It was when you were gone for groceries. I mean, they thought they were supposed to be here. We wanted it, they thought.
OZZIE No, no.
HARRIET Somebody called them to come here. They thought it had been us. They were supposed to look through David's luggage, they thought.
OZZIE They . . . were . . . what?
HARRIET That's what I mean. That's exactly what I—
OZZIE *Look through his luggage? There's nothing wrong with his luggage!*
HARRIET Isn't it incredible? Somebody called them—they didn't know who—no name was given and it sounded muffled through a handkerchief, they said. I said, "Well, it wasn't us." Told them, "Don't you worry; we're all all right here." It must have been a little joke by somebody.
OZZIE What about Dave?
HARRIET No, no.
OZZIE Or Ricky? Did you ask Ricky?
HARRIET Ricky?
OZZIE RICKY! RICKY!
RICK (*popping in from the kitchen, thinking he was called*) What's up, Dad?

OZZIE I DON'T KNOW.
RICK I thought you called.

(*He pops back out into the kitchen.*)

OZZIE (*to* HARRIET) You ask him; you ask him. I think the whole thing's preposterous—absolutely—
HARRIET (*as* RICK *reemerges to look and listen*) Ricky, do you know anything about anybody calling the police to come here?
OZZIE (*turning and moving for the stairs*) I'm going upstairs. I'll be upstairs.
RICK The police?

(*As* HARRIET *turns to look and half step after* OZZIE)

Oh, no, Mom, not me. Okay if I use the car?
HARRIET What?
FATHER DONALD (*encountering* OZZIE *in the upstairs hallway*) Gonna take care of old Dave right now.
OZZIE I'm going upstairs. I'll be upstairs.

(*He exits, as* HARRIET *stands looking up at them.*)

RICK Bye, Mom.
HARRIET What? Oh. (*looking back as* RICK *goes out the door*) BE CAREFUL!
FATHER DONALD (*after a slight hesitation*) Ozzie said to tell you he was going upstairs.
HARRIET What?
FATHER DONALD Ozzie said to tell you he was going upstairs.
HARRIET (*stares at him a moment*) Oh, Father, I'm so glad you're here.

(*And she exits into the kitchen, leaving* FATHER DONALD. *He nods, knocks on* DAVID'S *door.*)

FATHER DONALD Dave?

(*He opens the door, eases into the semidark of the room.*)

Dave? It's me . . . Dave . . .

(*Finding a light, he flicks it on.*)

Ohh, Dave, golly, you look just fine. Here I expected to see you all worn out and there you are looking so good. It's me, Dave, Father Donald. Let me shake your hand.

(DAVID'S *rising hand comes up far off from* FATHER DONALD. *The priest, his own hand extended, has to move nearly around the bed before he can shake* DAVID'S *hand.*)

No, no, David. Here. Over here. Can't see me, can you? There you go. Yes, sir, let me tell you, I'm proud. A lot of people might tell you that, I know, but I mean it, and I'll stand behind it if there's anything I can do for you—anything at all.

DAVID No. I'm all right.

FATHER DONALD And that's the amazing part of it, Dave, you are. You truly are. It's plain as day. Golleee, I just don't know how to tell you how glad I am to see you in such high fine spirits. Would you like my blessing? (*He gets to his feet.*) Let me just give you my blessing and then we'll talk things over a little and—

(DAVID *slashes with his cane and strikes the hand moving into the position to bless.*)

Ohhhhhhhhhhhhhh! (*wincing, teeth gritted*) Oh, Dave; oh, watch out what you're doing!

DAVID I know.

FATHER DONALD No, no, I mean, you swung it in the air, you—hit me.

DAVID Yes.

FATHER DONALD No, no, you don't understand, you—

DAVID I was trying to hit you, Father.

(FATHER DONALD *stares, taking this in.*)

FATHER DONALD What?

DAVID I didn't send for you.

FATHER DONALD I know, I know, your poor mother—your poor mother—

DAVID I don't want you here, Father; get out!

FATHER DONALD David!

DAVID Get out, I'm sick of you. You've been in one goddamn corner or another of this room all my life making signs at me, whispering, wanting to splash me with water or mark me with oil—some goddamn hocus-pocus. I feel reverence for the air and the air is empty, Father. Now get the fuck out of here.

FATHER DONALD No, no, no, no, David. No, no. I can't give that to you. You'll have to get that from somewhere else.

DAVID I don't want anything from you!

FATHER DONALD I'm supposed to react now in some foolish way—I see—some foolish, foolish way that will discredit me—isn't that right? Oh, of course it is. It's an excuse to dismiss my voice that you're seeking, an excuse for the self-destruction your anger has made you think you want, and I'm supposed to give it. I'm supposed to find all this you're doing obscene and sacrilegious instead of seeing it as the gesture of true despair that it is. You're trying to make me disappear, but it's not going to happen. No, no. No such luck, David. I understand you, you see. Everything about you.

DAVID Do you?

FATHER DONALD The way you're troubled.

DAVID I didn't know that, Father.

FATHER DONALD You say that sarcastically—"Do you? I didn't know that." As if to imply you're so complicated I couldn't ever understand you when I already have. You see, I've been looking into a few things, David, giving some things some thought. (*producing a magazine with a colorful cover*) I have in my hand a magazine—you can't see it, I know—but it's there. A psychiatric journal in which there is an article of some interest and it deals with soldiers and some of them carried on as you did and then there's some others who didn't. It's not all just a matter of hocus-pocus any longer.

DAVID Carried . . . on . . . Father?

FATHER DONALD That whore. That yellow whore. You understand. You knew I was bringing the truth when I came which is why you hit me.

DAVID I thought you didn't even know the problem. You came in here all bubbly and jolly asking how did I feel.

FATHER DONALD That was only a little ruse, David; a little maneuver to put you off your guard. I only did that to mislead you. That's right. Your mother gave me all the basics some weeks ago and I filled in the rest from what I know. You see, if it's a fight you want, it's what you'll get. Your soul is worth some time and sweat from me. You're valued by others, David, even if you don't value yourself. (*Waving the magazine in the air*) It's all here—right here—in these pages. It was demonstrated beyond any possible doubt that people—soldiers—who are compelled for some reason not even they themselves understand to establish personal sexual relationships with whores are inferior to those who don't; they're maladjusted, embittered, non-goal-oriented misfits. The sexual acceptance of another person, David, is intimate and extreme; this kind of acceptance of an alien race is in fact the rejection of one's own race—it is in fact the rejection of one's own self—it is sickness, David. Now I'm a religious man, a man of the spirit, but knowledge is knowledge and I must accept what is proven fact whether that fact come from science or philosophy or whatever. What kind of man are you that you think you can deny it? You're in despair, David, whether you think of it that way or not. It's only into a valley of ruin that you are trying to lock yourself. You can only die there, David. Accept me. Let God open your eyes; let Him. He will redeem you. Not I nor anyone, but only Him—yet if you reject me, you reject Him. My hand is His. His blessing.

(*The hand is rising as if the very words elevate it.*)

My blessing. Let me give you my blessing.

(*And* DAVID'S *cane hits like a snake.* FATHER DONALD *cries out in surprise and pain. He recovers and begs:*)

Let me bless you. (*His hand is again rising in blessing.*) Please!

(DAVID, *striking again, stands. He hits again and again.*)

David! David! (*Terrified*) Stop it. Let me bless you.

(DAVID *hits* FATHER DONALD's *arm, hits his leg.*)

DAVID I don't want you here!

FATHER DONALD You don't know what you're saying.

(*But now the blow seems about to come straight down on his head. He yells and covers his head with his arms. The blow hits. He picks up a chair, holds it up for protection.*)

Stop it. Stop it. Goddamnit, stop hitting me. Stop it. You are in despair.

(*He slams the chair down.*)

A man who hits a priest is in despair!

(*Whistling, the cane slams into his arm.*)

Ohhhhh, this pain—this terrible pain in my arm—I offer it to earn you your salvation.

DAVID Get out!

FATHER DONALD Death! Do you understand that. Death. Death is your choice. You are in despair.

(*He turns to leave.*)

DAVID And may God reward *you,* Father.

FATHER DONALD (*turning back, as* DAVID *flops down on the bed*) Oh yes; yes of course, you're so confident now, young and strong. Look at you—full of spunk, smiling. But all that'll change. Your tune'll change in time. What about pain, Dave? Physical pain. What do you do when it comes? Now you send me away, but in a little while you'll call me back, run down by time, lying with death on your bed . . . in an empty house . . . gagging on your own spit you cannot swallow; you'll call me then, nothing left to you but fear and Christ's black judging eyes about to find and damn you; you'll call.

(*Slight pause.*)

DAVID That's not impossible, Father.

FATHER DONALD I don't even like you; do you know that? I DON'T EVEN LIKE YOU!

DAVID Tell them I hit you when you go down.

FATHER DONALD (*near the door, thinking about trying to bless from there*) No. No, they've pain enough already.

DAVID Have they? You get the fuck out of here before I kill you.

(*As if he has read* FATHER DONALD's *mind and knows what the man is thinking,* DAVID's *cane has risen like a spear; it aims at the priest's heart.*)

FATHER DONALD (*moving not a muscle*) THOUGH I DO NOT MOVE MY HAND, I BLESS YOU! YOU ARE BLESSED!

(*And he exits hurriedly, heading straight down the hall toward the bathroom. Lights up downstairs: it seems a lovely afternoon as* RICK *and* HARRIET *enter from the kitchen, chatting.*)

HARRIET So the thing I want to do—I just think it would be so nice if we could get Dave a date with some nice girl.

RICK Oh, sure.

HARRIET Do you think that would be a good idea?

(OZZIE, *descending from the attic, pauses to peek into* DAVID's *room; he finds* DAVID *asleep, and, after a moment, continues on down.*)

RICK Sure.

HARRIET Do you know any girls you think might get along with David?

RICK No, but I still think it's really a good idea and I'll keep it in mind for all the girls I meet and maybe I'll meet one. Here comes Dad. Hi, Dad. Bye, Mom.

HARRIET Oh, Ozzie, did you see what they were doing?

OZZIE Dave's sleeping, Harriet; Father Donald's gone.

HARRIET What? He can't be gone.

OZZIE I thought maybe he was down here. How about the kitchen?

HARRIET No, no, I just came out of the kitchen. Where were you upstairs? Are you sure he wasn't in David's room?

OZZIE I was in the attic.

HARRIET Well, maybe he saw the light and came up to join you and you missed each other on the way up and down. Why don't you go check?

OZZIE I turned off all the lights, Harriet. The attic's dark now.

HARRIET Well, yell up anyway—

OZZIE But the attic's dark now, Harriet.

HARRIET Just in case.

OZZIE What are you trying to say? Father Donald's up in the attic in the dark? I mean, if he was up there and I turned off the lights, he'd have said something—"Hey, I'm here," or something. It's stupid to think he wouldn't.

(*And he sits down.*)

HARRIET No more stupid to think that than to think he'd leave without telling us what happened with David.

OZZIE All right, all right. (*Storming to the foot of the stairs*) HEEEEEEYYYYYYYYYYYYYY! HEEEEYYYYYYYY! UP THEEEEERRE! ANYBODY UP THERE?

(*There is a brief silence. He turns toward* HARRIET.)

DAVID (*on his bed in his room*) WHAT'S THAT, DAD?

OZZIE (*falters, looks about*) What?

DAVID WHAT'S UP, DAD?

OZZIE OH, DAVE, NO, NOT YOU.

DAVID WHY ARE YOU YELLING?

OZZIE NO, NO, WE JUST THOUGHT FATHER DONALD WAS UP THERE IN THE ATTIC, DAVE. DON'T YOU WORRY ABOUT IT.

DAVID I'M THE ONLY ONE UP HERE, DAD!

OZZIE BUT . . . YOU'RE NOT IN THE ATTIC, SEE?

DAVID I'M IN MY ROOM.

OZZIE I KNOW YOU'RE IN YOUR ROOM.

DAVID YOU WANT ME TO GO UP IN THE ATTIC?

OZZIE NO! GODDAMNIT, JUST—

DAVID I DON'T KNOW WHAT YOU WANT.

OZZIE I WANT YOU TO SHUT UP, DAVE, THAT'S WHAT I WANT, JUST—

FATHER DONALD (*appearing from off upstairs*) What's the matter? What's all the yelling?

HARRIET Oh, Father!

OZZIE Father, hello, hello.

HARRIET How did it go? Did it go all right?

FATHER DONALD (*coming down the steps, seeming as if nothing out of the ordinary has happened*) Fine, just fine.

HARRIET Oh, you're perspiring so though—look at you.

FATHER DONALD (*maneuvering for the door*) Well, I've got a lot on my mind. It happens. Nerves. I've other appointments. Many, many.

HARRIET You mean you're leaving? What are you saying?

FATHER DONALD I must.

HARRIET But we've got to talk.

FATHER DONALD Call me.

HARRIET Father . . . bless me! . . .

FATHER DONALD What? . . .

HARRIET Bless me. . . .

FATHER DONALD Of course.

(*She bows her head, and the priest blesses her, murmuring the Latin.*)

HARRIET Ohhh, Father, thank you so much. (*Touching his hand*) Shall I walk you to your car?

FATHER DONALD (*backing for the door*) Fine, fine. That's all right. Sure.

OZZIE (*nodding*) DAVE, SAY GOOD-BYE TO FATHER DONALD, HE'S LEAVING NOW.

FATHER DONALD GOOD-BYE, DAVE!

DAVID GOOD-BYE, FATHER!

(*Blackout as* HARRIET *and* FATHER DONALD *are going out the door. Music.*)

(OZZIE *is discovered in late night light, climbing the stairs to* DAVID'S *door, where, after hesitating an instant, he gently knocks.*)

OZZIE Dave, I'd like to come in . . . if I could. (*Easing in*) Awful dark; can I put on a light?

(*Silence.*)

I mean, we don't need one—not really. I just thought we might . . . I mean, first of all, I want to apologize for the way I hit you the other day. I don't know why I did it. I'm . . . gonna sit down here on the edge of the bed. Are you awake enough to understand? I am your father, you know, and I could command . . . if I wanted. I don't; but I could. I'm going to sit.

(*Slight pause.*)

I mean, it's so sad the way you just go on and on . . . and I'd like to have time for you, but you want so much; I have important things, too. I have plans; I'm older, you know; if I fail to fulfill them, who will do it: Not you, though you could. And Rick's too busy. Do you understand? There's no evidence in the world of me, no sign or trace, as if everything I've ever done were no more than smoke. My life has closed behind me like water. But I must not care about it. I must not. Though I have inside me a kind of grandeur I can't realize, many things and memories of a darker time when we were very different—harder—nearer to the air and we thought of nothing as a gift. But I can't make you see that. There's no way. It's what I am, but it's not what you are. Even if I had the guitar, I would only stand here telling my fingers what to do, but they would do nothing. You would not see. . . . I can't get beyond these hands. I jam in the fingers. I break on the bone. I am . . . lonely. I mean, oh, no, not exactly lonely, not really. That's a little strong, actually. . . .

(*Silence.*)

I mean . . . Dave . . . (*He pulls from his back pocket* DAVID'S *overseas cap.*) What's this?

DAVID What?

OZZIE This cap. What is it? I cut myself on it. I was rummaging in your stuff upstairs, your bags and stuff, and I grabbed it. It cut me.

DAVID (*reaching for the cap*) Oh . . . yes.

OZZIE There are razors sewn into it. Why is that?

DAVID To cut people.

(*Slowly he puts the cap on his head.*)

OZZIE Oh.

DAVID Here . . . I'll show you. . . . (*Getting slowly to his feet*) You're on the street, see. You walk . . . and see someone who's after you. . . . You wait. . . .

(*He tenses. His hand rises to the tip of the cap.*)

As they get near . . . slowly you remove the hat—they think you're going to toss it aside, see? You . . . *snap it! You snap it!*

(*Seizing the front edge of the cap between thumb and finger, he snaps it down. It whistles past* OZZIE, *who jumps.*)

It cuts them. They hold their face. However you want them, they're yours. You can stomp them, kick them. This is on the street. I'd like to do that to somebody, wouldn't you?

OZZIE Huh?

DAVID It'd be fun.

OZZIE Oh, sure. I . . .

DAVID Hank told you to buy this house, didn't he?

OZZIE What?

DAVID "Get that house," he said. "Get it."

OZZIE It's a good house. Solid. Not one of those prefabs, those—

DAVID It's a coffin. You made it big so you wouldn't know, but that's what it is, and not all the curtains and pictures and lamps in the world can change it. He threw you off a fast free train, Ozzie.

OZZIE I don't believe you saw him.

DAVID He told you gold, he gave you shit.

OZZIE I don't believe you saw him. You're a liar, David.

(ZUNG *appears.*)

DAVID Do you know, Dad, it seemed sometimes I would rise and slam with my fists into the walls of a city. Pointing at buildings, I turned them into fire. I took the fleeing people into my fingers and bent them to touch their heads to their heels, each screaming at the sight of their brain turning black. And now sometimes I miss them, all those screaming people. I wish they were here with us, you and Mom and Rick and Zung and me.

(*Pause.*)

OZZIE Mom and Rick and who and you, Dave?

DAVID Zung.

(ZUNG *is moving nearer to them now.*)

OZZIE Zung, Dave?

DAVID She's here. They were all just hunks of meat that had no mind to know of me until I cared for her. It was simple. We lived in a house. She didn't want to come back here, Dad; she wanted me to stay there. And in all the time I knew her, she cost me six dollars that I had to sneak into her purse. Surprised? In time I'll show you some things. You'll see them. I will be your father.

(*He tosses the cap at* OZZIE.)

OZZIE (*shaken, struggling to catch the cap*) Pardon, Dave?

DAVID What's wrong? You sound like something's terribly wrong?

OZZIE No. No, no. I'm fine. Your poor mother—she's why I'm here. Your poor mother, sick with grief. She's mine to care for, you know. It's me you're after, yet you torment her. No more. No more. That's what I came up here to tell you.

DAVID (*getting to his feet*) Good.

OZZIE You're phony, David—phony—trying to make up for the thousands you butchered, when if you were capable of love at all you would love us, your mother and me—not that we matter—instead of some poor little whore who isn't even here.

DAVID (*exiting the room*) I know.

OZZIE I want her happy.

DAVID (*as* OZZIE *follows a little into the hall*) I know.

(*And* DAVID *is gone.* HARRIET *enters slowly from the kitchen, sees* OZZIE, *then the room's open door.*)

HARRIET Did you have a nice talk?

OZZIE (*heading toward her*) Harriet, what would you say if I said I wanted some checking done?

HARRIET I don't know what you mean. In what way do you mean?

OZZIE Take a look at that. But just be careful.

HARRIET What is it?

OZZIE His cap. There are razor blades sewn in it; all along the edge.

HARRIET Ozzie . . . ohhh! Goodness.

OZZIE That's what I mean. And I was reading just yesterday—some of them bring back guns and knives. Bombs. We've got somebody living in this house who's killed people, Harriet, and that's a fact we've got to face. I mean, I think we ought to do some checking. You know that test where they check teeth against old X-rays. I think—

HARRIET Ohhh . . . my God! . . .

OZZIE I know, I know, it scares me, too, but what are we talking about? We're talking about bombs and guns and knives, and sometimes I don't even think it's David up there. I feel funny . . . sometimes . . . I mean, and I want his fingerprints taken. I think we should have his blood type—

HARRIET Oh, Ozzie, Ozzie, it was you.

OZZIE Huh?

HARRIET You did it. You got this out of his luggage, all his baggage upstairs. You broke in and searched and called the police.

OZZIE No. What?

HARRIET You told them to come here, and then you lied and said you didn't.

OZZIE What?

HARRIET You did, and then you lied and now you're lying again.

OZZIE Oh, no. No.

HARRIET What's wrong with you? What's happening to you?

OZZIE But I didn't do that. I didn't.

(DAVID *appears in the upstairs hallway, moving to return to his room.*)

I didn't. No, no. And even if I did, what would it mean but I changed my mind, that's all. Sure. (*looking up at* DAVID *moving in the hall toward his room*) I called and then changed my mind and said I didn't when I did, and since when is there anything wrong in that? It would mean only that I have a little problem of ambivalence. I got a minor problem of ambiguity goin' for me here, is all, and you're exaggerating everything all out of proportion. You're distorting everything! All of you! (*And he whirls to leave.*) If I have to lie to live, I will! (*He runs.*)

HARRIET Where are you going? Come back here, Ozzie. Where are you going?

OZZIE Kitchen. Kitchen.

(*He gallops away and out the front door. Blackout. Music.*)

(*Lights up. Bright afternoon. Harriet is alone, dusting. Rick, carrying books, enters from the kitchen and heads for the stairs to go to his room.*)

HARRIET One day, Ricky . . . there were these two kittens and a puppy all in our back yard fighting. The kittens were little fur balls, so angry, and the little puppy, yapping and yapping. I was just a girl, but I picked them up in my arms. I held them all in my arms and they got very, very quiet.

RICK I'm going up to my bedroom and study my history and English and trigonometry, Mom.

HARRIET Do you know, I've called Father Donald seven times now—seven times, and haven't got an answer. Isn't that funny? He's starting to act like Jesus. You never hear from him. Isn't that funny?

RICK I'm going up to my bedroom and study my history and English and trigonometry, Mom, okay?

HARRIET Fine, Ricky. Look in on David, would you?

RICK Sure.

HARRIET Good night.

RICK (*calling as he passes* DAVID'S *door*) Hi, Dave.
DAVID Hi, Rick.
RICK DAVE'S OKAY, MOM.

(*She is at the foot of the stairs.* RICK *goes from view. She turns back to her work, and the front door opens and* OZZIE *enters.*)

OZZIE (*excited, upset*) Harriet! Can you guess what happened? You'll never guess what happened.

(*She continues cleaning.*)

Harriet, wait. Stop.
HARRIET Ozzie, I've got work to do.
OZZIE But I want to tell you something.
HARRIET All right, tell me; I can clean and listen; I can do both.

(*As she moves away, he rushes toward her, stretching out the lapel of his jacket to show her a large stain on it. She must see.*)

OZZIE Lookit; look at that. What do you think that is? That spot on my coat, do you see it? That yellow?
HARRIET (*distressed, touching the spot*) Ohhhh, Ozzie! . . .
OZZIE And the red mark on my neck.
HARRIET (*wincing*) Ohh, Ozzie, what happened? A bee sting! You got stung by a bee!
OZZIE No, no; I was walking—thinking—trying to solve our problems. Somebody hit me with an egg. They threw it at me. I got hit with an egg.

(*She stares, incredulous.*)

That's right. I was just walking down the street and—bang—I was hit. I almost blacked out; I almost fell down.
HARRIET Ozzie, my God, who would do such a thing?
OZZIE I don't know. That's the whole point. I've racked my brain to understand and I can't. I was just walking along. That's all I was doing.
HARRIET You mean you didn't even see them?
OZZIE (*pacing, his excitement growing*) They were in a car. I saw the car. And I saw the hand, too. *A* hand. Somebody's hand. A very large hand. Incredibly large.
HARRIET What kind of car?
OZZIE I don't know. An old one—black—big high fenders.
HARRIET A Buick.
OZZIE I think so; yes. Cruising up and down, up and down.
HARRIET Was it near here? Why don't you sit down? (*Trying to help him sit, to calm and comfort him*) Sit down. Relax.

(*He obeys, hardly aware of what he is doing, sort of squatting on the couch, his body rigid with tension, as the story obsesses him.*)

OZZIE And I heard them, too. They were hollering.

HARRIET What did they say?

OZZIE I don't know. It was just all noise. I couldn't understand.

HARRIET (*as if the realization doubles the horror*) It was more than one? My God!

OZZIE I don't know. Two at least, at the very least. One to drive and one to throw. Maybe even three. A lookout sort of, peering up and down, and then he sees me. "There," he says; he points me out. I'm strolling along like a stupid ass, I don't even see them. The driver picks up speed.

(*And now he is rising from the couch, reliving the story, cocking his arm.*)

The thrower cocks his arm . . .

HARRIET Ozzie, please, can't you relax? You look awful.

OZZIE Nooo, I can't relax, goddamnit!

(*Off he goes, pacing again.*)

HARRIET You look all flushed and sweating; please.

OZZIE It just makes me so goddamn mad the more I think about it. It really does. GODDAMNIT! GODDAMNIT!

HARRIET Oh, you poor thing.

OZZIE Because it was calculated; it was calculated, Harriet, because that egg had been boiled to just the right point so it was hard enough to hurt but not so hard it wouldn't splatter. The filthy sonsabitches, but I'm gonna find 'em, I swear that to God, I'm gonna find 'em. I'm gonna kill 'em. I'm gonna cut out their hearts!

(RICK *appears at the top of the stairs.*)

RICK Hey! What's all the racket? What's—

OZZIE Ricky, come down here! . . . Goddamn 'em. . . .

HARRIET Ricky, somebody hit your father with an egg!

RICK Hit him? (*Descending hurriedly, worried*) Hit Dad?

OZZIE They just threw it! Where's Dave? Dave here?

(*He is suddenly looking around, moving for the stairs.*)

I wanna tell Dave. DAVE!

HARRIET Ozzie, give me your jacket!

(*She follows him part way up the stairs, tugging at the jacket.*)

OZZIE I wanna tell Dave!

(*He and* HARRIET *struggle to get the jacket off.*)

HARRIET I'll take the spot off.

OZZIE I gotta tell ole Dave!

(*And the jacket is in her arms. He races on up the stairs.*)

DAVE? DAVE! HEY, DAVE?

(*But* DAVID *is not in his room. While* HARRIET *descends and goes to a wall counter with drawers,* OZZIE *hurries off down the hallway. From a drawer* HARRIET *takes a spray container and begins to clean the jacket.*)

RICK (*wandering near to her*) Boy, that's something, huh. What you got there, Mom?

HARRIET (*as* RICK *watches*) Meyer Spot Remover, do you know it? It gives just a sprinkling . . . like snow, which brushed away, leaves the fabric clean and fresh like spring.

(OZZIE *and* DAVID *rush out from the hallway and down the stairs.* RICK *moves toward them to take a picture.*)

OZZIE But it happened—and then there's this car tearin' off up the street. "Christ Jesus," I said, "I just been hit with an egg. Jesus Christ, that's impossible." And the way I felt—the way I feel—Harriet, let's have some beer; let's have some good beer for the boys and me.

(*With a sigh, she moves to obey. As* OZZIE *continues, she brings beer, she brings peanuts.* OZZIE *now is pleased with his high energy, with his being the center of attention.*)

It took me back to when I was a kid. Ole Fat Kramer. He lived on my street and we used to fight every day. For fun. Monday he'd win, and Tuesday, I'd beat him silly, my knees on his shoulders, blam, blam, blam. Later on, he grew up, became a merchant marine, sailed all over the world, and then he used to race sailboats up and down both coasts—he had one he lived on—anything that floated, he wanted to sail. And he wasn't fat either. We just called him that . . . and boy, oh boy, if he was around now—ohhhh, would we go get those punks threw that egg at me. We'd run 'em into the ground. We'd kill 'em like dogs . . . poor stupid ugly dogs, we'd cut out their hearts.

RICK (*suddenly coughing and coughing—having gulped down beer—and getting to his feet*) Excuse me, Dad; excuse me. Listen, I've got to get going. You don't mind, do you? Got places to go; you're just talking nonsense anyway. (*He moves for the front door.*)

HARRIET Have a good time, Rick.

RICK I'm too pretty not to, Mom! (*And he is gone.*)

OZZIE Where is . . . he . . . going? Where does he always go? Why does he always go and have some place to go? Always! . . .

HARRIET Just you never mind, Ozzie. He's young and you're not. I'm going to do the dishes, but you just go right ahead with your little story and I'll listen from the kitchen.

(*Gathering the beer and glasses, she goes.*)

OZZIE (*following a little after her, not knowing quite what to do*) I . . . outran a bowling ball. . . . They bet I couldn't.

(*And he starts as if at a sound. He turns toward* DAVID.)

What are you . . . looking . . . at? What do you think you're seeing?

DAVID I'm not looking.

OZZIE I feel watched; looked at.

DAVID No.

OZZIE Observed.

DAVID I'm blind.

OZZIE Did you do it? Had you anything to do with it?

DAVID What?

OZZIE That egg.

DAVID I can't see.

OZZIE I think you did. I feel like you did it.

DAVID I don't have a car. I can't drive. How could I?

HARRIET (*hurrying in to clean up more of the party leftovers*) Ohh, it's so good to hear men's voices in the house again, my two favorite men in all the world—it's what I live for really. Would you like some coffee? Oh, of course you would. Let me put some on. Your humble servant at your command; I do your bidding, bid me be gone.

(*And she is gone without a pause, leaving* OZZIE *staring after her.*)

OZZIE I could run again if I wanted. I'd . . . like . . . to want to. Christ, Fat Kramer is probably dead . . . now . . . not bouncing about in the ocean in some rattletrap, tin-can joke of a ship . . . but dust . . . locked in a box . . . held in old . . . cold hands. . . . And I just stand here, don't I? and let you talk any way you want. And Ricky gets up in the middle of some sentence I'm saying and walks right out and I let him. Because I fear him as I fear her . . . and you. Because I know the time is close when I will be of no use to any of you any longer . . . and I am so frightened that if I do not seem inoffensive . . . and pleasant . . . if I am not careful to never disturb any of you unnecessarily, you will all abandon me. I can no longer compel recognition. I can no longer impose myself, make myself seen.

HARRIET (*entering now happily with a tray of coffee*) Here you go. One for each and tea for me. Cream for David . . . (*Setting a cup for* DAVID, *moving toward* OZZIE) and cream and sugar for—

OZZIE Christ how you must have beguiled me!

HARRIET Pardon?

OZZIE Beguiled and deceived!

HARRIET Pardon . . . Ozzie? . . .

OZZIE And I don't even remember. I say "must" because I don't remember, I was so innocent, so childish in my strength, never seeing that it was surrendering I was doing, innocently and easily giving to you the love that was to return in time as flesh to imprison, detain, disarm and begin . . . to kill.

HARRIET (*examining him, scolding him*) Ozzie, how many beers have you had? You've had too many beers!

OZZIE Get away!

(*He whirls to point at* DAVID *who sits on the floor facing upstage.*)

Shut up! You've said enough! Detain and kill! Take and give nothing. It's what you meant, isn't it. You said it yesterday, a warning, nearly exactly this. This is your meaning!

DAVID You're doing so well, Dad.

OZZIE (*not understanding*) What?

DAVID You're doing so well.

OZZIE No.

DAVID You are.

OZZIE Nooo, I'm doing awful. I'm doing terrible.

DAVID This is the way you start, Dad. We'll be runners. Dad and Dave!

OZZIE What's he saying?

HARRIET My God, you're shaking; you're shaking.

OZZIE I don't know what he's talking about. What's he talking about? (*to* HARRIET) Just let me alone. Just please let me be. I don't really mean these things I'm saying. They're not really important. They'll go away and I don't mean them; they're just coming out of me; I'm just saying them, but I don't mean them. Oh, please, please, go away.

(*And* DAVID, *behind them, pivots to go up the stairs. She whirls, drawn by his sudden movement.*)

HARRIET (*dismayed*) David? . . .

DAVID I'm going upstairs.

HARRIET Oh, yes. Of course, of course.

DAVID Just for a while.

HARRIET Fine. Good. Of course.

DAVID I'll see you all later.

(*And he quietly enters his room, lies down.*)

OZZIE (*coiled on the couch, constricted with pain*) I remember . . . there was a day . . . when I wanted to leave you, all of you, and I wanted desperately to leave, and Hank was there . . . with me. We'd been playing cards. "No," he told me. "No," I couldn't, he said. "Think of the children," he said. He meant something by that. He meant something and I understood it. But now . . . I don't. I no longer have it—that understanding. It's left me. What did he mean?

HARRIET (*approaching, a little fearful*) You're trembling again. Look at you.

OZZIE For a while . . . just a while, stay away. That's all I ask.

HARRIET (*reaching to touch him*) What?

OZZIE Stay the hell away from me!

HARRIET Stay away? How far away? Ozzie, how far away? I'll move over . . . (*And she scurries, frightened.*) . . . here. Is this far enough away? Ozzie . . .

OZZIE It's my hands, my feet. There's tiredness in me. I wake up each morning, it's in my fingers . . . sleep. . . .

HARRIET Ohhh, it's such a hateful thing in you the way you have no love for people different than yourself . . . even when your son has come home to tell you of them. You have no right to carry on this way. He didn't bring her back—didn't marry her—we have those two things to thank God for. You've got to stop thinking only of yourself. We don't matter, only the children. When are you going to straighten out your thinking? Promise. You've got to straighten out your thinking.

OZZIE I do. I know.

HARRIET We don't matter; we're nothing. You're nothing, Ozzie. Only the children.

OZZIE I know. I promise.

HARRIET (*moving toward the stairs*) All right . . . just . . . rest . . . for a little; I'll be back. . . .

OZZIE I promise, Harriet.

HARRIET (*more to herself than to him*) I'll go see how he is.

OZZIE (*coiled on the couch*) It's my hands; they hurt . . . I want to wrap them; my feet . . .

HARRIET I'll tell him for you. I'll explain—how you didn't mean those terrible things you said. I'll explain.

OZZIE It's going to be so cold; and I hurt . . . already . . . So cold; my ankles! . . .

HARRIET (*hesitating on the stairway*) Oh, Ozzie, Ozzie, we're all so worried, but I just think we must hope for the fine bright day coming when we'll be a family again, as long as we try for what is good, truly for one another, please.

(*And she goes upstairs. The front door pops open.*)

RICK Hi, Mom. Hi, Dad.

OZZIE Hi, Rick. Your mom's upstairs. You have a nice time? I bet you did.

RICK Fine; sure. How about you?

OZZIE Fine; sure.

RICK Whata you doin', restin'?

OZZIE Workin'. Measurin'. Not everybody can play the guitar, *you know.* I'm going to build a wall . . . I think—a wall. Pretty soon . . . or . . . six walls. Thinkin' through the blueprints, lookin' over the plans.

RICK (*moving for the kitchen*) I'm gonna get some fudge, Dad; you want some?

OZZIE No. Too busy.

RICK I had the greatest piece a tail tonight, Dad; I really did. What a beautiful piece a ass.

OZZIE Did you, Rick?

RICK She was beee-uuuuu-ti-ful.

OZZIE Who was it?

RICK Nobody you'd know, Dad.

OZZIE Oh. Where'd you do it—I mean, get it.

RICK In her car.

OZZIE You were careful, I hope.

RICK (*laughing a little*) C'mon, Dad.

OZZIE I mean, it wasn't any decent girl.

RICK Hell, no. . . .

(*He is still laughing, as* OZZIE *gets to his feet.*)

OZZIE (*starting for the door*) Had a dream of the guitar last night, Rick. It was huge as a building—all flecked with ice. You swung it in the air and I exploded.

RICK I did?

OZZIE Yes. I was gone.

RICK Fantastic.

OZZIE (*exaggeratedly happy, almost singing*) Good night.

(OZZIE *is gone out the door. Blackout. Music.*)

(*Late night.* HARRIET *comes down the hall toward* DAVID'S *room. She is wearing a bathrobe and carries a towel, soap, a basin of water. Giving just the lightest tap on the door, she enters, smiling.*)

HARRIET A little bath . . . David? A little sponge bath, all right? You must be all hot and sticky always in that bed. And we can talk. Why don't you take your shirt off? We've an awful lot to talk about. Take your shirt off, David. Your poor father . . . he has no patience, no strength. Something has to be done. . . . A little sponge bath would be so nice. Have you talked to him lately? I think he thinks you're angry, for instance, with . . . us . . . for some reason . . . I don't know. (*Tugging at his shirt a little*) Take your shirt off, David. You'll feel cool. That's all we've ever wanted, your father and me—

good sweet things for you and Rick—ease and lovely children, a car, a wife, a good job. Time to relax and go to church on Sundays . . . and on holidays all the children and grandchildren come together, mingling. It would be so wonderful—everyone so happy—turkey. Twinkling lights! (*She is puzzled, a little worried.*) David, are you going to take your shirt off for me?

DAVID They hit their children, did you know that? They hit them with sticks.

HARRIET What?

DAVID The yellow people. They punish the disobedience of their children with sticks. And then they sleep together, one family in a bed, limbs all entwined like puppies. They work. I've seen them . . . laugh. They go on picnics. They murder—out of petty jealousy. Young girls wet their cunts with spit when they are dry from wear and yet another GI stands in line. They spit on their hands and rub themselves, smiling, opening their arms.

HARRIET That's not true.

DAVID I saw—

HARRIET (*smiling, scolding him*) None of what you say. No. No. All you did was something normal and regular, can't you see? And hundreds of boys have done it before you. Thousands and thousands. Even now. Now. Now. Why do you have to be so sick and morbid about something so ordinary?

DAVID She wasn't always a whore. Not always. Not—

HARRIET If she is now, she was then, only you didn't know. You didn't know.

(*She is reaching for him. He eludes her, stands above her, as she is left sitting on the bed, looking up.*)

Oh, David, David, I'm sure she was a lovely little girl, but I would be insane if I didn't want you to marry someone of your own with whom you could be happy, if I didn't want grandchildren who could be free and welcome in their world. I couldn't want anything else and still think I loved you. David, think of their faces, their poor funny little faces. . . .

(*And the cane is moving, slowly moving along the floor; it grazes her ankle.*)

DAVID I know . . . I know. . . .

(*The cane moves now along her inner calf, rising under the hem of her robe, lifting. She tries to ignore it.*)

HARRIET The human face was not meant to be that way. A nose is a thinness—you know that. And lips that are not thin are ugly, and it is we who disappear, David. They don't change, and we are gone. It is our triumph, our whiteness. We disappear. What are you doing?

(*The cane has driven her back along the bed; no longer can it be ignored. It has pressed against her.*)

They take us back and down if our children are theirs—it is not a mingling of blood, it is theft.

(*And she hits the cane away. In revulsion she stands, wanting only to flee.*)

Oh, you don't mean these awful things you do. Your room stinks—odors come from under the door. You don't clean yourself. David, David, you've lost someone you love and it's pain for you, don't you see? I know, I know. But we will be the same, lost from you—you from us—and what will that gain for anyone? What?

(*Now the cane begins to scrape along the floor. It begins to lift toward her, and, shuddering, she flees down the hall.* DAVID *opens the door, listens. Stepping into the hall, he carefully shuts the door before moving down the stairs. In the living room, he moves to plant himself before the front door.* HARRIET, *wearing a raincoat over her robe and a scarf on her head, comes down the stairs, when she turns toward the door and she sees* DAVID, *she stops, nods hello, and stands as he begins to advance on her.*)

DAVID Do you remember? It was a Sunday when we had all gone to church and there was a young man there with his yellow wife and child. You spoke to us . . . Dad and Rick and me, as if we were conspirators. "I feel so sorry for that poor man—the baby looks like *her*," you said, and your mouth twisted as if you had been forced to swallow someone else's spit.

HARRIET No, no. You want only to hurt us, don't you? Isn't that right? That's all you want. Only to give us unhappiness. You cheat her, David. That lovely, lovely little girl you spoke of. She merits more to be done in her memory than cruelty.

(*She has seated herself on the couch, clinging to some kind of normalcy, an odd and eerie calmness on both of them now.*)

DAVID And I felt that I must go to her if I was to ever live, and I felt that to touch truly her secret stranger's tongue and mind would kill me. Now she will not forgive the way I was.

HARRIET (*standing up*) No. No, no. No, you don't know how badly I feel. I've got a fever, the start of a cold or flu. Let me be. I can't hardly . . . (*And she is moving away from him, back toward the stairs*) move . . . or stand up. I just want to flop somewhere and not have to move. I'm so weak . . . don't hurt me anymore. Don't hurt me—no more—I've got fever; please, fever; don't hurt me. (*She is on the stairs.*)

DAVID But I have so much to show you.

HARRIET (*stops to stare helplessly down at him*) Who are you? I don't know who you are.

DAVID David.

HARRIET Noooooo.

DAVID But I am.

HARRIET No, no. Oh, no.

(*Moving now as in a trance, she walks up the stairs and down the hallway, all slowly, while* ZUNG *comes forward in* DAVID'S *room, and* DAVID, *in the living room, calls after his mother.*)

DAVID But it's what you want, don't you see? You can see it. Her wrists are bound in coils of flowers. Flowers are strung in her hair. She hangs from the wind and men strike and kick her. They are blind so that they may not see her, yet they howl, wanting not to hurt her but only as I do, to touch and hold her . . . and they howl. I'm home. Little David. . . . Home.

(*And he is turning now to take possession of the house. As he speaks, he moves to take the space. A conqueror, he parades in the streets he has taken; among the chairs, around the lamp.*)

Little Davey . . . of all the toys and tops and sailor suits, the plastic cars and Tinkertoys. Drum-player, bed-wetter, home-run-hitter, I'm home . . . now . . . and I want to drink from the toilet, wash there.

(*As he climbs the stairs, he passes by* ZUNG, *who stands in his room looking out at him. He walks on down the hall in the direction* HARRIET *fled.*)

And you will join me. You . . . will . . . join me!

(*When he is gone,* ZUNG *sits to gaze down upon the living room, as the front door opens.* OZZIE, *dressed in a suit or perhaps even a tuxedo, enters from the outside. Under his arm he carries a packet of several hundred sheets of paper. He moves now with an absolute confidence, almost smugness, as he carefully sets down the papers and proceeds to arrange three items of furniture—perhaps two chairs and a footstool—in such a way that they face him. He is cocky. Now he addresses them.*)

HARRIET (*to the large chair*) Harriet. . . . (*nodding to the second chair*) David. . . . (*patting the footstool*) Ricky.

(*He looks them over, the three empty chairs, and then speaks in the manner of a chairman of the board addressing the members of his board, explaining his position and plan of action for total solution. This is a kind of commercial on the value of* OZZIE.)

I'm glad we've gotten finally together here, because the thing I've decided to do—and you all, hopefully, will understand my reasoning—is to *combat* the weariness beginning in me. It's like stepping into a hole, the way I feel each morning when I awaken, I see the day and the sun and I'm looking upward into the sky with a sense of looking down. A sense of hovering over a great pit into which I am about to fall. The sky. Foolishness and deceit, you say, and I know you're right—a trick of feeling inside me being played against me, seeking to diminish me and increase itself until it is larger than me filling me and who will I be then? It. That feeling of being nothing. At first . . . at first . . . I thought the thing to do would be to learn the guitar. . . . But *that* I realized in just the nick of time was a folly that would have taken me into the very agony of frustration I was seeking to avoid. The skill to play like Ricky does is a great gift and only Ricky has it. He has no acids rotting his heart. He is all lies and music, his brain small and scaly, the brain of a snake forever innocent of the fact that it crawls. Lucky Ricky. But there are other things that people can do. And I've come at last to see the one that I must try if I am to become strong again in my opinion of myself. (*holding up, with great confidence, one of the many packets of paper*) What I have here is an inventory of everything I own. Everything. Every stick of furniture, pot and pan, every sock, T-shirt, pen or pencil. The opposite is its price. For instance—here—that davenport—five hundred an' twelve dollars an' ninety-eight cents. That chair—a hundred twenty ninety-nine. That table . . . (*He hurries to the table.*) . . . this table—thirty-two twenty-nine. Et cetera. Et cetera. Now the idea is that you each carry a number of these at all times.

(*He is distributing more papers to the chairs, his control, however, diminishing, so that the papers are thrown about.*)

Two or three copies at all times, and you are to pass them out at the slightest provocation. Let people know who I am, what I've done. Someone says to you, "Who are you?" You say, "I'm Ozzie's son." "I'm Ozzie's wife." "Who?" they'll say. "Take a look at that!" you tell 'em. Spit it out, give 'em a copy, turn on your heel and walk right out. That's the way I want it; from all of you from here on out, that's the WAY I WANT IT!

(*And the room goes suddenly into eerie light.* ZUNG, *high behind him in* DAVID'S *room, is hit with a sudden light that makes* OZZIE *go rigid, as if some current from her has entered into him, and he turns slowly to look up at her.*)

Let him alone. Let David alone.

(HARRIET *is in the hallway.*)

HARRIET Is there any aspirin down there? I don't feel well . . . Ozzie. I don't feel well at all. David poked me with his cane and I don't like . . . what's . . . going on.

(OZZIE *is only staring at* ZUNG.)

I don't want what's happening to happen.

(*She has halted on the stairway.*)

It must be some awful flu, I'm so weak, or some awful cold. There's an odor . . .

OZZIE I'll go to the drugstore. My eyes hurt; funny . . .

HARRIET Oh, Ozzie . . . oh my God. It was awful. I can't help it. He's crazy—he—

OZZIE I don't want to hear about him. I don't want to hear. Oh, no, oh, no. I can't. No more, no more. Let him do what he wants. No more of him, no more. Just you—you're all that I can see. All that I care for or want.

(*He has moved to her as she moved down, and they embrace.*)

HARRIET David's crazy! . . .

OZZIE You're everything.

HARRIET Please . . .

OZZIE Listen; we must hide; please.

HARRIET (*moving to kneel and he, while helping her, kneels also*) Pray with me.

OZZIE We won't move. We'll hide by not moving.

HARRIET We must beg God to not turn against him; convince him. Ozzie, pray. . . .

OZZIE Yes! . . .

HARRIET Now! . . .

(*They pray: kneeling, murmuring, and it goes on and on. The front door opens.*)

RICK Hi, Mom. Hi, Dad.

(*They continue. He stops.*)

Hi . . . Mom. Hi, Dad. . . . (*very puzzled*) Hi . . . Mom. . . . Hi . . . Dad. . . .

(*He thinks and thinks.*)

DAVID!

(*He screams at* DAVID. *He goes running up to look in* DAVID's *room, but the room is empty.* DAVID, *in ragged combat fatigues, appears on the top of the stairs.* RICK, *frightened, backs away.*)

Dave . . . what have you got to say for yourself? What can you? Honest ta God, I've had it. I really have. I can't help it, even if you are sick, and I hate to complain, but you're getting them so mixed up they're not themselves anymore. Just a minute ago—one minute—they were on their knees, do you know that? Just a minute ago—right here on the living-room floor. Now what's the point of that? They're my mom and dad, too.

DAVID He doesn't know, does he? Dad? Did you hear him?

RICK (*as* OZZIE *and* HARRIET *are getting from their knees and struggling to sit on the couch*) Let Dad alone.

DAVID (*on the landing, looking down on them*) He doesn't know how when you finally see yourself, there's nothing really there to see . . . isn't that right? Mom?

RICK Dave, honest to God, I'm warning you, let them alone.

(DAVID *descends with* ZUNG *behind him. Calmly he speaks, growing slowly happy.*)

DAVID Do you know how north of here, on farms, gentle loving dogs are raised, while in the forests, other dogs run wild? And upon occasion, one of those that's wild is captured and put in among the others that are tame, bringing with it the memory of when they had all been wild—the dark and terror—that had made them wolves. Don't you hear them?

(*And there is a rumbling.*)

RICK What? Hear what?

(*It is windlike, the rumbling of many trucks.*)

DAVID Don't you hear the trucks? They're all over town, lined up from the center of town into the country. Don't you hear? They've stopped bringing back the blind. They're bringing back the dead now. The convoy's broken up. There's no control . . . they're walking from house to house, through the shrubbery, under the trees, carrying one of the dead in a bright blue rubber bag for which they have no papers, no name or number. No one knows whose it is. They're at the Jensens' now. Now Al Jensen's at the door, all his kids behind him trying to peek. Al looks for a long, long time into the open bag before he shakes his head. They zipper shut the bag and turn away. They've been to the Mayers', the Kellys', the Irwins' and Kresses'. They'll be here soon.

OZZIE Nooo.

DAVID And Dad's going to let them in. We're going to let them in.

HARRIET What's he saying?

DAVID He's going to knock.

OZZIE I DON'T KNOW.

DAVID Yes. Yes.

(*A knocking sound. Is it* DAVID *knocking with his fist against the door or table?*)

OZZIE Nooooo.

RICK Mom, he's driving Dad crazy.

(*Knocking loud: it seems to be at the front door.*)

OZZIE David, will I die?

(*He moves toward the door.*)

HARRIET Who do you suppose it could be so late?

RICK (*intercepting* OZZIE, *blocking the way to the door*) I don't think you should just go opening the door to anybody this time of the night, there's no telling who it might be.

DAVID We know who it is.

OZZIE Oh, David, why can't you wait? Why can't you rest?

(*But* DAVID *is the father now, and he will explain. He loves them all.*)

DAVID Look at her. See her, Dad. Tell her to go to the door. Tell her yes, it's your house, you want her to open the door and let them in. Tell her yes, the one with no name is ours. We'll put it in that chair. We can bring them all here. I want them all here, all the trucks and bodies. There's room. (*handing* RICK *the guitar*) Ricky can sing. We'll stack them along the walls . . .

OZZIE Nooo . . .

DAVID Pile them over the floor . . .

OZZIE No, no . . .

DAVID They will become the floor and they will become the walls, the chairs. We'll sit in them; sleep. We will call them "home." We will give them as gifts—call them "ring" and "pot" and "cup." No, no; it's not a thing to fear. . . . We will notice them no more than all the others.

(*He is gentle, happy, consoling to them.*)

OZZIE What others? There are no others. Oh . . . please die. Oh, wait. . . .

(*And he scurries to the TV where it sits beneath the stairs.*)

I'll get it fixed. I'll fix it. Who needs to hear it? We'll watch it. (*wildly turning TV channels*) I flick my rotten life. Oh, there's a good one. Look at that one. Ohhh, isn't that a good one? That's the best one. That's the best one.

DAVID They will call it madness. We will call it seeing.

(*Calmly he lifts* OZZIE.)

OZZIE I don't want to disappear.

DAVID Let her take you to the door. We will be runners. You will have eyes.

OZZIE I will be blind. I will disappear.

(*Knocking is heard again. Again.*)

DAVID You stand and she stands. "Let her go," you say; "she is garbage and filth and you must get her back if you wish to live. She is sickness, I must cherish her." Old voices you have trusted all your life as if they were your own, speaking always friendly. "She's all of everything impossible made possible!"

OZZIE Ricky . . . nooo! . . .

DAVID Don't call to Ricky. You love her. You will embrace her, see her and—

OZZIE He has no right to do this to me.

DAVID Don't call to Ricky!

OZZIE (*suddenly raging, rushing at* DAVID, *pushing him*) You have no right to do this.

RICK Noooooo!

(*Savagely he smashes his guitar down upon* DAVID, *who crumples.*)

Let Dad alone. Let him alone. He's sick of you. What the hell's the matter with you? He doesn't wanna talk anymore about all the stupid stuff you talk. He wants to talk about cake and cookies and cars and coffee. He's sick a you and he wants you to shut up. We hate you, goddamn you.

(*Silence:* DAVID *lies still.*)

ZUNG Chào ông!

(OZZIE *pivots, looks at her.*)

Chào ông! Hôm nay ông manh không?

OZZIE Oh, what is it that you want? I'm tired. I mean it. Forgive me. I'm sick of the sight of you, squatting all the time. In filth like animals, talking gibberish, your breath sick with rot. . . . And yet you look at me with those sad pleading eyes as if there is some real thing that can come between us when you're not even here. You are deceit.

(*His hands, rising, have driven to her throat. The fingers close.*)

I'm not David. I'm not silly and soft . . . little David. The sight of you sickens me. YOU HEAR ME, DAVID? Believe me. I am speaking my honest true feelings. I spit on you, the both of you; I piss on you and your eyes and pain. Flesh is lies. You are garbage and filth. You are darkness. I cast you down. Deceit. Animal. Dirty animal.

(*And he is over her. They are sprawled on the ground. Silence as no one moves. She lies like a rag beneath him.*)

RICK I saw this really funny movie last night. This really . . . funny, funny movie about this young couple and they were going to get a divorce but they didn't. It was really funny.

(*Ozzie is hiding the girl. In a proscenium production, he can drag her behind the couch; in three-quarter, he covers her with a blanket brought to him by* HARRIET *which matches the rug.*)

HARRIET What's that? What's that?

RICK This movie I saw.

HARRIET Anybody want to go for groceries? We need Kleenex, sugar, milk.

RICK What a really funny movie.

OZZIE I'll go; I'll go.

HARRIET Good. Good.

OZZIE I think I saw it on TV.

(*They are cleaning up the house now, putting the chairs back in order, dumping all of* OZZIE's *leaflets in the waste can.*)

HARRIET Did you enjoy it, Rick?

RICK Oh, yeh. I loved it.

OZZIE I laughed so much I almost got sick. It was really good. I laughed.

RICK I bet it was; I bet you did.

OZZIE Oh, I did.

(*Even* DAVID *helps with the cleaning: he gets himself off the floor and seated in a chair.*)

HARRIET How are you feeling, Ricky?

RICK Fine.

HARRIET Good.

RICK How do you feel?

HARRIET Oh, I'm all right. I feel fine.

OZZIE Me, too. I feel fine, too. What day is it anyway? Monday?

HARRIET Wednesday.

RICK Tuesday, Mom.

(*Now all three are seated on the couch.*)

OZZIE I thought it was Monday.

RICK Oh, no.

HARRIET No, no. You're home now, David. . . .

RICK (*moving to* DAVID, *who sits alone in a chair*) Hey, Dave, listen, will you. I mean I know it's not my place to speak out and give advice and everything because I'm the youngest, but I just gotta say my honest true feelings and I'd kill myself if I were you, Dave. You're in too much misery. I'd cut my wrists. Honestly speaking, brother to brother, you should have done it long ago.

(DAVID *is looking about.*)

You looking for her, Dave? You looking for her? She's not here.

DAVID What?

RICK Nooo. She's never been here. You just thought so. You decided not to bring her, Dave, remember? You decided, all things considered that you preferred to come back without her. Too much risk and inconvenience . . . you decided. Isn't that right? Sure. You know it is. You've always known.

(*Silence.* HARRIET *moves to look out the front door.*)

Do you want to use my razor, Dave? (*Pulling a straight razor from his pocket*) I have one right here and you can use it if you want.

(DAVID *seems to be looking at the razor.*)

Just take it if you want it, Dave.

HARRIET Go ahead, David. The front yard's empty. You don't have to be afraid. The streets, too . . . still and empty.

RICK It doesn't hurt like you think it will. Go ahead; just take it, Dave.

OZZIE You might as well.

RICK That's right.

OZZIE You'll feel better.

RICK I'll help you now, Dave, okay?

HARRIET I'll go get some pans and towels.

RICK (*moving about* DAVID, *patting him, buddying him*) Oh, you're so confused, you don't know what to do. It's just a good thing I got this razor, Boy, that's all I gotta say. You're so confused. You see, Dave, where you're wrong is your point of view, it's silly. It's just really comical because you think people are valuable or something and, given a chance like you were to mess with 'em, to take a young girl like that and turn her into a whore, you shouldn't, when of course you should or at least might . . . on whim . . . you see? I mean, you're all backwards, Dave—you're upside down. You don't know how to go easy and play—I bet you didn't have any fun the whole time you were over there—no fun at all—and it was there. I got this buddy Gerry, he was there, and he used to throw bags of cement at 'em from off the back a his truck. They'd go whizzin' through those villages, throwin' off these bags a cement. You could kill people, he says, you hit 'em right. Especially the kids. There was this once they knocked this ole man off his bicycle—fifty pounds a dry cement—and then the back a the truck got his legs. It was hysterical—can't you just see that, Dave? Him layin' there howlin', all the guys in the truck bowin' and wavin' and tippin' their hats. What a goddamn funny story, huh?

(HARRIET *has brought silver pans and towels with roosters on them. The towels cover the arms of the chair and* DAVID's *lap. The pans will catch the blood. All has been neatly placed.* DAVID, *with* RICKY's *help, cuts one wrist, then the other, as they talk.*)

DAVID I wanted . . . to kill you . . . all of you.

RICK I know, I know; but you're hurt; too weak.

DAVID I wanted for you to need what I had and I wouldn't give it.

HARRIET That's not possible.

OZZIE Nooooo.

DAVID I wanted to get you. Like poor bug-eyed fish flung up from the brief water to the lasting dirt, I would gut you.

HARRIET David, no, no, you didn't want that.

OZZIE No, no.

RICK I don't even know why you'd think you did.

OZZIE We kill you is what happens.

RICK That's right.

OZZIE And then, of course, we die, too. . . . Later on, I mean. And nothing stops it. Not words . . . or walls . . . or even guitars.

RICK Sure.

OZZIE That's what happens.

HARRIET It isn't too bad, is it?

RICK How bad is it?

OZZIE He's getting weaker.

HARRIET And in a little, it'll all be over. You'll feel so grand. No more funny talk.

RICK You can shower; put on clean clothes. I've got deodorant you can borrow. After Roses, Dave. The scent of a thousand roses.

(*He is preparing to take a picture—crouching, aiming.*)

HARRIET Take off your glasses, David.

OZZIE Do as you're told.

RICK (*as* DAVID's *hands are rising toward the glasses to remove them*) I bet when you were away there was only plain water to wash in, huh? You prob'ly hadda wash in the rain.

(*He takes the picture; there is a flash. A slide appears on the screen: a close-up of* DAVID, *nothing visible but his face. It is the slide that, appearing at the start of the play, was referred to as "somebody sick." Now it hovers, stricken, sightless, revealed.*)

Mom, I like David like this.

HARRIET He's happier.

OZZIE We're all happier.

RICK Too bad he's gonna die.

OZZIE No, no, he's not gonna die, Rick. He's only gonna nearly die. Only nearly.

RICK Ohhhhhhhhhhh.

HARRIET Mmmmmmmmmmmm.

(*And* RICK, *sitting, begins to play his guitar for* DAVID. *The music is alive and fast. It has a rhythm, a drive of happiness that is contagious. The lights slowly fade.*)

'NIGHT, MOTHER

(1983)

MARSHA NORMAN (1947–   )

Throughout history, the overwhelming domination by men of all phases of drama and theatre almost completely prevented women from participating in any manner except acting. In fact, it took more than two millenia for women to achieve acting roles: all characters in ancient Greek and Roman drama were played by men, and the theatre of Renaissance England cast young boys in all female roles until the theatres were closed in 1642. Seeing women on stage in England after the restoration of Charles II in 1660 was a novel, and to some a disturbing, turn of events. And until fairly recent times, the morals of women actors in general were seriously questioned.

The writing of plays, by long-established custom reserved for men, was seldom undertaken by women almost until the twentieth century. There exists the shadowy figure of Hroswitha in medieval times (see introduction to *The Second Shepherd's Play*), and a fairly prominent but second-rate author of Restoration comedy was Aphra Behn, who lived from 1640 to 1689. During the period of the American Revolution, the satires of Mercy Otis Warren were widely known, and Anna Cora Mowatt's *Fashion* of 1845 still remains playable, but not until the twentieth century, especially in America, did women play a significant role in the writing or production of drama.

We have already noted that Susan Glaspell was one of the most successful American woman dramatists in the early decades of the twentieth century (see the introduction to *Trifles*), and it was also a period in which women held highly important positions on all levels. In a field so thoroughly a male prerogative and at a time when women still could not vote, it was a remarkable achievement for women not only to gain recognition as playwrights but also to found an important theatre, the Neighborhood Playhouse. Begun in 1912 by Alice and Irene Lewisohn as a settlement-house project to bring good, accessible entertainment to a large immigrant population on New York's east side, it expanded into a major theatrical force with its own new theatre building in which the Lewisohns introduced plays by a wide variety of European and American writers. In its fifteen-year existence, all major administrative and operating positions were staffed by women.

Apart from Susan Glaspell, the most prolific and best-remembered was Rachel Crothers (1878–1958), a successful playwright, director, and producer from 1908 to 1937. Frequently treating women's conflicts between marriage and career, her otherwise realistic plots tended toward artificially romantic and sentimental endings. Her first success, *He and She* (1911), faced the problem of the talented wife who finally places the welfare of husband and daughter over pursuit of her own artistic career. The new freedoms of postwar women were dramatized in *Nice People* (1921), about rich New York "flappers," and in *Let Us Be Gay* (1929), involving a divorcée living the same kind of promiscuous life practiced by her husband. *When Ladies Meet* (1932) presents a wife and the "other woman" who decide between themselves that the man in their lives isn't really worth fighting for.

Edna St. Vincent Millay (1892–1950), a popular prize-winning poet, is best remembered for her highly stylized *Aria da Capo* (1919), a fanciful and bitter attack on humanity's inability to use reason to reconcile differences without war. Zoe Atkins (1886–1958) won the 1934–1935 Pulitzer Prize for drama for *The Old Maid,* depicting the sorrow of a mother who gave up the infant daughter who, now grown, regards her as a sour old spinster. Alice Gerstenberg (1885–1972), in *Overtones* (1915), used two separate actors to portray the split personality of her protagonist. Zona Gale won the Pulitzer for 1920–1921 with *Miss Lulu Bett,* dramatizing her own novel about a rebellious unmarried woman who loves a married man. Lula Vollmer's *Sun-Up* (1923) was a touching portrayal of North Carolina mountain folk, and Sophie Treadwell gained limited fame with *Machinal* in 1928, an expressionistic telling of the famous trial of a wife who murdered her husband.

For many years after Susan Glaspell's last appearance in 1930 with *Alison's House,* freely based on the life of Emily Dickinson, women dramatists made only rare appearances. The most famous was Lillian Hellman (1916–1984), who gained national attention and notoriety with *The Children's Hour* in 1934. Its subject of possible lesbianism involving two faculty members of a small private girls' school was a shocker on both sides of the Atlantic, banned both in Boston and in London. Hellman's greatest fame lies with her powerful portrayal of the predatory Hubbard family in the well-made realism of *The Little Foxes* (1939). The central figure of Regina Giddens, who would seek financial gain and social position at the expense of her husband's life, is one of the great American dramatic creations. The best of Hellman's plays with a war theme was *Watch on the Rhine* (1941), a sobering picture of the perils of an anti-Nazi German family living as refugees with their relatives in Washington. A "prequel" to *The Little Foxes* was *Another Part of the Forest* (1946), a chronicle of the Hubbard family before their appearance in the earlier play. *Toys in the Attic* (1960) with its suggestion of Southern decadence reminiscent of Tennessee Williams, involved two maiden aunts and their ne'er-do-well nephew married to a childlike bride whose mother seems to be keeping her black chauffeur as her lover.

Clare Boothe (1903–1987) gleefully savaged her own sex in *The Women* (1936), a stinging satire on the idle lives of sophisticated Park Avenue wives and mistresses. Mary Chase (1907–1981) wrote the Pulitzer Prize–winning tale of a gentle alcoholic and his six-foot, white-rabbit companion in *Harvey* (1945), one of the all-time Broadway successes.

It would not be until two decades later, in the 1960s, when the resurgence of women dramatists became evident.

Megan Terry (b. 1932) has witnessed publication and production of her works around the globe. She is noted for her "transformational" dramas, such as *Calm Down Mother* and *Keep Tightly Closed in a Cool Dry Place,* both written in 1965 and produced in New York's Open Theatre. Each presents a strong feminist message as she effectively deals with sexism and male domination in current American society. The first involves only three women, and the transformation occurs when they become, at various points throughout the play, among other things, two clerks and a customer, nursing home patients, call girls, and such abstractions as a subway car door and the sides of a triangle. In the second play, three convicts jailed for murder become General Custer and men, movie gangsters, drag queens, and a priest and altar boys.

Terry's best-known play is *Viet Rock: A Folk War Movie* produced first in 1966 and revived in 1987. Internationally famous, it was the first rock musical ever staged, and was the first theatre piece to deal with the Vietnam War, strongly protesting against it in both song and action.

The list of other women writers during the later years of the century, some equally as famous as Terry, others not so well known, is long and extremely impressive—indeed, too long for discussion of all of them here. Among them is Marie Irene Fornes (b. 1930), whose plays often show the influences of Samuel Beckett and the absurdists. *Fefu and Her Friends* won an Obie (the award for outstanding plays produced off Broadway) in 1977, invoking both sympathy and compassion for women in the male-dominated society. Adrienne Kennedy (b. 1931) gained attention with her Obie-winning *Funny House of a Negro* (1964), using some of Forne's transformational effects. The plight of an actual African-American Vietnam veteran driven to insanity and murder by his experiences in fighting and killing other minorities was the subject of *An Evening with Dead Essex* (1973). Rachel Owens (b. 1936) is best known for *Futz* (written in 1961 but not produced until 1967), a fanciful satire on misogyny involving the love of the central figure, Futz, for his pig. Jane Chambers (1937–1983) was the first to bring the lesbian community on stage with *A Late Snow* (1974), concerning the assorted complex sexual relationships among a group of five women stranded in a snowbound cabin. *Last Summer at Bluefish Cove* (1980) was produced at the first Gay American Art Festival. The central figure, Eva, gains the self-reliance denied her in her unsuccessful marriage through her evolving lesbian awareness.

Emily Mann (b. 1952), deeply concerned with morality, made innovative use of monologue, dialogue, music, film, and slides in *Still Life* (1980), based on personal interviews about a Vietnam veteran's brutalization by the war. Ntozake Shange (b. 1948 as Paulette Williams) received her greatest recognition with *for colored girls who have considered suicide/when the rainbow is enuf.* Produced in New York in 1976 after an extended tour around the country, it was the first play by an African-American woman since Hansberry to be produced on Broadway. It is based on a series of poems depicting the struggles of a black girl's growing up.

Beth Henley (b. 1952) began writing plays as early as the ninth grade. *Crimes of the Heart,* her best known, opened on Broadway in 1981 after having won the Pulitzer Prize during its previous brief off-Broadway run at the Manhattan Theatre Club. Henley was the first woman to receive the Pulitzer since Ketti Frings (for *Look Homeward, Angel* in 1958), and hers was the first play to receive the Pulitzer before its Broadway opening. *Crimes* presents the reunion of three sisters—Lenny, Meg, and Babe—who have suffered in the past from a father's abandonment, mother's suicide, and various forms of abuse from their Old Grandaddy, who supervised them as children. Furthermore, Babe, who has just shot her abusive husband and will probably enter a plea of temporary insanity, says she did it because she didn't like his looks. By the play's end, the three have somewhat assuaged the violence of their past as they establish new relationships with one another.

The fame of Tina Howe (b. 1937) rests mainly with *Painting Churches* (1983), an autobiographical play about a portrait artist who has returned home to paint the portrait of her parents (the family name is Church, hence the title), a staid couple who generally disapprove of their daughter's style of painting (purple skin, orange hair) and unconventional appearance in dress and hair style. But the parents eventually conclude that they like the portrait and end the play dancing a waltz.

If one were to judge by her childhood and adolescence, Marsha Norman would seem a most unlikely prospect as a dramatist. Her strict fundamentalist mother forbade her to watch television (and even radio was frowned upon) or to play with the neighborhood children, considered by her mother to be "inferior." Her college major in philosophy scarcely suggests a career in the theatre. While in college she worked in an Atlanta hospital pediatric burn unit and as a teacher of both disturbed and gifted children in Kentucky. But she did like to write and was encouraged by the artistic director of the Louisville Actors Theatre, resulting in her first play, *Getting Out* in 1977. It was suggested by her experiences with her disturbed teenage hospital patients. The play concerns the life of Arlene, a paroled prisoner (she had been imprisoned once for forgery and again for killing a cab driver who tried to attack her) attempting to gain her independence in the hostile outside world, which is still symbolically imprisoning her. On the stage at the same time is Arlie, portraying Arlene as a child, filling the audience in on her violent background, including rape by her father.

Norman's most important play to date and certainly the best known is *'night, Mother,* for which she won the 1983 Pulitzer Prize. It has won a variety of other artistic awards and has been played in such "exotic" places as Russia, South Africa, and New Guinea. Its appeal is universal.

What makes *'night, Mother,* this short two-character play ending in suicide, so appealing around the world? For one thing, its attraction lies in Norman's creation of an intensely realistic drama about two individuals with a relationship recognizable everywhere—ordinary, undistinguished people living what would seem to be a relatively comfortable, uncomplicated, unsophisticated, middle-class life. They live in an unprepossessing home, surrounded by familiar household items in the room and on the shelves. However, the central theme is the relationship between parent and child, both having experienced in one way or another disappointing lives that are discussed in some detail with the impending violence hanging over them. It is, at heart, a gripping situation.

'night, Mother turns things around in a significant way: instead of presenting the more common dramatic crisis situation between father and son, as compared with Arthur Miller and others, it uses a mother-daughter problem of considerable proportions. Moreover, it will not end in any compromise or any change of outlook as Jessie remains determined and Mama can do nothing whatever about it. Probably the most interesting aspect of the play and its building to the final catastrophe is the rationale behind Jessie's action. Nobody, even the most erudite of critics, has convincingly pinpointed the exact reason. The blunt, unwavering statement of intent does not supply what we all would like to know. There seems to be a veritable collage of reasons, but none seemingly adequate to explain her determination. Is it health? frustration? overwhelming loneliness? Is it a pointless, disappointing life, or just a tiring of life itself? Is it domestic parental problems, or a kind of revenge against the mother, or a future that appears blank and meaningless? Has there been a long period of acute depression and "nervous breakdown"? None of these explanations seems adequate, and even the cumulative evidence would scarcely seem to prompt the final irrevocable act. Perhaps this terrible ambiguity is what makes the play an ultimate success, as we all recognize that "real" life seldom, if ever, offers solutions or full explanations. There is no reason to expect that the art of the dramatist can do it, either.

'night, Mother MARSHA NORMAN

CHARACTERS

Jessie Cates, *in her late thirties or early forties, is pale and vaguely unsteady physically. It is only in the last year that Jessie has gained control of her mind and body, and tonight she is determined to hold on to that control. She wears pants and a long black sweater with deep pockets, which contain scraps of paper, and there may be a pencil behind her ear or a pen clipped to one of the pockets of the sweater.*

As a rule, Jessie doesn't feel much like talking. Other people have rarely found her quirky sense of humor amusing. She has a peaceful energy on this night, a sense of purpose, but is clearly aware of the time passing moment by moment. Oddly enough, Jessie has never been as communicative or as enjoyable as she is on this evening, but we must know she has not always been this way. There is a familiarity between these two women that comes from having lived together for a long time. There is a shorthand to the talk and a sense of routine comfort in the way they relate to each other physically. Naturally, there are also routine aggravations.

Thelma Cates, "Mama," *is Jessie's mother, in her late fifties or early sixties. She has begun to feel her age and so takes it easy when she can, or when it serves her purpose to let someone help her. But she speaks quickly and enjoys talking. She believes that things* are *what she says they are. Her sturdiness is more a mental quality than a physical one, finally. She is chatty and nosy, and this is* her *house.*

The play takes place in a relatively new house built way out on a country road, with a living room and connecting kitchen, and a center hall that leads off to the bedrooms. A pull cord in the hall ceiling releases a ladder which leads to the attic. One of these bedrooms opens directly onto the hall, and its entry should be visible to everyone in the audience. It should be, in fact, the focal point of the entire set, and the lighting should make it disappear completely at times and draw the entire set into it at others. It is a point of both threat and promise. It is an ordinary door that opens onto absolute nothingness. That door is the point of all the action, and the utmost care should be given to its design and construction.

The living room is cluttered with magazines and needlework catalogues, ashtrays and candy dishes. Examples of **Mama**'s *needlework are everywhere—pillows, afghans, and quilts, doilies and rugs, and they are quite nice examples. The house is more comfortable than messy, but there is quite a lot to keep in place here. It is more personal than charming. It is not quaint. Under no circumstances should the set and its dressing make a judgment about the intelligence or taste of* **Jessie** *and* **Mama.** *It should simply indicate that they are very specific real people who happen to live in a particular part of the country. Heavy accents, which would further distance the audience from* **Jessie** *and* **Mama,** *are also wrong.*

The time is the present, with the action beginning about 8:15. Clocks onstage in the kitchen and on a table in the living room should run throughout the performance and be visible to the audience.

There will be no intermission.

(MAMA *stretches to reach the cupcakes in a cabinet in the kitchen. She can't see them, but she can feel around for them, and she's eager to have one, so she's working pretty hard at it. This may be the most serious exercise* MAMA *ever gets. She finds a cupcake, the coconut-covered, raspberry-and-marshmallow-filled kind known as a snowball, but sees that there's one missing from the package. She calls to* JESSIE, *who is apparently somewhere else in the house.*)

MAMA (*unwrapping the cupcake*) Jessie, it's the last snowball, sugar. Put it on the list, O.K.? And we're out of Hershey bars, and where's that peanut brittle? I think maybe Dawson's been in it again. I ought to put a big mirror on the refrigerator door. That'll keep him out of my treats, won't it? You hear me, honey? (*then more to herself*) I hate it when the coconut falls off. Why does the coconut fall off?

(JESSIE *enters from her bedroom, carrying a stack of newspapers.*)

JESSIE We got any old towels?

MAMA There you are!

JESSIE (*holding a towel that was on the stack of newspapers*) Towels you don't want anymore. (*picking up* MAMA'S *snowball wrapper*) How about this swimming towel Loretta gave us? Beach towel, that's the name of it. You want it? (MAMA *shakes her head no.*)

MAMA What have you been doing in there?

JESSIE And a big piece of plastic like a rubber sheet or something. Garbage bags would do if there's enough.

MAMA Don't go making a big mess, Jessie. It's eight o'clock already.

JESSIE Maybe an old blanket or towels we got in a soap box sometime?

MAMA I said don't make a mess. Your hair is black enough, hon.

JESSIE (*continuing to search the kitchen cabinets, finding two or three more towels to add to her stack*) It's not for my hair, Mama. What about some old pillows anywhere, or a foam cushion out of a yard chair would be real good.

MAMA You haven't forgot what night it is, have you? (*holding up her fingernails*) They're all chipped, see? I've been waiting all week, Jess. It's Saturday night, sugar.

JESSIE I know. I got it on the schedule.

MAMA (*crossing to the living room*) You want me to wash 'em now or are you making your mess first? (*looking at the snowball*) We're out of these. Did I say that already?

JESSIE There's more coming tomorrow. I ordered you a whole case.

MAMA (*checking the* TV Guide) A whole case will go stale, Jessie.

JESSIE They can go in the freezer till you're ready for them. Where's Daddy's gun?

MAMA In the attic.

JESSIE Where in the attic? I looked your whole nap and couldn't find it anywhere.

MAMA One of his shoeboxes, I think.

JESSIE Full of shoes. I looked already.

MAMA Well, you didn't look good enough, then. There's that box from the ones he wore to the hospital. When he died, they told me I could have them back, but I never did like those shoes.

JESSIE (*pulling them out of her pocket*) I found the bullets. They were in an old milk can.

MAMA (*as* JESSIE *starts for the hall*) Dawson took the shotgun, didn't he? Hand me that basket, hon.

JESSIE (*getting the basket for her*) Dawson better not've taken that pistol.

MAMA (*stopping her again*) Now my glasses, please. (JESSIE *returns to get the glasses.*) I told him to take those rubber boots, too, but he said they were for fishing. I told him to take up fishing.

(JESSIE *reaches for the cleaning spray, and cleans* MAMA*'s glasses for her.*)

JESSIE He's just too lazy to climb up there, Mama. Or maybe he's just being smart. That floor's not very steady.

MAMA (*getting out a piece of knitting*) It's not a floor at all, hon, it's a board now and then. Measure this for me. I need six inches.

JESSIE (*as she measures*) Dawson could probably use some of those clothes up there. Somebody should have them. You ought to call the Salvation Army before the whole thing falls in on you. Six inches exactly.

MAMA It's plenty safe! As long as you don't go up there.

JESSIE (*turing to go again*) I'm careful.

MAMA What do you want the gun for, Jess?

JESSIE (*not returning this time; opening the ladder in the hall*) Protection. (*She steadies the ladder as* MAMA *talks.*)

MAMA You take the TV way too serious, hon. I've never seen a criminal in my life. This is way too far to come for what's out here to steal. Never seen a one.

JESSIE (*taking her first step up*) Except for Ricky.

MAMA Ricky is mixed up. That's not a crime.

JESSIE Get your hands washed. I'll be right back. And get 'em real dry. You dry your hands till I get back or it's no go, all right?

MAMA I thought Dawson told you not to go up those stairs.

JESSIE (*going up*) He did.

MAMA I don't like the idea of a gun, Jess.

JESSIE (*calling down from the attic*) Which shoebox, do you remember?

MAMA Black.

JESSIE The box was black?

MAMA The shoes were black.

JESSIE That doesn't help much, Mother.

MAMA I'm not trying to help, sugar. (*no answer*) We don't have anything anybody'd want, Jessie. I mean, I don't even want what we got, Jessie.

JESSIE Neither do I. Wash your hands. (MAMA *gets up and crosses to stand under the ladder.*)

MAMA You come down from there before you have a fit. I can't come up and get you, you know.

JESSIE I know.

MAMA We'll just hand it over to them when they come, how's that? Whatever they want, the criminals.

JESSIE That's a good idea, Mama.

MAMA Ricky will grow out of this and be a real fine boy, Jess. But I have to tell you, I wouldn't want Ricky to know we had a gun in the house.

JESSIE Here it is. I found it.

MAMA It's just something Ricky's going through. Maybe he's in with some bad people. He just needs some time, sugar. He'll get back in school or get a job or one day you'll get a call and he'll say he's sorry for all the trouble he's caused and invite you out for supper someplace dress-up.

JESSIE (*coming back down the steps*) Don't worry. It's not for him, it's for me.

MAMA I didn't think you would shoot your own boy, Jessie. I know you've felt like it, well, we've all felt like shooting somebody, but we don't do it. I just don't think we need . . .

JESSIE (*interrupting*) Your hands aren't washed. Do you want a manicure or not?

MAMA Yes, I do, but . . .

JESSIE (*crossing to the chair*) Then wash your hands and don't talk to me any more about Ricky. Those two rings he took were the last valuable things *I* had, so now he's started in on other people, door to door. I hope they put him away sometime. I'd turn him in myself if I knew where he was.

MAMA You don't mean that.

JESSIE Every word. Wash your hands and that's the last time I'm telling you.

(JESSIE *sits down with the gun and starts cleaning it, pushing the cylinder out, checking to see that the chambers and barrel are empty, then putting some oil on a small patch of cloth and pushing it through the barrel with the push rod that was in the box.* MAMA *goes to the kitchen and washes her hands, as instructed, trying not to show her concern about the gun.*)

MAMA I shoulda got you to bring down that milk can. Agnes Fletcher sold hers to somebody with a flea market for forty dollars apiece.

JESSIE I'll go back and get it in a minute. There's a wagon wheel up there, too. There's even a churn. I'll get it all if you want.

MAMA (*coming over, now, taking over now*) What are you doing?

JESSIE The barrel has to be clean, Mama. Old powder, dust gets in it . . .

MAMA What for?

JESSIE I told you.

MAMA (*reaching for the gun*) And I told you, we don't get criminals out here.

JESSIE (*quickly pulling it to her*) And I told you . . . (*then trying to be calm*) The gun is for me.

MAMA Well, you can have it if you want. When I die, you'll get it all, anyway.

JESSIE I'm going to kill myself, Mama.

MAMA (*returning to the sofa*) Very funny. Very funny.

JESSIE I am.

MAMA You are not! Don't even say such a thing, Jessie.

JESSIE How would you know if I didn't say it? You want it to be a surprise? You're lying there in your bed or maybe you're just brushing your teeth and you hear this . . . noise down the hall?

MAMA Kill yourself.

JESSIE Shoot myself. In a couple of hours.

MAMA It must be time for your medicine.

JESSIE Took it already.

MAMA What's the matter with you?

JESSIE Not a thing. Feel fine.

MAMA You feel fine. You're just going to kill yourself.

JESSIE Waited until I felt good enough, in fact.

MAMA Don't make jokes, Jessie. I'm too old for jokes.

JESSIE It's not a joke, Mama.

(MAMA *watches for a moment in silence.*)

MAMA That gun's no good, you know. He broke it right before he died. He dropped it in the mud one day.

JESSIE Seems O.K. (*She spins the chamber, cocks the pistol, and pulls the trigger. The gun is not yet loaded, so all we hear is the click, but it will definitely work. It's also obvious that* JESSIE *knows her way around a gun.* MAMA *cannot speak.*) I had Cecil's all ready in there, just in case I couldn't find this one, but I'd rather use Daddy's.

MAMA Those bullets are at least fifteen years old.

JESSIE (*pulling out another box*) These are from last week.

MAMA Where did you get those?

JESSIE Feed store Dawson told me about.

MAMA Dawson!

JESSIE I told him I was worried about prowlers. He said he thought it was a good idea. He told me what kind to ask for.

MAMA If he had any idea . . .

JESSIE He took it as a compliment. He thought I might be taking an interest in things. He got through telling me all about the bullets and then he said we ought to talk like this more often.

MAMA And where was I while this was going on?

JESSIE On the phone with Agnes. About the milk can, I guess. Anyway, I asked Dawson if he thought they'd send me some bullets and he said he'd just call for me, because he knew they'd send them if he told them to. And he was absolutely right. Here they are.

MAMA How could he do that?

JESSIE Just trying to help, Mama.

MAMA And then I told you where the gun was.

JESSIE (*smiling, enjoying this joke*) See? Everybody's doing what they can.

MAMA You told me it was for protection!

JESSIE It *is!* I'm still doing your nails, though. Want to try that new Chinaberry color?

MAMA Well, I'm calling Dawson right now. We'll just see what he has to say about this little stunt.

JESSIE Dawson doesn't have any more to do with this.

MAMA He's your brother.

JESSIE And that's all.

MAMA (*stands up, moves toward the phone*) Dawson will put a stop to this. Yes he will. He'll take the gun away.

JESSIE If you call him, I'll just have to do it before he gets here. Soon as you hang up the phone, I'll just walk in the bedroom and lock the door. Dawson will get here just in time to help you clean up. Go ahead, call him. Then call the police. Then call the funeral home. Then call Loretta and see if *she'll* do your nails.

MAMA You will not! This is crazy talk, Jessie!

(MAMA *goes directly to the telephone and starts to dial, but* JESSIE *is fast, coming up behind her and taking the receiver out of her hand, putting it back down.*)

JESSIE (*firm and quiet*) I said no. This is private. Dawson is not invited.

MAMA Just me.

JESSIE I don't want anybody else over here. Just you and me. If Dawson comes over, it'll make me feel stupid for not doing it ten years ago.

MAMA I think we better call the doctor. Or how about the ambulance. You like that one driver, I know. What's his name, Timmy? Get you somebody to talk to.

JESSIE (*going back to her chair*) I'm through talking, Mama. You're it. No more.

MAMA We're just going to sit around like every other night in the world and then you're going to kill yourself? (JESSIE *doesn't answer.*) You'll miss. (*Again there is no response.*) You'll just wind up a vegetable. How would you like that? Shoot your ear off? You know what the doctor said about getting excited. You'll cock the pistol and have a fit.

JESSIE I think I can kill myself, Mama.

MAMA You're not going to kill yourself, Jessie. You're not even upset! (JESSIE *smiles, or laughs quietly, and* MAMA *tries a different approach.*) People don't really kill themselves, Jessie. No, mam, doesn't make sense, unless you're retarded or deranged, and you're as normal as they come, Jessie, for the most part. We're all *afraid* to die.

JESSIE I'm not, Mama. I'm cold all the time, anyway.

MAMA That's ridiculous.

JESSIE It's exactly what I want. It's dark and quiet.

MAMA So is the back yard, Jessie! Close your eyes. Stuff cotton in your ears. Take a nap! It's quiet in your room. I'll leave the TV off all night.

JESSIE So quiet I don't know it's quiet. So nobody can get me.

MAMA You don't know what dead is like. It might not be quiet at all. What if it's like an alarm clock and you can't wake up so you can't shut it off. Ever.

JESSIE Dead is everybody and everything I ever knew, gone. Dead is dead quiet.

MAMA It's a sin. You'll go to hell.

JESSIE Uh-huh.

MAMA You will!

JESSIE Jesus was a suicide, if you ask me.

MAMA You'll go to hell just for saying that. Jessie!

JESSIE (*with a genuine surprise*) I didn't know I thought that.

MAMA Jessie!

(JESSIE *doesn't answer. She puts the now-loaded gun back in the box and crosses to the kitchen. But* MAMA *is afraid she's headed for the bedroom.*)

MAMA (*in a panic*) You can't use my towels! They're my towels. I've had them for a long time. I like my towels.

JESSIE I asked you if you wanted that swimming towel and you said you didn't.

MAMA And you can't use your father's gun, either. It's mine now, too. And you can't do it in my house.

JESSIE Oh, come on.

MAMA No. You can't do it. I won't let you. The house is in my name.

JESSIE I have to go in the bedroom and lock the door behind me so they won't arrest you for killing me. They'll probably test your hands for gunpowder, anyway, but you'll pass.

MAMA Not in my house!

JESSIE If I'd known you were going to act like this, I wouldn't have told you.

MAMA How am I supposed to act? Tell you to go ahead? O.K. by me, sugar? Might try it myself. What took you so long?

JESSIE There's just no point in fighting me over it, that's all. Want some coffee?

MAMA Your birthday's coming up, Jessie. Don't you want to know what we got you?

JESSIE You got me dusting powder, Loretta got me a new housecoat, pink probably, and Dawson got me new slippers, too small, but they go with the robe, he'll say. (MAMA *cannot speak.*) Right? (*Apparently* JESSIE *is right.*) Be back in a minute.

(JESSIE *takes the gun box, puts it on top of the stack of towels and garbage bags, and takes them into her bedroom.* MAMA, *alone for a moment, goes to the phone, picks up the receiver, looks toward the bedroom, starts to dial, and then replaces the receiver in its cradle as* JESSIE *walks back into the room.* JESSIE *wonders, silently. They have lived together for so long there is very rarely any reason for one to ask what the other was about to do.*)

MAMA I started to, but I didn't. I didn't call him.

JESSIE Good. Thank you.

MAMA (*starting over, a new approach*) What's this all about, Jessie?

JESSIE About?

(JESSIE *now begins the next task she had "on the schedule," which is refilling all the candy jars, taking the empty papers out of the boxes of chocolates, etc.* MAMA *generally snitches when* JESSIE *does this. Not tonight, though. Nevertheless,* JESSIE *offers.*)

MAMA What did I do?

JESSIE Nothing. Want a caramel?

MAMA (*ignoring the candy*) You're mad at me.

JESSIE Not a bit. I am worried about you, but I'm going to do what I can before I go. We're not just going to sit around tonight. I made a list of things.

MAMA What things?

JESSIE How the washer works. Things like that.

MAMA I know how the washer works. You put the clothes in. You put the soap in. You turn it on. You wait.

JESSIE You do something else. You don't just wait.

MAMA Whatever else you find to do, you're still mainly waiting. The waiting's the worst part of it. The waiting's what you pay somebody else to do, if you can.

JESSIE (*nodding*) O.K. Where do we keep the soap?

MAMA I could find it.

JESSIE See?

MAMA If you're mad about doing the wash, we can get Loretta to do it.

JESSIE Oh now, that might be worth staying to see.

MAMA She'd never in her life, would she?

JESSIE Nope.

MAMA What's the matter with her?

JESSIE She thinks she's better than we are. She's not.

MAMA Maybe if she didn't wear that yellow all the time.

JESSIE The washer repair number is on a little card taped to the side of the machine.

MAMA Loretta doesn't ever have to come over here again. Dawson can just leave her at home when he comes. And we don't ever have to see Dawson either if he bothers you. Does he bother you?

JESSIE Sure he does. Be sure you clean out the lint tray every time you use the dryer. But don't ever put your house shoes in, it'll melt the soles.

MAMA What does Dawson do, that bothers you?

JESSIE He just calls me Jess like he knows who he's talking to. He's always wondering what I do all day. I mean, I wonder that myself, but it's my day, so it's mine to wonder about, not his.

MAMA Family is just accident, Jessie. It's nothing personal, hon. They don't mean to get on your nerves. They don't even mean to be your family, they just are.

JESSIE They know too much.

MAMA About what?

JESSIE They know things about you, and they learned it before you had a chance to say whether you wanted them to know it or not. They were there when it happened and it don't belong to them, it belongs to you, only they got it. Like my mail-order bra got delivered to their house.

MAMA By accident!

JESSIE All the same . . . they opened it. They saw the little rosebuds on it. (*offering her another candy*) Chewy mint?

MAMA (*shaking her head no*) What do they know about you? I'll tell them never to talk about it again. Is it Ricky or Cecil or your fits or your hair is falling out or you drink too much coffee or you never go out of the house or what?

JESSIE I just don't like their talk. The account at the grocery is in Dawson's name when you call. The number's on a whole list of numbers on the back cover of the phone book.

MAMA Well! Now we're getting somewhere. They're none of them ever setting foot in this house again.

JESSIE It's not them, Mother. I wouldn't kill myself just to get away from them.

MAMA You leave the room when they come over, anyway.

JESSIE I stay as long as I can. Besides, it's you they come to see.

MAMA That's because I stay in the room when they come.

JESSIE It's not them.

MAMA Then what is it?

JESSIE (*checking the list on her note pad*) The grocery won't deliver on Saturday anymore. And if you want your order the same day, you have to call before ten. And they won't deliver less than fifteen dollars' worth. What I do is tell them what we need and tell them to add on cigarettes until it gets to fifteen dollars.

MAMA It's Ricky. You're trying to get through to him.

JESSIE If I thought I could do that, I would stay.

MAMA Make him sorry he hurt you, then. That's it, isn't it?

JESSIE He's hurt me, I've hurt him. We're about even.

MAMA You'll be telling him killing is O.K. with you, you know. Want him to start killing next? Nothing wrong with it. Mom did it.

JESSIE Only a matter of time, anyway, Mama. When the call comes, you let Dawson handle it.

MAMA Honey, nothing says those calls are always going to be some new trouble he's into. You could get one that he's got a job, that he's getting married, or how about he's joined the army, wouldn't that be nice?

JESSIE If you call the Sweet Tooth before you call the grocery, that Susie will take your fudge next door to the grocery and it'll all come out together. Be sure you talk to Susie, though. She won't let them put it in the bottom of a sack like that one time, remember?

MAMA Ricky could come over, you know. What if he calls us?

JESSIE It's not Ricky, Mama.

MAMA Or anybody could call us, Jessie.

JESSIE Not on Saturday night, Mama.

MAMA Then what is it? Are you sick? If your gums are swelling again, we can get you to the dentist in the morning.

JESSIE No. Can you order your medicine or do you want Dawson to? I've got a note to him. I'll add that to it if you want.

MAMA Your eyes don't look right. I thought so yesterday.

JESSIE That was just the ragweed. I'm not sick.

MAMA Epilepsy is sick, Jessie.

JESSIE It won't kill me. (*a pause*) If it would, I wouldn't have to.

MAMA You don't *have* to.

JESSIE No, I don't. That's what I like about it.

MAMA Well, I won't let you!

JESSIE It's not up to you.

MAMA Jessie!

JESSIE I want to hang a big sign around my neck, like Daddy's on the barn. GONE FISHING.

MAMA You don't like it here.

JESSIE (*smiling*) Exactly.

MAMA I meant here in my house.

JESSIE I know you did.

MAMA You never should have moved back in here with me. If you'd kept your little house or found another place when Cecil left you, you'd have made some new friends at least. Had a life to lead. Had your own things around you. Give Ricky a place to come see you. You never should've come here.

JESSIE Maybe.

MAMA But I didn't force you, did I?

JESSIE If it was a mistake, we made it together. You took me in. I appreciate that.

MAMA You didn't have any business being by yourself right then, but I can see how you might want a place of your own. A grown woman should . . .

JESSIE Mama . . . I'm just not having a very good time and I don't have any reason to think it'll get anything but worse. I'm tired. I'm hurt. I'm sad. I feel used.

MAMA Tired of what?

JESSIE It all.

MAMA What does that mean?

JESSIE I can't say it any better.

MAMA Well, you'll have to say it better because I'm not letting you alone till you do. What were those other things? Hurt . . . (*before* JESSIE *can answer*) You had this all ready to say to me, didn't you? Did you write this down? How long have you been thinking about this?

JESSIE Off and on, ten years. On all the time, since Christmas.

MAMA What happened at Christmas?

JESSIE Nothing.

MAMA So why Christmas?

JESSIE That's it. On the nose.

(*A pause.* MAMA *knows exactly what* JESSIE *means. She was there, too, after all.*)

JESSIE (*putting the candy sacks away*) See where all this is? Red hots up front, sour balls and horehound mixed together in this one sack. New packages of toffee and licorice right in back there.

MAMA Go back to your list. You're hurt by what?

JESSIE (MAMA *knows perfectly well.*) Mama . . .

MAMA O.K. Sad about what? There's nothing real sad going on right now. If it was after your divorce or something, that would make sense.

JESSIE (*looking at her list, then opening the drawer*) Now, this drawer has everything in it that there's no better place for. Extension cords, batteries for the radio, extra lighters, sandpaper, masking tape, Elmer's glue, thumbtacks, that kind of stuff. The mousetraps are under the sink, but you call Dawson if you've got one and let him do it.

MAMA Sad about what?

JESSIE The way things are.

MAMA Not good enough. What things?

JESSIE Oh, everything from you and me to Red China.

MAMA I think we can leave the Chinese out of this.

JESSIE (*crosses back into the living room*) There's extra light bulbs in a box in the hall closet. And we've got a couple of packages of fuses in the fuse box. There's candles and matches in the top of the broom closet, but if the lights go out, just call Dawson and sit tight. But don't open the refrigerator door. Things will stay cool in there as long as you keep the door shut.

MAMA I asked you a question.

JESSIE I read the paper. I don't like how things are. And they're not any better out there than they are in here.

MAMA If you're doing this because of the newspapers, I can sure fix that!

JESSIE There's just more of it on TV.

MAMA (*kicking the television set*) Take it out, then!

JESSIE You wouldn't do that.

MAMA Watch me.

JESSIE What would you do all day?

MAMA (*desperately*) Sing. (JESSIE *laughs.*) I would, too. You want to watch? I'll sing till morning to keep you alive, Jessie, please!

JESSIE No. (*then affectionately*) It's a funny idea, though. What do you sing?

MAMA (*Has no idea how to answer this.*) We've got a good life here!

JESSIE (*going back into the kitchen*) I called this morning and canceled the papers, except for Sunday, for your puzzles; you'll still get that one.

MAMA Let's get another dog, Jessie! You liked a big dog, now, didn't you? That King dog, didn't you?

JESSIE (*washing her hands*) I did like that King dog, yes.

MAMA I'm so dumb. He's the one run under the tractor.

JESSIE That makes him dumb, not you.

MAMA For bringing it up.

JESSIE It's O.K. Handi-Wipes and sponges under the sink.

MAMA We could get a new dog and keep him in the house. Dogs are cheap!

JESSIE (*getting big pill jars out of the cabinet*) No.

MAMA Something for you to take care of.

JESSIE I've had you, Mama.

MAMA (*frantically starting to fill pill bottles*) You do too much for me. I can fill pill bottles all day, Jessie, and change the shelf paper and wash the floor when I get through. You just watch me. You don't have to do another thing in this house if you don't want to. You don't have to take care of me, Jessie.

JESSIE I know that. You've just been letting me do it so I'll have something to do, haven't you?

MAMA (*realizing this was a mistake*) I don't do it as well as you. I just meant if it tires you out or makes you feel used . . .

JESSIE Mama, I know you used to ride the bus. Riding the bus and it's hot and bumpy and crowded and too noisy and more than anything in the world you want to get off and the only reason in the world you don't get off is it's still fifty blocks from where you're going? Well, I can get off right now if I want to, because even if I ride fifty more years and get off then, it's the same place when I step down to it. Whenever I feel like it, I can get off. As soon as I've had enough, it's my stop. I've had enough.

MAMA You're feeling sorry for yourself!

JESSIE The plumber's helper is under the sink, too.

MAMA You're not having a good time! Whoever promised you a good time? Do you think I've had a good time?

JESSIE I think you're pretty happy, yeah. You have things you like to do.

MAMA Like what?

JESSIE Like crochet.

MAMA I'll teach you to crochet.

JESSIE I can't do any of that nice work, Mama.

MAMA Good time don't come looking for you, Jessie. You could work some puzzles or put in a garden or go to the store. Let's call a taxi and go to the A&P!

JESSIE I shopped you up for about two weeks already. You're not going to need toilet paper till Thanksgiving.

MAMA (*interrupting*) You're acting like some little brat, Jessie. You're mad and everybody's boring and you don't have anything to do and you don't like me and you don't like going out and you don't like staying in and you never talk on the phone and you don't watch TV and you're miserable and it's your own sweet fault.

JESSIE And it's time I did something about it.

MAMA Not something like killing yourself. Something like . . . buying us all new dishes! I'd like that. Or maybe the doctor would let you get a driver's license now, or I know what let's do right this minute, let's rearrange the furniture.

JESSIE I'll do that. If you want. I always thought if the TV was somewhere else, you wouldn't get such a glare on it during the day. I'll do whatever you want before I go.

MAMA (*badly frightened by those words*) You could get a job!

JESSIE I took that telephone sales job and I didn't even make enough money to pay the phone bill, and I tried to work at the gift shop at the hospital and they said I made people real uncomfortable smiling at them the way I did.

MAMA You could keep books. You kept your dad's books.

JESSIE But nobody ever checked them.

MAMA When he died, they checked them.

JESSIE And that's when they took the books away from me.

MAMA That's because without him there wasn't any business, Jessie!

JESSIE (*putting the pill bottles away*) You know I couldn't work. I can't do anything. I've never been around people my whole life except when I went to the hospital. I could have a seizure any time. What good would a job do? The kind of job I could get would make me feel worse.

MAMA Jessie!

JESSIE It's true!

MAMA It's what you think is true!

JESSIE (*struck by the clarity of that*) That's right. It's what I think is true.

MAMA (*hysterically*) But I can't do anything about that!

JESSIE (*quietly*) No. You can't. (MAMA *slumps, if not physically, at least emotionally.*) And I can't do anything either, about my life, to change it, make it better, make me feel better about it. Like it better, make it work. But I can stop it. Shut it down, turn it off like the radio when there's nothing on I want to listen to. It's all I really have that belongs to me and I'm going to say what happens to it. And it's going to stop. And I'm going to stop it. So. Let's just have a good time.

MAMA Have a good time.

JESSIE We can't go on fussing all night. I mean, I could ask you things I always wanted to know and you could make me some hot chocolate. The old way.

MAMA (*in despair*) It takes cocoa, Jessie.

JESSIE (*gets it out of the cabinet*) I bought cocoa, Mama. And I'd like to have a caramel apple and do your nails.

MAMA You didn't eat a bite of supper.

JESSIE Does that mean I can't have a caramel apple?

MAMA Of course not. I mean . . . (*smiling a little*) Of course you can have a caramel apple.

JESSIE I thought I could.

MAMA I make the best caramel apples in the world.

JESSIE I know you do.

MAMA Or used to. And you don't get cocoa like mine anywhere anymore.

JESSIE It takes time, I know, but . . .

MAMA The salt is the trick.

JESSIE Trouble and everything.

MAMA (*backing away toward the stove*) It's no trouble. What trouble? You put it in the pan and stir it up. All right. Fine. Caramel apples. Cocoa. O.K.

(JESSIE *walks to the counter to retrieve her cigarettes as* MAMA *looks for the right pan. There are brief near-smiles, and maybe* MAMA *clears her throat. We have a truce, for the moment. A genuine but nevertheless uneasy one.* JESSIE, *who has been in constant motion since the beginning, now seems content to sit.*

MAMA *starts looking for a pan to make the cocoa, getting out all the pans in the cabinets in the process. It looks like she's making a mess on purpose so* JESSIE *will have to put them all away again.* MAMA *is buying time, or trying to, and entertaining.*)

JESSIE You talk to Agnes today?

MAMA She's calling me from a pay phone this week. God only knows why. She has a perfectly good Trimline at home.

JESSIE (*laughing*) Well, how is she?

MAMA How is she every day, Jessie? Nuts.

JESSIE Is she really crazy or just silly?

MAMA No, she's really crazy. She was probably using the pay phone because she had another little fire problem at home.

JESSIE Mother . . .

MAMA I'm serious! Agnes Fletcher's burned down every house she ever lived in. Eight fires, and she's due for a new one any day now.

JESSIE (*laughing*) No!

MAMA Wouldn't surprise me a bit.

JESSIE (*laughing*) Why didn't you tell me this before? Why isn't she locked up somewhere?

MAMA 'Cause nobody ever got hurt, I guess. Agnes woke everybody up to watch the fires as soon as she set 'em. One time she set out porch chairs and served lemonade.

JESSIE (*shaking her head*) Real lemonade?

MAMA The houses they lived in, you knew they were going to fall down anyway, so why wait for it, is all I could ever make out about it. Agnes likes a feeling of accomplishment.

JESSIE Good for her.

MAMA (*finding the pan she wants*) Why are you asking about Agnes? One cup or two?

JESSIE One. She's your friend. No marshmallows.

MAMA (*getting the milk, etc.*) You have to have marshmallows. That's the old way, Jess. Two or three? Three is better.

JESSIE Three, then. Her whole house burns up? Her clothes and pillows and everything? I'm not sure I believe this.

MAMA When she was a girl, Jess, not now. Long time ago. But she's still got it in her, I'm sure of it.

JESSIE She wouldn't burn her house down now. Where would she go? She can't get Buster to build her a new one, he's dead. How could she burn it up?

MAMA Be exciting, though, if she did. You never know.

JESSIE You do too know, Mama. She wouldn't do it.

MAMA (*forced to admit, but reluctant*) I guess not.

JESSIE What else? Why does she wear all those whistles around her neck?

MAMA Why does she have a house full of birds?

JESSIE I didn't know she had a house full of birds!

MAMA Well, she does. And she says they just follow her home. Well, I know for a fact she's still paying on the last parrot she bought. You gotta keep your life filled up, she says. She says a lot of stupid things. (JESSIE *laughs,* MAMA *continues, convinced she's getting somewhere.*) It's all that okra she eats. You can't just willy-nilly eat okra two meals a day and expect to get away with it. Made her crazy.

JESSIE She really eats okra twice a day? Where does she get it in the winter?

MAMA Well, she eats it a lot. Maybe not two meals, but . . .

JESSIE More than the average person.

MAMA (*beginning to get irritated*) I don't know how much okra the average person eats.

JESSIE Do you know how much okra Agnes eats?

MAMA No.

JESSIE How many birds does she have?

MAMA Two.

JESSIE Then what are the whistles for?

MAMA They're not real whistles. Just little plastic ones on a necklace she won playing Bingo, and I only told you about it because I thought I might get a laugh out of you for once even if it wasn't the truth, Jessie. Things don't have to be true to talk about 'em, you know.

JESSIE Why won't she come over here?

(MAMA *is suddenly quiet, but the cocoa and milk are in the pan now, so she lights the stove and starts stirring.*)

MAMA Well now, what a good idea. We should've had more cocoa. Cocoa is perfect.

JESSIE Except you don't like milk.

MAMA (*another attempt, but not as energetic*) I hate milk. Coats your throat as bad as okra. Something just downright disgusting about it.

JESSIE It's because of me, isn't it?

MAMA No, Jess.

JESSIE Yes, Mama.

MAMA O.K. Yes, then, but she's crazy. She's as crazy as they come. She's a lunatic.

JESSIE What is it exactly? Did I say something, sometime? Or did she see me have a fit and's afraid I might have another one if she came over, or what?

MAMA I guess.

JESSIE You guess what? What's she ever said? She must've given you some reason.

MAMA Your hands are cold.

JESSIE What difference does that make?

MAMA "Like a corpse," she says, "and I'm gonna be one soon enough as it is."

JESSIE That's crazy.

MAMA That's Agnes. "Jessie's shook the hand of death and I can't take the chance it's catching, Thelma, so I ain't comin' over, and you can understand or not, but I ain't comin'. I'll come up the driveway, but that's as far as I go."

JESSIE (*laughing, relieved*) I thought she didn't like me! She's scared of me! How about that! Scared of me.

MAMA I could make her come over here, Jessie. I could call her up right now and she could bring the birds and come visit. I didn't know you ever thought about her at all. I'll tell her she just has to come and she'll come, all right. She owes me one.

JESSIE No, that's all right. I just wondered about it. When I'm in the hospital, does she come over here?

MAMA Her kitchen is just a tiny thing. When she comes over here, she feels like . . . (*toning it down a little*) Well, we all like a change of scene, don't we?

JESSIE (*playing along*) Sure we do. Plus there's no birds diving around.

MAMA I hate those birds. She says I don't understand them. What's there to understand about birds?

JESSIE Why Agnes likes them, for one thing. Why they stay with her when they could be outside with the other birds. What their singing means. How they fly. What they think Agnes is.

MAMA Why do you have to know so much about things, Jessie? There's just not that much *to* things that I could ever see.

JESSIE That you could ever *tell*, you mean. You didn't have to lie to me about Agnes.

MAMA I didn't lie. You never asked before!

JESSIE You lied about setting fire to all those houses and about how many birds she has and how much okra she eats and why she won't come over here. If I have to keep dragging the truth out of you, this is going to take all night.

MAMA That's fine with me. I'm not a bit sleepy.

JESSIE Mama . . .

MAMA All right. Ask me whatever you want. Here.

(They come to an awkward stop, as the cocoa is ready and MAMA *pours it into the cups* JESSIE *has set on the table.)*

JESSIE *(as* MAMA *takes her first sip)* Did you love Daddy?

MAMA No.

JESSIE *(pleased that* MAMA *understands the rules better now)* I didn't think so. Were you really fifteen when you married him?

MAMA The way he told it? I'm sitting in the mud, he comes along, drags me in the kitchen, "She's been there ever since"?

JESSIE Yes.

MAMA No. It was a big fat lie, the whole thing. He just thought it was funnier that way. God, this milk in here.

JESSIE The cocoa helps.

MAMA *(pleased that they agree on this, at least)* Not enough, though, does it? You can still taste it, can't you?

JESSIE Yeah, it's pretty bad. I thought it was my memory that was bad, but it's not. It's the milk, all right.

MAMA It's a real waste of chocolate. You don't have to finish it.

JESSIE *(putting her cup down)* Thanks, though.

MAMA I should've known not to make it. I knew you wouldn't like it. You never did like it.

JESSIE You didn't ever love him, or he did something and you stopped loving him, or what?

MAMA He felt sorry for me. He wanted a plain country woman and that's what he married, and then he held it against me the rest of my life like I was supposed to change and surprise him somehow. Like I remember this one day he was standing on the porch and I told him to get a shirt on and he went in and got one and then he said, real peaceful, but to the point, "You're right, Thelma. If God had meant for people to go around without any clothes on, they'd have been born that way."

JESSIE *(sees* MAMA*'s hurt)* He didn't mean anything by that, Mama.

MAMA He never said a word he didn't have to, Jessie. That was probably all he'd said to me all day, Jessie. So if he said it, there was something to it, but I never did figure that one out. What did that mean?

JESSIE I don't know. I liked him better than you did, but I didn't know him any better.

MAMA How could I love him, Jessie. I didn't have a thing he wanted. (JESSIE *doesn't answer.*) He got his share, though. You loved him enough for both of us. You followed him around like some . . . Jessie, all the man ever did was farm and sit . . . and try to think of somebody to sell the farm to.

JESSIE Or make me a boyfriend out of pipe cleaners and sit back and smile like the stick man was about to dance and wasn't I going to get a kick out of that. Or sit up with a sick cow all night and leave me a chain of sleepy stick elephants on my bed in the morning.

MAMA Or just sit.

JESSIE I liked him sitting. Big old faded blue man in the chair. Quiet.

MAMA Agnes gets more talk out of her birds than I got from the two of you. He could've had that GONE FISHING sign around his neck in that chair. I saw him stare off at the water. I saw him look at the weather rolling in. I got where I could practically see the boat myself. But you, you knew what he was thinking about and you're going to tell me.

JESSIE I don't know, Mama! His life, I guess. His corn. His boots. Us. Things. You know.

MAMA No, I don't know, Jessie! You had those quiet little conversations after supper every night. What were you whispering about?

JESSIE We weren't whispering, you were just across the room.

MAMA What did you talk about?

JESSIE We talked about why black socks are warmer than blue socks. Is that something to go tell Mother? You were just jealous because I'd rather talk to him than wash the dishes with you.

MAMA I was jealous because you'd rather talk to him than anything! (JESSIE *reaches across the table for the small clock and starts to wind it.*) If I had died instead of him, he wouldn't have taken you in like I did.

JESSIE I wouldn't have expected him to.

MAMA Then what would you have done?

JESSIE Come visit.

MAMA Oh, I see. He died and left you stuck with me and you're mad about it.

JESSIE (*getting up from the table*) Not anymore. He didn't mean to. I didn't have to come here. We've been through this.

MAMA He felt sorry for you, too, Jessie, don't kid yourself about that. He said you were a runt and he said it from the day you were born and he said you didn't have a chance.

JESSIE (*getting the canister of sugar and starting to refill the sugar bowl*) I know he loved me.

MAMA What if he did? It didn't change anything.

JESSIE It didn't have to. I miss him.

MAMA He never really went fishing, you know. Never once. His tackle box was full of chewing tobacco and all he ever did was drive out to the lake and sit in his car. Dawson told me. And Bennie at the bait shop, he told Dawson. They all laughed about it. And he'd come back from fishing and all he'd have to show for it was . . . a whole pipe-cleaner *family*—chickens, pigs, a dog with a bad leg—it was creepy strange. It made me sick to look at them and I hid his pipe cleaners a couple of times but he always had more somewhere.

JESSIE I thought it might be better for you after he died. You'd get interested in things. Breathe better. Change somehow.

MAMA Into what? The Queen? A clerk in a shoe store? Why should I? Because he said to? Because you said to? (JESSIE *shakes her head.*) Well I wasn't here for his entertainment and I'm not here for yours either, Jessie. I don't know what I'm here for, but then I don't think about it. (*realizing what all this means*) But I bet you wouldn't be killing yourself if he were still alive. That's a fine thing to figure out, isn't it?

JESSIE (*filling the honey jar now*) That's not true.

MAMA Oh no? Then what were you asking about him for? Why did you want to know if I loved him?

JESSIE I didn't think you did, that's all.

MAMA Fine then. You were right. Do you feel better now?

JESSIE (*cleaning the honey jar carefully*) It feels good to be right about it.

MAMA It didn't matter whether I loved him. It didn't matter to me and it didn't matter to him. And it didn't mean we didn't get along. It wasn't important. We didn't talk about it. (*sweeping the pots off the cabinet*) Take all these pots out to the porch!

JESSIE What for?

MAMA Just leave me this one pan (*She jerks the silverware drawer open.*) Get me one knife, one fork, one big spoon, and the can opener, and put them out where I can get them. (*starts throwing knives and forks in one of the pans*)

JESSIE Don't do that! I just straightened that drawer!

MAMA (*throwing the pan in the sink*) And throw out all the plates and cups. I'll use paper. Loretta can have what she wants and Dawson can sell the rest.

JESSIE (*calmly*) What are you doing?

MAMA I'm not going to cook. I never liked it, anyway. I like candy. Wrapped in plastic or coming in sacks. And tuna. I like tuna. I'll eat tuna, thank you.

JESSIE (*taking the pan out of the sink*) What if you want to make apple butter? You can't make apple butter in that little pan. What if you leave carrots on cooking and burn up that pan?

MAMA I don't like carrots.

JESSIE What if the strawberries are good this year and you want to go picking with Agnes.

MAMA I'll tell her to bring a pan. You said you would do whatever I wanted! I don't want a bunch of pans cluttering up my cabinets I can't get down to, anyway. Throw them out. Every last one.

JESSIE (*gathering up the pots*) I'm putting them all back in. I'm not taking them to the porch. If you want them, they'll be here. You'll bend down and get them, like you got the one for the cocoa. And if somebody else comes over here to cook, they'll have something to cook in, and that's the end of it!

MAMA Who's going to come cook here?

JESSIE Agnes.

MAMA In my pots. Not on your life.

JESSIE There's no reason why the two of you couldn't just live here together. Be cheaper for both of you and somebody to talk to. And if the birds bothered you, well, one day when Agnes is out getting her hair done, you could take them all for a walk!

MAMA (*as* JESSIE *straightens the silverware*) So that's why you're pestering me about Agnes. You think you can rest easy if you get me a new babysitter? Well, I don't want to live with Agnes. I barely want to talk with Agnes. She's just around. We go back, that's all. I'm not letting Agnes near this place. You don't get off as easy as that, child.

JESSIE O.K., then. It's just something to think about.

MAMA I don't like things to think about. I like things to go on.

JESSIE (*closing the silverware drawer*) I want to know what Daddy said to you the night he died. You came storming out of his room and said I could wait it out with him if I wanted to, but you were going to watch *Gunsmoke*. What did he say to you?

MAMA He didn't have *anything* to say to me, Jessie. That's why I left. He didn't say a thing. It was his last chance not to talk to me and he took full advantage of it.

JESSIE (*after a moment*) I'm sorry you didn't love him. Sorry for you, I mean. He seemed like a nice man.

MAMA (*as* JESSIE *walks to the refrigerator*) Ready for your apple now?

JESSIE Soon as I'm through here, Mama.

MAMA You won't like the apple, either. It'll be just like the cocoa. You never liked eating at all, did you? Any of it! What have you been living on all these years, toothpaste?

JESSIE (*as she starts to clean out the refrigerator*) Now, you know the milkman comes on Wednesdays and Saturdays, and he leaves the order blank in an egg box, and you give the bills to Dawson once a month.

MAMA Do they still make that orangeade?

JESSIE It's not orangeade, it's just orange.

MAMA I'm going to get some. I thought they stopped making it. You just stopped ordering it.

JESSIE You should drink milk.

MAMA Not anymore, I'm not. That hot chocolate was the last. Hooray.

JESSIE (*getting the garbage can from under the sink*) I told them to keep delivering a quart a week no matter what you said. I told them you'd run out of Cokes and you'd have to drink it. I told them I knew you wouldn't pour it on the ground . . .

MAMA (*finishing her sentence*) And you told them you weren't going to be ordering anymore?

JESSIE I told them I was taking a little holiday and to look after you.

MAMA And they didn't think something was funny about that? You who doesn't go to the front steps? You, who only sees the driveway looking down from a stretcher passed out cold?

JESSIE (*enjoying this, but not laughing*) They said it was about time, but why didn't I take you with me? And I said I didn't think you'd want to go, and they said, "Yeah, everybody's got their own idea of vacation."

MAMA I guess you think that's funny.

JESSIE (*pulling jars out of the refrigerator*) You know there never was any reason to call the ambulance for me. All they ever did for me in the emergency room was let me wake up. I could've done that here. Now, I'll just call them out and you say yes or no. I know you like pickles. Ketchup?

MAMA Keep it.

JESSIE We've had this since last Fourth of July.

MAMA Keep the ketchup. Keep it all.

JESSIE Are you going to drink ketchup from the bottle or what? How can you want your food and not want your pots to cook it in? This stuff will all spoil in here, Mother.

MAMA Nothing I ever did was good enough for you and I want to know why.

JESSIE That's not true.

MAMA And I want to know why you've lived here this long feeling the way you do.

JESSIE You have no earthly idea how I feel.

MAMA Well, how could I? You're real far back there, Jessie.

JESSIE Back where?

MAMA What's it like over there, where you are? Do people always say the right thing or get whatever they want, or what?

JESSIE What are you talking about?

MAMA Why do you read the newspaper? Why don't you wear that sweater I made for you? Do you remember how I used to look, or am I just any old woman now? When you have a fit, do you see stars or what? How did you fall off the horse, really? Why did Cecil leave you? Where did you put my old glasses?

JESSIE (*stunned by* MAMA*'s intensity*) They're in the bottom drawer of your dresser in an old Milk of Magnesia box. Cecil left me because he made me choose between him and smoking.

MAMA Jessie, I know he wasn't that dumb.

JESSIE I never understood why he hated it so much when it's so good. Smoking is the only thing I know that's always just what you think it's going to be. Just like it was the last time, right there when you want it and real quiet.

MAMA Your fits made him sick and you know it.

JESSIE Say seizures, not fits. Seizures.

MAMA It's the same thing. A seizure in the hospital is a fit at home.

JESSIE They didn't bother him at all. Except he did feel responsible for it. It *was* his idea to go horseback riding that day. It was his idea I could do *anything* if I just made up my mind to. I fell off the horse because I didn't know how to hold on. Cecil left for pretty much the same reason.

MAMA He had a girl, Jessie. I walked right in on them in the toolshed.

JESSIE (*after a moment*) O.K. That's fair. (*lighting another cigarette*) Was she very pretty?

MAMA She was Agnes's girl, Carlene. Judge for yourself.

JESSIE (*as she walks to the living room*) I guess you and Agnes had a good talk about that, huh?

MAMA I never thought he was good enough for you. They moved here from Tennessee, you know.

JESSIE What are you talking about? You liked him better than I did. You flirted him out here to build your porch or I'd never even met him at all. You thought maybe he'd help you out around the place, come in and get some coffee and talk to you. God knows what you thought. All that curly hair.

MAMA He's the best carpenter I ever saw. That little house of yours will still be standing at the end of the world, Jessie.

JESSIE You didn't need a porch, Mama.

MAMA All right! I wanted you to have a husband.

JESSIE And I couldn't get one on my own, of course.

MAMA How were you going to get a husband never opening your mouth to a living soul?

JESSIE So I was quiet about it, so what?

MAMA So I should have let you just sit here? Sit like your daddy? Sit here?

JESSIE Maybe.

MAMA Well, I didn't think so.

JESSIE Well, what did you know?

MAMA I never said I knew much. How was I supposed to learn anything living out here? I didn't know enough to do half the things I did in my life. Things happen. You do what you can about them and you see what happens next. I married you off to the wrong man, I admit that. So I took you in when he left. I'm sorry.

JESSIE He wasn't the wrong man.

MAMA He didn't love you, Jessie, or he wouldn't have left.

JESSIE He wasn't the wrong man, Mama. I loved Cecil so much. And I tried to get more exercise and I tried to stay awake. I tried to learn to ride a horse. And I tried to stay outside with him, but he always knew I was trying, so it didn't work.

MAMA He was a selfish man. He told me once he hated to see people move into his houses after he built them. He knew they'd mess them up.

JESSIE I loved that bridge he built over the creek in back of the house. It didn't have to be anything special, a couple of boards would have been just fine, but he used that yellow pine and rubbed it so smooth . . .

MAMA He had responsibilities here. He had a wife and son here and he failed you.

JESSIE Or that baby bed he built for Ricky. I told him he didn't have to spend so much time on it, but he said it had to last, and the thing ended up weighing two hundred pounds and I couldn't move it. I said, "How long does a baby bed have to last, anyway?" But maybe he thought if it was strong enough, it might keep Ricky a baby.

MAMA Ricky is too much like Cecil.

JESSIE He is not. Ricky is as much like me as it's possible for any human to be. We even wear the same size pants. These are his, I think.

MAMA That's just the same size. That's not you're the same person.

JESSIE I see it on his face. I hear it when he talks. We look out at the world and we see the same thing: Not Fair. And the only difference between us is Ricky's out there trying to get even. And he knows not to trust anybody and he got it straight from me. And he knows not to try to get work, and guess where he got that. He walks around like there's loose boards in the floor, and you know who laid that floor, I did.

MAMA Ricky isn't through yet. You don't know how he'll turn out!

JESSIE (*going back to the kitchen*) Yes I do and so did Cecil. Ricky is the two of us together for all time in too small a space. And we're tearing each other apart, like always, inside that boy, and if you don't see it, then you're just blind.

MAMA Give him time, Jess.

JESSIE Oh, he'll have plenty of that. Five years for forgery, ten years for armed assault . . .

MAMA (*furious*) Stop that! (*then pleading*) Jessie, Cecil might be ready to try it again, honey, that happens sometimes. Go downtown. Find him. Talk to him. He didn't know what he had in you. Maybe he sees things different now, but you're not going to know that till you go see him. Or call him up! Right now! He might be home.

JESSIE And say what? Nothing's changed, Cecil, I'd just like to look at you, if you don't mind? No. He loved me, Mama. He just didn't know how things fall down around me like they do. I think he did the right thing. He gave himself another chance, that's all. But I did beg him to take me with him. I did tell him I would leave Ricky and you and everything I loved out here if only he would take me with him, but he couldn't and I understood that. (*pause*) I wrote that note I showed you. I wrote it. Not Cecil. I said "I'm sorry, Jessie, I can't fix it all for you." I said I'd always love me, not Cecil. But that's how he felt.

MAMA Then he should've taken you with him!

JESSIE (*picking up the garbage bag she has filled*) Mama, you don't pack your garbage when you move.

MAMA You will not call yourself garbage, Jessie.

JESSIE (*taking the bag to the big garbage can near the back door*) Just a say of saying it, Mama. Thinking about my list, that's all. (*opening the can, putting the garbage in, then securing the lid*) Well, a little more than that. I was trying to say it's all right that Cecil left. It was . . . a relief in a way. I never was what he wanted to see, so it was better when he wasn't looking at me all the time.

MAMA I'll make your apple now.

JESSIE No thanks. You get the manicure stuff and I'll be right there.

(JESSIE *ties up the big garbage bag in the can and replaces the small garbage bag under the sink, all the time trying desperately to regain her calm.* MAMA *watches, from a distance, her hand reaching unconsciously for the phone. Then she has a better idea. Or rather she thinks of the only other thing left and is willing to try it. Maybe she is even convinced it will work.*)

MAMA Jessie, I think your daddy had little . . .

JESSIE (*interrupting her*) Garbage night is Tuesday. Put it out as late as you can. The Davis's dogs get in it if you don't. (*replacing the garbage bag in the can under the sink*) And keep ordering the heavy black bags. It doesn't pay to buy the cheap ones. And I've got all the ties here with the hammers and all. Take them out of the box as soon as you open a new one and put them in this drawer. They'll get lost if you don't, and rubber bands or something else won't work.

MAMA I think your daddy had fits, too. I think he sat in his chair and had little fits. I read this a long time ago in a magazine, how little fits go, just little blackouts where maybe their eyes don't even close and people just call them "thinking spells."

JESSIE (*getting the slipcover out of the laundry basket*) I don't think you want this manicure we've been looking forward to. I washed this cover for the sofa, but it'll take both of us to get it back on.

MAMA I watched his eyes. I know that's what it was. The magazine said some people don't even know they've had one.

JESSIE Daddy would've known if he'd had fits, Mama.

MAMA The lady in this story had kept track of hers and she'd had eighty thousand of them in the last eleven years.

JESSIE Next time you wash this cover, it'll dry better if you put it on wet.

MAMA Jessie, listen to what I'm telling you. This lady had anywhere between five and five hundred fits a day and they lasted maybe fifteen seconds apiece, so that out of her life, she'd only lost about two weeks altogether, and she had a full-time secretary job and an IQ of 120.

JESSIE (*amused by* MAMA*'s approach*) You want to talk about fits, is that it?

MAMA Yes. I do. I want to say . . .

JESSIE (*interrupting*) Most of the time I wouldn't even know I'd had one, except I wake up with different clothes on, feeling like I've been run over. Sometimes I feel my head start to turn around or hear myself scream. And sometimes there *is* this dizzy stupid feeling a little before it, but if the TV's on, well, it's easy to miss.

(*As* JESSIE *and* MAMA *replace the slipcover on the sofa and the afghan on the chair, the physical struggle somehow mirrors the emotional one in the conversation.*)

MAMA I can tell when you're about to have one. Your eyes get this big! But, Jessie, you haven't . . .

JESSIE (*taking charge of this*) What do they look like? The seizures.

MAMA (*reluctant*) Different each time, Jess.

JESSIE O.K. Pick one, then. A good one. I think I want to know now.

MAMA There's not much to tell. You just . . . crumple, in a heap, like a puppet and somebody cut the strings all at once, or like the firing squad in some Mexican movie, you just slide down the wall, you know. You don't know what happens? How can you not know what happens?

JESSIE I'm busy.

MAMA That's not funny.

JESSIE I'm not laughing. My head turns around and I fall down and then what?

MAMA Well, your chest squeezes in and out, and you sound like you're gagging, sucking air in and out like you can't breathe.

JESSIE Do it for me. Make the sound for me.

MAMA I will not. It's awful-sounding.

JESSIE Yeah. It felt like it might be. What's next?

MAMA Your mouth bites down and I have to get your tongue out of the way fast, so you don't bite yourself.

JESSIE Or you. I bite you, too, don't I?

MAMA You got me once real good. I had to get a tetanus! But I know what to watch for now. And then you turn blue and the jerks start up. Like I'm standing there poking you with a cattle prod or you're sticking your finger in a light socket as fast as you can . . .

JESSIE Foaming like a mad dog the whole time.

MAMA It's bubbling, Jess, not foam like the washer overflowed, for God's sake; it's bubbling like a baby spitting up. I go get a wet washcloth, that's all. And then the jerks slow down and you wet yourself and it's over. Two minutes tops.

JESSIE How do I get to the bed?

MAMA How do you think?

JESSIE I'm too heavy for you now. How do you do it?

MAMA I call Dawson. But I get you cleaned up before he gets here and I make him leave before you wake up.

JESSIE You could just leave me on the floor.

MAMA I want you to wake up someplace nice, O.K.? (*then making a real effort*) But, Jessie, and this is the reason I even brought this up! You haven't had a seizure for a solid year. A whole year, do you realize that?

JESSIE Yeah, the phenobarb's about right now, I guess.

MAMA You bet it is. You might never have another one, ever! You might be through with it for all time!

JESSIE Could be.

MAMA You are. I know you are!

JESSIE I sure am feeling good. I really am. The double vision's gone and my gums aren't swelling. No rashes or anything. I'm feeling as good as I ever felt in my life. I'm even feeling like worrying or getting mad and I'm not afraid it will start a fit if I do, I just go ahead.

MAMA Of course you do! You can even scream at me, if you want to. I can take it. You don't have to act like you're just visiting here, Jessie. This is your house, too.

JESSIE The best part is, my memory's back.

MAMA Your memory's always been good. When couldn't you remember things? You're always reminding me what . . .

JESSIE Because I've made lists for everything. But now I remember what things mean on my lists. I see "dish towels," and I used to wonder whether I was supposed to wash them, buy them, or look for them because I wouldn't remember where I put them after I washed them, but now I know it means wrap them up, they're a present for Loretta's birthday.

MAMA (*finished with the sofa now*) You used to go looking for your lists, too, I've noticed that. You always know where they are now! (*then suddenly worried*) Loretta's birthday isn't coming up, is it?

JESSIE I made a list of all the birthdays for you. I even put yours on it. (*a small smile*) So you can call Loretta and remind her.

MAMA Let's take Loretta to Howard Johnson's and have those fried clams. I *know* you love that clam roll.

JESSIE (*slight pause*) I won't be here, Mama.

MAMA What have we just been talking about? You'll be here. You're well, Jessie. You're starting all over. You said it yourself. You're remembering things and . . .

JESSIE I won't be here. If I'd ever had a year like this, to think straight and all, before now, I'd be gone already.

MAMA (*not pleading, commanding*) No, Jessie.

JESSIE (*folding the rest of the laundry*) Yes, Mama. Once I started remembering, I could see what it all added up to.

MAMA The fits are over!

JESSIE It's not the fits, Mama.

MAMA Then it's me for giving them to you, but I didn't do it!

JESSIE It's not the fits! You said it yourself, the medicine takes care of the fits.

MAMA (*interrupting*) Your daddy gave you those fits, Jessie. He passed it down to you like your green eyes and your straight hair. It's not my fault!

JESSIE So what if he had little fits? It's not inherited. I fell off the horse. It was an accident.

MAMA The horse wasn't the first time, Jessie. You had a fit when you were five years old.

JESSIE I did not.

MAMA You did! You were eating a popsicle and down you went. He gave it to you. It's *his* fault, not mine.

JESSIE Well, you took your time telling me.

MAMA How do you tell that to a five-year-old?

JESSIE What did the doctor say?

MAMA He said kids have them all the time. He said there wasn't anything to do but wait for another one.

JESSIE But I didn't have another one.

(*Now there is a real silence.*)

JESSIE You mean to tell me I had fits all the time as a kid and you just told me I fell down or something and it wasn't till I had the fit when Cecil was looking that anybody bothered to find out what was the matter with me?

MAMA It wasn't *all the time,* Jessie. And they changed when you started to school. More like your daddy's. Oh, that was some swell time, sitting here with the two of you turning off and on like light bulbs some nights.

JESSIE How many fits did I have?

MAMA You never hurt yourself. I never let you out of my sight. I caught you every time.

JESSIE But you didn't tell anybody.

MAMA It was none of their business.

JESSIE You were ashamed.

MAMA I didn't want anybody to know. Least of all you.

JESSIE Least of all me. Oh, right. That was mine to know, Mama, not yours. Did Daddy know?

MAMA He thought you were . . . you fell down a lot. That's what he thought. You were careless. Or maybe he thought I beat you. I don't know what he thought. He didn't think about it.

JESSIE Because you didn't tell him!

MAMA If I told him about you, I'd have to tell him about him!

JESSIE I don't like this. I don't like this one bit.

MAMA I didn't think you'd like it. That's why I didn't tell you.

JESSIE If I'd known I was an epileptic, Mama, I wouldn't have ridden any horses.

MAMA Make you feel like a freak, is that what I should have done?

JESSIE Just get the manicure tray and sit down!

MAMA (*throwing it to the floor*) I don't want a manicure!

JESSIE Doesn't look like you do, no.

MAMA Maybe I did drop you, you don't know.

JESSIE If you say you didn't, you didn't.

MAMA (*beginning to break down*) Maybe I fed you the wrong thing. Maybe you had a fever sometime and I didn't know it soon enough. Maybe it's a punishment.

JESSIE For what?

MAMA I don't know. Because of how I felt about your father. Because I didn't want any more children. Because I smoked too much or didn't eat right when I was carrying you. It has to be something I did.

JESSIE It does not. It's just a sickness, not a curse. Epilepsy doesn't mean anything. It just is.

MAMA I'm not talking about the fits here, Jessie! I'm talking about this killing yourself. It has to be me that's the matter here. You wouldn't be doing this if it wasn't. I didn't tell you things or I married you off to the wrong man or I took you in and let your life get away from you or all of it put together. I don't know what I did, but I did it, I know. This is all my fault, Jessie, but I don't know what to do about it now!

JESSIE (*exasperated at having to say this again*) It doesn't have anything to do with you!

MAMA Everything you do has to do with me, Jessie. You can't do *anything,* wash your face or cut your finger, without doing it to me. That's right! You might as well kill me as you, Jessie, it's the same thing. This has to do with me, Jessie.

JESSIE Then what if it does! What if it has everything to do with you! What if you are all I have and you're not enough? What if I could take all the rest of it if only I didn't have you here? What if the only way I can get away from you for good is to kill myself? What if it is? I can *still* do it!

MAMA (*in desperate tears*) Don't leave me, Jessie! (JESSIE *stands for a moment, then turns for the bedroom.*) No! (*She grabs* JESSIE*'s arm.*)

JESSIE (*carefully taking her arm away*) I have a box of things I want people to have. I'm just going to go get it for you. You . . . just rest a minute.

(JESSIE *is gone.* MAMA *heads for the telephone, but she can't even pick up the receiver this time and, instead, stoops to clean up the bottles that have spilled out of the manicure tray.*

JESSIE *returns, carrying a box that groceries were delivered in. It probably says Hershey Kisses or Starkist Tuna.* MAMA *is still down on the floor cleaning up, hoping that maybe if she just makes it look nice enough,* JESSIE *will stay.*)

MAMA Jessie, how can I live here without you? I need you! You're supposed to tell me to stand up straight and say how nice I look in my pink dress, and drink my milk. You're supposed to go around and lock up so I know we're safe for the night, and when I wake up, you're supposed to be out there making the coffee and watching me get older every day, and you're supposed to help me die when the time comes. I can't do that by myself, Jessie. I'm not like you, Jessie. I hate the quiet and I don't want to die and I don't want you to go, Jessie. How can I . . . (*has to stop a moment*) How can I get up every day knowing you had to kill yourself to make it stop hurting and I was here all the time and I never even saw it. And then you gave me this chance to make it better, convince you to stay alive, and I couldn't do it. How can I live with myself after this, Jessie?

JESSIE I only told you so I could explain it, so you wouldn't blame yourself, so you wouldn't feel bad. There wasn't anything you could say to change my mind. I didn't want you to save me. I just wanted you to know.

MAMA Stay with me just a little longer. Just a few more years. I don't have that many more to go, Jessie. And as soon as I'm dead, you can do whatever you want. Maybe with me gone, you'll have all the quiet you want, right here in the house. And maybe one day you'll put in some begonias up the walk and get just the right rain for them all summer. And Ricky will be married by then and he'll bring your grandbabies over and you can sneak them a piece of candy when their daddy's not looking and then be real glad when they've gone home and left you to your quiet again.

JESSIE Don't you see, Mama, everything I do winds up like this. How could I think you would understand? How could I think you would want a manicure? We could hold hands for an hour and then I could go shoot myself? I'm sorry about tonight, Mama, but it's exactly why I'm doing it.

MAMA If you've got the guts to kill yourself, Jessie, you've got the guts to stay alive.

JESSIE I know that. So it's really just a matter of where I'd rather be.

MAMA Look, maybe I can't think of what you should do, but that doesn't mean there isn't something that would help. *You* find it. *You* think of it. You can keep trying. You can get brave and try some more. You don't have to give up!

JESSIE I'm *not* giving up! This *is* the other thing I'm trying. And I'm sure there are some other things that might work, but *might* work isn't good enough anymore. I need something that *will* work. *This* will work. That's why I picked it.

MAMA But something might happen. Something that could change everything. Who knows what it might be, but it might be worth waiting for! (JESSIE *doesn't respond.*) Try it for two more weeks. We could have more talks like tonight.

JESSIE No, Mama.

MAMA I'll pay more attention to you. Tell the truth when you ask me. Let you have your say.

JESSIE No, Mama! We wouldn't have more talks like tonight, because it's this next part that's made this last part so good, Mama. No, Mama. *This* is how I have my say. This is how I say what I thought about it *all* and I say no. To Dawson and Loretta and the Red Chinese and epilepsy and Ricky and Cecil and you. And me. And hope. I say no! (*then going to* MAMA *on the sofa*) Just let me go easy, Mama.

MAMA How can I let you go?

JESSIE You can because you have to. It's what you've always done.

MAMA You are my child!

JESSIE I am what became of your child. (MAMA *cannot answer.*) I found an old baby picture of me. And it was somebody else, not me. It was somebody pink and fat who never heard of sick or lonely, somebody who cried and got fed, and reached up and got held and kicked but didn't hurt anybody, and slept whenever she wanted to, just by closing her eyes. Somebody who mainly just laid there and laughed at the colors waving around over her head and chewed on a polka-dot whale and woke up knowing some new trick nearly every day, and rolled over and drooled on the sheet and felt your hand pulling my quilt back up over me. That's who I started out and this is who is left. (*There is no self-pity here.*) That's what this is about. It's somebody I lost, all right, it's my own self. Who I never was. Or who I tried to be and never got there. Somebody I waited for who never came. And never will. So, see, it doesn't much matter what else happens in the world or in this house, even. I'm what was worth waiting for and I didn't make it. Me . . .

who might have made a difference to me . . . I'm not going to show up, so there's no reason to stay, except to keep you company, and that's . . . not reason enough because I'm not . . . very good company. (*pause*) Am I.

MAMA (*knowing she must tell the truth*) No. And neither am I.

JESSIE I had this strange little thought, well, maybe it's not so strange. Anyway, after Christmas, after I decided to do this, I would wonder, sometimes, what might keep me here, what might be worth staying for, and you know what it was? It was maybe if there was something I really liked, like maybe if I really liked rice pudding or cornflakes for breakfast or something, that might be enough.

MAMA Rice pudding is good.

JESSIE Not to me.

MAMA And you're not afraid?

JESSIE Afraid of what?

MAMA I'm afraid of it, for me, I mean. When my time comes. I know it's coming, but . . .

JESSIE You don't know when. Like in a scary movie.

MAMA Yeah, sneaking up on me like some killer on the loose, hiding out in the back yard waiting for me to have my hands full someday and how am I supposed to protect myself anyhow when I don't know what he looks like and I don't know how he sounds coming up behind me like that or if it will hurt or take very long or what I don't get done before it happens.

JESSIE You've got plenty of time left.

MAMA I forget what for, right now.

JESSIE For whatever happens, I don't know. For the rest of your life. For Agnes burning down one more house or Dawson losing his hair or . . .

MAMA (*quickly*) Jessie. I can't just sit here and say O.K., kill yourself if you want to.

JESSIE Sure you can. You just did. Say it again.

MAMA (*really startled*) Jessie! (*quiet horror*) How dare you! (*furious*) How dare you! You think you can just leave whenever you want, like you're watching television here? No, you can't, Jessie. You make me feel like a fool for being alive, child, and you are so wrong! I like it here, and I will stay here until they make me go, until they drag me screaming and I mean screeching into my grave, and you're real smart to get away before then because, I mean, honey, you've never heard noise like that in your life. (JESSIE *turns away.*) Who am I talking to? You're gone already, aren't you? I'm looking right through you! I can't stop you because you're already gone! I guess you think they'll all have to talk about you now! I guess you think this will really confuse them. Oh yes, ever since Christmas you've been laughing to yourself and thinking, "Boy, are they all in for a surprise." Well, nobody's going to be a bit surprised, sweetheart. This is just like you. Do it the hard way, that's my girl, all right. (JESSIE *gets up and goes into the kitchen, but* MAMA *follows her.*) You know who they're going to feel sorry for? Me! How about that! Not you, me!

They're going to be *ashamed* of you. Yes. *Ashamed!* If somebody asks Dawson about it, he'll change the subject as fast as he can. He'll talk about how much he has to pay to park his car these days.

JESSIE Leave me alone.

MAMA It's the truth!

JESSIE I should've just left you a note!

MAMA (*screaming*) Yes! (*then suddenly understanding what she has said, nearly paralyzed by the thought of it, she turns slowly to face* JESSIE, *nearly whispering*) No. No. I . . . might not have thought of all the things you've said.

JESSIE It's O.K., Mama.

(MAMA *is nearly unconscious from the emotional devastation of these last few moments. She sits down at the kitchen table, hurt and angry and desperately afraid. But she looks almost numb. She is so far beyond what is known as pain that she is virtually unreachable and* JESSIE *knows this, and talks quietly, watching for signs of recovery.*)

JESSIE (*washes her hands in the sink*) I remember you liked that preacher who did Daddy's, so if you want to ask him to do the service, that's O.K. with me.

MAMA (*not an answer, just a word*) What.

JESSIE (*putting on hand lotion as she talks*) And pick some songs you like or let Agnes pick, she'll know exactly which ones. Oh, and I had your dress cleaned that you wore to Daddy's. You looked real good in that.

MAMA I don't remember, hon.

JESSIE And it won't be so bad once your friends start coming to the funeral home. You'll probably see people you haven't seen for years, but I thought about what you should say to get you over that nervous part when they first come in.

MAMA (*simply repeating*) Come in.

JESSIE Take them up to see their flowers, they'd like that. And when they say, "I'm so sorry, Thelma," you just say, "I appreciate your coming, Connie." And then ask how their garden was this summer or what they're doing for Thanksgiving or how their children . . .

MAMA I don't think I should ask about their children. I'll talk about what they have on, that's always good. And I'll have some crochet work with me.

JESSIE And Agnes will be there, so you might not have to talk at all.

MAMA Maybe if Connie Richards does come, I can get her to tell me where she gets that Irish yarn, she calls it. I know it doesn't come from Ireland. I think it just comes with a green wrapper.

JESSIE And be sure to invite enough people home afterward so you get enough food to feed them all and have some left for you. But don't let anybody take anything home, especially Loretta.

MAMA Loretta will get all the food set up, honey. It's only fair to let her have some macaroni or something.

JESSIE No, Mama. You have to be more selfish from now on. (*sitting at the table with* MAMA) Now, somebody's bound to ask you why I did it and you just say you don't know. That you loved me and you know I loved you and we just sat around tonight like every other night of our lives, and then I came over and kissed you and said, "'Night, Mother," and you heard me close my bedroom door and the next thing you heard was the shot. And whatever reason I had, well, you guess I just took them with me.

MAMA (*quietly*) It was something personal.

JESSIE Good. That's good, Mama.

MAMA That's what I'll say, then.

JESSIE Personal. Yeah.

MAMA Is that what I tell Dawson and Loretta, too? We sat around, you kissed me, "'Night, Mother"? They'll want to know more, Jessie. They won't believe it.

JESSIE Well, then, tell them what we did. I filled up the candy jars. I cleaned out the refrigerator. We made some hot chocolate and put the cover back on the sofa. You had no idea. All right? I really think it's better that way. If they know we talked about it, they really won't understand how you let me go.

MAMA I guess not.

JESSIE It's private. Tonight is private, yours and mine, and I don't want anybody else to have any of it.

MAMA O.K., then.

JESSIE (*standing behind* MAMA *now, holding her shoulders*) Now, when you hear the shot, I don't want you to come in. First of all, you won't be able to get in by yourself, but I don't want you trying. Call Dawson, then call the police, and then call Agnes. And then you'll need something to do till somebody gets here, so wash the hot-chocolate pan. You wash that pan till you hear the doorbell ring and I don't care if it's an hour, you keep washing that pan.

MAMA I'll make my calls and then I'll just sit. I won't need something to do. What will the police say?

JESSIE They'll do that gunpowder test, I guess, and ask you what happened, and by that time, the ambulance will be here and they'll come in and get me and you know how that goes. You stay out here with Dawson and Loretta. You keep Dawson out here. I want the police in the room first, not Dawson, O.K.?

MAMA What if Dawson and Loretta want me to go home with them?

JESSIE (*returning to the living room*) That's up to you.

MAMA I think I'll stay here. All they've got is Sanka.

JESSIE Maybe Agnes could come stay with you for a few days.

MAMA (*standing up, looking into the living room*) I'd rather be by myself, I think. (*walking toward the box* JESSIE *brought in earlier*) You want me to give people those things?

JESSIE (*They sit down on the sofa,* JESSIE *holding the box on her lap.*) I want Loretta to have my little calculator. Dawson bought it for himself, you know, but then he saw one he liked better and he couldn't bring both of them home with Loretta counting every penny the way she does, so he gave the first one to me. Be funny for her to have it now, don't you think? And all my house slippers are in a sack for her in my closet. Tell her I know they'll fit and I've never worn any of them, and make sure Dawson hears you tell her that. I'm glad he loves Loretta so much, but I wish he knew not everybody has her size feet.

MAMA (*taking the calculator*) O.K.

JESSIE (*reaching into the box again*) This letter is for Dawson, but it's mostly about you, so read it if you want. There's a list of presents for you for at least twenty more Christmases and birthdays, so if you want anything special you better add it to this list before you give it to him. Or if you want to be surprised, just don't read that page. This Christmas, you're getting mostly stuff for the house, like a new rug in your bathroom and needlework, but next Christmas, you're really going to cost him next Christmas. I think you'll like it a lot and you'd never think of it.

MAMA And you think he'll go for it?

JESSIE I think he'll feel like a real jerk if he doesn't. Me telling him to, like this and all. Now, this number's where you call Cecil. I called it last week and he answered, so I know he still lives there.

MAMA What do you want me to tell him?

JESSIE Tell him we talked about him and I only had good things to say about him, but mainly tell him to find Ricky and tell him what I did, and tell Ricky you have something for him, out here, from me, and to come get it. (*pulls a sack out of the box*)

MAMA (*The sack feels empty.*) What is it?

JESSIE (*taking it off*) My watch. (*putting it in the sack and taking a ribbon out of the sack to tie around the top of it*)

MAMA He'll sell it!

JESSIE That's the idea. I appreciate him not stealing it already. I'd like to buy him a good meal.

MAMA He'll buy dope with it!

JESSIE Well, then, I hope he gets some good dope with it, Mama. And the rest of this is for you. (*Handing* MAMA *the box now.* MAMA *picks up the things and looks at them.*)

MAMA (*surprised and pleased*) When did you do all this? During my naps, I guess.

JESSIE I guess. I tried to be quiet about it. (*as* MAMA *is puzzled by the presents*) Those are just little presents. For whenever you need one. They're not bought presents, just things I thought you might like to look at, pictures or things you think you've lost. Things you didn't know you had, even. You'll see.

MAMA I'm not sure I want them. They'll make me think of you.

JESSIE No they won't. They're just things, like a free tube of toothpaste I found hanging on the door one day.

MAMA Oh. All right, then.

JESSIE Well, maybe there's one nice present in there somewhere. It's Granny's ring she gave me and I thought you might like to have it, but I didn't think you'd wear if it I gave it to you right now.

MAMA (*taking the box to a table nearby*) No. Probably not. (*turning back to face her*) I'm ready for my manicure, I guess. Want me to wash my hands again?

JESSIE (*standing up*) It's time for me to go, Mama.

MAMA (*starting for her*) No, Jessie, you've got all night!

JESSIE (*as* MAMA *grabs her*) No, Mama.

MAMA It's not even ten o'clock.

JESSIE (*very calm*) Let me go, Mama.

MAMA I can't. You can't go. You can't do this. You didn't say it would be so soon, Jessie. I'm scared. I love you.

JESSIE (*takes her hands away*) Let go of me, Mama. I've said everything I had to say.

MAMA (*standing still a minute*) You said you wanted to do my nails.

JESSIE (*taking a small step backward*) I can't. It's too late.

MAMA It's not too late!

JESSIE I don't want you to wake Dawson and Loretta when you call. I want them to still be up and dressed so they can get right over.

MAMA (*As* JESSIE *backs up,* MAMA *moves in on her, but carefully.*) They wake up fast, Jessie, if they have to. They don't matter here, Jessie. You do. I do. We're not through yet. We've got a lot of things to take care of here. I don't know where my prescriptions are and you didn't tell me what to tell Dr. Davis when he calls or how much you want me to tell Ricky or who I call to rake the leaves or . . .

JESSIE Don't try and stop me, Mama, you can't do it.

MAMA (*grabbing her again, this time hard*) I can too! I'll stand in front of this hall and you can't get past me. (*They struggle.*) You'll have to knock me down to get away from me, Jessie. I'm not about to let you . . .

(MAMA *struggles with* JESSIE *at the door and in the struggle* JESSIE *gets away from her and—*

JESSIE (*almost a whisper*) 'Night, Mother. (*She vanishes into her bedroom and we hear the door lock just as* MAMA *gets to it.*)

MAMA (*screams*) Jessie! (*pounding on the door*) Jessie, you let me in there. Don't you do this, Jessie. I'm not going to stop screaming until you open this door, Jessie. Jessie! Jessie! What if I don't do any of the things you told me to do! I'll tell Cecil what a miserable man he was to make you feel the way he did and I'll give Ricky's watch to Dawson if I feel like it and the only way you can make sure I do what you want is to come out here and make me, Jessie! (*pounding again*) Jessie! Stop this! I didn't know! I was here with you all the time. How could I know you were so alone?

(*And* MAMA *stops for a moment, breathless and frantic, putting her ear to the door, and when she doesn't hear anything, she stands up straight again and screams once more.*)

Jessie! Please!

(*And we hear the shot, and it sounds like an answer, it sounds like No.*

MAMA *collapses against the door, tears streaming down her face, but not screaming anymore. In shock now.*)

Jessie, Jessie, child . . . Forgive me. (*pause*) I thought you were mine.

(*And she leaves the door and makes her way through the living room, around the furniture, as though she didn't know where it was, not knowing what to do. Finally, she goes to the stove in the kitchen and picks up the hot-chocolate pan and carries it with her to the telephone, and holds on to it while she dials the number. She looks down at the pan, holding it tight like her life depended on it. She hears Loretta answer.*)

MAMA Loretta, let me talk to Dawson, honey.

FENCES

(1985)

AUGUST WILSON (1945–)

In less than a decade after Lorraine Hansberry's stunning success with *A Raisin in the Sun,* the New York theatre welcomed a variety of plays by and about blacks that firmly established the increasing importance of African-American dramatists. Socially and politically, the status of blacks in America was changing rapidly, albeit far from peacefully, prompted first by the 1954 Supreme Court decision outlawing segregation in public schools, and followed by the Montgomery, Alabama, bus boycott in 1955 that precipitated Martin Luther King Jr. into public notice and brought about another court decision outlawing segregation in public transport. By 1960 the long series of lunch-counter sit-ins began in the South; in 1963 King delivered his "I have a dream" speech before 200,000 at the Lincoln Memorial; and in 1964 Congress passed the omnibus civil rights bill removing the last legal barriers that had prevented blacks from full participation in the rights and privileges always enjoyed by whites everywhere.

It was a time of rising black nationalism, as well, advocating not integration but black separatism, of the formation of the Black Muslims. It was a time that experienced the terrible riots in the black ghetto of Watts in Los Angeles in 1965 and in Newark and Detroit in 1967. But it was also a time (1967) in which African-American mayors were elected in Cleveland and Gary, Indiana, and Thurgood Marshall became the first black Supreme Court justice. In 1966 Edward Brooke of Massachusetts became the first black Senator since Reconstruction, and in 1968 Shirley Chisholm of New York became the first black woman elected to Congress, sadly the same year that saw the assassination of Dr. King in Memphis.

A great amount of writing by both blacks and whites reflected the combined national agonies of racial antagonism and the never-ending Vietnam War, which had sent such a large proportion of black draftees into the apparently pointless slaughter. One of the strongest voices was that of James Baldwin (1924–1987) whose two plays, *Blues for Mister Charlie* and *The Amen Corner,* were produced in 1964, although the latter had been written ten years earlier. Both are serious,

---

The factual material in this introduction was obtained from a variety of essays in *The Black American Writer,* Vol. II, ed. C. W. E. Bigsby, DeLand, FL, Everett/Edwards, 1969. Copyright by C. W. E. Bigsby.

even painful, studies of African Americans seeking meaning and identity in the struggles within the white world. *Blues for Mister Charlie* is based on the actual case of the murder of a southern black youth, Emmett Till, whose killers were tried and acquitted. *The Amen Corner* involves the struggles of Sister Margaret, a black evangelist, deserted by son and husband and eventually read out of her church. Both plays show Baldwin's ambivalent recognition of the need of love and affirmation through faith as well as vengeance. Sometimes shocking in what he had to say, Baldwin angered black militants and whites, but the plays established his importance in the creation of high-quality and challenging black drama.

In 1961 the actor and writer Ossie Davis (b. 1917) wrote a moderately successful satire called *Purlie Victorious,* a parody of black society in its assorted stereotypical portraits, headed by Purlie Victorious Judson, who is attempting to secure a sum of money from the local white cotton boss. Davis has a lot of fun with his straight-faced presentation of the Uncle Tom, the African-American nationalist, the leader of the race struggle, and the driven civil rights leader. As Davis admits, only a black could have dared write as he did, for it would have been highly offensive if written by a white.

In 1965 Douglas Turner Ward (b. 1930), in *Days of Absence,* expanded on the point that had been so successfully made by the Montgomery bus boycott. When Rosa Parks refused to move to the back of the bus and by her arrest sparked the whole affair, the blacks of this Alabama city united in a manner unimagined by the white citizenry in their virtually 100 percent refusal to ride segregated buses. Going about their business on foot or in organized car pools, the blacks showed how much the bus company relied on its black passengers. Now the buses were half or more empty, losing not only business but a lot of money as well. It was the first time that a white community had come to realize just how important the African-American consumer really was.

In *Days of Absence,* Ward goes a logical step further. One day the town awakes to discover that *all* blacks have left. Now there are no cooks, maids, janitors, or others whose menial jobs served the exploiting whites. The community quickly finds itself helpless, unable to function on the most basic levels. It is a good lesson for the whites while revealing to the blacks how powerful they can be. It is a funny play, full of white stereotypes. Ward himself called it "a reverse minstrel show done in whiteface," but it makes its point vividly.

Nearly all of the African-American drama discussed so far has been a fairly conventional body of work. Before the rise of black nationalism, there had been little basic differences between white and black drama in form and structure. Now there were voices, predominant among them LeRoi Jones, who wanted and wrote for a revolutionary theatre that would address the social situation in a manner far removed from the satires and fables of most black writers.

A true militant who embraced the concept of revolution, an avowed follower of Communist doctrine, Jones adopted the name by which he is now known, Imamu Amiri Baraka, and he has continually maintained his confrontational behavior. To meet and speak with him is to encounter a mild-mannered, cordial individual, easy to talk with, in dress and demeanor a seemingly thoroughly integrated member of the larger society around him. To read his published works and to hear him on the lecture platform is quite another matter. Never a man of nonviolence or accommodation, he has openly advocated revolution and the manning of the barricades in what he views as the inevitable shooting war between the races.

The most important of Baraka's plays are *The Slave, The Toilet,* and *Dutchman* (all 1964). They are not pleasant plays, replete with violence, foul language, and racial slurs, delivered in both directions. *The Slave* is probably the most chilling of the three. The war has started, and the recurrent explosions that flash through the windows of the living room of George and Grace Easley indicate that the battle outside is drawing nearer. George, liberal in all the proper ways, has long been a friend of Walker Vessels, leader of the revolt, to whom Grace was at one time married. In fact, Vessels' two daughters are asleep upstairs. But obviously things have gone wildly awry. All of the white liberal views are of no avail, and former friends are now enemies. In the course of events, the violence comes closer. A struggle between Easley and Vessels ends with Easley's death by gunshot; a collapsing beam kills Grace. Purporting to have come to claim his children, Vessels has already killed them and, wounded, he stumbles out into the dark as the explosions continue.

In *The Toilet,* Baraka deals with the search for identity among a group of African-American high school students, with the action taking place among the sinks and urinals of the boys' room. It is a brief and violent play. Apparently one of the gang members has received a "love" note from a white boy, who is beaten mercilessly and left bleeding on the grimy floor, where Foots, the object of the note (he may have written it himself) cradles the wounded victim in his arms as the curtain falls. One critic has seen the play as a plea for acceptance of the black in the white world, but this is hardly in keeping with Baraka's stated views. Others have seen it as a cry against the dominance of the African-American family by the matriarch, forcing a twisted turn toward homosexuality in an attempt to escape. Perhaps.

Dutchman is a frightening play, in many ways rivaling the terror in *The Slave.* It gains its force not so much from physical violence, which comes late and is brief, but through the vicious verbal assaults and counterthrusts. It is a powerful allegory, and should not in the least be taken on any literal realistic level. But the reality of its theme is clear enough; the struggle is deadly and never ending.

The setting is a subway car "heaped in modern myth" in the "flying underbelly" of the city. It is a subway car of death, a modern Flying Dutchman, the ghost ship an encounter with which on the high seas is always fatal. The two antagonists are primordial. One is named Clay, man created from dust. The other is Lula, the eternal sensual Edenic temptress who carries a supply of apples, which she continues to devour while offering them to the man beside her. And all the while the train speeds on. During the entire first scene, it never stops—unreal, ghostly, threatening.

Clay is the seemingly fully integrated black, neatly dressed, a proper citizen. Lula, in dress and language, is clearly the out-and-out strumpet. Lula engages in the usual stereotypical baiting, assuming that the handsome black, whose leg she fondles suggestively, would delight in having her sexually. Her taunts are increasingly racial, and she finally brings Clay out of his "polite" phase to react to her crudities by unleashing a lot of his own rage. Her ultimate reaction is to stab him and throw his body off the train. He cannot "fit in," and the world around him, as represented by both Lula and the other passengers, is unaffected by his murder.

By the time August Wilson's plays began to attract national attention in 1981 with the production of *Ma Rainey's Black Bottom* at the O'Neill Theatre Center in Waterford, Connecticut, blacks in American society had become a major force in a wide variety of areas. By the end of the 1980s, there were African-American mayors and police chiefs in several large cities, north and south–Detroit, Los Angeles, Atlanta, Houston, Chicago, New York–and an African-American black governor in Virginia. Their presence was felt in education, economics, law, the military, and, of course, college and professional athletics. The causes so fervently espoused by Baraka collapsed with the fall of the Berlin Wall in 1989 and the subsequent demise of communism as a world political power in the disintegration of the Soviet Union.

Still the status of the African American in the broader base of American society continued to remain second class. The legal barriers of overt discrimination were gone, but all the earlier promise that had seemed so hopeful, such as school desegregation, did not bring about a social Nirvana as African Americans on all levels continued to endure lower average incomes, limited opportunities in housing, and other more subtle methods of maintaining the color line and preventing full social assimilation. African-American dramatists, however, though remaining few, continued to gain prominence, especially in the person of August Wilson, together with Lloyd Richards of the O'Neill Center and Dean of the Yale School of Drama, who directed most of Wilson's plays. Their record has been impressive, with a long list of awards, including two Pulitzer Prizes.

Wilson, who considers himself more a poet than a dramatist, entered the theatre without, in his own words, knowing very much of what it was all about. He admits a very limited knowledge of the drama, having read very little Shakespeare and nothing at all of many of the great names such as Ibsen, Williams, or Miller. But he has had a long interest in things theatrical, having helped found the Pittsburgh Black Horizon Theatre in his hometown when only 21. After producing a couple of plays in St. Paul, to which he moved in 1977, his career was firmly launched with the acceptance of *Ma Rainey* by the O'Neill Center. It was the first (*Fences* is the second) in a planned series of ten plays intended to present various aspects of African-American culture and its inner conflicts, each dealing with a particular decade in black history, which, he has said, is "the most dramatic story of all mankind."

Ma Rainey was an African American (the term that Wilson prefers to use rather than "black") blues singer of the 1920s who had gained considerable fame before the later, and in many ways better known, Bessie Smith and Billie Holiday. There are two lines of development in the play, both concerned with two of Wilson's own deep interests: the civil rights movement of the 1960s and 1970s, in which he had actively participated, and the music of the blues. The first aspect is explored in a theme that Wilson carries through each of his plays, namely his strong feeling that African Americans must maintain their African-ness while they are attempting to gain a place in the white American society. Holding that blacks are inherently African and not American, Wilson firmly believes that the two cultures need not, nor indeed cannot, be successfully integrated, and that African Americans should not renounce their cultural background but build upon it. This viewpoint is made clear in the conflict between two of Ma Rainey's instrumentalists, Levee and Toledo. Toledo makes the point that "We done sold ourselves to the white man in order to be like him. We's imitation white men." Levee, on the other hand, wants to become a part of the society that is actually oppressing him by becoming a great jazz musician, willing to bow to the white man's ways. The conflict is unresolved and ends when Levee goes emotionally overboard and stabs Toledo.

The second theme, that of Ma Rainey's exploitation by white managers and recording studios, emphasizes her awareness of this fact and her own ability to handle it. Also her devotion to the traditional ways of rendering the blues prevents Levee's attempts to play them, especially the "Black Bottom," in more contemporary jazz style.

Fences, a Pulitzer Prize winner, presents the African-American patriarch, Troy, faced with a semirebellious son, Cory, and more or less held in check by his hard-working wife, Rose, who would like to see the rough dirt front yard enclosed by the fence that will give them all a sense of privacy in their own world. The unseen but always-present fences of an antagonistic white society kept Troy from realizing his potential as a powerful baseball player forced to remain in the Negro Leagues until it was too late. He is now kept in his place by being permitted to collect the garbage but not to drive the truck. It is increasingly a life of frustration. Reminders of his impotence as a male figure in society are Gabriel, maimed in body and mind by combat in the army then run entirely by whites, and Cory, who eventually enters the Marines. In a kind of revolt, Troy leaps the fence of propriety to father a child in an adulterous affair, but the child is brought back within the "fence" of the family by Rose's acceptance of her.

With the yard fence at last completed, there is a sense of finite accomplishment, although it is in no way "final." There *can* be no final resolution; the cultures will continue in their separate ways; Rose's family is as symbolically closed in as the white world closes them out.

In all of his plays, Wilson has remained in the well-made realistic tradition, in marked contrast to the style of Baraka. This is an interesting aspect in view of his avowed lack of acquaintance with, and thus presumed lack of influence from, the traditional realists as far back as Ibsen. But this does not limit his use of symbol and metaphor in making his points. The musical instruments in *Ma Rainey* reflect the characters and behavior of those who play them. The fence around Troy Maxson's yard is both symbol and metaphor of much that Troy endures; and the constant baseball imagery in Troy's speeches evokes the immediacy of his struggle in the terms of what he knows best. There have always been two strikes against him, but he is always trying to get ahead of the pitcher and hopefully knock it all right out of the park.

Fences AUGUST WILSON

When the sins of our fathers visit us
We do not have to play host.
We can banish them with forgiveness
As God, in His Largeness and Laws.

—AUGUST WILSON

CHARACTERS

TROY MAXSON
JIM BONO *TROY's friend*
ROSE *TROY's wife*
LYONS *TROY's oldest son by previous marriage*
GABRIEL *TROY's brother*
CORY *TROY and ROSE's son*
RAYNELL *TROY's daughter*

SETTING

The setting is the yard which fronts the only entrance to the MAXSON *household, an ancient two-story brick house set back off a small alley in a big-city neighborhood. The entrance to the house is gained by two or three steps leading to a wooden porch badly in need of paint.*

A relatively recent addition to the house and running its full width, the porch lacks congruence. It is a sturdy porch with a flat roof. One or two chairs of dubious value sit at one end where the kitchen window opens onto the porch. An old-fashioned icebox stands silent guard at the opposite end.

The yard is a small dirt yard, partially fenced, except for the last scene, with a wooden sawhorse, a pile of lumber, and other fence-building equipment set off to the side. Opposite is a tree from which hangs a ball made of rags. A baseball bat leans against the tree. Two oil drums serve as garbage receptacles and sit near the house at right to complete the setting.

Act I

Scene I

It is 1957. TROY *and* BONO *enter the yard, engaged in conversation.* TROY *is fifty-three years old, a large man with thick, heavy hands; it is this largeness that he strives to fill out and make an accommodation with. Together with his blackness, his largeness informs his sensibilities and the choices he has made in his life.*

Of the two men, **Bono** *is obviously the follower. His commitment to their friendship of thirty-odd years is rooted in his admiration of* **Troy**'*s honesty, capacity for hard work, and his strength, which* **Bono** *seeks to emulate.*

It is Friday night, payday, and the one night of the week the two men engage in a ritual of talk and drink. **Troy** *is usually the most talkative and at times he can be crude and almost vulgar, though he is capable of rising to profound heights of expression. The men carry lunch buckets and wear or carry burlap aprons and are dressed in clothes suitable to their jobs as garbage collectors.*

BONO Troy, you ought to stop that lying!

TROY I ain't lying! The nigger had a watermelon this big. (*He indicates with his hands.*) Talking about . . . "What watermelon, Mr. Rand?" I liked to fell out! "What watermelon, Mr. Rand?" . . . And it sitting there big as life.

BONO What did Mr. Rand say?

TROY Ain't said nothing. Figure if the nigger too dumb to know he carrying a watermelon, he wasn't gonna get much sense out of him. Trying to hide that great big old watermelon under his coat. Afraid to let the white man see him carry it home.

BONO I'm like you . . . I ain't got no time for them kind of people.

TROY Now what he look like getting mad cause he see the man from the union talking to Mr. Rand?

BONO He come to me talking about . . . "Maxson gonna get us fired." I told him to get away from me with that. He walked away from me calling you a troublemaker. What Mr. Rand say?

TROY Ain't said nothing. He told me to go down the Commissioner's office next Friday. They called me down there to see them.

BONO Well, as long as you got your complaint filed, they can't fire you. That's what one of them white fellows tell me.

TROY I ain't worried about them firing me. They gonna fire me cause I asked a question? That's all I did. I went to Mr. Rand and asked him, "Why?" "Why you got the white mens driving and the colored lifting?" Told him, "what's the matter, don't I count? You think only white fellows got sense enough to drive a truck. That ain't no paper job! Hell, anybody can drive a truck. How come you got all whites driving and the colored lifting?" He told me "take it to the union." Well, hell, that's what I done! Now they wanna come up with this pack of lies.

BONO I told Brownie if the man come and ask him any questions . . . just tell the truth! It ain't nothing but something they done trumped up on you cause you filed a complaint on them.

TROY Brownie don't understand nothing. All I want them to do is change the job description. Give everybody a chance to drive the truck. Brownie can't see that. He ain't got that much sense.

BONO How you figure he be making out with that gal be up at Taylors' all the time . . . that Alberta gal?

TROY Same as you and me. Getting just as much as we is. Which is to say nothing.

BONO It is, huh? I figure you doing a little better than me . . . and I ain't saying what I'm doing.

TROY Aw, nigger, look here . . . I know you. If you had got anywhere near that gal, twenty minutes later you be looking to tell somebody. And the first one you gonna tell . . . that you gonna want to brag to . . . is gonna be me.

BONO I ain't saying that. I see where you be eyeing her.

TROY I eye all the women. I don't miss nothing. Don't never let nobody tell you Troy Maxson don't eye the women.

BONO You been doing more than eyeing her. You done bought her a drink or two.

TROY Hell yeah, I bought her a drink! What that mean? I bought you one, too. What that mean cause I buy her a drink? I'm just being polite.

BONO It's alright to buy her one drink. That's what you call being polite. But when you wanna be buying two or three . . . that's what you call eyeing her.

TROY Look here, as long as you known me . . . you ever known me to chase after women?

BONO Hell yeah! Long as I done known you. You forgetting I knew you when.

TROY Naw, I'm talking about since I been married to Rose?

BONO Oh, not since you been married to Rose. Now, that's the truth, there. I can say that.

TROY Alright then! Case closed.

BONO I see you be walking up around Alberta's house. You supposed to be at Taylors' and you be walking up around there.

TROY What you watching where I'm walking for? I ain't watching after you.

BONO I seen you walking around there more than once.

TROY Hell, you liable to see me walking anywhere! That don't mean nothing cause you see me walking around there.

BONO Where she come from anyway? She just kinda showed up one day.

TROY Tallahassee. You can look at her and tell she one of them Florida gals. They got some big healthy women down there. Grow them right up out the ground. Got a little bit of Indian in her. Most of them niggers down in Florida got some Indian in them.

BONO I don't know about that Indian part. But she damn sure big and healthy. Woman wear some big stockings. Got them great big old legs and hips as wide as the Mississippi River.

TROY Legs don't mean nothing. You don't do nothing but push them out of the way. But them hips cushion the ride!

BONO Troy, you ain't got no sense.

TROY It's the truth! Like you riding on Goodyears!

(ROSE *enters from the house. She is ten years younger than* TROY, *her devotion to him stems from her recognition of the possibilities of her life without him: a succession of abusive men and their babies, a life of partying and running the streets, the*

Church, or aloneness with its attendant pain and frustration. She recognizes TROY*'s spirit as a fine and illuminating one and she either ignores or forgives his faults, only some of which she recognizes. Though she doesn't drink, her presence is an integral part of the Friday night rituals. She alternates between the porch and the kitchen, where supper preparations are under way.*)

ROSE What you all out here getting into?

TROY What you worried about what we getting into for? This is men talk, woman.

ROSE What I care what you all talking about? Bono, you gonna stay for supper?

BONO No, I thank you, Rose. But Lucille say she cooking up a pot of pigfeet.

TROY Pigfeet! Hell, I'm going home with you! Might even stay the night if you got some pigfeet. You got something in there to top them pigfeet, Rose?

ROSE I'm cooking up some chicken. I got some chicken and collard greens.

TROY Well, go on back in the house and let me and Bono finish what we was talking about. This is men talk. I got some talk for you later. You know what kind of talk I mean. You go on and powder it up.

ROSE Troy Maxson, don't you start that now!

TROY (*puts his arm around her*) Aw, woman . . . come here. Look here, Bono . . . when I met this woman . . . I got out that place, say, "Hitch up my pony, saddle up my mare . . . there's a woman out there for me somewhere. I looked here. Looked there. Saw Rose and latched on to her." I latched on to her and told her—I'm gonna tell you the truth—I told her, "Baby, I don't wanna marry, I just wanna be your man." Rose told me . . . tell him what you told me, Rose.

ROSE I told him if he wasn't the marrying kind, then move out the way so the marrying kind could find me.

TROY That's what she told me. "Nigger, you in my way. You blocking the view! Move out the way so I can find me a husband." I thought it over two or three days. Come back—

ROSE Ain't no two or three days nothing. You was back the same night.

TROY Come back, told her . . . "Okay, baby . . . but I'm gonna buy me a banty rooster and put him out there in the backyard . . . and when he see a stranger come he'll flap his wings and crow . . ." Look here, Bono, I could watch the front door by myself . . . it was that back door I was worried about.

ROSE Troy, you ought not talk like that. Troy ain't doing nothing but telling a lie.

TROY Only thing is . . . when we first got married . . . forget the rooster . . . we ain't had no yard!

BONO I hear you tell it. Me and Lucille was staying down there on Logan Street. Had two rooms with the outhouse in the back. I ain't mind the outhouse none. But when that goddamn wind blow through there in the winter . . . that's what I'm talking about! To this day I wonder why in the hell I ever stayed down there for six long years. But see, I didn't know I could do no better. I thought only white folks had inside toilets and things.

ROSE There's a lot of people don't know they can do no better than they doing now. That's just something you got to learn. A lot of folks still shop at Bella's.

TROY Ain't nothing wrong with shopping at Bella's. She got fresh food.

ROSE I ain't said nothing about if she got fresh food. I'm talking about what she charge. She charge ten cents more than the A&P.

TROY The A&P ain't never done nothing for me. I spends my money where I'm treated right. I go down to Bella, say, "I need a loaf of bread, I'll pay you Friday." She give it to me. What sense that make when I got money to go and spend it somewhere else and ignore the person who done right by me? That ain't in the Bible.

ROSE We ain't talking about what's in the Bible. What sense it make to shop there when she overcharge?

TROY You shop where you want to. I'll do my shopping where the people been good to me.

ROSE Well, I don't think it's right for her to overcharge. That's all I was saying.

BONO Look here . . . I got to get on. Lucille going be raising all kind of hell.

TROY Where you going, nigger? We ain't finished this pint. Come here, finish this pint.

BONO Well, hell, I am . . . if you ever turn the bottle loose.

TROY (*hands him the bottle*) The only thing I say about the A&P is I'm glad Cory got that job down there. Help him take care of his school clothes and things. Gabe done moved out and things getting tight around here. He got that job. . . . He can start to look out for himself.

ROSE Cory done went and got recruited by a college football team.

TROY I told that boy about that football stuff. The white man ain't gonna let him get nowhere with that football. I told him when he first come to me with it. Now you come telling me he done went and got more tied up in it. He ought to go and get recruited in how to fix cars or something where he can make a living.

ROSE He ain't talking about making no living playing football. It's just something the boys in school do. They gonna send a recruiter by to talk to you. He'll tell you he ain't talking about making no living playing football. It's a honor to be recruited.

TROY It ain't gonna get him nowhere. Bono'll tell you that.

BONO If he be like you in the sports . . . he's gonna be alright. Ain't but two men ever played baseball as good as you. That's Babe Ruth and Josh Gibson. Them's the only two men ever hit more home runs than you.

TROY What it ever get me? Ain't got a pot to piss in or a window to throw it out of.

ROSE Times have changed since you was playing baseball, Troy. That was before the war. Times have changed a lot since then.

TROY How in hell they done changed?

ROSE They got lots of colored boys playing ball now. Baseball and football.

BONO You right about that, Rose. Times have changed, Troy. You just come along too early.

TROY There ought not never have been no time called too early! Now you take that fellow . . . what's that fellow they had playing right field for the Yankees back then? You know who I'm talking about, Bono. Used to play right field for the Yankees.

ROSE Selkirk?

TROY Selkirk! That's it! Man batting .269, understand? .269. What kind of sense that make? I was hitting .432 with thirty-seven home runs! Man batting .269 and playing right field for the Yankees! I saw Josh Gibson's daughter yesterday. She walking around with raggedy shoes on her feet. Now I bet you Selkirk's daughter ain't walking around with raggedy shoes on her feet! I bet you that!

ROSE They got a lot of colored baseball players now. Jackie Robinson was the first. Folks had to wait for Jackie Robinson.

TROY I done seen a hundred niggers play baseball better than Jackie Robinson. Hell, I know some teams Jackie Robinson couldn't even make! What you talking about Jackie Robinson. Jackie Robinson wasn't nobody. I'm talking about if you could play ball then they ought to have let you play. Don't care what color you were. Come telling me I come along too early. If you could play . . . then they ought to have let you play.

(TROY *takes a long drink from the bottle.*)

ROSE You gonna drink yourself to death. You don't need to be drinking like that.

TROY Death ain't nothing. I done seen him. Done wrassled with him. You can't tell me nothing about death. Death ain't nothing but a fastball on the outside corner. And you know what I'll do to that! Lookee here, Bono . . . am I lying? You get one of them fastballs, about waist high, over the outside corner of the plate where you can get the meat of the bat on it . . . and good god! You can kiss it goodbye. Now, am I lying?

BONO Naw, you telling the truth there. I seen you do it.

TROY If I'm lying . . . that 450 feet worth of lying!

(*pause*)

That's all death is to me. A fastball on the outside corner.

ROSE I don't know why you want to get on talking about death.

TROY Ain't nothing wrong with talking about death. That's part of life. Everybody gonna die. You gonna die, I'm gonna die. Bono's gonna die. Hell, we all gonna die.

ROSE But you ain't got to talk about it. I don't like to talk about it.

TROY You the one brought it up. Me and Bono was talking about baseball . . . you tell me I'm gonna drink myself to death. Ain't that right, Bono? You know I don't drink this but one night out of the week. That's Friday night. I'm gonna drink just enough to where I can handle it. Then I cuts it loose. I leave it alone. So don't you worry about me drinking myself to death. 'Cause I ain't worried about Death. I done seen him. I done wrestled with him.

Look here, Bono . . . I looked up one day and Death was marching straight at me. Like Soldiers on Parade! The Army of Death was marching straight at me. The middle of July, 1941. It got real cold just like it be winter. It seem like Death himself reached out and touched me on the shoulder. He touch me just like I touch you. I got cold as ice and Death standing there grinning at me.

ROSE Troy, why don't you hush that talk.

TROY I say . . . What you want, Mr. Death? You be wanting me? You done brought your army to be getting me? I looked him dead in the eye. I wasn't fearing nothing. I was ready to tangle. Just like I'm ready to tangle now. The Bible say be ever vigilant. That's why I don't get but so drunk. I got to keep watch.

ROSE Troy was right down there in Mercy Hospital. You remember he had pneumonia? Laying there with a fever talking plumb out of his head.

TROY Death standing there staring at me . . . carrying that sickle in his hand. Finally he say, "You want bound over for another year?" See, just like that . . . "You want bound over for another year?" I told him, "Bound over hell! Let's settle this now!"

It seem like he kinda fell back when I said that, and all the cold went out of me. I reached down and grabbed that sickle and threw it just as far as I could throw it . . . and me and him commenced to wrestling. We wrestled for three days and three nights. I can't say where I found the strength from. Every time it seemed like he was gonna get the best of me, I'd reach way down deep inside myself and find the strength to do him one better.

ROSE Every time Troy tell that story he find different ways to tell it. Different things to make up about it.

TROY I ain't making up nothing. I'm telling you the facts of what happened. I wrestled with Death for three days and three nights and I'm standing here to tell you about it.

(*pause*)

Alright. At the end of the third night we done weakened each other to where we can't hardly move. Death stood up, throwed on his robe . . . had him a white robe with a hood on it. He throwed on that robe and went off to look for his sickle. Say, "I'll be back." Just like that. "I'll be back." I told him, say, "Yeah, but . . . you gonna have to find me!" I wasn't no fool. I wasn't going looking for him. Death ain't nothing to play with. And I know he's gonna get me. I know I got to join his army . . . his camp followers. But as long as I keep my strength and see him coming . . . as long as I keep up my vigilance . . . he's gonna have to fight to get me. I ain't going easy.

BONO Well, look here, since you got to keep up your vigilance . . . let me have the bottle.

TROY Aw hell, I shouldn't have told you that part. I should have left out that part.

ROSE Troy be talking that stuff and half the time don't even know what he be talking about.

TROY Bono know me better than that.

BONO That's right. I know you. I know you got some Uncle Remus in your blood. You got more stories than the devil got sinners.

TROY Aw hell, I done seen him too! Done talked with the devil.

ROSE Troy, don't nobody wanna be hearing all that stuff.

(LYONS *enters the yard from the street. Thirty-four years old,* TROY*'s son by a previous marriage, he sports a neatly trimmed goatee, sport coat, white shirt, tieless and buttoned at the collar. Though he fancies himself a musician, he is more caught up in the rituals and "idea" of being a musician than in the actual practice of the music. He has come to borrow money from* TROY, *and while he knows he will be successful, he is uncertain as to what extent his lifestyle will be held up to scrutiny and ridicule.*)

LYONS Hey, Pop.

TROY What you come "Hey, Popping" me for?

LYONS How you doing, Rose?

(*He kisses her.*)

Mr. Bono. How you doing?

BONO Hey, Lyons . . . how you been?

TROY He must have been doing alright. I ain't seen him around here last week.

ROSE Troy, leave your boy alone. He come by to see you and you wanna start all that nonsense.

TROY I ain't bothering Lyons.

(*offers him the bottle*)

Here . . . get you a drink. We got an understanding. I know why he come by to see me and he know I know.

LYONS Come on, Pop . . . I just stopped by to say hi . . . see how you was doing.

TROY You ain't stopped by yesterday.

ROSE You gonna stay for supper, Lyons? I got some chicken cooking in the oven.

LYONS No, Rose . . . thanks. I was just in the neighborhood and thought I'd stop by for a minute.

TROY You was in the neighborhood alright, nigger. You telling the truth there. You was in the neighborhood cause it's my payday.

LYONS Well, hell, since you mentioned it . . . let me have ten dollars.

TROY I'll be damned! I'll die and go to hell and play blackjack with the devil before I give you ten dollars.

BONO That's what I wanna know about . . . that devil you done seen.

LYONS What . . . Pop done seen the devil? You too much, Pops.

TROY Yeah, I done seen him. Talked to him too!

ROSE You ain't seen no devil. I done told you that man ain't had nothing to do with the devil. Anything you can't understand, you want to call it the devil.

TROY Look here, Bono . . . I went down to see Hertzberger about some furniture. Got three rooms for two-ninety-eight. That what it say on the radio. "Three rooms . . . two-ninety-eight." Even made up a little song about it. Go down there . . . man tell me I can't get no credit. I'm working every day and can't get no credit. What to do? I got an empty house with some raggedy furniture in it. Cory ain't got no bed. He's sleeping on a pile of rags on the floor. Working every day and can't get no credit. Come back here—Rose'll tell you—madder than hell. Sit down . . . try to figure what I'm gonna do. Come a knock on the door. Ain't been living here but three days. Who know I'm here? Open the door . . . devil standing there bigger than life. White fellow . . . got on good clothes and everything. Standing there with a clipboard in his hand. I ain't had to say nothing. First words come out of his mouth was . . . "I understand you need some furniture and can't get no credit." I liked to fell over. He say "I'll give you all the credit you want, but you got to pay the interest on it." I told him, "Give me three rooms worth and charge whatever you want." Next day a truck pulled up here and two men unloaded them three rooms. Man what drove the truck give me a book. Say send ten dollars, first of every month to the address in the book and everything will be alright. Say if I miss a payment the devil was coming back and it'll be hell to pay. That was fifteen years ago. To this day. . . the first of the month I send my ten dollars, Rose'll tell you.

ROSE Troy lying.

TROY I ain't never seen that man since. Now you tell me who else that could have been but the devil? I ain't sold my soul or nothing like that, you understand. Naw, I wouldn't have truck with the devil about nothing like that. I got my furniture and pays my ten dollars the first of the month just like clockwork.

BONO How long you say you been paying this ten dollars a month?

TROY Fifteen years!

BONO Hell, ain't you finished paying for it yet? How much the man done charged you.

TROY Aw hell, I done paid for it. I done paid for it ten times over! The fact is I'm scared to stop paying it.

ROSE Troy lying. We got that furniture from Mr. Glickman. He ain't paying no ten dollars a month to nobody.

TROY Aw hell, woman. Bono know I ain't that big a fool.

LYONS I was just getting ready to say . . . I know where there's a bridge for sale.

TROY Look here, I'll tell you this . . . it don't matter to me if he was the devil. It don't matter if the devil give credit. Somebody has got to give it.

ROSE It ought to matter. You going around talking about having truck with the devil . . . God's the one you gonna have to answer to. He's the one gonna be at the Judgment.

LYONS Yeah, well, look here, Pop . . . let me have that ten dollars. I'll give it back to you. Bonnie got a job working at the hospital.

TROY What I tell you, Bono? The only time I see this nigger is when he wants something. That's the only time I see him.

LYONS Come on, Pop, Mr. Bono don't want to hear all that. Let me have the ten dollars. I told you Bonnie working.

TROY What that mean to me? "Bonnie working." I don't care if she working. Go ask her for the ten dollars if she working. Talking about "Bonnie working." Why ain't you working?

LYONS Aw, Pop, you know I can't find no decent job. Where am I gonna get a job at? You know I can't get no job.

TROY I told you I know some people down there. I can get you on the rubbish if you want to work. I told you that the last time you came by here asking me for something.

LYONS Naw, Pop . . . thanks. That ain't for me. I don't wanna be carrying nobody's rubbish. I don't wanna be punching nobody's time clock.

TROY What's the matter, you too good to carry people's rubbish? Where you think that ten dollars you talking about come from? I'm just supposed to haul people's rubbish and give my money to you cause you too lazy to work. You too lazy to work and wanna know why you ain't got what I got.

ROSE What hospital Bonnie working at? Mercy?

LYONS She's down at Passavant working in the laundry.

TROY I ain't got nothing as it is. I give you that ten dollars and I got to eat beans the rest of the week. Naw . . . you ain't getting no ten dollars here.

LYONS You ain't got to be eating no beans. I don't know why you wanna say that.

TROY I ain't got no extra money. Gabe done moved over to Miss Pearl's paying her the rent and things done got tight around here. I can't afford to be giving you every payday.

LYONS I ain't asked you to give me nothing. I asked you to loan me ten dollars. I know you got ten dollars.

TROY Yeah, I got it. You know why I got it? Cause I don't throw my money away out there in the streets. You living the fast life . . . wanna be a musician . . .

running around in them clubs and things . . . then, you learn to take care of yourself. You ain't gonna find me going and asking nobody for nothing. I done spent too many years without.

LYONS You and me is two different people, Pop.

TROY I done learned my mistake and learned to do what's right by it. You still trying to get something for nothing. Life don't owe you nothing. You owe it to yourself. Ask Bono. He'll tell you I'm right.

LYONS You got your way of dealing with the world . . . I got mine. The only thing that matters to me is the music.

TROY Yeah, I can see that! It don't matter how you gonna eat . . . where your next dollar is coming from. You telling the truth there.

LYONS I know I got to eat. But I got to live too. I need something that gonna help me to get out of the bed in the morning. Make me feel like I belong in the world. I don't bother nobody. I just stay with my music cause that's the only way I can find to live in the world. Otherwise there ain't no telling what I might do. Now I don't come criticizing you and how you live. I just come by to ask you for ten dollars. I don't wanna hear all that about how I live.

TROY Boy, your mama did a hell of a job raising you.

LYONS You can't change me, Pop. I'm thirty-four years old. If you wanted to change me, you should have been there when I was growing up. I come by to see you . . . ask for ten dollars and you want to talk about how I was raised. You don't know nothing about how I was raised.

ROSE Let the boy have ten dollars, Troy.

TROY (*to* LYONS) What the hell you looking at me for? I ain't got no ten dollars. You know what I do with my money.

(*to* ROSE)

Give him ten dollars if you want him to have it.

ROSE I will. Just as soon as you turn it loose.

TROY (*handing* ROSE *the money*) There it is. Seventy-six dollars and forty-two cents. You see this, Bono? Now, I ain't gonna get but six of that back.

ROSE You ought to stop telling that lie. Here, Lyons.

(*She hands him the money.*)

LYONS Thanks, Rose. Look . . . I got to run . . . I'll see you later.

TROY Wait a minute. You gonna say, "thanks, Rose" and ain't gonna look to see where she got that ten dollars from? See how they do me, Bono?

LYONS I know she got it from you, Pop. Thanks. I'll give it back to you.

TROY There he go telling another lie. Time I see that ten dollars . . . he'll be owing me thirty more.

LYONS See you, Mr. Bono.

BONO Take care, Lyons!

LYONS Thanks, Pop. I'll see you again.

(LYONS *exits the yard.*)

TROY I don't know why he don't go and get him a decent job and take care of that woman he got.

BONO He'll be alright, Troy. The boy is still young.

TROY The *boy* is thirty-four years old.

ROSE Let's not get off into all that.

BONO Look here . . . I got to be going. I got to be getting on. Lucille gonna be waiting.

TROY (*puts his arm around* ROSE) See this woman, Bono? I love this woman. I love this woman so much it hurts. I love her so much . . . I done run out of ways of loving her. So I got to go back to basics. Don't you come by my house Monday morning talking about time to go to work . . . 'cause I'm still gonna be stroking!

ROSE Troy! Stop it now!

BONO I ain't paying him no mind, Rose. That ain't nothing but gin-talk. Go on, Troy. I'll see you Monday.

TROY Don't you come by my house, nigger! I done told you what I'm gonna be doing.

(*The lights go down to black.*)

Scene II

The lights come up on ROSE *hanging up clothes. She hums and sings softly to herself. It is the following morning.*

ROSE (*sings*) Jesus, be a fence all around me every day
Jesus, I want you to protect me as I travel on my way.
Jesus, be a fence all around me every day.

(TROY *enters from the house.*)

ROSE (*continued*) Jesus, I want you to protect me
As I travel on my way.

(*to* TROY)

'Morning. You ready for breakfast? I can fix it soon as I finish hanging up these clothes?

TROY I got the coffee on. That'll be alright. I'll just drink some of that this morning.

ROSE That 651 hit yesterday. That's the second time this month. Miss Pearl hit for a dollar . . . seem like those that need the least always get lucky. Poor folks can't get nothing.

TROY Them numbers don't know nobody. I don't know why you fool with them. You and Lyons both.

ROSE It's something to do.

TROY You ain't doing nothing but throwing your money away.

ROSE Troy, you know I don't play foolishly. I just play a nickel here and a nickel there.

TROY That's two nickels you done thrown away.

ROSE Now I hit sometimes . . . that makes up for it. It always comes in handy when I do hit. I don't hear you complaining then.

TROY I ain't complaining now. I just say it's foolish. Trying to guess out of six hundred ways which way the number gonna come. If I had all the money niggers, these Negroes, throw away on numbers for one week—just one week—I'd be a rich man.

ROSE Well, you wishing and calling it foolish ain't gonna stop folks from playing numbers. That's one thing for sure. Besides . . . some good things come from playing numbers. Look where Pope done bought him that restaurant off of numbers.

TROY I can't stand niggers like that. Man ain't had two dimes to rub together. He walking around with his shoes all run over bumming money for cigarettes. Alright. Got lucky there and hit the numbers . . .

ROSE Troy, I know all about it.

TROY Had good sense, I'll say that for him. He ain't throwed his money away. I seen niggers hit the numbers and go through two thousand dollars in four days. Man brought him that restaurant down there . . . fixed it up real nice . . . and then didn't want nobody to come in it! A Negro go in there and can't get no kind of service. I seen a white fellow come in there and order a bowl of stew. Pope picked all the meat out the pot for him. Man ain't had nothing but a bowl of meat! Negro come behind him and ain't got nothing but the potatoes and carrots. Talking about what numbers do for people, you picked a wrong example. Ain't done nothing but make a worser fool out of him than he was before.

ROSE Troy, you ought to stop worrying about what happened at work yesterday.

TROY I ain't worried. Just told me to be down there at the Commissioner's office on Friday. Everybody think they gonna fire me. I ain't worried about them firing me. You ain't got to worry about that.

(*pause*)

Where's Cory? Cory in the house? (*calls*) Cory?

ROSE He gone out.

TROY Out, huh? He gone out 'cause he know I want him to help me with this fence. I know how he is. That boy scared of work.

(GABRIEL *enters. He comes halfway down the alley and, hearing* TROY'S *voice, stops.*)

TROY (*continues*) He ain't done a lick of work in his life.

ROSE He had to go to football practice. Coach wanted them to get in a little extra practice before the season start.

TROY I got his practice . . . running out of here before he get his chores done.

ROSE Troy, what is wrong with you this morning? Don't nothing set right with you. Go on back in there and go to bed . . . get up on the other side.

TROY Why something got to be wrong with me? I ain't said nothing wrong with me.

ROSE You got something to say about everything. First it's the numbers . . . then it's the way the man runs his restaurant . . . then you done got on Cory. What's it gonna be next? Take a look up there and see if the weather suits you . . . or is it gonna be how you gonna put up the fence with the clothes hanging in the yard.

TROY You hit the nail on the head then.

ROSE I know you like I know the back of my hand. Go on in there and get you some coffee . . . see if that straighten you up. 'Cause you ain't right this morning.

(TROY *starts into the house and sees* GABRIEL. GABRIEL *starts singing.* TROY*'s brother, he is seven years younger than* TROY. *Injured in World War II, he has a metal plate in his head. He carries an old trumpet tied around his waist and believes with every fiber of his being that he is the Archangel Gabriel. He carries a chipped basket with an assortment of discarded fruits and vegetables he has picked up in the strip district and which he attempts to sell.*)

GABRIEL (*singing*)

Yes, ma'am, I got plums
You ask me how I sell them
Oh ten cents apiece
Three for a quarter
Come and buy now
'Cause I'm here today
And tomorrow I'll be gone

(GABRIEL *enters.*)

Hey, Rose!

ROSE How you doing, Gabe?

GABRIEL There's Troy . . . Hey, Troy!

TROY Hey, Gabe.

(*exit into kitchen*)

ROSE (*to* GABRIEL) What you got there?

GABRIEL You know what I got, Rose. I got fruits and vegetables.

ROSE (*looking in basket*) Where's all these plums you talking about?

GABRIEL I ain't got no plums today, Rose. I was just singing that. Have some tomorrow. Put me in a big order for plums. Have enough plums tomorrow for St. Peter and everybody.

(TROY *reenters from kitchen, crosses to steps.*)

(*to* ROSE)

Troy's mad at me.

TROY I ain't mad at you. What I got to be mad at you about? You ain't done nothing to me.

GABRIEL I just moved over to Miss Pearl's to keep out from in your way. I ain't mean no harm by it.

TROY Who said anything about that? I ain't said anything about that.

GABRIEL You ain't mad at me, is you?

TROY Naw . . . I ain't mad at you, Gabe. If I was mad at you I'd tell you about it.

GABRIEL Got me two rooms. In the basement. Got my own door too. Wanna see my key?

(*He holds up a key.*)

That's my own key! Ain't nobody else got a key like that. That's my key! My two rooms!

TROY Well, that's good, Gabe. You got your own key . . . that's good.

ROSE You hungry, Gabe? I was just fixing to cook Troy his breakfast.

GABRIEL I'll take some biscuits. You got some biscuits? Did you know when I was in heaven . . . every morning me and St. Peter would sit down by the gate and eat some big fat biscuits? Oh, yeah! We had us a good time. We'd sit there and eat us them biscuits and then St. Peter would go off to sleep and tell me to wake him up when it's time to open the gates for the judgment.

ROSE Well, come on . . . I'll make up a batch of biscuits.

(ROSE *exits into the house.*)

GABRIEL Troy . . . St. Peter got your name in the book. I seen it. It say . . . Troy Maxson. I say . . . I know him! He got the same name like what I got. That's my brother!

TROY How many times you gonna tell me that, Gabe?

GABRIEL Ain't got my name in the book. Don't have to have my name. I done died and went to heaven. He got your name though. One morning St. Peter was looking at his book . . . marking it up for the judgment . . . and he let me see your name. Got it in there under M. Got Rose's name . . . I ain't seen it like I seen yours . . . but I know it's in there. He got a great big book. Got everybody's name what was ever been born. That's what he told me. But I seen your name. Seen it with my own eyes.

TROY Go on in the house there. Rose going to fix you something to eat.

GABRIEL Oh, I ain't hungry. I done had breakfast with Aunt Jemimah. She come by and cooked me up a whole mess of flapjacks. Remember how we used to eat them flapjacks?

TROY Go on in the house and get you something to eat now.

GABRIEL I got to go sell my plums. I done sold some tomatoes. Got me two quarters. Wanna see?

(*He shows* TROY *his quarters.*)

I'm gonna save them and buy me a new horn so St. Peter can hear me when it's time to open the gates.

(GABRIEL *stops suddenly, listens.*)

Hear that? That's the hellhounds. I got to chase them out of here. Go on get out of here! Get out!

(GABRIEL *exits singing.*)

Better get ready for the judgment
Better get ready for the judgment
My Lord is coming down

(ROSE *enters from the house.*)

TROY He gone off somewhere.

GABRIEL (*offstage*)
Better get ready for the judgment
Better get ready for the judgment morning
Better get ready for the judgment
My God is coming down

ROSE He ain't eating right. Miss Pearl say she can't get him to eat nothing.

TROY What you want me to do about it, Rose? I done did everything I can for the man. I can't make him get well. Man got half his head blown away . . . what you expect?

ROSE Seem like something ought to be done to help him.

TROY Man don't bother nobody. He just mixed up from that metal plate he got in his head. Ain't no sense for him to go back into the hospital.

ROSE Least he be eating right. They can help him take care of himself.

TROY Don't nobody wanna be locked up, Rose. What you wanna lock him up for? Man go over there and fight the war . . . messin' around with them Japs, get half his head blown off . . . and they give him a lousy three thousand dollars. And I had to swoop down on that.

ROSE Is you fixing to go into that again?

TROY That's the only way I got a roof over my head . . . cause of that metal plate.

ROSE Ain't no sense you blaming yourself for nothing. Gabe wasn't in no condition to manage that money. You done what was right by him. Can't nobody say you ain't done what was right by him. Look how long you took care of him . . . till he wanted to have his own place and moved over there with Miss Pearl.

TROY That ain't what I'm saying, woman! I'm just stating the facts. If my brother didn't have that metal plate in his head . . . I wouldn't have a pot to piss in or a window to throw it out of. And I'm fifty-three years old. Now see if you can understand that!

(TROY *gets up from the porch and starts to exit the yard.*)

ROSE Where you going off to? You been running out of here every Saturday for weeks. I thought you was gonna work on this fence?

TROY I'm gonna walk down to Taylors'. Listen to the ball game. I'll be back in a bit. I'll work on it when I get back.

(*He exits the yard. The lights go to black.*)

Scene III

The lights come up on the yard. It is four hours later. **ROSE** *is taking down the clothes from the line.* **CORY** *enters carrying his football equipment.*

ROSE Your daddy like to had a fit with you running out of here this morning without doing your chores.

CORY I told you I had to go to practice.

ROSE He say you were supposed to help him with this fence.

CORY He been saying that the last four or five Saturdays, and then he don't never do nothing, but go down to Taylors'. Did you tell him about the recruiter?

ROSE Yeah, I told him.

CORY What he say?

ROSE He ain't said nothing too much. You get in there and get started on your chores before he gets back. Go on and scrub down them steps before he gets back here hollering and carrying on.

CORY I'm hungry. What you got to eat, Mama?

ROSE Go on and get started on your chores. I got some meat loaf in there. Go on and make you a sandwich . . . and don't leave no mess in there.

(CORY *exits into the house.* ROSE *continues to take down the clothes.* TROY *enters the yard and sneaks up and grabs her from behind.*)

Troy! Go on, now. You like to scared me to death. What was the score of the game? Lucille had me on the phone and I couldn't keep up with it.

TROY What I care about the game? Come here, woman.

(*He tries to kiss her.*)

ROSE I thought you went down Taylors' to listen to the game. Go on, Troy! You supposed to be putting up this fence.

TROY (*attempting to kiss her again*) I'll put it up when I finish with what is at hand.

ROSE Go on, Troy. I ain't studying you.

TROY (*chasing after her*) I'm studying you . . . fixing to do my homework!

ROSE Troy, you better leave me alone.

TROY Where's Cory? That boy brought his butt home yet?

ROSE He's in the house doing his chores.

TROY (*calling*) Cory! Get your butt out here, boy!

(ROSE *exits into the house with the laundry.* TROY *goes over to the pile of wood, picks up a board, and starts sawing.* CORY *enters from the house.*)

TROY You just now coming in here from leaving this morning?

CORY Yeah, I had to go to football practice.

TROY Yeah, what?

CORY Yessir.

TROY I ain't but two seconds off you noway. The garbage sitting in there overflowing . . . you ain't done none of your chores . . . and you come in here talking about "Yeah."

CORY I was just getting ready to do my chores now, Pop . . .

TROY Your first chore is to help me with this fence on Saturday. Everything else come after that. Now get that saw and cut them boards.

(CORY *takes the saw and begins cutting the boards.* TROY *continues working. There is a long pause.*)

CORY Hey, Pop . . . why don't you buy a TV?

TROY What I want with a TV? What I want one of them for?

CORY Everybody got one. Earl, Ba Bra . . . Jesse!

TROY I ain't asked you who had one. I say what I want with one?

CORY So you can watch it. They got lots of things on TV. Baseball games and everything. We could watch the World Series.

TROY Yeah . . . and how much this TV cost?

CORY I don't know. They got them on sale for around two hundred dollars.

TROY Two hundred dollars, huh?

CORY That ain't that much, Pop.

TROY Naw, it's just two hundred dollars. See that roof you got over your head at night? Let me tell you something about that roof. It's been over ten years since that roof was last tarred. See now . . . the snow come this winter and sit up there on that roof like it is . . . and it's gonna seep inside. It's just gonna be a little bit . . . ain't gonna hardly notice it. Then the next thing you know, it's gonna be leaking all over the house. Then the wood rot from all that water and you gonna need a whole new roof. Now, how much you think it cost to get that roof tarred?

CORY I don't know.

TROY Two hundred and sixty-four dollars . . . cash money. While you thinking about a TV, I got to be thinking about the roof . . . and whatever else go wrong around here. Now if you had two hundred dollars, what would you do . . . fix the roof or buy a TV?

CORY I'd buy a TV. Then when the roof started to leak . . . when it needed fixing . . . I'd fix it.

TROY Where you gonna get the money from? You done spent it for a TV. You gonna sit up and watch the water run all over your brand new TV.

CORY Aw, Pop. You got money. I know you do.

TROY Where I got it at, huh?

CORY You got it in the bank.

TROY You wanna see my bankbook? You wanna see that seventy-three dollars and twenty-two cents I got sitting up in there.

CORY You ain't got to pay for it all at one time. You can put a down payment on it and carry it on home with you.

TROY Not me. I ain't gonna owe nobody nothing if I can help it. Miss a payment and they come and snatch it right out your house. Then what you got? Now, soon as I get two hundred dollars clear, then I'll buy a TV. Right now, as soon as I get two hundred and sixty-four dollars, I'm gonna have this roof tarred.

CORY Aw . . . Pop!

TROY You go on and get you two hundred dollars and buy one if ya want it. I got better things to do with my money.

CORY I can't get no two hundred dollars. I ain't never seen two hundred dollars.

TROY I'll tell you what . . . you get you a hundred dollars and I'll put the other hundred with it.

CORY Alright, I'm gonna show you.

TROY You gonna show me how you can cut them boards right now.

(CORY *begins to cut the boards. There is a long pause.*)

CORY The Pirates won today. That makes five in a row.

TROY I ain't thinking about the Pirates. Got an all-white team. Got that boy . . . that Puerto Rican boy . . . Clemente. Don't even half-play him. That boy could be something if they give him a chance. Play him one day and sit him on the bench the next.

CORY He gets a lot of chances to play.

TROY I'm talking about playing regular. Playing every day so you can get your timing. That's what I'm talking about.

CORY They got some white guys on the team that don't play every day. You can't play everybody at the same time.

TROY If they got a white fellow sitting on the bench . . . you can bet your last dollar he can't play! The colored guy got to be twice as good before he get on the team. That's why I don't want you to get all tied up in them sports. Man on the team and what it get him? They got colored on the team and don't use them. Same as not having them. All them teams the same.

CORY The Braves got Hank Aaron and Wes Covington. Hank Aaron hit two home runs today. That makes forty-three.

TROY Hank Aaron ain't nobody. That's what you supposed to do. That's how you supposed to play the game. Ain't nothing to it. It's just a matter of timing . . . getting the right follow-through. Hell, I can hit forty-three home runs right now!

CORY Not off no major-league pitching, you couldn't.

TROY We had better pitching in the Negro leagues. I hit seven home runs off of Satchel Paige. You can't get no better than that!

CORY Sandy Koufax. He's leading the league in strikeouts.

TROY I ain't thinking of no Sandy Koufax.

CORY You got Warren Spahn and Lew Burdette. I bet you couldn't hit no home runs off of Warren Spahn.

TROY I'm through with it now. You go on and cut them boards.

(*pause*)

Your mama tell me you done got recruited by a college football team? Is that right?

CORY Yeah. Coach Zellman say the recruiter gonna be coming by to talk to you. Get you to sign the permission papers.

TROY I thought you supposed to be working down there at the A&P. Ain't you suppose to be working down there after school?

CORY Mr. Stawicki say he gonna hold my job for me until after the football season. Say starting next week I can work weekends.

TROY I thought we had an understanding about this football stuff? You suppose to keep up with your chores and hold that job down at the A&P. Ain't been around here all day on a Saturday. Ain't none of your chores done . . . and now you telling me you done quit your job.

CORY I'm gonna be working weekends.

TROY You damn right you are! And ain't no need for nobody coming around here to talk to me about signing nothing.

CORY Hey, Pop . . . you can't do that. He's coming all the way from North Carolina.

TROY I don't care where he coming from. The white man ain't gonna let you get nowhere with that football noway. You go on and get your book-learning so you can work yourself up in that A&P or learn how to fix cars or build houses or something, get you a trade. That way you have something can't nobody take away from you. You go on and learn how to put your hands to some good use. Besides hauling people's garbage.

CORY I get good grades, Pop. That's why the recruiter wants to talk with you. You got to keep up your grades to get recruited. This way I'll be going to college. I'll get a chance . . .

TROY First you gonna get your butt down there to the A&P and get your job back.

CORY Mr. Stawicki done already hired somebody else 'cause I told him I was playing football.

TROY You a bigger fool than I thought . . . to let somebody take away your job so you can play some football. Where you gonna get your money to take out your girlfriend and whatnot? What kind of foolishness is that to let somebody take away your job?

CORY I'm still gonna be working weekends.

TROY Naw . . . naw. You getting your butt out of here and finding you another job.

CORY Come on, Pop! I got to practice. I can't work after school and play football too. The team needs me. That's what Coach Zellman say . . .

TROY I don't care what nobody else say. I'm the boss . . . you understand? I'm the boss around here. I do the only saying what counts.

CORY Come on, Pop!

TROY I asked you . . . did you understand?

CORY Yeah . . .

TROY What?!

CORY Yessir.

TROY You go on down there to that A&P and see if you can get your job back. If you can't do both . . . then you quit the football team. You've got to take the crookeds with the straights.

CORY Yessir.

(*pause*)

Can I ask you a question?

TROY What the hell you wanna ask me? Mr. Stawicki the one you got the questions for.

CORY How come you ain't never liked me?

TROY Liked you? Who the hell say I got to like you? What law is there say I got to like you? Wanna stand up in my face and ask a damn fool-ass question like that. Talking about liking somebody. Come here, boy, when I talk to you.

(CORY *comes over to where* TROY *is working. He stands slouched over and* TROY *shoves him on his shoulder.*)

Straighten up, goddammit! I asked you a question . . . what law is there say I got to like you?

CORY None.

TROY Well, alright then! Don't you eat every day?

(*pause*)

Answer me when I talk to you! Don't you eat every day?

CORY Yeah.

TROY Nigger, as long as you in my house, you put that sir on the end of it when you talk to me!

CORY Yes . . . sir.

TROY You eat every day.

CORY Yessir!

TROY Got a roof over your head.

CORY Yessir!

TROY Got clothes on your back.

CORY Yessir.

TROY Why you think that is?

CORY Cause of you.

TROY Aw, hell I know it's 'cause of me . . . but why do you think that is?

CORY (*hesitant*) Cause you like me.

TROY Like you? I go out of here every morning . . . bust my butt . . . putting up with them crackers every day . . . cause I like you? You about the biggest fool I ever saw.

(*pause*)

It's my job. It's my responsibility! You understand that? A man got to take care of his family. You live in my house . . . sleep you behind on my bedclothes . . . fill you belly up with my food . . . cause you my son. You my flesh and blood. Not 'cause I like you! Cause it's my duty to take care of you. I owe a responsibility to you! Let's get this straight right here . . . before it go along any further . . . I ain't got to like you. Mr. Rand don't give me my money come payday cause he likes me. He gives me cause he owe me. I done give you everything I had to give you. I gave you your life! Me and your mama worked that out between us. And liking your black ass wasn't part of the bargain. Don't you try and go through life worrying about if somebody like you or not. You best be making sure they doing right by you. You understand what I'm saying, boy?

CORY Yessir.

TROY Then get the hell out of my face, and get on down to that A&P.

(ROSE *has been standing behind the screen door for much of the scene. She enters as* CORY *exits.*)

ROSE Why don't you let the boy go ahead and play football, Troy? Ain't no harm in that. He's just trying to be like you with the sports.

TROY I don't want him to be like me! I want him to move as far away from my life as he can get. You the only decent thing that ever happened to me. I wish him that. But I don't wish him a thing else from my life. I decided seventeen years ago that boy wasn't getting involved in no sports. Not after what they did to me in the sports.

ROSE Troy, why don't you admit you was too old to play in the major leagues? For once . . . why don't you admit that?

TROY What do you mean too old? Don't come telling me I was too old. I just wasn't the right color. Hell, I'm fifty-three years old and can do better than Selkirk's .269 right now!

ROSE How's was you gonna play ball when you were over forty? Sometimes I can't get no sense out of you.

TROY I got good sense, woman. I got sense enough not to let my boy get hurt over playing no sports. You been mothering that boy too much. Worried about if people like him.

ROSE Everything that boy do . . . he do for you. He wants you to say "Good job, son." That's all.

TROY Rose, I ain't got time for that. He's alive. He's healthy. He's got to make his own way. I made mine. Ain't nobody gonna hold his hand when he get out there in that world.

ROSE Times have changed from when you was young, Troy. People change. The world's changing around you and you can't even see it.

TROY (*slow, methodical*) Woman . . . I do the best I can do. I come in here every Friday. I carry a sack of potatoes and a bucket of lard. You all line up at the door with your hands out. I give you the lint from my pockets. I give you my sweat and my blood. I ain't got no tears. I done spent them. We go upstairs in that room at night . . . and I fall down on you and try to blast a hole into forever. I get up Monday morning . . . find my lunch on the table. I go out. Make my way. Find my strength to carry me through to the next Friday.

(*pause*)

That's all I got, Rose. That's all I got to give. I can't give nothing else.

(TROY *exits into the house. The lights go down to black.*)

Scene IV

It is Friday. Two weeks later. **CORY** *starts out of the house with his football equipment. The phone rings.*

CORY (*calling*) I got it!

(*He answers the phone and stands in the screen door talking.*)

Hello? Hey, Jesse. Naw . . . I was just getting ready to leave now.

ROSE (*calling*) Cory!

CORY I told you, man, them spikes is all tore up. You can use them if you want, but they ain't no good. Earl got some spikes.

ROSE (*calling*) Cory!

CORY (*calling to* ROSE) Mam? I'm talking to Jesse.

(*into phone*)

When she say that? (*pause*) Aw, you lying, man. I'm gonna tell her you said that.

ROSE (*calling*) Cory, don't you go nowhere!

CORY I got to go to the game, Ma!

(*into the phone*)

Yeah, hey, look, I'll talk to you later. Yeah, I'll meet you over Earl's house. Later. Bye, Ma.

(CORY *exits the house and starts out the yard.*)

ROSE Cory, where you going off to? You got that stuff all pulled out and thrown all over your room.

CORY (*in the yard*) I was looking for my spikes. Jesse wanted to borrow my spikes.

ROSE Get up there and get that cleaned up before your daddy get back in here.

CORY I got to go to the game! I'll clean it up *when I get back.*

(CORY *exits.*)

ROSE That's all he need to do is see that room all messed up.

(ROSE *exits into the house.* TROY *and* BONO *enter the yard.* TROY *is dressed in clothes other than his work clothes.*)

BONO He told him the same thing he told you. Take it to the union.

TROY Brownie ain't got that much sense. Man wasn't thinking about nothing. He wait until I confront them on it . . . then he wanna come crying seniority.

(*calls*)

Hey, Rose!

BONO I wish I could have seen Mr. Rand's face when he told you.

TROY He couldn't get it out of his mouth! Liked to bit his tongue! When they called me down there to the Commissioner's office . . . he thought they was gonna fire me. Like everybody else.

BONO I didn't think they was gonna fire you. I thought they was gonna put you on the warning paper.

TROY Hey, Rose!

(*to* BONO)

Yeah, Mr. Rand like to bit his tongue.

(TROY *breaks the seal on the bottle, takes a drink, and hands it to* BONO.)

BONO I see you run right down to Taylors' and told that Alberta gal.

TROY (*calling*) Hey Rose! (*to* BONO) I told everybody. Hey, Rose! I went down there to cash my check.

ROSE (*entering from the house*) Hush all that hollering, man! I know you out here. What they say down there at the Commissioner's office?

TROY You supposed to come when I call you, woman. Bono'll tell you that.

(*to* BONO)

Don't Lucille come when you call her?

ROSE Man, hush your mouth. I ain't no dog . . . talk about "come when you call me."

TROY (*puts his arm around* ROSE) You hear this, Bono? I had me an old dog used to get uppity like that. You say, "C'mere, Blue!" . . . and he just lay there and look at you. End up getting a stick and chasing him away trying to make him come.

ROSE I ain't studying you and your dog. I remember you used to sing that old song.

TROY (*He sings.*) Hear it ring! Hear it ring!
I had a dog his name was Blue.

ROSE Don't nobody wanna hear you sing that old song.

TROY (*sings*) You know Blue was mighty true.

ROSE Used to have Cory running around here singing that song.

BONO Hell, I remember that song myself.

TROY (*sings*) You know Blue was a good old dog.
Blue treed a possum in a hollow log.

That was my daddy's song. My daddy made up that song.

ROSE I don't care who made it up. Don't nobody wanna hear you sing it.

TROY (*makes a song like calling a dog*) Come here, woman.

ROSE You come in here carrying on, I reckon they ain't fired you. What they say down there at the Commissioner's office?

TROY Look here, Rose . . . Mr. Rand called me into his office today when I got back from talking to them people down there . . . it come from up top . . . he called me in and told me they was making me a driver.

ROSE Troy, you kidding!

TROY No I ain't. Ask Bono.

ROSE Well, that's great, Troy. Now you don't have to hassle them people no more.

(LYONS *enters from the street.*)

TROY Aw hell, I wasn't looking to see you today. I thought you was in jail. Got it all over the front page of the *Courier* about them raiding Sefus' place . . . where you be hanging out with all them thugs.

LYONS Hey, Pop . . . that ain't got nothing to do with me. I don't go down there gambling. I go down there to sit in with the band. I ain't got nothing to do with the gambling part. They got some good music down there.

TROY They got some rogues . . . is what they got.

LYONS How you been, Mr. Bono? Hi, Rose.

BONO I see where you playing down at the Crawford Grill tonight.

ROSE How come you ain't brought Bonnie like I told you. You should have brought Bonnie with you, she ain't been over in a month of Sundays.

LYONS I was just in the neighborhood . . . thought I'd stop by.

TROY Here he come . . .

BONO Your daddy got a promotion on the rubbish. He's gonna be the first colored driver. Ain't got to do nothing but sit up there and read the paper like them white fellows.

LYONS Hey, Pop . . . if you knew how to read you'd be alright.

BONO Naw . . . naw . . . you mean if the nigger knew how to *drive* he'd be all right. Been fighting with them people about driving and ain't even got a license. Mr. Rand know you ain't got no driver's license?

TROY Driving ain't nothing. All you do is point the truck where you want it to go. Driving ain't nothing.

BONO Do Mr. Rand know you ain't got no driver's license? That's what I'm talking about. I ain't asked if driving was easy. I asked if Mr. Rand know you ain't go no driver's license.

TROY He ain't got to know. The man ain't got to know my business. Time he find out, I have two or three driver's licenses.

LYONS (*going into his pocket*) Say, look here, Pop . . .

TROY I knew it was coming. Didn't I tell you, Bono? I know what kind of "Look here, Pop" that was. The nigger fixing to ask me for some money. It's Friday night. It's my payday. All them rogues down there on the avenue . . . the ones that ain't in jail . . . and Lyons is hopping in his shoes to get down there with them.

LYONS See, Pop . . . if you give somebody else a chance to talk sometime, you'd see that I was fixing to pay you back your ten dollars like I told you. Here . . . I told you I'd pay you when Bonnie got paid.

TROY Naw . . . you go ahead and keep that ten dollars. Put it in the bank. The next time you feel like you wanna come by here and ask me for something . . . you go on down there and get that.

LYONS Here's your ten dollars, Pop. I told you I don't want you to give me nothing. I just wanted to borrow ten dollars.

TROY Naw . . . you go on and keep that for the next time you want to ask me.

LYONS Come on, Pop . . . here go your ten dollars.

ROSE Why don't you go on and let the boy pay you back, Troy?

LYONS Here you go, Rose. If you don't take it I'm gonna have to hear about it for the next six months.

(*He hands her the money.*)

ROSE You can hand yours over here too, Troy.

TROY You see this, Bono. You see how they do me.

BONO Yeah, Lucille do me the same way.

(GABRIEL *is heard singing offstage. He enters.*)

GABRIEL Better get ready for the Judgment! Better get ready for . . . Hey! . . . Hey! There's Troy's boy!

LYONS How you doing, Uncle Gabe?

GABRIEL Lyons . . . The King of the Jungle! Rose . . . hey, Rose. Got a flower for you.

(*He takes a rose from his pocket.*)

Picked it myself. That's the same rose like you is!

ROSE That's right nice of you, Gabe.

LYONS What you been doing, Uncle Gabe?

GABRIEL Oh, I been chasing hellhounds and waiting on the time to tell St. Peter to open the gates.

LYONS You been chasing hellhounds, huh? Well . . . you doing the right thing, Uncle Gabe. Somebody got to chase them.

GABRIEL Oh, yeah . . . I know it. The devil's strong. The devil ain't no pushover. Hellhounds snipping at everybody's heels. But I got my trumpet waiting on the judgment time.

LYONS Waiting on the Battle of Armageddon, huh?

GABRIEL Ain't gonna be too much of a battle when God get to waving that Judgment sword. But the people's gonna have a hell of a time trying to get into heaven if them gates ain't open.

LYONS (*putting his arm around* GABRIEL) You hear this, Pop. Uncle Gabe, you alright!

GABRIEL (*laughing with* LYONS) Lyons! King of the Jungle.

ROSE You gonna stay for supper, Gabe. Want me to fix you a plate?

GABRIEL I'll take a sandwich, Rose. Don't want no plate. Just wanna eat with my hands. I'll take a sandwich.

ROSE How about you, Lyons? You staying? Got some short ribs cooking.

LYONS Naw, I won't eat nothing till after we finished playing.

(*pause*)

You ought to come down and listen to me play, Pop.

TROY I don't like that Chinese music. All that noise.

ROSE Go on in the house and wash up, Gabe . . . I'll fix you a sandwich.

GABRIEL (*to* LYONS, *as he exits*) Troy's mad at me.

LYONS What you mad at Uncle Gabe for, Pop.

ROSE He thinks Troy's mad at him cause he moved over to Miss Pearl's.

TROY I ain't mad at the man. He can live where he want to live at.

LYONS What he move over there for? Miss Pearl don't like nobody.

ROSE She don't mind him none. She treats him real nice. She just don't allow all that singing.

TROY She don't mind that rent he be paying . . . that's what she don't mind.

ROSE Troy, I ain't going through that with you no more. He's over there cause he want to have his own place. He can come and go as he please.

TROY Hell, he could come and go as he please here. I wasn't stopping him. I ain't put no rules on him.

ROSE It ain't the same thing, Troy. And you know it.

(GABRIEL *comes to the door.*)

Now, that's the last I wanna hear about that. I don't wanna hear nothing else about Gabe and Miss Pearl. And next week . . .

GABRIEL I'm ready for my sandwich, Rose.

ROSE And next week . . . when that recruiter come from that school . . . I want you to sign that paper and go on and let Cory play football. Then that'll be the last I have to hear about that.

TROY (*to* ROSE *as she exits into the house*) I ain't thinking about Cory nothing.

LYONS What . . . Cory got recruited? What school he going to?

TROY That boy walking around here smelling his piss . . . thinking he's grown. Thinking he's gonna do what he want, irrespective of what I say. Look here, Bono . . . I left the Commissioner's office and went down to the A&P . . . that boy ain't working down there. He lying to me. Telling me he got his job back . . . telling me he working weekends . . . telling me he working after school . . . Mr. Stawicki tell me he ain't working down there at all!

LYONS Cory just growing up. He's just busting at the seams trying to fill out your shoes.

TROY I don't care what he's doing. When he get to the point where he wanna disobey me . . . then it's time for him to move on. Bono'll tell you that. I bet he ain't never disobeyed his daddy without paying the consequences.

BONO I ain't never had a chance. My daddy came on through . . . but I ain't never knew him to see him . . . or what he had on his mind or where he went. Just moving on through. Searching out the New Land. That's what the old folks used to call it. See a fellow moving around from place to place . . . woman to woman . . . called it searching out the New Land. I can't say if he ever found it. I come along, didn't want no kids. Didn't know if I was gonna be in one place long enough to fix on them right as their daddy. I figured I was going searching too. As it turned out I been hooked up with Lucille near about as long as your daddy been with Rose. Going on sixteen years.

TROY Sometimes I wish I hadn't known my daddy. He ain't cared nothing about no kids. A kid to him wasn't nothing. All he wanted was for you to learn how to walk so he could start you to working. When it come time for eating . . . he ate first. If there was anything left over, that's what you got. Man would sit down and eat two chickens and give you the wing.

LYONS You ought to stop that, Pop. Everybody feed their kids. No matter how hard times is . . . everybody care about their kids. Make sure they have something to eat.

TROY The only thing my daddy cared about was getting them bales of cotton in to Mr. Lubin. That's the only thing that mattered to him. Sometimes I used to wonder why he was living. Wonder why the devil hadn't come and got him. "Get them bales of cotton in to Mr. Lubin" and find out he owe him money . . .

LYONS He should have just went on and left when he saw he couldn't get nowhere. That's what I would have done.

TROY How he gonna leave with eleven kids? And where he gonna go? He ain't knew how to do nothing but farm. No, he was trapped and I think he knew it. But I'll say this for him . . . he felt a responsibility toward us. Maybe he ain't treated us the way I felt he should have . . . but without that responsibility he could have walked off and left us . . . made his own way.

BONO A lot of them did. Back in those days what you talking about . . . they walk out their front door and just take on down one road or another and keep on walking.

LYONS There you go! That's what I'm talking about.

BONO Just keep on walking till you come to something else. Ain't you never heard of nobody having the walking blues? Well, that's what you call it when you just take off like that.

TROY My daddy ain't had them walking blues! What you talking about? He stayed right there with his family. But he was just as evil as he could be. My mama couldn't stand him. Couldn't stand that evilness. She run off when I was about eight. She sneaked off one night after he had gone to sleep. Told me she was coming back for me. I ain't never seen her no more. All his women run off and left him. He wasn't good for nobody.

When my turn come to head out, I was fourteen and got to sniffing around Joe Canewell's daughter. Had us an old mule we called Greyboy. My daddy sent me out to do some plowing and I tied up Greyboy and went to fooling around with Joe Canewell's daughter. We done found us a nice little spot, got real cozy with each other. She about thirteen and we done figured we was grown anyway . . . so we down there enjoying ourselves . . . ain't thinking about nothing. We didn't know Greyboy had got loose and wandered back to the house and my daddy was looking for me. We down there by the creek enjoying ourselves when my daddy come up on us. Surprised us. He had them leather straps off the mule and commenced to whupping me like there was no tomorrow. I jumped up, mad and embarrassed. I was scared of my daddy. When he commenced to whupping on me . . . quite naturally I run to get out of the way.

(*pause*)

Now I thought he was mad cause I ain't done my work. But I see where he was chasing me off so he could have the gal for himself. When I see what the matter of it was, I lost all fear of my daddy. Right there is where I become a man . . . at fourteen years of age.

(*pause*)

Now it was my turn to run him off. I picked up them same reins that he had used on me. I picked up them reins and commenced to whupping on him. The gal jumped up and run off . . . and when my daddy turned to face me, I could see why the devil had never come to get him . . . cause he was the devil himself. I don't know what happened. When I woke up, I was laying right there by the creek, and Blue . . . this old dog we had . . . was licking my face. I thought I was blind. I couldn't see nothing. Both my eyes were swollen shut. I layed there and cried. I didn't know what I was gonna do. The only thing I knew was the time had come for me to leave my daddy's house. And right there the world suddenly got big. And it was a long time before I could cut it down to where I could handle it.

Part of that cutting down was when I got to the place where I could feel him kicking in my blood and knew that the only thing that separated us was the matter of a few years.

(GABRIEL *enters from the house with a sandwich.*)

LYONS What you got there, Uncle Gabe?

GABRIEL Got me a ham sandwich. Rose gave me a ham sandwich.

TROY I don't know what happened to him. I done lost touch with everybody except Gabriel. But I hope he's dead. I hope he found some peace.

LYONS That's a heavy story, Pop. I didn't know you left home when you was fourteen.

TROY And didn't know nothing. The only part of the world I knew was the forty-two acres of Mr. Lubin's land. That's all I knew about life.

LYONS Fourteen's kinda young to be out on your own. (*phone rings*) I don't even think I was ready to be out on my own at fourteen. I don't know what I would have done.

TROY I got up from the creek and walked on down to Mobile. I was through with farming. Figured I could do better in the city. So I walked the two hundred miles to Mobile.

LYONS Wait a minute . . . you ain't walked no two hundred miles, Pop. Ain't nobody gonna walk no two hundred miles. You talking about some walking there.

BONO That's the only way you got anywhere back in them days.

LYONS Shhh. Damn if I wouldn't have hitched a ride with somebody!

TROY Who you gonna hitch it with? They ain't had no cars and things like they got now. We talking about 1918.

ROSE (*entering*) What you all out here getting into?

TROY (*to* ROSE) I'm telling Lyons how good he got it. He don't know nothing about this I'm talking.

ROSE Lyons, that was Bonnie on the phone. She say you supposed to pick her up.

LYONS Yeah, okay, Rose.

TROY I walked on down to Mobile and hitched up with some of them fellows that was heading this way. Got up here and found out . . . not only couldn't you get a job . . . you couldn't find no place to live. I thought I was in freedom. Shhh. Colored folks living down there on the riverbanks in whatever kind of shelter they could find for themselves. Right down there under the Brady Street Bridge. Living in shacks made of sticks and tarpaper. Messed around there and went from bad to worse. Started stealing. First it was food. Then I figured, hell, if I steal money I can buy me some food. Buy me some shoes too! One thing led to another. Met your mama. I was young and anxious to be a man. Met your mama and had you. What I do that for? Now I got to worry about feeding you and her. Got to steal three times as much. Went out one day looking for somebody to rob . . . that's what I was, a robber. I'll tell you the truth. I'm ashamed of it today. But it's the truth. Went to rob this fellow . . . pulled out my knife . . . and he pulled out a gun. Shot me in the chest. It felt just like somebody had taken a hot branding iron and laid it on me. When he shot me I jumped at him with my knife. They told me I killed him and they put me in the penitentiary and locked me up for fifteen years. That's where I met Bono. That's where I learned how to play baseball. Got out that place and your mama had taken you and went on to make life without me. Fifteen years was a long time for her to wait. But that fifteen years cured me of that robbing stuff. Rose'll tell you. She asked me when I met her if I had gotten all that foolishness out of my system. And I told her, "Baby, it's you and baseball all what count with me." You hear me, Bono? I meant it too. She say, "Which one comes first?" I told her, "Baby, ain't no doubt it's baseball . . . but you stick and get old with me and we'll both outlive this baseball." Am I right, Rose? And it's true.

ROSE Man, hush your mouth. You ain't said no such thing. Talking about, "Baby, you know you'll always be number one with me." That's what you was talking.

TROY You hear that, Bono. That's why I love her.

BONO Rose'll keep you straight. You get off the track, she'll straighten you up.

ROSE Lyons, you better get on up and get Bonnie. She waiting on you.

LYONS (*gets up to go*) Hey, Pop, why don't you come on down to the Grill and hear me play?

TROY I ain't going down there. I'm too old to be sitting around in them clubs.

BONO You got to be good to play down at the Grill.

LYONS Come on, Pop . . .

TROY I got to get up in the morning.

LYONS You ain't got to stay long.

TROY Naw, I'm gonna get my supper and go on to bed.

LYONS Well, I got to go. I'll see you again.

TROY Don't you come around my house on my payday.

ROSE Pick up the phone and let somebody know you coming. And bring Bonnie with you. You know I'm always glad to see her.

LYONS Yeah, I'll do that, Rose. You take care now. See you, Pop. See you, Mr. Bono. See you, Uncle Gabe.

GABRIEL Lyons! King of the Jungle!

(LYONS *exits.*)

TROY Is supper ready, woman? Me and you got some business to take care of. I'm gonna tear it up too.

ROSE Troy, I done told you now!

TROY (*puts his arm around* BONO) Aw hell, woman . . . this is Bono. Bono like family. I done known this nigger since . . . how long I done know you?

BONO It's been a long time.

TROY I done known this nigger since Skippy was a pup. Me and him done been through some times.

BONO You sure right about that.

TROY Hell, I done know him longer than I known you. And we still standing shoulder to shoulder. Hey, look here, Bono . . . a man can't ask for no more than that.

(*drinks to him*)

I love you, nigger.

BONO Hell, I love you too . . . but I got to get home see my woman. You got yours in hand. I got to go get mine.

(BONO *starts to exit as* CORY *enters the yard, dressed in his football uniform. He gives* TROY *a hard, uncompromising look.*)

CORY What you do that for, Pop?

(*He throws his helmet down in the direction of* TROY.)

ROSE What's the matter? Cory . . . what's the matter?

CORY Papa done went up to the school and told Coach Zellman I can't play football no more. Wouldn't even let me play the game. Told him to tell the recruiter not to come.

ROSE Troy . . .

TROY What you Troying me for. Yeah, I did it. And the boy know why I did it.

CORY Why you wanna do that to me? That was the one chance I had.

ROSE Ain't nothing wrong with Cory playing football, Troy.

TROY The boy lied to me. I told the nigger if he wanna play football . . . to keep up his chores and hold down that job at the A&P. That was the conditions. Stopped down there to see Mr. Stawicki . . .

CORY I can't work after school during the football season, Pop! I tried to tell you that Mr. Stawicki's holding my job for me. You don't never want to listen to nobody. And then you wanna go and do this to me!

TROY I ain't done nothing to you. You done it to yourself.

CORY Just cause you didn't have a chance! You just scared I'm gonna be better than you, that's all.

TROY Come here.

ROSE Troy . . .

(CORY *reluctantly crosses over to* TROY.)

TROY Alright! See. You done made a mistake.

CORY I didn't even do nothing!

TROY I'm gonna tell you what your mistake was. See . . . you swung at the ball and didn't hit it. That's strike one. See, you in the batter's box now. You swung and you missed. That's strike one. Don't you strike out!

(*Lights fade to black.*)

Act II

Scene I

The following morning. **CORY** *is at the tree hitting the ball with the bat. He tries to mimic* **TROY**, *but his swing is awkward, less sure.* **ROSE** *enters from the house.*

ROSE Cory, I want you to help me with this cupboard.

CORY I ain't quitting the team. I don't care what Poppa say.

ROSE I'll talk to him when he gets back. He had to go see about your Uncle Gabe. The police done arrested him. Say he was disturbing the peace. He'll be back directly. Come on in here and help me clean out the top of this cupboard.

(CORY *exits into the house.* ROSE *sees* TROY *and* BONO *coming down the alley.*)

Troy . . . what they say down there?

TROY Ain't said nothing. I give them fifty dollars and they let him go. I'll talk to you about it. Where's Cory?

ROSE He's in there helping me clean out these cupboards.

TROY Tell him to get his butt out here.

(TROY *and* BONO *go over to the pile of wood.* BONO *picks up the saw and begins sawing.*)

TROY (*to* BONO) All they want is the money. That makes six or seven times I done went down there and got him. See me coming they stick out their *hands.*

BONO Yeah. I know what you mean. That's all they care about . . . that money. They don't care about what's right.

(*pause*)

Nigger, why you got to go and get some hard wood? You ain't doing nothing but building a little old fence. Get you some soft pine wood. That's all you need.

TROY I know what I'm doing. This is outside wood. You put pine wood inside the house. Pine wood is inside wood. This here is outside wood. Now you tell me where the fence is gonna be?

BONO You don't need this wood. You can put it up with pine wood and it'll stand as long as you gonna be here looking at it.

TROY How you know how long I'm gonna be here, nigger? Hell, I might just live forever. Live longer than old man Horsely.

BONO That's what Magee used to say.

TROY Magee's a damn fool. Now you tell me who you ever heard of gonna pull their own teeth with a pair of rusty pliers.

BONO The old folks . . . my granddaddy used to pull his teeth with pliers. They ain't had no dentists for the colored folks back then.

TROY Get clean pliers! You understand? Clean pliers! Sterilize them! Besides we ain't living back then. All Magee had to do was walk over to Doc Goldblums.

BONO I see where you and that Tallahassee gal . . . that Alberta . . . I see where you all done got tight.

TROY What you mean "got tight"?

BONO I see where you be laughing and joking with her all the time.

TROY I laughs and jokes with all of them, Bono. You know me.

BONO That ain't the kind of laughing and joking I'm talking about.

(CORY *enters from the house.*)

CORY How you doing, Mr. Bono?

TROY Cory? Get that saw from Bono and cut some wood. He talking about the wood's too hard to cut. Stand back there, Jim, and let that young boy show you how it's done.

BONO He's sure welcome to it.

(CORY *takes the saw and begins to cut the wood.*)

Whew-e-e! Look at that. Big old strong boy. Look like Joe Louis. Hell, must be getting old the way I'm watching that boy whip through that wood.

CORY I don't see why Mama want a fence around the yard noways.

TROY Damn if I know either. What the hell she keeping out with it? She ain't got nothing nobody want.

BONO Some people build fences to keep people out . . . and other people build fences to keep people in. Rose wants to hold on to you all. She loves you.

TROY Hell, nigger, I don't need nobody to tell me my wife loves me, Cory . . . go on in the house and see if you can find that other saw.

CORY Where's it at?

TROY I said find it! Look for it till you find it!

(CORY *exits into the house.*)

What's that supposed to mean? Wanna keep us in?

BONO Troy . . . I done known you seem like damn near my whole life. You and Rose both. I done know both of you all for a long time. I remember when you met Rose. When you was hitting them baseball out the park. A lot of them old gals was after you then. You had the pick of the litter. When you picked Rose, I was happy for you. That was the first time I knew you had any sense. I said . . . My man Troy knows what he's doing . . . I'm gonna follow this nigger . . . he might take me somewhere. I been following you too. I done learned a whole heap of things about life watching you. I done learned how to tell where the shit lies. How to tell it from the alfalfa. You done learned me a lot of things. You showed me how to not make the same mistakes . . . to take life as it comes along and keep putting one foot in front of the other.

(*pause*)

Rose a good woman, Troy.

TROY Hell, nigger, I know she a good woman. I been married to her for eighteen years. What you got on your mind, Bono?

BONO I just say she a good woman. Just like I say anything. I ain't got to have nothing on my mind.

TROY You just gonna say she a good woman and leave it hanging out there like that? Why you telling me she a good woman?

BONO She loves you, Troy. Rose loves you.

TROY You saying I don't measure up. That's what you trying to say. I don't measure up cause I'm seeing this other gal. I know what you trying to say.

BONO I know what Rose means to you, Troy. I'm just trying to say I don't want to see you mess up.

TROY Yeah, I appreciate that, Bono. If you was messing around on Lucille I'd be telling you the same thing.

BONO Well, that's all I got to say. I just say that because I love you both.

TROY Hell, you know me . . . I wasn't out there looking for nothing. You can't find a better woman than Rose. I know that. But seems like this woman just stuck onto me where I can't shake her loose. I done wrestled with it, tried to throw her off me . . . but she just stuck on tighter. Now she's stuck on for good.

BONO You's in control . . . that's what you tell me all the time. You responsible for what you do.

TROY I ain't ducking the responsibility of it. As long as it sets right in my heart . . . then I'm okay. Cause that's all I listen to. It'll tell me right from wrong every time. And I ain't talking about doing Rose no bad turn. I love Rose. She done carried me a long ways and I love and respect her for that.

BONO I know you do. That's why I don't want to see you hurt her. But what you gonna do when she find out? What you got then? If you try and juggle both of them . . . sooner or later you gonna drop one of them. That's common sense.

TROY Yeah, I hear what you saying, Bono. I been trying to figure a way to work it out.

BONO Work it out right, Troy. I don't want to be getting all up between you and Rose's business . . . but work it so it come out right.

TROY Aw hell, I get all up between you and Lucille's business. When you gonna get that woman that refrigerator she been wanting? Don't tell me you ain't got no money now. I know who your banker is. Mellon don't need that money bad as Lucille want that refrigerator. I'll tell you that.

BONO Tell you what I'll do . . . when you finish building this fence for Rose . . . I'll buy Lucille that refrigerator.

TROY You done stuck your foot in your mouth now!

(TROY *grabs up a board and begins to saw.* BONO *starts to walk out the yard.*)

Hey, nigger . . . where you going?

BONO I'm going home. I know you don't expect me to help you now. I'm protecting my money. I wanna see you put that fence up by yourself. That's what I want to see. You'll be here another six months without me.

TROY Nigger, you ain't right.

BONO When it comes to my money . . . I'm right as fireworks on the Fourth of July.

TROY Alright, we gonna see now. You better get out your bankbook.

(BONO *exits, and* TROY *continues to work.* ROSE *enters from the house.*)

ROSE What they say down there? What's happening with Gabe?

TROY I went down there and got him out. Cost me fifty dollars. Say he was disturbing the peace. Judge set up a hearing for him in three weeks. Say to show cause why he shouldn't be recommitted.

ROSE What was he doing that cause them to arrest him?

TROY Some kids was teasing him and he run them off home. Say he was howling and carrying on. Some folks seen him and called the police. That's all it was.

ROSE Well, what's you say? What'd you tell the judge?

TROY Told him I'd look after him. It didn't make no sense to recommit the man. He stuck out his big greasy palm and told me to give him fifty dollars and take him on home.

ROSE Where's he at now? Where'd he go off to?

TROY He's gone on about his business. He don't need nobody to hold his hand.

ROSE Well, I don't know. Seem like that would be the best place for him if they did put him into the hospital. I know what you're gonna say. But that's what I think would be best.

TROY The man done had his life ruined fighting for what? And they wanna take and lock him up. Let him be free. He don't bother nobody.

ROSE Well, everybody got their own way of looking at it I guess. Come on and get your lunch. I got a bowl of lima beans and some cornbread in the oven. Come on get something to eat. Ain't no sense you fretting over Gabe.

(ROSE *turns to go into the house.*)

TROY Rose . . . got something to tell you.

ROSE Well, come on . . . wait till I get this food on the table.

TROY Rose!

(*She stops and turns around.*)

I don't know how to say this.

(*pause*)

I can't explain it none. It just sort of grows on you till it gets out of hand. It starts out like a little bush . . . and the next thing you know it's a whole forest.

ROSE Troy . . . what is you talking about?

TROY I'm talking, woman, let me talk. I'm trying to find a way to tell you . . . I'm gonna be a daddy. I'm gonna be somebody's daddy.

ROSE Troy . . . you're not telling me this? You're gonna be . . . what?

TROY Rose . . . now. . . see . . .

ROSE You telling me you gonna be somebody's daddy? You telling your *wife* this?

(GABRIEL *enters from the street. He carries a rose in his hand.*)

GABRIEL Hey, Troy! Hey, Rose!

ROSE I have to wait eighteen years to hear something like this.

GABRIEL Hey, Rose . . . I got a flower for you.

(*He hands it to her.*)

That's a rose. Same rose like you is.

ROSE Thanks, Gabe.

GABRIEL Troy, you ain't mad at me is you? Them bad mens come and put me away. You ain't mad at me is you?

TROY Naw, Gabe, I ain't mad at you.

ROSE Eighteen years and you wanna come with this.

GABRIEL (*takes a quarter out of his pocket*) See what I got? Got a brand new quarter.

TROY Rose . . . it's just . . .

ROSE Ain't nothing you can say, Troy. Ain't no way of explaining that.

GABRIEL Fellow that give me this quarter had a whole mess of them. I'm gonna keep this quarter till it stop shining.

ROSE Gabe, go on in the house there. I got some watermelon in the frigidaire. Go on and get you a piece.

GABRIEL Say, Rose . . . you know I was chasing hellhounds and them bad mens come and get me and take me away. Troy helped me. He come down there and told them they better let me go before he beat them up. Yeah, he did!

ROSE You go on and get you a piece of watermelon, Gabe. Them bad mens is gone now.

GABRIEL Okay, Rose . . . gonna get me some watermelon. The kind with the stripes on it.

(GABRIEL *exits into the house.*)

ROSE Why, Troy? Why? After all these years to come dragging this in to me now. It don't make no sense at your age. I could have expected this ten or fifteen years ago, but not now.

TROY Age ain't got nothing to do with it, Rose.

ROSE I done tried to be everything a wife should be. Everything a wife could be. Been married eighteen years and I got to live to see the day you tell me you been seeing another woman and done fathered a child by her. And you know I ain't never wanted no half nothing in my family. My whole family is half. Everybody got different fathers and mothers . . . my two sisters and my brother. Can't hardly tell who's who. Can't never sit down and talk about Papa and Mama. It's your papa and your mama and my papa and my mama . . .

TROY Rose . . . stop it now.

ROSE I ain't never wanted that for none of my children. And now you wanna drag your behind in here and tell me something like this.

TROY You ought to know. It's time for you to know.

ROSE Well, I don't want to know, goddamn it!

TROY I can't just make it go away. It's done now. I can't wish the circumstance of the thing away.

ROSE And you don't want to either. Maybe you want to wish me and my boy away. Maybe that's what you want? Well, you can't wish us away. I've got eighteen years of my life invested in you. You ought to have stayed upstairs in my bed where you belong.

TROY Rose . . . now listen to me . . . we can get a handle on this thing. We can talk this out . . . come to an understanding.

ROSE All of a sudden it's "we." Where was "we" at when you was down there rolling around with some godforsaken woman? "We" should have come to an understanding before you started making a damn fool of yourself. You're a day late and a dollar short when it comes to an understanding with me.

TROY It's just . . . She gives me a different idea . . . a different understanding about myself. I can step out of this house and get away from the pressures and problems . . . be a different man. I ain't got to wonder how I'm gonna pay the bills or get the roof fixed. I can just be a part of myself that I ain't never been.

ROSE What I want to know . . . is do you plan to continue seeing her. That's all you can say to me.

TROY I can sit up in her house and laugh. Do you understand what I'm saying. I can laugh out loud . . . and it feels good. It reaches all the way down to the bottom of my shoes.

(*pause*)

Rose, I can't give that up.

ROSE Maybe you ought to go on and stay down there with her . . . if she a better woman than me.

TROY It ain't about nobody being a better woman or nothing. Rose, you ain't the blame. A man couldn't ask for no woman to be a better wife than you've been. I'm responsible for it. I done locked myself into a pattern trying to take care of you all that I forgot about myself.

ROSE What the hell was I there for? That was my job, not somebody else's.

TROY Rose, I done tried all my life to live decent . . . to live a clean . . . hard . . . useful life. I tried to be a good husband to you. In every way I knew how. Maybe I come into the world backwards, I don't know. But . . . you born with two strikes on you before you come to the plate. You got to guard it closely . . . always looking for the curve-ball on the inside corner. You can't afford to let none get past you. You can't afford a call strike. If you going down . . . you going down swinging. Everything lined up against you. What you gonna do. I fooled them, Rose. I bunted. When I found you and Cory and a halfway decent job . . . I was safe. Couldn't nothing touch me. I wasn't gonna strike out no more. I wasn't going back to the penitentiary. I wasn't gonna lay in the streets with a bottle of wine. I was safe. I had me a family. A job. I wasn't gonna get that last strike. I was on first looking for one of them boys to knock me in. To get me home.

ROSE You should have stayed in my bed, Troy.

TROY Then when I saw that gal . . . she firmed up my backbone. And I got to thinking that if I tried . . . I just might be able to steal second. Do you understand after eighteen years I wanted to steal second.

ROSE You should have held me tight. You should have grabbed me and held on.

TROY I stood on first base for eighteen years and I thought . . . well, goddamn it . . . go on for it!

ROSE We're not talking about baseball! We're talking about you going off to lay in bed with another woman . . . and then bring it home to me. That's what we're talking about. We ain't talking about no baseball.

TROY Rose, you're not listening to me. I'm trying the best I can to explain it to you. It's not easy for me to admit that I been standing in the same place for eighteen years.

ROSE I been standing with you! I been right here with you, Troy. I got a life too. I gave eighteen years of my life to stand in the same spot with you. Don't you think I ever wanted other things? Don't you think I had dreams and hopes? What about my life? What about me. Don't you think it ever crossed my mind to want to know other men? That I wanted to lay up somewhere and forget about my responsibilities? That I wanted someone to make me laugh so I could feel good? You not the only one who's got wants and needs. But I held on to you, Troy. I took all my feelings, my wants and needs, my dreams . . . and I buried them inside you. I planted a seed and watched and prayed over it. I planted myself inside you and waited to bloom. And it didn't take me no eighteen years to find out the soil was hard and rocky and it wasn't never gonna bloom.

But I held on to you, Troy. I held you tighter. You was my husband. I owed you everything I had. Every part of me I could find to give you. And upstairs in that room . . . with the darkness falling in on me . . . I gave everything I had to try and erase the doubt that you wasn't the finest man in the world. And wherever you was going . . . I wanted to be there with you. Cause you was my husband. Cause that's the only way I was gonna survive as your wife. You always talking about what you give . . . and what you don't have to give. But you take too. You take . . . and don't even know nobody's giving!

(ROSE *turns to exit into the house;* TROY *grabs her arm.*)

TROY You say I take and don't give!

ROSE Troy! You're hurting me!

TROY You say I take and don't give.

ROSE Troy . . . you're hurting my arm! Let go!

TROY I done give you everything I got. Don't you tell that lie on me.

ROSE Troy!

TROY Don't you tell that lie on me!

(CORY *enters from the house.*)

CORY Mama!

ROSE Troy. You're hurting me.

TROY Don't you tell me about no taking and giving.

(CORY *comes up behind* TROY *and grabs him.* TROY, *surprised, is thrown off balance just as* CORY *throws a glancing blow that catches him on the chest and knocks him down.* TROY *is stunned, as is* CORY.)

ROSE Troy. Troy. No!

(TROY *gets to his feet and starts at* CORY.)

Troy . . . no. Please! Troy!

(ROSE *pulls on* TROY *to hold him back.* TROY *stops himself.*)

TROY (*to* CORY) Alright. That's strike two. You stay away from around me, boy. Don't you strike out. You living with a full count. Don't you strike out.

(TROY *exits out the yard as the lights go down.*)

Scene II

It is six months later, early afternoon. **TROY** *enters from the house and starts to exit the yard.* **ROSE** *enters from the house.*

ROSE Troy, I want to talk to you.

TROY All of a sudden, after all this time, you want to talk to me, huh? You ain't wanted to talk to me for months. You ain't wanted to talk to me last night. You ain't wanted no part of me then. What you wanna talk to me about now?

ROSE Tomorrow's Friday.

TROY I know what day tomorrow is. You think I don't know tomorrow's Friday? My whole life I ain't done nothing but look to see Friday coming and you got to tell me it's Friday.

ROSE I want to know if you're coming home.

TROY I always come home, Rose. You know that. There ain't never been a night I ain't come home.

ROSE That ain't what I mean . . . and you know it. I want to know if you're coming straight home after work.

TROY I figure I'd cash my check . . . hang out at Taylors' with the boys . . . maybe play a game of checkers . . .

ROSE Troy, I can't live like this. I won't live like this. You livin' on borrowed time with me. It's been going on six months now you ain't been coming home.

TROY I be here every night. Every night of the year. That's 365 days.

ROSE I want you to come home tomorrow after work.

TROY Rose . . . I don't mess up my pay. You know that now. I take my pay and I give it to you. I don't have no money but what you give me back. I just want to have a little time to myself . . . a little time to enjoy life.

ROSE What about me? When's my time to enjoy life?

TROY I don't know what to tell you, Rose. I'm doing the best I can.

ROSE You ain't been home from work but time enough to change your clothes and run out . . . and you wanna call that the best you can do?

TROY I'm going over to the hospital to see Alberta. She went into the hospital this afternoon. Look like she might have the baby early. I won't be gone long.

ROSE Well, you ought to know. They went over to Miss Pearl's and got Gabe today. She said you told them to go ahead and lock him up.

TROY I ain't said no such thing. Whoever told you that is telling a lie. Pearl ain't doing nothing but telling a big fat lie.

ROSE She ain't had to tell me. I read it on the papers.

TROY I ain't told them nothing of the kind.

ROSE I saw it right there on the papers.

TROY What it say, huh?

ROSE It said you told them to take him.

TROY Then they screwed that up, just the way they screw up everything. I ain't worried about what they got on the paper.

ROSE Say the government send part of his check to the hospital and the other part to you.

TROY I ain't got nothing to do with that if that's the way it works. I ain't made up the rules about how it work.

ROSE You did Gabe just like you did Cory. You wouldn't sign the paper for Cory . . . but you signed for Gabe. You signed that paper.

(*The telephone is heard ringing inside the house.*)

TROY I told you I ain't signed nothing, woman! The only thing I signed was the release form. Hell, I can't read, I don't know what they had on that paper! I ain't signed nothing about sending Gabe away.

ROSE I said send him to the hospital . . . you said let him be free . . . now you done went down there and signed him to the hospital for half his money. You went back on yourself, Troy. You gonna have to answer for that.

TROY See now . . . you been over there talking to Miss Pearl. She done got mad cause she ain't getting Gabe's rent money. That's all it is. She's liable to say anything.

ROSE Troy, I seen where you signed the paper.

TROY You ain't seen nothing I signed. What she doing got papers on my brother anyway? Miss Pearl telling a big fat lie. And I'm gonna tell her about it too! You ain't seen nothing I signed. Say . . . you ain't seen nothing I signed.

(ROSE *exits into the house to answer the telephone. Presently she returns.*)

ROSE Troy . . . that was the hospital. Alberta had the baby.

TROY What she have? What is it?

ROSE It's a girl.

TROY I better get on down to the hospital to see her.

ROSE Troy . . .

TROY Rose . . . I got to go see her now. That's only right . . . what's the matter . . . the baby's alright, ain't it?

ROSE Alberta died having the baby.

TROY Died . . . you say she's dead? Alberta's dead?

ROSE They said they done all they could. They couldn't do nothing for her.

TROY The baby? How's the baby?

ROSE They say it's healthy. I wonder who's gonna bury her.

TROY She had family, Rose. She wasn't living in the world by herself.

ROSE I know she wasn't living in the world by herself.

TROY Next thing you gonna want to know if she had any insurance.

ROSE Troy, you ain't got to talk like that.

TROY That's the first thing that jumped out your mouth. "Who's gonna bury her?" Like I'm fixing to take on that task for myself.

ROSE I am your wife. Don't push me away.

TROY I ain't pushing nobody away. Just give me some space. That's all. Just give me some room to breathe.

(ROSE *exits into the house.* TROY *walks about the yard.*)

TROY (*with a quiet rage that threatens to consume him*) Alright . . . Mr. Death. See now . . . I'm gonna tell you what I'm gonna do. I'm gonna take and build me a fence around this yard. See? I'm gonna build me a fence around what belongs to me. And then I want you to stay on the other side. See? You stay over there until you're ready for me. Then you come on. Bring your army. Bring your sickle. Bring your wrestling clothes. I ain't gonna fall down on my vigilance this time. You ain't gonna sneak up on me no more. When you ready for me . . . when the top of your list say Troy Maxson . . . that's when you come around here. You come up and knock on the front door. Ain't nobody else got nothing to do with this. This is between you and me. Man to man. You stay on the other side of that fence until you ready for me. Then you come up and knock on the front door. Anytime you want. I'll be ready for you.

(*The lights go down to black.*)

Scene III

The lights come up on the porch. It is late evening three days later. ROSE *sits listening to the ball game waiting for* TROY. *The final out of the game is made and* ROSE *switches off the radio.* TROY *enters the yard carrying an infant wrapped in blankets. He stands back from the house and calls.*

(ROSE *enters and stands on the porch. There is a long, awkward silence, the weight of which grows heavier with each passing second.*)

TROY Rose . . . I'm standing here with my daughter in my arms. She ain't but a wee bittie little old thing. She don't know nothing about grownups' business. She innocent . . . and she ain't go no mama.

ROSE What you telling me for, Troy?

(*She turns and exits into the house.*)

TROY Well . . . I guess we'll just sit out here on the porch.

(*He sits down on the porch. There is an awkward indelicateness about the way he handles the baby. His largeness engulfs and seems to swallow it. He speaks loud enough for* ROSE *to hear.*)

A man's got to do what's right for him. I ain't sorry for nothing I done. It felt right in my heart.

(*to the baby*)

What you smiling at? Your daddy's a big man. Got these great big old hands. But sometimes he's scared. And right now your daddy's scared cause we sitting out here and ain't got no home. Oh, I been homeless before. I ain't had no little baby with me. But I been homeless. You just be out on the road by your lonesome and you see one of them trains coming and you just kinda go like this . . .

(*He sings as a lullaby.*)

Please, Mr. Engineer let a man ride the line
Please, Mr. Engineer let a man ride the line
I ain't got no ticket please let me rid the blinds

(ROSE *enters from the house.* TROY *hearing her steps behind him, stands and faces her.*)

She's my daughter, Rose. My own flesh and blood. I can't deny her no more than I can deny them boys.

(*pause*)

You and them boys is my family. You and them and this child is all I got in the world. So I guess what I'm saying is . . . I'd appreciate it if you'd help me take care of her.

ROSE Okay, Troy . . . you're right. I'll take care of your baby for you . . . cause . . . like you say . . . she's innocent . . . and you can't visit the sins of the father upon the child. A motherless child has got a hard time.

(*She takes the baby from him.*)

From right now . . .this child got a mother. But you a womanless man.

(ROSE *turns and exits into the house with the baby. Lights go down to black.*)

Scene IV

It is two months later. LYONS *enters from the street. He knocks on the door and calls.*

LYONS Hey, Rose! (*pause*) Rose!

ROSE (*from inside the house*) Stop that yelling. You gonna wake up Raynell. I just got her to sleep.

LYONS I just stopped by to pay Papa this twenty dollars I owe him. Where's Papa at?

ROSE He should be here in a minute. I'm getting ready to go down to the church. Sit down and wait on him.

LYONS I got to go pick up Bonnie over her mother's house.

ROSE Well, sit it down there on the table. He'll get it.

LYONS (*enters the house and sets the money on the table*) Tell Papa I said thanks. I'll see you again.

ROSE Alright, Lyons. We'll see you.

(LYONS *starts to exit as* CORY *enters.*)

CORY Hey, Lyons.

LYONS What's happening, Cory. Say man, I'm sorry I missed your graduation. You know I had a gig and couldn't get away. Otherwise, I would have been there, man. So what you doing?

CORY I'm trying to find a job.

LYONS Yeah I know how that go, man. It's rough out here. Jobs are scarce.

CORY Yeah, I know.

LYONS Look here, I got to run. Talk to Papa . . . he know some people. He'll be able to help get you a job. Talk to him . . . see what he say.

CORY Yeah . . . alright, Lyons.

LYONS You take care. I'll talk to you soon. We'll find some time to talk.

(LYONS *exits the yard.* CORY *wanders over to the tree, picks up the bat and assumes a batting stance. He studies an imaginary pitcher and swings. Dissatisfied with the result, he tries again.* TROY *enters. They eye each other for a beat.* CORY *puts the bat down and exits the yard.* TROY *starts into the house as* ROSE *exits with* RAYNELL. *She is carrying a cake.*)

TROY I'm coming in and everybody's going out.

ROSE I'm taking this cake down to the church for the bakesale. Lyons was by to see you. He stopped by to pay you your twenty dollars. It's laying in there on the table.

TROY (*going into his pocket*) Well . . .here go this money.

ROSE Put it in there on the table, Troy. I'll get it.

TROY What time you coming back?

ROSE Ain't no use in you studying me. It don't matter what time I come back.

TROY I just asked you a question, woman. What's the matter . . . can't I ask you a question?

ROSE Troy, I don't want to go into it. Your dinner's in there on the stove. All you got to do is heat it up. And don't you be eating the rest of them cakes in there. I'm coming back for them. We having a bakesale at the church tomorrow.

(ROSE *exits the yard.* TROY *sits down on the steps, takes a pint bottle from his pocket, opens it and drinks. He begins to sing.*)

TROY

Hear it ring! Hear it ring!
Had an old dog his name was Blue
You know Blue was mighty true
You know Blue as a good old dog
Blue trees a possum in a hollow log
You know from that he was a good old dog

(BONO *enters the yard.*)

BONO Hey, Troy.

TROY Hey, what's happening, Bono?

BONO I just thought I'd stop by to see you.

TROY What you stop by and see me for? You ain't stopped by in a month of Sundays. Hell, I must owe you money or something.

BONO Since you got your promotion I can't keep up with you. Used to see you everyday. Now I don't even know what route you working.

TROY They keep switching me around. Got me out in Greentree now . . . hauling white folks' garbage.

BONO Greentree, huh? You lucky, at least you ain't got to be lifting them barrels. Damn if they ain't getting heavier. I'm gonna put in my two years and call it quits.

TROY I'm thinking about retiring myself.

BONO You got it easy. You can *drive* for another five years.

TROY It ain't the same, Bono. It ain't like working the back of the truck. Ain't got nobody to talk to . . . feel like you working by yourself. Naw, I'm thinking about retiring. How's Lucille?

BONO She alright. Her arthritis get to acting up on her sometime. Saw Rose on my way in. She going down to the church, huh?

TROY Yeah, she took up going down there. All them preachers looking for somebody to fatten their pockets.

(*pause*)

Got some gin here.

BONO Naw, thanks. I just stopped by to say hello.

TROY Hell, nigger . . . you can take a drink. I ain't never known you to say no to a drink. You ain't got to work tomorrow.

BONO I just stopped by. I'm fixing to go over to Skinner's. We got us a domino game going over his house every Friday.

TROY Nigger, you can't play no dominoes. I used to whup you four games out of five.

BONO Well, that learned me. I'm getting better.

TROY Yeah? Well, that's alright.

BONO Look here . . . I got to be getting on. Stop by sometime, huh?

TROY Yeah, I'll do that, Bono. Lucille told Rose you bought her a new refrigerator.

BONO Yeah, Rose told Lucille you had finally built your fence . . . so I figured we'd call it even.

TROY I knew you would.

BONO Yeah . . . okay. I'll be talking to you.

TROY Yeah, take care, Bono. Good to see you. I'm gonna stop over.

BONO Yeah. Okay, Troy.

(BONO *exits.* TROY *drinks from the bottle.*)

TROY

Old Blue died and I dig his grave
Let him down with a golden chain
Every night when I hear old Blue bark
I know Blue treed a possum in Noah's Ark.
Hear it ring! Hear it ring!

(CORY *enters the yard. They eye each other for a beat.* TROY *is sitting in the middle of the steps.* CORY walks over.)

CORY I got to get by.

TROY Say what? What's you say?

CORY You in my way. I got to get by.

TROY You got to get by where? This is my house. Bought and paid for. In full. Took me fifteen years. And if you wanna go in my house and I'm sitting on the steps . . . you say excuse me. Like your mama taught you.

CORY Come on, Pop . . . I got to get by.

(CORY *starts to maneuver his way past* TROY. TROY *grabs his leg and shoves him back.*)

TROY You just gonna walk over top of me?

CORY I live here too!

TROY (*advancing toward him*) You just gonna walk over top of me in my own house?

CORY I ain't scared of you.

TROY I ain't asked if you was scared of me. I asked you if you was fixing to walk over top of me in my own house? That's the question. You ain't gonna say excuse me? You just gonna walk over top of me?

CORY If you wanna put it like that.

TROY How else am I gonna put it?

CORY I was walking by you to go into the house cause you sitting on the steps drunk, singing to yourself. You can put it like that.

TROY Without saying excuse me???

(CORY *doesn't respond.*)

I asked you a question. Without saying excuse me???

CORY I ain't got to say excuse me to you. You don't count around here no more.

TROY Oh, I see . . . I don't count around here no more. You ain't got to say excuse me to your daddy. All of a sudden you done got so grown that your daddy don't count around here no more . . . Around here in his own house and yard that he done paid for with the sweat of his brow. You done got so grown to where you gonna take over. You gonna take over my house. Is that right? You gonna wear my pants. You gonna go in there and stretch out on my bed. You ain't got to say excuse me cause I don't count around here no more. Is that right?

CORY That's right. You always talking this dumb stuff. Now, why don't you just get out my way.

TROY I guess you got someplace to sleep and something to put in your belly. You got that, huh? You got that? That's what you need. You got that, huh?

CORY You don't know what I got. You ain't got to worry about what I got.

TROY You right! You one hundred percent right! I done spent the last seventeen years worrying about what you got. Now it's your turn, see? I'll tell you what to do. You grown . . . we done established that. You a man. Now, let's see you act like one. Turn your behind around and walk out this yard. And when you get out there in the alley . . . you can forget about this house. See? Cause this is my house. You go on and be a man and get your own house. You can forget about this. 'Cause this is mine. You go on and get yours cause I'm through with doing for you.

CORY You talking about what you did for me . . . what'd you ever give me?

TROY Them feet and bones! That pumping heart, nigger! I give you more than anybody else is ever gonna give you.

CORY You ain't never gave me nothing! You ain't never done nothing but hold me back. Afraid I was gonna be better than you. All you ever did was try and make me scared of you. I used to tremble every time you called my name. Every time I heard your footsteps in the house. Wondering all the time . . . what's Papa gonna say if I do this? . . . What's he gonna say if I do that? . . . What's Papa gonna say if I turn on the radio? And Mama, too . . .she tries . . . but she's scared of you.

TROY You leave your mama out of this. She ain't got nothing to do with this.

CORY I don't know how she stand you . . . after what you did to her.

TROY I told you to leave your mama out of this!

(*He advances toward* CORY.)

CORY What you gonna do . . . give me a whupping? You can't whup me no more. You're too old. You just an old man.

TROY (*shoves him on his shoulder*) Nigger! That's what you are. You just another nigger on the street to me!

CORY You crazy! You know that?

TROY Go on now! You got the devil in you. Get on away from me!

CORY You just a crazy old man . . . talking about I got the devil in me.

TROY Yeah, I'm crazy! If you don't get on the other side of that yard . . . I'm gonna show you how crazy I am! Go on . . . get the hell out of my yard.

CORY It ain't your yard. You took Uncle Gabe's money he got from the army to buy this house and then you put him out.

TROY (TROY *advances on* CORY.) Get your black ass out of my yard!

(TROY*'s advance backs* CORY *up against the tree.* CORY *grabs up the bat.*)

CORY I ain't going nowhere! Come on . . . put me out! I ain't scared of you.

TROY That's my bat!

CORY Come on!

TROY Put my bat down!

CORY Come on, put me out.

(CORY *swings at* TROY, *who backs across the yard.*)

What's the matter? You so bad . . . put me out!

(TROY *advances toward* CORY.)

CORY (*backing up*) Come on! Come on!

TROY You're gonna have to use it! You wanna draw that bat back on me . . . you're gonna have to use it.

CORY Come on! . . . Come on!

(CORY *swings the bat at* TROY *a second time. He misses.* TROY *continues to advance toward him.*)

TROY You're gonna have to kill me! You wanna draw that bat back on me. You're gonna have to kill me.

(CORY, *backed up against the tree, can go no farther.* TROY *taunts him. He sticks out his head and offers him a target.*)

Come on! Come on!

(CORY *is unable to swing the bat.* TROY *grabs it.*)

TROY Then I'll show you.

(CORY *and* TROY *struggle over the bat. The struggle is fierce and fully engaged.* TROY *ultimately is the stronger, and takes the bat from* CORY *and stands over him ready to swing. He stops himself.*)

Go on and get away from around my house.

(CORY, *stung by his defeat, picks himself up, walks slowly out of the yard and up the alley.*)

CORY Tell Mama I'll be back for my things.

TROY They'll be on the other side of that fence.

(CORY *exits.*)

TROY I can't taste nothing. Helluljah! I can't taste nothing no more. (TROY *assumes a batting posture and begins to taunt Death, the fastball in the outside corner.*) Come on! It's between you and me now! Come on! Anytime you want! Come on! I be ready for you . . . but I ain't gonna be easy.

(*The lights go down on the scene.*)

Scene V

The time is 1965. The lights come up in the yard. It is the morning of **TROY**'s *funeral. A funeral plaque with a light hangs beside the door. There is a small garden plot off to the side. There is noise and activity in the house as* **ROSE, GABRIEL** *and* **BONO** *have gathered. The door opens and* **RAYNELL**, *seven years old, enters dressed in a flannel nightgown. She crosses to the garden and pokes around with a stick.* **ROSE** *calls from the house.*

ROSE Raynell!

RAYNELL Mam?

ROSE What you doing out there?

RAYNELL Nothing.

(ROSE *comes to the door.*)

ROSE Girl, get in here and get dressed. What you doing?

RAYNELL Seeing if my garden growed.

ROSE I told you it ain't gonna grow overnight. You got to wait.

RAYNELL It don't look like it never gonna grow. Dag!

ROSE I told you a watched pot never boils. Get in here and get dressed.

RAYNELL This ain't even no pot, Mama.

ROSE You just have to give it a chance. It'll grow. Now you come on and do what I told you. We got to be getting ready. This ain't no morning to be playing around. You hear me?

RAYNELL Yes, mam.

(ROSE *exits into the house.* RAYNELL *continues to poke at her garden with a stick.* CORY *enters. He is dressed in a Marine corporal's uniform, and carries a duffel bag. His posture is that of a military man, and his speech has a clipped sternness.*)

CORY (*to* RAYNELL) Hi.

(*pause*)

I bet your name is Raynell.

RAYNELL Uh huh.

CORY Is your mama home?

(RAYNELL *runs up on the porch and calls through the screen door.*)

RAYNELL Mama . . . there's some man out here. Mama?

(ROSE *comes to the door.*)

ROSE Cory? Lord have mercy! Look here, you all!

(ROSE *and* CORY *embrace in a tearful reunion as* BONO *and* LYONS *enter from the house dressed in funeral clothes.*)

BONO Aw, looka here . . .

ROSE Done got all grown up!

CORY Don't cry, Mama. What you crying about?

ROSE I'm just so glad you made it.

CORY Hey Lyons. How you doing, Mr. Bono.

(LYONS *goes to embrace* CORY.)

LYONS Look at you, man. Look at you. Don't he look good, Rose. Got them Corporal stripes.

ROSE What took you so long.

CORY You know how the Marines are, Mama. They got to get all their paperwork straight before they let you do anything.

ROSE Well, I'm sure glad you made it. They let Lyons come. Your Uncle Gabe's still in the hospital. They don't know if they gonna let him out or not. I just talked to them a little while ago.

LYONS A Corporal in the United States Marines.

BONO Your daddy knew you had it in you. He used to tell me all the time.

LYONS Don't he look good, Mr. Bono?

BONO Yeah, he remind me of Troy when I first met him

(*pause*)

Say, Rose, Lucille's down at the church with the choir. I'm gonna go down and get the pallbearers lined up. I'll be back to get you all.

ROSE Thanks, Jim.

CORY See you, Mr. Bono.

LYONS (*with his arm around* RAYNELL) Cory . . . look at Raynell. Ain't she precious? She gonna break a whole lot of hearts.

ROSE Raynell, come and say hello to your brother. This is your brother, Cory. You remember Cory.

RAYNELL No, Mam.

CORY She don't remember me, Mama.

ROSE Well, we talk about you. She heard us talk about you. (*to* RAYNELL) This is your brother, Cory. Come on and say hello.

RAYNELL Hi.

CORY Hi. So you're Raynell. Mama told me a lot about you.

ROSE You all come on into the house and let me fix you some breakfast. Keep up your strength.

CORY I ain't hungry, Mama.

LYONS You can fix me something, Rose. I'll be in there in a minute.

ROSE Cory, you sure you don't want nothing. I know they ain't feeding you right.

CORY No, Mama . . . thanks. I don't feel like eating. I'll get something later.

ROSE Raynell . . . get on upstairs and get that dress on like I told you.

(ROSE *and* RAYNELL *exit into the house.*)

LYONS So . . . I hear you thinking about getting married.

CORY Yeah, I done found the right one, Lyons. It's about time.

LYONS Me and Bonnie been split up about four years now. About the time Papa retired. I guess she just got tired of all them changes I was putting her through.

(*pause*)

I always knew you was gonna make something out yourself. Your head was always in the right direction. So . . . you gonna stay in . . . make it a career . . . put in your twenty years?

CORY I don't know. I got six already, I think that's enough.

LYONS Stick with Uncle Sam and retire early. Ain't nothing out here. I guess Rose told you what happened with me. They got me down the workhouse. I thought I was being slick cashing other people's checks.

CORY How much time you doing?

LYONS They give me three years. I got that beat now. I ain't got but nine more months. It ain't so bad. You learn to deal with it like anything else. You got to take the crookeds with the straights. That's what Papa used to say. He used to say that when he struck out. I seen him strike out three times in a row . . . and the next time up he hit the ball over the grandstand. Right out there in Homestead Field. He wasn't satisfied hitting in the seats . . . he want to hit it over everything! After the game he had two hundred people standing around waiting to shake his hand. You got to take the crookeds with the straights. Yeah, Papa was something else.

CORY You still playing?

LYONS Cory . . . you know I'm gonna do that. There's some fellows down there we got us a band . . . we gonna try and stay together when we get out . . . but yeah, I'm still playing. It still helps me to get out of bed in the morning. As long as it do that I'm gonna be right there playing and trying to make some sense out of it.

ROSE (*calling*) Lyons, I got these eggs in the pan.

LYONS Let me go on and get these eggs, man. Get ready to go bury Papa.

(*pause*)

How you doing? You doing alright?

(CORY *nods.* LYONS *touches him on the shoulder and they share a moment of silent grief.* LYONS *exits into the house.* CORY *wanders about the yard.* RAYNELL *enters.*)

RAYNELL Hi.

CORY Hi.

RAYNELL Did you used to sleep in my room?

CORY Yeah . . . that used to be my room.

RAYNELL That's what Papa call it. "Cory's room." It got your football in the closet.

(ROSE *comes to the door.*)

ROSE Raynell, get in there and get them good shoes on.

RAYNELL Mama, can't I wear these. Them other one hurt my feet.

ROSE Well, they just gonna have to hurt your feet for a while. You ain't said they hurt your feet when you went down to the store and got them.

RAYNELL They didn't hurt then. My feet done got bigger.

ROSE Don't you give me no backtalk now. You get in there and get them shoes on.

(RAYNELL *exits into the house.*)

Ain't too much changed. He still got that piece of rag tied to that tree. He was out here swinging that bat. I was just ready to go back in the house. He swung that bat and then he just fell over. Seem like he swung it and stood there with this grin on his face . . . and then he just fell over. They carried him on down to the hospital, but I knew there wasn't no need . . . why don't you come on in the house?

CORY Mama . . . I got something to tell you. I don't know how to tell you this . . . but I've got to tell you . . . I'm not going to Papa's funeral.

ROSE Boy, hush your mouth. That's your daddy you talking about. I don't want hear that kind of talk this morning. I done raised you to come to this? You standing there all healthy and grown talking about you ain't going to your daddy's funeral?

CORY Mama . . . listen . . .

ROSE I don't want to hear it, Cory. You just get that thought out of your head.

CORY I can't drag Papa with me everywhere I go. I've got to say no to him. One time in my life I've got to say no.

ROSE Don't nobody have to listen to nothing like that. I know you and your daddy ain't seen eye to eye, but I ain't got to listen to that kind of talk this morning. Whatever was between you and your daddy . . . the time has come to put it aside. Just take it and set it over there on the shelf and forget about it. Disrespecting your daddy ain't gonna make you a man, Cory. You got to find a way to come to that on your own. Not going to your daddy's funeral ain't gonna make you a man.

CORY The whole time I was growing up . . . living in his house . . . Papa was like a shadow that followed you everywhere. It weighed on you and sunk into your flesh. It would wrap around you and lay there until you couldn't tell which one was you anymore. That shadow digging in your flesh. Trying to crawl in. Trying to live through you. Everywhere I looked, Troy Maxson was staring back at me . . . hiding under the bed . . . in the closet. I'm just saying I've got to find a way to get rid of that shadow, Mama.

ROSE You just like him. You got him in you good.

CORY Don't tell me that, Mama.

ROSE You Troy Maxson all over again.

CORY I don't want to be Troy Maxson. I want to be me.

ROSE You can't be nobody but who you are, Cory. That shadow wasn't nothing but you growing into yourself. You either got to grow into it or cut it down to fit you. But that's all you got to make life with. That's all you got to measure yourself against that world out there. Your daddy wanted you to be everything he wasn't . . . and at the same time he tried to make you into everything he was. I don't know if he was right or wrong . . . but I do know he meant to do more good than he meant to do harm. He wasn't always right. Sometimes when he touched he bruised. And sometimes when he took me in his arms he cut.

When I first met your daddy I thought . . . Here is a man I can lay down with and make a baby. That's the first thing I thought when I seen him. I was thirty years old and had done seen my share of men. But when he walked up to me and said, "I can dance a waltz that'll make you dizzy," I thought, Rose Lee, here is a man that you can open yourself up to and be filled to bursting. Here is a man that can fill all them empty spaces you been tipping around the edges of. One of them empty spaces was being somebody's mother.

I married your daddy and settled down to cooking his supper and keeping clean sheets on the bed. When your daddy walked through the house he was so big he filled it up. That was my first mistake. Not to make him leave some room for me. For my part in the matter. But at that time I wanted that. I wanted a house that I could sing in. And that's what your daddy gave me. I didn't know to keep up his strength I had to give up little pieces of mine. I did that. I took on his life as mine and mixed up the pieces so that you couldn't hardly tell which was which anymore. It was my choice. It was my life and I didn't have to live it like that. But that's what life offered me in the way of being a woman and I took it. I grabbed hold of it with both hands.

By the time Raynell came into the house, me and your daddy had done lost touch with one another. I didn't want to make my blessing off of nobody's misfortune . . . but I took on to Raynell like she was all them babies I had wanted and never had.

(*The phone rings.*)

Like I'd been blessed to relive a part of my life. And if the Lord see fit to keep up my strength . . . I'm gonna do her just like your daddy did you . . . I'm gonna give her the best of what's in me.

RAYNELL (*entering, still with her old shoes*) Mama . . . Reverend Tollivier on the phone.

(ROSE *exits into the house.*)

RAYNELL Hi.
CORY Hi.
RAYNELL You in the Army or the Marines?
CORY Marines.
RAYNELL Papa said it was the Army. Did you know Blue?
CORY Blue? Who's Blue?
RAYNELL Papa's dog what he sing about all the time.
CORY (*singing*)

Hear it ring! Hear it ring!
I had a dog his name was Blue
You know Blue was mighty true
You know Blue was a good old dog
Blue treed a possum in a hollow log
You know from that he was a good old dog.
Hear it ring! Hear it ring!

(RAYNELL *joins in singing.*)

CORY and RAYNELL

Blue treed a possum out on a limb
Blue looked at me and I looked at him
Grabbed that possum and put him in a sack
Blue stayed there till I came back

Old Blue's feets was big and round
Never allowed a possum to touch the ground.

Old Blue died and I dug his grave
I dug his grave with a silver spade
Let him down with a golden chain
And every night I call his name
Go on Blue, you good dog you
Go on Blue, you good dog you

RAYNELL Blue laid down and died like a man
Blue laid down and died . . .

BOTH Blue laid down and died like a man
Now he's treeing possums in the Promised Land
I'm gonna tell you this to let you know
Blue's gone where the good dogs go
When I hear old Blue bark
When I hear old Blue bark
Blue treed a possum in Noah's Ark
Blue treed a possum in Noah's Ark.

(ROSE *comes to the screen door.*)

ROSE Cory, we gonna be ready to go in a minute.

CORY (*to* RAYNELL) You go on in the house and change them shoes like Mama told you so we can go to Papa's funeral.

RAYNELL Okay, I'll be back.

(RAYNELL *exits into the house.* CORY *gets up and crosses over to the tree.* ROSE *stands in the screen door watching him.* GABRIEL *enters from the alley.*)

GABRIEL (*calling*) Hey, Rose!

ROSE Gabe?

GABRIEL I'm here, Rose. Hey Rose, I'm here!

(ROSE *enters from the house.*)

ROSE Lord . . . Look here, Lyons!

LYONS See, I told you, Rose . . . I told you they'd let him come.

CORY How you doing, Uncle Gabe?

LYONS How you doing, Uncle Gabe?

GABRIEL Hey, Rose. It's time. It's time to tell St. Peter to open the gates. Troy, you ready? You ready, Troy. I'm gonna tell St. Peter to open the gates. You get ready now.

(GABRIEL, *with great fanfare, braces himself to blow. The trumpet is without a mouthpiece. He puts the end of it into his mouth and blows with great force, like a man who has been waiting some twenty-odd years for this single moment. No sound comes out of the trumpet. He braces himself and blows again with the same result. A third time he blows. There is a weight of impossible description that falls away and leaves him bare and exposed to a frightful realization. It is a trauma that a sane and normal mind would be unable to withstand. He begins to dance. A slow, strange dance, eerie and lifegiving. A dance of atavistic signature and ritual.* LYONS *attempts to embrace him.* GABRIEL *pushes* LYONS *away. He begins to howl in what is an attempt at song, or perhaps a song turning back into itself in an attempt at speech. He finishes his dance and the gates of heaven stand open as wide as God's closet.)*

That's the way that go!

(BLACKOUT.)

SELECTED BIBLIOGRAPHY

This bibliography is designed to provide a list of basic critical and historical references pertinent to the study of dramatic literature in general and to the dramatists included in this volume in particular. References have been limited entirely to books. No attempt has been made to include items from periodicals, but several of the listed volumes contain essays from a variety of sources. Current material can always be secured through the various periodical indexes.

A number of the books included here are out of print, but they are standard works generally available in any college or university library. Many contain extensive bibliographies of their own. *The Oxford Companion to the Theatre* is a useful volume containing concise information about drama, dramatists, and theatre throughout history. It can be found on almost any library reference shelf.

General References

ANDERSON, MAXWELL. *The Essence of Tragedy.* Washington: Anderson House, 1938. A modern approach to tragedy by an important American dramatist.

BENTLEY, ERIC. *In Search of Theatre.* New York: Knopf, 1953.

———. *The Playwright as Thinker.* New York: Harcourt, Brace, 1946. Reprinted in Meridian Books, 1955.

———. *What Is Theatre?* Boston: Beacon Press, 1956.

These three volumes on all aspects of theatre and drama are by one of the foremost modern critics.

CORRIGAN, ROBERT W. *The Theatre in Search of a Fix.* New York: Dell, 1974.

FREEDLEY, GEORGE, and JOHN A. REEVES. *A History of the Theatre.* New York: Crown, 1955.

GASSNER, JOHN. *Masters of the Drama,* 3d ed. New York: Dover, 1954.

LEECH, CLIFFORD, and T. W. CRAIK, gen. eds. *The Revels History of Drama in English,* 8 vols. London: Methuen, 1975 and following. A compendium of extended essays by a variety of noted theatre and drama historians, covering the drama in English from its beginnings. See below for the volume on American drama.

MACGOWAN, KENNETH, and WILLIAM MELNITZ. *The Living Stage: A History of the World Theatre.* Englewood Cliffs, N.J.: Prentice-Hall, 1955.

NICOLL, ALLARDYCE. *The Development of the Theatre.* New York: Harcourt Brace, 1967.

———. *World Drama.* New York: Harcourt Brace, 1950.

STEINER, GEORGE. *The Death of Tragedy.* New York: Knopf, 1961.

SYPHER, WYLIE. *Comedy.* New York: Doubleday, 1956. Steiner's and Sypher's books are valuable studies in the concepts of tragedy and comedy throughout history. Steiner's first chapter is especially valuable. Sypher's volume is actually three separate studies: "An Essay on Comedy" by George Meredith and "Laughter" by Henri Bergson, both of which are very famous studies, and the third study, Sypher's own essay, "The Meaning of Comedy."

Classical Drama

Dover, Kenneth James. *Aristophanic Comedy.* Berkeley: Univ. of California Press, 1972.

Epps, Preston H. *The Poetics of Aristotle.* Chapel Hill: Univ. of N.C. Press, 1970. There are many versions of *The Poetics.* This is a convenient and very readable one.

Hadas, Moses. *Introduction to Classical Drama.* New York: Bantam, 1966. Written by one of America's foremost classical scholars.

Hamilton, Edith. *The Greek Way.* New York: The New American Library, reprinted from Little, Brown edition, Boston, 1942.

———. *Mythology.* New York: The New American Library, 1953, reprinted from Little, Brown edition, Boston, 1942. These are not about drama as such but are basic texts for the study of the Greek view of themselves, the gods, and tragedy. They are also fascinating reading.

Kitto, H. D. F. *Greek Tragedy.* Garden City, N.Y.: Doubleday, 1954.

Kott, Jan. *The Eating of the Gods: An Interpretation of Greek Tragedy.* New York: Vintage Books, Random House, 1974.

McLeish, Kenneth. *The Theatre of Aristophanes.* London: Thames and Hudson, 1980.

Murray, Gilbert. *Aristophanes: A Study.* Oxford: Clarendon Press, 1933.

Norwood, Gilbert. *Greek Comedy.* New York: Hill & Wang Dramabook, 1963.

———. *Greek Tragedy.* New York: Hill & Wang Dramabook, 1960.

O'Brien, Michael J. *20th Century Interpretations of Oedipus Rex.* Englewood Cliffs, NJ: Prentice-Hall, 1968.

Sandback, F. H. *The Comic Theatre of Greece and Rome.* New York: Norton, 1977.

Segal, Charles. *Oedipus Tyrannus: Tragic Heroism and the Limits of Knowledge.* New York: Twayne, 1993.

———. *Tragedy and Civilization: An Interpretation of Sophocles.* Cambridge: Harvard, 1981.

Medieval Drama, Shakespeare

The books on Shakespeare are, of course, legion. Students are advised to consult their school's library for items of particular interest. The following entries represent a basic list of works, by important Shakespearean scholars, providing a variety of studies on the dramatist and his theatre, with particular emphasis on *Hamlet.*

Bradley, A. C. *Shakespearean Tragedy.* New York: St. Martin's Press, 1966.

Chute, Marchette. *An Introduction to Shakespeare.* New York: Dutton, 1966.

———. *Shakespeare of London.* New York: Dutton, 1949.

Dean, Leonard F. *Shakespeare: Modern Essays in Criticism.* New York: Oxford, 1967.

Fluchere, Henri. *Shakespeare and the Elizabethans.* New York: Hill & Wang, 1956.

Granville-Barker, Harley. *A Companion to Shakespeare Studies.* New York: Macmillan, 1966. Originally published 1934.

———. *Prefaces to Shakespeare,* rev. ed. London: Batsford, 1972. Granville-Barker was one of the foremost Shakespearean scholars whose essays on individual plays are classic examples of criticism. Especially recommended is the preface to *Hamlet.*

Harbage, Alfred. *As They Liked It.* New York: Macmillan, 1947.

———. *Shakespeare's Audiences.* New York: Columbia Univ., 1941. These two studies by an outstanding American Shakespearean scholar are very interesting and readable accounts of what Elizabethan audiences were like and also what they liked.

HARRISON, TONY. *The Mysteries.* London: Faber and Faber, 1985.

HODGES, C. WALTER. *The Globe Restored.* London: Benn, 1953. A major study of what we know, and don't know, about the Elizabethan theatre structure. Numerous drawings and perspectives are of special interest. Now that the foundations of the Rose Theatre have been uncovered in London with the possibility of future discoveries, some of the conjectures may be disproven, but this still remains the best work of its kind.

JONES, ERNEST. *Hamlet and Oedipus.* New York: Doubleday, 1954. A comparative study of two of the drama's greatest tragic figures.

KNIGHT, L. C. *An Approach to Hamlet.* Stanford, CA: Stanford Univ. Press, 1961.

KOTT, JAN. *Shakespeare Our Contemporary.* New York: Norton, 1974.

LLOYD EVANS, GARETH. *The Upstart Crow: An Introduction to Shakespeare.* London: Dent, 1982. The title is taken from "A Groatsworth of Wit," by Robert Greene, a playwright contemporary of Shakespeare, who was contemptuous of this intruding "Shake-scene."

MILLS, JOHN A. *Hamlet on Stage: The Great Tradition.* Westport, CT: Greenwood Press, 1985.

POLLARD, ALFRED W. *English Miracle Plays, Moralities, and Interludes.* Oxford: Clarendon Press, 1927.

ROSE, MARTIAL, ed. *The Wakefield Mystery Plays.* Garden City, NY: Doubleday, 1962. The cycle from which *The Second Shepherd's Play* was taken.

SHAW, BERNARD. *Shaw on Shakespeare.* New York: Dutton, 1961. Shaw maintained that the world's three greatest dramatists all began with S—Sophocles, Shakespeare, Shaw.

SMITH, WARREN D. *Shakespeare's Playhouse Practice.* Hanover, NH: Univ. Press of New England, 1973.

TOLMAN, ALBERT H. *The Views about Hamlet.* New York: AMS Press, 1973.

WEBSTER, MARGARET. *Shakespeare Today.* London: Dent, 1957. Webster was the most famous American director of Shakespeare during her lifetime. Her book on the direction and production of Shakespeare's plays, *Shakespeare Without Tears,* is well worth reading.

Seventeenth-Century French and English Drama: Molière and Sheridan

AUBURN, MARK S. *Sheridan's Comedies.* Lincoln: U of Nebraska P, 1977.

DANZIGER, MARLIES K. *Oliver Goldsmith and Richard Brinsley Sheridan.* New York: Ungar, 1978. A discussion of the two playwrights who brought laughter back into 18th-century English comedy.

GUICHARNAUD, JACQUES. *Molière: A Collection of Critical Essays.* Englewood Cliffs, NJ: Prentice-Hall, 1964.

HALL, H. GASTON. *Comedy in Context: Essays on Molière.* Jackson: U of Mississippi, 1984.

KRUTCH, JOSEPH WOOD. *Comedy and Conscience after the Restoration.* New York: Columbia U P, 1949. The best single source of explanation and analysis of the British Restoration drama and its society.

LAWRENSON, T. E. *The French Stage of the 17th Century.* Manchester, Eng.: U of Manchester P, 1957.

REDFORD, BRUCE, ed. *The Origins of The School for Scandal.* Princeton, NJ: Princeton U P, 1986.

WILCOX, JOHN. *The Relation of Molière to Restoration Comedy.* New York: Columbia U P, 1938.

WILSON, JOHN HAROLD. *All the King's Ladies.* Chicago: U of Chicago Press, 1958. Discussion of women in the theatre during the Restoration, some of whom Charles II took as mistresses.

The Modern Era: General References

The following represent general histories and critical studies of the drama in Europe, England, and especially America during the last two centuries.

ADLER, THOMAS. *American Drama 1940–1960: A Critical History.* New York: Twayne, 1994.

BIGSBY, C. W. E. *Confrontation and Commitment: A Study of Contemporary American Drama.* Columbia: U of Missouri P, 1968.

———. *A Critical Introduction to Twentieth Century American Drama,* 3 vols. Cambridge, Eng.: Cambridge U P, 1982, 1984, 1985.

BOGARD, TRAVIS, et al. *The Revels History of Drama in English,* vol. 8. London: Methuen, 1975.

BROCKETT, OSCAR G., and ROBERT R. FINDLAY. *Century of Innovation: A History of European and American Theatre and Drama Since 1870.* Englewood Cliffs, NJ: Prentice-Hall, 1973.

DEUTSCH, HELEN, and STELLA HANAU. *The Provincetown.* New York: Farrar, Straus & Cudahy, 1931. A history of the theatre group that spawned Eugene O'Neill.

DRIVER, TOM F. *Romantic Quest and Modern Query: A History of the Modern Theatre.* New York: Dell, 1970.

ESSLIN, MARTIN. *The Theatre of the Absurd,* 3d rev. ed. London: Methuen, 1974. The book which contributed a new, and highly controversial, term to the study of modern drama.

GASSNER, JOHN. *Form and Idea in Modern Theatre.* New York: Dryden, 1956. An excellent critical account of modern theatrical styles, emphasizing realism and expressionism.

———. *The Theatre in Our Time.* New York: Crown, 1954. An extensive review of all phases of theatre in the forties and early fifties.

GORELIK, MORDECAI. *New Theatres for Old.* New York: Samuel French, 1940. The standard work treating the new movements in stage techniques of the first decades of the twentieth century. Written by one of America's greatest scene designers and stage craftsmen.

JONES, ROBERT EDMOND. *The Dramatic Imagination.* New York: Duell, Sloan & Pearce, 1941. Written by another of America's foremost scene designers. An excellent companion piece to Gorelik.

KRUTCH, JOSEPH WOOD. *The American Drama Since 1918.* New York: George Braziller, 1957.

———. *Modernism in Modern Drama.* Ithaca: Cornell U P, 1953.

MILLER, JORDAN Y., and WINIFRED FRASER. *American Drama Between the Wars.* Boston: Twayne, 1991. Historical and critical overview of the period when American drama achieved its place as world leader.

MOODY, RICHARD. *America Takes the Stage.* Bloomington: U of Indiana, 1955. Another excellent study of America's rise to world dominance.

NICOLL, ALLARDYCE. *The Theory of Drama.* London: Harrap, 1931. Though now over sixty years old, this remains a standard reference for any basic theatre library. Excellent discussions of tragedy and comedy.

RICHARDSON, GARY A. *American Drama from the Colonial Period through World War I: A Critical History.* New York: Twayne, 1993.

SIMONSON, LEE. *The Stage is Set.* New York: Harcourt, Brace, 1932. Though written a decade before Gorelik and Jones, this is a good companion to them in its discussion of theatrical and dramatic techniques seen from the scene designer's viewpoint.

VALENCY, MAURICE. *The Flower and the Castle: An Introduction to Modern Drama.* New York: Macmillan, 1963.

WILSON, GARFF B. *Three Hundred Years of American Drama and Theatre.* Englewood Cliffs, NJ: Prentice-Hall, 1973.

The Modern Era: Dramatists

In keeping with all other entries in this bibliography, all references are to books only. This does restrict material on the more contemporary writers such as Norman and Wilson, but because they remain active subjects for critical material in newspapers and periodicals, it is best that current periodical indexes be consulted for up-to-date entries.

CHEKHOV

BRUFORD, WALTER H. *Anton Chekhov.* London: Bowes & Bowes, 1957.

HINGLEY, RONALD. *Chekhov: A Biographical and Critical Study.* New York: Barnes & Noble, 1966.

TOUMANOVA, NINA. *Anton Chekhov, the Voice of Twilight Russia.* New York: Columbia U P, 1960.

GLASPELL

MAKOWSKY, VERONICA A. *Susan Glaspell's Century of American Women.* New York: Oxford U P, 1993.

WATERMAN, ARTHUR E. *Susan Glaspell.* New York: Twayne, 1966.

IBSEN

FJELDE, ROLF. *Ibsen: A Collection of Critical Essays.* Englewood Cliffs, NJ: Prentice-Hall, 1965.

HAUGEN, EINAR I. *Ibsen's Drama: Author to Audience.* Minneapolis: U of Minnesota P, 1979.

SHAFER, YVONNE. *Henrik Ibsen: Life, Work, and Criticism.* Fredericton, N.B., Canada: York Press, 1985.

SHAW, GEORGE BERNARD. *The Quintessence of Ibsenism.* Toronto: U of Toronto P, 1959. Shaw's classic study of the playwright, reflecting, of course, many of Shaw's views beyond Ibsen alone.

MILLER

BLOOM, HAROLD, ed. *Arthur Miller.* New York: Chelsea House, 1987. A collection of critical essays.

———. *Arthur Miller's Death of a Salesman.* New York: Chelsea House, 1988. A collection of critical essays.

———. *Willy Loman.* New York: Chelsea House, 1991.

MARTIN, ROBERT A. *Arthur Miller: New Perspectives.* Englewood Cliffs, NJ: Prentice-Hall, 1982.

MESERVE, WALTER J. *The Merrill Studies in Death of a Salesman.* Columbus, OH: Merrill, 1972.

WELLAND, DENNIS S. *Miller, the Playwright.* New York: Methuen, 1985.

NORMAN

KUNTZ, LINDA. *The Subject's Tragedy: Political Poetics, Feminist Theory, and Drama.* Ann Arbor: U of Michigan P, 1992. Contains criticism and interpretations of Norman's plays.

O'NEILL

ALEXANDER, DORIS. *The Tempering of Eugene O'Neill.* New York: Harcourt, Brace, 1962. An investigation of the many forces that led to O'Neill's development.

BOGARD, TRAVIS. *Contour in Time: The Plays of Eugene O'Neill.* New York: Oxford, 1972. A highly important study of each of O'Neill's plays.

FALK, DORIS V. *Eugene O'Neill and the Tragic Tension.* New Brunswick, NJ: Rutgers U P, 1958.

FLOYD, VIRGINIA. *The Plays of Eugene O'Neill: A New Assessment.* New York: Ungar, 1985.

GASSNER, JOHN. *O'Neill: A Collection of Critical Essays.* Englewood Cliffs, NJ: Prentice-Hall, 1964.

GELB, BARBARA and ARTHUR. *O'Neill.* New York: Dell, 1962. The first full-length biography to appear at the time of the O'Neill revival. An excellent one-volume treatment of the playwright's life.

MILLER, JORDAN Y. *Playwright's Progress: O'Neill and the Critics.* Chicago: Scott, Foresman, 1975. Reviews and critical essays concerning all of O'Neill's major works.

RALEIGH, JOHN H. *The Plays of Eugene O'Neill.* Carbondale, IL: Southern Illinois U P, 1965. A comprehensive overview of all of O'Neill's career.

SHEAFFER, LOUIS. *O'Neill, Son and Playwright.* Boston: Little, Brown, 1968.

———. *O'Neill, Son and Artist.* Boston: Little, Brown, 1973. These two volumes by Sheaffer are far and away the best accounts of O'Neill's remarkable life and career. Meticulously researched and generously illustrated. Superior in many ways to the Gelb volume. *Son and Artist* won the Pulitzer Prize.

Pinter

Bloom, Harold, ed. *Harold Pinter.* New York: Chelsea, 1987. A collection of critical essays.

Dukore, Bernard F. *Harold Pinter.* New York: Grove, 1982.

———. *Where Laughter Stops: Pinter's Tragicomedy.* Columbia: U of Missouri P, 1976.

Esslin, Martin. *Pinter the Playwright.* New York: Methuen, 1984.

Ganz, Arthur F., ed. *Pinter: A Collection of Critical Essays.* Englewood Cliffs, NJ: Prentice-Hall, 1972.

Hinshliffe, Arnold P. *Harold Pinter.* New York: Twayne, 1967. Revised 1981.

Rabe

Kolin, Philip C. *David Rabe: A Stage History.* New York: Garland, 1988.

Zimmerman, Toby S., ed. *David Rabe: A Casebook.* New York: Garland, 1991.

Shaw

Bentley, Eric. *Bernard Shaw.* New York: New Directions, 1957.

Chesterton, G. K. *George Bernard Shaw.* New York: Hill & Wang, 1956.

Hill, Eldon C. *George Bernard Shaw.* Boston: Twayne, 1978.

Mayne, Frederick. *The Wit and Satire of Bernard Shaw.* New York: St. Martin's, 1967.

Pearson, Hesketh. *George Bernard Shaw: A Full-length Portrait.* Garden City, NY: Garden City Publishing, 1946.

Wagenknecht, Edward. *A Guide to George Bernard Shaw.* New York: Russell & Russell, 1971.

Zimbardo, Rose A. *20th Century Interpretations of Major Barbara.* Englewood Cliffs, NJ: Prentice-Hall, 1970.

Williams

Donahue, Francis. *The Dramatic World of Tennessee Williams.* New York: Ungar, 1964.

Falk, Signi. *Tennessee Williams.* New York: Twayne, 1961. Revised 1978.

Jackson, Esther. *The Broken World of Tennessee Williams.* Madison: U of Wisconsin P, 1965.

Leavitt, Richard F. *The World of Tennessee Williams.* New York: Putnam, 1978.

Stanton, Stephen S. *Tennessee Williams: A Collection of Critical Essays.* Englewood Cliffs, NJ: Prentice-Hall, 1977.

Tischler, Nancy M. P. *Tennessee Williams: Rebellious Puritan.* New York: Citadel, 1965.

Williams, Edwina Dakin. *Remember Me to Tom.* New York: Putnam, 1963. A remembrance of the playwright written by his mother. He was known as Tom within his family.

Wilson

Nadel, Alan, ed. *May All Your Fences Have Gates.* Iowa City: U of Iowa P, 1994. A collection of essays on Wilson's drama.

SELECTED FILMOGRAPHY

The plays listed below are all on VHS videotape. A few are also obtainable in Beta format, but because of the predominance of VHS in audiovisual equipment, they have not been included. If Beta is preferred, contact the supplier of the tape you wish and ask if it is available.

All tapes listed are for *purchase* only; the suppliers do not rent them. Prices vary sharply from under $10 to over $200, and have been indicated when known. Again, contact the supplier for full information. Full names and addresses of suppliers are included at the end of the list.

If *rental* is preferred, check with your local video store. The larger outlets will be the most likely to carry these titles.

Although video equipment in the classroom has largely replaced conventional projectors, a few plays are available on 16mm sound film, generally for rental only, with purchase, if permitted, often quite costly. Most of them are obtainable through a great number of rental houses, but only four of the largest have been listed. Local school or public libraries should have catalogs for the major sources of 16mm films.

Plays are listed in the order in which they appear in this book.

Oedipus Rex

1957 Tyrone Guthrie's Stratford, Ontario, production, with Douglas Campbell.
Running time: 87 minutes
Home Vision
Also available in 16mm from Corinth Films
A fairly static filming of the play, *not* a film adaptation as such. However, it does give the sense of how the play might have originally been done and is well worth viewing.

1968 Christopher Plummer and Orson Welles
Running time: 97 minutes
Available in 16mm *only* from Swank

1978 Miami-Dade Community College production, hosted by José Ferrer.
Running time: 60 minutes
Films, Inc.
A somewhat shortened version performed by amateur players.

Hamlet

1948 The Laurence Olivier production, directed by Olivier, who also plays the lead.
Running time: 2 hours, 30 minutes

Purchase price: $19.95
Paramount; Baker & Taylor; Home Vision
Also available in 16mm from Budget; Films, Inc.; Swank. Can be purchased from Learning Corp.
The best-known and probably best made of all *Hamlet* films. The interpretation has raised conflicting public reactions from highest praise to severe criticism. It is not the complete play; Rosencrantz and Guildenstern have been entirely eliminated and the mouse-trap scene shortened, among other changes. The castle setting is imaginative and intriguing.

1969 Nicol Williamson and Anthony Hopkins
Running time: 2 hours
Purchase price: $19.95
Columbia Tristar
Also available in 16mm from Budget; Films, Inc.; Swank. Can be purchased from Learning Corp.

1979 Derek Jacobi, Claire Bloom
Running time: 3 hours, 45 minutes
Purchase price: $249.95
Ambrose
Full length and very expensive, but performed by some of England's best actors. It might be worth investigation as part of a permanent film library.

1990 Zeffirelli's production with Mel Gibson and Glenn Close.
Running time: 2 hours, 15 minutes
Purchase price: $19.98
Imaginative and controversial; *not* a faithful adaptation.

Tartuffe

1984 French adaptation with English subtitles. Cast not familiar to American audiences.
Running time: 2 hours, 20 minutes
Purchase price: $79.95
Applause, Connoisseur, Facets

1990 Anthony Shea, Nigel Hawthorne
Running time: 110 minutes
Purchase price: $39.95
Ingram, Turner

A Doll's House

1959 Julie Harris, Christopher Plummer, Jason Robards, Hume Cronyn
Running time: 89 minutes
Purchase price: $39.95

Facets, MGM/UA
A TV adaptation in black and white. The cast is outstanding.

1973 Jane Fonda, Trevor Howard
Running time: 98 minutes
Purchase price: $9.99
Listed as Beta only, but inquiry is suggested.
Prism, Starmaker
Also available in 16mm from Budget; Films, Inc.; Swank
A fairly faithful television adaptation with a highly competent cast.

1989 Claire Bloom, Anthony Hopkins, Ralph Richardson, Edith Evans
Running time: 98 minutes
Purchase price: $9.99
Hemdale
Also available in 16mm from Films, Inc.
Slightly longer than the Harris version, with an outstanding British cast.

Major Barbara

1941 Wendy Hiller, Rex Harrison, Robert Morley, Sybil Thorndike, Robert Newton
Running time: 90 minutes
Purchase price: $39.95
Facets, Home Video, Learning Corp.
Also in 16mm, uncut, 115 minutes running time, from Films, Inc. Can be purchased from Learning Corp.
A splendid British cast in a superb adaptation, approved by Shaw. The added exterior scenes are excellent. Highly recommended for purchase, especially the longer 16mm version. Actually filmed in London at the height of the World War II blitz.

Trifles

1979 Cast unknown.
Running time: 20 minutes
Centre Communications, Phoenix

Desire Under the Elms

1958 Anthony Perkins, Sophia Loren, Burl Ives
Running time: 114 minutes
Purchase price: $19.95
Barr, Facets, Paramount
Also available in 16mm from Films, Inc.
Fairly faithful adaptation, but with an added scene of Simeon and Peter's return from the West. Sophia Loren turns into a seducing Italian rather than Irish Abbie. Burl Ives is excellent as old Ephraim. Anthony Perkins is a reasonable Eben.

The Glass Menagerie

1987 Joanne Woodward
Running time: 2 hours, 15 minutes
Purchase price: $19.98
MCA/Universal, Knowledge

Death of a Salesman

1986 Dustin Hoffman
Running time: 2 hours, 15 minutes
Purchase price: $19.98
Facets, Lorimer, Warner
Hoffman's interpretation of Willy as a destroyed *little* man is much closer to Miller's original concept than Lee J. Cobb's large, hulking characterization in the original production.

The Dumb Waiter

1987 John Travolta, Tom Conti
Running time: 60 minutes
Purchase price: $79.95
Prism
Made for television with some changes, not necessarily for the better, but still an adequate interpretation.

A Raisin in the Sun

1961 Sidney Poitier, Claudia McNeil, Ruby Dee, Louis Gossett, Jr., Diana Sands
Running time: 2 hours, 20 minutes
Purchase price: $14.95
Columbia, Home Vision
Also available on 16mm from Budget; Films, Inc.; Swank
Superb rendition of the play with a top-drawer cast.

1989 Danny Glover and Esther Rolle
Running time: 2 hours, 50 minutes
Purchase price: $69.95
Fries

'night, Mother

1986 Sissy Spacek and Anne Bancroft
Running time: 97 minutes
Purchase price: $79.95
MCA/Universal

List of Videotape Distributors

Ambrose Video Publishing, Inc.
1290 Avenue of the Americas
New York, NY 10104
800-526-4663

Applause Productions, Inc.
85 Longview Road
Port Washington, NY 11050
516-883-2826

Baker & Taylor Video
501 S. Gladiolus
Momence, IL 60954
800-775-2300

Barr Entertainment
12801 Schabarum Ave.
Irwindale, CA 91706
800-582-2000

Centre Communications
1800 30th St., Suite 207
Boulder, CO 80301
800-886-1166

Columbia Tristar Home Video
3400 Riverside Drive
Burbank, CA 91505-4627
818-972-8193

Connoisseur Video Collection
1543 7th St., Suite 102
Santa Monica, CA 90401-2636
310-393-9000

Facets Multimedia, Inc.
1517 W. Fullerton Ave.
Chicago, IL 60614
312-281-9075

Films, Inc. Video
5547 N. Ravenswood Ave.
Chicago, IL 60640-1199
800-323-4222

Fries Home Video
6922 Hollywood Blvd, 12th Floor
Hollywood, CA 90028
213-466-2266

Hemdale Home Video
7966 Beverly Blvd.
Los Angeles, CA 90048
213-966-3758

Home Video Library
Better Homes & Gardens Books
PO Box 10670
Des Moines, IA 50381
800-678-2665

Home Vision Cinema
5547 N. Ravenswood Ave.
Chicago, IL 60640-1199
800-826-3456

Ingram International Films
10990 E. 55th Ave.
Denver, CO 80239
800-356-3577

Knowledge Unlimited, Inc.
Box 52
Madison, WI 53701-0052
800-356-2303

Learning Corporation of America
c/o Coronet/MTI
168 Walnut Road
Deerfield, IL 60015
800-621-2131

MCA/Universal Home Video
700 Universal City Plaza
Universal City, CA 91608-9955
818-777-6419

MGM/UA Home Video, Inc.
10000 W. Washington Blvd.
Culver City, CA 90232
310-280-6212

Paramount Home Video
Bluhdom Bldg, 1st Floor
5555 Melrose Ave.
Los Angeles, CA 90038
213-956-8090

Phoenix/BFA Films
PO Box 1850
New York, NY 10156-1850
800-221-1274

Prism Entertainment
1888 Century Park E.
Suite 1000
Los Angeles, CA 90067
310-277-3270

Starmaker Entertainment, Inc.
141 Industrial Way E.
Eatontown, NJ 07724
800-233-3738

Turner Home Entertainment Co.
1 CNN Center
N. Tower, 12th Floor
Atlanta, GA 30348
404-827-2000

Warner Home Video, Inc.
4000 Warner Blvd.
Burbank, CA 91522
818-954-6000

16mm Film Distributors

Budget Films
4590 Santa Monica Blvd.
Los Angeles, CA 90029
213-660-0187

Corinth Films
410 E. 62nd Street
New York, NY 10021
212-421-4770

Films, Inc.
1213 Wilmette Ave.
Suite 202
Wilmette, IL 60091
800-323-4222

Swank Motion
201 S. Jefferson Ave.
St. Louis, MO 63166
800-325-3344

INDEX